ALMANAC OF
BUSINESS
AND
INDUSTRIAL
FINANCIAL
RATIOS

2009 EDITION

LEO TROY, Ph.D.

.CCH
a Wolters Kluwer business

Editorial Staff

Production..Christopher Zwirek
Design ....Craig Arritola

This publication is designed to provide accurate and authoritative information in regard to the subject matter covered. It is sold with the understanding that the publisher is not engaged in rendering legal, accounting, or other professional service and that the author is not offering such advice in this publication. If legal advice or other professional assistance is required, the services of a competent professional person should be sought.

ISBN: 978-0-8080-1898-8

© 2008, CCH. All Rights Reserved.
4025 W. Peterson Avenue
Chicago, IL 60646-6085
1 800 248 3248
www.CCHGroup.com

No claim is made to original government works; however, within this Product or Publication, the following are subject to CCH's copyright: (1) the gathering, compilation, and arrangement of such government materials; (2) the magnetic translation and digital conversion of data, if applicable; (3) the historical, statutory and other notes and references; and (4) the commentary and other materials.

Printed in the United States of America

Dedicated

To Alexander, Suzannah, Dale, Ariel Sarah Troy, Abigayle Hannah Troy, and Rachel Ilana Troy

Preface

Now in its 40th Edition, the *Almanac of Business and Industrial Financial Ratios* provides a precise benchmark for evaluating an individual company's financial performance. The performance data is derived from the latest available IRS figures on U.S. and international companies, and tracks 50 operating and financial factors in nearly 200 industries. The *Almanac* provides competitive norms in actual dollar amounts for revenue and capital factors, as well as important average operating costs in percent of net sales. It also provides other critical financial factors in percentage, including debt ratio, return on assets, return on equity, profit margin, and more. Beyond its reliable insights into corporate behavior, the *Almanac* can be used by other countries looking to model their economies on American performance.

Also included with the text, in a special pocket provided in the inside cover of the book, is a CD-ROM that contains all the materials found in the book including the explanatory discussion, the data tables, and the supporting index. Also included on the CD, but not in the book itself, is a special template that allows the reader to add individual company data of interest to compare and contrast with data from the book.

2009 Edition Highlights

The 2009 Edition of the *Almanac of Business and Industrial Financial Ratios* has been updated to include the following:

- **Broad scope:** *2009 Almanac* features the North American Industry Classification System (NAICS), so you can benchmark or analyze results consistently with corporations in the United States, Canada, and Mexico.

- **Most industry types:** *2009 Almanac* highlights most industry types, including industries with advanced technologies and newly emerging industries such as paging and wireless communications.

- **A truer picture** of corporate financial performance, since the data isn't based on a mixed bag of averages that might include partnerships or sole proprietors. *2009 Almanac* features a homogeneous universe of American corporate financial performance.

- **Many classifications:** *2009 Almanac* analyzes 197 industries with 50 financial performance items.

- **Benchmarks:** *2009 Almanac* provides 13 benchmarks, including such critical measures as Receipts to Cash Flow, Debt to Total Assets, and Return on Equity both before and after taxes.

- **Analytical tables:** *Table I, Corporations with and without Net Income (All Corporations), and Table II, Corporations with Net Income.*

- **Easier apples-to-apples comparisons:** Each table is divided into 13 asset sizes.

- **More comprehensive:** Total receipts of all corporations covered by *2009 Almanac* is $25.5 trillion, making the *Almanac* the Anatomy of American Corporate Capitalism.

Leo Troy, Ph. D.

October 2008

About the Author

Dr. Leo Troy is Professor of Economics at Rutgers University. He has been a faculty member of Rutgers for 50 years. In addition to authoring the widely praised *Almanac*, he has written many other books and articles published in leading journals. Professor Troy has been the recipient of numerous awards including two from the National Science Foundation, and two Fulbright grants. In addition, he has received numerous awards from private foundations. Dr. Troy received his Ph.D. from Columbia University and is a member of Phi Beta Kappa. He is a veteran of World War II with three battle stars and the combat infantry badge. He is the father of two children and is also a grandfather of three girls, including twins.

Acknowledgments

I wish to acknowledge the contributions of five people in particular for the development of the 40th Edition of the *Almanac:* Phil Wilson, Alan Kovar of Brighton Best, Lawrence R. Chodor, CPA, CVA, Wiss & Company, Marvin Sunshine, and Karen Kane.

Philip is responsible for the programming, which dealt with a very large amount of data, covering both the current and trend information. Alan, drawing upon his knowledge and experience as a CPA and Partner of Wiss and Company of Livingston, N.J., contributed significantly to the new content of the book. To Marvin Sunshine, Esq, my appreciation for actions and support that helped make the *Almanac* a continuing publication. Karen Kane is acknowledged for her contributions to the graphics of this issue.

Special acknowledgement is due my late friends and colleagues, Stan Katz, CPA, and Professor Emeritus of Accounting, Rutgers University, John Gilmour. I thank, too, Professor of Accounting, Rutgers University, David Zaumeyer, Ph.D., CPA, for recommending several ratios that continue to be included in the *Almanac*. I thank Mr. Ka-Neng Au, Business Librarian, Rutgers University, for significant contributions to the *Almanac*.

I wish to recognize, too, the cooperation of members of the Statistics of Income Division of the Internal Revenue Service—in particular, Ken Szeflinksi, Martha A. Harris, and Phyllis J. Whiles of the Corporation Returns Analysis Section. Without their data and its reliability, the Almanac would not be possible. Responsibility for the use of their facts and figures is, of course, solely my own. In this regard, I recall the valuable assistance I received from Barry Rosenstein, MBA, CPA, in checking procedures, in earlier editions, and which have continued into the current one. Finally, I wish to recognize the help of Suzannah B. Troy in bringing about the 40th annual edition of the *Almanac*. I anticipate continuation of her valuable assistance in subsequent editions.

INTRODUCTION

QUESTIONS, ANSWERS AND COMMENTS ON THE ALMANAC
Some users have requested further information on the use of the Almanac's ratios and statistics. This Q & A addition to the Almanac is in response to that demand.

1. What are the general purposes of the Almanac?

The goal of the Almanac is to provide users with a reliable and comprehensive source of standard financial ratios and financial statistics on all corporations, public and private, including those filing 1120S returns in the United States. Excluded are all individual proprietorships and partnerships. The Almanac makes available key business and financial statistics, which are consistent and neutral (unbiased by any commercial publisher or trade association).

2. What is the source and reliability of the Almanac's results?

The Almanac's results are computed from the Department of the Treasury, Internal Revenue Service's statistical sampling of the tax returns of all corporations. Dividends received from foreign corporations are included in total receipts of those corporations affected. The statistics apply to the company rather than the establishment.

3. Are international comparisons available?

Yes. Because of the adoption of a common system of industrial classification by the U.S., Canada and Mexico, known as the North American Industrial Classification System of industries (NAICS), under the North American Free Trade Agreement, users in Canada and Mexico can compare and contrast their results with those corporations in the United States.

4. What about comparisons within the U.S?

These are the most important applications of the Almanac. Results are available for each and every corporation within the U.S., whether public or private, and include small business corporations, those which file the 1120S tax return. Therefore, users can compare their corporate performance with that of their industry and asset size group of corporate enterprise in the United States.

5. How many corporations are covered in the Almanac?

The Almanac's results are derived from more than 5.6 million corporation tax returns. Furthermore, the user can easily determine the number of enterprises for the total of each industry and by each of the 12 asset size groups. This makes for a total of 13 asset size comparisons.

6. What about differences in the size of corporations?

In addition to the results for each industry, the Almanac displays 12 columns of performance by the size of assets. Again, this makes for a total of 13 asset size comparisons.

7. Does the Almanac distinguish between the profitability of corporations?

In a word, yes. Each industry is divided between two tables: Table I reports the results of all corporations in an industry, that is, those with and without net income. It is followed by a second table for the same industry, Table II, which reports only those corporations with net income.

8. How many items of information are there for each industry?

There are 50 indicators of corporate performance in each table and each industry and for all asset size groups, except where the IRS' data sample is too small, or it does not supply the necessary information.

9. Who are the users of the Almanac?

Accountants, corporate managers, business consultants, investors evaluating a corporate takeover, entrepreneurs considering new businesses, lawyers, and students of accounting, business, and management.

10. What accounting time period is covered?

The Internal Revenue Service provides the most recent statistics publicly available for the Almanac. For the 2009 Almanac, these statistics apply to the accounting period from July 2005 through June 2006.

WHAT'S NEW IN THIS EDITION

Beginning with the year 2002, the *Almanac of Business and Industrial Financial Ratios* began using the North American Industry Classification System (NAICS). NAICS replaces the Internal Revenue Service's own system, which it had used for many years, an adaptation of Standard Industrial Classification (SIC); all previous *Almanacs* had used that adaptation.

The new industrial classification system is the product of the North American Free Trade Agreement (NAFTA), and it replaces the existing classification systems not only of the United States but also of Canada and Mexico. Hence, the new system applies uniformly to the three countries, and users of the *Almanac 2009*, utilizing the new international industrial classification system, can now compare their results with corporations in all three nations.

In the United States, the new manual was created by the Office of Management and Budget (OMB). The NAICS system gives special attention to industries producing and furnishing advanced technologies, new and emerging industries, as well as service industries in general. NAICS divides the economy into 21 sectors, five in the predominantly goods-producing area, and 16 in the service producing area.

INDUSTRY SECTORS

Particularly noteworthy is NAICS's introduction of an Information sector. This sector assembles the industries from Newspaper Publishers (511110) to Internet Service Providers, Web Portals, and Data Processing Services (518115). Within this span, NAICS and therefore the *Almanac* include such important industries as software publishing, database and directory publishing, satellite telecommunications, paging and cellular, and other wireless communications. NAICS and the *Almanac* also provide a category of industries on Professional, Scientific, and Technical Services, industries in which human capital is the major input. The sector includes Legal Services (541115) and Scientific Research and Development Services (541700), as well as Management, Scientific, and Technical Services (541600) and Computer Systems Design and Related Services (541515).

Other important sectors are the Arts, Entertainment, and Recreation including Amusement, Gambling, and Recreation (713105), and the Health Care and Social Assistance including

Offices of Physicians (621115), Hospitals, Nursing, and Residential Care Facilities (622005). Within Manufacturing, the key goods sector industry, there is now a category embracing Computer and Electronic Product Manufacturing. It spans industries such as Computer and Peripheral Equipment (334110) to Navigational, Measuring, Electromedical, and Control Instruments (334500).

The source of the IRS's data are the tax returns of all *active* public and private corporations. Because the *Almanac's* data are derived only from corporate tax returns, there is a mixture of corporate with the financial performance of partnerships and individual proprietorships; the *Almanac's* information constitutes a **homogeneous universe**. The tax returns are classified by the IRS on the basis of the business activity which accounts for a corporation's largest percentage of total receipts. Large corporations with dissimilar business activities are included in only one industry, despite operations that are unrelated to the industry in which they are grouped.

The data developed by the IRS are derived from a stratified probability sample of corporation income tax returns. Where the sample data from the sample are small and should those numbers be used in a denominator, the result is reported as a dot (·) in the *Almanac*. Returns of the largest corporations are generally in the sample from year to year, but comparability can be affected by consolidations and mergers, changes in the law and the tax forms, and changes in the industrial classification system used over the years.

Representative Industries

The *Almanac* reports on nearly 200 industries. Minor industries are denoted by a six-digit code; major industries are designated by a three-digit industry code; industrial sectors by a two-digit code; and industrial divisions by a two-digit code. When the data are the same for minor, major, sector, and industrial division, the IRS reports only the industrial division, and similarly for other identities applicable to the major and sectoral industries; the *Almanac* follows this procedure.

Almanac 2009 continues the previous coverage of reporting information: for all industries, **Table I, Corporations with and without Net Income** (that is, the entire universe of active reporting corporations), and **Table II, Corporations with Net Income**, a subset of the universe. In the *Almanac 2009*, Table I covers over 5.6 million enterprises (corporations), and Table II covers 3.3 million corporations with net income. This implies that 2.3 million corporations reported deficits. The IRS defines net income (or deficit) as the companies' net profit or loss from taxable sources of income reduced by allowable deductions. Total receipts of the 5.6 million corporations reported in *Almanac 2009* was $25.5 trillion, up by $2.8 trillion.

The *Almanac* continues to report performance results not only by the total for each industry, but by 12 other asset size groups (a total of 13 asset size groups), providing 50 items of data and/or ratios on corporate performance:

Total

Zero
$1 to $500,000
$500,001 to $1,000,000
$1,000,001 to $5,000,000
$5,000,001 to $10,000,000
$10,000,001 to $25,000,000
$25,000,001 to $50,000,000
$50,000,001 to $100,000,000
$100,000,001 to $250,000,000
$250,000,001 to $500,000,000
$500,000,001 to $2,500,000,000
$2,500,000,001 or more

All data in Tables I and II cover an accounting period identified on all tables and are the most recent information available from the IRS. For the *Almanac 2009*, the accounting period is July 2005 through June 2006. The dating of the data is counterbalanced by the most extensive industrial coverage available in any report on financial performance, the number of items of corporate performance, and their availability in thirteen asset size groups. Moreover, the timing of the data are also counterbalanced by the stability of the *Almanac's* values as past trends have indicated. Therefore, the *Almanac's* financial results are reliable in assessing current corporate performance.

Beyond its reliable insights into corporate behavior on a micro basis, its comprehensive and detailed coverage make the *Almanac* the **Anatomy of American Corporate Capitalism**. In this macro sense, it constitutes **the** example to those countries desirous of modeling their economies on the American performance.

HOW TO USE THE ALMANAC

On the micro level, the *Almanac* multiplies manyfold the power of financial analysis to evaluate an individual company's financial performance: In contrast to many standard reports, the *Almanac* gives management, and analysts independent of any company, more of the fundamental analytical tools needed to compare their company with companies in the same industry and of the same asset size. The *Almanac* can enhance the value of any company's annual report because it affords the analyst and the stockholder detailed background of financial information for comparison.

All items and ratios are listed in Both Table I and Table II. No figures are reported in the *Almanac* when the IRS has either suppressed the underlying data, or the sample size, or other reasons affecting a calculated result, and where the ratio/item was not applicable to an industry. The 50 tax-based items that provide that financial analysis are as follows:

1. Number of Enterprises

These are the count of corporate tax returns filed by active corporations on one of the Form 1120-series returns.

> SPECIAL NOTE: Net Sales is used to compute the percentage of items 3 to 7 to Net Sales for all industries, except Finance, Insurance, and Real Estate (FIRE). For the FIRE industries, Total Receipts are used to compute the percentage of items 3 to 7.

REVENUES ($ IN THOUSANDS), ITEMS 2 TO 9

2. Operating Income (Net Sales)

This is the IRS item Business Receipts, the gross operating receipts reduced by the cost of returned goods and allowances.

3. Interest

Taxable interest includes interest on U.S. Government obligations, loans, notes, mortgages, arbitrage bonds, nonexempt private activity bonds, corporate bonds, bank deposits, and tax refunds; interest received from tax-exempt state or local municipal bonds and ESOP loans are not included in this item.

4. Rents

These are the gross amounts received from the use or occupancy of property by corporations whose principal activities did not involve operating rental properties.

5. Royalties

These are gross payments received for the use of property rights before taking deductions.

6. Other Portfolio Income

These consist of cash, notes, and accounts receivable, less allowance for bad debts and inventories.

7. Other Receipts

These receipts include such items as income from minor operations, cash discounts, claims, license rights, judgments, and joint ventures.

8. Total Receipts

Total receipts are the sum of ten items: 1. Business receipts; 2. Interest; 3. Interest on government obligations: state and local; 4. Rents; 5. Royalties; 6. Net capital gains (excluding long-term gains from regulated investment companies); 7. Net gain, noncapital assets; 8. Dividends received from domestic corporations; 9. Dividends received from foreign corporations; 10. Other receipts.

9. Average Total Receipts

Total receipts divided by the number of enterprises.

OPERATING COSTS/OPERATING INCOME, ITEMS 10 TO 22

10. Cost of Operations

This is the IRS's Costs of Goods Sold; it consists of the costs incurred in producing the goods or furnishing the services that generated the corporations' business receipts.

11. Salaries and Wages

These include the amount of salaries and wages paid as well as bonuses and director's fees, but no contributions to pension plans (see item 16) nor compensation of officers (see item 20).

12. Taxes Paid

Excludes Federal Income Taxes; they are the amounts paid for ordinary state and local taxes, social security, payroll taxes, unemployment insurance taxes, excise taxes, import and tariff duties, and business license and privilege taxes.

13. Interest Paid

These amounts consist of interest paid on all business indebtedness.

14. Depreciation

The charges allowed are governed principally by the IRS rules in effect in 1997, basically enacted in 1986, but also include other modifications. Hence, depreciation could represent amounts computed by different sets of rules.

15. Amortization and Depletion

Most amortization is calculated on a straight-line basis. Depletion is allowed for the exhaustion of natural deposits and timber.

16. Pensions, Profit-Sharing, Stock Bonus, and Annuity Plans

These are amounts deducted during the current year for qualified pension, profit-sharing, or other funded deferred compensation plans.

17. Employee Benefits

These are employer contributions to death benefit, insurance, health, accident, and sickness, and other welfare plans.

18. Advertising

Amounts include promotion and publicity expenses.

19. Other Expenses

These include expenses for repairs, bad debts, rent paid on business property, domestic production activities, contributions and gifts, and expenses not allocable to specific deductible items.

20. Officers' Compensation

Salaries, wages, stock bonuses, bonds, and other forms of compensation are included in this item.

21. Operating Margin

This is the net income after all operating costs have been deducted.

22. Operating Margin Before Officers' Compensation

This measure takes into account the effect of Officers' Compensation on the operating margin.

SELECTED AVERAGE BALANCE SHEET ITEMS ($ IN THOUSANDS) ITEMS 23 TO 29

23. Average Net Receivables

The total of Notes and Accounts Receivable, less Allowance for Bad Debts, divided by the number of enterprises. Notes and Accounts Receivable are the gross amounts arising from business sales or services to customers on credit in the course of ordinary trade or business. This includes commercial paper, charge accounts, current intercompany receivables, property investment loans, and trade acceptances.

24. Average Inventories

Total inventories are divided by the number of enterprises. Inventories include finished goods, partially finished goods, new materials and supplies acquired for sale, merchandise on hand or in transit, and growing crops reported as assets by agricultural enterprises.

25. Average Net Property, Plant and Equipment

This includes depreciable assets less accumulated depreciation, depletable assets less accumulated depletion, and land; the sum is divided by the number of enterprises. Depreciable assets consist of end-of-year balance sheet tangible property, such as buildings and equipment used in trade or business, or held for the production of income, and that has a useful life of one year or more. The amount of accumulated depreciation represents the portion written off in the current year, as well as in prior years. Depletable assets represent the end-of-year value of mineral property, oil and gas wells, and other natural resources; standing timber; intangible development and drilling costs capitalized; and leases and leaseholds, subject to depletion. Accumulated depletion represents the cumulative adjustment of these assets.

26. Average Total Assets

Total Assets (and Total Liabilities) are amounts reported in the end-of-year balance sheet. Total Assets are net amounts after reduction from accumulated depreciation, accumulated amortization, accumulated depletion, and the reserve for bad debts. Total Liabilities include the claims of creditors and stockholders' equity, and were net after reduction by the cost of treasury stock. The average of total assets was obtained by dividing it by the number of enterprises.

27. Average of Notes and Loans Payable, and Mortgages

These liabilities were separated on the balance sheet according to the time to maturity of the obligations. Time to maturity was based on the date of the balance sheet, rather than the date of issue of the obligations. The total was divided by the number of enterprises.

28. Average of All Other Liabilities

These included accounts payable, and other liabilities including other current liabilities. The total was divided by the number of enterprises.

29. Average Net Worth

Net Worth represents the stockholders' equity in the corporation (total assets minus the claims of creditors). It consists of Capital Stock, Paid-In Capital Surplus, Retained Earnings Appropriated, Retained Earnings Unappropriated, less cost of treasury stock.

Selected Financial Ratios, Number of Times to One, Ratios 30 to 44

30. Current Ratio

The items that used Current Assets for this ratio are Cash; Notes and Accounts Receivable, Less: Allowance for Bad Debts; Inventories; Government Obligations; Tax-Exempt Securities; and Other Current Assets. For Current Liabilities, the following items were included: Accounts Payable; Mortgages and Notes Maturing in Less than 1 Year; and Other Current Liabilities.

This ratio, rated highest by CPAs as a measure of liquidity, gauges the ability of a company to meet its short-term financial obligations should it be compelled to liquidate its assets. However, it is not an absolute measure of the company's ability to meet its obligations. It is obtained by dividing current assets by current liabilities. The standard guideline has been a ratio of 2 to 1; however, some companies have found that in their experience, a ratio less than 2 to 1 is adequate, while others consider a larger one to be necessary. The ratio is affected by the method of valuation of inventory (LIFO or FIFO) and by inflation. The Almanac provides measures that can be treated as standards by size of asset.

31. Quick Ratio

This ratio is also known as the "Acid Test Ratio" because it is often used to estimate a company's general liquidity. There is some disagreement about the inclusion of inventory in the numerator because it may be slow moving, obsolete, or pledged to specific creditors, and, therefore, not be readily convertible into cash. The *Almanac* adopts a conservative approach and does not include the item in calculating the ratio. Excluding inventories and other current assets, the numerator is the same as that used in determining current assets. The denominator, current liabilities, is unchanged. The ratio of 1 to 1 has been considered a reasonable standard, but it is jeopardized because accounts and notes receivable may not be convertible into cash at face value and at short notice. The *Almanac* provides measures that can be treated as standards by size of asset.

32. Net Sales to Working Capital

This is an efficiency, or turnover, ratio that measures the rate at which current assets less current liabilities (Working Capital) is used in making sales. (In industries in Finance, Insurance, and Real Estate, total receipts rather than net sales is used.) A low ratio indicates a less efficient (profitable) use of working capital in making sales. The *Almanac* provides measures that can be treated as standards by size of asset. Working Capital is the difference between current assets and current liabilities.

33. Coverage Ratio

This ratio measures the number of times all interest paid by the company is covered by earnings before interest charges and taxes (EBIT). For that reason, the ratio is also known as the "times interest earned ratio." The ratio indicates the company's ability to service its debt based on its income.

34. Total Asset Turnover

The ratio is an efficiency ratio because it indicates the effectiveness of the company's use of its total assets in generating sales. It is measured by dividing net sales by total assets.

35. *Inventory Turnover*

Inventory turnover measures the liquidity of the inventory. It is computed by dividing the cost of goods sold by the average inventory. The result shows the number of times that the average inventory can be converted into receivables or cash. The ratio reflects both on the quality of the inventory and the efficiency of management. Typically, the higher the turnover rate, the more likely profits will be higher.

> Special Note: Inventory turnover is not computed for industries in Finance, Insurance, and Real Estate.

36. *Receivables Turnover*

This ratio measures the liquidity of accounts receivable. It indicates the average collection period throughout the year. It is obtained by dividing sales average by net receivables. It is not computed in the Finance, Insurance, and Real Estate industries (although it is calculated for all other industries even though conventional analysis typically omits it) for many of the industries in the *Almanac*.

37. *Total Liabilities to Net Worth*

This ratio indicates the extent to which the company's funds are supplied by short- and long-term creditors compared to its owners. It is an indicator of the company's long-term debt paying ability. The ratio is one of the most important bearing on the company's capital structure. Net worth is defined in ratio 29.

38. *Current Assets to Working Capital*

The dependence of Working Capital in part on current assets is important to understanding this part of the source of Working Capital. Current Assets are defined in ratio 30 and Working Capital is defined in ratio 32.

39. *Current Liabilities to Working Capital*

The dependence of Working Capital in part on current liabilities is important to understanding this part of the source of Working Capital. Current Liabilities are defined in ratio 30 and Working Capital is defined in ratio 32.

40. *Working Capital to Net Sales or Total Receipts*

The purpose of this ratio is to determine the working capital needed in relation to projected sales or receipts. Working Capital is defined in ratio 32.

41. *Inventory to Working Capital*

This ratio, by showing the proportion of Working Capital invested in Inventory, indicates the part of Current Assets that are least liquid. Inventories which exceed working capital indicate that current liabilities exceed liquid current assets. Working Capital is defined in ratio 32.

42. *Total Receipts to Cash Flow*

Cash Flow is the difference between cash receipts and cash disbursements. The ratio of total receipts to cash flow could suggest steps which management might take to improve the company's cash position.

43. Cost of Goods to Cash Flow

This ratio can be the basis for projections of cash requirements needed to fund projected costs of production. Cash flow is defined in ratio 42.

44. Cash Flow to Total Debt

This ratio indicates the extent to which a company could service its total debt from cash flow. It is analogous to the coverage ratio; refer to ratio 33. Cash flow is defined in ratio 42.

SELECTED FINANCIAL FACTORS (IN PERCENTAGES), ITEMS 45 TO 50

45. Debt Ratio (Total Liabilities to Total Assets)

This ratio indicates the company's ability to pay all its debts. It measures the creditors' and owners' of the company's ability to withstand losses. It is an indicator of the long-run solvency of the firm.

46. Return on Total Assets

The ratio combines the turnover and profit ratios (Sales/Total Assets x [times] Profit/Sales) and yields the return on investment (Total Assets). The result is the end product of the DuPont System of financial analysis. The system takes into account both operating income and operating assets. In Table I of each industry, the Return on Investment (ROI) is net income less deficit before income taxes divided by total assets. In Table II of each industry, the ROI is net income before income taxes divided by Total Assets. Total Assets are used because management has discretion in the investment of the resources provided by both the creditors and owners.

47. Return on Equity Before Income Taxes

This ratio measures the profitability of the company's operations to owners, before income taxes. For Table I this is net income, less deficit before income taxes and before credits. For Table II this is net income minus income tax before credits.

48. Return on Equity After Income Taxes

This ratio measures the profitability of the company's operations to owners, after income taxes. For Table I this is net income, less deficit and minus income tax before credits. For Table II this is net income minus income tax and before credits.

49. Profit Margin (Before Income Tax)

This is net income before income tax divided by net sales (or total receipts) and indicates the contribution of sales to the profitability of the company. Competition, capital structure, and operating characteristics cause the margin to vary within and among industries. For Table I, net income less deficit and before income taxes is the numerator; for Table II it is net income before tax.

50. Profit Margin (After Income Tax)

This ratio is the same as ratio 49 except that income taxes are taken into account.

Table of Contents

Page references to tables for industries with net income are in italic

PRINCIPAL BUSINESS ACTIVITY (BASED ON NAICS)

ALMANAC
of Business and
Industrial
FINANCIAL
RATIOS

40th ANNUAL EDITION
2009

Table I

Corporations with and without Net Income

AGRICULTURAL PRODUCTION

MONEY AMOUNTS AND SIZE OF ASSETS IN THOUSANDS OF DOLLARS

Item Description for Accounting Period 7/05 Through 6/06	Total	Zero Assets	Under 500	500 to 1,000	1,000 to 5,000	5,000 to 10,000	10,000 to 25,000	25,000 to 50,000	50,000 to 100,000	100,000 to 250,000	250,000 to 500,000	500,000 to 2,500,000	2,500,000 and over
Number of Enterprises **1**	101263	9934	61039	14175	14223	1156	462	125	84	49	10	3	3
Revenues ($ in Thousands)													
Net Sales **2**	88407346	1226277	11694389	6406449	18932641	7611513	8593108	4132521	7331994	8902515	2595627	1902040	9078270
Interest **3**	295149	8919	36949	26554	77672	23652	21024	16270	20264	29779	6852	2600	24613
Rents **4**	840841	16034	203680	188820	256277	61823	14525	9639	45177	27320	3978	8124	5445
Royalties **5**	118263	0	6335	8717	12915	6168	24130	7837	5348	14461	171	18780	13402
Other Portfolio Income **6**	2655173	224240	343957	172405	558391	99790	182860	117236	80391	176097	20123	33708	645973
Other Receipts **7**	9122058	328156	2228097	1227712	3532667	413020	598980	227814	134114	237155	82609	38112	73626
Total Receipts **8**	101438830	1803626	14513407	8030657	23370563	8215966	9434627	4511317	7617288	9387327	2709360	2003364	9841329
Average Total Receipts **9**	1002	182	238	567	1643	7107	20421	36091	90682	191578	270936	667788	3280443
Operating Costs/Operating Income (%)													
Cost of Operations **10**	50.6	74.1	19.3	31.6	33.4	42.8	62.2	65.4	65.1	76.1	86.6	56.8	78.0
Salaries and Wages **11**	8.8	4.7	11.1	9.2	12.3	11.2	7.4	6.5	6.9	5.5	1.3	13.7	4.6
Taxes Paid **12**	2.4	3.2	3.3	4.0	3.4	2.7	1.8	1.6	1.4	1.7	1.4	0.9	1.0
Interest Paid **13**	2.7	5.1	3.0	4.1	3.1	3.4	1.9	2.0	1.5	1.7	1.7	1.8	2.7
Depreciation **14**	5.5	5.5	8.3	10.0	8.2	5.3	2.9	3.4	3.3	2.9	3.3	1.6	2.0
Amortization and Depletion **15**	0.3	0.7	0.0	0.1	0.1	0.1	0.2	0.8	0.5	0.4	1.7	0.4	0.3
Pensions and Other Deferred Comp. **16**	0.3	0.0	0.1	0.6	0.3	0.5	0.2	0.2	0.2	0.3	0.1	0.4	0.1
Employee Benefits **17**	1.1	0.5	1.2	1.3	1.1	1.2	0.8	0.5	0.8	0.7	0.8	5.6	0.9
Advertising **18**	0.5	0.3	0.4	0.4	0.4	0.4	0.4	0.3	0.2	0.3	0.1	1.6	1.6
Other Expenses **19**	36.8	63.7	71.4	56.4	53.9	38.2	28.8	22.3	20.2	9.0	6.7	13.4	6.3
Officers' Compensation **20**	2.2	0.3	4.0	4.6	3.0	2.3	1.2	1.2	1.0	1.0	0.6	0.6	0.6
Operating Margin **21**	•	•	•	•	•	•	•	•	•	0.5	•	3.2	1.9
Operating Margin Before Officers' Comp. **22**	•	•	•	•	•	•	•	•	•	1.4	•	3.8	2.5

Selected Average Balance Sheet ($ in Thousands)

	C1	C2	C3	C4	C5	C6	C7	C8	C9	C10	C11	C12	C13
Net Receivables 23	96	0	3	24	89	268	1790	5162	9297	19821	23909	66348	1314592
Inventories 24	94	0	10	43	148	899	2264	5270	10570	17873	56606	222284	266135
Net Property, Plant and Equipment 25	438	0	88	423	1079	3734	6076	13505	29554	59501	117848	166598	589479
Total Assets 26	964	0	167	699	1914	6948	15276	35090	70397	157809	337931	703083	3902551
Notes and Loans Payable 27	483	0	150	349	1021	4871	7204	14996	27742	49989	75441	192787	1115704
All Other Liabilities 28	184	0	8	38	135	818	2786	6606	14856	35738	76703	186728	2756909
Net Worth 29	297	0	9	311	758	1258	5285	13489	27800	72081	185787	323568	29937

Selected Financial Ratios (Times to 1)

	C1	C2	C3	C4	C5	C6	C7	C8	C9	C10	C11	C12	C13
Current Ratio 30	1.4	•	1.4	1.6	1.5	1.1	1.4	1.3	1.4	1.7	1.5	1.7	1.1
Quick Ratio 31	0.8	•	0.9	0.9	0.8	0.4	0.7	0.7	0.7	0.9	0.4	0.9	0.9
Net Sales to Working Capital 32	10.7	•	15.9	8.3	8.0	58.0	10.9	8.5	10.5	6.9	6.4	5.6	34.2
Coverage Ratio 33	2.4	•	1.6	1.8	2.4	0.9	2.1	3.4	2.8	4.4	0.9	5.6	5.2
Total Asset Turnover 34	0.9	•	1.1	0.6	0.7	0.9	1.2	0.9	1.2	1.2	0.8	0.9	0.8
Inventory Turnover 35	4.7	•	3.6	3.3	3.0	3.1	5.1	4.1	5.4	7.7	4.0	1.6	8.9
Receivables Turnover 36	10.3	•	50.8	18.7	15.7	28.9	10.4	6.4	10.0	9.8	11.6	1.6	4.6
Total Liabilities to Net Worth 37	2.2	•	17.6	1.2	1.5	4.5	1.9	1.6	1.5	1.2	0.8	1.2	129.4
Current Assets to Working Capital 38	3.8	•	3.5	2.8	2.9	18.4	3.7	3.9	3.4	2.4	2.9	2.4	19.3
Current Liabilities to Working Capital 39	2.8	•	2.5	1.8	1.9	17.4	2.7	2.9	2.4	1.4	1.9	1.4	18.3
Working Capital to Net Sales 40	0.1	•	0.1	0.1	0.1	0.0	0.1	0.1	0.1	0.1	0.2	0.2	0.0
Inventory to Working Capital 41	1.1	•	0.8	0.8	0.9	9.4	1.3	1.4	1.3	0.6	1.4	0.6	3.0
Total Receipts to Cash Flow 42	3.4	7.3	2.1	2.3	2.3	3.5	4.0	4.5	5.0	8.9	27.9	5.9	6.8
Cost of Goods to Cash Flow 43	1.7	5.4	0.4	0.7	0.8	1.5	2.5	2.9	3.3	6.8	24.2	3.4	5.3
Cash Flow to Total Debt 44	0.4	•	0.6	0.5	0.5	0.3	0.5	0.3	0.4	0.2	0.1	0.3	0.1

Selected Financial Factors (in Percentages)

	C1	C2	C3	C4	C5	C6	C7	C8	C9	C10	C11	C12	C13
Debt Ratio 45	69.2		94.6	55.5	60.4	81.9	65.4	61.6	60.5	54.3	45.0	54.0	99.2
Return on Total Assets 46	5.8		5.6	4.7	5.1	3.0	4.8	6.6	5.2	8.6	1.2	9.1	10.7
Return on Equity Before Income Taxes 47	11.0		41.0	4.5	7.5	3.0	7.2	12.1	8.4	14.5	•	16.3	1123.8
Return on Equity After Income Taxes 48	8.5		30.2	3.9	6.6	•	4.9	9.2	5.7	10.9	•	14.3	925.7
Profit Margin (Before Income Tax) 49	3.8		1.9	3.1	4.2	•	2.0	4.9	2.7	5.8	•	8.3	11.1
Profit Margin (After Income Tax) 50	2.9		1.4	2.7	3.7	•	1.4	3.8	1.8	4.3	•	7.3	9.2

1

Table II

Corporations with Net Income

AGRICULTURAL PRODUCTION

MONEY AMOUNTS AND SIZE OF ASSETS IN THOUSANDS OF DOLLARS

Item Description for Accounting Period 7/05 Through 6/06	Total	Zero Assets	Under 500	500 to 1000	251 to 500	501 to 1,000	1,001 to 5,000	5,001 to 10,000	10,001 to 25,000	25,001 to 50,000	50,001 to 100,000	100,001 to 250,000	250,001 and over
Number of Enterprises 1	57057	4419	32962	8708	9873	684	238	80	49	•	•	3	3
Revenues ($ in Thousands)													
Net Sales 2	64636861	332477	7266230	4568522	14652708	4859433	5554256	3200478	4529838	•	•	1902040	9078270
Interest 3	240268	7349	28203	21614	63906	20745	18040	11165	14152	•	•	2600	24613
Rents 4	692732	15358	141591	171168	219119	50843	9756	4741	36644	•	•	8124	5445
Royalties 5	107445	0	5507	8102	12115	2565	24130	7585	771	•	•	18780	13402
Other Portfolio Income 6	2346271	222181	258783	132271	503458	89467	154545	94648	42309	•	•	33708	645973
Other Receipts 7	6723929	188339	1424782	962085	2638138	427422	428889	209129	90738	•	•	38112	73626
Total Receipts 8	74747506	765704	9125096	5863762	18089444	5450475	6189616	3527746	4714452	•	•	2003364	9841329
Average Total Receipts 9	1310	173	277	673	1832	7969	26007	44097	96213	•	•	667788	3280443
Operating Costs/Operating Income (%)													
Cost of Operations 10	50.7	37.6	14.5	34.8	29.7	43.5	65.8	62.7	65.3	•	•	56.8	78.0
Salaries and Wages 11	7.9	5.2	11.0	6.9	11.0	10.1	5.6	5.8	7.1	•	•	13.7	4.6
Taxes Paid 12	2.2	6.0	3.0	3.4	3.3	2.9	1.4	1.5	1.5	•	•	0.9	1.0
Interest Paid 13	2.3	7.3	2.5	3.4	2.5	3.6	1.2	1.5	1.3	•	•	1.8	2.7
Depreciation 14	4.9	14.8	7.1	9.5	7.5	5.3	2.4	2.8	3.1	•	•	1.6	2.0
Amortization and Depletion 15	0.2	0.1	0.0	0.0	0.1	0.1	0.2	0.6	0.3	•	•	0.4	0.3
Pensions and Other Deferred Comp. 16	0.3	0.1	0.2	0.8	0.4	0.2	0.2	0.3	0.3	•	•	0.4	0.1
Employee Benefits 17	1.0	1.0	0.8	1.4	1.1	1.0	0.5	0.5	0.8	•	•	5.6	0.9
Advertising 18	0.5	0.5	0.4	0.2	0.2	0.4	0.4	0.1	0.3	•	•	1.6	1.6
Other Expenses 19	31.9	50.5	64.1	50.6	51.6	35.3	23.6	23.2	15.6	•	•	13.4	6.3
Officers' Compensation 20	2.1	1.0	3.8	4.6	3.2	3.0	1.3	1.2	1.1	•	•	0.6	0.6
Operating Margin 21	•	•	•	•	•	•	•	•	3.5	•	•	3.2	1.9
Operating Margin Before Officers' Comp. 22	•	•	•	•	•	•	•	1.0	4.6	•	•	3.8	2.5

Selected Average Balance Sheet ($ in Thousands)

Net Receivables 23	138	0	4	29	90	309	1998	5863	9678	•	•	66348	1314592
Inventories 24	118	0	9	44	167	1385	2639	5976	9554	•	•	62312	266135
Net Property, Plant and Equipment 25	478	0	90	411	986	3653	5634	11690	28616	•	•	166598	589479
Total Assets 26	1154	0	181	697	1831	7140	15886	35974	70270	•	•	703083	3902551
Notes and Loans Payable 27	446	0	91	268	772	4404	5526	14188	24537	•	•	192787	1115704
All Other Liabilities 28	250	0	8	37	108	819	2836	6484	12896	•	•	186728	2756909
Net Worth 29	458	0	82	393	952	1917	7504	15303	32838	•	•	323568	29937

Selected Financial Ratios (Times to 1)

Current Ratio 30	1.5	•	1.9	2.0	1.7	1.1	1.4	1.6	1.7	•	•	1.7	1.1
Quick Ratio 31	0.9	•	1.3	1.3	0.9	0.4	0.7	0.9	0.9	•	•	0.9	0.9
Net Sales to Working Capital 32	8.6	•	9.0	6.7	7.1	26.5	12.1	6.3	7.6	•	•	5.6	34.2
Coverage Ratio 33	6.1	15.6	8.3	4.7	6.2	2.9	8.5	7.6	7.0	•	•	5.6	5.2
Total Asset Turnover 34	1.0	•	1.2	0.8	0.8	1.0	1.5	1.1	1.3	•	•	0.9	0.8
Inventory Turnover 35	4.9	•	3.4	4.2	2.6	2.2	5.8	4.2	6.3	•	•	5.8	8.9
Receivables Turnover 36	11.0	•	47.8	19.6	19.6	45.9	11.0	7.3	11.8	•	•	19.1	4.6
Total Liabilities to Net Worth 37	1.5	•	1.2	0.8	0.9	2.7	1.1	1.4	1.1	•	•	1.2	129.4
Current Assets to Working Capital 38	3.1	•	2.1	2.0	2.5	9.0	3.7	2.8	2.4	•	•	2.4	19.3
Current Liabilities to Working Capital 39	2.1	•	1.1	1.0	1.5	8.0	2.7	1.8	1.4	•	•	1.4	18.3
Working Capital to Net Sales 40	0.1	•	0.1	0.1	0.1	0.0	0.1	0.2	0.1	•	•	0.2	0.0
Inventory to Working Capital 41	0.9	•	0.4	0.5	0.8	5.2	1.1	1.0	0.8	•	•	0.6	3.0
Total Receipts to Cash Flow 42	3.0	0.9	1.7	2.1	2.0	2.9	3.7	3.5	4.9	•	•	5.9	6.8
Cost of Goods to Cash Flow 43	1.5	0.3	0.2	0.7	0.6	1.3	2.4	2.2	3.2	•	•	3.4	5.3
Cash Flow to Total Debt 44	0.5	•	1.3	0.8	0.8	0.5	0.8	0.6	0.5	•	•	0.3	0.1

Selected Financial Factors (in Percentages)

Debt Ratio 45	60.3	•	54.6	43.7	48.0	73.1	52.7	57.5	53.3	•	•	54.0	99.2
Return on Total Assets 46	13.6	•	25.3	12.1	12.5	10.4	14.7	12.8	11.6	•	•	9.1	10.7
Return on Equity Before Income Taxes 47	28.6	•	48.9	16.9	20.2	25.3	27.4	26.1	21.2	•	•	16.3	1123.8
Return on Equity After Income Taxes 48	25.7	•	46.7	16.0	19.1	22.1	24.4	22.2	17.3	•	•	14.3	925.7
Profit Margin (Before Income Tax) 49	11.6	106.2	18.2	12.7	12.9	6.8	8.8	10.0	7.5	•	•	8.3	11.1
Profit Margin (After Income Tax) 50	10.4	98.8	17.4	12.0	12.3	6.0	7.9	8.5	6.1	•	•	7.3	9.2

Table I

Corporations with and without Net Income

FORESTRY AND LOGGING

MONEY AMOUNTS AND SIZE OF ASSETS IN THOUSANDS OF DOLLARS

Item Description for Accounting Period 7/05 Through 6/06	Total	Zero Assets	Under 500	500 to 1,000	1,000 to 5,000	5,000 to 10,000	10,000 to 25,000	25,000 to 50,000	50,000 to 100,000	100,000 to 250,000	250,000 to 500,000	500,000 to 2,500,000	2,500,000 and over
Number of Enterprises **1**	11176	1296	7311	1244	1145	47	85	28	11	0	4	5	0
Revenues ($ in Thousands)													
Net Sales **2**	15564040	103333	4158027	1302736	4486215	51286	1584215	458979	1024630	0	228652	2165969	0
Interest **3**	66863	21	2065	478	3536	1182	1658	5405	2590	0	5773	44156	0
Rents **4**	67726	65	10916	600	7200	14	2745	21191	408	0	1570	23015	0
Royalties **5**	5302	0	0	3502	0	331	1223	0	0	0	0	247	0
Other Portfolio Income **6**	440622	18394	5041	19998	140511	17216	30683	6128	11706	0	90957	99987	0
Other Receipts **7**	234616	208	22952	1415	16155	2093	10782	7964	44684	0	47927	80434	0
Total Receipts **8**	16379169	122021	4199001	1328729	4653617	72122	1631306	499667	1084018	0	374879	2413808	0
Average Total Receipts **9**	1466	94	574	1068	4064	1535	19192	17845	98547	•	93720	482762	•
Operating Costs/Operating Income (%)													
Cost of Operations **10**	68.4	37.2	60.9	19.2	74.6	76.0	80.3	78.3	87.3	•	75.9	80.4	•
Salaries and Wages **11**	6.9	42.7	6.0	15.1	8.4	5.8	6.1	3.5	3.2	•	2.9	2.3	•
Taxes Paid **12**	2.0	2.5	1.8	2.6	2.1	7.9	1.6	3.4	1.1	•	4.5	1.8	•
Interest Paid **13**	2.4	0.1	1.1	3.5	1.2	4.2	0.9	4.7	1.0	•	5.6	7.6	•
Depreciation **14**	4.7	2.6	4.5	14.1	5.3	5.3	2.3	5.0	0.7	•	4.8	1.9	•
Amortization and Depletion **15**	0.5	0.0	0.0	0.1	0.0	0.2	0.2	1.0	0.2	•	20.3	1.0	•
Pensions and Other Deferred Comp. **16**	0.2	•	0.0	0.0	0.2	0.2	0.4	0.2	0.3	•	0.3	0.3	•
Employee Benefits **17**	0.8	2.0	1.1	0.3	0.7	1.0	1.0	2.1	1.0	•	1.1	0.1	•
Advertising **18**	0.1	0.0	0.0	0.1	0.2	0.2	0.3	0.2	0.1	•	0.1	0.1	•
Other Expenses **19**	13.7	27.5	17.8	38.8	10.4	15.3	5.1	11.2	6.3	•	20.4	6.7	•
Officers' Compensation **20**	2.3	0.0	3.4	3.8	2.4	1.5	2.5	1.8	1.0	•	1.1	0.3	•
Operating Margin **21**	•	•	3.5	2.5									
Operating Margin Before Officers' Comp. **22**	0.3	•	6.9	6.3	1.8								

Selected Average Balance Sheet ($ in Thousands)

Net Receivables 23	66	0	7	31	154	132	1481	1617	11053	•	4775	31316	•
Inventories 24	93	0	6	11	139	54	2441	1787	6015	•	5466	89633	•
Net Property, Plant and Equipment 25	528	0	59	552	1116	774	6619	16820	26674	•	87453	359003	•
Total Assets 26	1149	0	115	684	1981	9459	15622	34141	84162	•	299609	805956	•
Notes and Loans Payable 27	549	0	78	626	1381	299	3876	12284	23288	•	128551	350378	•
All Other Liabilities 28	216	0	11	22	195	203	2122	7038	14045	•	14814	296606	•
Net Worth 29	384	0	26	36	406	8957	9624	14820	46829	•	156245	158972	•

Selected Financial Ratios (Times to 1)

Current Ratio 30	1.6	•	2.5	0.9	1.2	5.8	2.2	1.2	1.1	•	4.1	1.6	•
Quick Ratio 31	0.8	•	2.0	0.6	0.6	0.5	0.9	0.6	0.8	•	3.5	0.6	•
Net Sales to Working Capital 32	13.6	•	21.7	•	31.8	0.8	5.2	13.9	32.6	•	1.3	9.6	•
Coverage Ratio 33	2.4	51.4	5.2	2.3	•	6.5	3.6	0.4	4.9	•	5.9	2.2	•
Total Asset Turnover 34	1.2	•	5.0	1.5	2.0	0.1	1.2	0.5	1.1	•	0.2	0.5	•
Inventory Turnover 35	10.3	•	58.6	18.4	21.0	15.2	6.1	7.2	13.5	•	7.9	3.9	•
Receivables Turnover 36	21.1	•	81.1	30.4	27.8	2.5	15.7	10.0	15.0	•	23.9	10.3	•
Total Liabilities to Net Worth 37	2.0	•	3.4	18.0	3.9	0.1	0.6	1.3	0.8	•	0.9	4.1	•
Current Assets to Working Capital 38	2.8	•	1.7	•	5.3	1.2	1.8	6.8	8.9	•	1.3	2.7	•
Current Liabilities to Working Capital 39	1.8	•	0.7	•	4.3	0.2	0.8	5.8	7.9	•	0.3	1.7	•
Working Capital to Net Sales 40	0.1	•	0.0	•	0.0	1.3	0.2	0.1	0.0	•	0.8	0.1	•
Inventory to Working Capital 41	0.6	•	0.2	•	1.0	0.0	0.9	1.5	1.6	•	0.1	0.1	•
Total Receipts to Cash Flow 42	7.6	12.2	5.3	2.8	16.5	26.6	21.0	15.6	11.7	•	3.4	8.9	•
Cost of Goods to Cash Flow 43	5.2	4.5	3.2	0.5	12.3	20.2	16.9	12.2	10.2	•	2.6	7.2	•
Cash Flow to Total Debt 44	0.2	•	1.2	0.6	0.2	0.1	0.1	0.1	0.2	•	0.1	0.1	•

Selected Financial Factors (in Percentages)

Debt Ratio 45	66.6	•	77.1	94.7	79.5	5.3	38.4	56.6	44.4	•	47.9	80.3	•
Return on Total Assets 46	6.8	•	27.4	12.1	•	3.2	3.7	1.0	5.1	•	6.3	8.9	•
Return on Equity Before Income Taxes 47	11.7	•	96.6	128.9	•	2.8	4.4	•	7.3	•	10.0	24.3	•
Return on Equity After Income Taxes 48	8.7	•	95.6	123.7	•	1.8	2.4	•	6.9	•	6.2	15.0	•
Profit Margin (Before Income Tax) 49	3.2	3.5	4.5	4.4	•	23.2	2.3	•	3.7	•	6.2	6.9	•
Profit Margin (After Income Tax) 50	2.4	3.0	4.4	4.3	•	14.6	1.2	•	3.4	•	5.5	•	•

Table II
Corporations with Net Income

FORESTRY AND LOGGING

MONEY AMOUNTS AND SIZE OF ASSETS IN THOUSANDS OF DOLLARS

Item Description for Accounting Period 7/05 Through 6/06	Total	Zero Assets	Under 500	500 to 1,000	1,000 to 5,000	5,000 to 10,000	10,000 to 25,000	25,000 to 50,000	50,000 to 100,000	100,000 to 250,000	250,000 to 500,000	500,000 to 2,500,000	2,500,000 and over
Number of Enterprises 1	6372	302	4888	713	394	7	49	7	•	0	•	•	0
Revenues ($ in Thousands)													
Net Sales 2	10442233	52234	3528656	928039	1418306	51286	1332293	194507	•	0	•	•	
Interest 3	58717	19	2064	423	2618	1182	1649	476	•	0	•	•	
Rents 4	59018	37	10916	600	5505	14	2660	15423	•	0	•	•	
Royalties 5	5301	0	0	3502	0	331	1222	0	•	0	•	•	
Other Portfolio Income 6	359350	2016	3683	10496	105451	17216	29411	381	•	0	•	•	
Other Receipts 7	200207	162	22826	358	12295	2652	7265	656	•	0	•	•	
Total Receipts 8	11124826	54468	3568145	943418	1544175	72681	1374500	211443	•	0	•	•	
Average Total Receipts 9	1746	180	730	1323	3919	10383	28051	30206	•	•	•	•	
Operating Costs/Operating Income (%)													
Cost of Operations 10	66.1	73.5	60.8	11.1	71.4	76.0	80.5	65.2	•	•	•	•	•
Salaries and Wages 11	6.1	2.0	6.4	16.7	5.7	5.8	6.0	4.9	•	•	•	•	•
Taxes Paid 12	1.9	0.4	1.5	2.9	2.7	7.7	1.3	3.4	•	•	•	•	•
Interest Paid 13	2.4	0.1	0.7	2.1	1.4	4.2	0.5	2.6	•	•	•	•	•
Depreciation 14	3.8	1.2	3.2	10.5	7.7	5.3	1.6	4.6	•	•	•	•	•
Amortization and Depletion 15	0.3	0.0	0.0	0.1	0.1	0.2	0.2	0.4	•	•	•	•	•
Pensions and Other Deferred Comp. 16	0.2	•	•	0.0	0.4	0.2	0.3	0.2	•	•	•	•	•
Employee Benefits 17	0.6	0.1	0.2	0.4	1.3	1.0	0.9	3.9	•	•	•	•	•
Advertising 18	0.2	0.0	0.1	0.1	0.5	0.2	0.3	0.2	•	•	•	•	•
Other Expenses 19	14.6	7.8	18.6	46.0	10.4	13.8	4.7	10.3	•	•	•	•	•
Officers' Compensation 20	1.8	0.1	2.3	2.6	2.2	1.5	2.2	1.9	•	•	•	•	•
Operating Margin 21	2.0	14.7	6.3	7.4	•	•	1.6	2.6	•	•	•	•	•
Operating Margin Before Officers' Comp. 22	3.8	14.8	8.6	10.1	•	•	3.8	4.4	•	•	•	•	•

Selected Average Balance Sheet ($ in Thousands)

Net Receivables 23	83	0	9	49	249	889	2231	1088
Inventories 24	131	0	7	10	346	244	2844	5686
Net Property, Plant and Equipment 25	479	0	56	518	1088	5195	4928	13467
Total Assets 26	1195	0	125	683	2017	7273	14653	31052
Notes and Loans Payable 27	571	0	73	588	991	2011	3735	12097
All Other Liabilities 28	305	0	11	28	190	1176	2603	4919
Net Worth 29	319	0	42	66	836	4087	8316	14035

Selected Financial Ratios (Times to 1)

Current Ratio 30	1.8	•	3.3	1.1	2.7	0.7	1.8	1.4
Quick Ratio 31	1.0	•	2.7	0.8	1.5	0.5	0.7	0.4
Net Sales to Working Capital 32	11.3	•	18.9	140.2	8.6	•	7.6	8.6
Coverage Ratio 33	4.5	140.6	12.0	5.3	4.7	7.1	10.1	5.3
Total Asset Turnover 34	1.4	•	5.8	1.9	1.8	1.0	1.9	0.9
Inventory Turnover 35	8.2	•	59.2	13.8	7.4	22.8	7.7	3.2
Receivables Turnover 36	19.4	•	73.4	23.3	13.6	16.5	17.3	11.4
Total Liabilities to Net Worth 37	2.7	•	2.0	9.3	1.4	0.8	0.8	1.2
Current Assets to Working Capital 38	2.2	•	1.4	16.5	1.6	•	2.2	3.3
Current Liabilities to Working Capital 39	1.2	•	0.4	15.5	0.6	•	1.2	2.3
Working Capital to Net Sales 40	0.1	•	0.1	0.0	0.1	•	0.1	0.1
Inventory to Working Capital 41	0.6	•	0.2	0.0	0.6	•	1.1	1.7
Total Receipts to Cash Flow 42	5.3	4.6	4.4	2.1	8.9	19.8	15.5	5.1
Cost of Goods to Cash Flow 43	3.5	3.4	2.7	0.2	6.4	15.1	12.5	3.3
Cash Flow to Total Debt 44	0.4	•	2.0	1.0	0.3	0.1	0.3	0.3

Selected Financial Factors (in Percentages)

Debt Ratio 45	73.3	•	66.9	90.3	58.6	43.8	43.3	54.8
Return on Total Assets 46	15.0	•	46.3	21.3	11.5	30.5	9.7	12.3
Return on Equity Before Income Taxes 47	43.7	•	128.2	177.0	21.7	46.6	15.4	22.1
Return on Equity After Income Taxes 48	37.4	•	127.3	172.1	21.2	31.2	11.5	20.4
Profit Margin (Before Income Tax) 49	8.5	19.0	7.4	9.0	5.0	26.0	4.7	11.2
Profit Margin (After Income Tax) 50	7.3	18.1	7.3	8.8	4.9	17.4	3.5	10.3

Table I

Corporations with and without Net Income

SUPPORT ACTIVITIES AND FISHING, HUNTING AND TRAPPING

MONEY AMOUNTS AND SIZE OF ASSETS IN THOUSANDS OF DOLLARS

Item Description for Accounting Period 7/05 Through 6/06	Total	Zero Assets	Under 500	500 to 1,000	1,000 to 5,000	5,000 to 10,000	10,000 to 25,000	25,000 to 50,000	50,000 to 100,000	100,000 to 250,000	250,000 to 500,000	500,000 to 2,500,000	2,500,000 and over
Number of Enterprises **1**	30001	6065	19773	2197	1565	258	106	27	7	4	0	0	0
Revenues ($ in Thousands)													
Net Sales **2**	21837837	872783	5525019	2939210	5344876	2500370	2061366	950835	513445	1129932	0	0	0
Interest **3**	23460	1206	1962	2357	8818	1256	1760	2671	2381	1048	0	0	0
Rents **4**	21079	769	8544	4795	3549	970	2451	0	0	0	0	0	0
Royalties **5**	328	0	0	0	0	0	0	0	0	328	0	0	0
Other Portfolio Income **6**	380495	173777	28549	24269	44779	31204	27078	2228	39681	8931	0	0	0
Other Receipts **7**	667683	4349	177480	239796	30239	65624	56027	53076	18019	23075	0	0	0
Total Receipts **8**	22930882	1052884	5741554	3210427	5432261	2599424	2148682	1008810	573526	1163314	•		
Average Total Receipts **9**	764	174	290	1461	3471	10075	20271	37363	81932	290828	•		
Operating Costs/Operating Income (%)													
Cost of Operations **10**	56.5	34.4	40.4	55.8	61.6	61.5	72.9	71.7	57.5	75.1	•	•	•
Salaries and Wages **11**	8.7	20.7	8.7	8.5	7.9	10.8	6.4	4.4	13.6	4.3	•	•	•
Taxes Paid **12**	2.3	4.7	2.8	1.6	2.2	1.8	1.8	1.1	2.3	2.9	•	•	•
Interest Paid **13**	1.3	1.1	1.3	0.7	1.2	1.2	1.3	1.7	2.6	2.8	•	•	•
Depreciation **14**	3.4	2.3	3.2	4.8	3.1	4.3	2.5	3.6	4.3	2.3	•	•	•
Amortization and Depletion **15**	0.1	0.0	0.1	0.0	0.3	0.0	0.1	0.1	0.1	0.3	•	•	•
Pensions and Other Deferred Comp. **16**	0.2	0.0	0.1	0.2	0.0	1.0	0.3	0.2	0.2	0.1	•	•	•
Employee Benefits **17**	0.6	0.1	0.7	0.7	0.5	0.9	0.6	0.6	1.9	0.4	•	•	•
Advertising **18**	0.5	0.1	0.8	0.1	0.1	1.1	0.2	0.1	0.8	0.4	•	•	•
Other Expenses **19**	23.8	41.2	35.6	25.3	21.4	14.9	11.7	17.2	13.5	11.5	•	•	•
Officers' Compensation **20**	3.5	1.3	5.6	7.2	1.9	3.6	1.3	0.8	1.7	0.6	•	•	•
Operating Margin **21**	•	•	0.7	•	•	•	0.9	•	1.6	•	•	•	•
Operating Margin Before Officers' Comp. **22**	2.6	•	6.3	2.3	1.6	2.5	2.2	•	3.3	•	•	•	•

Selected Average Balance Sheet ($ in Thousands)

Net Receivables 23	61	0	8	61	312	1148	3468	5947	11203	38690
Inventories 24	37	0	3	19	105	592	2039	5983	25531	75787
Net Property, Plant and Equipment 25	156	0	46	306	730	3175	4629	11413	14068	56997
Total Assets 26	405	0	100	711	1808	7048	14553	33528	71211	255580
Notes and Loans Payable 27	229	0	125	295	985	2236	5271	15207	36104	101330
All Other Liabilities 28	79	0	10	74	418	1045	3803	9122	23856	68476
Net Worth 29	97	0	-35	342	405	3766	5478	9199	11251	85773

Selected Financial Ratios (Times to 1)

Current Ratio 30	1.5	•	1.6	2.1	1.4	1.6	1.3	1.4	1.2	1.9
Quick Ratio 31	1.1	•	1.3	1.6	1.1	1.2	0.8	0.9	0.9	0.7
Net Sales to Working Capital 32	12.0	•	23.1	8.7	15.8	8.5	11.9	7.4	11.2	4.4
Coverage Ratio 33	4.2	14.2	4.6	7.2	2.1	3.4	4.9	3.7	6.1	2.0
Total Asset Turnover 34	1.8	•	2.8	1.9	1.9	1.4	1.3	1.1	1.0	1.1
Inventory Turnover 35	11.0	•	39.3	40.1	19.9	10.1	7.0	4.2	1.7	2.8
Receivables Turnover 36	13.5	•	37.5	30.3	14.2	8.6	6.1	5.4	4.5	14.6
Total Liabilities to Net Worth 37	3.2	•	1.1	1.1	3.5	0.9	1.7	2.6	5.3	2.0
Current Assets to Working Capital 38	2.8	•	2.8	1.9	3.3	2.6	4.4	3.3	5.2	2.1
Current Liabilities to Working Capital 39	1.8	•	1.8	0.9	2.3	1.6	3.4	2.3	4.2	1.1
Working Capital to Net Sales 40	0.1	•	0.0	0.1	0.1	0.1	0.1	0.1	0.1	0.2
Inventory to Working Capital 41	0.7	•	0.2	0.2	0.7	0.5	1.3	1.2	1.1	1.2
Total Receipts to Cash Flow 42	4.6	3.0	3.4	3.9	5.3	6.6	7.3	5.1	4.2	8.3
Cost of Goods to Cash Flow 43	2.6	1.0	1.4	2.2	3.3	4.1	5.4	3.6	2.4	6.2
Cash Flow to Total Debt 44	0.5	•	0.6	0.9	0.5	0.4	0.3	0.3	0.3	0.2

Selected Financial Factors (in Percentages)

Debt Ratio 45	76.0	•	134.5	51.9	77.6	46.6	62.4	72.6	84.2	66.4
Return on Total Assets 46	9.7	•	16.4	9.3	4.7	5.6	8.5	6.5	16.4	6.2
Return on Equity Before Income Taxes 47	30.7	•	•	16.6	11.2	7.4	18.0	17.5	86.5	9.1
Return on Equity After Income Taxes 48	27.9	•	•	15.9	10.7	7.0	17.5	16.5	78.8	2.0
Profit Margin (Before Income Tax) 49	4.1	14.7	4.6	4.2	1.3	2.9	5.1	4.6	13.3	2.8
Profit Margin (After Income Tax) 50	3.7	10.9	4.6	4.1	1.3	2.7	4.9	4.3	12.1	0.6

Table II

Corporations with Net Income

SUPPORT ACTIVITIES AND FISHING, HUNTING AND TRAPPING

MONEY AMOUNTS AND SIZE OF ASSETS IN THOUSANDS OF DOLLARS

Item Description for Accounting Period 7/05 Through 6/06	Total	Zero Assets	Under 500	500 to 1,000	1,000 to 5,000	5,000 to 10,000	10,000 to 25,000	25,000 to 50,000	50,000 to 100,000	100,000 to 250,000	250,000 to 500,000	500,000 to 2,500,000	2,500,000 and over
Number of Enterprises **1**	14508	2316	9505	1210	1189	185	75	19	•	•	0	0	0
Revenues ($ in Thousands)													
Net Sales **2**	17702162	413971	3841778	2412072	4808162	2056080	1676640	878887	•	•	0	0	0
Interest **3**	17344	1206	160	1717	7071	1207	1754	894	•	•	0	0	0
Rents **4**	13099	769	3543	4745	621	970	2451	0	•	•	0	0	0
Royalties **5**	328	0	0	0	0	0	0	0	•	•	0	0	0
Other Portfolio Income **6**	334547	170568	15582	12856	42813	24547	26828	412	•	•	0	0	0
Other Receipts **7**	545723	3673	166071	77905	68481	100606	42421	46154	•	•	0	0	0
Total Receipts **8**	18613203	590187	4027134	2509295	4927148	2183410	1750094	926347	•	•	0	0	0
Average Total Receipts **9**	1283	255	424	2074	4144	11802	23335	48755	•	•	•	•	•
Operating Costs/Operating Income (%)													
Cost of Operations **10**	59.8	63.4	43.1	62.1	62.6	58.5	70.6	72.0	•	•	•	•	•
Salaries and Wages **11**	7.2	1.9	5.4	6.0	7.9	13.1	7.2	4.2	•	•	•	•	•
Taxes Paid **12**	2.0	2.8	2.4	1.0	2.1	1.7	1.6	0.9	•	•	•	•	•
Interest Paid **13**	1.1	1.9	1.2	0.3	1.0	1.0	1.2	1.1	•	•	•	•	•
Depreciation **14**	2.7	2.5	2.6	2.4	2.6	4.6	2.1	2.1	•	•	•	•	•
Amortization and Depletion **15**	0.1	0.0	0.0	0.0	0.3	0.0	0.0	0.1	•	•	•	•	•
Pensions and Other Deferred Comp. **16**	0.3	0.0	0.1	0.3	0.0	1.2	0.3	0.2	•	•	•	•	•
Employee Benefits **17**	0.5	0.2	0.4	0.2	0.5	0.9	0.6	0.4	•	•	•	•	•
Advertising **18**	0.5	0.1	0.9	0.1	0.1	1.3	0.2	0.1	•	•	•	•	•
Other Expenses **19**	19.7	19.9	33.2	16.2	19.2	16.0	11.6	16.1	•	•	•	•	•
Officers' Compensation **20**	2.9	1.7	4.9	6.8	1.5	2.3	1.3	0.8	•	•	•	•	•
Operating Margin **21**	3.2	5.6	5.7	4.6	2.0	•	3.2	2.1	•	•	•	•	•
Operating Margin Before Officers' Comp. **22**	6.2	7.3	10.6	11.4	3.6	1.7	4.5	2.9	•	•	•	•	•

Selected Average Balance Sheet ($ in Thousands)

Net Receivables 23	96	0	11	95	251	1194	4101	7769
Inventories 24	65	0	3	24	121	781	2006	6795
Net Property, Plant and Equipment 25	192	0	60	174	650	2556	3172	10749
Total Assets 26	584	0	130	719	1711	7156	14060	34410
Notes and Loans Payable 27	271	0	151	136	710	2287	4849	14209
All Other Liabilities 28	131	0	12	101	422	1022	4457	11370
Net Worth 29	182	0	-33	481	579	3847	4753	8831

Selected Financial Ratios (Times to 1)

Current Ratio 30	1.6	•	2.1	2.4	1.2	2.1	1.3	1.4
Quick Ratio 31	1.1	•	1.8	2.2	0.9	1.6	0.8	0.8
Net Sales to Working Capital 32	11.5	•	16.5	8.8	28.9	6.0	12.4	8.2
Coverage Ratio 33	8.9	26.7	9.7	32.9	5.3	6.7	7.3	8.0
Total Asset Turnover 34	2.1	•	3.1	2.8	2.4	1.6	1.6	1.3
Inventory Turnover 35	11.3	•	53.1	52.6	21.0	8.3	7.9	4.9
Receivables Turnover 36	14.1	•	36.7	28.5	18.5	8.5	6.0	6.7
Total Liabilities to Net Worth 37	2.2	•	•	0.5	2.0	0.9	2.0	2.9
Current Assets to Working Capital 38	2.7	•	1.9	1.7	5.0	1.9	4.3	3.5
Current Liabilities to Working Capital 39	1.7	•	0.9	0.7	4.0	0.9	3.3	2.5
Working Capital to Net Sales 40	0.1	•	0.1	0.1	0.0	0.2	0.1	0.1
Inventory to Working Capital 41	0.7	•	0.1	0.1	1.2	0.4	1.2	1.4
Total Receipts to Cash Flow 42	4.4	2.6	3.1	4.5	4.8	5.2	6.2	4.5
Cost of Goods to Cash Flow 43	2.6	1.6	1.4	2.8	3.0	3.1	4.4	3.2
Cash Flow to Total Debt 44	0.7	•	0.8	1.9	0.7	0.6	0.4	0.4

Selected Financial Factors (in Percentages)

Debt Ratio 45	68.8	•	125.6	33.0	66.2	46.2	66.2	74.3
Return on Total Assets 46	19.7	•	36.6	24.8	13.1	10.3	14.0	11.5
Return on Equity Before Income Taxes 47	56.2	•	•	35.8	31.3	16.3	35.6	39.2
Return on Equity After Income Taxes 48	53.1	48.1	•	35.0	30.8	15.8	34.8	37.8
Profit Margin (Before Income Tax) 49	8.4	•	10.5	8.7	4.5	5.7	7.6	7.5
Profit Margin (After Income Tax) 50	7.9	40.1	10.5	8.4	4.4	5.5	7.4	7.2

Table I

Corporations with and without Net Income

OIL AND GAS EXTRACTION

MONEY AMOUNTS AND SIZE OF ASSETS IN THOUSANDS OF DOLLARS

Item Description for Accounting Period 7/05 Through 6/06	Total	Zero Assets	Under 500	500 to 1,000	1,000 to 5,000	5,000 to 10,000	10,000 to 25,000	25,000 to 50,000	50,000 to 100,000	100,000 to 250,000	250,000 to 500,000	500,000 to 2,500,000	2,500,000 and over
Number of Enterprises 1	17097	2238	10721	928	1828	550	368	187	89	82	38	49	19

Revenues ($ in Thousands)

	Total	Zero Assets	Under 500	500 to 1,000	1,000 to 5,000	5,000 to 10,000	10,000 to 25,000	25,000 to 50,000	50,000 to 100,000	100,000 to 250,000	250,000 to 500,000	500,000 to 2,500,000	2,500,000 and over
Net Sales 2	142424188	2115217	3127857	586404	5503620	2574035	3780347	2402456	3535675	5509285	5345094	17930937	90013262
Interest 3	1877104	49222	9975	3964	10578	7947	18190	26714	24183	102443	71170	193061	1359657
Rents 4	103865	181	5668	1027	13343	9530	7733	9507	14463	10184	5646	7133	19451
Royalties 5	951913	363	38543	2239	70642	16044	74601	14686	19622	44068	10737	96931	563438
Other Portfolio Income 6	10600016	195670	69209	6629	162678	101425	279698	163073	239499	221820	260215	799630	8100474
Other Receipts 7	8884346	230733	165093	62081	342819	222969	337609	289226	408820	320001	338560	960577	5205851
Total Receipts 8	164841432	2591386	3416345	662344	6103680	2931950	4498178	2905662	4242262	6207801	6031422	19988269	105262133
Average Total Receipts 9	9642	1158	319	714	3339	5331	12223	15538	47666	75705	158722	407924	5540112

Operating Costs/Operating Income (%)

	Total	Zero Assets	Under 500	500 to 1,000	1,000 to 5,000	5,000 to 10,000	10,000 to 25,000	25,000 to 50,000	50,000 to 100,000	100,000 to 250,000	250,000 to 500,000	500,000 to 2,500,000	2,500,000 and over
Cost of Operations 10	50.5	18.3	26.2	12.5	54.5	28.8	44.6	25.9	40.2	32.8	33.0	26.2	60.9
Salaries and Wages 11	4.0	6.8	9.1	3.9	7.1	5.2	7.4	6.9	7.7	5.4	5.3	4.5	2.9
Taxes Paid 12	3.1	1.1	3.9	5.4	2.6	4.6	3.3	4.9	3.6	3.5	3.4	4.0	2.8
Interest Paid 13	3.8	11.7	0.9	0.5	1.4	1.0	1.6	2.6	1.6	3.5	3.6	4.3	4.1
Depreciation 14	3.4	14.5	2.7	4.7	1.9	3.7	3.8	5.1	3.6	4.9	5.1	5.4	2.6
Amortization and Depletion 15	3.9	3.8	1.3	6.2	1.8	4.2	3.6	8.8	4.1	7.4	6.4	8.3	2.7
Pensions and Other Deferred Comp. 16	0.4	0.1	1.0	1.0	0.0	0.4	1.1	0.2	0.9	0.1	0.1	0.2	0.4
Employee Benefits 17	0.4	0.5	1.2	0.2	0.6	1.0	0.7	0.7	0.6	0.5	0.4	0.5	0.3
Advertising 18	0.0	0.0	0.1	0.0	0.2	0.0	0.1	0.2	0.1	0.0	0.0	0.0	0.0
Other Expenses 19	21.7	23.2	32.8	43.7	20.4	28.6	31.4	33.1	27.2	31.3	28.4	38.4	15.7
Officers' Compensation 20	1.3	3.7	8.6	4.1	2.3	3.1	3.1	2.9	2.4	2.0	1.0	1.2	0.7
Operating Margin 21	7.6	16.2	12.2	17.7	7.3	19.5	•	8.4	7.9	8.6	13.0	7.1	6.9
Operating Margin Before Officers' Comp. 22	8.9	19.9	20.8	21.8	9.5	22.6	2.5	11.3	10.3	10.6	14.1	8.2	7.6

Selected Average Balance Sheet ($ in Thousands)

	2014												
Net Receivables 23	2014	0	33	11	305	549	2557	3875	10119	18711	51656	101464	1166954
Inventories 24	132	0	2	1	26	29	147	179	1318	1788	1854	11344	62871
Net Property, Plant and Equipment 25	7556	0	41	157	570	1827	4672	13242	27287	71508	170122	644640	4000633
Total Assets 26	17736	0	131	676	2218	7638	15200	35805	69881	149944	347071	1049791	10395597
Notes and Loans Payable 27	4464	0	45	65	827	823	3481	8772	13391	39900	86844	265631	2637379
All Other Liabilities 28	5367	0	26	268	686	1572	4942	7649	19545	36508	82905	286375	3365460
Net Worth 29	7906	0	60	343	704	5243	6776	19384	36945	73536	177322	497785	4392759

Selected Financial Ratios (Times to 1)

Current Ratio 30	1.2	•	2.4	2.2	1.2	2.5	1.5	1.8	1.6	1.8		1.2	1.1
Quick Ratio 31	1.0	•	2.3	1.9	1.0	1.6	1.2	1.4	1.3	1.4		0.9	0.9
Net Sales to Working Capital 32	12.3	•	7.0	3.3	21.3	2.4	4.3	2.3	3.9	3.1		13.5	42.3
Coverage Ratio 33	7.5	4.5	25.3	57.0	14.0	35.2	12.4	12.0	18.1	7.0	8.5	5.7	7.2
Total Asset Turnover 34	0.5	•	2.2	0.9	1.4	0.6	0.7	0.4	0.6	0.4	0.4	0.3	0.5
Inventory Turnover 35	31.9	•	47.7	107.4	61.9	46.1	31.1	18.6	12.1	25.0	8.4	5.7	7.2
Receivables Turnover 36	4.9	•	9.7	24.4	7.1	7.9	4.8	3.7	4.4	4.3	3.2	4.1	45.9
Total Liabilities to Net Worth 37	1.2	•	1.2	1.0	2.1	0.5	1.2	0.8	0.9	1.0	1.0	1.1	4.9
Current Assets to Working Capital 38	5.3	•	1.7	1.8	6.6	1.7	3.1	2.3	2.7	2.5	2.2	7.4	1.4
Current Liabilities to Working Capital 39	4.3	•	0.7	0.8	5.6	0.7	2.1	1.3	1.7	1.5	1.2	6.4	14.9
Working Capital to Net Sales 40	0.1	•	0.1	0.3	0.0	0.4	0.2	0.4	0.3	0.3	0.1	0.1	13.9
Inventory to Working Capital 41	0.2	•	0.0	0.0	0.2	0.0	0.1	0.0	0.1	0.1	0.1	0.5	0.0
Total Receipts to Cash Flow 42	2.4	1.8	2.1	1.5	3.3	1.8	2.3	1.8	2.0	2.2	2.0	1.8	0.7
Cost of Goods to Cash Flow 43	1.2	0.3	0.5	0.2	1.8	0.5	1.0	0.5	0.8	0.7	0.7	0.5	2.8
Cash Flow to Total Debt 44	0.3	•	2.0	1.3	0.6	1.1	0.5	0.4	0.6	0.4	0.4	0.4	1.7

Selected Financial Factors (in Percentages)

Debt Ratio 45	55.4	•	54.2	49.2	68.2	31.4	55.4	45.9	47.1	51.0	48.9	52.6	57.7
Return on Total Assets 46	13.3	•	49.7	29.2	26.5	20.8	13.5	11.4	16.7	11.1	12.2	8.5	13.4
Return on Equity Before Income Taxes 47	25.9	•	104.2	56.5	77.4	29.4	27.8	19.3	29.8	19.3	21.1	14.7	27.4
Return on Equity After Income Taxes 48	19.3	•	97.5	54.9	74.7	28.0	25.8	16.3	25.4	14.9	16.8	10.8	19.2
Profit Margin (Before Income Tax) 49	24.6	40.8	21.4	30.7	18.1	33.0	18.3	29.2	27.7	21.2	26.6	20.0	25.4
Profit Margin (After Income Tax) 50	18.3	36.7	20.1	29.8	17.5	31.4	17.0	24.6	23.6	16.3	21.1	14.7	17.8

Table II

Corporations with Net Income

OIL AND GAS EXTRACTION

MONEY AMOUNTS AND SIZE OF ASSETS IN THOUSANDS OF DOLLARS

Item Description for Accounting Period 7/05 Through 6/06	Total	Zero Assets	Under 500	500 to 1,000	1,000 to 5,000	5,000 to 10,000	10,000 to 25,000	25,000 to 50,000	50,000 to 100,000	100,000 to 250,000	250,000 to 500,000	500,000 to 2,500,000	2,500,000 and over
Number of Enterprises **1**	10847	463	7418	597	1284	488	282	126	64	50	27	32	16
Revenues ($ in Thousands)													
Net Sales **2**	127475869	1784471	2491267	458727	3227718	2494331	3589177	2100835	2620278	4242542	4575469	13225287	86665767
Interest **3**	1732445	2544	9748	2045	8693	7559	12324	18434	18506	82116	58123	161296	1351057
Rents **4**	97715	52	5668	1027	13304	9530	7650	9024	11786	9504	5591	6613	17965
Royalties **5**	941964	70	35015	2239	69789	15516	74338	13284	19622	41000	10737	96916	563438
Other Portfolio Income **6**	10455584	188280	62377	6207	157995	101425	274234	150337	222266	175752	242586	786452	8087676
Other Receipts **7**	8750232	208668	187572	59083	294325	221127	275485	258753	393192	206046	201644	813520	5630815
Total Receipts **8**	149453809	2184085	2791647	529328	3771824	2849488	4233208	2550667	3285650	4756960	5094150	15090084	102316718
Average Total Receipts **9**	13778	4717	376	887	2938	5839	15011	20243	51338	95139	188672	471565	6394795
Operating Costs/Operating Income (%)													
Cost of Operations **10**	52.0	19.3	27.4	13.3	47.0	29.6	45.7	22.8	26.3	27.3	33.4	31.5	61.4
Salaries and Wages **11**	3.6	1.6	8.5	1.6	7.1	4.9	6.1	5.8	9.1	4.2	5.5	4.4	2.8
Taxes Paid **12**	3.2	0.5	3.5	4.4	3.3	4.6	3.1	5.0	4.4	3.7	3.7	4.1	2.9
Interest Paid **13**	3.5	7.5	0.4	0.4	1.5	0.7	1.1	1.7	1.3	2.2	2.6	3.2	4.1
Depreciation **14**	3.1	16.1	2.2	4.0	2.0	3.5	3.2	4.8	3.8	4.2	4.6	4.9	2.5
Amortization and Depletion **15**	3.2	2.0	1.6	7.9	2.0	3.8	2.3	6.8	3.7	5.5	4.2	6.1	2.6
Pensions and Other Deferred Comp. **16**	0.4	0.0	1.2	1.3	0.1	0.4	1.1	0.2	0.7	0.1	0.2	0.2	0.4
Employee Benefits **17**	0.4	0.5	1.1	0.1	0.5	1.0	0.6	0.7	0.5	0.5	0.4	0.5	0.3
Advertising **18**	0.0	0.0	0.1	*	0.2	0.0	0.1	0.2	0.2	0.0	0.0	0.0	0.0
Other Expenses **19**	18.8	13.6	27.2	27.4	16.2	23.3	26.1	25.8	27.1	27.0	22.5	30.7	15.4
Officers' Compensation **20**	1.1	0.1	7.1	2.8	1.7	2.9	2.9	2.5	2.5	1.6	0.9	1.2	0.7
Operating Margin **21**	10.7	38.8	19.7	36.8	18.4	25.2	7.7	23.7	20.5	23.5	22.0	13.3	7.0
Operating Margin Before Officers' Comp. **22**	11.9	38.8	26.8	39.7	20.1	28.1	10.6	26.2	23.0	25.1	22.9	14.5	7.7

Selected Average Balance Sheet ($ in Thousands)

Net Receivables 23	2869	0	42	3	343	562	2667	4169	11048	23671	64978	109122	1354814
Inventories 24	168	0	0	1	20	25	157	198	1585	1760	2427	8099	87628
Net Property, Plant and Equipment 25	9144	0	46	86	572	1472	3884	12980	23381	67632	159576	542632	4253242
Total Assets 26	22515	0	147	695	2283	7640	14624	36163	68316	148446	347028	993684	10900585
Notes and Loans Payable 27	5257	0	39	11	777	676	2846	5908	9590	33829	72960	196417	2706003
All Other Liabilities 28	6645	0	30	175	573	1171	4766	7702	17209	38525	84528	270803	3384412
Net Worth 29	10613	0	78	510	932	5793	7012	22553	41517	76091	189540	526464	4810170

Selected Financial Ratios (Times to 1)

Current Ratio 30	1.4	•	2.5	2.4	1.7	2.5	1.6	2.0	1.9	1.6	2.3	1.5	1.3
Quick Ratio 31	1.2	•	2.4	2.0	1.4	1.6	1.3	1.6	1.5	1.4	1.8	1.2	1.1
Net Sales to Working Capital 32	7.9	•	6.2	3.2	5.2	2.4	4.3	2.3	2.9	4.1	2.5	5.9	14.0
Coverage Ratio 33	9.3	9.5	76.9	148.4	25.1	53.9	24.2	27.7	36.6	16.9	14.1	10.1	7.6
Total Asset Turnover 34	0.5	•	2.3	1.1	1.1	0.7	0.9	0.5	0.6	0.6	0.5	0.4	0.5
Inventory Turnover 35	36.4	•	916.6	103.3	58.1	59.4	36.9	19.1	6.8	13.2	23.3	16.1	38.0
Receivables Turnover 36	4.8	•	8.5	24.1	5.2	9.2	6.2	4.2	4.3	4.1	5.2	7.6	8.0
Total Liabilities to Net Worth 37	1.1	•	0.9	0.4	1.4	0.3	1.1	0.6	0.6	1.0	0.8	0.9	1.3
Current Assets to Working Capital 38	3.3	•	1.7	1.7	2.4	1.7	2.6	2.0	2.1	2.6	1.8	3.1	5.0
Current Liabilities to Working Capital 39	2.3	•	0.7	0.7	1.4	0.7	1.6	1.0	1.1	1.6	0.8	2.1	4.0
Working Capital to Net Sales 40	0.1	•	0.2	0.3	0.2	0.4	0.2	0.4	0.3	0.2	0.4	0.2	0.1
Inventory to Working Capital 41	0.1	•	•	0.0	0.1	0.0	0.1	0.0	0.1	0.1	0.0	0.1	0.2
Total Receipts to Cash Flow 42	2.3	1.4	1.9	1.3	2.1	1.7	2.2	1.6	1.5	1.8	1.9	1.8	2.7
Cost of Goods to Cash Flow 43	1.2	0.3	0.5	0.2	1.0	0.5	1.0	0.4	0.4	0.5	0.6	0.6	1.7
Cash Flow to Total Debt 44	0.4	•	2.6	3.2	0.9	1.6	0.8	0.8	1.0	0.7	0.6	0.5	0.3

Selected Financial Factors (in Percentages)

Debt Ratio 45	52.9	•	47.0	26.7	59.2	24.2	52.0	37.6	39.2	48.7	45.4	47.0	55.9
Return on Total Assets 46	17.2	•	73.4	58.1	40.4	26.6	23.2	21.5	28.2	21.6	18.0	13.5	15.3
Return on Equity Before Income Taxes 47	32.5	•	136.8	78.7	94.9	34.5	46.4	33.2	45.1	39.6	30.6	23.0	30.1
Return on Equity After Income Taxes 48	24.8	•	129.3	77.0	92.1	33.0	44.0	29.3	39.7	32.5	24.9	17.4	21.1
Profit Margin (Before Income Tax) 49	29.4	63.7	31.7	52.2	35.2	39.1	25.6	45.0	45.7	35.5	34.2	29.3	26.7
Profit Margin (After Income Tax) 50	22.4	58.8	30.0	51.1	34.1	37.4	24.2	39.7	40.2	29.2	27.8	22.2	18.8

8

Table I

Corporations with and without Net Income

COAL MINING

MONEY AMOUNTS AND SIZE OF ASSETS IN THOUSANDS OF DOLLARS

Item Description for Accounting Period 7/05 Through 6/06	Total	Zero Assets	Under 500	500 to 1,000	1,000 to 5,000	5,000 to 10,000	10,000 to 25,000	25,000 to 50,000	50,000 to 100,000	100,000 to 250,000	250,000 to 500,000	500,000 to 2,500,000	2,500,000 and over
Number of Enterprises 1	987	9	596	57	141	90	38	25	10	8	0	10	3
Revenues ($ in Thousands)													
Net Sales 2	20480102	253496	73892	62436	1105167	1078598	1351284	1159851	938361	1435381	0	4991509	8030125
Interest 3	189251	230	462	0	746	664	1791	281	581	3105	0	57596	123798
Rents 4	35335	35	0	0	19038	171	1459	1	556	1456	0	2829	9791
Royalties 5	168158	769	0	0	0	196	3652	0	983	191	0	57537	104829
Other Portfolio Income 6	1785017	21434	32965	0	8494	7066	6302	8523	8463	1009	0	132544	1558216
Other Receipts 7	971909	26125	2095	0	6201	5439	2951	11393	17429	18187	0	606422	275667
Total Receipts 8	23629772	302089	109414	62436	1139646	1092134	1367439	1180049	966373	1459329	0	5848437	10102426
Average Total Receipts 9	23941	33565	184	1095	8083	12135	35985	47202	96637	182416	•	584844	3367475
Operating Costs/Operating Income (%)													
Cost of Operations 10	66.0	64.5	83.2	0.8	67.2	56.3	83.2	63.8	40.4	82.1	•	71.7	61.6
Salaries and Wages 11	3.6	8.4	10.8	4.4	2.2	6.8	1.7	3.0	7.7	1.0	•	5.4	2.3
Taxes Paid 12	6.8	5.8	26.2	5.7	5.5	5.0	2.4	4.6	4.9	1.6	•	7.7	8.6
Interest Paid 13	2.8	2.4	1.8	0.1	0.9	1.2	0.4	1.2	2.0	1.4	•	5.0	3.1
Depreciation 14	4.4	3.6	3.4	11.9	3.4	5.5	1.8	5.7	5.1	1.8	•	4.9	4.5
Amortization and Depletion 15	4.7	3.2	•	•	0.0	2.4	1.6	5.4	3.6	2.8	•	5.4	6.3
Pensions and Other Deferred Comp. 16	1.0	0.4	•	•	•	0.1	0.1	0.2	0.3	0.4	•	1.4	1.6
Employee Benefits 17	3.8	6.4	0.0	•	3.7	0.9	1.3	1.1	2.7	1.2	•	4.7	5.0
Advertising 18	0.1	0.0	•	•	0.2	0.0	0.0	0.0	0.0	0.0	•	0.1	0.1
Other Expenses 19	28.0	18.8	20.6	3.6	22.0	22.3	5.6	11.9	37.7	6.6	•	9.6	50.3
Officers' Compensation 20	1.0	0.1	41.5	0.7	0.3	0.7	0.6	0.7	0.1	•	•	1.4	0.8
Operating Margin 21	•	•	32.0	•	•	•	1.1	2.2	•	1.0	•	•	•
Operating Margin Before Officers' Comp. 22	•	•	73.5	•	•	•	1.8	2.8	•	1.1	•	•	•

Selected Average Balance Sheet ($ in Thousands)

Net Receivables 23	10035	0	19	0	381	740	2633	4596	10900	18516	82126	2826530
Inventories 24	1089	0	0	0	20	96	1302	838	2552	6181	19499	240103
Net Property, Plant and Equipment 25	13769	0	8	352	891	2717	4349	16445	26608	49536	394126	2671733
Total Assets 26	39659	0	153	813	2017	7756	14095	36056	67860	157406	993630	8237304
Notes and Loans Payable 27	8326	0	25	194	1219	1949	3179	9560	33300	62327	248403	1389666
All Other Liabilities 28	19419	0	65	385	897	1429	5412	11562	17346	37057	412015	4558716
Net Worth 29	11914	0	63	234	-99	4377	5504	14934	17213	58021	333213	2258922

Selected Financial Ratios (Times to 1)

Current Ratio 30	1.3	•	1.2	1.6	0.7	1.5	1.2	1.5	1.3	1.0	1.0	1.3
Quick Ratio 31	1.1	•	0.3	1.6	0.6	1.3	1.0	1.2	1.2	0.7	0.7	1.2
Net Sales to Working Capital 32	6.5	•	7.3	6.7	•	16.0	26.1	14.6	15.3	152.8	89.8	2.8
Coverage Ratio 33	•	3.4	2.2	339.5	•	1.3	6.9	4.2	•	2.9	0.8	•
Total Asset Turnover 34	0.5	•	0.8	1.3	3.9	1.5	2.5	1.3	1.4	1.1	0.5	0.3
Inventory Turnover 35	12.6	•	•	•	264.2	70.4	22.7	35.3	14.8	23.8	18.3	6.9
Receivables Turnover 36	3.0	5.1	•	38.5	•	17.6	27.0	11.7	6.9	14.6	5.2	1.6
Total Liabilities to Net Worth 37	2.3	•	1.4	2.5	•	0.8	1.6	1.4	2.9	1.7	2.0	2.6
Current Assets to Working Capital 38	4.6	•	6.1	2.8	•	3.0	5.1	3.2	3.9	33.6	34.5	3.9
Current Liabilities to Working Capital 39	3.6	•	5.1	1.8	•	2.0	4.1	2.2	2.9	32.6	33.5	2.9
Working Capital to Net Sales 40	0.2	•	0.1	0.1	•	0.0	0.0	0.1	0.1	0.0	0.0	0.4
Inventory to Working Capital 41	0.4	•	•	•	•	0.1	1.0	0.3	0.1	6.9	4.2	0.3
Total Receipts to Cash Flow 42	25.2	5.4	•	10.5	2.8	9.1	17.5	8.4	3.9	15.6	31.6	•
Cost of Goods to Cash Flow 43	16.6	3.5	•	7.0	0.0	5.1	14.6	5.4	1.6	12.8	22.6	•
Cash Flow to Total Debt 44	0.0	•	0.7	0.4	•	0.2	0.4	0.3	0.5	0.1	0.0	•

Selected Financial Factors (in Percentages)

Debt Ratio 45	70.0	•	58.7	71.3	104.9	43.6	61.0	58.6	74.6	63.1	66.5	72.6
Return on Total Assets 46	•	•	3.1	43.2	•	2.5	6.9	6.6	•	•	4.6	1.9
Return on Equity Before Income Taxes 47	•	•	4.0	150.0	211.1	1.1	15.0	12.2	•	8.3	•	•
Return on Equity After Income Taxes 48	•	•	4.0	102.0	309.7	0.6	12.5	11.5	•	7.7	•	•
Profit Margin (Before Income Tax) 49	5.7	2.1	2.1	32.0	•	0.4	2.3	3.9	•	2.7	•	•
Profit Margin (After Income Tax) 50	5.7	2.1	2.1	21.8	•	0.2	1.9	3.7	•	2.5	•	•

Table II
Corporations with Net Income

COAL MINING

MONEY AMOUNTS AND SIZE OF ASSETS IN THOUSANDS OF DOLLARS

Item Description for Accounting Period 7/05 Through 6/06	Total	Zero Assets	Under 500	500 to 1,000	1,000 to 5,000	5,000 to 10,000	10,000 to 25,000	25,000 to 50,000	50,000 to 100,000	100,000 to 250,000	250,000 to 500,000	500,000 to 2,500,000	2,500,000 and over
Number of Enterprises 1	378	5	122	57	84	54	25	15	5	•	0	•	0

Revenues ($ in Thousands)

	Total	Zero Assets	Under 500	500 to 1,000	1,000 to 5,000	5,000 to 10,000	10,000 to 25,000	25,000 to 50,000	50,000 to 100,000	100,000 to 250,000	250,000 to 500,000	500,000 to 2,500,000	2,500,000 and over
Net Sales 2	11760779	103789	212	62436	986847	689499	1112601	889200	590106	•	0	0	0
Interest 3	140274	0	409	0	733	287	1459	226	332	•	0	0	0
Rents 4	12867	0	0	0	0	0	0	1	556	•	0	0	0
Royalties 5	69239	0	0	0	0	0	0	0	833	•	0	0	0
Other Portfolio Income 6	201188	21424	32965	0	4378	6397	2767	7570	7560	•	0	0	0
Other Receipts 7	580355	7249	2084	0	6163	15917	2904	8805	3712	•	0	0	0
Total Receipts 8	12764702	132462	35670	62436	998121	712100	1119731	905802	603099	•	0	0	0
Average Total Receipts 9	33769	26492	292	1095	11882	13187	44789	60387	120620	•	•	•	•

Operating Costs/Operating Income (%)

	Total	Zero Assets	Under 500	500 to 1,000	1,000 to 5,000	5,000 to 10,000	10,000 to 25,000	25,000 to 50,000	50,000 to 100,000	100,000 to 250,000	250,000 to 500,000	500,000 to 2,500,000	2,500,000 and over
Cost of Operations 10	61.3	15.4	•	0.8	69.9	47.5	82.4	57.7	28.6	•	•	•	•
Salaries and Wages 11	3.4	13.7	3775.5	4.4	•	6.3	1.7	3.4	9.0	•	•	•	•
Taxes Paid 12	5.8	6.7	592.9	5.7	5.0	5.6	1.9	4.7	4.8	•	•	•	•
Interest Paid 13	2.6	1.8	571.2	0.1	0.0	0.9	0.4	1.0	1.6	•	•	•	•
Depreciation 14	4.0	3.3	150.5	11.9	1.6	5.6	1.7	5.0	4.2	•	•	•	•
Amortization and Depletion 15	3.7	4.4	•	•	0.0	3.6	1.7	6.9	4.5	•	•	•	•
Pensions and Other Deferred Comp. 16	1.1	0.9	•	•	•	0.1	0.1	0.2	0.3	•	•	•	•
Employee Benefits 17	4.5	2.7	4.2	•	3.8	1.3	0.9	1.1	2.4	•	•	•	•
Advertising 18	0.0	•	•	•	0.0	0.0	0.0	0.0	0.0	•	•	•	•
Other Expenses 19	15.6	38.5	4056.6	3.6	14.6	28.7	5.4	13.0	43.7	•	•	•	•
Officers' Compensation 20	0.7		•	41.5	0.6	0.3	0.8	0.6	0.4	•	•	•	•
Operating Margin 21	•	12.7	•	32.0	4.4	0.2	3.0	6.2	0.4	•	•	•	•
Operating Margin Before Officers' Comp. 22	•	12.7	•	73.5	5.0	0.5	3.8	6.9	0.8	•	•	•	•

Selected Average Balance Sheet ($ in Thousands)

Net Receivables 23	7401	0	93	0	565	519	3205	5695	10945
Inventories 24	769	0	0	0	14	108	1272	730	3231
Net Property, Plant and Equipment 25	15000	0	10	352	691	2371	4432	14952	28034
Total Assets 26	47999	0	174	813	1820	8383	14814	35530	68265
Notes and Loans Payable 27	11369	0	117	194	435	907	3500	10206	24254
All Other Liabilities 28	17623	0	151	385	1373	1142	7384	5986	18876
Net Worth 29	19007	0	-94	234	12	6334	3930	19338	25136

Selected Financial Ratios (Times to 1)

Current Ratio 30	1.8	•	0.6	1.6	0.7	3.3	1.1	1.5	1.0
Quick Ratio 31	1.5	•	0.4	1.6	0.6	2.8	0.8	1.3	0.7
Net Sales to Working Capital 32	5.9	•	•	6.7	•	6.8	53.1	15.9	356.8
Coverage Ratio 33	3.3	24.0	14.4	339.5	120.9	4.7	10.5	8.8	2.6
Total Asset Turnover 34	0.6	•	0.0	1.3	6.5	1.5	3.0	1.7	1.7
Inventory Turnover 35	24.8	•	•	•	584.1	55.9	28.8	46.8	10.4
Receivables Turnover 36	5.7	•	0.0	302.4	40.3	23.9	18.5	12.3	7.9
Total Liabilities to Net Worth 37	1.5	•	•	2.5	145.9	0.3	2.8	0.8	1.7
Current Assets to Working Capital 38	2.2	•	•	2.8	•	1.4	10.0	3.1	58.5
Current Liabilities to Working Capital 39	1.2	•	•	1.8	•	0.4	9.0	2.1	57.5
Working Capital to Net Sales 40	0.2	•	•	0.1	•	0.1	0.0	0.1	0.0
Inventory to Working Capital 41	0.2	•	•	•	•	0.0	2.3	0.2	7.9
Total Receipts to Cash Flow 42	6.2	1.5	0.4	2.8	8.9	6.0	13.9	6.0	2.9
Cost of Goods to Cash Flow 43	3.8	0.2	•	0.0	6.2	2.8	11.5	3.4	0.8
Cash Flow to Total Debt 44	0.2	•	0.0	0.7	0.7	1.0	0.3	0.6	1.0

Selected Financial Factors (in Percentages)

Debt Ratio 45	60.4	•	153.8	71.3	99.3	24.4	73.5	45.6	63.2
Return on Total Assets 46	5.5	•	82.3	43.2	36.3	6.4	12.2	15.2	7.3
Return on Equity Before Income Taxes 47	9.6	•	•	150.0	5287.2	6.7	41.4	24.8	12.4
Return on Equity After Income Taxes 48	7.9	•	•	102.0	3964.7	6.2	36.1	23.9	12.0
Profit Margin (Before Income Tax) 49	5.9	40.3	7675.5	32.0	5.6	3.3	3.7	8.1	2.6
Profit Margin (After Income Tax) 50	4.8	40.3	7675.5	21.8	4.2	3.1	3.2	7.8	2.6

Table I
Corporations with and without Net Income

METAL ORE MINING

Money Amounts and Size of Assets in Thousands of Dollars

Item Description for Accounting Period 7/05 Through 6/06	Total	Zero Assets	Under 500	500 to 1,000	1,000 to 5,000	5,000 to 10,000	10,000 to 25,000	25,000 to 50,000	50,000 to 100,000	100,000 to 250,000	250,000 to 500,000	500,000 to 2,500,000	2,500,000 and over
Number of Enterprises **1**	2002	18	1732	58	79	29	35	17	6	5	7	8	8
Revenues ($ in Thousands)													
Net Sales **2**	28274006	216	44454	22797	0	16853	245413	197189	110061	185977	1324774	3144524	22981748
Interest **3**	689827	99	418	0	1372	355	2295	4664	1121	4997	16211	63182	595113
Rents **4**	22643	65	6873	0	0	0	0	14	4	0	133	2	15552
Royalties **5**	176497	0	0	0	0	0	0	0	0	26299	2147	21980	126070
Other Portfolio Income **6**	1982312	10118	805	5	0	0	27108	4201	73	255	382	77105	1862261
Other Receipts **7**	943433	4	39067	0	3358	98	11853	168	143027	157	12978	1532	731191
Total Receipts **8**	32088718	10502	91617	22802	4730	17306	286669	206236	254286	217685	1356625	3308325	26311935
Average Total Receipts **9**	16028	583	53	393	60	597	8191	12132	42381	43537	193804	413541	3288992
Operating Costs/Operating Income (%)													
Cost of Operations **10**	49.8	·	0.5	·	·	44.6	95.9	46.7	72.1	60.8	70.3	55.3	47.4
Salaries and Wages **11**	1.8	1172.7	0.5	0.5	·	29.1	2.8	10.3	6.9	5.4	0.4	0.5	1.8
Taxes Paid **12**	2.1	60.6	12.0	1.0	·	3.1	0.1	2.9	2.8	3.0	0.4	2.9	2.0
Interest Paid **13**	3.1	13472.2	3.7	0.5	·	3.0	2.9	0.7	2.0	1.3	1.4	3.8	3.0
Depreciation **14**	4.7	1544.0	4.9	1.0	·	13.6	3.4	6.1	5.2	13.7	3.4	6.9	4.4
Amortization and Depletion **15**	11.6	0.5	3.3	0.0	·	95.1	3.8	8.4	7.4	16.9	7.0	14.3	11.5
Pensions and Other Deferred Comp. **16**	2.2	6.5	9.4	·	·	0.2	·	0.1	0.3	0.1	0.2	1.1	2.5
Employee Benefits **17**	1.1	78.7	0.1	·	·	3.2	·	1.4	0.2	0.1	2.2	0.2	1.1
Advertising **18**	0.1	635.6	0.1	·	·	3.3	0.0	0.0	0.0	·	0.0	0.0	0.1
Other Expenses **19**	12.8	4716.7	100.6	45.3	·	192.5	12.0	46.5	20.9	16.7	11.5	7.6	12.8
Officers' Compensation **20**	0.4	1416.7	51.5	0.9	·	9.8	0.7	1.5	2.8	8.7	0.3	0.2	0.2
Operating Margin **21**	10.3	·	·	50.8	·	·	·	·	·	·	3.1	7.4	13.1
Operating Margin Before Officers' Comp. **22**	10.8	·	·	51.7	·	·	·	·	·	·	3.4	7.6	13.3

Selected Average Balance Sheet ($ in Thousands)

Net Receivables 23	7321	0	4	0	4	3765	2333	931	6722	21461	85492	1701421
Inventories 24	1336	0	0	3	57	128	1903	1379	3402	33921	67607	228866
Net Property, Plant and Equipment 25	9282	9	549	753	5590	3006	15903	16083	94957	132707	318228	1736338
Total Assets 26	42838	117	691	1984	7130	16249	35545	65113	146467	316367	918966	9161578
Notes and Loans Payable 27	4336	75	4	243	4770	7589	13597	17947	12376	74680	226846	673633
All Other Liabilities 28	12990	41	7	135	5035	5024	18638	20638	68645	76040	352467	2683178
Net Worth 29	25512	1	680	1606	-2675	3637	3309	26528	65445	165647	339653	5804767

Selected Financial Ratios (Times to 1)

Current Ratio 30	1.6	•	1.0	0.8	5.3	1.7	0.9	2.6	0.5	1.7	2.4	1.6
Quick Ratio 31	1.3	•	1.0	0.8	4.6	1.6	0.7	1.4	0.5	0.6	1.7	1.3
Net Sales to Working Capital 32	3.3	•	12.0	•	•	3.3	•	3.1	•	6.1	2.2	3.2
Coverage Ratio 33	9.1	•	6.0	112.4	•	•	•	55.6	•	5.0	4.5	10.7
Total Asset Turnover 34	0.3	•	0.2	0.6	•	0.4	0.3	0.3	0.3	0.6	0.4	0.3
Inventory Turnover 35	5.3	•	•	•	•	52.3	2.8	9.6	6.7	3.9	3.2	5.9
Receivables Turnover 36	2.1	•	•	206.3	•	3.7	2.5	35.9	2.7	10.0	6.2	1.8
Total Liabilities to Net Worth 37	0.7	•	174.3	0.0	0.2	3.5	9.7	1.5	1.2	0.9	1.7	0.6
Current Assets to Working Capital 38	2.7	•	21.8	•	1.2	2.5	•	1.6	•	2.5	1.7	2.8
Current Liabilities to Working Capital 39	1.7	•	20.8	•	0.2	1.5	•	0.6	•	1.5	0.7	1.8
Working Capital to Net Sales 40	0.3	•	0.1	•	•	0.3	•	0.3	•	0.2	0.4	0.3
Inventory to Working Capital 41	0.3	•	•	0.0	•	0.1	•	0.1	•	1.3	0.3	0.3
Total Receipts to Cash Flow 42	3.1	•	1.0	1.1	•	15.3	4.6	0.8	•	7.3	5.1	2.8
Cost of Goods to Cash Flow 43	1.5	•	0.0	•	•	14.6	2.1	0.6	•	5.1	2.8	1.3
Cash Flow to Total Debt 44	0.3	•	0.2	33.0	•	0.0	0.1	0.6	•	0.2	0.1	0.3

Selected Financial Factors (in Percentages)

Debt Ratio 45	40.4	99.4	1.6	19.0	137.5	77.6	90.7	59.3	55.3	47.6	63.0	36.6
Return on Total Assets 46	9.3	•	4.8	29.2	•	•	•	31.8	•	4.1	7.3	10.1
Return on Equity Before Income Taxes 47	14.0	•	701.0	29.4	•	64.1	•	76.7	•	6.2	15.4	14.5
Return on Equity After Income Taxes 48	9.8	•	701.0	29.3	•	64.1	•	76.7	•	3.5	11.4	10.2
Profit Margin (Before Income Tax) 49	25.2	•	18.2	50.8	•	•	•	110.9	•	5.5	13.3	29.2
Profit Margin (After Income Tax) 50	17.8	•	18.2	50.6	•	•	•	110.9	•	3.0	9.9	20.7

Table II

Corporations with Net Income

METAL ORE MINING

MONEY AMOUNTS AND SIZE OF ASSETS IN THOUSANDS OF DOLLARS

Item Description for Accounting Period 7/05 Through 6/06	Total	Zero Assets	Under 500	500 to 1,000	1,000 to 5,000	5,000 to 10,000	10,000 to 25,000	25,000 to 50,000	50,000 to 100,000	100,000 to 250,000	250,000 to 500,000	500,000 to 2,500,000	2,500,000 and over
Number of Enterprises 1	550	•	417	•	31	0	11	5	3	0	4	5	•
Revenues ($ in Thousands)													
Net Sales 2	25336033	•	43760	•	0	0	209295	44017	6805	0	978762	2180265	•
Interest 3	562552	•	0	•	817	0	1584	2465	4281	0	9880	46250	•
Rents 4	15694	•	0	•	0	0	0	14	0	0	126	2	•
Royalties 5	171149	•	0	•	0	0	0	0	26299	0	476	19541	•
Other Portfolio Income 6	1973551	•	0	•	0	0	27108	798	56	0	7	76445	•
Other Receipts 7	893136	•	34097	•	0	0	11400	121	142096	0	5565	-23611	•
Total Receipts 8	28952115	•	77857	•	817	0	249387	47415	179537	0	994816	2298892	•
Average Total Receipts 9	52640	•	187	•	26	•	22672	9483	59846	•	248704	459778	•
Operating Costs/Operating Income (%)													
Cost of Operations 10	49.5	•	•	•	•	•	97.8	58.4	0.7	•	71.1	48.9	•
Salaries and Wages 11	1.2	•	•	•	•	•	2.2	0.1	12.1	•	0.0	0.1	•
Taxes Paid 12	1.9	•	6.6	•	•	•	0.0	4.5	26.6	•	0.0	2.3	•
Interest Paid 13	2.3	•	3.7	•	•	•	1.9	0.0	5.8	•	0.9	2.7	•
Depreciation 14	4.2	•	4.7	•	•	•	2.5	3.3	2.1	•	3.4	6.8	•
Amortization and Depletion 15	11.1	•	3.4	•	•	•	•	17.6	103.8	•	5.3	13.3	•
Pensions and Other Deferred Comp. 16	2.4	•	9.5	•	•	•	•	•	2.6	•	0.3	1.5	•
Employee Benefits 17	1.0	•	•	•	•	•	•	0.0	0.9	•	2.8	0.1	•
Advertising 18	0.1	•	0.1	•	•	•	0.0	•	•	•	•	0.0	•
Other Expenses 19	11.9	•	27.7	•	•	•	4.8	4.5	73.2	•	8.3	6.9	•
Officers' Compensation 20	0.3	•	38.5	•	•	•	•	•	86.3	•	0.3	0.2	•
Operating Margin 21	14.1	•	5.8	•	•	•	•	11.5	•	•	7.7	17.2	•
Operating Margin Before Officers' Comp. 22	14.5	•	44.3	•	•	•	•	11.5	•	•	7.9	17.4	•

Selected Average Balance Sheet ($ in Thousands)

	•	•	•	•	•	•	•	•	•	•
Net Receivables 23	23522	0	0	•	11949	283	4158	•	30918	84062
Inventories 24	3893	0	0	•	106	5338	751	•	14030	59418
Net Property, Plant and Equipment 25	28145	0	7	•	1852	7702	104739	•	148384	342620
Total Assets 26	121098	1000	247	•	17040	34546	152802	•	296697	1037129
Notes and Loans Payable 27	9494	0	78	•	1969	6363	1812	•	51026	176906
All Other Liabilities 28	40676	3	18	•	5813	13181	49617	•	58891	478959
Net Worth 29	70927	997	150	•	9258	15003	101373	•	186780	381264

Selected Financial Ratios (Times to 1)

	•	•	•	•	•	•	•	•	•	•
Current Ratio 30	1.5	4.0	41.8	•	3.0	2.0	0.7	•	1.1	1.9
Quick Ratio 31	1.2	4.0	41.8	•	3.0	1.2	0.7	•	0.7	1.4
Net Sales to Working Capital 32	4.0	1.3	•	•	1.7	1.2	•	•	51.8	3.1
Coverage Ratio 33	13.9	23.4	•	•	6.4	806.2	403.5	•	11.9	9.8
Total Asset Turnover 34	0.4	0.4	•	•	1.1	0.3	0.0	•	0.8	0.4
Inventory Turnover 35	5.9	•	176.1	•	•	1.0	0.0	•	12.4	3.6
Receivables Turnover 36	2.0	•	•	•	2.9	0.8	1.1	•	12.2	6.6
Total Liabilities to Net Worth 37	0.7	0.6	1.1	•	0.8	1.3	0.5	•	0.6	1.7
Current Assets to Working Capital 38	3.2	1.3	0.0	•	1.5	2.0	•	•	12.3	2.1
Current Liabilities to Working Capital 39	2.2	0.3	1.0	•	0.5	1.0	•	•	11.3	1.1
Working Capital to Net Sales 40	0.3	0.8	0.0	•	0.6	0.8	•	•	0.0	0.3
Inventory to Working Capital 41	0.3	•	•	•	0.0	0.8	0.0	•	3.7	0.4
Total Receipts to Cash Flow 42	2.8	1.0	•	•	6.8	4.4	0.0	•	5.9	3.4
Cost of Goods to Cash Flow 43	1.4	•	•	•	6.6	2.6	•	•	4.2	1.7
Cash Flow to Total Debt 44	0.3	1.1	6.1	•	0.4	0.1	1.1	•	0.4	0.2

Selected Financial Factors (in Percentages)

	•	•	•	•	•	•	•	•	•	•
Debt Ratio 45	41.4	39.1	0.3	•	45.7	56.6	33.7	•	37.0	63.2
Return on Total Assets 46	12.3	37.2	1.2	•	13.3	4.7	34.6	•	8.4	11.1
Return on Equity Before Income Taxes 47	19.5	58.4	1.2	•	20.6	10.7	52.0	•	12.2	27.1
Return on Equity After Income Taxes 48	14.1	58.4	1.1	•	16.9	10.6	50.4	•	8.2	21.5
Profit Margin (Before Income Tax) 49	30.0	83.7	•	•	10.0	18.3	2324.4	•	9.3	23.7
Profit Margin (After Income Tax) 50	21.7	83.7	•	•	8.2	18.1	2254.3	•	6.3	18.8

Table I
Corporations with and without Net Income

NONMETALLIC MINERAL MINING AND QUARRYING

MONEY AMOUNTS AND SIZE OF ASSETS IN THOUSANDS OF DOLLARS

Item Description for Accounting Period 7/05 Through 6/06	Total	Zero Assets	Under 500	500 to 1,000	1,000 to 5,000	5,000 to 10,000	10,000 to 25,000	25,000 to 50,000	50,000 to 100,000	100,000 to 250,000	250,000 to 500,000	500,000 to 2,500,000	2,500,000 and over
Number of Enterprises **1**	4637	5	3090	595	601	61	158	65	27	25	3	4	5
Revenues ($ in Thousands)													
Net Sales **2**	27871829	30582	565266	342720	2498203	549184	2530398	1917500	1904924	3580983	1187160	2906211	9858699
Interest **3**	103902	0	1160	74	894	694	4989	7012	6331	9253	730	17917	54846
Rents **4**	43339	0	0	391	766	294	5815	2424	6691	6364	512	9705	10375
Royalties **5**	54952	0	380	0	0	16704	334	1454	0	2498	101	11404	22077
Other Portfolio Income **6**	714798	11135	0	10586	10226	50912	14467	64988	20193	50356	856	88936	392146
Other Receipts **7**	616902	19	2465	823	29057	10187	20303	30293	21630	76894	13149	50153	361928
Total Receipts **8**	29405722	41736	569271	354594	2539146	627975	2576306	2023671	1959769	3726348	1202508	3084326	10700071
Average Total Receipts **9**	6342	8347	184	596	4225	10295	16306	31133	72584	149054	400836	771082	2140014
Operating Costs/Operating Income (%)													
Cost of Operations **10**	64.2	41.9	55.7	70.9	58.5	69.3	64.1	64.7	72.5	67.8	71.3	66.3	61.2
Salaries and Wages **11**	4.4	6.3	6.0	2.7	3.3	5.0	4.7	3.6	4.9	4.6	3.2	3.9	4.9
Taxes Paid **12**	2.8	19.2	2.7	4.8	3.1	2.9	3.1	2.6	2.0	1.6	1.8	1.6	3.7
Interest Paid **13**	3.5	0.2	0.5	2.0	1.6	2.6	1.6	1.1	1.5	2.1	2.5	5.0	5.7
Depreciation **14**	5.1	6.2	3.5	14.4	4.5	4.1	6.0	6.0	4.4	5.5	4.0	4.8	5.0
Amortization and Depletion **15**	2.8	1.6	1.9	1.0	1.1	1.3	2.4	2.3	1.8	2.8	2.3	5.1	3.2
Pensions and Other Deferred Comp. **16**	0.9	•	0.5	0.1	0.6	0.3	0.5	0.8	0.6	0.7	1.0	1.2	1.3
Employee Benefits **17**	2.0	7.7	0.1	2.2	2.3	2.3	1.9	1.3	2.5	2.4	3.4	1.6	1.8
Advertising **18**	0.2	0.2	0.5	0.8	0.2	0.3	0.2	0.2	0.2	0.2	0.1	0.2	0.1
Other Expenses **19**	12.5	2.4	34.5	15.7	17.6	19.1	9.2	9.2	8.3	8.7	9.1	7.5	15.1
Officers' Compensation **20**	1.2	1.0	4.7	2.1	2.1	1.8	2.4	2.1	1.3	1.1	0.8	1.3	0.4
Operating Margin **21**	0.3	13.2	•	•	5.0	•	4.0	5.9	•	2.5	0.5	1.5	•
Operating Margin Before Officers' Comp. **22**	1.5	14.2	•	•	7.1	•	6.4	8.1	1.3	3.6	1.3	2.8	•

Selected Average Balance Sheet ($ in Thousands)

Net Receivables 23	785	0	7	71	415	1126	2335	4094	10039	20591	46831	109440	252108
Inventories 24	537	0	0	35	186	822	1432	2256	7304	15593	45688	82190	176643
Net Property, Plant and Equipment 25	3243	0	19	412	1304	2448	6900	13990	32204	70139	217728	491416	1311680
Total Assets 26	7885	0	68	739	2476	7178	14820	34970	72063	157477	389247	1226938	3483454
Notes and Loans Payable 27	2348	0	32	455	916	4140	4029	6083	22235	41595	182000	550432	858841
All Other Liabilities 28	2426	0	16	194	442	2018	2204	5245	17496	36425	59774	281778	1463840
Net Worth 29	3111	0	20	90	1118	1020	8587	23643	32331	79457	147473	394728	1160772

Selected Financial Ratios (Times to 1)

Current Ratio 30	1.3	•	2.0	0.9	2.4	1.8	2.4	2.6	1.8	2.4	1.2	3.1	0.8
Quick Ratio 31	0.6	•	1.6	0.7	2.0	0.7	1.6	1.8	1.1	1.3	0.5	1.4	0.3
Net Sales to Working Capital 32	10.5	•	10.1	•	6.5	5.0	4.4	3.8	5.8	4.2	17.6	3.1	•
Coverage Ratio 33	2.8	245.6	•	•	5.1	3.0	4.5	10.9	2.9	4.1	1.7	2.5	2.3
Total Asset Turnover 34	0.8	•	2.7	0.8	1.7	1.3	1.1	0.8	1.0	0.9	1.0	0.6	0.6
Inventory Turnover 35	7.2	•	•	11.7	13.1	7.6	7.2	8.5	7.0	6.2	6.2	5.9	6.8
Receivables Turnover 36	6.1	•	29.5	6.9	12.9	4.8	7.3	8.2	7.0	7.8	6.6	5.4	4.5
Total Liabilities to Net Worth 37	1.5	•	2.5	7.2	1.2	6.0	0.7	0.5	1.2	1.0	1.6	2.1	2.0
Current Assets to Working Capital 38	4.2	•	2.0	•	1.7	2.2	1.7	1.6	2.2	1.7	5.5	1.5	•
Current Liabilities to Working Capital 39	3.2	•	1.0	•	0.7	1.2	0.7	0.6	1.2	0.7	4.5	0.5	•
Working Capital to Net Sales 40	0.1	•	0.1	•	0.2	0.2	0.2	0.3	0.2	0.2	0.1	0.3	•
Inventory to Working Capital 41	1.0	•	•	•	0.2	0.6	0.4	0.3	0.6	0.5	1.7	0.3	•
Total Receipts to Cash Flow 42	7.8	2.2	7.4	•	6.8	5.8	8.8	6.5	16.2	7.8	18.9	8.1	6.8
Cost of Goods to Cash Flow 43	5.0	0.9	4.1	•	4.0	4.0	5.6	4.2	11.8	5.3	13.5	5.4	4.2
Cash Flow to Total Debt 44	0.2	•	0.5	•	0.4	0.3	0.3	0.4	0.1	0.2	0.1	0.1	0.1

Selected Financial Factors (in Percentages)

Debt Ratio 45	60.5	•	71.2	87.8	54.8	85.8	42.1	32.4	55.1	49.5	62.1	67.8	66.7
Return on Total Assets 46	7.4	•	•	•	13.9	9.9	8.0	10.6	4.2	7.9	4.4	7.5	7.5
Return on Equity Before Income Taxes 47	12.1	•	•	•	24.7	46.7	10.8	14.2	6.1	11.9	4.8	14.2	12.8
Return on Equity After Income Taxes 48	9.1	•	•	•	24.3	41.0	9.5	12.4	3.7	9.1	4.1	9.9	8.7
Profit Margin (Before Income Tax) 49	6.3	49.6	•	•	6.7	5.3	5.8	11.4	2.8	6.6	1.8	7.7	7.5
Profit Margin (After Income Tax) 50	4.7	49.5	•	•	6.5	4.6	5.1	9.9	1.7	5.0	1.5	5.4	5.1

13

Table II
Corporations with Net Income

NONMETALLIC MINERAL MINING AND QUARRYING

MONEY AMOUNTS AND SIZE OF ASSETS IN THOUSANDS OF DOLLARS

Item Description for Accounting Period 7/05 Through 6/06	Total	Zero Assets	Under 500	500 to 1,000	1,000 to 5,000	5,000 to 10,000	10,000 to 25,000	25,000 to 50,000	50,000 to 100,000	100,000 to 250,000	250,000 to 500,000	500,000 to 2,500,000	2,500,000 and over
Number of Enterprises 1	1488	•	372	•	554	27	126	57	20	22	0	•	5
Revenues ($ in Thousands)													
Net Sales 2	24339640	•	264516	•	2360738	188879	2068634	1748243	1445815	3777618	0	•	9858699
Interest 3	95567	•	745	•	409	281	4466	6715	4707	8508	0	•	54846
Rents 4	35256	•	0	•	558	29	5638	2263	274	6552	0	•	10375
Royalties 5	54218	•	380	•	0	16704	334	1454	0	1900	0	•	22077
Other Portfolio Income 6	684233	•	0	•	9841	47096	6859	63953	16030	39350	0	•	392146
Other Receipts 7	548567	•	194	•	28785	8946	23523	22543	14687	42425	0	•	361928
Total Receipts 8	25757481	•	265835	•	2400331	261935	2109454	1845171	1481513	3876353	0	•	10700071
Average Total Receipts 9	17310	•	715	•	4333	9701	16742	32371	74076	176198	•	•	2140014
Operating Costs/Operating Income (%)													
Cost of Operations 10	63.7	•	83.2	•	56.7	56.2	61.6	64.3	73.4	69.1	•	•	61.2
Salaries and Wages 11	4.3	•	0.7	•	3.5	4.7	4.4	3.5	4.1	4.1	•	•	4.9
Taxes Paid 12	2.8	•	0.5	•	3.1	4.5	3.1	2.7	1.9	1.6	•	•	3.7
Interest Paid 13	3.4	•	•	•	1.5	1.7	1.3	1.0	1.5	1.8	•	•	5.7
Depreciation 14	4.9	•	0.2	•	4.6	3.1	6.2	5.7	4.1	4.4	•	•	5.0
Amortization and Depletion 15	2.8	•	0.0	•	1.1	2.3	2.4	2.4	1.8	2.4	•	•	3.2
Pensions and Other Deferred Comp. 16	1.0	•	1.1	•	0.7	0.3	0.4	0.9	0.6	0.9	•	•	1.3
Employee Benefits 17	1.8	•	•	•	2.5	0.8	1.8	1.4	1.6	2.0	•	•	1.8
Advertising 18	0.1	•	0.1	•	0.2	0.2	0.3	0.2	0.2	0.2	•	•	0.1
Other Expenses 19	11.9	•	9.4	•	18.2	32.5	8.7	8.6	6.2	7.8	•	•	15.1
Officers' Compensation 20	1.2	•	3.9	•	2.2	2.4	2.6	2.0	1.3	1.1	•	•	0.4
Operating Margin 21	2.0	•	0.9	•	5.8	•	7.2	7.4	3.5	4.7	•	•	•
Operating Margin Before Officers' Comp. 22	3.1	•	4.7	•	8.0	•	9.8	9.4	4.8	5.8	•	•	•

Selected Average Balance Sheet ($ in Thousands)

Net Receivables 23	2170	17	408	1244	2435	4347	10898	22937	•	252108
Inventories 24	1345	0	190	220	1256	2168	6276	15739	•	186726
Net Property, Plant and Equipment 25	8851	27	1370	1877	6916	13333	30450	81464	•	1311680
Total Assets 26	22029	170	2500	7664	14740	34444	70130	181634	•	3483454
Notes and Loans Payable 27	6163	13	870	4046	3478	5222	18986	52501	•	858841
All Other Liabilities 28	6803	87	415	1671	2119	5361	14517	31416	•	1463840
Net Worth 29	9062	69	1215	1948	9143	23861	36626	97717	•	1160772

Selected Financial Ratios (Times to 1)

Current Ratio 30	1.3	0.9	2.4	10.0	2.7	2.8	1.7	2.3	•	0.8
Quick Ratio 31	0.6	0.9	2.0	4.9	1.9	2.0	1.1	1.1	•	0.3
Net Sales to Working Capital 32	10.6	•	6.8	1.7	4.0	3.6	6.0	4.5	•	•
Coverage Ratio 33	3.4	•	5.9	18.4	7.9	14.5	5.0	5.1	•	2.3
Total Asset Turnover 34	0.7	4.2	1.7	0.9	1.1	0.9	1.0	0.9	•	0.6
Inventory Turnover 35	7.7	•	12.7	17.9	8.1	9.1	8.5	7.5	•	6.5
Receivables Turnover 36	8.9	82.5	13.4	2.7	7.4	8.9	7.8	9.8	•	15.6
Total Liabilities to Net Worth 37	1.4	1.5	1.1	2.9	0.6	0.4	0.9	0.9	•	2.0
Current Assets to Working Capital 38	4.4	•	1.7	1.1	1.6	1.6	2.4	1.8	•	•
Current Liabilities to Working Capital 39	3.4	•	0.7	0.1	0.6	0.6	1.4	0.8	•	•
Working Capital to Net Sales 40	0.1	•	0.1	0.6	0.2	0.3	0.2	0.2	•	•
Inventory to Working Capital 41	1.0	•	0.2	0.0	0.3	0.3	0.5	0.5	•	•
Total Receipts to Cash Flow 42	6.9	10.5	6.3	1.9	6.9	6.2	10.6	8.4	•	6.8
Cost of Goods to Cash Flow 43	4.4	8.8	3.6	1.1	4.3	4.0	7.8	5.8	•	4.2
Cash Flow to Total Debt 44	0.2	0.7	0.5	0.6	0.4	0.5	0.2	0.2	•	0.1

Selected Financial Factors (in Percentages)

Debt Ratio 45	58.9	59.5	51.4	74.6	38.0	30.7	47.8	46.2	•	66.7
Return on Total Assets 46	8.8	5.7	15.3	28.7	11.7	12.3	7.7	8.6	•	7.5
Return on Equity Before Income Taxes 47	15.1	14.0	26.2	107.0	16.5	16.5	11.8	12.9	•	12.8
Return on Equity After Income Taxes 48	11.9	12.6	25.7	100.1	15.0	14.5	8.8	10.2	•	8.7
Profit Margin (Before Income Tax) 49	8.4	1.4	7.5	29.8	9.2	12.9	6.0	7.3	•	7.5
Profit Margin (After Income Tax) 50	6.6	1.2	7.3	27.9	8.4	11.3	4.5	5.8	•	5.1

14

Table I

Corporations with and without Net Income

SUPPORT ACTIVITIES FOR MINING

MONEY AMOUNTS AND SIZE OF ASSETS IN THOUSANDS OF DOLLARS

Item Description for Accounting Period 7/05 Through 6/06		Total	Zero Assets	Under 500	500 to 1,000	1,000 to 5,000	5,000 to 10,000	10,000 to 25,000	25,000 to 50,000	50,000 to 100,000	100,000 to 250,000	250,000 to 500,000	500,000 to 2,500,000	2,500,000 and over
Number of Enterprises	1	7866	1200	4596	871	930	103	70	24	15	11	14	23	9
Revenues ($ in Thousands)														
Net Sales	2	60774902	1026731	4049412	1851441	6016373	1276106	1686052	883132	789166	1517557	2247785	14573663	24857484
Interest	3	931956	44274	1056	735	3704	1391	2969	708	6910	3644	28474	173766	664325
Rents	4	243866	13	823	0	4974	125	1345	0	728	9079	87788	118351	20640
Royalties	5	138662	0	22	0	18500	57	0	0	425	165	13902	54881	50709
Other Portfolio Income	6	1261982	2646	6322	1725	47931	3998	11706	5117	18156	70480	43730	463734	586439
Other Receipts	7	943400	23011	1099	26387	36991	64793	27024	18727	42555	14556	38206	140371	509681
Total Receipts	8	64294768	1096675	4058734	1880288	6128473	1346470	1729096	907684	857940	1615481	2459885	15524766	26689278
Average Total Receipts	9	8174	914	883	2159	6590	13073	24701	37820	57196	146862	175706	674990	2965475
Operating Costs/Operating Income (%)														
Cost of Operations	10	48.8	61.7	23.6	32.7	44.5	27.2	48.8	40.7	59.6	43.6	55.5	44.2	58.1
Salaries and Wages	11	10.9	7.8	12.2	20.3	14.8	22.8	6.7	15.3	12.4	11.1	9.1	9.4	9.8
Taxes Paid	12	2.4	2.1	2.7	3.4	2.6	3.3	1.7	3.9	1.9	1.6	3.8	2.1	2.3
Interest Paid	13	3.7	2.1	0.5	0.7	0.8	1.4	14.9	2.2	2.0	2.6	2.9	3.4	4.9
Depreciation	14	6.4	14.9	2.5	4.6	5.0	5.0	2.6	7.1	7.0	5.1	11.5	8.1	5.9
Amortization and Depletion	15	0.7	0.8	0.3	0.0	0.1	0.1	0.9	0.5	0.1	0.4	1.3	0.9	0.8
Pensions and Other Deferred Comp.	16	0.7	1.2	0.3	0.2	0.1	0.1	0.3	0.4	0.3	0.2	0.5	0.3	1.3
Employee Benefits	17	2.2	1.6	0.8	0.3	1.3	2.1	1.0	2.2	0.9	0.9	2.8	2.0	3.2
Advertising	18	0.1	0.1	0.2	0.2	0.1	0.4	0.1	0.2	0.1	0.1	0.1	0.1	0.1
Other Expenses	19	22.2	31.3	40.1	21.0	21.7	27.1	9.6	22.0	13.3	29.3	9.8	18.9	22.7
Officers' Compensation	20	1.7	1.4	5.4	8.3	2.6	3.1	1.5	1.1	1.1	1.0	1.2	1.0	0.8
Operating Margin	21	0.2	•	11.4	8.2	6.4	7.5	11.8	4.4	1.3	4.1	1.4	9.7	•
Operating Margin Before Officers' Comp.	22	1.9	•	16.8	16.5	9.0	10.6	13.3	5.5	2.4	5.1	2.7	10.7	•

Selected Average Balance Sheet ($ in Thousands)

Net Receivables 23	1601	0	6	117	421	1017	3852	8422	21744	40771	81051	185329	591458
Inventories 24	299	0	1	18	61	179	598	642	979	6205	5461	32965	142196
Net Property, Plant and Equipment 25	3714	0	71	261	991	2981	3362	14580	20849	59087	161186	494570	1361525
Total Assets 26	12013	0	137	767	2094	6796	15134	36677	70775	138244	367661	1174603	5984266
Notes and Loans Payable 27	3128	0	52	198	1272	3091	2630	12879	26360	57370	70954	276668	1535252
All Other Liabilities 28	2383	0	25	104	210	1193	2985	9080	23609	56554	79508	281253	1026304
Net Worth 29	6501	0	60	464	611	2513	9519	14719	20806	24320	217200	616683	3422710

Selected Financial Ratios (Times to 1)

Current Ratio 30	2.1	•	2.3	2.2	2.2	1.9	2.8	1.6	1.3	1.4	1.4	2.0	2.3
Quick Ratio 31	1.6	•	2.2	1.9	2.0	1.5	2.4	1.2	1.2	1.1	1.2	1.5	1.6
Net Sales to Working Capital 32	4.3	•	27.5	11.0	11.9	9.7	4.0	5.7	6.2	8.5	5.0	3.6	3.2
Coverage Ratio 33	3.0	•	26.2	15.1	11.9	10.1	2.0	4.3	6.1	5.0	4.8	6.7	0.7
Total Asset Turnover 34	0.6	•	6.4	2.8	3.1	1.8	1.6	1.0	0.7	1.0	0.4	0.5	0.7
Inventory Turnover 35	12.6	•	166.6	37.6	47.4	18.8	19.7	23.3	32.0	9.7	16.3	8.5	11.3
Receivables Turnover 36	5.6	•	97.7	19.7	14.8	16.4	7.2	4.6	3.6	3.8	2.5	4.5	4.9
Total Liabilities to Net Worth 37	0.8	•	1.3	0.7	2.4	1.7	0.6	1.5	2.4	4.7	0.7	0.9	0.7
Current Assets to Working Capital 38	1.9	•	1.7	1.8	1.8	2.1	1.5	2.6	4.1	3.6	3.5	2.0	1.8
Current Liabilities to Working Capital 39	0.9	•	0.7	0.8	0.8	1.1	0.5	1.6	3.1	2.6	2.5	1.0	0.8
Working Capital to Net Sales 40	0.2	•	0.0	0.1	0.1	0.1	0.3	0.2	0.2	0.1	0.2	0.3	0.3
Inventory to Working Capital 41	0.2	•	0.0	0.1	0.1	0.2	0.1	0.1	0.2	0.4	0.2	0.3	0.2
Total Receipts to Cash Flow 42	4.4	8.9	2.1	3.9	4.2	3.4	4.8	4.3	5.3	3.4	6.8	3.5	6.7
Cost of Goods to Cash Flow 43	2.2	5.5	0.5	1.3	1.9	0.9	2.4	1.8	3.2	1.5	3.8	1.5	3.9
Cash Flow to Total Debt 44	0.3	•	5.5	1.8	1.0	0.8	0.9	0.4	0.2	0.4	0.2	0.3	0.2

Selected Financial Factors (in Percentages)

Debt Ratio 45	45.9	•	56.2	39.5	70.8	63.0	37.1	59.9	70.6	82.4	40.9	47.5	42.8
Return on Total Assets 46	7.0	•	77.2	29.1	27.9	26.3	46.6	9.4	8.9	13.2	6.1	12.1	1.6
Return on Equity Before Income Taxes 47	8.5	•	169.6	44.9	87.6	64.0	36.2	17.9	25.4	59.9	8.1	19.6	•
Return on Equity After Income Taxes 48	6.0	•	168.4	43.8	77.1	53.9	32.7	15.4	17.9	47.1	6.1	14.7	•
Profit Margin (Before Income Tax) 49	7.2	•	11.6	9.8	8.3	13.0	14.3	7.2	10.1	10.6	11.0	19.1	•
Profit Margin (After Income Tax) 50	5.0	•	11.5	9.6	7.3	10.9	12.9	6.1	7.1	8.3	11.0	14.3	•

Table II

Corporations with Net Income

SUPPORT ACTIVITIES FOR MINING

MONEY AMOUNTS AND SIZE OF ASSETS IN THOUSANDS OF DOLLARS

Item Description for Accounting Period 7/05 Through 6/06	Total	Zero Assets	Under 500	500 to 1,000	1,000 to 5,000	5,000 to 10,000	10,000 to 25,000	25,000 to 50,000	50,000 to 100,000	100,000 to 250,000	250,000 to 500,000	500,000 to 2,500,000	2,500,000 and over
Number of Enterprises **1**	5075	434	2814	871	724	90	67	17	9	•	9	•	•
Revenues ($ in Thousands)													
Net Sales **2**	41655519	563040	3680490	1851441	3786093	1061023	1653701	768848	627596	•	1705331	•	•
Interest **3**	375893	8874	1056	735	3663	1272	2969	617	6058	•	22962	•	•
Rents **4**	235982	13	823	0	4974	125	1345	0	425	•	87788	•	•
Royalties **5**	54156	0	0	0	17769	57	0	0	28	•	4607	•	•
Other Portfolio Income **6**	963592	295	3046	1725	47640	3998	11693	4317	5558	•	43702	•	•
Other Receipts **7**	808030	2456	1099	26387	22117	61590	27020	10978	5050	•	28923	•	•
Total Receipts **8**	44093172	574678	3686514	1880288	3882256	1128065	1696728	784760	644715	•	1893313	•	•
Average Total Receipts **9**	8688	1324	1310	2159	5362	12534	25324	46162	71635	•	210368	•	•
Operating Costs/Operating Income (%)													
Cost of Operations **10**	37.5	50.1	20.6	32.7	27.7	23.5	47.8	36.5	56.9	•	49.4	•	•
Salaries and Wages **11**	12.8	13.6	11.9	20.3	20.6	24.2	6.7	15.8	9.3	•	9.7	•	•
Taxes Paid **12**	2.3	2.5	2.7	3.4	3.5	3.5	1.8	4.3	1.4	•	2.9	•	•
Interest Paid **13**	3.6	3.3	0.5	0.7	0.5	1.6	15.2	1.4	1.8	•	3.0	•	•
Depreciation **14**	7.7	6.9	2.6	4.6	3.6	5.2	2.7	6.7	6.2	•	12.9	•	•
Amortization and Depletion **15**	0.6	0.6	0.0	0.0	0.1	0.2	0.9	0.4	0.1	•	0.9	•	•
Pensions and Other Deferred Comp. **16**	0.7	1.6	0.4	0.2	0.2	0.1	0.3	0.5	0.4	•	0.3	•	•
Employee Benefits **17**	1.8	2.2	0.8	0.3	1.3	2.1	1.0	1.8	0.5	•	2.0	•	•
Advertising **18**	0.1	0.2	0.1	0.2	0.1	0.4	0.1	0.2	0.1	•	0.2	•	•
Other Expenses **19**	20.5	6.5	42.3	21.0	25.4	24.8	9.6	21.2	11.5	•	12.2	•	•
Officers' Compensation **20**	2.1	2.5	5.4	8.3	3.3	3.6	1.5	1.0	1.2	•	0.8	•	•
Operating Margin **21**	10.1	9.9	12.6	8.2	13.7	10.8	12.4	10.4	10.8	•	5.6	•	•
Operating Margin Before Officers' Comp. **22**	12.2	12.4	18.0	16.5	17.0	14.5	13.9	11.4	11.9	•	6.4	•	•

Selected Average Balance Sheet ($ in Thousands)

Net Receivables 23	1868	0	8	117	524	933	3920	8072	27344	72595
Inventories 24	307	0	2	18	56	151	594	462	1432	6726
Net Property, Plant and Equipment 25	5081	0	107	261	824	2940	3505	13487	17391	176857
Total Assets 26	12945	0	189	767	2014	6668	15375	36603	68834	372403
Notes and Loans Payable 27	3883	0	77	198	770	3089	2743	12403	31952	80097
All Other Liabilities 28	2825	0	32	104	198	996	2946	8576	16725	52720
Net Worth 29	6237	0	80	464	1046	2583	9685	15623	20157	239586

Selected Financial Ratios (Times to 1)

Current Ratio 30	1.9	•	2.4	2.2	2.8	2.2	2.8	1.7	1.7	1.5
Quick Ratio 31	1.5	•	2.2	1.9	2.5	1.8	2.4	1.3	1.6	1.3
Net Sales to Working Capital 32	4.7	•	32.3	11.0	7.5	8.7	4.1	6.7	4.2	5.1
Coverage Ratio 33	5.8	4.6	26.9	15.1	31.4	12.0	2.0	9.8	8.4	6.5
Total Asset Turnover 34	0.6	•	6.9	2.8	2.6	1.8	1.6	1.2	1.0	0.5
Inventory Turnover 35	10.0	•	157.1	37.9	25.8	18.3	19.9	35.7	27.7	13.9
Receivables Turnover 36	5.4	•	169.9	20.8	10.5	16.1	8.2	5.1	5.1	2.9
Total Liabilities to Net Worth 37	1.1	•	1.4	0.7	0.9	1.6	0.6	1.3	2.4	0.6
Current Assets to Working Capital 38	2.1	•	1.7	1.8	1.6	1.8	1.5	2.4	2.4	2.9
Current Liabilities to Working Capital 39	1.1	•	0.7	0.8	0.6	0.8	0.5	1.4	1.4	1.9
Working Capital to Net Sales 40	0.2	•	0.0	0.1	0.1	0.1	0.2	0.1	0.2	0.2
Inventory to Working Capital 41	0.2	•	0.1	0.1	0.1	0.2	0.1	0.1	0.1	0.2
Total Receipts to Cash Flow 42	3.3	6.2	1.9	3.9	3.0	2.9	4.7	3.7	4.8	4.7
Cost of Goods to Cash Flow 43	1.2	3.1	0.4	1.3	0.8	0.7	2.2	1.3	2.7	2.3
Cash Flow to Total Debt 44	0.4	•	6.2	1.8	1.8	1.0	0.9	0.6	0.3	0.3

Selected Financial Factors (in Percentages)

Debt Ratio 45	51.8	•	57.6	39.5	48.1	61.3	37.0	57.3	70.7	35.7
Return on Total Assets 46	13.2	•	91.8	29.1	43.6	33.1	48.4	17.2	15.5	10.1
Return on Equity Before Income Taxes 47	22.7	•	208.2	44.9	81.4	78.3	38.0	36.2	46.7	13.3
Return on Equity After Income Taxes 48	18.6	•	206.7	43.8	73.4	67.1	34.4	32.8	33.9	10.4
Profit Margin (Before Income Tax) 49	17.3	12.0	12.8	9.8	16.3	17.2	14.9	12.5	13.5	16.8
Profit Margin (After Income Tax) 50	14.1	10.1	12.7	9.6	14.7	14.7	13.5	11.3	9.8	13.1

Table I

Corporations with and without Net Income

ELECTRIC POWER GENERATION, TRANSMISSION AND DISTRIBUTION

MONEY AMOUNTS AND SIZE OF ASSETS IN THOUSANDS OF DOLLARS

Item Description for Accounting Period 7/05 Through 6/06	Total	Zero Assets	Under 500	500 to 1,000	1,000 to 5,000	5,000 to 10,000	10,000 to 25,000	25,000 to 50,000	50,000 to 100,000	100,000 to 250,000	250,000 to 500,000	500,000 to 2,500,000	2,500,000 and over
Number of Enterprises **1**	836	287	247	0	44	64	48	24	18	27	12	29	36
Revenues ($ in Thousands)													
Net Sales **2**	289887930	77112	3885	0	114181	146628	710617	1030291	1747680	2622902	1628352	13733550	268072731
Interest **3**	5567686	308929	0	0	368	9753	2352	10043	26996	48069	42514	399183	4719479
Rents **4**	2018531	45	0	0	0	1898	663	176	175	873	7533	46231	1960938
Royalties **5**	33666	0	0	0	0	0	563	0	38	0	0	23234	9831
Other Portfolio Income **6**	6590358	0	0	0	7047	29467	15574	1859	1490	62077	2402	140859	6329581
Other Receipts **7**	4604782	51162	-16483	0	-2244	17691	38397	26219	100239	74889	82710	744071	3488132
Total Receipts **8**	308702953	437248	-12598	0	119352	205437	768166	1068588	1876618	2808810	1763511	15087128	284580692
Average Total Receipts **9**	369262	1524	-51	•	2713	3210	16003	44524	104257	104030	146959	520246	7905019
Operating Costs/Operating Income (%)													
Cost of Operations **10**	64.5	2.1	24.2	•	11.6	38.3	85.7	70.4	85.7	23.7	46.9	64.6	64.9
Salaries and Wages **11**	3.7	5.1	20.6	•	27.4	13.6	2.3	10.8	2.6	1.8	4.8	4.2	3.6
Taxes Paid **12**	3.4	7.8	3.8	•	4.4	5.0	2.1	1.3	0.9	1.4	3.4	2.6	3.5
Interest Paid **13**	6.7	418.7	•	•	6.5	6.9	2.3	0.7	2.0	5.3	9.2	6.3	6.6
Depreciation **14**	6.0	69.3	•	•	6.8	23.7	2.4	1.2	1.5	4.0	8.2	7.0	6.0
Amortization and Depletion **15**	0.7	6.3	•	•	0.0	0.1	0.4	0.5	0.7	0.3	1.2	1.0	0.7
Pensions and Other Deferred Comp. **16**	1.1	0.6	•	•	4.7	0.7	0.7	0.2	0.1	0.3	0.9	0.8	1.2
Employee Benefits **17**	0.9	1.1	•	•	2.0	2.4	0.3	3.1	0.4	0.5	0.8	1.0	0.8
Advertising **18**	0.1	•	•	•	0.9	•	0.0	0.2	0.3	0.1	0.4	0.1	0.1
Other Expenses **19**	18.2	137.2	361.3	•	35.3	25.0	12.2	10.0	10.1	66.7	24.4	19.5	17.6
Officers' Compensation **20**	0.3	•	•	•	5.3	0.1	0.4	1.5	0.4	0.4	1.0	0.5	0.3
Operating Margin **21**	•	•	•	•	•	•	•	0.0	•	•	•	•	•
Operating Margin Before Officers' Comp. **22**	•	•	•	•	0.3	•	•	1.6	•	•	•	•	•

Selected Average Balance Sheet ($ in Thousands)

Net Receivables 23	69714	0	0	•	159	431	2225	5576	25042	10039	21552	86283	1514528
Inventories 24	10287	0	13	•	31	492	213	1032	1675	748	5762	21078	216489
Net Property, Plant and Equipment 25	376248	0	0	•	602	5418	5494	13927	19591	61956	169503	677349	8051923
Total Assets 26	804025	0	60	•	2681	8245	17744	35915	70793	151643	365386	1187780	17377555
Notes and Loans Payable 27	314473	0	36	•	729	4047	4573	11771	23706	96959	177270	561356	6684611
All Other Liabilities 28	299146	0	23	•	1636	55	5218	23305	21113	39896	103565	341818	6571729
Net Worth 29	190407	0	1	•	317	4143	7953	839	25974	14787	84550	284607	4121215

Selected Financial Ratios (Times to 1)

Current Ratio 30	0.9	•	7.0	•	1.3	1.2	1.1	0.7	2.1	1.1	1.5	1.1	0.9
Quick Ratio 31	0.5	•	0.1	•	0.5	1.0	0.8	0.3	1.9	0.9	1.1	0.8	0.5
Net Sales to Working Capital 32	•	•	0.2	•	8.0	9.2	16.8	•	5.5	52.6	5.3	18.4	•
Coverage Ratio 33	1.1	0.8	•	0.8	4.6	0.7	5.9	2.3	1.5	1.8	1.4	•	1.1
Total Asset Turnover 34	0.4	•	0.3	•	1.0	0.3	1.2	1.4	0.6	0.4	0.4	•	0.4
Inventory Turnover 35	21.8	•	0.3	•	9.7	1.8	29.3	111.2	13.7	11.0	14.5	•	22.3
Receivables Turnover 36	6.2	•	310.8	•	25.6	6.9	13.3	5.2	8.0	6.0	5.1	3.2	6.2
Total Liabilities to Net Worth 37	3.2	•	79.5	•	7.5	1.0	4.4	1.7	9.3	3.3	3.2	•	3.2
Current Assets to Working Capital 38	•	•	1.2	•	4.9	6.3	41.8	1.9	14.5	3.0	8.3	•	•
Current Liabilities to Working Capital 39	•	•	0.2	•	3.9	5.3	•	•	0.9	13.5	2.0	7.3	•
Working Capital to Net Sales 40	•	•	4.0	•	0.1	0.1	•	•	0.2	0.0	0.1	•	•
Inventory to Working Capital 41	•	•	0.2	•	0.2	0.5	0.2	•	0.0	0.9	0.2	0.8	0.1
Total Receipts to Cash Flow 42	7.4	2.0	•	•	3.2	3.5	11.6	9.1	9.7	1.6	3.5	7.0	0.8
Cost of Goods to Cash Flow 43	4.8	0.0	•	•	0.4	1.3	9.9	6.4	8.4	0.4	1.6	4.5	7.8
Cash Flow to Total Debt 44	0.1	•	•	•	0.3	0.2	0.1	0.1	0.2	0.4	0.1	0.1	5.1

Selected Financial Factors (in Percentages)

Debt Ratio 45	76.3	98.8	•	88.2	49.8	55.2	97.7	63.3	90.2	76.9	76.0	76.3	
Return on Total Assets 46	3.3	•	5.9	8.7	1.3	6.4	5.0	6.0	6.0	3.4	3.2		
Return on Equity Before Income Taxes 47	1.6	•	13.5	183.1	•	9.9	16.5	11.3	9.9	3.8	1.4		
Return on Equity After Income Taxes 48	•	•	11.3	135.9	•	6.4	11.7	8.6	11.7	1.8	•		
Profit Margin (Before Income Tax) 49	0.9	•	24.4	3.6	11.3	2.5	6.4	7.0	8.6	2.3	•		
Profit Margin (After Income Tax) 50	•	•	20.5	2.7	•	1.7	1.8	5.3	7.0	1.1	•		

Table II

Corporations with Net Income

ELECTRIC POWER GENERATION, TRANSMISSION AND DISTRIBUTION

MONEY AMOUNTS AND SIZE OF ASSETS IN THOUSANDS OF DOLLARS

Item Description for Accounting Period 7/05 Through 6/06	Total	Zero Assets	Under 500	500 to 1,000	1,000 to 5,000	5,000 to 10,000	10,000 to 25,000	25,000 to 50,000	50,000 to 100,000	100,000 to 250,000	250,000 to 500,000	500,000 to 2,500,000	2,500,000 and over
Number of Enterprises **1**	728	283	•	0	38	•	19	13	•	15	7	18	26
Revenues ($ in Thousands)													
Net Sales **2**	214278746	73375	•	0	99505	•	147146	874416	•	2144169	970660	8070694	200327965
Interest **3**	4029556	306114	•	0	299	•	1351	4981	•	26185	25311	185356	3464484
Rents **4**	1895812	23	•	0	0	•	663	146	•	396	6999	38290	1847268
Royalties **5**	30429	0	•	0	0	•	563	0	•	0	0	23194	6634
Other Portfolio Income **6**	3866920	0	•	0	7047	•	14701	0	•	61389	2359	74188	3676277
Other Receipts **7**	5743229	60324	•	0	-2573	•	39612	17979	•	35619	68699	330155	5092575
Total Receipts **8**	229844692	439836	•	0	104278	•	204036	897522	•	2267758	1074028	8721877	214415203
Average Total Receipts **9**	315721	1554	•	•	2744	•	10739	69040	•	151184	153433	484549	8246739
Operating Costs/Operating Income (%)													
Cost of Operations **10**	61.0	2.2	•	•	•	•	43.1	69.8	•	16.9	33.1	63.2	61.4
Salaries and Wages **11**	3.9	3.4	•	•	28.5	•	3.4	12.5	•	0.9	7.5	5.1	3.9
Taxes Paid **12**	3.5	7.5	•	•	3.9	•	6.1	1.3	•	1.2	3.8	2.9	3.6
Interest Paid **13**	6.7	439.4	•	•	0.3	•	3.8	0.3	•	2.8	7.9	5.3	6.7
Depreciation **14**	6.1	63.6	•	•	5.7	•	6.8	0.4	•	2.5	8.0	5.8	6.2
Amortization and Depletion **15**	0.8	6.6	•	•	•	•	1.5	0.0	•	0.3	2.0	1.2	0.7
Pensions and Other Deferred Comp. **16**	1.4	0.4	•	•	5.3	•	0.8	0.3	•	0.3	1.1	0.7	1.4
Employee Benefits **17**	0.7	1.1	•	•	2.0	•	0.4	3.6	•	0.4	0.9	1.2	0.7
Advertising **18**	0.1	•	•	•	0.7	•	•	0.3	•	0.0	0.7	0.1	0.1
Other Expenses **19**	17.3	26.8	•	•	29.7	•	27.0	8.0	•	74.7	28.1	14.4	16.8
Officers' Compensation **20**	0.3	•	•	•	4.7	•	1.1	1.4	•	0.2	1.4	0.6	0.3
Operating Margin **21**	•	•	•	•	18.9	•	6.1	2.1	•	•	5.5	•	•
Operating Margin Before Officers' Comp. **22**	•	•	•	•	23.7	•	7.2	3.6	•	•	6.9	•	•

Selected Average Balance Sheet ($ in Thousands)

Net Receivables 23	63673	0	170	1405	8576	11966	20511	81014	1700470
Inventories 24	7925	0	•	265	1449	2013	2244	16806	206037
Net Property, Plant and Equipment 25	319144	0	526	8639	4615	65748	139172	571712	8435375
Total Assets 26	710898	0	2656	20753	32575	145089	366760	1094052	18881476
Notes and Loans Payable 27	277057	0	598	4039	10033	99585	148037	444766	7324107
All Other Liabilities 28	243955	0	735	4333	29515	40254	147717	361900	6488576
Net Worth 29	189887	0	1323	12382	-6973	5250	71006	287386	5068792

Selected Financial Ratios (Times to 1)

Current Ratio 30	0.9	•	6.5	1.1	1.0	1.0	1.5	1.0	0.9
Quick Ratio 31	0.5	•	2.4	0.8	0.4	0.8	1.3	0.7	0.5
Net Sales to Working Capital 32	•	1.1	1.9	17.5	•	507.9	5.0	•	•
Coverage Ratio 33	1.8	•	74.6	12.9	16.8	2.9	3.0	2.4	1.8
Total Asset Turnover 34	0.4	•	1.0	0.4	2.1	1.0	0.4	0.4	0.4
Inventory Turnover 35	22.6	•	•	12.6	32.4	12.0	20.5	16.9	22.9
Receivables Turnover 36	6.6	•	30.9	3.9	8.1	13.5	6.8	6.6	6.6
Total Liabilities to Net Worth 37	2.7	•	1.0	0.7	•	26.6	4.2	2.8	2.7
Current Assets to Working Capital 38	•	•	1.2	10.1	•	109.6	2.9	•	•
Current Liabilities to Working Capital 39	•	•	0.2	9.1	•	108.6	1.9	•	•
Working Capital to Net Sales 40	•	•	0.5	0.1	•	0.0	0.2	•	•
Inventory to Working Capital 41	•	•	•	0.9	•	7.6	0.1	•	•
Total Receipts to Cash Flow 42	5.3	1.4	2.0	1.6	9.9	1.3	2.5	5.7	5.5
Cost of Goods to Cash Flow 43	3.2	0.0	0.7	0.7	6.9	0.2	0.8	3.6	3.4
Cash Flow to Total Debt 44	0.1	•	1.0	0.6	0.2	0.8	0.2	0.1	0.1

Selected Financial Factors (in Percentages)

Debt Ratio 45	73.3	•	50.2	40.3	121.4	96.4	80.6	73.7	73.2
Return on Total Assets 46	5.1	•	23.7	18.1	10.5	8.1	9.1	5.2	4.9
Return on Equity Before Income Taxes 47	8.6	•	47.0	28.0	•	146.7	31.6	11.7	8.1
Return on Equity After Income Taxes 48	6.3	•	32.2	23.4	•	122.1	26.1	8.5	6.0
Profit Margin (Before Income Tax) 49	5.6	48.4	23.7	44.8	4.8	5.4	16.2	7.5	5.3
Profit Margin (After Income Tax) 50	4.1	39.4	16.3	37.5	3.7	4.5	13.4	5.5	3.9

NATURAL GAS DISTRIBUTION

Table I
Corporations with and without Net Income

MONEY AMOUNTS AND SIZE OF ASSETS IN THOUSANDS OF DOLLARS

Item Description for Accounting Period 7/05 Through 6/06	Total	Zero Assets	Under 500	500 to 1,000	1,000 to 5,000	5,000 to 10,000	10,000 to 25,000	25,000 to 50,000	50,000 to 100,000	100,000 to 250,000	250,000 to 500,000	500,000 to 2,500,000	2,500,000 and over
Number of Enterprises **1**	680	9	348	27	155	41	38	11	10	9	6	9	16
Revenues ($ in Thousands)													
Net Sales **2**	102516965	12135	5533	51639	743773	815174	895539	899974	2327804	4387162	4104109	15913113	72361010
Interest **3**	1548135	351	0	55	1873	1818	828	2858	3076	4961	5520	73885	1452910
Rents **4**	70620	0	0	0	0	1	1565	0	1985	14	134	4376	62544
Royalties **5**	27015	0	0	0	0	0	0	0	32	0	575	0	26408
Other Portfolio Income **6**	2136121	30720	0	1959	0	1808	474	5293	720	61	1558	39742	2053786
Other Receipts **7**	6297533	188	0	439	3549	1839	7785	2010	-9608	63545	28908	15375	6183505
Total Receipts **8**	112596389	43394	5533	54092	749195	820640	906191	910135	2324009	4455743	4140804	16046491	82140163
Average Total Receipts **9**	165583	4822	16	2003	4834	20016	23847	82740	232401	495083	690134	1782943	5133760
Operating Costs/Operating Income (%)													
Cost of Operations **10**	75.5	•	•	53.0	71.8	78.6	87.4	94.8	93.0	95.8	90.6	81.2	71.3
Salaries and Wages **11**	3.2	•	•	2.4	4.6	1.8	2.3	1.2	0.7	0.5	1.1	1.4	3.9
Taxes Paid **12**	2.3	6.9	3.7	0.2	1.9	1.1	0.8	0.2	0.4	0.4	0.5	1.7	2.8
Interest Paid **13**	3.6	21.6	•	1.8	1.1	0.4	0.9	0.4	0.3	0.3	0.5	1.9	4.5
Depreciation **14**	4.0	13.8	•	6.9	3.8	1.7	1.6	0.1	0.9	0.8	0.9	3.1	4.8
Amortization and Depletion **15**	0.5	11.0	•	0.1	0.7	0.2	0.1	0.0	0.6	0.0	0.3	0.3	0.5
Pensions and Other Deferred Comp. **16**	0.6	•	•	•	1.3	0.3	0.4	0.0	0.1	0.1	0.1	0.5	0.7
Employee Benefits **17**	1.0	•	•	•	0.3	0.0	0.3	0.1	0.3	0.2	0.2	0.4	1.3
Advertising **18**	0.0	•	•	•	0.3	0.0	0.1	0.0	0.0	0.1	0.0	0.0	0.0
Other Expenses **19**	13.3	46.6	135.7	32.5	6.5	9.8	5.1	1.6	2.2	1.6	3.1	7.1	16.7
Officers' Compensation **20**	0.6	•	•	•	3.5	1.2	1.3	0.4	0.5	0.2	0.1	0.2	0.7
Operating Margin **21**	•	0.2	•	3.3	4.5	4.1	•	1.0	1.0	2.4	2.4	2.2	•
Operating Margin Before Officers' Comp. **22**	•	0.2	•	3.3	8.0	5.3	1.1	1.4	1.5	0.3	2.6	2.4	•

Selected Average Balance Sheet ($ in Thousands)

Item	1	2	3	4	5	6	7	8	9	10	11	12	13
Net Receivables 23	89868	0	104	240	409	192	3539	28248	11711	39834	91669	167678	3626032
Inventories 24	7842	0	0	53	126	53	859	2739	5920	8708	41643	89718	253258
Net Property, Plant and Equipment 25	118116	0	16	546	1434	3253	5732	497	28030	49160	107056	974269	4349151
Total Assets 26	312131	0	141	988	2518	6837	14602	36256	70650	159641	352963	1702313	11935428
Notes and Loans Payable 27	117255	0	11	3272	840	666	3820	7180	14177	32089	106396	445380	4636360
All Other Liabilities 28	190362	0	85	138	304	1236	6974	22404	24129	71143	150375	668810	7562526
Net Worth 29	4514	0	44	-2421	1373	4935	3808	6671	32343	56409	96193	588123	-263459

Selected Financial Ratios (Times to 1)

Item	1	2	3	4	5	6	7	8	9	10	11	12	13
Current Ratio 30	1.0	•	1.5	3.2	1.7	3.3	1.1	1.4	1.3	1.1	1.1	1.1	1.0
Quick Ratio 31	0.6	•	1.5	3.2	1.3	2.7	0.7	1.2	0.7	0.7	0.8	0.5	0.6
Net Sales to Working Capital 32	265.7	•	0.4	6.3	13.8	13.8	43.4	8.9	28.1	65.2	31.0	51.9	•
Coverage Ratio 33	2.5	12.9	•	5.5	5.7	13.8	2.1	6.0	3.9	6.5	7.3	2.6	2.4
Total Asset Turnover 34	0.5	•	0.1	1.9	1.9	2.9	1.6	2.3	3.3	3.1	1.9	1.0	0.4
Inventory Turnover 35	14.5	•	•	19.0	27.4	296.7	24.0	28.3	36.6	53.6	14.9	16.0	12.7
Receivables Turnover 36	1.9	•	0.3	12.6	15.5	124.3	6.9	4.6	17.7	12.2	11.8	13.3	1.4
Total Liabilities to Net Worth 37	68.1	2.2	•	0.8	0.4	2.8	4.4	1.2	1.8	2.7	1.9	•	•
Current Assets to Working Capital 38	276.3	3.1	•	1.5	2.5	1.4	3.8	4.1	10.3	8.6	12.8	•	•
Current Liabilities to Working Capital 39	275.3	2.1	•	0.5	1.5	0.4	2.8	3.1	9.3	7.6	11.8	•	•
Working Capital to Net Sales 40	0.0	2.5	•	0.2	0.1	0.1	0.1	0.0	0.0	0.0	0.0	•	•
Inventory to Working Capital 41	15.5	•	•	0.5	0.0	2.3	0.4	1.0	1.1	2.3	3.1	•	•
Total Receipts to Cash Flow 42	6.2	•	0.3	1.5	2.9	9.7	7.3	25.4	32.6	35.5	16.6	10.9	5.0
Cost of Goods to Cash Flow 43	4.7	•	•	1.6	7.0	5.7	22.2	30.9	33.1	31.4	15.0	8.9	3.6
Cash Flow to Total Debt 44	0.1	•	0.1	0.2	0.4	1.4	0.1	0.1	0.2	0.2	0.2	0.1	0.1

Selected Financial Factors (in Percentages)

Item	1	2	3	4	5	6	7	8	9	10	11	12	13
Debt Ratio 45	98.6	•	68.5	345.0	45.5	27.8	73.9	81.6	54.2	64.7	72.7	65.5	102.2
Return on Total Assets 46	4.3	•	•	18.9	12.1	14.7	2.9	5.9	3.7	6.3	7.5	5.1	4.2
Return on Equity Before Income Taxes 47	180.2	•	•	•	18.2	18.9	6.0	26.6	6.0	15.1	23.6	9.0	•
Return on Equity After Income Taxes 48	116.8	•	•	•	17.7	13.1	5.8	19.3	3.6	11.4	22.8	5.7	•
Profit Margin (Before Income Tax) 49	5.4	257.8	•	8.0	5.2	4.7	1.0	2.2	0.8	1.7	3.3	3.0	6.5
Profit Margin (After Income Tax) 50	3.5	249.0	•	8.0	5.1	3.3	0.9	1.6	0.5	1.3	3.2	1.9	4.1

Table II

Corporations with Net Income

NATURAL GAS DISTRIBUTION

MONEY AMOUNTS AND SIZE OF ASSETS IN THOUSANDS OF DOLLARS

Item Description for Accounting Period 7/05 Through 6/06	Total	Zero Assets	Under 500	500 to 1,000	1,000 to 5,000	5,000 to 10,000	10,000 to 25,000	25,000 to 50,000	50,000 to 100,000	100,000 to 250,000	250,000 to 500,000	500,000 to 2,500,000	2,500,000 and over
Number of Enterprises **1**	386	9	•	27	140	•	19	•	6	•	•	•	•
Revenues ($ in Thousands)													
Net Sales **2**	81195769	12135	•	51639	600185	•	749601	•	1830382	•	•	•	•
Interest **3**	780127	351	•	55	915	•	0	•	2370	•	•	•	•
Rents **4**	33093	0	•	0	0	•	0	•	1976	•	•	•	•
Royalties **5**	26860	0	•	0	0	•	0	•	0	•	•	•	•
Other Portfolio Income **6**	2039450	30720	•	1959	0	•	26	•	468	•	•	•	•
Other Receipts **7**	1895934	188	•	439	3550	•	6383	•	1721	•	•	•	•
Total Receipts **8**	85971233	43394	•	54092	604650	•	756010	•	1836917	•	•	•	•
Average Total Receipts **9**	222723	4822	•	2003	4319	•	39790	•	306153	•	•	•	•
Operating Costs/Operating Income (%)													
Cost of Operations **10**	73.8	•	•	53.0	65.1	•	92.6	•	93.5	•	•	•	•
Salaries and Wages **11**	3.2	•	•	2.4	5.7	•	1.4	•	0.6	•	•	•	•
Taxes Paid **12**	2.6	6.9	•	0.2	2.3	•	0.4	•	0.4	•	•	•	•
Interest Paid **13**	2.9	21.6	•	1.8	1.4	•	0.5	•	0.2	•	•	•	•
Depreciation **14**	4.0	13.8	•	6.9	4.7	•	0.9	•	0.7	•	•	•	•
Amortization and Depletion **15**	0.5	11.0	•	•	0.1	•	0.1	•	0.7	•	•	•	•
Pensions and Other Deferred Comp. **16**	0.6	•	•	•	0.8	•	0.4	•	0.0	•	•	•	•
Employee Benefits **17**	1.2	•	•	•	1.5	•	0.2	•	0.2	•	•	•	•
Advertising **18**	0.0	•	•	•	0.4	•	0.1	•	0.0	•	•	•	•
Other Expenses **19**	8.9	46.6	•	32.5	7.8	•	1.2	•	1.8	•	•	•	•
Officers' Compensation **20**	0.7	•	•	•	4.4	•	0.2	•	0.5	•	•	•	•
Operating Margin **21**	1.7	0.2	•	3.3	5.8	•	2.0	•	1.3	•	•	•	•
Operating Margin Before Officers' Comp. **22**	2.4	0.2	•	3.3	10.2	•	2.3	•	1.7	•	•	•	•

Selected Average Balance Sheet ($ in Thousands)

Net Receivables 23	29169	0	•	240	453	•	6148	10599
Inventories 24	12201	0	•	0	119	•	763	6293
Net Property, Plant and Equipment 25	168455	0	•	546	1588	•	4540	27187
Total Assets 26	302777	0	•	988	2523	•	16596	73074
Notes and Loans Payable 27	90383	0	•	3272	920	•	2655	7142
All Other Liabilities 28	131688	0	•	138	318	•	10683	24788
Net Worth 29	80707	0	•	-2421	1285	•	3258	41145

Selected Financial Ratios (Times to 1)

Current Ratio 30	1.0	•	•	3.2	1.6	•	1.2	1.7
Quick Ratio 31	0.4	•	•	3.2	1.3	•	0.9	0.9
Net Sales to Working Capital 32	397.6	12.9	•	6.3	12.3	•	29.9	19.9
Coverage Ratio 33	3.6	•	•	5.5	5.8	•	7.1	9.1
Total Asset Turnover 34	0.7	•	•	1.9	1.7	•	2.4	4.2
Inventory Turnover 35	12.7	•	•	23.5	•	•	47.9	45.3
Receivables Turnover 36	8.3	•	•	15.9	14.1	•	7.5	19.0
Total Liabilities to Net Worth 37	2.8	•	•	1.0	•	•	4.1	0.8
Current Assets to Working Capital 38	160.1	•	•	1.5	2.6	•	6.7	2.5
Current Liabilities to Working Capital 39	159.1	•	•	0.5	1.6	•	5.7	1.5
Working Capital to Net Sales 40	0.0	•	•	0.2	0.1	•	0.0	0.1
Inventory to Working Capital 41	26.9	•	•	•	0.6	•	0.7	0.5
Total Receipts to Cash Flow 42	7.3	0.3	•	2.9	7.9	•	25.3	31.3
Cost of Goods to Cash Flow 43	5.4	•	•	1.6	5.1	•	23.4	29.3
Cash Flow to Total Debt 44	0.1	•	•	0.2	0.4	•	0.1	0.3

Selected Financial Factors (in Percentages)

Debt Ratio 45	73.3	•	•	345.0	49.1	•	80.4	43.7
Return on Total Assets 46	7.3	•	•	18.9	13.5	•	8.0	7.6
Return on Equity Before Income Taxes 47	19.9	•	•	21.9	•	•	35.0	12.0
Return on Equity After Income Taxes 48	13.7	•	•	21.2	•	•	34.6	8.9
Profit Margin (Before Income Tax) 49	7.6	257.8	•	8.0	6.6	•	2.9	1.6
Profit Margin (After Income Tax) 50	5.2	249.0	•	8.0	6.4	•	2.9	1.2

Table I

Corporations with and without Net Income

WATER, SEWAGE AND OTHER SYSTEMS

MONEY AMOUNTS AND SIZE OF ASSETS IN THOUSANDS OF DOLLARS

Item Description for Accounting Period 7/05 Through 6/06	Total	Zero Assets	Under 500	500 to 1,000	1,000 to 5,000	5,000 to 10,000	10,000 to 25,000	25,000 to 50,000	50,000 to 100,000	100,000 to 250,000	250,000 to 500,000	500,000 to 2,500,000	2,500,000 and over
Number of Enterprises **1**	5984	296	4813	324	399	72	28	23	7	7	5	6	3
Revenues ($ in Thousands)													
Net Sales **2**	8042860	9165	751824	247343	435481	832992	235804	235832	90421	232153	492778	1143390	3335676
Interest **3**	183935	1505	1602	294	1062	3384	292	3204	4063	2700	2717	6076	157035
Rents **4**	18639	0	0	152	410	263	299	1534	155	1256	324	9287	4960
Royalties **5**	818	0	0	0	0	0	0	0	0	0	818	0	0
Other Portfolio Income **6**	85908	7452	29517	26347	1035	4200	473	350	1109	307	4261	7660	3200
Other Receipts **7**	232249	11571	46801	4346	13880	251	761	7899	4903	5806	29220	21985	84825
Total Receipts **8**	8564409	29693	829744	278482	451868	841090	237629	248819	100651	242222	530118	1188398	3585696
Average Total Receipts **9**	1431	100	172	860	1133	11682	8487	10818	14379	34603	106024	198066	1195232
Operating Costs/Operating Income (%)													
Cost of Operations **10**	29.2	86.4	3.1	40.1	45.8	13.3	55.7	42.5	28.5	27.4	41.2	43.0	26.7
Salaries and Wages **11**	11.1	1.8	11.8	8.2	7.0	44.6	8.0	3.6	7.6	8.3	14.9	3.9	6.3
Taxes Paid **12**	7.4	1.0	6.0	6.1	3.9	5.6	3.5	9.7	12.3	6.7	5.0	7.9	8.9
Interest Paid **13**	10.1	0.2	0.5	8.1	4.6	1.2	4.2	2.9	9.4	11.4	5.9	7.3	17.9
Depreciation **14**	9.8	7.1	5.0	6.5	10.7	1.9	5.7	9.9	10.5	15.3	7.9	12.3	12.3
Amortization and Depletion **15**	3.2	•	0.0	•	0.1	0.1	0.3	0.1	0.5	0.6	0.8	0.4	7.2
Pensions and Other Deferred Comp. **16**	1.2	•	1.1	0.7	0.0	0.0	0.5	0.6	1.9	2.3	0.9	2.0	1.6
Employee Benefits **17**	4.7	0.0	1.8	1.3	1.3	21.4	3.2	1.7	3.8	3.1	3.2	2.8	3.2
Advertising **18**	0.3	•	1.1	0.4	0.0	0.2	0.1	0.0	0.1	0.1	0.5	0.0	0.2
Other Expenses **19**	20.8	59.3	55.3	30.9	29.4	10.8	10.9	28.9	24.5	14.1	16.0	9.6	18.6
Officers' Compensation **20**	1.9	0.3	8.3	5.0	4.6	0.7	3.0	1.9	2.9	3.2	0.9	1.1	0.5
Operating Margin **21**	0.3	•	6.0	•	•	0.1	4.8	•	•	7.6	2.8	9.8	•
Operating Margin Before Officers' Comp. **22**	2.3	•	14.3	•	0.8	7.8	•	•	1.0	10.8	3.7	10.8	•

Selected Average Balance Sheet ($ in Thousands)

Net Receivables 23	179	0	14	75	98	900	1657	1624	1585	4709	32793	25455	143291
Inventories 24	34	0	0	89	8	28	105	109	320	6878	11569	7218	8513
Net Property, Plant and Equipment 25	3357	0	62	440	1912	3341	11562	21711	37722	139717	206449	568293	4044568
Total Assets 26	5888	0	122	723	2734	6757	16653	31201	61793	164579	353332	825204	7783968
Notes and Loans Payable 27	1947	0	20	106	1329	2856	5304	5430	20833	60783	159254	256118	2536047
All Other Liabilities 28	1733	0	23	125	1185	2515	7730	16594	24626	53359	98423	271186	2100403
Net Worth 29	2208	0	79	491	220	1386	3619	9177	16333	50437	95654	297899	3147518

Selected Financial Ratios (Times to 1)

Current Ratio 30	1.0	•	1.7	3.3	2.9	0.8	1.6	0.8	1.9	1.2	3.5	1.1	0.7
Quick Ratio 31	0.5	•	1.7	1.9	2.7	0.4	1.4	0.8	1.3	0.9	1.9	0.6	0.3
Net Sales to Working Capital 32	•	•	8.3	3.9	2.7	•	7.9	•	3.1	13.2	1.9	30.5	•
Coverage Ratio 33	1.7	700.3	37.2	1.6	0.2	1.9	2.3	2.3	2.0	2.0	2.8	2.9	1.2
Total Asset Turnover 34	0.2	•	1.3	1.1	0.4	1.7	0.5	0.3	0.2	0.2	0.3	0.2	0.1
Inventory Turnover 35	11.5	•	•	3.4	61.3	55.1	44.7	40.1	11.5	1.3	3.5	11.4	34.8
Receivables Turnover 36	8.1	•	22.7	9.3	11.3	17.5	5.9	12.6	11.0	7.6	4.6	2.9	15.5
Total Liabilities to Net Worth 37	1.7	•	0.5	0.5	11.4	3.9	3.6	2.4	2.8	2.3	2.7	1.8	1.5
Current Assets to Working Capital 38	•	•	2.4	1.4	1.5	•	2.6	•	2.2	5.5	1.4	10.7	•
Current Liabilities to Working Capital 39	•	•	1.4	0.4	0.5	•	1.6	•	1.2	4.5	0.4	9.7	•
Working Capital to Net Sales 40	•	•	0.1	0.3	0.4	0.1	0.1	•	0.3	0.1	0.5	0.0	•
Inventory to Working Capital 41	•	•	•	0.5	0.0	0.1	0.1	•	0.1	0.2	0.4	1.2	•
Total Receipts to Cash Flow 42	4.1	0.6	1.6	3.1	4.6	9.6	7.0	3.3	3.4	4.3	4.4	5.3	4.7
Cost of Goods to Cash Flow 43	1.2	0.5	0.1	1.2	2.1	1.3	3.9	1.4	1.0	1.2	1.8	2.3	1.3
Cash Flow to Total Debt 44	0.1	•	2.2	1.1	0.1	0.2	0.1	0.1	0.1	0.1	0.1	0.1	0.1

Selected Financial Factors (in Percentages)

Debt Ratio 45	62.5	•	35.0	32.0	92.0	79.5	78.3	70.6	73.6	69.4	72.9	63.9	59.6
Return on Total Assets 46	3.9	•	21.6	14.1	0.4	3.9	4.9	2.1	3.9	4.7	4.5	4.8	3.1
Return on Equity Before Income Taxes 47	4.1	•	32.3	8.1	•	9.1	13.0	4.0	7.4	7.8	10.7	8.8	1.5
Return on Equity After Income Taxes 48	3.2	•	30.4	5.8	•	4.7	7.8	1.6	4.3	5.7	9.3	5.8	1.2
Profit Margin (Before Income Tax) 49	6.8	167.9	16.4	5.2	•	1.1	5.6	3.6	9.4	11.8	10.4	13.7	4.1
Profit Margin (After Income Tax) 50	5.2	167.9	15.4	3.7	•	0.6	3.4	1.4	5.4	8.6	9.0	9.1	3.3

Table II

Corporations with Net Income

WATER, SEWAGE AND OTHER SYSTEMS

MONEY AMOUNTS AND SIZE OF ASSETS IN THOUSANDS OF DOLLARS

Item Description for Accounting Period 7/05 Through 6/06	Total	Zero Assets	Under 500	500 to 1,000	1,000 to 5,000	5,000 to 10,000	10,000 to 25,000	25,000 to 50,000	50,000 to 100,000	100,000 to 250,000	250,000 to 500,000	500,000 to 2,500,000	2,500,000 and over
Number of Enterprises **1**	4129	7	3584	261	163	49	24	20	•	•	•	•	3
Revenues ($ in Thousands)													
Net Sales **2**	6560070	2012	553092	208618	209690	165714	223183	235351	•	•	•	•	3335676
Interest **3**	175295	1505	871	169	1061	333	292	1528	•	•	•	•	157035
Rents **4**	18256	0	0	152	410	263	299	1534	•	•	•	•	4960
Royalties **5**	0	0	0	0	0	0	0	0	•	•	•	•	0
Other Portfolio Income **6**	80661	7452	26500	26347	1035	2899	473	350	•	•	•	•	3200
Other Receipts **7**	204195	11428	46800	3861	463	51	761	2729	•	•	•	•	84825
Total Receipts **8**	7038477	22397	627263	239147	212659	169260	225008	241492	•	•	•	•	3585696
Average Total Receipts **9**	1705	3200	175	916	1305	3454	9375	12075	•	•	•	•	1195232
Operating Costs/Operating Income (%)													
Cost of Operations **10**	31.0	4.8	4.2	47.5	50.0	28.1	58.9	42.6	•	•	•	•	26.7
Salaries and Wages **11**	6.2	8.0	9.3	9.7	5.9	7.1	7.2	3.2	•	•	•	•	6.3
Taxes Paid **12**	7.7	2.4	4.1	4.7	2.8	9.0	3.2	9.7	•	•	•	•	8.9
Interest Paid **13**	11.7	1.1	0.1	9.5	2.5	5.8	2.6	2.9	•	•	•	•	17.9
Depreciation **14**	10.8	32.4	4.4	5.8	8.5	8.0	4.8	9.9	•	•	•	•	12.3
Amortization and Depletion **15**	3.8	•	0.0	•	0.1	0.1	0.2	0.1	•	•	•	•	7.2
Pensions and Other Deferred Comp. **16**	1.4	•	0.8	0.5	0.0	0.1	0.5	0.6	•	•	•	•	1.6
Employee Benefits **17**	2.6	0.2	0.1	1.3	1.7	0.6	3.0	1.6	•	•	•	•	3.2
Advertising **18**	0.3	•	1.1	0.5	0.1	0.1	0.1	0.0	•	•	•	•	0.2
Other Expenses **19**	20.5	62.4	59.3	22.9	18.4	31.3	8.2	21.5	•	•	•	•	18.6
Officers' Compensation **20**	1.5	1.5	5.2	5.9	1.8	3.0	3.2	1.1	•	•	•	•	0.5
Operating Margin **21**	2.4	•	11.4	•	8.2	6.8	8.2	6.8	•	•	•	•	6.8
Operating Margin Before Officers' Comp. **22**	4.0	•	16.6	•	10.0	9.9	11.4	7.9	•	•	•	•	7.9

Selected Average Balance Sheet ($ in Thousands)

Net Receivables 23	209	0	12	93	99	1167	1834	1781	•	•	•	143291
Inventories 24	28	0	0	110	16	0	93	95	•	•	•	8513
Net Property, Plant and Equipment 25	4502	0	54	415	1701	4678	10425	22956	•	•	•	404568
Total Assets 26	7915	0	114	717	2313	6686	15535	30979	•	•	•	7783968
Notes and Loans Payable 27	2533	0	10	132	672	3844	4269	6106	•	•	•	2536047
All Other Liabilities 28	2226	0	13	104	387	1341	6422	11476	•	•	•	2100403
Net Worth 29	3156	0	90	480	1254	1501	4844	13398	•	•	•	3147518

Selected Financial Ratios (Times to 1)

Current Ratio 30	0.9	•	3.2	2.9	2.1	0.7	1.8	2.6	•	•	•	0.7
Quick Ratio 31	0.5	•	3.2	1.5	1.8	0.6	1.5	2.3	•	•	•	0.7
Net Sales to Working Capital 32	•	•	5.3	4.1	4.9	•	6.9	3.6	•	•	•	0.3
Coverage Ratio 33	1.8	915.9	232.5	1.7	4.9	2.6	4.5	4.3	•	•	•	1.2
Total Asset Turnover 34	0.2	•	1.4	1.1	0.6	0.5	0.6	0.4	•	•	•	0.1
Inventory Turnover 35	17.5	•	•	3.5	40.5	•	58.9	52.8	•	•	•	0.1
Receivables Turnover 36	11.6	•	14.5	11.2	10.5	3.9	7.5	8.7	•	•	•	34.8
Total Liabilities to Net Worth 37	1.5	•	0.3	0.5	0.8	3.5	2.2	1.3	•	•	•	15.5
Current Assets to Working Capital 38	•	•	1.5	1.5	1.9	•	2.3	1.6	•	•	•	1.5
Current Liabilities to Working Capital 39	•	•	0.5	0.5	0.9	•	1.3	0.6	•	•	•	0.6
Working Capital to Net Sales 40	•	0.2	0.2	0.2	0.2	•	0.1	0.3	•	•	•	0.3
Inventory to Working Capital 41	•	•	•	0.6	0.1	•	0.1	•	•	•	•	•
Total Receipts to Cash Flow 42	3.7	0.1	1.4	3.9	4.2	2.9	6.4	3.5	•	•	•	4.7
Cost of Goods to Cash Flow 43	1.2	0.0	0.1	1.8	2.1	0.8	3.8	1.5	•	•	•	1.3
Cash Flow to Total Debt 44	0.1	•	4.8	0.9	0.3	0.2	0.1	0.2	•	•	•	0.1

Selected Financial Factors (in Percentages)

Debt Ratio 45	60.1	•	20.8	32.9	45.8	77.6	68.8	56.8	•	•	•	59.6
Return on Total Assets 46	4.3	•	33.9	17.6	6.7	7.4	6.9	4.7	•	•	•	3.1
Return on Equity Before Income Taxes 47	4.9	•	42.6	10.5	9.8	20.2	17.3	8.2	•	•	•	1.5
Return on Equity After Income Taxes 48	3.9	•	40.3	7.5	7.3	14.2	12.8	6.3	•	•	•	1.2
Profit Margin (Before Income Tax) 49	9.7	1000.3	24.8	6.3	9.6	9.0	9.0	9.4	•	•	•	4.1
Profit Margin (After Income Tax) 50	7.8	1000.3	23.5	4.5	7.2	6.3	6.6	7.2	•	•	•	3.3

Table I

Corporations with and without Net Income

COMBINATION GAS AND ELECTRIC

MONEY AMOUNTS AND SIZE OF ASSETS IN THOUSANDS OF DOLLARS

Item Description for Accounting Period 7/05 Through 6/06	Total	Zero Assets	Under 500	500 to 1,000	1,000 to 5,000	5,000 to 10,000	10,000 to 25,000	25,000 to 50,000	50,000 to 100,000	100,000 to 250,000	250,000 to 500,000	500,000 to 2,500,000	2,500,000 and over
Number of Enterprises 1	36	0	0	0	0	0	0	3	0	0	3	0	30
Revenues ($ in Thousands)													
Net Sales 2	203692331	0	0	0	0	0	0	196195	0	0	1581950	0	201914186
Interest 3	3673244	0	0	0	0	0	0	389	0	0	4371	0	3668484
Rents 4	1010008	0	0	0	0	0	0	1	0	0	8227	0	1001780
Royalties 5	7871	0	0	0	0	0	0	0	0	0	0	0	7871
Other Portfolio Income 6	4073010	0	0	0	0	0	0	1416	0	0	1260	0	4070336
Other Receipts 7	10609442	0	0	0	0	0	0	1866	0	0	20606	0	10586968
Total Receipts 8	223065906	0	0	0	0	0	0	199867	0	0	1616414	0	221249625
Average Total Receipts 9	6196275	•	•	•	•	•	•	66622	•	•	538805	•	7374988
Operating Costs/Operating Income (%)													
Cost of Operations 10	54.6	•	•	•	•	•	•	72.4	•	•	67.8	•	54.5
Salaries and Wages 11	4.6	•	•	•	•	•	•	3.4	•	•	6.3	•	4.6
Taxes Paid 12	4.2	•	•	•	•	•	•	4.6	•	•	6.7	•	4.2
Interest Paid 13	6.2	•	•	•	•	•	•	2.0	•	•	5.2	•	6.2
Depreciation 14	6.8	•	•	•	•	•	•	4.0	•	•	11.1	•	6.7
Amortization and Depletion 15	0.4	•	•	•	•	•	•	0.7	•	•	1.8	•	0.4
Pensions and Other Deferred Comp. 16	1.1	•	•	•	•	•	•	0.1	•	•	1.0	•	1.1
Employee Benefits 17	1.2	•	•	•	•	•	•	1.0	•	•	2.9	•	1.2
Advertising 18	0.1	•	•	•	•	•	•	1.9	•	•	0.1	•	0.1
Other Expenses 19	24.0	•	•	•	•	•	•	8.3	•	•	16.1	•	24.0
Officers' Compensation 20	0.3	•	•	•	•	•	•	0.3	•	•	0.5	•	0.3
Operating Margin 21	•	•	•	•	•	•	•	1.1	•	•	•	•	•
Operating Margin Before Officers' Comp. 22	•	•	•	•	•	•	•	1.4	•	•	•	•	•

Selected Average Balance Sheet ($ in Thousands)

Net Receivables 23	1293484	13903	80415	1542749
Inventories 24	273881	352	23640	326241
Net Property, Plant and Equipment 25	6819974	41817	757024	8104085
Total Assets 26	15780682	93050	1279662	18799547
Notes and Loans Payable 27	5196993	49000	275790	6203913
All Other Liabilities 28	5501156	25869	431787	6555621
Net Worth 29	5082533	18181	572085	6040013

Selected Financial Ratios (Times to 1)

Current Ratio 30	1.0	1.3	1.1	1.0
Quick Ratio 31	0.6	1.1	0.6	0.6
Net Sales to Working Capital 32	64.0	16.9	26.7	64.9
Coverage Ratio 33	2.0	2.4		2.0
Total Asset Turnover 34	0.4	0.7	0.4	0.4
Inventory Turnover 35	11.3	134.7	15.1	11.2
Receivables Turnover 36	4.8	9.4	13.1	4.8
Total Liabilities to Net Worth 37	2.1	4.1	1.2	2.1
Current Assets to Working Capital 38	29.8	4.3	8.7	30.3
Current Liabilities to Working Capital 39	28.8	3.3	7.7	29.3
Working Capital to Net Sales 40	0.0	0.1	0.0	0.0
Inventory to Working Capital 41	3.2	0.1	0.0	3.3
Total Receipts to Cash Flow 42	3.9	11.8	1.2	3.9
Cost of Goods to Cash Flow 43	2.1	8.6	3.9	2.1
Cash Flow to Total Debt 44	0.1	0.1	2.1	0.1

Selected Financial Factors (in Percentages)

Debt Ratio 45	67.8	80.5	55.3	67.9
Return on Total Assets 46	4.4	3.4		4.4
Return on Equity Before Income Taxes 47	6.7		10.2	6.9
Return on Equity After Income Taxes 48	4.3		7.2	4.5
Profit Margin (Before Income Tax) 49	6.0		2.8	6.2
Profit Margin (After Income Tax) 50	3.8		2.0	4.0

Table II

Corporations with Net Income

COMBINATION GAS AND ELECTRIC

MONEY AMOUNTS AND SIZE OF ASSETS IN THOUSANDS OF DOLLARS

Item Description for Accounting Period 7/05 Through 6/06	Total	Zero Assets	Under 500	500 to 1,000	1,000 to 5,000	5,000 to 10,000	10,000 to 25,000	25,000 to 50,000	50,000 to 100,000	100,000 to 250,000	250,000 to 500,000	500,000 to 2,500,000	2,500,000 and over
Number of Enterprises 1	32	0	0	0	0	0	0	•	0	3	0	0	•
Revenues ($ in Thousands)													
Net Sales 2	191976558	0	0	0	0	0	0	•	0	879178	0	0	•
Interest 3	2320236	0	0	0	0	0	0	•	0	3974	0	0	•
Rents 4	948687	0	0	0	0	0	0	•	0	1030	0	0	•
Royalties 5	6499	0	0	0	0	0	0	•	0	0	0	0	•
Other Portfolio Income 6	3408051	0	0	0	0	0	0	•	0	853	0	0	•
Other Receipts 7	7210346	0	0	0	0	0	0	•	0	5513	0	0	•
Total Receipts 8	205870377	0	0	0	0	0	0	•	0	890548	0	0	•
Average Total Receipts 9	6433449	•	•	•	•	•	•	•	•	296849	•	•	•
Operating Costs/Operating Income (%)													
Cost of Operations 10	54.3	•	•	•	•	•	•	•	•	54.0	•	•	•
Salaries and Wages 11	4.6	•	•	•	•	•	•	•	•	2.0	•	•	•
Taxes Paid 12	4.1	•	•	•	•	•	•	•	•	3.6	•	•	•
Interest Paid 13	5.9	•	•	•	•	•	•	•	•	3.0	•	•	•
Depreciation 14	6.7	•	•	•	•	•	•	•	•	10.2	•	•	•
Amortization and Depletion 15	0.3	•	•	•	•	•	•	•	•	0.5	•	•	•
Pensions and Other Deferred Comp. 16	1.1	•	•	•	•	•	•	•	•	1.8	•	•	•
Employee Benefits 17	1.2	•	•	•	•	•	•	•	•	0.6	•	•	•
Advertising 18	0.1	•	•	•	•	•	•	•	•	0.5	•	•	•
Other Expenses 19	20.7	•	•	•	•	•	•	•	•	21.8	•	•	•
Officers' Compensation 20	0.3	•	•	•	•	•	•	•	•	0.7	•	•	•
Operating Margin 21	0.5	•	•	•	•	•	•	•	•	1.3	•	•	•
Operating Margin Before Officers' Comp. 22	0.8	•	•	•	•	•	•	•	•	2.0	•	•	•

Selected Average Balance Sheet ($ in Thousands)

Net Receivables 23	1407401	36597
Inventories 24	211335	9998
Net Property, Plant and Equipment 25	7061040	328532
Total Assets 26	16424583	543869
Notes and Loans Payable 27	5166680	170075
All Other Liabilities 28	5794857	208115
Net Worth 29	5463046	165679

Selected Financial Ratios (Times to 1)

Current Ratio 30	1.1	1.1
Quick Ratio 31	0.7	0.5
Net Sales to Working Capital 32	42.9	74.7
Coverage Ratio 33	2.3	1.9
Total Asset Turnover 34	0.4	0.5
Inventory Turnover 35	15.4	15.8
Receivables Turnover 36	5.2	16.0
Total Liabilities to Net Worth 37	2.0	2.3
Current Assets to Working Capital 38	19.8	20.9
Current Liabilities to Working Capital 39	18.8	19.9
Working Capital to Net Sales 40	0.0	0.0
Inventory to Working Capital 41	2.0	2.5
Total Receipts to Cash Flow 42	4.1	4.7
Cost of Goods to Cash Flow 43	2.2	2.6
Cash Flow to Total Debt 44	0.1	0.2

Selected Financial Factors (in Percentages)

Debt Ratio 45	66.7	69.5
Return on Total Assets 46	5.0	3.0
Return on Equity Before Income Taxes 47	8.6	4.5
Return on Equity After Income Taxes 48	6.1	3.0
Profit Margin (Before Income Tax) 49	7.8	2.5
Profit Margin (After Income Tax) 50	5.5	1.7

24

Table I

Corporations with and without Net Income

CONSTRUCTION OF BUILDINGS

MONEY AMOUNTS AND SIZE OF ASSETS IN THOUSANDS OF DOLLARS

Item Description for Accounting Period 7/05 Through 6/06	Total	Zero Assets	Under 500	500 to 1,000	1,000 to 5,000	5,000 to 10,000	10,000 to 25,000	25,000 to 50,000	50,000 to 100,000	100,000 to 250,000	250,000 to 500,000	500,000 to 2,500,000	2,500,000 and over
Number of Enterprises **1**	224109	32138	140337	18087	25705	4330	2409	622	275	116	34	44	12
Revenues ($ in Thousands)													
Net Sales **2**	624841005	5879865	77163452	32016834	111857768	53204565	66259653	41604933	33846402	30017775	17332665	60282874	95374220
Interest **3**	1801350	2503	21676	16836	67714	36913	50061	31384	21339	39124	28652	278504	1206645
Rents **4**	490392	58	28866	22641	83156	28754	25083	28659	23798	28784	51533	140834	28225
Royalties **5**	168085	0	0	0	0	7756	0	0	25	0	291	137871	22142
Other Portfolio Income **6**	1660625	10455	146815	89448	128589	63971	104418	42405	30570	111052	121959	410384	400566
Other Receipts **7**	8206113	-14391	620241	230889	1001908	596080	608419	331079	405498	295630	419082	1491807	2219863
Total Receipts **8**	637167570	5878490	77981050	32376648	113139135	53938039	67047634	42038460	34327632	30492365	17954182	62742274	99251661
Average Total Receipts **9**	2843	183	556	1790	4401	12457	27832	67586	124828	262865	528064	1425961	8270972
Operating Costs/Operating Income (%)													
Cost of Operations **10**	79.7	59.9	68.2	78.5	85.0	85.6	88.2	89.6	88.7	88.6	87.0	80.9	62.9
Salaries and Wages **11**	3.5	5.5	5.8	3.3	2.7	2.6	2.5	2.4	2.7	2.5	4.2	3.9	4.8
Taxes Paid **12**	1.1	1.9	1.8	1.3	1.1	0.9	0.7	0.6	0.6	0.6	0.7	1.2	1.4
Interest Paid **13**	0.7	0.6	0.5	0.8	0.6	0.5	0.5	0.5	0.3	0.4	0.5	1.2	1.4
Depreciation **14**	0.5	0.6	1.0	0.7	0.6	0.5	0.3	0.4	0.3	0.4	0.5	0.5	0.2
Amortization and Depletion **15**	0.0	0.0	0.0	0.0	0.0	0.0	0.0	0.0	0.0	0.0	0.0	0.2	0.1
Pensions and Other Deferred Comp. **16**	0.2	0.0	0.3	0.2	0.3	0.2	0.2	0.2	0.2	0.2	0.3	0.3	0.1
Employee Benefits **17**	0.5	0.5	1.0	0.6	0.4	0.5	0.5	0.4	0.4	0.2	0.3	0.4	0.3
Advertising **18**	0.3	0.2	0.4	0.4	0.2	0.2	0.2	0.2	0.2	0.2	0.3	0.4	0.5
Other Expenses **19**	7.4	21.2	13.2	7.9	4.4	4.2	3.0	2.5	2.7	2.2	2.3	4.8	17.9
Officers' Compensation **20**	1.9	4.4	4.7	3.0	2.5	2.4	1.5	1.2	1.0	0.8	0.6	0.9	0.6
Operating Margin **21**	4.0	5.2	3.1	3.4	2.3	2.4	2.3	2.2	2.7	3.8	3.1	5.3	9.8
Operating Margin Before Officers' Comp. **22**	6.0	9.6	7.8	6.4	4.7	4.8	3.8	3.3	3.7	4.6	3.6	6.2	10.4

Selected Average Balance Sheet ($ in Thousands)

Net Receivables 23	294	0	13	84	354	1601	3966	10100	20366	40384	74814	176969	841612
Inventories 24	418	0	15	180	545	1543	3191	6896	12906	33933	103560	225480	2896319
Net Property, Plant and Equipment 25	154	0	26	112	264	745	1398	3216	4915	13013	36772	153364	216628
Total Assets 26	1596	0	109	713	2130	6883	14924	34557	67116	151454	340920	1034517	7868179
Notes and Loans Payable 27	614	0	61	372	1002	2799	5598	11019	21340	48492	93766	277866	3099943
All Other Liabilities 28	552	0	25	190	754	2803	6482	16417	30339	60739	129544	395065	1848935
Net Worth 29	430	0	23	151	374	1281	2844	7120	15438	42224	117610	361587	2919301

Selected Financial Ratios (Times to 1)

Current Ratio 30	1.6	•	1.6	1.5	1.4	1.4	1.4	1.3	1.4	1.5	1.7	1.6	2.7
Quick Ratio 31	0.7	•	0.9	0.6	0.5	0.6	0.7	0.7	0.7	0.8	0.8	0.7	0.7
Net Sales to Working Capital 32	6.3	•	21.9	11.0	8.7	7.9	8.2	10.1	7.4	6.3	5.3	6.0	2.5
Coverage Ratio 33	9.1	10.1	9.9	7.1	6.7	8.4	7.9	8.1	10.0	10.3	10.5	8.7	10.9
Total Asset Turnover 34	1.7	•	5.1	2.5	2.0	1.8	1.9	1.9	1.8	1.7	1.5	1.3	1.0
Inventory Turnover 35	5.3	•	25.6	7.7	6.8	6.8	7.6	8.7	8.5	6.8	4.3	4.9	1.7
Receivables Turnover 36	10.4	•	40.2	20.5	12.3	8.6	7.6	7.2	6.7	7.2	6.4	9.1	11.5
Total Liabilities to Net Worth 37	2.7	•	3.8	3.7	4.7	4.2	3.9	3.9	3.3	2.6	1.9	1.9	1.7
Current Assets to Working Capital 38	2.6	•	2.7	3.2	3.4	3.5	3.6	4.2	3.3	2.8	2.5	2.7	1.6
Current Liabilities to Working Capital 39	1.6	•	1.7	2.2	2.4	2.5	2.6	3.2	2.3	1.8	1.5	1.7	0.6
Working Capital to Net Sales 40	0.2	•	0.0	0.1	0.1	0.1	0.1	0.1	0.1	0.2	0.2	0.2	0.4
Inventory to Working Capital 41	1.1	•	0.6	0.9	1.2	1.1	1.1	1.1	0.9	0.9	1.1	1.2	1.1
Total Receipts to Cash Flow 42	8.2	4.1	6.3	9.1	14.7	14.1	17.8	20.1	16.4	14.4	12.8	8.1	3.3
Cost of Goods to Cash Flow 43	6.5	2.4	4.3	7.2	12.5	12.1	15.7	18.0	14.6	12.7	11.2	6.6	2.1
Cash Flow to Total Debt 44	0.3	•	1.0	0.3	0.2	0.2	0.1	0.1	0.1	0.2	0.2	0.3	0.5

Selected Financial Factors (in Percentages)

Debt Ratio 45	73.0	•	79.1	78.8	82.4	81.4	80.9	79.4	77.0	72.1	65.5	65.0	62.9
Return on Total Assets 46	11.8	•	23.5	13.2	8.2	7.7	7.4	7.1	8.4	10.0	10.9	14.0	15.5
Return on Equity Before Income Taxes 47	38.9	•	101.2	53.5	39.5	36.5	34.0	30.0	33.0	32.5	28.6	35.5	37.8
Return on Equity After Income Taxes 48	31.9	•	99.4	52.5	38.3	34.1	32.1	28.6	31.2	30.1	26.8	27.1	24.6
Profit Margin (Before Income Tax) 49	6.0	5.1	4.2	4.6	3.4	3.8	3.5	3.2	4.1	5.3	6.6	9.4	13.9
Profit Margin (After Income Tax) 50	4.9	5.1	4.1	4.5	3.3	3.6	3.3	3.0	3.9	4.9	6.2	7.2	9.1

Table II
Corporations with Net Income

CONSTRUCTION OF BUILDINGS

MONEY AMOUNTS AND SIZE OF ASSETS IN THOUSANDS OF DOLLARS

Item Description for Accounting Period 7/05 Through 6/06	Total	Zero Assets	Under 500	500 to 1,000	1,000 to 5,000	5,000 to 10,000	10,000 to 25,000	25,000 to 50,000	50,000 to 100,000	100,000 to 250,000	250,000 to 500,000	500,000 to 2,500,000	2,500,000 and over
Number of Enterprises 1	141397	15142	89487	12958	17968	3094	1839	496	225	105	•	•	12

Revenues ($ in Thousands)

	Total	Zero Assets	Under 500	500 to 1,000	1,000 to 5,000	5,000 to 10,000	10,000 to 25,000	25,000 to 50,000	50,000 to 100,000	100,000 to 250,000	250,000 to 500,000	500,000 to 2,500,000	2,500,000 and over
Net Sales 2	549774456	3433267	60581061	25048843	94429525	44557624	57031160	36380622	30071131	28062240	•	•	95374220
Interest 3	1738360	1786	13028	13682	53268	31960	41860	25559	18878	38911	•	•	1206645
Rents 4	432490	58	15330	19050	61347	23813	21567	20002	22159	28784	•	•	28225
Royalties 5	168084	0	0	0	0	7755	0	0	25	0	•	•	22142
Other Portfolio Income 6	1533733	9596	100532	73556	112013	59042	84419	34300	25499	109626	•	•	400566
Other Receipts 7	8007568	29251	586495	206730	947416	548123	570798	290121	384104	327389	•	•	2219863
Total Receipts 8	561654691	3473958	61296446	25361861	95603569	45228317	57749804	36750604	30521796	28566950	•	•	99251661
Average Total Receipts 9	3972	229	685	1957	5321	14618	31403	74094	135652	272066	•	•	8270972

Operating Costs/Operating Income (%)

	Total	Zero Assets	Under 500	500 to 1,000	1,000 to 5,000	5,000 to 10,000	10,000 to 25,000	25,000 to 50,000	50,000 to 100,000	100,000 to 250,000	250,000 to 500,000	500,000 to 2,500,000	2,500,000 and over
Cost of Operations 10	79.0	47.0	66.9	76.3	84.8	85.0	87.8	88.8	88.1	88.3	•	•	62.9
Salaries and Wages 11	3.4	5.8	5.0	2.8	2.6	2.4	2.3	2.4	2.8	2.5	•	•	4.8
Taxes Paid 12	1.1	1.2	1.6	1.3	1.1	0.8	0.7	0.6	0.7	0.6	•	•	1.4
Interest Paid 13	0.7	0.4	0.3	0.7	0.5	0.4	0.4	0.4	0.5	0.6	•	•	1.4
Depreciation 14	0.4	0.5	0.8	0.6	0.5	0.5	0.3	0.3	0.3	0.4	•	•	0.2
Amortization and Depletion 15	0.1	0.0	0.0	0.0	0.0	0.0	0.0	0.0	0.0	0.0	•	•	0.1
Pensions and Other Deferred Comp. 16	0.2	•	0.2	0.2	0.3	0.2	0.2	0.2	0.2	0.2	•	•	0.1
Employee Benefits 17	0.5	0.2	1.0	0.6	0.3	0.5	0.5	0.4	0.4	0.2	•	•	0.3
Advertising 18	0.3	0.3	0.4	0.4	0.2	0.2	0.2	0.2	0.2	0.2	•	•	0.5
Other Expenses 19	7.2	24.4	12.8	8.0	3.7	4.0	2.7	2.3	2.4	2.1	•	•	17.9
Officers' Compensation 20	1.8	4.4	4.5	3.1	2.4	2.0	1.5	1.2	1.0	0.8	•	•	0.6
Operating Margin 21	5.4	15.7	6.4	5.9	3.6	4.0	3.5	3.3	3.5	4.2	•	•	9.8
Operating Margin Before Officers' Comp. 22	7.2	20.2	10.9	9.0	6.0	6.0	4.9	4.5	4.5	5.0	•	•	10.4

Selected Average Balance Sheet ($ in Thousands)

Net Receivables 23	402	0	11	88	379	1848	4278	10593	21362	41222	•	841612
Inventories 24	586	0	15	169	552	1565	3408	7206	14216	34810	•	2896319
Net Property, Plant and Equipment 25	180	0	22	87	239	623	1273	2641	3977	12452	•	216628
Total Assets 26	2141	0	105	706	2176	6919	14970	34707	67632	151793	•	7868179
Notes and Loans Payable 27	760	0	51	303	945	2315	4977	10048	20059	46433	•	3099943
All Other Liabilities 28	730	0	23	176	751	2842	6588	16562	31537	61921	•	1848935
Net Worth 29	651	0	31	227	480	1762	3406	8096	16036	43439	•	2919301

Selected Financial Ratios (Times to 1)

Current Ratio 30	1.7	•	1.7	1.7	1.5	1.4	1.3	1.4	1.6	•	2.7
Quick Ratio 31	0.7	•	1.0	0.7	0.6	0.7	0.7	0.7	0.8	•	0.7
Net Sales to Working Capital 32	6.0	•	24.4	8.9	8.5	8.1	9.9	9.3	8.5	•	2.5
Coverage Ratio 33	11.7	42.1	22.8	12.0	10.3	14.4	12.6	12.6	11.9	•	10.9
Total Asset Turnover 34	1.8	•	6.5	2.7	2.4	2.1	2.1	2.1	2.0	•	1.0
Inventory Turnover 35	5.2	•	31.0	8.8	8.1	7.8	9.0	8.0	8.3	•	1.7
Receivables Turnover 36	11.1	•	57.9	22.2	14.7	9.2	7.7	8.0	7.1	•	11.5
Total Liabilities to Net Worth 37	2.3	•	2.4	2.1	3.5	2.9	3.3	3.4	3.2	•	1.7
Current Assets to Working Capital 38	2.4	•	2.4	2.5	2.9	3.2	3.9	3.8	3.6	•	1.6
Current Liabilities to Working Capital 39	1.4	•	1.4	1.5	1.9	2.2	2.9	2.8	2.6	•	0.6
Working Capital to Net Sales 40	0.2	•	0.0	0.1	0.1	0.1	0.1	0.1	0.1	•	0.4
Inventory to Working Capital 41	1.0	•	0.6	0.5	1.0	0.9	1.1	1.1	0.9	•	1.1
Total Receipts to Cash Flow 42	7.3	2.5	5.3	7.3	12.8	11.7	16.9	15.4	15.0	•	3.3
Cost of Goods to Cash Flow 43	5.8	1.2	3.5	5.6	10.9	9.9	15.1	13.5	13.2	•	2.1
Cash Flow to Total Debt 44	0.4	•	1.7	0.6	0.2	0.2	0.2	0.2	0.2	•	0.5

Selected Financial Factors (in Percentages)

Debt Ratio 45	69.6	•	70.7	67.8	77.9	74.5	76.7	77.2	76.3	•	62.9
Return on Total Assets 46	15.0	•	50.9	21.5	13.0	12.3	9.9	10.6	10.8	•	15.5
Return on Equity Before Income Taxes 47	45.1	•	165.9	61.2	53.2	45.0	38.9	42.9	41.8	•	37.8
Return on Equity After Income Taxes 48	37.8	•	163.8	60.3	51.9	42.6	37.4	40.9	39.7	•	24.6
Profit Margin (Before Income Tax) 49	7.6	16.9	7.5	7.2	4.9	5.5	4.3	4.7	5.0	•	13.9
Profit Margin (After Income Tax) 50	6.3	16.8	7.4	7.1	4.7	5.2	4.1	4.5	4.8	•	9.1

Table I

Corporations with and without Net Income

HEAVY AND CIVIL ENGINEERING CONSTRUCTION

MONEY AMOUNTS AND SIZE OF ASSETS IN THOUSANDS OF DOLLARS

Item Description for Accounting Period 7/05 Through 6/06		Total	Zero Assets	Under 500	500 to 1,000	1,000 to 5,000	5,000 to 10,000	10,000 to 25,000	25,000 to 50,000	50,000 to 100,000	100,000 to 250,000	250,000 to 500,000	500,000 to 2,500,000	2,500,000 and over
Number of Enterprises	1	27269	3087	12626	3654	5449	1137	900	228	116	47	11	15	0
Revenues ($ in Thousands)														
Net Sales	2	177599780	980718	9593624	7433101	32267731	17572338	29245752	15737126	13370571	10965752	7088308	33344758	0
Interest	3	261192	3158	6990	3071	28528	18047	23506	11012	24640	11945	15886	114409	0
Rents	4	134001	1198	438	8173	14227	5671	28082	17909	10724	13120	4107	30352	0
Royalties	5	79924	0	0	0	0	0	1985	11	393	7302	8084	62148	0
Other Portfolio Income	6	991937	53764	106176	34476	178663	53354	118145	66060	99537	84259	13737	183768	0
Other Receipts	7	1941829	61209	51036	5171	87005	138578	142329	98098	177692	206297	30077	944338	0
Total Receipts	8	181008663	1100047	9758264	7483992	32576154	17787988	29559799	15930216	13683557	11288675	7160199	34679773	0
Average Total Receipts	9	6638	356	773	2048	5978	15645	32844	69869	117962	240185	650927	2311985	•
Operating Costs/Operating Income (%)														
Cost of Operations	10	75.0	70.6	44.3	57.5	61.1	77.6	80.1	82.0	80.1	84.3	86.1	84.5	•
Salaries and Wages	11	4.4	10.6	11.7	8.6	6.0	3.1	3.2	2.7	3.1	3.2	2.4	3.5	•
Taxes Paid	12	1.7	2.6	3.3	2.8	2.2	1.8	1.6	1.2	1.8	1.0	0.9	1.3	•
Interest Paid	13	0.7	1.1	0.9	0.8	0.6	0.7	0.6	0.5	0.6	1.2	1.1	0.8	•
Depreciation	14	2.7	4.1	2.9	5.1	3.5	2.7	2.6	2.5	2.9	2.8	2.0	1.6	•
Amortization and Depletion	15	0.2	0.3	0.0	0.0	0.0	0.0	0.0	0.1	0.3	0.2	0.3	0.5	•
Pensions and Other Deferred Comp.	16	0.4	0.3	0.6	0.7	0.3	0.9	0.4	0.5	0.3	0.4	0.3	0.3	•
Employee Benefits	17	1.0	2.0	1.7	1.1	0.9	1.6	1.1	1.2	1.0	1.0	1.0	0.5	•
Advertising	18	0.1	0.1	0.5	0.3	0.1	0.1	0.1	0.1	0.1	0.0	0.0	0.0	•
Other Expenses	19	9.5	18.1	21.3	15.8	18.7	6.6	5.8	4.8	6.6	5.7	4.6	5.8	•
Officers' Compensation	20	2.3	2.7	9.8	3.0	3.2	2.3	1.9	1.3	1.1	1.1	0.7	1.4	•
Operating Margin	21	1.9	•	3.0	4.2	3.3	2.6	2.7	3.2	2.1	•	0.6	•	•
Operating Margin Before Officers' Comp.	22	4.3	•	12.8	7.3	6.5	4.9	4.6	4.5	3.2	1.3	1.3	1.1	•

Selected Average Balance Sheet ($ in Thousands)

Net Receivables 23	992	0	20	182	701	2283	5586	13118	22786	42262	111244	389129
Inventories 24	100	0	4	17	74	434	450	857	2112	5318	14041	19822
Net Property, Plant and Equipment 25	899	0	64	301	777	1808	4161	8213	20396	36968	98099	368178
Total Assets 26	3307	0	163	706	2286	7139	15180	34338	69275	151086	348425	1633326
Notes and Loans Payable 27	783	0	122	262	682	1991	3487	6470	17610	46714	77315	210977
All Other Liabilities 28	1295	0	26	111	644	2594	5300	14406	22751	64786	113618	875279
Net Worth 29	1229	0	15	333	960	2554	6393	13462	28914	39586	157492	547071

Selected Financial Ratios (Times to 1)

Current Ratio 30	1.4	•	1.2	2.2	1.7	1.5	1.6	1.5	1.6	1.5	1.7	1.1
Quick Ratio 31	1.1	•	1.0	2.0	1.4	1.1	1.3	1.2	1.2	1.1	1.3	0.8
Net Sales to Working Capital 32	11.4	•	54.8	10.0	10.4	9.4	8.7	9.0	8.0	8.1	8.0	50.8
Coverage Ratio 33	6.3	0.8	6.4	6.8	7.9	6.7	7.5	10.6	7.8	2.7	2.6	5.5
Total Asset Turnover 34	2.0	•	4.7	2.9	2.6	2.2	2.1	2.0	1.7	1.5	1.8	1.4
Inventory Turnover 35	48.9	•	75.3	70.6	48.9	27.7	57.8	66.1	43.7	37.0	39.5	94.7
Receivables Turnover 36	7.1	•	31.6	12.3	8.4	6.8	6.3	5.9	5.8	5.6	6.7	8.4
Total Liabilities to Net Worth 37	1.7	•	9.8	1.1	1.4	1.8	1.4	1.6	1.4	2.8	1.2	2.0
Current Assets to Working Capital 38	3.3	•	5.1	1.8	2.4	2.9	2.6	3.0	2.7	2.9	2.4	18.7
Current Liabilities to Working Capital 39	2.3	•	4.1	0.8	1.4	1.9	1.6	2.0	1.7	1.9	1.4	17.7
Working Capital to Net Sales 40	0.1	•	0.0	0.1	0.1	0.1	0.1	0.1	0.1	0.1	0.1	0.0
Inventory to Working Capital 41	0.2	•	0.4	0.0	0.1	0.3	0.1	0.1	0.1	0.1	0.1	0.0
Total Receipts to Cash Flow 42	9.9	8.3	4.8	6.5	5.4	14.8	15.0	15.4	13.9	18.0	23.2	0.6
Cost of Goods to Cash Flow 43	7.4	5.9	2.1	3.8	3.3	11.5	12.0	12.7	11.2	15.2	20.0	12.7
Cash Flow to Total Debt 44	0.3	•	1.1	0.8	0.8	0.2	0.2	0.2	0.2	0.1	0.1	10.7

Selected Financial Factors (in Percentages)

Debt Ratio 45	62.8	•	90.8	52.8	58.0	64.2	57.9	60.8	58.3	73.8	54.8	66.5
Return on Total Assets 46	9.0	•	26.2	16.5	12.7	9.8	9.3	9.8	8.4	4.9	5.0	6.2
Return on Equity Before Income Taxes 47	20.4	•	238.9	29.9	26.3	23.4	19.1	22.6	17.5	11.6	6.8	15.1
Return on Equity After Income Taxes 48	17.9	•	229.1	29.0	24.4	21.0	17.3	20.8	15.8	9.9	5.1	11.1
Profit Margin (Before Income Tax) 49	3.8	•	4.7	4.9	4.3	3.9	3.8	4.4	4.4	2.0	1.7	3.7
Profit Margin (After Income Tax) 50	3.4	•	4.5	4.7	3.9	3.5	3.4	4.1	4.0	1.7	1.3	2.7

Table II
Corporations with Net Income

HEAVY AND CIVIL ENGINEERING CONSTRUCTION

MONEY AMOUNTS AND SIZE OF ASSETS IN THOUSANDS OF DOLLARS

Item Description for Accounting Period 7/05 Through 6/06	Total	Zero Assets	Under 500	500 to 1,000	1,000 to 5,000	5,000 to 10,000	10,000 to 25,000	25,000 to 50,000	50,000 to 100,000	100,000 to 250,000	250,000 to 500,000	500,000 to 2,500,000	2,500,000 and over
Number of Enterprises **1**	18927	1262	8397	2818	4420	915	758	200	95	•	8	•	0
Revenues ($ in Thousands)													
Net Sales **2**	153057756	823577	6563333	5811983	27737415	14950472	25467393	14235616	10772126	•	5402719	•	0
Interest **3**	226128	1547	4181	2200	23030	12966	18005	10233	19921	•	9815	•	0
Rents **4**	112667	1198	383	3640	10098	3915	20851	17788	9736	•	4102	•	0
Royalties **5**	71921	0	0	0	0	0	738	8	393	•	1374	•	0
Other Portfolio Income **6**	833181	30316	104635	21925	149307	47158	94419	56603	91309	•	12614	•	0
Other Receipts **7**	1809477	17561	41170	3224	74316	138146	118116	86037	152770	•	28741	•	0
Total Receipts **8**	156111130	874199	6713702	5842972	27994166	15152657	25719522	14406285	11046255	•	5459365	•	0
Average Total Receipts **9**	8248	693	800	2073	6334	16560	33931	72031	116276	•	682421	•	•
Operating Costs/Operating Income (%)													
Cost of Operations **10**	74.4	63.3	36.1	57.1	60.7	75.5	79.0	81.3	78.8	•	86.5	•	•
Salaries and Wages **11**	4.3	3.9	14.1	8.3	5.6	3.2	3.2	2.6	3.2	•	2.2	•	•
Taxes Paid **12**	1.7	1.7	3.1	2.8	2.2	1.9	1.6	1.2	1.9	•	1.0	•	•
Interest Paid **13**	0.6	1.0	0.6	0.9	0.6	0.5	0.5	0.4	0.5	•	0.6	•	•
Depreciation **14**	2.6	2.5	2.5	4.7	3.2	2.7	2.5	2.4	2.7	•	1.7	•	•
Amortization and Depletion **15**	0.2	0.3	0.0	0.0	0.0	0.0	0.0	0.1	0.1	•	0.3	•	•
Pensions and Other Deferred Comp. **16**	0.4	0.3	0.5	0.7	0.3	1.1	0.4	0.5	0.4	•	0.3	•	•
Employee Benefits **17**	1.0	1.4	0.9	1.2	0.9	1.7	1.0	1.3	1.0	•	1.1	•	•
Advertising **18**	0.1	0.1	0.6	0.1	0.1	0.1	0.1	0.1	0.1	•	0.0	•	•
Other Expenses **19**	9.0	13.6	22.7	13.8	18.3	6.6	5.6	4.9	6.6	•	2.6	•	•
Officers' Compensation **20**	2.4	0.9	11.5	3.4	3.3	2.5	1.8	1.3	0.9	•	0.8	•	•
Operating Margin **21**	3.5	11.0	7.3	7.0	4.8	4.2	4.2	4.0	3.8	•	2.7	•	•
Operating Margin Before Officers' Comp. **22**	5.8	11.9	18.9	10.4	8.2	6.7	6.1	5.3	4.7	•	3.5	•	•

Selected Average Balance Sheet ($ in Thousands)

Net Receivables 23	1211	0	22	189	749	2399	5663	13372	23477	122306
Inventories 24	104	0	4	21	74	335	380	577	1970	15999
Net Property, Plant and Equipment 25	1076	0	58	286	772	1674	4103	7999	18862	93787
Total Assets 26	4049	0	156	723	2354	7069	15124	34336	69293	340102
Notes and Loans Payable 27	812	0	88	247	615	1797	3169	5588	14165	71378
All Other Liabilities 28	1575	0	29	121	673	2407	5192	14565	24223	113050
Net Worth 29	1661	0	39	355	1066	2865	6763	14183	30904	155674

Selected Financial Ratios (Times to 1)

Current Ratio 30	1.5	•	1.6	2.4	1.8	1.7	1.5	1.5	1.6	1.7
Quick Ratio 31	1.2	•	1.2	2.2	1.5	1.3	1.4	1.2	1.3	1.4
Net Sales to Working Capital 32	10.7	•	28.5	8.7	9.9	7.8	8.5	9.2	7.0	8.6
Coverage Ratio 33	10.2	18.8	15.9	9.6	11.3	11.3	11.5	14.6	13.6	7.1
Total Asset Turnover 34	2.0	•	5.0	2.9	2.7	2.3	2.2	2.1	1.6	2.0
Inventory Turnover 35	58.1	•	75.4	55.7	51.7	36.8	69.8	100.3	45.4	36.5
Receivables Turnover 36	7.9	•	32.2	11.8	10.0	7.4	6.7	6.7	6.0	11.0
Total Liabilities to Net Worth 37	1.4	•	3.0	1.0	1.2	1.5	1.2	1.4	1.2	1.2
Current Assets to Working Capital 38	3.1	•	2.8	1.7	2.3	2.4	2.5	3.0	2.6	2.5
Current Liabilities to Working Capital 39	2.1	•	1.8	0.7	1.3	1.4	1.5	2.0	1.6	1.5
Working Capital to Net Sales 40	0.1	•	0.0	0.1	0.1	0.1	0.1	0.1	0.1	0.1
Inventory to Working Capital 41	0.1	•	0.3	0.0	0.1	0.2	0.1	0.1	0.1	0.2
Total Receipts to Cash Flow 42	8.7	4.0	3.6	6.2	4.9	12.2	12.5	13.7	11.1	20.3
Cost of Goods to Cash Flow 43	6.5	2.5	1.3	3.5	3.0	9.2	9.8	11.1	8.7	17.6
Cash Flow to Total Debt 44	0.4	•	1.8	0.9	1.0	0.3	0.3	0.3	0.3	0.2

Selected Financial Factors (in Percentages)

Debt Ratio 45	59.0	•	75.1	50.9	54.7	59.5	55.3	58.7	55.4	54.2
Return on Total Assets 46	12.1	•	51.2	24.0	16.9	14.2	12.6	11.4	11.1	8.7
Return on Equity Before Income Taxes 47	26.7	•	192.4	43.8	33.9	31.9	25.7	25.8	23.1	16.4
Return on Equity After Income Taxes 48	24.1	•	186.7	42.6	31.7	29.2	23.7	23.9	21.2	14.1
Profit Margin (Before Income Tax) 49	5.5	17.2	9.6	7.5	5.8	5.6	5.2	5.1	6.3	3.8
Profit Margin (After Income Tax) 50	4.9	16.5	9.3	7.3	5.4	5.1	4.8	4.8	5.8	3.3

Table I

Corporations with and without Net Income

LAND SUBDIVISION

MONEY AMOUNTS AND SIZE OF ASSETS IN THOUSANDS OF DOLLARS

Item Description for Accounting Period 7/05 Through 6/06	Total	Zero Assets	Under 500	500 to 1,000	1,000 to 5,000	5,000 to 10,000	10,000 to 25,000	25,000 to 50,000	50,000 to 100,000	100,000 to 250,000	250,000 to 500,000	500,000 to 2,500,000	2,500,000 and over
Number of Enterprises **1**	46219	4620	25464	5125	8745	1105	740	223	97	67	19	13	0
Revenues ($ in Thousands)													
Net Sales **2**	49546392	510774	4806492	2256664	13181108	4541188	5174753	3792676	2414405	3410386	2174654	7283292	0
Interest **3**	480989	49843	5639	3347	30078	37313	14857	19287	66141	43435	49022	162026	0
Rents **4**	589278	70798	18857	16442	27955	30508	38172	28221	66737	60960	46100	184529	0
Royalties **5**	4515	9	0	11	265	1876	10	1842	502	0	0	0	0
Other Portfolio Income **6**	1304756	72493	73156	6960	166561	100573	94373	43122	144420	104541	119311	379245	0
Other Receipts **7**	3082780	649156	69785	59779	464828	68674	527684	168601	448853	105240	171196	348985	0
Total Receipts **8**	55008710	1353073	4973929	2343203	13870795	4780132	5849849	4053749	3141058	3724562	2560283	8358077	0
Average Total Receipts **9**	1190	293	195	457	1586	4326	7905	18178	32382	55590	134752	642929	•
Operating Costs/Operating Income (%)													
Cost of Operations **10**	70.2	76.6	56.6	60.6	76.8	75.2	71.9	72.0	66.5	69.2	67.4	66.6	•
Salaries and Wages **11**	4.9	4.0	8.9	5.5	2.2	1.3	4.9	5.1	5.2	6.8	12.3	6.0	•
Taxes Paid **12**	1.9	15.2	2.1	2.6	1.0	0.9	1.5	1.5	1.8	1.9	1.5	3.3	•
Interest Paid **13**	3.3	9.9	1.8	6.1	1.9	4.0	2.9	2.9	4.4	3.7	3.9	4.7	•
Depreciation **14**	1.3	8.6	1.3	1.0	0.7	0.3	1.2	1.6	1.3	3.4	1.8	1.1	•
Amortization and Depletion **15**	0.1	0.0	0.0	0.0	0.1	0.1	0.1	0.1	0.2	0.2	0.2	0.2	•
Pensions and Other Deferred Comp. **16**	0.3	0.1	0.2	0.2	0.5	0.1	0.2	0.2	0.4	0.3	0.6	0.2	•
Employee Benefits **17**	0.5	0.2	1.1	0.8	0.2	0.2	0.4	0.3	0.4	0.6	0.4	1.0	•
Advertising **18**	0.6	0.2	0.4	0.2	0.5	0.5	0.6	0.7	0.8	1.1	0.8	0.7	•
Other Expenses **19**	10.3	21.8	12.9	19.0	7.6	9.8	11.7	7.7	16.6	10.1	12.8	8.0	•
Officers' Compensation **20**	1.9	0.8	4.7	1.9	1.7	1.0	2.7	1.9	2.2	1.8	1.2	0.9	•
Operating Margin **21**	4.8	•	9.9	2.1	6.7	6.5	2.0	6.1	0.3	1.0	•	7.3	•
Operating Margin Before Officers' Comp. **22**	6.7	•	14.6	4.0	8.4	7.5	4.7	8.0	2.5	2.8	•	8.2	•

Selected Average Balance Sheet ($ in Thousands)

	1	2	3	4	5	6	7	8	9	10	11	12	13
Net Receivables 23	170	0	9	59	212	418	1013	3316	3052	11527	45140	122604	•
Inventories 24	478	0	37	182	616	1884	3629	9140	17903	18640	77961	273142	•
Net Property, Plant and Equipment 25	485	0	33	181	451	1792	3986	8838	11546	37182	90696	346890	•
Total Assets 26	1996	0	145	723	2119	6885	14876	35729	70824	151535	366290	1212072	•
Notes and Loans Payable 27	1107	0	145	471	1161	4699	9039	23084	32692	71072	155047	538361	•
All Other Liabilities 28	371	0	69	92	306	826	2277	6015	12794	30376	92266	251671	•
Net Worth 29	518	0	-69	159	652	1360	3560	6631	25339	50087	118977	422040	•

Selected Financial Ratios (Times to 1)

	1	2	3	4	5	6	7	8	9	10	11	12	13
Current Ratio 30	2.1	•	1.3	2.2	2.3	2.3	2.3	2.0	2.8	2.0	2.5	1.6	•
Quick Ratio 31	0.6	•	0.5	0.6	0.7	0.6	0.6	0.6	0.7	0.7	0.9	0.5	•
Net Sales to Working Capital 32	2.0	•	10.2	2.1	2.2	2.1	1.6	1.7	1.0	1.6	1.0	2.9	•
Coverage Ratio 33	5.8	13.9	8.3	2.0	7.1	3.9	6.1	5.8	8.0	3.7	4.8	5.7	•
Total Asset Turnover 34	0.5	•	1.3	0.6	0.7	0.6	0.5	0.5	0.4	0.3	0.3	0.5	•
Inventory Turnover 35	1.6	•	2.9	1.5	1.9	1.6	1.4	1.3	0.9	1.9	1.0	1.4	•
Receivables Turnover 36	6.8	•	22.9	8.7	7.0	11.3	7.1	5.7	6.8	4.7	3.8	5.0	•
Total Liabilities to Net Worth 37	2.9	•	•	3.5	2.3	4.1	3.2	4.4	1.8	2.0	2.1	1.9	•
Current Assets to Working Capital 38	1.9	4.7	•	1.8	1.8	1.8	2.0	2.0	1.6	2.0	1.6	2.6	•
Current Liabilities to Working Capital 39	0.9	3.7	•	0.8	0.8	0.8	1.0	1.0	0.6	1.0	0.6	1.6	•
Working Capital to Net Sales 40	0.5	0.1	•	0.5	0.5	0.5	0.6	0.6	1.0	0.6	1.0	0.3	•
Inventory to Working Capital 41	1.0	1.9	•	0.8	0.9	0.9	0.9	1.0	0.9	0.7	0.7	1.5	•
Total Receipts to Cash Flow 42	4.4	0.8	4.2	4.5	5.6	5.4	4.3	5.4	2.5	5.6	4.2	4.1	•
Cost of Goods to Cash Flow 43	3.1	0.6	2.4	2.7	4.3	4.0	3.1	3.9	1.7	3.8	2.8	2.7	•
Cash Flow to Total Debt 44	0.2	•	0.2	0.2	0.2	0.1	0.1	0.1	0.2	0.1	0.1	0.2	•

Selected Financial Factors (in Percentages)

	1	2	3	4	5	6	7	8	9	10	11	12	13
Debt Ratio 45	74.1	•	147.7	77.9	69.2	80.2	76.1	81.4	64.2	66.9	67.5	65.2	•
Return on Total Assets 46	10.3	•	19.8	7.3	9.9	9.5	8.4	7.9	12.2	4.6	5.8	12.3	•
Return on Equity Before Income Taxes 47	32.7	•	•	16.5	27.6	35.7	29.4	35.3	29.8	10.3	14.1	29.2	•
Return on Equity After Income Taxes 48	28.2	•	•	15.9	26.8	33.9	27.6	32.4	27.5	8.2	11.6	19.4	•
Profit Margin (Before Income Tax) 49	15.8	127.5	13.4	6.0	11.9	11.8	14.9	13.8	30.4	10.1	14.7	22.0	•
Profit Margin (After Income Tax) 50	13.6	88.7	13.3	5.7	11.6	11.2	14.1	12.6	28.0	8.1	12.1	14.6	•

Table II
Corporations with Net Income

LAND SUBDIVISION

MONEY AMOUNTS AND SIZE OF ASSETS IN THOUSANDS OF DOLLARS

Item Description for Accounting Period 7/05 Through 6/06	Total	Zero Assets	Under 500	500 to 1,000	1,000 to 5,000	5,000 to 10,000	10,000 to 25,000	25,000 to 50,000	50,000 to 100,000	100,000 to 250,000	250,000 to 500,000	500,000 to 2,500,000	2,500,000 and over
Number of Enterprises 1	20729	1023	10452	2701	5060	774	445	129	74	47	11	13	0
Revenues ($ in Thousands)													
Net Sales 2	41440513	452623	4010227	1577527	9659588	4083366	4445120	3190687	2151946	2734022	1852116	7283292	0
Interest 3	438537	49796	4841	3131	24268	34635	8248	14726	59860	38076	38931	162026	0
Rents 4	523959	65035	18857	13922	26235	30508	31152	24569	53196	53398	21958	184529	0
Royalties 5	2518	9	0	11	71	83	0	1842	502	0	0	0	0
Other Portfolio Income 6	1278806	71860	72682	6960	160335	99661	88801	36703	140491	103260	118810	379245	0
Other Receipts 7	3026346	655899	67937	44895	451707	81124	480845	140170	384142	172723	197915	348985	0
Total Receipts 8	46710679	1295222	4174544	1646446	10322204	4329377	5054166	3408697	2790137	3102079	2229730	8358077	0
Average Total Receipts 9	2253	1266	399	610	2040	5594	11358	26424	37705	66002	202703	642929	•
Operating Costs/Operating Income (%)													
Cost of Operations 10	68.5	68.5	56.7	56.0	72.7	74.3	70.4	71.5	68.6	68.6	67.7	66.6	•
Salaries and Wages 11	4.3	4.3	7.9	2.4	1.8	1.3	3.9	4.5	4.1	4.8	12.2	6.0	•
Taxes Paid 12	1.8	16.5	1.6	2.4	1.0	0.9	1.3	1.3	1.7	1.5	1.5	3.3	•
Interest Paid 13	2.7	7.7	0.8	3.3	2.0	3.0	2.3	1.8	3.2	3.1	2.6	4.7	•
Depreciation 14	1.1	7.6	0.5	1.1	0.7	0.3	1.1	0.9	1.2	3.5	1.6	1.1	•
Amortization and Depletion 15	0.1	0.0	0.0	0.0	0.1	0.1	0.1	0.1	0.2	0.2	0.2	0.2	•
Pensions and Other Deferred Comp. 16	0.2	0.1	0.0	0.3	0.3	0.2	0.2	0.2	0.4	0.0	0.6	0.2	•
Employee Benefits 17	0.5	0.1	0.8	1.0	0.1	0.2	0.3	0.2	0.3	0.3	0.4	1.0	•
Advertising 18	0.5	0.2	0.1	0.3	0.5	0.5	0.5	0.7	0.7	0.6	0.8	0.7	•
Other Expenses 19	8.2	11.8	8.9	16.8	5.6	8.9	10.1	5.3	9.6	8.3	11.1	8.0	•
Officers' Compensation 20	1.8	0.7	3.3	1.5	1.9	0.9	2.7	2.1	2.1	1.3	1.2	0.9	•
Operating Margin 21	10.2	•	19.2	15.1	13.4	9.6	7.0	11.4	7.9	7.7	0.3	7.3	•
Operating Margin Before Officers' Comp. 22	11.9	•	22.6	16.6	15.3	10.4	9.7	13.5	10.0	9.0	1.4	8.2	•

Selected Average Balance Sheet ($ in Thousands)

Net Receivables 23	290	0	11	72	222	567	935	3495	3030	13851	72540	122604	•
Inventories 24	791	0	37	199	704	1896	4187	10372	20624	29023	110282	286360	•
Net Property, Plant and Equipment 25	686	0	31	238	424	1507	3218	7610	11112	33830	54892	346890	•
Total Assets 26	3094	0	177	756	2293	6781	14599	35967	70435	151136	381424	1212072	•
Notes and Loans Payable 27	1490	0	86	434	1120	4703	7529	17388	30884	67970	130097	538361	•
All Other Liabilities 28	541	0	18	81	326	568	2357	7011	12901	33597	86359	251671	•
Net Worth 29	1064	0	72	241	847	1510	4713	11568	26650	49569	164968	422040	•

Selected Financial Ratios (Times to 1)

Current Ratio 30	2.1	•	2.5	1.4	2.4	2.5	2.2	1.8	3.1	2.0	2.8	1.6	•
Quick Ratio 31	0.7	•	1.3	0.5	0.7	0.7	0.5	0.5	0.8	0.7	1.2	0.5	•
Net Sales to Working Capital 32	2.3	•	5.4	6.3	2.3	2.4	2.0	2.6	1.0	1.6	1.2	2.9	•
Coverage Ratio 33	9.3	22.8	30.4	6.9	11.1	6.2	9.9	11.7	12.8	7.7	9.0	5.7	•
Total Asset Turnover 34	0.6	•	2.2	0.8	0.8	0.8	0.7	0.7	0.4	0.4	0.4	0.5	•
Inventory Turnover 35	1.7	•	5.9	1.6	2.0	2.1	1.7	1.7	1.0	1.4	1.0	1.3	•
Receivables Turnover 36	7.9	•	31.7	8.5	9.9	11.8	10.3	7.4	10.0	8.4	4.6	9.1	•
Total Liabilities to Net Worth 37	1.9	•	1.4	2.1	1.7	3.5	2.1	2.1	1.6	2.0	1.3	1.9	•
Current Assets to Working Capital 38	1.9	•	1.7	3.8	1.7	1.7	1.8	2.3	1.5	2.0	1.6	2.6	•
Current Liabilities to Working Capital 39	0.9	•	0.7	2.8	0.7	0.7	0.8	1.3	0.5	1.0	0.6	1.6	•
Working Capital to Net Sales 40	0.4	•	0.2	0.2	0.4	0.4	0.5	0.4	1.0	0.6	0.8	0.3	•
Inventory to Working Capital 41	1.0	•	0.5	1.9	0.9	0.8	0.9	1.1	0.9	0.8	0.8	1.5	•
Total Receipts to Cash Flow 42	3.6	0.6	3.3	3.0	4.2	4.6	3.6	4.6	2.5	3.7	3.6	4.1	•
Cost of Goods to Cash Flow 43	2.5	0.4	1.9	1.7	3.1	3.4	2.5	3.3	1.7	2.5	2.4	2.7	•
Cash Flow to Total Debt 44	0.3	•	1.1	0.4	0.3	0.2	0.3	0.2	0.3	0.2	0.2	0.2	•

Selected Financial Factors (in Percentages)

Debt Ratio 45	65.6	•	59.0	68.1	63.1	77.7	67.7	67.8	62.2	67.2	56.7	65.2	•
Return on Total Assets 46	16.6	•	52.4	17.6	18.5	14.5	15.7	14.5	16.8	9.3	10.2	12.3	•
Return on Equity Before Income Taxes 47	43.0	•	123.5	47.2	45.5	54.5	43.8	41.2	40.9	24.7	21.1	29.2	•
Return on Equity After Income Taxes 48	38.1	•	123.2	46.4	44.4	52.2	41.6	38.3	38.0	21.8	17.9	19.4	•
Profit Margin (Before Income Tax) 49	22.9	168.7	23.3	19.5	20.2	15.6	20.7	19.3	37.5	21.0	20.6	22.0	•
Profit Margin (After Income Tax) 50	20.3	124.9	23.2	19.1	19.7	14.9	19.6	17.9	34.8	18.6	17.6	14.6	•

Table I

Corporations with and without Net Income

ELECTRICAL CONTRACTORS

MONEY AMOUNTS AND SIZE OF ASSETS IN THOUSANDS OF DOLLARS

Item Description for Accounting Period 7/05 Through 6/06	Total	Zero Assets	Under 500	500 to 1,000	1,000 to 5,000	5,000 to 10,000	10,000 to 25,000	25,000 to 50,000	50,000 to 100,000	100,000 to 250,000	250,000 to 500,000	500,000 to 2,500,000	2,500,000 and over
Number of Enterprises 1	51305	6709	37072	3273	3199	686	277	65	17	7	0	0	0
Revenues ($ in Thousands)													
Net Sales 2	75685472	565650	18971100	7565137	17419339	11820590	9124516	4918949	3022917	2277274	0	0	0
Interest 3	82040	0	5602	2044	13634	5325	3812	1990	9648	39985	0	0	0
Rents 4	17293	104	6705	1792	3931	1071	354	1418	107	1812	0	0	0
Royalties 5	269	0	0	0	0	1	268	0	0	0	0	0	0
Other Portfolio Income 6	140739	34131	19111	6507	34596	7568	6488	5732	3979	22624	0	0	0
Other Receipts 7	587502	511	41746	8840	-20700	52492	21631	11655	25116	446212	0	0	0
Total Receipts 8	76513315	600396	19044264	7584320	17450800	11887047	9157069	4939744	3061767	2787907	0	0	0
Average Total Receipts 9	1491	89	514	2317	5455	17328	33058	75996	180104	398272	•	•	•
Operating Costs/Operating Income (%)													
Cost of Operations 10	68.7	30.2	51.7	65.5	72.7	77.4	76.9	79.1	79.1	84.2	•	•	•
Salaries and Wages 11	6.9	6.5	10.0	8.0	5.8	4.1	5.3	4.9	6.8	10.2	•	•	•
Taxes Paid 12	2.7	2.1	3.2	3.2	2.9	2.3	2.3	2.4	1.7	2.3	•	•	•
Interest Paid 13	0.7	0.5	0.6	0.7	0.5	0.7	0.4	0.5	0.8	3.9	•	•	•
Depreciation 14	1.3	2.3	1.7	1.6	1.2	0.7	0.7	1.1	0.7	2.5	•	•	•
Amortization and Depletion 15	0.2	0.0	0.2	0.0	0.0	0.1	0.0	0.0	0.1	2.3	•	•	•
Pensions and Other Deferred Comp. 16	0.5	•	0.4	0.7	0.4	0.8	0.3	0.3	0.6	0.4	•	•	•
Employee Benefits 17	2.3	0.5	1.2	2.7	2.7	2.9	3.4	2.4	2.3	1.0	•	•	•
Advertising 18	0.3	0.6	0.4	0.4	0.3	0.2	0.1	0.2	0.1	0.2	•	•	•
Other Expenses 19	9.6	37.2	16.8	9.3	7.6	5.6	4.7	5.1	4.3	15.4	•	•	•
Officers' Compensation 20	4.5	9.4	8.7	4.5	3.8	2.9	2.5	1.9	1.5	1.0	•	•	•
Operating Margin 21	2.4	10.6	5.0	3.5	2.1	2.3	3.3	2.0	2.0	•	•	•	•
Operating Margin Before Officers' Comp. 22	7.0	20.0	13.7	8.0	5.9	5.2	5.8	3.9	3.4	•	•	•	•

Selected Average Balance Sheet ($ in Thousands)

Net Receivables 23	246	0	19	293	1008	4049	8031	16922	43012	128120
Inventories 24	24	0	7	69	107	238	460	755	1112	5603
Net Property, Plant and Equipment 25	72	0	26	110	254	659	1243	4314	5605	55816
Total Assets 26	540	0	95	743	2124	7261	14413	32903	70031	379805
Notes and Loans Payable 27	127	0	42	218	377	1465	2220	5825	11339	119533
All Other Liabilities 28	232	0	25	212	946	4024	6996	15093	39726	126476
Net Worth 29	182	0	28	313	801	1772	5198	11985	18966	133797

Selected Financial Ratios (Times to 1)

Current Ratio 30	1.6	•	1.7	2.4	1.6	1.2	1.6	1.5	1.5	2.3
Quick Ratio 31	1.3	•	1.4	1.9	1.3	1.0	1.3	1.2	1.2	1.8
Net Sales to Working Capital 32	9.4	•	20.7	6.9	8.3	14.9	7.2	8.8	9.2	2.3
Coverage Ratio 33	6.3	31.5	10.4	6.6	5.4	5.2	10.5	6.1	4.9	0.8
Total Asset Turnover 34	2.7	•	5.4	3.1	2.6	2.4	2.3	2.3	2.5	0.9
Inventory Turnover 35	41.7	•	39.5	22.0	36.9	56.1	55.0	79.2	126.5	48.9
Receivables Turnover 36	6.4	•	25.6	8.2	5.5	4.6	4.5	5.2	4.8	3.8
Total Liabilities to Net Worth 37	2.0	•	2.4	1.4	1.7	3.1	1.8	1.7	2.7	1.8
Current Assets to Working Capital 38	2.7	•	2.4	1.7	2.6	5.1	2.7	3.0	3.1	1.8
Current Liabilities to Working Capital 39	1.7	•	1.4	0.7	1.6	4.1	1.7	2.0	2.1	0.8
Working Capital to Net Sales 40	0.1	•	0.0	0.1	0.1	0.1	0.1	0.1	0.1	0.4
Inventory to Working Capital 41	0.2	•	0.3	0.3	0.2	0.2	0.1	0.1	0.1	0.1
Total Receipts to Cash Flow 42	9.1	2.2	5.1	9.7	12.6	14.5	14.6	19.0	16.9	9.7
Cost of Goods to Cash Flow 43	6.3	0.7	2.6	6.3	9.2	11.2	11.2	15.0	13.4	8.2
Cash Flow to Total Debt 44	0.5	•	1.5	0.6	0.3	0.2	0.2	0.2	0.2	0.1

Selected Financial Factors (in Percentages)

Debt Ratio 45	66.4	•	70.7	57.9	62.3	75.6	63.9	63.6	72.9	64.8
Return on Total Assets 46	11.4	•	31.9	13.7	7.2	8.3	9.2	6.7	10.4	2.6
Return on Equity Before Income Taxes 47	28.5	•	98.6	27.5	15.6	27.4	23.0	15.5	30.6	•
Return on Equity After Income Taxes 48	26.8	•	97.4	26.6	14.0	25.4	20.5	13.9	25.3	•
Profit Margin (Before Income Tax) 49	3.5	16.7	5.4	3.7	2.3	2.8	3.6	2.5	3.3	•
Profit Margin (After Income Tax) 50	3.3	16.5	5.3	3.6	2.1	2.6	3.2	2.2	2.7	•

31

Table II

Corporations with Net Income

ELECTRICAL CONTRACTORS

MONEY AMOUNTS AND SIZE OF ASSETS IN THOUSANDS OF DOLLARS

Item Description for Accounting Period 7/05 Through 6/06	Total	Zero Assets	Under 500	500 to 1,000	1,000 to 5,000	5,000 to 10,000	10,000 to 25,000	25,000 to 50,000	50,000 to 100,000	100,000 to 250,000	250,000 to 500,000	500,000 to 2,500,000	2,500,000 and over
Number of Enterprises 1	34617	4072	24797	2502	2371	566	238	•	•	3	0	0	0

Revenues ($ in Thousands)

Net Sales 2	60663864	480378	13917878	5897363	13986464	10755972	8329695	•	•	552872	0	0	0
Interest 3	33972	0	3209	1353	11618	4852	2657	•	•	7589	0	0	0
Rents 4	8625	0	0	1792	3931	1047	247	•	•	84	0	0	0
Royalties 5	269	0	0	0	0	1	268	•	•	0	0	0	0
Other Portfolio Income 6	72005	0	15701	6286	21600	3823	5901	•	•	9810	0	0	0
Other Receipts 7	505934	324	20926	7826	20629	39243	24749	•	•	359879	0	0	0
Total Receipts 8	61284669	480702	13957714	5914620	14044242	10804938	8363517	•	•	930234	0	0	0
Average Total Receipts 9	1770	118	563	2364	5923	19090	35141	•	•	310078	•	•	•

Operating Costs/Operating Income (%)

Cost of Operations 10	67.6	26.8	48.8	64.9	71.0	76.3	76.6	•	•	77.3	•	•	•
Salaries and Wages 11	6.5	6.7	9.9	7.8	5.4	4.1	5.2	•	•	23.9	•	•	•
Taxes Paid 12	2.7	2.1	3.0	3.2	3.0	2.3	2.3	•	•	3.6	•	•	•
Interest Paid 13	0.5	0.5	0.5	0.4	0.4	0.6	0.3	•	•	5.2	•	•	•
Depreciation 14	1.2	1.5	1.8	1.2	1.2	0.7	0.7	•	•	7.7	•	•	•
Amortization and Depletion 15	0.1	0.0	0.2	0.0	0.0	0.1	0.0	•	•	6.7	•	•	•
Pensions and Other Deferred Comp. 16	0.5	•	0.3	0.9	0.5	0.8	0.3	•	•	1.6	•	•	•
Employee Benefits 17	2.4	0.5	1.1	2.9	2.4	3.1	3.2	•	•	2.0	•	•	•
Advertising 18	0.3	0.7	0.4	0.3	0.4	0.2	0.1	•	•	0.5	•	•	•
Other Expenses 19	8.5	29.2	15.1	7.8	7.7	5.5	4.5	•	•	20.8	•	•	•
Officers' Compensation 20	4.5	7.8	8.8	4.4	3.8	3.0	2.4	•	•	3.0	•	•	•
Operating Margin 21	5.1	24.2	10.0	6.3	4.2	3.3	4.3	•	•	4.3	•	•	•
Operating Margin Before Officers' Comp. 22	9.6	32.0	18.8	10.6	8.0	6.3	6.6	•	•	6.6	•	•	•

Selected Average Balance Sheet ($ in Thousands)

Net Receivables 23	290	0	16	285	1041	4340	8327	153805
Inventories 24	24	0	7	69	113	164	363	8929
Net Property, Plant and Equipment 25	82	0	28	104	278	570	1237	102183
Total Assets 26	624	0	102	743	2144	7186	14672	587985
Notes and Loans Payable 27	116	0	38	135	329	1131	1968	155594
All Other Liabilities 28	266	0	24	213	948	4043	7047	165988
Net Worth 29	242	0	40	394	868	2013	5658	266403

Selected Financial Ratios (Times to 1)

Current Ratio 30	1.7	•	1.8	2.4	1.7	1.4	1.6	2.9
Quick Ratio 31	1.4	•	1.4	2.0	1.4	1.2	1.3	2.3
Net Sales to Working Capital 32	8.9	•	20.7	6.9	8.3	10.6	7.4	0.8
Coverage Ratio 33	14.2	50.7	23.5	18.5	12.5	7.7	15.9	4.1
Total Asset Turnover 34	2.8	•	5.5	3.2	2.8	2.6	2.4	0.3
Inventory Turnover 35	48.6	•	41.9	22.2	37.1	88.3	73.8	16.0
Receivables Turnover 36	6.8	•	32.8	9.4	5.9	5.1	4.8	2.4
Total Liabilities to Net Worth 37	1.6	•	1.5	0.9	1.5	2.6	1.6	1.2
Current Assets to Working Capital 38	2.5	•	2.2	1.7	2.5	3.4	2.7	1.5
Current Liabilities to Working Capital 39	1.5	•	1.2	0.7	1.5	2.4	1.7	0.5
Working Capital to Net Sales 40	0.1	•	0.0	0.1	0.1	0.1	0.1	1.2
Inventory to Working Capital 41	0.1	•	0.3	0.2	0.2	0.1	0.1	0.0
Total Receipts to Cash Flow 42	7.8	2.0	4.3	8.0	9.6	12.9	13.0	3.1
Cost of Goods to Cash Flow 43	5.3	0.5	2.1	5.2	6.8	9.9	9.9	2.4
Cash Flow to Total Debt 44	0.6	•	2.1	0.8	0.5	0.3	0.3	0.2

Selected Financial Factors (in Percentages)

Debt Ratio 45	61.2	•	60.6	46.9	59.5	72.0	61.4	54.7
Return on Total Assets 46	18.6	•	59.3	22.0	13.7	11.3	11.9	6.6
Return on Equity Before Income Taxes 47	44.5	•	144.2	39.2	31.1	35.1	28.9	11.0
Return on Equity After Income Taxes 48	42.6	•	142.9	38.3	29.1	33.0	26.1	10.5
Profit Margin (Before Income Tax) 49	6.1	24.2	10.3	6.6	4.6	3.7	4.7	15.9
Profit Margin (After Income Tax) 50	5.9	24.0	10.2	6.4	4.3	3.5	4.2	15.2

Table I

Corporations with and without Net Income

PLUMBING, HEATING, AND AIR-CONDITIONING CONTRACTORS

MONEY AMOUNTS AND SIZE OF ASSETS IN THOUSANDS OF DOLLARS

Item Description for Accounting Period 7/05 Through 6/06	Total	Zero Assets	Under 500	500 to 1,000	1,000 to 5,000	5,000 to 10,000	10,000 to 25,000	25,000 to 50,000	50,000 to 100,000	100,000 to 250,000	250,000 to 500,000	500,000 to 2,500,000	2,500,000 and over
Number of Enterprises **1**	73150	7751	56532	4186	3820	540	269	34	13	6	0	0	0

Revenues ($ in Thousands)

	Total	Zero Assets	Under 500	500 to 1,000	1,000 to 5,000	5,000 to 10,000	10,000 to 25,000	25,000 to 50,000	50,000 to 100,000	100,000 to 250,000	250,000 to 500,000	500,000 to 2,500,000	2,500,000 and over
Net Sales **2**	109038484	872675	37194373	10415885	28277083	10580616	10081003	3324493	2478779	5813576	0	0	0
Interest **3**	47872	984	8155	6071	17485	5470	4197	1317	0	4193	0	0	0
Rents **4**	17023	0	1538	7686	4700	2473	165	309	0	152	0	0	0
Royalties **5**	0	0	0	0	0	0	0	0	0	0	0	0	0
Other Portfolio Income **6**	195973	8322	75443	34250	44788	3189	7903	991	224	20866	0	0	0
Other Receipts **7**	239143	7304	50067	32205	63327	14922	33169	5459	4764	27923	0	0	0
Total Receipts **8**	109538495	889285	37329576	10496097	28407383	10606670	10126437	3332569	2483767	5866710	0	0	•
Average Total Receipts **9**	1497	115	660	2507	7436	19642	37645	98017	191059	977785	•	•	•

Operating Costs/Operating Income (%)

	Total	Zero Assets	Under 500	500 to 1,000	1,000 to 5,000	5,000 to 10,000	10,000 to 25,000	25,000 to 50,000	50,000 to 100,000	100,000 to 250,000	250,000 to 500,000	500,000 to 2,500,000	2,500,000 and over
Cost of Operations **10**	65.9	35.7	51.5	62.6	72.0	75.0	78.9	84.9	77.4	83.0	•	•	•
Salaries and Wages **11**	8.5	14.2	12.1	7.5	7.0	7.2	4.8	3.8	7.4	5.3	•	•	•
Taxes Paid **12**	2.9	4.6	3.6	3.5	2.4	2.4	2.4	2.2	1.6	2.2	•	•	•
Interest Paid **13**	0.5	0.8	0.6	0.5	0.4	0.4	0.4	0.3	0.3	0.5	•	•	•
Depreciation **14**	1.1	1.5	1.6	1.8	0.9	0.6	0.5	0.4	0.6	0.4	•	•	•
Amortization and Depletion **15**	0.0	0.2	0.0	0.0	0.0	0.0	0.0	0.0	0.1	0.4	•	•	•
Pensions and Other Deferred Comp. **16**	0.5	0.5	0.4	0.6	0.6	0.5	0.5	0.3	0.3	0.1	•	•	•
Employee Benefits **17**	2.0	0.5	1.9	2.0	2.1	1.7	2.6	0.9	2.2	1.6	•	•	•
Advertising **18**	0.6	0.5	1.0	0.8	0.4	0.3	0.2	0.1	0.1	0.1	•	•	•
Other Expenses **19**	10.6	35.5	16.1	12.3	8.3	6.2	4.5	2.7	6.6	4.7	•	•	•
Officers' Compensation **20**	4.9	6.3	7.5	5.5	4.2	3.0	2.6	1.2	1.0	1.5	•	•	•
Operating Margin **21**	2.6	•	3.6	2.8	1.7	2.7	2.7	3.4	2.3	0.1	•	•	•
Operating Margin Before Officers' Comp. **22**	7.5	6.0	11.2	8.4	5.9	5.6	5.2	4.6	3.3	1.5	•	•	•

Selected Average Balance Sheet ($ in Thousands)

Net Receivables 23	197	0	27	259	1148	4213	8348	21764	41210	276317
Inventories 24	22	0	8	42	134	370	513	1626	2769	3689
Net Property, Plant and Equipment 25	58	0	31	163	216	683	1114	2872	7024	18270
Total Assets 26	414		112	685	2161	7398	14799	36269	64586	462724
Notes and Loans Payable 27	105	0	59	222	464	1060	2198	3314	9114	36413
All Other Liabilities 28	191	0	33	209	1047	4140	8150	20428	37755	277761
Net Worth 29	117	0	20	254	649	2199	4450	12527	17717	148550

Selected Financial Ratios (Times to 1)

Current Ratio 30	1.5	•	1.6	2.1	1.6	1.3	1.4	1.4	1.4	1.4
Quick Ratio 31	1.2	•	1.3	1.7	1.3	1.0	1.2	1.2	1.2	1.2
Net Sales to Working Capital 32	13.3	•	25.5	9.8	11.3	12.3	9.5	10.2	11.8	8.4
Coverage Ratio 33	7.4	3.0	7.2	8.9	6.9	8.3	9.4	15.4	10.2	3.1
Total Asset Turnover 34	3.6	•	5.9	3.6	3.4	2.6	2.5	2.7	3.0	2.1
Inventory Turnover 35	44.1	•	40.2	37.1	39.7	39.7	57.7	51.0	53.3	218.1
Receivables Turnover 36	7.9	•	28.0	9.7	6.7	4.8	5.1	4.6	4.9	6.0
Total Liabilities to Net Worth 37	2.5	•	4.7	1.7	2.3	2.4	2.3	1.9	2.6	2.1
Current Assets to Working Capital 38	2.9	•	2.7	1.9	2.7	4.0	3.3	3.2	3.3	3.2
Current Liabilities to Working Capital 39	1.9	•	1.7	0.9	1.7	3.0	2.3	2.2	2.3	2.2
Working Capital to Net Sales 40	0.1	•	0.0	0.1	0.1	0.1	0.1	0.1	0.1	0.1
Inventory to Working Capital 41	0.2	•	0.4	0.2	0.2	0.2	0.1	0.1	0.2	0.1
Total Receipts to Cash Flow 42	8.7	3.1	5.7	7.6	12.1	13.6	16.0	19.0	12.7	27.8
Cost of Goods to Cash Flow 43	5.7	1.1	2.9	4.7	8.7	10.2	12.6	16.2	9.9	23.1
Cash Flow to Total Debt 44	0.6	•	1.3	0.8	0.4	0.3	0.2	0.2	0.3	0.1

Selected Financial Factors (in Percentages)

Debt Ratio 45	71.6	•	82.4	62.9	69.9	70.3	69.9	65.5	72.6	67.9
Return on Total Assets 46	12.8	•	27.4	14.8	8.8	8.8	8.8	10.4	8.1	3.2
Return on Equity Before Income Taxes 47	39.2	•	133.8	35.4	25.1	26.1	26.1	28.2	26.7	6.7
Return on Equity After Income Taxes 48	37.0	•	131.4	33.4	22.9	24.4	24.0	26.8	26.7	6.7
Profit Margin (Before Income Tax) 49	3.1	1.7	4.0	3.6	2.2	2.9	3.1	3.6	2.5	2.8
Profit Margin (After Income Tax) 50	2.9	1.7	3.9	3.4	2.0	2.7	2.8	3.4	1.0	0.4

Table II
Corporations with Net Income

PLUMBING, HEATING, AND AIR-CONDITIONING CONTRACTORS

MONEY AMOUNTS AND SIZE OF ASSETS IN THOUSANDS OF DOLLARS

Item Description for Accounting Period 7/05 Through 6/06	Total	Zero Assets	Under 500	500 to 1,000	1,000 to 5,000	5,000 to 10,000	10,000 to 25,000	25,000 to 50,000	50,000 to 100,000	100,000 to 250,000	250,000 to 500,000	500,000 to 2,500,000	2,500,000 and over
Number of Enterprises 1	50834	4147	39698	3334	2896	482	227	34	•	•	0	0	0
Revenues ($ in Thousands)													
Net Sales 2	88125457	424254	26593430	8736467	23535108	9437827	8648613	3324493	•	•	0	0	0
Interest 3	39316	984	6173	5797	15328	3960	3124	1317	•	•	0	0	0
Rents 4	16842	0	1538	7686	4562	2473	122	309	•	•	0	0	0
Royalties 5	0	0	0	0	0	0	0	0	•	•	0	0	0
Other Portfolio Income 6	158988	1924	65600	32774	26288	2657	7677	991	•	•	0	0	0
Other Receipts 7	209865	7304	39493	29618	56105	14162	31528	5459	•	•	0	0	0
Total Receipts 8	88550468	434466	26706234	8812342	23637391	9461079	8691064	3332569	•	•	•	•	•
Average Total Receipts 9	1742	105	673	2643	8162	19629	38287	98017	•	•	•	•	•
Operating Costs/Operating Income (%)													
Cost of Operations 10	65.6	28.5	49.0	61.0	71.8	73.6	77.7	84.9	•	•	•	•	•
Salaries and Wages 11	7.9	11.5	11.4	7.8	6.4	7.3	5.0	3.8	•	•	•	•	•
Taxes Paid 12	2.8	3.6	3.5	3.5	2.3	2.5	2.2	2.2	•	•	•	•	•
Interest Paid 13	0.4	0.3	0.5	0.4	0.3	0.4	0.3	0.3	•	•	•	•	•
Depreciation 14	1.0	1.1	1.6	1.6	0.8	0.6	0.6	0.4	•	•	•	•	•
Amortization and Depletion 15	0.0	•	0.0	0.0	0.0	0.0	0.0	0.0	•	•	•	•	•
Pensions and Other Deferred Comp. 16	0.5	1.0	0.4	0.7	0.6	0.6	0.6	0.3	•	•	•	•	•
Employee Benefits 17	2.0	0.4	2.1	2.0	2.0	1.8	2.6	0.9	•	•	•	•	•
Advertising 18	0.6	1.0	1.1	0.8	0.4	0.3	0.2	0.1	•	•	•	•	•
Other Expenses 19	9.8	32.4	15.5	11.6	7.8	6.6	4.5	2.7	•	•	•	•	•
Officers' Compensation 20	4.9	7.7	7.7	5.9	4.4	3.0	2.6	1.2	•	•	•	•	•
Operating Margin 21	4.5	12.4	7.1	4.7	3.2	3.3	3.8	3.4	•	•	•	•	•
Operating Margin Before Officers' Comp. 22	9.4	20.0	14.8	10.6	7.7	6.3	6.3	4.6	•	•	•	•	•

Selected Average Balance Sheet ($ in Thousands)

Net Receivables 23	239	0	26	253	1245	4356	8230	21764
Inventories 24	25	0	8	37	146	362	497	1213
Net Property, Plant and Equipment 25	63	0	34	133	194	701	1164	2872
Total Assets 26	492	0	118	686	2262	7601	14671	36269
Notes and Loans Payable 27	93	0	46	161	406	961	1998	3314
All Other Liabilities 28	222	0	28	207	1044	4260	7767	20428
Net Worth 29	177	0	43	318	812	2380	4906	12527

Selected Financial Ratios (Times to 1)

Current Ratio 30	1.6	•	1.9	2.2	1.7	1.4	1.5	1.4
Quick Ratio 31	1.3	•	1.6	1.8	1.4	1.1	1.2	1.2
Net Sales to Working Capital 32	11.5	•	18.9	9.2	10.1	10.9	8.9	10.2
Coverage Ratio 33	14.5	44.5	16.1	16.8	13.8	9.8	13.6	15.4
Total Asset Turnover 34	3.5	•	5.7	3.8	3.6	2.6	2.6	2.7
Inventory Turnover 35	45.9	•	41.8	42.8	39.9	39.8	59.5	68.4
Receivables Turnover 36	7.9	•	30.7	11.0	7.1	4.6	5.4	9.0
Total Liabilities to Net Worth 37	1.8	•	1.7	1.2	1.8	2.2	2.0	1.9
Current Assets to Working Capital 38	2.6	•	2.1	1.8	2.4	3.6	3.0	3.2
Current Liabilities to Working Capital 39	1.6	•	1.1	0.8	1.4	2.6	2.0	2.2
Working Capital to Net Sales 40	0.1	•	0.1	0.1	0.1	0.1	0.1	0.1
Inventory to Working Capital 41	0.2	•	0.3	0.2	0.2	0.2	0.1	0.1
Total Receipts to Cash Flow 42	7.9	2.5	4.9	6.8	10.8	12.0	13.5	19.0
Cost of Goods to Cash Flow 43	5.2	0.7	2.4	4.2	7.7	8.8	10.5	16.2
Cash Flow to Total Debt 44	0.7	•	1.8	1.0	0.5	0.3	0.3	0.2

Selected Financial Factors (in Percentages)

Debt Ratio 45	64.1	•	63.4	53.7	64.1	68.7	66.6	65.5
Return on Total Assets 46	18.9	•	45.6	22.8	14.2	10.1	11.9	10.4
Return on Equity Before Income Taxes 47	49.1	•	116.9	46.3	36.8	29.0	32.9	28.2
Return on Equity After Income Taxes 48	47.0	•	115.3	44.3	34.6	27.2	30.7	26.8
Profit Margin (Before Income Tax) 49	5.0	14.8	7.5	5.6	3.7	3.5	4.2	3.6
Profit Margin (After Income Tax) 50	4.8	14.7	7.4	5.4	3.5	3.3	3.9	3.4

Table I

Corporations with and without Net Income

OTHER SPECIALTY TRADE CONTRACTORS

Money Amounts and Size of Assets in Thousands of Dollars

Item Description for Accounting Period 7/05 Through 6/06	Total	Zero Assets	Under 500	500 to 1,000	1,000 to 5,000	5,000 to 10,000	10,000 to 25,000	25,000 to 50,000	50,000 to 100,000	100,000 to 250,000	250,000 to 500,000	500,000 to 2,500,000	2,500,000 and over
Number of Enterprises 1	329468	49405	243926	17133	15619	2020	1038	199	76	43	9	0	0

Revenues ($ in Thousands)

Item	Total	Zero Assets	Under 500	500 to 1,000	1,000 to 5,000	5,000 to 10,000	10,000 to 25,000	25,000 to 50,000	50,000 to 100,000	100,000 to 250,000	250,000 to 500,000	500,000 to 2,500,000	2,500,000 and over
Net Sales 2	390295719	7266662	136912148	41557641	96340307	32083894	35493268	15032638	10606554	11679021	3323588	0	0
Interest 3	213633	2272	27535	17236	43042	15210	21864	7716	12206	31643	34909	0	0
Rents 4	266755	6073	27676	11778	48245	6179	16334	14123	1511	38646	96189	0	0
Royalties 5	10617	0	460	0	1000	607	0	5333	35	2644	539	0	0
Other Portfolio Income 6	1069875	70877	356701	101193	222713	62750	69426	88976	26610	61671	8960	0	0
Other Receipts 7	1415157	41282	486625	119990	280611	39192	249191	78029	43549	58853	17832	0	0
Total Receipts 8	393271756	7387166	137811145	41807838	96935918	32207832	35850083	15226815	10690465	11872478	3482017	·	
Average Total Receipts 9	1194	150	565	2440	6206	15944	34538	76517	140664	276104	386891	·	

Operating Costs/Operating Income (%)

Item	Total	Zero Assets	Under 500	500 to 1,000	1,000 to 5,000	5,000 to 10,000	10,000 to 25,000	25,000 to 50,000	50,000 to 100,000	100,000 to 250,000	250,000 to 500,000	500,000 to 2,500,000	2,500,000 and over
Cost of Operations 10	66.4	49.0	55.6	64.4	71.5	76.6	78.1	77.7	78.7	77.7	72.9	·	
Salaries and Wages 11	7.3	11.8	10.3	7.4	5.8	4.5	4.3	4.2	4.8	5.9	5.9	·	
Taxes Paid 12	2.2	2.3	2.5	2.6	2.3	1.6	1.8	1.6	1.4	1.3	1.3	·	
Interest Paid 13	0.6	0.6	0.5	0.6	0.5	0.4	0.5	0.5	0.5	1.3	4.1	·	
Depreciation 14	1.8	2.2	1.9	2.2	1.6	1.3	1.4	1.6	1.2	2.2	3.1	·	
Amortization and Depletion 15	0.0	0.0	0.0	0.0	0.0	0.0	0.0	0.1	0.1	0.2	1.4	·	
Pensions and Other Deferred Comp. 16	0.4	0.1	0.3	0.5	0.3	0.6	0.5	0.3	0.3	0.2	0.2	·	
Employee Benefits 17	1.2	0.6	1.0	1.0	1.6	1.1	1.8	1.5	1.2	0.7	1.3	·	
Advertising 18	0.4	0.3	0.5	0.5	0.4	0.1	0.1	0.2	0.3	0.1	0.1	·	
Other Expenses 19	12.2	23.4	17.3	13.2	9.4	7.6	6.1	7.8	7.3	6.1	10.9	·	
Officers' Compensation 20	4.2	7.7	6.3	5.0	3.2	2.4	2.0	1.1	1.5	0.9	0.6	·	
Operating Margin 21	3.4	1.8	3.8	2.6	3.3	3.8	3.3	3.5	2.7	3.4	·		
Operating Margin Before Officers' Comp. 22	7.5	9.5	10.1	7.6	6.5	6.2	5.4	4.6	4.1	4.4	·		

Selected Average Balance Sheet ($ in Thousands)

Net Receivables 23	130	0	14	144	883	3313	7246	15888	32163	60456	101700
Inventories 24	17	0	4	42	124	288	634	1211	2230	4879	9105
Net Property, Plant and Equipment 25	82	0	31	243	431	965	2527	5694	9004	31935	66990
Total Assets 26	353	0	84	703	2070	6706	14739	33803	68059	150641	480878
Notes and Loans Payable 27	120	0	52	265	620	1427	3452	7611	11490	39468	238359
All Other Liabilities 28	126	0	17	168	739	3185	6653	14843	34510	66808	110309
Net Worth 29	107	0	14	269	711	2094	4634	11350	22058	44365	132210

Selected Financial Ratios (Times to 1)

Current Ratio 30	1.5	•	1.6	1.8	1.7	1.4	1.4	1.5	1.5	1.4	1.9
Quick Ratio 31	1.2	•	1.2	1.4	1.3	1.0	1.1	1.1	1.2	1.1	1.0
Net Sales to Working Capital 32	14.5	•	38.1	13.7	10.3	11.5	10.3	9.1	9.0	10.6	3.7
Coverage Ratio 33	8.1	6.5	9.5	6.8	8.2	10.5	9.2	9.8	7.8	4.8	1.7
Total Asset Turnover 34	3.4	•	6.7	3.5	3.0	2.4	2.3	2.2	2.1	1.8	0.8
Inventory Turnover 35	45.7	•	70.9	37.6	35.6	42.3	42.1	48.5	49.2	43.2	29.6
Receivables Turnover 36	9.8	•	43.3	15.5	7.1	5.6	5.4	5.2	4.8	5.6	4.7
Total Liabilities to Net Worth 37	2.3	•	4.9	1.6	1.9	2.2	2.2	2.0	2.1	2.4	2.6
Current Assets to Working Capital 38	2.8	•	2.8	2.2	2.5	3.7	3.3	3.1	3.2	3.7	2.1
Current Liabilities to Working Capital 39	1.8	•	1.8	1.2	1.5	2.7	2.3	2.1	2.2	2.7	1.1
Working Capital to Net Sales 40	0.1	•	0.0	0.1	0.1	0.1	0.1	0.1	0.1	0.1	0.3
Inventory to Working Capital 41	0.2	•	0.3	0.3	0.2	0.2	0.2	0.2	0.1	0.3	0.1
Total Receipts to Cash Flow 42	7.5	4.2	5.4	7.8	9.7	11.5	12.9	10.3	12.0	11.5	9.6
Cost of Goods to Cash Flow 43	5.0	2.1	3.0	5.0	6.9	8.8	10.1	8.0	9.4	8.9	7.0
Cash Flow to Total Debt 44	0.6	•	1.5	0.7	0.5	0.3	0.3	0.3	0.3	0.2	0.1

Selected Financial Factors (in Percentages)

Debt Ratio 45	69.7	•	83.0	61.7	65.7	68.8	68.6	66.4	67.6	70.5	72.5
Return on Total Assets 46	15.9	•	33.7	13.1	13.3	11.0	11.2	12.0	8.1	11.6	5.4
Return on Equity Before Income Taxes 47	45.9	•	177.6	29.2	34.0	32.0	31.9	32.0	21.7	31.1	8.3
Return on Equity After Income Taxes 48	43.6	•	175.0	28.0	32.2	29.3	29.5	29.5	19.2	26.9	4.0
Profit Margin (Before Income Tax) 49	4.1	3.4	4.5	3.2	3.9	4.2	4.3	4.8	3.4	5.1	3.0
Profit Margin (After Income Tax) 50	3.9	3.1	4.4	3.1	3.7	3.9	4.0	4.4	3.0	4.4	1.4

Table II
Corporations with Net Income

OTHER SPECIALTY TRADE CONTRACTORS

MONEY AMOUNTS AND SIZE OF ASSETS IN THOUSANDS OF DOLLARS

Item Description for Accounting Period 7/05 Through 6/06	Total	Zero Assets	Under 500	500 to 1,000	1,000 to 5,000	5,000 to 10,000	10,000 to 25,000	25,000 to 50,000	50,000 to 100,000	100,000 to 250,000	250,000 to 500,000	500,000 to 2,500,000	2,500,000 and over
Number of Enterprises **1**	222725	28953	165729	12876	12331	1690	859	•	59	36	•	0	0
Revenues ($ in Thousands)													
Net Sales **2**	324735236	4322671	108016467	33796992	82231360	28134965	31470812	•	9107781	10175617	•	•	0
Interest **3**	164887	2151	14845	15550	31050	13801	13775	•	11640	29290	•	•	0
Rents **4**	214463	5167	15572	1501	21303	5781	15596	•	1511	38646	•	•	0
Royalties **5**	9089	0	460	0	0	607	0	•	19	2644	•	•	0
Other Portfolio Income **6**	925321	70088	288743	89581	188680	50245	59860	•	26090	56682	•	•	0
Other Receipts **7**	1211266	35245	442519	109557	225367	23324	201104	•	40993	51663	•	•	0
Total Receipts **8**	327260262	4435322	108778606	34013181	82697760	28228723	31761147	•	9188034	10354542	•	•	0
Average Total Receipts **9**	1469	153	656	2642	6706	16703	36975	•	155729	287626	•	•	•
Operating Costs/Operating Income (%)													
Cost of Operations **10**	66.5	44.7	55.5	63.5	70.7	75.8	77.8	•	78.5	79.5	•	•	•
Salaries and Wages **11**	7.0	7.6	10.1	7.2	5.7	4.4	4.2	•	4.8	4.6	•	•	•
Taxes Paid **12**	2.1	2.0	2.3	2.4	2.2	1.5	1.7	•	1.4	1.1	•	•	•
Interest Paid **13**	0.5	0.7	0.4	0.4	0.5	0.4	0.4	•	0.4	1.4	•	•	•
Depreciation **14**	1.6	2.2	1.6	2.1	1.5	1.3	1.2	•	1.2	2.1	•	•	•
Amortization and Depletion **15**	0.0	0.1	0.0	0.0	0.0	0.0	0.0	•	0.1	0.1	•	•	•
Pensions and Other Deferred Comp. **16**	0.3	0.2	0.3	0.2	0.4	0.5	0.6	•	0.3	0.2	•	•	•
Employee Benefits **17**	1.2	0.7	0.9	1.0	1.5	1.0	1.7	•	1.1	0.4	•	•	•
Advertising **18**	0.3	0.3	0.5	0.4	0.3	0.1	0.1	•	0.3	0.1	•	•	•
Other Expenses **19**	11.1	21.4	15.8	13.1	9.0	7.4	5.7	•	6.5	4.9	•	•	•
Officers' Compensation **20**	3.9	9.6	5.9	4.7	3.3	2.4	2.1	•	1.5	1.0	•	•	•
Operating Margin **21**	5.5	10.5	6.6	4.9	5.0	5.1	4.6	•	3.8	4.7	•	•	•
Operating Margin Before Officers' Comp. **22**	9.4	20.1	12.5	9.6	8.2	7.5	6.7	•	5.3	5.6	•	•	•

Selected Average Balance Sheet ($ in Thousands)

Net Receivables 23	162	0	13	146	938	3425	7648	34671	61792
Inventories 24	19	0	4	42	124	216	543	1934	7624
Net Property, Plant and Equipment 25	89	0	31	215	401	1007	2405	9509	31049
Total Assets 26	416	0	89	704	2115	6667	14704	69626	148460
Notes and Loans Payable 27	122	0	44	235	606	1152	3083	9603	39908
All Other Liabilities 28	144	0	17	132	718	3171	6287	35617	60611
Net Worth 29	149	0	28	338	791	2344	5335	24406	47941

Selected Financial Ratios (Times to 1)

Current Ratio 30	1.7	·	1.9	2.4	1.8	1.5	1.5	1.5	1.5
Quick Ratio 31	1.3	·	1.5	1.9	1.4	1.2	1.3	1.2	1.2
Net Sales to Working Capital 32	12.8	·	30.6	11.0	9.5	10.5	9.3	9.3	9.1
Coverage Ratio 33	13.7	20.9	19.0	14.1	12.5	15.8	13.2	12.9	5.6
Total Asset Turnover 34	3.5	·	7.3	3.7	3.2	2.5	2.5	2.2	1.9
Inventory Turnover 35	51.4	·	80.5	39.3	38.1	58.4	52.5	62.7	29.5
Receivables Turnover 36	10.3	·	54.3	15.9	7.9	5.8	5.6	5.2	9.1
Total Liabilities to Net Worth 37	1.8	·	2.1	1.1	1.7	1.8	1.8	1.9	2.1
Current Assets to Working Capital 38	2.5	·	2.1	1.7	2.2	3.2	2.9	3.1	3.1
Current Liabilities to Working Capital 39	1.5	·	1.1	0.7	1.2	2.2	1.9	2.1	2.1
Working Capital to Net Sales 40	0.1	·	0.0	0.1	0.1	0.1	0.1	0.1	0.1
Inventory to Working Capital 41	0.2	·	0.2	0.2	0.2	0.1	0.1	0.1	0.1
Total Receipts to Cash Flow 42	6.9	3.2	4.9	6.6	8.6	10.4	11.5	11.0	10.8
Cost of Goods to Cash Flow 43	4.6	1.4	2.7	4.2	6.1	7.8	9.0	8.6	8.6
Cash Flow to Total Debt 44	0.8	·	2.2	1.1	0.6	0.4	0.3	0.3	0.3

Selected Financial Factors (in Percentages)

Debt Ratio 45	64.1	·	68.2	52.0	62.6	64.8	63.7	64.9	67.7
Return on Total Assets 46	23.7	·	56.8	22.3	19.0	14.6	14.8	11.3	14.9
Return on Equity Before Income Taxes 47	61.1	·	169.3	43.2	46.7	38.9	37.7	29.7	37.9
Return on Equity After Income Taxes 48	58.6	·	167.5	41.9	44.8	36.1	35.1	26.7	33.2
Profit Margin (Before Income Tax) 49	6.2	13.1	7.3	5.6	5.5	5.5	5.5	4.7	6.4
Profit Margin (After Income Tax) 50	6.0	12.6	7.3	5.4	5.3	5.1	5.1	4.2	5.6

Table I
Corporations with and without Net Income

ANIMAL FOOD AND GRAIN AND OILSEED MILLING

MONEY AMOUNTS AND SIZE OF ASSETS IN THOUSANDS OF DOLLARS

Item Description for Accounting Period 7/05 Through 6/06		Total	Zero Assets	Under 500	500 to 1,000	1,000 to 5,000	5,000 to 10,000	10,000 to 25,000	25,000 to 50,000	50,000 to 100,000	100,000 to 250,000	250,000 to 500,000	500,000 to 2,500,000	2,500,000 and over
Number of Enterprises	1	1617	264	556	212	346	86	64	37	20	19	4	5	4
Revenues ($ in Thousands)														
Net Sales	2	74660334	277422	237274	450309	1863402	1756986	2563643	2670375	2605571	3916813	1778969	2986757	53552811
Interest	3	466686	136	181	0	2980	1084	2843	2828	2207	5956	230	23046	425196
Rents	4	176939	24	442	0	47	0	1842	1584	538	126	0	479	171856
Royalties	5	547044	2	0	0	0	0	8	0	52	1179	0	40958	504843
Other Portfolio Income	6	1225734	1248	6950	0	1188	734	8810	1762	9181	3313	1232	62318	1129000
Other Receipts	7	1756503	57	14833	951	11786	825	6654	53248	25992	19117	4381	17278	1601383
Total Receipts	8	78833240	278889	259680	451260	1879403	1759629	2583800	2729797	2643541	3946504	1784812	3130836	57385089
Average Total Receipts	9	48753	1056	467	2129	5432	20461	40372	73778	132177	207711	446203	626167	14346272
Operating Costs/Operating Income (%)														
Cost of Operations	10	75.9	68.0	66.4	65.0	82.8	80.3	77.1	81.4	82.6	75.9	65.4	76.4	75.4
Salaries and Wages	11	3.4	13.2	20.8	8.6	4.5	4.3	4.2	4.7	3.3	4.2	4.7	1.9	3.0
Taxes Paid	12	0.9	1.0	6.2	2.7	0.7	1.4	1.1	0.9	0.8	1.1	1.3	0.9	0.8
Interest Paid	13	2.5	1.9	1.6	0.0	0.8	1.0	0.7	0.7	1.1	1.2	1.4	4.5	2.9
Depreciation	14	1.8	1.2	1.1	0.0	1.7	2.3	2.0	1.7	1.9	3.0	3.6	2.8	1.6
Amortization and Depletion	15	0.2	1.7	0.4	•	0.0	0.0	0.1	0.2	0.3	0.8	0.8	0.6	0.1
Pensions and Other Deferred Comp.	16	0.5	0.1	•	•	0.1	0.2	0.1	0.6	0.2	0.3	0.9	0.5	0.6
Employee Benefits	17	1.1	0.8	6.4	•	0.3	0.6	0.6	0.9	0.7	1.4	0.2	2.4	1.1
Advertising	18	6.2	9.9	0.5	0.0	0.5	0.8	0.4	0.4	0.2	1.0	3.7	1.2	8.2
Other Expenses	19	7.3	9.4	22.4	14.0	9.9	4.9	9.4	6.3	7.1	8.0	12.4	8.0	6.9
Officers' Compensation	20	0.6	13.1	1.8	7.1	1.6	1.0	1.0	0.8	0.5	0.9	0.6	1.6	0.3
Operating Margin	21	•	•	•	2.5	•	3.3	3.2	1.3	1.2	2.1	5.0	•	•
Operating Margin Before Officers' Comp.	22	0.2	•	•	9.6	•	4.2	4.2	2.0	1.7	3.0	5.6	0.7	•

Selected Average Balance Sheet ($ in Thousands)

Net Receivables 23	3026	30	132	400	2013	3703	6629	14414	18212	30124	164493	619422
Inventories 24	3455	42	140	600	1157	3443	6330	13432	20590	49998	34609	934744
Net Property, Plant and Equipment 25	7789	42	2	471	3904	6398	9703	23556	58804	160764	207912	2008402
Total Assets 26	39629	168	544	1835	8034	16224	33587	71912	155388	375885	941196	12416171
Notes and Loans Payable 27	14774	174	0	931	3688	5404	7126	24206	46784	159264	252395	4818138
All Other Liabilities 28	11450	101	139	779	1462	3604	10201	13931	37427	75446	224426	3753142
Net Worth 29	13405	-106	405	124	2884	7216	16260	33775	71177	141174	464375	3844892

Selected Financial Ratios (Times to 1)

Current Ratio 30	1.0	0.9	3.7	1.4	2.2	1.9	1.8	1.8	1.6	1.6	1.9	0.8
Quick Ratio 31	0.4	0.5	2.5	0.7	1.3	1.1	1.0	0.8	0.7	0.9	1.3	0.3
Net Sales to Working Capital 32	971.2	•	5.6	15.8	9.6	9.7	9.0	8.3	10.1	10.2	4.7	•
Coverage Ratio 33	3.3	•	12122.0	•	4.4	6.6	5.7	3.4	3.3	4.7	1.9	3.4
Total Asset Turnover 34	1.2	2.5	3.9	2.9	2.5	2.5	2.1	1.8	1.3	1.2	0.6	1.1
Inventory Turnover 35	10.1	6.8	9.9	7.4	14.2	9.0	9.3	8.0	7.6	5.8	13.2	10.8
Receivables Turnover 36	16.1	15.6	15.7	10.4	11.7	10.8	10.7	9.3	11.2	7.0	6.2	22.1
Total Liabilities to Net Worth 37	2.0	•	0.3	13.8	1.8	1.2	1.1	1.1	1.2	1.7	1.0	2.2
Current Assets to Working Capital 38	208.1	•	1.4	3.7	1.9	2.1	2.3	2.3	2.6	2.5	2.1	•
Current Liabilities to Working Capital 39	207.1	•	0.4	2.7	0.9	1.1	1.3	1.3	1.6	1.5	1.1	•
Working Capital to Net Sales 40	0.0	•	0.2	0.1	0.1	0.1	0.1	0.1	0.1	0.1	0.2	•
Inventory to Working Capital 41	76.0	•	0.4	1.6	0.6	0.7	0.9	1.0	1.1	0.9	0.3	•
Total Receipts to Cash Flow 42	9.6	•	8.2	18.2	13.3	8.7	12.2	11.8	10.5	6.1	10.1	9.2
Cost of Goods to Cash Flow 43	7.3	•	5.3	15.0	10.7	6.7	10.0	9.7	8.0	4.0	7.7	6.9
Cash Flow to Total Debt 44	0.2	•	1.9	0.2	0.3	0.5	0.3	0.3	0.2	0.3	0.1	0.2

Selected Financial Factors (in Percentages)

Debt Ratio 45	66.2	163.2	25.5	93.2	64.1	55.5	51.6	53.0	54.2	62.4	50.7	69.0
Return on Total Assets 46	9.5	•	10.5	•	11.2	11.7	9.1	6.8	5.4	7.9	5.4	10.6
Return on Equity Before Income Taxes 47	19.6	72.9	14.1	•	24.1	22.3	15.6	10.2	8.2	16.5	5.1	24.2
Return on Equity After Income Taxes 48	14.1	73.0	14.1	•	20.7	21.4	14.7	8.5	5.9	16.5	2.6	17.2
Profit Margin (Before Income Tax) 49	5.7	•	2.7	•	3.4	4.0	3.5	2.7	2.8	5.2	4.0	6.9
Profit Margin (After Income Tax) 50	4.1	•	2.7	•	2.9	3.9	3.3	2.2	2.0	5.2	2.1	4.9

Table II
Corporations with Net Income

ANIMAL FOOD AND GRAIN AND OILSEED MILLING

MONEY AMOUNTS AND SIZE OF ASSETS IN THOUSANDS OF DOLLARS

Item Description for Accounting Period 7/05 Through 6/06	Total	Zero Assets	Under 500	500 to 1,000	1,000 to 5,000	5,000 to 10,000	10,000 to 25,000	25,000 to 50,000	50,000 to 100,000	100,000 to 250,000	250,000 to 500,000	500,000 to 2,500,000	2,500,000 and over
Number of Enterprises **1**	820	10	92	212	296	86	54	30	17	12	•	•	4
Revenues ($ in Thousands)													
Net Sales **2**	70819743	180412	117277	450309	1733558	1756986	2287883	2162039	2078618	2790911	•	•	53552811
Interest **3**	462523	23	175	0	2836	1084	2292	2823	2202	5239	•	•	425196
Rents **4**	176388	24	0	0	47	0	1741	1584	531	126	•	•	171856
Royalties **5**	546913	0	0	0	0	0	8	0	52	1051	•	•	504843
Other Portfolio Income **6**	1196493	1248	0	0	1188	734	7194	1761	8860	2882	•	•	1129000
Other Receipts **7**	1731451	54	0	951	9395	825	5464	48016	28517	17120	•	•	1601383
Total Receipts **8**	74933511	181761	117452	451260	1747024	1759629	2304582	2216223	2118780	2817329	•	•	57385089
Average Total Receipts **9**	91382	18176	1277	2129	5902	20461	42677	73874	124634	234777	•	•	14346272
Operating Costs/Operating Income (%)													
Cost of Operations **10**	75.9	72.1	65.5	65.0	83.3	80.3	77.2	80.0	84.0	74.7	•	•	75.4
Salaries and Wages **11**	3.3	3.1	14.8	8.6	4.4	4.3	4.0	4.7	3.1	4.6	•	•	3.0
Taxes Paid **12**	0.9	1.0	7.9	2.7	0.6	1.4	1.1	1.0	0.9	1.2	•	•	0.8
Interest Paid **13**	2.5	0.1	0.3	0.0	0.6	1.0	0.7	0.5	1.2	1.0	•	•	2.9
Depreciation **14**	1.7	0.5	0.6	0.0	1.2	2.3	1.8	1.8	2.0	2.5	•	•	1.6
Amortization and Depletion **15**	0.2	0.6	•	•	0.0	0.0	0.0	0.0	0.3	0.8	•	•	0.1
Pensions and Other Deferred Comp. **16**	0.5	0.1	•	•	0.1	0.2	0.1	0.7	0.2	0.3	•	•	0.6
Employee Benefits **17**	1.1	0.6	3.9	•	0.2	0.6	0.6	1.0	0.8	1.6	•	•	1.1
Advertising **18**	6.5	11.8	0.4	0.0	0.5	0.8	0.3	0.4	0.3	1.2	•	•	8.2
Other Expenses **19**	7.0	6.1	4.1	14.0	6.9	4.9	9.1	6.1	4.9	6.9	•	•	6.9
Officers' Compensation **20**	0.5	0.2	2.3	7.1	1.7	1.0	1.0	0.9	0.5	0.9	•	•	0.3
Operating Margin **21**	0.0	3.8	0.1	2.5	0.5	3.3	4.0	2.8	1.8	4.2	•	•	•
Operating Margin Before Officers' Comp. **22**	0.5	4.0	2.4	9.6	2.2	4.2	4.9	3.7	2.3	5.2	•	•	•

Selected Average Balance Sheet ($ in Thousands)

Net Receivables 23	5511	0	30	132	431	2013	3723	6991	13386	18287	•	619422
Inventories 24	6235	0	50	149	461	1003	3372	5588	13639	22011	•	934744
Net Property, Plant and Equipment 25	14257	0	86	2	517	3904	6562	10520	23254	54730	•	2008402
Total Assets 26	74042	0	352	544	1850	8034	16326	34818	72120	151873	•	12416171
Notes and Loans Payable 27	26959	0	115	0	426	3688	4616	5766	24949	40293	•	4818138
All Other Liabilities 28	21616	0	68	139	619	1462	3706	10515	12618	39377	•	3753142
Net Worth 29	25466	0	169	405	806	2884	8003	18538	34553	72204	•	3844892

Selected Financial Ratios (Times to 1)

Current Ratio 30	1.0	•	2.4	3.7	2.2	2.2	2.0	2.1	1.9	1.7
Quick Ratio 31	0.4	•	0.8	2.5	1.1	1.3	1.2	1.2	0.8	0.8
Net Sales to Working Capital 32	•	•	13.0	5.6	8.3	9.6	8.9	7.4	7.4	10.3
Coverage Ratio 33	3.6	40.9	1.9	12122.0	3.2	4.4	8.1	11.2	4.1	6.2
Total Asset Turnover 34	1.2	•	3.6	3.9	3.2	2.5	2.6	2.1	1.7	1.5
Inventory Turnover 35	10.5	•	16.7	9.3	10.6	16.4	9.7	10.3	7.5	7.9
Receivables Turnover 36	17.0	•	44.2	32.2	12.5	17.1	11.6	11.9	9.9	11.5
Total Liabilities to Net Worth 37	1.9	•	1.1	0.3	1.3	1.8	1.0	0.9	1.1	1.1
Current Assets to Working Capital 38	•	•	1.7	1.4	1.8	1.9	2.0	1.9	2.1	2.4
Current Liabilities to Working Capital 39	•	•	0.7	0.4	0.8	0.9	1.0	0.9	1.1	1.4
Working Capital to Net Sales 40	•	•	0.1	0.2	0.1	0.1	0.1	0.1	0.1	0.1
Inventory to Working Capital 41	•	•	1.0	0.4	0.9	0.6	0.7	0.7	1.0	1.0
Total Receipts to Cash Flow 42	9.3	10.2	31.4	8.2	14.3	13.3	8.5	10.3	13.2	9.7
Cost of Goods to Cash Flow 43	7.0	7.4	20.6	5.3	11.9	10.7	6.6	8.2	11.1	7.2
Cash Flow to Total Debt 44	0.2	•	0.2	1.9	0.4	0.3	0.6	0.4	0.2	0.3

Selected Financial Factors (in Percentages)

Debt Ratio 45	65.6	•	52.1	25.5	56.5	64.1	51.0	46.8	52.1	52.5
Return on Total Assets 46	10.3	•	1.9	10.5	6.1	11.2	13.8	12.1	8.3	9.4
Return on Equity Before Income Taxes 47	21.7	•	1.9	14.1	9.6	24.1	24.8	20.6	13.1	16.5
Return on Equity After Income Taxes 48	16.0	•	1.6	14.1	8.9	20.7	23.9	19.7	11.2	12.8
Profit Margin (Before Income Tax) 49	6.4	4.5	0.3	2.7	1.3	3.4	4.7	5.3	3.7	5.1
Profit Margin (After Income Tax) 50	4.7	3.5	0.2	2.7	1.2	2.9	4.5	5.1	3.2	4.9

Table I

Corporations with and without Net Income

SUGAR AND CONFECTIONERY PRODUCT

MONEY AMOUNTS AND SIZE OF ASSETS IN THOUSANDS OF DOLLARS

Item Description for Accounting Period 7/05 Through 6/06	Total	Zero Assets	Under 500	500 to 1,000	1,000 to 5,000	5,000 to 10,000	10,000 to 25,000	25,000 to 50,000	50,000 to 100,000	100,000 to 250,000	250,000 to 500,000	500,000 to 2,500,000	2,500,000 and over
Number of Enterprises 1	1337	9	852	190	161	32	44	14	18	3	5	4	4
Revenues ($ in Thousands)													
Net Sales 2	39047160	241972	1045190	433791	620991	644453	1759305	626451	1924850	991625	1387913	2101251	27269367
Interest 3	179203	309	0	2	742	577	1021	713	573	33	12178	28006	135050
Rents 4	59032	0	0	0	0	429	816	4504	1272	5	65	25838	26102
Royalties 5	192641	0	0	0	0	0	79	2703	2	0	1072	2053	186732
Other Portfolio Income 6	1289654	0	0	1	0	605	297	1831	1238	7	2905	41039	1241729
Other Receipts 7	414970	3569	638	2903	11641	1630	19678	3281	6333	888	5763	118203	240447
Total Receipts 8	41182660	245850	1045828	436697	633374	647694	1781196	639483	1934268	992558	1409896	2316390	29099427
Average Total Receipts 9	30802	27317	1227	2298	3934	20240	40482	45677	107459	330853	281979	579098	7274857
Operating Costs/Operating Income (%)													
Cost of Operations 10	53.6	100.7	71.4	62.3	56.4	70.3	79.5	72.5	69.6	78.4	62.6	70.2	46.0
Salaries and Wages 11	6.1	2.6	5.2	12.5	9.6	4.7	3.8	3.5	6.6	3.1	8.0	4.8	6.4
Taxes Paid 12	1.3	0.3	3.6	1.7	2.4	1.5	1.1	1.5	1.6	0.9	1.6	1.0	1.2
Interest Paid 13	2.9	2.6	•	0.9	2.3	1.1	0.5	2.7	1.8	2.1	8.6	2.4	3.1
Depreciation 14	2.2	3.0	0.5	1.4	5.7	1.7	1.5	3.2	2.2	2.4	3.6	1.9	2.1
Amortization and Depletion 15	0.8	0.3	0.0	0.1	1.9	0.0	0.9	0.7	0.4	0.8	2.1	0.2	0.9
Pensions and Other Deferred Comp. 16	1.7	0.9	•	1.4	0.7	0.7	0.3	0.2	0.7	0.4	1.6	1.0	2.1
Employee Benefits 17	1.4	1.0	•	0.7	0.8	0.3	0.8	1.3	2.0	1.8	1.7	1.6	1.4
Advertising 18	5.2	0.1	0.8	0.0	1.5	1.8	0.5	0.7	2.2	0.8	2.9	3.1	6.8
Other Expenses 19	22.2	•	12.5	17.8	21.2	12.8	7.8	13.4	12.6	7.2	16.8	20.6	25.8
Officers' Compensation 20	0.7	0.1	0.6	4.7	4.1	2.6	1.7	1.2	1.3	1.0	1.3	0.2	0.4
Operating Margin 21	1.9	•	5.2	•	•	2.4	1.5	•	•	0.9	•	•	3.8
Operating Margin Before Officers' Comp. 22	2.6	•	5.9	1.1	•	5.0	3.2	0.4	2.0	•	•	•	4.2

Selected Average Balance Sheet ($ in Thousands)

Net Receivables 23	5883	0	94	375	308	1582	3362	6026	11255	31793	46524	210759	1502054
Inventories 24	2683	0	27	186	320	1750	3140	7331	16783	67817	49668	83255	523434
Net Property, Plant and Equipment 25	7191	0	21	153	395	3830	5306	14400	18739	43049	94163	297080	1705032
Total Assets 26	36774	0	183	848	1539	8473	16838	33664	64884	186297	365568	920031	9970874
Notes and Loans Payable 27	15530	0	5	693	1242	3305	3884	16697	21445	106779	367053	155835	4187962
All Other Liabilities 28	11361	0	77	252	525	2567	3722	6164	17193	32021	-119890	335548	3377861
Net Worth 29	9882	0	100	-97	-227	2601	9232	10803	26245	47497	118405	428648	2405052

Selected Financial Ratios (Times to 1)

Current Ratio 30	0.8	•	2.1	1.2	1.1	1.5	1.9	1.4	1.5	2.7	0.9	1.6	0.7
Quick Ratio 31	0.5	•	1.7	0.7	0.6	0.8	1.0	0.6	0.6	1.1	0.5	0.9	0.4
Net Sales to Working Capital 32	•	•	14.6	17.1	40.6	14.8	9.8	10.3	8.7	5.6	•	3.3	•
Coverage Ratio 33	3.9	•	•	•	•	3.6	6.6	1.5	0.8	1.5	•	2.3	4.9
Total Asset Turnover 34	0.8	•	6.7	2.7	2.5	2.4	2.4	1.3	1.6	1.8	0.8	0.6	0.7
Inventory Turnover 35	5.8	•	32.0	7.6	6.8	8.1	10.1	4.4	4.4	3.8	3.5	4.4	6.0
Receivables Turnover 36	5.3	•	15.1	6.3	15.5	13.3	14.4	8.6	10.1	7.6	6.4	2.6	4.8
Total Liabilities to Net Worth 37	2.7	•	0.8	•	•	2.3	0.8	2.1	1.5	2.9	2.1	1.1	3.1
Current Assets to Working Capital 38	•	•	1.9	5.0	10.2	3.1	2.2	3.6	2.9	1.6	•	2.6	•
Current Liabilities to Working Capital 39	•	•	0.9	4.0	9.2	2.1	1.2	2.6	1.9	0.6	•	1.6	•
Working Capital to Net Sales 40	•	•	0.1	0.1	0.0	0.1	0.1	0.1	0.1	0.2	•	0.3	•
Inventory to Working Capital 41	•	•	0.3	2.0	3.4	1.5	0.9	1.6	1.5	0.9	•	0.5	•
Total Receipts to Cash Flow 42	3.6	•	8.3	13.4	9.3	7.0	11.1	7.8	9.9	12.9	20.8	4.6	2.9
Cost of Goods to Cash Flow 43	1.9	•	6.0	8.4	5.3	4.9	8.8	5.6	6.9	10.1	13.0	3.2	1.3
Cash Flow to Total Debt 44	0.3	•	1.8	0.2	0.2	0.5	0.3	0.3	0.3	0.2	0.1	0.2	0.3

Selected Financial Factors (in Percentages)

Debt Ratio 45	73.1	•	45.2	111.4	114.8	69.3	45.2	67.9	59.6	74.5	67.6	53.4	75.9
Return on Total Assets 46	9.0	•	35.5	•	•	9.4	7.8	5.3	2.3	5.5	•	3.2	10.3
Return on Equity Before Income Taxes 47	24.8	•	64.7	68.9	78.5	22.2	12.1	5.3	•	7.1	•	3.9	34.0
Return on Equity After Income Taxes 48	17.6	•	64.7	80.4	86.9	16.9	10.7	4.6	•	4.4	•	1.7	24.6
Profit Margin (Before Income Tax) 49	8.4	•	5.3	•	•	2.9	2.8	1.3	•	1.0	•	3.2	12.0
Profit Margin (After Income Tax) 50	6.0	•	5.3	•	•	2.2	2.5	1.1	•	0.6	•	1.4	8.7

Table II

Corporations with Net Income

SUGAR AND CONFECTIONERY PRODUCT

MONEY AMOUNTS AND SIZE OF ASSETS IN THOUSANDS OF DOLLARS

Item Description for Accounting Period 7/05 Through 6/06	Total	Zero Assets	Under 500	500 to 1,000	1,000 to 5,000	5,000 to 10,000	10,000 to 25,000	25,000 to 50,000	50,000 to 100,000	100,000 to 250,000	250,000 to 500,000	500,000 to 2,500,000	2,500,000 and over
Number of Enterprises 1	1156	0	852	•	91	28	39	10	9	•	0	•	4
Revenues ($ in Thousands)													
Net Sales 2	34503627	0	1045190	•	304962	598922	1692771	441620	1125491	•	0	•	27269367
Interest 3	164990	0	0	•	737	568	729	640	339	•	0	•	135050
Rents 4	55234	0	0	•	0	429	816	2044	0	•	0	•	26102
Royalties 5	188863	0	0	•	0	0	79	0	0	•	0	•	186732
Other Portfolio Income 6	1285474	0	0	•	0	605	177	1739	202	•	0	•	1241729
Other Receipts 7	287123	0	638	•	0	374	19263	3031	904	•	0	•	240447
Total Receipts 8	36485311	0	1045828	•	305699	600898	1713835	449074	1126936	•	0	•	29099427
Average Total Receipts 9	31562	•	1227	•	3359	21461	43944	44907	125215	•	•	•	7274857
Operating Costs/Operating Income (%)													
Cost of Operations 10	51.3	•	71.4	•	58.4	69.4	79.2	68.8	70.3	•	•	•	46.0
Salaries and Wages 11	6.0	•	5.2	•	9.1	5.1	3.6	3.6	6.8	•	•	•	6.4
Taxes Paid 12	1.3	•	3.6	•	3.6	1.5	1.1	1.5	1.6	•	•	•	1.2
Interest Paid 13	2.7	•	•	•	0.8	1.1	0.5	2.3	0.7	•	•	•	3.1
Depreciation 14	2.0	•	0.5	•	1.9	1.2	1.3	2.5	1.4	•	•	•	2.1
Amortization and Depletion 15	0.8	•	0.0	•	•	0.0	0.9	0.5	0.0	•	•	•	0.9
Pensions and Other Deferred Comp. 16	1.8	•	•	•	1.5	0.7	0.3	0.2	0.7	•	•	•	2.1
Employee Benefits 17	1.3	•	•	•	1.3	0.3	0.8	1.8	2.2	•	•	•	1.4
Advertising 18	5.5	•	0.8	•	2.1	2.0	0.5	0.9	1.0	•	•	•	6.8
Other Expenses 19	22.9	•	12.5	•	9.9	12.6	7.0	15.5	10.8	•	•	•	25.8
Officers' Compensation 20	0.7	•	0.6	•	8.3	2.8	1.7	1.3	1.2	•	•	•	0.4
Operating Margin 21	3.7	•	5.2	•	3.2	3.2	3.1	1.2	3.3	•	•	•	3.8
Operating Margin Before Officers' Comp. 22	4.3	•	5.9	•	11.5	6.0	4.8	2.5	4.4	•	•	•	4.2

Selected Average Balance Sheet ($ in Thousands)

Net Receivables 23	5838	94	354	1779	3435	6874	14032	1502054
Inventories 24	2591	28	447	1921	2914	6909	21451	523434
Net Property, Plant and Equipment 25	6949	21	349	3694	5296	11981	18428	1705032
Total Assets 26	38310	183	1858	8784	17250	30356	66250	9970874
Notes and Loans Payable 27	15417	5	323	3442	3382	15986	15240	4187962
All Other Liabilities 28	12516	77	200	2336	3829	5902	14139	3377861
Net Worth 29	10377	100	1335	3007	10040	8468	36871	2405052

Selected Financial Ratios (Times to 1)

Current Ratio 30	0.8	2.1	3.6	1.8	1.9	1.8	2.2	0.7
Quick Ratio 31	0.5	1.7	2.0	0.9	1.0	0.9	0.9	0.4
Net Sales to Working Capital 32		14.6	3.8	10.6	10.4	6.3	5.6	
Coverage Ratio 33	4.9		5.6	4.3	10.0	2.3	5.9	4.9
Total Asset Turnover 34	0.8	6.7	1.8	2.4	2.5	1.5	1.9	0.7
Inventory Turnover 35	5.9	31.6	4.4	7.7	11.8	4.4		6.0
Receivables Turnover 36	5.4	26.0	10.3	12.5	16.6	8.3	8.3	4.8
Total Liabilities to Net Worth 37	2.7	0.8	0.4	1.9	0.7	2.6	0.8	3.1
Current Assets to Working Capital 38		1.9	1.4	2.3	2.1	2.3	1.9	
Current Liabilities to Working Capital 39		0.9	0.4	1.3	1.1	1.3	0.9	
Working Capital to Net Sales 40		0.1	0.3	0.1	0.1	0.2	0.2	
Inventory to Working Capital 41		0.3	0.5	1.0	0.9	0.9	1.0	
Total Receipts to Cash Flow 42	3.3	8.3	11.3	6.7	9.7	6.3	8.3	2.9
Cost of Goods to Cash Flow 43	1.7	6.0	6.6	4.7	7.7	4.3	5.8	1.3
Cash Flow to Total Debt 44	0.3	1.8	0.6	0.5	0.6	0.3	0.5	0.3

Selected Financial Factors (in Percentages)

Debt Ratio 45	72.9	45.2	28.2	65.8	41.8	72.1	44.3	75.9
Return on Total Assets 46	10.3	35.5	7.6	11.3	12.2	7.5	7.8	10.3
Return on Equity Before Income Taxes 47	30.3	64.7	8.7	25.2	18.8	15.1	11.6	34.0
Return on Equity After Income Taxes 48	22.4	64.7	6.2	20.0	17.4	13.9	11.5	24.6
Profit Margin (Before Income Tax) 49	10.5	5.3	3.5	3.5	4.4	2.9	3.4	12.0
Profit Margin (After Income Tax) 50	7.8	5.3	2.5	2.8	4.0	2.7	3.4	8.7

40

Table I

Corporations with and without Net Income

FRUIT AND VEGETABLE PRESERVING AND SPECIALTY FOOD

MONEY AMOUNTS AND SIZE OF ASSETS IN THOUSANDS OF DOLLARS

Item Description for Accounting Period 7/05 Through 6/06	Total	Zero Assets	Under 500	500 to 1,000	1,000 to 5,000	5,000 to 10,000	10,000 to 25,000	25,000 to 50,000	50,000 to 100,000	100,000 to 250,000	250,000 to 500,000	500,000 to 2,500,000	2,500,000 and over
Number of Enterprises **1**	860	4	482	0	174	13	100	26	28	17	3	8	5
Revenues ($ in Thousands)													
Net Sales **2**	39603105	237079	308028	0	667823	210051	3221586	1434688	3546645	4315734	1431510	9964474	14265486
Interest **3**	150783	0	0	0	594	132	1968	2278	2846	9312	2399	48056	83196
Rents **4**	26535	0	0	0	1505	0	1342	293	5877	7624	216	6453	3225
Royalties **5**	368657	0	0	0	844	0	0	0	106	0	0	35935	331772
Other Portfolio Income **6**	1432385	76	0	0	22962	0	1844	45550	1244	31748	1657	169528	1157775
Other Receipts **7**	932926	170	492	0	-7966	15	26693	25049	20589	48302	6659	66346	746681
Total Receipts **8**	42514391	237325	308520	0	685762	210198	3253333	1507858	3577307	4412720	1442441	10290792	16588135
Average Total Receipts **9**	49435	59331	640	•	3941	16169	32533	57995	127761	259572	480814	1286349	3317627
Operating Costs/Operating Income (%)													
Cost of Operations **10**	66.6	74.3	22.5	•	80.3	73.1	72.6	75.5	78.5	79.4	67.9	62.4	60.4
Salaries and Wages **11**	5.7	4.6	24.8	•	2.4	1.6	5.0	4.2	3.2	3.3	4.4	8.9	5.2
Taxes Paid **12**	1.3	0.5	4.1	•	2.5	1.7	1.4	1.6	1.0	2.1	0.7	1.5	1.0
Interest Paid **13**	2.5	1.0	0.2	•	0.6	0.5	1.6	1.9	1.9	1.4	1.5	2.6	3.3
Depreciation **14**	2.2	1.1	4.8	•	2.1	1.4	1.8	2.6	1.8	2.0	3.3	2.7	1.9
Amortization and Depletion **15**	1.0	0.1	0.2	•	0.0	0.1	0.2	0.3	0.3	0.1	0.5	1.8	1.4
Pensions and Other Deferred Comp. **16**	0.5	0.1	•	•	0.7	0.0	0.3	0.3	0.5	0.2	0.0	0.2	0.8
Employee Benefits **17**	1.2	1.2	•	•	2.2	1.4	0.7	1.3	1.1	1.0	1.9	1.9	0.7
Advertising **18**	2.8	2.9	0.0	•	0.9	1.1	1.7	1.1	0.7	0.5	4.5	5.6	2.6
Other Expenses **19**	15.7	11.2	50.4	•	4.3	9.8	10.4	10.3	9.3	8.8	10.9	12.9	23.4
Officers' Compensation **20**	0.8	2.3	0.0	•	6.2	4.8	1.7	1.3	1.0	0.6	0.6	0.3	0.5
Operating Margin **21**	•	0.9	•	•	•	4.5	2.6	•	0.8	0.5	3.7	•	•
Operating Margin Before Officers' Comp. **22**	0.5	3.1	•	•	4.1	9.3	4.3	1.0	1.8	1.1	4.3	•	•

Selected Average Balance Sheet ($ in Thousands)

Net Receivables 23	5226	0	15	334	1352	3691	5731	12482	21298	32366	65518	512061
Inventories 24	6502	0	0	591	3812	4705	11104	27116	46611	65776	147537	309138
Net Property, Plant and Equipment 25	8388	0	160	471	740	4549	10787	18654	58076	115147	282747	438447
Total Assets 26	51466	0	194	1956	5883	17295	32652	69871	166298	315087	1049704	5409028
Notes and Loans Payable 27	13817	0	142	502	2299	7335	11859	32013	44975	77787	392258	1124537
All Other Liabilities 28	13513	0	24	404	1899	6298	7739	18239	51833	87530	227661	1441516
Net Worth 29	24136	0	28	1051	1685	3662	13054	19619	69490	149771	429785	2842975

Selected Financial Ratios (Times to 1)

Current Ratio 30	1.3	0.9	2.5	1.7	1.1	1.7	1.8	1.6	1.7	1.9	1.0
Quick Ratio 31	0.6	0.9	1.1	0.5	0.5	0.7	0.6	0.4	0.9	0.7	0.6
Net Sales to Working Capital 32	13.6	•	4.6	8.1	44.7	7.1	6.9	7.0	10.1	8.7	262.1
Coverage Ratio 33	4.2	2.0	2.0	9.7	3.2	3.5	1.9	3.0	3.8	1.9	6.2
Total Asset Turnover 34	0.9	3.3	2.0	2.7	1.9	1.7	1.8	1.5	1.5	1.2	0.5
Inventory Turnover 35	4.7	4076.3	5.2	3.1	5.0	3.8	3.7	3.1	7.0	5.3	5.6
Receivables Turnover 36	5.6	81.5	13.8	3.7	10.9	8.5	11.1	12.2	29.5	20.3	2.7
Total Liabilities to Net Worth 37	1.1	6.0	0.9	2.5	3.7	1.5	2.6	1.4	1.1	1.4	0.9
Current Assets to Working Capital 38	4.5	•	1.7	2.5	14.6	2.4	2.3	2.7	2.4	2.2	102.3
Current Liabilities to Working Capital 39	3.5	•	0.7	1.5	13.6	1.4	1.3	1.7	1.4	1.2	101.3
Working Capital to Net Sales 40	0.1	•	0.2	0.1	0.0	0.1	0.1	0.1	0.1	0.1	0.0
Inventory to Working Capital 41	2.0	•	0.8	1.6	8.0	1.2	1.5	1.8	1.0	1.1	27.8
Total Receipts to Cash Flow 42	5.1	2.8	8.9	9.2	8.1	8.3	1.5	1.8	1.0	1.1	2.8
Cost of Goods to Cash Flow 43	3.4	0.6	6.6	6.7	5.9	6.3	8.7	11.0	6.9	9.5	1.7
Cash Flow to Total Debt 44	0.3	1.3	•	0.3	0.3	0.3	0.2	0.2	0.4	0.2	0.4

Selected Financial Factors (in Percentages)

Debt Ratio 45	53.1	85.8	46.3	71.4	78.8	60.0	71.9	58.2	52.5	59.1	47.4
Return on Total Assets 46	9.3	•	2.4	13.9	9.7	11.2	6.4	6.2	8.9	5.8	11.0
Return on Equity Before Income Taxes 47	15.1	•	2.3	43.4	31.6	20.1	10.7	9.9	13.9	6.6	17.5
Return on Equity After Income Taxes 48	10.7	•	0.3	42.5	26.8	15.9	8.3	7.5	9.3	2.9	12.7
Profit Margin (Before Income Tax) 49	7.9	1.0	0.6	4.5	3.6	4.8	1.7	2.7	4.4	2.3	17.4
Profit Margin (After Income Tax) 50	5.6	1.0	0.1	4.4	3.0	3.8	1.3	2.1	2.9	1.0	12.7

Table II
Corporations with Net Income

FRUIT AND VEGETABLE PRESERVING AND SPECIALTY FOOD

MONEY AMOUNTS AND SIZE OF ASSETS IN THOUSANDS OF DOLLARS

Item Description for Accounting Period 7/05 Through 6/06	Total	Zero Assets	Under 500	500 to 1,000	1,000 to 5,000	5,000 to 10,000	10,000 to 25,000	25,000 to 50,000	50,000 to 100,000	100,000 to 250,000	250,000 to 500,000	500,000 to 2,500,000	2,500,000 and over
Number of Enterprises **1**	307	4	0	0	135	•	85	22	20	14	3	•	•
Revenues ($ in Thousands)													
Net Sales **2**	33451366	237079	0	0	575586	•	2872846	1206665	2652428	3692825	1431510	•	•
Interest **3**	139574	0	0	0	444	•	1968	2145	964	3748	2399	•	•
Rents **4**	16993	0	0	0	196	•	1342	238	924	7624	216	•	•
Royalties **5**	360280	0	0	0	0	•	0	0	0	0	0	•	•
Other Portfolio Income **6**	1413958	76	0	0	22956	•	696	42447	1150	31646	1657	•	•
Other Receipts **7**	851024	170	0	0	3117	•	26342	14913	11498	46562	6659	•	•
Total Receipts **8**	36233195	237325	0	0	602299	•	2903194	1266408	2666964	3782405	1442441	•	•
Average Total Receipts **9**	118023	59331	•	•	4461	•	34155	57564	133348	270172	480814	•	•
Operating Costs/Operating Income (%)													
Cost of Operations **10**	64.7	74.3	•	•	79.8	•	73.1	74.9	78.7	78.5	67.9	•	•
Salaries and Wages **11**	5.9	4.6	•	•	1.6	•	5.1	3.9	2.4	3.4	4.4	•	•
Taxes Paid **12**	1.3	0.5	•	•	2.5	•	1.4	1.7	1.0	2.4	0.7	•	•
Interest Paid **13**	2.4	1.0	•	•	0.6	•	1.0	1.6	1.2	1.1	1.5	•	•
Depreciation **14**	2.1	1.1	•	•	1.6	•	1.8	2.8	1.9	2.0	3.3	•	•
Amortization and Depletion **15**	0.8	0.1	•	•	0.0	•	0.1	0.3	0.1	0.1	0.5	•	•
Pensions and Other Deferred Comp. **16**	0.4	0.1	•	•	0.8	•	0.3	0.3	0.6	0.2	0.0	•	•
Employee Benefits **17**	1.1	1.2	•	•	2.4	•	0.7	1.1	1.0	1.0	1.9	•	•
Advertising **18**	3.1	2.9	•	•	0.7	•	1.5	1.3	0.6	0.5	4.5	•	•
Other Expenses **19**	16.2	11.2	•	•	2.6	•	9.2	8.6	8.4	8.7	10.9	•	•
Officers' Compensation **20**	0.8	2.3	•	•	6.8	•	1.5	1.4	1.0	0.6	0.6	•	•
Operating Margin **21**	1.1	0.9	•	•	0.4	•	4.2	2.1	3.0	1.4	3.7	•	•
Operating Margin Before Officers' Comp. **22**	1.9	3.1	•	•	7.2	•	5.7	3.5	4.0	2.0	4.3	•	•

Selected Average Balance Sheet ($ in Thousands)

Net Receivables 23	12465	0	227	3953	5974	12726	20494	32366
Inventories 24	14155	0	620	4574	9882	28739	58791	46611
Net Property, Plant and Equipment 25	19273	0	347	4411	11322	21066	57529	115147
Total Assets 26	125211	0	1636	17290	33187	71032	166080	315087
Notes and Loans Payable 27	30364	0	292	5756	11763	24588	41901	77787
All Other Liabilities 28	32630	0	284	6434		16117	56194	87530
Net Worth 29	62217	0	1061	5101	14514	30327	67984	149771

Selected Financial Ratios (Times to 1)

Current Ratio 30	1.2		2.5	1.3	2.0	1.8	1.4	1.7
Quick Ratio 31	0.6		1.1	0.6	0.8	0.6	0.3	0.9
Net Sales to Working Capital 32	16.1		5.9	14.4	5.8	6.5	9.7	10.1
Coverage Ratio 33	5.4	2.0	8.8	6.3	5.4	4.0	4.5	3.8
Total Asset Turnover 34	0.9		2.6	2.0	1.7	1.9	1.6	1.5
Inventory Turnover 35	5.0		5.5	5.4	4.2	3.6	3.5	7.0
Receivables Turnover 36	5.3		19.5	11.7	9.4	11.1	14.1	29.5
Total Liabilities to Net Worth 37	1.0		0.5	2.4	1.3	1.3	1.4	1.1
Current Assets to Working Capital 38	5.3		1.7	4.7	2.0	2.2	3.5	2.4
Current Liabilities to Working Capital 39	4.3		0.7	3.7	1.0	1.2	2.5	1.4
Working Capital to Net Sales 40	0.1		0.2	0.1	0.2	0.2	0.1	0.1
Inventory to Working Capital 41	2.3		0.8	2.5	1.0	1.4	2.3	1.0
Total Receipts to Cash Flow 42	4.4	8.9	42.3	7.9	7.9	9.5	10.2	6.9
Cost of Goods to Cash Flow 43	2.8	6.6	33.8	5.8	5.9	7.5	8.0	4.7
Cash Flow to Total Debt 44	0.4		0.2	0.4	0.4	0.3	0.3	0.4

Selected Financial Factors (in Percentages)

Debt Ratio 45	50.3		35.2	70.5	56.3	57.3	59.1	52.5
Return on Total Assets 46	11.1		14.8	12.2	14.3	8.9	7.8	8.9
Return on Equity Before Income Taxes 47	18.2		20.2	34.8	26.5	15.5	14.8	13.9
Return on Equity After Income Taxes 48	13.5		17.7	30.8	22.0	13.4	11.9	9.3
Profit Margin (Before Income Tax) 49	10.4	1.0	5.0	5.3	7.0	3.6	3.8	4.4
Profit Margin (After Income Tax) 50	7.7	1.0	4.4	4.7	5.8	3.1	3.1	2.9

Table I

Corporations with and without Net Income

DAIRY PRODUCT

MONEY AMOUNTS AND SIZE OF ASSETS IN THOUSANDS OF DOLLARS

Item Description for Accounting Period 7/05 Through 6/06	Total	Zero Assets	Under 500	500 to 1,000	1,000 to 5,000	5,000 to 10,000	10,000 to 25,000	25,000 to 50,000	50,000 to 100,000	100,000 to 250,000	250,000 to 500,000	500,000 to 2,500,000	2,500,000 and over
Number of Enterprises **1**	791	3	498	0	94	74	47	34	21	10	4	6	0
Revenues ($ in Thousands)													
Net Sales **2**	35360800	0	186210	0	1270932	2046784	2209802	3098009	2711653	3284790	3027354	17525264	0
Interest **3**	70604	0	0	0	712	1711	234	804	3604	8980	6406	48153	0
Rents **4**	8648	0	0	0	0	2277	129	487	913	842	0	4000	0
Royalties **5**	10869	0	0	0	0	0	0	0	2719	8	0	8143	0
Other Portfolio Income **6**	209996	0	2051	0	1075	13893	10394	1521	4215	3702	305	172837	0
Other Receipts **7**	256052	10657	1	0	1548	1991	5188	13257	-5888	24813	8159	196331	0
Total Receipts **8**	35916969	10657	188262	0	1274267	2066656	2225747	3114078	2717216	3323135	3042224	17954728	0
Average Total Receipts **9**	45407	3552	378	•	13556	27928	47356	91591	129391	332314	760556	2992455	•
Operating Costs/Operating Income (%)													
Cost of Operations **10**	75.9	•	43.5	•	81.5	82.5	80.4	76.3	73.9	83.1	80.0	72.6	•
Salaries and Wages **11**	5.0	•	17.9	•	2.1	3.0	4.6	7.2	6.1	3.1	2.7	5.5	•
Taxes Paid **12**	1.0	•	4.9	•	1.6	1.1	1.1	1.3	1.2	0.8	0.8	1.0	•
Interest Paid **13**	1.2	•	1.0	•	0.4	0.3	0.5	0.7	0.8	1.4	1.2	1.6	•
Depreciation **14**	2.1	•	3.5	•	4.1	1.3	1.5	2.1	2.2	1.4	2.5	2.2	•
Amortization and Depletion **15**	0.5	•	0.4	•	•	0.0	0.0	0.2	0.1	0.5	0.1	0.9	•
Pensions and Other Deferred Comp. **16**	0.4	•	•	•	0.4	0.2	0.2	0.6	0.5	0.5	0.4	0.4	•
Employee Benefits **17**	1.0	•	2.7	•	1.2	0.7	0.4	1.3	1.4	1.1	0.8	1.0	•
Advertising **18**	1.7	•	1.0	•	0.0	0.9	0.9	0.9	1.7	1.7	4.0	1.8	•
Other Expenses **19**	11.4	•	33.4	•	7.3	6.1	6.3	8.5	8.9	5.8	7.1	15.5	•
Officers' Compensation **20**	0.7	•	4.1	•	1.1	2.0	1.6	0.7	0.5	0.8	0.2	0.5	•
Operating Margin **21**	•	•	•	•	0.3	1.9	2.3	0.3	2.8	•	0.3	•	•
Operating Margin Before Officers' Comp. **22**	•	•	•	•	1.4	3.9	3.9	1.0	3.3	0.7	0.5	•	•

Selected Average Balance Sheet ($ in Thousands)

Net Receivables 23	3407	0	8	878	2041	3395	6823	11783	24272	51114	228472
Inventories 24	2793	0	3	912	1053	3880	4622	11533	20408	50647	175920
Net Property, Plant and Equipment 25	7711	0	16	1364	2242	5806	14393	22184	45869	151971	583840
Total Assets 26	26866	0	130	3519	6431	15816	34257	68906	170397	333260	2331211
Notes and Loans Payable 27	12932	0	86	1294	1194	4406	9451	15938	76705	146341	1293404
All Other Liabilities 28	5063	0	5	828	2064	4066	8989	16965	37725	106118	352860
Net Worth 29	8871	0	38	1397	3174	7344	15818	36003	55968	80801	684946

Selected Financial Ratios (Times to 1)

Current Ratio 30	0.8		1.6	1.7	1.9	1.9	1.3	1.8	1.4	1.5	0.5
Quick Ratio 31	0.4		1.5	1.1	1.2	1.0	0.8	1.0	0.9	0.7	0.3
Net Sales to Working Capital 32			13.1	15.3	14.1	10.5	27.4	9.5	16.2	16.4	
Coverage Ratio 33	1.4			2.4	12.0	6.9	2.1	4.8	1.7	1.7	0.6
Total Asset Turnover 34	1.7		2.9	3.8	4.3	3.0	2.7	1.9	1.9	2.3	1.3
Inventory Turnover 35	12.1		47.0	12.1	21.7	9.7	15.0	8.3	13.4	12.0	12.1
Receivables Turnover 36	11.0		32.5	13.1	14.5	11.6	13.4	11.2	15.2	14.9	9.3
Total Liabilities to Net Worth 37	2.0		2.4	1.5	1.0	1.2	1.2	0.9	2.0	3.1	2.4
Current Assets to Working Capital 38			2.7	2.4	2.1	2.1	4.3	2.3	3.3	3.0	
Current Liabilities to Working Capital 39			1.7	1.4	1.1	1.1	3.3	1.3	2.3	2.0	
Working Capital to Net Sales 40			0.1	0.1	0.1	0.1	0.0	0.1	0.1	0.1	
Inventory to Working Capital 41			0.1	0.8	0.6	0.8	1.5	0.8	1.1	1.1	
Total Receipts to Cash Flow 42	12.1		9.3	15.8	13.8	12.1	12.8	9.4	18.2	15.4	11.1
Cost of Goods to Cash Flow 43	9.2		4.0	12.9	11.4	9.7	9.7	6.9	15.1	12.3	8.1
Cash Flow to Total Debt 44	0.2		0.4	0.4	0.6	0.5	0.4	0.4	0.2	0.2	0.2

Selected Financial Factors (in Percentages)

Debt Ratio 45	67.0		70.5	60.3	53.8	53.6	50.6	47.8	67.2	75.8	70.6
Return on Total Assets 46	2.9		3.9	4.1		10.5	13.6	7.1	4.9	4.4	1.2
Return on Equity Before Income Taxes 47	2.4			5.6	4.7	19.3	25.3	10.8	6.4	7.2	
Return on Equity After Income Taxes 48				5.1	4.0	19.1	21.0	8.0	4.8	7.1	
Profit Margin (Before Income Tax) 49	0.5			0.6	0.8	3.0	2.9	3.0	1.1	0.8	
Profit Margin (After Income Tax) 50	0.5				0.7	3.0	2.4	2.2	0.8	0.8	

43

Table II

Corporations with Net Income

DAIRY PRODUCT

MONEY AMOUNTS AND SIZE OF ASSETS IN THOUSANDS OF DOLLARS

Item Description for Accounting Period 7/05 Through 6/06	Total	Zero Assets	Under 500	500 to 1,000	1,000 to 5,000	5,000 to 10,000	10,000 to 25,000	25,000 to 50,000	50,000 to 100,000	100,000 to 250,000	250,000 to 500,000	500,000 to 2,500,000	2,500,000 and over
Number of Enterprises **1**	252	3	0	0	94	64	41	19	16	•	4	•	0

Revenues ($ in Thousands)

Item Description for Accounting Period 7/05 Through 6/06	Total	Zero Assets	Under 500	500 to 1,000	1,000 to 5,000	5,000 to 10,000	10,000 to 25,000	25,000 to 50,000	50,000 to 100,000	100,000 to 250,000	250,000 to 500,000	500,000 to 2,500,000	2,500,000 and over
Net Sales **2**	29465653	0	0	0	1270932	1856296	1938295	2054057	2047277	•	3027354	•	0
Interest **3**	62875	0	0	0	712	1279	233	569	3456	•	6406	•	0
Rents **4**	5285	0	0	0	0	2277	129	12	580	•	0	•	0
Royalties **5**	8974	0	0	0	0	0	0	0	2719	•	0	•	0
Other Portfolio Income **6**	206652	0	0	0	1075	13864	9961	896	4011	•	305	•	0
Other Receipts **7**	255668	10657	0	0	1548	1874	4996	10697	8242	•	8159	•	0
Total Receipts **8**	30005107	10657	0	0	1274267	1875590	1953614	2066231	2066285	•	3042224	•	0
Average Total Receipts **9**	119068	3552	•	•	13556	29306	47649	108749	129143	•	760556	•	•

Operating Costs/Operating Income (%)

Item Description for Accounting Period 7/05 Through 6/06	Total	Zero Assets	Under 500	500 to 1,000	1,000 to 5,000	5,000 to 10,000	10,000 to 25,000	25,000 to 50,000	50,000 to 100,000	100,000 to 250,000	250,000 to 500,000	500,000 to 2,500,000	2,500,000 and over
Cost of Operations **10**	79.1	•	•	•	81.5	81.5	79.3	75.3	73.1	•	80.0	•	•
Salaries and Wages **11**	4.3	•	•	•	2.1	3.2	4.6	6.7	5.8	•	2.7	•	•
Taxes Paid **12**	1.0	•	•	•	1.6	1.1	1.1	1.2	1.2	•	0.8	•	•
Interest Paid **13**	1.1	•	•	•	0.4	0.3	0.4	0.4	0.8	•	1.2	•	•
Depreciation **14**	2.1	•	•	•	4.1	1.3	1.5	2.1	2.3	•	2.5	•	•
Amortization and Depletion **15**	0.4	•	•	•	0.0	0.0	0.0	0.1	0.1	•	0.1	•	•
Pensions and Other Deferred Comp. **16**	0.4	•	•	•	0.4	0.2	0.2	0.5	0.4	•	0.4	•	•
Employee Benefits **17**	0.7	•	•	•	1.2	0.8	0.4	1.1	1.2	•	0.8	•	•
Advertising **18**	1.3	•	•	•	0.0	1.0	1.0	0.8	2.1	•	4.0	•	•
Other Expenses **19**	6.7	•	•	•	7.3	6.5	6.4	8.4	8.0	•	7.1	•	•
Officers' Compensation **20**	0.7	•	•	•	1.1	2.0	1.8	0.6	0.5	•	0.2	•	•
Operating Margin **21**	2.1	•	•	•	0.3	2.2	3.1	2.7	4.4	•	0.3	•	•
Operating Margin Before Officers' Comp. **22**	2.8	•	•	•	1.4	4.1	4.9	3.3	5.0	•	0.5	•	•

Selected Average Balance Sheet ($ in Thousands)

Net Receivables 23	9262	0	878	2174	3352	8385	12206	51114
Inventories 24	6815	0	541	964	3242	6428	10772	51839
Net Property, Plant and Equipment 25	18977	0	1364	2023	5846	14881	22767	151971
Total Assets 26	59500	0	3519	6197	16212	34039	71810	333260
Notes and Loans Payable 27	21967	0	1294	1379	4035	7760	16425	146341
All Other Liabilities 28	11185	0	828	2142	4128	8310	17013	106118
Net Worth 29	26348	0	1397	2677	8050	17969	38372	80801

Selected Financial Ratios (Times to 1)

Current Ratio 30	1.7		1.7	1.8	2.1	1.6	2.0	1.5
Quick Ratio 31	0.9		1.1	1.1	1.0	1.0	1.3	0.7
Net Sales to Working Capital 32	13.7		15.3	16.5	9.3	16.5	7.6	16.4
Coverage Ratio 33	4.6		2.4	12.0	10.0	8.7	7.6	1.7
Total Asset Turnover 34	2.0		3.8	4.7	2.9	3.2	1.8	2.3
Inventory Turnover 35	13.6		20.4	24.5	11.6	12.7	8.7	11.7
Receivables Turnover 36	10.6		20.0	16.7	13.4	11.6	10.4	29.6
Total Liabilities to Net Worth 37	1.3		1.5	1.3	1.0	0.9	0.9	3.1
Current Assets to Working Capital 38	2.5		2.4	2.3	1.9	2.6	2.0	3.0
Current Liabilities to Working Capital 39	1.5		1.4	1.3	0.9	1.6	1.0	2.0
Working Capital to Net Sales 40	0.1		0.1	0.1	0.1	0.1	0.1	0.1
Inventory to Working Capital 41	0.8		0.8	0.6	0.8	0.9	0.6	1.1
Total Receipts to Cash Flow 42	11.3		15.8	12.9	10.9	9.5	8.2	15.4
Cost of Goods to Cash Flow 43	9.0		12.9	10.5	8.7	7.2	6.0	12.3
Cash Flow to Total Debt 44	0.3		0.4	0.6	0.5	0.7	0.5	0.2

Selected Financial Factors (in Percentages)

Debt Ratio 45	55.7		60.3	56.8	50.3	47.2	46.6	75.8
Return on Total Assets 46	9.7		3.9	16.3	12.7	11.9	10.9	4.4
Return on Equity Before Income Taxes 47	17.2		5.6	34.6	23.0	19.9	17.7	7.2
Return on Equity After Income Taxes 48	13.2		5.1	28.7	22.7	18.8	14.3	7.1
Profit Margin (Before Income Tax) 49	3.9		0.6	3.2	3.9	3.3	5.3	0.8
Profit Margin (After Income Tax) 50	3.0		0.5	2.7	3.9	3.1	4.3	0.8

Table I
Corporations with and without Net Income

MEAT AND SEAFOOD PROCESSING

MONEY AMOUNTS AND SIZE OF ASSETS IN THOUSANDS OF DOLLARS

Item Description for Accounting Period 7/05 Through 6/06	Total	Zero Assets	Under 500	500 to 1,000	1,000 to 5,000	5,000 to 10,000	10,000 to 25,000	25,000 to 50,000	50,000 to 100,000	100,000 to 250,000	250,000 to 500,000	500,000 to 2,500,000	2,500,000 and over
Number of Enterprises 1	2363	32	1536	133	260	125	146	54	32	27	8	8	3
Revenues ($ in Thousands)													
Net Sales 2	107522967	129647	672840	237832	1667665	3490815	8737761	4268315	7062913	11019862	5228547	24307692	40699079
Interest 3	146892	2691	191	660	464	1679	3135	2628	1908	10062	9533	54849	59093
Rents 4	32439	0	0	147	1360	2945	346	388	26	1986	2589	2347	20305
Royalties 5	29960	0	0	0	0	0	0	0	0	0	55	25546	4359
Other Portfolio Income 6	878169	3720	5853	1533	8582	27243	25473	15048	2404	8302	35031	268198	476782
Other Receipts 7	728464	2016	17	27	11237	17951	11758	20055	21485	53254	113020	184715	292928
Total Receipts 8	109338891	138074	678901	240199	1689308	3540633	8778473	4306434	7088736	11093466	5388775	24843347	41552546
Average Total Receipts 9	46271	4315	442	1806	6497	28325	60127	79749	221523	410869	673597	3105418	13850849
Operating Costs/Operating Income (%)													
Cost of Operations 10	83.9	85.2	67.1	70.5	77.7	80.3	85.0	80.1	83.4	84.3	77.1	88.4	83.2
Salaries and Wages 11	3.4	4.8	7.9	4.5	6.3	5.2	3.7	4.5	3.1	3.0	2.4	3.9	2.8
Taxes Paid 12	1.0	1.5	2.9	2.9	1.8	1.1	1.0	1.2	0.9	0.9	1.2	0.6	1.0
Interest Paid 13	1.0	1.4	0.5	0.1	0.9	0.5	0.6	0.6	0.9	0.6	0.8	1.3	1.1
Depreciation 14	1.1	0.8	2.0	0.7	3.2	1.3	1.1	1.7	1.6	1.4	1.7	1.0	0.8
Amortization and Depletion 15	0.0	1.1	0.1	•	0.0	0.1	0.1	0.1	0.1	0.1	0.3	0.1	•
Pensions and Other Deferred Comp. 16	0.2	•	0.0	0.2	0.2	0.1	0.1	0.3	0.2	0.2	0.2	0.1	0.3
Employee Benefits 17	0.7	2.3	2.6	1.2	1.0	0.6	0.5	1.0	0.8	0.9	1.2	0.6	0.7
Advertising 18	0.7	0.5	0.5	3.2	0.3	0.1	0.5	0.6	1.7	0.5	2.0	0.3	0.7
Other Expenses 19	6.4	43.8	17.5	11.7	8.5	8.9	5.2	6.3	5.4	5.0	8.5	3.9	7.8
Officers' Compensation 20	0.5	1.5	5.9	4.7	2.1	1.6	0.8	1.0	0.4	0.4	1.0	0.2	0.2
Operating Margin 21	1.1	•	•	0.4	•	0.2	1.4	2.6	1.5	2.6	3.6	•	1.5
Operating Margin Before Officers' Comp. 22	1.6	•	•	5.0	0.1	1.8	2.2	3.6	2.0	3.0	4.6	•	1.7

Selected Average Balance Sheet ($ in Thousands)

Net Receivables 23	2761	0	15	112	518	1871	3923	6407	13219	27781	38990	231311	620821
Inventories 24	4163	0	3	95	201	593	2962	6662	17699	40102	50933	267685	1568264
Net Property, Plant and Equipment 25	6076	0	32	65	1341	2028	5126	11715	27874	56420	122587	333899	2082997
Total Assets 26	19275	0	56	761	2461	6611	15388	35942	73495	160950	338238	1401514	6363768
Notes and Loans Payable 27	7036	0	67	32	3434	2765	5460	9810	25683	51932	114777	459864	2377518
All Other Liabilities 28	5120	0	13	54	688	2135	3836	8421	18636	35556	87801	476334	1513618
Net Worth 29	7120	0	-24	675	-1661	1711	6091	17711	29176	73462	135660	465316	2472632

Selected Financial Ratios (Times to 1)

Current Ratio 30	1.5	•	0.3	3.3	2.1	1.1	1.5	1.7	1.3	1.7	1.1	2.0	1.3
Quick Ratio 31	0.6	•	0.3	2.0	1.6	0.8	0.8	0.8	0.6	0.8	0.4	0.7	0.4
Net Sales to Working Capital 32	15.4	•	•	9.1	14.5	81.3	21.2	11.2	24.6	12.0	38.0	7.2	29.6
Coverage Ratio 33	3.9	•	•	22.5	0.1	4.0	4.0	7.0	3.2	6.0	9.6	2.4	4.4
Total Asset Turnover 34	2.4	•	7.9	2.4	2.6	4.2	3.9	2.2	3.0	2.5	1.9	2.2	2.1
Inventory Turnover 35	9.2	•	108.7	13.3	24.8	37.8	17.2	9.5	10.4	8.6	9.9	10.0	7.2
Receivables Turnover 36	12.2	•	43.9	9.5	11.9	14.6	17.9	13.5	14.2	12.7	22.7	11.5	10.5
Total Liabilities to Net Worth 37	1.7	•	•	0.1	•	2.9	1.5	1.0	1.5	1.2	1.5	2.0	1.6
Current Assets to Working Capital 38	3.0	•	•	1.4	1.9	9.4	3.0	2.5	4.0	2.4	8.5	2.0	4.9
Current Liabilities to Working Capital 39	2.0	•	•	0.4	0.9	8.4	2.0	1.5	3.0	1.4	7.5	1.0	3.9
Working Capital to Net Sales 40	0.1	•	•	0.1	0.1	0.0	0.0	0.1	0.0	0.1	0.0	0.1	0.0
Inventory to Working Capital 41	1.3	•	•	0.5	0.3	1.5	1.1	1.1	2.0	1.1	3.6	0.6	2.8
Total Receipts to Cash Flow 42	12.5	•	13.2	11.2	17.6	12.0	17.1	11.9	15.1	14.0	6.9	22.3	9.6
Cost of Goods to Cash Flow 43	10.5	•	8.9	7.9	13.7	9.7	14.5	9.5	12.6	11.8	5.3	19.7	8.0
Cash Flow to Total Debt 44	0.3	•	0.4	1.9	0.1	0.5	0.4	0.4	0.3	0.3	0.5	0.1	0.4

Selected Financial Factors (in Percentages)

Debt Ratio 45	63.1	•	142.9	11.3	167.5	74.1	60.4	50.7	60.3	54.4	59.9	66.8	61.1
Return on Total Assets 46	9.0	•	•	2.8	0.3	9.2	9.8	9.1	8.4	9.8	14.8	6.7	10.1
Return on Equity Before Income Taxes 47	18.1	•	112.6	3.0	2.9	26.6	18.5	15.8	14.4	17.9	33.1	11.8	20.1
Return on Equity After Income Taxes 48	13.9	•	112.7	2.8	3.1	24.7	15.7	14.6	13.1	16.2	26.8	7.1	14.8
Profit Margin (Before Income Tax) 49	2.8	•	•	1.1	•	1.6	1.9	3.5	1.9	3.2	6.9	1.8	3.7
Profit Margin (After Income Tax) 50	2.2	•	•	1.1	•	1.5	1.6	3.3	1.7	2.9	5.6	1.1	2.7

Table II
Corporations with Net Income

MEAT AND SEAFOOD PROCESSING

MONEY AMOUNTS AND SIZE OF ASSETS IN THOUSANDS OF DOLLARS

Item Description for Accounting Period 7/05 Through 6/06	Total	Zero Assets	Under 500	500 to 1,000	1,000 to 5,000	5,000 to 10,000	10,000 to 25,000	25,000 to 50,000	50,000 to 100,000	100,000 to 250,000	250,000 to 500,000	500,000 to 2,500,000	2,500,000 and over
Number of Enterprises **1**	938	•	401	•	120	•	104	38	24	22	8	5	3
Revenues ($ in Thousands)													
Net Sales **2**	81703872	•	139075	•	1342270	•	6242721	3345115	5543927	9687469	5228547	7292527	40699079
Interest **3**	107914	•	4	•	167	•	1787	2454	776	8679	9533	24678	59093
Rents **4**	27751	•	0	•	1305	•	235	83	26	1058	2589	1993	20305
Royalties **5**	28901	•	0	•	0	•	0	0	0	0	55	24488	4359
Other Portfolio Income **6**	830124	•	5853	•	1550	•	18954	14594	1595	7718	35031	266194	476782
Other Receipts **7**	681833	•	0	•	1815	•	7453	23018	12852	47714	113020	167694	292928
Total Receipts **8**	83380395	•	144932	•	1347107	•	6271150	3385264	5559176	9752638	5388775	7777574	41552546
Average Total Receipts **9**	88892	•	361	•	11226	•	60300	89086	231632	443302	673597	1555515	13850849
Operating Costs/Operating Income (%)													
Cost of Operations **10**	81.0	•	46.8	•	79.0	•	82.7	80.5	82.5	84.1	77.1	66.9	83.2
Salaries and Wages **11**	3.8	•	23.8	•	5.6	•	4.2	3.7	2.8	3.0	2.4	11.5	2.8
Taxes Paid **12**	1.1	•	1.8	•	1.7	•	1.1	1.2	0.9	0.9	1.2	1.8	1.0
Interest Paid **13**	0.9	•	2.6	•	0.6	•	0.5	0.5	0.6	0.6	0.8	1.1	1.1
Depreciation **14**	1.2	•	1.0	•	1.6	•	1.0	1.5	1.7	1.4	1.7	2.4	0.8
Amortization and Depletion **15**	•	•	•	•	0.0	•	0.0	0.1	0.0	0.1	0.3	0.0	•
Pensions and Other Deferred Comp. **16**	0.3	•	0.0	•	0.1	•	0.2	0.3	0.2	0.1	0.2	0.4	0.3
Employee Benefits **17**	0.8	•	0.1	•	0.7	•	0.4	1.0	0.9	0.8	1.2	2.0	0.7
Advertising **18**	0.8	•	0.5	•	0.4	•	0.5	0.6	1.9	0.5	2.0	0.6	0.7
Other Expenses **19**	7.3	•	23.6	•	7.3	•	5.4	5.5	5.2	4.8	8.5	10.2	7.8
Officers' Compensation **20**	0.5	•	0.1	•	1.9	•	0.9	1.0	0.4	0.4	1.0	0.6	0.2
Operating Margin **21**	2.3	•	•	•	1.2	•	3.0	4.3	2.9	3.3	3.6	2.5	1.5
Operating Margin Before Officers' Comp. **22**	2.8	•	•	•	3.1	•	3.9	5.2	3.3	3.7	4.6	3.1	1.7

Selected Average Balance Sheet ($ in Thousands)

Net Receivables 23	4765	0	722	4454	7370	13861	28174	38990	70912	620821
Inventories 24	9102	9	361	3318	6758	17040	37015	61697	216384	1568264
Net Property, Plant and Equipment 25	13087	0	1029	4545	11985	30145	59077	122587	375443	2082997
Total Assets 26	40734	7	2260	15448	36795	77686	164698	338238	1415897	6363768
Notes and Loans Payable 27	12795	172	1091	4464	7749	23530	41920	114777	260458	2377518
All Other Liabilities 28	9848	6	455	4169	7567	18703	37073	87801	367043	1513618
Net Worth 29	18091	-171	714	6814	21478	35453	85704	135660	788395	2472632

Selected Financial Ratios (Times to 1)

Current Ratio 30	1.6	0.0	1.9	1.7	2.0	1.4	1.8	1.1	2.6	1.3
Quick Ratio 31	0.5	0.0	1.4	0.9	1.0	0.6	0.9	0.4	0.5	0.4
Net Sales to Working Capital 32	13.5	•	19.4	15.7	9.2	21.4	12.3	38.0	2.9	29.6
Coverage Ratio 33	6.0	2.6	3.5	7.7	13.0	6.3	8.1	9.6	9.9	4.4
Total Asset Turnover 34	2.1	47.8	4.9	3.9	2.4	3.0	2.7	1.9	1.0	2.1
Inventory Turnover 35	7.7	18.2	24.5	15.0	10.5	11.2	10.0	8.2	4.5	7.2
Receivables Turnover 36	12.4	40.3	15.5	16.1	14.1	16.1	31.3	33.5	41.1	10.5
Total Liabilities to Net Worth 37	1.3	•	2.2	1.3	0.7	1.2	0.9	1.5	0.8	1.6
Current Assets to Working Capital 38	2.8	•	2.1	2.5	2.1	3.5	2.3	8.5	1.6	4.9
Current Liabilities to Working Capital 39	1.8	•	1.1	1.5	1.1	2.5	1.3	7.5	0.6	3.9
Working Capital to Net Sales 40	0.1	•	0.1	0.1	0.1	0.0	0.1	0.0	0.4	0.0
Inventory to Working Capital 41	1.2	•	0.5	0.9	0.8	1.8	1.0	3.6	0.4	2.8
Total Receipts to Cash Flow 42	9.6	4.6	13.2	13.1	10.4	12.9	13.0	6.9	6.2	9.6
Cost of Goods to Cash Flow 43	7.8	2.1	10.4	10.8	8.4	10.7	10.9	5.3	4.1	8.0
Cash Flow to Total Debt 44	0.4	0.4	0.6	0.5	0.6	0.4	0.4	0.5	0.4	0.4

Selected Financial Factors (in Percentages)

Debt Ratio 45	55.6	2459.7	68.4	55.9	41.6	54.4	48.0	59.9	44.3	61.1
Return on Total Assets 46	11.3	314.7	10.8	15.4	14.4	11.1	12.0	14.8	10.7	10.1
Return on Equity Before Income Taxes 47	21.3	•	24.5	30.3	22.7	20.4	20.3	33.1	17.3	20.1
Return on Equity After Income Taxes 48	17.0	•	23.6	26.8	21.3	19.0	18.5	26.8	13.0	14.8
Profit Margin (Before Income Tax) 49	4.4	4.0	1.6	3.4	5.5	3.1	3.9	6.9	9.4	3.7
Profit Margin (After Income Tax) 50	3.5	4.0	1.5	3.0	5.2	2.9	3.6	5.6	7.0	2.7

Table I

Corporations with and without Net Income

BAKERIES AND TORTILLA

MONEY AMOUNTS AND SIZE OF ASSETS IN THOUSANDS OF DOLLARS

Item Description for Accounting Period 7/05 Through 6/06	Total	Zero Assets	Under 500	500 to 1,000	1,000 to 5,000	5,000 to 10,000	10,000 to 25,000	25,000 to 50,000	50,000 to 100,000	100,000 to 250,000	250,000 to 500,000	500,000 to 2,500,000	2,500,000 and over
Number of Enterprises 1	4261	299	2886	436	320	136	106	24	20	16	7	11	0
Revenues ($ in Thousands)													
Net Sales 2	92729326	150888	1656001	322834	1015878	2211078	3259252	2283541	3042525	3727639	3953309	71106382	0
Interest 3	673372	5	221	63	134	1317	1052	663	1296	6532	4251	657840	0
Rents 4	2012880	5	1337	0	4748	0	0	4046	267	58	282	2002138	0
Royalties 5	479461	0	0	0	0	0	0	0	1	1555	73169	404735	0
Other Portfolio Income 6	10539942	23877	0	0	233	134	1139	1228	3260	8591	4246	10497233	0
Other Receipts 7	2992653	768	17052	7148	14690	13274	11644	36246	14064	19290	61633	2796843	0
Total Receipts 8	109427634	175543	1674611	330045	1035683	2225803	3273087	2325724	3061413	3763665	4096890	87465171	•
Average Total Receipts 9	25681	587	580	757	3237	16366	30878	96905	153071	235229	585270	7951379	•
Operating Costs/Operating Income (%)													
Cost of Operations 10	52.8	56.9	48.6	55.4	52.7	75.3	66.3	60.1	65.7	69.5	57.5	49.6	•
Salaries and Wages 11	8.4	18.1	53.2	14.0	13.4	4.1	8.4	11.9	10.3	8.5	16.2	6.8	•
Taxes Paid 12	6.1	3.1	2.4	3.0	3.1	1.7	2.4	2.1	1.8	1.8	3.0	7.3	•
Interest Paid 13	3.5	2.5	0.5	1.6	1.2	0.8	0.9	1.2	0.7	2.4	0.9	4.2	•
Depreciation 14	2.9	3.7	2.8	2.5	2.3	3.4	2.8	2.4	2.7	4.0	2.7	2.9	•
Amortization and Depletion 15	0.5	1.2	0.0	0.5	0.1	0.0	0.2	0.3	0.1	1.3	0.6	0.5	•
Pensions and Other Deferred Comp. 16	2.0	0.8	0.0	•	0.3	0.5	0.2	1.4	1.7	0.8	1.4	2.3	•
Employee Benefits 17	2.8	6.9	1.8	1.8	1.4	2.7	2.1	3.1	3.4	3.5	2.9	2.9	•
Advertising 18	2.0	2.3	0.9	0.4	1.7	0.2	0.6	1.2	0.9	1.5	0.6	2.3	•
Other Expenses 19	18.2	21.6	•	20.8	20.2	7.9	10.9	13.3	8.4	11.0	12.3	20.9	•
Officers' Compensation 20	0.6	0.6	6.7	2.9	4.7	1.3	2.5	1.2	1.3	0.4	0.4	0.3	•
Operating Margin 21	0.2	•	•	•	•	2.2	2.7	1.7	3.0	•	1.3	0.1	•
Operating Margin Before Officers' Comp. 22	0.8	•	6.6	•	3.7	3.5	5.2	2.9	4.3	•	1.7	0.4	•

Selected Average Balance Sheet ($ in Thousands)

	•	•	•	•	•	•	•	•	•	•	•	•
Net Receivables 23	1483	0	13	16	207	1289	2742	7235	11697	19948	47353	425955
Inventories 24	1311	0	12	28	238	811	1384	3778	5279	9963	27706	423606
Net Property, Plant and Equipment 25	4262	0	63	194	796	4250	6911	16837	35210	57249	121110	1223463
Total Assets 26	35448	0	115	583	2076	8143	14683	38124	70718	157740	348841	12712199
Notes and Loans Payable 27	7489	0	115	346	786	3368	6012	14566	16999	69059	80893	2520096
All Other Liabilities 28	13016	0	23	81	239	1745	3052	11233	18923	82101	97969	4734129
Net Worth 29	14943		-22	156	1051	3030	5618	12325	34796	6581	169979	5457975

Selected Financial Ratios (Times to 1)

	•	•	•	•	•	•	•	•	•	•	•	•
Current Ratio 30	0.7	•	0.5	3.0	3.5	1.4	1.7	1.2	1.2	0.5	1.2	0.7
Quick Ratio 31	0.4	•	0.4	2.6	1.4	0.8	1.1	0.8	0.8	0.3	0.8	0.4
Net Sales to Working Capital 32	•	•	3.3	3.3	4.6	16.7	12.2	36.1	38.1	•	35.7	•
Coverage Ratio 33	7.6	0.5	3.1	0.6	1.7	4.8	4.5	4.0	6.3	•	6.2	8.0
Total Asset Turnover 34	0.6	•	5.0	1.3	1.5	2.0	2.1	2.5	2.2	1.5	1.6	0.5
Inventory Turnover 35	8.8	•	24.2	14.7	7.0	15.1	14.7	15.1	18.9	16.3	11.7	7.6
Receivables Turnover 36	11.6	•	42.9	19.6	9.1	15.6	12.5	14.2	14.2	14.7	12.8	11.0
Total Liabilities to Net Worth 37	1.4	•	2.7	1.0	1.7	1.6	2.1	1.0	23.0	•	1.1	1.3
Current Assets to Working Capital 38	•	•	•	1.5	1.4	3.6	2.5	6.0	6.3	•	6.9	•
Current Liabilities to Working Capital 39	•	•	•	0.5	0.4	2.6	1.5	5.0	5.3	•	5.9	•
Working Capital to Net Sales 40	•	•	•	0.3	0.2	0.1	0.0	0.0	0.0	•	0.0	•
Inventory to Working Capital 41	•	•	•	0.1	0.2	1.2	0.6	1.6	1.5	•	1.9	•
Total Receipts to Cash Flow 42	3.1	5.8	8.2	6.4	10.5	8.6	7.5	10.1	19.4	•	7.2	2.5
Cost of Goods to Cash Flow 43	1.6	3.3	4.5	3.4	7.9	5.7	4.5	6.6	13.5	•	4.2	1.2
Cash Flow to Total Debt 44	0.3	•	0.2	0.5	0.3	0.4	0.5	0.4	0.1	0.4	•	0.4

Selected Financial Factors (in Percentages)

	•	•	•	•	•	•	•	•	•	•	•	•
Debt Ratio 45	57.8	•	119.4	73.3	49.4	62.8	61.7	67.7	50.8	95.8	51.3	57.1
Return on Total Assets 46	16.4	•	7.4	1.2	3.1	7.2	8.5	11.9	9.2	•	9.5	17.2
Return on Equity Before Income Taxes 47	33.7	•	•	•	2.6	15.4	17.2	27.6	15.7	•	16.4	35.0
Return on Equity After Income Taxes 48	24.7	•	•	•	2.3	13.4	15.8	22.1	14.6	•	11.4	25.7
Profit Margin (Before Income Tax) 49	23.2	•	1.0	0.9	2.9	3.1	3.6	3.6	•	•	4.9	29.6
Profit Margin (After Income Tax) 50	17.0	•	1.0	0.8	2.5	2.9	2.9	3.3	•	•	3.4	21.7

Table II

Corporations with Net Income

BAKERIES AND TORTILLA

MONEY AMOUNTS AND SIZE OF ASSETS IN THOUSANDS OF DOLLARS

Item Description for Accounting Period 7/05 Through 6/06	Total	Zero Assets	Under 500	500 to 1,000	1,000 to 5,000	5,000 to 10,000	10,000 to 25,000	25,000 to 50,000	50,000 to 100,000	100,000 to 250,000	250,000 to 500,000	500,000 to 2,500,000	2,500,000 and over
Number of Enterprises **1**	2603	•	1906	•	245	81	91	17	17	7	•	6	0
Revenues ($ in Thousands)													
Net Sales **2**	79826182	•	1370224	•	728202	1539752	2902110	1442713	2779736	1882603	•	63505101	0
Interest **3**	647804	•	44	•	85	1276	1043	461	1149	2010	•	637423	0
Rents **4**	2007332	•	1337	•	557	0	0	3952	251	0	•	2001177	0
Royalties **5**	469269	•	0	•	0	0	0	0	1	1521	•	394578	0
Other Portfolio Income **6**	10432076	•	0	•	156	134	1076	1148	3164	5	•	10411996	0
Other Receipts **7**	2941770	•	8123	•	14692	10471	9263	32827	13312	6776	•	2785181	0
Total Receipts **8**	96324433	•	1379728	•	743692	1551633	2913492	1481101	2797613	1892915	•	79737456	0
Average Total Receipts **9**	37005	•	724	•	3035	19156	32016	87124	164565	270416	•	13289576	•
Operating Costs/Operating Income (%)													
Cost of Operations **10**	51.8	•	43.9	•	44.8	72.7	65.2	61.4	65.0	66.7	•	49.3	•
Salaries and Wages **11**	7.6	•	63.8	•	17.1	4.2	8.4	10.4	10.7	10.8	•	5.7	•
Taxes Paid **12**	6.7	•	2.3	•	3.4	1.3	2.4	2.1	1.9	1.7	•	7.8	•
Interest Paid **13**	3.8	•	0.5	•	1.4	0.7	0.8	1.5	0.6	1.7	•	4.5	•
Depreciation **14**	2.8	•	3.0	•	2.1	3.4	2.4	2.3	2.6	2.6	•	2.9	•
Amortization and Depletion **15**	0.4	•	0.0	•	0.2	0.0	0.2	0.4	0.0	0.6	•	0.4	•
Pensions and Other Deferred Comp. **16**	1.8	•	0.0	•	0.4	0.5	0.2	0.8	1.9	1.1	•	2.0	•
Employee Benefits **17**	2.5	•	1.5	•	1.2	2.2	2.1	1.7	3.4	3.9	•	2.5	•
Advertising **18**	2.0	•	0.2	•	1.6	0.2	0.7	1.5	0.9	0.8	•	2.3	•
Other Expenses **19**	18.8	•	•	•	21.1	7.1	10.5	11.9	8.2	8.1	•	21.7	•
Officers' Compensation **20**	0.7	•	7.5	•	5.9	1.8	2.7	1.7	1.4	0.3	•	0.3	•
Operating Margin **21**	1.1	•	2.1	•	1.0	5.9	4.4	4.4	3.4	1.6	•	0.6	•
Operating Margin Before Officers' Comp. **22**	1.8	•	9.6	•	6.9	7.8	7.1	6.1	4.8	1.8	•	0.9	•

Selected Average Balance Sheet ($ in Thousands)

Net Receivables 23	2012	12	178	1109	2722	6307	12491	9235	689333
Inventories 24	1936	10	115	883	1167	3626	5049	5645	741463
Net Property, Plant and Equipment 25	5613	80	551	4890	6117	15279	36463	46364	1909803
Total Assets 26	54691	139	2028	8826	14193	37323	72285	147857	22398796
Notes and Loans Payable 27	10914	166	674	3151	4216	13768	16230	78378	4302582
All Other Liabilities 28	20021	23	160	1686	3093	8651	20220	72329	8338592
Net Worth 29	23756	-50	1194	3990	6884	14904	35835	-2851	9757622

Selected Financial Ratios (Times to 1)

Current Ratio 30	0.7	0.5	6.8	1.9	1.7	1.5	1.3	0.3	0.7
Quick Ratio 31	0.4	0.3	2.3	1.2	1.2	1.0	0.9	0.1	0.4
Net Sales to Working Capital 32	•	•	3.3	10.7	12.0	17.0	30.1	•	•
Coverage Ratio 33	8.3	7.0	3.3	11.1	7.2	5.8	7.4	2.2	8.4
Total Asset Turnover 34	0.6	5.2	1.5	2.2	2.2	2.3	2.3	1.8	0.5
Inventory Turnover 35	8.2	32.4	11.6	15.6	17.8	14.4	21.1	31.8	7.0
Receivables Turnover 36	11.5	78.2	13.8	17.4	15.5	15.1	15.0	58.2	10.6
Total Liabilities to Net Worth 37	1.3	•	0.7	1.2	1.1	1.5	1.0	•	1.3
Current Assets to Working Capital 38	•	•	1.2	2.1	2.4	3.1	4.9	•	•
Current Liabilities to Working Capital 39	•	•	0.2	1.1	1.4	2.1	3.9	•	•
Working Capital to Net Sales 40	•	•	0.3	0.1	0.1	0.1	0.0	•	•
Inventory to Working Capital 41	•	•	0.1	0.7	0.6	0.8	1.1	•	•
Total Receipts to Cash Flow 42	2.7	•	5.6	7.8	7.7	6.3	9.9	13.1	2.3
Cost of Goods to Cash Flow 43	1.4	•	2.5	5.7	5.0	3.9	6.5	8.7	1.1
Cash Flow to Total Debt 44	0.4	•	0.6	0.5	0.6	0.6	0.5	0.1	0.4

Selected Financial Factors (in Percentages)

Debt Ratio 45	56.6	136.1	41.1	54.8	51.5	60.1	50.4	101.9	56.4
Return on Total Assets 46	17.6	16.7	6.6	15.9	12.5	19.4	10.5	6.9	17.9
Return on Equity Before Income Taxes 47	35.6	•	7.8	32.0	22.2	40.2	18.3	•	36.2
Return on Equity After Income Taxes 48	26.3	•	7.5	29.5	20.8	33.8	17.0	•	26.6
Profit Margin (Before Income Tax) 49	27.6	2.8	3.1	6.7	4.8	7.1	4.0	2.1	33.4
Profit Margin (After Income Tax) 50	20.4	2.7	3.0	6.2	4.5	5.9	3.7	1.8	24.6

Table I

Corporations with and without Net Income

OTHER FOOD

MONEY AMOUNTS AND SIZE OF ASSETS IN THOUSANDS OF DOLLARS

Item Description for Accounting Period 7/05 Through 6/06	Total	Zero Assets	Under 500	500 to 1,000	1,000 to 5,000	5,000 to 10,000	10,000 to 25,000	25,000 to 50,000	50,000 to 100,000	100,000 to 250,000	250,000 to 500,000	500,000 to 2,500,000	2,500,000 and over
Number of Enterprises 1	3728	128	2013	603	534	146	150	72	35	27	9	11	0
Revenues ($ in Thousands)													
Net Sales 2	76445974	18879	49130	783366	2644307	2237417	4203072	4684295	3892348	7383470	3225575	47324113	0
Interest 3	2115942	2074	45	0	2165	942	2493	2921	4935	11239	17594	2071532	0
Rents 4	137956	0	0	0	458	1609	2179	730	8409	834	8536	115201	0
Royalties 5	681039	0	0	0	0	679	0	4159	45767	8821	3151	618461	0
Other Portfolio Income 6	7641048	5315	16100	0	114	141	2762	13994	2461	7629	10147	7582384	0
Other Receipts 7	708633	3492	1	170	10227	37375	26158	15888	54761	68479	16898	475191	0
Total Receipts 8	87730592	29760	65276	783536	2657271	2278163	4236664	4721987	4008681	7480472	3281901	58186882	·
Average Total Receipts 9	23533	232	32	1299	4976	15604	28244	65583	114534	277055	364656	5289717	·
Operating Costs/Operating Income (%)													
Cost of Operations 10	73.1	30.8	25.1	52.0	70.4	70.6	72.5	73.4	66.9	71.4	66.1	75.1	·
Salaries and Wages 11	5.1	24.2	9.7	10.4	7.7	7.6	6.1	6.4	8.6	5.3	7.1	4.1	·
Taxes Paid 12	1.2	2.7	8.7	3.5	1.8	1.8	1.5	1.2	1.5	1.2	1.5	0.9	·
Interest Paid 13	4.4	93.7	8.1	2.5	0.7	1.0	0.9	0.9	1.4	1.3	2.9	6.2	·
Depreciation 14	1.7	3.9	2.2	1.9	1.7	1.7	2.3	1.6	2.5	2.0	2.9	1.4	·
Amortization and Depletion 15	0.4	0.5	0.1	0.1	0.1	0.3	0.3	0.3	0.9	0.6	0.4	0.4	·
Pensions and Other Deferred Comp. 16	0.6	·	0.0	·	0.3	0.6	0.3	0.3	0.5	0.3	0.4	0.7	·
Employee Benefits 17	0.9	3.9	0.0	0.6	0.5	1.4	1.2	1.4	1.6	1.1	1.9	0.7	·
Advertising 18	2.8	·	2.1	0.8	0.8	0.9	1.4	2.2	2.6	3.3	2.8	3.1	·
Other Expenses 19	9.4	28.3	74.2	14.3	8.9	9.4	8.2	9.0	11.9	9.9	11.5	9.0	·
Officers' Compensation 20	0.8	3.3	6.1	6.8	4.7	3.2	2.0	1.6	1.3	0.9	0.7	0.2	·
Operating Margin 21	·	·	·	7.1	2.4	1.6	3.4	1.6	0.3	2.8	1.7	·	·
Operating Margin Before Officers' Comp. 22	0.5	·	·	13.9	7.0	4.8	5.4	3.1	1.6	3.7	2.4	·	·

Selected Average Balance Sheet ($ in Thousands)

	•	•	•	•	•	•	•	•	•	•	•	•
Net Receivables **23**	44990	0	0	27	449	1444	3118	6669	9513	24725	29768	15003457
Inventories **24**	1536	0	2	22	352	1487	3099	8024	14013	25091	59065	232772
Net Property, Plant and Equipment **25**	3234	0	5	394	710	2093	6266	8259	21457	43471	112250	604864
Total Assets **26**	78224	0	9	772	1921	7385	15051	34395	71099	152138	362603	24949056
Notes and Loans Payable **27**	5519	0	9	214	877	2528	5281	9260	19325	44974	131312	1369038
All Other Liabilities **28**	50650	0	1	83	408	1755	4437	10107	20564	39977	73356	16767692
Net Worth **29**	22055	0	-1	475	636	3102	5333	15028	31209	67187	157935	6812327

Selected Financial Ratios (Times to 1)

	•	•	•	•	•	•	•	•	•	•	•	•
Current Ratio **30**	1.0	•	2.0	2.7	2.1	1.7	1.3	1.6	1.5	1.9	2.2	1.0
Quick Ratio **31**	0.9	•	1.5	2.5	1.2	1.0	0.8	0.7	0.6	1.0	0.7	0.9
Net Sales to Working Capital **32**	•	•	17.2	9.1	8.9	10.5	15.3	8.9	10.2	7.6	4.0	•
Coverage Ratio **33**	4.4	0.6	2.4	3.8	5.3	4.3	5.6	3.6	3.4	4.3	2.2	4.6
Total Asset Turnover **34**	0.3	•	2.8	1.7	2.6	2.1	1.9	1.9	1.6	1.8	1.0	0.2
Inventory Turnover **35**	9.8	•	3.2	30.6	9.9	7.3	6.6	6.0	5.3	7.8	4.0	13.9
Receivables Turnover **36**	0.5	•	2.2	46.1	13.1	8.1	8.9	9.9	11.4	12.3	12.5	0.3
Total Liabilities to Net Worth **37**	2.5	•	0.6	2.0	1.4	1.8	1.3	1.3	1.3	1.3	1.3	2.7
Current Assets to Working Capital **38**	•	•	2.0	1.6	1.9	2.5	4.2	2.7	2.9	2.1	1.8	•
Current Liabilities to Working Capital **39**	•	•	1.0	0.6	0.9	1.5	3.2	1.7	1.9	1.1	0.8	•
Working Capital to Net Sales **40**	•	•	0.1	0.1	0.1	0.1	0.1	0.1	0.1	0.1	0.3	•
Inventory to Working Capital **41**	•	•	0.3	0.2	0.6	0.9	1.6	1.2	1.3	0.7	0.6	•
Total Receipts to Cash Flow **42**	4.5	•	2.4	6.4	11.1	9.5	9.3	10.8	7.9	8.3	8.0	3.5
Cost of Goods to Cash Flow **43**	3.3	•	0.6	3.3	7.8	6.7	6.8	7.9	5.3	5.9	5.3	2.6
Cash Flow to Total Debt **44**	0.1	•	1.0	0.7	0.3	0.4	0.3	0.3	0.4	0.4	0.2	0.1

Selected Financial Factors (in Percentages)

	•	•	•	•	•	•	•	•	•	•	•	•
Debt Ratio **45**	71.8	•	111.4	38.5	66.9	58.0	64.6	56.3	56.1	55.8	56.4	72.7
Return on Total Assets **46**	5.1	•	54.6	16.1	9.1	9.3	9.4	6.2	7.3	9.6	6.3	4.9
Return on Equity Before Income Taxes **47**	14.1	•	•	19.4	22.2	17.1	21.9	10.2	11.7	16.6	7.8	14.1
Return on Equity After Income Taxes **48**	12.0	•	128.4	19.3	18.4	12.6	19.5	8.4	7.2	13.9	4.7	12.1
Profit Margin (Before Income Tax) **49**	15.2	•	11.4	7.1	2.9	3.5	4.2	2.4	3.3	4.1	3.4	22.3
Profit Margin (After Income Tax) **50**	12.9	•	•	7.1	2.4	2.6	3.7	1.9	2.0	3.4	2.1	19.2

Table II
Corporations with Net Income

OTHER FOOD

MONEY AMOUNTS AND SIZE OF ASSETS IN THOUSANDS OF DOLLARS

Item Description for Accounting Period 7/05 Through 6/06	Total	Zero Assets	Under 500	500 to 1,000	1,000 to 5,000	5,000 to 10,000	10,000 to 25,000	25,000 to 50,000	50,000 to 100,000	100,000 to 250,000	250,000 to 500,000	500,000 to 2,500,000	2,500,000 and over
Number of Enterprises 1	1427	122	4	•	345	128	118	47	22	23	6	•	0
Revenues ($ in Thousands)													
Net Sales 2	69959634	18879	21731	•	2364844	2080826	3498944	3193484	2621365	7046653	1962663	•	0
Interest 3	2106770	15	0	•	1686	926	2479	1741	2190	10870	16490	•	0
Rents 4	135143	0	0	•	458	1029	2179	547	7240	834	8113	•	0
Royalties 5	652783	0	0	•	0	679	0	2917	21374	8821	530	•	0
Other Portfolio Income 6	7639056	5138	16100	•	114	84	2649	12993	2011	7629	10147	•	0
Other Receipts 7	583444	3119	0	•	3591	36745	20314	10080	6428	67973	3118	•	0
Total Receipts 8	80676830	27151	37831	•	2370693	2120289	3526565	3221762	2660608	7142780	2001061	•	0
Average Total Receipts 9	56536	223	9458	•	6872	16565	29886	68548	120937	310556	333510	•	•
Operating Costs/Operating Income (%)													
Cost of Operations 10	73.2	30.8	24.0	•	71.2	70.2	73.1	69.7	65.5	71.6	64.1	•	•
Salaries and Wages 11	4.9	23.9	17.6	•	7.5	7.3	6.1	6.9	7.9	5.2	6.7	•	•
Taxes Paid 12	1.1	1.3	3.2	•	1.6	1.8	1.6	1.2	1.3	1.2	1.0	•	•
Interest Paid 13	4.5	6.0	•	•	0.4	0.6	0.8	0.7	1.1	1.1	1.9	•	•
Depreciation 14	1.5	3.9	0.6	•	1.4	1.5	1.8	1.5	2.4	1.9	3.1	•	•
Amortization and Depletion 15	0.4	0.5	•	•	0.1	0.0	0.3	0.2	0.5	0.4	0.6	•	•
Pensions and Other Deferred Comp. 16	0.6	•	•	•	0.4	0.6	0.3	0.4	0.7	0.4	0.6	•	•
Employee Benefits 17	0.8	3.9	0.1	•	0.4	1.3	1.1	1.5	1.3	1.1	1.0	•	•
Advertising 18	2.8	•	0.1	•	0.8	0.6	0.9	2.4	2.8	3.4	1.3	•	•
Other Expenses 19	9.1	22.5	12.8	•	7.4	8.5	7.1	8.3	9.8	9.7	12.3	•	•
Officers' Compensation 20	0.8	1.0	•	•	4.7	3.2	2.0	1.9	1.3	0.9	0.7	•	•
Operating Margin 21	0.4	6.3	41.6	•	4.1	4.4	5.0	5.5	5.4	3.0	6.7	•	•
Operating Margin Before Officers' Comp. 22	1.2	7.3	41.6	•	8.8	7.6	7.0	7.4	6.7	4.0	7.4	•	•

Selected Average Balance Sheet ($ in Thousands)

Net Receivables 23	117030	0	7	•	635	1541	3135	6737	10536	27627	32229
Inventories 24	3265	0	701	•	309	1528	3056	8603	17449	25693	30218
Net Property, Plant and Equipment 25	7154	0	78	•	698	2284	6169	7550	23502	46824	91368
Total Assets 26	199715	0	424	•	2178	7572	15097	34934	71922	156556	340642
Notes and Loans Payable 27	12241	0	326	•	582	1939	5536	7056	19874	45953	82288
All Other Liabilities 28	131170	0	6	•	470	1709	3645	9621	20679	43976	56670
Net Worth 29	56304	0	92	•	1126	3923	5915	18257	31368	66627	201684

Selected Financial Ratios (Times to 1)

Current Ratio 30	1.0	•	1.0	•	2.3	1.9	1.5	1.9	1.6	1.8	3.8
Quick Ratio 31	0.9	•	0.7	•	1.5	1.1	0.9	0.8	0.6	0.9	1.6
Net Sales to Working Capital 32	•	•	•	•	9.0	8.8	11.8	7.0	9.8	8.8	3.3
Coverage Ratio 33	4.8	9.4	•	•	12.4	12.0	8.3	10.2	7.0	5.0	5.6
Total Asset Turnover 34	0.2	•	12.8	•	3.1	2.1	2.0	1.9	1.7	2.0	1.0
Inventory Turnover 35	10.9	•	1.9	•	15.8	7.5	7.1	5.5	4.5	8.5	6.9
Receivables Turnover 36	0.5	•	1.0	•	17.1	8.1	10.0	10.1	11.1	13.1	20.3
Total Liabilities to Net Worth 37	2.5	•	3.6	•	0.9	0.9	1.6	0.9	1.3	1.3	0.7
Current Assets to Working Capital 38	•	•	•	•	1.7	2.1	3.2	2.2	2.8	2.2	1.4
Current Liabilities to Working Capital 39	•	•	•	•	0.7	1.1	2.2	1.2	1.8	1.2	0.4
Working Capital to Net Sales 40	•	•	•	•	0.1	0.1	0.1	0.1	0.1	0.1	0.3
Inventory to Working Capital 41	•	•	•	•	0.6	0.7	1.1	1.0	1.4	0.9	0.3
Total Receipts to Cash Flow 42	4.2	1.7	0.8	•	11.0	7.6	8.9	7.9	6.9	8.2	5.2
Cost of Goods to Cash Flow 43	3.1	0.5	0.2	•	7.9	5.4	6.5	5.5	4.5	5.9	3.3
Cash Flow to Total Debt 44	0.1	•	20.7	•	0.6	0.6	0.4	0.5	0.4	0.4	0.5

Selected Financial Factors (in Percentages)

Debt Ratio 45	71.8	•	78.3	•	48.3	48.2	60.8	47.7	56.4	57.4	40.8
Return on Total Assets 46	5.3	•	1910.6	•	14.9	14.8	12.9	13.7	13.3	10.7	10.1
Return on Equity Before Income Taxes 47	14.9	•	8786.7	•	26.5	26.1	28.9	23.7	26.2	20.2	14.0
Return on Equity After Income Taxes 48	12.8	•	6580.5	•	23.1	22.1	26.1	21.4	19.0	17.0	10.4
Profit Margin (Before Income Tax) 49	17.2	50.1	149.2	•	4.4	6.3	5.8	6.4	6.9	4.4	8.6
Profit Margin (After Income Tax) 50	14.8	48.3	111.7	•	3.8	5.3	5.2	5.8	5.0	3.7	6.4

50

Table I

Corporations with and without Net Income

SOFT DRINK AND ICE

Money Amounts and Size of Assets in Thousands of Dollars

Item Description for Accounting Period 7/05 Through 6/06	Total	Zero Assets	Under 500	500 to 1,000	1,000 to 5,000	5,000 to 10,000	10,000 to 25,000	25,000 to 50,000	50,000 to 100,000	100,000 to 250,000	250,000 to 500,000	500,000 to 2,500,000	2,500,000 and over
Number of Enterprises **1**	608	4	0	134	285	34	73	34	12	15	4	9	6

Revenues ($ in Thousands)

Item	Total	Zero Assets	Under 500	500 to 1,000	1,000 to 5,000	5,000 to 10,000	10,000 to 25,000	25,000 to 50,000	50,000 to 100,000	100,000 to 250,000	250,000 to 500,000	500,000 to 2,500,000	2,500,000 and over
Net Sales **2**	52497155	96238	0	197152	1114364	355195	2273228	2963052	1426945	3585371	1490416	9567341	29427853
Interest **3**	1057092	0	0	19	293	2096	1466	4399	1514	4254	6975	56694	979382
Rents **4**	84508	0	0	0	1855	0	3778	223	719	1225	175	5939	70594
Royalties **5**	1218615	0	0	0	0	0	0	0	0	0	583	45106	1172925
Other Portfolio Income **6**	8785864	7413	0	0	3546	22627	71953	37915	4206	5794	303	110856	8521250
Other Receipts **7**	2396137	1046	0	0	4810	28204	26387	20747	34790	86372	13580	422758	1757447
Total Receipts **8**	66039371	104697	0	197171	1124868	408122	2376812	3026336	1468174	3683016	1512032	10208694	41929451
Average Total Receipts **9**	108617	26174	•	1471	3947	12004	32559	89010	122348	245534	378008	1134299	6988242

Operating Costs/Operating Income (%)

Item	Total	Zero Assets	Under 500	500 to 1,000	1,000 to 5,000	5,000 to 10,000	10,000 to 25,000	25,000 to 50,000	50,000 to 100,000	100,000 to 250,000	250,000 to 500,000	500,000 to 2,500,000	2,500,000 and over
Cost of Operations **10**	52.9	65.0	•	46.9	71.6	76.8	73.4	67.7	72.7	66.3	57.9	48.9	47.3
Salaries and Wages **11**	11.6	13.7	•	7.9	7.9	7.3	7.7	8.4	10.4	10.0	14.1	10.2	13.1
Taxes Paid **12**	2.1	2.4	•	3.2	1.7	1.5	1.5	1.5	1.8	1.6	2.2	1.9	2.4
Interest Paid **13**	4.5	•	•	1.3	0.5	1.1	0.6	0.7	1.4	1.1	3.0	3.1	6.6
Depreciation **14**	3.1	2.0	•	3.8	1.3	1.3	2.4	2.2	2.5	3.2	3.5	4.0	3.1
Amortization and Depletion **15**	0.9	0.4	•	0.5	0.0	0.1	0.1	0.2	0.3	0.6	0.8	0.6	1.2
Pensions and Other Deferred Comp. **16**	1.0	1.4	•	1.5	0.4	0.6	0.6	0.5	0.4	0.5	1.0	0.2	1.5
Employee Benefits **17**	1.8	3.1	•	0.7	0.8	1.6	1.5	1.4	1.8	2.5	1.2	2.0	1.8
Advertising **18**	2.9	0.1	•	8.7	1.0	1.3	1.9	2.0	1.3	1.8	3.7	0.5	4.1
Other Expenses **19**	18.4	8.5	•	27.2	13.0	14.9	9.0	11.5	8.8	9.0	12.0	22.5	20.6
Officers' Compensation **20**	0.7	•	•	7.7	4.0	1.9	1.2	1.5	0.6	0.5	0.7	0.4	0.5
Operating Margin **21**	•	3.6	•	•	•	•	0.2	2.3	•	3.0	•	5.8	•
Operating Margin Before Officers' Comp. **22**	0.7	3.6	•	1.8	•	•	1.3	3.8	•	3.5	0.7	6.2	•

Selected Average Balance Sheet ($ in Thousands)

Net Receivables 23	17016	•	76	833	791	2543	7305	20109	18120	80636	139339	1257957
Inventories 24	3944	0	141	64	577	1452	4133	5089	12162	20621	48488	221437
Net Property, Plant and Equipment 25	21943	0	310	282	1401	4673	11709	21590	45273	154774	324547	1325700
Total Assets 26	154728	•	610	1587	6549	14371	37665	75799	155315	387827	1174982	12603822
Notes and Loans Payable 27	45740	0	349	313	4406	3111	9623	26286	34062	194999	436866	3572000
All Other Liabilities 28	48646	0	84	628	558	3878	10865	15981	29870	125817	288647	4162366
Net Worth 29	60342	0	177	646	1586	7382	17177	33532	91383	67011	449468	4869456

Selected Financial Ratios (Times to 1)

Current Ratio 30	1.5	•	2.4	1.2	2.4	1.6	1.8	1.7	1.7	1.3	1.8	1.5
Quick Ratio 31	1.1	•	0.9	1.1	1.7	1.1	1.2	1.3	1.1	1.0	1.3	1.1
Net Sales to Working Capital 32	7.1	•	9.5	19.4	6.9	13.2	10.5	7.9	11.6	14.4	7.5	5.9
Coverage Ratio 33	7.2	•	•	•	6.9	8.6	7.0	1.4	6.3	1.5	5.1	7.8
Total Asset Turnover 34	0.6	•	2.4	2.5	1.6	2.2	2.3	1.6	1.5	1.0	0.9	0.4
Inventory Turnover 35	11.6	•	4.9	43.8	13.9	15.7	14.3	17.0	13.0	10.5	10.7	10.5
Receivables Turnover 36	4.2	•	9.6	6.1	12.0	13.6	13.1	8.6	12.1	5.7	8.7	3.0
Total Liabilities to Net Worth 37	1.6	•	2.4	1.5	3.1	0.9	1.2	1.3	0.7	4.8	1.6	3.0
Current Assets to Working Capital 38	2.8	•	1.7	5.3	1.7	2.7	2.2	2.5	2.4	4.5	2.3	1.6
Current Liabilities to Working Capital 39	1.8	•	0.7	4.3	0.7	1.7	1.2	1.5	1.4	3.5	1.3	2.0
Working Capital to Net Sales 40	0.1	•	0.1	0.1	0.1	0.1	0.1	0.1	0.1	0.1	0.1	0.2
Inventory to Working Capital 41	0.3	•	1.0	0.3	0.4	0.6	0.6	0.4	0.6	0.7	0.4	0.2
Total Receipts to Cash Flow 42	2.4	5.5	7.8	9.2	6.3	10.4	7.6	13.3	7.6	9.6	3.2	1.7
Cost of Goods to Cash Flow 43	1.3	3.6	3.6	6.6	4.9	7.6	5.1	9.7	5.1	5.6	1.6	0.8
Cash Flow to Total Debt 44	0.4	•	0.4	0.5	0.3	0.4	0.6	0.2	0.5	0.1	0.5	0.4

Selected Financial Factors (in Percentages)

Debt Ratio 45	61.0	•	71.0	59.3	75.8	54.4	48.6	55.8	41.2	82.7	61.7	61.4
Return on Total Assets 46	18.2	•	•	•	12.1	11.9	11.5	3.0	10.3	4.2	14.1	19.9
Return on Equity Before Income Taxes 47	40.3	•	•	•	42.7	19.8	22.3	1.9	14.8	7.9	29.6	44.9
Return on Equity After Income Taxes 48	32.4	•	•	•	31.6	17.9	18.2	1.2	11.7	1.0	19.3	36.7
Profit Margin (Before Income Tax) 49	28.1	12.3	•	•	6.5	4.7	4.4	0.5	5.7	1.4	12.5	44.5
Profit Margin (After Income Tax) 50	22.6	12.3	•	•	4.8	4.2	3.6	0.3	4.5	0.2	8.2	36.5

Table II

Corporations with Net Income

SOFT DRINK AND ICE

MONEY AMOUNTS AND SIZE OF ASSETS IN THOUSANDS OF DOLLARS

Item Description for Accounting Period 7/05 Through 6/06	Total	Zero Assets	Under 500	500 to 1000	251 to 500	501 to 1,000	1,001 to 5,000	5,001 to 10,000	10,001 to 25,000	25,001 to 50,000	50,001 to 100,000	100,001 to 250,000	250,001 and over
Number of Enterprises **1**	302	4	0	117	21	•	67	25	8	15	•	•	6
Revenues ($ in Thousands)													
Net Sales **2**	49756094	96238	0	180063	297531	•	2212901	2586351	1053807	4585551	•	•	29427853
Interest **3**	1049697	0	0	19	149	•	1466	3732	1378	5098	•	•	979382
Rents **4**	77845	0	0	0	0	•	3778	223	719	1400	•	•	70594
Royalties **5**	1218031	0	0	0	0	•	0	0	0	0	•	•	1172925
Other Portfolio Income **6**	8772811	7413	0	0	1344	•	71953	27143	4149	6073	•	•	8521250
Other Receipts **7**	2400184	1046	0	0	4796	•	26332	16862	21879	92681	•	•	1757447
Total Receipts **8**	63274662	104697	0	180082	303820	•	2316430	2634311	1081932	4690803	•	•	41929451
Average Total Receipts **9**	209519	26174	•	1539	14468	•	34574	105372	135242	312720	•	•	6998242
Operating Costs/Operating Income (%)													
Cost of Operations **10**	52.4	65.0	•	48.0	81.6	•	73.3	66.8	70.5	65.2	•	•	47.3
Salaries and Wages **11**	11.8	13.7	•	7.1	4.6	•	7.5	7.7	8.9	11.6	•	•	13.1
Taxes Paid **12**	2.1	2.4	•	3.3	1.4	•	1.5	1.5	1.8	1.8	•	•	2.4
Interest Paid **13**	4.6	•	•	1.3	0.8	•	0.5	0.6	1.4	1.0	•	•	6.6
Depreciation **14**	3.0	2.0	•	4.0	2.1	•	2.2	2.1	2.7	2.8	•	•	3.1
Amortization and Depletion **15**	0.9	0.4	•	0.4	•	•	0.1	0.2	0.2	0.4	•	•	1.2
Pensions and Other Deferred Comp. **16**	1.1	1.4	•	1.3	0.6	•	0.6	0.5	0.4	0.6	•	•	1.5
Employee Benefits **17**	1.9	3.1	•	0.8	0.9	•	1.5	1.4	1.8	2.3	•	•	1.8
Advertising **18**	2.9	0.1	•	1.7	0.9	•	2.0	2.1	1.4	1.7	•	•	4.1
Other Expenses **19**	18.5	8.5	•	24.7	3.9	•	9.0	12.0	8.0	8.4	•	•	20.6
Officers' Compensation **20**	0.6	•	•	5.8	4.3	•	1.1	1.1	0.6	0.6	•	•	0.5
Operating Margin **21**	0.4	3.6	•	1.5	•	•	0.6	4.0	2.4	3.7	•	•	•
Operating Margin Before Officers' Comp. **22**	1.0	3.6	•	7.3	3.3	•	1.8	5.1	3.0	4.2	•	•	•

Selected Average Balance Sheet ($ in Thousands)

Net Receivables 23	32289	0	63	520	2694	8360	16271	27739	1257957
Inventories 24	6525	0	129	106	1178	4065	4411	12232	229620
Net Property, Plant and Equipment 25	39961	0	349	371	4432	12382	27466	55390	1325700
Total Assets 26	300575	0	618	3186	14600	42066	75593	181363	12603822
Notes and Loans Payable 27	86629	0	377	1326	2724	8090	23155	45936	3572000
All Other Liabilities 28	95370	0	62	278	4052	12012	17065	42550	4162366
Net Worth 29	118576	0	179	1582	7824	21964	35373	92876	4869456

Selected Financial Ratios (Times to 1)

Current Ratio 30	1.6	•	3.3	1.1	1.6	2.0	1.9	1.8	1.5
Quick Ratio 31	1.1	•	1.3	0.5	1.1	1.3	1.5	1.3	1.1
Net Sales to Working Capital 32	6.9	•	9.4	150.6	12.8	9.5	7.7	11.0	5.9
Coverage Ratio 33	7.6	•	2.1	2.4	10.9	10.7	4.5	6.9	7.8
Total Asset Turnover 34	0.5	•	2.5	4.4	2.3	2.5	1.7	1.7	0.4
Inventory Turnover 35	13.2	•	5.7	109.3	20.5	17.0	21.0	16.3	10.1
Receivables Turnover 36	4.5	•	13.2	54.5	16.7	15.5	12.1	13.1	7.8
Total Liabilities to Net Worth 37	1.5	•	2.4	1.0	0.9	0.9	1.1	1.0	7.8
Current Assets to Working Capital 38	2.8	•	1.4	16.9	2.6	2.0	2.1	2.2	1.6
Current Liabilities to Working Capital 39	1.8	•	0.4	15.9	1.6	1.0	1.1	1.2	3.0
Working Capital to Net Sales 40	0.1	•	0.1	0.0	0.1	0.1	0.1	0.1	2.0
Inventory to Working Capital 41	0.3	•	0.8	1.1	0.6	0.5	0.4	0.5	0.2
Total Receipts to Cash Flow 42	2.3	5.5	4.7	29.5	9.8	6.5	8.9	8.1	0.3
Cost of Goods to Cash Flow 43	1.2	3.6	2.3	24.1	7.2	4.3	6.2	5.3	1.7
Cash Flow to Total Debt 44	0.4	•	0.7	0.3	0.5	0.8	0.4	0.4	0.4

Selected Financial Factors (in Percentages)

Debt Ratio 45	60.6	•	71.0	50.3	46.4	47.8	53.2	48.8	61.4
Return on Total Assets 46	19.0	•	7.0	8.3	13.2	15.7	10.7	11.7	19.9
Return on Equity Before Income Taxes 47	41.8	•	12.9	9.7	22.4	27.3	17.7	19.5	44.9
Return on Equity After Income Taxes 48	33.7	•	11.6	8.5	20.4	22.9	16.7	15.2	36.7
Profit Margin (Before Income Tax) 49	30.1	12.3	1.5	1.1	5.3	5.8	4.8	5.9	44.5
Profit Margin (After Income Tax) 50	24.2	12.3	1.4	0.9	4.8	4.9	4.5	4.6	36.5

Table I

Corporations with and without Net Income

BREWERIES

MONEY AMOUNTS AND SIZE OF ASSETS IN THOUSANDS OF DOLLARS

Item Description for Accounting Period 7/05 Through 6/06	Total	Zero Assets	Under 500	500 to 1,000	1,000 to 5,000	5,000 to 10,000	10,000 to 25,000	25,000 to 50,000	50,000 to 100,000	100,000 to 250,000	250,000 to 500,000	500,000 to 2,500,000	2,500,000 and over
Number of Enterprises 1	445	0	340	58	17	10	11	0	6	0	0	0	3
Revenues ($ in Thousands)													
Net Sales 2	24136889	0	135144	30440	92426	91424	190663	0	717311	0	0	0	22879480
Interest 3	91744	0	0	418	0	0	6	0	945	0	0	0	90375
Rents 4	29700	0	0	0	0	37	0	0	424	0	0	0	29239
Royalties 5	377532	0	0	0	0	0	0	0	0	0	0	0	377532
Other Portfolio Income 6	212827	0	4436	0	0	0	17	0	5853	0	0	0	202523
Other Receipts 7	78273	0	0	0	0	1159	1636	0	8910	0	0	0	66566
Total Receipts 8	24926965	0	139580	30858	92426	92620	192322	0	733443	0	0	0	23645715
Average Total Receipts 9	56016	•	411	532	5437	9262	17484	0	122240	•	•	•	7881905
Operating Costs/Operating Income (%)													
Cost of Operations 10	41.9	•	27.1	71.3	89.2	73.0	54.1	•	51.0	•	•	•	41.2
Salaries and Wages 11	9.1	•	29.2	•	5.5	5.4	5.9	•	5.4	•	•	•	9.1
Taxes Paid 12	13.6	•	8.2	7.1	•	6.3	7.6	•	8.2	•	•	•	13.9
Interest Paid 13	2.7	•	6.3	•	0.1	1.3	3.2	•	0.1	•	•	•	2.8
Depreciation 14	3.9	•	6.0	•	•	4.0	7.7	•	1.9	•	•	•	4.0
Amortization and Depletion 15	0.4	•	0.5	•	•	0.5	0.2	•	0.1	•	•	•	0.4
Pensions and Other Deferred Comp. 16	1.9	•	•	•	0.4	0.4	0.2	•	0.7	•	•	•	2.0
Employee Benefits 17	1.5	•	1.6	•	•	2.5	1.6	•	0.7	•	•	•	1.5
Advertising 18	8.1	•	1.5	•	2.1	5.7	3.7	•	4.6	•	•	•	8.3
Other Expenses 19	8.7	•	28.2	21.3	6.7	7.6	7.9	•	14.4	•	•	•	8.4
Officers' Compensation 20	0.4	•	2.2	•	•	0.1	2.0	•	0.8	•	•	•	0.3
Operating Margin 21	7.9	•	•	0.3	•	•	6.0	•	12.2	•	•	•	8.0
Operating Margin Before Officers' Comp. 22	8.3	•	•	0.3	•	•	8.0	•	12.9	•	•	•	8.3

Selected Average Balance Sheet ($ in Thousands)

Net Receivables 23	4193	•	20	•	208	549	708	1006	•	10856	•	584855
Inventories 24	2082	•	74	•	0	662	1815	1097	•	4560	•	270277
Net Property, Plant and Equipment 25	24177	•	132	•	0	0	2632	12699	•	31880	•	3452269
Total Assets 26	64255	•	262	•	534	3684	5755	16086	•	86967	•	9218178
Notes and Loans Payable 27	34570	•	55	•	0	3450	3314	7865	•	12708	•	5036773
All Other Liabilities 28	14984	•	25	•	279	190	5944	2765	•	1266	•	2180929
Net Worth 29	14701	•	182	•	255	44	-3502	5455	•	72993	•	2000476

Selected Financial Ratios (Times to 1)

Current Ratio 30	0.8	•	1.3	•	1.9	9.6	0.3	0.7	•	5.2	•	0.8
Quick Ratio 31	0.5	•	0.3	•	1.8	6.5	0.1	0.3	•	4.6	•	0.5
Net Sales to Working Capital 32	•	•	18.3	•	2.1	3.3	•	•	•	3.5	•	•
Coverage Ratio 33	5.3	•	•	•	•	•	3.1	•	•	111.8	•	5.3
Total Asset Turnover 34	0.8	•	1.5	•	1.0	1.5	1.6	1.1	•	1.4	•	0.8
Inventory Turnover 35	10.9	•	1.5	•	•	7.3	3.7	8.5	•	13.4	•	11.6
Receivables Turnover 36	16.0	•	40.3	•	1.8	9.9	13.6	34.5	•	22.0	•	26.1
Total Liabilities to Net Worth 37	3.4	•	0.4	•	1.1	83.1	•	1.9	•	0.2	•	3.6
Current Assets to Working Capital 38	•	•	4.7	•	2.1	1.1	•	•	•	1.2	•	•
Current Liabilities to Working Capital 39	•	•	3.7	•	1.1	0.1	•	•	•	0.2	•	•
Working Capital to Net Sales 40	•	•	0.1	•	0.5	0.3	•	•	•	0.3	•	•
Inventory to Working Capital 41	•	•	3.4	•	•	0.4	•	•	•	0.1	•	•
Total Receipts to Cash Flow 42	5.7	•	9.2	•	58.2	33.3	74.9	7.6	•	3.6	•	5.8
Cost of Goods to Cash Flow 43	2.4	•	2.5	•	41.5	29.7	54.7	4.1	•	1.8	•	2.4
Cash Flow to Total Debt 44	0.2	•	0.5	•	0.0	0.0	0.0	0.2	•	2.4	•	0.2

Selected Financial Factors (in Percentages)

Debt Ratio 45	77.1	•	30.4	•	52.3	98.8	160.9	66.1	•	16.1	•	78.3
Return on Total Assets 46	12.1	•	•	•	1.7	•	•	10.9	•	19.7	•	12.1
Return on Equity Before Income Taxes 47	42.9	•	•	•	3.5	•	14.4	22.0	•	23.3	•	45.2
Return on Equity After Income Taxes 48	28.7	•	•	•	3.0	•	14.4	21.9	•	21.7	•	29.8
Profit Margin (Before Income Tax) 49	11.6	•	•	•	1.7	•	•	6.9	•	14.2	•	11.8
Profit Margin (After Income Tax) 50	7.8	•	•	•	1.5	•	•	6.9	•	13.2	•	7.8

Table II

Corporations with Net Income

BREWERIES

MANUFACTURING 312120

MONEY AMOUNTS AND SIZE OF ASSETS IN THOUSANDS OF DOLLARS

Item Description for Accounting Period 7/05 Through 6/06	Total	Zero Assets	Under 500	500 to 1,000	1,000 to 5,000	5,000 to 10,000	10,000 to 25,000	25,000 to 50,000	50,000 to 100,000	100,000 to 250,000	250,000 to 500,000	500,000 to 2,500,000	2,500,000 and over
Number of Enterprises **1**	74	0	0	58	0	0	7	0	6	0	0	0	3
Revenues ($ in Thousands)													
Net Sales **2**	23774910	0	0	30440	0	0	147678	0	717311	0	0	0	22879480
Interest **3**	91739	0	0	418	0	0	1	0	945	0	0	0	90375
Rents **4**	29663	0	0	0	0	0	0	0	424	0	0	0	29239
Royalties **5**	377532	0	0	0	0	0	0	0	0	0	0	0	377532
Other Portfolio Income **6**	208391	0	0	0	0	0	17	0	5853	0	0	0	202523
Other Receipts **7**	75884	0	0	0	0	0	406	0	8910	0	0	0	66566
Total Receipts **8**	24558119	0	0	30858	0	0	148102	0	733443	0	0	0	23645715
Average Total Receipts **9**	331866	•	•	532	•	•	21157	•	122240	•	•	•	7881905
Operating Costs/Operating Income (%)													
Cost of Operations **10**	41.6	•	•	71.3	•	•	51.1	•	51.0	•	•	•	41.2
Salaries and Wages **11**	9.0	•	•	•	•	•	4.7	•	5.4	•	•	•	9.1
Taxes Paid **12**	13.7	•	•	7.1	•	•	8.8	•	8.2	•	•	•	13.9
Interest Paid **13**	2.7	•	•	•	•	•	2.3	•	0.1	•	•	•	2.8
Depreciation **14**	3.9	•	•	•	•	•	7.4	•	1.9	•	•	•	4.0
Amortization and Depletion **15**	0.4	•	•	•	•	•	0.2	•	0.1	•	•	•	0.4
Pensions and Other Deferred Comp. **16**	1.9	•	•	•	•	•	0.3	•	0.7	•	•	•	2.0
Employee Benefits **17**	1.5	•	•	•	•	•	0.9	•	0.7	•	•	•	1.5
Advertising **18**	8.2	•	•	•	•	•	4.8	•	4.6	•	•	•	8.3
Other Expenses **19**	8.6	•	•	21.3	•	•	7.4	•	14.4	•	•	•	8.4
Officers' Compensation **20**	0.3	•	•	•	•	•	1.9	•	0.8	•	•	•	0.3
Operating Margin **21**	8.2	•	•	0.3	•	•	10.5	•	12.2	•	•	•	8.0
Operating Margin Before Officers' Comp. **22**	8.5	•	•	0.3	•	•	12.4	•	12.9	•	•	•	8.3

Selected Average Balance Sheet ($ in Thousands)

Net Receivables 23	24833	208	836	10856	584855
Inventories 24	11973	0	1107	4560	270277
Net Property, Plant and Equipment 25	143837	0	13690	31880	3452269
Total Assets 26	382764	534	16742	86967	9218178
Notes and Loans Payable 27	206008	0	8292	12708	5036773
All Other Liabilities 28	88969	279	2452	1266	2180929
Net Worth 29	87786	255	5999	72993	2000476

Selected Financial Ratios (Times to 1)

Current Ratio 30	0.9	1.9	1.0	5.2	0.8
Quick Ratio 31	0.6	1.8	0.5	4.6	0.5
Net Sales to Working Capital 32		2.1	6420.8	3.5	
Coverage Ratio 33	5.4		5.8	111.8	5.3
Total Asset Turnover 34	0.8	1.0	1.3	1.4	0.8
Inventory Turnover 35	11.2		9.7	13.4	11.6
Receivables Turnover 36	16.0	1.8	50.4	22.0	26.1
Total Liabilities to Net Worth 37	3.4	1.1	1.8	0.2	3.6
Current Assets to Working Capital 38		2.1	893.1	1.2	
Current Liabilities to Working Capital 39		1.1	892.1	0.2	
Working Capital to Net Sales 40		0.5	0.0	0.3	
Inventory to Working Capital 41			336.9	0.1	
Total Receipts to Cash Flow 42	5.7	58.2	6.0	3.6	5.8
Cost of Goods to Cash Flow 43	2.4	41.5	3.1	1.8	2.4
Cash Flow to Total Debt 44	0.2	0.0	0.3	2.4	0.2

Selected Financial Factors (in Percentages)

Debt Ratio 45	77.1	52.3	64.2	16.1	78.3
Return on Total Assets 46	12.3	1.7	16.5	19.7	12.1
Return on Equity Before Income Taxes 47	43.5	3.5	38.1	23.3	45.2
Return on Equity After Income Taxes 48	29.3	3.0	38.0	21.7	29.8
Profit Margin (Before Income Tax) 49	11.9	1.7	10.8	14.2	11.8
Profit Margin (After Income Tax) 50	8.0	1.5	10.8	13.2	7.8

Table I

Corporations with and without Net Income

WINERIES AND DISTILLERIES

MONEY AMOUNTS AND SIZE OF ASSETS IN THOUSANDS OF DOLLARS

Item Description for Accounting Period 7/05 Through 6/06	Total	Zero Assets	Under 500	500 to 1,000	1,000 to 5,000	5,000 to 10,000	10,000 to 25,000	25,000 to 50,000	50,000 to 100,000	100,000 to 250,000	250,000 to 500,000	500,000 to 2,500,000	2,500,000 and over
Number of Enterprises **1**	1513	•	555	275	480	90	•	27	22	8	6	0	4
Revenues ($ in Thousands)													
Net Sales **2**	20910962	•	20671	198175	518231	349776	•	559122	1095437	1013918	4431429	0	12296888
Interest **3**	135960	•	0	47	1811	1027	•	813	4891	425	11829	0	114902
Rents **4**	10928	•	0	0	535	0	•	240	254	1015	8015	0	868
Royalties **5**	480265	•	0	0	31770	0	•	2377	0	0	292	0	445826
Other Portfolio Income **6**	535897	•	0	0	537	351	•	2157	45220	216	1536	0	481015
Other Receipts **7**	302829	•	0	2533	4815	5709	•	8894	33986	-267	90926	0	134467
Total Receipts **8**	22376841	•	20671	200755	557699	356863	•	573603	1179788	1015307	4544027	0	13473966
Average Total Receipts **9**	14790	•	37	730	1162	3965	•	21245	53627	126913	757338	•	3368492
Operating Costs/Operating Income (%)													
Cost of Operations **10**	53.6	•	30.8	49.9	35.8	47.2	•	46.6	61.5	70.8	56.5	•	51.9
Salaries and Wages **11**	6.4	•	76.3	1.9	16.4	15.6	•	12.5	5.3	4.3	7.1	•	5.3
Taxes Paid **12**	10.9	•	3.9	5.7	5.2	5.8	•	3.8	7.9	4.4	15.0	•	11.3
Interest Paid **13**	5.4	•	56.1	4.3	0.9	3.3	•	2.2	2.7	2.6	1.4	•	7.8
Depreciation **14**	2.6	•	6.8	2.1	7.7	6.2	•	5.5	3.2	3.0	3.4	•	1.7
Amortization and Depletion **15**	1.5	•	2.1	0.0	0.1	0.1	•	0.4	0.8	1.5	0.5	•	2.1
Pensions and Other Deferred Comp. **16**	0.6	•	•	•	0.8	0.3	•	0.6	0.5	0.5	0.6	•	0.7
Employee Benefits **17**	1.3	•	7.3	0.8	2.5	1.4	•	1.6	0.6	1.2	1.1	•	1.3
Advertising **18**	5.8	•	4.2	3.9	3.2	1.0	•	0.8	3.1	1.3	3.0	•	8.0
Other Expenses **19**	9.8	•	95.5	4.3	33.0	14.6	•	13.3	13.2	5.4	7.7	•	9.1
Officers' Compensation **20**	1.2	•	•	20.1	2.5	1.3	•	1.6	1.6	1.5	0.3	•	1.0
Operating Margin **21**	0.9	•	•	7.1	•	3.1	•	11.1	•	3.6	3.4	•	0.9
Operating Margin Before Officers' Comp. **22**	2.1	•	•	27.2	•	4.5	•	12.7	1.2	5.1	3.6	•	0.9

Selected Average Balance Sheet ($ in Thousands)

Net Receivables 23	2721	0	15	183	219	3238	6881	18402	124114	706420
Inventories 24	4389	35	442	601	2809	9640	17998	60581	168606	722284
Net Property, Plant and Equipment 25	3471	55	207	430	2761	14676	22912	42742	171962	527274
Total Assets 26	20559	114	675	1756	6924	35895	65612	145570	746760	5138120
Notes and Loans Payable 27	9899	225	492	183	4289	7068	24319	60747	195282	2895408
All Other Liabilities 28	3598	3	33	86	308	5867	10043	32177	155981	917761
Net Worth 29	7062	-114	150	1486	2327	22961	31250	52647	395497	1324950

Selected Financial Ratios (Times to 1)

Current Ratio 30	2.7	10.7	7.1	8.2	6.6	2.6	2.3	1.8	2.1	2.9
Quick Ratio 31	1.0	10.2	1.3	1.6	1.3	0.9	0.7	0.5	0.6	1.3
Net Sales to Working Capital 32	2.6	1.3	1.8	1.0	1.1	1.9	3.0	3.7	3.2	2.7
Coverage Ratio 33	2.5	•	2.9	0.4	2.6	7.3	3.8	2.5	5.2	2.3
Total Asset Turnover 34	0.7	0.3	1.1	0.6	0.6	0.6	0.8	0.9	1.0	0.6
Inventory Turnover 35	1.7	0.3	0.8	0.6	0.7	1.0	1.7	1.5	2.5	2.2
Receivables Turnover 36	4.2	544.0	16.0	5.8	12.6	6.6	14.5	5.9	9.4	3.3
Total Liabilities to Net Worth 37	1.9	•	3.5	0.2	2.0	0.6	1.1	1.8	0.9	2.9
Current Assets to Working Capital 38	1.6	1.1	1.2	1.1	1.2	1.6	1.8	2.3	1.9	1.5
Current Liabilities to Working Capital 39	0.6	0.1	0.2	0.1	0.2	0.6	0.8	1.3	0.9	0.5
Working Capital to Net Sales 40	0.4	0.8	0.6	1.0	0.9	0.5	0.3	0.3	0.3	0.4
Inventory to Working Capital 41	0.8	0.0	1.0	0.9	0.8	0.9	1.1	1.6	1.1	0.6
Total Receipts to Cash Flow 42	6.4	•	11.8	3.9	5.7	4.1	6.4	13.1	8.3	6.0
Cost of Goods to Cash Flow 43	3.5	•	5.9	1.4	2.7	1.9	3.9	9.3	4.7	3.1
Cash Flow to Total Debt 44	0.2	•	0.1	1.0	0.1	0.4	0.2	0.1	0.3	0.1

Selected Financial Factors (in Percentages)

Debt Ratio 45	65.7	200.4	77.8	15.4	66.4	36.0	52.4	63.8	47.0	74.2
Return on Total Assets 46	9.1	•	13.5	0.2	4.7	9.1	7.6	5.6	7.2	10.5
Return on Equity Before Income Taxes 47	15.8	59.6	40.2	•	8.6	12.3	11.7	9.2	11.0	22.6
Return on Equity After Income Taxes 48	12.1	59.6	40.2	•	5.3	11.4	8.8	8.0	8.3	17.3
Profit Margin (Before Income Tax) 49	8.1	•	8.4	•	5.1	13.6	7.3	3.8	5.9	9.7
Profit Margin (After Income Tax) 50	6.2	•	8.4	•	3.2	12.6	5.5	3.3	4.4	7.4

55

Table II

Corporations with Net Income

WINERIES AND DISTILLERIES

MONEY AMOUNTS AND SIZE OF ASSETS IN THOUSANDS OF DOLLARS

Item Description for Accounting Period 7/05 Through 6/06	Total	Zero Assets	Under 500	500 to 1,000	1,000 to 5,000	5,000 to 10,000	10,000 to 25,000	25,000 to 50,000	50,000 to 100,000	100,000 to 250,000	250,000 to 500,000	500,000 to 2,500,000	2,500,000 and over
Number of Enterprises **1**	501	0	0	243	109	•	25	•	13	•	6	0	4
Revenues ($ in Thousands)													
Net Sales **2**	20005626	0	0	176643	311178	•	336368	•	813184	•	4431429	0	12296888
Interest **3**	131573	0	0	47	1811	•	36	•	1063	•	11829	0	114902
Rents **4**	10522	0	0	0	535	•	0	•	77	•	8015	0	868
Royalties **5**	480265	0	0	0	31770	•	0	•	0	•	292	0	445826
Other Portfolio Income **6**	530643	0	0	0	537	•	222	•	44624	•	1536	0	481015
Other Receipts **7**	297031	0	0	2235	3661	•	20480	•	25881	•	90926	0	134467
Total Receipts **8**	21455660	0	0	178925	349492	•	357106	•	884829	•	4544027	0	13473966
Average Total Receipts **9**	42826	•	•	736	3206	•	14284	•	68064	•	757338	•	3368492
Operating Costs/Operating Income (%)													
Cost of Operations **10**	53.4	•	•	49.2	29.6	•	49.6	•	58.1	•	56.5	•	51.9
Salaries and Wages **11**	6.1	•	•	•	15.1	•	9.6	•	6.0	•	7.1	•	5.3
Taxes Paid **12**	11.2	•	•	5.8	4.7	•	4.0	•	7.9	•	15.0	•	11.3
Interest Paid **13**	5.5	•	•	3.4	1.2	•	2.2	•	2.6	•	1.4	•	7.8
Depreciation **14**	2.4	•	•	2.1	4.9	•	5.1	•	2.5	•	3.4	•	1.7
Amortization and Depletion **15**	1.5	•	•	•	0.1	•	0.1	•	1.1	•	0.5	•	2.1
Pensions and Other Deferred Comp. **16**	0.6	•	•	•	1.4	•	0.5	•	0.4	•	0.6	•	0.7
Employee Benefits **17**	1.2	•	•	0.8	1.6	•	1.4	•	0.7	•	1.1	•	1.3
Advertising **18**	5.9	•	•	3.2	2.4	•	0.6	•	3.1	•	3.0	•	8.0
Other Expenses **19**	8.9	•	•	3.5	27.0	•	12.0	•	10.7	•	7.7	•	9.1
Officers' Compensation **20**	1.2	•	•	22.6	4.0	•	2.0	•	1.8	•	0.3	•	1.0
Operating Margin **21**	2.0	•	•	9.4	7.9	•	13.0	•	5.2	•	3.4	•	•
Operating Margin Before Officers' Comp. **22**	3.2	•	•	32.0	12.0	•	15.0	•	7.0	•	3.6	•	0.9

Selected Average Balance Sheet ($ in Thousands)

Net Receivables 23	7889	12	238	1409	8744	124114	706420
Inventories 24	11160	461	883	6523	20506	262027	711923
Net Property, Plant and Equipment 25	8994	197	580	7823	15886	171962	527274
Total Assets 26	58230	643	2453	19865	65135	746760	5138120
Notes and Loans Payable 27	28841	436	623	4323	23271	195282	2895408
All Other Liabilities 28	10601	16	324	3875	13368	155981	917761
Net Worth 29	19187	192	1506	11668	28496	395497	1324950

Selected Financial Ratios (Times to 1)

Current Ratio 30	2.6	7.4	3.1	1.8	2.1	2.1	2.9
Quick Ratio 31	1.0	1.4	0.8	0.3	0.6	0.6	1.3
Net Sales to Working Capital 32	2.7	1.9	2.8	3.2	3.4	3.2	2.7
Coverage Ratio 33	2.7	4.1	17.9	9.9	6.4	5.2	2.3
Total Asset Turnover 34	0.7	1.1	1.2	0.7	1.0	1.0	0.6
Inventory Turnover 35	1.9	0.8	1.0	1.0	1.8	1.6	2.2
Receivables Turnover 36	5.3	36.0	12.5	8.8	7.7	11.9	8.7
Total Liabilities to Net Worth 37	2.0	2.4	0.6	0.7	1.3	0.9	2.9
Current Assets to Working Capital 38	1.6	1.2	1.5	2.3	1.9	1.9	1.5
Current Liabilities to Working Capital 39	0.6	0.2	0.5	1.3	0.9	0.9	0.5
Working Capital to Net Sales 40	0.4	0.5	0.4	0.3	0.3	0.3	0.4
Inventory to Working Capital 41	0.8	0.9	1.0	1.8	1.2	1.1	0.6
Total Receipts to Cash Flow 42	6.2	9.0	2.6	3.6	5.4	8.3	6.0
Cost of Goods to Cash Flow 43	3.3	4.4	0.8	1.8	3.1	4.7	3.1
Cash Flow to Total Debt 44	0.2	0.2	1.2	0.5	0.3	0.3	0.1

Selected Financial Factors (in Percentages)

Debt Ratio 45	67.0	70.2	38.6	41.3	56.3	47.0	74.2
Return on Total Assets 46	10.2	16.0	25.0	14.4	16.0	7.2	10.5
Return on Equity Before Income Taxes 47	19.6	40.6	38.4	22.1	30.8	11.0	22.6
Return on Equity After Income Taxes 48	15.5	40.6	33.7	20.7	25.5	8.3	17.3
Profit Margin (Before Income Tax) 49	9.4	10.7	20.2	19.1	14.0	5.9	9.7
Profit Margin (After Income Tax) 50	7.4	10.7	17.8	18.0	11.6	4.4	7.4

Table I

Corporations with and without Net Income

TOBACCO MANUFACTURING

MONEY AMOUNTS AND SIZE OF ASSETS IN THOUSANDS OF DOLLARS

Item Description for Accounting Period 7/05 Through 6/06		Total	Zero Assets	Under 500	500 to 1,000	1,000 to 5,000	5,000 to 10,000	10,000 to 25,000	25,000 to 50,000	50,000 to 100,000	100,000 to 250,000	250,000 to 500,000	500,000 to 2,500,000	2,500,000 and over
Number of Enterprises	1	23	•	0	0	0	0	•	7	0	0	3	7	0
Revenues ($ in Thousands)														
Net Sales	2	17937601	•	0	0	0	0	•	381751	0	0	732297	1661787	0
Interest	3	275758	•	0	0	0	0	•	1445	0	0	25078	245693	0
Rents	4	9869	•	0	0	0	0	•	0	0	0	1148	8675	0
Royalties	5	111240	•	0	0	0	0	•	0	0	0	4781	106293	0
Other Portfolio Income	6	550295	•	0	0	0	0	•	68	0	0	160940	389287	0
Other Receipts	7	176247	•	0	0	0	0	•	1953	0	0	4486	153245	0
Total Receipts	8	19061010	•	0	0	0	0	•	385217	0	0	928730	17514980	0
Average Total Receipts	9	828740	•	•	•	•	•	•	55031	•	•	309577	2502140	•
Operating Costs/Operating Income (%)														
Cost of Operations	10	47.8	•	•	•	•	•	•	57.6	•	•	47.6	47.6	•
Salaries and Wages	11	4.5	•	•	•	•	•	•	4.6	•	•	3.8	4.5	•
Taxes Paid	12	15.6	•	•	•	•	•	•	17.2	•	•	9.8	15.5	•
Interest Paid	13	2.7	•	•	•	•	•	•	1.5	•	•	3.7	2.7	•
Depreciation	14	1.0	•	•	•	•	•	•	2.1	•	•	1.0	1.0	•
Amortization and Depletion	15	0.3	•	•	•	•	•	•	0.1	•	•	0.1	0.3	•
Pensions and Other Deferred Comp.	16	0.5	•	•	•	•	•	•	0.2	•	•	0.7	0.5	•
Employee Benefits	17	2.3	•	•	•	•	•	•	0.5	•	•	2.6	2.3	•
Advertising	18	1.6	•	•	•	•	•	•	1.0	•	•	0.7	1.6	•
Other Expenses	19	10.8	•	•	•	•	•	•	14.4	•	•	11.3	10.7	•
Officers' Compensation	20	0.5	•	•	•	•	•	•	2.0	•	•	0.9	0.4	•
Operating Margin	21	12.4	•	•	•	•	•	•	•	•	•	17.8	12.7	•
Operating Margin Before Officers' Comp.	22	12.9	•	•	•	•	•	•	0.7	•	•	18.7	13.2	•

Selected Average Balance Sheet ($ in Thousands)

Net Receivables 23	22997	2720	17787	63616
Inventories 24	97108	9976	78171	295843
Net Property, Plant and Equipment 25	86720	5602	17116	271346
Total Assets 26	1061351	43759	335052	3291077
Notes and Loans Payable 27	253527	17883	51561	793002
All Other Liabilities 28	357120	8504	91149	1123382
Net Worth 29	450703	17372	192341	1374694

Selected Financial Ratios (Times to 1)

Current Ratio 30	2.7	1.4	3.4	2.7
Quick Ratio 31	1.3	0.6	1.9	1.3
Net Sales to Working Capital 32	4.7	9.1	1.4	5.1
Coverage Ratio 33	7.8	0.7	13.0	7.7
Total Asset Turnover 34	0.7	1.2	0.7	0.7
Inventory Turnover 35	3.8	3.2	1.5	3.8
Receivables Turnover 36	12.7	40.1	4.3	74.6
Total Liabilities to Net Worth 37	1.4	1.5	0.7	1.4
Current Assets to Working Capital 38	1.6	3.6	1.4	1.6
Current Liabilities to Working Capital 39	0.6	2.6	0.4	0.6
Working Capital to Net Sales 40	0.2	0.1	0.7	0.2
Inventory to Working Capital 41	0.6	1.7	0.2	0.6
Total Receipts to Cash Flow 42	3.6	15.8	2.1	3.7
Cost of Goods to Cash Flow 43	1.7	9.1	1.0	1.8
Cash Flow to Total Debt 44	0.4	0.1	0.8	0.3

Selected Financial Factors (in Percentages)

Debt Ratio 45	57.5	60.3	42.6	58.2
Return on Total Assets 46	15.5	1.3	35.2	14.8
Return on Equity Before Income Taxes 47	31.8	•	56.7	30.9
Return on Equity After Income Taxes 48	23.5	•	50.5	22.3
Profit Margin (Before Income Tax) 49	18.4	•	44.7	17.9
Profit Margin (After Income Tax) 50	13.6	•	39.8	12.9

Table II

Corporations with Net Income

TOBACCO MANUFACTURING

MONEY AMOUNTS AND SIZE OF ASSETS IN THOUSANDS OF DOLLARS

Item Description for Accounting Period 7/05 Through 6/06	Total	Zero Assets	Under 500	500 to 1,000	1,000 to 5,000	5,000 to 10,000	10,000 to 25,000	25,000 to 50,000	50,000 to 100,000	100,000 to 250,000	250,000 to 500,000	500,000 to 2,500,000	2,500,000 and over
Number of Enterprises **1**	19	0	0	0	0	0	4	·	0	0	3	·	0
Revenues ($ in Thousands)													
Net Sales **2**	17804998	0	0	0	0	0	178555	·	0	0	732297	·	0
Interest **3**	270771	0	0	0	0	0	0	·	0	0	25078	·	0
Rents **4**	9823	0	0	0	0	0	0	·	0	0	1148	·	0
Royalties **5**	111075	0	0	0	0	0	0	·	0	0	4781	·	0
Other Portfolio Income **6**	550295	0	0	0	0	·0	0	·	0	0	160940	·	0
Other Receipts **7**	175731	0	0	0	0	0	16279	·	0	0	4486	·	0
Total Receipts **8**	18922693	0	0	0	0	0	194834	·	0	0	928730	·	0
Average Total Receipts **9**	995931	·	·	·	·	·	48708	·	·	·	309577	·	·
Operating Costs/Operating Income (%)													
Cost of Operations **10**	47.7	·	·	·	·	·	32.4	·	·	·	47.6	·	·
Salaries and Wages **11**	4.5	·	·	·	·	·	6.7	·	·	·	3.8	·	·
Taxes Paid **12**	15.5	·	·	·	·	·	45.7	·	·	·	9.8	·	·
Interest Paid **13**	2.7	·	·	·	·	·	0.3	·	·	·	3.7	·	·
Depreciation **14**	1.0	·	·	·	·	·	0.4	·	·	·	1.0	·	·
Amortization and Depletion **15**	0.3	·	·	·	·	·	0.0	·	·	·	0.1	·	·
Pensions and Other Deferred Comp. **16**	0.5	·	·	·	·	·	0.4	·	·	·	0.7	·	·
Employee Benefits **17**	2.3	·	·	·	·	·	1.0	·	·	·	2.6	·	·
Advertising **18**	1.6	·	·	·	·	·	1.3	·	·	·	0.7	·	·
Other Expenses **19**	10.8	·	·	·	·	·	11.5	·	·	·	11.3	·	·
Officers' Compensation **20**	0.5	·	·	·	·	·	2.1	·	·	·	0.9	·	·
Operating Margin **21**	12.7	·	·	·	·	·	·	·	·	·	17.8	·	·
Operating Margin Before Officers' Comp. **22**	13.2	·	·	·	·	·	0.4	·	·	·	18.7	·	·

Selected Average Balance Sheet ($ in Thousands)

Net Receivables 23	27682	2803	17787
Inventories 24	113525	5751	36210
Net Property, Plant and Equipment 25	104045	1148	17116
Total Assets 26	1279764	15515	335052
Notes and Loans Payable 27	304383	62	51561
All Other Liabilities 28	431052	4280	91149
Net Worth 29	544329	11172	192341

Selected Financial Ratios (Times to 1)

Current Ratio 30	2.7	2.8	3.4
Quick Ratio 31	1.3	1.3	1.9
Net Sales to Working Capital 32	4.6	5.7	1.4
Coverage Ratio 33	8.0	26.3	13.0
Total Asset Turnover 34	0.7	2.9	0.7
Inventory Turnover 35	3.9	2.5	3.2
Receivables Turnover 36	13.3	31.8	27.4
Total Liabilities to Net Worth 37	1.4	0.4	0.7
Current Assets to Working Capital 38	1.6	1.5	1.4
Current Liabilities to Working Capital 39	0.6	0.5	0.4
Working Capital to Net Sales 40	0.2	0.2	0.7
Inventory to Working Capital 41	0.6	0.7	0.2
Total Receipts to Cash Flow 42	3.6	5.6	2.1
Cost of Goods to Cash Flow 43	1.7	1.8	1.0
Cash Flow to Total Debt 44	0.4	1.8	0.8

Selected Financial Factors (in Percentages)

Debt Ratio 45	57.5	28.0	42.6
Return on Total Assets 46	15.7	22.1	35.2
Return on Equity Before Income Taxes 47	32.2	29.5	56.7
Return on Equity After Income Taxes 48	23.9	29.5	50.5
Profit Margin (Before Income Tax) 49	18.7	7.4	44.7
Profit Margin (After Income Tax) 50	13.9	7.4	39.8

58

TEXTILE MILLS

Table I

Corporations with and without Net Income

MONEY AMOUNTS AND SIZE OF ASSETS IN THOUSANDS OF DOLLARS

Item Description for Accounting Period 7/05 Through 6/06	Total	Zero Assets	Under 500	500 to 1,000	1,000 to 5,000	5,000 to 10,000	10,000 to 25,000	25,000 to 50,000	50,000 to 100,000	100,000 to 250,000	250,000 to 500,000	500,000 to 2,500,000	2,500,000 and over
Number of Enterprises 1	1783	230	955	61	360	41	73	19	20	14	7	3	0
Revenues ($ in Thousands)													
Net Sales 2	14595404	12065	760404	228902	1069492	549408	1978151	969356	1851940	2863177	2519118	1793392	0
Interest 3	100765	0	0	183	2964	1205	1430	1892	2367	12343	3466	74915	0
Rents 4	8313	0	0	0	1696	1515	616	694	795	454	2544	0	0
Royalties 5	37617	0	0	0	0	0	0	0	65	1383	0	36169	0
Other Portfolio Income 6	120362	0	0	2	20694	7390	686	1201	4887	45077	5685	34742	0
Other Receipts 7	142138	0	15	265	11112	425	3811	2610	36380	45079	34621	7813	0
Total Receipts 8	15004599	12065	760419	229352	1105958	559943	1984694	975753	1896434	2967513	2565434	1947031	0
Average Total Receipts 9	8415	52	796	3760	3072	13657	27188	51355	94822	211965	366491	649010	•
Operating Costs/Operating Income (%)													
Cost of Operations 10	78.5	56.6	74.9	73.8	73.9	77.9	82.1	83.5	79.9	73.1	76.9	86.7	•
Salaries and Wages 11	4.7	32.9	1.7	1.8	5.2	4.6	5.1	4.3	4.9	6.8	4.0	3.3	•
Taxes Paid 12	1.8	5.4	1.4	3.6	2.3	1.3	1.6	1.9	1.8	1.4	2.1	1.8	•
Interest Paid 13	2.6	0.4	3.6	0.3	1.5	0.3	1.5	1.8	1.9	2.5	2.3	6.8	•
Depreciation 14	2.7	0.4	0.2	1.0	2.7	1.8	2.0	2.1	3.2	3.4	2.7	3.4	•
Amortization and Depletion 15	0.3	•	0.0	•	0.5	0.3	0.1	0.1	0.4	0.4	0.2	0.5	•
Pensions and Other Deferred Comp. 16	0.5	0.1	0.1	0.0	0.0	0.5	0.1	0.3	1.2	0.4	0.6	0.9	•
Employee Benefits 17	1.2	0.9	0.0	3.0	2.3	1.4	1.0	1.4	0.9	1.5	0.7	1.0	•
Advertising 18	0.3	3.5	0.1	0.3	0.2	0.1	0.1	0.3	0.7	0.2	0.3	0.1	•
Other Expenses 19	8.9	21.6	14.9	7.0	14.6	7.9	5.9	12.7	8.0	10.3	8.1	4.7	•
Officers' Compensation 20	1.7	39.4	5.4	8.4	4.3	1.9	1.0	0.8	1.1	1.0	1.3	0.7	•
Operating Margin 21	•	•	•	0.8	•	2.1	•	•	•	•	0.6	•	•
Operating Margin Before Officers' Comp. 22	•	•	3.2	9.2	•	4.0	0.4	•	•	0.1	1.9	•	•

Selected Average Balance Sheet ($ in Thousands)

Net Receivables 23	1132	0	93	319	416	1878	3786	6581	10358	23170	60886	108209	·
Inventories 24	1269	0	2	127	368	2136	4223	8277	13028	32048	76278	107856	·
Net Property, Plant and Equipment 25	1839	0	19	64	451	1303	5335	11119	24981	55901	109502	130608	·
Total Assets 26	6656	0	145	558	1903	7394	16466	34622	74922	161562	371562	829728	·
Notes and Loans Payable 27	2255	0	84	300	731	1180	5830	18547	25206	50382	99515	308711	·
All Other Liabilities 28	1547	0	108	554	401	1731	3876	8536	17715	42930	64264	185003	·
Net Worth 29	2854	0	-48	-297	771	4483	6760	7538	32000	67952	207783	336014	·

Selected Financial Ratios (Times to 1)

Current Ratio 30	1.7	·	0.9	0.7	2.0	3.1	1.6	1.4	2.2	1.7	1.8	1.7	·
Quick Ratio 31	0.9	·	0.9	0.5	1.2	2.0	0.8	0.8	1.0	0.8	0.9	0.9	·
Net Sales to Working Capital 32	6.6	·	·	·	5.0	3.8	6.9	8.1	4.9	7.5	5.8	6.9	·
Coverage Ratio 33	0.9	·	·	4.4	·	12.9	0.8	·	0.1	2.1	2.1	0.8	·
Total Asset Turnover 34	1.2	·	5.5	6.7	1.6	1.8	1.6	1.5	1.2	1.3	1.0	0.7	·
Inventory Turnover 35	5.1	·	306.1	21.8	6.0	4.9	5.3	5.1	5.7	4.7	3.6	4.8	·
Receivables Turnover 36	6.3	·	8.6	12.5	6.6	5.5	7.1	6.9	10.3	8.1	4.5	4.1	·
Total Liabilities to Net Worth 37	1.3	·	·	·	1.5	0.6	1.4	3.6	1.3	1.4	0.8	1.5	·
Current Assets to Working Capital 38	2.4	·	·	·	2.0	1.5	2.6	3.3	1.8	2.5	2.3	2.5	·
Current Liabilities to Working Capital 39	1.4	·	·	·	1.0	0.5	1.6	2.3	0.8	1.5	1.3	1.5	·
Working Capital to Net Sales 40	0.2	·	·	·	0.2	0.3	0.1	0.1	0.2	0.1	0.2	0.1	·
Inventory to Working Capital 41	0.9	·	·	·	0.6	0.5	0.9	1.3	0.8	1.1	1.0	1.0	·
Total Receipts to Cash Flow 42	16.0	·	15.2	20.9	16.0	10.3	22.6	29.8	21.1	10.6	10.5	78.8	·
Cost of Goods to Cash Flow 43	12.5	·	11.4	15.4	11.8	8.1	18.6	24.9	16.9	7.8	8.1	68.4	·
Cash Flow to Total Debt 44	0.1	·	0.3	0.2	0.2	0.4	0.1	0.1	0.2	0.1	0.2	0.0	·

Selected Financial Factors (in Percentages)

Debt Ratio 45	57.1	·	132.7	153.3	59.5	39.4	58.9	78.2	57.3	57.9	44.1	59.5	·
Return on Total Assets 46	2.8	·	7.6	8.3	·	7.8	1.9	·	0.2	6.6	4.6	4.0	·
Return on Equity Before Income Taxes 47	·	·	36.3	·	11.9	·	·	·	·	8.1	4.3	·	·
Return on Equity After Income Taxes 48	·	·	36.4	·	9.4	·	·	·	·	5.2	3.2	·	·
Profit Margin (Before Income Tax) 49	·	·	·	1.0	4.0	·	·	·	·	2.7	2.5	·	·
Profit Margin (After Income Tax) 50	·	·	·	0.8	3.1	·	·	·	·	1.7	1.8	·	·

Table II

Corporations with Net Income

TEXTILE MILLS

MONEY AMOUNTS AND SIZE OF ASSETS IN THOUSANDS OF DOLLARS

Item Description for Accounting Period 7/05 Through 6/06	Total	Zero Assets	Under 500	500 to 1,000	1,000 to 5,000	5,000 to 10,000	10,000 to 25,000	25,000 to 50,000	50,000 to 100,000	100,000 to 250,000	250,000 to 500,000	500,000 to 2,500,000	2,500,000 and over
Number of Enterprises 1	619	0	272	·	179	·	46	8	8	7	·	·	0
Revenues ($ in Thousands)													
Net Sales 2	8184735	0	520752	·	740334	·	1362386	311677	703864	1594193	·	·	0
Interest 3	21290	0	0	·	2273	·	1228	1268	559	9031	·	·	0
Rents 4	6861	0	0	·	1506	·	616	260	2	453	·	·	0
Royalties 5	1044	0	0	·	0	·	0	0	0	1044	·	·	0
Other Portfolio Income 6	90807	0	0	·	5730	·	439	473	732	43623	·	·	0
Other Receipts 7	91956	0	15	·	9223	·	3170	371	3730	39962	·	·	0
Total Receipts 8	8396693	0	520767	·	759066	·	1367839	314049	708887	1688306	·	·	0
Average Total Receipts 9	13565	·	1915	·	4241	·	29736	39256	88611	241187	·	·	·
Operating Costs/Operating Income (%)													
Cost of Operations 10	75.5	·	82.6	·	70.3	·	79.9	75.8	75.7	70.1	·	·	·
Salaries and Wages 11	4.8	·	0.4	·	4.4	·	5.6	4.7	7.0	6.7	·	·	·
Taxes Paid 12	1.6	·	0.3	·	2.4	·	1.8	1.2	2.0	1.2	·	·	·
Interest Paid 13	1.6	·	4.4	·	1.0	·	1.1	0.7	0.5	1.3	·	·	·
Depreciation 14	2.3	·	0.0	·	2.3	·	1.2	2.4	2.1	2.9	·	·	·
Amortization and Depletion 15	0.2	·	0.0	·	0.6	·	0.0	0.0	0.0	0.2	·	·	·
Pensions and Other Deferred Comp. 16	0.3	·	0.1	·	0.0	·	0.1	0.2	0.7	0.3	·	·	·
Employee Benefits 17	1.1	·	0.0	·	2.7	·	0.5	0.9	0.9	1.3	·	·	·
Advertising 18	0.3	·	·	·	0.2	·	0.1	0.1	1.3	0.3	·	·	·
Other Expenses 19	8.2	·	7.1	·	13.0	·	5.7	8.2	5.3	11.3	·	·	·
Officers' Compensation 20	1.7	·	3.1	·	4.0	·	0.9	1.4	1.0	1.0	·	·	·
Operating Margin 21	2.5	·	2.0	·	·	·	3.0	4.3	3.5	3.3	·	·	·
Operating Margin Before Officers' Comp. 22	4.1	·	5.2	·	3.1	·	4.0	5.7	4.6	4.4	·	·	·

Selected Average Balance Sheet ($ in Thousands)

Net Receivables 23	1734	188	631	4648	5531	7272	18036
Inventories 24	2104	0	479	4449	7934	20241	31782
Net Property, Plant and Equipment 25	2535	1	552	3178	9011	17785	53469
Total Assets 26	9553	201	2236	15308	31384	77070	160646
Notes and Loans Payable 27	2187	14	658	4026	3939	14763	26703
All Other Liabilities 28	2155	327	533	3730	4759	9592	45312
Net Worth 29	5211	-140	1044	7553	22687	52716	88631

Selected Financial Ratios (Times to 1)

Current Ratio 30	1.9	0.6	2.3	1.9	2.5	3.0	1.6
Quick Ratio 31	1.0	0.6	1.3	1.0	1.5	1.3	0.7
Net Sales to Working Capital 32	6.0		4.6	5.3	3.1	3.5	10.3
Coverage Ratio 33	4.2	1.5	2.6	4.0	8.2	8.9	7.9
Total Asset Turnover 34	1.4	9.5	1.9	1.9	1.2	1.1	1.4
Inventory Turnover 35	4.7		6.1	5.3	3.7	3.3	5.0
Receivables Turnover 36	6.0	20.3	6.7	7.1	6.0	8.1	9.2
Total Liabilities to Net Worth 37	0.8		1.1	1.0	0.4	0.5	0.8
Current Assets to Working Capital 38	2.1		1.7	2.2	1.7	1.5	2.6
Current Liabilities to Working Capital 39	1.1		0.7	1.2	0.7	0.5	1.6
Working Capital to Net Sales 40	0.2		0.2	0.2	0.3	0.3	0.1
Inventory to Working Capital 41	0.8		0.6	0.7	0.6	0.6	1.2
Total Receipts to Cash Flow 42	8.9	11.0	9.8	12.3	7.9	12.9	6.1
Cost of Goods to Cash Flow 43	6.8	9.1	6.9	9.8	6.0	9.8	4.3
Cash Flow to Total Debt 44	0.3	0.5	0.4	0.3	0.6	0.3	0.5

Selected Financial Factors (in Percentages)

Debt Ratio 45	45.5	169.4	53.3	50.7	27.7	31.6	44.8
Return on Total Assets 46	9.2	61.0	4.7	8.7	7.1	5.3	15.0
Return on Equity Before Income Taxes 47	12.8		6.2	13.3	8.7	6.9	23.8
Return on Equity After Income Taxes 48	11.1		5.5	12.8	8.7	6.1	19.4
Profit Margin (Before Income Tax) 49	5.1	2.1	1.6	3.4	5.1	4.2	9.2
Profit Margin (After Income Tax) 50	4.4	2.0	1.4	3.3	5.1	3.7	7.5

Table I

Corporations with and without Net Income

TEXTILE PRODUCT MILLS

MONEY AMOUNTS AND SIZE OF ASSETS IN THOUSANDS OF DOLLARS

Item Description for Accounting Period 7/05 Through 6/06	Total	Zero Assets	Under 500	500 to 1,000	1,000 to 5,000	5,000 to 10,000	10,000 to 25,000	25,000 to 50,000	50,000 to 100,000	100,000 to 250,000	250,000 to 500,000	500,000 to 2,500,000	2,500,000 and over
Number of Enterprises 1	2270	452	774	450	385	14	109	49	13	13	4	7	0
Revenues ($ in Thousands)													
Net Sales 2	29667591	47181	195724	620986	1367403	189070	4322613	2666702	1641495	2869511	1623041	14123864	0
Interest 3	65836	935	5	395	829	7	3122	2280	1213	9414	1604	46033	0
Rents 4	10532	675	25	0	2159	0	1312	999	1366	2441	157	1398	0
Royalties 5	37309	434	0	0	0	0	884	0	9	128	30	35824	0
Other Portfolio Income 6	312057	31551	0	0	24884	0	26551	3003	3772	20263	27300	174732	0
Other Receipts 7	533709	47	555	0	4434	259	15906	9562	3492	32385	2966	464104	0
Total Receipts 8	30627034	80823	196309	621381	1399709	189336	4370388	2682546	1651347	2934142	1655098	14845955	0
Average Total Receipts 9	13492	179	254	1381	3636	13524	40095	54746	127027	225703	413774	2120851	•
Operating Costs/Operating Income (%)													
Cost of Operations 10	70.2	68.4	74.2	67.5	64.3	66.7	74.9	75.0	74.7	78.0	70.6	66.4	•
Salaries and Wages 11	9.6	0.6	8.8	5.3	9.4	3.9	8.2	6.3	5.9	5.1	4.8	13.0	•
Taxes Paid 12	1.9	5.1	1.4	2.0	2.8	1.4	1.6	2.1	2.1	1.5	1.7	2.0	•
Interest Paid 13	2.0	0.4	1.2	1.7	0.9	3.1	1.9	1.1	1.4	2.0	3.1	2.3	•
Depreciation 14	2.1	•	0.3	2.9	2.2	0.6	1.5	2.3	2.0	2.2	3.4	2.0	•
Amortization and Depletion 15	0.3	•	•	1.1	0.0	•	0.2	0.2	0.2	0.2	1.3	0.3	•
Pensions and Other Deferred Comp. 16	0.5	•	0.0	0.0	0.4	0.9	0.3	0.3	0.5	0.4	0.7	0.6	•
Employee Benefits 17	1.8	•	1.1	0.8	1.4	0.2	1.5	1.6	2.2	1.9	1.0	2.1	•
Advertising 18	0.8	•	0.2	0.4	0.9	0.2	0.5	0.6	0.6	0.9	2.7	0.8	•
Other Expenses 19	10.8	126.8	12.3	17.7	16.4	4.8	9.0	6.6	7.8	8.5	9.1	12.1	•
Officers' Compensation 20	1.2	7.1	2.4	4.1	2.2	13.9	1.8	1.9	0.7	0.9	1.5	0.6	•
Operating Margin 21	•	•	•	•	•	4.4	•	2.1	1.8	•	•	•	•
Operating Margin Before Officers' Comp. 22	•	•	0.5	0.5	1.2	18.2	0.3	4.0	2.5	•	1.5	•	•

Selected Average Balance Sheet ($ in Thousands)

Net Receivables 23	1452	0	18	144	401	1701	3167	6876	18681	26498	43239	228134
Inventories 24	1939	0	8	259	528	3997	4749	8861	18634	37912	64260	296367
Net Property, Plant and Equipment 25	1963	0	2	248	247	296	2855	10462	17852	30690	129099	324562
Total Assets 26	10888	0	45	852	1775	5765	16039	33553	72008	153201	364542	2250764
Notes and Loans Payable 27	4661	0	231	574	734	3332	13626	8483	22556	45384	171154	906407
All Other Liabilities 28	2436	0	21	132	290	646	5582	9444	22163	53738	70608	427565
Net Worth 29	3791	0	-207	146	751	1786	-3169	15626	27289	54080	122779	916792

Selected Financial Ratios (Times to 1)

Current Ratio 30	1.8	•	1.2	1.1	2.0	4.4	1.0	1.8	1.6	1.5	2.0	2.2
Quick Ratio 31	0.9	•	0.8	0.5	0.7	1.8	0.4	0.8	0.7	0.7	0.8	1.2
Net Sales to Working Capital 32	6.4	•	32.2	45.5	4.8	3.7	250.2	6.1	7.6	7.8	6.7	4.7
Coverage Ratio 33	1.9	•	•	2.5	2.4	2.4	0.8	3.4	1.3	1.4	1.7	2.3
Total Asset Turnover 34	1.2	•	5.6	1.6	2.0	2.3	0.8	1.6	2.8	1.4	1.7	2.3
Inventory Turnover 35	4.7	•	23.9	3.6	4.3	2.3	2.5	4.6	5.1	4.5	1.1	0.9
Receivables Turnover 36	9.9	•	7.5	7.1	8.8	5.7	6.3	8.0	7.2	7.6	8.8	11.4
Total Liabilities to Net Worth 37	1.9	•	•	4.8	1.4	2.2	•	1.1	1.6	1.8	2.0	1.5
Current Assets to Working Capital 38	2.3	•	5.5	15.6	2.0	1.3	71.5	2.2	2.6	2.8	2.0	1.8
Current Liabilities to Working Capital 39	1.3	•	4.5	14.6	1.0	0.3	70.5	1.2	1.6	1.8	1.0	0.8
Working Capital to Net Sales 40	0.2	•	0.0	0.0	0.2	0.3	0.0	0.2	0.1	0.1	0.1	0.2
Inventory to Working Capital 41	1.0	•	1.8	8.7	0.7	0.7	34.6	1.1	1.1	1.4	0.9	0.7
Total Receipts to Cash Flow 42	10.1	16.9	12.3	10.4	7.3	12.3	14.7	13.0	11.8	16.1	10.4	8.3
Cost of Goods to Cash Flow 43	7.1	11.6	9.1	7.0	4.7	8.2	11.0	9.7	8.8	12.6	7.4	5.5
Cash Flow to Total Debt 44	0.2	0.1	0.1	0.2	0.5	0.3	0.1	0.2	0.2	0.1	0.2	0.2

Selected Financial Factors (in Percentages)

Debt Ratio 45	65.2	•	557.9	82.9	57.7	69.0	119.8	53.4	62.1	64.7	66.3	59.3
Return on Total Assets 46	4.7	•	•	•	4.5	17.9	3.6	6.2	7.1	3.8	5.8	4.9
Return on Equity Before Income Taxes 47	6.6	1.9	•	•	6.5	34.0	5.0	9.4	12.1	2.5	7.0	6.8
Return on Equity After Income Taxes 48	3.8	2.2	•	4.0	33.2	9.1	8.5	11.0	12.1	2.5	5.5	3.9
Profit Margin (Before Income Tax) 49	1.9	•	•	1.4	4.5	2.7	0.6	2.6	•	0.1	2.1	3.1
Profit Margin (After Income Tax) 50	1.1	•	•	0.8	4.4	2.4	0.0	2.4	•	0.1	1.6	1.8

Table II

Corporations with Net Income

TEXTILE PRODUCT MILLS

MONEY AMOUNTS AND SIZE OF ASSETS IN THOUSANDS OF DOLLARS

Item Description for Accounting Period 7/05 Through 6/06	Total	Zero Assets	Under 500	500 to 1,000	1,000 to 5,000	5,000 to 10,000	10,000 to 25,000	25,000 to 50,000	50,000 to 100,000	100,000 to 250,000	250,000 to 500,000	500,000 to 2,500,000	2,500,000 and over
Number of Enterprises 1	738	0	66	·	283	·	72	32	8	·	0	3	0

Revenues ($ in Thousands)

Net Sales 2	17227126	0	195724	·	914347	·	2225799	1956854	947014	·	0	7284573	0
Interest 3	16569	0	5	·	555	·	2066	743	1070	·	0	3726	0
Rents 4	6167	0	25	·	2137	·	0	460	1366	·	0	294	0
Royalties 5	23738	0	0	·	0	·	0	0	9	·	0	23571	0
Other Portfolio Income 6	228344	0	0	·	24866	·	2644	1051	3768	·	0	153992	0
Other Receipts 7	460798	0	555	·	3555	·	8434	5024	1335	·	0	412960	0
Total Receipts 8	17962742	0	196309	·	945460	·	2238943	1964132	954562	·	0	7879116	0
Average Total Receipts 9	24340	·	2974	·	3341	·	31096	61379	119320	·	·	2626372	·

Operating Costs/Operating Income (%)

Cost of Operations 10	67.2	·	74.2	·	62.5	·	74.1	73.0	72.6	·	·	61.0	·
Salaries and Wages 11	10.7	·	8.8	·	9.7	·	6.1	6.2	6.0	·	·	17.1	·
Taxes Paid 12	1.8	·	1.2	·	2.5	·	1.3	2.2	2.0	·	·	2.0	·
Interest Paid 13	1.2	·	1.2	·	0.7	·	0.7	0.7	0.9	·	·	1.7	·
Depreciation 14	1.6	·	0.3	·	2.4	·	1.3	1.7	1.7	·	·	1.4	·
Amortization and Depletion 15	0.2	·	·	·	0.0	·	0.0	0.2	0.2	·	·	0.3	·
Pensions and Other Deferred Comp. 16	0.5	·	0.0	·	0.1	·	0.4	0.4	0.6	·	·	0.5	·
Employee Benefits 17	1.5	·	1.1	·	0.9	·	1.1	1.6	2.2	·	·	1.7	·
Advertising 18	1.0	·	0.2	·	0.8	·	0.2	0.4	0.8	·	·	0.9	·
Other Expenses 19	10.7	·	9.1	·	18.2	·	7.7	5.4	5.8	·	·	13.4	·
Officers' Compensation 20	1.5	·	2.4	·	1.8	·	2.7	2.1	0.9	·	·	0.6	·
Operating Margin 21	2.1	·	1.6	·	0.3	·	4.4	6.2	6.4	·	·	·	·
Operating Margin Before Officers' Comp. 22	3.6	·	3.9	·	2.1	·	7.1	8.3	7.3	·	·	·	·

Selected Average Balance Sheet ($ in Thousands)

Net Receivables 23	1663	214	368	2975	7424	16595	39260
Inventories 24	3713	166	444	4486	10169	18904	401344
Net Property, Plant and Equipment 25	3204	18	183	2784	8215	14685	377425
Total Assets 26	18977	430	1660	15056	33472	73939	2761268
Notes and Loans Payable 27	7285	299	596	2518	6120	12473	1315605
All Other Liabilities 28	3706	226	266	4683	7793	19632	427892
Net Worth 29	7986	-96	798	7855	19559	41833	1017771

Selected Financial Ratios (Times to 1)

Current Ratio 30	1.8	1.0	2.0	2.3	2.6	2.0	1.4
Quick Ratio 31	0.6	0.6	0.7	1.0	1.2	1.0	0.2
Net Sales to Working Capital 32	7.5	287.0	4.5	5.0	4.4	5.2	16.1
Coverage Ratio 33	6.4	2.6	6.1	8.5	10.1	9.6	6.0
Total Asset Turnover 34	1.2	6.9	1.9	2.1	1.8	1.6	0.9
Inventory Turnover 35	4.2	13.2	4.5	5.1	4.4	4.5	3.7
Receivables Turnover 36	13.2	27.7	7.6	10.4	8.0	7.3	123.7
Total Liabilities to Net Worth 37	1.4		1.1	0.9	0.7	0.8	1.7
Current Assets to Working Capital 38	2.2	39.5	2.0	1.7	1.6	2.0	3.5
Current Liabilities to Working Capital 39	1.2	38.5	1.0	0.7	0.6	1.0	2.5
Working Capital to Net Sales 40	0.1	0.0	0.2	0.2	0.2	0.2	0.1
Inventory to Working Capital 41	1.3	16.1	0.6	0.8	0.8	0.8	2.7
Total Receipts to Cash Flow 42	6.8	11.9	5.9	9.2	9.6	8.8	5.5
Cost of Goods to Cash Flow 43	4.6	8.9	3.7	6.8	7.0	6.4	3.3
Cash Flow to Total Debt 44	0.3	0.5	0.6	0.5	0.5	0.4	0.3

Selected Financial Factors (in Percentages)

Debt Ratio 45	57.9	122.4	51.9	47.8	41.6	43.4	63.1
Return on Total Assets 46	9.8	20.8	8.7	11.6	13.3	13.4	8.7
Return on Equity Before Income Taxes 47	19.7		15.1	19.6	20.5	21.3	19.7
Return on Equity After Income Taxes 48	15.6		12.0	17.1	19.5	20.1	13.6
Profit Margin (Before Income Tax) 49	6.7	1.9	3.7	5.0	6.6	7.5	8.2
Profit Margin (After Income Tax) 50	5.3	1.6	3.0	4.3	6.2	7.1	5.7

Table I

Corporations with and without Net Income

APPAREL KNITTING MILLS

MONEY AMOUNTS AND SIZE OF ASSETS IN THOUSANDS OF DOLLARS

Item Description for Accounting Period 7/05 Through 6/06	Total	Zero Assets	Under 500	500 to 1,000	1,000 to 5,000	5,000 to 10,000	10,000 to 25,000	25,000 to 50,000	50,000 to 100,000	100,000 to 250,000	250,000 to 500,000	500,000 to 2,500,000	2,500,000 and over
Number of Enterprises **1**	375	246	0	0	70	17	21	9	4	6	0	0	0
Revenues ($ in Thousands)													
Net Sales **2**	3570108	0	0	0	316974	364939	524020	766671	357928	1239576	0	0	0
Interest **3**	9701	0	0	0	798	412	1447	38	278	6728	0	0	0
Rents **4**	344	0	0	0	1	0	15	97	9	222	0	0	0
Royalties **5**	10484	0	0	0	0	0	0	0	10083	401	0	0	0
Other Portfolio Income **6**	4277	0	0	0	138	0	223	168	3154	595	0	0	0
Other Receipts **7**	13294	0	0	0	2370	795	2646	1839	448	5196	0	0	0
Total Receipts **8**	3608208	0	0	0	320281	366146	528351	768813	371900	1252718	0	0	0
Average Total Receipts **9**	9622	0	•	•	4575	21538	25160	85424	92975	208786	•	•	•
Operating Costs/Operating Income (%)													
Cost of Operations **10**	76.7	•	•	•	75.1	75.3	79.4	84.7	79.6	70.5	•	•	•
Salaries and Wages **11**	5.3	•	•	•	3.3	5.6	5.5	3.9	6.1	6.1	•	•	•
Taxes Paid **12**	2.0	•	•	•	4.6	1.8	2.1	2.2	1.5	1.3	•	•	•
Interest Paid **13**	1.8	•	•	•	1.0	1.0	1.1	1.2	1.0	3.1	•	•	•
Depreciation **14**	1.3	•	•	•	0.4	1.4	0.8	1.1	2.2	1.7	•	•	•
Amortization and Depletion **15**	0.4	•	•	•	0.1	0.0	0.0	0.1	0.2	1.1	•	•	•
Pensions and Other Deferred Comp. **16**	0.2	•	•	•	0.0	0.1	0.1	0.3	0.1	0.2	•	•	•
Employee Benefits **17**	0.8	•	•	•	0.8	1.0	2.1	0.7	0.3	0.5	•	•	•
Advertising **18**	1.5	•	•	•	1.1	0.0	0.4	0.2	1.5	3.2	•	•	•
Other Expenses **19**	6.2	•	•	•	9.8	8.1	4.3	3.0	8.5	6.9	•	•	•
Officers' Compensation **20**	2.0	•	•	•	5.3	5.2	2.8	1.1	1.0	0.8	•	•	•
Operating Margin **21**	1.8	•	•	•	•	0.4	1.4	1.7	•	4.5	•	•	•
Operating Margin Before Officers' Comp. **22**	3.9	•	•	•	3.9	5.7	4.2	2.7	•	5.3	•	•	•

Selected Average Balance Sheet ($ in Thousands)

Net Receivables 23	1124	0	•	596	333	3751	8411	13121	27881
Inventories 24	1819	0	•	672	2779	5191	13248	22515	44684
Net Property, Plant and Equipment 25	944	0	•	364	1107	1516	4880	18142	26876
Total Assets 26	5989	0	•	2513	6755	14861	39510	69416	168304
Notes and Loans Payable 27	1877	0	•	429	1182	3927	10485	11651	71739
All Other Liabilities 28	1140	0	•	648	2555	2324	10329	9854	26266
Net Worth 29	2972	0	•	1436	3018	8610	18695	47910	70300

Selected Financial Ratios (Times to 1)

Current Ratio 30	1.9	•	•	2.5	2.1	2.3	2.0	2.2	1.6
Quick Ratio 31	0.8	•	•	1.3	0.2	1.2	0.9	1.1	0.6
Net Sales to Working Capital 32	5.6	•	•	5.4	7.5	4.4	5.3	4.6	6.8
Coverage Ratio 33	2.7	•	•	0.6	1.7	2.9	2.7	2.8	2.9
Total Asset Turnover 34	1.6	•	•	1.8	3.2	1.7	2.2	1.3	1.2
Inventory Turnover 35	4.0	•	•	5.1	5.8	3.8	5.4	3.2	3.3
Receivables Turnover 36	8.3	•	•	15.2	128.8	5.5	10.2	5.5	8.3
Total Liabilities to Net Worth 37	1.0	•	•	0.8	1.2	0.7	1.1	0.4	1.4
Current Assets to Working Capital 38	2.1	•	•	1.7	1.9	1.8	2.0	1.8	2.7
Current Liabilities to Working Capital 39	1.1	•	•	0.7	0.9	0.8	1.0	0.8	1.7
Working Capital to Net Sales 40	0.2	•	•	0.2	0.1	0.2	0.2	0.2	0.1
Inventory to Working Capital 41	1.1	•	•	0.8	1.0	0.7	1.0	0.8	1.6
Total Receipts to Cash Flow 42	13.3	•	•	12.7	17.7	20.0	25.3	12.6	9.0
Cost of Goods to Cash Flow 43	10.2	•	•	9.6	13.3	15.9	21.4	10.0	6.3
Cash Flow to Total Debt 44	0.2	•	•	0.3	0.3	0.2	0.2	0.3	0.2

Selected Financial Factors (in Percentages)

Debt Ratio 45	50.4	•	•	42.9	55.3	42.1	52.7	31.0	58.2
Return on Total Assets 46	7.5	•	•	1.1	5.6	5.5	6.7	3.5	10.9
Return on Equity Before Income Taxes 47	9.5	•	•	•	5.3	6.3	9.0	3.3	17.0
Return on Equity After Income Taxes 48	6.8	•	•	•	5.3	5.9	8.6	1.8	11.5
Profit Margin (Before Income Tax) 49	3.0	•	•	0.7	0.7	2.2	2.0	1.8	5.8
Profit Margin (After Income Tax) 50	2.1	•	•	0.7	•	2.0	1.9	0.9	3.9

Table II

Corporations with Net Income

APPAREL KNITTING MILLS

Money Amounts and Size of Assets in Thousands of Dollars

Item Description for Accounting Period 7/05 Through 6/06	Total	Zero Assets	Under 500	500 to 1,000	1,000 to 5,000	5,000 to 10,000	10,000 to 25,000	25,000 to 50,000	50,000 to 100,000	100,000 to 250,000	250,000 to 500,000	500,000 to 2,500,000	2,500,000 and over
Number of Enterprises 1	63	0	0	0	21	5	•	•	•	•	0	0	0
Revenues ($ in Thousands)													
Net Sales 2	2722015	0	0	0	65507	189092	•	•	•	•	0	0	0
Interest 3	9691	0	0	0	798	412	•	•	•	•	0	0	0
Rents 4	340	0	0	0	1	0	•	•	•	•	0	0	0
Royalties 5	10484	0	0	0	0	0	•	•	•	•	0	0	0
Other Portfolio Income 6	4189	0	0	0	138	0	•	•	•	•	0	0	0
Other Receipts 7	10178	0	0	0	0	676	•	•	•	•	0	0	0
Total Receipts 8	2756897	0	0	0	66444	190180	•	•	•	•	0	0	0
Average Total Receipts 9	43760	•	•	•	3164	38036	•	•	•	•	•	•	•
Operating Costs/Operating Income (%)													
Cost of Operations 10	74.3	•	•	•	64.3	68.7	•	•	•	•	•	•	•
Salaries and Wages 11	5.7	•	•	•	1.3	6.1	•	•	•	•	•	•	•
Taxes Paid 12	1.7	•	•	•	5.2	0.8	•	•	•	•	•	•	•
Interest Paid 13	1.7	•	•	•	0.6	0.3	•	•	•	•	•	•	•
Depreciation 14	1.4	•	•	•	0.7	0.0	•	•	•	•	•	•	•
Amortization and Depletion 15	0.4	•	•	•	•	•	•	•	•	•	•	•	•
Pensions and Other Deferred Comp. 16	0.2	•	•	•	0.1	0.1	•	•	•	•	•	•	•
Employee Benefits 17	0.8	•	•	•	0.5	0.3	•	•	•	•	•	•	•
Advertising 18	1.9	•	•	•	4.0	0.0	•	•	•	•	•	•	•
Other Expenses 19	5.5	•	•	•	6.7	5.6	•	•	•	•	•	•	•
Officers' Compensation 20	2.0	•	•	•	3.3	8.8	•	•	•	•	•	•	•
Operating Margin 21	4.5	•	•	•	13.6	9.2	•	•	•	•	•	•	•
Operating Margin Before Officers' Comp. 22	6.5	•	•	•	16.9	18.0	•	•	•	•	•	•	•

Selected Average Balance Sheet ($ in Thousands)

Net Receivables 23	5083	447	110
Inventories 24	8182	723	1695
Net Property, Plant and Equipment 25	4335	139	23
Total Assets 26	27726	2568	9173
Notes and Loans Payable 27	8113	36	0
All Other Liabilities 28	4741	598	2317
Net Worth 29	14871	1934	6856

Selected Financial Ratios (Times to 1)

Current Ratio 30	1.9	1.1	3.9
Quick Ratio 31	0.8	0.9	0.1
Net Sales to Working Capital 32	5.6	39.4	5.6
Coverage Ratio 33	4.4	28.2	35.2
Total Asset Turnover 34	1.6	1.2	4.1
Inventory Turnover 35	3.9	2.8	15.3
Receivables Turnover 36	8.4	3.4	685.1
Total Liabilities to Net Worth 37	0.9	0.3	0.3
Current Assets to Working Capital 38	2.1	8.8	1.3
Current Liabilities to Working Capital 39	1.1	7.8	0.3
Working Capital to Net Sales 40	0.2	0.0	0.2
Inventory to Working Capital 41	1.0	1.4	0.2
Total Receipts to Cash Flow 42	10.2	5.6	6.7
Cost of Goods to Cash Flow 43	7.6	3.6	4.6
Cash Flow to Total Debt 44	0.3	0.9	2.4

Selected Financial Factors (in Percentages)

Debt Ratio 45	46.4	24.7	25.3
Return on Total Assets 46	11.7	18.9	41.6
Return on Equity Before Income Taxes 47	16.9	24.2	54.0
Return on Equity After Income Taxes 48	13.6	16.2	54.0
Profit Margin (Before Income Tax) 49	5.8	15.0	9.8
Profit Margin (After Income Tax) 50	4.7	10.0	9.8

Table I

Corporations with and without Net Income

CUT AND SEW APPAREL CONTRACTORS AND MFRS.

MONEY AMOUNTS AND SIZE OF ASSETS IN THOUSANDS OF DOLLARS

Item Description for Accounting Period 7/05 Through 6/06		Total	Zero Assets	Under 500	500 to 1,000	1,000 to 5,000	5,000 to 10,000	10,000 to 25,000	25,000 to 50,000	50,000 to 100,000	100,000 to 250,000	250,000 to 500,000	500,000 to 2,500,000	2,500,000 and over
Number of Enterprises	1	6725	1204	4090	203	841	188	113	42	16	13	6	5	4
Revenues ($ in Thousands)														
Net Sales	2	45309535	356523	1650726	232253	4547485	2838357	4847840	2841997	1855018	2639331	2281018	5236277	15982711
Interest	3	226613	612	35	0	4152	202	2211	1293	621	9237	93	59676	148480
Rents	4	27648	252	0	0	141	0	615	1852	0	459	160	2854	21314
Royalties	5	954079	228	0	0	940	0	16067	258	0	795	1834	238784	695175
Other Portfolio Income	6	486379	13966	0	0	690	655	36726	1102	3110	2193	3545	61823	362569
Other Receipts	7	909418	9479	6846	14	11855	8108	68396	26738	25461	39618	45961	151966	514975
Total Receipts	8	47913672	381060	1657607	232267	4565263	2847322	4971855	2873240	1884210	2691633	2332611	5751380	17725224
Average Total Receipts	9	7125	316	405	1144	5428	15145	43999	68410	117763	207049	388768	1150276	4431306
Operating Costs/Operating Income (%)														
Cost of Operations	10	64.5	56.3	36.7	58.8	69.4	66.5	74.2	66.1	71.7	68.3	60.8	66.9	60.9
Salaries and Wages	11	9.5	18.4	12.6	9.7	6.6	11.9	6.9	8.9	8.8	10.4	9.5	8.5	10.5
Taxes Paid	12	2.0	4.7	3.4	2.1	1.1	2.6	2.4	2.2	2.1	1.5	1.6	3.4	1.4
Interest Paid	13	2.4	2.2	0.4	2.3	1.0	1.0	1.1	1.0	1.0	3.1	1.0	2.9	3.9
Depreciation	14	0.9	1.2	1.2	2.2	0.5	1.2	0.4	0.6	1.1	1.1	1.2	1.3	1.0
Amortization and Depletion	15	0.5	0.1	0.0	0.0	0.2	0.0	0.1	0.4	0.1	0.5	0.2	0.8	0.8
Pensions and Other Deferred Comp.	16	0.6	0.0	0.0	•	0.4	0.1	0.3	0.4	0.3	0.3	0.8	0.3	1.1
Employee Benefits	17	1.0	1.6	0.9	0.6	0.5	0.5	0.6	0.7	1.3	1.1	1.2	1.5	1.3
Advertising	18	2.5	0.6	0.5	1.1	1.1	2.1	0.8	1.6	1.4	1.4	3.7	3.2	3.8
Other Expenses	19	14.2	25.0	43.8	13.7	11.3	12.2	7.5	9.5	7.8	7.8	10.5	15.5	16.9
Officers' Compensation	20	2.3	6.4	5.0	2.4	3.4	2.6	4.1	3.5	1.9	1.6	1.8	1.2	1.3
Operating Margin	21	•	•	•	7.0	4.4	•	1.7	5.1	2.5	2.8	7.8	•	•
Operating Margin Before Officers' Comp.	22	1.9	•	•	9.3	7.8	1.8	5.8	8.6	4.3	4.5	9.6	•	•

Selected Average Balance Sheet ($ in Thousands)

Net Receivables 23	948	0	14	146	398	1247	4556	6383	14606	27113	92398	163542	744235
Inventories 24	964	0	24	338	622	2094	4978	13092	29546	31580	70986	179216	520920
Net Property, Plant and Equipment 25	470	0	15	236	174	1561	1291	3094	8952	16144	35628	102593	314382
Total Assets 26	5276	0	95	701	2114	6779	15756	32567	72626	148315	355340	907749	4747331
Notes and Loans Payable 27	1269	0	50	253	770	1638	4399	8078	14656	56734	42568	192745	1074210
All Other Liabilities 28	1705	0	36	306	458	2203	5782	8119	9755	28747	112401	294174	1697281
Net Worth 29	2302	0	9	142	886	2938	5575	16369	48215	62834	200371	420831	1975840

Selected Financial Ratios (Times to 1)

Current Ratio 30	1.5	•	1.3	0.7	2.2	1.9	1.6	2.3	3.7	2.3	2.1	1.9	1.1
Quick Ratio 31	0.8	•	0.6	0.5	0.9	0.8	0.7	0.9	1.4	1.1	1.2	0.9	0.6
Net Sales to Working Capital 32	8.2	•	35.5	•	6.9	6.4	9.0	4.6	3.2	4.5	3.9	4.9	38.2
Coverage Ratio 33	3.4	•	•	4.0	5.6	0.5	5.0	7.3	4.8	2.6	10.8	2.6	3.2
Total Asset Turnover 34	1.3	•	4.2	1.6	2.6	2.2	2.7	2.1	1.6	1.4	1.1	1.2	0.8
Inventory Turnover 35	4.5	•	6.2	2.0	6.0	4.8	6.4	3.4	2.8	4.4	3.3	3.9	4.7
Receivables Turnover 36	7.3	•	48.0	2.6	14.1	13.4	11.0	9.7	6.5	6.6	4.9	6.6	5.6
Total Liabilities to Net Worth 37	1.3	•	9.4	3.9	1.4	1.3	1.8	1.0	0.5	1.4	0.8	1.2	1.4
Current Assets to Working Capital 38	2.9	•	4.6	•	1.8	2.1	2.6	1.8	1.4	1.8	1.9	2.1	1.4
Current Liabilities to Working Capital 39	1.9	•	3.6	•	0.8	1.1	1.6	0.8	0.4	0.8	0.9	1.1	13.7
Working Capital to Net Sales 40	0.1	•	0.0	•	0.1	0.2	0.1	0.2	0.3	0.2	0.3	0.2	12.7
Inventory to Working Capital 41	1.2	•	1.8	•	1.0	1.0	1.0	0.9	0.7	0.7	0.3	0.2	0.0
Total Receipts to Cash Flow 42	6.0	17.3	3.0	6.7	7.3	10.3	10.8	7.4	10.2	10.6	5.2	6.2	5.0
Cost of Goods to Cash Flow 43	3.9	9.7	1.1	4.0	5.1	6.9	8.0	4.9	7.3	7.2	3.2	4.2	2.8
Cash Flow to Total Debt 44	0.4	•	1.6	0.3	0.6	0.4	0.6	0.8	0.5	0.2	0.5	0.3	0.3

Selected Financial Factors (in Percentages)

Debt Ratio 45	56.4	•	90.4	79.7	58.1	56.7	64.6	49.7	33.6	57.6	43.6	53.6	58.4
Return on Total Assets 46	10.3	•	•	15.1	14.9	1.2	14.8	8.0	10.9	11.9	8.5	•	10.7
Return on Equity Before Income Taxes 47	16.6	•	56.0	29.2	•	32.9	25.4	9.6	15.9	19.1	11.2	•	17.7
Return on Equity After Income Taxes 48	12.9	•	55.7	28.8	•	30.2	23.8	8.4	13.5	18.2	11.2	•	17.7
Profit Margin (Before Income Tax) 49	5.7	•	7.0	4.8	•	4.3	6.1	4.0	4.9	10.1	8.4	•	12.1
Profit Margin (After Income Tax) 50	4.4	•	6.9	4.7	•	3.9	5.7	3.5	4.2	9.6	4.5	•	8.7

Table II

Corporations with Net Income

CUT AND SEW APPAREL CONTRACTORS AND MFRS.

MONEY AMOUNTS AND SIZE OF ASSETS IN THOUSANDS OF DOLLARS

Item Description for Accounting Period 7/05 Through 6/06	Total	Zero Assets	Under 500	500 to 1,000	1,000 to 5,000	5,000 to 10,000	10,000 to 25,000	25,000 to 50,000	50,000 to 100,000	100,000 to 250,000	250,000 to 500,000	500,000 to 2,500,000	2,500,000 and over
Number of Enterprises 1	3703	474	2042	203	704	120	91	34	•	9	6	5	•
Revenues ($ in Thousands)													
Net Sales 2	39068719	150923	1068971	232253	4360689	1987252	3931167	2541105	•	2240881	2281018	5236277	•
Interest 3	113882	2	35	0	4117	202	1823	1249	•	9013	93	59676	•
Rents 4	26010	144	0	0	0	0	615	1852	•	431	160	2854	•
Royalties 5	786594	111	0	0	0	0	16067	163	•	535	1834	238784	•
Other Portfolio Income 6	437833	1423	0	0	690	127	36682	1094	•	868	3545	61823	•
Other Receipts 7	851494	-1	505	14	17323	2345	64916	27259	•	15445	45961	151966	•
Total Receipts 8	41284532	152602	1069511	232267	4382819	1989926	4051270	2572722	•	2267173	2332611	5751380	•
Average Total Receipts 9	11149	322	524	1144	6226	16583	44519	75668	•	251908	388768	1150276	•
Operating Costs/Operating Income (%)													
Cost of Operations 10	63.8	55.5	18.1	58.8	69.1	68.1	72.7	65.5	•	65.6	60.8	66.9	•
Salaries and Wages 11	9.2	0.9	14.0	9.7	6.8	9.9	6.5	9.0	•	9.5	9.5	8.5	•
Taxes Paid 12	2.0	7.0	2.1	2.1	1.1	3.0	2.8	2.2	•	1.7	1.6	3.4	•
Interest Paid 13	1.4	0.0	0.5	2.3	0.8	0.6	0.9	0.8	•	3.3	1.0	2.9	•
Depreciation 14	0.9	0.6	0.8	2.2	0.4	1.5	0.4	0.5	•	1.2	1.2	1.3	•
Amortization and Depletion 15	0.5	•	0.0	0.0	0.2	0.0	0.1	0.2	•	0.5	0.2	0.8	•
Pensions and Other Deferred Comp. 16	0.5	0.0	•	•	0.4	0.1	0.4	0.4	•	0.3	0.8	0.3	•
Employee Benefits 17	1.1	2.3	0.6	0.6	0.5	0.3	0.5	0.7	•	1.3	1.2	1.5	•
Advertising 18	2.4	0.1	0.8	1.1	1.1	2.5	0.9	1.3	•	1.6	3.7	3.2	•
Other Expenses 19	14.1	9.5	57.0	13.7	11.3	9.3	6.6	9.3	•	8.0	10.5	15.5	•
Officers' Compensation 20	2.2	9.7	2.9	2.4	3.3	1.9	4.7	3.7	•	1.8	1.8	1.2	•
Operating Margin 21	2.0	14.5	3.1	7.0	4.9	2.9	3.5	6.3	•	5.2	7.8	•	•
Operating Margin Before Officers' Comp. 22	4.2	24.2	6.0	9.3	8.3	4.7	8.2	10.0	•	7.0	9.6	•	•

Selected Average Balance Sheet ($ in Thousands)

Net Receivables 23	1499	0	19	146	463	1395	4560	6434	31667	92398	163542	•
Inventories 24	1433	0	34	209	626	2135	4588	13200	34465	64809	192568	•
Net Property, Plant and Equipment 25	725	0	13	236	191	2061	1344	3127	20780	35628	102593	•
Total Assets 26	7296	0	91	701	2287	7166	15609	31786	156651	355340	907749	•
Notes and Loans Payable 27	1399	0	30	253	644	1274	3941	6123	70184	42568	192745	•
All Other Liabilities 28	1960	0	21	306	523	2345	5071	8447	23089	112401	294174	•
Net Worth 29	3937	0	41	142	1119	3547	6597	17216	63378	200371	420831	•

Selected Financial Ratios (Times to 1)

Current Ratio 30	2.0	•	2.9	0.7	2.1	2.1	1.7	2.3	2.4	2.1	1.9	•
Quick Ratio 31	1.0	•	1.5	0.5	0.9	1.1	0.8	0.9	1.2	1.2	0.9	•
Net Sales to Working Capital 32	5.8	•	11.5	•	7.7	6.5	8.6	4.9	5.0	3.9	4.9	•
Coverage Ratio 33	6.6	7867.7	7.5	4.0	8.3	5.7	8.0	10.1	2.9	10.8	2.6	•
Total Asset Turnover 34	1.4	•	5.7	1.6	2.7	2.3	2.8	2.4	1.6	1.1	1.2	•
Inventory Turnover 35	4.7	•	2.8	3.2	6.8	5.3	6.8	3.7	4.7	3.6	3.6	•
Receivables Turnover 36	7.4	•	43.4	2.7	14.8	14.2	11.2	11.0	15.7	8.2	12.8	•
Total Liabilities to Net Worth 37	0.9	•	1.2	3.9	1.0	1.0	1.4	0.8	1.5	0.8	1.2	•
Current Assets to Working Capital 38	2.0	•	1.5	•	1.9	1.9	2.5	1.7	1.7	1.9	2.1	•
Current Liabilities to Working Capital 39	1.0	•	0.5	•	0.9	0.9	1.5	0.7	0.7	0.9	1.1	•
Working Capital to Net Sales 40	0.2	•	0.1	•	0.1	0.2	0.1	0.2	0.2	0.3	0.2	•
Inventory to Working Capital 41	0.8	•	0.6	•	1.0	0.8	0.9	0.9	0.7	0.7	0.9	•
Total Receipts to Cash Flow 42	5.3	4.4	1.8	6.7	6.9	9.2	9.6	6.8	9.2	5.2	6.2	•
Cost of Goods to Cash Flow 43	3.4	2.5	0.3	4.0	4.8	6.3	7.0	4.4	6.0	3.2	4.2	•
Cash Flow to Total Debt 44	0.6	•	5.7	0.3	0.8	0.5	0.5	0.8	0.3	0.5	0.3	•

Selected Financial Factors (in Percentages)

Debt Ratio 45	46.0	•	55.5	79.7	51.1	50.5	57.7	45.8	59.5	43.6	53.6	•
Return on Total Assets 46	13.3	•	20.7	15.1	16.8	8.5	20.7	19.6	15.2	11.9	8.5	•
Return on Equity Before Income Taxes 47	20.9	•	40.4	56.0	30.2	14.1	42.9	32.6	24.9	19.1	11.2	•
Return on Equity After Income Taxes 48	17.0	•	39.0	55.7	29.8	13.7	40.1	30.7	21.4	18.2	8.4	•
Profit Margin (Before Income Tax) 49	7.8	15.6	3.1	7.0	5.5	3.0	6.6	7.5	6.3	10.1	4.5	•
Profit Margin (After Income Tax) 50	6.3	15.6	3.0	6.9	5.4	2.9	6.1	7.1	5.4	9.6	3.4	•

66

Table I

Corporations with and without Net Income

APPAREL ACCESSORIES AND OTHER APPAREL

MONEY AMOUNTS AND SIZE OF ASSETS IN THOUSANDS OF DOLLARS

Item Description for Accounting Period 7/05 Through 6/06	Total	Zero Assets	Under 500	500 to 1,000	1,000 to 5,000	5,000 to 10,000	10,000 to 25,000	25,000 to 50,000	50,000 to 100,000	100,000 to 250,000	250,000 to 500,000	500,000 to 2,500,000	2,500,000 and over
Number of Enterprises 1	2754	274	1303	639	430	24	50	17	12	5	0	0	0

Revenues ($ in Thousands)

	Total	Zero Assets	Under 500	500 to 1,000	1,000 to 5,000	5,000 to 10,000	10,000 to 25,000	25,000 to 50,000	50,000 to 100,000	100,000 to 250,000	250,000 to 500,000	500,000 to 2,500,000	2,500,000 and over
Net Sales 2	10068691	252119	597636	1105944	2764756	486025	1278219	1143722	1029494	1410777	0	0	0
Interest 3	12848	0	0	595	1054	16	852	1111	7093	2127	0	0	0
Rents 4	851	0	0	0	256	0	259	2	288	47	0	0	0
Royalties 5	16501	0	0	0	0	0	0	0	2321	14180	0	0	0
Other Portfolio Income 6	27623	1829	4	0	12263	2	8497	688	3220	1120	0	0	0
Other Receipts 7	145095	0	-1	18715	21329	1216	48187	3782	25489	26376	0	0	0
Total Receipts 8	10271609	253948	597639	1125254	2799658	487259	1336014	1149305	1067905	1454627	0	0	0
Average Total Receipts 9	3730	927	459	1761	6511	20302	26720	67606	88992	290925	•	•	•

Operating Costs/Operating Income (%)

	Total	Zero Assets	Under 500	500 to 1,000	1,000 to 5,000	5,000 to 10,000	10,000 to 25,000	25,000 to 50,000	50,000 to 100,000	100,000 to 250,000	250,000 to 500,000	500,000 to 2,500,000	2,500,000 and over
Cost of Operations 10	66.1	35.2	72.1	67.0	69.7	67.2	67.6	71.4	65.1	56.4	•	•	•
Salaries and Wages 11	9.3	10.6	8.6	6.5	10.8	6.7	10.7	6.7	10.1	9.8	•	•	•
Taxes Paid 12	2.5	1.0	0.8	2.4	1.6	1.9	2.4	2.3	1.9	6.4	•	•	•
Interest Paid 13	1.2	0.0	0.4	0.6	0.7	0.9	1.2	1.5	2.6	2.3	•	•	•
Depreciation 14	0.9	3.7	0.3	0.9	0.7	0.5	0.8	1.0	1.2	0.9	•	•	•
Amortization and Depletion 15	0.2	•	0.0	0.1	0.0	0.0	0.1	0.0	0.8	0.9	•	•	•
Pensions and Other Deferred Comp. 16	0.3	•	0.5	0.9	0.1	0.1	0.4	0.1	0.3	0.1	•	•	•
Employee Benefits 17	1.1	5.1	0.0	1.1	0.8	1.0	1.1	1.0	1.2	1.5	•	•	•
Advertising 18	1.4	•	0.2	0.9	0.7	0.6	1.5	0.9	2.4	4.1	•	•	•
Other Expenses 19	12.3	42.6	5.3	16.4	10.6	9.5	10.5	11.2	15.1	11.6	•	•	•
Officers' Compensation 20	2.3	0.0	3.4	7.0	1.1	2.8	2.3	1.9	2.4	1.0	•	•	•
Operating Margin 21	2.3	1.7	8.3	•	3.3	8.8	1.3	2.2	•	5.2	•	•	•
Operating Margin Before Officers' Comp. 22	4.6	1.7	11.7	3.1	4.4	11.6	3.7	4.0	•	6.2	•	•	•

Selected Average Balance Sheet ($ in Thousands)

Net Receivables 23	428	0	45	186	530	2058	4620	7628	15610	35351
Inventories 24	605	0	39	261	989	2325	5102	12980	21538	39187
Net Property, Plant and Equipment 25	178	0	15	34	252	607	1518	4066	7032	19204
Total Assets 26	1796	0	92	731	2675	6266	15834	34415	71601	164546
Notes and Loans Payable 27	656	0	47	170	569	2332	4841	10045	35442	99706
All Other Liabilities 28	566	0	38	388	1042	1813	3105	8213	23130	39205
Net Worth 29	574	0	7	173	1064	2121	7888	16157	13029	25634

Selected Financial Ratios (Times to 1)

Current Ratio 30	2.1	•	2.0	2.1	1.6	2.3	2.3		1.7	2.3
Quick Ratio 31	0.9	•	1.9	1.2	0.6	0.6	1.0	0.8	0.7	1.2
Net Sales to Working Capital 32	5.2	•	12.0	5.4	5.5	10.2	3.6	4.5	4.9	4.4
Coverage Ratio 33	4.5	202.7	20.6	•	7.5	11.6	6.0	2.7	1.3	4.5
Total Asset Turnover 34	2.0	•	5.0	2.4	2.4	3.2	1.6	2.0	1.2	1.7
Inventory Turnover 35	4.0	•	8.6	4.4	4.5	5.9	3.4	3.7	2.6	4.1
Receivables Turnover 36	8.5	•	5.2	12.1	24.3	19.7	6.4	7.4	4.9	12.0
Total Liabilities to Net Worth 37	2.1	•	12.9	3.2	1.5	2.0	1.0	1.1	4.5	5.4
Current Assets to Working Capital 38	1.9	•	2.0	2.0	1.9	2.8	1.8	1.8	2.4	1.7
Current Liabilities to Working Capital 39	0.9	•	1.0	1.0	0.9	1.8	0.8	0.8	1.4	0.7
Working Capital to Net Sales 40	0.2	•	0.1	0.2	0.2	0.1	0.3	0.2	0.2	0.2
Inventory to Working Capital 41	0.8	•	0.1	0.8	0.8	1.2	0.8	0.8	1.2	0.7
Total Receipts to Cash Flow 42	7.4	2.8	8.4	9.9	8.4	5.9	7.4	8.3	7.6	6.0
Cost of Goods to Cash Flow 43	4.9	1.0	6.1	6.6	5.9	4.0	5.0	5.9	5.0	3.4
Cash Flow to Total Debt 44	0.4	•	0.6	0.3	0.5	0.8	0.4	0.4	0.2	0.3

Selected Financial Factors (in Percentages)

Debt Ratio 45	68.0	•	92.8	76.3	60.2	66.2	50.2	53.1	81.8	84.4
Return on Total Assets 46	11.3	•	43.5	12.7	32.1	11.3	8.2	•	4.0	18.2
Return on Equity Before Income Taxes 47	27.4	•	575.3	27.7	86.6	18.9	11.1	•	4.9	90.9
Return on Equity After Income Taxes 48	23.9	•	575.0	27.0	84.9	16.9	8.0	•	•	81.0
Profit Margin (Before Income Tax) 49	4.3	2.4	8.3	•	4.6	9.1	5.8	2.7	0.7	8.3
Profit Margin (After Income Tax) 50	3.8	2.3	8.3	•	4.5	8.9	5.2	1.9	•	7.4

Table II

Corporations with Net Income

APPAREL ACCESSORIES AND OTHER APPAREL

MONEY AMOUNTS AND SIZE OF ASSETS IN THOUSANDS OF DOLLARS

Item Description for Accounting Period 7/05 Through 6/06	Total	Zero Assets	Under 500	500 to 1,000	1,000 to 5,000	5,000 to 10,000	10,000 to 25,000	25,000 to 50,000	50,000 to 100,000	100,000 to 250,000	250,000 to 500,000	500,000 to 2,500,000	2,500,000 and over
Number of Enterprises 1	1619	20	742	376	394	24	•	11	6	•	0	0	0
Revenues ($ in Thousands)													
Net Sales 2	8229961	115534	574642	704576	2601425	486025	•	838663	560956	•	0	0	0
Interest 3	4727	0	0	595	1054	16	•	142	525	•	0	0	0
Rents 4	722	0	0	0	256	0	•	0	161	•	0	0	0
Royalties 5	14296	0	0	0	0	0	•	0	116	•	0	0	0
Other Portfolio Income 6	22553	1829	4	0	12263	2	•	7	3220	•	0	0	0
Other Receipts 7	140122	-1	-1	18112	21096	1216	•	2080	23499	•	0	0	0
Total Receipts 8	8412381	117362	574645	723283	2636094	487259	•	840892	588477	•	0	0	0
Average Total Receipts 9	5196	5868	774	1924	6691	20302	•	76445	98080	•	•	•	•
Operating Costs/Operating Income (%)													
Cost of Operations 10	65.9	70.4	73.8	63.8	69.8	67.2	•	68.6	62.7	•	•	•	•
Salaries and Wages 11	8.9	0.1	7.1	5.7	11.2	6.7	•	6.4	5.9	•	•	•	•
Taxes Paid 12	2.4	0.0	0.8	1.7	1.5	1.9	•	2.4	1.5	•	•	•	•
Interest Paid 13	0.8	•	0.0	0.5	0.7	0.9	•	1.0	0.8	•	•	•	•
Depreciation 14	0.8	6.9	0.3	1.3	0.7	0.5	•	0.7	0.6	•	•	•	•
Amortization and Depletion 15	0.2	•	0.0	0.0	0.0	0.0	•	0.0	0.3	•	•	•	•
Pensions and Other Deferred Comp. 16	0.2	•	0.5	1.2	0.1	0.1	•	0.1	0.1	•	•	•	•
Employee Benefits 17	1.1	11.0	0.0	1.7	0.8	1.0	•	1.1	0.5	•	•	•	•
Advertising 18	1.4	•	0.1	1.0	0.7	0.6	•	0.8	3.1	•	•	•	•
Other Expenses 19	10.7	5.9	5.0	13.6	9.9	9.5	•	10.6	13.0	•	•	•	•
Officers' Compensation 20	2.3	•	3.5	7.4	1.0	2.8	•	2.0	3.8	•	•	•	•
Operating Margin 21	5.2	5.7	8.8	2.1	3.7	8.8	•	6.5	7.7	•	•	•	•
Operating Margin Before Officers' Comp. 22	7.5	5.7	12.3	9.5	4.6	11.6	•	8.5	11.5	•	•	•	•

Selected Average Balance Sheet ($ in Thousands)

Net Receivables 23	574	0	78	215	526	2058	•	8435	13071
Inventories 24	780	0	2	263	1041	2325	•	14248	37923
Net Property, Plant and Equipment 25	206	0	26	49	271	607	•	3494	2904
Total Assets 26	2311	0	155	707	2792	6266	•	33536	65609
Notes and Loans Payable 27	696	0	31	55	561	2332	•	11337	17978
All Other Liabilities 28	695	0	45	436	1100	1813	•	7913	9922
Net Worth 29	920	0	80	216	1131	2121	•	14286	37710

Selected Financial Ratios (Times to 1)

Current Ratio 30	2.3	•	2.9	2.9	2.1	1.6	•	2.7	2.1
Quick Ratio 31	1.0	•	2.8	2.3	0.6	0.6	•	1.0	0.6
Net Sales to Working Capital 32	5.0	•	9.2	4.4	5.5	10.2	•	4.1	3.8
Coverage Ratio 33	9.8	•	5631.2	11.3	8.2	11.6	•	8.0	17.5
Total Asset Turnover 34	2.2	•	5.0	2.7	2.4	3.2	•	2.3	1.4
Inventory Turnover 35	4.3	•	370.4	4.5	4.4	5.9	•	3.7	1.5
Receivables Turnover 36	9.1	•	6.7	12.9	13.0	19.7	•	18.1	3.7
Total Liabilities to Net Worth 37	1.5	•	1.0	2.3	1.5	2.0	•	1.3	0.7
Current Assets to Working Capital 38	1.8	•	1.5	1.5	1.9	2.8	•	1.6	1.9
Current Liabilities to Working Capital 39	0.8	•	0.5	0.5	0.9	1.8	•	0.6	0.9
Working Capital to Net Sales 40	0.2	•	0.1	0.2	0.2	0.1	•	0.2	0.3
Inventory to Working Capital 41	0.7	•	0.0	0.3	0.9	1.2	•	0.8	0.9
Total Receipts to Cash Flow 42	6.5	12.4	8.3	6.5	8.6	5.9	•	6.3	4.1
Cost of Goods to Cash Flow 43	4.3	8.8	6.1	4.2	6.0	4.0	•	4.3	2.6
Cash Flow to Total Debt 44	0.6	•	1.2	0.6	0.5	0.8	•	0.6	0.8

Selected Financial Factors (in Percentages)

Debt Ratio 45	60.2	•	48.8	69.5	59.5	66.2	•	57.4	42.5
Return on Total Assets 46	18.1	•	44.0	13.8	13.5	32.1	•	17.5	19.1
Return on Equity Before Income Taxes 47	40.9	•	85.9	41.3	29.2	86.6	•	36.0	31.3
Return on Equity After Income Taxes 48	37.2	•	85.8	36.3	28.4	84.9	•	30.7	23.5
Profit Margin (Before Income Tax) 49	7.4	7.3	8.8	4.8	5.0	9.1	•	6.7	12.6
Profit Margin (After Income Tax) 50	6.7	7.2	8.8	4.2	4.9	8.9	•	5.8	9.5

Table I

Corporations with and without Net Income

LEATHER AND ALLIED PRODUCT MANUFACTURING

MONEY AMOUNTS AND SIZE OF ASSETS IN THOUSANDS OF DOLLARS

Item Description for Accounting Period 7/05 Through 6/06	Total	Zero Assets	Under 500	500 to 1,000	1,000 to 5,000	5,000 to 10,000	10,000 to 25,000	25,000 to 50,000	50,000 to 100,000	100,000 to 250,000	250,000 to 500,000	500,000 to 2,500,000	2,500,000 and over
Number of Enterprises 1	2661	898	1470	63	154	0	44	11	13	0	4	4	0

Revenues ($ in Thousands)

	Total	Zero Assets	Under 500	500 to 1,000	1,000 to 5,000	5,000 to 10,000	10,000 to 25,000	25,000 to 50,000	50,000 to 100,000	100,000 to 250,000	250,000 to 500,000	500,000 to 2,500,000	2,500,000 and over
Net Sales 2	9759341	40401	243963	2890	542333	0	1238448	957273	1925789	0	1487431	3320811	0
Interest 3	22509	531	26	0	402	0	1451	849	2594	0	8846	7810	0
Rents 4	4519	13	308	0	0	0	536	207	442	0	2919	94	0
Royalties 5	76731	0	0	0	0	0	0	1189	1878	0	34575	39089	0
Other Portfolio Income 6	109326	2	0	0	1164	0	282	4804	161	0	60632	42284	0
Other Receipts 7	88837	849	125	0	68	0	6273	4420	25226	0	13617	38257	0
Total Receipts 8	10061263	41796	244422	2890	543967	0	1246990	968742	1956090	0	1608020	3448345	0
Average Total Receipts 9	3781	47	166	46	3532	•	28341	88067	150468	•	402005	862086	•

Operating Costs/Operating Income (%)

	Total	Zero Assets	Under 500	500 to 1,000	1,000 to 5,000	5,000 to 10,000	10,000 to 25,000	25,000 to 50,000	50,000 to 100,000	100,000 to 250,000	250,000 to 500,000	500,000 to 2,500,000	2,500,000 and over
Cost of Operations 10	63.7	92.6	40.3	22.5	63.6	•	71.7	63.5	65.5	•	72.7	57.2	•
Salaries and Wages 11	9.6	0.8	8.2	92.2	10.1	•	8.4	9.6	7.9	•	7.0	12.3	•
Taxes Paid 12	1.8	3.9	1.9	8.6	3.0	•	1.5	1.8	2.1	•	1.4	1.6	•
Interest Paid 13	1.4	0.0	0.2	•	0.1	•	0.9	0.8	1.6	•	2.9	1.2	•
Depreciation 14	1.2	2.1	0.3	252.7	0.8	•	0.8	0.7	0.8	•	1.5	1.5	•
Amortization and Depletion 15	0.3	•	0.3	28.2	0.0	•	0.1	0.1	0.1	•	0.3	0.6	•
Pensions and Other Deferred Comp. 16	0.4	0.0	0.1	•	0.6	•	0.2	0.7	0.2	•	0.7	0.5	•
Employee Benefits 17	1.3	3.2	•	42.5	0.3	•	1.7	1.5	1.5	•	2.5	0.6	•
Advertising 18	2.5	0.0	1.1	8.6	0.7	•	1.9	3.7	1.8	•	2.5	3.1	•
Other Expenses 19	12.6	5.3	35.2	133.1	18.9	•	7.1	12.2	11.9	•	12.4	12.4	•
Officers' Compensation 20	2.2	•	6.4	•	3.2	•	4.5	1.0	2.8	•	1.3	1.2	•
Operating Margin 21	3.1	•	6.0	•	1.2	•	1.2	4.4	3.9	•	•	7.8	•
Operating Margin Before Officers' Comp. 22	5.3	•	12.4	•	2.0	•	5.7	5.4	6.6	•	•	9.0	•

Selected Average Balance Sheet ($ in Thousands)

Net Receivables 23	593	0	17	0	48	•	5035	12188	38174	•	56079	117703	•
Inventories 24	613	0	29	262	399	•	4538	13682	21691	•	46053	166708	•
Net Property, Plant and Equipment 25	316	0	8	180	199	•	1730	3495	8233	•	39525	102122	•
Total Assets 26	2533	0	78	528	1536	•	15956	38041	92837	•	349255	658207	•
Notes and Loans Payable 27	692	0	33	3115	65	•	3721	7285	18869	•	126443	147932	•
All Other Liabilities 28	836	0	4	100	777	•	3294	11425	27530	•	224344	141277	•
Net Worth 29	1006	0	41	-2686	694	•	8941	19331	46439	•	-1532	368998	•

Selected Financial Ratios (Times to 1)

Current Ratio 30	2.1	•	15.3	•	1.4	•	2.9	2.8	2.8	•	1.2	2.7	•
Quick Ratio 31	1.0	•	7.3	•	0.4	•	1.5	1.3	1.7	•	0.4	1.3	•
Net Sales to Working Capital 32	4.1	•	2.6	0.2	9.6	•	3.5	4.5	3.1	•	8.4	3.8	•
Coverage Ratio 33	5.8	•	32.0	•	•	•	3.0	8.1	4.4	•	2.9	10.6	•
Total Asset Turnover 34	1.4	•	2.1	0.1	2.3	•	1.8	2.3	1.6	•	1.1	1.3	•
Inventory Turnover 35	3.8	•	2.3	0.0	5.6	•	4.4	4.0	4.5	•	5.9	2.8	•
Receivables Turnover 36	6.1	•	12.0	5.2	45.0	•	7.1	6.6	5.8	•	13.3	5.5	•
Total Liabilities to Net Worth 37	1.5	•	0.9	•	1.2	•	0.8	1.0	1.0	•	•	0.8	•
Current Assets to Working Capital 38	1.9	•	1.1	1.0	3.2	•	1.5	1.5	1.5	•	5.5	1.6	•
Current Liabilities to Working Capital 39	0.9	•	0.1	•	2.2	•	0.5	0.5	0.5	•	4.5	0.6	•
Working Capital to Net Sales 40	0.2	•	0.4	5.2	0.1	•	0.3	0.2	0.3	•	0.1	0.3	•
Inventory to Working Capital 41	0.7	•	0.6	0.9	1.1	•	0.7	0.7	0.6	•	1.0	0.7	•
Total Receipts to Cash Flow 42	6.6	•	2.7	•	7.1	•	12.8	6.3	6.3	•	8.7	5.5	•
Cost of Goods to Cash Flow 43	4.2	•	1.1	•	4.5	•	9.2	4.0	4.1	•	6.3	3.1	•
Cash Flow to Total Debt 44	0.4	•	1.7	•	0.6	•	0.3	0.7	0.5	•	0.1	0.5	•

Selected Financial Factors (in Percentages)

Debt Ratio 45	60.3	•	47.7	608.7	54.8	•	44.0	49.2	50.0	•	100.4	43.9	•
Return on Total Assets 46	11.6	•	13.6	•	•	•	4.9	15.4	11.2	•	8.9	16.2	•
Return on Equity Before Income Taxes 47	24.1	•	25.3	8.3	•	•	5.8	26.6	17.3	•	•	26.2	•
Return on Equity After Income Taxes 48	20.3	•	25.3	8.3	•	•	5.0	25.6	15.2	•	•	21.8	•
Profit Margin (Before Income Tax) 49	6.6	•	6.2	•	•	•	1.9	5.9	5.4	•	5.5	11.6	•
Profit Margin (After Income Tax) 50	5.6	•	6.2	•	•	•	1.6	5.7	4.8	•	4.2	9.7	•

Table II
Corporations with Net Income

LEATHER AND ALLIED PRODUCT MANUFACTURING

MONEY AMOUNTS AND SIZE OF ASSETS IN THOUSANDS OF DOLLARS

Item Description for Accounting Period 7/05 Through 6/06	Total	Zero Assets	Under 500	500 to 1,000	1,000 to 5,000	5,000 to 10,000	10,000 to 25,000	25,000 to 50,000	50,000 to 100,000	100,000 to 250,000	250,000 to 500,000	500,000 to 2,500,000	2,500,000 and over
Number of Enterprises 1	919	•	828	0	36	0	28	•	9	0	4	•	0
Revenues ($ in Thousands)													
Net Sales 2	7914160	•	120722	0	325732	0	842520	•	1145948	0	1487431	•	0
Interest 3	19307	•	0	0	402	0	1338	•	1580	0	8846	•	0
Rents 4	3787	•	0	0	0	0	159	•	442	0	2919	•	0
Royalties 5	75916	•	0	0	0	0	0	•	1878	0	34575	•	0
Other Portfolio Income 6	107750	•	0	0	0	0	102	•	47	0	60632	•	0
Other Receipts 7	61311	•	0	0	34	0	2316	•	3427	0	13617	•	0
Total Receipts 8	8182231	•	120722	0	326168	0	846435	•	1153322	0	1608020	•	0
Average Total Receipts 9	8903	•	146	•	9060	•	30230	•	128147	•	402005	•	•
Operating Costs/Operating Income (%)													
Cost of Operations 10	61.9	•	26.2	•	74.9	•	66.6	•	57.6	•	72.7	•	•
Salaries and Wages 11	9.8	•	2.6	•	11.1	•	9.1	•	8.1	•	7.0	•	•
Taxes Paid 12	1.7	•	1.0	•	2.1	•	1.5	•	2.4	•	1.4	•	•
Interest Paid 13	1.3	•	•	•	0.0	•	0.9	•	1.9	•	2.9	•	•
Depreciation 14	1.2	•	0.1	•	0.8	•	0.8	•	0.7	•	1.5	•	•
Amortization and Depletion 15	0.3	•	0.5	•	•	•	0.1	•	0.1	•	0.3	•	•
Pensions and Other Deferred Comp. 16	0.4	•	0.1	•	1.0	•	0.2	•	0.1	•	0.7	•	•
Employee Benefits 17	1.1	•	•	•	0.4	•	1.9	•	0.7	•	2.5	•	•
Advertising 18	2.9	•	2.1	•	0.5	•	2.5	•	2.7	•	2.5	•	•
Other Expenses 19	11.9	•	40.9	•	6.9	•	6.4	•	10.7	•	12.4	•	•
Officers' Compensation 20	2.2	•	3.8	•	2.0	•	5.3	•	4.3	•	1.3	•	•
Operating Margin 21	5.2	•	22.8	•	0.2	•	4.5	•	10.5	•	1.3	•	•
Operating Margin Before Officers' Comp. 22	7.4	•	26.6	•	2.2	•	9.8	•	14.8	•	•	•	•

Selected Average Balance Sheet ($ in Thousands)

Net Receivables 23	1430	1	37	5775	42972	56079
Inventories 24	1415	4	770	4811	26643	46053
Net Property, Plant and Equipment 25	747	0	324	1727	8308	39525
Total Assets 26	5601	3	2359	15535	95846	349255
Notes and Loans Payable 27	1185	23	31	5081	22637	126443
All Other Liabilities 28	2001	0	728	4001	22187	224344
Net Worth 29	2415	-20	1600	6453	51021	-1532

Selected Financial Ratios (Times to 1)

Current Ratio 30	2.0	50.2	2.3	2.4	3.0	1.2
Quick Ratio 31	1.0	39.7	0.9	1.3	1.9	0.4
Net Sales to Working Capital 32	4.2	44.6	9.2	4.1	2.4	8.4
Coverage Ratio 33	8.0	•	7.8	6.3	6.7	2.9
Total Asset Turnover 34	1.5	43.7	3.8	1.9	1.3	1.1
Inventory Turnover 35	3.8	9.2	8.8	4.2	2.8	5.9
Receivables Turnover 36	5.8	14.1	139.6	6.2	5.9	13.3
Total Liabilities to Net Worth 37	1.3	•	0.5	1.4	0.9	•
Current Assets to Working Capital 38	2.0	1.0	1.8	1.7	1.5	5.5
Current Liabilities to Working Capital 39	1.0	0.0	0.8	0.7	0.5	4.5
Working Capital to Net Sales 40	0.2	0.0	0.1	0.2	0.4	0.1
Inventory to Working Capital 41	0.7	0.2	1.0	0.7	0.5	1.0
Total Receipts to Cash Flow 42	6.0	1.6	19.8	9.7	4.9	8.7
Cost of Goods to Cash Flow 43	3.7	0.4	14.8	6.4	2.8	6.3
Cash Flow to Total Debt 44	0.5	3.8	0.6	0.3	0.6	0.1

Selected Financial Factors (in Percentages)

Debt Ratio 45	56.9	704.3	32.2	58.5	46.8	100.4
Return on Total Assets 46	16.1	997.0	1.3	11.4	17.4	8.9
Return on Equity Before Income Taxes 47	32.6	•	1.6	23.1	27.8	•
Return on Equity After Income Taxes 48	28.0	•	1.4	21.2	25.0	•
Profit Margin (Before Income Tax) 49	9.1	22.8	0.3	5.0	11.1	5.5
Profit Margin (After Income Tax) 50	7.9	22.8	0.2	4.6	10.0	4.2

70

Table I

Corporations with and without Net Income

WOOD PRODUCT MANUFACTURING

MONEY AMOUNTS AND SIZE OF ASSETS IN THOUSANDS OF DOLLARS

Item Description for Accounting Period 7/05 Through 6/06	Total	Zero Assets	Under 500	500 to 1,000	1,000 to 5,000	5,000 to 10,000	10,000 to 25,000	25,000 to 50,000	50,000 to 100,000	100,000 to 250,000	250,000 to 500,000	500,000 to 2,500,000	2,500,000 and over
Number of Enterprises **1**	14326	1066	7908	1111	3187	482	328	116	66	34	12	14	0
Revenues ($ in Thousands)													
Net Sales **2**	108389808	943291	6499119	2359656	17245477	7498097	11163312	7159579	7149619	7518649	6688965	34164044	0
Interest **3**	831768	726	1001	1119	9000	7691	4101	6300	8148	27722	29559	736402	0
Rents **4**	44689	93	475	2017	5393	4063	9601	5439	5805	3978	2838	4987	0
Royalties **5**	42981	0	0	441	0	0	371	1233	124	8170	141	32500	0
Other Portfolio Income **6**	1564996	19351	45169	17691	99096	20785	39825	21576	51904	13648	23990	1211962	0
Other Receipts **7**	1049059	7124	3139	27716	62684	139471	65554	32554	69756	71605	232016	337439	0
Total Receipts **8**	111923301	970585	6548903	2408640	17421650	7670107	11282764	7226681	7285356	7643772	6977509	36487334	0
Average Total Receipts **9**	7813	910	828	2168	5466	15913	34399	62299	110384	224817	581459	2606238	•
Operating Costs/Operating Income (%)													
Cost of Operations **10**	74.4	72.8	56.8	73.1	69.2	76.7	77.3	81.1	80.0	78.5	76.0	75.2	•
Salaries and Wages **11**	5.9	4.7	11.7	5.1	7.4	5.2	4.6	3.5	4.4	4.5	5.4	5.8	•
Taxes Paid **12**	1.7	0.8	3.0	2.3	2.5	2.0	1.7	1.6	1.4	1.2	1.4	1.1	•
Interest Paid **13**	2.4	3.5	0.7	1.3	0.9	0.8	0.9	0.8	1.2	1.7	1.1	5.3	•
Depreciation **14**	1.8	11.3	1.9	2.0	1.8	1.9	1.9	2.3	2.0	2.7	2.1	1.1	•
Amortization and Depletion **15**	0.6	0.3	0.1	0.0	0.0	0.0	0.0	0.1	0.3	0.2	0.6	1.4	•
Pensions and Other Deferred Comp. **16**	0.5	0.4	0.0	0.0	0.1	0.1	0.3	0.4	0.4	0.2	1.0	0.9	•
Employee Benefits **17**	1.1	0.4	1.1	1.4	1.4	1.2	1.0	1.0	1.0	0.6	1.0	1.1	•
Advertising **18**	0.6	0.3	0.5	0.4	0.2	0.4	0.3	0.3	0.5	0.7	0.9	0.8	•
Other Expenses **19**	7.2	10.9	13.0	13.1	9.5	8.2	6.3	3.7	5.7	6.4	8.0	5.6	•
Officers' Compensation **20**	1.9	1.8	7.4	2.8	3.3	1.9	1.3	1.2	0.6	0.8	0.4	1.2	•
Operating Margin **21**	2.1	•	3.9	•	3.6	1.6	4.3	3.8	2.4	2.4	2.1	0.3	•
Operating Margin Before Officers' Comp. **22**	3.9	•	11.3	1.4	6.9	3.5	5.6	5.0	3.0	3.2	2.5	1.5	•

Selected Average Balance Sheet ($ in Thousands)

Net Receivables 23	2338	0	41	139	499	1571	2864	5120	8830	23916	48543	1939807
Inventories 24	724	0	26	224	448	2021	4278	8417	15906	23820	44129	196474
Net Property, Plant and Equipment 25	1951	0	56	141	498	1774	4798	12199	21517	54275	107052	1240468
Total Assets 26	10161	0	159	695	2097	6834	14529	32704	67010	144135	328297	7981074
Notes and Loans Payable 27	2027	0	95	423	878	1976	4924	9467	21134	55151	56824	1242918
All Other Liabilities 28	3566	0	28	118	555	1427	2759	6052	13760	33971	83580	3114689
Net Worth 29	4568	0	36	154	664	3432	6846	17185	32115	55012	187894	3623466

Selected Financial Ratios (Times to 1)

Current Ratio 30	1.1	•	2.6	1.8	1.9	1.9	2.0	1.9	1.7	1.8	1.8	0.9
Quick Ratio 31	0.8	•	1.7	0.7	1.2	0.9	0.9	0.8	0.7	1.0	0.8	0.8
Net Sales to Working Capital 32	25.2	•	13.4	9.5	8.0	7.8	7.9	7.8	7.9	7.5	8.4	•
Coverage Ratio 33	3.3	•	7.8	1.5	6.2	5.6	6.9	6.7	4.6	3.4	6.9	2.4
Total Asset Turnover 34	0.7	•	5.2	3.1	2.6	2.3	2.3	1.9	1.6	1.5	1.7	0.3
Inventory Turnover 35	7.8	•	17.7	6.9	8.4	5.9	6.1	5.9	5.4	7.3	9.6	9.3
Receivables Turnover 36	5.2	•	18.5	12.0	12.5	9.6	12.3	11.6	11.5	11.0	15.2	2.3
Total Liabilities to Net Worth 37	1.2	•	3.4	2.2	1.0	1.1	1.1	0.9	1.1	1.6	0.7	1.2
Current Assets to Working Capital 38	12.3	•	1.6	2.2	2.1	2.2	2.0	2.2	2.4	2.2	2.2	•
Current Liabilities to Working Capital 39	11.3	•	0.6	1.2	1.1	1.2	1.0	1.2	1.4	1.2	1.2	•
Working Capital to Net Sales 40	0.0	•	0.1	0.1	0.1	0.1	0.1	0.1	0.1	0.1	0.1	•
Inventory to Working Capital 41	2.5	•	0.4	1.0	0.7	1.0	1.0	1.0	1.2	0.8	0.8	•
Total Receipts to Cash Flow 42	9.3	28.2	7.4	10.9	8.8	10.2	9.6	13.8	11.8	10.9	7.7	8.6
Cost of Goods to Cash Flow 43	6.9	20.5	4.2	8.0	6.1	7.8	7.4	11.2	9.4	8.5	5.8	6.4
Cash Flow to Total Debt 44	0.1	•	0.9	0.4	0.4	0.4	0.5	0.3	0.3	0.2	0.5	0.1

Selected Financial Factors (in Percentages)

Debt Ratio 45	55.0	•	77.5	77.8	68.3	49.8	52.9	47.5	52.1	61.8	42.8	54.6
Return on Total Assets 46	5.8	•	27.4	6.0	14.3	10.7	14.7	10.5	9.2	8.8	12.6	3.9
Return on Equity Before Income Taxes 47	9.0	•	106.2	8.8	37.7	17.6	26.7	17.0	15.1	16.2	18.8	5.0
Return on Equity After Income Taxes 48	7.8	•	104.3	3.2	36.3	15.5	24.8	14.9	13.0	12.7	15.7	4.1
Profit Margin (Before Income Tax) 49	5.4	•	4.6	0.6	4.6	3.9	5.4	4.7	4.5	4.0	6.3	7.4
Profit Margin (After Income Tax) 50	4.7	•	4.5	0.2	4.5	3.4	5.0	4.1	3.8	3.2	5.3	6.1

71

Table II
Corporations with Net Income

WOOD PRODUCT MANUFACTURING

MONEY AMOUNTS AND SIZE OF ASSETS IN THOUSANDS OF DOLLARS

Item Description for Accounting Period 7/05 Through 6/06	Total	Zero Assets	Under 500	500 to 1,000	1,000 to 5,000	5,000 to 10,000	10,000 to 25,000	25,000 to 50,000	50,000 to 100,000	100,000 to 250,000	250,000 to 500,000	500,000 to 2,500,000	2,500,000 and over
Number of Enterprises 1	9961	556	5436	617	2512	369	273	100	53	26	9	11	0
Revenues ($ in Thousands)													
Net Sales 2	92441415	368892	4494538	1185137	15233650	5766846	9748102	6374899	6333242	6364715	5243987	31307408	0
Interest 3	818541	202	232	1063	7071	7604	3648	6254	4404	26576	28907	732577	0
Rents 4	39187	0	0	0	3069	3985	9601	5407	5670	3630	2838	4987	0
Royalties 5	38866	0	0	0	0	0	371	1233	35	4586	141	32500	0
Other Portfolio Income 6	1500277	14511	44070	14905	90554	17782	31764	19933	40427	10602	23975	1191756	0
Other Receipts 7	912188	2493	1861	19111	60065	127691	58776	29016	59067	65316	225912	262879	0
Total Receipts 8	95730474	386098	4540701	1220216	15394409	5923908	9852262	6436742	6442845	6475425	5525760	33532107	0
Average Total Receipts 9	9611	694	835	1978	6128	16054	36089	64367	121563	249055	613973	3048373	•
Operating Costs/Operating Income (%)													
Cost of Operations 10	73.6	70.4	52.1	59.8	67.6	76.0	76.9	80.1	79.2	77.4	76.4	75.0	•
Salaries and Wages 11	5.8	9.9	10.8	6.1	7.9	4.3	4.5	3.5	4.4	4.9	4.2	6.0	•
Taxes Paid 12	1.6	0.5	2.8	3.3	2.4	1.6	1.7	1.6	1.4	1.3	1.6	1.1	•
Interest Paid 13	2.4	1.6	0.5	1.0	0.6	0.7	0.7	0.8	0.9	1.4	0.7	5.5	•
Depreciation 14	1.6	5.8	2.0	2.5	1.6	2.1	1.7	2.3	1.7	2.1	1.6	1.0	•
Amortization and Depletion 15	0.6	0.1	0.1	0.0	0.0	0.0	0.0	0.1	0.2	0.2	0.6	1.5	•
Pensions and Other Deferred Comp. 16	0.6	0.0	0.0	0.0	0.2	0.2	0.3	0.5	0.4	0.2	1.2	1.0	•
Employee Benefits 17	1.0	0.1	0.7	1.6	1.5	1.2	1.0	1.0	0.9	0.6	0.9	1.0	•
Advertising 18	0.6	0.2	0.7	0.3	0.2	0.2	0.3	0.3	0.6	0.7	0.8	0.9	•
Other Expenses 19	6.8	9.8	13.4	17.2	9.8	6.3	6.0	3.6	5.8	6.7	8.0	5.0	•
Officers' Compensation 20	1.9	0.7	9.0	5.2	3.3	2.0	1.3	1.2	0.6	0.9	0.4	1.2	•
Operating Margin 21	3.5	0.9	7.9	2.9	4.9	5.5	5.6	5.0	4.0	3.6	3.6	0.8	•
Operating Margin Before Officers' Comp. 22	5.4	1.6	16.9	8.1	8.2	7.5	6.9	6.2	4.6	4.5	4.0	2.0	•

Selected Average Balance Sheet ($ in Thousands)

Net Receivables 23	3231	0	38	220	567	1533	3093	5283	9368	27556	51258	2436892	•
Inventories 24	835	0	20	184	415	2084	4287	7693	15861	24147	43106	226619	•
Net Property, Plant and Equipment 25	2469	0	56	112	467	1858	4533	12264	19669	49344	102210	1514092	•
Total Assets 26	13589	0	141	715	2129	6869	14574	32800	66735	147249	327113	9882164	•
Notes and Loans Payable 27	2369	0	59	282	680	1484	4414	8625	19274	49510	47206	1459072	•
All Other Liabilities 28	4900	0	19	155	581	1356	2744	6118	14097	36658	95695	3883940	•
Net Worth 29	6320	0	63	278	869	4030	7416	18057	33364	61081	184213	4539152	•

Selected Financial Ratios (Times to 1)

Current Ratio 30	1.1	•	2.9	2.3	2.1	2.3	2.2	2.0	1.8	1.9	1.7	0.9	•
Quick Ratio 31	0.8	•	2.1	1.1	1.4	1.2	1.0	0.9	0.8	1.2	0.8	0.7	•
Net Sales to Working Capital 32	37.1	•	14.9	6.2	7.9	6.6	7.3	7.6	7.4	7.2	9.5	•	•
Coverage Ratio 33	4.0	4.5	20.0	6.7	10.1	13.3	10.2	8.7	7.4	4.7	13.4	2.5	•
Total Asset Turnover 34	0.7	•	5.9	2.7	2.8	2.3	2.5	1.9	1.8	1.7	1.8	0.3	•
Inventory Turnover 35	8.2	•	22.0	6.3	9.9	5.7	6.4	6.6	6.0	7.8	10.3	9.4	•
Receivables Turnover 36	4.8	•	19.9	7.2	12.9	9.3	12.4	12.5	13.4	11.2	14.7	2.1	•
Total Liabilities to Net Worth 37	1.2	•	1.2	1.6	1.5	0.7	1.0	0.8	1.0	1.4	0.8	1.2	•
Current Assets to Working Capital 38	19.3	•	1.5	1.8	1.9	1.8	1.9	2.0	2.2	2.1	2.5	•	•
Current Liabilities to Working Capital 39	18.3	•	0.5	0.8	0.9	0.8	0.9	1.0	1.2	1.1	1.5	•	•
Working Capital to Net Sales 40	0.0	•	0.1	0.2	0.1	0.2	0.1	0.1	0.1	0.1	0.1	•	•
Inventory to Working Capital 41	3.4	•	0.3	0.5	0.6	0.8	0.9	0.9	1.2	0.6	0.8	•	•
Total Receipts to Cash Flow 42	8.2	10.0	5.7	6.0	7.8	8.0	8.8	12.0	10.1	9.4	6.3	8.3	•
Cost of Goods to Cash Flow 43	6.1	7.1	3.0	3.6	5.3	6.1	6.8	9.6	8.0	7.3	4.8	6.2	•
Cash Flow to Total Debt 44	0.2	•	1.9	0.7	0.6	0.7	0.6	0.4	0.4	0.3	0.6	0.1	•

Selected Financial Factors (in Percentages)

Debt Ratio 45	53.5	•	55.3	61.1	59.2	41.3	49.1	44.9	50.0	58.5	43.7	54.1	•
Return on Total Assets 46	6.6	•	55.0	18.4	18.7	20.1	18.1	13.0	12.2	11.3	17.2	4.0	•
Return on Equity Before Income Taxes 47	10.6	•	117.0	40.3	41.4	31.7	32.0	20.9	21.1	21.4	28.2	5.2	•
Return on Equity After Income Taxes 48	9.3	•	115.4	34.6	40.0	29.4	29.9	18.5	18.6	17.3	24.1	4.3	•
Profit Margin (Before Income Tax) 49	7.2	5.5	8.9	5.8	5.9	8.2	6.7	5.9	5.9	5.3	8.9	8.3	•
Profit Margin (After Income Tax) 50	6.4	4.5	8.8	5.0	5.7	7.6	6.2	5.2	5.2	4.3	7.6	6.9	•

Table I

Corporations with and without Net Income

PULP, PAPER, AND PAPERBOARD MILLS

MONEY AMOUNTS AND SIZE OF ASSETS IN THOUSANDS OF DOLLARS

Item Description for Accounting Period 7/05 Through 6/06	Total	Zero Assets	Under 500	500 to 1,000	1,000 to 5,000	5,000 to 10,000	10,000 to 25,000	25,000 to 50,000	50,000 to 100,000	100,000 to 250,000	250,000 to 500,000	500,000 to 2,500,000	2,500,000 and over
Number of Enterprises **1**	182	·	·	0	31	·	25	18	11	17	7	22	7
Revenues ($ in Thousands)													
Net Sales **2**	100514129	·	·	0	893443	·	889553	847022	1062859	2979549	2934218	24521786	63515967
Interest **3**	1038390	·	·	0	15	·	590	433	1352	14722	3750	199422	811807
Rents **4**	58422	·	·	0	0	·	0	1032	65	383	2329	10284	43973
Royalties **5**	164609	·	·	0	0	·	276	0	0	0	188	44345	119781
Other Portfolio Income **6**	5033481	·	·	0	0	·	8083	2868	568	27326	149394	116141	4721535
Other Receipts **7**	1228476	·	·	0	0	·	3449	45859	13638	31183	11794	213043	899939
Total Receipts **8**	108037507	·	·	0	893458	·	901951	897214	1078482	3053163	3101673	25105021	70113002
Average Total Receipts **9**	593613	·	·	·	28821	·	36078	49845	98044	179598	443096	1141137	10016143
Operating Costs/Operating Income (%)													
Cost of Operations **10**	77.7	·	·	·	94.0	·	76.8	84.3	77.8	83.9	79.0	80.9	75.7
Salaries and Wages **11**	4.3	·	·	·	0.5	·	4.4	3.3	3.7	2.9	9.5	3.5	4.6
Taxes Paid **12**	1.3	·	·	·	0.1	·	1.9	1.1	0.9	0.9	1.2	1.2	1.4
Interest Paid **13**	4.0	·	·	·	0.5	·	1.7	1.4	1.5	4.1	1.5	3.3	4.6
Depreciation **14**	3.3	·	·	·	0.0	·	2.1	2.8	2.0	4.4	3.9	4.7	2.6
Amortization and Depletion **15**	0.4	·	·	·	·	·	0.2	0.0	0.2	0.3	0.9	0.4	0.3
Pensions and Other Deferred Comp. **16**	0.6	·	·	·	·	·	0.4	0.8	0.8	0.5	2.6	0.5	0.6
Employee Benefits **17**	1.8	·	·	·	·	·	1.5	1.0	2.1	1.0	4.0	1.6	1.8
Advertising **18**	0.3	·	·	·	0.0	·	0.1	0.2	0.2	0.3	0.3	0.3	0.3
Other Expenses **19**	7.8	·	·	·	4.2	·	9.2	16.9	9.0	5.0	1.4	6.0	9.0
Officers' Compensation **20**	0.3	·	·	·	2.5	·	1.0	1.5	0.5	0.7	0.3	0.4	0.1
Operating Margin **21**	·	·	·	·	·	·	0.6	·	1.3	0.3	·	·	·
Operating Margin Before Officers' Comp. **22**	·	·	·	·	0.8	·	1.6	·	1.8	·	·	·	·

Selected Average Balance Sheet ($ in Thousands)

Net Receivables 23	59413	·	1240	·	3008	5867	15202	21287	21934	119158	1039197
Inventories 24	46945	·	0	·	2317	5567	11422	18589	40339	108723	750779
Net Property, Plant and Equipment 25	279659	·	7	·	6418	12321	25700	69116	225661	624690	4817813
Total Assets 26	792066	·	1284	·	16177	32600	57988	172532	348692	1166270	15887636
Notes and Loans Payable 27	302770	·	2597	·	5941	29124	18760	100530	97503	421521	6063932
All Other Liabilities 28	188202	·	10	·	4805	8912	15716	53401	85453	336824	3552925
Net Worth 29	301094	·	-1323	·	5431	-5436	23513	18601	165736	407925	6270779

Selected Financial Ratios (Times to 1)

Current Ratio 30	1.0	122.8	·	1.8	1.2	2.2	1.4	1.8	1.6	0.8
Quick Ratio 31	0.5	122.8	·	1.0	0.7	1.3	0.6	0.8	0.7	0.4
Net Sales to Working Capital 32	612.0	23.4	·	10.9	22.6	6.1	8.6	9.6	8.5	·
Coverage Ratio 33	2.5	·	·	2.2	·	2.8	0.7	1.9	0.9	3.1
Total Asset Turnover 34	0.7	22.5	·	2.2	1.4	1.7	1.0	1.2	1.0	0.6
Inventory Turnover 35	9.1	·	·	11.8	7.1	6.6	7.9	8.2	8.3	9.1
Receivables Turnover 36	9.1	46.5	·	11.9	7.9	7.9	9.8	14.8	8.0	8.9
Total Liabilities to Net Worth 37	1.6	·	·	2.0	·	1.5	8.3	1.1	1.9	1.5
Current Assets to Working Capital 38	165.6	·	·	2.3	7.2	1.9	3.3	2.2	2.6	·
Current Liabilities to Working Capital 39	164.6	·	·	1.3	6.2	0.9	2.3	1.2	1.6	·
Working Capital to Net Sales 40	0.0	·	·	0.1	0.0	0.2	0.1	0.1	0.1	·
Inventory to Working Capital 41	54.0	·	·	0.8	2.2	0.6	1.1	1.0	1.0	·
Total Receipts to Cash Flow 42	9.2	41.3	·	10.7	35.7	9.5	53.3	27.8	·	6.5
Cost of Goods to Cash Flow 43	7.1	38.9	·	8.3	30.1	7.4	44.8	22.5	·	4.9
Cash Flow to Total Debt 44	0.1	0.3	·	0.3	0.0	0.3	0.0	0.1	·	0.1

Selected Financial Factors (in Percentages)

Debt Ratio 45	62.0	203.1	·	66.4	116.7	59.5	89.2	52.5	65.0	60.5
Return on Total Assets 46	6.9	·	·	8.1	·	7.2	2.7	3.2	2.8	8.1
Return on Equity Before Income Taxes 47	10.9	38.1	·	13.0	63.5	11.5	·	·	·	·
Return on Equity After Income Taxes 48	8.7	38.1	·	9.3	64.7	10.2	·	3.2	·	13.8
Profit Margin (Before Income Tax) 49	5.9	·	·	2.0	·	2.8	·	3.0	·	11.3
Profit Margin (After Income Tax) 50	4.7	·	·	1.4	·	2.5	·	1.2	·	7.8

Table II

Corporations with Net Income

PULP, PAPER, AND PAPERBOARD MILLS

MONEY AMOUNTS AND SIZE OF ASSETS IN THOUSANDS OF DOLLARS

Item Description for Accounting Period 7/05 Through 6/06	Total	Zero Assets	Under 500	500 to 1,000	1,000 to 5,000	5,000 to 10,000	10,000 to 25,000	25,000 to 50,000	50,000 to 100,000	100,000 to 250,000	250,000 to 500,000	500,000 to 2,500,000	2,500,000 and over
Number of Enterprises **1**	69	•	0	0	0	0	19	9	8	10	•	11	•

Revenues ($ in Thousands)

Item Description for Accounting Period 7/05 Through 6/06	Total	Zero Assets	Under 500	500 to 1,000	1,000 to 5,000	5,000 to 10,000	10,000 to 25,000	25,000 to 50,000	50,000 to 100,000	100,000 to 250,000	250,000 to 500,000	500,000 to 2,500,000	2,500,000 and over
Net Sales **2**	78483969	•	0	0	0	0	616349	551086	760124	1591285	•	8753559	•
Interest **3**	929335	•	0	0	0	0	106	295	1201	13952	•	95563	•
Rents **4**	37541	•	0	0	0	0	0	1032	0	383	•	5310	•
Royalties **5**	119563	•	0	0	0	0	0	0	0	0	•	4882	•
Other Portfolio Income **6**	497319	•	0	0	0	0	4335	2621	556	24834	•	91973	•
Other Receipts **7**	991491	•	0	0	0	0	1768	568	11565	15094	•	56496	•
Total Receipts **8**	85540218	•	0	0	0	0	622558	555602	773446	1645548	•	9007783	•
Average Total Receipts **9**	1239713	•	•	•	•	•	32766	61734	96681	164555	•	818889	•

Operating Costs/Operating Income (%)

Item Description for Accounting Period 7/05 Through 6/06	Total	Zero Assets	Under 500	500 to 1,000	1,000 to 5,000	5,000 to 10,000	10,000 to 25,000	25,000 to 50,000	50,000 to 100,000	100,000 to 250,000	250,000 to 500,000	500,000 to 2,500,000	2,500,000 and over
Cost of Operations **10**	76.0	•	•	•	•	•	71.5	84.3	77.4	79.4	•	74.2	•
Salaries and Wages **11**	4.6	•	•	•	•	•	5.2	2.3	2.5	4.0	•	4.6	•
Taxes Paid **12**	1.4	•	•	•	•	•	1.2	0.9	0.6	1.0	•	1.4	•
Interest Paid **13**	4.1	•	•	•	•	•	1.0	0.8	1.2	3.0	•	2.9	•
Depreciation **14**	2.8	•	•	•	•	•	2.3	1.3	2.0	2.6	•	4.2	•
Amortization and Depletion **15**	0.3	•	•	•	•	•	0.1	0.0	0.3	0.2	•	0.3	•
Pensions and Other Deferred Comp. **16**	0.7	•	•	•	•	•	0.2	1.1	0.5	0.7	•	0.6	•
Employee Benefits **17**	1.8	•	•	•	•	•	1.2	0.9	1.5	1.1	•	1.4	•
Advertising **18**	0.3	•	•	•	•	•	0.1	0.1	0.2	0.5	•	0.1	•
Other Expenses **19**	8.5	•	•	•	•	•	10.5	5.4	10.3	6.5	•	8.1	•
Officers' Compensation **20**	0.2	•	•	•	•	•	0.9	1.0	0.7	0.9	•	0.6	•
Operating Margin **21**	•	•	•	•	•	•	5.8	1.9	2.9	0.1	•	1.6	•
Operating Margin Before Officers' Comp. **22**	•	•	•	•	•	•	6.6	2.9	3.6	1.0	•	2.1	•

Selected Average Balance Sheet ($ in Thousands)

Net Receivables 23	125858	•	3348	7805	13954	18643	•	105152
Inventories 24	89535	•	2168	5254	13780	18287	•	92608
Net Property, Plant and Equipment 25	594535	•	6687	11260	26664	54869	•	586787
Total Assets 26	1776742	•	15897	32041	58234	165377	•	987712
Notes and Loans Payable 27	652257	•	5548	10093	13345	64280	•	287209
All Other Liabilities 28	393699	•	3741	7920	14412	51453	•	267303
Net Worth 29	730786	•	6607	14027	30477	49644	•	433199

Selected Financial Ratios (Times to 1)

Current Ratio 30	0.9	•	1.9	1.5	2.4	2.1	•	1.6
Quick Ratio 31	0.5	•	1.2	0.8	1.3	0.8	•	0.8
Net Sales to Working Capital 32	•	•	9.1	11.8	5.2	4.5	•	7.8
Coverage Ratio 33	3.1	•	7.7	4.5	5.0	2.2	•	2.6
Total Asset Turnover 34	0.6	•	2.0	1.9	1.6	1.0	•	0.8
Inventory Turnover 35	9.7	•	10.7	9.8	5.3	6.9	•	6.4
Receivables Turnover 36	10.5	•	10.5	8.9	8.3	10.6	•	7.3
Total Liabilities to Net Worth 37	1.4	•	1.4	1.3	0.9	2.3	•	1.3
Current Assets to Working Capital 38	•	•	2.1	3.1	1.7	1.9	•	2.6
Current Liabilities to Working Capital 39	•	•	1.1	2.1	0.7	0.9	•	1.6
Working Capital to Net Sales 40	•	•	0.1	0.1	0.2	0.2	•	0.1
Inventory to Working Capital 41	•	•	0.7	0.9	0.6	0.6	•	0.9
Total Receipts to Cash Flow 42	7.2	•	6.4	14.1	7.4	13.4	•	11.0
Cost of Goods to Cash Flow 43	5.5	•	4.6	11.9	5.7	10.6	•	8.1
Cash Flow to Total Debt 44	0.2	•	0.5	0.2	0.5	0.1	•	0.1

Selected Financial Factors (in Percentages)

Debt Ratio 45	58.9	•	58.4	56.2	47.7	70.0	•	56.1
Return on Total Assets 46	8.1	•	15.9	6.7	9.6	6.4	•	6.0
Return on Equity Before Income Taxes 47	13.5	•	33.2	11.9	14.6	11.8	•	8.3
Return on Equity After Income Taxes 48	11.1	•	29.3	11.8	13.2	10.2	•	6.5
Profit Margin (Before Income Tax) 49	8.6	•	6.8	2.7	4.7	3.7	•	4.5
Profit Margin (After Income Tax) 50	7.1	•	6.0	2.7	4.2	3.2	•	3.5

Table I

Corporations with and without Net Income

CONVERTED PAPER PRODUCT

MONEY AMOUNTS AND SIZE OF ASSETS IN THOUSANDS OF DOLLARS

Item Description for Accounting Period 7/05 Through 6/06	Total	Zero Assets	Under 500	500 to 1,000	1,000 to 5,000	5,000 to 10,000	10,000 to 25,000	25,000 to 50,000	50,000 to 100,000	100,000 to 250,000	250,000 to 500,000	500,000 to 2,500,000	2,500,000 and over
Number of Enterprises **1**	3395	•	•	592	914	•	187	75	23	18	6	10	4
Revenues ($ in Thousands)													
Net Sales **2**	73980294	•	•	1214499	6009563	•	6057363	4661671	2541146	4172679	1987329	11495469	30156535
Interest **3**	1684515	•	•	25	709	•	7123	13674	2538	5267	641	79069	1573079
Rents **4**	67929	•	•	3	2598	•	2784	4914	80	71	425	3706	51159
Royalties **5**	830413	•	•	0	1844	•	7	14	0	871	2953	27823	796901
Other Portfolio Income **6**	4946135	•	•	648	17283	•	6114	356150	3407	13300	24723	324757	4057123
Other Receipts **7**	2335866	•	•	454	31865	•	36001	59760	19388	16389	22573	141555	1878666
Total Receipts **8**	83845152	•	•	1215629	6063862	•	6109392	5096183	2566559	4208577	2038644	12072379	38513463
Average Total Receipts **9**	24697	•	•	2053	6634	•	32671	67949	111590	233810	339774	1207238	9628366
Operating Costs/Operating Income (%)													
Cost of Operations **10**	68.1	•	•	75.8	69.6	•	73.2	76.0	74.4	70.3	70.2	72.8	61.7
Salaries and Wages **11**	9.2	•	•	6.3	8.5	•	5.9	5.9	6.8	5.3	7.2	5.9	13.4
Taxes Paid **12**	1.7	•	•	1.2	2.4	•	2.1	1.8	1.5	1.5	2.1	1.6	1.3
Interest Paid **13**	3.5	•	•	0.8	1.2	•	1.2	1.4	1.5	1.4	1.0	3.7	5.7
Depreciation **14**	3.1	•	•	2.3	2.5	•	2.3	2.5	3.2	2.2	3.5	3.9	3.3
Amortization and Depletion **15**	0.6	•	•	0.1	0.1	•	0.2	0.2	0.1	0.3	0.2	1.8	0.7
Pensions and Other Deferred Comp. **16**	1.1	•	•	0.4	0.3	•	0.3	0.8	0.4	0.3	0.7	1.0	1.9
Employee Benefits **17**	2.6	•	•	0.7	1.8	•	1.4	1.6	2.0	1.7	1.9	3.5	3.2
Advertising **18**	0.8	•	•	0.2	0.2	•	0.1	0.2	0.3	0.7	0.9	0.3	1.5
Other Expenses **19**	9.0	•	•	10.0	8.5	•	8.7	7.1	8.1	11.6	8.8	7.0	9.3
Officers' Compensation **20**	1.1	•	•	3.1	3.0	•	1.8	1.4	1.3	0.5	1.0	0.3	0.5
Operating Margin **21**	•	•	•	•	1.8	•	2.7	1.2	0.3	4.2	2.4	•	•
Operating Margin Before Officers' Comp. **22**	0.3	•	•	2.1	4.9	•	4.5	2.5	1.6	4.7	3.4	•	•

Selected Average Balance Sheet ($ in Thousands)

Net Receivables 23	2833	273	3990	8577	14174	27521	47508	144920	1104974
Inventories 24	1800	65	2743	5942	17662	25644	61468	97047	567411
Net Property, Plant and Equipment 25	5828	105	5380	11361	26227	43144	130363	410914	2538938
Total Assets 26	32216	667	15149	34707	71090	144419	362431	1076447	20594603
Notes and Loans Payable 27	8423	372	6284	11598	24135	42765	89276	547060	4273653
All Other Liabilities 28	12163	187	3983	8058	18120	44062	78232	244226	8660291
Net Worth 29	11630	108	4882	15051	28835	57592	194922	285161	7660660

Selected Financial Ratios (Times to 1)

Current Ratio 30	0.7	2.3	1.7	1.5	1.6	1.9	1.8	1.7	0.5
Quick Ratio 31	0.4	2.0	1.2	0.8	0.7	1.1	0.8	0.8	0.3
Net Sales to Working Capital 32	•	6.6	11.1	12.2	8.6	7.4	5.1	8.5	•
Coverage Ratio 33	5.1	•	3.3	3.9	1.9	4.4	6.0	2.0	6.1
Total Asset Turnover 34	0.7	3.1	2.7	2.1	1.6	1.6	0.9	1.1	0.4
Inventory Turnover 35	8.2	23.8	13.9	8.6	4.7	6.4	3.8	8.6	8.2
Receivables Turnover 36	8.1	7.2	18.2	8.8	7.5	7.1	6.5	8.4	7.4
Total Liabilities to Net Worth 37	1.8	5.2	1.8	2.1	1.5	1.5	0.9	2.8	1.7
Current Assets to Working Capital 38	•	1.8	2.3	3.1	2.7	2.2	2.2	2.5	•
Current Liabilities to Working Capital 39	•	0.8	1.3	2.1	1.7	1.2	1.2	1.5	•
Working Capital to Net Sales 40	•	0.2	0.1	0.1	0.1	0.1	0.2	0.1	•
Inventory to Working Capital 41	•	0.2	0.6	1.1	1.3	0.7	0.9	0.8	•
Total Receipts to Cash Flow 42	5.3	17.8	12.9	11.0	14.9	7.0	8.1	11.9	3.1
Cost of Goods to Cash Flow 43	3.6	13.5	8.9	8.0	11.1	4.9	5.7	8.6	1.9
Cash Flow to Total Debt 44	0.2	0.2	0.3	0.3	0.2	0.4	0.2	0.1	0.2

Selected Financial Factors (in Percentages)

Debt Ratio 45	63.9	83.9	63.9	67.8	56.6	59.4	60.1	46.2	73.5	62.8
Return on Total Assets 46	11.9	•	10.5	10.3	21.3	4.3	10.2	5.6	7.7	12.8
Return on Equity Before Income Taxes 47	26.6	•	20.4	23.7	43.2	5.1	19.9	8.7	14.2	28.7
Return on Equity After Income Taxes 48	20.0	•	19.6	21.1	30.9	2.8	17.4	7.1	10.2	21.6
Profit Margin (Before Income Tax) 49	14.2	•	2.7	3.6	10.5	1.3	4.9	5.1	3.5	29.2
Profit Margin (After Income Tax) 50	10.7	•	2.6	3.2	7.5	0.7	4.3	4.2	2.5	22.0

Table II

Corporations with Net Income

CONVERTED PAPER PRODUCT

MONEY AMOUNTS AND SIZE OF ASSETS IN THOUSANDS OF DOLLARS

Item Description for Accounting Period 7/05 Through 6/06	Total	Zero Assets	Under 500	500 to 1,000	1,000 to 5,000	5,000 to 10,000	10,000 to 25,000	25,000 to 50,000	50,000 to 100,000	100,000 to 250,000	250,000 to 500,000	500,000 to 2,500,000	2,500,000 and over
Number of Enterprises 1	2489	101	867	359	699	200	155	60	15	•	•	7	4

Revenues ($ in Thousands)

Item	Total	Zero Assets	Under 500	500 to 1,000	1,000 to 5,000	5,000 to 10,000	10,000 to 25,000	25,000 to 50,000	50,000 to 100,000	100,000 to 250,000	250,000 to 500,000	500,000 to 2,500,000	2,500,000 and over
Net Sales 2	63072595	183345	1444515	721475	4948525	2487035	5221045	3855487	1830704	•	•	7200697	30156535
Interest 3	167233	0	0	25	604	1232	6402	13559	1936	•	•	75684	1573079
Rents 4	65667	0	0	3	993	2157	2742	4434	80	•	•	3602	51159
Royalties 5	828430	0	0	0	0	0	7	14	0	•	•	27798	796901
Other Portfolio Income 6	4885390	121735	132	648	4413	19963	4800	354996	3121	•	•	280681	4057123
Other Receipts 7	2194998	24704	17	453	29178	22538	31336	56623	11622	•	•	102611	1878666
Total Receipts 8	72725313	329784	1444664	722604	4983713	2552925	5266332	4285113	1847463	•	•	7691073	38513463
Average Total Receipts 9	29219	3265	1666	2013	7130	12665	33976	71419	123164	•	•	1098725	9628366

Operating Costs/Operating Income (%)

Item	Total	Zero Assets	Under 500	500 to 1,000	1,000 to 5,000	5,000 to 10,000	10,000 to 25,000	25,000 to 50,000	50,000 to 100,000	100,000 to 250,000	250,000 to 500,000	500,000 to 2,500,000	2,500,000 and over
Cost of Operations 10	67.0	75.7	81.2	64.0	67.9	67.0	71.9	75.7	74.6	•	•	73.4	61.7
Salaries and Wages 11	9.7	5.4	1.3	7.7	8.4	7.5	6.2	5.7	6.1	•	•	6.1	13.4
Taxes Paid 12	1.7	31.8	1.3	1.8	2.2	2.2	2.1	1.9	1.6	•	•	1.5	1.3
Interest Paid 13	3.6	0.4	0.2	0.1	0.9	1.4	1.2	1.2	1.0	•	•	3.8	5.7
Depreciation 14	2.9	2.8	0.0	1.9	2.1	3.4	2.3	2.2	2.7	•	•	3.4	3.3
Amortization and Depletion 15	0.5	1.1	•	0.0	0.1	0.1	0.1	0.2	0.1	•	•	0.7	0.7
Pensions and Other Deferred Comp. 16	1.2	0.4	0.0	•	0.3	0.3	0.2	0.7	0.3	•	•	1.1	1.9
Employee Benefits 17	2.5	0.0	1.0	1.2	1.9	1.7	1.3	1.5	1.8	•	•	2.9	3.2
Advertising 18	0.9	0.1	0.1	0.2	0.3	0.2	0.2	0.2	0.3	•	•	0.4	1.5
Other Expenses 19	8.6	11.6	8.4	13.3	7.5	7.8	8.7	6.8	6.9	•	•	6.3	9.3
Officers' Compensation 20	1.1	3.0	3.3	4.7	3.3	2.4	1.9	1.4	1.5	•	•	0.5	0.5
Operating Margin 21	0.4	•	3.1	4.9	5.0	6.0	3.8	2.6	3.0	•	•	•	•
Operating Margin Before Officers' Comp. 22	1.5	•	6.4	9.6	8.3	8.4	5.7	4.0	4.5	•	•	0.2	•

Selected Average Balance Sheet ($ in Thousands)

Net Receivables 23	3364	0	112	280	672	1419	4059	8825	16092	•	131307	1104974
Inventories 24	1984	0	23	65	357	918	2589	5878	19933	•	94560	605348
Net Property, Plant and Equipment 25	6835	0	12	120	762	2541	5447	10661	26180	•	394598	2538938
Total Assets 26	41223	0	211	762	2214	6593	15466	34139	73141	•	1045320	20594603
Notes and Loans Payable 27	9806	0	43	174	858	2660	6131	9651	19702	•	452322	4273653
All Other Liabilities 28	15826	0	82	187	618	1313	3976	7945	19093	•	221891	8660291
Net Worth 29	15591	0	86	401	737	2620	5359	16543	34346	•	371107	7660660

Selected Financial Ratios (Times to 1)

Current Ratio 30	0.7	•	1.7	3.2	1.6	1.8	1.5	1.8	1.9	•	1.6	0.5
Quick Ratio 31	0.4	•	1.3	2.8	1.2	1.1	0.9	1.1	0.9	•	0.7	0.3
Net Sales to Working Capital 32	•	•	21.4	4.5	13.4	7.9	11.4	7.6	6.7	•	8.6	•
Coverage Ratio 33	5.9	111.1	13.6	39.4	7.2	6.7	4.9	12.6	4.9	•	2.9	6.1
Total Asset Turnover 34	0.6	•	7.9	2.6	3.2	1.9	4.9	1.9	1.7	•	1.0	0.4
Inventory Turnover 35	8.6	•	58.4	19.8	13.5	9.1	9.4	8.3	4.6	•	8.0	7.7
Receivables Turnover 36	8.5	•	29.6	9.1	9.2	9.9	9.5	8.7	7.6	•	9.6	13.6
Total Liabilities to Net Worth 37	1.6	•	1.5	0.9	2.0	1.5	1.9	1.1	1.1	•	1.8	1.7
Current Assets to Working Capital 38	•	•	2.5	1.5	2.6	2.3	2.8	2.3	2.1	•	2.7	•
Current Liabilities to Working Capital 39	•	•	1.5	0.5	1.6	1.3	1.8	1.3	1.1	•	1.7	•
Working Capital to Net Sales 40	•	•	0.0	0.2	0.1	0.1	0.1	0.1	0.1	•	0.1	•
Inventory to Working Capital 41	•	•	0.5	0.1	0.6	0.7	1.0	0.8	1.0	•	0.9	•
Total Receipts to Cash Flow 42	4.6	1.9	17.1	7.2	9.6	8.0	9.9	5.5	10.8	•	8.9	3.1
Cost of Goods to Cash Flow 43	3.1	1.4	13.9	4.6	6.5	5.3	7.1	4.1	8.1	•	6.5	1.9
Cash Flow to Total Debt 44	0.2	•	0.8	0.8	0.5	0.4	0.3	0.7	0.3	•	0.2	0.2

Selected Financial Factors (in Percentages)

Debt Ratio 45	62.2	•	59.3	47.4	66.7	60.3	65.3	51.5	53.0	•	64.5	62.8
Return on Total Assets 46	13.1	•	26.4	13.7	21.2	17.4	12.7	28.1	8.3	•	10.6	12.8
Return on Equity Before Income Taxes 47	28.7	•	60.0	25.4	54.9	37.2	29.3	53.5	14.1	•	19.5	28.7
Return on Equity After Income Taxes 48	21.9	•	60.0	25.4	53.7	35.2	26.4	39.5	11.2	•	15.1	21.6
Profit Margin (Before Income Tax) 49	17.6	47.5	3.1	5.1	5.7	7.8	4.7	13.8	4.0	•	7.0	29.2
Profit Margin (After Income Tax) 50	13.5	4.5	3.1	5.1	5.6	7.4	4.2	10.2	3.2	•	5.4	22.0

Table I

Corporations with and without Net Income

PRINTING AND RELATED SUPPORT ACTIVITIES

MONEY AMOUNTS AND SIZE OF ASSETS IN THOUSANDS OF DOLLARS

Item Description for Accounting Period 7/05 Through 6/06	Total	Zero Assets	Under 500	500 to 1,000	1,000 to 5,000	5,000 to 10,000	10,000 to 25,000	25,000 to 50,000	50,000 to 100,000	100,000 to 250,000	250,000 to 500,000	500,000 to 2,500,000	2,500,000 and over
Number of Enterprises 1	32671	3016	22163	2852	3629	486	329	112	37	22	8	17	0
Revenues ($ in Thousands)													
Net Sales 2	90556289	958626	10973385	5345672	15249190	6122251	8867944	6114771	3629679	4226894	3762404	25305475	0
Interest 3	182282	8122	1503	6624	9256	3629	7334	3165	2382	9846	20046	110375	0
Rents 4	135659	642	84	10941	4938	10356	1611	830	998	3292	386	101581	0
Royalties 5	321449	1422	1638	0	0	3272	2927	2724	65	16875	15463	277062	0
Other Portfolio Income 6	517778	26697	18531	35978	19408	23830	16155	31335	9454	18551	30467	287371	0
Other Receipts 7	709687	27190	10593	18703	121982	50020	69375	32230	20329	18483	9797	330984	0
Total Receipts 8	92423144	1022699	11005734	5417918	15404774	6213358	8965346	6185055	3662907	4293941	3838563	26412848	0
Average Total Receipts 9	2829	339	497	1900	4245	12785	27250	55224	98997	195179	479820	1553697	•
Operating Costs/Operating Income (%)													
Cost of Operations 10	61.3	60.9	48.1	51.5	59.7	62.7	68.3	68.8	65.6	58.8	65.9	64.6	•
Salaries and Wages 11	10.1	15.8	11.0	11.6	11.8	9.6	9.2	9.6	7.1	10.0	7.7	9.7	•
Taxes Paid 12	2.4	2.2	2.9	2.6	3.0	2.5	2.3	2.3	2.1	2.1	1.8	2.0	•
Interest Paid 13	1.9	2.4	0.7	1.7	1.6	1.6	1.5	1.5	2.1	3.4	2.9	2.5	•
Depreciation 14	3.4	2.7	2.4	3.5	3.7	3.5	3.5	3.3	4.7	3.5	3.3	3.4	•
Amortization and Depletion 15	0.4	0.6	0.2	0.2	0.2	0.1	0.3	0.5	0.6	1.2	1.7	0.5	•
Pensions and Other Deferred Comp. 16	0.6	0.3	0.2	0.4	0.4	0.3	0.4	0.5	0.6	0.7	1.3	0.8	•
Employee Benefits 17	1.8	3.6	1.1	0.9	1.5	1.4	1.4	2.3	1.9	2.0	2.9	2.3	•
Advertising 18	0.8	0.6	1.0	0.4	0.5	0.3	0.6	0.4	3.4	1.3	0.2	0.8	•
Other Expenses 19	12.0	12.9	20.4	17.5	10.8	12.5	7.9	7.2	7.3	14.3	10.2	10.8	•
Officers' Compensation 20	3.2	4.5	7.7	7.6	5.3	4.2	2.3	1.9	1.6	1.1	0.7	0.4	•
Operating Margin 21	2.1	•	4.4	2.1	1.5	1.2	2.4	1.6	3.0	1.6	1.6	2.1	•
Operating Margin Before Officers' Comp. 22	5.3	•	12.0	9.7	6.8	5.4	4.7	3.5	4.6	2.7	2.3	2.5	•

Selected Average Balance Sheet ($ in Thousands)

Net Receivables 23	369	0	22	207	550	1971	3987	8374	13852	26123	52850	250332	•
Inventories 24	138	0	5	46	145	1117	1741	4089	8671	13306	27064	61622	•
Net Property, Plant and Equipment 25	551	0	45	270	795	2364	5673	11345	21746	40117	96547	388280	•
Total Assets 26	1944	0	104	714	1957	7022	15205	34152	66583	165148	385883	1802588	•
Notes and Loans Payable 27	745	0	95	421	919	2649	5899	12281	24951	71207	131659	561520	•
All Other Liabilities 28	611	0	37	142	464	1822	4048	10287	17587	45877	105605	657169	•
Net Worth 29	589	0	-28	151	574	2550	5257	11584	24045	48065	148618	583898	•

Selected Financial Ratios (Times to 1)

Current Ratio 30	1.2	•	1.2	2.0	1.5	1.6	1.5	1.4	1.6	1.3	1.3	0.9	•
Quick Ratio 31	0.9	•	1.0	1.7	1.1	1.0	1.0	1.0	1.0	0.8	0.9	0.7	•
Net Sales to Working Capital 32	20.8	•	57.6	10.0	13.2	8.4	11.3	10.8	8.3	14.4	17.6	•	•
Coverage Ratio 33	3.2	1.1	7.3	3.0	2.6	2.7	3.4	2.8	2.9	2.0	2.3	3.6	•
Total Asset Turnover 34	1.4	•	4.8	2.6	2.1	1.8	1.8	1.6	1.5	1.2	1.2	0.8	•
Inventory Turnover 35	12.3	•	47.3	21.2	17.3	7.1	10.6	9.2	7.4	8.5	11.4	15.6	•
Receivables Turnover 36	7.4	•	20.9	8.5	8.4	6.6	6.9	6.8	7.2	9.2	9.9	6.6	•
Total Liabilities to Net Worth 37	2.3	•	•	3.7	2.4	1.8	1.9	1.9	1.8	2.4	1.6	2.1	•
Current Assets to Working Capital 38	5.2	•	5.8	2.0	3.1	2.8	3.2	3.3	2.6	4.2	4.0	•	•
Current Liabilities to Working Capital 39	4.2	•	4.8	1.0	2.1	1.8	2.2	2.3	1.6	3.2	3.0	•	•
Working Capital to Net Sales 40	0.0	•	0.0	0.1	0.1	0.1	0.1	0.1	0.1	0.1	0.1	•	•
Inventory to Working Capital 41	1.0	•	0.5	0.3	0.5	0.7	0.7	0.9	0.8	1.1	1.1	•	•
Total Receipts to Cash Flow 42	8.2	12.4	5.5	6.5	10.6	9.4	11.4	13.2	10.6	7.3	9.9	7.1	•
Cost of Goods to Cash Flow 43	5.0	7.6	2.7	3.3	6.3	5.9	7.8	9.1	6.9	4.3	6.5	4.6	•
Cash Flow to Total Debt 44	0.3	0.7	0.5	0.5	0.3	0.3	0.2	0.2	0.2	0.2	0.2	0.2	•

Selected Financial Factors (in Percentages)

Debt Ratio 45	69.7	•	126.5	78.8	70.6	63.7	65.4	66.1	63.9	70.9	61.5	67.6	•
Return on Total Assets 46	8.7	•	25.7	13.6	8.8	7.7	8.8	6.8	8.8	7.7	7.9	7.4	•
Return on Equity Before Income Taxes 47	19.7	•	•	42.5	18.6	13.3	17.9	12.9	15.9	13.0	11.5	16.6	•
Return on Equity After Income Taxes 48	16.3	•	•	41.2	17.5	11.3	16.2	11.6	13.9	10.9	7.1	12.0	•
Profit Margin (Before Income Tax) 49	4.2	0.1	4.7	3.4	2.5	2.7	3.5	2.7	3.9	3.2	3.6	6.5	•
Profit Margin (After Income Tax) 50	3.5	•	4.6	3.3	2.4	2.3	3.2	2.5	3.4	2.7	2.2	4.7	•

Table II
Corporations with Net Income

PRINTING AND RELATED SUPPORT ACTIVITIES

MONEY AMOUNTS AND SIZE OF ASSETS IN THOUSANDS OF DOLLARS

Item Description for Accounting Period 7/05 Through 6/06	Total	Zero Assets	Under 500	500 to 1,000	1,000 to 5,000	5,000 to 10,000	10,000 to 25,000	25,000 to 50,000	50,000 to 100,000	100,000 to 250,000	250,000 to 500,000	500,000 to 2,500,000	2,500,000 and over
Number of Enterprises **1**	18007	1273	11680	1861	2429	358	265	75	31	14	•	•	0

Revenues ($ in Thousands)

	Total	Zero Assets	Under 500	500 to 1,000	1,000 to 5,000	5,000 to 10,000	10,000 to 25,000	25,000 to 50,000	50,000 to 100,000	100,000 to 250,000	250,000 to 500,000	500,000 to 2,500,000	2,500,000 and over
Net Sales **2**	68692000	140755	7732269	3881507	10398660	4641907	7297328	4226069	3176899	2709932	•	•	0
Interest **3**	150938	49	905	6568	5297	2715	6547	2233	2333	9223	•	•	0
Rents **4**	127649	1	0	10941	2319	5718	1611	826	998	3292	•	•	0
Royalties **5**	310579	0	0	0	0	3238	2901	2701	65	16851	•	•	0
Other Portfolio Income **6**	475471	26697	16778	35978	14734	12174	14315	9690	9452	17876	•	•	0
Other Receipts **7**	593760	14719	8398	4665	99509	32947	47703	32699	20071	16644	•	•	0
Total Receipts **8**	70350397	182221	7758350	3939659	10520519	4698699	7370405	4274218	3209818	2773818	•	•	•
Average Total Receipts **9**	3907	143	664	2117	4331	13125	27813	56990	103543	198130	•	•	•

Operating Costs/Operating Income (%)

	Total	Zero Assets	Under 500	500 to 1,000	1,000 to 5,000	5,000 to 10,000	10,000 to 25,000	25,000 to 50,000	50,000 to 100,000	100,000 to 250,000	250,000 to 500,000	500,000 to 2,500,000	2,500,000 and over
Cost of Operations **10**	60.1	69.9	47.8	46.4	57.8	61.4	66.7	67.2	65.6	51.5	•	•	•
Salaries and Wages **11**	9.9	4.2	9.1	13.2	11.1	10.4	9.3	9.6	7.1	12.5	•	•	•
Taxes Paid **12**	2.3	2.6	2.5	2.5	3.0	2.4	2.3	2.1	2.0	1.9	•	•	•
Interest Paid **13**	1.8	1.5	0.4	1.7	1.3	1.2	1.3	0.8	1.3	2.3	•	•	•
Depreciation **14**	3.3	4.4	2.0	2.8	3.3	3.5	3.3	3.3	4.6	3.6	•	•	•
Amortization and Depletion **15**	0.4	0.1	0.1	0.1	0.1	0.1	0.2	0.2	0.4	1.0	•	•	•
Pensions and Other Deferred Comp. **16**	0.6	0.2	0.2	0.6	0.4	0.4	0.5	0.4	0.6	0.5	•	•	•
Employee Benefits **17**	1.8	1.7	0.8	0.7	1.5	1.5	1.5	2.1	1.8	2.1	•	•	•
Advertising **18**	0.9	0.0	0.6	0.3	0.7	0.2	0.5	0.5	3.9	1.8	•	•	•
Other Expenses **19**	11.5	10.9	19.4	16.8	10.9	11.7	7.5	6.8	7.4	17.2	•	•	•
Officers' Compensation **20**	3.1	5.3	8.0	8.6	5.1	3.3	2.4	1.9	1.5	1.2	•	•	•
Operating Margin **21**	4.5	•	8.9	6.5	4.8	3.9	4.5	5.1	3.9	4.4	•	•	•
Operating Margin Before Officers' Comp. **22**	7.6	4.4	16.9	15.0	9.9	7.2	6.9	6.9	5.4	5.6	•	•	•

Selected Average Balance Sheet ($ in Thousands)

Net Receivables 23	506	0	28	232	525	1990	3993	8752	14512	22584
Inventories 24	176	0	5	28	147	927	1606	4516	9431	12491
Net Property, Plant and Equipment 25	761	0	44	254	747	2444	5613	11230	19849	37376
Total Assets 26	2800	0	123	736	1907	6734	15264	34580	65043	161549
Notes and Loans Payable 27	929	0	71	254	779	2378	5146	8429	19416	47096
All Other Liabilities 28	821	0	28	122	393	1505	3793	8732	18427	44781
Net Worth 29	1050	0	24	360	735	2851	6325	17418	27200	69672

Selected Financial Ratios (Times to 1)

Current Ratio 30	1.3	•	2.0	2.9	1.7	1.9	1.6	1.8	1.7	1.3
Quick Ratio 31	1.0	•	1.7	2.6	1.3	1.4	1.1	1.2	1.1	0.8
Net Sales to Working Capital 32	16.6	•	19.9	7.8	9.8	6.8	10.0	7.0	7.5	14.5
Coverage Ratio 33	4.9	19.6	22.4	5.7	5.5	5.3	5.3	8.5	4.7	3.9
Total Asset Turnover 34	1.4	•	5.4	2.8	2.2	1.9	1.8	1.6	1.6	1.2
Inventory Turnover 35	13.0	•	62.3	34.4	16.9	8.6	11.4	8.4	7.1	8.0
Receivables Turnover 36	7.6	•	23.4	8.1	8.9	7.4	7.7	6.6	14.1	12.2
Total Liabilities to Net Worth 37	1.7	•	4.1	1.0	1.6	1.4	1.4	1.0	1.4	1.3
Current Assets to Working Capital 38	4.2	•	2.0	1.5	2.3	2.1	2.8	2.2	2.4	4.4
Current Liabilities to Working Capital 39	3.2	•	1.0	0.5	1.3	1.1	1.8	1.2	1.4	3.4
Working Capital to Net Sales 40	0.1	•	0.1	0.1	0.1	0.1	0.1	0.1	0.1	0.1
Inventory to Working Capital 41	0.8	•	0.2	0.1	0.4	0.5	0.6	0.6	0.7	1.2
Total Receipts to Cash Flow 42	6.7	2.8	4.5	5.1	8.0	7.9	9.6	9.3	9.5	5.1
Cost of Goods to Cash Flow 43	4.0	2.0	2.2	2.3	4.6	4.9	6.4	6.2	6.2	2.6
Cash Flow to Total Debt 44	0.3	•	1.5	1.1	0.5	0.4	0.3	0.4	0.3	0.4

Selected Financial Factors (in Percentages)

Debt Ratio 45	62.5	•	80.5	51.1	61.5	57.7	58.6	49.6	58.2	56.9
Return on Total Assets 46	11.8	•	52.0	27.3	16.3	12.2	12.2	11.4	9.8	10.9
Return on Equity Before Income Taxes 47	25.2	•	254.0	46.2	34.6	23.3	23.9	20.0	18.4	18.8
Return on Equity After Income Taxes 48	21.7	•	251.6	45.3	33.3	20.9	22.2	18.8	16.3	16.6
Profit Margin (Before Income Tax) 49	6.9	28.5	9.3	8.0	5.9	5.1	5.5	6.2	4.9	6.8
Profit Margin (After Income Tax) 50	6.0	23.2	9.2	7.8	5.7	4.6	5.1	5.8	4.3	6.0

Table I

Corporations with and without Net Income

PETROLEUM REFINERIES (INCLUDING INTEGRATED)

MONEY AMOUNTS AND SIZE OF ASSETS IN THOUSANDS OF DOLLARS

Item Description for Accounting Period 7/05 Through 6/06	Total	Zero Assets	Under 500	500 to 1,000	1,000 to 5,000	5,000 to 10,000	10,000 to 25,000	25,000 to 50,000	50,000 to 100,000	100,000 to 250,000	250,000 to 500,000	500,000 to 2,500,000	2,500,000 and over
1 Number of Enterprises	1067	255	644	3	98	5	10	6	8	10	0	10	18
Revenues ($ in Thousands)													
2 Net Sales	1514778119	18718668	0	8317	0	47504	605056	847630	1569483	5932889	0	25368215	1461680357
3 Interest	15572735	8280	0	0	437	0	338	464	3827	7506	0	68488	15483393
4 Rents	1414105	70	0	0	0	0	298	0	154	4683	0	13679	1395221
5 Royalties	890706	0	0	0	0	0	0	0	0	11604	0	41	879061
6 Other Portfolio Income	20642602	8394	0	0	0	1	1621	204	12806	36111	0	80885	20502581
7 Other Receipts	33073543	1210402	1135	0	81794	2300	2506	1257	35951	112583	0	204422	31142195
8 Total Receipts	1586371810	19945814	1135	8317	82231	49805	609819	849555	1622221	6105376	0	25735730	1531361808
9 Average Total Receipts	1486759	78219	2	2772	839	9961	60982	141592	202778	610538	•	2573573	85075656
Operating Costs/Operating Income (%)													
10 Cost of Operations	87.2	96.3	•	86.3	•	36.3	83.2	90.2	86.3	92.1	•	85.8	87.1
11 Salaries and Wages	1.4	0.3	•	28.3	•	16.2	2.4	1.8	1.6	1.0	•	2.1	1.4
12 Taxes Paid	1.7	0.4	•	9.2	•	1.4	0.8	0.4	0.9	0.8	•	1.1	1.7
13 Interest Paid	1.2	0.3	•	12.9	•	1.5	0.8	0.8	0.8	0.6	•	0.7	1.2
14 Depreciation	0.9	1.0	•	3.5	•	1.4	0.6	1.7	1.3	1.0	•	1.2	0.9
15 Amortization and Depletion	0.3	0.1	•	•	•	•	0.3	0.1	0.1	0.0	•	0.8	0.3
16 Pensions and Other Deferred Comp.	0.2	0.1	•	•	•	0.5	0.1	0.2	0.2	0.1	•	0.2	0.2
17 Employee Benefits	0.1	0.0	•	•	•	1.2	0.1	0.1	0.3	0.2	•	0.2	0.1
18 Advertising	0.1	0.0	•	•	•	0.0	0.0	0.2	0.0	0.1	•	0.1	0.1
19 Other Expenses	4.1	0.5	•	58.5	•	9.2	12.8	7.3	3.9	2.5	•	4.4	4.2
20 Officers' Compensation	0.1	0.5	•	19.6	•	5.8	1.1	0.6	0.6	0.5	•	0.5	0.0
21 Operating Margin	2.8	0.5	•	•	•	26.4	•	•	3.9	1.1	•	3.1	2.8
22 Operating Margin Before Officers' Comp.	2.8	1.0	•	•	•	32.2	•	•	4.5	1.6	•	3.6	2.8

Selected Average Balance Sheet ($ in Thousands)

Net Receivables 23	961688	0	0	107	4	2219	4785	15112	21023	43431	148708	56882313
Inventories 24	23494	0	0	94	6	797	1657	2851	11064	20252	98233	1312371
Net Property, Plant and Equipment 25	174723	0	0	488	49	1997	5333	15975	19646	57289	323418	10127744
Total Assets 26	1848859	0	34	816	1421	9603	17610	39381	78425	226281	869331	108906205
Notes and Loans Payable 27	149687	0	64	4539	0	2347	5061	17050	10935	26650	174585	8744276
All Other Liabilities 28	1112850	0	0	1188	-9	4063	6527	20780	30604	116661	351092	65681954
Net Worth 29	586122	0	-30	-4911	1430	3193	6022	1552	36885	82969	343654	34479975

Selected Financial Ratios (Times to 1)

Current Ratio 30	1.0	•	0.9	0.3	•	1.4	1.5	1.0	1.4	1.1	1.5	1.0
Quick Ratio 31	1.0	•	0.9	0.2	•	0.8	1.0	0.8	1.0	0.6	1.0	1.0
Net Sales to Working Capital 32	39.6	•	•	•	•	5.5	18.7	252.5	13.4	69.2	15.7	40.2
Coverage Ratio 33	8.4	24.1	0.5	•	•	21.6	•	•	10.2	8.2	7.8	8.3
Total Asset Turnover 34	0.8	•	•	3.4	•	1.0	3.4	3.6	2.5	2.6	2.9	0.7
Inventory Turnover 35	52.7	•	•	25.5	•	4.3	30.4	44.7	15.3	27.0	22.2	53.9
Receivables Turnover 36	1.9	•	•	52.0	•	8.6	16.2	12.5	11.4	21.7	22.5	1.8
Total Liabilities to Net Worth 37	2.2	•	•	•	•	2.0	1.9	24.4	1.1	1.7	1.5	2.2
Current Assets to Working Capital 38	29.7	•	•	•	1.0	3.4	3.0	39.4	3.2	13.9	2.9	31.1
Current Liabilities to Working Capital 39	28.7	•	•	•	•	2.4	2.0	38.4	2.2	12.9	1.9	30.1
Working Capital to Net Sales 40	0.0	•	•	•	•	0.2	0.1	0.0	0.1	0.0	0.1	0.0
Inventory to Working Capital 41	0.7	•	•	•	•	0.5	0.8	4.4	0.7	4.4	0.8	0.7
Total Receipts to Cash Flow 42	9.4	13.5	•	•	•	2.5	9.4	29.1	9.9	18.2	13.0	9.3
Cost of Goods to Cash Flow 43	8.2	12.9	•	•	•	0.9	7.8	26.3	8.6	16.7	11.1	8.1
Cash Flow to Total Debt 44	0.1	•	•	•	•	0.6	0.6	0.1	0.5	0.2	0.4	0.1

Selected Financial Factors (in Percentages)

Debt Ratio 45	68.3	•	189.2	701.8	•	66.7	65.8	96.1	53.0	63.3	60.5	68.3
Return on Total Assets 46	7.8	•	2.5	•	56.9	32.4	•	•	20.1	12.1	15.1	7.7
Return on Equity Before Income Taxes 47	21.7	•	3.2	•	56.5	92.8	•	•	38.6	29.0	33.2	21.4
Return on Equity After Income Taxes 48	14.2	•	3.2	•	53.0	92.8	•	•	34.5	18.2	22.8	14.0
Profit Margin (Before Income Tax) 49	9.0	7.0	•	•	•	31.2	•	•	7.3	4.1	4.5	9.1
Profit Margin (After Income Tax) 50	5.9	4.7	•	•	•	31.2	•	•	6.5	2.5	3.1	5.9

Table II
Corporations with Net Income

PETROLEUM REFINERIES (INCLUDING INTEGRATED)

MONEY AMOUNTS AND SIZE OF ASSETS IN THOUSANDS OF DOLLARS

Item Description for Accounting Period 7/05 Through 6/06	Total	Zero Assets	Under 500	500 to 1,000	1,000 to 5,000	5,000 to 10,000	10,000 to 25,000	25,000 to 50,000	50,000 to 100,000	100,000 to 250,000	250,000 to 500,000	500,000 to 2,500,000	2,500,000 and over
Number of Enterprises **1**	408	255	0	0	98	5	3	•	•	•	0	•	18

Revenues ($ in Thousands)

Item	Total	Zero Assets	Under 500	500 to 1,000	1,000 to 5,000	5,000 to 10,000	10,000 to 25,000	25,000 to 50,000	50,000 to 100,000	100,000 to 250,000	250,000 to 500,000	500,000 to 2,500,000	2,500,000 and over
Net Sales **2**	1511146613	18718668	0	0	0	47504	216933	•	•	•	0	•	•1461680357
Interest **3**	15550414	8280	0	0	437	0	131	•	•	•	0	•	15483393
Rents **4**	1409414	70	0	0	0	0	0	•	•	•	0	•	1395221
Royalties **5**	890706	0	0	0	0	0	0	•	•	•	0	•	879061
Other Portfolio Income **6**	2061818	8394	0	0	0	0	696	•	•	•	0	•	20502581
Other Receipts **7**	32987572	1210402	0	0	81794	2300	0	•	•	•	0	•	31421195
Total Receipts **8**	1582603337	19945814	0	0	82231	49805	217760	•	•	•	0	•	•1531361808
Average Total Receipts **9**	3878930	78219	•	•	839	9961	72587	•	•	•	•	•	85075656

Operating Costs/Operating Income (%)

Item	Total	Zero Assets	Under 500	500 to 1,000	1,000 to 5,000	5,000 to 10,000	10,000 to 25,000	25,000 to 50,000	50,000 to 100,000	100,000 to 250,000	250,000 to 500,000	500,000 to 2,500,000	2,500,000 and over
Cost of Operations **10**	87.2	96.3	•	•	•	36.3	83.6	•	•	•	•	•	87.1
Salaries and Wages **11**	1.4	0.3	•	•	•	16.2	3.3	•	•	•	•	•	1.4
Taxes Paid **12**	1.7	0.4	•	•	•	1.4	0.9	•	•	•	•	•	1.7
Interest Paid **13**	1.2	0.3	•	•	•	1.5	0.0	•	•	•	•	•	1.2
Depreciation **14**	0.9	1.0	•	•	•	1.4	1.4	•	•	•	•	•	0.9
Amortization and Depletion **15**	0.3	0.1	•	•	•	•	0.7	•	•	•	•	•	0.3
Pensions and Other Deferred Comp. **16**	0.2	0.1	•	•	•	0.5	•	•	•	•	•	•	0.2
Employee Benefits **17**	0.1	0.0	•	•	•	1.2	0.4	•	•	•	•	•	0.1
Advertising **18**	0.1	0.0	•	•	•	0.0	•	•	•	•	•	•	0.1
Other Expenses **19**	4.1	0.5	•	•	•	9.2	7.8	•	•	•	•	•	4.2
Officers' Compensation **20**	0.1	0.5	•	•	•	5.8	0.3	•	•	•	•	•	0.0
Operating Margin **21**	2.8	0.5	•	•	•	26.4	1.6	•	•	•	•	•	2.8
Operating Margin Before Officers' Comp. **22**	2.8	1.0	•	•	•	32.2	1.9	•	•	•	•	•	2.8

Selected Average Balance Sheet ($ in Thousands)

Net Receivables 23	2514128	0	4	2219	4681	56882313
Inventories 24	60155	0	0	671	2965	1421342
Net Property, Plant and Equipment 25	455868	0	49	1997	8149	10127744
Total Assets 26	4830762	0	1421	9603	22015	108906205
Notes and Loans Payable 27	390527	0	0	2347	26	8744276
All Other Liabilities 28	2908291	0	-9	4063	4282	65681954
Net Worth 29	1531945	0	1430	3193	17707	34479975

Selected Financial Ratios (Times to 1)

Current Ratio 30	1.0			1.4	2.7	1.0
Quick Ratio 31	1.0			0.8	1.9	1.0
Net Sales to Working Capital 32	39.5			5.5	10.0	40.2
Coverage Ratio 33	8.4	24.1		21.6	620.4	8.3
Total Asset Turnover 34	0.8			1.0	3.3	0.7
Inventory Turnover 35	53.7			5.1	20.4	49.7
Receivables Turnover 36	1.9			4.7	30.9	2.9
Total Liabilities to Net Worth 37	2.2			2.0	0.2	2.2
Current Assets to Working Capital 38	29.7		1.0	3.4	1.6	31.1
Current Liabilities to Working Capital 39	28.7			2.4	0.6	30.1
Working Capital to Net Sales 40	0.0			0.2	0.1	0.0
Inventory to Working Capital 41	0.7			0.5	0.4	0.7
Total Receipts to Cash Flow 42	9.4	13.5		2.5	12.2	0.7
Cost of Goods to Cash Flow 43	8.2	12.9		0.9	10.2	9.3
Cash Flow to Total Debt 44	0.1			0.6	1.4	0.1

Selected Financial Factors (in Percentages)

Debt Ratio 45	68.3			66.7	19.6	68.3
Return on Total Assets 46	7.8		56.9	32.4	6.6	7.7
Return on Equity Before Income Taxes 47	21.8		56.5	92.8	8.2	21.4
Return on Equity After Income Taxes 48	14.2		53.0	92.8	8.0	14.0
Profit Margin (Before Income Tax) 49	9.0	7.0		31.2	2.0	9.1
Profit Margin (After Income Tax) 50	5.9	4.7		31.2	2.0	5.9

Table I

Corporations with and without Net Income

ASPHALT PAVING, ROOFING, OTHER PETROLEUM AND COAL PRODUCTS

MONEY AMOUNTS AND SIZE OF ASSETS IN THOUSANDS OF DOLLARS

Item Description for Accounting Period 7/05 Through 6/06	Total	Zero Assets	Under 500	500 to 1,000	1,000 to 5,000	5,000 to 10,000	10,000 to 25,000	25,000 to 50,000	50,000 to 100,000	100,000 to 250,000	250,000 to 500,000	500,000 to 2,500,000	2,500,000 and over
Number of Enterprises 1	786	233	97	52	239	53	68	15	12	8	5	3	0
Revenues ($ in Thousands)													
Net Sales 2	15212321	243770	102141	158579	772597	665273	2171784	845529	1208995	2458086	1533243	5052325	0
Interest 3	33716	533	0	13	465	110	3644	1132	2847	4120	17197	3655	0
Rents 4	8096	0	0	0	777	0	6308	0	331	0	681	0	0
Royalties 5	5218	1236	0	0	0	5	0	0	9	2118	1851	0	0
Other Portfolio Income 6	70325	3314	0	0	382	559	4325	5963	818	5827	43196	5940	0
Other Receipts 7	253021	207	-20349	28	35088	59822	8633	6480	33889	19375	44479	65367	0
Total Receipts 8	15582697	249060	81792	158620	809309	725769	2194694	859104	1246889	2489526	1640647	5127287	•
Average Total Receipts 9	19825	1069	843	3050	3386	13694	32275	57274	103907	311191	328129	1709096	•
Operating Costs/Operating Income (%)													
Cost of Operations 10	76.3	82.8	•	64.9	43.6	84.8	75.4	77.2	81.1	87.4	75.5	75.8	•
Salaries and Wages 11	5.0	2.8	•	8.0	19.2	4.7	4.8	3.6	4.2	3.2	2.0	5.2	•
Taxes Paid 12	1.0	0.8	•	1.6	2.6	1.2	1.5	1.3	1.0	0.6	1.4	0.5	•
Interest Paid 13	2.1	1.9	•	0.1	3.6	2.3	0.7	1.1	1.2	0.8	9.1	1.6	•
Depreciation 14	1.9	3.9	•	3.9	3.7	3.2	1.9	2.2	1.6	0.8	2.7	1.7	•
Amortization and Depletion 15	0.3	1.6	•	•	0.0	0.4	0.2	0.1	0.5	0.5	1.1	0.1	•
Pensions and Other Deferred Comp. 16	0.4	2.9	•	0.0	0.5	0.2	0.3	0.5	0.1	0.2	0.9	0.2	•
Employee Benefits 17	0.9	1.0	•	•	0.8	1.0	0.9	1.1	0.5	0.5	1.5	1.0	•
Advertising 18	0.4	0.1	•	0.0	0.4	0.1	0.5	0.3	1.0	0.1	0.1	0.5	•
Other Expenses 19	8.4	7.5	2.5	12.1	21.2	4.0	7.5	6.0	7.3	3.5	9.1	10.3	•
Officers' Compensation 20	0.9	2.3	•	8.6	1.7	1.4	1.8	1.5	0.8	0.6	0.6	0.2	•
Operating Margin 21	2.3	•	97.5	0.7	2.7	•	4.5	5.2	0.7	1.8	•	2.7	•
Operating Margin Before Officers' Comp. 22	3.2	•	97.5	9.4	4.4	•	6.3	6.7	1.5	2.4	•	3.0	•

Selected Average Balance Sheet ($ in Thousands)

Net Receivables 23	2674	0	0	276	528	1993	4627	6463	19668	38675	57436	203756	•
Inventories 24	1458	0	0	126	495	2314	5832	14922	10574	46463	122010		•
Net Property, Plant and Equipment 25	3738	0	0	296	1102	3841	4554	10196	15392	32974	111551	329045	•
Total Assets 26	11417	0	10	673	2245	7701	16276	34564	76318	141072	389045	792814	•
Notes and Loans Payable 27	5119	0	143	153	3190	4263	8663	18696	34892	256814	293674		•
All Other Liabilities 28	3567	0	1618	295	1423	3749	9764	23672	30710	112278	240051		•
Net Worth 29	2731	0	-1751	226	-2368	1954	9368	16137	33950	75471	19953	259089	•

Selected Financial Ratios (Times to 1)

Current Ratio 30	1.8	•	1.1	0.7	1.3	2.1	2.1	1.8	1.8	1.6	2.5	•
Quick Ratio 31	1.1	•	1.1	0.5	1.0	1.4	1.1	1.3	1.1	0.7	1.4	•
Net Sales to Working Capital 32	8.2	101.1	94.4	•	19.1	6.4	5.6	4.8	10.5	6.4	7.1	•
Coverage Ratio 33	3.2	•	7.5	3.1	3.5	9.5	7.3	4.1	5.1	1.3	3.6	•
Total Asset Turnover 34	1.7	101.1	4.5	1.4	1.6	2.0	1.6	1.3	2.2	0.8	2.1	•
Inventory Turnover 35	10.1	•	•	11.2	21.5	10.4	7.5	7.7	18.0	5.0	10.5	•
Receivables Turnover 36	7.8	1309.5	5.1	5.1	6.5	7.8	7.5	5.4	10.2	6.3	8.8	•
Total Liabilities to Net Worth 37	3.2	•	2.0	•	2.9	0.7	1.1	1.2	0.9	18.5	2.1	•
Current Assets to Working Capital 38	2.3	1.0	11.4	•	4.7	2.0	1.9	2.2	2.3	2.7	1.7	•
Current Liabilities to Working Capital 39	1.3	0.0	10.4	•	3.7	1.0	0.9	1.2	1.3	1.7	0.7	•
Working Capital to Net Sales 40	0.1	•	0.0	•	0.1	0.2	0.2	0.2	0.1	0.2	0.1	•
Inventory to Working Capital 41	0.7	•	•	•	0.9	0.5	0.6	0.6	0.6	1.1	0.6	•
Total Receipts to Cash Flow 42	8.7	90.1	1.2	9.7	4.7	11.4	8.8	9.3	9.7	16.7	12.1	7.4 •
Cost of Goods to Cash Flow 43	6.7	74.6	6.3	2.0	9.6	6.7	7.2	7.8	14.6	9.1	5.6	•
Cash Flow to Total Debt 44	0.3	0.5	0.7	0.2	0.2	0.5	0.3	0.2	0.3	0.1	0.4	•

Selected Financial Factors (in Percentages)

Debt Ratio 45	76.1	•	66.5	205.5	74.6	42.4	53.3	55.5	46.5	94.9	67.3	•
Return on Total Assets 46	11.7	16914.2	4.0	15.8	13.3	12.2	12.7	6.6	8.5	9.6	12.3	•
Return on Equity Before Income Taxes 47	33.6	7844.7	10.2	•	37.3	18.9	23.5	11.2	12.7	46.7	27.1	•
Return on Equity After Income Taxes 48	29.1	•	8.7	•	34.0	16.2	18.4	10.5	9.8	32.4	23.8	•
Profit Margin (Before Income Tax) 49	4.7	77.6	0.8	7.4	5.8	5.6	6.7	3.8	3.1	3.0	4.2	•
Profit Margin (After Income Tax) 50	4.1	77.6	0.6	7.2	5.3	4.8	5.3	3.5	2.4	2.1	3.7	•

Table II
Corporations with Net Income

ASPHALT PAVING, ROOFING, OTHER PETROLEUM AND COAL PRODUCTS

MONEY AMOUNTS AND SIZE OF ASSETS IN THOUSANDS OF DOLLARS

Item Description for Accounting Period 7/05 Through 6/06	Total	Zero Assets	Under 500	500 to 1,000	1,000 to 5,000	5,000 to 10,000	10,000 to 25,000	25,000 to 50,000	50,000 to 100,000	100,000 to 250,000	250,000 to 500,000	500,000 to 2,500,000	2,500,000 and over
Number of Enterprises 1	491	0	97	52	208	44	56	•	•	•	•	3	0
Revenues ($ in Thousands)													
Net Sales 2	12853701	0	102141	158579	672256	561958	1853621	•	•	•	•	5052325	0
Interest 3	29872	0	0	13	465	107	3460	•	•	•	•	3655	0
Rents 4	7914	0	0	0	777	0	6129	•	•	•	•	0	0
Royalties 5	1860	0	0	0	0	5	0	•	•	•	•	0	0
Other Portfolio Income 6	64784	0	0	0	196	0	3990	•	•	•	•	5940	0
Other Receipts 7	231134	0	-20349	28	34023	59258	8494	•	•	•	•	65367	0
Total Receipts 8	13189265	0	81792	158620	707717	621328	1875694	•	•	•	•	5127287	0
Average Total Receipts 9	26862	•	843	3050	3402	14121	33495	•	•	•	•	1709096	•
Operating Costs/Operating Income (%)													
Cost of Operations 10	74.9	•	•	64.9	38.0	89.1	73.2	•	•	•	•	75.8	•
Salaries and Wages 11	5.2	•	•	8.0	20.3	1.9	5.4	•	•	•	•	5.2	•
Taxes Paid 12	1.0	•	•	1.6	2.8	0.9	1.6	•	•	•	•	0.5	•
Interest Paid 13	1.7	•	•	0.1	3.8	2.7	0.6	•	•	•	•	1.6	•
Depreciation 14	2.0	•	•	3.9	3.9	3.5	1.9	•	•	•	•	1.7	•
Amortization and Depletion 15	0.3	•	•	0.0	0.0	0.4	0.2	•	•	•	•	0.1	•
Pensions and Other Deferred Comp. 16	0.3	•	•	0.0	0.5	0.1	0.3	•	•	•	•	0.2	•
Employee Benefits 17	0.9	•	•	0.9	0.9	0.9	1.0	•	•	•	•	1.0	•
Advertising 18	0.5	•	•	0.0	0.5	0.0	0.6	•	•	•	•	0.5	•
Other Expenses 19	8.7	•	2.5	12.1	22.6	3.7	7.9	•	•	•	•	10.3	•
Officers' Compensation 20	0.8	•	•	8.6	1.6	0.3	1.4	•	•	•	•	0.2	•
Operating Margin 21	3.8	•	97.5	0.7	5.1	•	5.9	•	•	•	•	2.7	•
Operating Margin Before Officers' Comp. 22	4.5	•	97.5	9.4	6.7	•	7.3	•	•	•	•	3.0	•

Selected Average Balance Sheet ($ in Thousands)

Net Receivables 23	3609	0	276	532	2005	4280	203756
Inventories 24	1781	0	0	329	2219		122010
Net Property, Plant and Equipment 25	5182	0	52	1251	4287	4793	329045
Total Assets 26	15102	10	296	673	2344	8083/16643	792814
Notes and Loans Payable 27	6507	143	153	3394	5046	2956	293674
All Other Liabilities 28	5008	1618	295	1555	1638	3897	240051
Net Worth 29	3587	-1751	226	-2605	1399	9790	259089

Selected Financial Ratios (Times to 1)

Current Ratio 30	1.7		1.1	0.6	1.0	2.0	2.5
Quick Ratio 31	1.0		1.1	0.5	0.8	1.3	1.4
Net Sales to Working Capital 32	9.2	101.1	94.4	199.9	6.9	7.1	
Coverage Ratio 33	4.6		7.5	3.8	3.6	12.7	3.6
Total Asset Turnover 34	1.7	101.1	4.5	1.4	1.6	2.0	2.1
Inventory Turnover 35	11.0		23.8	34.6	10.9	10.5	
Receivables Turnover 36	8.2		22.1	12.1	6.8	8.9	8.8
Total Liabilities to Net Worth 37	3.2		2.0	4.8	0.7	2.1	
Current Assets to Working Capital 38	2.5		11.4	44.8	2.0	2.0	1.7
Current Liabilities to Working Capital 39	1.5		1.0	10.4	43.8	1.0	0.7
Working Capital to Net Sales 40	0.1		0.0	0.0	0.0	0.1	0.1
Inventory to Working Capital 41	0.8			7.2			0.6
Total Receipts to Cash Flow 42	7.5		9.7	1.2	4.0	10.5	7.4
Cost of Goods to Cash Flow 43	5.6		6.3	1.5	9.3	5.4	5.6
Cash Flow to Total Debt 44	0.3		0.7	0.5	0.2	0.2	0.4

Selected Financial Factors (in Percentages)

Debt Ratio 45	76.2	16914.2	66.2	211.2	82.7	66.5	41.2 / 67.3
Return on Total Assets 46	14.1	7844.7	4.0	19.5	15.2	4.0	15.4 / 12.3
Return on Equity Before Income Taxes 47	46.5		10.2		63.4		24.1 / 27.1
Return on Equity After Income Taxes 48	41.0		8.7		57.8		20.9 / 23.8
Profit Margin (Before Income Tax) 49	6.4	77.6	0.8	10.4	6.9		7.1 / 4.2
Profit Margin (After Income Tax) 50	5.6	77.6	0.6	10.2	6.3		6.2 / 3.7

Table I

Corporations with and without Net Income

BASIC CHEMICAL

MONEY AMOUNTS AND SIZE OF ASSETS IN THOUSANDS OF DOLLARS

Item Description for Accounting Period 7/05 Through 6/06	Total	Zero Assets	Under 500	500 to 1,000	1,000 to 5,000	5,000 to 10,000	10,000 to 25,000	25,000 to 50,000	50,000 to 100,000	100,000 to 250,000	250,000 to 500,000	500,000 to 2,500,000	2,500,000 and over
Number of Enterprises 1	1129	355	83	215	148	117	65	38	21	21	14	32	21

Revenues ($ in Thousands)

	Total	Zero Assets	Under 500	500 to 1,000	1,000 to 5,000	5,000 to 10,000	10,000 to 25,000	25,000 to 50,000	50,000 to 100,000	100,000 to 250,000	250,000 to 500,000	500,000 to 2,500,000	2,500,000 and over
Net Sales 2	153036607	2038966	81522	494487	750608	1029202	2129982	1838480	2012554	4464249	5100472	33660872	99435214
Interest 3	2695840	19270	0	0	1271	1549	1437	1941	2359	28467	33368	354309	2251867
Rents 4	291964	25	0	0	0	34	1469	2324	397	13241	641	15329	258505
Royalties 5	3641476	22479	0	0	0	0	0	505	1814	9377	10397	258184	3338720
Other Portfolio Income 6	7362100	5091	0	0	7021	1613	15386	6756	29221	41087	102078	998732	6155115
Other Receipts 7	5403563	32383	0	11821	1007	21894	5307	18621	18580	95636	647958	579259	397097
Total Receipts 8	172431550	2118214	81522	506308	759907	1054292	2153581	1868627	2064925	4652057	5894914	35866685	115410518
Average Total Receipts 9	152729	5967	982	2355	5135	9011	33132	49174	98330	221527	421065	1120834	5495739

Operating Costs/Operating Income (%)

	Total	Zero Assets	Under 500	500 to 1,000	1,000 to 5,000	5,000 to 10,000	10,000 to 25,000	25,000 to 50,000	50,000 to 100,000	100,000 to 250,000	250,000 to 500,000	500,000 to 2,500,000	2,500,000 and over
Cost of Operations 10	73.8	76.9	74.5	58.6	73.5	73.5	76.5	67.8	78.1	79.7	59.7	72.5	74.6
Salaries and Wages 11	5.5	4.1	3.1	3.7	7.0	4.8	4.7	7.5	4.6	5.1	8.0	6.3	5.1
Taxes Paid 12	1.2	0.9	2.6	1.0	2.0	2.5	1.5	1.7	1.4	0.8	1.4	1.1	1.2
Interest Paid 13	5.0	2.5	0.1	0.2	0.7	1.6	0.6	1.0	1.4	1.9	2.0	3.1	6.4
Depreciation 14	3.5	3.3	0.1	0.6	2.2	4.4	2.3	3.2	1.9	2.2	3.2	3.3	3.7
Amortization and Depletion 15	1.9	0.8	2.1	•	0.0	0.1	0.2	0.7	0.5	0.7	1.0	0.9	2.5
Pensions and Other Deferred Comp. 16	1.3	0.2	0.0	•	0.4	0.5	0.6	0.7	0.2	0.5	0.6	0.9	1.6
Employee Benefits 17	2.2	1.4	4.2	1.1	0.9	0.8	1.3	1.1	1.2	0.6	2.2	2.3	2.3
Advertising 18	0.5	0.2	0.0	0.1	0.3	0.1	0.2	0.3	0.3	0.1	0.4	1.7	0.1
Other Expenses 19	10.9	9.4	6.6	16.2	10.5	6.8	6.1	10.1	7.8	9.5	26.1	9.9	10.7
Officers' Compensation 20	0.6	0.4	11.2	8.3	4.6	1.9	1.5	1.9	1.0	0.8	0.7	0.7	0.4
Operating Margin 21	•	0.0	•	10.3	3.1	5.0	4.6	4.0	1.6	•	•	•	•
Operating Margin Before Officers' Comp. 22	•	0.4	6.6	18.6	2.4	5.0	6.1	5.9	2.6	•	•	•	•

Selected Average Balance Sheet ($ in Thousands)

Net Receivables 23	53892	0	138	324	728	1486	4356	7350	19073	29639	58611	161566	2519323
Inventories 24	13875	0	166	116	283	1073	3742	5395	13608	18032	35106	155188	423251
Net Property, Plant and Equipment 25	44908	0	8	29	297	2923	5857	11671	15836	49005	125920	343465	1684195
Total Assets 26	247572	0	333	618	2258	7132	16772	36103	72482	166118	372963	1298423	10663607
Notes and Loans Payable 27	101856	0	1	123	631	5733	5898	7533	26047	64984	99229	440534	4577939
All Other Liabilities 28	75429	0	69	182	755	2190	4624	7611	25448	41415	116964	484784	3123903
Net Worth 29	70287	0	262	313	873	-791	6250	20958	20987	59719	156770	373105	2961765

Selected Financial Ratios (Times to 1)

Current Ratio 30	1.1	•	4.1	2.2	1.9	1.5	2.1	1.9	1.6	1.6	1.7	1.4	1.0
Quick Ratio 31	0.8	•	2.1	1.3	1.4	0.7	1.1	1.1	0.8	1.0	1.0	0.7	0.8
Net Sales to Working Capital 32	14.8	•	4.6	7.2	7.1	6.3	6.3	6.0	6.2	7.9	6.3	7.9	29.8
Coverage Ratio 33	2.5	2.5	•	59.9	•	4.4	9.9	6.8	4.0	2.2	6.5	2.3	2.5
Total Asset Turnover 34	0.5	•	3.0	3.7	2.2	1.2	2.0	1.3	1.3	1.3	1.0	0.8	0.4
Inventory Turnover 35	7.2	•	4.4	11.6	13.2	6.0	6.7	6.1	5.5	9.4	6.2	4.9	8.4
Receivables Turnover 36	2.7	•	2.9	8.1	5.6	6.0	7.0	6.6	5.3	8.0	8.3	6.9	2.1
Total Liabilities to Net Worth 37	2.5	•	0.3	1.0	1.6	•	1.7	0.7	2.5	1.8	1.4	2.5	2.6
Current Assets to Working Capital 38	9.2	•	1.3	1.8	2.2	2.8	1.9	2.1	2.8	2.7	2.5	3.2	22.3
Current Liabilities to Working Capital 39	8.2	•	0.3	0.8	1.2	1.8	0.9	1.1	1.8	1.7	1.5	2.2	21.3
Working Capital to Net Sales 40	0.1	•	0.2	0.1	0.1	0.2	0.2	0.2	0.2	0.1	0.2	0.1	0.0
Inventory to Working Capital 41	1.6	•	0.6	0.4	0.4	1.0	0.8	0.7	0.9	0.7	0.8	1.2	2.9
Total Receipts to Cash Flow 42	7.0	8.2	•	4.2	14.8	9.2	9.7	7.2	10.3	9.9	3.0	10.1	6.5
Cost of Goods to Cash Flow 43	5.2	6.3	•	2.5	10.8	6.8	7.4	4.9	8.0	7.9	1.8	7.3	4.9
Cash Flow to Total Debt 44	0.1	•	•	1.8	0.2	0.1	0.3	0.4	0.2	0.2	0.6	0.1	0.1

Selected Financial Factors (in Percentages)

Debt Ratio 45	71.6	•	21.3	49.3	61.4	111.1	62.7	41.9	71.0	64.1	58.0	71.3	72.2
Return on Total Assets 46	7.0	•	•	47.8	8.7	•	12.5	8.9	7.5	5.5	12.7	5.9	7.0
Return on Equity Before Income Taxes 47	15.1	•	•	92.8	•	•	30.1	13.1	19.4	8.4	25.5	11.5	15.2
Return on Equity After Income Taxes 48	12.4	•	•	92.5	•	•	23.9	11.3	15.5	4.7	16.7	7.9	12.9
Profit Margin (Before Income Tax) 49	7.8	3.7	•	12.7	5.4	•	5.7	5.7	4.3	2.4	11.0	4.1	9.5
Profit Margin (After Income Tax) 50	6.4	3.3	•	12.6	•	4.5	4.6	4.9	3.4	1.3	7.2	2.8	8.1

Table II
Corporations with Net Income

BASIC CHEMICAL

MONEY AMOUNTS AND SIZE OF ASSETS IN THOUSANDS OF DOLLARS

Item Description for Accounting Period 7/05 Through 6/06	Total	Zero Assets	Under 500	500 to 1,000	1,000 to 5,000	5,000 to 10,000	10,000 to 25,000	25,000 to 50,000	50,000 to 100,000	100,000 to 250,000	250,000 to 500,000	500,000 to 2,500,000	2,500,000 and over
Number of Enterprises 1	655	66	•	215	115	104	55	30	11	•	10	•	13
Revenues ($ in Thousands)													
Net Sales 2	117607476	1882785	•	494487	680832	1028053	1958421	1478535	1154900	•	4877275	•	78839637
Interest 3	2052974	19060	•	0	1228	1549	1360	931	1855	•	32345	•	1676174
Rents 4	199641	25	•	0	0	34	1469	2324	360	•	641	•	173059
Royalties 5	3137581	22479	•	0	0	0	0	505	1321	•	10230	•	2932705
Other Portfolio Income 6	6946629	5091	•	0	7021	1613	15335	4131	19281	•	102078	•	5848409
Other Receipts 7	4106505	32382	•	11821	998	21894	5300	10947	13553	•	641778	•	2924050
Total Receipts 8	134050806	1961822	•	506308	690079	1053143	1981885	1497373	1191270	•	5664347	•	92394034
Average Total Receipts 9	204658	29725	•	2355	6001	10126	36034	49912	108297	•	566435	•	7107233
Operating Costs/Operating Income (%)													
Cost of Operations 10	74.3	76.9	•	58.6	70.9	73.5	76.3	63.8	74.3	•	59.0	•	77.1
Salaries and Wages 11	5.0	4.3	•	3.7	6.9	4.7	4.3	8.5	4.7	•	7.8	•	4.2
Taxes Paid 12	1.2	0.9	•	1.0	1.7	2.5	1.4	1.9	1.5	•	1.4	•	1.2
Interest Paid 13	3.9	2.6	•	0.2	0.6	0.7	0.6	1.0	1.1	•	1.8	•	4.8
Depreciation 14	3.6	2.7	•	0.6	1.9	4.2	2.1	3.0	2.0	•	3.0	•	3.9
Amortization and Depletion 15	2.1	0.7	•	•	0.0	0.1	0.2	0.3	0.4	•	1.0	•	2.8
Pensions and Other Deferred Comp. 16	1.0	0.2	•	•	0.4	0.5	0.7	0.5	0.2	•	0.6	•	1.1
Employee Benefits 17	2.3	1.5	•	1.1	0.9	0.8	1.2	1.2	1.3	•	2.2	•	2.4
Advertising 18	0.6	0.2	•	0.1	0.3	0.1	0.2	0.2	0.3	•	0.4	•	0.1
Other Expenses 19	9.9	8.8	•	16.2	10.0	6.7	5.8	9.3	6.5	•	26.3	•	9.1
Officers' Compensation 20	0.5	0.4	•	8.3	5.0	1.9	1.6	2.1	0.8	•	0.7	•	0.3
Operating Margin 21	•	0.8	•	10.3	1.2	4.3	5.8	8.1	6.8	•	•	•	•
Operating Margin Before Officers' Comp. 22	•	1.1	•	18.6	6.2	6.2	7.4	10.3	7.7	•	•	•	•

Selected Average Balance Sheet ($ in Thousands)

Net Receivables 23	78960	0	•	324	729	1617	4484	7647	21209	•	68572 •	3566374
Inventories 24	14515	0	•	116	211	923	4013	6786	12946	•	50890 •	370443
Net Property, Plant and Equipment 25	52323	0	•	29	247	2933	5094	10853	16988	•	124473 •	1887864
Total Assets 26	315280	0	•	618	2356	7242	16997	35306	71486	•	387790 •	13169394
Notes and Loans Payable 27	123938	0	•	123	463	4633	5030	7998	21466	•	72128 •	5377342
All Other Liabilities 28	92917	0	•	182	665	2350	4829	7995	15982	•	140596 •	3834932
Net Worth 29	98425	0	•	313	1228	259	7138	19313	34037	•	175066 •	3957121

Selected Financial Ratios (Times to 1)

Current Ratio 30	1.1	•	2.2	2.2	1.5	2.2	1.9	2.1	• 1.5	•	1.0
Quick Ratio 31	0.8	•	1.3	1.7	0.7	1.1	1.1	1.3	• 0.9	•	0.8
Net Sales to Working Capital 32	20.0	•	7.2	6.8	7.7	6.1	5.8	4.9	• 8.7	•	0.8
Coverage Ratio 33	3.8	2.8	59.9	5.0	10.4	12.1	10.3	10.1	• 8.2	•	3.6
Total Asset Turnover 34	0.6	•	3.7	2.5	1.4	2.1	1.4	1.5	• 1.3	•	0.5
Inventory Turnover 35	9.2	•	11.6	19.9	7.9	6.8	4.6	6.0	• 5.7	•	12.6
Receivables Turnover 36	3.6	•	8.1	11.6	8.4	7.4	12.9	5.6	• 14.2	•	2.8
Total Liabilities to Net Worth 37	2.2	•	1.0	0.9	27.0	1.4	0.8	1.1	• 1.2	•	2.3
Current Assets to Working Capital 38	13.0	•	1.8	1.8	3.1	1.9	2.1	1.9	• 2.8	•	2.3
Current Liabilities to Working Capital 39	12.0	•	0.8	0.8	2.1	0.9	1.1	0.9	• 1.8	•	1.9
Working Capital to Net Sales 40	0.0	•	0.1	0.1	0.2	0.9	0.2	0.2	• 0.1	•	0.1
Inventory to Working Capital 41	2.0	•	0.4	0.4	1.0	0.8	0.8	0.6	• 0.9	•	0.2
Total Receipts to Cash Flow 42	6.0	7.9	4.2	10.5	8.4	8.9	5.9	7.0	• 2.8	•	6.0
Cost of Goods to Cash Flow 43	4.5	6.1	2.5	7.4	6.2	6.8	3.8	5.2	• 1.7	•	4.6
Cash Flow to Total Debt 44	0.1	•	1.8	0.5	0.4	0.2	0.5	0.4	• 0.8	•	0.1

Selected Financial Factors (in Percentages)

Debt Ratio 45	68.8	•	49.3	47.9	96.4	58.0	45.3	52.4	• 54.9	•	70.0
Return on Total Assets 46	8.6	•	47.8	7.9	10.1	16.1	14.6	16.3	• 18.1	•	8.0
Return on Equity Before Income Taxes 47	20.5	•	92.8	12.2	254.5	35.1	24.0	30.8	• 35.3	•	19.3
Return on Equity After Income Taxes 48	17.2	•	92.5	10.5	217.0	28.7	21.5	26.2	• 24.3	•	16.6
Profit Margin (Before Income Tax) 49	11.2	4.7	12.7	2.5	6.7	7.0	9.4	10.0	• 12.7	•	12.6
Profit Margin (After Income Tax) 50	9.4	4.3	12.6	2.2	5.7	5.8	8.4	8.5	• 8.7	•	10.8

Table I

Corporations with and without Net Income

RESIN, SYNTHETIC RUBBER AND FIBERS AND FILAMENTS

MONEY AMOUNTS AND SIZE OF ASSETS IN THOUSANDS OF DOLLARS

Item Description for Accounting Period 7/05 Through 6/06	Total	Zero Assets	Under 500	500 to 1,000	1,000 to 5,000	5,000 to 10,000	10,000 to 25,000	25,000 to 50,000	50,000 to 100,000	100,000 to 250,000	250,000 to 500,000	500,000 to 2,500,000	2,500,000 and over
Number of Enterprises **1**	930	3	474	164	130	88	26	11	14	5	6	9	0
Revenues ($ in Thousands)													
Net Sales **2**	37321382	9198	0	71291	732623	1305782	721739	718970	1410030	1008498	2608868	28734382	0
Interest **3**	2079119	0	0	0	21	475	323	437	11922	10321	9001	2046619	0
Rents **4**	71466	0	0	0	0	0	0	43	906	0	2028	68489	0
Royalties **5**	721485	0	0	0	0	11985	0	50	24	4532	1909	702986	0
Other Portfolio Income **6**	8668151	0	0	0	303	31	205	222	3726	12190	17373	8650102	0
Other Receipts **7**	2403071	763	0	0	1770	514	22624	4665	1574	2768	26975	2341418	0
Total Receipts **8**	51280674	9961	0	71291	734717	1318787	744891	724387	1428182	1038309	2666154	42543996	0
Average Total Receipts **9**	55141	3320	0	435	5652	14986	28650	65853	102013	207662	444359	4727111	•
Operating Costs/Operating Income (%)													
Cost of Operations **10**	72.5	61.3	•	95.4	65.1	65.0	76.4	73.6	80.5	79.8	75.2	71.9	•
Salaries and Wages **11**	2.2	9.2	•	11.1	6.0	10.4	4.0	4.8	3.5	2.7	3.4	1.5	•
Taxes Paid **12**	0.8	1.4	•	5.1	3.4	1.5	1.3	1.1	1.3	1.3	1.6	0.5	•
Interest Paid **13**	7.5	1.6	•	•	0.4	1.2	1.2	1.5	2.2	5.7	2.0	9.2	•
Depreciation **14**	3.9	6.1	•	3.3	3.8	0.8	2.7	2.2	2.5	2.2	3.7	4.2	•
Amortization and Depletion **15**	0.2	•	•	0.0	•	0.0	0.1	0.2	0.2	0.1	0.2	0.3	•
Pensions and Other Deferred Comp. **16**	0.4	1.7	•	•	0.7	0.7	0.1	1.0	0.4	0.6	0.9	0.3	•
Employee Benefits **17**	3.4	1.6	•	5.4	4.4	0.2	0.8	2.7	1.9	1.3	1.4	3.9	•
Advertising **18**	0.3	0.1	•	6.1	0.1	0.4	0.1	0.2	0.2	0.1	0.1	0.3	•
Other Expenses **19**	16.8	43.4	•	58.6	11.3	11.8	8.8	5.6	5.2	7.9	4.5	19.5	•
Officers' Compensation **20**	0.3	7.4	•	6.0	3.6	0.9	1.4	1.1	0.7	0.3	0.6	0.1	•
Operating Margin **21**	•	•	•	•	1.2	7.1	3.1	6.0	1.4	•	6.5	7.2	•
Operating Margin Before Officers' Comp. **22**	•	•	•	•	4.8	8.1	4.4	7.1	2.1	•	7.2	•	•

Selected Average Balance Sheet ($ in Thousands)

Net Receivables 23	9567	0	0	5	549	1985	3306	9543	13044	19358	49087	876236
Inventories 24	4898	0	0	36	632	1096	3015	6823	9502	18855	39086	251945
Net Property, Plant and Equipment 25	13757	0	2	69	551	1096	5925	16047	23745	60862	145628	1196918
Total Assets 26	108554	0	9	564	2140	6172	16462	39294	69946	156347	375457	10573636
Notes and Loans Payable 27	12592	0	18	662	399	938	5274	13699	16095	53796	137735	1094500
All Other Liabilities 28	40986	0	0	139	259	1722	5620	12468	21991	26802	73019	4082838
Net Worth 29	54976	0	-9	-237	1482	3513	5568	13128	31860	75750	164703	5396298

Selected Financial Ratios (Times to 1)

Current Ratio 30	2.0	•	3.6	3.3	1.8	1.2	1.6	1.8	1.8	1.5	2.5	2.0
Quick Ratio 31	1.3	•	0.9	1.7	1.1	0.6	1.0	0.9	0.9	0.7	1.3	1.3
Net Sales to Working Capital 32	4.2	•	1.2	5.1	8.0	21.4	9.8	6.6	6.6	10.3	5.9	3.7
Coverage Ratio 33	5.3	•	•	4.7	7.9	6.3	5.6	2.4	2.4	1.2	6.6	5.4
Total Asset Turnover 34	0.4	•	0.8	2.6	2.4	1.7	1.7	1.4	1.4	1.3	1.2	0.3
Inventory Turnover 35	5.9	•	11.4	5.8	8.8	7.0	7.0	8.5	8.5	8.5	8.4	9.1
Receivables Turnover 36	4.5	•	192.7	20.5	11.0	8.8	6.2	9.4	9.4	9.3	10.8	6.4
Total Liabilities to Net Worth 37	1.0	•	•	0.4	0.8	2.0	2.0	1.2	1.2	1.1	1.3	1.0
Current Assets to Working Capital 38	2.0	1.0	1.4	1.4	2.2	6.2	2.7	2.3	2.3	3.1	1.7	2.0
Current Liabilities to Working Capital 39	1.0	•	0.4	0.4	1.2	5.2	1.7	1.3	1.3	2.1	0.7	1.0
Working Capital to Net Sales 40	0.2	•	0.8	0.2	0.1	0.0	0.1	0.2	0.2	0.1	0.2	0.3
Inventory to Working Capital 41	0.5	•	0.1	0.6	0.8	2.7	0.9	0.7	0.7	1.1	0.6	0.5
Total Receipts to Cash Flow 42	2.3	5.8	14.4	14.4	5.5	7.4	8.7	14.3	13.9	7.9	0.6	0.5
Cost of Goods to Cash Flow 43	1.7	3.6	9.4	9.4	3.6	5.7	6.4	11.5	11.1	6.0	1.4	1.9
Cash Flow to Total Debt 44	0.3	•	0.6	0.6	1.0	0.3	0.3	0.2	0.2	0.3	0.3	0.3

Selected Financial Factors (in Percentages)

Debt Ratio 45	49.4	•	193.3	142.0	30.7	43.1	66.2	66.6	54.5	51.6	56.1	49.0
Return on Total Assets 46	14.7	•	•	•	4.9	22.4	12.5	13.7	7.6	8.5	15.3	14.9
Return on Equity Before Income Taxes 47	23.6	•	100.8	167.3	5.6	34.4	31.2	33.6	9.8	2.3	29.6	23.9
Return on Equity After Income Taxes 48	20.2	•	100.8	167.3	5.5	32.5	23.5	28.2	7.7	•	19.4	20.6
Profit Margin (Before Income Tax) 49	32.4	•	•	•	1.5	8.1	6.3	6.7	3.1	0.9	11.2	40.3
Profit Margin (After Income Tax) 50	27.7	•	•	•	1.4	7.7	4.7	5.7	2.4	•	7.3	34.8

Table II
Corporations with Net Income

RESIN, SYNTHETIC RUBBER AND FIBERS AND FILAMENTS

MONEY AMOUNTS AND SIZE OF ASSETS IN THOUSANDS OF DOLLARS

Item Description for Accounting Period 7/05 Through 6/06	Total	Zero Assets	Under 500	500 to 1,000	1,000 to 5,000	5,000 to 10,000	10,000 to 25,000	25,000 to 50,000	50,000 to 100,000	100,000 to 250,000	250,000 to 500,000	500,000 to 2,500,000	2,500,000 and over
Number of Enterprises **1**	275	0	0	0	130	88	20	•	11	•	•	•	0
Revenues ($ in Thousands)													
Net Sales **2**	34925181	0	0	0	732623	1305782	617373	•	1198624	•	•	•	0
Interest **3**	2074882	0	0	0	21	475	303	•	10099	•	•	•	0
Rents **4**	71087	0	0	0	0	0	0	•	662	•	•	•	0
Royalties **5**	721450	0	0	0	0	11985	0	•	24	•	•	•	0
Other Portfolio Income **6**	8681460	0	0	0	303	31	10	•	1757	•	•	•	0
Other Receipts **7**	2400432	0	0	0	1770	514	22438	•	1539	•	•	•	0
Total Receipts **8**	48874492	0	0	0	734717	1318787	640124	•	1212705	•	•	•	0
Average Total Receipts **9**	177725	•	•	•	5652	14986	32006	•	110246	•	•	•	•
Operating Costs/Operating Income (%)													
Cost of Operations **10**	71.6	•	•	•	65.1	65.0	73.8	•	80.2	•	•	•	•
Salaries and Wages **11**	2.2	•	•	•	6.0	10.4	4.0	•	3.4	•	•	•	•
Taxes Paid **12**	0.8	•	•	•	3.4	1.5	1.5	•	1.3	•	•	•	•
Interest Paid **13**	7.7	•	•	•	0.4	1.2	1.2	•	1.4	•	•	•	•
Depreciation **14**	3.9	•	•	•	3.8	0.8	2.5	•	2.8	•	•	•	•
Amortization and Depletion **15**	0.2	•	•	•	•	0.0	0.1	•	0.1	•	•	•	•
Pensions and Other Deferred Comp. **16**	0.3	•	•	•	0.7	0.7	0.2	•	0.2	•	•	•	•
Employee Benefits **17**	3.4	•	•	•	4.4	0.2	0.9	•	1.1	•	•	•	•
Advertising **18**	0.3	•	•	•	0.1	0.4	0.1	•	0.3	•	•	•	•
Other Expenses **19**	17.4	•	•	•	11.3	11.8	9.6	•	4.2	•	•	•	•
Officers' Compensation **20**	0.3	•	•	•	3.6	0.9	1.4	•	0.6	•	•	•	•
Operating Margin **21**	•	•	•	•	1.2	7.1	4.6	•	4.6	•	•	•	•
Operating Margin Before Officers' Comp. **22**	•	•	•	•	4.8	8.1	6.0	•	5.2	•	•	•	•

Selected Average Balance Sheet ($ in Thousands)

Net Receivables 23	31280	549	1985	3511	13204
Inventories 24	15405	605	1033	2724	10798
Net Property, Plant and Equipment 25	42704	551	1096	4941	26241
Total Assets 26	357524	2140	6172	16529	70828
Notes and Loans Payable 27	36927	399	938	4431	9511
All Other Liabilities 28	137003	259	1722	6350	19764
Net Worth 29	183595	1482	3513	5748	41553

Selected Financial Ratios (Times to 1)

Current Ratio 30	2.0	3.3	1.8	1.3	2.0
Quick Ratio 31	1.3	1.7	1.1	0.7	1.1
Net Sales to Working Capital 32	4.1	5.1	8.0	15.4	6.0
Coverage Ratio 33	5.5	4.7	7.9	8.0	5.1
Total Asset Turnover 34	0.4	2.6	2.4	1.9	1.5
Inventory Turnover 35	5.9	6.1	9.3	8.4	8.1
Receivables Turnover 36	4.4	11.4	11.3	9.6	10.0
Total Liabilities to Net Worth 37	0.9	0.4	0.8	1.9	0.7
Current Assets to Working Capital 38	2.0	1.4	2.2	4.2	2.0
Current Liabilities to Working Capital 39	1.0	0.4	1.2	3.2	1.0
Working Capital to Net Sales 40	0.2	0.2	0.1	0.1	0.2
Inventory to Working Capital 41	0.5	0.6	0.8	1.7	0.6
Total Receipts to Cash Flow 42	2.2	14.4	5.5	6.2	10.7
Cost of Goods to Cash Flow 43	1.6	9.4	3.6	4.6	8.6
Cash Flow to Total Debt 44	0.3	0.6	1.0	0.5	0.3

Selected Financial Factors (in Percentages)

Debt Ratio 45	48.6	30.7	43.1	65.2	41.3
Return on Total Assets 46	15.2	4.9	22.4	17.7	11.0
Return on Equity Before Income Taxes 47	24.2	5.6	34.4	44.6	15.1
Return on Equity After Income Taxes 48	20.8	5.5	32.5	34.9	13.0
Profit Margin (Before Income Tax) 49	35.0	1.5	8.1	8.3	5.8
Profit Margin (After Income Tax) 50	30.0	1.4	7.7	6.5	5.0

Table I
Corporations with and without Net Income

PHARMACEUTICAL AND MEDICINE

MONEY AMOUNTS AND SIZE OF ASSETS IN THOUSANDS OF DOLLARS

Item Description for Accounting Period 7/05 Through 6/06	Total	Zero Assets	Under 500	500 to 1,000	1,000 to 5,000	5,000 to 10,000	10,000 to 25,000	25,000 to 50,000	50,000 to 100,000	100,000 to 250,000	250,000 to 500,000	500,000 to 2,500,000	2,500,000 and over
Number of Enterprises **1**	1415	9	639	134	104	189	104	58	47	48	19	33	31
Revenues ($ in Thousands)													
Net Sales **2**	284218465	61427	103645	281323	226169	2439542	1737635	1720605	2046978	5735043	2791775	26852223	240222100
Interest **3**	6960120	77681	1	157	844	4397	14679	22082	35881	55465	60717	347773	6340444
Rents **4**	711069	61	553	0	48	461	457	316	1900	4077	946	11779	690471
Royalties **5**	20164906	100843	0	0	6173	827	21004	31192	32349	155246	31345	327641	19458287
Other Portfolio Income **6**	104505611	0	0	0	13646	12229	65001	25967	35226	19069	142824	1196692	102994955
Other Receipts **7**	25268648	310147	417	13861	9449	52049	50351	19175	54865	353284	156575	1246532	23001943
Total Receipts **8**	441828819	550159	104616	295341	256329	2509505	1889127	1819337	2207199	6322184	3184182	29982640	392708200
Average Total Receipts **9**	312247	61129	164	2204	2465	13278	18165	31368	46962	131712	167589	908565	12668006
Operating Costs/Operating Income (%)													
Cost of Operations **10**	49.6	32.8	32.9	67.9	68.6	68.2	56.3	54.4	53.3	40.7	32.4	45.8	50.1
Salaries and Wages **11**	15.2	10.9	11.6	10.8	19.5	7.7	12.8	14.0	19.2	11.9	19.8	14.1	15.4
Taxes Paid **12**	1.6	9.3	1.4	3.4	3.5	2.2	2.5	2.4	2.7	2.2	1.5	1.8	1.6
Interest Paid **13**	3.8	0.3	0.9	1.4	3.4	0.9	1.9	2.6	1.9	1.7	3.4	2.7	4.1
Depreciation **14**	2.5	2.1	9.3	1.1	4.3	3.4	3.2	3.3	4.0	2.5	2.2	2.0	2.5
Amortization and Depletion **15**	1.5	5.7	0.0	2.5	0.1	0.8	0.6	2.2	3.6	1.6	3.7	2.1	1.4
Pensions and Other Deferred Comp. **16**	1.7	0.1	0.8	0.0	0.4	0.2	0.3	0.5	0.6	1.3	0.4	0.9	1.9
Employee Benefits **17**	2.0	1.3	*	0.5	2.0	1.3	1.7	1.6	3.2	1.7	3.1	1.6	2.1
Advertising **18**	4.6	0.4	0.3	2.8	1.3	0.3	2.1	4.3	2.9	2.1	5.1	2.6	5.0
Other Expenses **19**	26.2	564.6	25.7	29.7	42.3	13.6	28.7	25.1	36.3	31.0	34.9	23.7	26.2
Officers' Compensation **20**	0.7	1.3	4.7	4.4	11.0	4.4	5.6	4.0	3.3	1.6	3.2	1.4	0.4
Operating Margin **21**	*	*	12.3	*	*	*	*	*	*	1.5	*	1.2	*
Operating Margin Before Officers' Comp. **22**	*	*	17.1	*	1.4	*	*	*	*	3.1	*	2.6	*

Selected Average Balance Sheet ($ in Thousands)

Net Receivables 23	170040	0	8	82	703	1701	2588	4445	10229	19460	48423	195586	7447717
Inventories 24	24344	0	7	220	447	1062	2149	4932	7630	16490	25180	126284	898704
Net Property, Plant and Equipment 25	49035	0	48	95	556	2227	3837	6556	12072	25526	29254	158684	1951573
Total Assets 26	681373	0	91	696	2254	7754	16880	36557	72008	150228	350916	1199090	29083338
Notes and Loans Payable 27	218957	0	34	1048	934	4944	4326	13560	15900	31624	59436	305787	9480916
All Other Liabilities 28	186624	0	13	370	772	2433	4867	7793	25815	35415	105865	312686	7976563
Net Worth 29	275793	0	44	-721	549	377	7687	15204	30294	83189	185614	580618	11625859

Selected Financial Ratios (Times to 1)

Current Ratio 30	1.2	•	1.8	1.5	1.9	1.8	1.8	1.7	2.3	2.5	2.0	2.3	1.2
Quick Ratio 31	0.9	•	1.3	0.6	1.5	1.2	1.2	1.1	1.5	1.4	1.1	1.3	0.9
Net Sales to Working Capital 32	3.8	1019.1	13.0	12.7	2.9	6.3	3.6	3.2	2.0	2.6	1.8	2.5	4.2
Coverage Ratio 33	14.2	•	15.6	•	•	0.8	•	•	•	8.5	2.8	6.0	15.2
Total Asset Turnover 34	0.3	•	1.8	3.0	1.0	1.7	1.0	0.8	0.6	0.8	0.4	0.7	0.3
Inventory Turnover 35	4.1	•	7.9	6.5	3.3	8.3	4.4	3.3	3.0	3.0	1.9	3.0	4.3
Receivables Turnover 36	1.4	•	20.8	19.8	3.2	10.3	6.9	6.6	4.2	6.4	3.5	4.6	1.2
Total Liabilities to Net Worth 37	1.5	•	1.1	•	3.1	19.6	1.2	1.4	1.4	0.8	0.9	1.1	1.5
Current Assets to Working Capital 38	5.2	•	2.2	3.2	2.1	2.3	2.2	2.3	1.8	1.7	2.0	1.8	6.2
Current Liabilities to Working Capital 39	4.2	•	1.2	2.2	1.1	1.3	1.2	1.3	0.8	0.7	1.0	0.8	5.2
Working Capital to Net Sales 40	0.3	•	0.1	0.1	0.3	0.2	0.3	0.3	0.5	0.4	0.6	0.4	0.2
Inventory to Working Capital 41	0.5	•	0.6	1.6	0.3	0.6	0.5	0.5	0.3	0.4	0.3	0.5	0.5
Total Receipts to Cash Flow 42	1.5	0.1	3.1	34.3	•	10.6	7.1	7.4	12.8	2.5	2.8	3.0	1.3
Cost of Goods to Cash Flow 43	0.7	0.0	1.0	23.3	•	7.2	4.0	4.0	6.8	1.0	0.9	1.4	0.7
Cash Flow to Total Debt 44	0.3	•	1.1	0.0	•	0.2	0.3	0.2	0.1	0.7	0.3	0.4	0.3

Selected Financial Factors (in Percentages)

Debt Ratio 45	59.5	•	51.6	203.6	75.7	95.1	54.5	58.4	57.9	44.6	47.1	51.6	60.0
Return on Total Assets 46	15.9	•	25.2	•	•	1.3	•	•	•	11.8	4.0	10.9	16.5
Return on Equity Before Income Taxes 47	36.5	•	48.7	56.8	•	•	•	•	•	18.9	4.9	18.8	38.4
Return on Equity After Income Taxes 48	31.1	•	41.7	57.6	•	•	•	•	•	9.2	0.8	13.0	33.1
Profit Margin (Before Income Tax) 49	50.1	266.8	13.2	•	•	•	•	•	•	13.1	6.2	13.4	57.7
Profit Margin (After Income Tax) 50	42.7	117.0	11.3	•	•	•	•	•	•	6.4	1.1	9.3	49.7

Table II
Corporations with Net Income

PHARMACEUTICAL AND MEDICINE

MONEY AMOUNTS AND SIZE OF ASSETS IN THOUSANDS OF DOLLARS

Item Description for Accounting Period 7/05 Through 6/06	Total	Zero Assets	Under 500	500 to 1,000	1,000 to 5,000	5,000 to 10,000	10,000 to 25,000	25,000 to 50,000	50,000 to 100,000	100,000 to 250,000	250,000 to 500,000	500,000 to 2,500,000	2,500,000 and over
Number of Enterprises **1**	612	6	•	88	8	140	65	28	15	31	10	24	•

Revenues ($ in Thousands)

	Total	Zero Assets	Under 500	500 to 1,000	1,000 to 5,000	5,000 to 10,000	10,000 to 25,000	25,000 to 50,000	50,000 to 100,000	100,000 to 250,000	250,000 to 500,000	500,000 to 2,500,000	2,500,000 and over
Net Sales **2**	277222553	57678	•	265764	71062	1854285	1376676	1324226	1215136	4593735	2354704	23790053	•
Interest **3**	6708755	77602	•	8	133	1589	4839	5881	5044	22579	39647	210988	•
Rents **4**	704796	61	•	0	48	320	441	316	1651	937	922	9076	•
Royalties **5**	19924275	100843	•	0	6173	0	20016	630	2731	151162	8389	176043	•
Other Portfolio Income **6**	104415571	0	•	0	13319	11855	64973	21542	12167	6357	142800	1147602	•
Other Receipts **7**	24458435	310107	•	13499	7189	4323	40921	25832	3980	232451	21398	796379	•
Total Receipts **8**	433434385	546291	•	279271	97924	1872372	1507866	1378427	1240709	5007221	2567860	26130141	•
Average Total Receipts **9**	708226	91048	•	3174	12240	13374	23198	49230	82714	161523	256786	1088756	•

Operating Costs/Operating Income (%)

	Total	Zero Assets	Under 500	500 to 1,000	1,000 to 5,000	5,000 to 10,000	10,000 to 25,000	25,000 to 50,000	50,000 to 100,000	100,000 to 250,000	250,000 to 500,000	500,000 to 2,500,000	2,500,000 and over
Cost of Operations **10**	49.7	31.1	•	68.3	44.0	64.4	56.6	50.1	53.1	40.4	28.5	47.6	•
Salaries and Wages **11**	14.9	9.9	•	7.9	10.1	6.4	9.2	10.5	10.7	8.4	17.1	11.9	•
Taxes Paid **12**	1.6	9.8	•	2.8	3.2	2.1	2.4	2.0	2.2	2.0	1.0	1.7	•
Interest Paid **13**	3.8	0.3	•	0.7	2.5	0.6	1.5	1.0	0.9	1.2	2.2	2.3	•
Depreciation **14**	2.4	1.8	•	0.7	1.1	3.1	2.5	2.2	2.6	2.1	1.4	1.9	•
Amortization and Depletion **15**	1.4	5.7	•	0.0	0.0	0.2	0.5	0.4	0.8	1.1	2.4	1.1	•
Pensions and Other Deferred Comp. **16**	1.7	0.1	•	0.0	0.7	0.2	0.3	0.5	0.8	0.4	0.5	0.9	•
Employee Benefits **17**	2.0	0.8	•	0.1	1.5	1.0	1.6	1.3	2.3	1.3	2.1	1.4	•
Advertising **18**	4.7	0.4	•	0.0	0.0	0.3	2.2	4.8	3.9	1.9	5.0	2.6	•
Other Expenses **19**	25.6	598.0	•	16.9	26.9	9.3	16.7	14.1	12.8	25.2	26.9	21.3	•
Officers' Compensation **20**	0.5	1.3	•	2.1	10.3	4.2	2.8	3.2	1.3	1.4	2.1	0.9	•
Operating Margin **21**	•	•	•	0.5	•	8.2	3.6	9.8	8.7	14.5	10.9	6.5	•
Operating Margin Before Officers' Comp. **22**	•	•	•	2.6	10.0	12.5	6.4	12.9	10.0	15.9	13.0	7.4	•

Selected Average Balance Sheet ($ in Thousands)

Net Receivables 23	390484	0	•	118	630	1864	3381	7052	17998	25377	74135	233351	•
Inventories 24	52010	0	•	320	1950	1246	2464	6936	13740	19216	36286	137819	•
Net Property, Plant and Equipment 25	109023	0	•	86	706	1986	4488	7353	15982	25586	29902	169659	•
Total Assets 26	1544874	0	•	721	3631	7508	17235	36595	75684	150920	364123	1295110	•
Notes and Loans Payable 27	495044	0	•	274	1646	4894	4965	6600	11842	25944	41660	267256	•
All Other Liabilities 28	423135	0	•	140	4518	2029	4532	8356	21756	33466	145026	333406	•
Net Worth 29	626696	0	•	308	-2533	585	7738	21639	42086	91509	177437	694448	•

Selected Financial Ratios (Times to 1)

Current Ratio 30	1.2	•	•	4.5	0.6	2.4	1.7	2.5	1.9	2.4	1.5	2.1	•
Quick Ratio 31	0.9	•	•	1.3	0.5	1.6	1.1	1.6	1.1	1.4	1.0	1.2	•
Net Sales to Working Capital 32	4.1	1039.3	•	6.3	•	4.7	5.4	3.3	4.2	3.1	4.3	3.0	•
Coverage Ratio 33	14.9	•	•	9.6	22.0	15.3	9.7	14.9	13.3	21.6	11.2	8.4	•
Total Asset Turnover 34	0.3	•	•	4.2	2.4	1.8	1.2	1.3	1.1	1.0	0.6	0.8	•
Inventory Turnover 35	4.3	•	•	6.4	2.0	6.8	4.9	3.4	3.1	3.1	1.8	3.4	•
Receivables Turnover 36	1.4	•	•	19.1	2.6	9.3	7.3	6.4	4.3	6.2	4.0	5.3	•
Total Liabilities to Net Worth 37	1.5	•	•	1.3	•	11.8	1.2	0.7	0.8	0.6	1.1	0.9	•
Current Assets to Working Capital 38	5.5	•	•	1.3	•	1.7	2.5	1.7	2.2	1.7	3.1	1.9	•
Current Liabilities to Working Capital 39	4.5	•	•	0.3	•	0.7	1.5	0.7	1.2	0.7	2.1	0.9	•
Working Capital to Net Sales 40	0.2	•	•	0.2	•	0.2	0.2	0.3	0.2	0.3	0.2	0.3	•
Inventory to Working Capital 41	0.5	•	•	0.8	•	0.5	0.7	0.5	0.6	0.4	0.5	0.6	•
Total Receipts to Cash Flow 42	1.4	0.1	•	6.2	2.4	6.6	4.5	3.9	4.7	2.1	2.2	2.9	•
Cost of Goods to Cash Flow 43	0.7	0.0	•	4.2	1.1	4.3	2.6	1.9	2.5	0.9	0.6	1.4	•
Cash Flow to Total Debt 44	0.3	•	•	1.2	0.6	0.3	0.5	0.8	0.5	1.2	0.6	0.6	•

Selected Financial Factors (in Percentages)

Debt Ratio 45	59.4	•	•	57.3	169.8	92.2	55.1	40.9	44.4	39.4	51.3	46.4	•
Return on Total Assets 46	16.5	•	•	26.2	133.9	17.3	18.1	19.2	12.5	26.1	15.7	14.7	•
Return on Equity Before Income Taxes 47	37.9	•	•	55.0	•	207.6	36.2	30.3	20.8	41.1	29.3	24.1	•
Return on Equity After Income Taxes 48	32.4	•	•	52.3	•	198.9	31.5	27.0	16.5	27.5	21.2	17.6	•
Profit Margin (Before Income Tax) 49	52.4	288.0	•	5.6	52.2	9.2	13.2	13.9	10.8	25.4	22.1	16.9	•
Profit Margin (After Income Tax) 50	44.8	128.5	•	5.3	46.6	8.8	11.5	12.3	8.6	17.0	16.0	12.3	•

Table I

Corporations with and without Net Income

PAINT, COATING, AND ADHESIVE

MONEY AMOUNTS AND SIZE OF ASSETS IN THOUSANDS OF DOLLARS

Item Description for Accounting Period 7/05 Through 6/06	Total	Zero Assets	Under 500	500 to 1,000	1,000 to 5,000	5,000 to 10,000	10,000 to 25,000	25,000 to 50,000	50,000 to 100,000	100,000 to 250,000	250,000 to 500,000	500,000 to 2,500,000	2,500,000 and over
Number of Enterprises **1**	1214	0	83	109	796	102	58	26	16	10	0	10	5
Revenues ($ in Thousands)													
Net Sales **2**	42630293	0	68953	106478	2947545	1919650	1863516	1709375	1368140	2350054	0	8384445	21912136
Interest **3**	327057	0	0	1040	319	658	151	592	849	12549	0	101909	208991
Rents **4**	14389	0	0	0	0	0	0	737	10	1349	0	6932	5361
Royalties **5**	410742	0	0	0	0	0	0	338	1157	17377	0	54899	336971
Other Portfolio Income **6**	692805	0	0	132	1629	303	2444	18907	599	76434	0	113679	478677
Other Receipts **7**	328116	0	158	0	8547	2193	7540	4466	12897	10189	0	136224	145902
Total Receipts **8**	44403402	0	69111	107650	2958040	1922804	1873651	1734415	1383652	2467952	0	8798088	23088038
Average Total Receipts **9**	36576	•	833	988	3716	18851	32304	66708	86478	246795	•	879809	4617608
Operating Costs/Operating Income (%)													
Cost of Operations **10**	63.4	•	68.7	63.3	63.2	66.8	70.1	64.0	72.1	66.8	•	69.0	59.5
Salaries and Wages **11**	10.2	•	8.8	7.0	8.1	6.0	10.1	8.3	6.6	10.0	•	10.0	11.4
Taxes Paid **12**	1.8	•	4.6	3.0	2.0	3.2	1.6	1.6	1.5	1.5	•	1.5	1.8
Interest Paid **13**	2.2	•	0.2	2.9	0.9	0.9	1.0	0.4	1.3	1.3	•	4.5	2.1
Depreciation **14**	1.7	•	0.7	1.3	0.9	1.9	1.0	1.3	2.0	1.5	•	2.5	1.6
Amortization and Depletion **15**	0.6	•	•	0.1	0.1	0.0	0.2	0.2	0.3	1.2	•	0.7	0.6
Pensions and Other Deferred Comp. **16**	1.6	•	•	0.0	0.5	0.3	0.4	0.3	0.9	2.1	•	1.5	2.2
Employee Benefits **17**	1.8	•	4.3	1.1	1.1	1.9	0.8	1.6	1.3	1.7	•	2.1	1.9
Advertising **18**	1.3	•	•	0.5	1.1	0.2	1.1	1.3	0.4	1.0	•	0.4	1.9
Other Expenses **19**	13.2	•	22.8	20.6	13.8	12.3	9.2	11.2	10.6	10.9	•	11.7	14.5
Officers' Compensation **20**	1.2	•	4.1	3.5	6.1	3.4	2.2	2.1	1.4	0.9	•	0.4	0.4
Operating Margin **21**	1.0	•	•	•	2.2	3.1	2.2	7.7	1.7	1.0	•	•	2.1
Operating Margin Before Officers' Comp. **22**	2.2	•	•	0.0	8.3	6.5	4.4	9.8	3.1	1.9	•	•	2.6

Selected Average Balance Sheet ($ in Thousands)

Net Receivables 23	5560	82	147	492	2313	3992	10046	13979	40703	162116	670986
Inventories 24	3301	150	612	355	980	4588	7666	11150	22543	91396	349792
Net Property, Plant and Equipment 25	5942	28	66	274	2141	2386	7111	19832	30454	217125	730212
Total Assets 26	32300	263	765	1680	7237	14795	34635	71475	186309	1076881	4299380
Notes and Loans Payable 27	7850	112	724	670	2625	4156	4538	20465	53163	417371	649817
All Other Liabilities 28	13795	134	105	575	2365	4229	7719	17271	61289	327898	2282339
Net Worth 29	10654	17	-65	435	2248	6411	22378	33739	71857	331612	1367224

Selected Financial Ratios (Times to 1)

Current Ratio 30	1.5	1.7	3.8	1.9	1.0	1.8	2.7	1.5	1.6	1.6	1.4
Quick Ratio 31	0.8	0.6	1.1	1.2	0.6	1.0	1.7	0.8	0.9	0.9	0.7
Net Sales to Working Capital 32	8.7	8.4	2.3	7.1	373.6	6.8	4.7	8.1	7.6	5.5	12.3
Coverage Ratio 33	3.5		0.2	3.7	4.7	3.5	25.7	3.1	5.7	1.1	5.1
Total Asset Turnover 34	1.1	3.2	1.3	2.2	2.6	2.2	1.9	1.2	1.3	0.8	1.0
Inventory Turnover 35	6.7	3.8	1.0	6.6	12.8	4.9	5.5	5.5	7.0	6.3	7.5
Receivables Turnover 36	6.6	20.2	2.3	15.1	9.8	7.3	6.8	6.7	6.7	5.8	6.8
Total Liabilities to Net Worth 37	2.0	14.4		2.9	2.2	1.3	0.5	1.1	1.6	2.2	2.1
Current Assets to Working Capital 38	3.0	2.4	1.4	2.2	79.1	2.2	1.6	3.0	2.8	2.7	3.9
Current Liabilities to Working Capital 39	2.0	1.4	0.4	1.2	78.1	1.2	0.6	2.0	1.8	1.7	2.9
Working Capital to Net Sales 40	0.1	0.1	0.4	0.1	0.0	0.1	0.2	0.1	0.1	0.2	0.1
Inventory to Working Capital 41	0.9	1.5	0.9	0.7	27.1	0.9	0.5	1.2	0.8	0.7	1.1
Total Receipts to Cash Flow 42	6.4	20.4	6.7	7.2	10.3	11.3	5.4	8.1	9.0	9.9	5.1
Cost of Goods to Cash Flow 43	4.1	14.0	4.3	4.5	6.9	7.9	3.5	5.8	6.0	6.8	3.1
Cash Flow to Total Debt 44	0.3	0.2	0.2	0.4	0.4	0.3	1.0	0.3	0.2	0.1	0.3

Selected Financial Factors (in Percentages)

Debt Ratio 45	67.0	93.5	108.4	74.1	68.9	56.7	35.4	52.8	61.4	69.2	68.2
Return on Total Assets 46	8.6		0.6	7.7	10.8	8.0	19.8	4.9	9.5	3.9	10.7
Return on Equity Before Income Taxes 47	18.7		35.9	21.7	27.5	13.3	29.5	7.1	20.3	1.3	27.0
Return on Equity After Income Taxes 48	13.1		35.9	21.4	24.3	11.7	24.0	6.2	15.3		18.7
Profit Margin (Before Income Tax) 49	5.7		2.5	3.3	2.6	6.2	2.8	6.2	0.5		8.4
Profit Margin (After Income Tax) 50	4.0		2.5	2.9	2.3	8.2	2.4		4.7		5.8

Table II
Corporations with Net Income

PAINT, COATING, AND ADHESIVE

MONEY AMOUNTS AND SIZE OF ASSETS IN THOUSANDS OF DOLLARS

Item Description for Accounting Period 7/05 Through 6/06	Total	Zero Assets	Under 500	500 to 1,000	1,000 to 5,000	5,000 to 10,000	10,000 to 25,000	25,000 to 50,000	50,000 to 100,000	100,000 to 250,000	250,000 to 500,000	500,000 to 2,500,000	2,500,000 and over
Number of Enterprises **1**	616	0	•	0	418	98	43	•	12	10	0	5	5
Revenues ($ in Thousands)													
Net Sales **2**	35272053	0	•	0	2143895	1906588	1367690	•	1032081	2350054	0	2903606	21912136
Interest **3**	264539	0	•	0	318	657	94	•	710	12549	0	40630	208991
Rents **4**	13163	0	•	0	0	0	0	•	10	1349	0	5706	5361
Royalties **5**	383905	0	•	0	0	0	0	•	1157	17377	0	28061	336971
Other Portfolio Income **6**	619455	0	•	0	1629	303	1826	•	521	76434	0	41159	478677
Other Receipts **7**	204782	0	•	0	12492	2147	2055	•	8643	10189	0	18434	145902
Total Receipts **8**	36757897	0	•	0	2158334	1909695	1371665	•	1043122	2467952	0	3037596	23088038
Average Total Receipts **9**	59672	•	•	•	5163	19487	31899	•	86927	246795	•	607519	4617608
Operating Costs/Operating Income (%)													
Cost of Operations **10**	61.6	•	•	•	62.6	66.5	68.6	•	71.5	66.8	•	61.5	59.5
Salaries and Wages **11**	10.5	•	•	•	5.7	6.0	10.3	•	6.1	10.0	•	13.9	11.4
Taxes Paid **12**	1.8	•	•	•	1.8	3.2	1.4	•	1.5	1.5	•	2.2	1.8
Interest Paid **13**	1.7	•	•	•	0.2	0.9	1.0	•	1.5	1.3	•	2.1	2.1
Depreciation **14**	1.6	•	•	•	0.4	1.8	0.9	•	2.3	1.5	•	2.1	1.6
Amortization and Depletion **15**	0.5	•	•	•	0.0	0.0	0.3	•	0.3	1.2	•	0.5	0.6
Pensions and Other Deferred Comp. **16**	1.7	•	•	•	0.7	0.3	0.5	•	0.5	2.1	•	1.3	2.2
Employee Benefits **17**	1.8	•	•	•	1.0	1.9	0.7	•	1.1	1.7	•	2.8	1.9
Advertising **18**	1.5	•	•	•	1.3	0.2	1.4	•	0.4	1.0	•	0.6	1.9
Other Expenses **19**	13.1	•	•	•	11.8	12.3	8.3	•	10.5	10.9	•	9.7	14.5
Officers' Compensation **20**	1.3	•	•	•	7.6	3.4	2.3	•	1.2	0.9	•	0.7	0.4
Operating Margin **21**	2.9	•	•	•	6.9	3.5	4.3	•	3.1	1.0	•	2.7	2.1
Operating Margin Before Officers' Comp. **22**	4.1	•	•	•	14.5	6.9	6.6	•	4.3	1.9	•	3.4	2.6

Selected Average Balance Sheet ($ in Thousands)

Net Receivables 23	8397	580	2311	4286	14082	40703	69655	670986
Inventories 24	4923	375	951	4531	10379	25561	51731	397219
Net Property, Plant and Equipment 25	8567	149	2128	2406	21155	30454	103560	730212
Total Assets 26	49558	1632	7254	14822	72518	186309	685730	4299380
Notes and Loans Payable 27	8642	160	2561	4530	22866	53163	132124	649817
All Other Liabilities 28	22911	522	2364	4515	15444	61289	213094	2282339
Net Worth 29	18005	950	2329	5777	34208	71857	340512	1367224

Selected Financial Ratios (Times to 1)

Current Ratio 30	1.5	2.4	1.0	1.8	1.6	1.6	1.8	1.4
Quick Ratio 31	0.8	1.6	0.6	1.0	0.9	0.9	1.3	0.7
Net Sales to Working Capital 32	9.5	6.6	532.4	6.8	7.4	7.6	5.0	12.3
Coverage Ratio 33	5.5	36.6	5.3	5.3	3.7	5.7	4.3	5.1
Total Asset Turnover 34	1.2	3.1	2.7	2.1	1.2	1.3	0.8	1.0
Inventory Turnover 35	7.2	8.6	13.6	4.8	5.9	6.1	6.9	6.6
Receivables Turnover 36	7.4	9.3	13.1	7.1	7.6	11.5	16.7	13.1
Total Liabilities to Net Worth 37	1.8	0.7	2.1	1.6	1.1	1.6	1.0	2.1
Current Assets to Working Capital 38	3.1	1.7	109.9	2.2	2.6	2.8	2.2	3.9
Current Liabilities to Working Capital 39	2.1	0.7	108.9	1.2	1.6	1.8	1.2	2.9
Working Capital to Net Sales 40	0.1	0.2	0.0	0.1	0.1	0.1	0.2	0.1
Inventory to Working Capital 41	0.9	0.5	38.8	0.9	1.0	0.8	0.4	1.1
Total Receipts to Cash Flow 42	5.8	5.8	9.9	10.2	7.3	9.0	7.0	5.1
Cost of Goods to Cash Flow 43	3.6	3.7	6.6	7.0	5.2	6.0	4.3	3.1
Cash Flow to Total Debt 44	0.3	1.3	0.4	0.3	0.3	0.2	0.2	0.3

Selected Financial Factors (in Percentages)

Debt Ratio 45	63.7	41.8	67.9	61.0	52.8	61.4	50.3	68.2
Return on Total Assets 46	10.8	24.2	12.2	11.8	6.8	9.5	7.4	10.7
Return on Equity Before Income Taxes 47	24.3	40.4	30.9	24.6	10.5	20.3	11.4	27.0
Return on Equity After Income Taxes 48	17.8	40.1	27.6	22.2	9.2	15.3	7.8	18.7
Profit Margin (Before Income Tax) 49	7.7	7.5	3.7	4.5	4.2	6.2	6.7	8.4
Profit Margin (After Income Tax) 50	5.6	7.4	3.3	4.0	3.7	4.7	4.6	5.8

Table I

Corporations with and without Net Income

SOAP, CLEANING COMPOUND, AND TOILET PREPARATION

MONEY AMOUNTS AND SIZE OF ASSETS IN THOUSANDS OF DOLLARS

Item Description for Accounting Period 7/05 Through 6/06	Total	Zero Assets	Under 500	500 to 1,000	1,000 to 5,000	5,000 to 10,000	10,000 to 25,000	25,000 to 50,000	50,000 to 100,000	100,000 to 250,000	250,000 to 500,000	500,000 to 2,500,000	2,500,000 and over
Number of Enterprises 1	1357	8	629	389	183	24	50	25	13	10	7	9	11

Revenues ($ in Thousands)

Item Description for Accounting Period 7/05 Through 6/06	Total	Zero Assets	Under 500	500 to 1,000	1,000 to 5,000	5,000 to 10,000	10,000 to 25,000	25,000 to 50,000	50,000 to 100,000	100,000 to 250,000	250,000 to 500,000	500,000 to 2,500,000	2,500,000 and over
Net Sales 2	117308254	39093	417839	695526	1473590	223936	1630303	1401344	1286891	1986732	3291137	11517487	93344376
Interest 3	741293	1939	52	79	231	149	1403	4356	1314	2719	3961	80241	644851
Rents 4	85571	0	0	0	2338	0	270	460	100	237	1469	44884	35814
Royalties 5	2623348	41	0	0	5352	0	2370	255	124	4110	24812	397286	2188999
Other Portfolio Income 6	4235881	10322	0	0	4578	25	614	3767	3679	4773	19739	703482	3484907
Other Receipts 7	1870214	18758	12986	254	11081	920	8023	22829	1599	52452	10756	257082	1473464
Total Receipts 8	126864561	70153	430877	695859	1497170	225030	1642983	1433011	1293707	2051023	3351874	13000462	101172411
Average Total Receipts 9	93489	8769	685	1789	8181	9376	32860	57320	99516	205102	478839	1444496	9197492

Operating Costs/Operating Income (%)

Item Description for Accounting Period 7/05 Through 6/06	Total	Zero Assets	Under 500	500 to 1,000	1,000 to 5,000	5,000 to 10,000	10,000 to 25,000	25,000 to 50,000	50,000 to 100,000	100,000 to 250,000	250,000 to 500,000	500,000 to 2,500,000	2,500,000 and over
Cost of Operations 10	60.5	63.5	64.1	52.7	63.6	65.2	66.3	65.3	59.5	48.5	61.4	44.1	62.6
Salaries and Wages 11	6.8	14.0	4.1	16.5	7.4	8.9	9.5	8.9	8.4	7.2	8.6	12.8	5.8
Taxes Paid 12	1.2	13.8	3.1	2.8	2.0	2.0	1.6	1.6	2.0	1.0	1.6	1.9	1.1
Interest Paid 13	2.6	1.9	5.6	0.7	0.5	1.3	0.8	1.3	1.7	1.8	1.5	3.1	2.7
Depreciation 14	2.0	3.2	1.3	1.7	0.6	3.4	1.4	1.2	1.6	1.9	2.3	1.5	2.1
Amortization and Depletion 15	1.3	25.8	0.0	0.0	0.0	0.0	0.2	0.6	0.6	0.6	1.0	0.9	1.4
Pensions and Other Deferred Comp. 16	1.3	33.3	2.0	0.1	1.0	0.4	0.3	0.2	0.4	0.6	0.2	1.4	1.4
Employee Benefits 17	2.1	3.3	0.1	2.0	0.8	0.5	1.9	1.4	1.1	0.7	1.3	2.6	2.1
Advertising 18	5.9	5.5	0.1	0.7	1.0	1.7	1.2	3.1	2.4	14.5	4.3	6.0	6.1
Other Expenses 19	14.1	79.1	20.0	22.2	16.3	13.6	11.3	12.3	14.8	15.7	15.0	25.0	12.6
Officers' Compensation 20	0.8	27.7	11.4	7.4	3.6	1.7	1.9	2.8	4.0	0.8	0.7	1.6	0.4
Operating Margin 21	1.3	•	•	•	3.3	1.4	3.8	1.3	3.5	6.6	2.0	•	1.6
Operating Margin Before Officers' Comp. 22	2.1	•	•	0.7	6.9	3.1	5.7	4.1	7.5	7.4	2.8	0.6	2.0

Selected Average Balance Sheet ($ in Thousands)

Net Receivables 23	16992	0	59	198	835	1235	4247	8520	15486	29537	60435	159269	1816591
Inventories 24	5430	0	156	201	522	2467	3745	8340	10386	23714	55428	168695	396768
Net Property, Plant and Equipment 25	12846	0	39	104	428	3115	3711	7693	11059	26465	80457	171883	1301674
Total Assets 26	120137	0	337	811	3290	6655	14460	35915	64249	162085	363595	1537323	12843523
Notes and Loans Payable 27	46020	0	242	732	597	1828	4030	11129	17554	50070	97215	640080	4928183
All Other Liabilities 28	28150	0	145	191	884	1735	4349	7615	16546	37942	95808	424922	2939387
Net Worth 29	45967	0	-49	-112	1809	3093	6082	17171	30148	74073	170571	472320	4975954

Selected Financial Ratios (Times to 1)

Current Ratio 30	1.0	•	2.1	2.1	2.3	1.6	1.6	2.1	1.8	1.9	1.4	1.1	0.9
Quick Ratio 31	0.6	•	0.7	1.0	1.2	0.7	0.8	1.1	1.0	1.0	0.6	0.5	0.7
Net Sales to Working Capital 32	•	•	4.3	4.8	5.8	7.5	8.9	5.2	6.5	6.4	9.9	51.9	•
Coverage Ratio 33	5.4	•	•	9.6	2.5	6.9	3.6	3.5	6.5	3.6	5.8	5.4	•
Total Asset Turnover 34	0.7	•	2.0	2.2	2.4	1.4	2.3	1.6	1.5	1.2	1.3	0.8	0.7
Inventory Turnover 35	9.6	•	2.7	4.7	9.8	2.5	5.8	4.4	5.7	4.1	5.2	3.3	13.4
Receivables Turnover 36	5.2	•	9.2	9.9	9.5	5.8	8.2	7.0	6.9	7.5	7.5	9.3	4.7
Total Liabilities to Net Worth 37	1.6	•	•	0.8	1.2	1.4	1.1	1.1	1.2	1.1	2.3	1.6	•
Current Assets to Working Capital 38	•	•	1.9	1.8	2.7	2.7	1.9	2.2	2.2	2.2	3.3	20.6	•
Current Liabilities to Working Capital 39	•	•	0.9	0.8	1.7	1.7	0.9	1.2	1.2	1.2	2.3	19.6	•
Working Capital to Net Sales 40	•	•	0.2	0.2	0.2	0.1	0.1	0.2	0.2	0.2	0.1	0.0	•
Inventory to Working Capital 41	•	•	0.6	0.9	0.4	1.4	1.0	0.8	0.8	0.8	1.1	7.3	•
Total Receipts to Cash Flow 42	4.7	•	12.6	8.9	5.5	7.8	7.1	7.2	5.9	4.2	6.1	3.0	4.9
Cost of Goods to Cash Flow 43	2.8	•	8.1	4.7	3.5	5.1	4.7	4.7	3.5	2.0	3.7	1.3	3.0
Cash Flow to Total Debt 44	0.2	•	0.1	0.2	1.0	0.3	0.5	0.4	0.5	0.5	0.4	0.4	0.2

Selected Financial Factors (in Percentages)

Debt Ratio 45	61.7	•	114.6	113.8	45.0	53.5	57.9	52.2	53.1	54.3	53.1	69.3	61.3
Return on Total Assets 46	10.1	•	•	12.9	4.4	12.1	7.5	9.0	14.2	7.1	15.1	9.8	•
Return on Equity Before Income Taxes 47	21.6	•	118.8	106.9	21.0	5.8	24.6	11.4	13.7	26.3	11.0	40.7	20.6
Return on Equity After Income Taxes 48	14.8	•	118.8	107.7	19.0	2.1	22.0	8.7	10.5	20.9	6.6	29.3	14.0
Profit Margin (Before Income Tax) 49	11.5	•	•	4.7	1.9	4.6	3.5	4.2	9.8	4.0	15.0	12.1	•
Profit Margin (After Income Tax) 50	7.9	•	•	4.3	0.7	4.1	2.7	3.2	7.8	2.4	10.8	8.2	•

SOAP, CLEANING COMPOUND, AND TOILET PREPARATION

Table II

Corporations with Net Income

MONEY AMOUNTS AND SIZE OF ASSETS IN THOUSANDS OF DOLLARS

Item Description for Accounting Period 7/05 Through 6/06	Total	Zero Assets	Under 500	500 to 1,000	1,000 to 5,000	5,000 to 10,000	10,000 to 25,000	25,000 to 50,000	50,000 to 100,000	100,000 to 250,000	250,000 to 500,000	500,000 to 2,500,000	2,500,000 and over
Number of Enterprises **1**	448	0	0	205	131	21	35	17	8	10	·	·	6
Revenues ($ in Thousands)													
Net Sales **2**	110001154	0	0	402073	1201058	171877	1086917	962047	1027561	1986732	·	·	9414067
Interest **3**	630564	0	0	79	121	149	1403	3993	1178	2719	·	·	74096
Rents **4**	84067	0	0	0	1109	0	270	460	100	237	·	·	44650
Royalties **5**	2532721	0	0	0	5352	0	2370	144	124	4110	·	·	391383
Other Portfolio Income **6**	4169502	0	0	0	4216	25	601	968	3137	4773	·	·	690629
Other Receipts **7**	1796307	0	0	254	10552	749	3278	12635	1898	52452	·	·	251174
Total Receipts **8**	119214315	0	0	402406	1222408	172800	1094839	980247	1033998	2051023	·	·	10865999
Average Total Receipts **9**	266103	·	·	1963	9331	8229	31281	57662	129250	205102	·	·	1811000
Operating Costs/Operating Income (%)													
Cost of Operations **10**	60.5	·	·	50.5	59.0	54.9	56.9	62.0	58.6	48.5	·	·	41.4
Salaries and Wages **11**	6.6	·	·	13.4	7.2	10.9	11.7	8.4	8.0	7.2	·	·	14.1
Taxes Paid **12**	1.2	·	·	2.8	2.0	2.0	1.8	1.6	2.0	1.0	·	·	2.1
Interest Paid **13**	2.3	·	·	0.8	0.4	1.1	0.7	0.9	1.2	1.8	·	·	2.0
Depreciation **14**	2.0	·	·	1.7	0.6	2.3	1.5	1.0	1.4	1.9	·	·	1.4
Amortization and Depletion **15**	1.2	·	·	0.0	0.0	0.0	0.1	0.4	0.1	0.6	·	·	0.9
Pensions and Other Deferred Comp. **16**	1.3	·	·	0.2	1.0	0.5	0.3	0.3	0.5	0.6	·	·	1.4
Employee Benefits **17**	2.0	·	·	2.7	0.5	0.4	1.6	1.6	1.3	0.7	·	·	2.6
Advertising **18**	6.1	·	·	0.1	1.1	2.2	1.7	3.5	2.1	14.5	·	·	5.8
Other Expenses **19**	14.0	·	·	18.8	18.5	16.0	14.0	10.6	13.6	15.7	·	·	26.8
Officers' Compensation **20**	0.6	·	·	7.0	3.3	2.0	2.7	3.8	3.9	0.8	·	·	1.8
Operating Margin **21**	2.2	·	·	1.9	6.3	7.7	7.1	5.8	7.5	6.6	·	·	·
Operating Margin Before Officers' Comp. **22**	2.8	·	·	8.9	9.7	9.7	9.7	9.7	11.3	7.4	·	·	1.4

Selected Average Balance Sheet ($ in Thousands)

Net Receivables 23	48364	285	954	1194	3553	9631	20806	29537	178748
Inventories 24	14354	148	554	1960	3378	9209	10872	24365	216685
Net Property, Plant and Equipment 25	36429	68	480	3005	4039	7517	13534	26465	201161
Total Assets 26	333062	661	3689	6368	14488	37030	64525	162085	1673272
Notes and Loans Payable 27	122504	631	270	1442	3424	8736	19960	50070	589461
All Other Liabilities 28	79210	120	953	1443	3687	7028	21223	37942	519711
Net Worth 29	131347	-90	2465	3484	7377	21266	23342	74073	564100

Selected Financial Ratios (Times to 1)

Current Ratio 30	1.0	2.9	3.0	2.1	2.1	2.7	1.8	1.9	1.0
Quick Ratio 31	0.6	1.7	1.6	1.0	1.0	1.4	1.0	1.0	0.5
Net Sales to Working Capital 32			4.6	4.8	6.3	4.1	7.0	6.4	208.0
Coverage Ratio 33	6.4	3.6	22.0	8.2	11.4	9.6	8.1	6.5	10.4
Total Asset Turnover 34	0.7	3.0	2.5	1.3	2.1	1.5	2.0	1.2	0.9
Inventory Turnover 35	10.3	6.7	9.8	2.3	5.2	3.8	6.9	4.0	3.0
Receivables Turnover 36	5.2	6.6	8.9	6.8	9.0	6.1	8.2	13.5	17.6
Total Liabilities to Net Worth 37	1.5		0.5	0.8	1.0	0.7	1.8	1.2	2.0
Current Assets to Working Capital 38		1.5	1.5	1.9	1.9	1.6	2.3	2.2	80.0
Current Liabilities to Working Capital 39		0.5	0.5	0.9	0.9	0.6	1.3	1.2	79.0
Working Capital to Net Sales 40		0.2	0.2	0.2	0.2	0.2	0.1	0.2	0.0
Inventory to Working Capital 41		0.4	0.3	1.0	0.7	0.7	0.8	0.8	28.7
Total Receipts to Cash Flow 42	4.5	6.0	4.2	4.6	5.1	6.1	5.0	4.2	2.7
Cost of Goods to Cash Flow 43	2.7	3.0	2.5	2.5	2.9	3.8	2.9	2.0	1.1
Cash Flow to Total Debt 44	0.3	0.4	1.8	0.6	0.9	0.6	0.6	0.5	0.5

Selected Financial Factors (in Percentages)

Debt Ratio 45	60.6	113.6	33.2	45.3	49.1	42.6	63.8	54.3	66.3
Return on Total Assets 46	11.0	8.2	20.4	12.1	18.3	13.1	18.8	14.2	19.2
Return on Equity Before Income Taxes 47	23.5		29.2	19.4	32.8	20.4	45.6	26.3	51.4
Return on Equity After Income Taxes 48	16.3	27.1	27.1	15.6	29.7	17.2	39.0	20.9	37.0
Profit Margin (Before Income Tax) 49	12.6	2.0	7.9	8.2	7.8	7.7	8.3	9.8	18.5
Profit Margin (After Income Tax) 50	8.7	1.9	7.3	6.6	7.1	6.5	7.1	7.8	13.3

Table I

Corporations with and without Net Income

CHEMICAL PRODUCT AND PREPARATION

MONEY AMOUNTS AND SIZE OF ASSETS IN THOUSANDS OF DOLLARS

Item Description for Accounting Period 7/05 Through 6/06	Total	Zero Assets	Under 500	500 to 1,000	1,000 to 5,000	5,000 to 10,000	10,000 to 25,000	25,000 to 50,000	50,000 to 100,000	100,000 to 250,000	250,000 to 500,000	500,000 to 2,500,000	2,500,000 and over
Number of Enterprises 1	3126	182	1915	360	306	89	118	49	40	29	15	19	5
Revenues ($ in Thousands)													
Net Sales 2	57056281	619901	809163	400827	1466671	1230521	3327084	2466355	3301822	5678331	5574758	15660453	16520397
Interest 3	283303	2403	491	205	2434	2448	3771	2856	12534	45879	17716	124243	68325
Rents 4	27031	655	0	1289	682	4797	1965	91	548	476	3495	8365	4667
Royalties 5	441993	0	0	0	152	0	64	12084	944	12245	24718	202073	189714
Other Portfolio Income 6	2232933	20	1	0	1711	12002	11695	36851	18253	39644	327608	1158559	626588
Other Receipts 7	1011504	-47209	3445	338	-2696	6752	16787	36454	14615	118426	76668	434005	353916
Total Receipts 8	61053045	575770	813100	402659	1468954	1256520	3361366	2554691	3348716	5895001	6024963	17587698	17763607
Average Total Receipts 9	19531	3164	425	1118	4801	14118	28486	52137	83718	203276	401664	925668	3552721
Operating Costs/Operating Income (%)													
Cost of Operations 10	71.0	78.1	51.3	43.2	55.7	58.7	70.8	73.5	70.4	67.4	78.8	70.7	73.4
Salaries and Wages 11	6.9	6.1	2.0	18.7	8.9	13.7	5.7	6.9	8.2	8.8	6.4	5.9	6.7
Taxes Paid 12	1.4	1.2	2.7	4.1	2.2	2.2	1.5	1.3	1.5	1.8	1.4	1.5	0.8
Interest Paid 13	2.2	0.8	0.8	2.9	0.8	0.9	0.9	0.8	1.5	2.9	2.1	3.0	2.4
Depreciation 14	2.6	0.6	1.8	4.8	1.6	1.8	1.7	2.0	2.0	2.0	2.0	3.3	2.8
Amortization and Depletion 15	0.8	0.4	0.0	•	0.0	0.2	0.2	0.3	0.6	0.8	1.1	1.2	0.9
Pensions and Other Deferred Comp. 16	1.0	0.5	0.4	0.6	0.4	0.4	0.3	0.5	0.6	0.7	0.5	1.1	1.7
Employee Benefits 17	1.5	1.1	0.5	2.3	1.8	1.5	0.8	1.0	1.5	2.0	0.9	2.0	1.1
Advertising 18	1.0	0.0	0.2	2.5	0.1	1.5	0.6	0.5	0.7	0.3	0.3	2.2	0.7
Other Expenses 19	12.4	9.9	22.3	21.3	20.4	13.7	11.7	10.8	11.0	11.6	6.8	13.2	13.2
Officers' Compensation 20	1.2	0.3	11.3	7.3	5.2	4.3	2.1	1.8	1.8	0.9	0.7	0.8	0.3
Operating Margin 21	•	0.9	6.7	•	2.9	0.9	3.7	0.6	0.1	0.8	•	•	
Operating Margin Before Officers' Comp. 22	•	1.2	18.0	•	8.1	5.2	5.8	2.4	1.9	1.7	•	•	

Selected Average Balance Sheet ($ in Thousands)

Net Receivables 23	3343	0	55	133	530	1619	4031	6726	13915	33478	82203	161323	671723
Inventories 24	2244	0	8	180	453	1577	3372	7898	11851	23544	40454	103808	426599
Net Property, Plant and Equipment 25	4565	0	17	203	374	2161	4468	8859	13978	31579	81465	258760	1056784
Total Assets 26	20352	0	102	633	2120	7724	15577	37022	70954	148559	338851	1151551	4819849
Notes and Loans Payable 27	6345	0	110	418	527	1866	4746	8841	20491	68400	109305	372486	1326526
All Other Liabilities 28	7635	0	53	132	511	1822	3761	9040	18395	63289	90600	363433	2335399
Net Worth 29	6371	0	-62	83	1082	4036	7069	19141	32068	16870	138946	415632	1157924

Selected Financial Ratios (Times to 1)

Current Ratio 30	1.2	•	1.1	1.1	2.4	2.4	1.9	1.9	1.6	1.4	1.5	1.4	0.8
Quick Ratio 31	0.6	•	1.0	0.5	1.4	1.1	1.0	1.0	0.9	0.7	1.0	0.7	0.4
Net Sales to Working Capital 32	13.8	•	51.5	24.6	5.9	4.8	5.9	5.5	5.8	10.1	7.6	6.6	•
Coverage Ratio 33	3.4	•	10.4	•	5.0	4.2	6.0	6.3	2.0	2.7	4.7	3.7	2.9
Total Asset Turnover 34	0.9	•	4.1	1.8	2.3	1.8	1.8	1.4	1.2	1.3	1.1	0.7	0.7
Inventory Turnover 35	5.8	•	26.1	2.7	5.9	5.1	5.9	4.7	4.9	5.6	7.2	5.6	5.7
Receivables Turnover 36	5.7	•	8.7	7.7	10.1	9.0	7.1	6.7	6.0	6.6	4.3	5.0	5.8
Total Liabilities to Net Worth 37	2.2	•	•	6.6	1.0	0.9	1.2	0.9	1.2	7.8	1.4	1.8	3.2
Current Assets to Working Capital 38	6.0	•	10.3	7.8	1.7	1.7	2.2	2.2	2.7	3.7	3.0	3.4	•
Current Liabilities to Working Capital 39	5.0	•	9.3	6.8	0.7	0.7	1.2	1.2	1.7	2.7	2.0	2.4	•
Working Capital to Net Sales 40	0.1	•	0.0	0.0	0.2	0.2	0.2	0.2	0.2	0.1	0.1	0.2	•
Inventory to Working Capital 41	1.9	•	1.3	3.8	0.5	0.6	0.7	0.9	0.9	1.3	0.7	0.9	•
Total Receipts to Cash Flow 42	6.9	62.3	4.0	10.2	5.1	7.4	7.0	8.0	9.1	7.3	12.7	5.8	6.5
Cost of Goods to Cash Flow 43	4.9	48.6	2.1	4.4	2.8	4.3	4.9	5.9	6.4	4.9	10.0	4.1	4.8
Cash Flow to Total Debt 44	0.2	•	0.6	0.2	0.9	0.5	0.5	0.4	0.2	0.2	0.1	0.2	0.1

Selected Financial Factors (in Percentages)

Debt Ratio 45	68.7	•	160.7	86.9	49.0	47.8	54.6	48.3	54.8	88.6	59.0	63.9	76.0
Return on Total Assets 46	6.8	•	32.9	•	8.6	7.1	10.2	7.2	3.6	10.0	10.7	7.7	4.7
Return on Equity Before Income Taxes 47	15.4	•	•	•	13.5	10.4	18.8	11.7	4.1	55.2	20.7	15.6	13.0
Return on Equity After Income Taxes 48	12.2	•	•	•	11.2	8.1	15.0	9.1	1.2	41.4	13.7	12.9	11.5
Profit Margin (Before Income Tax) 49	5.4	•	7.2	•	3.0	3.0	4.7	4.5	1.6	4.8	7.7	7.9	4.5
Profit Margin (After Income Tax) 50	4.3	•	7.1	•	2.5	2.4	3.8	3.5	0.5	3.6	5.1	6.5	4.0

Table II
Corporations with Net Income

CHEMICAL PRODUCT AND PREPARATION

MONEY AMOUNTS AND SIZE OF ASSETS IN THOUSANDS OF DOLLARS

Item Description for Accounting Period 7/05 Through 6/06	Total	Zero Assets	Under 500	500 to 1,000	1,000 to 5,000	5,000 to 10,000	10,000 to 25,000	25,000 to 50,000	50,000 to 100,000	100,000 to 250,000	250,000 to 500,000	500,000 to 2,500,000	2,500,000 and over
Number of Enterprises **1**	1756	6	1166	60	246	69	95	35	27	22	10	15	5
Revenues ($ in Thousands)													
Net Sales **2**	49644205	557991	686971	61713	1337911	966654	2967157	2016048	2519138	4512116	3417480	14080629	16520397
Interest **3**	238220	2403	459	1	2189	1681	3338	2484	7090	32154	16416	101681	68325
Rents **4**	25914	655	0	1170	682	4573	1965	62	548	476	3233	7881	4667
Royalties **5**	428819	0	0	0	0	0	64	12084	534	11866	21932	192625	189714
Other Portfolio Income **6**	2076954	20	0	0	1711	9559	11695	32424	14872	38447	318628	1023011	626588
Other Receipts **7**	989489	20726	3205	1	2992	6690	16775	30847	6094	103589	52159	392495	353916
Total Receipts **8**	53403601	581795	690635	62885	1345485	989157	3000994	2093949	2548276	4698648	3829848	15798322	17763607
Average Total Receipts **9**	30412	96966	592	1048	5469	14336	31589	59827	94381	213575	382985	1053221	3552721
Operating Costs/Operating Income (%)													
Cost of Operations **10**	70.2	78.4	49.3	35.0	54.3	57.3	71.3	73.1	68.6	66.0	75.5	69.3	73.4
Salaries and Wages **11**	6.7	5.6	0.3	14.1	8.9	12.5	5.0	6.6	7.9	8.5	6.3	6.2	6.7
Taxes Paid **12**	1.4	1.3	2.7	4.7	2.1	2.3	1.5	1.2	1.6	1.9	1.7	1.5	0.8
Interest Paid **13**	2.0	0.9	0.9	2.8	0.8	0.6	0.7	0.6	0.8	2.3	1.4	2.7	2.4
Depreciation **14**	2.5	0.7	1.4	3.0	1.6	1.8	1.7	1.6	1.7	2.3	2.0	3.2	2.8
Amortization and Depletion **15**	0.8	0.5	•	•	0.0	0.1	0.2	0.3	0.2	0.7	0.9	1.1	0.9
Pensions and Other Deferred Comp. **16**	1.1	0.6	0.5	3.6	0.5	0.5	0.3	0.5	0.7	0.8	0.7	1.0	1.7
Employee Benefits **17**	1.5	1.0	0.0	3.5	1.7	1.5	0.8	0.8	1.5	2.2	0.9	2.1	1.1
Advertising **18**	1.1	0.0	0.1	0.9	0.1	1.5	0.4	0.5	0.6	0.3	0.3	2.5	0.7
Other Expenses **19**	12.3	7.3	20.2	6.3	20.5	12.6	10.4	10.1	9.7	11.3	7.1	13.1	13.2
Officers' Compensation **20**	1.1	0.4	12.0	22.7	5.1	4.3	2.2	1.9	1.5	0.8	0.8	0.8	0.3
Operating Margin **21**	•	3.4	12.6	3.3	4.3	5.0	5.6	2.7	5.1	2.9	2.5	•	•
Operating Margin Before Officers' Comp. **22**	0.4	3.8	24.5	26.0	9.4	9.3	7.8	4.7	6.6	3.7	3.3	•	•

Selected Average Balance Sheet ($ in Thousands)

Net Receivables **23**	4950	0	82	89	442	1604	4283	7629	14687	34732	91230	151138	671723
Inventories **24**	3032	0	9	644	365	1691	3457	8601	12132	23751	37505	118124	576712
Net Property, Plant and Equipment **25**	6832	0	17	126	388	1887	4315	7355	14737	35896	53835	271114	1056784
Total Assets **26**	30934	0	143	706	2073	7474	15947	35878	68258	149252	346994	1174597	4819849
Notes and Loans Payable **27**	9169	0	89	462	569	1311	4352	7585	16697	60673	97172	378029	1326526
All Other Liabilities **28**	12007	0	23	155	533	1795	3623	9018	13558	60516	90862	390011	2335399
Net Worth **29**	9757	0	30	89	971	4368	7972	19275	38003	28064	158960	406557	1157924

Selected Financial Ratios (Times to 1)

Current Ratio **30**	1.2	•	1.9	0.6	2.1	2.6	2.0	2.0	1.9	1.6	1.3	0.8	
Quick Ratio **31**	0.6	•	1.7	0.2	1.3	1.1	1.1	1.0	1.1	0.9	0.6	0.4	
Net Sales to Working Capital **32**	16.4	•	10.2	8.0	4.5	5.5	5.7	5.2	7.4	6.1	8.4	•	
Coverage Ratio **33**	4.7	9.4	15.7	2.9	7.1	13.8	10.5	12.0	8.7	4.1	12.3	4.4	2.9
Total Asset Turnover **34**	0.9	•	4.1	1.5	2.6	1.9	2.0	1.6	1.4	1.4	1.0	0.8	0.7
Inventory Turnover **35**	6.5	32.5	0.6	8.1	2.6	4.7	6.4	4.9	5.3	5.7	6.9	5.5	4.2
Receivables Turnover **36**	6.6	•	8.0	2.0	13.5	9.4	8.1	6.6	7.1	7.0	4.4	4.7	9.8
Total Liabilities to Net Worth **37**	2.2	•	3.7	6.9	1.1	0.7	1.0	0.9	0.8	4.3	1.2	1.9	3.2
Current Assets to Working Capital **38**	6.9	•	2.2	•	1.9	1.6	2.0	2.0	2.1	2.7	2.8	3.9	•
Current Liabilities to Working Capital **39**	5.9	1.2	•	0.9	0.6	1.0	1.0	1.1	1.7	1.8	2.9	•	
Working Capital to Net Sales **40**	0.1	0.1	•	0.1	0.2	0.2	0.2	0.2	0.1	0.2	0.1	•	
Inventory to Working Capital **41**	2.2	0.2	•	0.6	0.6	0.7	0.8	0.7	0.9	0.7	1.0	•	
Total Receipts to Cash Flow **42**	6.1	7.8	3.5	9.6	4.6	6.1	6.6	7.0	6.9	6.1	7.8	5.4	6.5
Cost of Goods to Cash Flow **43**	4.3	6.1	1.7	3.4	2.5	3.5	4.7	5.1	4.8	4.0	5.9	3.8	4.8
Cash Flow to Total Debt **44**	0.2	•	1.5	0.2	1.1	0.7	0.6	0.5	0.4	0.3	0.2	0.2	0.1

Selected Financial Factors (in Percentages)

Debt Ratio **45**	68.5	•	78.7	87.3	53.2	41.6	50.0	46.3	44.3	81.2	54.2	65.4	76.0
Return on Total Assets **46**	8.6	•	57.8	11.6	14.8	14.8	14.6	11.9	9.7	13.1	16.7	9.6	4.7
Return on Equity Before Income Taxes **47**	21.5	•	253.9	59.7	27.1	23.5	26.5	20.3	15.5	52.6	33.5	21.4	13.0
Return on Equity After Income Taxes **48**	17.8	•	252.8	50.6	23.9	20.9	22.2	16.8	11.9	41.9	24.4	17.9	11.5
Profit Margin (Before Income Tax) **49**	7.4	7.7	13.1	5.2	4.8	7.3	6.8	6.8	6.3	7.2	15.6	9.3	4.5
Profit Margin (After Income Tax) **50**	6.1	5.2	13.0	4.4	4.3	6.5	5.7	5.6	4.8	5.7	11.4	7.8	4.0

Table I
Corporations with and without Net Income

PLASTICS PRODUCT

MONEY AMOUNTS AND SIZE OF ASSETS IN THOUSANDS OF DOLLARS

Item Description for Accounting Period 7/05 Through 6/06		Total	Zero Assets	Under 500	500 to 1,000	1,000 to 5,000	5,000 to 10,000	10,000 to 25,000	25,000 to 50,000	50,000 to 100,000	100,000 to 250,000	250,000 to 500,000	500,000 to 2,500,000	2,500,000 and over
Number of Enterprises	1	10359	1128	4046	1378	2482	477	420	173	108	91	27	24	5
Revenues ($ in Thousands)														
Net Sales	2	11534497	1008096	1642754	2883791	11224067	5824077	12430806	9683542	10801418	18361995	9664651	20427308	11390991
Interest	3	446825	1277	1124	1492	4662	1516	8254	9179	15782	46927	41834	190971	123808
Rents	4	42193	149	629	0	674	2182	1382	2169	3555	10480	8374	7654	4945
Royalties	5	213296	4252	0	18182	0	834	6943	21	6348	6206	40170	44415	85924
Other Portfolio Income	6	986287	46	21732	15075	31993	5679	15335	138701	39922	65414	208600	219811	223981
Other Receipts	7	1040719	12784	32223	2127	74581	26227	51915	45885	88083	192015	36326	49764	428789
Total Receipts	8	118072817	1026604	1698462	2920667	11335977	5860515	12514635	9879497	10955108	18683037	9999955	20939923	12258438
Average Total Receipts	9	11398	910	420	2119	4567	12286	29797	57107	101436	205308	370369	872497	2451688
Operating Costs/Operating Income (%)														
Cost of Operations	10	72.2	71.8	65.7	59.8	64.4	68.6	73.6	71.0	74.4	75.6	77.8	76.8	65.0
Salaries and Wages	11	5.4	5.7	7.4	6.5	6.6	7.5	5.6	6.3	5.6	4.2	4.0	4.8	5.4
Taxes Paid	12	1.7	1.2	2.5	2.2	2.4	1.8	1.9	1.8	1.8	1.6	1.2	1.4	1.1
Interest Paid	13	2.6	1.2	1.5	0.6	0.9	1.0	1.4	1.7	1.6	2.1	3.4	4.8	5.5
Depreciation	14	2.6	1.7	1.0	0.9	2.4	2.5	2.5	2.9	2.9	2.4	3.2	3.2	2.2
Amortization and Depletion	15	0.4	0.5	0.2	0.2	0.1	0.1	0.2	0.3	0.5	0.5	0.7	0.8	0.4
Pensions and Other Deferred Comp.	16	0.5	0.4	0.0	0.5	0.2	0.4	0.4	0.5	0.5	0.4	0.3	0.5	1.1
Employee Benefits	17	1.5	4.4	0.6	1.0	1.5	1.2	1.7	1.7	1.7	1.4	1.4	1.3	1.6
Advertising	18	0.5	1.2	0.2	0.4	0.4	1.3	0.5	0.4	0.5	0.4	0.2	0.3	1.0
Other Expenses	19	9.7	14.6	26.9	13.3	10.9	8.9	7.6	8.7	8.3	7.9	7.4	7.6	18.4
Officers' Compensation	20	1.6	3.1	4.6	5.7	4.9	3.0	1.9	1.5	1.1	0.7	0.7	0.4	0.6
Operating Margin	21	1.3	•	•	8.8	5.4	3.7	2.9	3.2	1.1	2.8	•	•	•
Operating Margin Before Officers' Comp.	22	2.9	•	•	14.5	10.3	6.6	4.8	4.7	2.2	3.5	0.4	•	•

Selected Average Balance Sheet ($ in Thousands)

Net Receivables 23	1709	0	155	538	1424	3817	9059	15129	27053	56968	117951	740963
Inventories 24	1172	0	135	432	1212	3512	6622	12324	22698	33500	94591	198746
Net Property, Plant and Equipment 25	2259	0	106	602	2053	4860	11919	22142	40978	94331	236849	447152
Total Assets 26	9381	140	687	2107	6501	15774	35729	68977	151831	351918	950639	4188479
Notes and Loans Payable 27	4083	0	159	778	2227	5747	12746	24584	53546	141010	501767	2161607
All Other Liabilities 28	3105	60	174	576	1376	4778	9280	17305	42902	121283	238712	2241860
Net Worth 29	2192	9	354	753	2897	5248	13703	27089	55383	89624	210160	-214988

Selected Financial Ratios (Times to 1)

Current Ratio 30	1.4	•	1.1	2.6	1.8	1.5	1.5	1.5	1.6	1.6	1.6	0.8	
Quick Ratio 31	0.8	•	0.8	1.7	1.1	0.9	0.9	0.8	0.9	0.8	0.8	0.6	
Net Sales to Working Capital 32	10.2	•	87.8	6.8	7.5	7.9	9.2	8.4	8.3	9.1	7.2	7.2	•
Coverage Ratio 33	2.4	•	•	16.6	8.3	5.4	3.6	4.1	2.6	3.2	1.9	1.2	2.0
Total Asset Turnover 34	1.2	•	2.9	3.0	2.1	1.9	1.9	1.6	1.4	1.3	1.0	0.9	0.5
Inventory Turnover 35	6.9	•	9.4	9.3	6.7	6.9	6.2	6.0	6.0	6.7	8.3	6.9	7.5
Receivables Turnover 36	6.6	•	9.1	13.3	8.3	8.9	7.6	6.4	6.7	7.6	6.9	7.2	3.2
Total Liabilities to Net Worth 37	3.3	•	13.8	0.9	1.8	1.2	2.0	1.6	1.5	1.7	2.9	3.5	•
Current Assets to Working Capital 38	3.5	•	16.3	1.6	2.2	2.2	2.9	2.8	2.9	2.8	2.6	2.6	•
Current Liabilities to Working Capital 39	2.5	•	15.3	0.6	1.2	1.2	1.9	1.8	1.9	1.8	1.6	1.6	•
Working Capital to Net Sales 40	0.1	•	0.0	0.1	0.1	0.1	0.1	0.1	0.1	0.1	0.1	0.1	•
Inventory to Working Capital 41	1.1	•	4.0	0.4	0.7	0.8	1.1	1.0	1.0	1.1	0.7	0.8	•
Total Receipts to Cash Flow 42	9.1	13.2	17.0	5.3	7.2	9.0	10.9	8.9	11.1	9.5	12.0	16.5	4.5
Cost of Goods to Cash Flow 43	6.6	9.5	11.2	3.1	4.6	6.2	8.0	6.3	8.3	7.2	9.3	12.7	2.9
Cash Flow to Total Debt 44	0.2	•	0.2	1.2	0.5	0.4	0.3	0.3	0.2	0.2	0.2	0.1	0.1

Selected Financial Factors (in Percentages)

Debt Ratio 45	76.6	93.2	48.5	64.2	55.4	66.7	61.6	60.7	63.5	74.5	77.9	105.1
Return on Total Assets 46	7.5	•	32.6	15.7	9.8	9.2	10.9	6.1	8.8	6.7	4.9	6.1
Return on Equity Before Income Taxes 47	18.8	•	59.5	38.6	18.0	20.1	21.4	9.5	16.6	12.8	3.0	•
Return on Equity After Income Taxes 48	15.8	•	58.6	37.1	17.1	17.7	18.7	7.4	13.6	10.5	1.5	•
Profit Margin (Before Income Tax) 49	3.7	•	10.1	6.4	4.3	3.6	5.2	2.6	4.5	3.2	0.7	5.7
Profit Margin (After Income Tax) 50	3.1	•	9.9	6.2	4.1	3.1	4.6	2.0	3.7	2.6	0.4	4.1

Table II

Corporations with Net Income

PLASTICS PRODUCT

MONEY AMOUNTS AND SIZE OF ASSETS IN THOUSANDS OF DOLLARS

Item Description for Accounting Period 7/05 Through 6/06		Total	Zero Assets	Under 500	500 to 1,000	1,000 to 5,000	5,000 to 10,000	10,000 to 25,000	25,000 to 50,000	50,000 to 100,000	100,000 to 250,000	250,000 to 500,000	500,000 to 2,500,000	2,500,000 and over
Number of Enterprises	1	5722	436	1382	988	1958	335	303	132	82	70	•	•	•
Revenues ($ in Thousands)														
Net Sales	2	89178893	519023	471496	2266827	9346540	4522535	9465738	8039017	8418657	15929252			
Interest	3	378814	431	1097	853	4368	913	5978	6744	11769	31758			
Rents	4	24768	149	629	0	674	2002	1236	2043	1275	8240			
Royalties	5	183815	7	0	18182	0	0	1629	21	5949	3575			
Other Portfolio Income	6	805041	46	663	656	30623	4498	12581	137878	28837	59358			
Other Receipts	7	952985	2387	29121	1872	56863	26522	41071	17949	80419	155196			
Total Receipts	8	91524316	522043	503006	2288390	9439068	4556470	9528233	8203652	8546906	16187379			
Average Total Receipts	9	15995	1197	364	2316	4821	13601	31446	62149	104231	231248			
Operating Costs/Operating Income (%)														
Cost of Operations	10	70.5	71.8	39.1	59.2	63.1	64.9	71.9	70.1	72.6	75.8			
Salaries and Wages	11	5.2	6.2	12.4	5.2	6.7	8.0	5.2	6.1	5.7	3.9			
Taxes Paid	12	1.7	1.2	4.5	1.7	2.3	1.7	1.9	1.8	1.8	1.6			
Interest Paid	13	2.2	1.0	0.7	0.5	0.6	0.5	0.8	1.2	1.2	1.6			
Depreciation	14	2.4	1.5	2.4	0.5	2.1	1.8	2.3	2.7	2.6	2.3			
Amortization and Depletion	15	0.3	0.2	0.1	0.1	0.1	0.1	0.1	0.1	0.2	0.3			
Pensions and Other Deferred Comp.	16	0.5	0.3	0.0	0.6	0.2	0.4	0.4	0.5	0.5	0.3			
Employee Benefits	17	1.4	0.7	1.6	1.0	1.5	1.2	1.6	1.5	1.7	1.3			
Advertising	18	0.5	0.9	0.4	0.5	0.4	1.7	0.5	0.4	0.5	0.4			
Other Expenses	19	9.5	9.3	22.9	12.7	10.8	8.9	6.9	8.1	7.7	7.3			
Officers' Compensation	20	1.6	3.0	8.0	5.2	4.5	3.4	1.9	1.5	1.2	0.7			
Operating Margin	21	4.1	4.1	7.9	12.9	7.6	7.4	6.4	5.9	4.4	4.4			
Operating Margin Before Officers' Comp.	22	5.7	7.0	15.9	18.1	12.2	10.7	8.3	7.5	5.6	5.1			

Selected Average Balance Sheet ($ in Thousands)

Net Receivables 23	2088	0	31	144	548	1583	4110	9505	15540	30301
Inventories 24	1533	0	21	143	407	1223	3591	6574	11492	26920
Net Property, Plant and Equipment 25	2891	0	26	104	522	1748	5002	11535	22114	42230
Total Assets 26	12262	0	120	691	2050	6503	16050	35906	69662	151114
Notes and Loans Payable 27	4895	0	37	78	638	1503	4608	11346	21916	48489
All Other Liabilities 28	3904	0	26	188	540	1088	3842	8912	16087	42178
Net Worth 29	3463	0	57	424	872	3912	7600	15648	31659	60447

Selected Financial Ratios (Times to 1)

Current Ratio 30	1.6	•	1.7	2.6	2.0	2.8	1.9	1.7	1.7	1.6
Quick Ratio 31	0.9	•	1.2	1.7	1.3	1.7	1.1	1.0	0.9	0.8
Net Sales to Working Capital 32	8.6	•	10.7	7.2	7.1	5.6	6.7	7.4	7.0	9.0
Coverage Ratio 33	4.1	5.9	21.4	28.0	14.7	16.3	9.5	7.4	5.9	4.7
Total Asset Turnover 34	1.3	•	2.8	3.3	2.3	2.1	1.9	1.7	1.5	1.5
Inventory Turnover 35	7.2	•	6.5	9.5	7.4	7.2	6.3	6.5	6.5	6.4
Receivables Turnover 36	8.2	•	22.1	15.8	9.0	9.3	7.7	7.0	7.5	15.0
Total Liabilities to Net Worth 37	2.5	•	1.1	0.6	1.4	0.7	1.1	1.3	1.2	1.5
Current Assets to Working Capital 38	2.8	•	2.5	1.6	2.0	1.6	2.1	2.4	2.4	2.7
Current Liabilities to Working Capital 39	1.8	•	1.5	0.6	1.0	0.6	1.1	1.4	1.4	1.7
Working Capital to Net Sales 40	0.1	•	0.1	0.1	0.1	0.2	0.1	0.1	0.1	0.1
Inventory to Working Capital 41	0.9	•	0.6	0.4	0.6	0.5	0.8	0.8	0.8	1.1
Total Receipts to Cash Flow 42	7.1	8.8	3.3	4.5	6.2	6.7	8.2	7.5	8.4	8.7
Cost of Goods to Cash Flow 43	5.0	6.3	1.3	2.7	3.9	4.4	5.9	5.3	6.1	6.6
Cash Flow to Total Debt 44	0.2	•	1.6	1.9	0.7	0.8	0.5	0.4	0.3	0.3

Selected Financial Factors (in Percentages)

Debt Ratio 45	71.8	•	52.5	38.6	57.5	39.8	52.6	56.4	54.6	60.0
Return on Total Assets 46	11.5	•	43.6	47.5	21.6	17.9	15.4	15.6	10.6	11.5
Return on Equity Before Income Taxes 47	31.0	•	87.5	74.7	47.3	27.9	29.1	31.0	19.4	22.6
Return on Equity After Income Taxes 48	27.5	•	80.1	73.6	45.6	27.0	26.8	27.9	16.9	19.1
Profit Margin (Before Income Tax) 49	6.9	4.7	14.6	13.8	8.6	8.1	7.1	8.0	6.0	6.0
Profit Margin (After Income Tax) 50	6.1	3.5	13.4	13.6	8.3	7.8	6.5	7.2	5.2	5.1

Table I

Corporations with and without Net Income

RUBBER PRODUCT

MONEY AMOUNTS AND SIZE OF ASSETS IN THOUSANDS OF DOLLARS

Item Description for Accounting Period 7/05 Through 6/06	Total	Zero Assets	Under 500	500 to 1,000	1,000 to 5,000	5,000 to 10,000	10,000 to 25,000	25,000 to 50,000	50,000 to 100,000	100,000 to 250,000	250,000 to 500,000	500,000 to 2,500,000	2,500,000 and over
Number of Enterprises 1	693	12	52	104	347	64	44	30	19	7	6	5	4
Revenues ($ in Thousands)													
Net Sales 2	48133243	35331	41266	144165	2206790	1230017	1307754	1778186	1980010	1568412	2233770	6829022	28778519
Interest 3	294097	663	0	86	1277	1216	758	2040	2527	6096	21246	25476	232712
Rents 4	21309	0	0	0	0	0	995	548	2243	13	1151	4948	11412
Royalties 5	536856	1983	0	0	809	0	0	660	42	10089	3410	114830	405032
Other Portfolio Income 6	839506	0	0	0	44921	0	12274	1727	8654	39003	25536	408489	298900
Other Receipts 7	461474	-1406	1210	448	3884	4236	12316	19269	12340	22082	66388	26224	294486
Total Receipts 8	50286485	36571	42476	144699	2257681	1235469	1334097	1802430	2005816	1645695	2351501	7408989	30021061
Average Total Receipts 9	72563	3048	817	1391	6506	19304	30320	60081	105569	235099	391917	1481798	7505265
Operating Costs/Operating Income (%)													
Cost of Operations 10	70.6	68.2	59.3	82.1	66.2	76.5	73.6	74.8	75.6	74.4	72.7	75.6	68.3
Salaries and Wages 11	6.5	1.7	17.5	3.8	6.9	4.7	7.4	7.3	5.0	3.9	6.3	5.2	7.1
Taxes Paid 12	1.3	1.5	3.1	1.5	2.1	1.3	2.0	2.0	2.1	1.3	1.5	0.8	1.3
Interest Paid 13	2.3	2.8	6.9	1.3	0.5	0.6	1.0	2.0	1.9	1.7	4.2	1.8	2.6
Depreciation 14	2.5	0.9	11.8	0.2	1.1	2.1	2.9	2.1	2.7	1.8	1.7	2.0	2.8
Amortization and Depletion 15	0.7	2.1	0.0	•	0.1	0.0	0.1	0.4	0.5	0.9	1.8	0.8	0.7
Pensions and Other Deferred Comp. 16	1.5	•	•	•	0.6	0.0	0.6	0.4	1.0	2.0	0.8	0.8	2.0
Employee Benefits 17	3.4	2.0	0.4	•	1.3	0.9	2.3	1.6	2.8	4.2	2.0	3.8	3.8
Advertising 18	1.1	0.2	1.3	•	0.1	0.1	0.4	0.5	0.5	0.7	0.9	1.1	1.4
Other Expenses 19	12.3	14.5	38.8	12.3	11.2	7.3	8.9	6.8	6.8	12.5	9.9	6.8	14.9
Officers' Compensation 20	0.6	1.8	6.0	2.3	6.2	1.3	1.7	1.1	0.8	0.8	0.4	0.5	0.1
Operating Margin 21	•	4.4	•	•	3.5	5.1	•	1.1	0.2	•	•	0.8	•
Operating Margin Before Officers' Comp. 22	•	6.1	•	•	9.7	6.4	0.9	2.1	1.0	•	•	1.2	•

Selected Average Balance Sheet ($ in Thousands)

Net Receivables 23	9989	0	24	162	733	2281	3961	8602	12646	22913	47910	172891	1129800
Inventories 24	9102	0	60	173	711	913	4789	6650	12333	21791	60324	191879	965803
Net Property, Plant and Equipment 25	12380	0	270	390	359	2707	5134	9288	18141	40299	52592	345711	1262874
Total Assets 26	56437	0	475	872	2462	7567	15825	33953	69404	166119	398111	1277825	6170713
Notes and Loans Payable 27	17423	0	162	305	442	1734	4469	15150	26558	63189	206093	222917	1955092
All Other Liabilities 28	26630	0	692	133	728	2102	6144	11603	19132	64026	83010	420841	3496295
Net Worth 29	12384	0	-380	434	1291	3731	5212	7200	23714	38905	109008	634067	719327

Selected Financial Ratios (Times to 1)

Current Ratio 30	1.5	•	0.8	2.3	2.1	1.4	1.4	1.4	1.7	1.2	1.6	2.3	1.4
Quick Ratio 31	0.9	•	0.7	1.3	1.5	1.1	0.8	0.8	0.9	0.6	0.8	1.3	0.8
Net Sales to Working Capital 32	8.5	•	•	5.1	6.7	16.0	10.7	11.2	8.0	25.7	7.5	5.4	9.4
Coverage Ratio 33	1.8	3.8	•	•	11.7	9.9	2.2	2.2	1.8	1.5	1.7	6.6	0.9
Total Asset Turnover 34	1.2	•	1.7	1.6	2.6	2.5	1.9	1.7	1.5	1.3	0.9	1.1	1.2
Inventory Turnover 35	5.4	•	7.8	6.6	5.9	16.1	4.6	6.7	6.4	7.6	4.5	5.4	5.1
Receivables Turnover 36	6.5	•	6.7	9.5	7.0	7.6	5.7	8.2	7.5	12.5	6.9	6.1	6.2
Total Liabilities to Net Worth 37	3.6	•	•	1.0	0.9	1.0	2.0	3.7	1.9	3.3	2.7	1.0	7.6
Current Assets to Working Capital 38	2.9	•	•	1.8	1.9	3.8	3.3	3.8	2.4	6.5	2.7	1.8	3.3
Current Liabilities to Working Capital 39	1.9	•	•	0.8	0.9	2.8	2.3	2.8	1.4	5.5	1.7	0.8	2.3
Working Capital to Net Sales 40	0.1	•	•	0.2	0.1	0.1	0.1	0.1	0.1	0.0	0.1	0.2	0.1
Inventory to Working Capital 41	1.1	•	•	0.7	0.4	0.7	1.2	1.4	0.9	2.6	1.1	0.6	1.3
Total Receipts to Cash Flow 42	8.9	4.5	•	25.6	6.5	9.7	12.6	13.3	15.1	12.2	8.7	6.7	9.1
Cost of Goods to Cash Flow 43	6.3	3.1	•	21.0	4.3	7.5	9.3	9.9	11.4	9.1	6.4	5.1	6.2
Cash Flow to Total Debt 44	0.2	•	•	0.1	0.8	0.5	0.2	0.2	0.2	0.1	0.1	0.3	0.1

Selected Financial Factors (in Percentages)

Debt Ratio 45	78.1	•	180.0	50.3	47.5	50.7	67.1	78.8	65.8	76.6	72.6	50.4	88.3
Return on Total Assets 46	5.1	•	•	•	16.3	15.6	4.2	7.6	5.1	3.4	6.6	12.6	2.6
Return on Equity Before Income Taxes 47	10.7	•	88.6	•	28.5	28.5	6.9	19.8	6.6	4.6	9.6	21.6	•
Return on Equity After Income Taxes 48	8.5	•	88.6	•	27.2	25.2	5.6	14.1	4.2	3.7	7.5	17.6	•
Profit Margin (Before Income Tax) 49	1.9	7.9	•	•	5.8	5.5	1.2	2.4	1.5	0.8	2.8	10.0	•
Profit Margin (After Income Tax) 50	1.5	6.4	•	•	5.5	4.9	1.0	1.7	1.0	0.6	2.2	8.2	•

Table II
Corporations with Net Income

RUBBER PRODUCT

MONEY AMOUNTS AND SIZE OF ASSETS IN THOUSANDS OF DOLLARS

Item Description for Accounting Period 7/05 Through 6/06	Total	Zero Assets	Under 500	500 to 1,000	1,000 to 5,000	5,000 to 10,000	10,000 to 25,000	25,000 to 50,000	50,000 to 100,000	100,000 to 250,000	250,000 to 500,000	500,000 to 2,500,000	2,500,000 and over
Number of Enterprises 1	510	12	0	52	319	61	21	16	13	•	•	•	0
Revenues ($ in Thousands)													
Net Sales 2	32090372	35331	0	120304	2206790	1228801	748322	1036278	1515203	•	•	•	0
Interest 3	139528	663	0	86	1277	1201	296	574	2413	•	•	•	0
Rents 4	17877	0	0	0	0	0	0	440	2243	•	•	•	0
Royalties 5	158942	1983	0	0	0	0	0	1	42	•	•	•	0
Other Portfolio Income 6	601023	0	0	0	44921	0	4326	917	4541	•	•	•	0
Other Receipts 7	284726	-1406	0	448	3283	4237	6119	5989	13359	•	•	•	0
Total Receipts 8	33292468	36571	0	120838	2256271	1234239	759063	1044199	1537801	•	•	•	0
Average Total Receipts 9	65279	3048	•	2324	7073	20233	36146	65262	118292	•	•	•	•
Operating Costs/Operating Income (%)													
Cost of Operations 10	71.2	68.2	•	80.4	66.2	76.6	73.4	71.7	75.4	•	•	•	•
Salaries and Wages 11	6.0	1.7	•	4.5	6.9	4.7	5.8	7.9	5.1	•	•	•	•
Taxes Paid 12	1.2	1.5	•	1.6	2.1	1.3	1.8	1.9	2.0	•	•	•	•
Interest Paid 13	1.8	2.8	•	0.7	0.5	0.4	0.4	0.5	1.0	•	•	•	•
Depreciation 14	2.1	0.9	•	0.1	1.1	2.1	1.6	1.5	2.1	•	•	•	•
Amortization and Depletion 15	0.4	2.1	•	•	0.0	0.0	0.1	0.1	0.4	•	•	•	•
Pensions and Other Deferred Comp. 16	1.1	•	•	•	0.6	0.0	0.3	0.4	1.1	•	•	•	•
Employee Benefits 17	3.0	2.0	•	•	1.3	0.9	1.5	1.8	2.6	•	•	•	•
Advertising 18	1.3	0.2	•	•	0.1	0.1	0.4	0.3	0.6	•	•	•	•
Other Expenses 19	10.9	14.5	•	8.5	11.2	6.3	7.8	5.7	6.4	•	•	•	•
Officers' Compensation 20	0.8	1.8	•	2.8	6.2	1.3	1.6	1.2	0.8	•	•	•	•
Operating Margin 21	0.3	4.4	•	1.4	3.6	6.3	5.3	7.1	2.7	•	•	•	•
Operating Margin Before Officers' Comp. 22	1.1	6.1	•	4.2	9.8	7.6	6.9	8.2	3.4	•	•	•	•

Selected Average Balance Sheet ($ in Thousands)

Net Receivables 23	9321	0	•	323	694	2392	4542	10040	13890
Inventories 24	8106	0	•	347	711	958	6353	8627	14810
Net Property, Plant and Equipment 25	10676	0	•	84	390	2818	4497	7651	17718
Total Assets 26	48334	0	•	851	2507	7629	16451	35772	74418
Notes and Loans Payable 27	10021	0	•	211	481	1448	2553	7419	17417
All Other Liabilities 28	21062	0	•	266	581	2187	3790	10428	20449
Net Worth 29	17252	0	•	374	1445	3994	10107	17925	36552

Selected Financial Ratios (Times to 1)

Current Ratio 30	1.7	•	•	1.8	2.5	1.5	3.0	1.7	2.0
Quick Ratio 31	1.0	•	•	0.8	1.8	1.2	1.6	1.0	1.1
Net Sales to Working Capital 32	7.6	•	•	6.8	6.1	12.5	4.7	6.8	6.4
Coverage Ratio 33	3.4	3.8	•	3.6	11.9	18.7	17.6	16.2	5.0
Total Asset Turnover 34	1.3	•	•	2.7	2.8	2.6	2.2	1.8	1.6
Inventory Turnover 35	5.5	•	•	5.4	6.4	16.1	4.1	5.4	5.9
Receivables Turnover 36	6.2	•	•	8.0	7.7	7.6	5.2	7.1	7.3
Total Liabilities to Net Worth 37	1.8	•	•	1.3	0.7	0.9	0.6	1.0	1.0
Current Assets to Working Capital 38	2.5	•	•	2.2	1.7	2.9	1.5	2.4	2.0
Current Liabilities to Working Capital 39	1.5	•	•	1.2	0.7	1.9	0.5	1.4	1.0
Working Capital to Net Sales 40	0.1	•	•	0.1	0.2	0.1	0.2	0.1	0.2
Inventory to Working Capital 41	0.9	•	•	1.2	0.4	0.5	0.6	0.9	0.8
Total Receipts to Cash Flow 42	7.6	4.5	•	19.9	6.5	9.6	8.0	8.3	11.0
Cost of Goods to Cash Flow 43	5.4	3.1	•	16.0	4.3	7.3	5.8	6.0	8.3
Cash Flow to Total Debt 44	0.3	•	•	0.2	1.0	0.6	0.7	0.4	0.3

Selected Financial Factors (in Percentages)

Debt Ratio 45	64.3	•	•	56.1	42.3	47.6	38.6	49.9	50.9
Return on Total Assets 46	7.8	•	•	6.8	17.7	18.7	15.5	15.0	8.2
Return on Equity Before Income Taxes 47	15.3	•	•	11.2	28.1	33.9	23.8	28.2	13.2
Return on Equity After Income Taxes 48	13.1	•	•	9.5	26.8	30.6	22.4	23.9	11.0
Profit Margin (Before Income Tax) 49	4.2	7.9	•	1.8	5.9	6.7	6.8	7.8	4.2
Profit Margin (After Income Tax) 50	3.6	6.4	•	1.5	5.6	6.1	6.6	6.6	3.4

Table I

Corporations with and without Net Income

CLAY, REFRACTORY AND OTHER NONMETALLIC MINERAL PRODUCT

MONEY AMOUNTS AND SIZE OF ASSETS IN THOUSANDS OF DOLLARS

Item Description for Accounting Period 7/05 Through 6/06	Total	Zero Assets	Under 500	500 to 1,000	1,000 to 5,000	5,000 to 10,000	10,000 to 25,000	25,000 to 50,000	50,000 to 100,000	100,000 to 250,000	250,000 to 500,000	500,000 to 2,500,000	2,500,000 and over
Number of Enterprises **1**	2525	•	1480	541	325	•	64	31	18	10	3	8	0
Revenues ($ in Thousands)													
Net Sales **2**	22253771	•	592560	1073252	1332983	•	1258933	1572355	1674880	1449927	1009481	11557897	0
Interest **3**	258802	•	1599	1172	281	•	861	1628	1715	4042	829	241581	0
Rents **4**	31344	•	0	171	0	•	523	39	969	639	36	28390	0
Royalties **5**	291337	•	0	0	0	•	2179	0	446	1598	551	279984	0
Other Portfolio Income **6**	229033	•	2559	271	57	•	12635	6909	17591	26607	1460	152084	0
Other Receipts **7**	292233	•	700	7141	2712	•	16331	8204	64054	28085	7543	133865	0
Total Receipts **8**	23356520	•	597418	1082007	1336033	•	1291462	1589135	1759655	1510898	1019900	12393801	0
Average Total Receipts **9**	9250	•	404	2000	4111	•	20179	51262	97759	151090	339967	1549225	•
Operating Costs/Operating Income (%)													
Cost of Operations **10**	68.3	•	60.1	62.3	65.7	•	71.2	68.3	70.0	62.7	61.0	70.8	•
Salaries and Wages **11**	6.8	•	8.9	5.6	8.8	•	6.0	6.5	9.5	9.5	6.3	6.1	•
Taxes Paid **12**	1.7	•	3.0	3.1	2.7	•	2.0	2.0	2.2	2.4	1.1	1.1	•
Interest Paid **13**	3.3	•	0.3	0.7	1.0	•	0.8	1.1	1.4	1.3	0.9	5.4	•
Depreciation **14**	2.8	•	2.5	1.1	2.9	•	2.5	3.4	3.1	3.2	4.5	2.7	•
Amortization and Depletion **15**	1.0	•	0.0	0.2	0.5	•	0.4	0.2	0.6	0.4	0.3	1.6	•
Pensions and Other Deferred Comp. **16**	0.6	•	0.0	0.2	0.5	•	0.5	0.6	0.7	1.2	0.1	0.7	•
Employee Benefits **17**	1.7	•	0.7	0.7	1.0	•	1.2	1.7	1.6	2.5	1.1	2.0	•
Advertising **18**	0.6	•	0.4	0.1	0.5	•	0.4	0.6	0.7	0.6	0.2	0.6	•
Other Expenses **19**	10.0	•	18.6	9.9	9.4	•	7.1	9.0	10.3	8.8	9.2	10.2	•
Officers' Compensation **20**	1.8	•	10.1	6.3	6.3	•	2.2	2.1	0.9	1.1	1.4	0.5	•
Operating Margin **21**	1.4	•	•	9.8	0.7	•	5.6	4.5	•	6.3	13.9	•	•
Operating Margin Before Officers' Comp. **22**	3.2	•	5.5	16.1	7.1	•	7.8	6.6	7.5	7.5	15.3	•	•

Selected Average Balance Sheet ($ in Thousands)

Net Receivables 23	3571	51	146	238	2828	6729	13471	34580	49050	954496
Inventories 24	908	13	27	752	3557	7501	13161	38691	53092	97163
Net Property, Plant and Equipment 25	2051	25	189	471	4490	11603	29828	52792	141277	338174
Total Assets 26	14792	170	704	1662	14892	34718	75652	151578	356022	3754195
Notes and Loans Payable 27	5442	165	262	580	3593	9824	22484	32228	56248	1458305
All Other Liabilities 28	7111	23	91	271	4010	6166	23702	43700	63993	2030242
Net Worth 29	2239	-19	351	811	7288	18728	29465	75650	235780	265648

Selected Financial Ratios (Times to 1)

Current Ratio 30	1.3	1.4	3.0	2.5	1.7	1.8	2.2	3.4	1.2	
Quick Ratio 31	0.7	1.1	2.8	1.0	0.9	0.8	1.2	2.0	0.7	
Net Sales to Working Capital 32	5.1	11.2	6.7	7.6	6.6	5.6	3.6	2.7	5.1	
Coverage Ratio 33	3.0	•	15.1	1.9	12.6	3.9	9.5	17.0	2.1	
Total Asset Turnover 34	0.6	2.4	2.8	2.5	1.3	1.2	1.0	0.9	0.4	
Inventory Turnover 35	6.6	18.9	46.2	3.6	3.9	4.9	2.3	3.9	10.5	
Receivables Turnover 36	2.6	11.7	15.3	7.9	6.3	9.0	3.2	13.7	1.6	
Total Liabilities to Net Worth 37	5.6	•	1.0	1.0	1.0	1.6	1.0	0.5	13.1	
Current Assets to Working Capital 38	4.3	3.9	1.5	1.7	2.5	2.3	1.8	1.4	6.6	
Current Liabilities to Working Capital 39	3.3	2.9	0.5	0.7	1.5	1.3	0.8	0.4	5.6	
Working Capital to Net Sales 40	0.2	0.1	0.1	0.1	0.2	0.2	0.3	0.4	0.2	
Inventory to Working Capital 41	0.6	0.5	0.1	0.9	1.1	1.1	0.7	0.4	0.4	
Total Receipts to Cash Flow 42	7.4	8.8	5.5	210.9	7.7	8.9	5.7	4.5	7.5	
Cost of Goods to Cash Flow 43	5.1	5.3	3.4	138.6	5.5	6.2	3.6	2.7	5.3	
Cash Flow to Total Debt 44	0.1	0.2	1.0	0.0	0.3	0.2	0.3	0.6	0.1	

Selected Financial Factors (in Percentages)

Debt Ratio 45	84.9	111.0	50.2	51.2	51.1	46.1	50.1	33.8	92.9	
Return on Total Assets 46	5.9	•	31.9	4.7	14.1	9.8	11.7	14.9	4.3	
Return on Equity Before Income Taxes 47	26.0	80.3	59.8	4.7	26.6	15.2	12.5	21.1	31.4	
Return on Equity After Income Taxes 48	20.5	82.5	59.4	4.6	24.0	12.0	11.3	15.7	13.8	24.6
Profit Margin (Before Income Tax) 49	6.6	•	10.6	0.9	9.9	5.6	4.0	11.0	14.8	5.8
Profit Margin (After Income Tax) 50	5.2	•	10.5	0.9	8.9	4.4	3.6	8.2	9.7	4.5

99

CLAY, REFRACTORY AND OTHER NONMETALLIC MINERAL PRODUCT

Table II
Corporations with Net Income

MONEY AMOUNTS AND SIZE OF ASSETS IN THOUSANDS OF DOLLARS

Item Description for Accounting Period 7/05 Through 6/06	Total	Zero Assets	Under 500	500 to 1,000	1,000 to 5,000	5,000 to 10,000	10,000 to 25,000	25,000 to 50,000	50,000 to 100,000	100,000 to 250,000	250,000 to 500,000	500,000 to 2,500,000	2,500,000 and over
Number of Enterprises 1	1745	•	860	489	255	16	50	24	13	•	3	•	0
Revenues ($ in Thousands)													
Net Sales 2	20021491	•	516636	988425	1028319	210812	1193894	1314423	1129478	•	1009481	•	0
Interest 3	251932	•	1007	1110	257	0	852	1228	1504	•	829	•	0
Rents 4	31091	•	0	171	0	576	271	39	969	•	36	•	0
Royalties 5	279476	•	0	0	0	6323	2179	0	213	•	551	•	0
Other Portfolio Income 6	207225	•	2559	271	57	0	12493	6864	1155	•	1460	•	0
Other Receipts 7	283303	•	639	7140	936	21266	13942	7914	59414	•	7543	•	0
Total Receipts 8	21074518	•	520841	997117	1029569	238977	1223631	1330468	1192733	•	1019900	•	0
Average Total Receipts 9	12077	•	606	2039	4038	14936	24473	55436	91749	•	339967	•	•
Operating Costs/Operating Income (%)													
Cost of Operations 10	68.1	•	53.2	62.8	62.6	58.7	70.8	67.2	72.3	•	61.0	•	•
Salaries and Wages 11	6.5	•	6.0	4.7	11.0	5.6	5.9	6.6	6.7	•	6.3	•	•
Taxes Paid 12	1.6	•	2.8	3.0	2.4	3.3	1.9	2.0	2.0	•	1.1	•	•
Interest Paid 13	3.2	•	0.3	0.7	0.7	1.4	0.8	0.9	1.3	•	0.9	•	•
Depreciation 14	2.7	•	2.8	1.1	1.5	2.0	2.0	2.2	3.4	•	4.5	•	•
Amortization and Depletion 15	1.0	•	•	0.2	0.7	0.2	0.4	0.2	0.7	•	0.3	•	•
Pensions and Other Deferred Comp. 16	0.7	•	0.0	0.2	0.6	0.0	0.6	0.6	1.0	•	0.1	•	•
Employee Benefits 17	1.6	•	0.8	0.5	1.3	0.8	1.2	1.3	1.1	•	1.1	•	•
Advertising 18	0.6	•	0.3	0.2	0.6	1.9	0.3	0.6	0.1	•	0.2	•	•
Other Expenses 19	9.5	•	16.0	9.4	8.2	12.8	6.8	7.9	7.2	•	9.2	•	•
Officers' Compensation 20	1.8	•	10.2	6.3	7.5	6.4	2.2	2.3	1.2	•	1.4	•	•
Operating Margin 21	2.8	•	7.7	10.8	3.0	6.8	7.1	8.1	3.1	•	13.9	•	•
Operating Margin Before Officers' Comp. 22	4.6	•	17.9	17.1	10.5	13.2	9.3	10.4	4.3	•	15.3	•	•

Selected Average Balance Sheet ($ in Thousands)

Net Receivables 23	4902	48	117	227	1020	3007	7112	11925	49050
Inventories 24	939	17	21	719	2052	3659	8108	13069	53092
Net Property, Plant and Equipment 25	2570	27	200	176	1182	3820	10992	29215	141277
Total Assets 26	20086	218	714	1377	6615	15193	35970	71773	356022
Notes and Loans Payable 27	6992	18	225	386	1560	2955	8924	16341	56248
All Other Liabilities 28	9923	10	85	319	1343	3651	6369	20872	63993
Net Worth 29	3171	190	403	672	3712	8587	20677	34559	235780

Selected Financial Ratios (Times to 1)

Current Ratio 30	1.3	23.7	3.0	2.3	1.6	2.1	2.7	2.0	3.4
Quick Ratio 31	0.7	19.6	2.8	0.9	0.7	1.1	1.4	0.9	2.0
Net Sales to Working Capital 32	5.0	3.5	7.0	8.1	8.3	5.7	4.0	5.3	2.7
Coverage Ratio 33	3.6	33.3	17.0	5.7	15.1	15.3	11.5	7.7	17.0
Total Asset Turnover 34	0.6	2.8	2.8	2.9	2.0	1.6	1.5	1.2	0.9
Inventory Turnover 35	8.3	18.7	59.7	3.5	3.8	4.6	4.5	4.8	3.9
Receivables Turnover 36	3.9	15.4	25.0	7.2	25.8	7.8	8.1	14.6	13.7
Total Liabilities to Net Worth 37	5.3	0.1	0.8	1.1	0.8	0.8	0.7	1.1	0.5
Current Assets to Working Capital 38	4.4	1.0	1.5	1.8	2.7	1.9	1.6	2.0	1.4
Current Liabilities to Working Capital 39	3.4	0.0	0.5	0.8	1.7	0.9	0.6	1.0	0.4
Working Capital to Net Sales 40	0.2	0.3	0.1	0.1	0.1	0.2	0.2	0.2	0.4
Inventory to Working Capital 41	0.5	0.2	0.1	1.0	1.3	0.9	0.6	0.8	0.4
Total Receipts to Cash Flow 42	6.8	4.8	5.4	377.8	3.3	7.1	6.3	6.9	4.5
Cost of Goods to Cash Flow 43	4.6	2.6	3.4	236.4	2.0	5.0	4.2	5.0	2.7
Cash Flow to Total Debt 44	0.1	4.5	1.2	0.0	1.4	0.5	0.6	0.3	0.6

Selected Financial Factors (in Percentages)

Debt Ratio 45	84.2	12.8	43.5	51.2	43.9	43.5	42.5	51.8	33.8
Return on Total Assets 46	6.6	24.3	35.1	11.0	43.0	19.2	15.6	12.1	14.9
Return on Equity Before Income Taxes 47	30.1	27.0	58.5	18.7	71.5	31.7	24.8	21.9	21.1
Return on Equity After Income Taxes 48	24.5	26.7	58.1	18.5	62.6	28.9	21.2	20.4	13.8
Profit Margin (Before Income Tax) 49	8.3	8.6	11.7	3.1	20.1	11.4	9.4	8.7	14.8
Profit Margin (After Income Tax) 50	6.8	8.4	11.6	3.1	17.6	10.4	8.0	8.1	9.7

Table I
Corporations with and without Net Income

GLASS AND GLASS PRODUCT

MONEY AMOUNTS AND SIZE OF ASSETS IN THOUSANDS OF DOLLARS

Item Description for Accounting Period 7/05 Through 6/06		Total	Zero Assets	Under 500	500 to 1,000	1,000 to 5,000	5,000 to 10,000	10,000 to 25,000	25,000 to 50,000	50,000 to 100,000	100,000 to 250,000	250,000 to 500,000	500,000 to 2,500,000	2,500,000 and over
Number of Enterprises	1	1776	•	800	523	322	•	32	9	9	6	5	7	0
Revenues ($ in Thousands)														
Net Sales	2	23813264	•	745964	517635	1668422	•	776836	530235	714191	1415784	2307237	14188734	0
Interest	3	183059	•	136	0	1757	•	711	1196	1054	3970	8044	165880	0
Rents	4	14472	•	0	0	0	•	104	506	165	1700	14	11920	0
Royalties	5	103593	•	0	0	0	•	0	309	117	14750	7451	80966	0
Other Portfolio Income	6	82551	•	0	0	563	•	455	857	4902	2150	19673	48326	0
Other Receipts	7	205923	•	150	2005	4237	•	2584	1224	15239	24322	32192	122519	0
Total Receipts	8	24402862	•	746250	519640	1674979	•	780690	534327	735668	1462676	2374611	14618345	0
Average Total Receipts	9	13740	•	933	994	5202	•	24397	59370	81741	243779	474922	2088335	•
Operating Costs/Operating Income (%)														
Cost of Operations	10	67.4	•	37.0	35.7	61.5	•	68.2	68.7	74.7	68.5	65.3	70.0	•
Salaries and Wages	11	7.1	•	22.7	27.6	7.6	•	6.7	8.0	6.3	8.9	7.2	5.3	•
Taxes Paid	12	2.4	•	3.4	1.8	2.1	•	2.4	2.4	3.0	2.9	2.7	2.2	•
Interest Paid	13	3.4	•	0.7	1.5	0.8	•	1.5	1.0	1.7	1.3	1.8	4.9	•
Depreciation	14	3.9	•	0.5	11.5	2.0	•	3.5	2.2	3.9	3.1	2.5	4.5	•
Amortization and Depletion	15	0.3	•	0.0	0.0	0.0	•	0.6	0.1	0.3	0.1	0.4	0.4	•
Pensions and Other Deferred Comp.	16	1.4	•	•	•	0.1	•	0.2	0.3	7.5	1.0	0.6	1.7	•
Employee Benefits	17	3.1	•	1.5	1.4	1.3	•	1.6	0.7	4.8	1.7	4.3	3.6	•
Advertising	18	0.6	•	1.8	1.1	0.5	•	1.0	0.2	0.4	2.3	0.7	0.3	•
Other Expenses	19	11.4	•	22.6	38.6	9.3	•	9.9	8.6	12.2	8.9	11.7	10.8	•
Officers' Compensation	20	1.4	•	9.5	3.3	8.5	•	1.1	1.4	0.9	0.6	0.5	0.2	•
Operating Margin	21	•	•	0.4	•	6.3	•	3.3	6.2	•	0.6	2.3	•	•
Operating Margin Before Officers' Comp.	22	•	•	9.9	•	14.8	•	4.4	7.6	•	1.2	2.8	•	•

Selected Average Balance Sheet ($ in Thousands)

Net Receivables 23	1247	56	71	696	2546	8228	11840	22412	95689	130231
Inventories 24	1657	30	319	436	3295	6877	11417	29703	50899	257876
Net Property, Plant and Equipment 25	3876	18	328	796	5976	8126	18885	45549	108606	730182
Total Assets 26	15518	198	903	2357	15118	38485	65661	141807	413382	3058260
Notes and Loans Payable 27	6440	209	1576	1084	8248	7974	26201	32720	138950	1220251
All Other Liabilities 28	4153	86	25	472	3595	10652	19130	44311	126192	821455
Net Worth 29	4925	-97	-697	802	3276	19859	20331	64776	148240	1016553

Selected Financial Ratios (Times to 1)

Current Ratio 30	1.1	2.1	0.6	2.6	1.0	1.7	1.2	1.9	1.8	0.8
Quick Ratio 31	0.4	1.7	0.1	1.6	0.5	1.0	0.7	1.0	1.0	0.2
Net Sales to Working Capital 32	56.8	9.9	•	5.9	•	6.6	13.5	6.2	5.8	•
Coverage Ratio 33	1.1	1.6	•	9.8	3.5	7.9	•	4.0	4.0	0.8
Total Asset Turnover 34	0.9	4.7	1.1	2.2	1.6	1.5	1.2	1.7	1.1	0.7
Inventory Turnover 35	5.5	11.6	1.1	7.3	5.0	5.9	5.2	5.4	5.9	5.5
Receivables Turnover 36	9.7	33.1	28.0	7.8	8.5	7.7	7.2	9.6	5.8	11.7
Total Liabilities to Net Worth 37	2.2	•	•	1.9	3.6	0.9	2.2	1.2	1.8	2.0
Current Assets to Working Capital 38	16.3	1.9	•	1.6	•	2.4	5.3	2.1	2.3	•
Current Liabilities to Working Capital 39	15.3	0.9	•	0.6	•	1.4	4.3	1.1	1.3	•
Working Capital to Net Sales 40	0.0	0.1	•	0.2	•	0.2	0.1	0.2	0.2	•
Inventory to Working Capital 41	7.1	0.3	•	0.5	0.8	0.8	1.9	0.7	0.7	•
Total Receipts to Cash Flow 42	13.2	6.0	148.4	7.3	9.0	7.3	•	9.4	7.4	18.1
Cost of Goods to Cash Flow 43	8.9	2.2	53.0	4.5	6.1	5.0	6.4	6.4	4.9	12.7
Cash Flow to Total Debt 44	0.1	0.5	0.0	0.5	0.2	0.4	0.3	0.3	0.2	0.1

Selected Financial Factors (in Percentages)

Debt Ratio 45	68.3	148.9	177.2	66.0	78.3	48.4	69.0	54.3	64.1	66.8
Return on Total Assets 46	3.1	5.2	•	16.4	8.5	12.1	•	8.6	7.8	2.6
Return on Equity Before Income Taxes 47	0.6	•	31.6	43.3	28.0	20.6	•	14.2	16.3	•
Return on Equity After Income Taxes 48	•	•	31.6	39.8	26.5	15.6	•	11.1	12.0	•
Profit Margin (Before Income Tax) 49	0.2	0.4	•	6.7	3.8	6.9	•	3.9	5.2	•
Profit Margin (After Income Tax) 50	•	0.4	•	6.2	3.6	5.3	•	3.0	3.8	•

Table II

Corporations with Net Income

GLASS AND GLASS PRODUCT

MONEY AMOUNTS AND SIZE OF ASSETS IN THOUSANDS OF DOLLARS

Item Description for Accounting Period 7/05 Through 6/06	Total	Zero Assets	Under 500	500 to 1000	251 to 500	501 to 1,000	1,001 to 5,000	5,001 to 10,000	10,001 to 25,000	25,001 to 50,000	50,001 to 100,000	100,001 to 250,000	250,001 and over
Number of Enterprises **1**	1043	•	462	•	307	58	22	•	•	•	5	4	0

Revenues ($ in Thousands)

	Total	Zero Assets	Under 500	500 to 1000	251 to 500	501 to 1,000	1,001 to 5,000	5,001 to 10,000	10,001 to 25,000	25,001 to 50,000	50,001 to 100,000	100,001 to 250,000	250,001 and over
Net Sales **2**	17085552	•	170709	•	1619845	856468	599069	•	•	•	2307237	9442436	0
Interest **3**	82998	•	136	•	944	134	54	•	•	•	8044	69684	0
Rents **4**	3945	•	0	•	0	63	104	•	•	•	14	1726	0
Royalties **5**	29113	•	0	•	0	0	0	•	•	•	7451	21354	0
Other Portfolio Income **6**	72396	•	0	•	201	65	205	•	•	•	19673	42657	0
Other Receipts **7**	93249	•	63	•	1048	469	1541	•	•	•	32192	30883	0
Total Receipts **8**	17367253	•	170908	•	1622038	857199	600973	•	•	•	2374611	9608740	•
Average Total Receipts **9**	16651	•	370	•	5284	14779	27317	•	•	•	474922	2402185	•

Operating Costs/Operating Income (%)

	Total	Zero Assets	Under 500	500 to 1000	251 to 500	501 to 1,000	1,001 to 5,000	5,001 to 10,000	10,001 to 25,000	25,001 to 50,000	50,001 to 100,000	100,001 to 250,000	250,001 and over
Cost of Operations **10**	66.0	•	33.8	•	60.9	77.2	65.0	•	•	•	65.3	67.2	•
Salaries and Wages **11**	6.7	•	24.5	•	7.7	6.9	7.2	•	•	•	7.2	6.2	•
Taxes Paid **12**	2.3	•	2.9	•	2.0	1.5	2.8	•	•	•	2.7	2.2	•
Interest Paid **13**	1.7	•	2.3	•	0.7	0.5	1.1	•	•	•	1.8	2.0	•
Depreciation **14**	3.7	•	0.8	•	1.8	1.1	2.5	•	•	•	2.5	4.5	•
Amortization and Depletion **15**	0.4	•	0.1	•	0.0	0.0	0.4	•	•	•	0.4	0.5	•
Pensions and Other Deferred Comp. **16**	1.5	•	•	•	0.1	0.1	0.2	•	•	•	0.6	2.4	•
Employee Benefits **17**	2.8	•	5.7	•	1.1	0.7	1.8	•	•	•	4.3	3.1	•
Advertising **18**	0.6	•	0.1	•	0.4	0.2	1.3	•	•	•	0.7	0.4	•
Other Expenses **19**	10.0	•	5.3	•	9.0	5.4	10.6	•	•	•	11.7	9.9	•
Officers' Compensation **20**	1.3	•	2.9	•	8.3	2.2	1.0	•	•	•	0.5	0.1	•
Operating Margin **21**	3.0	•	21.5	•	7.7	4.1	6.1	•	•	•	2.3	1.4	•
Operating Margin Before Officers' Comp. **22**	4.3	•	24.5	•	16.0	6.3	7.1	•	•	•	2.8	1.5	•

Selected Average Balance Sheet ($ in Thousands)

Net Receivables 23	1569	•	27	•	725	2017	2642	•	95689
Inventories 24	1849	•	26	•	444	1810	2478	•	52904
Net Property, Plant and Equipment 25	4303	•	6	•	780	1293	5355	•	108606
Total Assets 26	15491	•	63	•	2294	6779	13957	•	413382
Notes and Loans Payable 27	4061	•	66	•	1051	1593	5563	•	138950
All Other Liabilities 28	4487	•	30	•	424	1790	3708	•	126192
Net Worth 29	6943	•	-34	•	819	3396	4687	•	148240

(continued)

	last col
Net Receivables 23	122262
Inventories 24	283715
Net Property, Plant and Equipment 25	759948
Total Assets 26	2805920
Notes and Loans Payable 27	646298
All Other Liabilities 28	839233
Net Worth 29	1320389

Selected Financial Ratios (Times to 1)

Current Ratio 30	1.3	•	1.9	•	2.9	2.5	1.4	•	1.8	0.9
Quick Ratio 31	0.5	•	1.8	•	1.8	1.3	0.8	•	1.0	0.2
Net Sales to Working Capital 32	17.0	•	13.8	•	5.6	5.5	12.7	•	5.8	•
Coverage Ratio 33	3.8	•	10.3	•	12.0	8.8	7.0	•	4.0	2.6
Total Asset Turnover 34	1.1	•	5.9	•	2.3	2.2	2.0	•	1.1	0.8
Inventory Turnover 35	5.8	•	4.8	•	7.2	6.3	7.1	•	5.7	5.6
Receivables Turnover 36	10.3	•	6.6	•	7.8	14.6	11.0	•	9.6	14.2
Total Liabilities to Net Worth 37	1.2	•	•	•	1.8	1.0	2.0	•	1.8	1.1
Current Assets to Working Capital 38	4.8	•	2.1	•	1.5	1.7	3.3	•	2.3	•
Current Liabilities to Working Capital 39	3.8	•	1.1	•	0.5	0.7	2.3	•	1.3	•
Working Capital to Net Sales 40	0.1	•	0.1	•	0.2	0.2	0.1	•	0.2	•
Inventory to Working Capital 41	2.1	•	0.1	•	0.5	0.7	1.3	•	0.7	•
Total Receipts to Cash Flow 42	9.1	•	4.2	•	6.8	11.0	7.2	•	7.4	11.5
Cost of Goods to Cash Flow 43	6.0	•	1.4	•	4.2	8.5	4.7	•	4.9	7.7
Cash Flow to Total Debt 44	0.2	•	0.9	•	0.5	0.4	0.4	•	0.2	0.1

Selected Financial Factors (in Percentages)

Debt Ratio 45	55.2	•	153.6	•	64.3	49.9	66.4	•	64.1	52.9
Return on Total Assets 46	6.8	•	141.6	•	19.8	10.3	14.5	•	7.8	4.4
Return on Equity Before Income Taxes 47	11.2	•	•	•	50.7	18.3	37.0	•	16.3	5.8
Return on Equity After Income Taxes 48	9.5	•	•	•	47.2	16.9	35.5	•	12.0	4.8
Profit Margin (Before Income Tax) 49	4.7	•	21.7	•	7.9	4.2	6.4	•	5.2	3.2
Profit Margin (After Income Tax) 50	4.0	•	21.7	•	7.3	3.9	6.1	•	3.8	2.7

Table I

Corporations with and without Net Income

CEMENT, CONCRETE, LIME AND GYPSUM PRODUCT

MONEY AMOUNTS AND SIZE OF ASSETS IN THOUSANDS OF DOLLARS

Item Description for Accounting Period 7/05 Through 6/06	Total	Zero Assets	Under 500	500 to 1,000	1,000 to 5,000	5,000 to 10,000	10,000 to 25,000	25,000 to 50,000	50,000 to 100,000	100,000 to 250,000	250,000 to 500,000	500,000 to 2,500,000	2,500,000 and over
Number of Enterprises **1**	4852	259	1805	1031	1194	273	152	58	23	23	12	13	9
Revenues ($ in Thousands)													
Net Sales **2**	72883083	1784665	1257097	2079418	6401732	3395092	3851308	3424055	2439105	4007492	4226458	12075060	27941601
Interest **3**	915195	5338	718	1637	8249	5027	3962	1516	1475	11048	28320	61581	786323
Rents **4**	51781	721	0	2411	10731	1597	2611	269	1831	6486	3519	12184	9421
Royalties **5**	52218	284	0	0	0	156	15	0	30	1334	16999	13271	20129
Other Portfolio Income **6**	2314004	62412	0	53459	80554	29047	17127	6893	3977	17000	28397	152642	1862496
Other Receipts **7**	707122	13729	8199	14863	83350	7284	16945	23558	5382	45099	90213	209493	189007
Total Receipts **8**	76923403	1867149	1266014	2151788	6584616	3438203	3891968	3456291	2451800	4088459	4390178	12527959	30808977
Average Total Receipts **9**	15854	7209	701	2087	5515	12594	25605	59591	106600	177759	365848	963689	3423220
Operating Costs/Operating Income (%)													
Cost of Operations **10**	64.7	64.0	43.7	57.5	67.9	70.7	70.1	70.1	72.5	67.8	65.5	63.4	62.8
Salaries and Wages **11**	5.7	5.5	12.6	11.8	5.9	5.4	5.6	6.0	3.8	4.4	5.9	4.3	5.8
Taxes Paid **12**	2.3	1.7	5.3	2.2	2.9	2.1	2.3	1.9	1.6	2.5	2.6	2.1	2.2
Interest Paid **13**	3.3	1.8	1.1	0.9	1.3	1.2	0.8	0.8	0.6	1.5	2.0	2.4	6.0
Depreciation **14**	3.9	4.2	3.8	3.8	3.4	2.8	3.4	3.5	3.7	4.0	3.5	4.9	3.8
Amortization and Depletion **15**	0.7	0.4	0.1	0.1	0.1	0.0	0.3	0.1	0.2	0.7	1.6	1.6	0.6
Pensions and Other Deferred Comp. **16**	0.7	0.4	•	0.6	0.4	0.5	0.5	0.6	0.4	0.8	0.6	1.0	0.8
Employee Benefits **17**	2.0	2.2	0.3	0.9	1.5	1.4	1.5	1.4	1.9	2.2	1.6	1.9	2.5
Advertising **18**	0.3	0.2	0.4	0.5	0.4	0.3	0.4	0.3	0.4	0.4	0.8	0.1	0.3
Other Expenses **19**	10.3	15.2	22.7	19.7	13.9	8.2	8.2	7.5	4.7	5.8	9.4	8.9	10.8
Officers' Compensation **20**	1.0	0.3	2.8	2.5	3.3	3.1	1.9	1.3	1.8	0.7	0.5	0.4	0.2
Operating Margin **21**	5.1	4.2	7.1	•	•	4.3	5.1	6.5	8.5	9.2	6.1	9.0	4.2
Operating Margin Before Officers' Comp. **22**	6.1	4.5	9.9	1.9	2.3	7.4	7.0	7.7	10.3	9.9	6.6	9.4	4.4

Selected Average Balance Sheet ($ in Thousands)

Net Receivables 23	2681	0	28	182	722	1706	3420	9038	16216	25864	50026	174450	729027
Inventories 24	1023	0	10	85	291	877	1748	4202	6512	12562	20480	75943	235263
Net Property, Plant and Equipment 25	6428	0	128	245	969	3187	6209	14984	30621	59417	152423	539462	1772215
Total Assets 26	16940	0	225	738	2517	7106	14432	34563	67812	148668	347261	1227709	5197143
Notes and Loans Payable 27	4577	0	103	321	1088	3361	4310	8723	11731	38896	111626	424871	1143009
All Other Liabilities 28	6244	0	23	144	597	1611	3154	6723	15134	32501	68860	259119	2532968
Net Worth 29	6118	0	99	274	832	2135	6968	19117	40947	77272	166775	543718	1521166

Selected Financial Ratios (Times to 1)

Current Ratio 30	1.1	•	1.4	2.2	1.7	1.8	1.9	2.1	2.0	1.7	1.4		0.8
Quick Ratio 31	0.7	•	1.1	1.7	1.2	1.2	1.3	1.4	1.3	1.1	0.8		0.5
Net Sales to Working Capital 32	40.9	•	47.1	8.5	9.3	8.4	6.8	6.5	6.3	8.2	9.1		•
Coverage Ratio 33	4.3	5.9	8.0	4.1	2.4	5.7	8.2	10.2	16.0	8.6	6.0		3.5
Total Asset Turnover 34	0.9	•	3.1	2.7	2.1	1.8	1.7	1.6	1.2	1.0	0.8		0.6
Inventory Turnover 35	9.5	•	29.6	13.7	12.5	10.0	9.9	11.8	9.4	11.3	7.8		0.6
Receivables Turnover 36	6.2	•	49.6	22.2	6.9	8.1	6.4	6.5	7.1	8.4	5.6		8.3
Total Liabilities to Net Worth 37	1.8	•	1.3	1.7	2.0	1.1	0.8	0.7	0.9	1.1	1.3		5.1
Current Assets to Working Capital 38	15.2	•	3.6	1.9	2.4	2.3	2.1	1.9	2.0	2.5	3.5		2.4
Current Liabilities to Working Capital 39	14.2	•	2.6	0.9	1.4	1.3	1.1	0.9	1.0	1.5	2.5		•
Working Capital to Net Sales 40	0.0	•	0.0	0.1	0.1	0.1	0.1	0.2	0.2	0.1	0.1		•
Inventory to Working Capital 41	2.9	•	0.7	0.4	0.5	0.6	0.5	0.4	0.5	0.6	0.8		•
Total Receipts to Cash Flow 42	5.6	4.9	4.1	5.4	9.1	8.4	8.3	8.3	6.7	6.4	5.1		4.6
Cost of Goods to Cash Flow 43	3.6	3.1	1.8	3.1	6.2	5.9	5.8	6.0	4.6	4.2	3.2		2.9
Cash Flow to Total Debt 44	0.2	•	1.4	0.8	0.4	0.3	0.4	0.5	0.5	0.4	0.3		0.2

Selected Financial Factors (in Percentages)

Debt Ratio 45	63.9	•	55.9	62.9	66.9	70.0	51.7	44.7	39.6	48.0	52.0	55.7	70.7
Return on Total Assets 46	12.5	•	27.5	10.4	6.6	11.9	12.3	14.0	15.0	14.8	12.1	11.6	12.4
Return on Equity Before Income Taxes 47	26.6	•	54.6	21.2	11.9	32.6	22.3	22.9	23.3	25.2	21.1	22.0	30.2
Return on Equity After Income Taxes 48	20.2	•	53.9	20.4	10.7	27.1	20.4	20.2	20.8	19.8	14.4	14.8	22.9
Profit Margin (Before Income Tax) 49	10.8	8.8	7.8	2.9	1.8	5.6	6.1	9.0	11.2	10.0	11.2	12.9	14.8
Profit Margin (After Income Tax) 50	8.2	7.1	7.7	2.8	1.7	4.7	5.6	6.5	8.0	6.8	8.7		11.2

Table II
Corporations with Net Income

CEMENT, CONCRETE, LIME AND GYPSUM PRODUCT

MONEY AMOUNTS AND SIZE OF ASSETS IN THOUSANDS OF DOLLARS

Item Description for Accounting Period 7/05 Through 6/06	Total	Zero Assets	Under 500	500 to 1,000	1,000 to 5,000	5,000 to 10,000	10,000 to 25,000	25,000 to 50,000	50,000 to 100,000	100,000 to 250,000	250,000 to 500,000	500,000 to 2,500,000	2,500,000 and over
Number of Enterprises 1	3551	11	1370	•	666	219	128	54	•	•	12	•	•
Revenues ($ in Thousands)													
Net Sales 2	65807662	1532224	1208442	•	4089428	3247851	3418508	3321680	•	•	4226458	•	•
Interest 3	788650	5222	718	•	5465	4604	3942	1420	•	•	28320	•	•
Rents 4	46430	522	0	•	7845	1597	1596	269	•	•	3519	•	•
Royalties 5	50531	284	0	•	0	156	15	0	•	•	13271	•	•
Other Portfolio Income 6	2247666	50667	0	•	56026	29047	16097	6850	•	•	28397	•	•
Other Receipts 7	596666	13765	8192	•	17211	7210	14575	22015	•	•	90213	•	•
Total Receipts 8	69537605	1602684	1217352	•	4175975	3290465	3454733	3352234	•	•	4390178	•	•
Average Total Receipts 9	19583	145699	889	•	6270	15025	26990	62078	•	•	365848	•	•
Operating Costs/Operating Income (%)													
Cost of Operations 10	63.3	64.6	43.3	•	60.7	70.1	68.7	69.7	•	•	65.5	•	•
Salaries and Wages 11	5.8	4.9	12.7	•	6.4	5.3	6.0	5.9	•	•	5.9	•	•
Taxes Paid 12	2.2	1.8	5.5	•	2.6	2.1	2.3	1.9	•	•	2.6	•	•
Interest Paid 13	3.1	1.8	1.0	•	0.9	1.0	0.7	0.7	•	•	2.0	•	•
Depreciation 14	3.8	4.0	3.3	•	3.1	2.4	3.3	3.1	•	•	3.5	•	•
Amortization and Depletion 15	0.6	0.4	0.1	•	0.1	0.0	0.1	0.1	•	•	1.6	•	•
Pensions and Other Deferred Comp. 16	0.7	0.4	•	•	0.6	0.5	0.5	0.6	•	•	0.6	•	•
Employee Benefits 17	2.0	2.5	0.3	•	1.7	1.4	1.5	1.4	•	•	1.6	•	•
Advertising 18	0.3	0.1	0.4	•	0.4	0.3	0.3	0.3	•	•	0.8	•	•
Other Expenses 19	10.3	10.2	22.1	•	15.6	8.2	8.1	7.4	•	•	9.4	•	•
Officers' Compensation 20	1.0	0.2	3.0	•	3.3	3.2	2.0	1.3	•	•	0.5	•	•
Operating Margin 21	6.8	9.2	8.3	•	4.6	5.4	6.5	7.5	•	•	6.1	•	•
Operating Margin Before Officers' Comp. 22	7.7	9.4	11.2	•	7.9	8.6	8.5	8.8	•	•	6.6	•	•

Selected Average Balance Sheet ($ in Thousands)

Net Receivables 23	3400	0	29	•	727	1982	3606	9422	•	•	•	•	50026
Inventories 24	1208	0	12	•	230	899	1763	3836	•	•	•	•	23526
Net Property, Plant and Equipment 25	7799	0	160	•	965	2882	5909	13597	•	•	•	•	152423
Total Assets 26	21141	0	271	•	2569	7495	14308	33406	•	•	•	•	347261
Notes and Loans Payable 27	5373	0	102	•	875	2855	3749	8154	•	•	•	•	111626
All Other Liabilities 28	8074	0	26	•	581	1866	2847	6725	•	•	•	•	68860
Net Worth 29	7694	0	143	•	1113	2773	7712	18527	•	•	•	•	166775

Selected Financial Ratios (Times to 1)

Current Ratio 30	1.1	•	1.6	•	1.7	1.8	2.0	2.0	•	•	•	•	1.7
Quick Ratio 31	0.7	•	1.3	•	1.4	1.3	1.5	1.4	•	•	•	•	1.1
Net Sales to Working Capital 32	51.7	•	37.6	•	10.1	8.5	7.0	6.6	•	•	•	•	8.2
Coverage Ratio 33	5.0	8.5	9.7	•	8.1	7.9	11.0	12.3	•	•	•	•	6.0
Total Asset Turnover 34	0.9	•	3.3	•	2.4	2.0	1.9	1.8	•	•	•	•	1.0
Inventory Turnover 35	9.7	•	32.2	•	16.2	11.6	10.4	11.2	•	•	•	•	9.8
Receivables Turnover 36	6.4	•	40.2	•	7.5	8.4	6.9	7.9	•	•	•	•	14.1
Total Liabilities to Net Worth 37	1.7	•	0.9	•	1.3	1.7	0.9	0.8	•	•	•	•	1.1
Current Assets to Working Capital 38	19.8	•	2.6	•	2.3	2.3	2.0	2.0	•	•	•	•	2.5
Current Liabilities to Working Capital 39	18.8	•	1.6	•	1.3	1.3	1.0	1.0	•	•	•	•	1.5
Working Capital to Net Sales 40	0.0	•	0.0	•	0.1	0.1	0.1	0.2	•	•	•	•	0.1
Inventory to Working Capital 41	3.7	•	0.6	•	0.3	0.5	0.4	0.4	•	•	•	•	0.6
Total Receipts to Cash Flow 42	5.1	4.6	3.9	•	6.1	7.6	7.6	7.8	•	•	•	•	6.4
Cost of Goods to Cash Flow 43	3.2	3.0	1.7	•	3.7	5.4	5.2	5.4	•	•	•	•	4.2
Cash Flow to Total Debt 44	0.3	•	1.8	•	0.7	0.4	0.5	0.5	•	•	•	•	0.3

Selected Financial Factors (in Percentages)

Debt Ratio 45	63.6	•	47.1	•	56.7	63.0	46.1	44.5	•	•	•	•	52.0
Return on Total Assets 46	13.8	•	32.8	•	18.3	15.3	15.4	16.8	•	•	•	•	12.1
Return on Equity Before Income Taxes 47	30.3	•	55.7	•	37.1	36.1	25.9	27.9	•	•	•	•	21.1
Return on Equity After Income Taxes 48	23.4	•	55.0	•	35.5	30.9	23.9	24.9	•	•	•	•	14.4
Profit Margin (Before Income Tax) 49	12.6	13.8	9.0	•	6.7	6.8	7.5	8.4	•	•	•	•	10.0
Profit Margin (After Income Tax) 50	9.7	11.7	8.9	•	6.4	5.8	6.9	7.5	•	•	•	•	6.8

Table I

Corporations with and without Net Income

IRON, STEEL MILLS AND STEEL PRODUCT

MONEY AMOUNTS AND SIZE OF ASSETS IN THOUSANDS OF DOLLARS

Item Description for Accounting Period 7/05 Through 6/06	Total	Zero Assets	Under 500	500 to 1,000	1,000 to 5,000	5,000 to 10,000	10,000 to 25,000	25,000 to 50,000	50,000 to 100,000	100,000 to 250,000	250,000 to 500,000	500,000 to 2,500,000	2,500,000 and over
Number of Enterprises **1**	3688	11	2408	400	344	198	145	62	42	40	10	21	7
Revenues ($ in Thousands)													
Net Sales **2**	118685428	341288	2062981	1044647	1851056	2724597	4502299	4302863	4436069	10779897	6646139	35558317	44435275
Interest **3**	545102	20	10	697	423	743	2140	2131	8180	51380	24442	127166	327770
Rents **4**	46157	0	0	0	0	19	460	986	3066	6402	1312	11906	22006
Royalties **5**	342313	0	0	0	0	0	0	0	4871	3804	0	232177	101460
Other Portfolio Income **6**	940593	69869	33483	4675	3068	9782	5168	8544	164336	11970	2649	204970	422079
Other Receipts **7**	1637806	20264	5963	2948	7793	22512	9949	16123	43830	67986	67375	829320	543744
Total Receipts **8**	122197399	431441	2102437	1052967	1862340	2757653	4520016	4330647	4660352	10921439	6741917	36963856	45852334
Average Total Receipts **9**	33134	39222	873	2632	5414	13928	31173	69849	110961	273036	674192	1760184	6550333
Operating Costs/Operating Income (%)													
Cost of Operations **10**	77.1	86.9	63.1	72.5	74.3	76.6	78.8	79.9	79.3	80.2	81.7	79.2	74.2
Salaries and Wages **11**	2.9	2.6	16.1	4.0	6.6	4.6	3.8	3.4	3.7	2.8	2.5	3.2	1.7
Taxes Paid **12**	1.4	0.7	2.5	1.9	1.9	1.6	1.4	1.3	1.4	1.2	1.2	1.1	1.7
Interest Paid **13**	1.4	2.2	0.7	0.8	0.9	0.5	0.9	0.8	1.2	1.9	1.2	1.5	1.4
Depreciation **14**	2.2	0.7	1.4	1.7	1.8	1.8	1.5	1.7	2.2	1.7	1.3	1.6	3.0
Amortization and Depletion **15**	0.3	0.3	0.1	0.0	0.0	0.1	0.3	0.1	0.1	0.3	0.2	0.2	0.5
Pensions and Other Deferred Comp. **16**	1.4	0.2	•	0.9	0.1	0.8	0.4	0.5	0.4	0.9	0.7	0.7	2.8
Employee Benefits **17**	1.3	0.0	1.1	1.2	0.7	1.1	1.3	1.6	1.1	1.1	1.3	1.1	1.5
Advertising **18**	0.1	0.1	0.2	0.3	0.3	0.1	0.1	0.2	0.1	0.2	0.0	0.1	0.0
Other Expenses **19**	6.2	3.5	15.0	7.8	7.7	3.3	5.3	4.3	4.7	4.7	4.4	5.4	7.7
Officers' Compensation **20**	0.7	0.4	3.0	3.6	5.3	1.8	1.8	1.6	1.1	0.5	0.6	0.3	0.3
Operating Margin **21**	5.0	2.5	•	5.1	0.4	7.9	4.4	4.7	4.6	4.5	4.9	5.5	5.3
Operating Margin Before Officers' Comp. **22**	5.7	2.9	•	8.7	5.7	9.7	6.1	6.3	5.7	5.0	5.6	5.8	5.6

Selected Average Balance Sheet ($ in Thousands)

Net Receivables 23	3824	0	87	181	794	1570	4517	8707	14637	31424	75988	223154	675000
Inventories 24	4228	0	18	107	917	1341	3432	8480	17403	45839	106272	245859	730045
Net Property, Plant and Equipment 25	6541	0	36	228	339	1826	3491	8702	17905	40079	87213	357369	1670009
Total Assets 26	22413	0	183	749	2254	6228	15985	33759	68665	163131	351819	1211238	5305371
Notes and Loans Payable 27	5112	0	131	260	1542	929	4682	10176	16027	58508	85514	252880	1032836
All Other Liabilities 28	8219	0	52	81	683	1379	5275	9554	24486	55758	112920	456095	2045707
Net Worth 29	9083	0	-0	408	29	3920	6028	14028	28152	48864	153385	502263	2226828

Selected Financial Ratios (Times to 1)

Current Ratio 30	2.1	•	1.6	4.9	2.1	3.4	1.7	1.7	1.8	2.1	2.1	2.1	2.4
Quick Ratio 31	1.1	•	1.2	3.4	1.1	2.3	0.9	1.0	0.8	0.9	1.1	1.1	1.2
Net Sales to Working Capital 32	5.3	•	17.9	8.0	5.5	4.6	7.8	8.1	6.2	6.1	5.8	5.1	4.7
Coverage Ratio 33	6.7	14.2	•	8.3	2.1	20.7	6.4	7.4	8.8	4.1	6.4	7.2	7.0
Total Asset Turnover 34	1.4	•	4.7	3.5	2.4	2.2	1.9	2.1	1.5	1.7	1.9	1.4	1.2
Inventory Turnover 35	5.9	•	29.4	17.7	4.4	7.9	7.1	6.5	4.8	4.7	5.1	5.5	6.5
Receivables Turnover 36	8.8	•	13.1	11.9	6.7	8.1	8.1	8.4	7.2	9.0	8.3	8.2	9.5
Total Liabilities to Net Worth 37	1.5	•	0.8	78.0	1.7	0.6	1.7	1.4	1.4	1.3	1.4	1.4	1.4
Current Assets to Working Capital 38	1.9	•	2.8	1.3	1.9	1.4	2.5	2.4	2.4	2.3	1.9	1.9	1.4
Current Liabilities to Working Capital 39	0.9	•	1.8	0.3	0.9	0.4	1.5	1.4	1.4	1.3	0.9	0.9	0.7
Working Capital to Net Sales 40	0.2	•	0.1	0.2	0.2	0.2	0.1	0.1	0.2	0.2	0.2	0.2	0.7
Inventory to Working Capital 41	0.7	•	0.4	0.3	0.9	0.4	0.9	1.0	0.9	1.0	0.9	0.8	0.5
Total Receipts to Cash Flow 42	8.2	3.1	12.2	8.7	14.0	9.1	11.8	11.9	10.2	10.4	10.2	7.4	7.4
Cost of Goods to Cash Flow 43	6.3	2.7	7.7	6.3	10.4	6.9	9.3	9.5	8.1	8.4	8.3	5.8	5.5
Cash Flow to Total Debt 44	0.3	•	0.4	0.9	0.2	0.7	0.3	0.3	0.3	0.2	0.3	0.3	0.3

Selected Financial Factors (in Percentages)

Debt Ratio 45	59.5	•	100.1	45.5	98.7	37.1	62.3	58.4	59.0	56.4	58.5	58.0	
Return on Total Assets 46	13.4	•	4.6	23.4	4.6	21.1	10.9	12.7	16.8	14.2	15.5	11.8	
Return on Equity Before Income Taxes 47	28.2	•	3907.1	37.7	191.8	31.9	24.4	26.5	36.2	27.6	32.1	24.0	
Return on Equity After Income Taxes 48	21.0	•	4169.3	37.2	80.9	30.9	21.0	23.8	31.0	19.8	32.1	24.0	
Profit Margin (Before Income Tax) 49	8.0	28.9	•	5.9	1.0	9.1	5.4	9.7	23.6	19.8	22.7	17.7	
Profit Margin (After Income Tax) 50	5.9	27.1	•	5.8	0.4	8.8	4.8	4.1	8.3	6.4	9.5	8.4	6.2

MANUFACTURING
331115

Table II

Corporations with Net Income

IRON, STEEL MILLS AND STEEL PRODUCT

MONEY AMOUNTS AND SIZE OF ASSETS IN THOUSANDS OF DOLLARS

Item Description for Accounting Period 7/05 Through 6/06	Total	Zero Assets	Under 500	500 to 1,000	1,000 to 5,000	5,000 to 10,000	10,000 to 25,000	25,000 to 50,000	50,000 to 100,000	100,000 to 250,000	250,000 to 500,000	500,000 to 2,500,000	2,500,000 and over
Number of Enterprises **1**	1834	3	•	342	242	185	112	50	38	34	•	18	7
Revenues ($ in Thousands)													
Net Sales **2**	108506287	303274	•	906767	1460807	2569658	3872699	3832857	3905784	9547281	•	31256005	44435275
Interest **3**	503746	20	•	691	415	653	1232	2125	7824	45782	•	111891	327770
Rents **4**	40603	0	•	0	0	19	426	986	2828	6261	•	7295	22006
Royalties **5**	341874	0	•	0	0	0	0	0	4871	3366	•	232177	101460
Other Portfolio Income **6**	920148	69869	•	2431	3068	9207	4219	8377	161412	10451	•	195567	422079
Other Receipts **7**	1564824	19984	•	899	7793	22483	9470	10591	42388	55527	•	785832	543744
Total Receipts **8**	111877482	393147	•	910788	1472083	2602020	3888046	3854936	4125107	9668668	•	32588767	45852334
Average Total Receipts **9**	61002	131049	•	2663	6083	14065	34715	77099	108555	284373	•	1810487	6550333
Operating Costs/Operating Income (%)													
Cost of Operations **10**	76.5	87.6	•	71.8	71.2	76.2	77.9	80.2	78.2	80.4	•	77.4	74.2
Salaries and Wages **11**	2.8	1.4	•	4.4	7.4	4.6	3.7	3.0	3.5	2.7	•	3.5	1.7
Taxes Paid **12**	1.4	0.3	•	1.8	1.8	1.5	1.3	1.1	1.5	1.2	•	1.2	1.7
Interest Paid **13**	1.3	1.6	•	0.9	0.5	0.4	0.8	0.8	1.3	1.5	•	1.3	1.4
Depreciation **14**	2.2	0.4	•	1.7	2.1	1.8	1.4	1.4	2.2	1.6	•	1.7	3.0
Amortization and Depletion **15**	0.3	0.0	•	0.1	0.0	0.1	0.2	0.1	0.1	0.2	•	0.2	0.5
Pensions and Other Deferred Comp. **16**	1.5	0.2	•	1.0	0.1	0.4	0.4	0.5	0.5	1.0	•	0.7	2.8
Employee Benefits **17**	1.3	0.0	•	0.9	0.5	1.1	1.1	1.6	1.2	1.1	•	1.1	1.5
Advertising **18**	0.1	0.0	•	0.3	0.2	0.1	0.1	0.0	0.1	0.2	•	0.1	0.0
Other Expenses **19**	6.1	2.0	•	6.7	6.0	3.3	4.8	3.5	4.5	3.8	•	5.7	7.7
Officers' Compensation **20**	0.6	0.2	•	2.9	6.0	1.9	1.9	1.6	1.2	0.4	•	0.3	0.3
Operating Margin **21**	6.0	6.2	•	7.6	4.2	8.7	6.4	6.1	5.7	5.8	•	6.8	5.3
Operating Margin Before Officers' Comp. **22**	6.6	6.4	•	10.6	10.3	10.6	8.3	7.8	6.9	6.3	•	7.1	5.6

Selected Average Balance Sheet ($ in Thousands)

Item	C1		C2	C3	C4	C5	C6	C7	C8		C9	C10
Net Receivables 23	7084	•	150	958	1587	4866	8945	14671	32336	•	236210	675000
Inventories 24	7696	•	90	654	1352	3718	8786	16939	47284	•	264059	739745
Net Property, Plant and Equipment 25	12372	•	258	446	1788	3682	8090	17895	39856	•	380972	1670009
Total Assets 26	42016	•	748	2392	6236	16051	34471	69725	163664	•	1281765	5305371
Notes and Loans Payable 27	8701	•	294	430	845	3876	9403	15655	53210	•	243756	1032836
All Other Liabilities 28	15040	•	59	724	1351	5699	9277	24024	50698	•	448477	2045707
Net Worth 29	18276	•	395	1238	4040	6476	15791	30045	59756	•	589532	2226828

Selected Financial Ratios (Times to 1)

Item	C1		C2	C3	C4	C5	C6	C7	C8		C9	C10
Current Ratio 30	2.2	•	2.2	2.4	3.7	1.7	1.8	1.9	2.0	•	2.2	2.4
Quick Ratio 31	1.1	•	1.1	1.5	2.5	0.9	0.9	1.0	0.9	•	1.1	1.2
Net Sales to Working Capital 32	5.0	•	8.7	5.5	4.4	8.2	7.7	5.4	5.5	•	4.7	4.7
Coverage Ratio 33	8.2	22.8	9.8	10.8	24.8	9.9	9.9	10.0	5.9	•	9.3	7.0
Total Asset Turnover 34	1.4	•	3.5	2.5	2.2	2.2	2.2	1.5	1.7	•	1.4	1.2
Inventory Turnover 35	5.9	•	21.1	6.6	7.8	7.2	7.0	4.7	4.8	•	5.1	6.4
Receivables Turnover 36	8.8	•	35.4	6.3	8.1	8.4	9.8	7.2	9.3	•	8.0	18.8
Total Liabilities to Net Worth 37	1.3	•	0.9	0.9	0.5	1.5	1.2	1.3	1.7	•	1.2	1.4
Current Assets to Working Capital 38	1.8	•	1.2	1.7	1.4	2.4	2.3	2.1	2.0	•	1.8	1.7
Current Liabilities to Working Capital 39	0.8	•	0.2	0.7	0.4	1.4	1.3	1.1	1.0	•	0.8	0.7
Working Capital to Net Sales 40	0.2	•	0.1	0.2	0.2	0.1	0.1	0.2	0.2	•	0.2	0.2
Inventory to Working Capital 41	0.7	•	0.3	0.6	0.4	0.9	1.0	0.8	0.9	•	0.7	0.5
Total Receipts to Cash Flow 42	7.6	2.6	7.7	10.8	8.4	9.7	11.0	9.1	9.9	•	6.5	7.4
Cost of Goods to Cash Flow 43	5.8	2.3	5.5	7.7	6.4	7.6	8.8	7.1	7.9	•	5.0	5.5
Cash Flow to Total Debt 44	0.3	•	1.0	0.5	0.7	0.4	0.4	0.3	0.3	•	0.4	0.3

Selected Financial Factors (in Percentages)

Item	C1		C2	C3	C4	C5	C6	C7	C8		C9	C10
Debt Ratio 45	56.5	•	47.2	48.2	35.2	54.2	59.7	56.9	63.5	•	54.0	58.0
Return on Total Assets 46	14.5	•	31.9	13.8	23.1	16.6	16.3	18.6	14.7	•	16.8	11.8
Return on Equity Before Income Taxes 47	29.3	•	54.2	24.2	34.2	32.5	36.2	38.8	33.5	•	32.6	24.0
Return on Equity After Income Taxes 48	22.2	•	53.6	20.6	33.2	29.5	32.2	33.4	25.3	•	23.3	17.7
Profit Margin (Before Income Tax) 49	9.1	35.8	8.1	5.0	9.9	6.7	11.3	7.1		•	11.1	8.4
Profit Margin (After Income Tax) 50	6.8	33.8	8.0	4.2	9.7	6.1	9.8	5.4		•	7.9	6.2

Table I
Corporations with and without Net Income

NONFERROUS METAL PRODUCTION AND PROCESSING

MONEY AMOUNTS AND SIZE OF ASSETS IN THOUSANDS OF DOLLARS

Item Description for Accounting Period 7/05 Through 6/06	Total	Zero Assets	Under 500	500 to 1,000	1,000 to 5,000	5,000 to 10,000	10,000 to 25,000	25,000 to 50,000	50,000 to 100,000	100,000 to 250,000	250,000 to 500,000	500,000 to 2,500,000	2,500,000 and over
Number of Enterprises 1	1167	9	341	213	350	39	88	46	33	15	12	18	3
Revenues ($ in Thousands)													
Net Sales 2	75916597	293434	364413	538462	2975816	941448	3700862	3874682	3307763	4339783	5512756	24212918	25854261
Interest 3	1346545	3360	137	9	1750	342	1349	1577	6358	7385	67429	146562	1110288
Rents 4	48814	0	0	0	5496	0	1037	39	115	585	1693	18793	21056
Royalties 5	88954	0	0	0	0	2602	404	7217	26	0	678	22878	55149
Other Portfolio Income 6	1857884	39	10654	0	5108	533	2160	3744	3243	863	43425	557053	1231062
Other Receipts 7	1194696	18856	20	3481	-27220	5659	10893	5139	307832	14897	103287	278867	472983
Total Receipts 8	80453490	315689	375224	541952	2960950	950584	3716705	3892398	3625337	4363513	5729268	25237071	28744799
Average Total Receipts 9	68940	35077	1100	2544	8460	24374	42235	84617	109859	290901	477439	1402060	9581600
Operating Costs/Operating Income (%)													
Cost of Operations 10	82.9	79.2	55.9	55.9	82.9	83.8	83.3	84.4	81.4	83.5	84.2	82.8	83.5
Salaries and Wages 11	3.2	2.9	13.5	10.4	1.9	3.5	2.5	2.9	4.9	1.8	2.0	3.9	2.8
Taxes Paid 12	0.9	0.9	1.3	2.6	0.8	1.0	1.2	1.1	1.3	0.8	0.9	0.9	0.8
Interest Paid 13	2.9	2.9	•	1.1	0.7	0.7	1.0	0.9	1.1	1.0	2.4	1.9	5.5
Depreciation 14	1.9	2.9	1.1	1.0	0.6	1.3	1.4	1.8	2.0	1.9	2.2	1.7	2.4
Amortization and Depletion 15	0.8	0.2	•	0.2	0.0	0.1	0.1	0.1	0.2	0.1	0.3	0.3	1.9
Pensions and Other Deferred Comp. 16	0.7	0.5	•	0.2	0.5	0.3	0.3	0.2	0.4	0.2	0.9	1.2	0.4
Employee Benefits 17	1.0	0.7	0.6	1.0	0.6	1.0	1.4	1.0	1.8	1.0	1.5	0.9	0.7
Advertising 18	0.2	0.2	1.2	2.9	0.1	0.1	0.1	0.1	0.1	0.0	0.0	0.1	0.2
Other Expenses 19	6.4	7.6	24.2	7.2	4.0	4.9	3.8	4.8	12.5	3.2	5.1	6.0	7.6
Officers' Compensation 20	0.5	1.2	1.1	4.6	0.9	0.7	1.5	1.0	1.2	0.4	0.9	0.3	0.0
Operating Margin 21	•	0.9	1.3	12.7	6.9	2.5	3.6	1.5	•	6.0	•	•	•
Operating Margin Before Officers' Comp. 22	•	2.1	2.4	17.3	7.8	3.2	5.1	2.5	•	6.5	0.4	0.2	•

Selected Average Balance Sheet ($ in Thousands)

Net Receivables 23	34549	0	73	119	681	1505	5452	10736	15707	38050	75545	203375	11113835
Inventories 24	5936	0	5	72	741	750	3796	9300	11362	32607	72200	109935	716714
Net Property, Plant and Equipment 25	13602	0	48	23	416	2617	3552	9734	19054	38417	87116	243380	2737547
Total Assets 26	114618	0	161	612	2288	6769	15892	36941	66276	152965	363021	1032575	33995550
Notes and Loans Payable 27	32949	0	63	455	933	3765	5701	11089	19932	51467	123765	479928	8431504
All Other Liabilities 28	34925	0	35	166	704	1466	6147	12502	23942	53460	107634	493174	9176595
Net Worth 29	46743	0	63	-8	651	1538	4044	13350	22401	48037	131622	59473	16687451

Selected Financial Ratios (Times to 1)

Current Ratio 30	1.2	•	1.1	2.3	1.4	1.6	1.7	1.4	1.6	2.1	1.7	1.0	1.0
Quick Ratio 31	0.9	•	1.0	2.1	0.7	1.0	1.0	0.7	0.9	1.0	0.9	0.9	0.9
Net Sales to Working Capital 32	10.9	•	97.4	7.7	16.7	18.3	8.8	12.0	7.6	9.8	5.1	7.8	29.6
Coverage Ratio 33	2.8	3.9	•	13.4	9.8	5.6	5.2	3.1	3.3	7.4	2.5	3.2	2.3
Total Asset Turnover 34	0.6	•	6.6	4.1	3.7	3.6	2.6	2.3	1.5	1.9	1.3	1.3	0.3
Inventory Turnover 35	9.1	•	119.8	19.7	9.5	27.0	9.2	7.6	7.2	7.4	5.4	10.1	10.0
Receivables Turnover 36	2.2	•	13.2	29.2	13.1	22.7	8.7	8.8	7.3	7.3	6.7	9.2	0.9
Total Liabilities to Net Worth 37	1.5	•	1.6	•	2.5	3.4	2.9	1.8	2.0	2.2	1.8	16.4	1.1
Current Assets to Working Capital 38	7.5	•	9.1	1.8	3.5	2.6	2.4	3.4	2.8	2.6	1.9	2.4	42.6
Current Liabilities to Working Capital 39	6.5	•	8.1	0.8	2.5	1.6	1.4	2.4	1.8	1.6	0.9	1.4	41.6
Working Capital to Net Sales 40	0.1	•	0.0	0.1	0.1	0.1	0.1	0.1	0.1	0.2	0.1	0.1	0.0
Inventory to Working Capital 41	1.0	•	0.2	0.1	1.5	0.9	0.9	1.5	1.0	0.8	0.8	0.0	0.0
Total Receipts to Cash Flow 42	11.9	6.6	5.1	5.2	11.6	14.1	14.2	17.7	7.8	10.9	12.9	14.3	10.8
Cost of Goods to Cash Flow 43	9.9	5.2	2.9	2.9	9.6	11.8	11.9	14.9	9.1	9.1	10.9	11.9	9.0
Cash Flow to Total Debt 44	0.1	•	2.1	0.8	0.4	0.3	0.2	0.2	0.3	0.2	0.1	0.1	0.0

Selected Financial Factors (in Percentages)

Debt Ratio 45	59.2	•	60.9	101.3	71.6	77.3	74.6	63.9	66.2	68.6	63.7	94.2	51.8
Return on Total Assets 46	4.6	•	27.9	59.8	26.6	14.9	13.2	6.6	5.7	14.4	7.5	7.8	3.2
Return on Equity Before Income Taxes 47	7.2	•	71.4	•	84.0	54.0	41.7	12.3	11.9	39.6	12.3	92.3	3.7
Return on Equity After Income Taxes 48	5.3	•	67.1	•	82.1	46.9	37.2	8.7	6.8	27.9	7.2	77.8	2.4
Profit Margin (Before Income Tax) 49	5.2	8.5	4.2	13.4	6.4	3.4	4.0	2.0	2.7	6.6	3.5	4.1	2.4
Profit Margin (After Income Tax) 50	3.8	6.0	3.9	13.4	6.3	3.0	3.6	1.4	1.5	4.6	2.1	3.4	4.6

Table II

Corporations with Net Income

NONFERROUS METAL PRODUCTION AND PROCESSING

MONEY AMOUNTS AND SIZE OF ASSETS IN THOUSANDS OF DOLLARS

Item Description for Accounting Period 7/05 Through 6/06	Total	Zero Assets	Under 500	500 to 1,000	1,000 to 5,000	5,000 to 10,000	10,000 to 25,000	25,000 to 50,000	50,000 to 100,000	100,000 to 250,000	250,000 to 500,000	500,000 to 2,500,000	2,500,000 and over
Number of Enterprises 1	1053	9	•	183	321	36	73	31	•	•	8	•	3
Revenues ($ in Thousands)													
Net Sales 2	66649353	293434	•	474176	2917326	874528	2961058	2709610	•	•	3970613	•	25854261
Interest 3	1266023	3360	•	9	273	231	1269	1210	•	•	66140	•	1110288
Rents 4	45274	0	•	0	2334	0	1034	39	•	•	1693	•	21056
Royalties 5	88551	0	•	0	0	2602	1	7217	•	•	678	•	55149
Other Portfolio Income 6	1775421	39	•	0	5108	13	1135	3659	•	•	2012	•	1231062
Other Receipts 7	853073	18856	•	3481	-27229	490	11217	308	•	•	90054	•	472983
Total Receipts 8	70677695	315689	•	477666	2897812	877864	2975714	2722043	•	•	4131190	•	28744799
Average Total Receipts 9	67120	35077	•	2610	9027	24385	40763	87808	•	•	516399	•	9581600
Operating Costs/Operating Income (%)													
Cost of Operations 10	82.2	79.2	•	51.3	82.6	85.3	81.6	82.5	•	•	81.0	•	83.5
Salaries and Wages 11	3.1	2.9	•	11.8	1.9	2.6	2.6	2.9	•	•	2.5	•	2.8
Taxes Paid 12	0.9	0.9	•	2.9	0.8	0.9	1.2	1.1	•	•	0.8	•	0.8
Interest Paid 13	2.9	2.9	•	0.2	0.7	0.7	0.9	0.8	•	•	2.3	•	5.5
Depreciation 14	1.9	2.9	•	0.3	0.6	1.3	1.2	1.6	•	•	2.0	•	2.4
Amortization and Depletion 15	0.9	0.2	•	0.0	0.0	0.1	0.0	0.1	•	•	0.2	•	1.9
Pensions and Other Deferred Comp. 16	0.7	0.5	•	0.2	0.5	0.3	0.2	0.3	•	•	1.1	•	0.4
Employee Benefits 17	0.9	0.7	•	1.2	0.6	0.8	1.2	1.0	•	•	1.4	•	0.7
Advertising 18	0.2	0.2	•	3.3	0.1	0.1	0.1	0.1	•	•	0.0	•	0.2
Other Expenses 19	6.0	7.6	•	7.8	3.9	3.4	4.0	5.1	•	•	5.0	•	7.6
Officers' Compensation 20	0.4	1.2	•	5.2	0.9	0.7	1.6	1.1	•	•	0.3	•	0.0
Operating Margin 21	•	0.9	•	15.8	7.3	3.9	5.2	3.4	•	•	3.3	•	•
Operating Margin Before Officers' Comp. 22	0.3	2.1	•	21.0	8.2	4.6	6.8	4.6	•	•	3.6	•	•

Selected Average Balance Sheet ($ in Thousands)

Net Receivables 23	36969	0	•	98	713	1608	5712	10738	76320	•	11113835
Inventories 24	5411	0	•	5	612	703	3596	9014	71147	•	716714
Net Property, Plant and Equipment 25	13347	0	•	16	449	2541	3450	10050	88934	•	2737547
Total Assets 26	120777	0	•	612	2335	6443	15966	37707	383474	•	33995550
Notes and Loans Payable 27	33540	0	•	68	841	3098	4288	10418	134999	•	8431504
All Other Liabilities 28	36638	0	•	172	738	1553	4926	11274	99720	•	9176595
Net Worth 29	50598	0	•	372	755	1793	6752	16015	148754	•	16387451

Selected Financial Ratios (Times to 1)

Current Ratio 30	1.1	•	•	2.9	1.3	1.5	1.9	1.5	1.9	•	1.0
Quick Ratio 31	0.9	•	•	2.9	0.7	0.9	1.1	0.8	0.8	•	0.9
Net Sales to Working Capital 32	11.6	•	•	6.7	20.9	21.9	7.2	10.7	5.7	•	29.6
Coverage Ratio 33	3.2	3.9	•	96.0	10.0	6.8	7.2	6.2	4.2	•	2.3
Total Asset Turnover 34	0.5	•	•	4.2	3.9	3.8	2.5	2.3	1.3	•	0.3
Inventory Turnover 35	9.6	•	•	248.2	12.3	29.5	9.2	8.0	5.6	•	10.0
Receivables Turnover 36	2.0	•	•	52.8	15.8	24.9	8.6	9.3	7.3	•	0.9
Total Liabilities to Net Worth 37	1.4	•	•	0.6	2.1	2.6	1.4	1.4	1.6	•	1.1
Current Assets to Working Capital 38	8.5	•	•	1.5	4.1	3.0	2.1	3.0	2.1	•	42.6
Current Liabilities to Working Capital 39	7.5	•	•	0.5	3.1	2.0	1.1	2.0	1.1	•	41.6
Working Capital to Net Sales 40	0.1	•	•	0.1	0.0	0.0	0.1	0.1	0.2	•	0.0
Inventory to Working Capital 41	1.1	•	•	0.0	1.9	1.0	0.7	1.3	1.0	•	2.2
Total Receipts to Cash Flow 42	11.0	6.6	•	4.3	11.4	14.8	11.2	13.1	8.8	•	10.8
Cost of Goods to Cash Flow 43	9.0	5.2	•	2.2	9.4	12.6	9.1	10.8	7.1	•	9.0
Cash Flow to Total Debt 44	0.1	•	•	2.5	0.5	0.4	0.4	0.3	0.2	•	0.0

Selected Financial Factors (in Percentages)

Debt Ratio 45	58.1	•	•	39.3	67.6	72.2	57.7	57.5	61.2	•	51.8
Return on Total Assets 46	5.0	•	•	70.8	28.9	19.1	16.8	10.7	12.5	•	3.2
Return on Equity Before Income Taxes 47	8.2	•	•	115.4	80.3	58.6	34.2	21.2	24.6	•	3.7
Return on Equity After Income Taxes 48	6.2	•	•	115.4	78.5	52.1	31.0	16.9	17.9	•	2.4
Profit Margin (Before Income Tax) 49	6.5	8.5	•	16.5	6.7	4.3	5.7	3.9	7.4	•	7.0
Profit Margin (After Income Tax) 50	5.0	6.0	•	16.5	3.8	3.8	5.2	3.1	5.4	•	4.6

Table I

Corporations with and without Net Income

FOUNDRIES

MONEY AMOUNTS AND SIZE OF ASSETS IN THOUSANDS OF DOLLARS

Item Description for Accounting Period 7/05 Through 6/06		Total	Zero Assets	Under 500	500 to 1,000	1,000 to 5,000	5,000 to 10,000	10,000 to 25,000	25,000 to 50,000	50,000 to 100,000	100,000 to 250,000	250,000 to 500,000	500,000 to 2,500,000	2,500,000 and over
Number of Enterprises	1	1679	18	1205	57	231	71	45	23	10	4	8	6	0
Revenues ($ in Thousands)														
Net Sales	2	22291981	98990	830078	143516	1826173	806672	1115472	1353545	974419	720312	4491115	10031688	0
Interest	3	38610	1151	0	38	1383	401	714	172	676	238	11924	21913	0
Rents	4	2872	0	0	0	730	209	1315	14	112	79	210	203	0
Royalties	5	16331	0	0	0	0	886	0	7	0	0	13322	2117	0
Other Portfolio Income	6	70443	0	0	0	1486	291	365	11716	2057	0	27726	26805	0
Other Receipts	7	279270	2	86	1	55570	12115	1936	4734	18916	951	28508	156448	0
Total Receipts	8	22799507	100143	830164	143555	1885342	820574	1119802	1370188	996180	721580	4572805	10239174	0
Average Total Receipts	9	13579	5564	689	2519	8162	11557	24884	59573	99618	180395	571601	1706529	•
Operating Costs/Operating Income (%)														
Cost of Operations	10	75.7	71.9	60.9	69.6	68.4	80.0	73.9	75.1	74.8	72.7	80.3	76.5	•
Salaries and Wages	11	5.1	10.5	7.4	•	5.8	5.0	4.5	3.6	4.5	4.0	4.4	5.5	•
Taxes Paid	12	1.8	2.7	3.3	1.9	3.8	2.1	2.5	2.1	2.5	1.8	1.5	1.1	•
Interest Paid	13	1.6	1.2	0.8	0.3	0.7	2.1	1.0	1.1	1.0	2.4	1.4	2.1	•
Depreciation	14	2.5	1.3	1.6	5.3	2.2	3.2	2.5	2.7	2.9	2.9	2.6	2.4	•
Amortization and Depletion	15	0.2	0.9	1.0	•	0.0	0.2	0.1	0.0	0.3	0.1	0.4	0.2	•
Pensions and Other Deferred Comp.	16	0.6	0.1	0.0	•	0.3	0.6	0.5	0.5	0.5	1.5	0.6	0.7	•
Employee Benefits	17	2.4	1.8	1.1	•	4.9	1.8	1.4	3.0	1.0	1.8	2.2	2.4	•
Advertising	18	0.1	0.0	0.3	0.4	0.1	0.2	0.1	0.2	0.0	0.0	0.1	0.1	•
Other Expenses	19	5.3	16.8	11.3	8.8	9.9	3.2	5.5	5.1	5.2	6.0	3.1	4.9	•
Officers' Compensation	20	1.5	3.8	7.7	12.3	4.5	2.6	2.3	1.3	1.8	0.3	0.3	0.8	•
Operating Margin	21	3.1	•	4.6	1.3	•	•	5.7	5.3	5.5	6.3	3.2	3.2	•
Operating Margin Before Officers' Comp.	22	4.7	•	12.3	13.7	3.9	1.7	7.9	6.6	7.3	6.6	3.5	4.0	•

Selected Average Balance Sheet ($ in Thousands)

Net Receivables 23	1884	0	68	165	1225	1697	3438	8122	14333	24886	90394	226827
Inventories 24	1386	0	44	106	538	1312	2981	5104	13076	14822	49938	207126
Net Property, Plant and Equipment 25	2953	0	22	255	880	3216	4776	12610	25993	52300	125246	418295
Total Assets 26	10850	0	188	573	3403	7269	12600	32662	75179	140617	368221	1846266
Notes and Loans Payable 27	2929	0	175	184	656	2593	3867	8025	20606	65430	109434	443152
All Other Liabilities 28	2683	0	51	158	818	2206	3155	9725	19824	39272	99631	428495
Net Worth 29	5238	0	-38	231	1928	2469	5578	14911	34750	35916	159156	974619

Selected Financial Ratios (Times to 1)

Current Ratio 30	1.6	•	2.7	1.6	1.7	1.4	1.5	1.4	1.5	1.1	1.9	1.6
Quick Ratio 31	0.9	•	1.8	1.0	1.2	0.8	0.9	0.9	0.9	0.6	1.2	0.8
Net Sales to Working Capital 32	8.8	•	8.0	23.1	9.0	11.4	9.9	11.5	7.9	32.3	6.8	8.9
Coverage Ratio 33	4.1	•	7.0	5.8	4.8	1.4	6.8	7.0	8.7	3.7	4.5	3.6
Total Asset Turnover 34	1.2	•	3.7	4.4	2.3	1.6	2.0	1.8	1.3	1.3	1.5	0.9
Inventory Turnover 35	7.3	•	9.6	16.5	10.1	6.9	6.1	8.7	5.6	8.8	9.0	6.2
Receivables Turnover 36	7.8	•	11.8	30.5	8.0	7.2	5.0	8.0	5.4	14.5	7.4	8.1
Total Liabilities to Net Worth 37	1.1	•	•	1.5	0.8	1.9	1.3	1.2	1.2	2.9	1.3	0.9
Current Assets to Working Capital 38	2.7	•	1.6	2.6	2.4	3.6	2.8	3.2	3.1	8.4	2.2	2.8
Current Liabilities to Working Capital 39	1.7	•	0.6	1.6	1.4	2.6	1.8	2.2	2.1	7.4	1.2	1.8
Working Capital to Net Sales 40	0.1	•	0.1	0.0	0.1	0.1	0.1	0.1	0.1	0.0	0.1	0.1
Inventory to Working Capital 41	1.0	•	0.5	1.0	0.7	1.4	0.8	1.1	1.0	2.7	0.7	1.2
Total Receipts to Cash Flow 42	11.4	18.6	8.8	13.7	10.9	28.3	10.3	9.7	8.7	9.8	15.5	10.8
Cost of Goods to Cash Flow 43	8.7	13.3	5.3	9.6	7.5	22.7	7.6	7.3	6.5	7.1	12.4	8.3
Cash Flow to Total Debt 44	0.2	•	0.3	0.5	0.5	0.1	0.3	0.3	0.3	0.2	0.2	0.2

Selected Financial Factors (in Percentages)

Debt Ratio 45	51.7	•	120.3	59.8	43.3	66.0	55.7	54.3	53.8	74.5	56.8	47.2
Return on Total Assets 46	8.2	•	19.8	7.3	7.5	4.5	14.0	13.7	11.0	11.4	9.7	6.8
Return on Equity Before Income Taxes 47	12.8	•	•	15.0	10.5	3.5	26.9	25.6	21.0	32.5	17.6	9.3
Return on Equity After Income Taxes 48	10.4	•	•	12.7	10.3	1.7	22.4	25.4	17.5	23.1	13.5	7.3
Profit Margin (Before Income Tax) 49	5.0	•	4.6	1.4	2.6	0.8	6.1	6.5	7.5	6.5	5.0	5.4
Profit Margin (After Income Tax) 50	4.1	•	4.6	1.2	2.5	0.4	5.0	6.4	6.2	4.6	3.8	4.2

Table II
Corporations with Net Income

FOUNDRIES

MONEY AMOUNTS AND SIZE OF ASSETS IN THOUSANDS OF DOLLARS

Item Description for Accounting Period 7/05 Through 6/06	Total	Zero Assets	Under 500	500 to 1,000	1,000 to 5,000	5,000 to 10,000	10,000 to 25,000	25,000 to 50,000	50,000 to 100,000	100,000 to 250,000	250,000 to 500,000	500,000 to 2,500,000	2,500,000 and over
Number of Enterprises **1**	1087	0	717	57	197	31	42	19	•	•	•	•	0

Revenues ($ in Thousands)

	Total	Zero Assets	Under 500	500 to 1,000	1,000 to 5,000	5,000 to 10,000	10,000 to 25,000	25,000 to 50,000	50,000 to 100,000	100,000 to 250,000	250,000 to 500,000	500,000 to 2,500,000	2,500,000 and over
Net Sales **2**	19592927	0	607356	143516	1437278	472832	1043580	1088335	•	•	•	•	0
Interest **3**	17659	0	0	38	399	399	714	113	•	•	•	•	0
Rents **4**	2141	0	0	0	0	209	1315	14	•	•	•	•	0
Royalties **5**	16331	0	0	0	0	886	0	7	•	•	•	•	0
Other Portfolio Income **6**	69075	0	0	0	1089	162	365	11689	•	•	•	•	0
Other Receipts **7**	210670	0	0	1	54085	7229	1936	2727	•	•	•	•	0
Total Receipts **8**	19908803	0	607356	143555	1492851	481717	1047910	1102885	•	•	•	•	0
Average Total Receipts **9**	18315	•	847	2519	7578	15539	24950	58047	•	•	•	•	•

Operating Costs/Operating Income (%)

	Total	Zero Assets	Under 500	500 to 1,000	1,000 to 5,000	5,000 to 10,000	10,000 to 25,000	25,000 to 50,000	50,000 to 100,000	100,000 to 250,000	250,000 to 500,000	500,000 to 2,500,000	2,500,000 and over
Cost of Operations **10**	74.6	•	63.2	69.6	64.4	75.1	73.1	73.1	•	•	•	•	•
Salaries and Wages **11**	5.1	•	4.8	•	5.9	6.5	4.5	3.6	•	•	•	•	•
Taxes Paid **12**	1.7	•	2.7	1.9	3.3	2.4	2.6	2.2	•	•	•	•	•
Interest Paid **13**	1.4	•	0.7	0.3	0.7	0.7	1.0	1.0	•	•	•	•	•
Depreciation **14**	2.4	•	1.4	5.3	2.2	3.0	2.7	2.6	•	•	•	•	•
Amortization and Depletion **15**	0.2	•	0.9	•	•	0.0	0.1	0.0	•	•	•	•	•
Pensions and Other Deferred Comp. **16**	0.6	•	•	•	0.2	1.0	0.5	0.6	•	•	•	•	•
Employee Benefits **17**	2.3	•	0.7	•	5.2	1.5	1.4	3.3	•	•	•	•	•
Advertising **18**	0.1	•	0.3	0.4	0.1	0.2	0.1	0.2	•	•	•	•	•
Other Expenses **19**	5.0	•	10.0	8.8	13.3	4.5	5.6	4.4	•	•	•	•	•
Officers' Compensation **20**	1.5	•	7.7	12.3	5.3	2.8	2.2	1.5	•	•	•	•	•
Operating Margin **21**	5.0	•	7.4	1.3	•	2.3	6.1	7.4	•	•	•	•	•
Operating Margin Before Officers' Comp. **22**	6.5	•	15.2	13.7	4.8	5.1	8.3	8.9	•	•	•	•	•

Selected Average Balance Sheet ($ in Thousands)

Net Receivables 23	2530	82	165	1117	2488	3399	8263
Inventories 24	1725	29	106	496	1367	2802	4910
Net Property, Plant and Equipment 25	3857	13	255	872	2807	5093	11675
Total Assets 26	14845	170	573	3274	8266	12762	32246
Notes and Loans Payable 27	3440	78	184	565	1416	3768	7057
All Other Liabilities 28	3608	47	158	829	2564	3308	8577
Net Worth 29	7797	45	231	1880	4286	5685	16611

Selected Financial Ratios (Times to 1)

Current Ratio 30	1.8	3.3	1.6	1.5	1.9	1.5	1.7
Quick Ratio 31	1.0	2.6	1.0	1.0	1.1	0.9	1.1
Net Sales to Working Capital 32	7.6	7.8	23.1	11.3	6.8	10.3	8.3
Coverage Ratio 33	5.7	11.0	5.8	6.1	7.0	7.3	10.2
Total Asset Turnover 34	1.2	5.0	4.4	2.2	1.8	1.9	1.8
Inventory Turnover 35	7.8	18.4	16.5	9.5	8.4	6.5	8.5
Receivables Turnover 36	8.6	20.7	30.5	8.1	8.0	5.6	8.1
Total Liabilities to Net Worth 37	0.9	2.8	1.5	0.7	0.9	1.2	0.9
Current Assets to Working Capital 38	2.3	1.4	2.6	3.0	2.2	2.8	2.4
Current Liabilities to Working Capital 39	1.3	0.4	1.6	2.0	1.2	1.8	1.4
Working Capital to Net Sales 40	0.1	0.1	0.0	0.1	0.1	0.1	0.1
Inventory to Working Capital 41	0.9	0.3	1.0	0.9	0.7	0.8	0.8
Total Receipts to Cash Flow 42	9.8	7.7	13.7	7.7	12.4	9.8	8.1
Cost of Goods to Cash Flow 43	7.3	4.8	9.6	5.0	9.3	7.2	5.9
Cash Flow to Total Debt 44	0.3	0.9	0.5	0.7	0.3	0.4	0.5

Selected Financial Factors (in Percentages)

Debt Ratio 45	47.5	73.5	59.8	42.6	48.1	55.4	48.5
Return on Total Assets 46	9.8	40.7	7.3	9.0	9.0	14.7	17.2
Return on Equity Before Income Taxes 47	15.4	139.7	15.0	13.1	14.8	28.5	30.1
Return on Equity After Income Taxes 48	12.8	139.7	12.7	12.9	12.4	23.8	29.9
Profit Margin (Before Income Tax) 49	6.6	7.4	1.4	3.4	4.2	6.5	8.7
Profit Margin (After Income Tax) 50	5.6	7.4	1.2	3.3	3.5	5.4	8.7

Table I

Corporations with and without Net Income

FORGING AND STAMPING

MONEY AMOUNTS AND SIZE OF ASSETS IN THOUSANDS OF DOLLARS

Item Description for Accounting Period 7/05 Through 6/06	Total	Zero Assets	Under 500	500 to 1,000	1,000 to 5,000	5,000 to 10,000	10,000 to 25,000	25,000 to 50,000	50,000 to 100,000	100,000 to 250,000	250,000 to 500,000	500,000 to 2,500,000	2,500,000 and over
Number of Enterprises **1**	2786	.	1286	.	621	192	136	50	26	17	7	0	0
Revenues ($ in Thousands)													
Net Sales **2**	21958052	.	481243	.	3300391	2328721	3976264	2831975	2554559	3296629	2445617	0	0
Interest **3**	123478	.	394	.	1725	630	1033	889	2871	1395	114320	0	0
Rents **4**	2791	.	1	.	0	0	60	1807	42	636	246	0	0
Royalties **5**	3647	.	0	.	2	0	0	2	0	0	3644	0	0
Other Portfolio Income **6**	55874	.	33	.	1092	16	5618	8406	17530	2754	20219	0	0
Other Receipts **7**	203961	.	1	.	29642	24865	26273	16497	17927	28732	57777	0	0
Total Receipts **8**	22347803	.	481672	.	3332852	2354232	4009248	2859576	2592929	3330146	2641823	0	0
Average Total Receipts **9**	8021	.	375	.	5367	12262	29480	57192	99728	195891	377403	.	.
Operating Costs/Operating Income (%)													
Cost of Operations **10**	73.5	.	69.9	.	67.5	70.6	80.0	77.0	75.7	76.9	67.2	.	.
Salaries and Wages **11**	4.5	.	7.8	.	4.7	6.0	3.2	4.8	3.9	3.4	6.5	.	.
Taxes Paid **12**	2.0	.	3.1	.	2.6	2.3	1.8	1.9	1.9	1.4	1.6	.	.
Interest Paid **13**	1.6	.	0.1	.	0.7	1.0	0.8	1.0	1.0	1.3	6.7	.	.
Depreciation **14**	2.6	.	2.3	.	2.7	1.4	2.2	2.9	3.2	2.9	3.2	.	.
Amortization and Depletion **15**	0.4	.	.	.	0.0	0.0	0.1	0.1	0.2	0.3	2.2	.	.
Pensions and Other Deferred Comp. **16**	0.6	.	0.2	.	0.9	0.4	0.5	0.7	0.4	0.3	1.3	.	.
Employee Benefits **17**	1.8	.	1.3	.	2.2	1.1	1.6	1.7	2.0	2.0	2.3	.	.
Advertising **18**	0.2	.	0.0	.	0.2	0.3	0.1	0.1	0.1	0.2	0.2	.	.
Other Expenses **19**	7.6	.	11.0	.	9.7	9.1	4.4	6.6	4.6	5.5	11.4	.	.
Officers' Compensation **20**	2.5	.	3.2	.	5.2	3.4	1.9	1.1	1.4	1.7	0.8	.	.
Operating Margin **21**	2.8	.	1.1	.	3.7	4.4	3.5	2.0	5.5	4.0	.	.	.
Operating Margin Before Officers' Comp. **22**	5.3	.	4.3	.	8.8	7.8	5.4	3.1	6.9	5.7	.	.	.

Selected Average Balance Sheet ($ in Thousands)

Net Receivables 23	1158	32	634	1511	4017	8738	16103	34482	60759
Inventories 24	890	11	536	1484	3291	6468	13113	27226	55354
Net Property, Plant and Equipment 25	1421	27	663	1359	4111	11592	23827	44289	95258
Total Assets 26	5087	133	2356	6433	14011	34812	69532	142084	440345
Notes and Loans Payable 27	1583	28	822	1593	4291	10216	18501	40923	169433
All Other Liabilities 28	1316	8	683	1815	3522	8628	17295	41284	108246
Net Worth 29	2188	97	851	3025	6197	15968	33736	59877	162667

Selected Financial Ratios (Times to 1)

Current Ratio 30	1.6	12.4	1.7	1.8	1.9	1.6	1.7	1.7	1.1
Quick Ratio 31	0.9	10.9	0.9	0.9	1.2	0.9	1.0	1.0	0.6
Net Sales to Working Capital 32	7.6	4.3	9.0	7.2	6.8	7.8	6.2	7.1	33.4
Coverage Ratio 33	3.8	11.0	7.3	6.7	6.3	3.8	7.8	4.8	1.7
Total Asset Turnover 34	1.5	2.8	2.3	1.9	2.1	1.6	1.4	1.4	0.8
Inventory Turnover 35	6.5	24.8	6.7	5.8	7.1	6.7	5.7	5.5	4.2
Receivables Turnover 36	7.1	23.2	8.5	8.6	7.3	6.3	5.9	5.2	11.5
Total Liabilities to Net Worth 37	1.3	0.4	1.8	1.1	1.3	1.2	1.1	1.4	1.7
Current Assets to Working Capital 38	2.5	1.1	2.5	2.2	2.1	2.6	2.4	2.5	13.5
Current Liabilities to Working Capital 39	1.5	0.1	1.5	1.2	1.1	1.6	1.4	1.5	12.5
Working Capital to Net Sales 40	0.1	0.2	0.1	0.1	0.1	0.1	0.2	0.1	0.0
Inventory to Working Capital 41	0.9	0.1	1.0	1.0	0.7	0.9	0.8	0.8	5.3
Total Receipts to Cash Flow 42	10.1	15.4	9.8	8.4	13.3	12.7	10.4	10.8	7.2
Cost of Goods to Cash Flow 43	7.4	10.8	6.6	6.0	10.6	9.8	7.9	8.3	4.8
Cash Flow to Total Debt 44	0.3	0.7	0.4	0.4	0.3	0.2	0.2	0.2	0.2

Selected Financial Factors (in Percentages)

Debt Ratio 45	57.0	26.6	63.9	53.0	55.8	54.1	51.5	57.9	63.1
Return on Total Assets 46	9.5	3.8	12.2	12.2	10.6	6.5	11.2	8.6	9.1
Return on Equity Before Income Taxes 47	16.4	4.7	29.1	22.1	20.2	10.4	20.2	16.1	10.1
Return on Equity After Income Taxes 48	14.6	4.2	27.6	20.5	18.8	8.3	17.4	13.2	9.2
Profit Margin (Before Income Tax) 49	4.6	1.2	4.7	5.5	4.3	2.9	6.9	5.0	4.7
Profit Margin (After Income Tax) 50	4.0	1.1	4.4	5.1	4.0	2.3	6.0	4.1	4.3

Table II
Corporations with Net Income

FORGING AND STAMPING

MONEY AMOUNTS AND SIZE OF ASSETS IN THOUSANDS OF DOLLARS

Item Description for Accounting Period 7/05 Through 6/06	Total	Zero Assets	Under 500	500 to 1,000	1,000 to 5,000	5,000 to 10,000	10,000 to 25,000	25,000 to 50,000	50,000 to 100,000	100,000 to 250,000	250,000 to 500,000	500,000 to 2,500,000	2,500,000 and over
Number of Enterprises **1**	2162	•	896	392	502	172	121	32	•	13	•	0	0
Revenues ($ in Thousands)													
Net Sales **2**	18022961	•	386513	696951	2905095	1965896	3478022	1889268	•	2664393	•	0	0
Interest **3**	62273	•	393	207	1369	630	991	588	•	1279	•	0	0
Rents **4**	1033	•	0	0	0	0	14	95	•	636	•	0	0
Royalties **5**	3354	•	0	0	2	0	0	2	•	0	•	0	0
Other Portfolio Income **6**	48088	•	0	205	1028	16	4092	3867	•	2508	•	0	0
Other Receipts **7**	157390	•	1	2224	28707	24445	20641	8421	•	27938	•	0	0
Total Receipts **8**	18295099	•	386907	699587	2936201	1990987	3503760	1902241	•	2696754	•	0	0
Average Total Receipts **9**	8462	•	432	1785	5849	11576	28957	59445	•	207443	•	•	•
Operating Costs/Operating Income (%)													
Cost of Operations **10**	72.4	•	63.1	60.9	67.8	67.5	78.9	75.2	•	74.0	•	•	•
Salaries and Wages **11**	4.2	•	9.6	1.7	4.1	6.7	3.2	4.3	•	3.7	•	•	•
Taxes Paid **12**	1.9	•	3.8	2.1	2.3	2.2	1.8	1.8	•	1.2	•	•	•
Interest Paid **13**	1.2	•	0.1	0.7	0.7	1.0	0.6	0.8	•	1.3	•	•	•
Depreciation **14**	2.5	•	2.6	1.3	2.8	1.5	2.1	2.5	•	2.9	•	•	•
Amortization and Depletion **15**	0.3	•	•	0.1	0.0	0.1	0.1	0.2	•	0.3	•	•	•
Pensions and Other Deferred Comp. **16**	0.6	•	0.2	0.3	1.0	0.5	0.5	0.6	•	0.4	•	•	•
Employee Benefits **17**	1.8	•	1.6	1.5	1.9	1.3	1.6	1.7	•	2.3	•	•	•
Advertising **18**	0.2	•	0.0	0.3	0.2	0.4	0.1	0.1	•	0.3	•	•	•
Other Expenses **19**	7.0	•	11.9	19.8	9.7	9.3	4.1	5.1	•	5.8	•	•	•
Officers' Compensation **20**	2.6	•	4.0	10.5	4.5	3.8	2.0	1.1	•	1.9	•	•	•
Operating Margin **21**	5.2	•	3.1	1.0	4.9	5.8	5.0	6.6	•	6.0	•	•	•
Operating Margin Before Officers' Comp. **22**	7.8	•	7.1	11.5	9.4	9.6	7.0	7.6	•	7.8	•	•	•

Selected Average Balance Sheet ($ in Thousands)

Net Receivables 23	1200	46	220	675	1440	3977	8602	35772
Inventories 24	881	27	176	457	1387	3122	7234	22368
Net Property, Plant and Equipment 25	1387	34	86	702	1289	3816	10961	46807
Total Assets 26	5148	174	795	2479	6321	13805	35139	146614
Notes and Loans Payable 27	1406	31	237	882	1317	3728	8503	38605
All Other Liabilities 28	1297	11	159	717	1784	3333	7820	45808
Net Worth 29	2445	132	399	879	3220	6743	18816	62202

Selected Financial Ratios (Times to 1)

Current Ratio 30	1.7	11.6	3.5	1.6	1.9	2.1	1.8	1.5
Quick Ratio 31	1.0	10.0	2.4	0.9	0.9	1.3	1.1	0.9
Net Sales to Working Capital 32	7.2	3.8	3.7	10.4	6.9	6.1	6.8	8.6
Coverage Ratio 33	6.3	25.8	2.9	9.4	8.4	9.9	10.0	6.4
Total Asset Turnover 34	1.6	2.5	2.2	2.3	1.8	2.1	1.7	1.4
Inventory Turnover 35	6.9	10.2	6.1	8.6	5.6	7.3	6.1	6.8
Receivables Turnover 36	7.6	6.1	16.2	9.8	8.5	7.8	5.9	6.1
Total Liabilities to Net Worth 37	1.1	0.3	1.0	1.8	1.0	1.0	0.9	1.4
Current Assets to Working Capital 38	2.4	1.1	1.4	2.8	2.1	1.9	2.2	2.9
Current Liabilities to Working Capital 39	1.4	0.1	0.4	1.8	1.1	0.9	1.2	1.9
Working Capital to Net Sales 40	0.1	0.3	0.3	0.1	0.1	0.2	0.1	0.1
Inventory to Working Capital 41	0.8	0.1	0.4	1.0	1.0	0.7	0.8	0.8
Total Receipts to Cash Flow 42	8.7	10.5	6.2	8.8	7.1	11.4	9.1	8.6
Cost of Goods to Cash Flow 43	6.3	6.6	3.8	6.0	4.8	9.0	6.8	6.4
Cash Flow to Total Debt 44	0.4	1.0	0.7	0.4	0.5	0.4	0.4	0.3

Selected Financial Factors (in Percentages)

Debt Ratio 45	52.5	23.8	49.8	64.5	49.1	51.2	46.5	57.6
Return on Total Assets 46	12.8	8.2	4.6	15.7	14.6	13.4	13.5	11.9
Return on Equity Before Income Taxes 47	22.7	10.4	6.0	39.5	25.2	24.6	22.7	23.6
Return on Equity After Income Taxes 48	20.7	9.8	5.4	37.7	23.6	23.2	20.1	19.9
Profit Margin (Before Income Tax) 49	6.7	3.2	1.3	6.0	7.1	5.8	7.2	7.2
Profit Margin (After Income Tax) 50	6.1	3.0	1.2	5.7	6.6	5.4	6.4	6.0

Table I

Corporations with and without Net Income

CUTLERY, HARDWARE, SPRING AND WIRE MACHINE SHOPS, NUT, BOLT

MONEY AMOUNTS AND SIZE OF ASSETS IN THOUSANDS OF DOLLARS

Item Description for Accounting Period 7/05 Through 6/06	Total	Zero Assets	Under 500	500 to 1,000	1,000 to 5,000	5,000 to 10,000	10,000 to 25,000	25,000 to 50,000	50,000 to 100,000	100,000 to 250,000	250,000 to 500,000	500,000 to 2,500,000	2,500,000 and over
Number of Enterprises **1**	20988	2276	13059	1958	2891	377	273	81	28	25	11	8	0

Revenues ($ in Thousands)

	Total	Zero Assets	Under 500	500 to 1,000	1,000 to 5,000	5,000 to 10,000	10,000 to 25,000	25,000 to 50,000	50,000 to 100,000	100,000 to 250,000	250,000 to 500,000	500,000 to 2,500,000	2,500,000 and over
Net Sales **2**	62628406	2272023	5684461	2796667	11778479	4390983	6602179	4165719	2896798	4045377	5347545	12648175	0
Interest **3**	1443535	463	3197	2906	13743	6545	5093	13987	4419	15867	20580	1356735	0
Rents **4**	21156	25	0	6	7416	537	310	2273	1850	3557	1142	4039	0
Royalties **5**	147502	0	14	0	44	0	56	604	527	2622	7744	135891	0
Other Portfolio Income **6**	668812	23184	6105	23007	31074	9985	5591	25252	9797	12160	55356	467302	0
Other Receipts **7**	876243	21096	11129	17502	58180	22039	33713	17569	18699	168392	30829	477095	0
Total Receipts **8**	65785654	2316791	5704906	2840088	11888936	4430089	6646942	4225404	2932090	4247975	5463196	15089237	0
Average Total Receipts **9**	3134	1018	437	1451	4112	11751	24348	52165	104718	169919	496654	1886155	·

Operating Costs/Operating Income (%)

	Total	Zero Assets	Under 500	500 to 1,000	1,000 to 5,000	5,000 to 10,000	10,000 to 25,000	25,000 to 50,000	50,000 to 100,000	100,000 to 250,000	250,000 to 500,000	500,000 to 2,500,000	2,500,000 and over
Cost of Operations **10**	64.9	78.0	50.8	53.7	64.8	67.3	69.7	74.3	74.7	70.0	71.5	58.3	·
Salaries and Wages **11**	7.0	4.7	9.2	4.5	6.3	3.7	5.6	4.8	6.1	8.0	6.5	10.6	·
Taxes Paid **12**	2.3	1.2	3.2	3.5	3.0	2.9	2.3	1.9	1.9	1.7	1.4	1.6	·
Interest Paid **13**	3.9	0.9	0.9	1.5	1.5	0.8	1.0	1.5	1.2	2.4	3.4	13.0	·
Depreciation **14**	2.7	1.7	3.3	4.0	3.5	3.5	3.0	3.0	2.4	2.4	2.2	1.6	·
Amortization and Depletion **15**	0.7	0.6	0.0	0.1	0.1	0.0	0.2	0.4	0.5	0.6	1.0	2.3	·
Pensions and Other Deferred Comp. **16**	0.6	1.5	0.6	0.6	0.5	0.7	0.7	0.4	0.6	0.6	1.1	0.6	·
Employee Benefits **17**	2.0	1.7	1.4	1.8	1.7	1.6	1.9	1.9	1.6	2.1	2.1	2.9	·
Advertising **18**	0.7	0.1	0.5	0.4	0.2	0.4	0.7	0.5	0.6	1.0	0.8	1.7	·
Other Expenses **19**	11.3	8.5	19.6	14.6	9.5	6.9	7.7	7.0	5.7	9.1	9.9	16.6	·
Officers' Compensation **20**	3.1	1.1	6.2	9.9	5.7	5.0	2.5	1.3	1.5	1.0	0.6	0.5	·
Operating Margin **21**	0.7	0.0	4.4	5.5	3.1	7.3	4.7	3.0	3.2	1.1	·	·	·
Operating Margin Before Officers' Comp. **22**	3.8	1.1	10.6	15.4	8.8	12.3	7.2	4.3	4.7	2.2	0.1	·	·

Selected Average Balance Sheet ($ in Thousands)

	1	2	3	4	5	6	7	8	9	10	11	12	
Net Receivables 23	549	0	25	136	475	1398	3441	8145	13808	30679	73402	684254	•
Inventories 24	330	0	20	88	373	1242	3841	7073	18848	26992	56721	188000	•
Net Property, Plant and Equipment 25	430	0	34	224	617	2019	4398	9551	19458	32748	74694	180802	•
Total Assets 26	2810	0	121	694	2045	7020	15277	33838	70153	166050	377971	3787927	•
Notes and Loans Payable 27	1018	0	89	350	1054	1364	4284	10644	17668	53820	204093	1229827	•
All Other Liabilities 28	688	0	25	168	683	1018	2984	8359	16807	30573	120959	922070	•
Net Worth 29	1104	0	7	176	308	4638	8009	14835	35678	81657	52920	1636030	•

Selected Financial Ratios (Times to 1)

	1	2	3	4	5	6	7	8	9	10	11	12	
Current Ratio 30	2.1	•	2.2	2.3	1.2	2.8	2.2	1.9	2.1	2.0	1.8	2.9	•
Quick Ratio 31	1.3	•	1.5	0.8	1.8	1.1	1.0	1.0	1.1	0.8	2.1		•
Net Sales to Working Capital 32	4.9	•	10.5	6.7	19.0	4.4	4.9	5.8	5.3	4.4	6.4	2.2	•
Coverage Ratio 33	2.6	3.3	6.2	5.6	3.7	11.7	6.2	4.0	4.5	3.7	1.6	1.9	•
Total Asset Turnover 34	1.1	•	3.6	2.1	2.0	1.7	1.6	1.5	1.5	1.0	1.3	0.4	•
Inventory Turnover 35	5.9	•	11.0	8.7	7.1	6.3	4.4	5.4	4.1	4.2	6.1	4.9	•
Receivables Turnover 36	6.1	•	18.4	10.2	8.6	8.2	7.1	7.1	6.7	5.5	8.4	2.9	•
Total Liabilities to Net Worth 37	1.5	•	16.3	2.9	5.6	0.5	0.9	1.3	1.0	1.0	6.1	1.3	•
Current Assets to Working Capital 38	1.9	•	1.8	1.8	5.4	1.6	1.8	2.1	1.9	2.0	2.3	1.5	•
Current Liabilities to Working Capital 39	0.9	•	0.8	0.8	4.4	0.6	0.8	1.1	0.9	1.0	1.3	0.5	•
Working Capital to Net Sales 40	0.2	•	0.1	0.1	0.1	0.2	0.2	0.2	0.2	0.2	0.2	0.5	•
Inventory to Working Capital 41	0.6	•	0.5	0.5	1.7	0.5	0.8	0.9	0.9	0.7	0.9	0.3	•
Total Receipts to Cash Flow 42	6.9	12.7	5.5	5.6	9.6	8.1	8.9	10.2	11.2	7.2	11.1	4.0	•
Cost of Goods to Cash Flow 43	4.5	9.9	2.8	3.0	6.2	5.4	6.2	7.6	8.4	5.0	7.9	2.3	•
Cash Flow to Total Debt 44	0.3	•	0.7	0.5	0.2	0.6	0.4	0.3	0.3	0.3	0.1	0.2	•

Selected Financial Factors (in Percentages)

	1	2	3	4	5	6	7	8	9	10	11	12	
Debt Ratio 45	60.7	•	94.2	74.7	85.0	33.9	47.6	56.2	49.1	50.8	86.0	56.8	•
Return on Total Assets 46	10.6	•	20.6	17.7	11.0	14.8	10.1	9.2	8.3	8.4	6.9	10.2	•
Return on Equity Before Income Taxes 47	16.5	•	298.5	57.3	53.3	20.5	16.1	15.7	12.7	12.5	17.5	11.1	•
Return on Equity After Income Taxes 48	13.7	•	294.6	55.1	45.5	19.3	14.5	13.6	10.5	9.9	11.8	8.2	•
Profit Margin (Before Income Tax) 49	6.1	2.0	4.8	7.1	4.0	8.1	5.3	4.5	4.4	6.3	1.9	11.4	•
Profit Margin (After Income Tax) 50	5.1	2.0	4.7	6.8	3.4	7.7	4.8	3.9	3.6	5.0	1.3	8.5	•

Table II

Corporations with Net Income

CUTLERY, HARDWARE, SPRING AND WIRE MACHINE SHOPS, NUT, BOLT

MONEY AMOUNTS AND SIZE OF ASSETS IN THOUSANDS OF DOLLARS

Item Description for Accounting Period 7/05 Through 6/06	Total	Zero Assets	Under 500	500 to 1,000	1,000 to 5,000	5,000 to 10,000	10,000 to 25,000	25,000 to 50,000	50,000 to 100,000	100,000 to 250,000	250,000 to 500,000	500,000 to 2,500,000	2,500,000 and over
Number of Enterprises 1	13823	1869	7843	1186	2303	292	217	58	22	•	7	•	0
Revenues ($ in Thousands)													
Net Sales 2	50861724	1984963	3921358	2097563	9889281	3542139	5507723	3271881	2308338	•	3606401	•	0
Interest 3	1426809	248	2268	1009	12504	6140	4131	13457	3333	•	17685	•	0
Rents 4	18361	0	0	6	7132	0	294	1855	1845	•	829	•	0
Royalties 5	146194	0	0	0	44	0	42	604	95	•	7744	•	0
Other Portfolio Income 6	647132	11999	5997	22561	30457	9985	4937	19853	8963	•	55092	•	0
Other Receipts 7	825706	19977	5402	2283	51535	19345	28925	13787	13848	•	27953	•	0
Total Receipts 8	53925926	2017187	3935025	2123422	10000953	3577609	5546052	3321437	2336422	•	3715704	•	0
Average Total Receipts 9	3901	1079	502	1790	4343	12252	25558	57266	106201	•	530815	•	•
Operating Costs/Operating Income (%)													
Cost of Operations 10	63.9	80.2	52.6	51.1	62.8	66.0	68.2	74.5	73.9	•	68.9	•	•
Salaries and Wages 11	7.0	4.2	6.8	3.8	6.6	3.0	5.6	4.9	5.7	•	7.6	•	•
Taxes Paid 12	2.2	0.8	2.6	3.1	3.0	2.8	2.3	1.7	1.9	•	1.5	•	•
Interest Paid 13	4.3	0.5	0.5	1.5	1.4	0.5	1.0	1.0	1.2	•	3.6	•	•
Depreciation 14	2.4	1.5	2.6	4.3	3.2	3.0	2.8	2.2	2.1	•	2.1	•	•
Amortization and Depletion 15	0.7	0.5	0.0	0.0	0.1	0.0	0.1	0.3	0.6	•	1.1	•	•
Pensions and Other Deferred Comp. 16	0.6	0.4	0.8	0.7	0.6	0.7	0.6	0.4	0.5	•	1.5	•	•
Employee Benefits 17	2.0	0.9	1.2	1.7	1.7	1.5	1.9	1.7	1.7	•	2.2	•	•
Advertising 18	0.6	0.0	0.5	0.5	0.2	0.4	0.7	0.6	0.6	•	1.0	•	•
Other Expenses 19	10.8	7.4	16.9	11.5	8.9	6.2	7.6	6.7	5.4	•	8.6	•	•
Officers' Compensation 20	3.1	0.9	6.2	8.5	6.1	5.9	2.5	1.2	1.6	•	0.7	•	•
Operating Margin 21	2.3	2.6	9.2	13.5	5.5	10.0	6.8	4.9	4.7	•	1.3	•	•
Operating Margin Before Officers' Comp. 22	5.4	3.5	15.4	21.9	11.5	15.9	9.3	6.1	6.3	•	2.0	•	•

Selected Average Balance Sheet ($ in Thousands)

Net Receivables 23	707	0	24	127	455	1352	3687	9143	13171	84613
Inventories 24	373	0	20	112	370	1201	3805	7970	16699	72146
Net Property, Plant and Equipment 25	491	0	32	263	588	1820	4401	8428	19142	77907
Total Assets 26	3669	0	115	744	2045	7132	15306	34547	70005	393693
Notes and Loans Payable 27	1284	0	84	430	951	804	4262	8571	16312	222898
All Other Liabilities 28	830	0	22	157	399	941	3081	8897	17229	121367
Net Worth 29	1555	0	9	158	695	5386	7963	17079	36463	49427

Selected Financial Ratios (Times to 1)

Current Ratio 30	2.5	•	2.6	2.2	2.0	2.2	2.1	2.3	2.1
Quick Ratio 31	1.6	•	2.0	1.5	1.3	1.1	1.1	1.1	1.0
Net Sales to Working Capital 32	4.2	•	10.9	7.7	7.2	4.9	5.0	5.0	4.9
Coverage Ratio 33	3.1	9.0	21.0	11.0	5.7	8.8	7.5	5.9	2.2
Total Asset Turnover 34	1.0	•	4.3	2.4	2.1	1.7	1.6	1.5	1.3
Inventory Turnover 35	6.3	•	13.0	8.1	7.3	4.6	5.3	4.6	4.9
Receivables Turnover 36	6.2	•	20.9	10.9	9.7	6.7	7.3	8.1	12.2
Total Liabilities to Net Worth 37	1.4	•	11.9	3.7	1.9	0.9	1.0	0.9	0.3
Current Assets to Working Capital 38	1.7	•	1.6	1.8	2.0	1.8	1.9	1.8	1.9
Current Liabilities to Working Capital 39	0.7	•	0.6	0.8	1.0	0.8	0.9	0.8	0.9
Working Capital to Net Sales 40	0.2	•	0.1	0.1	0.1	0.2	0.2	0.2	0.2
Inventory to Working Capital 41	0.5	•	0.3	0.5	0.6	0.8	0.8	0.8	0.7
Total Receipts to Cash Flow 42	5.9	10.6	4.8	4.4	8.1	7.6	8.6	6.8	9.8
Cost of Goods to Cash Flow 43	3.8	8.5	2.5	2.2	5.1	5.2	6.4	4.5	7.2
Cash Flow to Total Debt 44	0.3	•	1.0	0.7	0.4	0.5	0.4	1.0	0.3

Selected Financial Factors (in Percentages)

Debt Ratio 45	57.6	•	92.2	78.7	66.0	48.0	50.6	47.9	87.4
Return on Total Assets 46	13.1	•	43.3	38.4	16.6	13.9	12.3	10.8	10.6
Return on Equity Before Income Taxes 47	20.9	•	530.5	164.4	40.1	23.8	21.5	17.2	46.6
Return on Equity After Income Taxes 48	17.9	•	525.6	160.4	35.8	21.7	19.0	14.5	37.0
Profit Margin (Before Income Tax) 49	8.8	4.3	9.5	14.7	6.5	7.5	6.5	6.0	4.5
Profit Margin (After Income Tax) 50	7.6	4.2	9.4	14.4	5.8	6.8	5.7	5.0	3.5

Table I

Corporations with and without Net Income

ARCHITECTURAL AND STRUCTURAL METALS

MONEY AMOUNTS AND SIZE OF ASSETS IN THOUSANDS OF DOLLARS

Item Description for Accounting Period 7/05 Through 6/06	Total	Zero Assets	Under 500	500 to 1,000	1,000 to 5,000	5,000 to 10,000	10,000 to 25,000	25,000 to 50,000	50,000 to 100,000	100,000 to 250,000	250,000 to 500,000	500,000 to 2,500,000	2,500,000 and over
Number of Enterprises 1	7482	318	3451	1358	1760	300	197	47	19	19	6	9	0
Revenues ($ in Thousands)													
Net Sales 2	43381836	372403	2433414	2928789	8845964	4168649	5998292	3048196	2074874	5531232	2392563	5587460	0
Interest 3	84936	2258	4036	2140	3647	3438	5310	1135	1293	10924	5738	45016	0
Rents 4	23793	13	803	0	908	924	2922	44	141	985	2656	14398	0
Royalties 5	11236	102	0	0	652	0	0	62	392	0	386	9642	0
Other Portfolio Income 6	195371	1663	2892	130	32153	3832	2047	6189	507	15012	10722	120226	0
Other Receipts 7	433047	6700	30954	14304	14626	34695	42021	-392	29564	13805	14592	232176	0
Total Receipts 8	44130219	383139	2472099	2945363	8897950	4211538	6050592	3055234	2106771	5571958	2426657	6008918	0
Average Total Receipts 9	5898	1205	716	2169	5056	14038	30714	65005	110883	293261	404443	667658	·
Operating Costs/Operating Income (%)													
Cost of Operations 10	71.2	69.2	67.2	70.9	67.5	77.0	75.4	73.8	73.7	73.6	72.8	65.0	·
Salaries and Wages 11	6.7	11.2	6.0	5.2	6.6	3.8	6.0	6.4	5.5	7.9	6.8	9.7	·
Taxes Paid 12	2.1	1.7	3.6	2.6	2.6	2.0	1.8	1.8	1.7	1.8	1.8	2.0	·
Interest Paid 13	1.6	3.0	0.5	0.9	0.9	1.1	0.8	0.7	1.2	1.1	3.3	5.0	·
Depreciation 14	2.0	1.2	1.8	1.1	1.8	2.3	1.5	1.2	1.5	1.7	2.3	4.2	·
Amortization and Depletion 15	0.2	1.3	0.0	0.0	0.0	0.1	0.1	0.1	0.1	0.2	0.8	0.7	·
Pensions and Other Deferred Comp. 16	0.5	0.4	0.5	0.2	0.3	0.4	0.4	0.4	0.5	0.5	0.5	1.2	·
Employee Benefits 17	1.9	2.2	0.9	2.3	3.0	1.2	1.6	1.8	1.2	1.6	1.3	2.1	·
Advertising 18	0.5	0.8	0.3	0.2	0.4	0.2	0.3	0.4	0.9	0.8	0.8	0.6	·
Other Expenses 19	8.3	15.1	12.1	9.9	10.5	6.1	5.7	5.9	8.7	6.0	8.3	10.0	·
Officers' Compensation 20	2.2	2.0	5.9	3.7	3.6	3.0	1.7	1.3	0.9	0.7	0.9	0.9	·
Operating Margin 21	2.7	·	1.3	3.0	3.0	2.9	4.7	6.3	4.0	4.2	0.4	·	·
Operating Margin Before Officers' Comp. 22	5.0	·	7.2	6.7	6.6	5.9	6.4	7.6	4.9	4.8	1.3	·	·

Selected Average Balance Sheet ($ in Thousands)

Net Receivables 23	•	1062	0	61	355	734	2262	5225	10292	20510	44121	113999	206885
Inventories 24	•	527	0	18	149	378	1360	2922	6040	15612	27632	49541	69317
Net Property, Plant and Equipment 25	•	823	0	28	83	503	1975	3536	8698	15503	41034	69225	208569
Total Assets 26	•	3830	0	172	826	2123	6937	15156	33888	71823	161944	329828	1125231
Notes and Loans Payable 27	•	1322	0	63	307	936	2515	4131	7704	17506	33164	127171	439231
All Other Liabilities 28	•	1183	0	57	247	511	2201	4617	9297	22012	49046	135477	361052
Net Worth 29	•	1326	0	53	272	676	2221	6408	16887	32305	79733	67179	324947

Selected Financial Ratios (Times to 1)

Current Ratio 30	•	1.8	2.0	2.1	1.9	1.4	1.7	2.0	1.8	1.9	1.5	1.8
Quick Ratio 31	•	1.2	1.7	1.5	1.3	0.9	1.1	1.2	1.1	1.1	1.0	1.2
Net Sales to Working Capital 32	•	6.6	11.0	6.2	7.5	10.5	7.5	5.9	5.9	6.5	6.1	4.0
Coverage Ratio 33	•	3.9	7.2	5.1	5.1	4.6	8.0	10.7	5.7	5.3	1.6	2.4
Total Asset Turnover 34	•	1.5	4.1	2.6	2.4	2.0	2.0	1.9	1.5	1.8	1.2	0.6
Inventory Turnover 35	•	7.8	26.8	10.2	9.0	7.9	7.9	7.9	5.2	7.8	5.9	5.8
Receivables Turnover 36	•	5.9	12.4	7.8	7.6	7.4	6.2	6.7	5.2	6.2	4.6	3.1
Total Liabilities to Net Worth 37	•	1.9	2.3	2.0	2.1	2.1	1.4	1.0	1.2	1.0	3.9	2.5
Current Assets to Working Capital 38	•	2.3	2.0	1.9	2.1	3.3	2.5	2.0	2.2	2.1	2.9	2.3
Current Liabilities to Working Capital 39	•	1.3	1.0	0.9	1.1	2.3	1.5	1.0	1.2	1.1	1.9	1.3
Working Capital to Net Sales 40	•	0.2	0.1	0.2	0.1	0.1	0.1	0.2	0.2	0.2	0.2	0.3
Inventory to Working Capital 41	•	0.6	0.3	0.5	0.6	1.0	0.7	0.6	0.8	0.5	0.9	0.5
Total Receipts to Cash Flow 42	•	9.6	12.5	8.9	10.0	9.3	11.8	10.1	9.2	7.8	10.8	12.1	7.6
Cost of Goods to Cash Flow 43	•	6.8	8.7	6.0	7.1	6.2	9.1	7.6	6.8	5.8	8.0	8.8	4.9
Cash Flow to Total Debt 44	•	0.2	0.7	0.4	0.4	0.3	0.3	0.4	0.4	0.3	0.1	0.1

Selected Financial Factors (in Percentages)

Debt Ratio 45	•	65.4	69.3	67.1	68.2	68.0	57.7	50.2	55.0	50.8	79.6	71.1
Return on Total Assets 46	•	9.3	13.7	11.6	10.5	10.0	12.8	13.8	10.3	10.9	6.1	6.5
Return on Equity Before Income Taxes 47	•	20.0	38.4	28.1	26.5	24.5	26.4	25.1	18.8	17.9	10.7	13.2
Return on Equity After Income Taxes 48	•	16.7	36.9	25.8	23.9	20.5	24.9	22.0	17.0	13.8	3.1	9.4
Profit Margin (Before Income Tax) 49	•	4.6	2.9	3.6	3.6	3.9	5.6	6.5	5.6	4.9	1.8	6.9
Profit Margin (After Income Tax) 50	•	3.8	2.8	3.2	3.2	3.3	5.3	5.7	5.0	3.8	0.5	4.9

Table II

Corporations with Net Income

ARCHITECTURAL AND STRUCTURAL METALS

MONEY AMOUNTS AND SIZE OF ASSETS IN THOUSANDS OF DOLLARS

Item Description for Accounting Period 7/05 Through 6/06	Total	Zero Assets	Under 500	500 to 1,000	1,000 to 5,000	5,000 to 10,000	10,000 to 25,000	25,000 to 50,000	50,000 to 100,000	100,000 to 250,000	250,000 to 500,000	500,000 to 2,500,000	2,500,000 and over
Number of Enterprises **1**	5499	16	2692	1054	1282	208	163	•	14	15	•	9	0
Revenues ($ in Thousands)													
Net Sales **2**	36608965	188101	2277775	2446657	6879140	3095761	5419727	•	1607621	4542379	•	5587460	0
Interest **3**	77830	1469	3238	678	3108	3429	4807	•	1094	9476	•	45016	0
Rents **4**	22968	13	803	0	309	924	2922	•	141	759	•	14398	0
Royalties **5**	11085	97	0	0	652	0	0	•	392	0	•	9642	0
Other Portfolio Income **6**	183513	815	2892	103	32015	3590	1874	•	505	14929	•	120226	0
Other Receipts **7**	388527	248	30386	1489	11148	21385	34980	•	29242	7515	•	232176	0
Total Receipts **8**	37292888	190743	2315094	2448927	6926372	3125089	5464310	•	1638995	4575058	•	6008918	0
Average Total Receipts **9**	6782	11921	860	2323	5403	15024	33523	•	117071	305004	•	667658	•
Operating Costs/Operating Income (%)													
Cost of Operations **10**	70.4	72.7	67.7	70.8	65.8	73.2	74.8	•	73.0	74.1	•	65.0	•
Salaries and Wages **11**	6.5	11.0	5.3	4.9	6.4	4.1	5.7	•	4.9	7.3	•	9.7	•
Taxes Paid **12**	2.1	1.4	3.5	2.5	2.2	2.5	1.8	•	1.7	1.8	•	2.0	•
Interest Paid **13**	1.5	1.8	0.4	0.9	0.9	0.8	0.7	•	1.0	1.1	•	5.0	•
Depreciation **14**	2.0	1.4	1.8	1.0	1.8	2.4	1.4	•	1.4	1.7	•	4.2	•
Amortization and Depletion **15**	0.2	0.4	0.0	0.0	0.0	0.0	0.1	•	0.1	0.1	•	0.7	•
Pensions and Other Deferred Comp. **16**	0.6	0.7	0.5	0.2	0.3	0.5	0.4	•	0.4	0.6	•	1.2	•
Employee Benefits **17**	1.6	2.8	1.0	1.7	2.0	1.3	1.6	•	0.8	1.5	•	2.1	•
Advertising **18**	0.5	0.6	0.3	0.2	0.4	0.2	0.3	•	1.1	0.8	•	0.6	•
Other Expenses **19**	7.7	•	9.8	9.2	9.9	5.8	5.6	•	8.4	5.0	•	10.0	•
Officers' Compensation **20**	2.3	2.6	6.0	3.6	3.8	3.4	1.7	•	0.9	0.6	•	0.9	•
Operating Margin **21**	4.7	5.4	3.8	4.9	6.6	5.7	6.0	•	6.3	5.6	•	•	•
Operating Margin Before Officers' Comp. **22**	7.0	8.0	9.8	8.5	10.4	9.1	7.7	•	7.2	6.2	•	•	•

Selected Average Balance Sheet ($ in Thousands)

	1	2	3	4	5	6	7	8	9	10
Net Receivables 23	1210	0	68	376	818	2635	5546	21392	43164	206885
Inventories 24	537	0	16	130	333	1266	2936	18059	25594	75681
Net Property, Plant and Equipment 25	959	0	31	81	560	2102	3320	17068	44401	208569
Total Assets 26	4449	0	190	847	2154	7241	15007	72524	168712	1125231
Notes and Loans Payable 27	1468	0	56	330	1008	2063	3610	16156	32536	439231
All Other Liabilities 28	1338	0	58	248	492	1996	4618	23206	50026	361052
Net Worth 29	1644	0	76	268	654	3182	6779	33161	86150	324947

Selected Financial Ratios (Times to 1)

	1	2	3	4	5	6	7	8	9	10
Current Ratio 30	1.9	•	2.3	2.3	2.1	1.7	1.8	1.8	1.9	1.8
Quick Ratio 31	1.3	•	1.9	1.7	1.5	1.2	1.2	1.0	1.1	1.2
Net Sales to Working Capital 32	6.3	•	10.7	6.1	6.8	7.9	7.4	6.2	6.7	4.0
Coverage Ratio 33	5.6	4.7	14.4	6.7	9.6	8.9	11.2	9.4	6.8	2.4
Total Asset Turnover 34	1.5	•	4.5	2.7	2.5	2.1	2.2	1.6	1.8	0.6
Inventory Turnover 35	8.7	•	34.8	12.7	10.6	8.6	8.5	4.6	8.8	5.3
Receivables Turnover 36	6.7	•	14.4	8.2	7.2	7.5	7.0	5.0	7.3	6.0
Total Liabilities to Net Worth 37	1.7	•	1.5	2.2	2.3	1.3	1.2	1.2	1.0	2.5
Current Assets to Working Capital 38	2.1	•	1.8	1.8	1.9	2.4	2.3	2.3	2.1	2.3
Current Liabilities to Working Capital 39	1.1	•	0.8	0.8	0.9	1.4	1.3	1.3	1.1	1.3
Working Capital to Net Sales 40	0.2	•	0.1	0.2	0.1	0.1	0.1	0.2	0.1	0.3
Inventory to Working Capital 41	0.5	•	0.3	0.4	0.5	0.6	0.7	0.8	0.5	0.5
Total Receipts to Cash Flow 42	8.3	25.2	8.1	9.6	7.1	9.2	9.0	6.5	10.4	7.6
Cost of Goods to Cash Flow 43	5.9	18.3	5.5	6.8	4.7	6.7	6.8	4.7	7.7	4.9
Cash Flow to Total Debt 44	0.3	•	0.9	0.4	0.5	0.4	0.4	0.5	0.4	0.1

Selected Financial Factors (in Percentages)

	1	2	3	4	5	6	7	8	9	10
Debt Ratio 45	63.1	•	59.8	68.3	69.6	56.1	54.8	54.3	48.9	71.1
Return on Total Assets 46	12.3	•	26.0	16.2	20.3	15.4	16.5	14.5	13.3	6.5
Return on Equity Before Income Taxes 47	27.2	•	60.2	43.4	59.9	31.2	33.3	28.3	22.3	13.2
Return on Equity After Income Taxes 48	23.6	•	58.9	40.3	56.2	27.2	31.7	26.0	17.5	9.4
Profit Margin (Before Income Tax) 49	6.7	6.8	5.4	5.0	7.3	6.7	6.8	8.2	6.3	6.9
Profit Margin (After Income Tax) 50	5.8	5.6	5.3	4.7	6.8	5.8	6.5	7.5	5.0	4.9

116

Table I

Corporations with and without Net Income

BOILER, TANK, AND SHIPPING CONTAINER

MONEY AMOUNTS AND SIZE OF ASSETS IN THOUSANDS OF DOLLARS

Item Description for Accounting Period 7/05 Through 6/06	Total	Zero Assets	Under 500	500 to 1,000	1,000 to 5,000	5,000 to 10,000	10,000 to 25,000	25,000 to 50,000	50,000 to 100,000	100,000 to 250,000	250,000 to 500,000	500,000 to 2,500,000	2,500,000 and over
Number of Enterprises **1**	420	•	0	•	221	20	59	13	11	5	4	0	4
Revenues ($ in Thousands)													
Net Sales **2**	20368166	•	0	•	989570	170177	1880816	959697	942208	1130872	3266355	0	10700196
Interest **3**	39122	•	0	•	199	475	5443	377	2415	8470	2248	0	19495
Rents **4**	21279		0		4386	0	0	216	0	129	4817	0	11730
Royalties **5**	130931		0		0	0	0	0	271	176	4919	0	125565
Other Portfolio Income **6**	706079		0		439	29	12219	429	1655	1221	65391	0	624694
Other Receipts **7**	228927		0		1233	208	37177	3656	2754	15025	18227	0	147744
Total Receipts **8**	21494504		0		995827	170889	1935655	964375	949303	1155893	3361957	0	11629424
Average Total Receipts **9**	51177		•	•	4506	8544	32808	74183	86300	231179	840489	•	2907356
Operating Costs/Operating Income (%)													
Cost of Operations **10**	79.7	•	•	•	71.4	62.6	74.7	77.2	71.5	79.5	79.3	•	82.7
Salaries and Wages **11**	4.1	•	•	•	7.9	2.5	5.4	3.9	6.7	4.6	2.4	•	3.5
Taxes Paid **12**	1.3	•	•	•	2.8	1.2	1.6	2.0	1.5	1.5	1.4	•	0.9
Interest Paid **13**	2.4	•	•	•	1.5	2.8	1.2	0.6	2.5	3.0	3.3	•	2.4
Depreciation **14**	1.8	•	•	•	0.9	2.1	1.2	1.0	2.0	2.1	3.3	•	1.6
Amortization and Depletion **15**	0.4	•	•	•	0.1	0.0	0.5	0.1	1.1	0.2	0.5	•	0.4
Pensions and Other Deferred Comp. **16**	1.7	•	•	•	0.5	0.1	0.3	0.1	0.4	0.4	0.9	•	2.8
Employee Benefits **17**	1.9	•	•	•	2.1	0.2	1.2	2.6	1.0	1.6	1.3	•	2.2
Advertising **18**	0.2	•	•	•	0.6	0.4	0.6	0.2	0.3	0.2	0.1	•	0.0
Other Expenses **19**	5.1	•	•	•	5.2	14.9	7.7	7.5	8.5	5.1	4.0	•	3.9
Officers' Compensation **20**	1.2	•	•	•	4.2	2.1	2.1	1.7	1.0	0.9	0.2	•	1.1
Operating Margin **21**	0.2	•	•	•	2.8	11.2	3.3	2.9	3.5	1.0	3.2	•	•
Operating Margin Before Officers' Comp. **22**	1.4	•	•	•	7.0	13.3	5.4	4.7	4.5	1.8	3.4	•	•

Selected Average Balance Sheet ($ in Thousands)

Net Receivables 23	9392	596	1466	4635	14487	19105	31899	70691	662788
Inventories 24	4346	591	922	3350	5465	8988	29739	91902	193591
Net Property, Plant and Equipment 25	9898	261	3447	2063	6936	16013	37443	192898	668434
Total Assets 26	53754	1733	6572	15408	37270	73483	165799	695064	4046052
Notes and Loans Payable 27	17278	860	3253	3420	5536	32684	60568	318310	1129078
All Other Liabilities 28	23680	260	1309	4850	11065	17681	78947	226859	1971978
Net Worth 29	12795	613	2010	7137	20668	23119	26284	149896	944996

Selected Financial Ratios (Times to 1)

Current Ratio 30	1.1	3.5	1.4	1.9	2.0	1.7	1.1	1.3	0.9
Quick Ratio 31	0.7	2.0	0.8	1.1	1.3	1.1	0.5	0.6	0.7
Net Sales to Working Capital 32	26.9	4.5	10.5	6.3	5.3	6.2	19.8	16.1	•
Coverage Ratio 33	3.6	3.3	5.2	6.0	6.2	2.9	2.1	2.9	4.2
Total Asset Turnover 34	0.9	2.6	1.3	2.1	2.0	1.2	1.4	1.2	0.7
Inventory Turnover 35	8.9	5.4	5.8	7.1	10.4	6.8	6.0	7.1	11.4
Receivables Turnover 36	5.4	6.7	7.0	7.0	6.4	4.8	6.3	12.0	4.3
Total Liabilities to Net Worth 37	3.2	1.8	2.3	1.2	0.8	2.2	5.3	3.6	3.3
Current Assets to Working Capital 38	10.0	1.4	3.6	2.1	2.0	2.5	7.8	4.1	•
Current Liabilities to Working Capital 39	9.0	0.4	2.6	1.1	1.0	1.5	6.8	3.1	•
Working Capital to Net Sales 40	0.0	0.2	0.1	0.2	0.2	0.2	0.1	0.1	•
Inventory to Working Capital 41	2.5	0.5	1.4	0.7	0.4	0.6	3.4	1.8	•
Total Receipts to Cash Flow 42	11.4	17.0	3.9	7.8	11.9	9.0	14.1	11.4	11.7
Cost of Goods to Cash Flow 43	9.1	12.1	2.5	5.9	9.2	6.5	11.2	9.1	9.7
Cash Flow to Total Debt 44	0.1	0.2	0.5	0.5	0.4	0.2	0.1	0.1	0.1

Selected Financial Factors (in Percentages)

Debt Ratio 45	76.2	64.7	69.4	53.7	44.5	68.5	84.1	78.4	76.6
Return on Total Assets 46	7.7	12.6	18.6	15.3	8.0	8.4	8.5	11.3	6.7
Return on Equity Before Income Taxes 47	23.1	24.8	49.0	27.6	12.1	17.5	27.5	34.4	22.0
Return on Equity After Income Taxes 48	18.8	20.4	48.8	25.9	10.1	11.2	18.1	26.9	18.3
Profit Margin (Before Income Tax) 49	6.1	3.4	11.6	6.2	3.4	4.7	3.2	6.3	7.8
Profit Margin (After Income Tax) 50	4.9	2.8	11.5	5.8	2.8	3.0	2.1	4.9	6.5

Table II

Corporations with Net Income

BOILER, TANK, AND SHIPPING CONTAINER

MONEY AMOUNTS AND SIZE OF ASSETS IN THOUSANDS OF DOLLARS

Item Description for Accounting Period 7/05 Through 6/06	Total	Zero Assets	Under 500	500 to 1,000	1,000 to 5,000	5,000 to 10,000	10,000 to 25,000	25,000 to 50,000	50,000 to 100,000	100,000 to 250,000	250,000 to 500,000	500,000 to 2,500,000	2,500,000 and over
Number of Enterprises 1	264	•	0	•	157	20	56	9	•	•	4	0	0

Revenues ($ in Thousands)

Item Description for Accounting Period 7/05 Through 6/06	Total	Zero Assets	Under 500	500 to 1,000	1,000 to 5,000	5,000 to 10,000	10,000 to 25,000	25,000 to 50,000	50,000 to 100,000	100,000 to 250,000	250,000 to 500,000	500,000 to 2,500,000	2,500,000 and over
Net Sales 2	16906388	•	0	•	802435	170177	1665403	746607	•	•	3266355	0	0
Interest 3	34136	•	0	•	83	475	2836	35	•	•	2248	0	0
Rents 4	20739	•	0	•	4386	0	0	216	•	•	4817	0	0
Royalties 5	33932	•	0	•	0	0	0	0	•	•	4919	0	0
Other Portfolio Income 6	490185	•	0	•	96	29	1946	355	•	•	65391	0	0
Other Receipts 7	179166	•	0	•	1171	208	4970	3075	•	•	18227	0	0
Total Receipts 8	17664546	•	0	•	808171	170889	1675155	750288	•	•	3361957	0	0
Average Total Receipts 9	66911	•	•	•	5148	8544	29913	83365	•	•	840489	•	•

Operating Costs/Operating Income (%)

Item Description for Accounting Period 7/05 Through 6/06	Total	Zero Assets	Under 500	500 to 1,000	1,000 to 5,000	5,000 to 10,000	10,000 to 25,000	25,000 to 50,000	50,000 to 100,000	100,000 to 250,000	250,000 to 500,000	500,000 to 2,500,000	2,500,000 and over
Cost of Operations 10	78.8	•	•	•	70.7	62.6	73.6	77.9	•	•	79.3	•	•
Salaries and Wages 11	4.2	•	•	•	7.4	2.5	5.7	3.8	•	•	2.4	•	•
Taxes Paid 12	1.2	•	•	•	2.8	1.2	1.7	1.7	•	•	1.4	•	•
Interest Paid 13	1.8	•	•	•	0.8	2.8	0.6	0.7	•	•	3.3	•	•
Depreciation 14	2.1	•	•	•	0.9	2.1	0.9	1.1	•	•	3.3	•	•
Amortization and Depletion 15	0.2	•	•	•	0.1	0.0	0.0	0.2	•	•	0.5	•	•
Pensions and Other Deferred Comp. 16	0.8	•	•	•	0.7	0.1	0.4	0.2	•	•	0.9	•	•
Employee Benefits 17	1.9	•	•	•	2.0	0.2	1.3	0.9	•	•	1.3	•	•
Advertising 18	0.2	•	•	•	0.7	0.4	0.7	0.2	•	•	0.1	•	•
Other Expenses 19	4.2	•	•	•	5.2	14.9	6.2	6.3	•	•	4.0	•	•
Officers' Compensation 20	1.1	•	•	•	3.3	2.1	2.1	1.7	•	•	0.2	•	•
Operating Margin 21	3.6	•	•	•	5.4	11.2	6.7	5.4	•	•	3.2	•	•
Operating Margin Before Officers' Comp. 22	4.7	•	•	•	8.7	13.3	8.8	7.0	•	•	3.4	•	•

Selected Average Balance Sheet ($ in Thousands)

Net Receivables 23	12288	674	1466	4697	13550	70691
Inventories 24	5526	703	1171	3115	6956	90412
Net Property, Plant and Equipment 25	13642	314	3447	1969	8291	192898
Total Assets 26	71787	1934	6572	15140	39152	695064
Notes and Loans Payable 27	12497	519	3253	2822	6003	318310
All Other Liabilities 28	37082	316	1309	4979	11390	226859
Net Worth 29	22208	1099	2010	7339	21759	149896

Selected Financial Ratios (Times to 1)

Current Ratio 30	1.0	3.1	1.4	1.9	2.2	1.3
Quick Ratio 31	0.7	1.6	0.8	1.0	1.3	0.6
Net Sales to Working Capital 32	69.1	4.9	10.5	5.9	5.2	16.1
Coverage Ratio 33	5.7	9.2	5.2	12.8	9.1	2.9
Total Asset Turnover 34	0.9	2.6	1.3	2.0	2.1	1.2
Inventory Turnover 35	9.1	5.1	4.6	7.0	9.3	7.2
Receivables Turnover 36	5.7	6.8	11.6	8.0	7.5	23.1
Total Liabilities to Net Worth 37	2.2	0.8	2.3	1.1	0.8	3.6
Current Assets to Working Capital 38	25.6	1.5	3.6	2.1	1.8	4.1
Current Liabilities to Working Capital 39	24.6	0.5	2.6	1.1	0.8	3.1
Working Capital to Net Sales 40	0.0	0.2	0.1	0.2	0.2	0.1
Inventory to Working Capital 41	6.3	0.6	1.4	0.7	0.5	1.8
Total Receipts to Cash Flow 42	9.2	11.9	3.9	8.1	9.4	11.4
Cost of Goods to Cash Flow 43	7.2	8.4	2.5	6.0	7.3	9.1
Cash Flow to Total Debt 44	0.1	0.5	0.5	0.5	0.5	0.1

Selected Financial Factors (in Percentages)

Debt Ratio 45	69.1	43.2	69.4	51.5	44.4	78.4
Return on Total Assets 46	9.0	18.2	18.6	15.5	13.9	11.3
Return on Equity Before Income Taxes 47	23.9	28.6	49.0	29.5	22.2	34.4
Return on Equity After Income Taxes 48	19.9	25.2	48.8	27.7	19.4	26.9
Profit Margin (Before Income Tax) 49	8.3	6.2	11.6	7.3	5.8	6.3
Profit Margin (After Income Tax) 50	6.9	5.4	11.5	6.8	5.1	4.9

Table I

Corporations with and without Net Income

COATING, ENGRAVING, HEAT TREATING, AND ALLIED ACTIVITIES

MONEY AMOUNTS AND SIZE OF ASSETS IN THOUSANDS OF DOLLARS

Item Description for Accounting Period 7/05 Through 6/06	Total	Zero Assets	Under 500	500 to 1,000	1,000 to 5,000	5,000 to 10,000	10,000 to 25,000	25,000 to 50,000	50,000 to 100,000	100,000 to 250,000	250,000 to 500,000	500,000 to 2,500,000	2,500,000 and over
Number of Enterprises **1**	4185	19	3058	158	772	88	48	22	7	9	0	3	0

Revenues ($ in Thousands)

	Total	Zero Assets	Under 500	500 to 1,000	1,000 to 5,000	5,000 to 10,000	10,000 to 25,000	25,000 to 50,000	50,000 to 100,000	100,000 to 250,000	250,000 to 500,000	500,000 to 2,500,000	2,500,000 and over
Net Sales **2**	13997404	50871	2097789	298060	2761618	815423	1059046	1005184	700062	1436147	0	3773204	0
Interest **3**	49027	2	1034	2	2403	1355	2888	965	363	7049	0	32968	0
Rents **4**	12822	2	5165	0	5084	418	858	643	12	22	0	617	0
Royalties **5**	51419	0	0	0	0	0	2685	0	165	12396	0	36172	0
Other Portfolio Income **6**	191920	1936	23732	529	2966	3687	8316	4675	2984	14895	0	128197	0
Other Receipts **7**	70746	7	193	1931	30556	5990	4942	13199	2384	1978	0	9570	0
Total Receipts **8**	14373338	52818	2127913	300522	2802627	826873	1078735	1024666	705970	1472487	0	3980728	0
Average Total Receipts **9**	3434	2780	696	1902	3630	9396	22474	46576	100853	163610	•	1326909	•

Operating Costs/Operating Income (%)

	Total	Zero Assets	Under 500	500 to 1,000	1,000 to 5,000	5,000 to 10,000	10,000 to 25,000	25,000 to 50,000	50,000 to 100,000	100,000 to 250,000	250,000 to 500,000	500,000 to 2,500,000	2,500,000 and over
Cost of Operations **10**	59.5	64.7	29.8	44.2	50.8	64.4	65.9	66.0	75.1	70.3	•	71.8	•
Salaries and Wages **11**	8.6	21.1	14.5	1.9	9.7	2.3	6.9	6.5	6.5	5.0	•	9.2	•
Taxes Paid **12**	3.0	1.8	4.7	1.7	4.7	3.9	3.1	2.8	2.1	2.1	•	1.2	•
Interest Paid **13**	2.1	2.8	0.6	0.9	0.9	1.1	2.1	1.5	2.0	4.4	•	3.3	•
Depreciation **14**	3.1	1.8	2.0	5.2	3.7	3.7	3.6	4.1	3.0	5.4	•	1.8	•
Amortization and Depletion **15**	0.5	0.0	0.1	•	0.0	0.0	0.4	0.3	0.3	1.6	•	1.0	•
Pensions and Other Deferred Comp. **16**	0.6	0.1	0.3	0.0	0.7	1.5	0.4	0.4	0.5	0.9	•	0.5	•
Employee Benefits **17**	2.1	1.2	2.2	3.7	2.9	1.6	2.3	2.0	1.3	2.0	•	1.4	•
Advertising **18**	0.5	0.1	0.3	0.1	0.3	0.1	0.2	0.2	0.2	0.3	•	1.2	•
Other Expenses **19**	14.1	36.6	24.9	42.3	17.7	11.4	7.8	8.1	6.0	7.7	•	10.9	•
Officers' Compensation **20**	5.5	1.7	17.7	4.4	8.5	3.1	2.9	2.3	0.9	0.7	•	1.3	•
Operating Margin **21**	0.4	•	3.1	•	•	6.9	4.5	5.7	1.9	•	•	•	•
Operating Margin Before Officers' Comp. **22**	5.9	•	20.8	•	8.4	10.0	7.4	8.1	2.8	0.3	•	•	•

Selected Average Balance Sheet ($ in Thousands)

Net Receivables 23	480	0	48	213	437	1150	3363	7292	13737	23219	•	254282
Inventories 24	233	0	14	26	119	398	1427	4015	11437	14516	•	180950
Net Property, Plant and Equipment 25	678	0	60	393	608	2911	6294	14845	24745	53709	•	193480
Total Assets 26	2536	0	177	746	1963	6316	15391	36015	73148	178759	•	1410964
Notes and Loans Payable 27	994	0	120	575	528	2278	6338	10606	28712	79952	•	545157
All Other Liabilities 28	620	0	33	69	552	949	3343	7167	19432	42500	•	379258
Net Worth 29	922	0	24	102	884	3088	5710	18242	25003	56308	•	486549

Selected Financial Ratios (Times to 1)

Current Ratio 30	2.0	•	2.6	2.0	2.1	1.7	1.9	1.9	1.4	1.9	•	2.0
Quick Ratio 31	1.2	•	2.1	1.6	1.3	1.2	1.5	1.1	0.8	1.0	•	1.2
Net Sales to Working Capital 32	6.4	•	11.5	10.8	6.7	10.2	7.0	6.4	10.0	5.7	•	4.5
Coverage Ratio 33	2.5	•	8.2	•	2.4	8.8	4.1	6.0	2.4	1.5	•	1.6
Total Asset Turnover 34	1.3	•	3.9	2.5	1.8	1.5	1.4	1.3	1.4	0.9	•	0.9
Inventory Turnover 35	8.5	•	14.2	32.0	15.3	15.0	10.2	7.5	6.6	7.7	•	5.0
Receivables Turnover 36	7.9	•	13.1	11.0	7.8	9.1	5.7	6.7	8.4	8.1	•	9.9
Total Liabilities to Net Worth 37	1.7	•	6.4	6.3	1.2	1.0	1.7	1.0	1.9	2.2	•	1.9
Current Assets to Working Capital 38	2.0	•	1.6	2.0	1.9	2.5	2.1	2.1	3.3	2.1	•	2.0
Current Liabilities to Working Capital 39	1.0	•	0.6	1.0	0.9	1.5	1.1	1.1	2.3	1.1	•	1.0
Working Capital to Net Sales 40	0.2	•	0.1	0.1	0.1	0.1	0.1	0.2	0.1	0.2	•	0.2
Inventory to Working Capital 41	0.5	•	0.3	0.1	0.2	0.4	0.3	0.6	1.2	0.7	•	0.6
Total Receipts to Cash Flow 42	7.5	•	4.7	3.5	7.3	5.9	8.5	7.6	13.2	12.9	•	9.7
Cost of Goods to Cash Flow 43	4.5	•	1.4	1.6	3.7	3.8	5.6	5.0	9.9	9.1	•	7.0
Cash Flow to Total Debt 44	0.3	•	1.0	0.8	0.5	0.5	0.3	0.3	0.2	0.1	•	0.1

Selected Financial Factors (in Percentages)

Debt Ratio 45	63.6	•	86.5	86.4	55.0	51.1	62.9	49.3	65.8	68.5	•	65.5
Return on Total Assets 46	6.8	•	19.8	•	4.1	13.8	12.0	11.6	6.6	5.8	•	4.6
Return on Equity Before Income Taxes 47	11.3	•	129.0	•	5.2	24.9	24.3	19.1	11.1	5.9	•	4.8
Return on Equity After Income Taxes 48	9.6	•	125.6	•	3.5	21.4	22.4	17.1	8.5	2.3	•	4.4
Profit Margin (Before Income Tax) 49	3.1	•	4.5	•	1.3	8.3	6.3	7.6	2.8	2.1	•	1.9
Profit Margin (After Income Tax) 50	2.6	•	4.4	•	0.9	7.1	5.8	6.8	2.1	0.8	•	1.7

Table II
Corporations with Net Income

COATING, ENGRAVING, HEAT TREATING, AND ALLIED ACTIVITIES

MONEY AMOUNTS AND SIZE OF ASSETS IN THOUSANDS OF DOLLARS

Item Description for Accounting Period 7/05 Through 6/06	Total	Zero Assets	Under 500	500 to 1,000	1,000 to 5,000	5,000 to 10,000	10,000 to 25,000	25,000 to 50,000	50,000 to 100,000	100,000 to 250,000	250,000 to 500,000	500,000 to 2,500,000	2,500,000 and over
Number of Enterprises 1	2840	·	2148	·	479	84	37	·	3	6	3	0	0
Revenues ($ in Thousands)													
Net Sales 2	11262004	·	1746100	·	2130445	772386	934550	·	352357	915427	3293683	0	0
Interest 3	40056	·	1011	·	2178	1319	2716	·	170	2096	29600	0	0
Rents 4	10289	·	5165	·	2565	418	858	·	0	22	617	0	0
Royalties 5	51419	·	0	·	0	0	2685	·	165	12290	36279	0	0
Other Portfolio Income 6	161588	·	927	·	2966	3687	8304	·	242	14885	123961	0	0
Other Receipts 7	42325	·	23	·	8753	5982	4197	·	782	1573	7559	0	0
Total Receipts 8	11567681	·	1753226	·	2146907	783792	953310	·	353716	946293	3491699	0	0
Average Total Receipts 9	4073	·	816	·	4482	9331	25765	·	117905	157716	1163900	·	·
Operating Costs/Operating Income (%)													
Cost of Operations 10	58.0	·	30.0	·	50.4	61.5	67.3	·	72.7	63.9	68.6	·	·
Salaries and Wages 11	8.4	·	11.6	·	10.0	2.4	6.2	·	4.9	5.9	9.7	·	·
Taxes Paid 12	2.8	·	4.2	·	4.0	3.9	3.1	·	1.5	3.1	1.2	·	·
Interest Paid 13	1.9	·	0.4	·	0.4	1.1	0.9	·	0.9	3.8	4.0	·	·
Depreciation 14	2.8	·	1.9	·	3.4	3.7	3.3	·	1.3	5.9	1.7	·	·
Amortization and Depletion 15	0.6	·	0.0	·	0.0	0.0	0.1	·	0.3	1.4	1.4	·	·
Pensions and Other Deferred Comp. 16	0.7	·	0.4	·	0.9	1.6	0.4	·	0.7	1.2	0.6	·	·
Employee Benefits 17	1.9	·	2.0	·	2.2	1.7	2.3	·	0.7	2.9	1.3	·	·
Advertising 18	0.6	·	0.2	·	0.4	0.1	0.2	·	0.2	0.1	1.5	·	·
Other Expenses 19	12.8	·	21.5	·	15.0	12.0	6.3	·	5.1	7.4	12.2	·	·
Officers' Compensation 20	5.8	·	18.4	·	8.7	3.3	3.2	·	1.2	1.1	1.5	·	·
Operating Margin 21	3.6	·	9.4	·	4.6	8.6	6.8	·	10.6	3.2	·	·	·
Operating Margin Before Officers' Comp. 22	9.4	·	27.8	·	13.3	11.9	10.0	·	11.8	4.4	·	·	·

Selected Average Balance Sheet ($ in Thousands)

Net Receivables 23	524	60	545	1151	3859	16427	22900	167752
Inventories 24	267	15	75	338	1503	23696	19944	154636
Net Property, Plant and Equipment 25	764	63	725	2917	6096	25439	64055	140412
Total Assets 26	3033	208	2155	6369	15950	71552	157395	1352572
Notes and Loans Payable 27	1051	52	295	2251	3872	19394	66814	570214
All Other Liabilities 28	653	32	306	732	3005	18727	32153	354002
Net Worth 29	1330	123	1554	3386	9073	33431	58429	428355

Selected Financial Ratios (Times to 1)

Current Ratio 30	2.3	3.6	2.9	1.7	2.1	2.9	1.9	2.3
Quick Ratio 31	1.5	3.0	2.4	1.2	1.7	1.6	1.1	1.2
Net Sales to Working Capital 32	6.0	9.5	6.8	9.5	6.4	4.4	5.3	4.5
Coverage Ratio 33	4.3	24.8	14.9	10.0	10.6	12.7	2.7	1.6
Total Asset Turnover 34	1.3	3.9	2.1	1.4	1.6	1.6	1.0	0.8
Inventory Turnover 35	8.6	15.9	29.7	16.7	11.3	3.6	4.9	4.9
Receivables Turnover 36	8.9	16.0	8.6	16.0	6.2	4.3	13.3	13.1
Total Liabilities to Net Worth 37	1.3	0.7	0.4	0.9	0.8	1.1	1.7	2.2
Current Assets to Working Capital 38	1.8	1.4	1.5	2.3	1.9	1.5	2.1	1.8
Current Liabilities to Working Capital 39	0.8	0.4	0.5	1.3	0.9	0.5	1.1	0.8
Working Capital to Net Sales 40	0.2	0.1	0.1	0.1	0.2	0.2	0.2	0.2
Inventory to Working Capital 41	0.5	0.2	0.2	0.3	0.3	0.5	0.7	0.6
Total Receipts to Cash Flow 42	6.5	4.0	6.5	5.2	7.6	6.8	8.8	8.4
Cost of Goods to Cash Flow 43	3.8	1.2	3.3	3.2	5.1	5.0	5.6	5.7
Cash Flow to Total Debt 44	0.4	2.4	1.1	0.6	0.5	0.5	0.2	0.1

Selected Financial Factors (in Percentages)

Debt Ratio 45	56.2	40.7	27.9	46.8	43.1	53.3	62.9	68.3
Return on Total Assets 46	10.8	40.1	11.8	16.2	15.3	19.6	10.1	5.2
Return on Equity Before Income Taxes 47	18.8	64.8	15.2	27.5	24.3	38.6	17.2	6.2
Return on Equity After Income Taxes 48	17.1	63.9	13.6	24.1	22.8	33.9	11.9	5.7
Profit Margin (Before Income Tax) 49	6.3	9.8	5.3	10.1	8.7	11.0	6.6	2.4
Profit Margin (After Income Tax) 50	5.7	9.7	4.8	8.9	8.2	9.7	4.6	2.2

Table I

Corporations with and without Net Income

OTHER FABRICATED METAL PRODUCT

MONEY AMOUNTS AND SIZE OF ASSETS IN THOUSANDS OF DOLLARS

Item Description for Accounting Period 7/05 Through 6/06		Total	Zero Assets	Under 500	500 to 1,000	1,000 to 5,000	5,000 to 10,000	10,000 to 25,000	25,000 to 50,000	50,000 to 100,000	100,000 to 250,000	250,000 to 500,000	500,000 to 2,500,000	2,500,000 and over
Number of Enterprises	1	18499	940	10884	2121	3202	671	363	149	78	44	20	18	9
Revenues ($ in Thousands)														
Net Sales	2	145165747	9457292	6552319	3946016	17766408	9303357	10376568	8431197	7776558	7601757	10082578	15329047	38542650
Interest	3	2910189	35853	1770	2480	6020	5425	10071	11124	13486	27299	24167	265432	2507061
Rents	4	103134	3118	55	318	4161	1185	4244	1937	1623	1789	6842	5288	72572
Royalties	5	1371212	248574	0	0	0	25	1152	856	6080	16531	25890	23144	1048961
Other Portfolio Income	6	6027722	2818945	23238	21554	52378	29161	14113	23978	36467	45521	81600	349432	2531337
Other Receipts	7	1656221	67452	16194	57747	115137	51199	58826	45565	106269	44704	96176	196112	800841
Total Receipts	8	157234225	12631234	6593576	4028115	17944104	9390352	10464974	8514657	7940483	7737601	10317253	16168455	45503422
Average Total Receipts	9	8500	13437	606	1899	5604	13995	28829	57145	101801	175855	515863	898248	5055936
Operating Costs/Operating Income (%)														
Cost of Operations	10	68.3	66.2	51.4	64.5	67.6	73.1	70.7	71.0	71.4	68.2	75.1	69.8	67.2
Salaries and Wages	11	6.5	5.7	11.9	8.8	5.7	5.7	6.5	6.5	6.3	7.3	5.7	7.8	5.8
Taxes Paid	12	2.0	0.3	3.4	2.8	2.7	2.0	2.2	1.7	1.7	1.6	1.9	1.8	2.0
Interest Paid	13	3.4	1.3	0.9	1.0	0.9	0.8	0.8	1.4	1.7	1.9	1.6	4.2	8.1
Depreciation	14	2.1	1.9	2.5	1.6	1.8	2.0	1.8	2.0	2.2	2.5	1.6	2.2	2.5
Amortization and Depletion	15	0.6	0.3	0.1	0.3	0.1	0.1	0.1	0.2	0.3	0.4	0.2	0.6	1.7
Pensions and Other Deferred Comp.	16	1.1	0.8	0.2	0.5	0.6	0.5	0.8	0.4	0.8	1.0	0.7	1.1	2.2
Employee Benefits	17	2.1	0.4	1.5	1.3	1.6	1.3	1.8	1.5	1.8	2.0	1.6	3.1	3.0
Advertising	18	1.0	5.0	0.3	0.3	0.6	0.4	0.4	0.6	0.6	0.6	0.5	0.4	1.4
Other Expenses	19	9.0	9.0	14.6	11.9	8.8	5.6	7.1	8.3	7.1	8.3	7.6	6.9	11.2
Officers' Compensation	20	2.0	0.5	8.6	6.2	5.0	3.4	2.2	1.7	1.3	1.3	0.6	0.5	0.5
Operating Margin	21	1.7	8.8	4.7	0.8	4.6	5.2	5.5	4.6	5.0	4.8	2.8	1.6	•
Operating Margin Before Officers' Comp.	22	3.8	9.2	13.4	7.0	9.5	8.5	7.8	6.3	6.2	6.1	3.4	2.1	•

Selected Average Balance Sheet ($ in Thousands)

Net Receivables 23	1241	0	37	188	632	1970	4495	8091	15226	28016	65692	138862	1081476
Inventories 24	939	0	21	141	604	1617	3988	8344	15007	27655	73301	125519	557406
Net Property, Plant and Equipment 25	1194	0	57	139	507	1667	3450	8545	16688	35077	71242	135355	1022773
Total Assets 26	12869	0	172	667	2301	6852	15725	35191	70171	155829	335954	903633	19615369
Notes and Loans Payable 27	4815	0	117	251	806	2221	4069	10112	19101	51290	105800	302254	7655538
All Other Liabilities 28	1740	0	47	143	592	1742	4155	8845	20672	36154	115614	245835	1725985
Net Worth 29	6314	8	273	903	2889	7500	16233	30398	68385	114541	355544	10233846	

Selected Financial Ratios (Times to 1)

Current Ratio 30	1.5	•	1.4	2.2	1.9	2.1	1.9	1.9	1.9	2.2	2.1	1.8	1.1
Quick Ratio 31	0.8	•	0.9	1.3	1.1	1.2	1.1	1.0	1.0	1.0	0.9	1.0	0.6
Net Sales to Working Capital 32	7.7	•	21.3	7.8	7.3	5.3	5.7	5.8	5.4	4.2	5.4	4.9	17.2
Coverage Ratio 33	4.1	33.0	6.9	3.7	7.2	8.5	8.9	4.9	5.1	4.7	4.2	2.8	2.6
Total Asset Turnover 34	0.6	•	3.5	2.8	2.4	2.0	1.8	1.6	1.4	1.1	1.5	0.9	0.2
Inventory Turnover 35	5.7	•	14.9	8.5	6.2	6.3	5.1	4.8	4.7	4.3	5.2	4.7	5.2
Receivables Turnover 36	6.3	•	16.4	10.1	8.1	7.5	6.6	7.4	6.7	6.3	7.5	7.0	3.7
Total Liabilities to Net Worth 37	1.0	•	21.3	1.4	1.5	1.4	1.1	1.2	1.3	1.3	1.9	1.5	0.9
Current Assets to Working Capital 38	3.1	•	3.5	1.8	2.1	1.9	2.2	2.1	2.2	1.8	1.9	2.2	10.5
Current Liabilities to Working Capital 39	2.1	•	2.5	0.8	1.1	0.9	1.2	1.1	1.2	0.8	0.9	1.2	9.5
Working Capital to Net Sales 40	0.1	•	0.0	0.1	0.1	0.2	0.2	0.2	0.2	0.2	0.2	0.2	0.1
Inventory to Working Capital 41	0.9	•	0.7	0.6	0.8	0.7	0.8	0.9	0.8	0.7	0.8	0.8	2.1
Total Receipts to Cash Flow 42	6.0	2.0	6.3	9.7	8.7	10.2	8.5	8.1	8.0	7.5	9.6	8.4	4.9
Cost of Goods to Cash Flow 43	4.1	1.3	3.3	6.2	5.9	7.5	6.0	5.8	5.7	5.1	7.2	5.8	3.3
Cash Flow to Total Debt 44	0.2	•	0.6	0.5	0.5	0.3	0.4	0.4	0.3	0.3	0.2	0.2	0.1

Selected Financial Factors (in Percentages)

Debt Ratio 45	50.9	•	95.5	59.1	60.8	57.8	52.3	53.9	56.7	56.1	65.9	60.7	47.8
Return on Total Assets 46	8.3	•	22.0	10.7	15.6	14.0	13.0	11.4	12.4	9.8	10.2	11.0	4.6
Return on Equity Before Income Taxes 47	12.8	•	418.1	19.2	34.2	29.3	24.3	19.6	23.1	17.6	22.8	17.9	5.5
Return on Equity After Income Taxes 48	10.3	•	402.8	18.7	32.7	27.3	21.7	16.5	19.0	14.3	17.5	12.1	4.0
Profit Margin (Before Income Tax) 49	10.3	42.4	5.4	2.8	5.6	6.1	6.4	5.6	7.0	7.0	5.2	7.5	13.1
Profit Margin (After Income Tax) 50	8.3	35.1	5.2	2.7	5.3	5.7	5.7	4.7	5.8	5.7	4.0	5.0	9.6

121

Table II

Corporations with Net Income

OTHER FABRICATED METAL PRODUCT

MONEY AMOUNTS AND SIZE OF ASSETS IN THOUSANDS OF DOLLARS

Item Description for Accounting Period 7/05 Through 6/06	Total	Zero Assets	Under 500	500 to 1,000	1,000 to 5,000	5,000 to 10,000	10,000 to 25,000	25,000 to 50,000	50,000 to 100,000	100,000 to 250,000	250,000 to 500,000	500,000 to 2,500,000	2,500,000 and over
Number of Enterprises 1	15535	520	9857	1394	2602	587	312	119	70	33	16	•	•
Revenues ($ in Thousands)													
Net Sales 2	129947350	9370401	6232211	2955232	15104094	8334192	9142252	7048106	6954852	6504223	8646524	•	•
Interest 3	2891514	35741	1762	1469	3801	5319	9016	10020	13473	18890	21576	•	•
Rents 4	100327	3118	51	318	3972	162	4244	1318	1623	993	6666	•	•
Royalties 5	1344306	248139	0	0	0	25	265	590	6080	8043	9122	•	•
Other Portfolio Income 6	5963471	2818474	23231	21409	45636	13146	12308	19385	32979	33668	81340	•	•
Other Receipts 7	1531729	66415	16103	43101	95417	38649	47568	30344	105515	37203	58193	•	•
Total Receipts 8	141778697	12542288	6273358	3021529	15252920	8391493	9215653	7109763	7114522	6603020	8823421	•	•
Average Total Receipts 9	9126	24120	636	2168	5862	14296	29537	59746	101636	200092	551464	•	•
Operating Costs/Operating Income (%)													
Cost of Operations 10	67.5	66.2	50.4	62.8	66.0	72.1	70.1	70.6	70.0	68.0	74.8	•	•
Salaries and Wages 11	6.5	5.5	12.2	9.4	5.8	5.6	6.5	6.4	6.5	7.0	6.1	•	•
Taxes Paid 12	1.9	0.3	3.4	2.9	2.5	2.1	2.2	1.6	1.7	1.6	1.7	•	•
Interest Paid 13	3.4	1.2	0.9	0.6	0.8	0.8	0.6	0.9	1.5	0.9	1.1	•	•
Depreciation 14	2.1	1.9	2.6	1.3	1.7	1.9	1.7	1.8	2.2	2.3	1.6	•	•
Amortization and Depletion 15	0.7	0.3	0.1	0.2	0.1	0.0	0.1	0.2	0.3	0.2	0.2	•	•
Pensions and Other Deferred Comp. 16	0.8	0.8	0.2	0.6	0.7	0.4	0.6	0.5	0.7	1.1	0.7	•	•
Employee Benefits 17	2.1	0.3	1.5	1.4	1.7	1.3	1.7	1.3	1.8	2.1	1.7	•	•
Advertising 18	1.1	5.0	0.3	0.2	0.6	0.4	0.4	0.7	0.5	0.5	0.4	•	•
Other Expenses 19	9.2	8.6	14.7	11.6	8.3	5.4	6.2	7.0	7.1	8.2	6.5	•	•
Officers' Compensation 20	2.0	0.5	8.7	6.4	5.3	3.3	2.3	1.7	1.4	1.1	0.7	•	•
Operating Margin 21	2.7	9.4	5.1	2.7	6.6	6.8	7.5	7.4	6.3	7.1	4.7	•	•
Operating Margin Before Officers' Comp. 22	4.8	9.9	13.8	9.1	11.9	10.1	9.8	9.1	7.6	8.2	5.3	•	•

Selected Average Balance Sheet ($ in Thousands)

Net Receivables 23	1314	0	39	209	650	2048	4402	8190	15060	31554	65721
Inventories 24	973	0	19	142	533	1591	3838	8443	14230	29676	76732
Net Property, Plant and Equipment 25	1263	0	58	107	478	1669	3313	8043	16796	37007	70826
Total Assets 26	14579	0	179	681	2303	6837	15733	35063	70995	151787	334700
Notes and Loans Payable 27	5363	0	128	142	732	2063	3227	7716	16734	35298	86388
All Other Liabilities 28	1791	0	49	153	571	1646	3825	7661	21156	37595	101536
Net Worth 29	7424	0	2	386	1001	3128	8681	19686	33104	78894	146776

Selected Financial Ratios (Times to 1)

Current Ratio 30	1.5	•	1.4	2.8	2.1	2.3	2.1	2.3	2.0	2.2	2.1
Quick Ratio 31	0.8	•	0.9	1.7	1.3	1.2	1.2	1.2	1.0	1.1	0.9
Net Sales to Working Capital 32	7.6	•	23.7	6.6	7.0	5.0	5.1	4.8	5.0	4.4	5.9
Coverage Ratio 33	4.5	36.8	7.2	9.5	9.9	10.9	13.9	10.0	6.6	11.3	7.3
Total Asset Turnover 34	0.6	•	3.5	3.1	2.5	2.1	1.9	1.7	1.4	1.3	1.6
Inventory Turnover 35	5.8	•	16.5	9.4	7.2	6.4	5.4	4.9	4.9	4.5	5.3
Receivables Turnover 36	6.3	•	20.9	11.7	9.0	7.7	7.1	7.9	7.0	6.4	8.0
Total Liabilities to Net Worth 37	1.0	•	96.8	0.8	1.3	1.2	0.8	0.8	1.1	0.9	1.3
Current Assets to Working Capital 38	3.1	•	3.8	1.5	1.9	1.8	1.9	1.8	2.0	1.9	1.9
Current Liabilities to Working Capital 39	2.1	•	2.8	0.5	0.9	0.8	0.9	0.8	1.0	0.9	0.9
Working Capital to Net Sales 40	0.1	•	0.0	0.2	0.1	0.2	0.2	0.2	0.2	0.2	0.2
Inventory to Working Capital 41	0.9	•	0.8	0.5	0.6	0.7	0.7	0.7	0.8	0.7	0.9
Total Receipts to Cash Flow 42	5.4	2.0	6.1	8.9	7.6	9.1	7.8	7.2	7.1	6.6	9.0
Cost of Goods to Cash Flow 43	3.6	1.3	3.1	5.6	5.0	6.6	5.5	5.1	5.0	4.5	6.8
Cash Flow to Total Debt 44	0.2	•	0.6	0.8	0.6	0.4	0.5	0.5	0.4	0.4	0.3

Selected Financial Factors (in Percentages)

Debt Ratio 45	49.1	•	99.0	43.3	56.6	54.2	44.8	43.9	53.4	48.0	56.1
Return on Total Assets 46	8.9	•	23.7	16.9	21.1	17.2	16.6	15.7	14.1	12.7	12.7
Return on Equity Before Income Taxes 47	13.6	•	1996.6	26.7	43.7	34.1	28.0	25.1	25.6	22.4	25.1
Return on Equity After Income Taxes 48	11.1	•	1925.1	26.2	42.1	32.0	25.3	21.9	21.4	18.6	19.9
Profit Margin (Before Income Tax) 49	12.1	43.3	5.8	4.9	7.5	7.5	8.3	8.4	8.5	9.0	6.8
Profit Margin (After Income Tax) 50	9.8	36.0	5.6	4.8	7.3	7.0	7.5	7.3	7.1	7.4	5.4

Table I

Corporations with and without Net Income

AGRICULTURE, CONSTRUCTION, AND MINING MACHINERY

MONEY AMOUNTS AND SIZE OF ASSETS IN THOUSANDS OF DOLLARS

Item Description for Accounting Period 7/05 Through 6/06	Total	Zero Assets	Under 500	500 to 1,000	1,000 to 5,000	5,000 to 10,000	10,000 to 25,000	25,000 to 50,000	50,000 to 100,000	100,000 to 250,000	250,000 to 500,000	500,000 to 2,500,000	2,500,000 and over
Number of Enterprises **1**	2485	283	648	104	1048	153	125	50	18	23	11	12	9
Revenues ($ in Thousands)													
Net Sales **2**	108210188	165788	263191	88324	5333830	1852472	3210080	2882133	2123683	3689612	4739936	15273283	68587855
Interest **3**	3649269	155	28	636	2504	1296	2949	4517	3691	8320	21541	135572	3468061
Rents **4**	905820	928	0	0	170	0	5165	4832	51	522	925	697	892529
Royalties **5**	700192	0	0	0	0	0	79	0	1048	1624	13692	79054	604696
Other Portfolio Income **6**	2666753	345	0	0	119933	593	11728	3564	4599	99756	45563	507356	1873316
Other Receipts **7**	2237414	22838	18	18	17646	18912	18580	22780	13342	63642	10255	171474	1877926
Total Receipts **8**	118369636	190054	263219	88978	5474083	1873273	3248581	2917826	2146414	3863476	4831912	16167436	77304383
Average Total Receipts **9**	47634	672	406	856	5223	12244	25989	58357	119245	167977	439265	1347286	8589376
Operating Costs/Operating Income (%)													
Cost of Operations **10**	72.8	66.4	66.0	53.7	73.8	64.6	71.1	69.1	70.4	68.7	75.9	76.4	72.5
Salaries and Wages **11**	6.5	7.5	6.4	11.8	7.0	8.6	7.6	8.2	5.4	8.6	6.7	6.1	6.3
Taxes Paid **12**	0.9	1.0	2.6	10.5	1.7	2.5	1.9	1.8	1.3	1.7	1.3	0.9	0.6
Interest Paid **13**	3.6	3.3	3.9	0.0	0.7	0.6	1.5	1.4	1.9	2.5	1.4	2.2	4.7
Depreciation **14**	1.8	0.8	2.4	0.1	1.3	1.3	1.3	1.5	1.4	1.8	1.5	1.1	2.1
Amortization and Depletion **15**	0.8	1.8	0.0	•	0.1	0.2	0.2	0.2	0.2	0.7	0.6	0.4	1.1
Pensions and Other Deferred Comp. **16**	0.6	0.3	0.2	0.8	0.3	0.1	0.6	0.6	0.4	0.6	0.3	0.6	0.6
Employee Benefits **17**	2.0	2.5	0.9	25.3	1.2	1.6	2.1	1.4	1.4	1.6	1.2	1.4	2.3
Advertising **18**	0.4	0.6	0.5	0.7	0.6	2.2	0.8	1.0	0.8	0.6	0.4	0.5	0.2
Other Expenses **19**	11.3	13.9	9.8	29.1	7.2	12.3	7.4	8.7	9.0	10.0	6.5	7.8	13.1
Officers' Compensation **20**	0.7	0.5	6.3	7.0	3.4	3.3	2.1	1.9	0.8	0.6	0.4	0.7	0.3
Operating Margin **21**	•	1.3	1.1	•	2.7	2.6	3.3	4.4	6.9	2.6	3.8	2.0	•
Operating Margin Before Officers' Comp. **22**	•	1.9	7.5	•	6.2	6.0	5.4	6.3	7.7	3.2	4.2	2.6	•

Selected Average Balance Sheet ($ in Thousands)

Net Receivables 23	20185	0	66	51	547	1473	3400	7480	17302	24611	75346	286538	4818766
Inventories 24	5345	0	30	577	746	2009	4664	9426	17863	42622	65735	168252	779355
Net Property, Plant and Equipment 25	5905	0	139	32	300	1070	2577	6358	11315	24764	60582	145750	1141480
Total Assets 26	61556	0	258	675	2287	6288	14423	33952	69288	140395	346379	1301606	13551680
Notes and Loans Payable 27	26102	0	263	87	736	1293	4254	10621	19864	50697	69590	288168	6322683
All Other Liabilities 28	18143	0	44	166	556	1311	4054	8946	23822	33704	92181	473444	3933601
Net Worth 29	17312	0	-50	422	995	3684	6115	14385	25602	55994	184607	539994	3295396

Selected Financial Ratios (Times to 1)

Current Ratio 30	1.6	•	1.6	2.7	2.6	2.5	1.9	1.8	1.8	1.8	2.4	1.5	1.5
Quick Ratio 31	1.1	•	1.2	1.8	1.3	1.2	0.9	0.8	0.9	0.8	1.2	0.8	1.2
Net Sales to Working Capital 32	3.8	•	9.3	3.0	4.8	4.5	5.2	5.7	5.8	4.8	3.7	7.1	3.2
Coverage Ratio 33	3.5	5.9	1.3	•	8.5	7.6	4.0	5.1	5.1	3.9	5.2	5.0	3.2
Total Asset Turnover 34	0.7	•	1.6	1.3	2.2	1.9	1.8	1.7	1.7	1.1	1.2	1.0	0.6
Inventory Turnover 35	5.9	•	8.9	0.8	5.0	3.9	3.9	4.2	4.7	2.6	5.0	5.8	7.1
Receivables Turnover 36	2.5	•	4.4	5.4	10.6	10.8	8.3	8.5	7.3	5.5	6.4	4.9	1.8
Total Liabilities to Net Worth 37	2.6	•	•	0.6	1.3	0.7	1.4	1.4	1.7	1.5	0.9	1.4	3.1
Current Assets to Working Capital 38	2.7	•	2.6	1.6	1.6	1.7	2.1	2.2	2.2	2.3	1.7	3.2	2.9
Current Liabilities to Working Capital 39	1.7	•	1.6	0.6	0.6	0.7	1.1	1.2	1.2	1.3	0.7	2.2	1.9
Working Capital to Net Sales 40	0.3	•	0.1	0.3	0.2	0.2	0.2	0.2	0.2	0.2	0.3	0.1	0.3
Inventory to Working Capital 41	0.5	•	0.6	0.5	0.8	0.8	1.0	1.1	1.0	1.1	0.7	1.0	0.4
Total Receipts to Cash Flow 42	5.6	3.7	15.0	•	9.3	7.1	9.7	7.7	6.2	6.3	9.0	7.0	4.9
Cost of Goods to Cash Flow 43	4.1	2.5	9.9	•	6.8	4.6	6.9	5.3	4.4	4.4	6.8	5.3	3.5
Cash Flow to Total Debt 44	0.2	•	0.1	•	0.4	0.7	0.3	0.4	0.4	0.3	0.3	0.2	0.2

Selected Financial Factors (in Percentages)

Debt Ratio 45	71.9	•	119.3	37.5	56.5	41.4	57.6	57.6	63.0	60.1	46.7	58.5	75.7
Return on Total Assets 46	9.0	•	7.9	•	13.5	8.3	10.7	11.9	16.8	11.3	9.3	10.7	8.5
Return on Equity Before Income Taxes 47	22.9	•	•	•	27.3	12.3	19.0	22.6	36.6	21.1	14.1	20.8	24.1
Return on Equity After Income Taxes 48	17.2	•	•	•	26.4	10.3	16.1	18.1	32.6	17.6	9.1	16.5	17.6
Profit Margin (Before Income Tax) 49	9.1	15.9	1.1	•	5.3	3.8	4.5	5.6	8.0	7.4	9.1	8.8	10.4
Profit Margin (After Income Tax) 50	6.9	13.7	1.0	•	5.2	3.1	3.8	4.5	7.1	6.1	3.9	7.0	7.6

Table II
Corporations with Net Income

AGRICULTURE, CONSTRUCTION, AND MINING MACHINERY

MONEY AMOUNTS AND SIZE OF ASSETS IN THOUSANDS OF DOLLARS

Item Description for Accounting Period 7/05 Through 6/06		Total	Zero Assets	Under 500	500 to 1,000	1,000 to 5,000	5,000 to 10,000	10,000 to 25,000	25,000 to 50,000	50,000 to 100,000	100,000 to 250,000	250,000 to 500,000	500,000 to 2,500,000	2,500,000 and over
Number of Enterprises	1	1776	•	282	70	858	74	105	40	18	20	•	•	•
Revenues ($ in Thousands)														
Net Sales	2	99866316	•	139690	88102	4709844	1042348	2565193	2392451	2123683	3456796	•	•	•
Interest	3	3526837	•	28	564	1176	1296	2590	2698	3691	8015	•	•	•
Rents	4	901692	•	0	0	170	0	2001	4832	51	486	•	•	•
Royalties	5	621833	•	0	0	0	0	79	0	1048	1624	•	•	•
Other Portfolio Income	6	2653509	•	0	0	118523	205	11665	2295	4599	99754	•	•	•
Other Receipts	7	2048380	•	0	19	12596	17151	18418	19961	13342	61799	•	•	•
Total Receipts	8	109620567	•	139718	88685	4842309	1061000	2599946	2422237	2146414	3628474	•	•	•
Average Total Receipts	9	61723	•	495	1267	5644	14338	24761	60556	119245	181424	•	•	•
Operating Costs/Operating Income (%)														
Cost of Operations	10	72.9	•	73.3	53.9	73.3	67.9	71.6	68.7	70.4	68.8	•	•	•
Salaries and Wages	11	6.3	•	9.5	11.8	7.1	7.1	6.5	8.1	5.4	8.5	•	•	•
Taxes Paid	12	0.9	•	2.8	10.5	1.7	2.3	1.9	1.8	1.3	1.5	•	•	•
Interest Paid	13	3.5	•	4.3	0.0	0.7	0.7	1.2	1.3	1.9	2.6	•	•	•
Depreciation	14	1.7	•	1.6	0.0	1.3	1.2	1.2	1.4	1.4	1.8	•	•	•
Amortization and Depletion	15	0.8	•	0.0	•	0.0	0.3	0.1	0.1	0.2	0.6	•	•	•
Pensions and Other Deferred Comp.	16	0.6	•	0.1	0.8	0.3	0.2	0.7	0.7	0.4	0.5	•	•	•
Employee Benefits	17	2.0	•	1.6	1.0	1.2	1.4	2.2	1.3	1.4	1.7	•	•	•
Advertising	18	0.4	•	0.0	0.7	0.6	0.8	0.8	0.9	0.8	0.6	•	•	•
Other Expenses	19	11.4	•	0.1	9.1	6.8	10.1	6.3	7.7	9.0	9.9	•	•	•
Officers' Compensation	20	0.6	•	2.3	7.0	3.3	2.9	1.9	2.0	0.8	0.6	•	•	•
Operating Margin	21	•	•	4.4	5.1	3.8	5.0	5.4	6.0	6.9	3.0	•	•	•
Operating Margin Before Officers' Comp.	22	•	•	6.7	12.1	7.0	7.9	7.3	8.0	7.7	3.6	•	•	•

Selected Average Balance Sheet ($ in Thousands)

Net Receivables 23	24696	143	76	542	1993	3419	7214	17302	27034
Inventories 24	6522	6	648	587	1751	4508	10359	20521	37036
Net Property, Plant and Equipment 25	7212	161	35	318	1076	2472	6731	11315	22284
Total Assets 26	76693	339	702	2335	6585	14131	33932	69288	144151
Notes and Loans Payable 27	34045	394	129	726	2146	3826	9530	19864	53419
All Other Liabilities 28	21406	77	117	502	1237	3539	8599	23822	34107
Net Worth 29	21241	-132	455	1108	3202	6766	15803	25602	56625

Selected Financial Ratios (Times to 1)

Current Ratio 30	1.6	1.4	5.6	2.8	2.5	2.0	1.8	1.8	1.9
Quick Ratio 31	1.1	1.4	3.8	1.4	1.4	1.0	0.8	0.9	0.9
Net Sales to Working Capital 32	3.7	9.3	2.3	4.8	4.5	4.7	5.7	5.8	4.5
Coverage Ratio 33	3.8	2.0	5069.0	10.6	11.0	6.8	6.6	5.1	4.1
Total Asset Turnover 34	0.7	1.5	1.8	2.4	2.1	1.7	1.8	1.7	1.2
Inventory Turnover 35	6.3	63.3	1.0	6.9	5.5	3.9	4.0	4.0	3.2
Receivables Turnover 36	2.5	2.6	6.6	13.5	10.9	7.9	8.5	13.6	6.6
Total Liabilities to Net Worth 37	2.6	•	0.5	1.1	1.1	1.1	1.1	1.7	1.5
Current Assets to Working Capital 38	2.6	3.3	1.2	1.6	1.6	2.0	2.2	2.2	2.1
Current Liabilities to Working Capital 39	1.6	2.3	0.2	0.6	0.6	1.0	1.2	1.2	1.1
Working Capital to Net Sales 40	0.3	0.1	0.4	0.2	0.2	0.2	0.2	0.2	0.2
Inventory to Working Capital 41	0.5	0.1	0.4	0.7	0.7	0.9	1.1	1.0	1.0
Total Receipts to Cash Flow 42	5.3	23.8	7.1	8.4	6.5	8.5	7.3	6.2	6.1
Cost of Goods to Cash Flow 43	3.9	17.5	3.8	6.1	4.4	6.1	5.0	4.4	4.2
Cash Flow to Total Debt 44	0.2	0.0	0.7	0.5	0.6	0.4	0.5	0.4	0.3

Selected Financial Factors (in Percentages)

Debt Ratio 45	72.3	139.0	35.1	52.6	51.4	52.1	53.4	63.0	60.7
Return on Total Assets 46	10.0	12.7	10.3	17.1	16.0	13.7	15.1	16.8	12.8
Return on Equity Before Income Taxes 47	26.7	•	15.9	32.6	29.9	24.5	27.5	36.6	24.5
Return on Equity After Income Taxes 48	20.2	•	12.7	31.6	25.0	21.3	22.5	32.6	20.5
Profit Margin (Before Income Tax) 49	10.1	4.4	5.8	6.6	6.8	6.8	7.3	8.0	8.0
Profit Margin (After Income Tax) 50	7.6	4.1	4.6	6.4	5.7	5.9	5.9	7.1	6.7

Table I

Corporations with and without Net Income

INDUSTRIAL MACHINERY

MONEY AMOUNTS AND SIZE OF ASSETS IN THOUSANDS OF DOLLARS

Item Description for Accounting Period 7/05 Through 6/06	Total	Zero Assets	Under 500	500 to 1,000	1,000 to 5,000	5,000 to 10,000	10,000 to 25,000	25,000 to 50,000	50,000 to 100,000	100,000 to 250,000	250,000 to 500,000	500,000 to 2,500,000	2,500,000 and over
Number of Enterprises **1**	3626	61	1932	123	898	275	149	87	38	36	12	12	3
Revenues ($ in Thousands)													
Net Sales **2**	48104532	260899	879524	207966	3764684	3590163	3584219	4229770	2923658	5803003	3803284	6539739	12517623
Interest **3**	402610	4337	81	8	3193	2291	4802	18768	13831	44810	18299	112699	179491
Rents **4**	38110	189	0	1876	444	3910	2864	7688	1554	9638	7200	427	2320
Royalties **5**	184706	0	0	0	112	0	14955	4320	6414	25347	37855	36459	59244
Other Portfolio Income **6**	1108745	1993	1171	4	3173	11587	23694	19737	43165	37301	22243	238673	706002
Other Receipts **7**	937941	15015	30549	10170	61508	20285	22966	38682	12437	49277	88531	44993	543531
Total Receipts **8**	50776644	282433	911325	220024	3833114	3628236	3653500	4318965	3001059	5969376	3977412	6972990	14008211
Average Total Receipts **9**	14003	4630	472	1789	4269	13194	24520	49643	78975	165816	331451	581082	4669404
Operating Costs/Operating Income (%)													
Cost of Operations **10**	66.4	64.0	58.4	79.9	64.1	65.3	68.7	69.5	71.7	67.1	68.3	62.0	66.3
Salaries and Wages **11**	10.3	9.3	5.6	4.4	10.9	8.1	9.7	7.0	8.3	11.6	9.0	11.9	12.0
Taxes Paid **12**	1.8	1.3	3.7	2.9	3.4	2.7	2.3	2.1	2.2	1.5	1.5	1.9	0.7
Interest Paid **13**	1.9	3.7	1.6	0.4	0.9	1.2	1.0	1.3	1.5	1.8	1.7	4.5	1.6
Depreciation **14**	2.0	1.1	1.8	0.5	1.8	1.0	1.4	1.9	1.9	2.0	1.4	3.1	2.3
Amortization and Depletion **15**	0.6	2.3	0.1	0.0	0.1	0.2	0.3	0.3	0.6	1.1	0.6	1.9	0.2
Pensions and Other Deferred Comp. **16**	0.9	0.1	0.0	•	0.8	0.8	0.6	1.0	0.9	1.2	0.6	1.7	0.5
Employee Benefits **17**	2.2	5.1	2.3	1.2	2.8	1.5	2.0	1.6	1.8	2.9	2.7	2.3	1.9
Advertising **18**	0.6	0.2	0.6	0.0	1.3	0.3	0.7	0.8	0.4	0.6	0.5	0.5	0.5
Other Expenses **19**	10.1	19.5	15.5	10.2	10.0	8.9	8.6	9.0	7.9	11.5	8.0	12.5	9.9
Officers' Compensation **20**	1.9	16.0	8.5	6.3	4.4	6.6	2.1	1.5	1.2	1.1	0.9	1.1	0.4
Operating Margin **21**	1.3	•	2.0	•	•	3.4	2.7	4.0	1.5	•	4.6	•	3.8
Operating Margin Before Officers' Comp. **22**	3.3	•	10.5	0.5	3.9	10.0	4.7	5.5	2.7	•	5.6	•	4.2

Selected Average Balance Sheet ($ in Thousands)

Net Receivables **23**	2898	0	48	376	612	4114	9036	16867	40065	63221	166970	1006639
Inventories **24**	1813	0	47	195	712	4118	7352	11389	23058	34155	63702	582840
Net Property, Plant and Equipment **25**	1700	0	15	70	437	2457	6843	11726	21320	43235	61687	676590
Total Assets **26**	15568	0	147	742	2094	15459	35682	69894	162659	344928	938518	7557766
Notes and Loans Payable **27**	3192	0	52	216	504	3498	8378	15532	46516	83629	232427	958395
All Other Liabilities **28**	4447	0	47	672	568	5095	10962	22011	61046	93777	385110	1477315
Net Worth **29**	7928	0	48	-146	1022	6865	16342	32351	55098	167522	320981	5122057

Selected Financial Ratios (Times to 1)

Current Ratio **30**	2.2	•	2.4	0.9	2.3	2.0	1.8	1.9	1.5	2.0	2.0	1.4	3.2
Quick Ratio **31**	1.5	•	1.3	0.8	1.2	1.2	1.0	1.1	0.9	1.3	1.0		2.5
Net Sales to Working Capital **32**	3.2	•	6.1	•	4.9	5.0	5.1	4.5	5.3	3.3	4.3	6.7	1.6
Coverage Ratio **33**	5.0	•	4.6	0.8	2.4	4.7	5.8	5.6	3.8	1.3	6.7	2.0	11.9
Total Asset Turnover **34**	0.9	•	3.1	2.3	2.0	1.6	1.6	1.4	1.1	1.0	0.9	0.6	2.0
Inventory Turnover **35**	4.9	•	5.7	6.9	3.8	6.1	4.0	4.6	4.8	4.7	6.3	5.3	0.6
Receivables Turnover **36**	4.7	•	12.5	2.9	6.8	5.7	5.7	4.8	4.8	4.9	5.2	3.3	4.7
Total Liabilities to Net Worth **37**	1.0	•	2.0	•	1.0	1.5	1.3	1.2	1.2	2.0	1.1	1.9	4.2
Current Assets to Working Capital **38**	1.9	•	1.7	•	1.8	2.0	2.3	2.1	2.9	2.0	2.0	3.4	0.5
Current Liabilities to Working Capital **39**	0.9	•	0.7	•	0.8	1.0	1.3	1.1	1.9	1.0	1.0	2.4	1.5
Working Capital to Net Sales **40**	0.3	•	0.2	•	0.2	0.2	0.2	0.2	0.2	0.3	0.2	0.1	0.5
Inventory to Working Capital **41**	0.4	•	0.7	•	0.8	0.6	0.9	0.8	0.8	0.6	0.5	0.8	0.6
Total Receipts to Cash Flow **42**	6.8	34.6	5.9	12.3	12.6	8.9	8.6	7.2	10.5	10.4	6.4	7.7	0.2
Cost of Goods to Cash Flow **43**	4.5	22.1	3.4	9.8	8.1	5.8	5.9	5.0	7.5	7.0	4.4	4.8	4.3
Cash Flow to Total Debt **44**	0.3	•	0.8	0.2	0.3	0.3	0.3	0.2	0.2	0.1	0.3	0.1	2.8

Selected Financial Factors (in Percentages)

Debt Ratio **45**	49.1	•	67.2	119.7	51.2	60.5	55.6	54.2	53.7	66.1	51.4	65.8	32.2
Return on Total Assets **46**	8.0	•	22.2	0.8	4.4	9.2	8.6	10.1	6.1	2.4	10.2	5.4	10.3
Return on Equity Before Income Taxes **47**	12.6	•	52.9	0.7	5.3	18.4	16.0	18.1	9.8	1.8	17.9	8.0	14.0
Return on Equity After Income Taxes **48**	9.0	•	52.9	0.8	3.4	17.6	13.7	14.3	6.8	0.1	12.8	4.5	10.0
Profit Margin (Before Income Tax) **49**	7.5	•	5.6	1.3	4.5	4.6	6.1	4.1	0.6	9.5	4.7		17.1
Profit Margin (After Income Tax) **50**	5.4	•	5.6	0.8	4.3	3.9	4.8	2.9	0.0	6.8	2.7		12.3

Table II
Corporations with Net Income

INDUSTRIAL MACHINERY

MONEY AMOUNTS AND SIZE OF ASSETS IN THOUSANDS OF DOLLARS

Item Description for Accounting Period 7/05 Through 6/06	Total	Zero Assets	Under 500	500 to 1,000	1,000 to 5,000	5,000 to 10,000	10,000 to 25,000	25,000 to 50,000	50,000 to 100,000	100,000 to 250,000	250,000 to 500,000	500,000 to 2,500,000	2,500,000 and over
Number of Enterprises **1**	2077	52	882	120	515	251	115	75	27	18	12	7	3
Revenues ($ in Thousands)													
Net Sales **2**	38099463	152095	296008	197464	2193265	3290196	2900932	3778888	2246377	3178654	3803284	3544677	12517623
Interest **3**	275156	529	30	1	2616	1166	3213	18684	12439	18395	18299	20293	179491
Rents **4**	31403	189	0	1876	398	13	2655	7430	1321	8001	7200	0	2320
Royalties **5**	127714	0	0	0	112	0	6414	4320	4729	5346	37855	9693	59244
Other Portfolio Income **6**	1056350	1158	1171	0	2375	11135	21397	19042	42261	19118	22243	210450	706002
Other Receipts **7**	871169	13339	27337	10079	59990	16086	18497	37283	9409	22128	88531	24959	543531
Total Receipts **8**	40461255	167310	324546	209420	2258756	3318596	2953108	3865647	2316536	3251642	3977412	3810072	14008211
Average Total Receipts **9**	19481	3218	368	1745	4386	13221	25679	51542	85798	180647	331451	544296	4669404
Operating Costs/Operating Income (%)													
Cost of Operations **10**	66.6	68.0	51.4	78.7	67.6	64.1	68.7	69.3	72.6	67.4	68.3	58.8	66.3
Salaries and Wages **11**	9.8	6.5	3.4	4.2	6.4	8.2	8.6	6.9	7.6	9.4	9.0	13.6	12.0
Taxes Paid **12**	1.6	0.9	4.1	3.0	3.3	2.7	2.2	2.0	2.1	1.4	1.5	1.5	0.7
Interest Paid **13**	1.4	1.1	1.6	0.3	0.9	0.4	0.8	1.2	1.1	1.3	1.7	2.3	1.6
Depreciation **14**	2.0	1.0	2.8	0.5	1.9	1.0	1.4	1.8	1.4	2.0	1.4	4.0	2.3
Amortization and Depletion **15**	0.4	2.5	•	•	0.0	0.1	0.2	0.3	0.3	0.5	0.6	1.3	0.2
Pensions and Other Deferred Comp. **16**	0.7	•	•	•	0.7	0.9	0.6	1.1	0.9	0.7	0.6	1.5	0.5
Employee Benefits **17**	2.0	5.8	2.7	1.3	2.6	1.4	1.8	1.3	1.8	2.8	2.7	1.7	1.9
Advertising **18**	0.5	0.0	0.2	0.0	0.7	0.3	0.7	0.8	0.4	0.3	0.5	0.6	0.5
Other Expenses **19**	8.7	18.3	15.9	9.6	7.6	8.5	7.8	8.8	5.8	9.3	8.0	7.5	9.9
Officers' Compensation **20**	1.8	0.1	5.9	6.6	4.9	6.9	2.2	1.6	1.2	1.1	0.9	1.3	0.4
Operating Margin **21**	4.5	•	12.1	•	3.4	5.5	5.0	5.0	4.7	3.8	4.6	5.9	3.8
Operating Margin Before Officers' Comp. **22**	6.3	•	18.0	2.4	8.3	12.4	7.2	6.6	5.9	4.9	5.6	7.2	4.2

Selected Average Balance Sheet ($ in Thousands)

Net Receivables 23	3856	45	383	507	1982	4249	9292	18478	45180	63221	127062	1006639
Inventories 24	2221	26	125	578	1337	3877	6346	9139	21329	36328	57932	519264
Net Property, Plant and Equipment 25	2422	15	70	402	975	2561	7009	10601	23766	43235	67769	676590
Total Assets 26	22132	100	742	1941	7899	15526	35911	68702	153049	344928	986802	7757766
Notes and Loans Payable 27	3953	32	104	578	2643	3409	7268	10892	46983	83629	178934	958395
All Other Liabilities 28	5541	71	681	490	1583	4554	11594	21874	51356	93777	321432	1477315
Net Worth 29	12638	-3	-42	873	3672	7563	17050	35937	54710	167522	486436	5122057

Selected Financial Ratios (Times to 1)

Current Ratio 30	2.2	•	0.9	2.6	2.3	1.9	2.0	1.6	2.2	2.0	1.0	3.2
Quick Ratio 31	1.6	•	0.8	1.4	1.4	1.0	1.1	1.0	1.3	1.3	0.6	2.5
Net Sales to Working Capital 32	3.0	•	•	4.9	4.6	5.0	4.5	5.0	3.6	4.3	•	1.6
Coverage Ratio 33	9.4	6.3	6.8	8.1	16.4	9.0	7.1	8.2	5.8	6.7	7.9	11.9
Total Asset Turnover 34	0.8	•	2.2	2.2	1.7	1.6	1.4	1.2	1.2	0.9	0.5	0.6
Inventory Turnover 35	5.5	•	10.4	5.0	6.3	4.5	5.5	6.6	5.6	6.0	5.1	5.3
Receivables Turnover 36	5.3	•	4.0	8.4	5.9	6.1	6.7	5.2	5.4	10.0	4.4	8.3
Total Liabilities to Net Worth 37	0.8	•	•	1.2	1.2	1.1	1.1	0.9	1.8	1.1	1.0	0.5
Current Assets to Working Capital 38	1.8	7.0	•	1.6	1.8	2.2	2.0	2.6	1.9	2.0	•	1.5
Current Liabilities to Working Capital 39	0.8	6.0	•	0.6	0.8	1.2	1.0	1.6	0.9	1.0	•	0.5
Working Capital to Net Sales 40	0.3	0.0	•	0.2	0.2	0.2	0.2	0.2	0.3	0.2	•	0.6
Inventory to Working Capital 41	0.4	1.9	•	0.7	0.5	0.8	0.7	0.6	0.5	0.5	•	0.2
Total Receipts to Cash Flow 42	5.7	4.8	10.4	8.6	7.8	7.7	6.8	8.8	7.8	6.4	5.1	4.3
Cost of Goods to Cash Flow 43	3.8	3.3	8.2	5.8	5.0	5.3	4.7	6.4	5.3	4.4	3.0	2.8
Cash Flow to Total Debt 44	0.3	•	0.2	0.5	0.4	0.4	0.4	0.3	0.2	0.3	0.2	0.4

Selected Financial Factors (in Percentages)

Debt Ratio 45	42.9	•	105.7	55.0	53.5	51.3	52.5	47.7	64.3	51.4	50.7	32.2
Return on Total Assets 46	10.6	78.6	4.9	15.9	11.2	12.4	11.9	10.9	9.0	10.2	9.4	10.3
Return on Equity Before Income Taxes 47	16.6	103.2	•	31.0	22.7	22.5	21.5	18.2	20.9	17.9	16.7	14.0
Return on Equity After Income Taxes 48	12.7	21.8	•	27.2	22.0	19.8	17.2	14.5	17.4	12.8	12.8	10.0
Profit Margin (Before Income Tax) 49	11.4	5.7	1.9	6.4	6.4	6.8	7.3	7.9	6.5	9.5	16.0	17.1
Profit Margin (After Income Tax) 50	8.7	5.0	1.9	5.6	6.2	5.9	5.8	6.3	5.4	6.8	12.3	12.3

Table I

Corporations with and without Net Income

COMMERCIAL AND SERVICE INDUSTRY MACHINERY

MONEY AMOUNTS AND SIZE OF ASSETS IN THOUSANDS OF DOLLARS

Item Description for Accounting Period 7/05 Through 6/06	Total	Zero Assets	Under 500	500 to 1,000	1,000 to 5,000	5,000 to 10,000	10,000 to 25,000	25,000 to 50,000	50,000 to 100,000	100,000 to 250,000	250,000 to 500,000	500,000 to 2,500,000	2,500,000 and over
Number of Enterprises **1**	1994	436	577	285	518	63	48	21	19	14	4	6	4
Revenues ($ in Thousands)													
Net Sales **2**	38699813	234640	243822	696118	2897872	723928	1116660	1175268	1475102	2666767	1188994	3586134	22694508
Interest **3**	1208878	827	91	67	907	1194	2186	3632	3962	19344	5528	27670	1143470
Rents **4**	200069	0	3007	0	3319	0	0	39	6613	5953	842	89310	90985
Royalties **5**	1481045	62	0	0	0	0	89	0	104	1550	744	25646	1452851
Other Portfolio Income **6**	1356144	54489	0	4811	5525	3128	119	13188	2596	37079	15332	72369	1147510
Other Receipts **7**	1336285	3546	2334	762	13917	5752	4794	8376	7223	30645	42597	18687	1197650
Total Receipts **8**	44282234	293564	249254	701758	2921540	734002	1123848	1200503	1495600	2761338	1287164	3786689	27726974
Average Total Receipts **9**	22208	673	432	2462	5640	11651	23414	57167	78716	197238	321791	631115	6931744
Operating Costs/Operating Income (%)													
Cost of Operations **10**	59.5	64.1	55.0	60.4	59.8	61.6	66.0	71.6	63.1	66.0	65.8	67.8	55.8
Salaries and Wages **11**	16.1	16.7	13.5	3.5	17.5	9.0	8.7	9.2	10.6	9.2	12.7	9.4	19.6
Taxes Paid **12**	2.3	24.5	2.5	2.3	2.5	2.3	2.2	1.8	2.4	1.7	1.4	2.1	2.2
Interest Paid **13**	4.8	3.9	0.6	0.2	0.4	1.3	0.8	0.8	1.6	1.9	5.4	2.2	6.9
Depreciation **14**	4.5	5.2	0.4	0.6	1.0	2.2	2.0	1.8	2.0	1.8	4.1	3.7	6.0
Amortization and Depletion **15**	0.6	0.0	•	0.0	0.1	0.1	0.3	0.2	0.8	0.3	2.9	0.5	0.7
Pensions and Other Deferred Comp. **16**	0.9	0.6	1.3	0.0	0.7	0.0	0.6	0.4	1.2	0.6	0.3	1.0	1.1
Employee Benefits **17**	3.7	0.7	4.8	1.4	2.3	3.4	1.9	2.4	2.8	1.9	2.3	3.0	4.6
Advertising **18**	1.6	1.4	1.0	0.6	1.0	0.8	1.2	0.3	1.3	1.0	0.9	0.6	2.1
Other Expenses **19**	13.4	15.8	9.9	25.1	9.2	14.6	10.9	7.9	13.4	11.3	8.5	10.0	15.0
Officers' Compensation **20**	1.5	16.7	5.7	9.2	4.1	2.7	2.3	1.9	1.6	2.2	1.1	0.8	0.7
Operating Margin **21**	•	•	5.4	•	1.4	2.0	3.1	1.7	•	2.3	•	•	•
Operating Margin Before Officers' Comp. **22**	•	•	11.1	5.8	5.5	4.7	5.4	3.5	1.0	4.4	•	•	•

Selected Average Balance Sheet ($ in Thousands)

Net Receivables 23	6843	0	18	239	841	1141	3486	9356	14406	38876	34818	184518	2657518
Inventories 24	1872	0	54	243	797	1917	5416	7947	14625	33593	40092	99622	299043
Net Property, Plant and Equipment 25	3592	0	48	87	533	2248	2752	7225	11581	24403	43945	117713	1241816
Total Assets 26	34124	0	146	911	3171	6914	14610	32488	68310	163949	316339	790363	13359466
Notes and Loans Payable 27	13469	0	35	138	976	1944	4401	3902	20234	54969	138692	141116	5830026
All Other Liabilities 28	13180	0	28	535	1219	3222	22462	17747	21305	40442	66039	406118	5038633
Net Worth 29	7476	0	83	238	975	1747	-12252	10840	26771	68537	111608	243128	2790808

Selected Financial Ratios (Times to 1)

Current Ratio 30	1.1	•	2.1	1.3	1.7	1.6	0.5	1.7	1.5	1.5	2.0	1.2	1.0
Quick Ratio 31	0.7	•	0.9	0.8	0.9	0.8	0.2	1.0	0.9	0.8	0.8	0.8	0.7
Net Sales to Working Capital 32	20.1	•	8.6	12.8	5.7	7.4	•	5.2	6.1	6.6	6.0	9.7	53.9
Coverage Ratio 33	2.5	•	14.2	•	7.1	3.6	5.7	5.8	1.5	4.1	1.6	3.0	2.5
Total Asset Turnover 34	0.6	•	2.9	2.7	1.8	1.7	1.6	1.7	1.1	1.2	0.9	0.8	0.4
Inventory Turnover 35	6.2	•	4.3	6.1	4.2	3.7	2.8	5.0	3.3	3.7	4.9	4.1	10.6
Receivables Turnover 36	2.8	•	46.8	20.4	7.2	9.4	4.9	8.3	4.7	4.9	3.5	2.4	2.2
Total Liabilities to Net Worth 37	3.6	•	0.8	2.8	2.3	3.0	2.0	2.0	1.6	1.4	1.8	2.3	3.9
Current Assets to Working Capital 38	13.3	•	1.9	4.0	2.4	2.8	•	2.3	2.9	3.0	2.0	5.8	43.7
Current Liabilities to Working Capital 39	12.3	•	0.9	3.0	1.4	1.8	•	1.3	1.9	2.0	1.0	4.8	42.7
Working Capital to Net Sales 40	0.0	•	0.1	0.1	0.2	0.1	•	0.2	0.2	0.2	0.2	0.1	0.0
Inventory to Working Capital 41	1.9	•	1.1	1.3	1.0	1.2	0.9	0.9	1.1	1.0	0.8	1.2	3.0
Total Receipts to Cash Flow 42	6.3	•	6.1	7.2	11.5	6.1	7.6	9.8	8.1	6.5	11.5	9.3	5.3
Cost of Goods to Cash Flow 43	3.8	•	3.3	4.3	6.9	3.8	5.0	7.0	5.1	4.3	7.6	6.3	3.0
Cash Flow to Total Debt 44	0.1	•	1.1	0.5	0.2	0.4	0.1	0.3	0.2	0.3	0.1	0.1	0.1

Selected Financial Factors (in Percentages)

Debt Ratio 45	78.1	•	43.1	73.9	69.2	74.7	183.9	66.6	60.8	58.2	64.7	69.2	79.6
Return on Total Assets 46	6.9	•	23.9	•	4.5	7.8	7.2	7.9	2.6	9.0	7.9	5.0	7.2
Return on Equity Before Income Taxes 47	18.9	•	39.0	•	12.6	22.2	•	19.6	2.2	16.4	8.0	11.0	20.9
Return on Equity After Income Taxes 48	14.2	•	38.6	•	10.9	19.5	•	17.8	0.1	11.9	7.9	10.5	15.5
Profit Margin (Before Income Tax) 49	7.3	•	7.7	•	2.2	3.4	•	3.8	0.8	5.9	3.0	4.5	10.3
Profit Margin (After Income Tax) 50	5.5	•	7.6	•	1.9	3.0	2.7	3.4	0.0	4.3	3.0	4.3	7.6

Table II
Corporations with Net Income

COMMERCIAL AND SERVICE INDUSTRY MACHINERY

MONEY AMOUNTS AND SIZE OF ASSETS IN THOUSANDS OF DOLLARS

Item Description for Accounting Period 7/05 Through 6/06		Total	Zero Assets	Under 500	500 to 1,000	1,000 to 5,000	5,000 to 10,000	10,000 to 25,000	25,000 to 50,000	50,000 to 100,000	100,000 to 250,000	250,000 to 500,000	500,000 to 2,500,000	2,500,000 and over
Number of Enterprises	1	1127	9	483	212	302	38	35	16	12	•	0	•	4
Revenues ($ in Thousands)														
Net Sales	2	34898519	172696	196145	580533	2011088	455946	957245	820474	1015371	•	0	•	22694508
Interest	3	1196228	121	0	2	749	176	1486	2693	2203	•	0	•	1143470
Rents	4	188571	0	0	0	395	0	0	39	1664	•	0	•	90985
Royalties	5	1479489	62	0	0	0	0	89	0	74	•	0	•	1452851
Other Portfolio Income	6	1322298	54444	0	0	5320	3048	119	13114	2525	•	0	•	1147510
Other Receipts	7	1311687	3034	153	0	13868	887	4440	5370	6328	•	0	•	1197650
Total Receipts	8	40396792	230357	196298	580535	2031420	460057	963379	841690	1028165	•	0	•	27726974
Average Total Receipts	9	35845	25595	406	2738	6727	12107	27525	52606	85680	•	•	•	6931744
Operating Costs/Operating Income (%)														
Cost of Operations	10	58.8	69.3	54.5	55.2	64.6	60.5	65.9	69.5	58.6	•	•	•	55.8
Salaries and Wages	11	16.0	12.9	14.0	1.8	11.0	9.1	8.2	9.3	8.4	•	•	•	19.6
Taxes Paid	12	2.1	0.2	2.3	2.3	2.0	2.7	2.1	2.1	2.2	•	•	•	2.2
Interest Paid	13	5.0	1.0	•	0.2	0.3	0.8	0.5	0.9	1.2	•	•	•	6.9
Depreciation	14	4.7	1.1	0.1	0.6	1.1	2.4	1.3	1.5	2.0	•	•	•	6.0
Amortization and Depletion	15	0.6	•	•	•	0.0	0.2	0.0	0.1	0.5	•	•	•	0.7
Pensions and Other Deferred Comp.	16	1.0	0.7	1.5	0.0	0.6	0.0	0.7	0.6	1.5	•	•	•	1.1
Employee Benefits	17	3.8	0.5	5.5	1.7	2.4	0.5	1.8	1.6	3.0	•	•	•	4.6
Advertising	18	1.7	1.9	0.8	0.4	1.1	1.0	0.9	0.4	1.4	•	•	•	2.1
Other Expenses	19	13.5	21.6	7.9	22.9	7.2	12.1	9.7	6.8	12.1	•	•	•	15.0
Officers' Compensation	20	1.3	0.6	3.9	9.6	4.3	3.2	2.2	2.5	2.0	•	•	•	0.7
Operating Margin	21	•	•	9.5	5.4	5.4	7.5	6.8	4.7	7.1	•	•	•	•
Operating Margin Before Officers' Comp.	22	•	•	13.4	15.0	9.7	10.8	9.0	7.2	9.1	•	•	•	•

Selected Average Balance Sheet ($ in Thousands)

Net Receivables 23	11053	0	5	145	678	1148	4320	8638	14462	•	2657518
Inventories 24	2605	0	52	323	916	1855	5392	7904	17027	•	320102
Net Property, Plant and Equipment 25	5815	0	18	77	452	1474	1964	5642	13255	•	1241816
Total Assets 26	57114	0	101	895	3109	6580	15160	31418	70269	•	13659466
Notes and Loans Payable 27	22678	0	1	63	349	1424	3331	5121	18059	•	5830026
All Other Liabilities 28	20778	0	23	232	615	2205	4979	13056	16840	•	5038633
Net Worth 29	13659	0	76	601	2145	2951	6850	13241	35370	•	2790808

Selected Financial Ratios (Times to 1)

Current Ratio 30	1.1	•	3.5	2.9	3.2	1.8	1.9	2.1	1.5	•	1.0
Quick Ratio 31	0.8	•	1.2	1.4	1.8	0.9	1.0	1.2	0.9	•	0.7
Net Sales to Working Capital 32	13.3	•	6.8	5.4	4.3	5.9	4.6	3.8	6.4	•	53.9
Coverage Ratio 33	2.8	25.2	•	37.2	21.2	11.2	15.6	9.0	8.1	•	2.5
Total Asset Turnover 34	0.5	•	4.0	3.1	2.1	1.8	1.8	1.6	1.2	•	0.4
Inventory Turnover 35	7.0	•	4.3	4.7	4.7	3.9	3.3	4.5	2.9	•	9.9
Receivables Turnover 36	2.8	•	149.0	37.7	7.6	8.9	5.7	7.8	4.5	•	4.3
Total Liabilities to Net Worth 37	3.2	•	0.3	0.5	0.4	1.2	1.2	1.4	1.0	•	3.9
Current Assets to Working Capital 38	9.0	•	1.4	1.5	1.5	2.2	2.1	1.9	2.9	•	43.7
Current Liabilities to Working Capital 39	8.0	•	0.4	0.5	0.5	1.2	1.1	0.9	1.9	•	42.7
Working Capital to Net Sales 40	0.1	•	0.1	0.2	0.2	0.2	0.2	0.3	0.2	•	0.0
Inventory to Working Capital 41	1.2	•	0.9	0.6	0.6	1.0	0.9	0.7	1.1	•	3.0
Total Receipts to Cash Flow 42	5.7	2.2	6.2	5.4	9.1	5.5	6.3	7.9	5.3	•	5.3
Cost of Goods to Cash Flow 43	3.4	1.5	3.4	3.0	5.9	3.3	4.2	5.5	3.1	•	3.0
Cash Flow to Total Debt 44	0.1	•	2.7	1.7	0.8	0.6	0.5	0.4	0.5	•	0.1

Selected Financial Factors (in Percentages)

Debt Ratio 45	76.1	•	24.0	32.9	31.0	55.2	54.8	57.9	49.7	•	79.6
Return on Total Assets 46	7.7	•	38.5	17.0	14.4	16.8	14.3	13.3	11.5	•	7.2
Return on Equity Before Income Taxes 47	20.7	•	50.7	24.7	19.9	34.2	29.7	28.1	20.1	•	20.9
Return on Equity After Income Taxes 48	16.1	•	50.2	24.7	18.6	31.5	25.0	26.1	17.5	•	15.5
Profit Margin (Before Income Tax) 49	9.1	24.3	9.5	5.4	6.4	8.4	7.4	7.3	8.4	•	10.3
Profit Margin (After Income Tax) 50	7.1	22.0	9.4	5.4	6.0	7.7	6.3	6.7	7.3	•	7.6

Table I

Corporations with and without Net Income

VENTILATION, HEATING, A.C. & COMMERCIAL REFRIGERATION EQUIP.

MONEY AMOUNTS AND SIZE OF ASSETS IN THOUSANDS OF DOLLARS

Item Description for Accounting Period 7/05 Through 6/06	Total	Zero Assets	Under 500	500 to 1,000	1,000 to 5,000	5,000 to 10,000	10,000 to 25,000	25,000 to 50,000	50,000 to 100,000	100,000 to 250,000	250,000 to 500,000	500,000 to 2,500,000	2,500,000 and over
Number of Enterprises 1	838	35	•	•	166	55	67	49	18	15	0	8	3

Revenues ($ in Thousands)

	Total	Zero Assets	Under 500	500 to 1,000	1,000 to 5,000	5,000 to 10,000	10,000 to 25,000	25,000 to 50,000	50,000 to 100,000	100,000 to 250,000	250,000 to 500,000	500,000 to 2,500,000	2,500,000 and over
Net Sales 2	36491627	2960724	•	•	567340	536825	2158503	3218370	1792089	2943072	0	11551214	10106585
Interest 3	111113	7653	•	•	216	1689	4223	3480	3269	32233	0	24671	33460
Rents 4	6915	2	•	•	399	0	521	505	537	2883	0	942	1041
Royalties 5	117317	5890	•	•	0	0	1474	3991	3322	1755	0	8540	92345
Other Portfolio Income 6	639952	5509	•	•	32	138	2247	12415	5827	20152	0	71260	522370
Other Receipts 7	560763	18686	•	•	2180	2725	13220	18609	6203	10023	0	420910	65464
Total Receipts 8	37927687	2998464	•	•	570167	541377	2180188	3257370	1811247	3010118	0	12077537	10821265
Average Total Receipts 9	45260	85670	•	•	3435	9843	32540	66477	100625	200675	•	1509692	3607088

Operating Costs/Operating Income (%)

	Total	Zero Assets	Under 500	500 to 1,000	1,000 to 5,000	5,000 to 10,000	10,000 to 25,000	25,000 to 50,000	50,000 to 100,000	100,000 to 250,000	250,000 to 500,000	500,000 to 2,500,000	2,500,000 and over
Cost of Operations 10	74.4	80.0	•	•	67.2	74.8	69.3	70.2	69.7	71.9	•	73.6	79.2
Salaries and Wages 11	6.8	8.1	•	•	7.7	8.0	8.6	8.7	6.8	6.9	•	5.6	6.7
Taxes Paid 12	1.1	0.5	•	•	2.9	1.8	1.4	2.1	1.5	1.5	•	1.2	0.3
Interest Paid 13	2.2	1.5	•	•	0.7	0.4	0.7	0.7	1.7	2.9	•	2.3	3.3
Depreciation 14	1.0	1.5	•	•	1.4	1.2	1.1	1.3	1.7	1.7	•	1.0	0.5
Amortization and Depletion 15	0.7	0.3	•	•	0.2	0.1	0.1	0.1	0.4	0.7	•	0.5	1.7
Pensions and Other Deferred Comp. 16	0.8	1.4	•	•	0.1	1.0	0.7	0.5	0.6	1.3	•	1.0	0.4
Employee Benefits 17	1.6	1.6	•	•	2.5	1.0	1.7	2.0	1.7	2.4	•	1.3	1.7
Advertising 18	1.0	0.6	•	•	0.9	0.9	0.5	0.5	0.8	1.2	•	1.2	1.1
Other Expenses 19	8.3	8.9	•	•	11.5	4.0	9.1	7.4	9.0	8.8	•	9.4	6.1
Officers' Compensation 20	1.4	3.4	•	•	9.3	3.5	1.9	1.8	1.2	0.9	•	1.3	0.2
Operating Margin 21	0.6	•	•	•	•	3.4	5.0	4.8	5.0	1.3	•	1.8	•
Operating Margin Before Officers' Comp. 22	2.0	•	•	•	4.9	6.9	6.9	6.5	6.2	0.8	•	3.1	•

Selected Average Balance Sheet ($ in Thousands)

Net Receivables 23	6737	0	•	521	2464	4780	11193	17818	32472	• 156718 815784
Inventories 24	3872	0	•	523	1072	3850	6042	10549	18827	• 189842 292321
Net Property, Plant and Equipment 25	3909	0	•	153	954	2825	7464	12576	27461	• 108517 363594
Total Assets 26	42370	0	•	1560	6783	14332	35298	69110	174583	• 1480762 5425268
Notes and Loans Payable 27	9199	0	•	510	1267	2467	7689	18339	59155	• 285824 1157239
All Other Liabilities 28	20103	0	•	342	2200	4640	10115	20676	48452	• 621454 3217948
Net Worth 29	13068	0	•	707	3315	7225	17493	30096	66976	• 573484 1050079

Selected Financial Ratios (Times to 1)

Item	All											
Current Ratio 30	1.2	•	3.2	2.4	1.9	1.9	2.2	1.6	•	1.2	0.9	
Quick Ratio 31	0.7	•	1.7	1.8	1.1	1.2	1.4	0.9	•	0.8	0.5	
Net Sales to Working Capital 32	18.3	•	3.9	3.0	6.6	6.0	4.3	8.5	•	19.7	•	
Coverage Ratio 33	3.2	•	•	12.4	9.6	9.7	4.7	1.9	•	3.7	3.1	
Total Asset Turnover 34	1.0	•	2.2	1.4	2.2	1.9	1.4	1.1	•	1.0	0.6	
Inventory Turnover 35	8.4	•	4.4	6.8	5.8	7.6	6.6	7.5	•	5.6	9.1	
Receivables Turnover 36	6.8	•	6.7	5.9	6.5	7.4	6.2	8.8	•	4.8	8.3	
Total Liabilities to Net Worth 37	2.2	•	1.2	1.0	1.0	1.0	1.3	1.6	•	1.6	4.2	
Current Assets to Working Capital 38	5.8	•	1.4	1.7	2.1	2.1	1.8	2.7	•	5.2	•	
Current Liabilities to Working Capital 39	4.8	•	0.4	0.7	1.1	1.1	0.8	1.7	•	4.2	•	
Working Capital to Net Sales 40	0.1	•	0.3	0.3	0.2	0.2	0.2	0.1	•	0.1	•	
Inventory to Working Capital 41	1.5	•	0.7	0.3	0.7	0.6	0.5	1.0	•	1.5	•	
Total Receipts to Cash Flow 42	8.9	111.1	79.6	18.7	7.2	8.7	7.2	12.9	•	6.9	9.1	
Cost of Goods to Cash Flow 43	6.6	88.9	53.5	14.0	5.0	6.1	5.0	9.3	•	5.1	7.2	
Cash Flow to Total Debt 44	0.2	•	0.1	0.2	0.6	0.4	0.4	0.1	•	0.2	0.1	

Selected Financial Factors (in Percentages)

Item	All										
Debt Ratio 45	69.2	•	54.7	51.1	49.6	50.4	56.5	61.6	•	61.3	80.6
Return on Total Assets 46	7.2	•	•	6.6	15.0	12.5	11.1	6.0	•	8.2	6.4
Return on Equity Before Income Taxes 47	16.1	•	•	12.5	26.7	22.6	20.1	7.2	•	15.6	22.4
Return on Equity After Income Taxes 48	11.2	•	•	11.2	22.5	18.6	15.3	1.7	•	10.9	16.3
Profit Margin (Before Income Tax) 49	4.8	•	•	4.2	6.0	6.0	6.1	2.5	•	6.2	7.0
Profit Margin (After Income Tax) 50	3.4	•	•	3.8	5.1	5.0	4.6	0.6	•	4.3	5.1

Table II

Corporations with Net Income

VENTILATION, HEATING, A.C. & COMMERCIAL REFRIGERATION EQUIP.

MONEY AMOUNTS AND SIZE OF ASSETS IN THOUSANDS OF DOLLARS

Item Description for Accounting Period 7/05 Through 6/06	Total	Zero Assets	Under 500	500 to 1,000	1,000 to 5,000	5,000 to 10,000	10,000 to 25,000	25,000 to 50,000	50,000 to 100,000	100,000 to 250,000	250,000 to 500,000	500,000 to 2,500,000	2,500,000 and over
Number of Enterprises **1**	667	•	242	57	147	44	61	•	15	12	0	•	0

Revenues ($ in Thousands)

Item	Total	Zero Assets	Under 500	500 to 1,000	1,000 to 5,000	5,000 to 10,000	10,000 to 25,000	25,000 to 50,000	50,000 to 100,000	100,000 to 250,000	250,000 to 500,000	500,000 to 2,500,000	2,500,000 and over
Net Sales **2**	30606902	•	317874	153571	524735	533246	2046089	•	1403543	2245655	•	•	0
Interest **3**	83739	•	144	0	30	1468	4191	•	2344	31492	0	•	0
Rents **4**	6013	•	84	0	0	0	444	•	537	2459	0	•	0
Royalties **5**	110785	•	0	0	0	0	1474	•	3295	1580	0	•	0
Other Portfolio Income **6**	625658	•	0	0	0	138	988	•	5827	12251	0	•	0
Other Receipts **7**	518345	•	1684	125	890	2726	12477	•	3504	8921	0	•	0
Total Receipts **8**	31951442	•	319786	153696	525655	537578	2065663	•	1419050	2302358	0	•	0
Average Total Receipts **9**	47903	•	1321	2696	3576	12218	33863	•	94603	191863	•	•	•

Operating Costs/Operating Income (%)

Item	Total	Zero Assets	Under 500	500 to 1,000	1,000 to 5,000	5,000 to 10,000	10,000 to 25,000	25,000 to 50,000	50,000 to 100,000	100,000 to 250,000	250,000 to 500,000	500,000 to 2,500,000	2,500,000 and over
Cost of Operations **10**	73.8	•	52.5	73.6	65.5	74.8	69.4	•	65.2	68.5	•	•	•
Salaries and Wages **11**	6.6	•	5.9	4.3	7.9	8.0	8.2	•	7.7	6.9	•	•	•
Taxes Paid **12**	1.1	•	1.1	2.9	2.9	1.8	1.4	•	1.7	1.5	•	•	•
Interest Paid **13**	1.6	•	•	0.6	0.6	0.4	0.7	•	1.3	1.4	•	•	•
Depreciation **14**	1.0	•	0.6	2.5	1.3	1.1	1.0	•	1.6	1.8	•	•	•
Amortization and Depletion **15**	0.4	•	•	•	0.2	0.1	0.1	•	0.5	0.5	•	•	•
Pensions and Other Deferred Comp. **16**	0.8	•	0.9	0.4	0.0	1.0	0.7	•	0.8	1.5	•	•	•
Employee Benefits **17**	1.6	•	0.1	1.5	1.9	1.0	1.6	•	1.9	2.8	•	•	•
Advertising **18**	1.1	•	0.4	0.1	0.7	0.9	0.5	•	0.8	1.4	•	•	•
Other Expenses **19**	7.9	•	22.6	2.4	8.2	1.9	9.2	•	9.7	7.1	•	•	•
Officers' Compensation **20**	1.2	•	2.2	10.0	8.4	3.5	1.6	•	1.4	0.9	•	•	•
Operating Margin **21**	3.0	•	13.9	1.6	2.4	5.5	5.7	•	7.6	5.6	•	•	•
Operating Margin Before Officers' Comp. **22**	4.2	•	16.1	11.6	10.8	9.0	7.3	•	9.0	6.5	•	•	•

Selected Average Balance Sheet ($ in Thousands)

Net Receivables 23	7807	28	377	528	2024	5051	18078	34151
Inventories 24	3986	0	287	555	1368	3737	10246	19147
Net Property, Plant and Equipment 25	4430	152	55	162	1193	2733	12639	29963
Total Assets 26	40295	268	773	1493	7254	14472	66492	177572
Notes and Loans Payable 27	7988	0	209	558	1584	2389	15800	33972
All Other Liabilities 28	19285	29	381	345	2714	4733	14409	45510
Net Worth 29	13021	239	182	589	2955	7349	36283	98090

Selected Financial Ratios (Times to 1)

Current Ratio 30	1.2	3.9	1.6	3.2	2.0	2.0	3.0	1.8
Quick Ratio 31	0.7	3.7	0.9	1.6	1.5	1.2	1.9	1.1
Net Sales to Working Capital 32	18.9	15.1	11.2	4.2	4.0	6.2	3.4	6.5
Coverage Ratio 33	5.7	.	3.8	5.4	18.0	10.3	7.8	6.8
Total Asset Turnover 34	1.1	4.9	3.5	2.4	1.7	2.3	1.4	1.1
Inventory Turnover 35	8.5	.	6.9	4.2	6.6	6.2	6.0	6.7
Receivables Turnover 36	6.5	92.8	14.3	6.7	12.0	6.9	10.4	5.8
Total Liabilities to Net Worth 37	2.1	0.1	3.2	1.5	1.5	1.0	0.8	0.8
Current Assets to Working Capital 38	6.5	1.3	2.8	1.5	2.0	2.0	1.5	2.2
Current Liabilities to Working Capital 39	5.5	0.3	1.8	0.5	1.0	1.0	0.5	1.2
Working Capital to Net Sales 40	0.1	0.1	0.1	0.2	0.2	0.2	0.3	0.2
Inventory to Working Capital 41	1.6	.	1.2	0.7	0.5	0.7	0.4	0.7
Total Receipts to Cash Flow 42	7.2	2.9	39.0	14.1	14.5	6.9	5.8	7.2
Cost of Goods to Cash Flow 43	5.3	1.5	28.7	9.3	10.9	4.8	3.8	4.9
Cash Flow to Total Debt 44	0.2	15.2	0.1	0.3	0.2	0.7	0.5	0.3

Selected Financial Factors (in Percentages)

Debt Ratio 45	67.7	11.0	76.4	60.5	59.3	49.2	45.4	44.8
Return on Total Assets 46	10.6	70.9	8.1	7.5	11.1	16.9	14.0	10.2
Return on Equity Before Income Taxes 47	27.1	79.7	25.3	15.5	25.8	30.1	22.4	15.7
Return on Equity After Income Taxes 48	20.9	79.7	25.3	13.4	24.0	25.6	17.7	11.1
Profit Margin (Before Income Tax) 49	7.7	14.5	1.7	2.6	6.3	6.6	8.7	8.2
Profit Margin (After Income Tax) 50	5.9	14.5	1.7	2.2	5.9	5.6	6.9	5.8

Table I

Corporations with and without Net Income

METALWORKING MACHINERY

MONEY AMOUNTS AND SIZE OF ASSETS IN THOUSANDS OF DOLLARS

Item Description for Accounting Period 7/05 Through 6/06	Total	Zero Assets	Under 500	500 to 1,000	1,000 to 5,000	5,000 to 10,000	10,000 to 25,000	25,000 to 50,000	50,000 to 100,000	100,000 to 250,000	250,000 to 500,000	500,000 to 2,500,000	2,500,000 and over
Number of Enterprises 1	6754	125	4179	619	1479	142	129	53	14	11	0	4	0
Revenues ($ in Thousands)													
Net Sales 2	2491244	47862	1938864	790987	5570764	1593785	2883864	2170386	1130721	2528747	0	6255265	0
Interest 3	93429	5	241	1900	5204	1423	2064	1761	2654	35431	0	42746	0
Rents 4	19028	0	0	0	8248	1704	2127	241	802	4800	0	1105	0
Royalties 5	13240	0	0	0	0	0	3348	501	1	3177	0	6212	0
Other Portfolio Income 6	2128262	0	358	187	23214	9400	24028	4898	14569	50234	0	2001371	0
Other Receipts 7	346238	1951	16096	3413	25779	3856	30726	14391	7707	99950	0	142374	0
Total Receipts 8	2751441	49818	1955559	796487	5633209	1610168	2946157	2192178	1156454	2722339	0	8449073	0
Average Total Receipts 9	4073	399	468	1287	3809	11339	22838	41362	82604	247485	•	2112268	•
Operating Costs/Operating Income (%)													
Cost of Operations 10	65.7	104.4	34.7	59.4	67.9	66.6	69.1	69.9	68.5	70.0	•	68.5	•
Salaries and Wages 11	7.7	16.5	11.2	6.3	5.1	4.2	7.6	6.6	8.0	10.8	•	9.0	•
Taxes Paid 12	2.9	2.2	4.4	4.7	3.8	2.8	2.4	2.7	2.5	1.8	•	2.1	•
Interest Paid 13	2.1	1.2	2.1	1.3	0.9	0.9	1.2	1.4	1.0	2.7	•	4.3	•
Depreciation 14	2.5	1.1	4.0	3.3	2.9	3.4	2.9	2.7	2.7	1.2	•	1.4	•
Amortization and Depletion 15	0.3	0.0	0.2	•	0.0	0.0	0.0	0.4	0.4	0.2	•	0.8	•
Pensions and Other Deferred Comp. 16	0.6	•	0.1	0.6	0.4	0.7	0.7	0.5	1.6	0.6	•	0.8	•
Employee Benefits 17	2.2	3.4	2.7	3.1	2.0	2.4	2.0	2.3	2.4	1.4	•	2.6	•
Advertising 18	0.4	0.1	0.1	0.1	0.2	0.2	0.4	0.4	0.4	0.5	•	0.7	•
Other Expenses 19	11.0	140.2	30.0	11.5	7.6	7.4	8.0	8.0	8.7	8.9	•	11.7	•
Officers' Compensation 20	2.8	0.7	6.5	8.2	5.0	3.7	2.3	1.8	1.3	0.7	•	0.6	•
Operating Margin 21	1.7	•	4.0	1.4	4.0	7.6	3.4	3.3	2.6	1.2	•	•	•
Operating Margin Before Officers' Comp. 22	4.6	•	10.5	9.6	9.1	11.4	5.7	5.1	3.9	1.9	•	•	•

Selected Average Balance Sheet ($ in Thousands)

Net Receivables 23	658	0	54	188	623	1756	3787	9338	13486	59995	•	274825
Inventories 24	493	0	21	145	400	1425	3088	7753	14585	47241	•	206590
Net Property, Plant and Equipment 25	574	0	48	121	615	2168	4383	8454	16255	29392	•	204849
Total Assets 26	3423	0	159	642	2218	6838	15204	34645	72073	205987	•	2683745
Notes and Loans Payable 27	1027	0	145	299	680	1735	4555	11126	11017	48329	•	757988
All Other Liabilities 28	997	0	45	106	478	1728	4070	10853	18381	63925	•	866552
Net Worth 29	1399	0	-31	237	1060	3376	6579	12666	42675	93734	•	1059205

Selected Financial Ratios (Times to 1)

Current Ratio 30	1.5	•	1.5	2.6	1.9	2.0	1.6	1.5	2.0	1.9	•	1.0
Quick Ratio 31	0.8	•	1.1	1.9	1.2	1.1	0.9	0.8	1.0	1.1	•	0.5
Net Sales to Working Capital 32	7.6	•	12.3	4.4	5.8	5.5	6.3	5.4	4.2	3.7	•	
Coverage Ratio 33	6.8	•	3.3	2.6	6.9	10.8	5.7	4.0	6.3	4.6	•	8.7
Total Asset Turnover 34	1.1	•	2.9	2.0	1.7	1.6	1.5	1.2	1.1	1.1	•	0.6
Inventory Turnover 35	4.9	•	7.6	5.2	6.4	5.2	5.0	3.7	3.8	3.4	•	5.2
Receivables Turnover 36	5.2	•	9.5	6.9	6.3	6.6	6.2	4.7	4.9	4.7	•	3.8
Total Liabilities to Net Worth 37	1.4	•		1.7	1.1	1.0	1.3	1.7	0.7	1.2	•	1.5
Current Assets to Working Capital 38	3.2	•	2.9	1.6	2.1	2.0	2.6	2.9	2.0	2.1	•	
Current Liabilities to Working Capital 39	2.2	•	1.9	0.6	1.1	1.0	1.6	1.9	1.0	1.1	•	
Working Capital to Net Sales 40	0.1	•	0.1	0.2	0.2	0.2	0.2	0.2	0.2	0.3	•	
Inventory to Working Capital 41	1.1	•	0.6	0.4	0.7	0.7	1.0	1.2	0.8	0.8	•	
Total Receipts to Cash Flow 42	6.6	•	3.5	10.1	10.2	7.3	9.0	9.3	8.5	6.7	•	4.7
Cost of Goods to Cash Flow 43	4.3	•	1.2	6.0	6.9	4.9	6.2	6.5	5.8	4.7	•	3.2
Cash Flow to Total Debt 44	0.3	•	0.7	0.3	0.3	0.4	0.3	0.2	0.2	0.3	•	0.2

Selected Financial Factors (in Percentages)

Debt Ratio 45	59.1	•	119.4	63.1	52.2	50.6	56.7	63.4	40.8	54.5	•	60.5
Return on Total Assets 46	15.7	•	20.3	6.9	10.1	15.7	9.8	6.8	7.0	13.8	•	21.9
Return on Equity Before Income Taxes 47	32.7	•		11.3	18.1	28.8	18.7	14.0	9.9	23.7	•	49.2
Return on Equity After Income Taxes 48	25.8	•		10.7	17.1	26.5	17.0	12.0	8.3	20.1	•	36.3
Profit Margin (Before Income Tax) 49	12.4	•	4.8	2.1	5.1	8.7	5.5	4.3	5.2	9.7	•	33.3
Profit Margin (After Income Tax) 50	9.8	•	4.8	2.0	4.8	8.0	5.0	3.7	4.4	8.2	•	24.6

Table II
Corporations with Net Income

METALWORKING MACHINERY

MONEY AMOUNTS AND SIZE OF ASSETS IN THOUSANDS OF DOLLARS

Item Description for Accounting Period 7/05 Through 6/06	Total	Zero Assets	Under 500	500 to 1,000	1,000 to 5,000	5,000 to 10,000	10,000 to 25,000	25,000 to 50,000	50,000 to 100,000	100,000 to 250,000	250,000 to 500,000	500,000 to 2,500,000	2,500,000 and over
Number of Enterprises 1	4081	13	2281	452	1041	120	109	41	·	·	0	·	0
Revenues ($ in Thousands)													
Net Sales 2	21123142	12264	1447795	632260	4336750	1446805	2433842	1716477	·	·	0	·	0
Interest 3	86245	5	126	967	4024	708	1865	1724	·	·	0	·	0
Rents 4	17072	0	0	0	8057	1150	2095	241	·	·	0	·	0
Royalties 5	13239	0	0	0	0	0	3348	501	·	·	0	·	0
Other Portfolio Income 6	2108076	0	358	70	15174	8506	22108	4831	·	·	0	·	0
Other Receipts 7	315010	1731	13720	3181	14090	3331	15690	9338	·	·	0	·	0
Total Receipts 8	23662784	14000	1461999	636478	4378095	1460500	2478948	1733112	·	·	0	·	0
Average Total Receipts 9	5798	1077	641	1408	4206	12171	22743	42271	·	·	·	·	·
Operating Costs/Operating Income (%)													
Cost of Operations 10	65.9	60.1	33.8	57.4	66.0	66.0	68.2	68.1	·	·	·	·	·
Salaries and Wages 11	7.0	8.4	7.1	7.1	5.0	3.3	7.1	6.5	·	·	·	·	·
Taxes Paid 12	2.8	0.6	4.7	4.6	3.5	3.0	2.2	2.8	·	·	·	·	·
Interest Paid 13	2.1	2.5	1.8	1.2	0.7	0.9	1.0	1.3	·	·	·	·	·
Depreciation 14	2.4	3.0	3.0	3.9	3.1	3.4	2.7	2.6	·	·	·	·	·
Amortization and Depletion 15	0.3	0.2	0.0	·	0.0	0.0	0.0	0.4	·	·	·	·	·
Pensions and Other Deferred Comp. 16	0.7	·	0.0	0.6	0.5	0.6	0.7	0.6	·	·	·	·	·
Employee Benefits 17	2.2	0.1	2.6	2.9	1.7	2.5	1.9	2.0	·	·	·	·	·
Advertising 18	0.4	0.3	0.1	0.1	0.1	0.2	0.4	0.5	·	·	·	·	·
Other Expenses 19	9.8	10.5	33.1	11.3	6.5	7.6	7.4	7.5	·	·	·	·	·
Officers' Compensation 20	2.8	·	7.4	8.4	5.2	3.4	2.5	1.9	·	·	·	·	·
Operating Margin 21	3.8	14.4	6.5	2.5	7.8	9.3	6.0	5.9	·	·	·	·	·
Operating Margin Before Officers' Comp. 22	6.6	14.4	13.9	10.9	13.0	12.6	8.4	7.7	·	·	·	·	·

Selected Average Balance Sheet ($ in Thousands)

Net Receivables 23	909	0	83	201	627	1983	3947	9041
Inventories 24	611	0	19	135	290	1272	2885	6883
Net Property, Plant and Equipment 25	789	0	49	146	679	2313	4042	8388
Total Assets 26	4813	0	209	665	2100	6712	15290	34970
Notes and Loans Payable 27	1305	0	162	307	455	1679	3765	10288
All Other Liabilities 28	1404	0	55	103	431	1683	3696	9123
Net Worth 29	2103	0	-9	255	1214	3350	7830	15560

Selected Financial Ratios (Times to 1)

Current Ratio 30	1.5	•	1.9	3.1	2.2	2.0	1.9	1.8
Quick Ratio 31	0.8	•	1.5	2.3	1.5	1.3	1.1	0.9
Net Sales to Working Capital 32	7.5	•	8.6	4.1	5.7	5.9	5.0	4.4
Coverage Ratio 33	8.8	12.5	5.2	3.7	14.4	12.0	9.2	6.2
Total Asset Turnover 34	1.1	•	3.0	2.1	2.0	1.8	1.5	1.2
Inventory Turnover 35	5.6	•	11.3	5.9	9.5	6.3	5.3	4.1
Receivables Turnover 36	5.5	•	10.7	9.7	8.0	6.8	6.7	5.7
Total Liabilities to Net Worth 37	1.3	•	•	1.6	0.7	1.0	1.0	1.2
Current Assets to Working Capital 38	3.1	•	2.1	1.5	1.9	2.0	2.1	2.3
Current Liabilities to Working Capital 39	2.1	•	1.1	0.5	0.9	1.0	1.1	1.3
Working Capital to Net Sales 40	0.1	•	0.1	0.2	0.2	0.2	0.2	0.2
Inventory to Working Capital 41	1.0	•	0.2	0.3	0.5	0.6	0.8	1.0
Total Receipts to Cash Flow 42	5.9	2.6	2.9	9.8	7.7	6.5	7.8	7.9
Cost of Goods to Cash Flow 43	3.9	1.6	1.0	5.6	5.1	4.3	5.3	5.4
Cash Flow to Total Debt 44	0.3	•	1.0	0.3	0.6	0.6	0.4	0.3

Selected Financial Factors (in Percentages)

Debt Ratio 45	56.3	•	104.2	61.7	42.2	50.1	48.8	55.5
Return on Total Assets 46	19.5	•	28.2	9.2	18.6	20.0	12.7	9.8
Return on Equity Before Income Taxes 47	39.6	•	•	17.4	30.0	36.7	22.1	18.5
Return on Equity After Income Taxes 48	32.0	•	•	16.7	28.7	33.9	20.4	16.4
Profit Margin (Before Income Tax) 49	16.1	28.5	7.5	3.2	8.7	10.2	7.8	6.9
Profit Margin (After Income Tax) 50	13.0	28.5	7.4	3.0	8.4	9.4	7.2	6.1

Table I

Corporations with and without Net Income

ENGINE, TURBINE AND POWER TRANSMISSION EQUIPMENT

MONEY AMOUNTS AND SIZE OF ASSETS IN THOUSANDS OF DOLLARS

Item Description for Accounting Period 7/05 Through 6/06		Total	Zero Assets	Under 500	500 to 1,000	1,000 to 5,000	5,000 to 10,000	10,000 to 25,000	25,000 to 50,000	50,000 to 100,000	100,000 to 250,000	250,000 to 500,000	500,000 to 2,500,000	2,500,000 and over
Number of Enterprises	1	257	3	•	•	121	25	29	11	6	12	0	8	4
Revenues ($ in Thousands)														
Net Sales	2	48972066	599924	•	•	572732	328969	624072	403260	411970	2993037	0	7208098	35763778
Interest	3	737030	8269	•	•	702	204	953	1409	10081	22505	0	78586	613883
Rents	4	498546	322	•	•	0	0	0	361	0	1345	0	31224	465294
Royalties	5	675440	1607	•	•	273	0	0	0	68	7526	0	27230	638735
Other Portfolio Income	6	441870	0	•	•	211	1445	297	213	164	8608	0	141981	288950
Other Receipts	7	315231	13691	•	•	254	2165	1646	1094	1535	25411	0	171732	97705
Total Receipts	8	51640183	623813	•	•	574172	332783	626968	406337	423818	3058432	0	7658851	37868345
Average Total Receipts	9	200935	207938	•	•	4745	13311	21620	36940	70636	254869	•	957356	9467086
Operating Costs/Operating Income (%)														
Cost of Operations	10	72.4	64.2	•	•	64.8	62.8	69.6	74.4	78.2	70.7	•	73.9	72.6
Salaries and Wages	11	13.8	15.5	•	•	5.7	10.4	6.7	6.2	7.6	8.0	•	7.3	16.0
Taxes Paid	12	1.5	2.2	•	•	2.0	2.4	2.6	1.3	2.4	2.0	•	1.5	1.4
Interest Paid	13	2.4	0.8	•	•	1.2	2.4	1.6	1.1	3.2	2.0	•	3.9	2.2
Depreciation	14	2.8	0.7	•	•	2.7	1.8	2.6	3.3	2.5	2.3	•	2.7	2.9
Amortization and Depletion	15	0.4	0.1	•	•	0.1	0.1	0.4	0.8	1.7	0.3	•	1.3	0.3
Pensions and Other Deferred Comp.	16	2.6	1.0	•	•	1.3	0.0	0.3	0.3	0.4	0.8	•	1.2	3.1
Employee Benefits	17	1.8	3.8	•	•	1.9	1.3	1.8	1.9	2.0	2.6	•	1.3	1.7
Advertising	18	0.6	0.1	•	•	0.5	0.1	0.2	0.1	0.6	0.5	•	0.8	0.6
Other Expenses	19	2.9	13.3	•	•	7.0	9.8	10.3	4.5	14.9	7.5	•	6.2	1.2
Officers' Compensation	20	0.6	0.4	•	•	1.9	1.7	2.5	0.9	1.4	0.8	•	0.4	0.5
Operating Margin	21	•	•	•	•	10.8	7.1	1.3	5.1	•	2.4	•	•	•
Operating Margin Before Officers' Comp.	22	•	•	•	•	12.7	8.7	3.8	6.1	•	3.2	•	•	•

Selected Average Balance Sheet ($ in Thousands)

Net Receivables 23	31908	0	•	626	2154	3034	9206	12226	46108	•	252425	1308785
Inventories 24	21764	0	•	567	1028	4721	9062	9689	27481	•	147388	904076
Net Property, Plant and Equipment 25	27289	0	•	885	1038	3171	10085	9767	44975	•	198759	1121872
Total Assets 26	198564	0	•	2894	6653	15422	37635	72569	225099	•	1119880	9381956
Notes and Loans Payable 27	38472	0	•	1393	3609	3426	7064	18750	60921	•	365107	1421587
All Other Liabilities 28	100926	0	•	461	1872	4624	10741	36635	63972	•	443769	5261308
Net Worth 29	59166	0	•	1040	1172	7372	19830	17184	100206	•	311005	2699062

Selected Financial Ratios (Times to 1)

Current Ratio 30	1.4	•	•	1.8	2.4	1.9	2.3	1.7	1.7	•	1.6	1.2
Quick Ratio 31	0.7	•	•	0.9	1.5	1.0	1.2	1.2	1.0	•	0.9	0.6
Net Sales to Working Capital 32	9.2	•	•	6.6	5.0	4.5	2.6	4.0	5.2	•	4.4	14.1
Coverage Ratio 33	2.6	3.2	•	10.0	4.4	2.1	6.3	•	3.4	•	2.6	2.6
Total Asset Turnover 34	1.0	•	•	1.6	2.0	1.4	1.0	0.9	1.1	•	0.8	1.0
Inventory Turnover 35	6.3	•	•	5.4	8.0	3.2	3.0	5.5	6.4	•	4.5	7.2
Receivables Turnover 36	6.3	•	•	9.2	8.2	5.7	5.3	5.5	7.0	•	4.4	6.8
Total Liabilities to Net Worth 37	2.4	•	•	1.8	4.7	1.1	0.9	3.2	1.2	•	2.6	2.5
Current Assets to Working Capital 38	3.8	•	•	2.2	1.7	2.1	1.8	2.5	2.3	•	2.6	5.4
Current Liabilities to Working Capital 39	2.8	•	•	1.2	0.7	1.1	0.8	1.5	1.3	•	1.6	4.4
Working Capital to Net Sales 40	0.1	•	•	0.2	0.2	0.2	0.4	0.2	0.2	•	0.2	0.1
Inventory to Working Capital 41	1.1	•	•	1.0	0.6	0.9	0.8	0.5	0.8	•	0.8	1.4
Total Receipts to Cash Flow 42	22.0	7.8	•	6.3	6.2	9.4	11.4	93.2	9.7	•	9.6	44.0
Cost of Goods to Cash Flow 43	16.0	5.0	•	4.1	3.9	6.6	8.5	72.9	6.8	•	7.1	31.9
Cash Flow to Total Debt 44	0.1	•	•	0.4	0.4	0.3	0.2	0.0	0.2	•	0.1	0.0

Selected Financial Factors (in Percentages)

Debt Ratio 45	70.2	•	•	64.1	82.4	52.2	47.3	76.3	55.5	•	72.2	71.2
Return on Total Assets 46	6.0	•	•	20.0	21.0	4.7	6.8	•	7.5	•	8.0	5.4
Return on Equity Before Income Taxes 47	12.5	•	•	50.2	92.5	5.2	10.8	•	11.9	•	17.5	11.4
Return on Equity After Income Taxes 48	8.6	•	•	37.1	76.8	1.4	8.1	•	8.2	•	13.1	7.7
Profit Margin (Before Income Tax) 49	3.9	1.8	•	11.0	8.2	1.8	5.9	•	4.8	•	6.0	3.4
Profit Margin (After Income Tax) 50	2.7	1.8	•	8.2	6.8	0.5	4.4	•	3.3	•	4.5	2.3

Table II
Corporations with Net Income

ENGINE, TURBINE AND POWER TRANSMISSION EQUIPMENT

MONEY AMOUNTS AND SIZE OF ASSETS IN THOUSANDS OF DOLLARS

Item Description for Accounting Period 7/05 Through 6/06	Total	Zero Assets	Under 500	500 to 1,000	1,000 to 5,000	5,000 to 10,000	10,000 to 25,000	25,000 to 50,000	50,000 to 100,000	100,000 to 250,000	250,000 to 500,000	500,000 to 2,500,000	2,500,000 and over
Number of Enterprises 1	197	•	0	32	85	25	20	•	•	•	0	•	•
Revenues ($ in Thousands)													
Net Sales 2	45698622	•	0	64924	526486	328969	579917	•	•	•	0	•	•
Interest 3	718715	•	0	437	520	204	204	•	•	•	0	•	•
Rents 4	497298	•	0	0	0	0	0	•	•	•	0	•	•
Royalties 5	654128	•	0	0	0	0	0	•	•	•	0	•	•
Other Portfolio Income 6	405316	•	0	0	211	1445	294	•	•	•	0	•	•
Other Receipts 7	285930	•	0	0	255	2165	1436	•	•	•	0	•	•
Total Receipts 8	48260009	•	0	65361	527472	332783	581851	•	•	•	0	•	•
Average Total Receipts 9	244975	•	•	2043	6206	13311	29093	•	•	•	•	•	•
Operating Costs/Operating Income (%)													
Cost of Operations 10	72.9	•	•	25.1	63.7	62.8	67.8	•	•	•	•	•	•
Salaries and Wages 11	13.6	•	•	25.0	5.5	10.4	5.2	•	•	•	•	•	•
Taxes Paid 12	1.4	•	•	2.7	2.0	2.4	2.5	•	•	•	•	•	•
Interest Paid 13	2.3	•	•	0.0	1.1	2.4	1.5	•	•	•	•	•	•
Depreciation 14	2.8	•	•	3.6	2.8	1.8	2.5	•	•	•	•	•	•
Amortization and Depletion 15	0.4	•	•	•	0.1	0.1	0.3	•	•	•	•	•	•
Pensions and Other Deferred Comp. 16	2.6	•	•	0.6	1.4	0.0	0.3	•	•	•	•	•	•
Employee Benefits 17	1.6	•	•	0.4	1.9	1.3	1.9	•	•	•	•	•	•
Advertising 18	0.7	•	•	0.7	0.5	0.1	0.2	•	•	•	•	•	•
Other Expenses 19	1.8	•	•	16.0	7.1	9.8	9.0	•	•	•	•	•	•
Officers' Compensation 20	0.6	•	•	5.0	1.7	1.7	2.1	•	•	•	•	•	•
Operating Margin 21	•	•	•	20.8	12.2	7.1	6.8	•	•	•	•	•	•
Operating Margin Before Officers' Comp. 22	•	•	•	25.9	13.9	8.7	8.9	•	•	•	•	•	•

Selected Average Balance Sheet ($ in Thousands)

Net Receivables 23	35328		4	871	2154	4033
Inventories 24	25971		0	779	1615	5060
Net Property, Plant and Equipment 25	34042		37	1014	1038	3912
Total Assets 26	231584		820	3262	6653	17093
Notes and Loans Payable 27	43943		21	1176	3609	4261
All Other Liabilities 28	116541		5	526	1872	6240
Net Worth 29	71101		794	1561	1172	6592

Selected Financial Ratios (Times to 1)

Current Ratio 30	1.4	145.1	2.1	2.4	1.4
Quick Ratio 31	0.7	129.6	1.1	1.5	0.6
Net Sales to Working Capital 32	9.3	2.7	5.5	5.0	8.9
Coverage Ratio 33	3.1	451.4	12.4	4.4	5.8
Total Asset Turnover 34	1.0	2.5	1.9	2.0	1.7
Inventory Turnover 35	6.5	.	5.1	5.1	3.9
Receivables Turnover 36	6.9	1073.1	9.5	12.2	6.9
Total Liabilities to Net Worth 37	2.3	0.0	1.1	4.7	1.6
Current Assets to Working Capital 38	3.6	1.0	1.9	1.7	3.3
Current Liabilities to Working Capital 39	2.6	0.0	0.9	0.7	2.3
Working Capital to Net Sales 40	0.1	0.4	0.2	0.2	0.1
Inventory to Working Capital 41	1.1	.	0.9	0.6	1.5
Total Receipts to Cash Flow 42	21.9	3.1	5.8	6.2	6.8
Cost of Goods to Cash Flow 43	15.9	0.8	3.7	3.9	4.6
Cash Flow to Total Debt 44	0.1	25.0	0.6	0.4	0.4

Selected Financial Factors (in Percentages)

Debt Ratio 45	69.3	3.2	52.2	82.4	61.4
Return on Total Assets 46	7.3	53.3	25.5	21.0	14.6
Return on Equity Before Income Taxes 47	16.2	55.0	49.0	92.5	31.4
Return on Equity After Income Taxes 48	11.9	36.3	36.6	76.8	25.3
Profit Margin (Before Income Tax) 49	5.0	21.5	12.3	8.2	7.1
Profit Margin (After Income Tax) 50	3.7	14.2	9.2	6.8	5.8

Table I
Corporations with and without Net Income

OTHER GENERAL PURPOSE MACHINERY

MONEY AMOUNTS AND SIZE OF ASSETS IN THOUSANDS OF DOLLARS

Item Description for Accounting Period 7/05 Through 6/06	Total	Zero Assets	Under 500	500 to 1,000	1,000 to 5,000	5,000 to 10,000	10,000 to 25,000	25,000 to 50,000	50,000 to 100,000	100,000 to 250,000	250,000 to 500,000	500,000 to 2,500,000	2,500,000 and over
Number of Enterprises 1	7288	309	5331	442	704	211	147	61	27	23	12	15	7
Revenues ($ in Thousands)													
Net Sales 2	65256901	288357	1582638	707032	3070220	2494952	3999799	2584519	2708356	4362246	5054195	10805226	27599360
Interest 3	1335516	932	1536	789	2300	6468	1598	3467	4331	16796	17462	128241	1151596
Rents 4	14961	4	0	1084	630	522	1331	580	631	2262	2518	528	4871
Royalties 5	661699	544	0	0	5946	0	51	222	47	6610	8705	123611	515964
Other Portfolio Income 6	1877339	97	0	0	6490	749	35803	4536	25737	153708	263064	184889	1202262
Other Receipts 7	666828	90	4963	1042	27712	13770	32245	16488	52026	21698	41080	85023	370697
Total Receipts 8	69813244	290024	1589137	709947	3113298	2516461	4070827	2609812	2791128	4563320	5387024	11327518	30844750
Average Total Receipts 9	9579	939	298	1606	4422	11926	27693	42784	103375	198405	448919	755168	4406393
Operating Costs/Operating Income (%)													
Cost of Operations 10	68.1	61.3	37.2	62.3	65.0	66.4	71.4	71.3	73.8	71.3	66.3	64.4	70.6
Salaries and Wages 11	8.8	10.2	13.8	8.0	9.7	9.0	7.8	8.0	6.3	8.3	9.3	10.7	8.1
Taxes Paid 12	1.7	2.0	4.1	2.8	2.3	2.4	2.0	1.9	1.5	1.6	2.0	1.6	1.4
Interest Paid 13	3.9	1.0	0.6	0.8	1.1	1.2	0.7	1.6	1.4	1.4	1.6	2.7	6.9
Depreciation 14	1.8	1.9	3.6	1.4	2.0	1.6	1.5	1.8	2.0	1.5	2.0	1.8	1.8
Amortization and Depletion 15	0.8	6.0	0.1	0.0	0.1	0.3	0.1	0.8	0.5	0.9	0.5	1.3	0.8
Pensions and Other Deferred Comp. 16	0.9	•	0.3	0.7	0.6	0.5	0.5	0.7	0.5	0.8	0.7	1.3	1.0
Employee Benefits 17	2.4	3.1	3.8	1.1	2.2	2.1	2.1	1.7	1.5	1.8	2.2	3.3	2.4
Advertising 18	0.6	0.4	0.9	1.2	0.5	0.7	0.5	0.4	0.4	0.7	0.9	0.4	0.6
Other Expenses 19	10.8	34.2	23.6	12.8	10.7	9.1	6.9	7.3	12.2	7.2	9.2	11.6	11.3
Officers' Compensation 20	1.6	0.7	10.5	7.0	5.0	3.4	2.4	1.6	1.1	1.1	3.3	0.7	0.4
Operating Margin 21	•	•	1.5	2.0	0.6	3.4	4.2	2.9	•	3.3	1.9	0.1	•
Operating Margin Before Officers' Comp. 22	0.1	•	12.0	9.0	5.7	6.8	6.6	4.4	•	4.4	5.3	0.8	•

Selected Average Balance Sheet ($ in Thousands)

Net Receivables 23	1523	0	23	138	697	1862	4017	6809	19490	33784	82670	154996	629472
Inventories 24	1062	0	22	264	571	1762	3986	6763	14728	25215	54528	83239	407635
Net Property, Plant and Equipment 25	1022	0	41	158	326	1510	2992	6111	13590	24000	55476	81088	428560
Total Assets 26	15436	0	119	668	1939	7475	15002	33807	73872	161209	361325	935755	11469553
Notes and Loans Payable 27	3607	0	99	192	1065	2534	3848	9479	22559	36280	65226	221823	2527589
All Other Liabilities 28	4703	0	40	180	935	2475	4970	9603	24601	52215	107855	336321	3325996
Net Worth 29	7126	0	-20	295	-62	2466	6185	14726	26712	72714	188243	377611	5615968

Selected Financial Ratios (Times to 1)

Current Ratio 30	1.4	•	1.6	2.4	1.6	1.5	1.7	1.7	1.5	1.5	1.7	1.7	1.1
Quick Ratio 31	0.7	•	•	1.2	1.0	0.8	0.9	0.9	0.8	0.8	1.0	1.0	0.6
Net Sales to Working Capital 32	8.6	•	11.6	5.9	8.2	6.8	6.0	5.2	7.2	7.3	5.1	4.8	24.0
Coverage Ratio 33	2.6	•	•	4.1	2.9	4.6	9.5	3.4	2.5	6.6	6.6	3.1	2.1
Total Asset Turnover 34	0.6	•	2.5	2.4	2.2	1.6	1.8	1.3	1.4	1.2	1.2	0.8	0.3
Inventory Turnover 35	5.7	•	4.9	3.8	5.0	4.5	4.9	4.5	5.0	5.4	5.1	5.6	6.8
Receivables Turnover 36	6.0	•	13.8	12.0	5.9	6.1	6.9	6.9	5.9	6.4	5.0	5.3	5.9
Total Liabilities to Net Worth 37	1.2	•	•	1.3	•	2.0	1.4	1.3	1.8	1.2	0.9	1.5	1.0
Current Assets to Working Capital 38	3.7	•	2.8	1.7	2.7	2.9	2.4	2.4	3.0	3.1	2.4	2.4	9.9
Current Liabilities to Working Capital 39	2.7	•	1.8	0.7	1.7	1.9	1.4	1.4	2.0	2.1	1.4	1.4	8.9
Working Capital to Net Sales 40	0.1	•	0.1	0.2	0.1	0.1	0.2	0.2	0.1	0.1	0.2	0.2	0.0
Inventory to Working Capital 41	1.1	•	1.2	0.8	1.0	1.0	0.9	0.9	1.1	1.0	0.7	0.6	2.7
Total Receipts to Cash Flow 42	7.1	8.1	5.8	7.8	9.9	8.9	9.2	11.0	8.5	9.3	6.3	6.6	6.5
Cost of Goods to Cash Flow 43	4.9	5.0	2.2	4.9	6.4	5.9	6.6	7.8	6.3	6.6	4.2	4.3	4.6
Cash Flow to Total Debt 44	0.2	•	0.4	0.5	0.2	0.3	0.3	0.2	0.2	0.2	0.4	0.2	0.1

Selected Financial Factors (in Percentages)

Debt Ratio 45	53.8	116.8	55.8	103.2	67.0	58.8	56.4	63.8	54.9	47.9	59.6	51.0
Return on Total Assets 46	5.8	6.3	7.6	7.0	8.7	12.0	6.8	4.6	11.3	12.3	6.5	4.9
Return on Equity Before Income Taxes 47	7.7	•	13.1	•	20.6	26.1	11.0	7.5	21.3	20.0	11.0	5.1
Return on Equity After Income Taxes 48	5.9	•	9.9	•	16.9	22.6	8.7	3.0	15.9	15.2	8.7	3.9
Profit Margin (Before Income Tax) 49	6.1	1.9	2.4	2.0	4.3	5.9	3.8	2.0	8.2	9.0	5.8	7.3
Profit Margin (After Income Tax) 50	4.7	1.9	1.8	1.5	3.5	5.1	3.0	0.8	6.1	6.8	4.5	5.6

135

Table II
Corporations with Net Income

OTHER GENERAL PURPOSE MACHINERY

MONEY AMOUNTS AND SIZE OF ASSETS IN THOUSANDS OF DOLLARS

Item Description for Accounting Period 7/05 Through 6/06		Total	Zero Assets	Under 500	500 to 1,000	1,000 to 5,000	5,000 to 10,000	10,000 to 25,000	25,000 to 50,000	50,000 to 100,000	100,000 to 250,000	250,000 to 500,000	500,000 to 2,500,000	2,500,000 and over
Number of Enterprises	1	3759	19	2481	327	531	166	122	47	22	19	•	11	•
Revenues ($ in Thousands)														
Net Sales	2	53486336	9134	949064	534907	2658906	2031166	3350906	2154717	2085080	3474135	•	8410541	•
Interest	3	920607	0	0	738	2013	6452	1291	2802	4150	16137	•	45375	•
Rents	4	13471	0	0	1084	224	377	1081	575	631	1924	•	211	•
Royalties	5	640713	0	0	0	5946	0	51	222	47	4881	•	117220	•
Other Portfolio Income	6	1807409	0	0	0	2570	749	32390	4516	21208	149427	•	177299	•
Other Receipts	7	448800	260	0	805	26943	7002	28870	13606	39069	15813	•	47772	•
Total Receipts	8	57317336	9394	949064	537534	2696602	2045746	3414589	2176438	2150185	3662317	•	8798418	•
Average Total Receipts	9	15248	494	383	1644	5078	12324	27988	46307	97736	192754	•	799856	•
Operating Costs/Operating Income (%)														
Cost of Operations	10	66.5	75.2	24.2	58.4	65.3	64.0	68.9	70.8	69.0	67.6	•	62.2	•
Salaries and Wages	11	8.9	1.2	16.8	9.5	9.0	9.2	7.9	7.7	7.1	8.5	•	11.2	•
Taxes Paid	12	1.8	2.5	3.8	3.0	2.1	2.6	1.9	1.8	1.5	1.7	•	1.6	•
Interest Paid	13	2.8	0.7	0.5	0.8	0.6	0.9	0.6	1.2	1.2	1.7	•	2.2	•
Depreciation	14	1.8	•	2.2	1.6	1.8	1.6	1.3	1.8	1.6	1.8	•	1.9	•
Amortization and Depletion	15	0.7	•	•	0.0	0.0	0.1	0.1	0.2	0.3	1.1	•	1.4	•
Pensions and Other Deferred Comp.	16	1.0	•	0.5	1.0	0.6	0.6	0.4	0.7	0.7	1.0	•	1.3	•
Employee Benefits	17	2.5	1.6	1.6	1.3	2.1	1.8	2.1	1.7	1.5	1.8	•	3.7	•
Advertising	18	0.6	•	0.3	0.9	0.6	0.7	0.6	0.4	0.5	0.8	•	0.4	•
Other Expenses	19	10.8	15.2	20.1	12.6	9.9	8.9	6.9	6.4	11.0	7.9	•	11.1	•
Officers' Compensation	20	1.6	0.8	11.6	6.6	4.9	3.6	2.6	1.6	1.1	1.2	•	0.8	•
Operating Margin	21	1.0	2.8	18.4	4.3	3.1	6.1	6.6	5.7	4.6	4.6	•	2.3	•
Operating Margin Before Officers' Comp.	22	2.5	3.6	30.1	10.9	8.0	9.7	9.2	7.2	5.6	5.9	•	3.1	•

Selected Average Balance Sheet ($ in Thousands)

Net Receivables 23	2464	0	28	151	730	1966	4078	7197	17794	28047	164469
Inventories 24	1696	0	13	120	531	1514	3934	6679	13972	23667	80850
Net Property, Plant and Equipment 25	1599	0	30	185	281	1394	2631	6673	13588	25797	86084
Total Assets 26	22254	93	598	1924	7502	14548	33340	72137	163578	972222	
Notes and Loans Payable 27	4306	0	52	198	536	2381	3605	8999	19470	38908	227009
All Other Liabilities 28	6798	14	176	1105	2428	4373	8314	21444	44528	258945	
Net Worth 29	11150	26	224	283	2693	6570	16027	31222	80142	486268	

Selected Financial Ratios (Times to 1)

Current Ratio 30	1.4	•	2.9	2.0	1.9	1.7	1.8	2.0	1.5	1.6	1.6
Quick Ratio 31	0.8	•	2.6	1.4	1.2	0.9	0.9	1.0	0.8	0.8	1.1
Net Sales to Working Capital 32	8.2	•	9.7	8.4	7.2	5.5	5.7	4.7	7.0	6.8	5.5
Coverage Ratio 33	4.1	9.0	37.2	7.0	8.0	8.8	16.1	6.7	7.6	7.0	4.6
Total Asset Turnover 34	0.6	•	4.1	2.7	2.6	1.6	1.9	1.4	1.3	1.1	0.8
Inventory Turnover 35	5.6	•	7.1	7.9	6.1	5.2	4.8	4.9	4.7	5.2	5.9
Receivables Turnover 36	5.8	•	11.8	21.6	6.5	6.2	7.2	7.6	5.9	6.6	6.1
Total Liabilities to Net Worth 37	1.0	•	2.6	1.7	5.8	1.8	1.2	1.1	1.3	1.0	1.0
Current Assets to Working Capital 38	3.5	•	1.5	2.0	2.2	2.4	2.2	2.0	3.0	2.8	2.6
Current Liabilities to Working Capital 39	2.5	•	0.5	1.0	1.2	1.4	1.2	1.0	2.0	1.8	1.6
Working Capital to Net Sales 40	0.1	•	0.1	0.1	0.1	0.2	0.2	0.2	0.1	0.1	0.2
Inventory to Working Capital 41	1.0	•	0.2	0.6	0.7	0.8	0.9	0.8	1.1	0.9	0.7
Total Receipts to Cash Flow 42	6.0	5.8	3.2	6.7	8.4	7.5	7.5	8.7	5.9	7.7	6.0
Cost of Goods to Cash Flow 43	4.0	4.3	0.8	3.9	5.5	4.8	5.2	6.2	4.1	5.2	3.8
Cash Flow to Total Debt 44	0.2	1.8	1.8	0.6	0.4	0.3	0.5	0.3	0.3	0.4	0.3

Selected Financial Factors (in Percentages)

Debt Ratio 45	49.9	•	71.9	62.5	85.3	64.1	54.8	51.9	56.7	51.0	50.0
Return on Total Assets 46	7.4	•	77.9	15.3	13.3	12.5	17.0	10.8	11.9	13.5	8.0
Return on Equity Before Income Taxes 47	11.2	•	270.1	34.9	79.0	30.9	35.3	19.1	23.9	23.7	12.5
Return on Equity After Income Taxes 48	9.0	•	270.1	29.1	68.5	26.6	31.3	16.3	19.1	17.8	10.0
Profit Margin (Before Income Tax) 49	8.8	5.6	18.4	4.8	4.5	6.8	8.5	6.7	7.9	10.4	7.9
Profit Margin (After Income Tax) 50	7.1	5.2	18.4	4.0	3.9	5.9	7.5	5.7	6.3	7.8	6.4

Table I

Corporations with and without Net Income

COMPUTER AND PERIPHERAL EQUIPMENT

MONEY AMOUNTS AND SIZE OF ASSETS IN THOUSANDS OF DOLLARS

Item Description for Accounting Period 7/05 Through 6/06	Total	Zero Assets	Under 500	500 to 1,000	1,000 to 5,000	5,000 to 10,000	10,000 to 25,000	25,000 to 50,000	50,000 to 100,000	100,000 to 250,000	250,000 to 500,000	500,000 to 2,500,000	2,500,000 and over
Number of Enterprises **1**	3133	647	1411	318	422	89	110	49	21	22	16	19	8
Revenues ($ in Thousands)													
Net Sales **2**	169284760	1086976	639931	580562	2071100	1018522	1690784	2325278	1879429	2738339	4785157	24464930	126003752
Interest **3**	2001505	1109	24	290	3607	3371	21553	9261	11439	17000	70736	215375	1647739
Rents **4**	1139347	0	0	0	0	0	874	293	348	263	329	42827	1094414
Royalties **5**	18403664	0	0	0	0	0	2	30981	1694	233083	162457	189571	17785876
Other Portfolio Income **6**	37459229	3711	0	23	35	1191	15843	67124	17184	77433	378854	1421632	35476198
Other Receipts **7**	4039695	82296	8828	477	17354	-225	53429	13367	6280	14000	56150	576631	3211109
Total Receipts **8**	232328200	1174092	648783	581352	2092096	1022859	1782485	2446304	1916374	3080118	5453683	26910966	185219088
Average Total Receipts **9**	74155	1815	460	1828	4958	11493	16204	49925	91256	140005	340855	1416367	23152386
Operating Costs/Operating Income (%)													
Cost of Operations **10**	66.2	87.3	54.4	65.2	54.4	60.0	74.0	66.5	64.7	67.7	64.8	74.7	64.6
Salaries and Wages **11**	15.2	13.7	7.3	23.1	12.8	18.4	21.3	17.0	16.0	12.4	16.8	10.3	16.0
Taxes Paid **12**	1.9	1.0	4.0	3.0	4.0	2.5	2.1	2.1	1.4	1.3	2.0	1.2	2.0
Interest Paid **13**	1.2	0.3	3.5	0.4	1.0	1.9	1.7	0.4	0.8	2.5	1.4	0.5	1.3
Depreciation **14**	3.1	0.5	1.6	0.3	1.6	1.4	2.4	1.4	2.2	1.7	2.5	1.7	3.5
Amortization and Depletion **15**	1.2	0.3	0.1	0.2	0.4	3.2	1.3	0.7	1.0	1.1	3.0	0.6	1.3
Pensions and Other Deferred Comp. **16**	2.0	0.4	0.5	0.3	0.4	0.1	0.3	0.2	0.1	0.3	0.3	0.2	2.6
Employee Benefits **17**	1.9	0.5	2.2	0.4	1.0	1.5	2.7	1.4	1.7	1.8	1.5	0.9	2.1
Advertising **18**	1.8	0.4	0.4	0.3	1.2	1.1	1.3	1.7	0.8	1.5	1.7	2.0	1.9
Other Expenses **19**	20.3	9.8	20.9	14.4	14.8	15.8	11.2	12.3	15.8	14.3	15.5	9.1	23.4
Officers' Compensation **20**	0.7	0.8	12.4	1.9	4.1	3.8	3.4	2.1	1.5	1.3	1.5	0.5	0.5
Operating Margin **21**	•	•	•	•	4.3	•	•	•	•	•	•	•	•
Operating Margin Before Officers' Comp. **22**	•	5.2	•	•	8.4	•	•	•	•	•	•	•	•

Selected Average Balance Sheet ($ in Thousands)

Net Receivables 23	10923	0	34	19	654	2135	3427	6397	13362	38301	57445	195846	3406108
Inventories 24	3252	0	20	63	562	1255	2077	5196	10994	16341	34776	70745	852101
Net Property, Plant and Equipment 25	6327	0	23	52	393	477	1536	2243	7422	8389	20206	109716	2067333
Total Assets 26	63751	0	101	671	2675	7200	15470	33878	69630	155737	365720	1211031	20061794
Notes and Loans Payable 27	10600	0	195	220	1867	8810	2244	4564	16378	31452	62481	120767	3311587
All Other Liabilities 28	27615	0	106	243	750	3368	3902	11477	24209	58510	139618	484109	8932058
Net Worth 29	25535	0	-200	208	58	-4978	9324	17837	29043	65776	163621	606155	7818149

Selected Financial Ratios (Times to 1)

Current Ratio 30	1.4	•	0.6	1.5	2.5	1.3	2.1	2.7	1.5	1.6	1.7	1.6	1.3
Quick Ratio 31	0.8	•	0.5	1.1	1.6	0.9	1.5	1.9	0.9	1.1	1.2	0.9	0.8
Net Sales to Working Capital 32	6.4	•	14.0	4.2	9.7	2.6	3.1	6.4	3.2	•	•	5.6	7.2
Coverage Ratio 33	24.2	•	•	6.1	•	•	•	•	•	4.2	4.1	19.3	28.3
Total Asset Turnover 34	0.8	•	4.5	2.7	1.8	1.6	1.0	1.4	1.3	0.8	0.8	1.1	0.8
Inventory Turnover 35	11.0	•	12.5	18.9	4.7	5.5	5.5	6.1	5.3	5.2	5.6	13.6	11.9
Receivables Turnover 36	4.8	•	10.9	143.6	7.9	5.5	4.7	6.5	6.2	3.7	5.5	7.1	4.4
Total Liabilities to Net Worth 37	1.5	•	•	2.2	45.4	0.7	0.9	0.9	1.4	1.4	1.2	1.0	1.6
Current Assets to Working Capital 38	3.7	•	•	3.0	1.7	4.3	1.9	1.6	2.9	2.6	2.4	2.8	4.3
Current Liabilities to Working Capital 39	2.7	•	•	2.0	0.7	3.3	0.9	0.6	1.9	1.6	1.4	1.8	3.3
Working Capital to Net Sales 40	0.2	•	•	0.1	0.2	0.1	0.4	0.3	0.2	0.3	0.3	0.2	0.1
Inventory to Working Capital 41	0.4	•	•	0.7	0.5	1.1	0.4	0.3	0.7	0.5	0.4	0.3	0.4
Total Receipts to Cash Flow 42	2.5	69.0	10.0	295.0	5.7	23.2	13.7	11.1	5.3	6.7	6.9	2.0	•
Cost of Goods to Cash Flow 43	1.7	60.3	5.4	192.2	3.1	13.9	9.1	7.2	3.6	4.3	5.2	1.3	•
Cash Flow to Total Debt 44	0.6	•	0.2	0.0	0.3	0.0	0.2	0.2	0.3	0.2	0.3	0.6	•

Selected Financial Factors (in Percentages)

Debt Ratio 45	59.9	•	298.0	69.0	97.8	169.1	39.7	47.4	58.3	57.8	55.3	49.9	61.0
Return on Total Assets 46	23.9	•	•	•	11.6	•	•	•	•	8.5	4.7	9.7	28.3
Return on Equity Before Income Taxes 47	57.2	•	13.2	•	449.6	21.2	•	•	•	15.4	7.9	18.3	70.0
Return on Equity After Income Taxes 48	49.7	•	15.0	•	438.9	23.5	•	•	•	10.6	6.7	15.0	61.2
Profit Margin (Before Income Tax) 49	27.1	•	•	•	5.3	•	•	•	•	8.2	4.3	8.6	34.7
Profit Margin (After Income Tax) 50	23.5	•	•	•	5.2	•	•	•	•	5.6	3.7	7.0	30.4

Table II

Corporations with Net Income

COMPUTER AND PERIPHERAL EQUIPMENT

MONEY AMOUNTS AND SIZE OF ASSETS IN THOUSANDS OF DOLLARS

Item Description for Accounting Period 7/05 Through 6/06	Total	Zero Assets	Under 500	500 to 1,000	1,000 to 5,000	5,000 to 10,000	10,000 to 25,000	25,000 to 50,000	50,000 to 100,000	100,000 to 250,000	250,000 to 500,000	500,000 to 2,500,000	2,500,000 and over
Number of Enterprises 1	1938	488	806	211	286	29	33	28	9	12	13	14	8
Revenues ($ in Thousands)													
Net Sales 2	160859679	689328	517452	461193	1495477	446255	998546	1784024	1060539	1797082	3708319	21897712	126003752
Interest 3	1885237	544	11	0	1543	353	4024	3734	3116	8896	63028	152249	1647739
Rents 4	1128601	0	0	0	0	0	0	293	348	263	329	32955	1094414
Royalties 5	18346263	0	0	0	0	0	0	30981	1354	227230	154859	145963	17785876
Other Portfolio Income 6	37349825	0	0	0	0	15	7361	63809	12674	54134	354880	1380755	35476198
Other Receipts 7	3822679	65643	8706	0	15890	1320	20009	6436	3640	5757	53144	431024	3211109
Total Receipts 8	223392284	755515	526169	461193	1512910	447943	1029940	1889277	1081671	2093362	4334559	24040658	185219088
Average Total Receipts 9	115269	1548	653	2186	5290	15446	31210	67474	120186	174447	333428	1717190	23152386
Operating Costs/Operating Income (%)													
Cost of Operations 10	66.1	90.5	59.2	71.7	53.7	47.1	76.1	69.0	71.6	67.6	62.0	74.6	64.6
Salaries and Wages 11	14.8	11.5	3.5	13.4	7.7	12.3	8.9	12.1	7.6	12.0	17.1	9.4	16.0
Taxes Paid 12	1.9	0.8	3.6	1.9	4.1	1.5	1.2	1.6	1.1	1.4	2.1	1.2	2.0
Interest Paid 13	1.1	0.0	0.4	0.1	1.0	0.8	1.3	0.2	0.9	0.9	0.9	0.2	1.3
Depreciation 14	3.1	0.7	1.7	0.2	1.9	0.5	0.7	0.9	1.2	1.5	2.4	1.5	3.5
Amortization and Depletion 15	1.1	•	•	•	0.3	0.7	0.3	0.3	0.3	0.4	1.9	0.5	1.3
Pensions and Other Deferred Comp. 16	2.1	0.5	0.4	•	0.3	0.1	0.2	0.1	0.2	0.4	0.3	0.2	2.6
Employee Benefits 17	1.8	0.4	0.6	0.5	0.3	1.4	1.4	1.1	0.6	0.9	1.5	0.7	2.1
Advertising 18	1.8	0.5	0.3	0.2	1.3	0.8	0.9	1.9	0.0	1.2	1.5	1.8	1.9
Other Expenses 19	20.4	13.9	13.9	9.4	11.9	12.5	2.5	8.5	13.6	12.3	15.4	8.4	23.4
Officers' Compensation 20	0.6	1.6	12.6	•	2.0	4.5	1.9	1.9	0.5	1.2	1.6	0.5	0.5
Operating Margin 21	•	•	3.9	2.5	15.6	17.8	4.6	2.6	2.2	0.1	•	0.9	•
Operating Margin Before Officers' Comp. 22	•	•	16.4	2.5	17.7	22.3	6.6	4.5	2.8	1.4	•	1.4	•

Selected Average Balance Sheet ($ in Thousands)

Net Receivables 23	16826	0	48	0	720	1684	4778	7679	15042	37577	56218	241121	3406108
Inventories 24	4591	0	14	26	672	1586	3323	5681	14829	20908	24710	71907	864509
Net Property, Plant and Equipment 25	9848	0	36	62	475	353	2157	2691	9644	9599	20211	124780	2067333
Total Assets 26	96950	0	144	580	2618	6864	14291	33968	73451	162016	374262	1236782	20061794
Notes and Loans Payable 27	14947	0	54	128	599	1771	2799	3921	24226	10286	40880	79077	3311587
All Other Liabilities 28	42386	0	64	283	874	1844	3910	14368	21246	67021	99831	532080	8932058
Net Worth 29	39616	0	27	170	1145	3249	7582	15678	27979	84709	233552	625625	7818149

Selected Financial Ratios (Times to 1)

Current Ratio 30	1.4	·	1.2	0.6	2.8	2.0	2.1	2.4	1.7	1.8	2.8	1.6	1.3
Quick Ratio 31	0.8	·	1.0	0.5	1.8	1.3	1.3	1.6	1.0	1.3	1.9	0.9	0.8
Net Sales to Working Capital 32	6.4	100.9	51.7	·	4.3	6.8	5.5	4.4	6.5	2.8	2.0	5.6	7.2
Coverage Ratio 33	28.2	·	15.8	28.4	17.7	23.0	7.0	50.8	5.6	22.5	13.6	47.8	28.3
Total Asset Turnover 34	0.9	·	4.4	3.8	2.0	2.2	2.1	1.9	1.6	0.9	0.8	1.3	0.8
Inventory Turnover 35	11.9	·	28.1	61.1	4.2	4.6	6.9	7.7	5.7	4.8	7.2	16.2	11.8
Receivables Turnover 36	5.0	·	26.7	·	7.1	5.4	5.6	10.2	7.0	4.3	6.8	8.0	9.2
Total Liabilities to Net Worth 37	1.4	·	4.4	2.4	1.3	1.1	0.9	1.2	1.6	0.9	0.6	1.0	1.6
Current Assets to Working Capital 38	3.7	·	7.2	·	1.6	2.0	1.9	1.7	2.4	2.2	1.6	2.6	4.3
Current Liabilities to Working Capital 39	2.7	·	6.2	·	0.6	1.0	0.9	0.7	1.4	1.2	0.6	1.6	3.3
Working Capital to Net Sales 40	0.2	·	0.0	·	0.2	0.1	0.2	0.2	0.2	0.4	0.5	0.2	0.1
Inventory to Working Capital 41	0.4	·	1.1	·	0.5	0.7	0.6	0.5	0.7	0.4	0.2	0.3	0.4
Total Receipts to Cash Flow 42	2.4	25.2	7.0	12.0	3.8	3.5	12.2	8.0	6.5	3.7	4.3	6.2	2.0
Cost of Goods to Cash Flow 43	1.6	22.8	4.1	8.6	2.0	1.6	9.3	5.5	4.6	2.5	2.7	4.6	1.3
Cash Flow to Total Debt 44	0.6	·	0.8	0.4	0.9	1.2	0.4	0.4	0.4	0.5	0.5	0.4	0.6

Selected Financial Factors (in Percentages)

Debt Ratio 45	59.1	·	81.6	70.7	56.3	52.7	46.9	53.8	61.9	47.7	37.6	49.4	61.0
Return on Total Assets 46	26.3	·	26.4	9.9	35.5	42.5	19.2	16.4	8.2	18.5	9.7	14.2	28.3
Return on Equity Before Income Taxes 47	62.0	·	134.1	32.8	76.6	86.0	31.0	34.8	17.6	33.8	14.4	27.5	70.0
Return on Equity After Income Taxes 48	54.2	·	109.8	32.8	75.8	74.9	28.8	28.4	13.9	27.0	13.3	23.1	61.2
Profit Margin (Before Income Tax) 49	29.6	3.0	5.6	2.5	16.8	18.1	7.8	8.6	4.2	19.1	11.8	11.0	34.7
Profit Margin (After Income Tax) 50	25.9	2.2	4.6	2.5	16.6	15.8	7.2	7.0	3.3	15.3	10.9	9.2	30.4

138

Table I

Corporations with and without Net Income

COMMUNICATIONS EQUIPMENT

MONEY AMOUNTS AND SIZE OF ASSETS IN THOUSANDS OF DOLLARS

Item Description for Accounting Period 7/05 Through 6/06	Total	Zero Assets	Under 500	500 to 1,000	1,000 to 5,000	5,000 to 10,000	10,000 to 25,000	25,000 to 50,000	50,000 to 100,000	100,000 to 250,000	250,000 to 500,000	500,000 to 2,500,000	2,500,000 and over
Number of Enterprises **1**	1438	31	513	212	412	54	66	50	24	27	17	15	16
Revenues ($ in Thousands)													
Net Sales **2**	122777067	571269	190591	87157	1545115	623069	1053068	2060996	1410943	5653059	3688451	13231078	92262270
Interest **3**	150948	10817	226	1620	8535	2941	5492	20260	11585	45585	57072	134565	1206249
Rents **4**	237165	8506	0	1327	580	0	0	506	27	10	881	3033	222296
Royalties **5**	451812	0	0	0	0	0	0	333	4345	19248	15882	29755	444948
Other Portfolio Income **6**	6244284	28350	0	0	5169	182	160	617	35735	281375	24318	63885	5804490
Other Receipts **7**	1671771	6703	62	6560	237996	820	25222	9223	10348	22315	43895	59955	1248677
Total Receipts **8**	13695047	625645	190879	96664	1797395	627012	1083942	2091935	1472983	6021592	3830499	13522271	105593230
Average Total Receipts **9**	95239	20182	372	456	4363	11611	16423	41839	61374	223022	225323	901485	6599577
Operating Costs/Operating Income (%)													
Cost of Operations **10**	67.8	48.8	39.2	29.3	49.5	65.6	63.0	55.5	53.2	74.9	57.3	78.9	67.2
Salaries and Wages **11**	15.5	16.6	9.6	38.1	30.9	26.1	24.7	19.3	18.9	11.3	17.9	8.0	16.1
Taxes Paid **12**	1.6	2.6	4.2	5.8	3.3	3.0	3.5	2.8	1.8	1.2	1.6	1.0	1.6
Interest Paid **13**	1.8	23.1	0.3	4.8	1.2	1.9	3.3	1.3	2.4	0.7	3.3	1.2	1.7
Depreciation **14**	2.5	15.4	0.8	2.5	2.0	1.4	3.6	1.9	2.8	1.3	2.9	1.6	2.6
Amortization and Depletion **15**	1.2	3.2	0.0	0.0	2.1	3.2	3.8	1.1	2.6	0.4	2.0	0.5	1.2
Pensions and Other Deferred Comp. **16**	1.3	0.6	0.2	2.7	0.5	0.1	0.6	0.2	0.3	0.3	0.2	0.2	1.6
Employee Benefits **17**	1.5	3.0	0.5	4.0	2.9	2.4	2.9	2.3	3.3	1.3	5.0	1.0	1.4
Advertising **18**	1.0	0.4	0.2	2.2	0.8	1.1	0.8	0.8	0.6	0.5	0.5	0.6	1.2
Other Expenses **19**	11.4	30.1	28.1	38.2	37.6	22.5	20.2	16.9	22.5	9.3	12.3	9.0	10.8
Officers' Compensation **20**	0.9	2.0	14.9	7.9	7.7	4.7	4.0	2.0	3.2	1.1	1.8	0.3	0.7
Operating Margin **21**	•	•	2.0	•	•	•	•	•	•	•	•	•	•
Operating Margin Before Officers' Comp. **22**	•	•	16.9	•	•	•	•	•	•	•	•	•	•

Selected Average Balance Sheet ($ in Thousands)

Net Receivables 23	17007	0	16	62	535	1347	2794	8503	10539	29091	52796	138741	1219699
Inventories 24	6195	0	111	80	455	1619	3338	5045	8745	18476	26630	93028	345624
Net Property, Plant and Equipment 25	9288	0	9	76	132	691	2137	3256	6288	11394	27199	77793	678275
Total Assets 26	126772	0	245	584	2727	6714	15376	35364	67173	151031	360742	1105176	9336198
Notes and Loans Payable 27	18763	0	62	1148	739	2522	6408	3325	16696	13770	84687	208323	1271149
All Other Liabilities 28	48374	0	17	157	997	3227	6376	14550	19173	50583	89394	330155	3718074
Net Worth 29	59635	0	167	-721	990	964	2592	17489	31304	86678	186661	566698	4346975

Selected Financial Ratios (Times to 1)

Current Ratio 30	1.8	•	3.0	2.2	2.2	1.7	1.6	1.9	2.4	2.1	2.1	1.6	1.8
Quick Ratio 31	1.1	•	1.4	1.7	1.6	1.1	1.0	1.3	1.5	1.2	1.4	0.8	1.0
Net Sales to Working Capital 32	3.4	•	2.4	2.3	3.0	5.2	4.0	3.4	2.4	4.3	2.3	4.3	3.3
Coverage Ratio 33	4.0	•	7.4	•	•	•	•	•	•	7.3	0.8	1.0	5.7
Total Asset Turnover 34	0.7	•	1.5	0.7	1.4	1.7	1.0	1.2	0.9	1.4	0.6	0.8	0.6
Inventory Turnover 35	9.3	•	1.3	1.5	4.1	4.7	3.0	4.5	3.6	8.5	4.7	7.5	11.3
Receivables Turnover 36	5.2	•	27.3	9.6	7.1	8.4	4.5	6.2	4.9	7.8	3.3	5.7	5.1
Total Liabilities to Net Worth 37	1.1	•	0.5	•	1.8	6.0	4.9	1.0	1.1	0.7	0.9	1.0	1.1
Current Assets to Working Capital 38	2.2	•	1.5	1.9	1.8	2.5	2.6	2.1	1.7	1.9	1.9	2.5	2.3
Current Liabilities to Working Capital 39	1.2	•	0.5	0.9	0.8	1.5	1.6	1.1	0.7	0.9	0.9	1.5	1.3
Working Capital to Net Sales 40	0.3	•	0.4	0.4	0.3	0.2	0.3	0.3	0.4	0.2	0.4	0.2	0.3
Inventory to Working Capital 41	0.3	•	0.8	0.3	0.4	0.5	0.7	0.5	0.3	0.4	0.2	0.4	0.3
Total Receipts to Cash Flow 42	7.0	•	3.8	13.4	11.8	•	•	8.3	8.9	12.2	12.1	13.6	5.9
Cost of Goods to Cash Flow 43	4.7	•	1.5	3.9	5.8	•	•	4.6	4.7	9.1	6.9	10.7	4.0
Cash Flow to Total Debt 44	0.2	•	1.2	0.0	0.2	•	•	0.3	0.2	0.3	0.1	0.1	0.2

Selected Financial Factors (in Percentages)

Debt Ratio 45	53.0	•	32.0	223.4	63.7	85.6	83.1	50.5	53.4	42.6	48.3	48.7	53.4
Return on Total Assets 46	4.7	•	3.7	•	•	•	•	•	7.1	1.6	•	1.0	6.0
Return on Equity Before Income Taxes 47	7.5	•	4.7	14.0	•	•	•	•	10.6	•	•	•	10.6
Return on Equity After Income Taxes 48	5.7	•	4.7	14.0	•	•	•	•	9.1	•	•	•	8.7
Profit Margin (Before Income Tax) 49	5.2	•	2.1	•	•	•	•	•	4.4	•	•	•	8.0
Profit Margin (After Income Tax) 50	4.0	•	2.1	•	•	•	•	•	3.8	•	•	•	6.5

Table II

Corporations with Net Income

COMMUNICATIONS EQUIPMENT

MONEY AMOUNTS AND SIZE OF ASSETS IN THOUSANDS OF DOLLARS

Item Description for Accounting Period 7/05 Through 6/06	Total	Zero Assets	Under 500	500 to 1,000	1,000 to 5,000	5,000 to 10,000	10,000 to 25,000	25,000 to 50,000	50,000 to 100,000	100,000 to 250,000	250,000 to 500,000	500,000 to 2,500,000	2,500,000 and over
Number of Enterprises 1	793	•	407	78	190	15	19	30	8	17	•	•	7
Revenues ($ in Thousands)													
Net Sales 2	98480966	•	50217	75597	973763	325199	541976	1504204	549032	3881274	•	•	9806743
Interest 3	915725	•	192	1612	1514	0	3	5347	1940	12863	•	•	29109
Rents 4	175582	•	0	1327	0	0	0	124	0	0	•	•	2821
Royalties 5	2232220	•	0	0	0	0	0	333	3856	19248	•	•	27431
Other Portfolio Income 6	5731386	•	0	0	324	0	16	364	35725	256525	•	•	50731
Other Receipts 7	1260314	•	63	-1	221314	-611	16876	5889	5073	5219	•	•	16334
Total Receipts 8	108796193	•	50472	78535	1196915	324588	558871	1516261	595626	4175129	•	•	9933169
Average Total Receipts 9	137196	•	124	1007	6300	21639	29414	50542	74453	245596	•	•	1419024
Operating Costs/Operating Income (%)													
Cost of Operations 10	68.2	•	53.6	33.8	53.5	57.3	63.5	54.8	50.8	73.7	•	•	80.1
Salaries and Wages 11	13.9	•	11.2	30.1	15.6	14.4	10.9	14.9	10.2	10.5	•	•	6.1
Taxes Paid 12	1.4	•	3.1	3.7	2.2	2.5	2.4	2.4	1.7	1.2	•	•	1.0
Interest Paid 13	1.0	•	1.3	0.6	0.7	0.1	0.9	0.7	3.6	0.4	•	•	0.7
Depreciation 14	2.4	•	1.9	1.3	1.2	0.8	1.2	1.3	1.8	1.1	•	•	1.1
Amortization and Depletion 15	0.9	•	0.1	•	0.3	0.0	0.0	0.4	1.1	0.4	•	•	0.3
Pensions and Other Deferred Comp. 16	1.0	•	0.7	3.2	0.6	0.3	0.3	0.3	0.4	0.3	•	•	0.1
Employee Benefits 17	1.2	•	1.7	4.6	1.3	1.3	2.1	2.2	3.0	1.4	•	•	0.8
Advertising 18	1.1	•	0.8	2.4	0.6	0.4	0.3	0.7	0.6	0.6	•	•	0.5
Other Expenses 19	8.4	•	10.9	14.8	30.0	2.9	5.4	12.4	14.6	8.8	•	•	7.5
Officers' Compensation 20	0.8	•	6.3	7.2	4.4	3.0	2.9	1.5	2.6	0.8	•	•	0.3
Operating Margin 21	•	•	8.3	•	•	17.0	10.2	8.4	9.6	0.9	•	•	1.6
Operating Margin Before Officers' Comp. 22	0.4	•	14.6	5.6	•	20.0	13.1	10.0	12.3	1.7	•	•	2.0

Selected Average Balance Sheet ($ in Thousands)

Net Receivables 23	20243	3	87	639	2134	5174	10154	10104	32769	160457
Inventories 24	7753	112	165	645	3229	5873	5500	10839	15323	129535
Net Property, Plant and Equipment 25	10517	6	14	112	1671	2880	3902	7127	11685	59158
Total Assets 26	147310	213	696	2415	8139	15579	35747	62462	144638	1021773
Notes and Loans Payable 27	20848	78	1026	1011	564	4608	2197	40364	14913	138809
All Other Liabilities 28	57157	10	66	492	2167	2880	18205	15463	49895	319021
Net Worth 29	69305	125	-396	912	5408	8091	15345	6634	79831	563942

Selected Financial Ratios (Times to 1)

Current Ratio 30	1.7	2.3	10.3	1.8	2.9	2.5	1.8	2.2	2.2	1.4
Quick Ratio 31	1.0	1.1	8.3	1.1	1.6	1.4	1.1	1.6	1.3	0.7
Net Sales to Working Capital 32	4.6	1.0	1.6	5.4	5.2	3.9	3.9	3.7	4.5	10.1
Coverage Ratio 33	10.7	7.9	4.8	20.0	161.1	16.1	15.0	6.1	22.7	5.3
Total Asset Turnover 34	0.8	0.6	1.4	2.1	2.7	1.8	1.4	1.1	1.6	1.4
Inventory Turnover 35	10.9	0.6	2.0	4.2	3.8	3.1	5.0	3.2	11.0	8.7
Receivables Turnover 36	7.3	80.2	13.0	9.7	8.8	4.7	6.7	3.6	9.4	7.2
Total Liabilities to Net Worth 37	1.1	0.7		1.6	0.5	0.9	1.3	8.4	0.8	0.8
Current Assets to Working Capital 38	2.5	1.7	1.1	2.2	1.5	1.7	2.2	1.8	1.9	3.4
Current Liabilities to Working Capital 39	1.5	0.7	0.1	1.2	0.5	0.7	1.2	0.8	0.9	2.4
Working Capital to Net Sales 40	0.2	1.0	0.6	0.2	0.2	0.3	0.3	0.3	0.2	0.1
Inventory to Working Capital 41	0.3	0.9	0.2	0.8	0.4	0.6	0.6	0.4	0.4	1.0
Total Receipts to Cash Flow 42	6.0	7.1	7.5	2.6	5.4	5.8	5.0	3.4	9.8	10.6
Cost of Goods to Cash Flow 43	4.1	3.8	2.5	1.4	3.1	3.7	2.7	1.7	7.2	8.5
Cash Flow to Total Debt 44	0.3	0.2	0.1	1.3	1.5	0.7	0.5	0.4	0.4	0.3

Selected Financial Factors (in Percentages)

Debt Ratio 45	53.0	41.4	156.9	62.2	33.6	48.1	57.1	89.4	44.8	44.8
Return on Total Assets 46	9.3	5.8	4.0	27.9	45.0	26.1	13.8	23.9	14.0	5.0
Return on Equity Before Income Taxes 47	18.0	8.7		70.3	67.3	47.1	30.1	188.6	24.3	7.4
Return on Equity After Income Taxes 48	15.2	8.7		59.0	67.3	47.0	24.9	164.2	21.8	5.7
Profit Margin (Before Income Tax) 49	10.0	8.8	2.3	12.5	16.8	13.4	9.2	18.2	8.5	3.0
Profit Margin (After Income Tax) 50	8.5	8.8	2.2	10.5	16.8	13.3	7.6	15.9	7.6	2.3

Table I
Corporations with and without Net Income

AUDIO AND VIDEO EQUIP., REPRODUCING MAGNETIC & OPTICAL MEDIA

MONEY AMOUNTS AND SIZE OF ASSETS IN THOUSANDS OF DOLLARS

Item Description for Accounting Period 7/05 Through 6/06	Total	Zero Assets	Under 500	500 to 1,000	1,000 to 5,000	5,000 to 10,000	10,000 to 25,000	25,000 to 50,000	50,000 to 100,000	100,000 to 250,000	250,000 to 500,000	500,000 to 2,500,000	2,500,000 and over
Number of Enterprises 1	1431	35	692	123	360	70	71	32	17	14	7	10	0
Revenues ($ in Thousands)													
Net Sales 2	23685035	90754	26053	79181	1244277	735052	1420305	1726180	1364280	2327431	2268030	12403493	0
Interest 3	249885	1771	9	473	1075	3072	5025	3150	9945	15175	20651	189539	0
Rents 4	6265	0	0	798	0	984	0	159	333	537	75	3379	0
Royalties 5	413687	0	0	0	0	28	0	401	1357	300	0	411600	0
Other Portfolio Income 6	1364972	0	0	90	438	115	15143	1075	1105	19495	10192	1317319	0
Other Receipts 7	669053	2274	1	74	38922	310818	12995	32041	6803	3214	115423	146487	0
Total Receipts 8	26388897	94799	26063	80616	1284712	1050069	1453468	1763006	1383823	2366152	2414371	14471817	0
Average Total Receipts 9	18441	2709	38	655	3569	15001	20471	55094	81401	169011	344910	1447182	•
Operating Costs/Operating Income (%)													
Cost of Operations 10	61.6	74.4	56.4	46.4	54.8	83.3	65.0	63.7	58.1	64.3	38.7	64.3	•
Salaries and Wages 11	11.9	8.5	5.9	16.1	17.2	15.0	14.4	10.6	17.2	10.7	11.1	10.9	•
Taxes Paid 12	1.4	1.3	2.8	1.9	3.6	1.8	2.0	1.5	1.8	1.3	1.2	1.1	•
Interest Paid 13	2.0	1.7	4.2	5.6	1.8	0.8	1.3	1.0	1.8	1.8	1.1	2.6	•
Depreciation 14	2.8	2.1	4.7	15.5	1.4	1.5	2.6	3.8	2.3	2.6	1.2	3.3	•
Amortization and Depletion 15	0.9	0.3	0.2	•	0.5	0.2	1.1	0.8	•	0.6	0.5	1.3	•
Pensions and Other Deferred Comp. 16	0.4	0.3	•	1.3	0.1	0.1	0.1	0.3	0.1	0.6	0.5	0.5	•
Employee Benefits 17	2.1	0.7	1.5	0.1	2.5	1.4	2.4	2.2	2.6	1.3	1.4	2.2	•
Advertising 18	1.6	3.9	2.4	0.3	2.4	0.2	0.6	1.2	2.7	1.9	0.6	1.8	•
Other Expenses 19	20.4	17.3	73.6	21.6	17.7	41.4	15.9	14.4	16.8	13.2	39.2	19.0	•
Officers' Compensation 20	1.2	10.1	•	6.1	4.8	2.5	3.8	1.4	2.3	0.8	1.1	0.4	•
Operating Margin 21	•	•	•	•	•	•	•	•	•	1.1	•	3.6	•
Operating Margin Before Officers' Comp. 22	•	•	•	•	•	0.5	•	0.5	1.9	1.9	4.7	•	•

Selected Average Balance Sheet ($ in Thousands)

Net Receivables 23	3333	0	2	71	304	2277	4026	9627	14367	28168	57577	285525	•
Inventories 24	1656	0	32	37	338	924	2190	6655	13242	25909	28281	100280	•
Net Property, Plant and Equipment 25	2008	0	0	150	174	1736	2440	4437	7235	28940	23392	166337	•
Total Assets 26	18966	0	4	671	1630	7156	15316	35718	78857	172624	360544	1745586	•
Notes and Loans Payable 27	4816	0	20	613	748	2099	3683	21568	17834	44112	57679	410919	•
All Other Liabilities 28	6008	0	34	120	436	2810	5833	17336	19234	52229	110458	540490	•
Net Worth 29	8143	0	-51	-62	446	2248	5800	-3186	41789	76282	192407	794178	•

Selected Financial Ratios (Times to 1)

Current Ratio 30	1.6	•	0.2	2.3	1.7	1.6	1.4	1.3	2.2	2.5	1.7	1.4	•
Quick Ratio 31	0.9	•	0.1	1.9	1.2	1.1	0.9	0.8	1.5	1.5	1.2	0.8	•
Net Sales to Working Capital 32	5.2	•	•	3.7	6.5	6.1	7.1	9.4	2.9	2.8	5.1	5.8	•
Coverage Ratio 33	3.6	•	•	•	•	•	•	2.1	•	2.7	10.1	4.8	•
Total Asset Turnover 34	0.9	•	9.3	1.0	2.1	1.5	1.3	1.5	1.0	1.0	0.9	0.7	•
Inventory Turnover 35	6.2	•	0.7	8.1	5.6	9.5	5.9	5.2	3.5	4.1	4.4	8.0	•
Receivables Turnover 36	5.4	•	16.5	12.8	8.7	5.8	6.1	6.2	4.8	5.9	5.8	5.0	•
Total Liabilities to Net Worth 37	1.3	•	•	•	2.7	2.2	1.6	•	0.9	1.3	0.9	1.2	•
Current Assets to Working Capital 38	2.8	•	•	1.8	2.5	2.6	3.5	4.5	1.8	1.7	2.5	3.3	•
Current Liabilities to Working Capital 39	1.8	•	•	0.8	1.5	1.6	2.5	3.5	0.8	0.7	1.5	2.3	•
Working Capital to Net Sales 40	0.2	•	•	0.3	0.2	0.2	0.1	0.1	0.3	0.4	0.2	0.2	•
Inventory to Working Capital 41	0.5	•	•	0.3	0.5	0.6	1.0	1.1	0.5	0.4	0.4	0.5	•
Total Receipts to Cash Flow 42	4.5	1463.8	4.6	•	9.4	2.9	19.8	7.7	9.8	7.1	2.1	4.1	•
Cost of Goods to Cash Flow 43	2.8	1088.4	2.6	•	5.2	2.4	12.8	4.9	5.7	4.5	0.8	2.6	•
Cash Flow to Total Debt 44	0.3	•	0.1	•	0.3	0.7	0.1	0.2	0.2	0.2	0.9	0.3	•

Selected Financial Factors (in Percentages)

Debt Ratio 45	57.1	•	1352.5	109.2	72.6	68.6	62.1	108.9	47.0	55.8	46.6	54.5	•
Return on Total Assets 46	6.4	•	•	•	•	•	•	3.3	•	4.5	9.7	8.8	•
Return on Equity Before Income Taxes 47	10.7	•	38.1	136.2	•	•	•	•	•	6.4	16.3	15.4	•
Return on Equity After Income Taxes 48	7.3	•	38.1	136.2	•	•	•	•	•	3.2	9.5	12.5	•
Profit Margin (Before Income Tax) 49	5.3	•	•	•	•	•	•	1.1	•	2.9	9.7	9.8	•
Profit Margin (After Income Tax) 50	3.6	•	•	•	•	•	•	0.3	•	1.5	5.6	8.0	•

Table II
Corporations with Net Income

AUDIO AND VIDEO EQUIP., REPRODUCING MAGNETIC & OPTICAL MEDIA

MONEY AMOUNTS AND SIZE OF ASSETS IN THOUSANDS OF DOLLARS

Item Description for Accounting Period 7/05 Through 6/06	Total	Zero Assets	Under 500	500 to 1,000	1,000 to 5,000	5,000 to 10,000	10,000 to 25,000	25,000 to 50,000	50,000 to 100,000	100,000 to 250,000	250,000 to 500,000	500,000 to 2,500,000	2,500,000 and over
Number of Enterprises **1**	698	0	293	0	290	30	38	20	7	9	4	7	0
Revenues ($ in Thousands)													
Net Sales **2**	13816210	0	7633	0	1138659	267240	972295	1055080	672212	2045863	1674087	5983140	0
Interest **3**	202442	0	0	0	20	2193	1364	1390	2613	9701	9189	175971	0
Rents **4**	679	0	0	0	0	205	0	159	110	206	0	0	0
Royalties **5**	345793	0	0	0	0	28	0	401	274	300	0	344790	0
Other Portfolio Income **6**	1293882	0	0	0	412	115	1049	941	840	19412	10192	1260920	0
Other Receipts **7**	460657	0	0	0	37534	310817	11152	30281	6158	2500	10849	51368	0
Total Receipts **8**	16119663	0	7633	0	1176625	580598	985860	1088252	682207	2077982	1704317	7816189	0
Average Total Receipts **9**	23094	•	26	•	4057	19353	25944	54413	97458	230887	426079	1116598	•
Operating Costs/Operating Income (%)													
Cost of Operations **10**	51.4	•	52.7	•	53.3	85.6	70.0	53.5	54.0	62.7	27.7	48.6	•
Salaries and Wages **11**	13.0	•	•	•	14.7	27.0	9.0	11.1	12.2	10.7	8.3	15.2	•
Taxes Paid **12**	1.4	•	0.6	•	3.4	0.9	1.5	1.6	1.7	1.2	1.0	1.1	•
Interest Paid **13**	2.3	•	•	•	0.2	0.6	1.4	0.8	2.9	1.8	0.5	3.8	•
Depreciation **14**	2.4	•	•	•	0.8	0.8	1.1	2.3	1.0	1.8	0.9	3.9	•
Amortization and Depletion **15**	1.0	•	•	•	0.0	0.5	0.3	0.2	0.3	0.5	0.3	1.8	•
Pensions and Other Deferred Comp. **16**	0.5	•	•	•	0.1	0.1	0.1	0.5	0.0	0.6	0.3	0.8	•
Employee Benefits **17**	2.2	•	•	•	2.2	0.4	0.8	3.0	1.7	1.3	1.0	3.1	•
Advertising **18**	2.3	•	•	•	2.4	0.4	0.1	1.7	2.6	2.1	0.5	3.4	•
Other Expenses **19**	22.3	•	39.7	•	12.6	89.1	9.2	13.1	10.7	12.0	43.7	23.8	•
Officers' Compensation **20**	1.3	•	•	•	4.1	1.4	3.4	1.9	3.0	0.7	0.5	0.5	•
Operating Margin **21**	•	•	7.0	•	6.1	•	3.1	10.2	9.9	4.6	15.3	•	•
Operating Margin Before Officers' Comp. **22**	1.1	•	7.0	•	10.2	•	6.5	12.1	12.9	5.3	15.8	•	•

Selected Average Balance Sheet ($ in Thousands)

Net Receivables 23	2848	4	301	2402	4021	8905	14092	31706	29402	142117
Inventories 24	1662	1	373	1237	2537	6165	16910	30178	29600	62090
Net Property, Plant and Equipment 25	2334	0	88	1410	2280	4962	5053	20428	20200	153625
Total Assets 26	20940	5	1472	7204	13861	36748	79768	174320	331038	1322586
Notes and Loans Payable 27	4744	6	512	1454	5571	6118	34044	56293	14186	283112
All Other Liabilities 28	5550	0	258	2475	4018	8667	19255	47474	99414	348490
Net Worth 29	10645	-1	702	3274	4273	21963	26469	70553	217438	690983

Selected Financial Ratios (Times to 1)

Current Ratio 30	2.0		3.7	1.9	1.2	2.5	2.8	2.5	2.1	1.9
Quick Ratio 31	1.1		2.7	1.4	0.7	1.7	1.9	1.3	1.2	0.9
Net Sales to Working Capital 32	3.7	4.8	4.2	4.1	17.0	3.2	2.7	3.6	5.6	3.2
Coverage Ratio 33	8.3		48.4	17.2	4.3	17.0	4.9	4.5	32.0	7.8
Total Asset Turnover 34	0.9	4.8	2.7	1.2	1.8	1.4	1.2	1.3	1.3	0.6
Inventory Turnover 35	6.1	10.3	5.6	6.2	7.1	4.6	3.1	4.7	3.9	6.7
Receivables Turnover 36	8.8	13.0	11.8	3.5	8.4	6.5	5.0	7.8	28.5	12.0
Total Liabilities to Net Worth 37	1.0		1.1	1.2	2.2	0.7	2.0	1.5	0.5	0.9
Current Assets to Working Capital 38	2.0	1.0	1.4	2.1	5.9	1.7	1.6	1.6	1.9	2.1
Current Liabilities to Working Capital 39	1.0		0.4	1.1	4.9	0.7	0.6	0.6	0.9	1.1
Working Capital to Net Sales 40	0.3	0.2	0.2	0.2	0.1	0.3	0.4	0.3	0.2	0.3
Inventory to Working Capital 41	0.4	0.2	0.3	0.3	2.1	0.4	0.5	0.5	0.4	0.2
Total Receipts to Cash Flow 42	2.7	2.1	5.3	1.0	8.4	4.1	4.8	6.0	1.7	2.2
Cost of Goods to Cash Flow 43	1.4	1.1	2.8	0.9	5.9	2.2	2.6	3.8	0.5	1.1
Cash Flow to Total Debt 44	0.7	2.0	1.0	2.2	0.3	0.9	0.4	0.4	2.2	0.6

Selected Financial Factors (in Percentages)

Debt Ratio 45	49.2	113.9	52.3	54.5	69.2	40.2	66.8	59.5	34.3	47.8
Return on Total Assets 46	18.3	33.9	25.8	13.7	10.9	20.2	17.1	10.6	21.7	19.2
Return on Equity Before Income Taxes 47	31.6		52.9	28.3	27.2	31.9	40.9	20.5	31.9	32.0
Return on Equity After Income Taxes 48	26.3		51.5	22.5	20.8	28.5	35.0	15.0	21.3	27.3
Profit Margin (Before Income Tax) 49	17.0	7.0	9.5	10.4	4.5	13.3	11.3	6.4	16.6	25.8
Profit Margin (After Income Tax) 50	14.1	7.0	9.2	8.3	3.5	11.8	9.7	4.7	11.1	22.1

Table I

Corporations with and without Net Income

SEMICONDUCTOR AND OTHER ELECTRONIC COMPONENT

MONEY AMOUNTS AND SIZE OF ASSETS IN THOUSANDS OF DOLLARS

Item Description for Accounting Period 7/05 Through 6/06	Total	Zero Assets	Under 500	500 to 1,000	1,000 to 5,000	5,000 to 10,000	10,000 to 25,000	25,000 to 50,000	50,000 to 100,000	100,000 to 250,000	250,000 to 500,000	500,000 to 2,500,000	2,500,000 and over
Number of Enterprises 1	6036	968	2157	354	1741	301	219	91	47	55	36	43	24
Revenues ($ in Thousands)													
Net Sales 2	232125729	336558	781266	475383	8939237	3584542	3821657	3540956	3270383	8705911	10423923	31561914	156684000
Interest 3	3293061	1534	1493	2404	6349	6740	19788	23298	27826	64844	160435	493389	2484961
Rents 4	74693	0	0	1141	736	395	172	1689	5238	1708	13725	11786	38102
Royalties 5	4263781	266	0	0	0	0	118	3415	30247	140433	215327	453865	3420111
Other Portfolio Income 6	16353468	69330	0	0	14178	1901	27603	30627	14294	174661	283819	3933233	11803824
Other Receipts 7	4110519	4881	577	4709	27614	13340	28817	61920	48138	159640	113531	1388467	2258882
Total Receipts 8	260221251	412569	783336	483637	8988114	3606918	3898155	3661905	3396126	9247197	11210760	37842654	176689880
Average Total Receipts 9	43112	426	363	1366	5163	11983	17800	40241	72258	168131	311410	880062	7362078
Operating Costs/Operating Income (%)													
Cost of Operations 10	69.3	52.6	48.3	32.0	59.8	62.0	66.8	68.0	65.7	70.3	65.0	69.9	70.5
Salaries and Wages 11	9.8	40.1	6.4	20.8	13.6	11.6	12.8	11.8	14.8	11.1	12.0	14.6	8.1
Taxes Paid 12	1.1	4.4	2.9	5.1	3.3	2.8	2.3	1.8	1.8	1.7	1.5	1.4	0.8
Interest Paid 13	1.7	0.5	0.6	0.1	0.9	1.3	1.7	1.0	1.7	1.0	1.3	1.9	1.9
Depreciation 14	3.8	2.0	0.3	2.5	2.0	2.1	3.0	2.3	4.0	2.5	4.4	4.4	4.0
Amortization and Depletion 15	1.1	0.9	1.0	0.1	0.2	0.5	1.0	1.0	0.8	0.9	1.3	1.7	1.1
Pensions and Other Deferred Comp. 16	0.5	0.2	•	1.4	0.7	0.4	0.4	0.5	0.3	0.3	0.4	0.6	0.6
Employee Benefits 17	1.5	1.3	0.1	0.9	1.5	1.8	2.0	2.2	2.1	1.4	1.8	2.0	1.4
Advertising 18	1.4	0.8	0.0	0.2	0.7	0.7	0.5	0.7	0.7	0.7	0.3	0.4	1.9
Other Expenses 19	9.0	34.5	29.9	30.4	11.1	13.4	14.5	12.2	14.8	11.6	11.8	9.9	7.7
Officers' Compensation 20	1.0	10.4	12.5	22.2	4.2	3.7	3.2	2.2	1.7	1.2	2.1	1.1	0.4
Operating Margin 21	•	•	•	2.0	•	•	•	•	•	•	•	•	1.8
Operating Margin Before Officers' Comp. 22	0.6	•	10.4	6.4	6.2	3.2	•	0.3	•	•	•	•	2.2

Selected Average Balance Sheet ($ in Thousands)

Net Receivables 23	8499	0	12	203	717	1692	2727	7999	14931	37559	52949	143891	1552571
Inventories 24	3233	0	15	184	557	1974	2583	5153	10973	23535	27466	68396	461730
Net Property, Plant and Equipment 25	6715	0	8	99	571	1183	2370	4624	13888	20547	54287	154328	1158978
Total Assets 26	46580	0	114	637	2378	7515	14792	35137	74113	165636	356736	1139273	8059268
Notes and Loans Payable 27	5609	0	61	558	821	2519	4412	7477	14328	21879	49131	233456	667137
All Other Liabilities 28	13027	0	10	132	722	1789	3141	9918	23709	42343	74290	252643	2424795
Net Worth 29	27944	0	43	-53	835	3207	7238	17742	36076	101413	233315	653174	4967337

Selected Financial Ratios (Times to 1)

Current Ratio 30	2.0	•	5.1	1.2	1.7	2.6	1.9	2.1	1.9	2.7	2.4	2.5	1.9
Quick Ratio 31	1.4	•	3.4	1.0	1.0	1.5	1.1	1.4	1.3	1.8	1.5	1.7	1.3
Net Sales to Working Capital 32	3.4	•	8.7	14.0	7.5	3.6	3.9	3.2	3.5	2.3	2.7	2.1	3.8
Coverage Ratio 33	8.5	•	•	•	3.9	1.1	•	0.7	•	4.8	6.0	7.6	9.8
Total Asset Turnover 34	0.8	•	•	2.1	2.2	1.6	1.2	1.1	0.9	1.0	0.8	0.6	0.8
Inventory Turnover 35	8.2	•	12.0	2.3	5.5	3.7	4.5	5.1	4.2	4.7	6.9	7.5	10.0
Receivables Turnover 36	5.1	•	27.1	4.4	8.1	7.4	7.1	6.0	4.9	4.2	6.1	4.3	5.0
Total Liabilities to Net Worth 37	0.7	•	1.6	•	1.8	1.3	1.0	1.0	1.1	0.6	0.5	0.7	0.6
Current Assets to Working Capital 38	2.0	•	1.2	5.2	2.4	1.6	2.1	1.9	2.1	1.6	1.7	1.7	2.2
Current Liabilities to Working Capital 39	1.0	•	0.2	4.2	1.4	0.6	1.1	0.9	1.1	0.6	0.7	0.7	1.2
Working Capital to Net Sales 40	0.3	•	0.1	0.1	0.1	0.3	0.3	0.3	0.3	0.4	0.4	0.5	0.3
Inventory to Working Capital 41	0.3	•	0.4	0.7	0.9	0.5	0.6	0.5	0.5	0.3	0.3	0.2	0.2
Total Receipts to Cash Flow 42	5.3	44.8	5.3	14.0	10.2	9.8	19.5	11.2	14.0	7.9	6.7	5.2	4.8
Cost of Goods to Cash Flow 43	3.7	23.6	2.6	4.5	6.1	6.1	13.0	7.6	9.2	5.6	4.3	3.6	3.4
Cash Flow to Total Debt 44	0.4	•	1.0	0.1	0.3	0.3	0.1	0.2	0.1	0.3	0.4	0.3	0.4

Selected Financial Factors (in Percentages)

Debt Ratio 45	40.0	•	62.3	108.3	64.9	57.3	51.1	49.5	51.3	38.8	34.6	42.7	38.4
Return on Total Assets 46	12.3	•	•	•	7.3	2.3	•	0.9	•	4.4	6.4	9.4	14.8
Return on Equity Before Income Taxes 47	18.0	•	•	355.1	15.5	0.4	•	•	•	5.7	8.1	14.2	21.6
Return on Equity After Income Taxes 48	13.6	•	•	360.0	12.5	•	•	•	•	4.0	6.3	11.6	16.3
Profit Margin (Before Income Tax) 49	13.1	•	•	•	2.5	0.1	•	•	•	3.7	6.5	12.7	16.4
Profit Margin (After Income Tax) 50	9.9	•	•	•	2.0	•	•	•	•	2.6	5.1	10.3	12.4

143

Table II
Corporations with Net Income

SEMICONDUCTOR AND OTHER ELECTRONIC COMPONENT

MONEY AMOUNTS AND SIZE OF ASSETS IN THOUSANDS OF DOLLARS

Item Description for Accounting Period 7/05 Through 6/06	Total	Zero Assets	Under 500	500 to 1,000	1,000 to 5,000	5,000 to 10,000	10,000 to 25,000	25,000 to 50,000	50,000 to 100,000	100,000 to 250,000	250,000 to 500,000	500,000 to 2,500,000	2,500,000 and over
Number of Enterprises **1**	3577	624	1073	199	1180	207	112	55	21	32	26	28	18
Revenues ($ in Thousands)													
Net Sales **2**	190272935	135349	391234	444915	6317334	2853500	2624339	2762006	1784652	5633411	8236376	20538918	138550901
Interest **3**	2348220	81	1483	649	3522	3189	2576	11040	14046	42206	122726	293010	1853692
Rents **4**	56788	0	0	1141	522	293	170	1563	417	845	6317	7846	37674
Royalties **5**	3882342	95	0	0	0	0	0	3086	29882	58361	205555	252641	3332722
Other Portfolio Income **6**	15934894	68149	0	0	13185	1257	21744	24326	2036	166425	243224	3725108	11669442
Other Receipts **7**	3045998	1158	391	4701	7290	8057	16845	59444	17751	99106	72394	1166751	1592108
Total Receipts **8**	215541177	204832	393108	451406	6341853	2866296	2665674	2861465	1848784	6000354	8886592	25984274	157036539
Average Total Receipts **9**	60258	328	366	2268	5374	13847	23801	52027	88037	187511	341792	928010	8724252
Operating Costs/Operating Income (%)													
Cost of Operations **10**	68.5	53.1	53.2	33.9	58.0	58.8	64.5	67.0	62.8	68.5	63.2	65.6	70.2
Salaries and Wages **11**	9.2	29.2	2.1	13.0	10.5	9.6	7.4	9.8	10.8	9.4	11.0	16.4	7.9
Taxes Paid **12**	1.0	1.7	4.2	3.0	3.4	2.7	1.7	1.6	1.5	1.5	1.5	1.5	0.7
Interest Paid **13**	1.2	0.0	0.0	0.1	0.8	1.0	0.9	0.9	0.9	0.5	1.0	1.1	1.3
Depreciation **14**	3.5	1.3	0.4	1.3	1.5	1.7	2.0	1.8	2.5	1.8	4.2	4.4	3.6
Amortization and Depletion **15**	0.7	0.5	0.6	0.1	0.3	0.2	0.2	0.3	0.4	0.3	1.0	1.0	0.7
Pensions and Other Deferred Comp. **16**	0.6	0.3	•	1.5	0.9	0.5	0.5	0.5	0.4	0.4	0.4	0.5	0.6
Employee Benefits **17**	1.5	2.1	0.2	0.2	1.2	1.3	1.6	1.8	1.7	1.1	1.7	2.1	1.4
Advertising **18**	1.7	0.4	0.1	0.2	0.8	0.9	0.4	0.5	0.8	0.8	0.2	0.5	2.1
Other Expenses **19**	7.5	11.5	13.9	26.0	9.2	10.1	9.5	9.7	12.4	9.6	10.7	8.6	6.6
Officers' Compensation **20**	1.0	15.3	16.3	20.9	4.4	3.3	2.8	1.9	1.3	1.2	2.4	1.5	0.4
Operating Margin **21**	3.9	8.9	8.9	•	9.0	9.9	8.4	4.3	4.5	5.0	2.7	•	4.5
Operating Margin Before Officers' Comp. **22**	4.8	•	25.2	20.8	13.4	13.2	11.2	6.2	5.9	6.2	5.1	•	4.9

Selected Average Balance Sheet ($ in Thousands)

Net Receivables 23	11767	0	24	344	818	1947	3307	9241	16511	35067	61935	142409	1815674
Inventories 24	3772	0	27	327	442	1903	3360	5973	13589	26444	21973	58223	469172
Net Property, Plant and Equipment 25	8732	0	3	59	529	1157	2410	4754	11381	20936	63136	172248	1247267
Total Assets 26	60165	0	143	689	2293	7452	14181	34028	77265	172750	365728	1139560	8813521
Notes and Loans Payable 27	5550	0	36	18	792	2335	3006	7166	10703	12278	28249	145059	680501
All Other Liabilities 28	16386	0	19	190	641	1523	3607	10122	20107	37282	84494	231172	2568702
Net Worth 29	3829	0	88	481	861	3594	7568	16740	46455	123190	252984	763330	5564319

Selected Financial Ratios (Times to 1)

Current Ratio 30	2.1	•	5.1	2.9	1.7	3.4	2.0	2.0	2.5	3.1	2.5	3.2	1.8
Quick Ratio 31	1.4	•	3.6	2.2	1.1	2.0	1.1	1.1	1.6	2.1	1.8	2.2	1.3
Net Sales to Working Capital 32	3.4	•	4.7	5.9	7.9	3.4	4.8	4.1	3.0	2.2	2.9	1.7	3.9
Coverage Ratio 33	17.1	782.4	364.8	12.5	12.9	11.8	13.4	10.4	9.7	23.5	12.8	22.4	16.8
Total Asset Turnover 34	0.9	•	2.6	3.2	2.3	1.8	1.7	1.5	1.1	1.0	0.9	0.6	0.9
Inventory Turnover 35	9.7	•	7.3	2.3	7.0	4.3	4.5	5.6	3.9	4.6	9.1	8.3	11.5
Receivables Turnover 36	5.6	•	19.3	4.2	7.8	7.9	7.5	7.1	5.4	4.6	7.5	5.1	5.5
Total Liabilities to Net Worth 37	0.6	•	0.6	0.4	1.7	1.1	0.9	1.0	0.7	0.4	0.4	0.5	0.6
Current Assets to Working Capital 38	1.9	•	1.2	1.5	2.4	1.4	2.0	2.0	1.7	1.5	1.7	1.5	2.2
Current Liabilities to Working Capital 39	0.9	•	0.2	0.5	1.4	0.4	1.0	1.0	0.7	0.5	0.7	0.5	1.2
Working Capital to Net Sales 40	0.3	•	0.2	0.2	0.1	0.3	0.2	0.2	0.3	0.5	0.3	0.6	0.3
Inventory to Working Capital 41	0.2	•	0.4	0.3	0.7	0.4	0.8	0.6	0.4	0.3	0.3	0.2	0.2
Total Receipts to Cash Flow 42	4.3	2.4	5.4	5.6	6.6	5.7	5.9	6.6	5.4	5.2	5.1	3.4	4.3
Cost of Goods to Cash Flow 43	3.0	1.3	2.9	1.9	3.8	3.4	3.8	4.4	3.4	3.5	3.2	2.2	3.0
Cash Flow to Total Debt 44	0.6	•	1.2	1.9	0.6	0.6	0.6	0.4	0.5	0.7	0.6	0.6	0.6

Selected Financial Factors (in Percentages)

Debt Ratio 45	36.5	•	38.3	30.1	62.5	51.8	46.6	50.8	39.9	28.7	30.8	33.0	36.9
Return on Total Assets 46	17.7	•	24.0	5.0	23.8	20.9	19.0	13.1	9.9	12.6	10.8	16.4	18.5
Return on Equity Before Income Taxes 47	26.3	•	38.9	6.5	58.4	39.6	32.9	24.0	14.8	16.9	14.4	23.4	27.6
Return on Equity After Income Taxes 48	20.8	•	36.0	5.6	54.1	34.8	27.9	21.4	11.7	14.5	12.2	19.9	21.4
Profit Margin (Before Income Tax) 49	18.9	35.8	9.4	1.4	9.4	10.3	10.6	8.0	8.1	11.8	11.5	24.4	20.0
Profit Margin (After Income Tax) 50	15.0	33.3	8.7	1.2	8.7	9.1	9.0	7.1	6.4	10.1	9.7	20.7	15.4

Table I

Corporations with and without Net Income

NAVIGATIONAL, MEASURING, ELECTROMEDICAL, AND CONTROL

MONEY AMOUNTS AND SIZE OF ASSETS IN THOUSANDS OF DOLLARS

Item Description for Accounting Period 7/05 Through 6/06	Total	Zero Assets	Under 500	500 to 1,000	1,000 to 5,000	5,000 to 10,000	10,000 to 25,000	25,000 to 50,000	50,000 to 100,000	100,000 to 250,000	250,000 to 500,000	500,000 to 2,500,000	2,500,000 and over
Number of Enterprises 1	2750	364	589	703	653	181	107	45	34	33	9	23	9
Revenues ($ in Thousands)													
Net Sales 2	58010683	539678	139637	1379790	3352031	1695953	2507794	2084922	2618589	4808355	2182181	14060374	22641381
Interest 3	916591	1865	113	417	6340	1641	5358	2916	13541	39380	28142	101654	715224
Rents 4	83558	0	0	1224	205	5189	128	1168	7471	730	812	8916	57714
Royalties 5	413716	3480	0	0	101	2231	0	8440	13	9502	608	65667	323675
Other Portfolio Income 6	4039435	5	0	3048	595	8545	6136	15192	23210	43470	67758	1643651	2227826
Other Receipts 7	1455847	18603	-1	16218	33882	25961	10732	27870	21042	22283	19911	350455	908888
Total Receipts 8	64919830	563631	139749	1400697	3393154	1739520	2530148	2140508	2683866	4923720	2299412	16230717	26874708
Average Total Receipts 9	23607	1548	237	1992	5196	9611	23646	47567	78937	149204	255490	705683	2986079
Operating Costs/Operating Income (%)													
Cost of Operations 10	60.7	58.5	40.9	51.5	58.4	59.5	58.7	56.2	60.3	52.6	58.7	58.9	65.6
Salaries and Wages 11	13.8	7.4	5.5	12.1	15.7	13.7	11.3	14.3	12.1	16.4	12.6	16.2	12.4
Taxes Paid 12	2.1	1.0	2.9	2.8	3.1	2.9	2.4	2.3	2.4	2.3	2.1	1.5	2.0
Interest Paid 13	2.8	1.6	2.9	0.6	1.0	1.3	0.7	1.3	1.6	1.3	1.3	1.9	4.9
Depreciation 14	2.0	1.2	0.9	0.7	1.5	2.2	1.3	1.6	1.6	2.1	2.0	2.3	2.0
Amortization and Depletion 15	1.3	0.5	•	0.0	0.0	0.2	0.1	1.0	0.7	0.8	1.1	1.4	2.1
Pensions and Other Deferred Comp. 16	1.7	1.2	0.0	0.3	0.3	0.4	0.7	0.9	0.7	0.6	0.3	1.1	3.0
Employee Benefits 17	2.7	1.5	3.3	1.9	5.0	2.2	1.7	3.3	1.9	2.6	1.2	2.3	3.2
Advertising 18	0.8	0.2	2.8	0.3	1.0	1.4	1.0	0.8	1.6	1.5	0.8	0.6	0.5
Other Expenses 19	12.3	22.6	54.8	13.2	13.2	13.7	13.4	13.7	14.6	16.3	17.3	13.7	8.7
Officers' Compensation 20	1.7	3.2	16.4	7.5	4.6	3.9	3.6	2.0	1.9	1.6	1.6	1.5	0.5
Operating Margin 21	•	1.1	•	8.9	•	•	5.2	2.7	0.5	2.0	1.0	•	•
Operating Margin Before Officers' Comp. 22	•	4.3	•	16.4	0.8	2.5	8.9	4.6	2.5	3.5	2.5	0.1	•

Selected Average Balance Sheet ($ in Thousands)

Net Receivables 23	4214	0	7	147	958	1928	3800	8006	16239	29499	73476	147656	461891
Inventories 24	2594	0	9	202	652	2063	2644	5776	11734	19738	35659	82304	264314
Net Property, Plant and Equipment 25	2747	0	2	32	406	646	2782	4583	8378	21147	31924	91989	362207
Total Assets 26	33711	0	113	799	2539	7554	15076	36538	73370	165707	354865	967623	5820369
Notes and Loans Payable 27	8501	0	124	306	822	1820	2771	8285	11881	18954	28448	228238	1668657
All Other Liabilities 28	7378	0	69	97	861	1815	3252	11709	15424	39093	81602	205972	1236521
Net Worth 29	17833	0	-81	396	857	3918	9053	16544	46064	107661	244814	533413	2915191

Selected Financial Ratios (Times to 1)

Current Ratio 30	1.6	•	0.8	6.0	1.9	2.5	2.5	1.8	2.4	2.6	3.0	1.8	1.0
Quick Ratio 31	1.0	•	0.6	4.8	1.1	1.6	1.5	1.0	1.4	1.5	2.1	1.2	0.6
Net Sales to Working Capital 32	5.1	•	•	4.0	5.5	3.2	3.7	5.2	2.7	2.7	1.7	3.3	48.7
Coverage Ratio 33	5.3	4.5	•	17.8	•	1.9	9.6	5.2	3.3	4.4	5.8	9.0	4.6
Total Asset Turnover 34	0.6	•	2.1	2.5	2.0	1.2	1.6	1.3	1.0	0.9	0.7	0.6	0.4
Inventory Turnover 35	4.9	10.9	5.0	•	4.6	2.7	5.2	4.5	4.0	3.9	4.0	4.4	6.2
Receivables Turnover 36	5.3	10.6	12.0	•	5.6	4.2	7.3	6.4	5.4	5.4	3.3	4.2	6.0
Total Liabilities to Net Worth 37	0.9	•	1.0	1.0	2.0	0.9	0.7	1.2	0.6	0.5	0.4	0.8	1.0
Current Assets to Working Capital 38	2.8	•	1.2	1.2	2.1	1.7	1.7	2.2	1.7	1.6	1.5	2.3	23.3
Current Liabilities to Working Capital 39	1.8	•	0.2	0.2	1.1	1.1	0.7	1.2	0.7	0.6	0.5	1.3	22.3
Working Capital to Net Sales 40	0.2	•	0.3	0.3	0.2	0.6	0.3	0.2	0.4	0.4	0.6	0.3	0.0
Inventory to Working Capital 41	0.6	•	0.2	0.2	0.7	0.7	0.5	0.6	0.4	0.4	0.2	0.4	5.3
Total Receipts to Cash Flow 42	5.2	5.3	5.3	5.3	12.2	9.1	5.5	6.0	6.8	5.6	5.2	4.0	5.3
Cost of Goods to Cash Flow 43	3.2	2.2	2.7	2.7	7.1	5.4	3.2	3.4	4.1	2.9	3.0	2.4	3.5
Cash Flow to Total Debt 44	0.3	0.2	0.9	0.9	0.3	0.3	0.7	0.4	0.4	0.4	0.4	0.3	0.2

Selected Financial Factors (in Percentages)

Debt Ratio 45	47.1	•	171.5	50.4	66.3	48.1	40.0	54.7	37.2	35.0	31.0	44.9	49.9
Return on Total Assets 46	9.2	•	•	27.0	•	3.0	10.7	8.5	5.5	4.9	5.3	10.7	9.7
Return on Equity Before Income Taxes 47	14.1	•	89.6	51.4	•	2.8	16.0	15.2	6.2	5.9	6.4	17.3	15.2
Return on Equity After Income Taxes 48	11.9	•	90.7	50.9	•	1.8	14.0	11.9	3.6	3.8	3.8	15.0	13.2
Profit Margin (Before Income Tax) 49	11.9	5.5	•	10.4	•	1.2	6.2	5.4	3.7	4.3	6.5	15.1	17.6
Profit Margin (After Income Tax) 50	10.0	4.7	•	10.3	•	0.8	5.4	4.3	2.1	2.8	3.9	13.1	15.3

Table II
Corporations with Net Income

NAVIGATIONAL, MEASURING, ELECTROMEDICAL, AND CONTROL

MONEY AMOUNTS AND SIZE OF ASSETS IN THOUSANDS OF DOLLARS

Item Description for Accounting Period 7/05 Through 6/06	Total	Zero Assets	Under 500	500 to 1,000	1,000 to 5,000	5,000 to 10,000	10,000 to 25,000	25,000 to 50,000	50,000 to 100,000	100,000 to 250,000	250,000 to 500,000	500,000 to 2,500,000	2,500,000 and over
Number of Enterprises 1	2163	•	303	683	455	145	93	33	26	27	•	•	20
Revenues ($ in Thousands)													
Net Sales 2	53968697	•	92489	1373878	2520948	1504864	2291395	1708492	2231783	4242559	•	13385905	•
Interest 3	880804	•	107	174	5247	313	2168	2447	12091	31449	•	93700	•
Rents 4	82710	•	0	1224	205	5186	128	1088	7471	730	•	8152	•
Royalties 5	404124	•	0	0	101	0	0	1370	13	9502	•	65376	•
Other Portfolio Income 6	4027196	•	0	3038	244	8518	4075	14650	21810	42496	•	1638941	•
Other Receipts 7	1353845	•	0	16212	32735	14943	9250	13781	20278	18187	•	284886	•
Total Receipts 8	60717376	•	92596	1394526	2559480	1533824	2307016	1741828	2293446	4344923	•	15476960	•
Average Total Receipts 9	28071	•	306	2042	5625	10578	24807	52783	88209	160923	•	773848	•
Operating Costs/Operating Income (%)													
Cost of Operations 10	60.5	•	17.7	50.7	51.8	60.3	57.9	53.3	59.3	53.7	•	58.4	•
Salaries and Wages 11	13.2	•	0.1	12.1	16.5	11.9	10.7	14.1	11.1	14.0	•	15.6	•
Taxes Paid 12	2.0	•	2.4	2.7	2.7	2.6	2.3	2.3	2.1	2.3	•	1.5	•
Interest Paid 13	2.8	•	0.0	0.5	0.8	0.9	0.7	0.9	0.6	1.2	•	1.9	•
Depreciation 14	1.9	•	1.3	0.7	1.6	1.4	1.2	1.1	1.5	2.0	•	2.3	•
Amortization and Depletion 15	1.4	•	•	0.0	0.0	0.1	0.1	0.8	0.3	0.7	•	1.3	•
Pensions and Other Deferred Comp. 16	1.8	•	0.1	0.3	0.3	0.5	0.6	1.0	0.9	0.7	•	1.2	•
Employee Benefits 17	2.6	•	5.0	1.9	3.1	2.2	1.6	3.5	2.0	2.5	•	2.1	•
Advertising 18	0.7	•	•	0.3	0.9	1.5	1.1	0.8	1.4	1.6	•	0.6	•
Other Expenses 19	11.5	•	47.0	12.9	13.5	11.0	11.7	12.6	13.9	14.2	•	13.3	•
Officers' Compensation 20	1.6	•	22.1	7.3	5.0	3.0	3.5	2.0	1.9	1.5	•	1.6	•
Operating Margin 21	0.1	•	4.2	10.6	3.8	4.5	8.6	7.6	4.9	5.4	•	0.2	•
Operating Margin Before Officers' Comp. 22	1.7	•	26.3	17.9	8.7	7.6	12.2	9.6	6.9	6.9	•	1.8	•

Selected Average Balance Sheet ($ in Thousands)

Net Receivables 23	4834	12	149	887	2097	3881	8356	16670	30771	155727
Inventories 24	2602	9	111	773	2361	2607	5776	11742	21232	84713
Net Property, Plant and Equipment 25	3217	3	31	442	664	2960	4768	9283	22702	96991
Total Assets 26	38780	203	799	2627	7732	14823	36484	73658	166503	1000253
Notes and Loans Payable 27	10064	0	305	734	1802	2794	6912	8710	16457	235382
All Other Liabilities 28	8706	5	94	865	1563	3315	11964	15988	41413	216357
Net Worth 29	20010	198	400	1028	4367	8715	17608	48959	108633	548513

Selected Financial Ratios (Times to 1)

Current Ratio 30	1.5	17.0	6.1	2.2	2.6	2.4	1.9	2.8	2.8	1.8
Quick Ratio 31	1.0	14.6	4.9	1.2	1.6	1.4	1.1	1.7	1.6	1.2
Net Sales to Working Capital 32	5.5	3.7	4.1	5.1	3.6	4.2	4.9	2.6	2.9	3.5
Coverage Ratio 33	6.2	108.8	23.9	7.3	8.6	15.2	11.6	13.5	7.3	10.0
Total Asset Turnover 34	0.6	1.5	2.5	2.1	1.3	1.7	1.4	1.2	0.9	0.7
Inventory Turnover 35	5.8	6.2	9.2	3.7	2.7	5.5	4.8	4.3	4.0	4.6
Receivables Turnover 36	6.3	7.8	27.1	7.1	4.1	7.8	7.2	6.0	5.7	4.6
Total Liabilities to Net Worth 37	0.9	0.0	1.0	1.6	0.8	0.7	1.1	0.5	0.5	0.8
Current Assets to Working Capital 38	2.9	1.1	1.2	1.9	1.6	1.7	2.1	1.6	1.6	2.3
Current Liabilities to Working Capital 39	1.9	0.1	0.2	0.9	0.6	0.7	1.1	0.6	0.6	1.3
Working Capital to Net Sales 40	0.2	0.3	0.2	0.2	0.3	0.2	0.2	0.4	0.3	0.3
Inventory to Working Capital 41	0.7	0.1	0.2	0.8	0.6	0.5	0.6	0.4	0.4	0.4
Total Receipts to Cash Flow 42	4.8	2.2	4.9	6.1	7.1	5.1	4.9	5.4	5.2	3.8
Cost of Goods to Cash Flow 43	2.9	0.4	2.5	3.2	4.3	2.9	2.6	3.2	2.8	2.2
Cash Flow to Total Debt 44	0.3	27.0	1.0	0.6	0.4	0.8	0.6	0.6	0.5	0.4

Selected Financial Factors (in Percentages)

Debt Ratio 45	48.4	2.5	49.9	60.9	43.5	41.2	51.7	33.5	34.8	45.2
Return on Total Assets 46	11.1	6.5	31.8	12.9	9.9	16.7	15.0	10.0	8.5	12.7
Return on Equity Before Income Taxes 47	18.1	6.6	60.9	28.5	15.4	26.5	28.5	14.0	11.3	20.8
Return on Equity After Income Taxes 48	15.6	5.7	60.3	22.3	14.3	24.2	24.2	10.8	8.8	18.2
Profit Margin (Before Income Tax) 49	14.5	4.3	12.1	5.3	6.5	9.4	9.7	8.0	7.8	17.0
Profit Margin (After Income Tax) 50	12.5	3.7	12.0	4.1	6.0	8.6	8.2	6.2	6.1	14.9

Table I

Corporations with and without Net Income

ELECTRICAL LIGHTING EQUIPMENT AND HOUSEHOLD APPLIANCE

MONEY AMOUNTS AND SIZE OF ASSETS IN THOUSANDS OF DOLLARS

Item Description for Accounting Period 7/05 Through 6/06	Total	Zero Assets	Under 500	500 to 1,000	1,000 to 5,000	5,000 to 10,000	10,000 to 25,000	25,000 to 50,000	50,000 to 100,000	100,000 to 250,000	250,000 to 500,000	500,000 to 2,500,000	2,500,000 and over
Number of Enterprises 1	1520	26	1175	0	64	106	82	22	9	20	6	4	5
Revenues ($ in Thousands)													
Net Sales 2	135269987	1766560	163388	0	457696	1073081	2602400	1255086	848284	4562839	2618411	4514424	115407817
Interest 3	36835507	53703	0	0	441	16	1972	285	10346	8038	676	4427	36755602
Rents 4	29959	0	0	0	0	0	3804	688	33	3795	383	17289	3968
Royalties 5	1914640	1969	0	0	0	0	0	1141	61	24381	191	7737	1879160
Other Portfolio Income 6	10403135	11117	0	0	0	20	6793	1365	10093	23162	5681	60601	10284302
Other Receipts 7	14474051	54572	3472	0	1481	2789	5207	2525	2516	62285	28651	19281	14291275
Total Receipts 8	198927279	1887921	166860	0	459618	1075906	2620176	1261090	871333	4684500	2653993	4623759	178622124
Average Total Receipts 9	130873	72612	142	•	7182	10150	31953	57322	96815	234225	442332	1155940	35724425
Operating Costs/Operating Income (%)													
Cost of Operations 10	65.6	76.3	50.3	•	60.9	69.8	65.9	73.6	61.3	64.4	66.5	66.2	65.3
Salaries and Wages 11	12.5	4.4	14.1	•	8.0	11.8	8.1	5.0	11.0	8.6	4.1	14.9	13.1
Taxes Paid 12	1.1	1.1	2.7	•	1.4	2.5	1.9	1.7	1.6	1.6	1.2	2.1	1.0
Interest Paid 13	29.4	2.6	2.0	•	0.8	1.5	1.1	0.9	1.3	1.1	1.5	1.8	34.3
Depreciation 14	8.4	1.4	0.6	•	1.0	0.9	1.1	1.6	1.9	1.5	1.8	1.5	9.6
Amortization and Depletion 15	1.5	0.6	0.2	•	0.2	0.2	0.1	0.1	0.6	0.5	0.4	0.3	1.7
Pensions and Other Deferred Comp. 16	0.6	0.3	•	•	0.1	0.0	0.4	0.4	0.7	0.8	0.2	1.2	0.6
Employee Benefits 17	2.0	1.8	0.3	•	1.0	1.4	1.7	0.9	2.6	1.9	1.8	2.0	2.0
Advertising 18	1.0	0.7	1.8	•	0.3	0.8	1.3	1.8	1.9	3.2	8.0	0.9	0.8
Other Expenses 19	20.5	11.2	32.9	•	25.9	13.2	13.3	7.9	14.3	10.5	10.3	8.6	22.1
Officers' Compensation 20	0.4	1.2	6.7	•	3.1	0.6	2.0	1.7	1.5	1.1	0.3	0.1	0.3
Operating Margin 21	•	•	•	•	•	•	3.0	4.4	1.3	4.9	3.7	0.3	•
Operating Margin Before Officers' Comp. 22	•	•	•	•	0.4	•	5.0	6.1	2.7	6.0	4.0	0.4	•

Selected Average Balance Sheet ($ in Thousands)

Net Receivables 23	117317	0	6	•	797	2157	4062	10322	18874	44497	54092	210839	35049559
Inventories 24	6353	0	24	•	2363	2632	4205	7113	15786	32675	52124	181392	1387799
Net Property, Plant and Equipment 25	32939	0	1	•	324	804	2652	6312	12023	26549	61366	144276	9603716
Total Assets 26	822110	0	54	•	3455	6306	15991	34850	67358	164742	326224	1308435	247096833
Notes and Loans Payable 27	282899	0	24	•	410	2926	4550	9209	18120	36106	101478	250690	85313778
All Other Liabilities 28	122133	0	29	•	640	2028	4279	12509	18556	51316	94652	293278	36358444
Net Worth 29	417079	0	2	•	2406	1352	7162	13132	30682	77321	130094	764466	125424611

Selected Financial Ratios (Times to 1)

Current Ratio 30	0.8	•	1.2	•	2.1	1.4	1.9	1.9	1.9	2.3	2.2	1.7	0.7
Quick Ratio 31	0.6	•	0.6	•	1.0	0.6	0.9	1.0	1.2	1.4	1.1	0.9	0.6
Net Sales to Working Capital 32	•	•	20.6	•	5.3	7.6	6.1	4.7	4.8	4.0	4.9	5.7	•
Coverage Ratio 33	1.2	3.1	•	•	•	•	4.4	6.4	4.0	8.1	4.2	2.7	1.2
Total Asset Turnover 34	0.1	•	2.6	•	2.1	1.6	2.0	1.6	1.4	1.4	1.3	0.9	0.1
Inventory Turnover 35	9.2	•	2.9	•	1.8	2.7	5.0	5.9	3.7	4.5	5.6	4.1	10.9
Receivables Turnover 36	0.6	•	45.3	•	6.2	9.4	9.1	6.3	5.0	5.5	9.0	5.3	0.6
Total Liabilities to Net Worth 37	1.0	•	33.5	•	0.4	3.7	1.2	1.7	1.2	1.1	1.5	0.7	1.0
Current Assets to Working Capital 38	•	•	6.9	•	1.9	3.7	2.1	2.1	2.2	1.8	1.8	2.4	•
Current Liabilities to Working Capital 39	•	•	5.9	•	0.9	2.7	1.1	1.1	1.2	0.8	0.8	1.4	•
Working Capital to Net Sales 40	•	•	0.0	•	0.2	0.1	0.2	0.2	0.2	0.3	0.2	0.2	•
Inventory to Working Capital 41	•	•	3.6	•	1.0	2.0	1.0	0.6	0.7	0.6	0.7	0.9	•
Total Receipts to Cash Flow 42	5.2	6.4	7.8	•	4.7	10.3	6.7	8.7	6.5	6.0	7.2	10.2	4.9
Cost of Goods to Cash Flow 43	3.4	4.9	3.9	•	2.9	7.2	4.4	6.4	4.0	3.9	4.8	6.8	3.2
Cash Flow to Total Debt 44	0.0	•	0.3	•	1.5	0.2	0.5	0.3	0.4	0.4	0.3	0.2	0.0

Selected Financial Factors (in Percentages)

Debt Ratio 45	49.3	•	97.1	•	30.4	78.6	55.2	62.3	54.4	53.1	60.1	41.6	49.2
Return on Total Assets 46	3.8	•	•	•	•	•	9.4	9.5	7.4	12.1	8.6	4.0	3.8
Return on Equity Before Income Taxes 47	1.3	•	•	•	•	9.4	16.3	21.2	12.2	22.5	16.4	4.3	1.1
Return on Equity After Income Taxes 48	0.9	•	•	•	•	•	14.4	18.7	10.5	19.8	13.9	4.9	0.8
Profit Margin (Before Income Tax) 49	5.9	5.4	•	•	3.7	4.9	4.9	7.6	4.0	4.9	2.7	2.9	6.2
Profit Margin (After Income Tax) 50	4.1	3.4	•	•	3.3	4.3	3.4	6.7	3.4	4.9	4.1	1.8	4.2

147

ELECTRICAL LIGHTING EQUIPMENT AND HOUSEHOLD APPLIANCE

Table II

Corporations with Net Income

MONEY AMOUNTS AND SIZE OF ASSETS IN THOUSANDS OF DOLLARS

Item Description for Accounting Period 7/05 Through 6/06	Total	Zero Assets	Under 500	500 to 1,000	1,000 to 5,000	5,000 to 10,000	10,000 to 25,000	25,000 to 50,000	50,000 to 100,000	100,000 to 250,000	250,000 to 500,000	500,000 to 2,500,000	2,500,000 and over
Number of Enterprises 1	714	·	497	0	48	23	67	19	6	·	·	0	5
Revenues ($ in Thousands)													
Net Sales 2	132314357	·	104590	0	452301	326872	2330999	984981	766075	·	·	0	115407817
Interest 3	36824838	·	0	0	5	1	1786	271	1795	·	·	0	36755602
Rents 4	27183	·	0	0	0	0	3804	688	33	·	·	0	3968
Royalties 5	1906087	·	0	0	0	0	0	1141	61	·	·	0	1879160
Other Portfolio Income 6	10397810	·	0	0	0	20	6793	1307	10093	·	·	0	10284302
Other Receipts 7	14437340	·	0	0	1371	236	4542	1204	1066	·	·	0	14291275
Total Receipts 8	195907615	·	104590	0	453677	327129	2347924	989592	779123	·	·	0	178622124
Average Total Receipts 9	274380	·	210	·	9452	14223	35044	52084	129854	·	·	·	3572425
Operating Costs/Operating Income (%)													
Cost of Operations 10	65.3	·	44.8	·	61.6	67.2	65.3	70.4	60.4	·	·	·	65.3
Salaries and Wages 11	12.6	·	3.0	·	5.5	9.0	8.4	6.1	11.0	·	·	·	13.1
Taxes Paid 12	1.1	·	3.6	·	1.1	1.8	1.9	1.9	1.6	·	·	·	1.0
Interest Paid 13	30.1	·	0.8	·	0.7	1.1	1.0	1.1	1.2	·	·	·	34.3
Depreciation 14	8.6	·	0.9	·	0.6	0.6	1.0	1.8	1.5	·	·	·	9.6
Amortization and Depletion 15	1.5	·	·	·	0.1	·	0.1	0.1	0.4	·	·	·	1.7
Pensions and Other Deferred Comp. 16	0.6	·	·	·	0.1	0.1	0.5	0.4	0.8	·	·	·	0.6
Employee Benefits 17	2.0	·	·	·	0.8	0.8	1.4	0.7	2.5	·	·	·	2.0
Advertising 18	1.0	·	0.7	·	0.3	1.1	1.3	1.2	2.0	·	·	·	0.8
Other Expenses 19	20.7	·	36.5	·	22.2	15.4	12.5	7.3	13.8	·	·	·	22.1
Officers' Compensation 20	0.4	·	6.8	·	2.3	1.8	2.1	2.1	1.5	·	·	·	0.3
Operating Margin 21	·	·	3.0	·	4.7	1.0	4.6	6.7	3.2	·	·	·	·
Operating Margin Before Officers' Comp. 22	·	·	9.7	·	7.0	2.8	6.7	8.8	4.7	·	·	·	·

Selected Average Balance Sheet ($ in Thousands)

Net Receivables 23	248904	2	1063	1937	4423	8457	23856		35049559
Inventories 24	12128	26	3136	5032	4195	6028	17264		1544272
Net Property, Plant and Equipment 25	69474	2	287	424	2498	6111	11586		9603716
Total Assets 26	1744554	65	3317	8192	15786	33524	74439		247096833
Notes and Loans Payable 27	601234	8	357	3025	4351	8528	21510		85313778
All Other Liabilities 28	258629	43	728	2928	4553	11750	18543		36358444
Net Worth 29	884690	15	2231	2239	6882	13246	34386		125424611

Selected Financial Ratios (Times to 1)

Current Ratio 30	0.8	1.0	2.1	1.5	1.9	1.9	2.2		0.7
Quick Ratio 31	0.6	0.4	0.9	0.4	0.9	0.9	1.4		0.6
Net Sales to Working Capital 32			5.9	5.4	6.0	4.7	4.4		1.2
Coverage Ratio 33	1.2	4.9	8.1	1.9	6.4	7.4	5.2		1.2
Total Asset Turnover 34	0.1	3.2	2.8	1.7	2.2	1.5	1.7		0.1
Inventory Turnover 35	10.0	3.6	1.9	1.9	5.4	6.1	4.5		9.8
Receivables Turnover 36	0.6	48.3	6.2	7.4	9.7	8.2	10.7		1.3
Total Liabilities to Net Worth 37	1.0	3.5	0.5	2.7	1.3	1.5	1.2		1.0
Current Assets to Working Capital 38			1.9	2.9	2.1	2.1	1.8		
Current Liabilities to Working Capital 39			0.9	1.9	1.1	1.1	0.8		
Working Capital to Net Sales 40			0.2	0.2	0.2	0.2	0.2		
Inventory to Working Capital 41			1.1	2.0	1.0	0.6	0.6		
Total Receipts to Cash Flow 42	5.1	3.9	3.9	6.4	6.3	7.6	6.2		4.9
Cost of Goods to Cash Flow 43	3.3	1.8	2.4	4.3	4.1	5.4	3.8		3.2
Cash Flow to Total Debt 44	0.0	1.1	2.2	0.4	0.6	0.3	0.5		0.0

Selected Financial Factors (in Percentages)

Debt Ratio 45	49.3	77.8	32.7	72.7	56.4	60.5	53.8		49.2
Return on Total Assets 46	3.8	12.0	16.2	3.8	13.9	12.8	10.4		3.8
Return on Equity Before Income Taxes 47	1.3	43.3	21.2	6.8	27.0	28.0	18.2		1.1
Return on Equity After Income Taxes 48	0.9	43.3	20.4	4.9	24.7	25.2	16.0		0.8
Profit Margin (Before Income Tax) 49	6.2	3.0	5.0	1.1	5.3	7.2	4.9		6.2
Profit Margin (After Income Tax) 50	4.3	3.0	4.8	0.8	4.9	6.4	4.3		4.2

Table I

Corporations with and without Net Income

ELECTRICAL EQUIPMENT

MONEY AMOUNTS AND SIZE OF ASSETS IN THOUSANDS OF DOLLARS

Item Description for Accounting Period 7/05 Through 6/06	Total	Zero Assets	Under 500	500 to 1,000	1,000 to 5,000	5,000 to 10,000	10,000 to 25,000	25,000 to 50,000	50,000 to 100,000	100,000 to 250,000	250,000 to 500,000	500,000 to 2,500,000	2,500,000 and over
Number of Enterprises 1	2091	620	581	308	341	125	51	22	12	14	6	7	4
Revenues ($ in Thousands)													
Net Sales 2	43093259	744743	174955	530413	1965411	1530886	1331902	903074	965297	2856422	2377295	6725949	22986909
Interest 3	499619	578	303	23	1715	1861	2274	124	4579	13013	15511	75801	382839
Rents 4	81758	0	0	0	519	278	2375	255	408	0	521	1027	76373
Royalties 5	148029	6	0	0	0	0	127	0	1935	510	6161	19092	120198
Other Portfolio Income 6	2453385	9337	4803	523	633	2406	40651	1297	2991	143757	31430	613401	1602155
Other Receipts 7	630112	20385	4965	30	35112	8695	8486	-2726	4746	18734	14149	75907	441633
Total Receipts 8	46905162	775049	185026	530989	2003390	1544126	1385815	902024	979956	3032436	2445067	7511177	25610107
Average Total Receipts 9	22432	1250	318	1724	5875	12353	27173	41001	81663	216603	407511	1073025	6402527
Operating Costs/Operating Income (%)													
Cost of Operations 10	68.4	70.2	56.8	58.8	66.9	66.1	64.8	74.3	65.9	64.8	61.9	68.6	70.1
Salaries and Wages 11	7.3	4.7	11.1	3.6	9.6	7.5	9.6	7.0	9.6	9.3	7.4	7.5	6.7
Taxes Paid 12	1.8	0.7	3.3	2.7	1.9	2.0	2.6	1.6	1.6	2.0	2.4	1.1	1.9
Interest Paid 13	2.5	0.3	0.8	0.9	1.0	0.1	0.5	1.7	1.7	1.0	1.4	1.7	3.7
Depreciation 14	1.7	1.8	2.6	2.6	1.2	0.8	1.8	1.5	2.8	2.0	2.2	1.8	1.7
Amortization and Depletion 15	1.2	0.4	0.0	0.1	0.1	0.0	0.1	0.2	1.9	1.0	0.6	1.6	1.6
Pensions and Other Deferred Comp. 16	1.2	0.5	•	0.1	1.2	0.9	1.1	0.9	1.0	1.1	1.7	0.8	1.4
Employee Benefits 17	2.5	1.9	3.3	0.8	0.5	1.4	2.4	1.1	1.9	1.6	1.6	2.5	3.1
Advertising 18	0.5	0.2	0.6	0.3	0.4	0.4	0.3	0.7	0.5	0.9	0.5	1.0	0.4
Other Expenses 19	9.9	12.8	28.3	16.6	10.1	6.3	9.7	6.7	10.8	10.4	15.2	12.3	8.5
Officers' Compensation 20	1.1	2.7	14.2	7.5	2.0	5.1	3.1	1.6	1.3	0.9	1.2	0.6	0.5
Operating Margin 21	1.8	3.9	•	6.1	5.1	9.2	4.0	2.7	1.0	4.8	3.8	0.6	0.7
Operating Margin Before Officers' Comp. 22	2.9	6.6	•	13.6	7.1	14.3	7.1	4.2	2.3	5.7	5.0	1.2	1.2

Selected Average Balance Sheet ($ in Thousands)

	1	2	3	4	5	6	7	8	9	10	11	12	13
Net Receivables 23	4278	0	48	194	540	1577	4311	8726	14425	32144	88570	312770	1180346
Inventories 24	2018	0	45	220	1163	1514	3673	8167	12430	22335	51335	134408	370433
Net Property, Plant and Equipment 25	2558	0	6	102	406	662	2002	6352	13592	26936	84431	124272	733468
Total Assets 26	31287	0	137	768	2419	6447	15075	35285	71756	165640	360845	1318171	11839176
Notes and Loans Payable 27	3247	0	45	181	931	383	1867	9706	21359	28288	43834	158682	1001737
All Other Liabilities 28	7193	0	47	260	497	2144	4742	10760	11983	48430	128296	420253	2371129
Net Worth 29	20847	0	45	326	990	3919	8466	14818	38413	88922	188716	739236	8466310

Selected Financial Ratios (Times to 1)

	1	2	3	4	5	6	7	8	9	10	11	12	13
Current Ratio 30	1.2	•	1.8	1.9	3.1	3.6	2.6	2.0	2.2	2.0	1.8	1.9	0.8
Quick Ratio 31	0.7	•	1.1	0.8	1.1	2.4	1.6	1.0	1.2	1.1	1.2	1.4	0.5
Net Sales to Working Capital 32	15.8	•	6.1	6.3	4.5	3.5	3.8	4.1	4.5	4.0	4.6	3.2	•
Coverage Ratio 33	5.8	24.9	•	7.5	8.0	71.3	16.6	2.5	3.2	11.7	6.5	9.4	4.9
Total Asset Turnover 34	0.7	•	2.2	2.2	2.4	1.9	1.7	1.2	1.1	1.2	1.1	0.7	0.5
Inventory Turnover 35	7.0	•	3.8	4.6	3.3	5.3	4.6	3.7	4.3	5.9	4.8	4.9	10.9
Receivables Turnover 36	4.3	•	12.4	8.2	11.5	15.5	5.5	4.7	5.7	7.5	6.2	2.9	3.9
Total Liabilities to Net Worth 37	0.5	•	2.0	1.4	0.6	0.8	4.7	1.4	0.9	0.9	0.8	2.9	0.4
Current Assets to Working Capital 38	6.8	•	2.2	2.2	1.4	1.6	2.0	0.8	1.8	2.0	2.2	2.1	0.4
Current Liabilities to Working Capital 39	5.8	•	1.2	1.2	0.5	1.2	1.0	0.6	0.8	1.0	1.2	1.1	•
Working Capital to Net Sales 40	0.1	•	0.2	0.2	0.2	0.3	0.6	0.2	0.2	0.2	0.2	0.3	•
Inventory to Working Capital 41	1.6	•	0.9	1.0	0.9	0.4	0.4	0.9	0.6	0.5	0.7	0.4	•
Total Receipts to Cash Flow 42	5.4	6.3	16.8	5.2	6.6	6.5	7.5	11.8	8.4	5.9	5.0	4.3	5.3
Cost of Goods to Cash Flow 43	3.7	4.4	9.5	3.0	4.5	4.3	4.8	8.8	5.6	3.8	3.1	3.0	3.7
Cash Flow to Total Debt 44	0.4	•	0.2	0.8	0.6	0.7	0.5	0.2	0.3	0.4	0.5	0.4	0.3

Selected Financial Factors (in Percentages)

	1	2	3	4	5	6	7	8	9	10	11	12	13
Debt Ratio 45	33.4	•	66.9	57.5	59.0	39.2	43.8	58.0	46.5	46.3	47.7	43.9	28.5
Return on Total Assets 46	9.6	•	16.0	19.0	14.8	19.4	4.8	6.0	14.9	9.7	11.4	8.6	
Return on Equity Before Income Taxes 47	11.9	•	32.6	40.6	31.5	24.7	6.9	7.7	25.5	15.6	18.1	9.6	
Return on Equity After Income Taxes 48	9.6	•	31.5	36.8	29.0	21.0	5.2	4.7	22.8	10.4	14.6	7.6	
Profit Margin (Before Income Tax) 49	12.1	8.3	6.2	7.0	10.1	8.0	2.5	3.7	11.1	7.4	13.9	14.2	
Profit Margin (After Income Tax) 50	9.7	7.8	6.0	6.3	9.3	6.8	1.9	2.2	9.9	5.0	11.2	11.2	

149

Table II

Corporations with Net Income

ELECTRICAL EQUIPMENT

MONEY AMOUNTS AND SIZE OF ASSETS IN THOUSANDS OF DOLLARS

Item Description for Accounting Period 7/05 Through 6/06	Total	Zero Assets	Under 500	500 to 1,000	1,000 to 5,000	5,000 to 10,000	10,000 to 25,000	25,000 to 50,000	50,000 to 100,000	100,000 to 250,000	250,000 to 500,000	500,000 to 2,500,000	2,500,000 and over
Number of Enterprises 1	1251	372	105	308	280	91	43	15	9	•	6	•	•
Revenues ($ in Thousands)													
Net Sales 2	37301835	632007	99422	530413	1600905	1371502	1209168	595708	687150	•	2377295	•	•
Interest 3	468881	410	0	23	1706	653	1564	118	2515	•	15511	•	•
Rents 4	73907	0	0	0	519	0	2375	0	408	•	521	•	•
Royalties 5	141703	6	0	0	0	0	0	0	1935	•	6161	•	•
Other Portfolio Income 6	2412173	6913	0	523	319	301	40471	1275	2991	•	31430	•	•
Other Receipts 7	568332	19768	0	30	34985	5079	8471	2231	4643	•	14149	•	•
Total Receipts 8	40966831	659104	99422	530989	1638434	1377535	1262049	599332	699642	•	2445067	•	•
Average Total Receipts 9	32747	1772	947	1724	5852	15138	29350	39955	77738	•	407511	•	•
Operating Costs/Operating Income (%)													
Cost of Operations 10	67.3	74.6	69.9	58.8	65.0	63.2	63.1	69.9	67.4	•	61.9	•	•
Salaries and Wages 11	7.1	3.3	•	3.6	10.0	7.0	9.7	7.4	10.7	•	7.4	•	•
Taxes Paid 12	1.8	0.5	2.2	2.7	2.1	2.0	2.5	1.6	1.6	•	2.4	•	•
Interest Paid 13	2.6	0.4	0.8	0.9	1.0	0.1	0.5	1.2	0.9	•	1.4	•	•
Depreciation 14	1.8	1.3	3.2	2.6	1.3	0.7	1.9	1.6	2.9	•	2.2	•	•
Amortization and Depletion 15	1.3	0.5	•	0.1	0.1	0.0	0.0	0.1	0.4	•	0.6	•	•
Pensions and Other Deferred Comp. 16	1.3	0.0	•	0.1	1.4	1.0	1.2	0.4	0.9	•	1.7	•	•
Employee Benefits 17	2.5	1.7	3.1	0.8	0.5	1.4	2.3	0.8	1.4	•	1.6	•	•
Advertising 18	0.5	0.1	•	0.3	0.4	0.4	0.3	1.0	0.3	•	0.5	•	•
Other Expenses 19	9.5	8.3	11.6	16.6	8.5	5.1	9.1	7.3	9.1	•	15.2	•	•
Officers' Compensation 20	1.2	2.8	7.5	7.5	2.5	5.3	3.3	1.9	1.3	•	1.2	•	•
Operating Margin 21	3.2	6.6	1.6	6.1	7.2	13.8	6.0	6.9	3.1	•	3.8	•	•
Operating Margin Before Officers' Comp. 22	4.3	9.4	9.0	13.6	9.7	19.1	9.3	8.8	4.4	•	5.0	•	•

Selected Average Balance Sheet ($ in Thousands)

Net Receivables 23	6265	0	179	194	443	1916	4199	7073	14614	88570
Inventories 24	2862	0	164	152	1138	1494	3517	6299	11570	56544
Net Property, Plant and Equipment 25	3811	0	2	102	420	485	2261	4813	15676	84431
Total Assets 26	47664	0	355	768	2396	6311	15467	31427	67745	360845
Notes and Loans Payable 27	4838	0	220	181	833	441	1950	4076	13565	43834
All Other Liabilities 28	9277	0	156	260	398	1414	3656	8777	13096	128296
Net Worth 29	33549	0	-21	326	1164	4456	9862	18575	41084	188716

Selected Financial Ratios (Times to 1)

Current Ratio 30	1.2	•	1.6	1.9	4.1	3.6	2.9	2.6	2.4	1.8
Quick Ratio 31	0.8	•	0.8	0.8	1.4	2.3	1.8	1.4	1.4	1.2
Net Sales to Working Capital 32	13.4	•	7.5	6.3	4.1	3.8	3.8	4.2	4.2	4.6
Coverage Ratio 33	6.6	29.7	2.9	7.5	10.3	100.3	22.4	7.2	7.9	6.5
Total Asset Turnover 34	0.6	•	2.7	2.2	2.4	2.4	1.8	1.3	1.1	1.1
Inventory Turnover 35	7.0	•	4.0	6.7	3.3	6.4	5.0	4.4	4.4	4.3
Receivables Turnover 36	4.1	•	10.6	12.3	12.8	8.1	6.7	5.6	6.1	8.9
Total Liabilities to Net Worth 37	0.4	•	•	1.4	1.1	0.4	0.6	0.7	0.6	0.9
Current Assets to Working Capital 38	5.6	•	2.8	2.2	1.3	1.4	1.5	1.6	1.7	2.2
Current Liabilities to Working Capital 39	4.6	•	1.8	1.2	0.3	0.4	0.5	0.6	0.7	1.2
Working Capital to Net Sales 40	0.1	•	0.1	0.2	0.2	0.3	0.3	0.2	0.2	0.2
Inventory to Working Capital 41	1.4	•	1.3	1.0	0.8	0.4	0.4	0.7	0.6	0.7
Total Receipts to Cash Flow 42	4.9	6.6	12.9	5.2	6.3	5.4	6.7	7.1	8.1	5.0
Cost of Goods to Cash Flow 43	3.3	4.9	9.0	3.0	4.1	3.4	4.2	5.0	5.4	3.1
Cash Flow to Total Debt 44	0.4	•	0.2	0.8	0.7	1.5	0.8	0.4	0.4	0.5

Selected Financial Factors (in Percentages)

Debt Ratio 45	29.6	•	105.8	57.5	51.4	29.4	36.2	40.9	39.4	47.7
Return on Total Assets 46	10.8	6.4	16.0	25.2	34.4	19.8	10.8	8.5	9.7
Return on Equity Before Income Taxes 47	13.0	•	•	32.6	46.9	48.2	29.6	15.7	12.2	15.6
Return on Equity After Income Taxes 48	10.6	•	•	31.5	43.0	45.1	25.8	13.8	8.4	10.4
Profit Margin (Before Income Tax) 49	14.6	11.6	1.6	6.2	9.5	14.2	10.4	7.4	6.6	7.4
Profit Margin (After Income Tax) 50	11.9	11.0	1.6	6.0	8.7	13.3	9.0	6.5	4.5	5.0

Table I

Corporations with and without Net Income

OTHER ELECTRICAL EQUIPMENT AND COMPONENT

MONEY AMOUNTS AND SIZE OF ASSETS IN THOUSANDS OF DOLLARS

Item Description for Accounting Period 7/05 Through 6/06	Total	Zero Assets	Under 500	500 to 1,000	1,000 to 5,000	5,000 to 10,000	10,000 to 25,000	25,000 to 50,000	50,000 to 100,000	100,000 to 250,000	250,000 to 500,000	500,000 to 2,500,000	2,500,000 and over
Number of Enterprises 1	4417	364	1702	620	796	510	211	95	48	33	16	18	4
Revenues ($ in Thousands)													
Net Sales 2	57954811	272857	632914	1587925	3787559	6211599	5560040	4572010	4619795	3819238	4989336	12157881	9743658
Interest 3	505352	2189	60	250	960	4522	5402	15855	11949	32978	63101	227314	140774
Rents 4	28677	0	0	146	1278	60	333	663	1341	2230	535	6378	15712
Royalties 5	211475	0	4869	0	0	0	2957	628	11751	22763	18882	26156	123469
Other Portfolio Income 6	1326637	12317	10	3518	15213	4487	25137	19715	16648	31036	18869	223027	956660
Other Receipts 7	748946	38101	2707	69636	10906	33033	47003	33351	29146	53017	86727	61772	283546
Total Receipts 8	60775898	325464	640560	1661475	3815916	6253701	5640872	4642222	4690630	3961262	5177450	12702528	11263819
Average Total Receipts 9	13760	894	376	2680	4794	12262	26734	48865	97721	120038	323591	705696	2815955
Operating Costs/Operating Income (%)													
Cost of Operations 10	67.7	99.2	39.0	64.0	63.0	69.0	69.6	68.8	70.8	64.7	73.9	67.6	65.5
Salaries and Wages 11	10.2	13.5	16.6	14.6	13.1	9.8	9.2	9.5	9.1	11.3	6.9	9.1	12.0
Taxes Paid 12	1.9	2.6	3.0	2.4	3.1	2.2	2.0	2.3	1.7	1.6	1.8	1.4	1.5
Interest Paid 13	2.5	2.3	0.2	6.0	1.7	0.9	1.0	1.4	1.2	2.2	2.7	4.1	3.2
Depreciation 14	2.0	0.8	0.6	2.4	2.2	1.4	1.6	2.2	1.9	2.3	2.3	2.2	2.0
Amortization and Depletion 15	0.9	0.3	•	0.1	0.5	0.3	0.3	0.4	0.4	1.7	1.3	1.6	1.1
Pensions and Other Deferred Comp. 16	0.6	0.0	0.0	0.0	0.2	0.3	0.4	0.6	0.2	0.4	0.4	0.9	1.0
Employee Benefits 17	1.8	0.1	1.4	0.2	1.8	1.2	1.8	2.4	1.8	2.4	1.8	2.5	0.9
Advertising 18	1.0	2.3	2.2	1.1	0.5	0.6	0.7	0.5	0.7	0.5	0.7	0.7	2.6
Other Expenses 19	10.7	13.3	34.4	14.2	11.4	8.1	9.2	8.5	6.6	13.5	11.4	12.3	10.1
Officers' Compensation 20	1.8	4.8	8.3	4.6	4.4	3.2	2.6	1.9	1.8	1.5	0.6	0.6	0.5
Operating Margin 21	•	•	•	•	•	3.0	1.7	1.5	3.8	•	•	•	•
Operating Margin Before Officers' Comp. 22	0.9	•	2.6	2.6	2.6	6.2	4.3	3.4	5.6	•	•	•	0.0

Selected Average Balance Sheet ($ in Thousands)

	1	2	3	4	5	6	7	8	9	10	11	12	13
Net Receivables 23	2295	0	43	210	669	1923	3969	7769	17351	24374	90104	138784	316980
Inventories 24	1657	0	16	200	732	1982	3849	8061	15261	17219	43119	73626	170080
Net Property, Plant and Equipment 25	1581	0	13	36	465	1302	2550	6064	12958	20585	44235	96074	262740
Total Assets 26	15603	0	126	722	2341	7243	15150	34112	71679	154669	373477	1006125	5907425
Notes and Loans Payable 27	3916	0	110	1609	972	2126	3746	7708	18784	32046	104041	274414	1041968
All Other Liabilities 28	4639	0	179	321	823	2224	4504	8423	17608	30345	118588	326367	1707112
Net Worth 29	7048	0	-163	-1209	546	2893	6900	17981	35287	92278	150848	405344	3158344

Selected Financial Ratios (Times to 1)

	1	2	3	4	5	6	7	8	9	10	11	12	13
Current Ratio 30	1.8	•	1.2	1.8	1.3	1.8	1.9	2.5	2.3	2.5	1.9	1.6	1.7
Quick Ratio 31	1.0	•	1.0	0.9	0.7	0.9	1.1	1.3	1.2	1.4	1.2	1.0	0.6
Net Sales to Working Capital 32	4.7	•	19.3	9.7	11.2	5.5	5.4	3.7	3.9	2.4	3.4	5.4	5.2
Coverage Ratio 33	2.7	•	•	0.2	0.4	5.0	4.3	3.2	5.6	1.9	1.0	1.4	6.1
Total Asset Turnover 34	0.8	•	2.9	3.5	2.0	1.7	1.7	1.4	1.3	0.7	0.8	0.7	0.4
Inventory Turnover 35	5.4	•	9.2	8.2	4.1	4.2	4.8	4.1	4.5	4.4	5.3	6.2	9.4
Receivables Turnover 36	6.0	•	11.6	13.8	6.9	7.3	6.7	6.2	5.5	4.8	3.3	5.3	9.2
Total Liabilities to Net Worth 37	1.2	•	•	•	3.3	1.5	1.2	0.9	1.0	0.7	1.5	1.5	0.9
Current Assets to Working Capital 38	2.2	•	5.2	2.3	3.9	2.3	2.1	1.7	1.8	1.7	2.2	2.7	2.4
Current Liabilities to Working Capital 39	1.2	•	4.2	1.3	2.9	1.3	1.1	0.7	0.8	0.7	1.2	1.7	1.4
Working Capital to Net Sales 40	0.2	•	0.1	0.1	0.1	0.2	0.2	0.3	0.3	0.4	0.3	0.2	0.2
Inventory to Working Capital 41	0.6	•	0.9	1.0	1.7	1.0	0.8	0.6	0.6	0.4	0.4	0.6	0.5
Total Receipts to Cash Flow 42	8.2	•	6.7	19.2	14.9	9.8	10.3	10.3	9.8	8.5	9.9	8.7	4.4
Cost of Goods to Cash Flow 43	5.6	•	2.6	12.3	9.4	6.8	7.1	7.1	7.0	5.5	7.3	5.9	2.9
Cash Flow to Total Debt 44	0.2	•	0.2	0.1	0.2	0.3	0.3	0.3	0.3	0.2	0.1	0.1	0.2

Selected Financial Factors (in Percentages)

	1	2	3	4	5	6	7	8	9	10	11	12	13
Debt Ratio 45	54.8	•	229.1	267.4	76.7	60.1	54.5	47.3	50.8	40.3	59.6	59.7	46.5
Return on Total Assets 46	5.7	•	•	3.8	1.3	7.7	7.2	6.3	8.7	3.1	2.3	4.0	8.1
Return on Equity Before Income Taxes 47	8.0	•	10.1	10.4	•	15.5	12.1	8.2	14.6	2.4	•	3.1	12.7
Return on Equity After Income Taxes 48	5.8	•	10.6	10.5	•	13.0	9.7	5.8	12.4	•	•	1.5	10.6
Profit Margin (Before Income Tax) 49	4.3	•	•	•	•	3.7	3.2	3.1	5.3	•	•	1.9	16.4
Profit Margin (After Income Tax) 50	3.1	•	•	•	•	3.1	2.5	2.2	4.5	•	•	0.9	13.7

Table II
Corporations with Net Income

OTHER ELECTRICAL EQUIPMENT AND COMPONENT

MONEY AMOUNTS AND SIZE OF ASSETS IN THOUSANDS OF DOLLARS

Item Description for Accounting Period 7/05 Through 6/06	Total	Zero Assets	Under 500	500 to 1000	251 to 500	501 to 1,000	1,001 to 5,000	5,001 to 10,000	10,001 to 25,000	25,001 to 50,000	50,001 to 100,000	100,001 to 250,000	250,001 and over
Number of Enterprises 1	2512	·	1160	135	457	395	156	69	38	21	·	11	·
Revenues ($ in Thousands)													
Net Sales 2	42125963	·	210064	248254	2479040	5142188	3997840	3775281	3942317	3145420	·	8737553	·
Interest 3	303884	·	35	154	886	1849	2286	6857	7828	24372	·	96334	·
Rents 4	21145	·	0	146	1278	60	0	663	781	1210	·	1018	·
Royalties 5	155516	·	0	0	0	0	2957	0	4730	19107	·	20180	·
Other Portfolio Income 6	1268923	·	10	147	11406	4336	24640	12109	12129	26173	·	216083	·
Other Receipts 7	482588	·	9	673	5663	22732	36243	19780	27549	25464	·	13525	·
Total Receipts 8	44358019	·	210118	249374	2498273	5171165	4063966	3814690	3995334	3241746	·	9084693	·
Average Total Receipts 9	17658	·	181	1847	5467	13092	26051	55285	105140	154369	·	825881	·
Operating Costs/Operating Income (%)													
Cost of Operations 10	66.3	·	44.8	69.3	59.4	67.5	64.6	68.3	69.1	64.7	·	66.2	·
Salaries and Wages 11	9.3	·	9.3	5.4	12.2	9.4	9.2	8.5	8.0	9.4	·	7.7	·
Taxes Paid 12	1.8	·	1.5	2.1	3.1	2.2	2.0	2.1	1.6	1.4	·	1.4	·
Interest Paid 13	1.7	·	0.5	0.3	0.9	0.8	0.8	1.0	1.1	1.4	·	2.5	·
Depreciation 14	1.8	·	1.5	4.6	2.0	1.2	1.3	1.9	1.8	1.7	·	1.8	·
Amortization and Depletion 15	0.5	·	·	·	0.1	0.1	0.2	0.4	0.4	0.6	·	0.9	·
Pensions and Other Deferred Comp. 16	0.6	·	·	·	0.3	0.4	0.5	0.6	0.2	0.4	·	0.8	·
Employee Benefits 17	1.8	·	0.0	1.2	2.3	1.2	1.9	2.4	1.7	2.1	·	2.7	·
Advertising 18	1.1	·	3.1	0.5	0.4	0.6	0.7	0.5	0.8	0.6	·	0.9	·
Other Expenses 19	9.0	·	25.5	8.9	9.0	7.4	8.1	6.7	7.7	10.8	·	11.0	·
Officers' Compensation 20	1.6	·	1.5	6.5	5.1	3.0	2.8	1.4	1.6	1.2	·	0.6	·
Operating Margin 21	4.6	·	12.4	1.2	5.3	6.4	8.0	6.3	6.1	5.8	·	3.4	·
Operating Margin Before Officers' Comp. 22	6.1	·	13.8	7.7	10.4	9.3	10.7	7.8	7.6	7.0	·	4.0	·

Selected Average Balance Sheet ($ in Thousands)

Net Receivables 23	2939	19	235	810	2065	3915	8390	18665	31085	169960
Inventories 24	2003	9	388	824	1647	4018	8208	16997	19669	85167
Net Property, Plant and Equipment 25	1947	17	57	465	1404	2407	5878	13562	22470	105293
Total Assets 26	18993	73	751	2549	7172	14904	34132	71804	161020	931134
Notes and Loans Payable 27	3463	60	121	686	1908	2919	6153	17878	25565	227934
All Other Liabilities 28	5477	31	99	814	1808	3639	8189	18331	35459	302215
Net Worth 29	10053	-17	531	1048	3456	8346	19790	35596	99995	400985

Selected Financial Ratios (Times to 1)

Current Ratio 30	2.2	1.8	4.3	1.5	2.3	2.4	2.6	2.3	2.3	2.4
Quick Ratio 31	1.2	1.4	2.4	0.9	1.2	1.4	1.4	1.2	1.3	1.6
Net Sales to Working Capital 32	3.9	7.2	3.5	8.6	4.6	4.3	3.8	4.1	2.8	3.1
Coverage Ratio 33	7.0	27.7	7.7	7.6	9.4	12.6	8.6	7.8	7.7	4.1
Total Asset Turnover 34	0.9	2.5	2.4	2.1	1.8	1.7	1.6	1.4	0.9	0.9
Inventory Turnover 35	5.5	9.1	3.3	3.9	5.3	4.1	4.5	4.2	4.9	6.2
Receivables Turnover 36	6.3	9.0	4.3	6.2	8.4	6.4	7.1	11.1	5.3	9.3
Total Liabilities to Net Worth 37	0.9	•	0.4	1.4	1.1	0.8	0.7	1.0	0.6	1.3
Current Assets to Working Capital 38	1.9	2.2	1.3	2.9	1.8	1.7	1.6	1.8	1.7	1.7
Current Liabilities to Working Capital 39	0.9	1.2	0.3	1.9	0.8	0.7	0.6	0.8	0.7	0.7
Working Capital to Net Sales 40	0.3	0.1	0.3	0.1	0.2	0.2	0.3	0.2	0.4	0.3
Inventory to Working Capital 41	0.5	0.3	0.5	1.2	0.7	0.7	0.6	0.7	0.4	0.3
Total Receipts to Cash Flow 42	5.9	3.0	15.3	8.2	7.6	6.4	8.0	7.4	5.5	6.0
Cost of Goods to Cash Flow 43	3.9	1.3	10.6	4.9	5.1	4.1	5.5	5.1	3.6	4.0
Cash Flow to Total Debt 44	0.3	0.7	0.5	0.4	0.5	0.6	0.5	0.4	0.4	0.3

Selected Financial Factors (in Percentages)

Debt Ratio 45	47.1	123.4	29.3	58.9	51.8	44.0	42.0	50.4	37.9	56.9
Return on Total Assets 46	10.5	31.7	4.7	14.9	14.1	18.1	13.4	12.3	9.7	8.6
Return on Equity Before Income Taxes 47	17.0	•	5.8	31.4	26.1	29.7	20.4	21.6	13.6	15.1
Return on Equity After Income Taxes 48	14.3	•	4.9	25.5	23.4	27.0	17.4	18.8	9.7	12.6
Profit Margin (Before Income Tax) 49	10.2	12.4	1.7	6.1	6.9	9.7	7.4	7.4	9.1	7.6
Profit Margin (After Income Tax) 50	8.6	11.8	1.4	4.9	6.2	8.8	6.3	6.5	6.5	6.3

Table I

Corporations with and without Net Income

MOTOR VEHICLES AND PARTS

MONEY AMOUNTS AND SIZE OF ASSETS IN THOUSANDS OF DOLLARS

Item Description for Accounting Period 7/05 Through 6/06	Total	Zero Assets	Under 500	500 to 1,000	1,000 to 5,000	5,000 to 10,000	10,000 to 25,000	25,000 to 50,000	50,000 to 100,000	100,000 to 250,000	250,000 to 500,000	500,000 to 2,500,000	2,500,000 and over
Number of Enterprises 1	4958	53	2619	302	1010	243	257	167	100	92	39	54	21
Revenues ($ in Thousands)													
Net Sales 2	615864275	1065336	3378121	406618	6122490	3219518	7876532	10333058	13410425	23360395	20928223	68444351	457319207
Interest 3	39622133	3771	145	245	2777	2264	5855	16569	18570	49095	119653	427319	38975871
Rents 4	18860149	187	0	0	421	166	969	3914	3061	15107	12137	10865	18813324
Royalties 5	12928574	5079	0	0	690	0	921	7522	7897	10715	92968	185505	12617276
Other Portfolio Income 6	21939624	11615	7337	5709	31413	16545	86476	9803	22444	75422	38050	1331695	20303115
Other Receipts 7	23722714	13036	77812	958	12933	35564	47045	99733	98797	291307	167494	602969	22275065
Total Receipts 8	732937469	1099024	3463415	413530	6170724	3274057	8017798	10470599	13561194	23802041	21358525	71002704	570303858
Average Total Receipts 9	147829	20736	1322	1369	6110	13473	31198	62698	135612	258718	547654	1314865	27157327
Operating Costs/Operating Income (%)													
Cost of Operations 10	80.5	74.5	79.9	68.9	73.5	83.3	76.9	78.4	80.2	83.3	82.5	80.7	80.5
Salaries and Wages 11	3.9	6.6	2.6	4.3	7.9	3.4	4.7	4.8	3.4	3.9	3.9	4.2	3.9
Taxes Paid 12	0.9	1.3	2.2	4.3	2.3	1.7	1.9	1.7	1.4	1.4	1.1	1.3	0.8
Interest Paid 13	6.3	1.4	0.3	3.5	1.4	0.8	1.0	1.1	1.4	1.2	2.0	2.4	7.8
Depreciation 14	6.5	2.1	0.3	2.3	2.2	1.6	1.8	2.9	2.8	2.7	2.5	2.4	8.0
Amortization and Depletion 15	0.9	0.5	0.0	0.1	0.1	0.1	0.2	0.2	0.3	0.4	0.4	0.6	1.1
Pensions and Other Deferred Comp. 16	0.8	0.2	•	0.1	0.6	0.3	0.3	0.4	0.3	0.3	0.4	1.5	0.8
Employee Benefits 17	1.8	2.3	1.0	0.4	1.6	1.1	1.7	1.7	1.6	1.7	1.3	2.1	1.8
Advertising 18	1.9	0.2	0.5	0.2	0.9	0.3	0.4	0.3	0.4	0.2	0.2	0.3	2.4
Other Expenses 19	11.7	15.4	10.5	16.0	8.8	6.8	8.2	7.0	5.9	4.3	5.0	6.2	13.6
Officers' Compensation 20	0.3	0.8	2.3	4.4	2.0	2.1	1.8	0.8	0.7	0.4	0.4	0.3	0.1
Operating Margin 21	•	•	0.5	•	•	•	1.1	0.7	1.6	0.2	0.3	•	•
Operating Margin Before Officers' Comp. 22	•	2.8	2.8	•	0.6	0.5	2.9	1.5	2.3	0.6	0.7	•	•

Selected Average Balance Sheet ($ in Thousands)

Net Receivables 23	86028	0	7	129	574	1666	3586	8583	18070	31414	78103	189252	19293658
Inventories 24	8131	0	79	358	709	1925	3843	6154	13530	24099	55067	104659	1210980
Net Property, Plant and Equipment 25	38351	0	24	115	605	1468	3785	12832	26962	46189	83389	210856	7827655
Total Assets 26	257770	0	102	737	2466	6154	14947	36178	75627	150685	359465	1011421	55885737
Notes and Loans Payable 27	101827	0	172	296	1327	2923	5512	12514	31388	48703	131384	395663	22126302
All Other Liabilities 28	109240	0	40	328	1580	2094	4442	11481	24644	49929	123471	345581	24081376
Net Worth 29	46703	0	-110	113	-441	1137	4992	12183	19595	52054	104610	270178	9678059

Selected Financial Ratios (Times to 1)

Current Ratio 30	1.4	•	0.9	1.6	1.0	1.5	1.5	1.3	1.2	1.1	1.2	1.2	1.4
Quick Ratio 31	1.1	•	0.1	0.5	0.5	0.7	0.8	0.8	0.7	0.6	0.7	0.7	1.1
Net Sales to Working Capital 32	3.7	•	•	6.5	104.3	8.8	9.5	13.8	17.9	37.3	18.9	17.0	2.9
Coverage Ratio 33	1.7	•	12.1	0.2	0.6	1.1	3.9	3.0	3.0	2.7	2.3	1.8	1.7
Total Asset Turnover 34	0.5	•	12.6	1.8	2.5	2.2	2.1	1.7	1.8	1.7	1.5	1.3	0.4
Inventory Turnover 35	12.3	•	13.0	2.6	6.3	5.7	6.1	7.9	8.0	8.8	8.0	9.8	14.5
Receivables Turnover 36	1.3	•	138.0	6.6	11.3	9.4	8.7	8.4	7.7	8.2	7.5	7.3	1.0
Total Liabilities to Net Worth 37	4.5	•	•	5.5	•	4.4	2.0	2.0	2.9	1.9	2.4	2.7	4.8
Current Assets to Working Capital 38	3.7	•	•	2.7	28.4	3.1	2.9	4.4	5.2	10.7	6.0	5.7	3.6
Current Liabilities to Working Capital 39	2.7	•	•	1.7	27.4	2.1	1.9	3.4	4.2	9.7	5.0	4.7	2.6
Working Capital to Net Sales 40	0.3	•	0.2	0.0	0.0	0.1	0.1	0.1	0.1	0.0	0.1	0.1	0.3
Inventory to Working Capital 41	0.3	•	•	1.8	13.3	1.5	1.3	1.5	1.9	3.5	2.0	1.4	0.2
Total Receipts to Cash Flow 42	7.5	9.8	8.3	12.2	29.4	21.7	10.7	13.4	13.5	19.5	15.5	15.3	6.4
Cost of Goods to Cash Flow 43	6.0	7.3	6.6	8.4	21.6	18.1	8.2	10.5	10.8	16.3	12.8	12.3	5.1
Cash Flow to Total Debt 44	0.1	•	0.7	0.2	0.1	0.1	0.3	0.2	0.2	0.1	0.1	0.1	0.1

Selected Financial Factors (in Percentages)

Debt Ratio 45	81.9	•	207.5	84.7	117.9	81.5	66.6	66.3	74.1	65.5	70.9	73.3	82.7
Return on Total Assets 46	5.1	•	41.9	1.2	2.1	2.0	7.8	5.4	7.3	5.6	6.8	5.4	5.0
Return on Equity Before Income Taxes 47	11.4	•	•	•	7.8	1.0	17.4	10.8	18.7	10.0	13.1	9.1	11.4
Return on Equity After Income Taxes 48	8.0	•	•	•	12.8	•	13.2	7.9	13.1	6.1	7.7	5.4	8.1
Profit Margin (Before Income Tax) 49	4.3	•	3.0	•	•	0.1	2.8	2.1	2.7	2.1	2.6	1.9	5.1
Profit Margin (After Income Tax) 50	3.0	•	3.0	•	•	2.1	1.6	1.5	1.9	1.3	1.5	1.2	3.6

153

Table II

Corporations with Net Income

MOTOR VEHICLES AND PARTS

MONEY AMOUNTS AND SIZE OF ASSETS IN THOUSANDS OF DOLLARS

Item Description for Accounting Period 7/05 Through 6/06	Total	Zero Assets	Under 500	500 to 1,000	1,000 to 5,000	5,000 to 10,000	10,000 to 25,000	25,000 to 50,000	50,000 to 100,000	100,000 to 250,000	250,000 to 500,000	500,000 to 2,500,000	2,500,000 and over
Number of Enterprises 1	2634	12	1085	217	702	135	167	115	66	64	25	33	12

Revenues ($ in Thousands)

	Total	Zero Assets	Under 500	500 to 1,000	1,000 to 5,000	5,000 to 10,000	10,000 to 25,000	25,000 to 50,000	50,000 to 100,000	100,000 to 250,000	250,000 to 500,000	500,000 to 2,500,000	2,500,000 and over
Net Sales 2	399035581	545183	2991250	227143	4307664	2451851	5639299	7461428	9741241	16947985	14614833	39529689	294578015
Interest 3	21553645	2760	4	175	1537	1684	5353	9397	9602	37539	30281	88104	21367209
Rents 4	13798200	117	0	0	207	91	788	1134	2151	10644	5364	4209	13773497
Royalties 5	3698777	5070	0	0	690	0	921	7522	4754	8429	92581	85377	3493432
Other Portfolio Income 6	18905352	9538	7337	5709	31413	16545	85999	5783	11786	43402	25766	1147534	17514542
Other Receipts 7	10253088	1444	77302	935	10464	34121	42467	41007	94384	208548	137525	190854	9414034
Total Receipts 8	467244643	564112	3075893	233962	4351975	2504292	5774827	7526271	9863918	17256547	14906350	41045767	360140729
Average Total Receipts 9	177390	47009	2835	1078	6199	18550	34580	65446	149453	269634	596254	1243811	30011727

Operating Costs/Operating Income (%)

	Total	Zero Assets	Under 500	500 to 1,000	1,000 to 5,000	5,000 to 10,000	10,000 to 25,000	25,000 to 50,000	50,000 to 100,000	100,000 to 250,000	250,000 to 500,000	500,000 to 2,500,000	2,500,000 and over
Cost of Operations 10	80.2	67.7	83.3	53.3	68.2	81.6	75.2	75.9	79.2	82.6	81.2	78.9	80.6
Salaries and Wages 11	3.6	6.4	0.5	3.2	7.9	2.4	4.6	4.8	2.9	3.6	3.8	4.4	3.4
Taxes Paid 12	1.0	1.4	2.0	6.9	2.6	1.5	1.6	1.6	1.4	1.3	1.2	1.2	0.8
Interest Paid 13	5.0	0.3	0.2	4.9	0.8	0.6	0.7	0.9	1.0	0.8	0.7	1.1	6.4
Depreciation 14	5.6	1.8	0.2	3.3	1.9	1.2	1.3	2.7	2.4	2.4	2.7	2.3	6.8
Amortization and Depletion 15	0.3	0.6	0.0	•	0.2	0.0	0.1	0.1	0.3	0.3	0.2	0.3	0.3
Pensions and Other Deferred Comp. 16	0.6	0.2	•	0.2	0.9	0.3	0.3	0.5	0.3	0.3	0.4	0.5	0.7
Employee Benefits 17	1.7	3.0	0.5	0.3	2.0	0.7	1.5	1.8	1.5	1.7	1.2	1.9	1.7
Advertising 18	1.7	0.0	0.2	0.1	0.5	0.2	0.5	0.3	0.5	0.2	0.2	0.2	2.2
Other Expenses 19	9.2	9.7	9.8	17.2	8.5	5.3	8.0	5.8	5.7	3.5	4.0	6.0	10.5
Officers' Compensation 20	0.3	0.1	1.3	4.8	2.2	2.4	1.7	0.9	0.6	0.4	0.4	0.3	0.1
Operating Margin 21	•	8.7	2.0	5.7	4.1	3.7	4.6	4.8	4.1	3.0	4.0	2.8	•
Operating Margin Before Officers' Comp. 22	•	8.8	3.3	10.5	6.3	6.2	6.3	5.7	4.8	3.4	4.4	3.2	•

Selected Average Balance Sheet ($ in Thousands)

Net Receivables 23	109124	0	11	86	558	1972	3834	8743	16982	32159	85337	194951	22779462
Inventories 24	11087	0	82	362	657	2416	3841	6081	14491	25333	56557	93575	1652313
Net Property, Plant and Equipment 25	48619	0	34	106	485	1229	3205	11659	25341	44934	94627	201852	9337079
Total Assets 26	289905	0	104	705	2380	6413	14687	35550	75126	145283	356985	937586	58345471
Notes and Loans Payable 27	100257	0	347	267	867	1793	3769	9677	26929	35135	92848	238500	20569346
All Other Liabilities 28	120181	0	54	337	583	1946	4246	11011	25710	50302	123444	288109	24689066
Net Worth 29	69467	0	-298	102	930	2674	6672	14862	22487	59846	140692	410977	13087059

Selected Financial Ratios (Times to 1)

Current Ratio 30	1.5	•	0.6	1.3	1.6	1.7	1.9	1.5	1.4	1.4	1.4	1.3	1.5
Quick Ratio 31	1.1	•	0.1	0.4	0.7	0.8	1.0	0.9	0.8	0.8	0.8	0.8	1.2
Net Sales to Working Capital 32	2.8	•	•	7.9	9.8	8.6	7.2	9.9	12.4	13.4	10.5	10.6	2.2
Coverage Ratio 33	2.7	43.3	25.2	2.8	7.1	10.9	10.6	7.6	6.2	7.2	9.2	7.5	2.4
Total Asset Turnover 34	0.5	•	26.6	1.5	2.6	2.8	2.3	1.8	2.0	1.8	1.6	1.3	0.4
Inventory Turnover 35	11.0	•	28.1	1.5	6.4	6.1	6.6	8.1	8.1	8.6	8.4	10.1	12.0
Receivables Turnover 36	1.2	•	158.6	5.4	12.7	10.4	9.2	8.8	8.8	8.3	7.8	7.0	0.9
Total Liabilities to Net Worth 37	3.2	•	•	5.9	1.6	1.4	1.2	1.4	2.3	1.4	1.5	1.3	3.5
Current Assets to Working Capital 38	2.9	•	•	3.9	2.6	2.4	2.1	3.1	3.3	3.8	3.3	3.9	2.9
Current Liabilities to Working Capital 39	1.9	•	•	2.9	1.6	1.4	1.1	2.1	2.3	2.8	2.3	2.9	1.9
Working Capital to Net Sales 40	0.4	•	•	0.1	0.1	0.1	0.1	0.1	0.1	0.1	0.1	0.1	0.5
Inventory to Working Capital 41	0.2	•	•	2.8	1.3	1.3	0.9	1.0	1.3	1.2	1.1	0.9	0.1
Total Receipts to Cash Flow 42	6.6	4.9	7.6	5.2	12.0	11.1	7.4	10.0	9.9	13.4	10.8	8.7	5.9
Cost of Goods to Cash Flow 43	5.3	3.3	6.3	2.8	8.2	9.0	5.6	7.6	7.9	11.1	8.8	6.9	4.8
Cash Flow to Total Debt 44	0.1	•	0.9	0.3	0.4	0.4	0.6	0.3	0.3	0.2	0.3	0.3	0.1

Selected Financial Factors (in Percentages)

Debt Ratio 45	76.0	•	386.7	85.6	60.9	58.3	54.6	58.2	70.1	58.8	60.6	56.2	77.6
Return on Total Assets 46	7.0	•	133.5	20.1	15.5	18.3	17.8	12.3	12.7	10.1	10.9	10.3	6.6
Return on Equity Before Income Taxes 47	18.5	•	•	89.3	34.0	39.9	35.4	25.5	35.6	21.2	24.7	20.4	17.5
Return on Equity After Income Taxes 48	14.3	•	•	85.2	30.6	36.0	30.5	22.1	28.3	16.3	18.4	16.4	13.3
Profit Margin (Before Income Tax) 49	8.5	12.2	4.8	8.7	5.2	5.9	7.0	5.8	5.4	4.8	5.9	7.0	9.3
Profit Margin (After Income Tax) 50	6.5	9.1	4.8	4.6	4.6	5.3	6.0	5.1	4.3	3.7	4.4	5.6	7.1

Table I

Corporations with and without Net Income

AEROSPACE PRODUCT AND PARTS

MONEY AMOUNTS AND SIZE OF ASSETS IN THOUSANDS OF DOLLARS

Item Description for Accounting Period 7/05 Through 6/06	Total	Zero Assets	Under 500	500 to 1,000	1,000 to 5,000	5,000 to 10,000	10,000 to 25,000	25,000 to 50,000	50,000 to 100,000	100,000 to 250,000	250,000 to 500,000	500,000 to 2,500,000	2,500,000 and over
Number of Enterprises 1	1537	·	1051	·	78	118	90	56	21	13	6	20	9
Revenues ($ in Thousands)													
Net Sales 2	233041951	·	708543	·	469842	1201278	1999002	1961323	1570322	1886506	1710022	17810394	203616917
Interest 3	2360388	·	511	·	126	991	915	6926	4211	8936	21694	198725	2117324
Rents 4	1281672	·	0	·	0	0	435	1561	1570	4738	452	51391	1221168
Royalties 5	2034574	·	0	·	0	0	0	13	0	1565	942	43254	1988800
Other Portfolio Income 6	6189182	·	0	·	800	0	12934	256	13341	27505	2764	587149	5543055
Other Receipts 7	3251742	·	1535	·	4008	37363	13997	45241	69815	15918	28677	134483	2900647
Total Receipts 8	248159509	·	710589	·	474776	1239632	2027283	2015320	1659259	1945168	1764551	18825396	217387911
Average Total Receipts 9	161457	·	676	·	6087	10505	22525	35988	79012	149628	294092	941270	24154212
Operating Costs/Operating Income (%)													
Cost of Operations 10	71.0	·	57.0	·	76.8	66.8	64.7	68.5	67.5	67.3	67.5	72.2	71.1
Salaries and Wages 11	7.2	·	13.4	·	4.3	9.4	6.0	8.5	11.0	5.3	8.7	7.9	7.1
Taxes Paid 12	1.3	·	4.1	·	1.0	1.8	2.8	2.2	2.5	2.2	2.6	1.9	1.2
Interest Paid 13	2.2	·	0.2	·	0.9	0.5	1.2	1.4	2.6	2.0	5.4	4.9	2.0
Depreciation 14	2.0	·	0.8	·	2.1	2.6	2.8	1.8	3.7	2.6	2.0	3.0	1.8
Amortization and Depletion 15	1.2	·	0.1	·	0.3	0.0	0.4	0.2	0.5	0.9	2.0	1.0	1.3
Pensions and Other Deferred Comp. 16	1.6	·	·	·	0.2	0.2	0.5	0.5	0.5	0.3	0.6	0.9	1.7
Employee Benefits 17	2.8	·	0.3	·	0.6	2.9	2.7	1.5	3.1	2.5	1.3	2.2	2.9
Advertising 18	0.2	·	0.7	·	0.1	0.2	0.3	0.4	0.6	0.2	0.3	0.2	0.2
Other Expenses 19	11.4	·	22.0	·	6.4	11.6	11.9	11.3	10.8	8.2	10.3	8.4	11.7
Officers' Compensation 20	0.3	·	1.0	·	4.6	1.2	3.3	2.4	1.2	1.4	1.5	0.7	0.1
Operating Margin 21	·	·	0.4	·	2.7	2.7	3.4	1.4	·	7.1	·	·	·
Operating Margin Before Officers' Comp. 22	·	·	1.4	·	7.3	4.0	6.6	3.8	8.5	8.5	·	·	·

Selected Average Balance Sheet ($ in Thousands)

Net Receivables 23	21881	66	537	1470	3249	6582	8872	18974	50656	164337	3184283
Inventories 24	16395	14	1022	2578	4971	7201	14555	41211	66232	131645	2224551
Net Property, Plant and Equipment 25	26546	36	701	1200	3436	4939	17198	29621	47502	234768	3806111
Total Assets 26	182782	154	2395	6305	15896	34566	77889	154771	338040	1320452	27150271
Notes and Loans Payable 27	50869	137	1059	2507	4341	8161	23510	40249	173932	547028	7087835
All Other Liabilities 28	81846	34	565	865	3551	10175	20305	39456	113024	468376	12637784
Net Worth 29	50067	-17	771	2933	8003	16230	34074	75067	51084	305047	7424652

Selected Financial Ratios (Times to 1)

Current Ratio 30	1.1	2.1	2.2	2.0	2.2	2.4	1.6	2.5	1.2	1.5	1.1
Quick Ratio 31	0.6	1.8	1.0	0.7	0.9	1.2	0.7	1.2	0.6	0.8	0.6
Net Sales to Working Capital 32	22.4	11.3	6.3	4.0	4.0	2.7	5.3	2.5	11.2	5.5	47.7
Coverage Ratio 33	3.7	3.9	5.3	12.7	5.1	4.0	1.5	6.0	1.2	1.6	4.2
Total Asset Turnover 34	0.8	4.4	2.5	1.6	1.4	1.0	1.0	0.9	0.8	0.7	0.8
Inventory Turnover 35	6.6	27.7	4.5	2.6	2.9	3.3	3.5	2.4	2.9	4.9	7.2
Receivables Turnover 36	6.8	16.4	7.1	8.5	7.6	6.7	8.6	7.4	5.4	5.7	6.8
Total Liabilities to Net Worth 37	2.7		2.1	1.1	1.0	1.1	1.3	1.1	5.6	3.3	2.7
Current Assets to Working Capital 38	8.7	1.9	1.8	2.0	1.9	1.7	2.6	1.7	5.7	2.8	17.7
Current Liabilities to Working Capital 39	7.7	0.9	0.8	1.0	0.9	0.7	1.6	0.7	4.7	1.8	16.7
Working Capital to Net Sales 40	0.0	0.1	0.2	0.3	0.3	0.4	0.2	0.4	0.1	0.2	0.0
Inventory to Working Capital 41	2.9	0.2	1.0	1.3	0.9	0.7	1.0	0.8	2.4	1.1	5.7
Total Receipts to Cash Flow 42	7.0	8.1	11.5	7.3	7.2	7.4	10.3	6.0	10.7	11.4	6.7
Cost of Goods to Cash Flow 43	5.0	4.6	8.8	4.8	4.7	5.1	6.9	4.0	7.2	8.3	4.8
Cash Flow to Total Debt 44	0.2	0.5	0.3	0.4	0.4	0.3	0.2	0.3	0.1	0.1	0.2

Selected Financial Factors (in Percentages)

Debt Ratio 45	72.6	111.0	67.8	53.5	49.6	53.0	56.3	51.5	84.9	76.9	72.7
Return on Total Assets 46	6.7	4.0	11.5	10.4	8.3	5.7	3.7	11.3	5.5	5.2	6.9
Return on Equity Before Income Taxes 47	17.8		29.1	20.5	13.2	9.0	2.9	19.4	6.7	8.4	19.1
Return on Equity After Income Taxes 48	13.7		25.8	20.5	11.1	6.8	2.3	16.1	5.2	5.7	14.7
Profit Margin (Before Income Tax) 49	5.9	0.7	3.7	5.9	4.8	4.2	1.3	10.0	1.2	2.9	6.3
Profit Margin (After Income Tax) 50	4.5	0.7	3.3	5.9	4.0	3.1	1.0	8.3	0.9	2.0	4.8

Table II
Corporations with Net Income

AEROSPACE PRODUCT AND PARTS

MONEY AMOUNTS AND SIZE OF ASSETS IN THOUSANDS OF DOLLARS

Item Description for Accounting Period 7/05 Through 6/06	Total	Zero Assets	Under 500	500 to 1,000	1,000 to 5,000	5,000 to 10,000	10,000 to 25,000	25,000 to 50,000	50,000 to 100,000	100,000 to 250,000	250,000 to 500,000	500,000 to 2,500,000	2,500,000 and over
Number of Enterprises 1	708	0	356	57	•	59	72	36	15	9	•	•	9
Revenues ($ in Thousands)													
Net Sales 2	224316788	0	172431	72022	•	758537	1617814	1403852	1192401	1390607	•	•	203616917
Interest 3	2276473	0	90	0	•	0	659	3865	1643	4290	•	•	2117324
Rents 4	1257738	0	0	0	•	0	435	815	1569	4376	•	•	1221168
Royalties 5	2033723	0	0	0	•	0	0	13	0	1565	•	•	1988800
Other Portfolio Income 6	6176815	0	0	284	•	0	12648	197	8499	25158	•	•	5543055
Other Receipts 7	3169152	0	1534	0	•	3327	12468	41373	60205	12939	•	•	2900647
Total Receipts 8	239230689	0	174055	72306	•	761864	1644024	1450115	1264317	1438935	•	•	217387911
Average Total Receipts 9	337896	•	489	1269	•	12913	22834	40281	84288	159882	•	•	24154212
Operating Costs/Operating Income (%)													
Cost of Operations 10	70.8	•	43.0	66.1	•	57.4	61.4	67.8	65.0	66.4	•	•	71.1
Salaries and Wages 11	7.1	•	4.8	•	•	8.6	6.3	6.6	7.7	3.4	•	•	7.1
Taxes Paid 12	1.2	•	2.3	1.0	•	1.5	2.6	1.8	2.2	2.5	•	•	1.2
Interest Paid 13	2.1	•	1.0	1.9	•	0.1	1.2	0.8	1.3	1.5	•	•	2.0
Depreciation 14	1.9	•	1.7	1.3	•	2.2	2.6	1.3	2.8	2.5	•	•	1.8
Amortization and Depletion 15	1.3	•	0.2	•	•	0.0	0.5	0.2	0.3	0.8	•	•	1.3
Pensions and Other Deferred Comp. 16	1.6	•	•	2.8	•	0.4	0.5	0.5	0.4	0.4	•	•	1.7
Employee Benefits 17	2.8	•	1.3	•	•	1.1	2.3	1.5	2.7	2.0	•	•	2.9
Advertising 18	0.2	•	0.4	0.7	•	0.3	0.3	0.3	0.6	0.1	•	•	0.2
Other Expenses 19	11.4	•	36.3	14.2	•	12.7	10.1	7.8	8.3	7.5	•	•	11.7
Officers' Compensation 20	0.2	•	4.2	11.4	•	1.9	3.6	2.8	1.4	1.6	•	•	0.1
Operating Margin 21	•	•	4.7	0.6	•	13.8	8.6	8.5	7.2	11.4	•	•	•
Operating Margin Before Officers' Comp. 22	•	•	8.9	12.0	•	15.7	12.3	11.3	8.6	13.0	•	•	•

Selected Average Balance Sheet ($ in Thousands)

Net Receivables 23	45721	·	6	44	·	1620	3592	7245	8262	16758 ·	3184283
Inventories 24	28342	·	41	594	·	2775	4616	7886	17780	37485 ·	1833582
Net Property, Plant and Equipment 25	54524	·	49	3	·	1654	3644	4208	13908	27238 ·	3806111
Total Assets 26	382510	·	133	682	·	7015	16275	35410	77304	150648 ·	27150271
Notes and Loans Payable 27	104595	·	100	438	·	1052	3215	5147	16366	30626 ·	7087835
All Other Liabilities 28	170064	·	34	1	·	1301	3362	10214	14966	27875 ·	12637784
Net Worth 29	107851	·	-1	243	·	4661	9698	20049	45971	92148 ·	7424652

Selected Financial Ratios (Times to 1)

Current Ratio 30	1.1	·	0.8	13.4	·	4.1	2.4	2.8	2.2	3.1 ·	1.1
Quick Ratio 31	0.6	·	0.3	0.9	·	1.5	1.1	1.4	1.0	1.4 ·	0.6
Net Sales to Working Capital 32	23.2	·	·	2.0	·	3.2	3.6	2.5	4.2	2.6 ·	47.7
Coverage Ratio 33	4.1	·	6.9	1.5	·	150.9	9.7	15.1	11.0	10.6 ·	4.2
Total Asset Turnover 34	0.8	·	3.6	1.9	·	1.8	1.4	1.1	1.0	1.0 ·	0.8
Inventory Turnover 35	7.9	·	5.1	1.4	·	2.7	3.0	3.4	2.9	2.7 ·	8.8
Receivables Turnover 36	8.6	·	71.2	31.2	·	9.6	7.6	6.7	9.4	8.4 ·	9.0
Total Liabilities to Net Worth 37	2.5	·	·	1.8	·	0.5	0.7	0.8	0.7	0.6 ·	2.7
Current Assets to Working Capital 38	9.0	·	·	1.1	·	1.3	1.7	1.6	1.8	1.5 ·	17.7
Current Liabilities to Working Capital 39	8.0	·	·	0.1	·	0.3	0.7	0.6	0.8	0.5 ·	16.7
Working Capital to Net Sales 40	0.0	·	·	0.5	·	0.3	0.3	0.4	0.2	0.4 ·	0.0
Inventory to Working Capital 41	3.0	·	·	1.0	·	0.8	0.9	0.6	0.9	0.7 ·	5.7
Total Receipts to Cash Flow 42	6.7	·	3.5	7.1	·	4.1	5.7	5.6	5.1	4.7 ·	6.7
Cost of Goods to Cash Flow 43	4.8	·	1.5	4.7	·	2.4	3.5	3.8	3.3	3.1 ·	4.8
Cash Flow to Total Debt 44	0.2	·	1.0	0.4	·	1.3	0.6	0.5	0.5	0.6 ·	0.2

Selected Financial Factors (in Percentages)

Debt Ratio 45	71.8	·	100.7	64.3	·	33.6	40.4	43.4	40.5	38.8 ·	72.7
Return on Total Assets 46	7.2	·	24.1	5.4	·	26.2	15.7	13.9	14.8	16.6 ·	6.9
Return on Equity Before Income Taxes 47	19.2	·	·	5.2	·	39.2	23.7	22.9	22.6	24.5 ·	19.1
Return on Equity After Income Taxes 48	15.1	·	·	4.4	·	39.2	21.5	20.0	22.0	20.6 ·	14.7
Profit Margin (Before Income Tax) 49	6.5	·	5.7	1.0	·	14.2	10.2	11.8	13.1	14.6 ·	6.3
Profit Margin (After Income Tax) 50	5.1	·	5.7	0.9	·	14.2	9.3	10.3	12.7	13.1 ·	4.8

156

Table I

Corporations with and without Net Income

SHIP AND BOAT BUILDING

MONEY AMOUNTS AND SIZE OF ASSETS IN THOUSANDS OF DOLLARS

Item Description for Accounting Period 7/05 Through 6/06	Total	Zero Assets	Under 500	500 to 1,000	1,000 to 5,000	5,000 to 10,000	10,000 to 25,000	25,000 to 50,000	50,000 to 100,000	100,000 to 250,000	250,000 to 500,000	500,000 to 2,500,000	2,500,000 and over
Number of Enterprises **1**	2908	404	1977	0	381	28	62	27	14	9	5	0	0

Revenues ($ in Thousands)

Item	Total	Zero Assets	Under 500	500 to 1,000	1,000 to 5,000	5,000 to 10,000	10,000 to 25,000	25,000 to 50,000	50,000 to 100,000	100,000 to 250,000	250,000 to 500,000	500,000 to 2,500,000	2,500,000 and over
Net Sales **2**	34620515	5132	2067947	0	3198473	461875	1821647	1935902	1813728	1593078	21722734	0	0
Interest **3**	39856	487	44	0	2183	167	590	1970	403	3421	30591	0	0
Rents **4**	42766	0	0	0	5779	218	490	3567	20	145	32547	0	0
Royalties **5**	7468	0	0	0	0	0	0	3070	0	0	4398	0	0
Other Portfolio Income **6**	191184	2342	5794	0	5322	238	516	2456	8669	2144	163703	0	0
Other Receipts **7**	220346	10	4731	0	18473	3799	17351	12417	27226	-246	136583	0	0
Total Receipts **8**	35122135	7971	2078516	0	3230230	466297	1840594	1959382	1850046	1598542	22090556	0	0
Average Total Receipts **9**	12078	20	1051	•	8478	16653	29687	72570	132146	177616	4418111	•	•

Operating Costs/Operating Income (%)

Item	Total	Zero Assets	Under 500	500 to 1,000	1,000 to 5,000	5,000 to 10,000	10,000 to 25,000	25,000 to 50,000	50,000 to 100,000	100,000 to 250,000	250,000 to 500,000	500,000 to 2,500,000	2,500,000 and over
Cost of Operations **10**	76.9	83.2	63.3	•	73.8	73.7	79.8	78.5	74.1	75.6	78.7	•	•
Salaries and Wages **11**	3.9	•	10.9	•	7.5	5.0	3.1	4.6	3.2	5.4	2.7	•	•
Taxes Paid **12**	1.9	0.8	2.1	•	2.1	1.1	1.1	1.4	2.2	2.2	2.0	•	•
Interest Paid **13**	0.8	•	0.4	•	0.5	3.0	0.9	0.6	0.5	1.5	0.8	•	•
Depreciation **14**	1.0	24.0	1.2	•	1.5	1.2	2.1	1.8	1.6	2.3	0.7	•	•
Amortization and Depletion **15**	0.7	•	0.2	•	0.0	0.0	0.1	0.1	0.1	0.2	1.1	•	•
Pensions and Other Deferred Comp. **16**	0.4	•	0.1	•	0.1	0.0	0.3	0.3	0.8	0.4	0.4	•	•
Employee Benefits **17**	2.2	3.0	3.0	•	1.7	1.4	1.2	0.7	3.2	2.3	2.3	•	•
Advertising **18**	0.5	•	0.6	•	1.4	1.1	0.8	1.5	0.8	0.6	0.3	•	•
Other Expenses **19**	5.9	17.7	11.1	•	7.6	5.9	7.9	6.3	8.8	2.8	4.9	•	•
Officers' Compensation **20**	1.2	•	3.7	•	3.2	1.8	1.5	1.1	1.5	0.9	0.6	•	•
Operating Margin **21**	4.5	•	3.3	•	0.7	5.7	1.2	3.3	3.3	5.8	5.5	•	•
Operating Margin Before Officers' Comp. **22**	5.7	•	7.1	•	3.9	7.5	2.7	4.3	4.7	6.7	6.1	•	•

Selected Average Balance Sheet ($ in Thousands)

Net Receivables 23	873	0	61	•	444	739	1854	4563	10889	12675	345076
Inventories 24	1234	0	9	•	1181	2306	3502	7778	14343	14347	459796
Net Property, Plant and Equipment 25	1330	0	55	•	672	2043	5296	9254	21074	43655	436039
Total Assets 26	8712	0	217	•	3030	7558	15895	33312	66667	159874	3856335
Notes and Loans Payable 27	1983	0	99	•	967	3057	6857	11094	11557	58855	740699
All Other Liabilities 28	2885	0	39	•	1095	1889	5696	13156	19596	37969	1303660
Net Worth 29	3843	0	79	•	968	2612	3343	9063	35514	63351	1811975

Selected Financial Ratios (Times to 1)

Current Ratio 30	1.5	•	2.8	•	1.5	1.1	1.3	1.3	1.8	2.3	1.4
Quick Ratio 31	0.6	•	2.5	•	0.4	0.5	0.5	0.5	0.8	0.7	0.7
Net Sales to Working Capital 32	9.5	•	14.3	•	11.6	32.0	15.0	13.7	7.7	4.1	9.3
Coverage Ratio 33	8.9	•	11.6	•	4.5	3.3	3.5	8.7	11.1	4.9	10.7
Total Asset Turnover 34	1.4	•	4.8	•	2.8	2.2	1.8	2.2	1.9	1.1	1.1
Inventory Turnover 35	7.4	•	75.1	•	5.2	5.3	6.7	7.2	6.7	9.3	7.4
Receivables Turnover 36	13.7	•	23.0	•	23.5	25.7	16.6	13.3	17.9	12.5	12.2
Total Liabilities to Net Worth 37	1.3	•	1.8	•	2.1	1.9	3.8	2.7	0.9	1.5	1.1
Current Assets to Working Capital 38	3.0	•	1.6	•	3.2	7.9	4.0	4.0	2.2	1.7	3.3
Current Liabilities to Working Capital 39	2.0	•	0.6	•	2.2	6.9	3.0	3.0	1.2	0.7	2.3
Working Capital to Net Sales 40	0.1	•	0.1	•	0.1	0.0	0.1	0.1	0.1	0.2	0.1
Inventory to Working Capital 41	1.1	•	0.2	•	2.1	3.3	1.9	1.6	0.9	0.2	1.1
Total Receipts to Cash Flow 42	10.3	•	9.2	•	16.2	8.5	12.7	10.7	8.0	13.2	9.9
Cost of Goods to Cash Flow 43	8.0	•	5.8	•	12.0	6.3	10.2	8.4	5.9	10.0	7.8
Cash Flow to Total Debt 44	0.2	•	0.8	•	0.3	0.4	0.2	0.3	0.5	0.1	0.2

Selected Financial Factors (in Percentages)

Debt Ratio 45	55.9	•	63.8	•	68.0	65.4	79.0	72.8	46.7	60.4	53.0
Return on Total Assets 46	9.2	•	20.3	•	6.2	21.1	5.8	10.9	11.2	8.4	9.0
Return on Equity Before Income Taxes 47	18.5	•	51.3	•	15.1	42.3	19.7	35.4	19.1	16.8	17.4
Return on Equity After Income Taxes 48	13.0	•	50.6	•	13.4	42.3	12.2	29.4	17.9	12.7	11.4
Profit Margin (Before Income Tax) 49	6.0	29.6	3.9	•	1.7	6.7	2.2	4.5	5.2	6.0	7.3
Profit Margin (After Income Tax) 50	4.2	17.9	3.8	•	1.5	6.7	1.4	3.7	4.9	4.6	4.7

Table II
Corporations with Net Income

SHIP AND BOAT BUILDING

MONEY AMOUNTS AND SIZE OF ASSETS IN THOUSANDS OF DOLLARS

Item Description for Accounting Period 7/05 Through 6/06	Total	Zero Assets	Under 500	500 to 1,000	1,000 to 5,000	5,000 to 10,000	10,000 to 25,000	25,000 to 50,000	50,000 to 100,000	100,000 to 250,000	250,000 to 500,000	500,000 to 2,500,000	2,500,000 and over
Number of Enterprises 1	2121	404	1331	0	297	•	33	17	•	•	•	0	0
Revenues ($ in Thousands)													
Net Sales 2	30931054	5132	1385095	0	2890242	•	1134367	1488566	•	•	•	0	0
Interest 3	31051	487	44	0	1581	•	498	882	•	•	•	0	0
Rents 4	40736	0	0	0	5779	•	0	3567	•	•	•	0	0
Royalties 5	7460	0	0	0	0	•	0	3070	•	•	•	0	0
Other Portfolio Income 6	184959	2342	1648	0	4247	•	101	2117	•	•	•	0	0
Other Receipts 7	202680	10	3837	0	17712	•	13836	11521	•	•	•	0	0
Total Receipts 8	31397940	7971	1390624	0	2919561	•	1148802	1509723	•	•	•	0	0
Average Total Receipts 9	14803	20	1045	•	9830	•	34812	88807	•	•	•	•	•
Operating Costs/Operating Income (%)													
Cost of Operations 10	76.6	83.2	46.8	•	74.6	•	76.3	74.9	•	•	•	•	•
Salaries and Wages 11	3.8	•	14.4	•	7.3	•	3.6	5.2	•	•	•	•	•
Taxes Paid 12	2.0	0.8	2.9	•	1.8	•	1.0	1.5	•	•	•	•	•
Interest Paid 13	0.7	•	0.5	•	0.5	•	0.7	0.5	•	•	•	•	•
Depreciation 14	0.9	24.0	1.6	•	1.5	•	1.4	1.6	•	•	•	•	•
Amortization and Depletion 15	0.8	•	0.0	•	0.0	•	0.1	0.1	•	•	•	•	•
Pensions and Other Deferred Comp. 16	0.4	•	0.2	•	0.1	•	0.4	0.4	•	•	•	•	•
Employee Benefits 17	2.2	•	4.3	•	1.5	•	0.7	0.6	•	•	•	•	•
Advertising 18	0.5	•	0.5	•	1.5	•	1.0	1.0	•	•	•	•	•
Other Expenses 19	5.2	17.7	14.8	•	6.5	•	6.3	6.5	•	•	•	•	•
Officers' Compensation 20	1.2	•	5.6	•	3.0	•	1.4	1.3	•	•	•	•	•
Operating Margin 21	5.8	•	8.4	•	1.6	•	7.1	6.4	•	•	•	•	•
Operating Margin Before Officers' Comp. 22	6.9	•	14.0	•	4.6	•	8.5	7.6	•	•	•	•	•

Selected Average Balance Sheet ($ in Thousands)

Net Receivables 23	1094	0	87	490	2289	5237
Inventories 24	1481	0	12	1167	3582	9008
Net Property, Plant and Equipment 25	1511	0	57	804	3446	10702
Total Assets 26	10605	0	262	3377	14514	34896
Notes and Loans Payable 27	2081	0	106	1171	3677	7764
All Other Liabilities 28	3546	0	46	1044	3521	11124
Net Worth 29	4978	0	110	1163	7316	16007

Selected Financial Ratios (Times to 1)

Current Ratio 30	1.5		3.5	1.5	2.0	1.9
Quick Ratio 31	0.7		3.2	0.4	0.9	0.9
Net Sales to Working Capital 32	9.0		9.5	11.2	8.0	8.8
Coverage Ratio 33	11.5		20.3	6.5	12.2	17.5
Total Asset Turnover 34	1.4		4.0	2.9	2.4	2.5
Inventory Turnover 35	7.5		41.3	6.2	7.3	7.3
Receivables Turnover 36	13.5		23.8	31.2	16.8	13.3
Total Liabilities to Net Worth 37	1.1		1.4	1.9	1.0	1.2
Current Assets to Working Capital 38	2.9		1.4	2.9	2.0	2.1
Current Liabilities to Working Capital 39	1.9		0.4	1.9	1.0	1.1
Working Capital to Net Sales 40	0.1		0.1	0.1	0.1	0.1
Inventory to Working Capital 41	1.0		0.1	1.9	0.8	0.8
Total Receipts to Cash Flow 42	9.7		5.6	16.4	7.3	7.9
Cost of Goods to Cash Flow 43	7.4		2.6	12.3	5.6	5.9
Cash Flow to Total Debt 44	0.3		1.2	0.3	0.7	0.6

Selected Financial Factors (in Percentages)

Debt Ratio 45	53.1		58.1	65.6	49.6	54.1
Return on Total Assets 46	11.1		36.8	9.0	21.6	20.7
Return on Equity Before Income Taxes 47	21.5		83.3	22.1	39.4	42.6
Return on Equity After Income Taxes 48	15.7		82.6	20.3	32.9	37.2
Profit Margin (Before Income Tax) 49	7.4	29.6	8.8	2.6	8.4	7.8
Profit Margin (After Income Tax) 50	5.4	17.9	8.7	2.4	7.0	6.8

158

Table I

Corporations with and without Net Income

OTHER TRANSPORTATION EQUIPMENT AND RAILROAD ROLLING STOCK

MONEY AMOUNTS AND SIZE OF ASSETS IN THOUSANDS OF DOLLARS

Item Description for Accounting Period 7/05 Through 6/06	Total	Zero Assets	Under 500	500 to 1,000	1,000 to 5,000	5,000 to 10,000	10,000 to 25,000	25,000 to 50,000	50,000 to 100,000	100,000 to 250,000	250,000 to 500,000	500,000 to 2,500,000	2,500,000 and over
Number of Enterprises 1	1103	•	513	•	285	64	46	26	8	10	5	7	3

Revenues ($ in Thousands)

Net Sales 2	30602560	•	166405	•	1512682	995472	1243755	1899085	791206	2466854	3658167	5808455	11893128
Interest 3	840671	•	2	•	1229	0	1654	1924	555	4714	2854	16527	811185
Rents 4	207438	•	0	•	0	0	70	0	63	5	588	53667	153045
Royalties 5	56578	•	0	•	0	0	0	0	48	4543	57	3512	48419
Other Portfolio Income 6	180392	•	508	•	0	100	3301	1307	1932	7057	28486	24987	103083
Other Receipts 7	597514	•	7808	•	17410	2493	10508	18567	1564	15814	11969	99295	410494
Total Receipts 8	32485153	•	174723	•	1531321	998065	1259288	1920883	795368	2498987	3702121	6006443	13419354
Average Total Receipts 9	29452	•	341	•	5373	15595	27376	73880	99421	249899	740424	858063	4473118

Operating Costs/Operating Income (%)

Cost of Operations 10	74.4	•	79.3	•	79.1	72.2	74.0	78.3	76.5	80.5	83.1	80.1	66.0
Salaries and Wages 11	5.4	•	1.1	•	3.5	8.8	5.4	5.6	6.1	2.9	3.8	5.6	6.2
Taxes Paid 12	1.3	•	0.5	•	1.5	1.5	2.1	2.0	1.5	1.2	0.8	0.7	1.6
Interest Paid 13	2.5	•	2.2	•	0.8	0.5	0.7	0.9	1.3	2.0	0.7	1.6	4.6
Depreciation 14	2.2	•	1.0	•	2.1	0.9	1.4	1.1	0.9	1.5	1.7	2.1	2.9
Amortization and Depletion 15	0.5	•	0.1	•	0.1	0.0	0.1	0.1	1.0	0.3	0.4	0.5	0.7
Pensions and Other Deferred Comp. 16	0.9	•	0.0	•	0.1	0.1	0.8	0.2	1.5	0.8	0.5	1.4	1.1
Employee Benefits 17	2.7	•	0.1	•	0.4	2.0	1.8	1.7	1.9	1.9	1.3	2.2	4.3
Advertising 18	0.9	•	3.3	•	0.4	0.3	0.6	0.5	0.5	0.5	1.8	0.8	1.0
Other Expenses 19	8.5	•	16.5	•	2.5	8.0	8.7	4.2	7.3	3.2	4.7	5.4	13.7
Officers' Compensation 20	0.9	•	3.0	•	4.3	1.1	2.2	2.3	1.2	0.6	0.1	1.0	0.3
Operating Margin 21	•	•	•	•	5.2	4.5	2.2	3.3	0.4	4.6	1.1	•	•
Operating Margin Before Officers' Comp. 22	0.7	•	•	•	9.5	5.6	4.4	5.6	1.6	5.2	1.2	•	•

Selected Average Balance Sheet ($ in Thousands)

Item	1	2	3	4	5	6	7	8	9	10	11
Net Receivables 23	4905	39	772	1743	3125	8088	19782	28235	70229	147736	954452
Inventories 24	4167	18	559	3171	4658	9102	16415	31508	112695	268269	585087
Net Property, Plant and Equipment 25	4200	54	328	826	3147	7035	7608	19520	85517	117422	865825
Total Assets 26	23683	137	2444	6178	16528	35945	66362	152734	361374	802600	4563673
Notes and Loans Payable 27	5327	162	1359	1085	3270	8606	17365	34382	99791	243917	723506
All Other Liabilities 28	11909	24	5442	2057	4822	14060	16728	57036	166339	397938	2150312
Net Worth 29	6448	-49	-4357	3036	8435	13278	32269	61317	95244	160745	1689856

Selected Financial Ratios (Times to 1)

Item	1	2	3	4	5	6	7	8	9	10	11
Current Ratio 30	1.7	•	1.3	2.5	1.9	1.4	2.0	1.8	1.2	1.1	2.4
Quick Ratio 31	0.9	•	0.8	1.0	1.1	0.7	1.2	0.7	0.5	0.4	1.3
Net Sales to Working Capital 32	4.5	•	11.2	4.8	5.0	10.7	4.9	5.5	21.9	37.7	2.3
Coverage Ratio 33	3.4	0.1	8.6	10.9	5.8	6.0	1.6	3.9	4.1	2.4	3.3
Total Asset Turnover 34	1.2	2.4	2.2	2.5	1.6	2.0	1.5	1.6	2.0	1.0	0.9
Inventory Turnover 35	5.0	14.0	7.5	3.5	4.3	6.3	4.6	6.3	5.4	2.5	4.5
Receivables Turnover 36	4.9	16.6	8.6	9.9	7.5	10.9	5.9	8.0	9.7	1.7	8.3
Total Liabilities to Net Worth 37	2.7	•	•	1.0	1.0	1.7	1.1	1.5	2.8	4.0	1.7
Current Assets to Working Capital 38	2.4	•	4.1	1.7	2.1	3.3	2.0	2.2	6.5	20.4	1.7
Current Liabilities to Working Capital 39	1.4	•	3.1	0.7	1.1	2.3	1.0	1.2	5.5	19.4	0.7
Working Capital to Net Sales 40	0.2	•	0.1	0.2	0.2	0.1	0.2	0.2	0.0	0.0	0.4
Inventory to Working Capital 41	0.7	•	1.4	0.9	0.9	1.7	0.6	0.8	3.2	9.3	0.3
Total Receipts to Cash Flow 42	8.3	•	9.4	13.5	9.4	13.3	14.6	12.3	18.1	17.9	4.9
Cost of Goods to Cash Flow 43	6.2	•	7.4	10.7	6.8	10.4	11.2	9.9	15.1	14.3	3.3
Cash Flow to Total Debt 44	0.2	•	0.2	0.1	0.5	0.4	0.2	0.2	0.2	0.1	0.3

Selected Financial Factors (in Percentages)

Item	1	2	3	4	5	6	7	8	9	10	11
Debt Ratio 45	72.8	135.8	278.3	50.9	49.0	63.1	51.4	59.9	73.6	80.0	63.0
Return on Total Assets 46	10.0	0.5	15.8	13.2	6.8	10.9	3.2	12.7	6.2	3.9	13.1
Return on Equity Before Income Taxes 47	25.8	13.0	•	24.5	10.9	24.5	2.5	23.6	17.9	11.5	24.7
Return on Equity After Income Taxes 48	17.7	13.0	•	24.0	9.2	19.0	•	16.6	16.7	5.5	16.5
Profit Margin (Before Income Tax) 49	6.0	•	6.4	4.8	3.4	4.5	0.8	5.9	2.3	2.2	10.5
Profit Margin (After Income Tax) 50	4.1	•	5.8	4.7	2.9	3.4	•	4.1	2.2	1.1	7.0

Table II

Corporations with Net Income

OTHER TRANSPORTATION EQUIPMENT AND RAILROAD ROLLING STOCK

MONEY AMOUNTS AND SIZE OF ASSETS IN THOUSANDS OF DOLLARS

Item Description for Accounting Period 7/05 Through 6/06	Total	Zero Assets	Under 500	500 to 1,000	1,000 to 5,000	5,000 to 10,000	10,000 to 25,000	25,000 to 50,000	50,000 to 100,000	100,000 to 250,000	250,000 to 500,000	500,000 to 2,500,000	2,500,000 and over
Number of Enterprises 1	444	0	106	67	•	•	32	22	•	•	5	•	3
Revenues ($ in Thousands)													
Net Sales 2	28559128	0	80533	66618	•	•	965593	1752236	•	•	3658167	•	11893128
Interest 3	836167	0	2	1	•	•	417	1789	•	•	2854	•	811185
Rents 4	207404	0	0	0	•	•	36	0	•	•	588	•	153045
Royalties 5	52035	0	0	0	•	•	0	0	•	•	57	•	48419
Other Portfolio Income 6	179342	0	508	9617	•	•	3187	950	•	•	28486	•	103083
Other Receipts 7	581191	0	7808	0	•	•	2031	17823	•	•	11969	•	410494
Total Receipts 8	30415267	0	88851	76236	•	•	971264	1772798	•	•	3702121	•	13419354
Average Total Receipts 9	68503	•	838	1138	•	•	30352	80582	•	•	740424	•	4473118
Operating Costs/Operating Income (%)													
Cost of Operations 10	73.3	•	62.6	71.1	•	•	69.5	77.3	•	•	83.1	•	66.0
Salaries and Wages 11	5.4	•	2.2	0.1	•	•	5.1	5.4	•	•	3.8	•	6.2
Taxes Paid 12	1.3	•	0.2	0.4	•	•	2.1	1.9	•	•	0.8	•	1.6
Interest Paid 13	2.5	•	2.2	5.7	•	•	0.5	0.8	•	•	0.7	•	4.6
Depreciation 14	2.1	•	1.6	12.4	•	•	1.3	1.0	•	•	1.7	•	2.9
Amortization and Depletion 15	0.4	•	0.0	•	•	•	0.1	0.0	•	•	0.4	•	0.7
Pensions and Other Deferred Comp. 16	0.9	•	0.0	•	•	•	0.9	0.2	•	•	0.5	•	1.1
Employee Benefits 17	2.8	•	0.2	0.3	•	•	2.0	1.5	•	•	1.3	•	4.3
Advertising 18	0.9	•	0.9	0.2	•	•	0.5	0.5	•	•	1.8	•	1.0
Other Expenses 19	8.4	•	13.5	14.9	•	•	7.4	4.5	•	•	4.7	•	13.7
Officers' Compensation 20	0.9	•	6.1	1.3	•	•	2.1	2.2	•	•	0.1	•	0.3
Operating Margin 21	0.9	•	10.2	•	•	•	8.5	4.8	•	•	1.1	•	•
Operating Margin Before Officers' Comp. 22	1.8	•	16.3	•	•	•	10.7	7.0	•	•	1.2	•	•

Selected Average Balance Sheet ($ in Thousands)

Net Receivables 23	11166	188	2	3194	8841	70229	954452
Inventories 24	8423	25	0	5430	8265	107763	585087
Net Property, Plant and Equipment 25	9859	62	344	3439	6930	85517	865825
Total Assets 26	52620	308	756	15268	35688	361374	4563673
Notes and Loans Payable 27	9870	255	1103	3108	7976	99791	723506
All Other Liabilities 28	23498	114	10	3692	13714	166339	2150312
Net Worth 29	19252	-61	-356	8468	13999	95244	1689856

Selected Financial Ratios (Times to 1)

Current Ratio 30	2.0	1.4	42.1	2.2	1.5	1.2	2.4
Quick Ratio 31	1.0	1.2	41.8	1.1	0.7	0.5	1.3
Net Sales to Working Capital 32	4.0	12.7	2.5	5.1	11.0	21.9	2.3
Coverage Ratio 33	4.0	10.2	2.4	21.1	8.8	4.1	3.3
Total Asset Turnover 34	1.2	2.5	1.3	2.0	2.2	2.0	0.9
Inventory Turnover 35	5.6	19.0	1822.1	3.9	7.4	5.6	4.5
Receivables Turnover 36	5.3	8.1	1074.5	8.0	11.8	20.8	8.3
Total Liabilities to Net Worth 37	1.7	•	•	0.8	1.5	2.8	1.7
Current Assets to Working Capital 38	2.0	3.7	1.0	1.8	3.2	6.5	1.7
Current Liabilities to Working Capital 39	1.0	2.7	0.0	0.8	2.2	5.5	0.7
Working Capital to Net Sales 40	0.3	0.1	0.4	0.2	0.1	0.0	0.4
Inventory to Working Capital 41	0.6	0.4	0.0	0.8	1.5	3.2	0.3
Total Receipts to Cash Flow 42	7.5	3.1	5.0	6.6	10.7	18.1	4.9
Cost of Goods to Cash Flow 43	5.5	1.9	3.5	4.6	8.3	15.1	3.3
Cash Flow to Total Debt 44	0.3	0.7	0.2	0.7	0.3	0.2	0.3

Selected Financial Factors (in Percentages)

Debt Ratio 45	63.4	119.8	147.1	44.5	60.8	73.6	63.0
Return on Total Assets 46	12.2	56.1	18.0	18.9	15.0	6.2	13.1
Return on Equity Before Income Taxes 47	24.8	•	•	32.5	33.9	17.9	24.7
Return on Equity After Income Taxes 48	18.1	•	•	30.0	27.7	16.7	16.5
Profit Margin (Before Income Tax) 49	7.4	20.5	8.0	9.1	6.0	2.3	10.5
Profit Margin (After Income Tax) 50	5.4	20.5	8.0	8.4	4.9	2.2	7.0

Table I

Corporations with and without Net Income

FURNITURE AND RELATED PRODUCT MANUFACTURING

MONEY AMOUNTS AND SIZE OF ASSETS IN THOUSANDS OF DOLLARS

Item Description for Accounting Period 7/05 Through 6/06	Total	Zero Assets	Under 500	500 to 1,000	1,000 to 5,000	5,000 to 10,000	10,000 to 25,000	25,000 to 50,000	50,000 to 100,000	100,000 to 250,000	250,000 to 500,000	500,000 to 2,500,000	2,500,000 and over
Number of Enterprises 1	12126	1394	8274	997	916	257	161	58	29	20	6	11	3

Revenues ($ in Thousands)

	Total	Zero Assets	Under 500	500 to 1,000	1,000 to 5,000	5,000 to 10,000	10,000 to 25,000	25,000 to 50,000	50,000 to 100,000	100,000 to 250,000	250,000 to 500,000	500,000 to 2,500,000	2,500,000 and over
Net Sales 2	74142230	654947	4638816	2259746	6524844	4686173	5676726	3791030	4273423	4831792	3339527	15910616	17554589
Interest 3	148970	125	1032	405	4659	4473	2495	2635	3790	3038	15527	40733	70059
Rents 4	57949	0	629	0	164	309	2139	270	1222	1457	11277	11443	25402
Royalties 5	62856	0	0	0	0	694	1054	270	1060	4148	3470	46923	5235
Other Portfolio Income 6	362374	153	250	944	2498	5559	3756	9254	3041	12878	39224	121483	163334
Other Receipts 7	975266	11842	46663	2855	33078	20882	45960	12504	50696	21959	22707	524265	181858
Total Receipts 8	75749645	667067	4687390	2263950	6565243	4718090	5732130	3819599	4333232	4875272	3431732	16655463	18000477
Average Total Receipts 9	6247	479	567	2271	7167	18358	35603	65855	149422	243764	571955	1514133	6000159

Operating Costs/Operating Income (%)

	Total	Zero Assets	Under 500	500 to 1,000	1,000 to 5,000	5,000 to 10,000	10,000 to 25,000	25,000 to 50,000	50,000 to 100,000	100,000 to 250,000	250,000 to 500,000	500,000 to 2,500,000	2,500,000 and over
Cost of Operations 10	66.4	62.6	58.1	63.4	65.5	62.5	71.3	71.9	75.0	72.1	71.2	64.4	64.8
Salaries and Wages 11	7.5	15.7	9.5	6.9	9.9	10.6	7.2	7.0	5.6	5.6	5.1	7.4	6.8
Taxes Paid 12	2.1	3.7	3.2	2.3	2.7	2.5	1.9	1.9	1.8	1.6	1.7	2.2	1.9
Interest Paid 13	1.4	0.7	0.6	0.7	0.8	1.1	0.8	0.8	2.0	1.3	1.7	1.4	2.2
Depreciation 14	1.4	1.2	0.9	1.6	1.4	1.1	1.6	1.5	1.1	1.7	1.9	1.3	1.3
Amortization and Depletion 15	0.3	0.7	0.1	0.1	0.0	0.1	0.1	0.1	0.2	1.0	0.3	0.5	0.2
Pensions and Other Deferred Comp. 16	0.5	0.6	0.1	0.2	0.2	0.6	0.4	0.4	0.3	0.4	0.7	0.5	0.7
Employee Benefits 17	1.9	0.2	0.9	1.2	1.4	1.3	2.1	1.8	2.2	2.1	1.8	1.9	2.3
Advertising 18	2.0	0.5	0.5	0.1	1.7	0.9	0.9	1.4	1.3	1.4	2.0	3.5	2.4
Other Expenses 19	12.2	15.5	17.0	19.6	11.5	9.7	9.6	9.2	8.8	10.2	12.3	13.8	12.0
Officers' Compensation 20	1.8	1.8	8.9	3.7	2.6	5.5	1.7	1.4	0.9	1.0	0.6	0.7	0.2
Operating Margin 21	2.7	•	0.2	0.2	2.1	4.1	2.4	2.5	0.8	1.5	0.9	2.3	5.4
Operating Margin Before Officers' Comp. 22	4.5	•	9.1	4.0	4.8	9.6	4.1	3.9	1.7	2.5	1.5	3.1	5.5

Selected Average Balance Sheet ($ in Thousands)

Net Receivables 23	803	0	32	365	781	1777	3896	8184	17907	31869	67519	249824	841079
Inventories 24	556	0	21	168	766	2200	4095	8441	18823	34833	52631	150542	511638
Net Property, Plant and Equipment 25	706	0	29	84	536	1097	4173	9439	17664	36424	90634	163807	883384
Total Assets 26	3920	0	117	777	2399	7248	15030	35031	72660	141388	351592	1019765	6338197
Notes and Loans Payable 27	1294	0	53	332	1125	2566	4084	8920	31643	42598	110057	330421	1994508
All Other Liabilities 28	1084	0	35	295	1079	2369	3319	7802	20758	46417	60360	270571	1700434
Net Worth 29	1542	0	28	150	195	2313	7627	18308	20260	52372	181175	418772	2634254

Selected Financial Ratios (Times to 1)

Current Ratio 30	1.6	•	1.5	1.6	1.6	2.1	2.0	2.2	2.1	1.5	1.9	1.8	1.1
Quick Ratio 31	0.8	•	1.1	1.1	0.9	1.1	1.1	1.1	1.0	0.7	1.0	1.1	0.5
Net Sales to Working Capital 32	9.5	•	22.2	9.1	11.2	6.6	7.4	5.7	6.3	9.1	7.9	6.7	32.2
Coverage Ratio 33	4.5	•	3.0	1.6	4.4	5.1	5.0	4.9	2.1	2.7	3.3	5.9	4.9
Total Asset Turnover 34	1.6	•	4.8	2.9	3.0	2.5	2.3	1.9	2.0	1.7	1.6	1.4	0.9
Inventory Turnover 35	7.3	•	15.5	8.5	6.1	5.2	6.1	5.6	5.9	5.0	7.5	6.2	7.4
Receivables Turnover 36	9.1	•	16.1	5.7	8.9	9.5	8.6	8.6	8.9	8.2	9.3	6.4	13.9
Total Liabilities to Net Worth 37	1.5	•	3.2	4.2	11.3	2.1	1.0	0.9	2.6	1.7	0.9	1.4	1.4
Current Assets to Working Capital 38	2.8	•	2.8	2.6	2.8	1.9	2.1	1.8	1.9	2.9	2.2	2.3	10.4
Current Liabilities to Working Capital 39	1.8	•	1.8	1.6	1.8	0.9	1.1	0.8	0.9	1.9	1.2	1.3	9.4
Working Capital to Net Sales 40	0.1	•	0.0	0.1	0.1	0.2	0.1	0.2	0.2	0.1	0.1	0.2	0.0
Inventory to Working Capital 41	0.9	•	0.8	0.5	1.0	0.8	0.8	0.7	0.9	1.3	0.9	0.6	2.8
Total Receipts to Cash Flow 42	7.0	10.5	7.6	11.2	9.7	9.1	9.0	9.3	10.5	9.3	7.1	5.3	5.5
Cost of Goods to Cash Flow 43	4.6	6.6	4.4	7.1	6.4	5.7	6.4	6.7	7.9	6.7	5.1	3.4	3.6
Cash Flow to Total Debt 44	0.4	•	0.3	0.3	0.3	0.4	0.5	0.4	0.3	0.3	0.5	0.4	0.3

Selected Financial Factors (in Percentages)

Debt Ratio 45	60.7	•	76.1	80.7	91.9	68.1	49.3	47.7	72.1	63.0	48.5	58.9	58.3
Return on Total Assets 46	10.0	•	8.9	3.3	10.6	14.8	9.8	7.6	8.4	6.3	8.7	11.9	9.8
Return on Equity Before Income Taxes 47	19.7	•	25.0	6.3	100.8	37.3	15.4	11.6	15.8	10.7	11.8	24.2	18.6
Return on Equity After Income Taxes 48	14.8	•	23.2	5.4	93.1	34.0	13.6	10.0	12.7	7.0	7.1	18.8	12.4
Profit Margin (Before Income Tax) 49	5.0	•	1.2	0.4	2.8	4.7	3.3	3.2	2.2	2.3	3.8	7.0	8.4
Profit Margin (After Income Tax) 50	3.7	•	1.2	0.4	2.5	4.3	2.9	2.8	1.7	1.5	2.3	5.5	5.6

Table II
Corporations with Net Income

FURNITURE AND RELATED PRODUCT MANUFACTURING

MONEY AMOUNTS AND SIZE OF ASSETS IN THOUSANDS OF DOLLARS

Item Description for Accounting Period 7/05 Through 6/06	Total	Zero Assets	Under 500	500 to 1,000	1,000 to 5,000	5,000 to 10,000	10,000 to 25,000	25,000 to 50,000	50,000 to 100,000	100,000 to 250,000	250,000 to 500,000	500,000 to 2,500,000	2,500,000 and over
Number of Enterprises **1**	6746	685	4517	541	560	227	118	47	20	14	•	•	3
Revenues ($ in Thousands)													
Net Sales **2**	63622568	452487	3032022	1512115	4331591	4112446	4109515	3184245	3172552	3490522	•	•	17554589
Interest **3**	145475	29	514	403	4501	3593	1909	2589	3043	2755	•	•	70059
Rents **4**	53659	0	0	0	164	309	90	3704	989	282	•	•	25402
Royalties **5**	56946	0	0	0	0	0	610	270	437	0	•	•	5235
Other Portfolio Income **6**	349070	153	0	944	2175	1792	3167	8933	3005	4928	•	•	163334
Other Receipts **7**	839513	9710	2007	1931	25340	9381	20816	8407	21467	11632	•	•	181858
Total Receipts **8**	65067231	462379	3034543	1515393	4363771	4127521	4136107	3208148	3201493	3510119	•	•	18000477
Average Total Receipts **9**	9645	675	672	2801	7792	18183	35052	68258	160075	250723	•	•	6000159
Operating Costs/Operating Income (%)													
Cost of Operations **10**	65.6	60.2	55.7	66.8	63.7	59.3	69.4	70.3	73.6	72.9	•	•	64.8
Salaries and Wages **11**	7.4	15.3	9.9	8.7	9.1	11.3	7.6	7.4	5.3	4.6	•	•	6.8
Taxes Paid **12**	2.1	4.3	2.5	2.8	2.4	2.5	1.8	1.9	1.7	1.5	•	•	1.9
Interest Paid **13**	1.3	•	0.5	0.4	0.5	1.1	0.6	0.8	1.0	0.9	•	•	2.2
Depreciation **14**	1.4	1.3	0.6	2.0	1.4	1.1	1.6	1.6	1.1	1.5	•	•	1.3
Amortization and Depletion **15**	0.2	•	0.0	0.1	0.0	0.1	0.0	0.1	0.1	0.1	•	•	0.2
Pensions and Other Deferred Comp. **16**	0.5	0.6	0.2	0.2	0.3	0.7	0.4	0.5	0.3	0.4	•	•	0.7
Employee Benefits **17**	1.9	0.1	0.6	1.2	1.6	1.3	1.7	1.7	2.2	2.3	•	•	2.3
Advertising **18**	2.0	0.1	0.4	0.2	1.4	0.9	0.8	1.3	1.2	0.9	•	•	2.4
Other Expenses **19**	11.7	8.7	17.2	11.9	11.4	9.0	8.5	9.2	7.6	8.2	•	•	12.0
Officers' Compensation **20**	1.6	1.3	7.8	3.4	2.8	6.2	1.8	1.3	0.9	1.2	•	•	0.2
Operating Margin **21**	4.4	8.2	4.8	2.1	5.4	6.3	5.7	4.0	5.1	5.5	•	•	5.4
Operating Margin Before Officers' Comp. **22**	6.0	9.5	12.6	5.6	8.2	12.5	7.6	5.3	6.0	6.7	•	•	5.5

Selected Average Balance Sheet ($ in Thousands)

Net Receivables 23	1258	0	34	353	743	1804	4045	8832	19292	35134	•	841079
Inventories 24	793	0	21	227	654	2118	3825	8512	17987	36468	•	511638
Net Property, Plant and Equipment 25	1089	0	21	105	529	887	4087	10043	19715	35192	•	883384
Total Assets 26	6220	0	112	785	2370	7213	14918	35866	77657	146320	•	6338197
Notes and Loans Payable 27	1823	0	32	238	597	2554	3024	7830	20198	38056	•	1994508
All Other Liabilities 28	1617	0	31	240	787	2245	3127	8110	16315	26693	•	1700434
Net Worth 29	2780	0	49	307	985	2414	8768	19926	41144	81571	•	2643254

Selected Financial Ratios (Times to 1)

Current Ratio 30	1.6	•	1.7	2.0	1.9	2.4	2.2	2.3	2.4	2.7	•	1.1
Quick Ratio 31	0.9	•	1.2	1.5	1.1	1.3	1.3	1.3	1.2	1.4	•	0.5
Net Sales to Working Capital 32	8.8	•	23.1	9.5	9.6	5.8	6.4	5.4	5.8	4.7	•	32.2
Coverage Ratio 33	6.4	•	11.6	6.3	13.4	6.9	12.0	7.2	6.7	7.7	•	4.9
Total Asset Turnover 34	1.5	•	6.0	3.6	3.3	2.5	2.3	1.9	2.0	1.7	•	0.9
Inventory Turnover 35	7.8	•	18.0	8.2	7.5	5.1	6.3	5.6	6.5	5.0	•	7.4
Receivables Turnover 36	9.5	•	15.7	7.6	9.5	20.1	8.2	8.3	9.5	7.6	•	13.9
Total Liabilities to Net Worth 37	1.2	•	1.3	1.6	1.4	2.0	0.7	0.8	0.9	0.8	•	1.4
Current Assets to Working Capital 38	2.6	•	2.5	2.0	2.1	1.7	1.8	1.8	1.7	1.6	•	10.4
Current Liabilities to Working Capital 39	1.6	•	1.5	1.0	1.1	0.7	0.8	0.8	0.7	0.6	•	9.4
Working Capital to Net Sales 40	0.1	•	0.0	0.1	0.1	0.2	0.2	0.2	0.2	0.2	•	0.0
Inventory to Working Capital 41	0.8	•	0.6	0.5	0.7	0.7	0.6	0.6	0.8	0.7	•	2.8
Total Receipts to Cash Flow 42	6.2	5.6	5.8	9.4	7.4	8.4	7.7	8.1	8.1	7.7	•	5.5
Cost of Goods to Cash Flow 43	4.1	3.4	3.2	6.3	4.7	5.0	5.4	5.7	6.0	5.6	•	3.6
Cash Flow to Total Debt 44	0.4	•	1.8	0.6	0.8	0.5	0.7	0.5	0.5	0.5	•	0.3

Selected Financial Factors (in Percentages)

Debt Ratio 45	55.3	•	56.4	61.0	58.4	66.5	41.2	44.4	47.0	44.3	•	58.3
Return on Total Assets 46	12.3	•	32.1	10.0	21.8	19.6	16.2	10.5	14.3	11.7	•	9.8
Return on Equity Before Income Taxes 47	23.1	•	67.3	21.5	48.4	50.1	25.3	16.3	22.9	18.3	•	18.6
Return on Equity After Income Taxes 48	18.2	•	65.4	20.8	45.9	46.5	23.3	14.5	20.7	14.9	•	12.4
Profit Margin (Before Income Tax) 49	6.8	10.4	4.9	2.4	6.2	6.7	6.4	4.8	5.9	6.0	•	8.4
Profit Margin (After Income Tax) 50	5.4	10.4	4.7	2.3	5.9	6.2	5.9	4.3	5.4	4.9	•	5.6

Table I

Corporations with and without Net Income

MEDICAL EQUIPMENT AND SUPPLIES

MONEY AMOUNTS AND SIZE OF ASSETS IN THOUSANDS OF DOLLARS

Item Description for Accounting Period 7/05 Through 6/06	Total	Zero Assets	Under 500	500 to 1,000	1,000 to 5,000	5,000 to 10,000	10,000 to 25,000	25,000 to 50,000	50,000 to 100,000	100,000 to 250,000	250,000 to 500,000	500,000 to 2,500,000	2,500,000 and over
Number of Enterprises 1	7922	80	5501	421	1256	190	196	98	56	46	30	33	13

Revenues ($ in Thousands)

Item Description for Accounting Period 7/05 Through 6/06	Total	Zero Assets	Under 500	500 to 1,000	1,000 to 5,000	5,000 to 10,000	10,000 to 25,000	25,000 to 50,000	50,000 to 100,000	100,000 to 250,000	250,000 to 500,000	500,000 to 2,500,000	2,500,000 and over
Net Sales 2	99900314	785591	1947672	853030	6063221	1831908	4002114	4081532	3379757	6222105	7608079	20832819	42292485
Interest 3	1503928	16273	1324	1405	3591	16477	19626	19861	24545	30774	58631	125578	1185842
Rents 4	55694	657	0	1	644	0	440	1099	2930	6988	14055	20725	8156
Royalties 5	3062341	2296	0	0	12	795	8529	21275	3869	1722	38109	130716	2855018
Other Portfolio Income 6	10886077	146073	0	46708	2835	13083	33182	27322	62389	43991	390043	1566930	8554520
Other Receipts 7	2867185	12556	557	19	24488	26329	60279	31737	14133	40733	83095	193592	2379670
Total Receipts 8	118275539	963446	1949553	901163	6094791	1888592	4124170	4182826	3487623	6346313	8192012	22869360	57275691
Average Total Receipts 9	14930	12043	354	2141	4853	9940	21042	42682	62279	137963	273067	693011	4405822

Operating Costs/Operating Income (%)

Item Description for Accounting Period 7/05 Through 6/06	Total	Zero Assets	Under 500	500 to 1,000	1,000 to 5,000	5,000 to 10,000	10,000 to 25,000	25,000 to 50,000	50,000 to 100,000	100,000 to 250,000	250,000 to 500,000	500,000 to 2,500,000	2,500,000 and over
Cost of Operations 10	50.0	39.9	36.3	52.6	61.5	52.4	53.2	51.8	45.2	48.1	42.2	47.6	51.9
Salaries and Wages 11	15.8	26.6	13.1	10.5	10.6	24.2	18.7	17.7	17.6	17.1	16.1	13.8	16.4
Taxes Paid 12	1.9	2.3	3.2	4.0	3.6	3.0	2.3	2.4	2.2	1.9	2.0	1.7	1.5
Interest Paid 13	3.0	7.7	1.0	0.9	0.8	1.4	1.4	1.6	1.3	1.8	1.5	2.4	4.7
Depreciation 14	2.3	3.6	2.1	1.5	1.2	1.6	2.1	2.5	2.9	2.1	2.3	2.6	2.4
Amortization and Depletion 15	1.5	1.3	0.1	0.9	0.2	1.0	0.6	1.0	1.1	1.2	1.2	1.2	2.2
Pensions and Other Deferred Comp. 16	1.2	0.3	0.5	0.2	0.3	0.3	0.4	0.5	0.4	0.4	0.6	1.0	2.0
Employee Benefits 17	2.8	11.9	2.7	1.1	1.2	1.6	2.0	2.3	2.8	2.2	2.6	2.4	3.4
Advertising 18	1.3	1.9	0.7	0.6	1.5	1.7	1.4	3.2	2.9	1.7	1.0	1.3	0.9
Other Expenses 19	20.0	27.4	21.2	25.7	12.6	26.4	19.8	19.9	21.2	17.8	22.1	19.1	20.8
Officers' Compensation 20	1.9	12.2	14.7	4.7	4.8	4.1	4.1	2.8	2.6	1.7	1.6	1.4	0.6
Operating Margin 21	•	4.4	•	1.8	•	•	•	•	•	4.0	6.6	5.7	•
Operating Margin Before Officers' Comp. 22	0.1	•	19.1	1.8	6.6	•	•	•	2.4	5.7	8.2	7.1	•

Selected Average Balance Sheet ($ in Thousands)

Net Receivables 23	2650	0	8	246	612	1436	3109	6595	11211	31508	53455	121404	835730
Inventories 24	1550	0	12	147	435	1155	2815	5720	7734	17478	27941	84476	416095
Net Property, Plant and Equipment 25	2012	0	21	97	268	727	2255	5736	10538	18694	39895	120949	589723
Total Assets 26	18833	0	73	678	1802	7159	15404	35947	70113	160751	350347	994133	6438793
Notes and Loans Payable 27	4501	0	49	218	500	1649	4086	7560	11513	30354	55772	226443	1663785
All Other Liabilities 28	5421	0	16	238	458	1380	3462	9688	12009	49489	69579	195879	2214542
Net Worth 29	8911	0	8	221	844	4129	7855	18699	46591	80908	224996	571811	2560467

Selected Financial Ratios (Times to 1)

Current Ratio 30	1.7	•	1.3	1.4	2.1	2.9	2.1	2.5	3.0	2.0	3.0	2.0	1.4
Quick Ratio 31	1.0	•	0.8	0.8	1.3	1.9	1.2	1.5	1.8	1.3	1.7	1.1	0.8
Net Sales to Working Capital 32	3.9	•	40.2	13.4	6.4	2.6	3.9	3.1	2.5	3.2	2.3	3.6	4.6
Coverage Ratio 33	7.1	•	5.4	3.9	4.0	•	•	•	3.4	4.3	10.7	7.9	8.0
Total Asset Turnover 34	0.7	•	4.8	3.0	2.7	1.3	1.3	1.2	0.9	0.8	0.7	0.6	0.5
Inventory Turnover 35	4.1	•	10.9	7.3	6.8	4.4	3.9	3.8	3.5	3.7	3.8	3.6	4.1
Receivables Turnover 36	4.6	•	30.1	9.9	8.3	7.1	6.7	6.6	5.0	4.0	5.6	4.6	3.7
Total Liabilities to Net Worth 37	1.1	•	7.9	2.1	1.1	0.7	1.0	0.9	0.5	1.0	0.6	0.7	1.5
Current Assets to Working Capital 38	2.4	•	4.9	3.4	1.9	1.5	1.9	1.7	1.5	2.0	1.5	2.0	3.3
Current Liabilities to Working Capital 39	1.4	•	3.9	2.4	0.9	0.5	0.9	0.7	0.5	1.0	0.5	1.0	2.3
Working Capital to Net Sales 40	0.3	•	0.0	0.1	0.2	0.4	0.3	0.3	0.4	0.3	0.4	0.3	0.2
Inventory to Working Capital 41	0.5	•	1.7	0.8	0.6	0.3	0.6	0.5	0.3	0.4	0.3	0.5	0.6
Total Receipts to Cash Flow 42	3.0	•	5.0	5.6	8.8	12.1	7.6	7.1	4.9	4.6	2.9	3.1	2.1
Cost of Goods to Cash Flow 43	1.5	•	1.8	3.0	5.4	6.3	4.1	3.7	2.2	2.2	1.2	1.5	1.1
Cash Flow to Total Debt 44	0.4	•	1.1	0.8	0.6	0.3	0.4	0.3	0.5	0.4	0.7	0.5	0.4

Selected Financial Factors (in Percentages)

Debt Ratio 45	52.7	•	88.7	67.3	53.2	42.3	49.0	48.0	33.5	49.7	35.8	42.5	60.2
Return on Total Assets 46	14.4	•	26.8	11.0	8.3	•	•	•	3.8	6.6	11.9	11.9	18.9
Return on Equity Before Income Taxes 47	26.2	•	193.0	25.1	13.2	•	•	•	4.0	10.0	16.8	18.1	41.6
Return on Equity After Income Taxes 48	21.0	•	192.5	23.6	12.6	•	•	•	2.2	6.6	12.6	13.1	35.1
Profit Margin (Before Income Tax) 49	18.5	•	4.5	2.7	2.3	•	•	•	3.1	6.0	14.9	16.4	32.8
Profit Margin (After Income Tax) 50	14.9	•	4.5	2.6	2.2	•	•	•	1.7	4.0	11.2	11.9	27.7

Table II
Corporations with Net Income

MEDICAL EQUIPMENT AND SUPPLIES

MONEY AMOUNTS AND SIZE OF ASSETS IN THOUSANDS OF DOLLARS

Item Description for Accounting Period 7/05 Through 6/06	Total	Zero Assets	Under 500	500 to 1,000	1,000 to 5,000	5,000 to 10,000	10,000 to 25,000	25,000 to 50,000	50,000 to 100,000	100,000 to 250,000	250,000 to 500,000	500,000 to 2,500,000	2,500,000 and over
Number of Enterprises 1	5849	58	4113	316	1005	67	110	52	34	32	26	24	13
Revenues ($ in Thousands)													
Net Sales 2	87788410	115510	1499412	693157	5021497	889799	2872807	2725725	2579487	4790279	7030681	17277570	42292485
Interest 3	1393206	7384	1278	597	1703	3075	4181	6052	11855	19704	54878	96657	1185842
Rents 4	50498	0	0	1	0	0	134	1029	2694	4417	14055	20013	8156
Royalties 5	2987478	0	0	0	0	772	8161	2124	3701	621	38109	78971	2855018
Other Portfolio Income 6	10647482	56885	0	46708	2242	314	1197	23021	37854	17851	389808	1517082	8554520
Other Receipts 7	2765980	-368	124	19	19622	15229	47448	18482	20035	33281	66908	165530	2379670
Total Receipts 8	105633054	179411	1500814	740482	5045064	909189	2933928	2776433	2665626	4866153	7594439	19155823	57275691
Average Total Receipts 9	18060	3093	365	2343	5020	13570	26672	53393	78107	152067	292094	798159	4405822
Operating Costs/Operating Income (%)													
Cost of Operations 10	49.7	30.5	34.7	52.3	57.8	52.3	55.6	51.3	48.3	48.7	42.1	45.3	51.9
Salaries and Wages 11	14.7	37.3	11.7	6.1	9.5	9.2	12.5	13.5	13.7	13.8	15.7	13.3	16.4
Taxes Paid 12	1.9	4.2	3.3	4.1	3.7	3.1	1.9	2.3	2.0	1.9	2.0	1.7	1.5
Interest Paid 13	2.9	0.8	0.8	0.3	0.7	0.8	0.6	0.6	0.9	1.4	1.4	1.8	4.7
Depreciation 14	2.2	1.1	1.5	0.9	0.9	1.2	1.4	2.1	2.4	2.0	2.3	2.6	2.4
Amortization and Depletion 15	1.4	1.1	0.0	1.1	0.0	0.3	0.4	0.2	0.7	1.1	1.0	0.7	2.2
Pensions and Other Deferred Comp. 16	1.3	0.3	0.5	0.2	0.2	0.3	0.4	0.6	0.5	0.5	0.6	1.1	2.0
Employee Benefits 17	2.8	1.5	2.7	1.2	1.0	1.0	1.3	2.1	2.7	2.4	2.5	2.5	3.4
Advertising 18	1.2	5.6	0.7	0.5	1.7	1.4	1.3	3.0	2.9	1.9	1.1	1.4	0.9
Other Expenses 19	18.9	19.3	15.5	22.1	12.0	13.3	13.9	13.1	14.8	15.6	21.0	19.0	20.8
Officers' Compensation 20	1.6	4.8	14.9	4.8	4.7	3.8	3.2	2.5	2.2	1.6	1.7	1.1	0.6
Operating Margin 21	1.5	•	13.6	6.2	7.8	13.3	7.5	8.8	9.0	9.3	8.5	9.4	•
Operating Margin Before Officers' Comp. 22	3.1	•	28.5	11.1	12.5	17.1	10.7	11.3	11.2	10.8	10.2	10.6	•

Selected Average Balance Sheet ($ in Thousands)

Net Receivables 23	3181	0	10	243	582	1651	3836	7665	11474	35343	53776	132734	835730
Inventories 24	1688	0	12	86	383	2272	3282	5984	8583	19436	27384	95920	457030
Net Property, Plant and Equipment 25	2433	0	21	70	237	736	2550	7350	11932	21181	43231	137502	589723
Total Assets 26	22412	0	70	618	1711	7486	14884	36623	70432	164975	351494	1013581	6438793
Notes and Loans Payable 27	4939	0	30	153	351	988	3382	3752	8484	26570	38064	165628	1663785
All Other Liabilities 28	6659	0	15	264	387	1398	3699	10289	13192	44515	71448	202564	2214542
Net Worth 29	10814	0	26	201	973	5100	7803	22582	48756	93890	241982	645389	2560467

Selected Financial Ratios (Times to 1)

Current Ratio 30	1.7	•	1.5	1.3	2.5	3.4	2.2	2.3	3.0	2.0	2.8	2.3	1.4
Quick Ratio 31	1.0	•	1.0	0.7	1.5	1.4	1.3	1.4	1.6	1.3	1.8	1.2	0.8
Net Sales to Working Capital 32	4.0	•	24.1	18.0	6.0	3.0	4.6	4.0	3.1	3.5	2.7	3.3	4.6
Coverage Ratio 33	9.2	64.9	17.2	40.7	13.5	20.6	16.2	19.9	15.1	9.0	13.6	12.6	8.0
Total Asset Turnover 34	0.7	•	5.2	3.6	2.9	1.8	1.8	1.4	1.1	0.9	0.8	0.7	0.5
Inventory Turnover 35	4.4	•	10.9	13.3	7.5	3.1	4.4	4.5	4.3	3.7	4.2	3.4	3.7
Receivables Turnover 36	5.4	•	23.8	18.1	9.4	5.4	7.1	7.1	6.4	3.9	6.2	4.6	7.8
Total Liabilities to Net Worth 37	1.1	•	1.7	2.1	0.8	0.5	0.9	0.6	0.4	0.8	0.5	0.6	1.5
Current Assets to Working Capital 38	2.4	•	3.1	4.0	1.7	1.4	1.8	1.8	1.5	2.0	1.5	1.7	3.3
Current Liabilities to Working Capital 39	1.4	•	2.1	3.0	0.7	0.4	0.8	0.8	0.5	1.0	0.5	0.7	2.3
Working Capital to Net Sales 40	0.2	•	0.0	0.1	0.2	0.3	0.2	0.2	0.3	0.3	0.4	0.3	0.2
Inventory to Working Capital 41	0.5	•	0.9	0.7	0.5	0.6	0.5	0.4	0.4	0.3	0.4	0.3	0.2
Total Receipts to Cash Flow 42	2.6	5.6	4.2	4.3	6.0	3.7	4.8	4.6	4.0	2.8	2.8	2.7	2.1
Cost of Goods to Cash Flow 43	1.3	1.7	1.5	2.3	3.4	2.0	2.4	2.6	2.0	2.0	1.2	1.2	1.1
Cash Flow to Total Debt 44	0.5	•	2.0	1.2	1.5	0.8	0.8	0.9	0.5	0.9	0.5	0.7	0.4

Selected Financial Factors (in Percentages)

Debt Ratio 45	51.8	•	63.3	67.5	43.1	31.9	47.6	38.3	30.8	43.1	31.2	36.3	60.2
Return on Total Assets 46	18.0	•	75.4	47.5	26.2	28.9	18.0	16.1	14.0	11.0	14.3	16.4	18.9
Return on Equity Before Income Taxes 47	33.3	•	193.5	142.7	42.6	40.4	32.2	24.8	18.9	17.3	19.2	23.8	41.6
Return on Equity After Income Taxes 48	27.5	•	193.2	140.5	41.9	37.9	27.5	21.2	16.1	13.1	14.7	17.8	35.1
Profit Margin (Before Income Tax) 49	24.0	48.8	13.7	13.1	8.3	15.5	21.2	10.7	12.2	10.8	17.2	21.3	32.8
Profit Margin (After Income Tax) 50	19.8	37.7	13.7	12.9	8.2	14.5	9.6	9.1	10.4	8.2	13.1	16.0	27.7

Table I

Corporations with and without Net Income

OTHER MISCELLANEOUS MANUFACTURING

MONEY AMOUNTS AND SIZE OF ASSETS IN THOUSANDS OF DOLLARS

Item Description for Accounting Period 7/05 Through 6/06	Total	Zero Assets	Under 500	500 to 1,000	1,000 to 5,000	5,000 to 10,000	10,000 to 25,000	25,000 to 50,000	50,000 to 100,000	100,000 to 250,000	250,000 to 500,000	500,000 to 2,500,000	2,500,000 and over
Number of Enterprises **1**	24197	213	18391	2013	2279	457	480	167	83	56	24	27	5
Revenues ($ in Thousands)													
Net Sales **2**	108991831	1476183	7019916	3488655	13093280	5622175	12714719	8618633	6946510	10125622	7939584	19311476	12635079
Interest **3**	807574	3702	1600	3123	7663	4644	12294	28473	11789	26309	79771	128264	499941
Rents **4**	45935	0	277	943	2278	864	3784	1304	3873	2447	18744	6244	5176
Royalties **5**	722416	13854	58	0	1	1218	2223	5367	34695	19055	24868	180550	440528
Other Portfolio Income **6**	1657892	34273	28940	4150	44030	31633	45496	118231	64375	71155	95362	442377	677869
Other Receipts **7**	2119304	24184	56920	959	169314	27740	83349	121308	88435	55685	112316	105258	1273838
Total Receipts **8**	114344952	1552196	7107711	3497830	13316566	5688274	12861865	8893316	7149677	10300273	8270645	20174169	15532431
Average Total Receipts **9**	4726	7287	386	1738	5843	12447	26796	53253	86141	183933	344610	747191	3106486
Operating Costs/Operating Income (%)													
Cost of Operations **10**	64.4	66.2	42.8	66.1	67.7	64.4	67.9	68.4	66.7	61.7	65.1	68.8	60.0
Salaries and Wages **11**	9.2	13.2	17.9	5.1	8.1	10.2	8.7	8.3	8.1	8.8	8.3	7.1	11.8
Taxes Paid **12**	1.8	1.8	3.1	2.1	2.2	1.7	2.0	1.8	1.8	1.5	1.7	1.2	1.9
Interest Paid **13**	2.5	4.7	1.2	1.4	1.0	2.0	1.4	1.6	2.5	1.9	3.6	3.1	5.7
Depreciation **14**	1.8	1.3	1.1	1.4	1.3	1.8	1.5	1.7	2.1	2.2	2.3	1.9	2.4
Amortization and Depletion **15**	0.7	1.3	0.2	0.1	0.1	0.2	0.4	0.5	0.7	0.7	1.2	0.9	1.4
Pensions and Other Deferred Comp. **16**	0.6	0.2	0.5	0.1	0.5	0.5	0.3	0.5	0.5	0.4	0.6	0.4	1.4
Employee Benefits **17**	1.5	1.4	1.2	1.2	1.2	2.0	1.5	1.8	1.6	1.6	1.9	1.8	1.1
Advertising **18**	1.6	1.3	1.4	0.9	0.7	0.8	1.3	1.7	2.6	2.0	2.1	1.6	2.7
Other Expenses **19**	13.1	15.8	19.7	14.1	14.9	12.7	10.7	11.2	11.9	11.7	11.1	11.1	17.2
Officers' Compensation **20**	2.5	1.6	9.3	5.1	5.1	2.6	2.4	1.9	3.3	1.3	0.9	0.5	0.3
Operating Margin **21**	0.2	•	1.6	2.8	•	1.0	1.9	0.7	•	6.2	1.3	1.6	•
Operating Margin Before Officers' Comp. **22**	2.7	•	10.9	7.9	2.2	3.6	4.2	2.6	1.6	7.5	2.2	2.1	•

Selected Average Balance Sheet ($ in Thousands)

Net Receivables 23	645	0	29	200	654	1683	3830	8886	16274	31201	59030	120563	263534
Inventories 24	604	0	32	167	732	2290	4098	8436	12845	27708	50076	88511	279866
Net Property, Plant and Equipment 25	529	0	19	141	440	2804	6156	12134	27401	63666	78912	403936	
Total Assets 26	3710	109	699	2391	6885	15368	34008	68350	160641	361374	901031	3406069	
Notes and Loans Payable 27	1312	77	348	934	2351	5131	10617	26379	49709	150510	323051	973913	
All Other Liabilities 28	1053	48	237	660	2018	4550	9473	23095	35738	96041	229167	1103518	
Net Worth 29	1346	-16	114	797	2515	5687	13918	18877	75194	114823	348814	1328637	

Selected Financial Ratios (Times to 1)

Current Ratio 30	1.6	•	1.2	1.8	2.1	1.8	1.8	1.4	1.9	1.5	1.6	1.1	
Quick Ratio 31	0.8	•	0.7	0.9	1.1	0.9	0.9	0.8	1.0	0.7	0.9	0.4	
Net Sales to Working Capital 32	7.1	•	30.7	7.8	6.4	5.5	5.9	5.2	7.3	5.0	6.9	6.1	29.9
Coverage Ratio 33	3.1	0.3	3.4	3.2	•	2.1	3.1	3.4	1.5	5.2	2.5	3.1	4.2
Total Asset Turnover 34	1.2	•	3.5	2.5	2.4	1.8	1.7	1.5	1.2	1.1	0.9	0.8	0.7
Inventory Turnover 35	4.8	•	5.1	6.8	5.3	3.5	4.4	4.2	4.3	4.0	4.3	5.6	5.4
Receivables Turnover 36	7.0	•	12.7	10.7	9.2	7.4	7.1	5.6	5.6	5.4	6.1	6.1	7.3
Total Liabilities to Net Worth 37	1.8	•	•	5.1	2.0	1.7	1.7	1.4	2.6	2.1	1.6	1.6	
Current Assets to Working Capital 38	2.8	•	6.1	2.3	1.9	2.3	2.3	2.2	3.4	3.2	2.7	12.4	
Current Liabilities to Working Capital 39	1.8	•	5.1	1.3	0.9	1.3	1.3	1.2	2.4	2.2	1.7	11.4	
Working Capital to Net Sales 40	0.1	•	0.0	0.1	0.2	0.2	0.2	0.2	0.1	0.1	0.2	0.0	
Inventory to Working Capital 41	1.0	•	2.2	1.0	0.8	1.1	1.0	0.8	1.2	0.7	0.8	3.1	
Total Receipts to Cash Flow 42	6.4	10.3	7.7	6.0	8.5	8.8	9.6	8.2	9.1	5.6	6.9	6.3	3.1
Cost of Goods to Cash Flow 43	4.1	6.8	5.1	2.6	5.5	6.0	6.5	5.6	6.1	3.5	4.5	4.3	1.9
Cash Flow to Total Debt 44	0.3	•	0.4	0.5	0.3	0.3	0.4	0.3	0.2	0.2	0.2	0.4	

Selected Financial Factors (in Percentages)

Debt Ratio 45	63.7	•	114.2	83.7	66.7	63.5	63.0	59.1	72.4	53.2	68.2	61.3	61.0
Return on Total Assets 46	9.6	•	14.2	10.9	•	7.5	7.7	8.5	4.6	11.2	8.3	7.7	17.6
Return on Equity Before Income Taxes 47	18.0	•	•	45.9	•	10.8	14.0	14.8	5.7	19.3	15.9	13.6	34.3
Return on Equity After Income Taxes 48	13.6	•	•	44.9	•	9.2	11.1	11.6	3.3	16.5	12.6	10.3	24.8
Profit Margin (Before Income Tax) 49	5.4	•	2.9	3.0	•	2.2	3.0	4.0	1.3	8.0	5.5	6.6	18.0
Profit Margin (After Income Tax) 50	4.1	•	2.8	3.0	•	1.9	2.4	3.1	0.7	6.8	4.4	5.0	13.0

Table II
Corporations with Net Income

OTHER MISCELLANEOUS MANUFACTURING

MONEY AMOUNTS AND SIZE OF ASSETS IN THOUSANDS OF DOLLARS

Item Description for Accounting Period 7/05 Through 6/06	Total	Zero Assets	Under 500	500 to 1,000	1,000 to 5,000	5,000 to 10,000	10,000 to 25,000	25,000 to 50,000	50,000 to 100,000	100,000 to 250,000	250,000 to 500,000	500,000 to 2,500,000	2,500,000 and over
Number of Enterprises **1**	12833	75	8869	1850	1125	306	353	117	53	43	17	20	5
Revenues ($ in Thousands)													
Net Sales **2**	82348677	900421	4732618	3247927	7174121	4247106	9603873	6576783	4861575	8493178	6184316	13691679	12635079
Interest **3**	765314	1844	344	2943	5097	2528	8766	25451	6625	23456	75440	112878	499941
Rents **4**	37780	0	0	943	1834	862	2235	1057	2117	2357	16865	4333	5176
Royalties **5**	656014	0	58	0	1	0	1006	5360	7286	10382	24686	166706	440528
Other Portfolio Income **6**	1584148	33388	27787	4087	40681	26635	38106	116172	43384	60499	94317	421222	677869
Other Receipts **7**	1846994	21842	54238	18944	63427	12750	64042	88501	27586	41162	103192	77477	1273838
Total Receipts **8**	87238927	957495	4815045	3274844	7285161	4289881	9718028	6813324	4948573	8631034	6498816	14474295	15532431
Average Total Receipts **9**	6798	12767	543	1770	6476	14019	27530	58234	93369	200722	382283	723715	3106486
Operating Costs/Operating Income (%)													
Cost of Operations **10**	61.6	72.4	38.8	65.2	62.8	62.0	66.1	67.3	61.8	59.5	62.9	63.4	60.0
Salaries and Wages **11**	9.4	5.4	20.5	4.7	7.5	9.3	8.3	7.5	8.1	9.1	9.2	7.9	11.8
Taxes Paid **12**	1.9	2.1	3.3	2.1	2.6	1.5	2.0	1.8	1.8	1.5	1.7	1.5	1.9
Interest Paid **13**	2.4	2.3	0.9	1.4	0.5	1.2	1.0	1.2	1.9	1.4	2.9	3.4	5.7
Depreciation **14**	1.8	1.1	1.2	1.4	1.3	1.7	1.5	1.5	2.0	2.0	2.2	1.8	2.4
Amortization and Depletion **15**	0.6	0.9	0.1	0.1	0.0	0.1	0.3	0.4	0.4	0.6	0.9	1.0	1.4
Pensions and Other Deferred Comp. **16**	0.6	0.2	0.3	0.1	0.9	0.5	0.3	0.5	0.5	0.4	0.7	0.5	1.4
Employee Benefits **17**	1.5	1.0	1.2	0.8	1.5	2.0	1.5	1.3	1.5	1.6	2.0	2.0	1.1
Advertising **18**	1.8	0.6	0.8	0.8	1.0	0.6	1.2	1.6	2.9	2.0	2.6	2.0	2.7
Other Expenses **19**	12.4	9.6	18.6	14.5	11.1	11.0	9.7	10.2	9.4	11.5	11.2	12.1	17.2
Officers' Compensation **20**	2.3	1.3	7.6	5.1	6.0	2.6	2.4	2.0	3.9	1.4	0.8	0.6	0.3
Operating Margin **21**	3.6	3.2	6.6	3.7	4.9	7.5	5.6	4.8	5.7	8.9	2.8	3.8	•
Operating Margin Before Officers' Comp. **22**	5.9	4.5	14.2	8.8	10.9	10.1	8.0	6.8	9.6	10.3	3.7	4.4	•

Selected Average Balance Sheet ($ in Thousands)

Net Receivables 23	923	0	42	195	678	1844	4087	9891	17468	32915	66851	119554	263534
Inventories 24	817	0	32	216	887	2482	3954	8565	14249	28660	55110	75521	257739
Net Property, Plant and Equipment 25	746	0	27	143	440	1286	2839	5745	11419	29165	63231	77498	403936
Total Assets 26	5407	128	691	2414	6952	15195	33873	69748	161302	364765	947212		3406069
Notes and Loans Payable 27	1684	85	351	546	2001	3939	7609	22053	43839	130519	327793		973913
All Other Liabilities 28	1530	60	201	834	1850	4068	9108	18593	37711	107548	238394		1103518
Net Worth 29	2194	-17	138	1033	3101	7188	17156	29102	79752	126698	381025		1328637

Selected Financial Ratios (Times to 1)

Current Ratio 30	1.7	•	1.3	1.9	2.1	2.1	2.0	2.1	1.9	2.1	1.7	1.6	1.1
Quick Ratio 31	0.9	•	1.0	1.0	1.2	1.0	1.1	1.2	1.1	1.1	0.8	1.0	0.4
Net Sales to Working Capital 32	6.4	•	23.9	7.1	6.8	4.8	5.1	4.5	4.6	4.4	5.3	5.9	29.9
Coverage Ratio 33	5.1	5.2	10.2	4.2	12.7	8.1	7.5	8.1	4.8	8.5	3.7	4.0	4.2
Total Asset Turnover 34	1.2	•	4.2	2.5	2.6	2.0	1.8	1.7	1.3	1.2	1.0	0.7	0.7
Inventory Turnover 35	4.8	•	6.5	5.3	4.5	3.5	4.6	4.4	4.0	4.1	4.2	5.7	5.9
Receivables Turnover 36	7.0	•	12.6	18.0	8.7	7.1	7.0	5.6	5.7	5.7	6.1	6.2	19.2
Total Liabilities to Net Worth 37	1.5	•	•	4.0	1.3	1.2	1.1	1.0	1.4	1.0	1.9	1.5	1.6
Current Assets to Working Capital 38	2.5	•	4.1	2.1	1.9	1.9	2.0	1.9	2.1	1.9	2.5	2.6	12.4
Current Liabilities to Working Capital 39	1.5	•	3.1	1.1	0.9	0.9	1.0	0.9	1.1	0.9	1.5	1.6	11.4
Working Capital to Net Sales 40	0.2	•	0.0	0.1	0.1	0.2	0.2	0.2	0.2	0.2	0.2	0.2	0.0
Inventory to Working Capital 41	0.8	•	1.0	0.9	0.8	0.8	0.8	0.6	0.8	0.6	0.8	0.8	3.1
Total Receipts to Cash Flow 42	5.1	5.5	4.6	6.6	7.1	6.0	7.0	6.4	6.8	4.9	5.9	5.0	3.1
Cost of Goods to Cash Flow 43	3.2	4.0	1.8	4.3	4.5	3.7	4.6	4.3	4.2	2.9	3.7	3.1	1.9
Cash Flow to Total Debt 44	0.4	•	0.8	0.5	0.7	0.6	0.5	0.5	0.3	0.5	0.3	0.2	0.4

Selected Financial Factors (in Percentages)

Debt Ratio 45	59.4	•	113.3	80.0	57.2	55.4	52.7	49.4	58.3	50.6	65.3	59.8	61.0
Return on Total Assets 46	14.5	•	38.6	15.0	18.4	19.3	14.0	16.2	12.4	14.7	10.9	9.8	17.6
Return on Equity Before Income Taxes 47	28.7	•	•	56.9	39.6	37.9	25.7	28.1	23.6	26.3	22.9	18.2	34.3
Return on Equity After Income Taxes 48	23.7	•	•	56.0	35.7	35.9	22.7	24.4	21.2	22.8	18.7	14.1	24.8
Profit Margin (Before Income Tax) 49	9.8	9.6	8.4	4.5	6.4	6.8	6.8	8.6	7.5	10.6	8.0	10.1	18.0
Profit Margin (After Income Tax) 50	8.1	8.2	8.2	4.4	5.8	6.0	7.5	7.5	6.7	9.2	6.5	7.8	13.0

Table I

Corporations with and without Net Income

MOTOR VEHICLE AND MOTOR VEHICLE PARTS AND SUPPLIES

MONEY AMOUNTS AND SIZE OF ASSETS IN THOUSANDS OF DOLLARS

Item Description for Accounting Period 7/05 Through 6/06	Total	Zero Assets	Under 500	500 to 1,000	1,000 to 5,000	5,000 to 10,000	10,000 to 25,000	25,000 to 50,000	50,000 to 100,000	100,000 to 250,000	250,000 to 500,000	500,000 to 2,500,000	2,500,000 and over
Number of Enterprises 1	14644	1723	6893	2345	2623	489	343	112	47	30	14	18	6
Revenues ($ in Thousands)													
Net Sales 2	248367301	2463934	7357002	5207459	14224548	10433934	12444347	9309320	6804787	7777608	12920196	41101562	118322603
Interest 3	2050345	3824	1698	1550	11717	8883	8757	6939	8221	18774	57329	135860	1786793
Rents 4	540632	33	0	3045	2979	778	10858	28168	6104	2494	5679	46466	434028
Royalties 5	42000	0	0	0	0	0	0	459	0	2845	978	19594	18124
Other Portfolio Income 6	990113	1809	228	753	9641	11673	17599	21205	15451	6320	28457	285088	591890
Other Receipts 7	3187286	10726	15057	119568	68126	43959	67763	61423	33590	38416	31352	400946	2296359
Total Receipts 8	255177677	2480326	7373985	5332375	14317011	10499227	12549324	9427514	6868153	7846457	13043991	41989516	123449797
Average Total Receipts 9	17425	1440	1070	2274	5458	21471	36587	84174	146131	261549	931714	2332751	20574966
Operating Costs/Operating Income (%)													
Cost of Operations 10	81.1	78.0	80.5	79.3	73.6	83.6	79.3	77.0	79.2	79.5	84.9	84.2	81.2
Salaries and Wages 11	4.0	3.8	4.6	7.1	6.7	4.8	7.1	7.8	6.9	5.3	4.2	3.5	2.7
Taxes Paid 12	0.8	0.8	1.3	1.3	1.6	1.0	1.2	1.2	1.1	1.0	0.7	0.8	0.6
Interest Paid 13	0.9	0.4	0.4	0.5	0.8	0.7	0.7	0.8	0.8	1.1	0.5	0.7	1.1
Depreciation 14	2.7	0.9	0.5	0.4	0.6	0.4	0.8	1.1	0.9	0.8	1.0	1.1	4.8
Amortization and Depletion 15	0.1	0.1	0.1	0.0	0.0	0.1	0.1	0.2	0.1	0.1	0.1	0.2	0.1
Pensions and Other Deferred Comp. 16	0.2	0.1	0.1	0.1	0.3	0.1	0.2	0.2	0.2	0.2	0.2	0.1	0.3
Employee Benefits 17	0.5	0.2	0.2	0.7	0.5	0.5	0.6	0.9	0.7	0.8	0.7	0.5	0.3
Advertising 18	2.7	3.1	0.5	0.3	1.2	0.3	0.4	0.5	0.3	0.7	0.9	2.5	4.2
Other Expenses 19	5.5	13.1	9.6	7.8	10.1	5.5	6.3	7.4	6.4	7.0	4.6	6.2	3.9
Officers' Compensation 20	0.7	0.7	2.5	2.7	3.3	1.8	1.5	1.3	0.8	0.7	0.5	0.2	0.1
Operating Margin 21	0.8	•	•	•	1.3	1.2	1.7	1.5	2.7	2.9	1.7	0.0	0.7
Operating Margin Before Officers' Comp. 22	1.5	•	2.3	2.3	4.6	3.0	3.3	2.8	3.4	3.6	2.2	0.2	0.7

Selected Average Balance Sheet ($ in Thousands)

Net Receivables 23	2853	0	32	162	466	2080	4202	9378	17135	32938	60476	226061	4955008
Inventories 24	1936	0	90	285	815	3147	5998	12659	26702	58644	93544	347285	1555449
Net Property, Plant and Equipment 25	2522	0	15	89	240	362	2028	4965	9139	15801	68793	165051	4952860
Total Assets 26	10357	0	178	678	1826	7118	15456	33744	68598	150827	352323	1194262	16220829
Notes and Loans Payable 27	3240	0	75	190	651	2093	5751	12210	22817	45484	89925	321342	5154923
All Other Liabilities 28	4416	0	61	245	471	2859	5334	10918	20244	49374	106678	492273	7532430
Net Worth 29	2701	0	41	243	703	2165	4371	10617	25537	55969	155720	380647	3533477

Selected Financial Ratios (Times to 1)

Current Ratio 30	1.4	•	2.4	1.8	2.1	1.5	1.4	1.6	1.6	1.5	1.7	1.2	1.3
Quick Ratio 31	0.7	•	1.1	0.8	0.9	0.6	0.6	0.7	0.7	0.6	0.7	0.5	0.8
Net Sales to Working Capital 32	9.5	•	12.1	9.2	7.2	10.2	9.6	9.2	7.7	8.1	10.9	16.7	8.3
Coverage Ratio 33	5.0	•	1.1	5.3	3.4	3.7	4.4	4.5	5.6	4.5	6.0	4.3	5.5
Total Asset Turnover 34	1.6	•	6.0	3.3	3.0	3.0	2.3	2.5	2.1	1.7	2.6	1.9	1.2
Inventory Turnover 35	7.1	•	9.6	6.2	4.9	5.7	4.8	5.1	4.3	3.5	8.4	5.5	10.3
Receivables Turnover 36	6.3	•	23.7	15.6	12.7	11.0	9.2	9.2	8.2	8.3	13.7	12.0	4.2
Total Liabilities to Net Worth 37	2.8	•	3.3	1.8	1.6	2.3	2.5	2.2	1.7	1.7	1.3	2.1	3.6
Current Assets to Working Capital 38	3.6	•	1.7	2.3	1.9	3.0	3.3	2.8	2.8	3.2	2.4	5.3	3.9
Current Liabilities to Working Capital 39	2.6	•	0.7	1.3	0.9	2.0	2.3	1.8	1.8	2.2	1.4	4.3	2.9
Working Capital to Net Sales 40	0.1	•	0.1	0.1	0.1	0.1	0.1	0.1	0.1	0.1	0.1	0.1	0.1
Inventory to Working Capital 41	1.1	•	0.9	1.2	1.1	1.7	1.7	1.4	1.4	1.7	1.2	2.7	0.7
Total Receipts to Cash Flow 42	12.6	9.2	14.4	12.6	10.3	18.0	13.7	12.4	12.2	10.8	15.6	13.3	12.1
Cost of Goods to Cash Flow 43	10.2	7.1	11.6	10.0	7.5	15.1	10.9	9.6	9.7	8.6	13.3	11.2	9.9
Cash Flow to Total Debt 44	0.2	•	0.5	0.4	0.5	0.2	0.2	0.3	0.3	0.3	0.3	0.2	0.1

Selected Financial Factors (in Percentages)

Debt Ratio 45	73.9	•	76.8	64.1	61.5	69.6	71.7	68.5	62.8	62.9	55.8	68.1	78.2
Return on Total Assets 46	7.2	•	2.8	8.2	8.3	7.5	7.8	8.7	9.2	8.3	8.1	5.4	7.4
Return on Equity Before Income Taxes 47	22.2	•	1.3	18.5	15.2	17.9	21.3	21.4	20.4	17.5	15.3	13.0	27.8
Return on Equity After Income Taxes 48	16.8	•	•	17.6	13.1	14.7	19.3	18.7	16.9	13.4	12.0	8.1	20.8
Profit Margin (Before Income Tax) 49	3.5	•	0.1	2.0	2.0	1.8	2.6	2.7	3.6	3.8	2.6	2.2	5.0
Profit Margin (After Income Tax) 50	2.7	•	•	1.9	1.7	1.5	2.3	2.4	3.0	2.9	2.0	1.4	3.7

167

Table II

Corporations with Net Income

MOTOR VEHICLE AND MOTOR VEHICLE PARTS AND SUPPLIES

MONEY AMOUNTS AND SIZE OF ASSETS IN THOUSANDS OF DOLLARS

Item Description for Accounting Period 7/05 Through 6/06	Total	Zero Assets	Under 500	500 to 1,000	1,000 to 5,000	5,000 to 10,000	10,000 to 25,000	25,000 to 50,000	50,000 to 100,000	100,000 to 250,000	250,000 to 500,000	500,000 to 2,500,000	2,500,000 and over
Number of Enterprises 1	10045	678	4834	•	2035	459	257	101	42	26	•	14	6
Revenues ($ in Thousands)													
Net Sales 2	226020375	2110727	6536851	•	11366194	10095623	9585592	8352386	6356313	6833426	•	30598882	118322603
Interest 3	2019845	3719	767	•	7094	8204	6616	6376	8132	11755	•	124982	1786793
Rents 4	535806	33	0	•	2853	396	10517	27563	6104	1602	•	44859	434028
Royalties 5	42000	0	0	•	0	0	0	459	0	2845	•	19594	18124
Other Portfolio Income 6	962400	353	28	•	8596	11486	15130	20786	15393	6050	•	263898	591890
Other Receipts 7	3126762	26916	13101	•	62652	41017	61608	54678	27909	32589	•	364725	2296359
Total Receipts 8	232707188	2141748	6550747	•	11447389	10156726	9679463	8462248	6413851	6888267	•	31417040	123449797
Average Total Receipts 9	23166	3159	1355	•	5625	22128	37663	83785	152711	264933	•	2244074	20574966
Operating Costs/Operating Income (%)													
Cost of Operations 10	81.1	77.9	82.1	•	71.7	83.4	78.5	77.3	79.7	80.7	•	84.4	81.2
Salaries and Wages 11	3.8	2.2	3.1	•	6.8	4.8	7.1	7.3	6.6	4.8	•	3.7	2.7
Taxes Paid 12	0.8	0.5	1.1	•	1.6	1.0	1.2	1.2	1.1	0.9	•	0.9	0.6
Interest Paid 13	0.9	0.3	0.3	•	0.7	0.6	0.8	0.7	0.7	0.8	•	0.8	1.1
Depreciation 14	2.9	1.0	0.5	•	0.6	0.3	0.8	1.1	1.0	0.8	•	1.0	4.8
Amortization and Depletion 15	0.1	0.0	0.1	•	0.0	0.0	0.1	0.1	0.1	0.1	•	0.2	0.1
Pensions and Other Deferred Comp. 16	0.2	0.1	0.1	•	0.3	0.1	0.2	0.2	0.2	0.1	•	0.1	0.3
Employee Benefits 17	0.4	0.2	0.2	•	0.4	0.5	0.7	0.9	0.7	0.7	•	0.4	0.3
Advertising 18	2.8	3.6	0.5	•	1.2	0.3	0.4	0.4	0.3	0.7	•	2.4	4.2
Other Expenses 19	5.0	12.1	7.8	•	10.3	5.4	5.9	6.8	6.0	6.1	•	5.0	3.9
Officers' Compensation 20	0.6	0.6	2.2	•	3.6	1.9	1.5	1.4	0.8	0.6	•	0.2	0.1
Operating Margin 21	1.3	1.5	2.0	•	2.8	1.6	2.9	2.5	3.0	3.7	•	0.8	0.7
Operating Margin Before Officers' Comp. 22	1.9	2.1	4.2	•	6.3	3.5	4.4	3.9	3.8	4.3	•	1.0	0.7

Selected Average Balance Sheet ($ in Thousands)

Net Receivables 23	3918	0	33	•	502	2102	4099	8922	16859	32533	•	211151	4955008
Inventories 24	2241	0	87	•	828	3006	6367	12085	26393	53609	•	529053	1559390
Net Property, Plant and Equipment 25	3510	0	17	•	281	322	2200	4836	9722	15726	•	140043	4952860
Total Assets 26	14083	0	191	•	1856	7074	15624	33015	69614	144367	•	1207767	16220829
Notes and Loans Payable 27	4385	0	74	•	673	1934	5630	10142	22326	37760	•	341634	5154923
All Other Liabilities 28	6008	0	42	•	496	2815	4668	10935	20129	48662	•	485177	7532430
Net Worth 29	3690	0	76	•	687	2325	5327	11938	27159	57945	•	380957	3553477

Selected Financial Ratios (Times to 1)

Current Ratio 30	1.4	•	3.5	•	1.9	1.6	1.6	1.6	1.6	1.6	•	1.3	1.3
Quick Ratio 31	0.8	•	1.7	•	0.9	0.6	0.7	0.7	0.7	0.7	•	0.5	0.8
Net Sales to Working Capital 32	9.1	•	11.5	•	8.1	9.7	8.4	8.9	7.5	7.3	•	14.5	8.3
Coverage Ratio 33	5.7	9.8	9.6	•	6.1	4.5	6.1	6.6	6.6	6.7	•	5.3	5.5
Total Asset Turnover 34	1.6	•	7.1	•	3.0	3.1	2.4	2.5	2.2	1.8	•	1.8	1.2
Inventory Turnover 35	8.1	•	12.8	•	4.8	6.1	4.6	5.3	4.6	4.0	•	3.5	10.3
Receivables Turnover 36	8.7	•	29.1	•	12.8	11.5	8.9	9.7	8.8	16.2	•	6.4	8.0
Total Liabilities to Net Worth 37	2.8	•	1.5	•	1.7	2.0	1.9	1.8	1.6	1.5	•	2.2	3.6
Current Assets to Working Capital 38	3.5	•	1.4	•	2.1	2.8	2.8	2.7	2.6	2.8	•	4.8	3.9
Current Liabilities to Working Capital 39	2.5	•	0.4	•	1.1	1.8	1.8	1.7	1.6	1.8	•	3.8	2.9
Working Capital to Net Sales 40	0.1	•	0.1	•	0.1	0.1	0.1	0.1	0.1	0.1	•	0.1	0.1
Inventory to Working Capital 41	1.0	•	0.7	•	1.1	1.5	1.5	1.4	1.3	1.5	•	2.6	0.7
Total Receipts to Cash Flow 42	12.1	7.1	12.6	•	8.7	17.1	12.1	11.3	12.1	10.7	•	13.2	12.1
Cost of Goods to Cash Flow 43	9.8	5.5	10.3	•	6.3	14.3	9.5	8.8	9.7	8.7	•	11.1	9.9
Cash Flow to Total Debt 44	0.2	•	0.9	•	0.5	0.3	0.3	0.3	0.3	0.3	•	0.2	0.1

Selected Financial Factors (in Percentages)

Debt Ratio 45	73.8	•	60.4	•	63.0	67.1	65.9	63.8	61.0	59.9	•	68.5	78.2
Return on Total Assets 46	8.2	•	17.4	•	12.5	8.8	11.0	11.3	10.0	9.7	•	7.7	7.4
Return on Equity Before Income Taxes 47	25.9	•	39.4	•	28.3	20.9	27.1	26.6	21.8	20.5	•	19.9	27.8
Return on Equity After Income Taxes 48	20.1	•	37.5	•	25.5	17.7	24.9	23.9	18.2	15.9	•	13.6	20.8
Profit Margin (Before Income Tax) 49	4.2	2.9	2.2	•	3.5	2.2	3.9	3.8	3.9	4.5	•	3.5	5.0
Profit Margin (After Income Tax) 50	3.3	2.7	2.1	•	3.1	1.9	3.6	3.5	3.3	3.5	•	2.4	3.7

Table I

Corporations with and without Net Income

LUMBER AND OTHER CONSTRUCTION MATERIALS

MONEY AMOUNTS AND SIZE OF ASSETS IN THOUSANDS OF DOLLARS

Item Description for Accounting Period 7/05 Through 6/06	Total	Zero Assets	Under 500	500 to 1,000	1,000 to 5,000	5,000 to 10,000	10,000 to 25,000	25,000 to 50,000	50,000 to 100,000	100,000 to 250,000	250,000 to 500,000	500,000 to 2,500,000	2,500,000 and over
Number of Enterprises **1**	14652	1368	6712	1297	3572	1058	407	149	55	19	8	6	0
Revenues ($ in Thousands)													
Net Sales **2**	14049374	532835	6993751	3972247	29107437	24400685	18943324	16687846	10952930	6955843	7197073	14749403	0
Interest **3**	117110	34	3217	2245	22985	8323	7265	13381	7289	4182	4213	43977	0
Rents **4**	47347	0	0	8819	4972	7040	17304	1214	2026	1048	1670	3253	0
Royalties **5**	39956	0	0	0	0	63	0	0	4	76	0	39814	0
Other Portfolio Income **6**	1161872	74837	4325	16989	17841	14347	20863	11641	7066	9911	5450	978605	0
Other Receipts **7**	899561	6264	3613	6779	163877	122239	119689	78391	57909	74812	26564	239421	0
Total Receipts **8**	142759220	613970	7004906	4007079	29311112	24552697	19108445	16792473	11027224	7045872	7234970	16054473	0
Average Total Receipts **9**	9743	449	1044	3089	8207	23207	46949	112701	200495	370835	904371	2675746	·
Operating Costs/Operating Income (%)													
Cost of Operations **10**	80.4	79.5	70.7	75.5	78.5	82.2	80.8	82.1	79.9	80.4	86.0	82.7	·
Salaries and Wages **11**	5.9	3.7	5.7	5.9	6.4	4.8	6.4	5.9	6.5	6.8	4.7	5.7	·
Taxes Paid **12**	1.0	1.4	1.3	1.3	1.1	1.1	1.0	0.9	1.0	0.9	0.8	1.0	·
Interest Paid **13**	0.6	0.7	0.2	0.5	0.5	0.6	0.6	0.6	0.7	0.9	0.5	1.1	·
Depreciation **14**	0.7	0.7	0.4	1.1	0.6	0.6	0.8	0.7	0.8	1.0	0.7	1.0	·
Amortization and Depletion **15**	0.1	0.5	0.0	0.0	0.0	0.0	0.0	0.0	0.1	0.1	0.2	0.2	·
Pensions and Other Deferred Comp. **16**	0.3	0.4	0.7	0.3	0.4	0.3	0.3	0.2	0.2	0.3	0.3	0.3	·
Employee Benefits **17**	0.6	1.2	0.6	0.4	0.5	0.7	0.6	0.4	0.7	0.4	0.6	0.8	·
Advertising **18**	0.2	0.5	0.5	0.3	0.3	0.2	0.2	0.3	0.3	0.2	0.2	0.1	·
Other Expenses **19**	5.9	4.6	13.4	8.4	6.0	5.4	4.9	5.0	5.5	5.4	4.3	5.5	·
Officers' Compensation **20**	1.7	8.0	3.5	4.7	2.5	1.9	1.5	0.9	0.9	0.6	0.4	0.8	·
Operating Margin **21**	2.5	·	2.9	1.7	3.2	2.3	2.8	2.9	3.4	2.9	1.3	0.8	·
Operating Margin Before Officers' Comp. **22**	4.3	6.9	6.5	6.3	5.8	4.2	4.3	3.9	4.3	3.5	1.7	1.7	·

Selected Average Balance Sheet ($ in Thousands)

	•	•	•	•	•	•	•	•	•	•	•	•
Net Receivables 23	1074	0	17	298	868	2854	5221	13699	22293	56031	84945	330550
Inventories 24	892	0	38	259	747	2567	5176	10134	26566	38046	35042	169048
Net Property, Plant and Equipment 25	561	0	22	97	250	987	2233	5383	11584	23751	62274	452705
Total Assets 26	3246	0	139	778	2420	7207	15327	35603	72914	142307	296183	1452610
Notes and Loans Payable 27	1015	0	37	202	652	2083	4839	11967	24989	49557	90656	507061
All Other Liabilities 28	977	0	38	181	779	2105	4222	10690	21297	46909	111509	424640
Net Worth 29	1253	0	64	395	989	3018	6267	12946	26627	45841	94018	520909

Selected Financial Ratios (Times to 1)

	•	•	•	•	•	•	•	•	•	•	•	•
Current Ratio 30	1.8	•	2.3	2.7	2.0	2.0	1.8	1.6	1.9	1.5	1.2	1.6
Quick Ratio 31	1.0	•	1.4	1.6	1.1	1.1	0.9	0.9	0.8	0.9	0.8	1.1
Net Sales to Working Capital 32	9.4	•	19.1	7.6	7.8	8.0	9.1	10.7	8.0	9.9	29.1	10.8
Coverage Ratio 33	7.7	22.0	16.1	6.6	9.6	5.8	6.8	6.8	6.5	5.7	4.5	10.5
Total Asset Turnover 34	3.0	•	7.5	3.9	3.4	3.2	3.0	3.1	2.7	2.6	3.0	1.7
Inventory Turnover 35	8.6	•	19.5	8.9	8.6	7.4	7.3	9.1	6.0	7.7	22.1	12.0
Receivables Turnover 36	9.6	•	54.4	11.5	10.3	8.8	8.8	9.3	8.6	6.6	13.1	8.2
Total Liabilities to Net Worth 37	1.6	•	1.2	1.0	1.4	1.4	1.4	1.8	1.7	2.1	2.2	1.8
Current Assets to Working Capital 38	2.3	•	1.8	1.6	2.0	2.1	2.3	2.7	2.2	2.8	5.0	2.8
Current Liabilities to Working Capital 39	1.3	•	0.8	0.6	1.0	1.1	1.3	1.7	1.2	1.8	4.0	1.8
Working Capital to Net Sales 40	0.1	•	0.1	0.1	0.1	0.1	0.1	0.1	0.1	0.1	0.0	0.1
Inventory to Working Capital 41	0.9	•	0.7	0.6	0.8	0.9	1.0	1.0	1.0	1.1	1.6	0.8
Total Receipts to Cash Flow 42	11.8	5.7	7.7	12.5	12.1	14.1	14.0	13.8	12.6	12.3	19.1	7.1
Cost of Goods to Cash Flow 43	9.5	4.5	5.4	9.5	9.5	11.6	11.3	11.3	10.1	9.9	16.5	5.9
Cash Flow to Total Debt 44	0.4	1.8	0.6	0.6	0.5	0.4	0.4	0.4	0.3	0.3	0.2	0.4

Selected Financial Factors (in Percentages)

	•	•	•	•	•	•	•	•	•	•	•	•
Debt Ratio 45	61.4	•	54.0	49.2	59.1	58.1	59.1	63.6	63.5	67.8	68.3	64.1
Return on Total Assets 46	14.3	•	24.7	11.8	14.8	11.2	13.1	13.1	13.0	13.1	7.3	19.1
Return on Equity Before Income Taxes 47	32.2	•	50.3	19.7	32.4	22.2	27.4	30.8	30.1	33.6	17.9	48.2
Return on Equity After Income Taxes 48	28.8	•	48.2	18.1	30.8	20.3	25.1	28.1	27.5	29.6	13.3	39.4
Profit Margin (Before Income Tax) 49	4.2	14.2	3.1	2.5	3.9	2.9	3.7	3.6	4.0	4.2	1.9	10.2
Profit Margin (After Income Tax) 50	3.8	13.9	3.0	2.3	3.7	2.7	3.4	3.2	3.7	3.7	1.4	8.4

169

Table II
Corporations with Net Income

LUMBER AND OTHER CONSTRUCTION MATERIALS

MONEY AMOUNTS AND SIZE OF ASSETS IN THOUSANDS OF DOLLARS

Item Description for Accounting Period 7/05 Through 6/06	Total	Zero Assets	Under 500	500 to 1,000	1,000 to 5,000	5,000 to 10,000	10,000 to 25,000	25,000 to 50,000	50,000 to 100,000	100,000 to 250,000	250,000 to 500,000	500,000 to 2,500,000	2,500,000 and over
Number of Enterprises **1**	10634	540	4357	1209	3075	872	368	134	50	19	•	•	0
Revenues ($ in Thousands)													
Net Sales **2**	129094858	257271	6396513	3761088	26889697	21119932	17345809	15348038	10140723	6955843	•	•	0
Interest **3**	92070	34	1089	2033	20398	7747	6177	12455	6569	4182	•	•	0
Rents **4**	42569	0	0	8048	4770	6462	16799	1129	294	1048	•	•	0
Royalties **5**	39956	0	0	0	0	63	0	0	4	76	•	•	0
Other Portfolio Income **6**	1118824	74815	1621	16989	16493	11468	14468	9311	6883	9911	•	•	0
Other Receipts **7**	689548	4960	2905	6760	160289	106677	109267	77243	54302	74812	•	•	0
Total Receipts **8**	131077825	337080	6402128	3794918	27071647	21252349	17492520	15448176	10208775	7045872	•	•	0
Average Total Receipts **9**	12326	624	1469	3139	8804	24372	47534	115285	204176	370835			
Operating Costs/Operating Income (%)													
Cost of Operations **10**	80.5	71.4	71.6	75.3	78.1	82.5	80.3	82.2	79.2	80.4	•	•	•
Salaries and Wages **11**	5.8	4.5	5.2	6.0	6.5	4.4	6.4	5.8	6.7	6.8	•	•	•
Taxes Paid **12**	1.0	1.0	1.1	1.3	1.1	0.8	1.1	0.8	1.0	0.9	•	•	•
Interest Paid **13**	0.5	1.4	0.2	0.4	0.5	0.5	0.6	0.6	0.7	0.9	•	•	•
Depreciation **14**	0.7	1.2	0.3	1.1	0.6	0.5	0.8	0.7	0.8	1.0	•	•	•
Amortization and Depletion **15**	0.1	1.1	0.0	0.0	0.0	0.1	0.0	0.0	0.1	0.1	•	•	•
Pensions and Other Deferred Comp. **16**	0.3	0.3	0.6	0.3	0.4	0.3	0.3	0.3	0.2	0.3	•	•	•
Employee Benefits **17**	0.5	0.2	0.6	0.4	0.5	0.4	0.6	0.4	0.7	0.4	•	•	•
Advertising **18**	0.2	0.9	0.5	0.3	0.3	0.2	0.2	0.2	0.3	0.2	•	•	•
Other Expenses **19**	5.5	6.4	12.5	8.3	5.8	5.4	5.0	4.7	5.6	5.4	•	•	•
Officers' Compensation **20**	1.7	5.1	2.9	4.7	2.5	1.9	1.4	0.9	1.0	0.6	•	•	•
Operating Margin **21**	3.2	6.5	4.5	1.9	3.7	3.1	3.3	3.4	3.8	2.9	•	•	•
Operating Margin Before Officers' Comp. **22**	4.9	11.6	7.4	6.6	6.3	5.0	4.8	4.4	4.7	3.5	•	•	•

Selected Average Balance Sheet ($ in Thousands)

Net Receivables 23	1343	0	20	292	877	2916	5316	14235	23178	56031
Inventories 24	1082	0	33	248	720	2691	5115	10081	26198	40066
Net Property, Plant and Equipment 25	584	0	21	99	274	914	2237	4827	11327	23751
Total Assets 26	3743	0	146	774	2491	7155	15243	34899	72870	142307
Notes and Loans Payable 27	1087	0	32	198	643	2146	4528	11233	25592	49557
All Other Liabilities 28	1119	0	51	185	764	1802	4082	10128	20126	46909
Net Worth 29	1538	0	62	390	1084	3206	6633	13539	27152	45841

Selected Financial Ratios (Times to 1)

Current Ratio 30	1.8	•	1.9	2.7	2.0	2.1	1.8	1.6	1.9	1.5
Quick Ratio 31	1.0	•	1.2	1.6	1.2	1.2	1.0	0.9	0.9	0.9
Net Sales to Working Capital 32	9.4	•	28.7	7.7	8.1	7.6	8.7	10.6	7.8	9.9
Coverage Ratio 33	9.8	27.8	25.2	7.5	11.4	7.7	8.5	8.1	7.0	5.7
Total Asset Turnover 34	3.2	•	10.1	4.0	3.5	3.4	3.1	3.3	2.8	2.6
Inventory Turnover 35	9.0	•	32.2	9.4	9.5	7.4	7.4	9.3	6.1	7.3
Receivables Turnover 36	9.7	•	75.7	12.4	11.4	8.6	8.7	9.2	8.4	13.1
Total Liabilities to Net Worth 37	1.4	•	1.3	1.0	1.3	1.2	1.3	1.6	1.7	2.1
Current Assets to Working Capital 38	2.2	•	2.1	1.6	2.0	1.9	2.2	2.6	2.1	2.8
Current Liabilities to Working Capital 39	1.2	•	1.1	0.6	1.0	0.9	1.2	1.6	1.1	1.8
Working Capital to Net Sales 40	0.1	•	0.0	0.1	0.1	0.1	0.1	0.1	0.1	0.1
Inventory to Working Capital 41	0.9	•	0.7	0.6	0.8	0.8	0.9	0.9	1.0	1.1
Total Receipts to Cash Flow 42	11.4	2.4	7.1	12.3	11.6	12.6	13.1	13.4	12.0	12.3
Cost of Goods to Cash Flow 43	9.2	1.7	5.1	9.2	9.1	10.4	10.5	11.0	9.5	9.9
Cash Flow to Total Debt 44	0.5	•	2.5	0.7	0.5	0.5	0.4	0.4	0.4	0.3

Selected Financial Factors (in Percentages)

Debt Ratio 45	58.9	•	57.4	49.6	56.5	55.2	56.5	61.2	62.7	67.8
Return on Total Assets 46	17.5	•	48.2	13.0	17.3	14.3	14.6	15.3	14.4	13.1
Return on Equity Before Income Taxes 47	38.2	•	108.7	22.3	36.3	27.9	29.6	34.6	33.0	33.6
Return on Equity After Income Taxes 48	34.3	•	105.4	20.5	34.6	25.8	27.1	31.8	30.1	29.6
Profit Margin (Before Income Tax) 49	4.8	37.5	4.6	2.8	4.5	3.7	4.2	4.1	4.4	4.2
Profit Margin (After Income Tax) 50	4.3	36.9	4.5	2.6	4.3	3.4	3.8	3.8	4.0	3.7

Table I

Corporations with and without Net Income

PROFESSIONAL AND COMMERCIAL EQUIPMENT AND SUPPLIES

MONEY AMOUNTS AND SIZE OF ASSETS IN THOUSANDS OF DOLLARS

Item Description for Accounting Period 7/05 Through 6/06		Total	Zero Assets	Under 500	500 to 1,000	1,000 to 5,000	5,000 to 10,000	10,000 to 25,000	25,000 to 50,000	50,000 to 100,000	100,000 to 250,000	250,000 to 500,000	500,000 to 2,500,000	2,500,000 and over
Number of Enterprises	1	31444	4106	20326	2847	3126	470	339	89	54	40	17	22	7
Revenues ($ in Thousands)														
Net Sales	2	184196484	6771805	10593738	6416113	19320642	15584294	15360184	6519025	8391554	12419107	10827184	31322554	40670284
Interest	3	624159	3205	2035	4022	11760	6898	7846	16059	13586	22729	34850	154539	346629
Rents	4	194795	822	0	413	5716	495	1519	10190	3205	10670	17170	33552	111043
Royalties	5	262215	1118	0	0	36	13902	1133	0	12784	90481	0	51999	90761
Other Portfolio Income	6	384361	568	4819	3739	12223	1939	7541	27701	16450	18216	3784	228447	58935
Other Receipts	7	1453228	22432	24077	151811	119284	159275	130166	57078	121680	42489	48881	308073	267982
Total Receipts	8	187115242	6799950	10624669	6576098	19469661	15766803	15508389	6630053	8559259	12603692	10931869	32099164	41545634
Average Total Receipts	9	5951	1656	523	2310	6228	33546	45747	74495	158505	315092	643051	1459053	5935091
Operating Costs/Operating Income (%)														
Cost of Operations	10	76.3	89.5	61.2	63.6	69.7	84.3	78.4	75.2	74.8	80.5	80.6	72.8	80.1
Salaries and Wages	11	8.1	3.7	7.9	11.6	10.2	7.1	8.2	9.8	10.2	5.8	6.9	10.4	6.3
Taxes Paid	12	1.0	0.5	1.8	1.5	1.5	0.7	1.0	1.1	1.1	0.8	1.0	1.0	0.7
Interest Paid	13	0.9	0.2	0.6	0.7	0.6	0.4	0.4	0.7	0.7	0.7	0.8	1.5	1.4
Depreciation	14	1.0	0.2	0.7	0.6	0.7	0.4	0.7	0.8	0.9	0.7	0.6	1.7	1.3
Amortization and Depletion	15	0.2	0.0	0.0	0.0	0.1	0.0	0.1	0.4	0.3	0.1	0.5	0.5	0.3
Pensions and Other Deferred Comp.	16	0.2	0.0	0.2	0.2	0.3	0.1	0.2	0.2	0.3	0.1	0.1	0.4	0.2
Employee Benefits	17	0.8	0.1	0.5	1.0	0.9	0.5	0.6	0.8	1.2	0.6	0.5	1.1	0.9
Advertising	18	0.8	0.4	0.7	1.6	0.6	0.4	0.7	0.5	0.7	1.3	1.2	1.0	0.8
Other Expenses	19	8.1	5.9	14.9	12.8	10.1	5.3	7.8	10.1	8.3	7.4	6.8	7.4	7.0
Officers' Compensation	20	1.6	0.5	8.5	4.5	3.9	0.9	1.5	1.0	0.9	0.5	0.5	0.7	0.2
Operating Margin	21	1.0	•	3.0	2.0	1.5	•	0.4	•	0.8	1.5	0.4	1.6	0.8
Operating Margin Before Officers' Comp.	22	2.5	•	11.4	6.5	5.4	0.8	1.9	0.3	1.7	2.0	0.9	2.2	0.9

Selected Average Balance Sheet ($ in Thousands)

Net Receivables 23	793	0	28	211	831	2584	11577	22375	47953	100795	230860	987579
Inventories 24	460	0	27	189	473	2606	9413	18279	27731	62011	112015	426754
Net Property, Plant and Equipment 25	227	0	13	96	309	572	3691	8054	10123	19487	89194	200933
Total Assets 26	3076	0	102	726	2220	7107	36349	72395	143679	316386	989107	5295758
Notes and Loans Payable 27	852	0	84	190	679	2478	6747	18774	35988	87498	291057	1303970
All Other Liabilities 28	1136	0	31	279	924	3449	17029	26947	59636	111677	340131	1823024
Net Worth 29	1088	0	-13	257	617	1180	12572	26674	48056	117210	357918	2168765

Selected Financial Ratios (Times to 1)

Current Ratio 30	1.4	•	1.8	1.8	1.6	1.4	1.5	1.4	1.6	1.5	1.3	1.5	1.3
Quick Ratio 31	0.8	•	1.0	1.1	1.0	0.7	1.0	0.8	0.9	0.9	0.7	0.9	0.7
Net Sales to Working Capital 32	11.5	•	13.6	8.7	10.1	19.4	10.5	9.9	8.2	9.0	15.1	9.2	13.0
Coverage Ratio 33	3.9	•	6.7	7.9	5.1	4.0	4.3	2.4	5.0	5.4	2.7	3.7	3.2
Total Asset Turnover 34	1.9	•	5.1	3.1	2.8	4.7	3.0	2.0	2.1	2.2	2.0	1.4	1.1
Inventory Turnover 35	9.7	•	11.6	7.6	9.1	10.7	9.8	5.8	6.4	9.0	8.3	9.3	10.9
Receivables Turnover 36	7.7	•	19.5	11.6	7.2	12.7	8.2	6.3	6.1	7.2	5.8	6.5	6.7
Total Liabilities to Net Worth 37	1.8	•	1.8	2.6	5.0	2.0	1.9	1.7	2.0	1.7	1.8	1.4	
Current Assets to Working Capital 38	3.3	•	2.2	2.2	2.8	3.6	2.9	3.5	2.7	2.9	4.7	3.1	4.4
Current Liabilities to Working Capital 39	2.3	•	1.2	1.2	1.8	2.6	1.9	2.5	1.7	1.9	3.7	2.1	3.4
Working Capital to Net Sales 40	0.1	•	0.1	0.1	0.1	0.1	0.1	0.1	0.1	0.1	0.1	0.1	0.1
Inventory to Working Capital 41	0.9	•	0.8	0.7	0.7	1.6	0.9	1.2	0.9	0.9	1.5	0.8	0.9
Total Receipts to Cash Flow 42	10.9	23.6	7.1	6.9	9.7	18.3	12.7	10.6	10.5	10.8	13.8	10.1	11.3
Cost of Goods to Cash Flow 43	8.4	21.1	4.4	4.4	6.8	15.4	10.0	8.0	7.8	8.7	11.1	7.4	9.0
Cash Flow to Total Debt 44	0.3	•	0.6	0.7	0.4	0.3	0.3	0.3	0.3	0.3	0.2	0.2	0.2

Selected Financial Factors (in Percentages)

Debt Ratio 45	64.6	•	112.3	64.5	72.2	83.4	65.4	67.0	63.2	66.6	63.0	63.8	59.0
Return on Total Assets 46	6.7	•	19.4	16.0	7.8	6.6	3.4	5.3	7.5	8.3	4.5	7.9	5.1
Return on Equity Before Income Taxes 47	14.0	•	•	39.4	22.6	29.8	5.7	12.4	16.2	20.2	7.7	15.9	8.5
Return on Equity After Income Taxes 48	10.6	•	•	37.3	20.0	23.9	2.2	9.7	13.3	14.0	5.0	11.7	5.7
Profit Margin (Before Income Tax) 49	2.6	•	3.3	4.5	2.3	1.1	1.0	1.4	2.8	3.1	1.4	4.0	3.2
Profit Margin (After Income Tax) 50	2.0	•	3.2	4.3	2.0	0.9	0.4	1.1	2.3	2.2	0.9	2.9	2.1

Table II
Corporations with Net Income

PROFESSIONAL AND COMMERCIAL EQUIPMENT AND SUPPLIES

MONEY AMOUNTS AND SIZE OF ASSETS IN THOUSANDS OF DOLLARS

Item Description for Accounting Period 7/05 Through 6/06	Total	Zero Assets	Under 500	500 to 1,000	1,000 to 5,000	5,000 to 10,000	10,000 to 25,000	25,000 to 50,000	50,000 to 100,000	100,000 to 250,000	250,000 to 500,000	500,000 to 2,500,000	2,500,000 and over
Number of Enterprises 1	18947	2107	11180	2351	2513	376	248	60	44	31	12	17	7
Revenues ($ in Thousands)													
Net Sales 2	160951430	5520221	7860019	5804740	17001708	14260557	11915652	4870282	6900181	10196956	8079929	27870901	40670284
Interest 3	555588	2196	1438	3476	8517	5569	4293	6729	10425	13074	20350	132891	346629
Rents 4	181733	578	0	8	4373	366	548	2579	931	10641	17157	33510	111043
Royalties 5	237474	1118	0	0	36	13902	1133	0	12784	66252	0	51487	90761
Other Portfolio Income 6	370066	109	4819	1712	12000	1921	6858	27350	15224	17404	3772	219964	58935
Other Receipts 7	1031846	21768	17943	124664	107516	66002	47058	34186	119206	33706	36239	155576	267982
Total Receipts 8	163328137	5545990	7884219	5934600	17134150	14348317	11975542	4941126	7058751	10338033	8157447	28464329	41545634
Average Total Receipts 9	8620	2632	705	2524	6818	38160	48288	82352	160426	333485	679787	1674372	5935091
Operating Costs/Operating Income (%)													
Cost of Operations 10	76.1	91.1	59.8	63.0	69.8	84.5	77.7	74.7	73.2	78.9	77.3	73.2	80.1
Salaries and Wages 11	7.9	2.6	6.9	11.6	9.8	6.7	8.0	8.6	10.5	5.7	7.3	10.1	6.3
Taxes Paid 12	1.0	0.3	1.8	1.4	1.4	0.7	0.9	1.1	1.2	0.8	1.1	0.9	0.7
Interest Paid 13	0.8	0.3	0.5	0.5	0.5	0.2	0.4	0.6	0.7	0.6	0.9	1.0	1.4
Depreciation 14	1.0	0.1	0.6	0.6	0.7	0.3	0.6	0.8	0.9	0.8	0.7	1.7	1.3
Amortization and Depletion 15	0.2	0.0	0.0	0.0	0.1	0.0	0.1	0.4	0.3	0.1	0.6	0.3	0.3
Pensions and Other Deferred Comp. 16	0.2	0.0	0.3	0.2	0.3	0.1	0.3	0.3	0.3	0.2	0.2	0.4	0.2
Employee Benefits 17	0.8	0.1	0.3	0.9	0.8	0.4	0.6	0.8	1.2	0.7	0.5	1.1	0.9
Advertising 18	0.8	0.3	0.6	1.6	0.5	0.3	0.7	0.5	0.5	1.5	1.2	1.1	0.8
Other Expenses 19	7.4	4.0	13.4	11.9	9.0	4.6	6.3	7.7	8.5	7.6	7.6	6.8	7.0
Officers' Compensation 20	1.5	0.5	9.0	4.1	4.0	0.8	1.5	1.1	0.9	0.5	0.4	0.5	0.2
Operating Margin 21	2.3	0.7	6.7	4.0	3.1	1.3	3.0	3.5	1.9	2.7	2.1	2.9	0.8
Operating Margin Before Officers' Comp. 22	3.8	1.1	15.6	8.1	7.1	2.2	4.5	4.6	2.8	3.1	2.5	3.4	0.9

Selected Average Balance Sheet ($ in Thousands)

Net Receivables **23**	1129	0	26	222	883	2688	6846	11992	21535	51539	91975	257000	987579
Inventories **24**	626	0	28	181	467	2622	3762	10956	17901	27989	60073	141570	421078
Net Property, Plant and Equipment **25**	328	0	15	101	310	588	1384	4367	7644	12241	25889	104027	200933
Total Assets **26**	4355	0	111	736	2310	7236	15088	35907	72340	142141	319071	977662	5295758
Notes and Loans Payable **27**	1068	0	59	188	580	2025	3098	6993	16186	34415	80242	226922	1303970
All Other Liabilities **28**	1598	0	39	222	950	3171	6975	14103	27769	59460	115940	349571	1823024
Net Worth **29**	1689	0	14	326	780	2040	5016	14811	28385	48266	122890	401169	2168765

Selected Financial Ratios (Times to 1)

Current Ratio **30**	1.5	·	1.8	2.3	1.6	1.5	1.5	1.7	1.6	1.6	1.3	1.5	1.3
Quick Ratio **31**	0.9	·	1.0	1.4	1.1	0.8	1.0	0.9	0.8	1.0	0.8	0.9	0.7
Net Sales to Working Capital **32**	11.6	·	18.2	7.7	10.0	19.0	11.3	7.6	8.6	9.0	14.9	9.5	13.0
Coverage Ratio **33**	5.7	5.6	14.7	12.6	8.9	9.8	11.0	9.4	7.4	7.8	4.4	5.9	3.2
Total Asset Turnover **34**	2.0	·	6.3	3.4	2.9	5.2	3.2	2.3	2.2	2.3	2.1	1.7	1.1
Inventory Turnover **35**	10.3	·	14.9	8.6	10.1	12.2	9.9	5.5	6.4	9.3	8.7	8.5	11.0
Receivables Turnover **36**	8.2	·	24.8	12.5	7.7	16.0	7.9	6.2	6.7	7.9	6.8	12.8	11.8
Total Liabilities to Net Worth **37**	1.6	·	7.1	1.3	2.0	2.5	1.4	1.4	1.5	1.9	1.6	1.4	1.4
Current Assets to Working Capital **38**	3.2	·	2.3	1.8	2.7	3.1	3.0	2.5	2.8	2.7	4.2	3.1	4.4
Current Liabilities to Working Capital **39**	2.2	·	1.3	0.8	1.7	2.1	2.0	1.5	1.8	1.7	3.2	2.1	3.4
Working Capital to Net Sales **40**	0.1	·	0.1	0.1	0.1	0.1	0.1	0.1	0.1	0.1	0.1	0.1	0.1
Inventory to Working Capital **41**	0.9	·	0.7	0.6	0.7	1.4	0.9	0.9	0.9	0.9	1.5	0.8	0.9
Total Receipts to Cash Flow **42**	10.2	24.2	6.2	6.3	9.0	17.8	11.5	9.0	9.2	9.5	10.4	9.7	11.3
Cost of Goods to Cash Flow **43**	7.8	22.0	3.7	4.0	6.3	15.0	8.9	6.7	7.5	8.1	7.1	9.0	
Cash Flow to Total Debt **44**	0.3	·	1.2	1.0	0.5	0.4	0.4	0.4	0.4	0.4	0.3	0.3	0.2

Selected Financial Factors (in Percentages)

Debt Ratio **45**	61.2	·	87.6	55.7	66.3	71.8	66.8	58.8	60.8	66.0	61.5	59.0	59.0
Return on Total Assets **46**	9.1	·	47.3	22.7	12.8	11.3	12.4	12.7	10.5	11.1	8.4	10.1	5.1
Return on Equity Before Income Taxes **47**	19.5	·	355.0	47.0	33.7	36.0	33.9	27.5	23.1	28.4	16.9	20.4	8.5
Return on Equity After Income Taxes **48**	15.8	·	348.6	45.1	31.2	31.7	30.1	23.1	19.8	20.4	13.3	15.6	5.7
Profit Margin (Before Income Tax) **49**	3.9	1.1	7.0	6.2	3.9	1.9	3.5	5.0	4.2	4.2	3.1	5.0	3.2
Profit Margin (After Income Tax) **50**	3.1	1.0	6.9	6.0	3.6	1.7	3.1	4.2	3.6	3.0	2.4	3.8	2.1

Table I

Corporations with and without Net Income

METAL AND MINERAL (EXCEPT PETROLEUM)

MONEY AMOUNTS AND SIZE OF ASSETS IN THOUSANDS OF DOLLARS

Item Description for Accounting Period 7/05 Through 6/06	Total	Zero Assets	Under 500	500 to 1,000	1,000 to 5,000	5,000 to 10,000	10,000 to 25,000	25,000 to 50,000	50,000 to 100,000	100,000 to 250,000	250,000 to 500,000	500,000 to 2,500,000	2,500,000 and over
Number of Enterprises 1	3702	15	1564	395	905	386	214	89	60	39	16	14	3

Revenues ($ in Thousands)

	Total	Zero Assets	Under 500	500 to 1,000	1,000 to 5,000	5,000 to 10,000	10,000 to 25,000	25,000 to 50,000	50,000 to 100,000	100,000 to 250,000	250,000 to 500,000	500,000 to 2,500,000	2,500,000 and over
Net Sales 2	123673370	255688	1458319	904341	6178796	8837524	8971245	8849679	10881433	16134207	10299532	38840180	12062424
Interest 3	558762	566	935	1027	3316	2477	3954	6487	6054	25932	31198	134707	342108
Rents 4	35703	0	0	0	151	0	2163	578	1278	2724	13257	15544	7
Royalties 5	1803	0	0	0	367	0	0	0	0	456	150	358	473
Other Portfolio Income 6	524085	26	5501	3704	4128	1978	26983	5206	6163	19904	72011	244656	133826
Other Receipts 7	706174	807	344	1437	7500	70152	33361	38122	65076	37631	106865	133826	211054
Total Receipts 8	125499897	257087	1465099	910509	6194258	8912131	9037706	8900072	10960004	16220854	10523013	39369271	12749892
Average Total Receipts 9	33901	17139	937	2305	6844	23088	42232	100001	182667	415919	657688	2812091	4249964

Operating Costs/Operating Income (%)

	Total	Zero Assets	Under 500	500 to 1,000	1,000 to 5,000	5,000 to 10,000	10,000 to 25,000	25,000 to 50,000	50,000 to 100,000	100,000 to 250,000	250,000 to 500,000	500,000 to 2,500,000	2,500,000 and over
Cost of Operations 10	88.3	84.6	72.3	73.4	78.5	86.5	83.6	86.2	88.3	90.8	82.7	91.2	94.5
Salaries and Wages 11	2.9	2.7	2.8	3.1	5.3	2.9	4.2	3.2	2.4	2.1	3.9	2.7	2.0
Taxes Paid 12	0.6	0.4	1.2	1.7	1.1	0.7	0.7	0.6	0.6	0.5	1.0	0.4	0.3
Interest Paid 13	1.0	0.4	0.8	1.0	0.5	0.5	0.6	0.6	0.6	0.6	0.7	0.9	3.7
Depreciation 14	0.5	0.1	0.8	0.6	0.8	0.4	0.5	0.3	0.5	0.3	0.8	0.4	0.8
Amortization and Depletion 15	0.1	0.0	0.0	0.1	0.0	0.0	0.0	0.0	0.0	0.1	0.2	0.1	0.7
Pensions and Other Deferred Comp. 16	0.2	0.0	0.2	0.5	0.4	0.2	0.2	0.2	0.1	0.2	0.4	0.2	0.0
Employee Benefits 17	0.5	0.3	0.9	0.6	0.6	0.3	0.4	0.4	0.4	0.3	0.9	0.6	0.9
Advertising 18	0.1	0.1	0.1	0.2	0.1	0.1	0.1	0.1	0.1	0.0	0.0	0.0	0.0
Other Expenses 19	3.4	8.3	8.6	10.4	7.3	3.3	4.2	3.9	2.4	2.1	6.0	2.1	4.1
Officers' Compensation 20	0.9	0.3	8.8	3.8	3.4	1.6	1.5	1.1	0.9	0.4	0.4	0.2	0.3
Operating Margin 21	1.5	2.9	3.4	4.6	1.9	3.5	3.8	3.6	3.7	2.6	2.8	1.2	•
Operating Margin Before Officers' Comp. 22	2.3	3.1	12.2	8.4	5.3	5.1	5.3	4.6	4.6	3.0	3.2	1.3	•

Selected Average Balance Sheet ($ in Thousands)

Net Receivables 23	3654	0	41	101	751	2395	4821	12700	22039	42996	81900	240889	658223
Inventories 24	3966	0	28	249	861	2095	6136	13637	28029	49333	102681	286249	390320
Net Property, Plant and Equipment 25	2165	0	25	39	143	572	1683	3070	6000	12246	50007	179086	944313
Total Assets 26	14865	0	162	785	2288	6725	15317	35033	67588	150650	349092	1109213	4120217
Notes and Loans Payable 27	4052	0	44	70	719	1857	3388	12486	20732	38065	56010	337384	1117318
All Other Liabilities 28	6338	0	33	122	780	1962	6083	13594	23810	63242	119658	416249	2584517
Net Worth 29	4475	0	85	592	790	2907	5846	8953	23046	49343	173424	355580	418382

Selected Financial Ratios (Times to 1)

Current Ratio 30	1.5	•	1.9	4.7	2.2	1.6	1.7	1.6	1.7	1.5	2.0	1.4	1.2
Quick Ratio 31	0.7	•	1.3	3.1	1.3	1.0	0.8	0.8	0.7	0.6	1.1	0.6	0.5
Net Sales to Working Capital 32	9.9	•	18.1	4.2	6.1	11.1	8.1	9.3	8.1	9.5	5.6	14.2	16.2
Coverage Ratio 33	4.0	10.3	5.8	5.7	5.3	9.1	8.5	8.0	8.5	6.0	8.2	3.9	0.5
Total Asset Turnover 34	2.2	•	5.8	2.9	3.0	3.4	2.7	2.8	2.7	2.7	1.8	2.5	1.0
Inventory Turnover 35	7.4	•	24.2	6.7	6.2	9.5	5.7	6.3	5.7	7.6	5.2	8.8	9.7
Receivables Turnover 36	8.8	•	22.3	16.4	9.0	10.9	8.1	8.1	8.6	9.6	7.6	11.2	5.0
Total Liabilities to Net Worth 37	2.3	•	0.9	0.3	1.9	1.3	1.6	2.9	1.9	2.1	1.0	2.1	8.8
Current Assets to Working Capital 38	2.9	•	2.1	1.3	1.8	2.6	2.5	2.8	2.5	2.8	2.0	3.5	7.1
Current Liabilities to Working Capital 39	1.9	•	1.1	0.3	0.8	1.6	1.5	1.8	1.5	1.8	1.0	2.5	6.1
Working Capital to Net Sales 40	0.1	•	0.1	0.2	0.2	0.1	0.1	0.1	0.1	0.1	0.2	0.1	0.1
Inventory to Working Capital 41	1.2	•	0.5	0.4	0.7	1.0	1.2	1.2	1.3	1.4	0.7	1.5	1.7
Total Receipts to Cash Flow 42	18.5	8.9	9.6	7.7	12.9	14.5	13.4	14.1	15.9	21.5	11.0	25.6	98.2
Cost of Goods to Cash Flow 43	16.3	7.6	7.0	5.6	10.1	12.6	11.2	12.2	14.1	19.5	9.1	23.4	92.8
Cash Flow to Total Debt 44	0.2	•	1.3	1.5	0.4	0.4	0.3	0.3	0.3	0.2	0.3	0.1	0.0

Selected Financial Factors (in Percentages)

Debt Ratio 45	69.9	•	47.3	24.6	65.5	56.8	61.8	74.4	65.9	67.2	50.3	67.9	89.8
Return on Total Assets 46	9.0	•	27.1	17.3	8.0	16.6	14.2	13.4	13.6	10.0	10.5	8.9	1.9
Return on Equity Before Income Taxes 47	22.4	•	42.5	18.9	18.8	34.2	32.8	45.8	35.1	25.4	18.6	20.6	•
Return on Equity After Income Taxes 48	17.5	•	40.8	18.8	15.6	32.2	29.5	39.4	29.2	18.4	13.6	15.7	•
Profit Margin (Before Income Tax) 49	3.0	3.4	3.9	4.9	2.2	4.3	4.6	4.1	4.5	3.0	5.0	2.6	•
Profit Margin (After Income Tax) 50	2.3	2.9	3.7	4.9	1.8	4.1	4.1	3.5	3.7	2.2	3.7	2.0	•

Table II
Corporations with Net Income

METAL AND MINERAL (EXCEPT PETROLEUM)

MONEY AMOUNTS AND SIZE OF ASSETS IN THOUSANDS OF DOLLARS

Item Description for Accounting Period 7/05 Through 6/06	Total	Zero Assets	Under 500	500 to 1,000	1,000 to 5,000	5,000 to 10,000	10,000 to 25,000	25,000 to 50,000	50,000 to 100,000	100,000 to 250,000	250,000 to 500,000	500,000 to 2,500,000	2,500,000 and over
Number of Enterprises **1**	3420	7	1509	•	746	364	198	83	54	36	•	•	0
Revenues ($ in Thousands)													
Net Sales **2**	115561067	255688	1295804	•	5278644	8449262	8498405	8112046	10172332	15114811	•	•	0
Interest **3**	346787	549	450	•	2727	2354	3328	6487	5871	24288	•	•	0
Rents **4**	20435	0	0	•	151	0	636	578	1278	2724	•	•	0
Royalties **5**	682	0	0	•	0	0	0	0	0	456	•	•	0
Other Portfolio Income **6**	503409	26	5383	•	4127	1978	25540	5053	5569	16044	•	•	0
Other Receipts **7**	633210	805	344	•	5092	69799	29708	27734	62358	54575	•	•	0
Total Receipts **8**	117065590	257068	1301981	•	5290741	8523393	8557617	8151898	10247408	15212898	•	•	0
Average Total Receipts **9**	34230	36724	863	•	7092	23416	43220	98216	189767	422580	•	•	•
Operating Costs/Operating Income (%)													
Cost of Operations **10**	88.1	84.6	73.2	•	76.6	86.9	83.6	85.4	88.3	90.6	•	•	•
Salaries and Wages **11**	2.9	2.7	2.5	•	5.8	2.8	4.1	3.3	2.4	2.1	•	•	•
Taxes Paid **12**	0.6	0.4	1.2	•	1.2	0.7	0.7	0.6	0.6	0.5	•	•	•
Interest Paid **13**	0.8	0.4	0.9	•	0.3	0.5	0.6	0.6	0.5	0.6	•	•	•
Depreciation **14**	0.4	0.1	0.9	•	0.7	0.4	0.5	0.3	0.4	0.3	•	•	•
Amortization and Depletion **15**	0.1	0.0	0.0	•	0.0	0.0	0.0	0.0	0.0	0.1	•	•	•
Pensions and Other Deferred Comp. **16**	0.2	0.0	0.2	•	0.4	0.2	0.2	0.2	0.1	0.3	•	•	•
Employee Benefits **17**	0.5	0.3	1.0	•	0.6	0.3	0.4	0.4	0.3	0.3	•	•	•
Advertising **18**	0.1	0.1	0.2	•	0.1	0.1	0.1	0.1	0.1	0.0	•	•	•
Other Expenses **19**	3.1	8.2	9.0	•	6.9	3.1	4.0	3.9	2.1	2.1	•	•	•
Officers' Compensation **20**	0.8	0.3	7.0	•	3.6	1.3	1.5	1.1	0.9	0.4	•	•	•
Operating Margin **21**	2.5	3.0	3.9	•	3.8	3.7	4.2	4.1	4.3	2.7	•	•	•
Operating Margin Before Officers' Comp. **22**	3.3	3.2	10.9	•	7.4	5.1	5.7	5.2	5.2	3.2	•	•	•

Selected Average Balance Sheet ($ in Thousands)

Net Receivables 23	3518	0	31	•	752	2392	4873	12894	21337	42089
Inventories 24	3911	0	17	•	866	2137	6172	13471	29572	61781
Net Property, Plant and Equipment 25	1379	0	24	•	117	529	1652	2906	5150	12960
Total Assets 26	13612	0	150	•	2263	6692	15231	35230	67580	151228
Notes and Loans Payable 27	3942	0	45	•	483	1867	3211	12616	19375	38040
All Other Liabilities 28	5112	0	27	•	734	1951	6094	13461	22758	65987
Net Worth 29	4558	0	77	•	1046	2874	5926	9153	25447	47201

Selected Financial Ratios (Times to 1)

Current Ratio 30	1.6	•	1.9	2.4	1.6	1.7	1.6	1.7	1.6
Quick Ratio 31	0.7	•	1.3	1.4	1.0	0.9	0.8	0.7	0.6
Net Sales to Working Capital 32	9.5	•	18.9	6.1	11.6	8.1	8.6	7.7	9.3
Coverage Ratio 33	5.7	10.5	5.8	13.8	9.6	9.7	9.1	10.7	6.6
Total Asset Turnover 34	2.5	•	5.7	3.1	3.5	2.8	2.8	2.8	2.8
Inventory Turnover 35	7.6	•	36.4	6.3	9.4	5.8	6.2	5.6	6.2
Receivables Turnover 36	9.3	•	23.0	9.5	10.9	8.3	8.2	8.9	20.0
Total Liabilities to Net Worth 37	2.0	•	0.9	1.2	1.3	1.6	2.8	1.7	2.2
Current Assets to Working Capital 38	2.7	•	2.1	1.7	2.6	2.5	2.7	2.3	2.8
Current Liabilities to Working Capital 39	1.7	•	1.1	0.7	1.6	1.5	1.7	1.3	1.8
Working Capital to Net Sales 40	0.1	•	0.1	0.2	0.1	0.1	0.1	0.1	0.1
Inventory to Working Capital 41	1.1	•	0.5	0.7	1.0	1.1	1.1	1.2	1.4
Total Receipts to Cash Flow 42	16.6	8.9	8.8	11.0	14.5	13.1	13.1	15.1	20.3
Cost of Goods to Cash Flow 43	14.6	7.6	6.4	8.4	12.6	10.9	11.2	13.3	18.4
Cash Flow to Total Debt 44	0.2	•	1.4	0.5	0.4	0.4	0.3	0.3	0.2

Selected Financial Factors (in Percentages)

Debt Ratio 45	66.5	•	48.3	53.8	57.1	61.1	74.0	62.3	68.8
Return on Total Assets 46	11.4	•	30.6	13.4	17.8	15.5	14.3	15.6	10.9
Return on Equity Before Income Taxes 47	28.1	•	49.1	27.0	37.2	35.7	49.1	37.6	29.6
Return on Equity After Income Taxes 48	22.9	•	47.1	24.0	35.1	32.2	42.3	31.6	21.7
Profit Margin (Before Income Tax) 49	3.8	3.5	4.4	4.0	4.6	4.9	4.6	5.1	3.3
Profit Margin (After Income Tax) 50	3.1	3.0	4.2	3.6	4.3	4.4	4.0	4.3	2.4

Table I

Corporations with and without Net Income

ELECTRICAL GOODS

MONEY AMOUNTS AND SIZE OF ASSETS IN THOUSANDS OF DOLLARS

Item Description for Accounting Period 7/05 Through 6/06		Total	Zero Assets	Under 500	500 to 1,000	1,000 to 5,000	5,000 to 10,000	10,000 to 25,000	25,000 to 50,000	50,000 to 100,000	100,000 to 250,000	250,000 to 500,000	500,000 to 2,500,000	2,500,000 and over
Number of Enterprises	1	22600	2610	12169	2756	3413	857	402	185	96	49	27	29	7
Revenues ($ in Thousands)														
Net Sales	2	268787030	4097013	9286004	5587067	25816369	15232593	17145327	15280319	15190890	17154065	19723653	52465685	71808045
Interest	3	681135	1051	3942	4809	8126	6058	9134	21858	28831	28197	34820	243296	291012
Rents	4	177333	1	0	0	1620	4659	4273	3687	7238	16156	2537	52883	84280
Royalties	5	798161	785	0	0	0	0	287	219	5069	1058	13164	22831	754747
Other Portfolio Income	6	705148	1140	4674	19278	15288	10526	7301	14524	36125	183856	111103	132953	168380
Other Receipts	7	2385997	13372	79611	37408	90421	122713	93460	175202	97352	204987	94484	500135	876853
Total Receipts	8	273534804	4113362	9374231	5648562	25931824	15376549	17259782	15495809	15365505	17588319	19979761	53417783	73983317
Average Total Receipts	9	12103	1576	770	2050	7598	17942	42935	83761	160057	358945	739991	1841993	10569045
Operating Costs/Operating Income (%)														
Cost of Operations	10	81.0	90.0	69.7	78.3	66.9	77.7	81.1	80.4	81.3	84.5	88.9	86.6	80.8
Salaries and Wages	11	6.7	4.1	9.7	5.5	16.7	8.6	6.8	6.9	6.6	5.4	3.7	5.5	4.4
Taxes Paid	12	0.7	0.4	1.5	1.1	1.1	1.1	0.9	1.0	0.9	0.7	0.6	0.6	0.5
Interest Paid	13	0.7	0.2	0.6	0.7	0.4	0.7	0.4	0.5	0.7	0.5	0.4	1.0	0.9
Depreciation	14	0.6	0.3	0.5	0.4	0.3	0.5	0.4	0.5	0.5	0.4	0.6	0.6	0.7
Amortization and Depletion	15	1.5	0.5	0.0	0.0	0.0	0.0	0.1	0.1	0.2	0.1	0.3	0.2	5.2
Pensions and Other Deferred Comp.	16	0.2	0.0	0.4	0.2	0.3	0.3	0.2	0.2	0.3	0.3	0.1	0.2	0.2
Employee Benefits	17	0.6	0.3	0.7	0.4	0.5	0.7	0.5	0.6	0.6	0.5	0.4	0.7	0.5
Advertising	18	1.1	0.1	0.5	0.5	0.4	0.4	0.4	0.5	0.6	0.8	0.6	0.5	2.8
Other Expenses	19	5.9	3.8	11.4	8.5	9.0	7.5	5.5	6.4	5.6	6.2	4.7	4.0	5.2
Officers' Compensation	20	0.9	0.4	5.2	4.0	2.5	2.0	1.4	1.0	0.9	0.4	0.3	0.2	0.1
Operating Margin	21	0.1	•	•	0.4	1.8	0.5	2.2	1.9	1.9	0.2	•	0.0	•
Operating Margin Before Officers' Comp.	22	1.1	0.2	5.0	4.5	4.3	2.5	3.6	2.9	2.8	0.6	•	0.2	•

Selected Average Balance Sheet ($ in Thousands)

Net Receivables 23	1759	0	207	40	869	2335	5967	12427	25339	63791	100575	312507	1671867
Inventories 24	1203	0	185	41	715	2430	4870	10046	18508	36636	65621	202219	945737
Net Property, Plant and Equipment 25	398	0	111	15	184	578	1176	2627	5555	8308	23035	75203	382343
Total Assets 26	5637	0	718	149	2212	7291	15353	35498	68955	150399	330090	1009405	6411625
Notes and Loans Payable 27	1212	0	306	112	684	2038	3627	8138	15909	31349	36686	149706	1392121
All Other Liabilities 28	2603	0	237	53	906	2993	6755	13577	29055	71742	162355	461979	3222917
Net Worth 29	1821	0	175	-16	622	2260	4971	13783	23991	47308	131049	397720	1796587

Selected Financial Ratios (Times to 1)

Current Ratio 30	1.5	•	1.6	1.6	1.6	1.8	1.5	1.7	1.5	1.5	1.5	1.5	1.3
Quick Ratio 31	0.8	•	1.0	0.9	1.0	0.9	0.9	1.0	0.9	1.0	0.9	0.9	0.6
Net Sales to Working Capital 32	9.3	•	16.5	9.4	10.1	6.5	9.6	6.9	8.4	8.3	9.9	8.9	10.0
Coverage Ratio 33	3.9	2.1	2.3	3.3	6.0	3.0	8.0	7.7	5.8	6.5	2.9	3.0	3.0
Total Asset Turnover 34	2.1	•	5.1	2.8	3.4	2.4	2.8	2.3	2.3	2.3	2.2	1.8	1.6
Inventory Turnover 35	8.0	•	12.9	8.6	7.1	5.7	7.1	6.6	6.9	8.1	9.9	7.7	8.8
Receivables Turnover 36	7.4	•	17.3	12.4	8.7	7.9	7.2	6.8	6.6	5.9	7.4	6.3	7.5
Total Liabilities to Net Worth 37	2.1	•	•	3.1	2.6	2.2	2.1	1.6	1.9	2.2	1.5	1.5	2.6
Current Assets to Working Capital 38	3.1	•	2.6	2.7	2.5	2.3	3.0	2.4	2.9	2.9	3.2	3.0	4.1
Current Liabilities to Working Capital 39	2.1	•	1.6	1.7	1.5	1.3	2.0	1.4	1.9	1.9	2.2	2.0	3.1
Working Capital to Net Sales 40	0.1	•	0.1	0.1	0.1	0.2	0.1	0.1	0.1	0.1	0.1	0.1	0.1
Inventory to Working Capital 41	1.0	•	0.9	0.9	0.9	1.0	1.1	0.9	1.1	0.9	0.9	0.9	1.0
Total Receipts to Cash Flow 42	15.1	29.1	11.3	12.7	10.5	13.4	13.8	11.9	13.1	12.3	22.1	21.0	16.8
Cost of Goods to Cash Flow 43	12.3	26.1	7.9	9.9	7.0	10.4	11.2	9.6	10.6	10.4	19.7	18.2	13.6
Cash Flow to Total Debt 44	0.2	0.4	0.3	0.3	0.5	0.3	0.3	0.3	0.3	0.2	0.2	0.1	0.1

Selected Financial Factors (in Percentages)

Debt Ratio 45	67.7	•	110.8	75.7	71.9	69.0	67.6	61.2	65.2	68.5	60.3	60.6	72.0
Return on Total Assets 46	5.7	•	6.6	6.2	9.0	5.4	9.2	9.0	8.9	7.6	2.7	5.5	4.2
Return on Equity Before Income Taxes 47	13.2	•	•	17.9	26.8	11.7	24.9	20.1	21.2	20.5	4.5	9.3	9.9
Return on Equity After Income Taxes 48	10.4	•	•	16.1	23.9	9.6	22.1	17.0	17.5	17.5	1.0	7.2	7.2
Profit Margin (Before Income Tax) 49	2.0	0.3	0.7	1.5	2.2	1.5	2.9	3.3	3.2	2.8	0.8	2.1	1.7
Profit Margin (After Income Tax) 50	1.6	•	0.6	1.4	2.0	1.2	2.6	2.8	2.7	2.4	0.2	1.6	1.3

175

Table II
Corporations with Net Income

ELECTRICAL GOODS

MONEY AMOUNTS AND SIZE OF ASSETS IN THOUSANDS OF DOLLARS

Item Description for Accounting Period 7/05 Through 6/06	Total	Zero Assets	Under 500	500 to 1,000	1,000 to 5,000	5,000 to 10,000	10,000 to 25,000	25,000 to 50,000	50,000 to 100,000	100,000 to 250,000	250,000 to 500,000	500,000 to 2,500,000	2,500,000 and over
Number of Enterprises 1	15229	1405	7894	1818	2841	610	353	148	74	38	14	25	7
Revenues ($ in Thousands)													
Net Sales 2	234480518	3805405	7856274	4065359	22585649	12790438	15805903	12835863	12547457	13579746	11516497	45283882	71808045
Interest 3	599046	885	1931	2626	7402	3722	8182	14168	14598	22320	11178	221022	291012
Rents 4	163223	1	0	0	1597	2068	1472	3411	7141	15987	1491	45775	84280
Royalties 5	789643	785	0	0	0	0	10	0	5032	1058	5726	22286	754747
Other Portfolio Income 6	661632	973	4518	19278	15186	1866	6851	11282	33981	182479	102734	114107	168380
Other Receipts 7	2116517	11407	35478	27052	72641	79480	90266	134097	63330	181238	52758	491914	876853
Total Receipts 8	238810579	3819456	7898201	4114315	22682475	12877574	15912684	12998821	12671539	13982828	11690384	46178986	73983317
Average Total Receipts 9	15681	2718	1001	2263	7984	21111	45078	87830	171237	367969	835027	1847159	10569045
Operating Costs/Operating Income (%)													
Cost of Operations 10	80.4	90.5	71.7	79.0	66.1	77.3	81.0	78.9	80.5	83.1	87.9	86.0	80.8
Salaries and Wages 11	6.6	3.2	7.5	4.4	17.6	8.1	6.6	7.3	6.6	5.6	4.1	5.3	4.4
Taxes Paid 12	0.7	0.3	1.3	1.0	1.1	1.1	0.9	0.9	0.9	0.8	0.7	0.6	0.5
Interest Paid 13	0.7	0.3	0.1	0.5	0.4	0.5	0.4	0.4	0.5	0.5	0.2	1.0	0.9
Depreciation 14	0.5	0.2	0.3	0.4	0.3	0.4	0.4	0.5	0.5	0.4	0.5	0.6	0.7
Amortization and Depletion 15	1.7	0.5	0.0	0.0	0.0	0.0	0.1	0.1	0.1	0.1	0.1	0.2	5.2
Pensions and Other Deferred Comp. 16	0.2	0.0	0.5	0.2	0.4	0.3	0.2	0.2	0.3	0.3	0.1	0.2	0.2
Employee Benefits 17	0.5	0.3	0.5	0.3	0.4	0.6	0.6	0.6	0.6	0.5	0.4	0.6	0.5
Advertising 18	1.2	0.1	0.3	0.6	0.4	0.4	0.4	0.4	0.6	0.9	0.5	0.4	2.8
Other Expenses 19	5.5	2.9	8.4	7.3	8.2	6.5	5.1	6.1	5.2	6.5	2.9	4.3	5.2
Officers' Compensation 20	0.9	0.3	5.3	3.8	2.4	2.0	1.4	1.1	1.0	0.3	0.3	0.1	0.1
Operating Margin 21	1.1	1.5	4.0	2.5	2.9	2.9	3.0	3.4	3.3	1.1	2.1	0.7	•
Operating Margin Before Officers' Comp. 22	1.9	1.8	9.3	6.3	5.2	4.9	4.4	4.5	4.2	1.4	2.5	0.8	•

Selected Average Balance Sheet ($ in Thousands)

Net Receivables 23	2248	0	40	238	919	2867	6009	13020	27330	62687	103425	301037	1671867
Inventories 24	1493	0	34	174	701	2359	4820	9872	19779	35385	88820	203351	1081098
Net Property, Plant and Equipment 25	516	0	8	144	185	636	1175	2860	5495	9068	30075	77230	382343
Total Assets 26	7136	0	139	721	2291	7398	15506	34852	69629	151536	316397	975723	6441625
Notes and Loans Payable 27	1436	0	44	173	666	1879	3388	7419	15679	23528	21702	151022	1392121
All Other Liabilities 28	3263	0	50	265	845	3177	6659	12720	27324	68484	151223	437689	3222917
Net Worth 29	2437	0	45	283	781	2342	5460	14713	26626	59525	143472	387013	1796587

Selected Financial Ratios (Times to 1)

Current Ratio 30	1.5	•	2.2	2.0	1.7	1.7	1.6	1.8	1.7	1.5	1.6	1.6	1.3
Quick Ratio 31	0.8	•	1.4	1.3	1.0	0.9	0.9	1.0	1.0	1.0	1.0	1.0	0.6
Net Sales to Working Capital 32	9.0	•	14.3	8.0	9.4	8.1	9.3	6.6	7.0	8.2	10.1	7.9	10.0
Coverage Ratio 33	5.6	8.2	64.1	8.9	9.6	7.8	10.1	12.0	10.2	9.9	17.9	3.8	3.0
Total Asset Turnover 34	2.2	•	7.2	3.1	3.5	2.8	2.9	2.5	2.4	2.4	2.6	1.9	1.6
Inventory Turnover 35	8.3	•	21.0	10.1	7.5	6.9	7.5	6.9	6.9	8.4	8.1	7.7	7.7
Receivables Turnover 36	7.6	•	26.8	12.0	8.8	7.7	7.8	7.0	6.6	11.4	6.7	6.4	12.3
Total Liabilities to Net Worth 37	1.9	•	2.1	1.5	1.9	2.2	1.8	1.4	1.6	1.5	1.2	1.5	2.6
Current Assets to Working Capital 38	3.0	•	1.8	2.0	2.3	2.5	2.8	2.2	2.4	2.9	2.8	2.7	4.1
Current Liabilities to Working Capital 39	2.0	•	0.8	1.0	1.3	1.5	1.8	1.2	1.4	1.9	1.8	1.7	3.1
Working Capital to Net Sales 40	0.1	•	0.1	0.1	0.1	0.1	0.1	0.2	0.1	0.1	0.1	0.1	0.1
Inventory to Working Capital 41	0.9	•	0.6	0.7	0.8	0.9	1.0	0.8	0.9	0.8	0.9	0.8	1.0
Total Receipts to Cash Flow 42	13.7	23.2	9.6	11.0	10.0	11.2	13.1	10.6	11.9	10.3	17.3	17.2	16.8
Cost of Goods to Cash Flow 43	11.0	21.0	6.9	8.7	6.6	8.7	10.6	8.4	9.6	8.6	15.2	14.8	13.6
Cash Flow to Total Debt 44	0.2	•	1.1	0.5	0.5	0.4	0.3	0.4	0.3	0.4	0.3	0.2	0.1

Selected Financial Factors (in Percentages)

Debt Ratio 45	65.9	•	67.8	60.8	65.9	68.3	64.8	57.8	61.8	60.7	54.7	60.3	72.0
Return on Total Assets 46	8.0	•	33.4	12.9	12.7	11.7	11.7	12.7	12.0	10.6	11.1	7.3	4.2
Return on Equity Before Income Taxes 47	19.1	•	102.0	29.2	33.5	32.1	30.0	27.7	28.3	24.3	23.1	13.6	9.9
Return on Equity After Income Taxes 48	16.1	•	99.2	27.5	30.7	29.3	27.1	24.1	24.0	21.2	17.0	11.1	7.2
Profit Margin (Before Income Tax) 49	3.0	1.8	4.6	3.7	3.3	3.6	3.7	4.7	4.4	4.0	4.0	2.9	1.7
Profit Margin (After Income Tax) 50	2.5	1.5	4.4	3.5	3.0	3.3	3.3	4.1	3.8	3.5	3.0	2.4	1.3

Table I

Corporations with and without Net Income

HARDWARE, PLUMBING, HEATING EQUIPMENT, AND SUPPLIES

MONEY AMOUNTS AND SIZE OF ASSETS IN THOUSANDS OF DOLLARS

Item Description for Accounting Period 7/05 Through 6/06	Total	Zero Assets	Under 500	500 to 1,000	1,000 to 5,000	5,000 to 10,000	10,000 to 25,000	25,000 to 50,000	50,000 to 100,000	100,000 to 250,000	250,000 to 500,000	500,000 to 2,500,000	2,500,000 and over
Number of Enterprises **1**	14347	1187	7394	2080	2629	565	324	91	46	21	0	9	0
Revenues ($ in Thousands)													
Net Sales **2**	94228884	286353	4511459	5041529	15158698	10185200	12596342	7682440	7035724	8251289	0	23479848	0
Interest **3**	128473	478	204	3549	22892	5489	7456	6060	5163	6075	0	71107	0
Rents **4**	18445	0	220	543	3180	1266	1555	1048	5464	2580	0	2588	0
Royalties **5**	73195	0	0	0	0	5	0	3475	529	8811	0	60376	0
Other Portfolio Income **6**	143501	8413	11245	374	52896	649	33336	8063	13466	6840	0	8222	0
Other Receipts **7**	1589932	753	17661	23020	151490	293747	74480	70751	57652	133285	0	767092	0
Total Receipts **8**	96182430	295997	4540789	5069015	15389156	10486356	12713169	7771837	7117998	8408880	0	24389233	0
Average Total Receipts **9**	6704	249	614	2437	5854	18560	39238	85405	154739	400423	·	2709915	·
Operating Costs/Operating Income (%)													
Cost of Operations **10**	74.0	63.0	65.7	65.3	72.6	70.3	75.5	75.9	76.1	76.4	·	77.3	·
Salaries and Wages **11**	9.2	6.0	9.1	11.8	9.2	11.3	8.8	9.1	8.5	8.6	·	8.6	·
Taxes Paid **12**	1.4	1.8	1.9	1.6	1.7	1.6	1.3	1.3	1.2	1.2	·	1.1	·
Interest Paid **13**	0.9	0.5	0.2	0.7	0.5	0.7	0.7	0.7	0.7	0.7	·	1.5	·
Depreciation **14**	0.6	1.4	0.6	0.7	0.6	0.9	0.4	0.5	0.6	0.8	·	0.7	·
Amortization and Depletion **15**	0.1	0.1	0.1	0.1	0.1	0.0	0.1	0.1	0.2	0.2	·	0.2	·
Pensions and Other Deferred Comp. **16**	0.5	0.2	0.6	0.5	0.7	0.4	0.3	0.5	0.4	0.4	·	0.5	·
Employee Benefits **17**	0.9	1.1	0.9	1.2	0.7	1.0	0.7	0.7	1.0	0.9	·	1.0	·
Advertising **18**	0.5	0.2	0.9	0.2	0.4	0.8	0.5	0.5	0.4	0.6	·	0.2	·
Other Expenses **19**	8.3	15.4	13.6	8.5	8.7	8.8	5.7	6.8	6.7	6.5	·	9.8	·
Officers' Compensation **20**	2.2	2.8	4.3	8.0	4.4	3.2	2.3	1.0	1.0	0.7	·	0.1	·
Operating Margin **21**	1.4	7.6	2.2	1.4	0.5	0.9	3.8	2.8	3.2	3.0	·	·	·
Operating Margin Before Officers' Comp. **22**	3.6	10.4	6.5	9.4	4.9	4.1	6.1	3.8	4.2	3.7	·	·	·

Selected Average Balance Sheet ($ in Thousands)

Net Receivables 23	834	0	42	253	662	2196	4955	10712	20972	52056	390040	•
Inventories 24	880	0	23	200	738	2863	6108	12606	21545	52192	340651	•
Net Property, Plant and Equipment 25	289	0	9	81	155	706	1190	3514	9043	32525	143997	•
Total Assets 26	2775	0	113	698	2150	6831	15536	33898	65538	185062	1444679	•
Notes and Loans Payable 27	813	0	71	243	442	1827	3866	10430	16947	63632	458396	•
All Other Liabilities 28	997	0	56	276	802	2078	4668	8488	22264	57770	613376	•
Net Worth 29	965	0	-14	179	907	2926	7002	14980	26328	63660	372906	•

Selected Financial Ratios (Times to 1)

Current Ratio 30	1.7	•	1.3	1.5	2.0	2.0	2.0	2.0	1.8	1.8	1.4	•
Quick Ratio 31	0.9	•	0.9	0.9	1.0	0.9	0.9	0.9	0.9	0.9	0.8	•
Net Sales to Working Capital 32	7.6	•	28.8	12.9	6.5	6.3	6.0	5.9	6.8	6.4	10.4	•
Coverage Ratio 33	5.0	23.3	17.0	3.7	5.0	6.6	7.9	6.7	6.9	7.7	2.9	•
Total Asset Turnover 34	2.4	•	5.4	3.5	2.7	2.6	2.5	2.5	2.3	2.1	1.8	•
Inventory Turnover 35	5.5	•	17.2	7.9	5.7	4.4	4.8	5.1	5.4	5.7	5.9	•
Receivables Turnover 36	8.2	•	16.6	9.8	9.0	8.2	8.2	7.7	7.8	9.0	7.2	•
Total Liabilities to Net Worth 37	1.9	•	•	2.9	1.4	1.3	1.2	1.3	1.5	1.9	2.9	•
Current Assets to Working Capital 38	2.3	•	4.2	2.8	2.0	2.0	2.0	2.0	2.2	2.2	3.3	•
Current Liabilities to Working Capital 39	1.3	•	3.2	1.8	1.0	1.0	1.0	1.0	1.2	1.2	2.3	•
Working Capital to Net Sales 40	0.1	•	0.0	0.1	0.2	0.2	0.2	0.2	0.1	0.2	0.1	•
Inventory to Working Capital 41	1.0	•	1.1	0.9	0.9	0.9	1.0	0.9	1.1	1.0	1.4	•
Total Receipts to Cash Flow 42	10.2	4.1	7.2	12.2	11.4	9.6	12.0	11.4	10.9	10.4	9.0	•
Cost of Goods to Cash Flow 43	7.5	2.6	4.7	8.0	8.3	6.8	9.1	8.7	8.3	7.9	7.0	•
Cash Flow to Total Debt 44	0.4	•	0.4	0.4	0.5	0.4	0.4	0.4	0.4	0.3	0.3	•

Selected Financial Factors (in Percentages)

Debt Ratio 45	65.2	•	112.1	74.4	57.8	57.2	54.9	55.8	59.8	65.6	74.2	•
Return on Total Assets 46	10.2	•	16.2	9.2	6.8	12.0	13.7	11.5	11.8	12.1	7.9	•
Return on Equity Before Income Taxes 47	23.4	•	•	26.2	12.9	23.9	26.5	22.2	25.2	30.5	19.9	•
Return on Equity After Income Taxes 48	19.6	•	•	22.6	9.3	22.2	23.9	19.1	20.8	25.8	14.6	•
Profit Margin (Before Income Tax) 49	3.4	10.9	2.8	1.9	2.0	3.9	4.8	3.9	4.3	4.9	2.8	•
Profit Margin (After Income Tax) 50	2.9	10.4	2.7	1.7	1.5	3.6	4.3	3.4	3.6	4.2	2.1	•

Table II
Corporations with Net Income

HARDWARE, PLUMBING, HEATING EQUIPMENT, AND SUPPLIES

MONEY AMOUNTS AND SIZE OF ASSETS IN THOUSANDS OF DOLLARS

Item Description for Accounting Period 7/05 Through 6/06	Total	Zero Assets	Under 500	500 to 1,000	1,000 to 5,000	5,000 to 10,000	10,000 to 25,000	25,000 to 50,000	50,000 to 100,000	100,000 to 250,000	250,000 to 500,000	500,000 to 2,500,000	2,500,000 and over
Number of Enterprises **1**	9554	711	4097	1679	2101	507	306	83	42	•	0	•	0
Revenues ($ in Thousands)													
Net Sales **2**	85776021	211265	3428865	3618687	13508941	9450334	12158315	7084926	6663377	•	0	•	0
Interest **3**	122864	478	201	2659	19847	5154	7456	5635	4266	•	0	•	0
Rents **4**	13003	0	220	543	2588	1225	1555	968	2705	•	0	•	0
Royalties **5**	70529	0	0	0	0	5	0	3475	529	•	0	•	0
Other Portfolio Income **6**	127580	1651	11245	374	52294	555	33269	8061	13210	•	0	•	0
Other Receipts **7**	1472177	753	17537	22284	145547	281988	72527	64622	49130	•	0	•	0
Total Receipts **8**	87582174	214147	3458068	3644547	13729217	9739261	12273122	7167687	6733217	•	0	•	0
Average Total Receipts **9**	9167	301	844	2171	6535	19210	40108	86358	160315	•	•	•	•
Operating Costs/Operating Income (%)													
Cost of Operations **10**	74.6	56.4	66.7	66.4	72.8	69.6	75.5	75.8	75.6	•	•	•	•
Salaries and Wages **11**	9.1	4.1	6.6	11.3	9.0	11.6	8.7	8.9	8.5	•	•	•	•
Taxes Paid **12**	1.4	1.8	1.9	1.7	1.7	1.6	1.3	1.3	1.2	•	•	•	•
Interest Paid **13**	0.8	0.5	0.1	0.8	0.4	0.6	0.7	0.6	0.7	•	•	•	•
Depreciation **14**	0.6	1.5	0.3	0.8	0.6	0.9	0.4	0.5	0.6	•	•	•	•
Amortization and Depletion **15**	0.1	0.0	0.0	0.0	0.0	0.0	0.1	0.1	0.1	•	•	•	•
Pensions and Other Deferred Comp. **16**	0.5	0.3	0.4	0.3	0.7	0.5	0.3	0.5	0.4	•	•	•	•
Employee Benefits **17**	0.9	1.5	0.1	1.4	0.7	1.1	0.7	0.7	1.0	•	•	•	•
Advertising **18**	0.5	0.2	1.0	0.2	0.4	0.8	0.5	0.5	0.4	•	•	•	•
Other Expenses **19**	7.5	13.6	12.4	9.3	8.0	8.7	5.6	6.7	6.8	•	•	•	•
Officers' Compensation **20**	2.0	3.4	3.7	4.1	4.4	3.4	2.2	1.0	1.0	•	•	•	•
Operating Margin **21**	2.1	16.6	6.7	3.6	1.3	1.4	4.0	3.2	3.6	•	•	•	•
Operating Margin Before Officers' Comp. **22**	4.0	20.0	10.4	7.7	5.7	4.7	6.2	4.3	4.6	•	•	•	•

Selected Average Balance Sheet ($ in Thousands)

Net Receivables 23	1150	0	63	247	713	2262	5021	10957	20605
Inventories 24	1173	0	18	210	797	2783	6118	12695	22122
Net Property, Plant and Equipment 25	404	0	12	91	161	698	1216	3500	9692
Total Assets 26	3778	0	134	705	2151	6716	15731	34018	66390
Notes and Loans Payable 27	1049	0	20	216	398	1488	3858	10041	17242
All Other Liabilities 28	1316	0	63	272	775	2067	4678	8266	21852
Net Worth 29	1413	0	51	216	978	3161	7195	15710	27296

Selected Financial Ratios (Times to 1)

Current Ratio 30	1.8	•	1.7	1.6	2.1	2.1	2.0	2.0	1.8
Quick Ratio 31	0.9	•	1.4	1.0	1.0	1.1	0.9	0.9	0.9
Net Sales to Working Capital 32	7.3	•	16.6	10.4	6.5	6.2	6.1	5.9	6.9
Coverage Ratio 33	6.0	36.1	101.5	6.2	7.8	8.8	8.6	7.9	7.7
Total Asset Turnover 34	2.4	•	6.2	3.1	3.0	2.8	2.5	2.5	2.4
Inventory Turnover 35	5.7	•	30.3	6.8	5.9	4.7	4.9	5.1	5.4
Receivables Turnover 36	8.3	•	18.0	8.6	9.4	8.6	8.4	7.7	8.2
Total Liabilities to Net Worth 37	1.7	•	1.6	2.3	1.2	1.1	1.2	1.2	1.4
Current Assets to Working Capital 38	2.2	•	2.4	2.6	1.9	1.9	2.0	2.0	2.3
Current Liabilities to Working Capital 39	1.2	•	1.4	1.6	0.9	0.9	1.0	1.0	1.3
Working Capital to Net Sales 40	0.1	•	0.1	0.1	0.2	0.2	0.2	0.2	0.1
Inventory to Working Capital 41	1.0	•	0.4	0.8	0.9	0.9	1.0	0.9	1.1
Total Receipts to Cash Flow 42	10.2	3.4	5.7	8.9	11.1	9.2	11.8	11.0	10.5
Cost of Goods to Cash Flow 43	7.6	1.9	3.8	5.9	8.1	6.4	8.9	8.3	7.9
Cash Flow to Total Debt 44	0.4	1.8	1.8	0.5	0.5	0.6	0.4	0.4	0.4

Selected Financial Factors (in Percentages)

Debt Ratio 45	62.6	•	61.7	69.3	54.5	52.9	54.3	53.8	58.9
Return on Total Assets 46	11.9	•	47.5	15.6	9.9	13.9	14.3	12.6	12.7
Return on Equity Before Income Taxes 47	26.5	•	122.7	42.5	19.0	26.1	27.7	23.8	26.9
Return on Equity After Income Taxes 48	22.6	•	121.0	38.8	14.9	24.4	25.0	20.5	22.2
Profit Margin (Before Income Tax) 49	4.2	18.0	7.5	4.3	2.9	4.4	5.0	4.4	4.6
Profit Margin (After Income Tax) 50	3.5	17.3	7.4	3.9	2.3	4.1	4.5	3.8	3.8

Table I
Corporations with and without Net Income

MACHINERY, EQUIPMENT, AND SUPPLIES

MONEY AMOUNTS AND SIZE OF ASSETS IN THOUSANDS OF DOLLARS

Item Description for Accounting Period 7/05 Through 6/06	Total	Zero Assets	Under 500	500 to 1,000	1,000 to 5,000	5,000 to 10,000	10,000 to 25,000	25,000 to 50,000	50,000 to 100,000	100,000 to 250,000	250,000 to 500,000	500,000 to 2,500,000	2,500,000 and over
Number of Enterprises 1	49836	3028	30146	5083	8663	1604	811	278	105	70	28	17	3
Revenues ($ in Thousands)													
Net Sales 2	225566451	4333278	16091820	10228694	47039416	27867428	25594144	17539658	12288424	16554374	12732726	23169086	12130402
Interest 3	534402	5406	7918	5040	35931	17662	20309	33723	30955	53821	23387	117902	182349
Rents 4	231955	117	0	7458	26663	16617	15556	11840	9330	36273	71804	11686	24610
Royalties 5	13685	0	0	0	0	7	0	558	2496	7742	554	1661	667
Other Portfolio Income 6	1551779	61864	2696	40212	102081	44426	190929	155129	141541	173276	225422	182465	231735
Other Receipts 7	2510689	11290	493303	89960	426063	229051	199948	201645	133385	327229	225467	104541	68812
Total Receipts 8	230411961	4411955	16595737	10371364	47630154	28175191	26020886	17942553	12606131	17152715	13279360	23587341	12638575
Average Total Receipts 9	4623	1457	551	2040	5498	17566	32085	64542	120058	245039	474263	1387491	4212858
Operating Costs/Operating Income (%)													
Cost of Operations 10	75.3	92.9	67.0	68.8	73.1	78.6	77.1	77.3	76.9	77.2	74.1	77.0	73.7
Salaries and Wages 11	7.2	2.0	5.4	7.3	8.4	6.9	7.7	7.4	7.5	6.2	7.6	5.9	8.8
Taxes Paid 12	1.2	0.4	1.7	1.7	1.4	1.2	1.1	1.1	1.1	0.9	1.0	1.0	1.5
Interest Paid 13	0.9	0.3	0.5	0.7	0.7	0.7	0.9	0.8	1.3	1.1	1.3	1.1	1.7
Depreciation 14	1.4	0.6	0.7	1.3	1.0	0.9	1.6	1.5	2.1	2.0	4.1	1.6	1.1
Amortization and Depletion 15	0.1	0.1	0.0	0.1	0.1	0.1	0.1	0.1	0.2	0.2	0.2	0.3	0.2
Pensions and Other Deferred Comp. 16	0.4	0.2	0.7	0.3	0.4	0.3	0.3	0.3	0.5	0.3	0.4	0.6	0.8
Employee Benefits 17	0.9	0.4	0.8	0.6	0.8	0.8	0.9	0.7	0.8	1.3	1.7	0.9	1.0
Advertising 18	0.4	0.0	0.4	0.5	0.4	0.4	0.4	0.5	0.4	0.5	0.3	0.5	0.9
Other Expenses 19	7.6	3.1	12.9	11.5	8.2	6.2	6.6	6.9	7.4	6.7	7.1	6.2	7.0
Officers' Compensation 20	2.2	0.8	7.7	4.6	3.5	2.2	1.6	1.2	1.0	0.8	0.5	0.4	0.4
Operating Margin 21	2.3	•	2.2	2.7	2.0	1.8	1.9	2.3	0.8	2.8	1.6	4.5	3.0
Operating Margin Before Officers' Comp. 22	4.5	0.0	9.9	7.3	5.5	3.9	3.5	3.5	1.9	3.6	2.2	4.9	3.3

Selected Average Balance Sheet ($ in Thousands)

Net Receivables 23	568	0	37	183	615	2052	3779	9148	18647	37262	67001	174056	867205
Inventories 24	717	0	34	227	813	2620	6214	11396	22457	52250	120359	230545	519662
Net Property, Plant and Equipment 25	316	0	16	96	259	639	2202	4944	11842	23225	66422	154438	337486
Total Assets 26	2213	0	121	743	2190	6988	14972	34255	69104	161628	355316	812090	2892464
Notes and Loans Payable 27	684	0	53	249	700	2121	5274	10715	25597	48782	125649	158749	717289
All Other Liabilities 28	760	0	33	256	737	3170	5012	12266	21574	52861	131189	307273	584163
Net Worth 29	769	0	34	239	753	1697	4686	11274	21933	59985	98477	346067	1591012

Selected Financial Ratios (Times to 1)

Current Ratio 30	1.6	•	2.3	1.8	1.8	1.3	1.5	1.5	1.6	1.6	1.4	1.7	1.7
Quick Ratio 31	0.7	•	1.5	0.8	0.8	0.6	0.6	0.7	0.7	0.7	0.5	0.7	0.9
Net Sales to Working Capital 32	7.6	•	9.4	8.0	7.1	12.2	8.3	7.6	6.5	6.0	6.8	6.4	5.1
Coverage Ratio 33	5.9	4.4	11.1	7.0	5.6	5.2	5.1	6.9	3.6	7.0	5.4	6.5	5.2
Total Asset Turnover 34	2.0	•	4.4	2.7	2.5	2.5	2.1	1.8	1.7	1.5	1.3	1.7	1.4
Inventory Turnover 35	4.8	•	10.5	6.1	4.9	5.2	3.9	4.3	4.0	3.5	2.8	4.6	5.7
Receivables Turnover 36	8.3	•	14.2	11.3	9.2	8.8	8.4	8.0	6.7	6.5	6.8	5.6	9.3
Total Liabilities to Net Worth 37	1.9	•	2.5	2.1	1.9	3.1	2.2	2.0	2.2	1.7	2.6	1.3	0.8
Current Assets to Working Capital 38	2.7	•	1.7	2.3	2.3	4.0	3.1	3.1	2.7	2.8	3.4	2.4	2.4
Current Liabilities to Working Capital 39	1.7	•	0.7	1.3	1.3	3.0	2.1	2.1	1.7	1.8	2.4	1.4	1.4
Working Capital to Net Sales 40	0.1	•	0.1	0.1	0.1	0.1	0.1	0.1	0.2	0.2	0.1	0.2	0.2
Inventory to Working Capital 41	1.3	•	0.6	1.0	1.1	2.0	1.7	1.5	1.3	1.4	2.0	1.0	0.7
Total Receipts to Cash Flow 42	9.8	27.4	6.8	7.5	10.4	12.6	11.4	9.9	11.0	8.6	8.8	9.0	8.6
Cost of Goods to Cash Flow 43	7.3	25.4	4.5	5.1	7.6	9.9	8.8	7.7	8.5	6.6	6.6	7.0	6.3
Cash Flow to Total Debt 44	0.3	•	0.9	0.5	0.4	0.3	0.3	0.3	0.2	0.3	0.2	0.3	0.4

Selected Financial Factors (in Percentages)

Debt Ratio 45	65.2	•	71.6	67.9	65.6	75.7	68.7	67.1	68.3	62.9	72.3	57.4	45.0
Return on Total Assets 46	10.8	25.7	13.0	9.8	8.8	9.4	10.0	7.9	11.0	9.3	11.0	12.5	12.4
Return on Equity Before Income Taxes 47	25.9	82.3	34.7	23.5	29.2	24.1	25.9	18.1	25.3	27.2	24.8	18.2	
Return on Equity After Income Taxes 48	21.7	81.0	32.2	21.5	25.6	21.8	21.7	14.9	20.7	22.2	17.5	12.1	
Profit Margin (Before Income Tax) 49	4.4	1.0	5.3	4.1	3.3	2.9	3.6	4.6	3.4	6.4	5.9	6.3	7.2
Profit Margin (After Income Tax) 50	3.7	0.9	5.2	3.8	3.0	2.5	3.2	3.9	2.8	5.3	4.8	4.4	4.8

Table II
Corporations with Net Income

MACHINERY, EQUIPMENT, AND SUPPLIES

MONEY AMOUNTS AND SIZE OF ASSETS IN THOUSANDS OF DOLLARS

Item Description for Accounting Period 7/05 Through 6/06	Total	Zero Assets	Under 500	500 to 1,000	1,000 to 5,000	5,000 to 10,000	10,000 to 25,000	25,000 to 50,000	50,000 to 100,000	100,000 to 250,000	250,000 to 500,000	500,000 to 2,500,000	2,500,000 and over
Number of Enterprises **1**	33100	519	19603	3958	6584	1289	707	242	88	65	•	•	3
Revenues ($ in Thousands)													
Net Sales **2**	201555740	3855867	13748448	8999710	39298491	24274089	22878919	15782094	10436179	16087482	•	•	12130402
Interest **3**	502841	4324	5269	3464	30731	15250	18843	30019	28249	50244	•	•	182349
Rents **4**	212534	0	0	7138	23329	13649	14494	11094	9330	36045	•	•	24610
Royalties **5**	13480	0	0	0	0	7	0	558	2496	7742	•	•	667
Other Portfolio Income **6**	1449605	59748	1677	7911	94922	35690	177551	149719	137865	168564	•	•	231735
Other Receipts **7**	2380271	8974	497719	70960	401735	201200	180954	189225	112827	316680	•	•	68812
Total Receipts **8**	206114471	3928913	14253113	9089183	39849208	24539885	23270761	16162709	10726946	16666757	•	•	12638575
Average Total Receipts **9**	6227	7570	727	2296	6052	19038	32915	66788	121897	256412	•	•	4212858
Operating Costs/Operating Income (%)													
Cost of Operations **10**	75.0	95.1	66.8	68.6	72.0	78.4	76.5	76.7	76.9	77.0	•	•	73.7
Salaries and Wages **11**	7.0	1.2	4.9	7.2	8.4	6.5	7.6	7.4	7.2	6.2	•	•	8.8
Taxes Paid **12**	1.2	0.2	1.7	1.6	1.4	1.1	1.1	1.1	1.1	0.9	•	•	1.5
Interest Paid **13**	0.8	0.1	0.5	0.5	0.6	0.6	0.8	0.8	1.2	1.0	•	•	1.7
Depreciation **14**	1.4	0.4	0.6	0.9	1.0	0.9	1.6	1.5	2.1	2.0	•	•	1.1
Amortization and Depletion **15**	0.1	0.0	0.0	0.0	0.1	0.0	0.1	0.1	0.1	0.2	•	•	0.2
Pensions and Other Deferred Comp. **16**	0.4	0.1	0.8	0.3	0.5	0.4	0.3	0.3	0.5	0.3	•	•	0.8
Employee Benefits **17**	0.9	0.2	0.7	0.6	0.8	0.7	0.9	0.7	0.8	1.3	•	•	1.0
Advertising **18**	0.4	0.0	0.4	0.5	0.4	0.4	0.4	0.4	0.3	0.5	•	•	0.9
Other Expenses **19**	7.2	12.1	8.1	10.8	8.1	5.8	6.4	6.9	7.0	6.4	•	•	7.0
Officers' Compensation **20**	2.2	7.9	4.6	3.7	3.7	2.3	1.7	1.2	0.9	0.8	•	•	0.4
Operating Margin **21**	3.2	0.6	3.7	4.3	3.1	2.9	2.6	3.0	1.9	3.4	•	•	3.0
Operating Margin Before Officers' Comp. **22**	5.4	0.8	11.6	9.0	6.7	5.1	4.3	4.2	2.8	4.2	•	•	3.3

Selected Average Balance Sheet ($ in Thousands)

Net Receivables 23	745	0	48	175	642	2137	3760	9244	18379	38636	867205
Inventories 24	912	0	39	216	843	2710	6105	11044	21949	51758	519662
Net Property, Plant and Equipment 25	415	0	19	76	255	649	2285	4847	11787	22134	337486
Total Assets 26	2900	0	145	743	2261	7089	14963	34107	68644	163895	2892464
Notes and Loans Payable 27	856	0	48	236	650	2028	5145	10979	24179	48983	717289
All Other Liabilities 28	936	0	37	238	686	2591	4838	11236	20538	52556	584163
Net Worth 29	1108	0	60	269	925	2469	4979	11891	23928	62356	1591012

Selected Financial Ratios (Times to 1)

Current Ratio 30	1.7	•	2.7	1.9	1.9	1.6	1.5	1.5	1.5	1.6	1.7
Quick Ratio 31	0.7	•	1.8	0.9	1.0	0.7	0.6	0.7	0.7	0.7	0.9
Net Sales to Working Capital 32	7.1	•	9.1	8.2	6.6	8.4	8.1	7.5	6.5	6.2	5.1
Coverage Ratio 33	7.4	23.2	15.6	10.8	8.0	7.4	6.1	8.0	5.0	7.7	5.2
Total Asset Turnover 34	2.1	•	4.8	3.1	2.6	2.7	2.2	1.9	1.7	1.5	1.4
Inventory Turnover 35	5.0	•	12.0	7.2	5.1	5.4	4.1	4.5	4.2	3.7	5.7
Receivables Turnover 36	8.8	•	15.0	12.6	10.0	9.1	9.0	8.7	7.0	7.0	9.3
Total Liabilities to Net Worth 37	1.6	•	1.4	1.8	1.4	1.9	2.0	1.9	1.9	1.6	0.8
Current Assets to Working Capital 38	2.5	•	1.6	2.1	2.1	2.7	3.0	3.1	2.7	2.8	2.4
Current Liabilities to Working Capital 39	1.5	•	0.6	1.1	1.1	1.7	2.0	2.1	1.7	1.8	1.4
Working Capital to Net Sales 40	0.1	•	0.1	0.1	0.2	0.1	0.1	0.1	0.2	0.2	0.2
Inventory to Working Capital 41	1.2	•	0.5	0.9	1.0	1.0	1.6	1.5	1.4	1.5	0.7
Total Receipts to Cash Flow 42	9.1	23.1	6.3	7.1	9.2	11.6	10.8	9.2	9.9	8.4	8.6
Cost of Goods to Cash Flow 43	6.8	21.9	4.2	4.9	6.6	9.1	8.2	7.1	7.6	6.4	6.3
Cash Flow to Total Debt 44	0.4	•	1.3	0.7	0.5	0.4	0.3	0.3	0.3	0.3	0.4

Selected Financial Factors (in Percentages)

Debt Ratio 45	61.8	•	58.6	63.8	59.1	65.2	66.7	65.1	65.1	62.0	45.0
Return on Total Assets 46	13.1	•	38.2	18.0	13.4	12.2	11.1	11.8	10.1	12.2	12.4
Return on Equity Before Income Taxes 47	29.8	•	86.5	45.1	28.7	30.2	27.9	29.7	23.2	27.8	18.2
Return on Equity After Income Taxes 48	25.3	•	85.3	42.2	26.6	27.1	25.4	25.1	19.7	23.1	12.1
Profit Margin (Before Income Tax) 49	5.4	2.5	7.4	5.3	4.5	4.0	4.3	5.4	4.7	7.0	7.2
Profit Margin (After Income Tax) 50	4.6	2.4	7.3	5.0	4.1	3.6	3.9	4.6	4.0	5.8	4.8

Table I

Corporations with and without Net Income

FURNITURE, SPORTS, TOYS, JEWELRY, OTHER DURABLE GOODS

MONEY AMOUNTS AND SIZE OF ASSETS IN THOUSANDS OF DOLLARS

Item Description for Accounting Period 7/05 Through 6/06	Total	Zero Assets	Under 500	500 to 1,000	1,000 to 5,000	5,000 to 10,000	10,000 to 25,000	25,000 to 50,000	50,000 to 100,000	100,000 to 250,000	250,000 to 500,000	500,000 to 2,500,000	2,500,000 and over
Number of Enterprises 1	72454	7801	48897	6579	6443	1319	931	264	109	66	22	18	3
Revenues ($ in Thousands)													
Net Sales 2	243041249	4572762	18277387	11748948	42710931	21322628	35222470	22796464	14814153	20690133	8632948	27218631	15033793
Interest 3	331406	8262	3997	12241	15456	10484	28011	22820	28245	39711	24775	64039	73366
Rents 4	93319	157	3413	2739	13127	4430	3101	3877	5871	5249	2919	31575	16863
Royalties 5	372519	84	528	2996	33274	5503	1274	11632	26828	51622	33207	111198	94372
Other Portfolio Income 6	3703939	12836	45967	28917	84482	26395	23971	83218	29729	85298	378174	478703	2426248
Other Receipts 7	2348318	50565	241036	59229	325125	86698	187610	137700	133001	272791	419369	275969	159225
Total Receipts 8	249890750	4644666	18572328	11855070	43182395	21456138	35466437	23055711	15037827	21144804	9491392	28180115	17803867
Average Total Receipts 9	3449	595	380	1802	6702	16267	38095	87332	137962	320376	431427	1565562	5934622
Operating Costs/Operating Income (%)													
Cost of Operations 10	77.4	80.1	63.4	71.4	73.3	75.3	80.1	80.5	77.7	81.6	76.6	81.3	89.9
Salaries and Wages 11	5.8	4.3	6.0	7.7	6.9	6.5	5.9	5.4	6.1	4.6	7.5	4.4	4.1
Taxes Paid 12	1.1	1.3	1.4	1.6	1.3	1.3	0.9	0.9	1.0	0.8	1.2	0.7	0.5
Interest Paid 13	0.8	0.9	0.5	0.6	0.6	0.8	0.7	0.8	1.1	1.1	1.6	0.6	0.9
Depreciation 14	0.6	0.8	0.7	0.7	0.6	0.7	0.4	0.6	0.8	0.6	1.0	0.7	0.5
Amortization and Depletion 15	0.2	0.4	0.1	0.1	0.0	0.1	0.1	0.2	0.2	0.3	0.2	0.2	0.9
Pensions and Other Deferred Comp. 16	0.2	0.6	0.6	0.1	0.3	0.1	0.1	0.2	0.2	0.1	0.1	0.2	0.2
Employee Benefits 17	0.5	0.7	0.6	0.3	0.4	0.4	0.4	0.4	0.7	0.1	1.1	0.5	0.1
Advertising 18	1.3	1.2	1.0	0.7	0.7	0.9	1.0	1.3	1.3	0.6	2.3	1.9	2.1
Other Expenses 19	9.2	9.7	18.2	13.1	10.5	9.3	6.9	7.1	9.0	6.8	11.0	6.9	5.9
Officers' Compensation 20	2.0	3.4	6.0	3.7	3.5	2.2	1.5	1.1	0.9	0.6	1.3	0.4	0.4
Operating Margin 21	0.9	•	1.4	0.0	2.0	2.3	1.9	1.4	1.0	0.8	•	2.3	•
Operating Margin Before Officers' Comp. 22	3.0	•	7.3	3.7	4.5	5.6	3.4	2.5	2.0	1.5		2.7	•

Selected Average Balance Sheet ($ in Thousands)

Net Receivables 23	398	0	13	180	728	2000	5240	11798	20576	45215	71648	184963	514295
Inventories 24	422	0	35	232	919	2772	5255	11304	22697	37074	71901	136256	315418
Net Property, Plant and Equipment 25	136	0	12	60	267	818	1027	3272	8837	11366	28417	74538	189118
Total Assets 26	1440	0	89	668	2420	6957	14905	35174	72211	145618	312792	775539	3115115
Notes and Loans Payable 27	413	0	47	242	611	2266	4052	11976	22941	52804	91722	131376	595075
All Other Liabilities 28	553	0	33	229	999	2719	6271	12729	27832	49572	116331	258082	1396388
Net Worth 29	474	0	8	197	810	1971	4582	10469	21438	43241	104740	386081	1123652

Selected Financial Ratios (Times to 1)

Current Ratio 30	1.6	•	1.7	2.0	1.6	1.5	1.5	1.6	1.6	1.6	1.4	1.6	1.4
Quick Ratio 31	0.8	•	0.9	1.0	0.8	0.7	0.8	0.8	0.9	0.9	0.7	0.8	0.6
Net Sales to Working Capital 32	8.7	•	13.0	6.4	9.3	7.9	8.6	7.0	8.0	7.0	7.0	8.6	9.5
Coverage Ratio 33	5.9	•	7.1	2.6	6.2	4.5	4.8	4.4	3.3	3.7	4.8	10.9	16.2
Total Asset Turnover 34	2.3	•	4.2	2.7	2.7	2.3	2.5	2.5	1.9	2.2	1.3	1.9	1.6
Inventory Turnover 35	6.1	•	6.7	5.5	5.3	4.4	5.8	6.1	4.7	6.9	4.2	9.0	14.3
Receivables Turnover 36	8.6	•	23.4	11.5	9.6	7.5	7.5	7.5	6.5	7.3	4.5	9.2	9.8
Total Liabilities to Net Worth 37	2.0	•	9.9	2.4	2.0	2.5	2.3	2.4	2.4	2.4	2.0	1.0	1.8
Current Assets to Working Capital 38	2.8	•	2.4	2.0	2.8	2.8	2.9	2.7	2.7	2.6	3.4	2.6	3.7
Current Liabilities to Working Capital 39	1.8	•	1.4	1.0	1.8	1.8	1.9	1.9	1.7	1.6	2.4	1.6	2.7
Working Capital to Net Sales 40	0.1	•	0.1	0.2	0.1	0.1	0.1	0.1	0.1	0.1	0.1	0.1	0.1
Inventory to Working Capital 41	1.1	•	1.1	1.0	1.2	1.3	1.3	1.2	1.1	1.0	1.2	0.8	0.6
Total Receipts to Cash Flow 42	9.6	17.2	6.3	9.5	9.3	10.7	12.7	12.4	10.3	11.9	7.0	8.6	6.8
Cost of Goods to Cash Flow 43	7.4	13.8	4.0	6.8	6.8	8.1	10.2	10.0	8.0	9.7	5.4	7.0	6.1
Cash Flow to Total Debt 44	0.4	•	0.7	0.4	0.4	0.3	0.3	0.3	0.3	0.3	0.3	0.5	0.4

Selected Financial Factors (in Percentages)

Debt Ratio 45	67.1	•	90.8	70.4	66.5	71.7	69.3	70.2	70.3	70.3	66.5	50.2	63.9
Return on Total Assets 46	10.8	•	14.7	3.9	10.2	8.6	8.4	8.5	6.9	9.1	9.8	12.9	24.3
Return on Equity Before Income Taxes 47	27.3	•	137.9	8.2	25.7	23.5	21.6	22.1	16.0	22.3	23.3	23.6	63.3
Return on Equity After Income Taxes 48	23.6	•	132.2	6.8	24.3	21.3	19.3	18.4	12.1	17.2	18.2	17.6	59.7
Profit Margin (Before Income Tax) 49	3.9	•	3.0	0.9	3.1	2.9	2.6	2.7	2.5	3.1	6.2	6.0	14.2
Profit Margin (After Income Tax) 50	3.3	•	2.9	0.8	3.0	2.6	2.3	2.2	1.9	2.4	4.9	4.5	13.4

Table II

Corporations with Net Income

FURNITURE, SPORTS, TOYS, JEWELRY, OTHER DURABLE GOODS

MONEY AMOUNTS AND SIZE OF ASSETS IN THOUSANDS OF DOLLARS

Item Description for Accounting Period 7/05 Through 6/06	Total	Zero Assets	Under 500	500 to 1,000	1,000 to 5,000	5,000 to 10,000	10,000 to 25,000	25,000 to 50,000	50,000 to 100,000	100,000 to 250,000	250,000 to 500,000	500,000 to 2,500,000	2,500,000 and over
Number of Enterprises **1**	40124	2170	25707	4725	5216	1114	800	216	90	•	15	•	3
Revenues ($ in Thousands)													
Net Sales **2**	208764301	935230	13980884	9193630	37300089	18460153	31152724	20262013	12603818	•	6111182	•	15033793
Interest **3**	291800	1953	2308	4766	12951	9695	27173	13168	27243	•	22894	•	73366
Rents **4**	78708	0	3413	180	5788	3202	2196	3877	5708	•	696	•	16863
Royalties **5**	288363	25	0	0	0	4383	1184	8758	25688	•	33207	•	94372
Other Portfolio Income **6**	3634781	6559	41166	27874	73795	26287	22987	73654	23341	•	377100	•	2426248
Other Receipts **7**	2114483	12041	222958	46775	308958	63697	154350	111475	122190	•	411180	•	159225
Total Receipts **8**	215172436	955808	14250729	9273225	37701581	18567417	31360614	20472945	12807988	•	6956259	•	17803867
Average Total Receipts **9**	5363	440	554	1963	7228	16667	39201	94782	142311	•	463751	•	5934622
Operating Costs/Operating Income (%)													
Cost of Operations **10**	77.9	50.2	64.6	71.8	72.6	75.1	80.7	81.4	77.4	•	75.4	•	89.9
Salaries and Wages **11**	5.5	5.4	5.5	7.4	6.9	6.0	5.5	4.8	5.7	•	8.2	•	4.1
Taxes Paid **12**	1.0	1.9	1.0	1.5	1.3	1.3	0.9	0.8	1.1	•	1.4	•	0.5
Interest Paid **13**	0.7	0.8	0.3	0.4	0.6	0.8	0.6	0.6	0.9	•	2.0	•	0.9
Depreciation **14**	0.6	0.6	0.6	0.6	0.6	0.8	0.4	0.5	0.7	•	1.2	•	0.5
Amortization and Depletion **15**	0.2	0.4	0.1	0.0	0.0	0.0	0.1	0.1	0.1	•	0.4	•	0.9
Pensions and Other Deferred Comp. **16**	0.2	2.9	0.6	0.1	0.3	0.1	0.1	0.2	0.2	•	0.1	•	0.2
Employee Benefits **17**	0.4	1.7	0.4	0.3	0.3	0.4	0.4	0.4	0.6	•	1.0	•	0.1
Advertising **18**	1.1	3.1	0.7	0.5	0.6	0.8	0.7	1.1	1.3	•	2.3	•	2.1
Other Expenses **19**	8.1	17.2	14.4	11.5	10.0	8.5	6.1	6.1	8.3	•	10.8	•	5.9
Officers' Compensation **20**	2.0	7.2	5.9	3.7	3.6	2.3	1.5	1.0	0.9	•	1.0	•	0.4
Operating Margin **21**	2.4	8.5	5.9	2.2	3.2	3.8	3.0	3.0	2.8	•	3.0	•	•
Operating Margin Before Officers' Comp. **22**	4.4	15.7	11.8	5.8	6.8	6.1	4.5	4.1	3.7	•	4.1	•	•

Selected Average Balance Sheet ($ in Thousands)

Net Receivables 23	608	0	18	200	794	2068	5406	12569	20984	54196	514295
Inventories 24	604	0	38	230	938	2576	5122	11208	22222	78436	338598
Net Property, Plant and Equipment 25	201	0	16	47	277	828	991	3226	8172	27469	189118
Total Assets 26	2169	0	116	647	2468	6867	14901	34930	71891	321802	3115115
Notes and Loans Payable 27	560	0	41	228	579	2309	3549	10178	19755	116083	595075
All Other Liabilities 28	806	0	42	214	990	2657	6193	12687	24640	100970	1396388
Net Worth 29	802	0	32	205	899	1900	5159	12065	27496	104749	1123652

Selected Financial Ratios (Times to 1)

Current Ratio 30	1.6	•	2.0	2.0	1.6	1.6	1.6	1.6	1.7	1.5	1.4
Quick Ratio 31	0.8	•	1.1	1.0	0.9	0.7	0.8	0.9	0.8	0.7	0.6
Net Sales to Working Capital 32	8.4	•	12.4	6.8	9.1	7.8	8.2	8.5	6.4	6.8	9.5
Coverage Ratio 33	9.1	14.8	23.9	7.9	8.6	6.3	7.3	7.6	5.8	6.4	16.2
Total Asset Turnover 34	2.4	•	4.7	3.0	2.9	2.4	2.6	2.7	1.9	1.3	1.6
Inventory Turnover 35	6.7	•	9.4	6.1	5.5	4.8	6.1	6.8	4.9	3.9	13.3
Receivables Turnover 36	8.8	•	23.4	10.8	9.6	7.5	7.7	7.7	6.8	4.4	19.5
Total Liabilities to Net Worth 37	1.7	•	2.6	2.2	1.7	2.6	1.9	1.9	1.6	2.1	1.8
Current Assets to Working Capital 38	2.6	•	2.0	2.0	2.6	2.7	2.7	2.6	2.5	2.9	3.7
Current Liabilities to Working Capital 39	1.6	•	1.0	1.0	1.6	1.7	1.7	1.6	1.5	1.9	2.7
Working Capital to Net Sales 40	0.1	•	0.1	0.1	0.1	0.1	0.1	0.1	0.2	0.1	0.1
Inventory to Working Capital 41	1.0	•	0.8	0.9	1.1	1.2	1.2	1.1	1.0	1.1	0.6
Total Receipts to Cash Flow 42	8.9	4.1	5.6	8.6	8.8	9.7	12.2	11.5	9.1	5.4	6.8
Cost of Goods to Cash Flow 43	6.9	2.0	3.6	6.2	6.4	7.3	9.8	9.3	7.0	4.1	6.1
Cash Flow to Total Debt 44	0.4	•	1.2	0.5	0.5	0.3	0.3	0.4	0.3	0.3	0.4

Selected Financial Factors (in Percentages)

Debt Ratio 45	63.0	•	72.6	68.4	63.6	72.3	65.4	65.5	61.8	67.4	63.9
Return on Total Assets 46	15.0	•	38.5	10.4	14.0	12.7	11.0	12.6	10.3	15.8	24.3
Return on Equity Before Income Taxes 47	36.1	•	134.5	28.7	33.9	38.5	27.5	31.7	22.3	40.9	63.3
Return on Equity After Income Taxes 48	32.2	•	133.2	26.8	32.4	35.7	25.1	27.7	18.6	33.4	59.7
Profit Margin (Before Income Tax) 49	5.6	11.1	7.8	3.0	4.3	4.4	3.6	4.1	4.4	10.5	14.2
Profit Margin (After Income Tax) 50	5.0	10.3	7.8	2.8	4.1	4.1	3.3	3.6	3.7	8.6	13.4

PAPER AND PAPER PRODUCT

Table I

Corporations with and without Net Income

MONEY AMOUNTS AND SIZE OF ASSETS IN THOUSANDS OF DOLLARS

Item Description for Accounting Period 7/05 Through 6/06	Total	Zero Assets	Under 500	500 to 1,000	1,000 to 5,000	5,000 to 10,000	10,000 to 25,000	25,000 to 50,000	50,000 to 100,000	100,000 to 250,000	250,000 to 500,000	500,000 to 2,500,000	2,500,000 and over
Number of Enterprises 1	9488	862	6522	951	883	78	98	51	16	16	6	4	0
Revenues ($ in Thousands)													
Net Sales 2	51801324	706164	3542421	1582797	7460034	1466581	5406542	5765408	3541980	9258505	2823963	10246927	0
Interest 3	23310	3	284	142	1675	2078	2304	4484	919	2937	210	8273	0
Rents 4	10824	0	0	0	4959	279	54	289	802	393	0	4048	0
Royalties 5	20338	0	0	0	7484	0	0	1159	0	0	3899	7796	0
Other Portfolio Income 6	60321	0	27	0	20007	2874	1223	1195	798	1424	17449	15326	0
Other Receipts 7	397419	138742	28452	1738	50155	8973	38874	14327	5454	75115	4082	31509	0
Total Receipts 8	52313536	844909	3571184	1584677	7544314	1480785	5448997	5786862	3549953	9338374	2849603	10313879	0
Average Total Receipts 9	5514	980	548	1666	8544	18984	55602	113468	221872	583648	474934	2578470	•
Operating Costs/Operating Income (%)													
Cost of Operations 10	82.9	86.7	69.4	61.1	77.4	80.5	83.0	86.2	83.6	89.7	87.4	85.4	•
Salaries and Wages 11	5.5	7.3	5.5	9.3	7.7	5.2	5.9	5.5	5.5	3.5	5.2	4.8	•
Taxes Paid 12	0.8	1.1	1.1	1.5	1.2	1.4	0.8	0.7	0.7	0.4	0.5	0.7	•
Interest Paid 13	0.8	2.8	0.5	1.1	0.4	0.7	0.4	0.6	0.6	0.7	1.7	1.4	•
Depreciation 14	0.4	0.4	0.4	0.3	0.4	0.8	0.3	0.3	0.3	0.2	0.4	0.7	•
Amortization and Depletion 15	0.2	0.4	0.1	0.0	0.0	0.1	0.1	0.1	0.0	0.2	0.5	0.5	•
Pensions and Other Deferred Comp. 16	0.2	•	0.2	0.0	0.4	0.4	0.2	0.2	0.2	0.1	0.1	0.2	•
Employee Benefits 17	0.5	1.3	0.3	0.4	0.6	0.4	0.5	0.6	0.4	0.2	0.5	0.5	•
Advertising 18	0.3	0.4	0.5	1.0	0.1	0.4	0.9	0.1	0.2	0.0	0.1	0.4	•
Other Expenses 19	6.4	10.4	12.9	16.8	7.0	5.8	5.4	4.8	6.0	4.8	3.7	5.9	•
Officers' Compensation 20	1.5	0.3	5.3	4.6	3.6	2.6	1.1	0.6	1.2	0.3	0.6	0.1	•
Operating Margin 21	0.5	•	3.8	3.9	1.1	1.9	1.3	0.3	1.3	•	•	•	•
Operating Margin Before Officers' Comp. 22	2.0	•	9.1	8.5	4.7	4.4	2.5	0.9	2.5	0.3	•	•	•

Selected Average Balance Sheet ($ in Thousands)

Net Receivables 23	646	0	27	214	872	1767	6891	15474	29720	70943	69373	337576	•
Inventories 24	369	0	12	205	614	1885	4421	8741	22196	27382	22434	201392	•
Net Property, Plant and Equipment 25	158	0	14	29	153	1015	1498	2568	5439	10553	11716	140228	•
Total Assets 26	1755	0	89	629	2095	6986	15474	33282	68108	148336	377840	1033162	•
Notes and Loans Payable 27	673	0	47	362	582	2147	4334	12091	19173	53458	202310	409830	•
All Other Liabilities 28	698	0	50	134	1020	1470	6771	14184	27120	69840	91701	415563	•
Net Worth 29	383	0	-9	132	494	3369	4369	7008	21815	25037	83830	207768	•

Selected Financial Ratios (Times to 1)

Current Ratio 30	1.5	•	1.0	3.5	1.6	2.0	1.4	1.4	1.7	1.5	1.1	1.3	•
Quick Ratio 31	0.9	•	0.7	2.0	1.0	1.1	0.9	0.9	1.0	1.0	0.9	0.8	•
Net Sales to Working Capital 32	14.5	•	•	4.3	12.6	7.0	14.0	13.9	8.9	14.7	42.0	20.1	•
Coverage Ratio 33	2.9	4.1	10.3	4.6	7.3	5.3	6.0	2.1	3.8	2.3	1.2	1.0	•
Total Asset Turnover 34	3.1	•	6.1	2.6	4.0	2.7	3.6	3.4	3.3	3.9	1.2	2.5	•
Inventory Turnover 35	12.3	•	32.5	5.0	10.7	8.0	10.4	11.1	8.3	19.0	18.3	10.9	•
Receivables Turnover 36	8.7	•	18.0	8.9	10.4	10.3	7.6	8.1	6.2	8.1	13.6	7.6	•
Total Liabilities to Net Worth 37	3.6	•	•	3.8	3.2	1.1	2.5	3.7	2.1	4.9	3.5	4.0	•
Current Assets to Working Capital 38	3.2	•	•	1.4	2.7	2.0	3.3	3.4	2.4	3.0	10.1	4.5	•
Current Liabilities to Working Capital 39	2.2	•	•	0.4	1.7	1.0	2.3	2.4	1.4	2.0	9.1	3.5	•
Working Capital to Net Sales 40	0.1	•	•	0.2	0.1	0.1	0.1	0.1	0.1	0.1	0.0	0.0	•
Inventory to Working Capital 41	1.0	•	•	0.6	0.9	0.7	1.0	1.1	0.8	0.8	2.0	1.5	•
Total Receipts to Cash Flow 42	15.5	6.1	7.0	5.4	14.3	14.2	15.5	25.1	15.9	21.5	35.8	21.4	•
Cost of Goods to Cash Flow 43	12.9	5.3	4.9	3.3	11.0	11.4	12.9	21.7	13.3	19.3	31.3	18.3	•
Cash Flow to Total Debt 44	0.3	0.8	0.6	0.4	0.4	0.1	0.3	0.2	0.3	0.2	0.0	0.1	•

Selected Financial Factors (in Percentages)

Debt Ratio 45	78.2	•	110.0	79.0	76.4	51.8	71.8	78.9	68.0	83.1	77.8	79.9	•
Return on Total Assets 46	7.2	•	31.2	13.5	10.6	9.5	9.0	4.3	6.8	5.8	2.5	3.4	•
Return on Equity Before Income Taxes 47	21.6	•	•	50.2	38.8	15.9	26.6	10.9	15.5	19.0	1.8	•	
Return on Equity After Income Taxes 48	18.3	•	•	50.2	37.3	13.8	23.6	7.5	14.6	15.4	1.1	•	
Profit Margin (Before Income Tax) 49	1.5	8.6	4.6	4.0	2.3	2.9	2.1	0.7	1.5	0.8	0.3	•	
Profit Margin (After Income Tax) 50	1.3	8.6	4.3	4.0	2.2	2.5	1.9	0.5	1.4	0.7	0.2	•	

Table II
Corporations with Net Income

PAPER AND PAPER PRODUCT

MONEY AMOUNTS AND SIZE OF ASSETS IN THOUSANDS OF DOLLARS

Item Description for Accounting Period 7/05 Through 6/06	Total	Zero Assets	Under 500	500 to 1,000	1,000 to 5,000	5,000 to 10,000	10,000 to 25,000	25,000 to 50,000	50,000 to 100,000	100,000 to 250,000	250,000 to 500,000	500,000 to 2,500,000	2,500,000 and over
Number of Enterprises 1	5729	196	4293	368	639	·	93	36	13	·	·	·	0
Revenues ($ in Thousands)													
Net Sales 2	41383903	642710	3008957	439732	7021115	·	5092463	4233726	2706494	·	·	·	0
Interest 3	14744	3	284	0	1470	·	2237	1271	917	·	·	·	0
Rents 4	6776	0	0	0	4959	·	54	289	802	·	·	·	0
Royalties 5	7676	0	0	0	7484	·	0	0	0	·	·	·	0
Other Portfolio Income 6	41506	0	27	0	14735	·	1223	1043	763	·	·	·	0
Other Receipts 7	360137	138745	25515	1043	47750	·	34633	5255	6877	·	·	·	0
Total Receipts 8	41814742	781458	3034783	440775	7097513	·	5130610	4241584	2715853	·	·	·	0
Average Total Receipts 9	7299	3987	707	1198	11107	·	55168	117822	208912	·	·	·	·
Operating Costs/Operating Income (%)													
Cost of Operations 10	82.6	89.8	70.2	53.1	78.3	·	82.2	86.9	82.0	·	·	·	·
Salaries and Wages 11	5.5	4.0	5.9	4.9	7.5	·	6.2	5.1	6.0	·	·	·	·
Taxes Paid 12	0.8	0.8	1.0	0.7	1.2	·	0.8	0.7	0.8	·	·	·	·
Interest Paid 13	0.7	3.0	0.5	0.0	0.3	·	0.4	0.5	0.5	·	·	·	·
Depreciation 14	0.4	0.3	0.3	0.1	0.4	·	0.3	0.3	0.3	·	·	·	·
Amortization and Depletion 15	0.1	0.4	0.1	·	0.0	·	0.0	0.1	0.0	·	·	·	·
Pensions and Other Deferred Comp. 16	0.2	·	0.2	·	0.3	·	0.2	0.1	0.2	·	·	·	·
Employee Benefits 17	0.5	1.5	0.3	0.0	0.6	·	0.5	0.4	0.3	·	·	·	·
Advertising 18	0.3	0.3	0.6	1.7	0.1	·	1.0	0.1	0.2	·	·	·	·
Other Expenses 19	5.7	10.2	12.4	14.1	6.2	·	5.1	3.7	6.4	·	·	·	·
Officers' Compensation 20	1.4	0.4	3.6	6.0	3.6	·	1.2	0.7	1.4	·	·	·	·
Operating Margin 21	1.7	·	5.0	19.4	1.5	·	2.1	1.6	1.9	·	·	·	·
Operating Margin Before Officers' Comp. 22	3.1	·	8.5	25.4	5.0	·	3.3	2.3	3.3	·	·	·	·

Selected Average Balance Sheet ($ in Thousands)

Net Receivables 23	843	0	33	269	1129	•	6880	15640	28518
Inventories 24	415	0	13	123	485	•	4228	9299	19432
Net Property, Plant and Equipment 25	224	0	18	29	142	•	1509	2006	5881
Total Assets 26	2253	0	117	582	2288	•	15512	32001	67742
Notes and Loans Payable 27	726	0	53	214	544	•	3959	9289	17815
All Other Liabilities 28	961	0	61	67	1208	•	6732	14340	25530
Net Worth 29	566	0	2	301	537	•	4820	8372	24598

Selected Financial Ratios (Times to 1)

Current Ratio 30	1.4	•	1.1	8.2	1.5	•	1.5	1.5	1.9
Quick Ratio 31	0.9	•	0.8	6.3	1.0	•	0.9	0.9	1.0
Net Sales to Working Capital 32	17.0	•	147.4	2.5	17.2	•	12.7	13.3	7.7
Coverage Ratio 33	4.9	4.6	12.3	561.1	9.8	•	8.2	4.8	5.8
Total Asset Turnover 34	3.2	•	6.0	2.1	4.8	•	3.5	3.7	3.1
Inventory Turnover 35	14.4	•	36.9	5.1	17.8	•	10.6	11.0	8.8
Receivables Turnover 36	9.1	•	21.6	8.9	10.9	•	7.8	7.7	6.0
Total Liabilities to Net Worth 37	3.0	•	51.0	0.9	3.3	•	2.2	2.8	1.8
Current Assets to Working Capital 38	3.6	•	14.8	1.1	3.1	•	3.0	3.1	2.2
Current Liabilities to Working Capital 39	2.6	•	13.8	0.1	2.1	•	2.0	2.1	1.2
Working Capital to Net Sales 40	0.1	•	0.0	0.4	0.1	•	0.1	0.1	0.1
Inventory to Working Capital 41	1.0	•	3.5	0.3	0.8	•	1.0	1.0	0.7
Total Receipts to Cash Flow 42	14.3	5.4	6.6	3.1	14.6	•	14.4	22.8	13.7
Cost of Goods to Cash Flow 43	11.8	4.9	4.6	1.6	11.4	•	11.8	19.8	11.2
Cash Flow to Total Debt 44	0.3	•	0.9	1.4	0.4	•	0.4	0.2	0.4

Selected Financial Factors (in Percentages)

Debt Ratio 45	74.9	•	98.1	48.3	76.5	•	68.9	73.8	63.7
Return on Total Assets 46	11.0	•	38.0	40.3	13.7	•	11.5	8.3	8.3
Return on Equity Before Income Taxes 47	34.8	•	1815.6	77.9	52.6	•	32.4	25.1	18.9
Return on Equity After Income Taxes 48	31.1	•	1718.4	77.9	50.7	•	29.5	21.2	17.8
Profit Margin (Before Income Tax) 49	2.7	10.8	5.8	19.6	2.6	•	2.8	1.8	2.2
Profit Margin (After Income Tax) 50	2.4	10.8	5.5	19.6	2.5	•	2.6	1.5	2.1

Table I

Corporations with and without Net Income

DRUGS AND DRUGGISTS' SUNDRIES

MONEY AMOUNTS AND SIZE OF ASSETS IN THOUSANDS OF DOLLARS

Item Description for Accounting Period 7/05 Through 6/06	Total	Zero Assets	Under 500	500 to 1,000	1,000 to 5,000	5,000 to 10,000	10,000 to 25,000	25,000 to 50,000	50,000 to 100,000	100,000 to 250,000	250,000 to 500,000	500,000 to 2,500,000	2,500,000 and over
Number of Enterprises **1**	5569	793	2978	341	995	167	143	47	29	31	14	19	12
Revenues ($ in Thousands)													
Net Sales **2**	378973955	895457	939007	891101	6131105	2442390	5899271	3605822	4944841	8221167	14447638	21757679	308798478
Interest **3**	1230233	11375	337	1113	1939	5004	10040	3721	11222	23247	32642	117728	1011864
Rents **4**	539938	0	0	0	131	0	0	1375	375	162	1828	7670	528397
Royalties **5**	1961857	3820	0	4218	0	0	4424	18747	4443	51329	2761	530467	1341648
Other Portfolio Income **6**	2462785	155	0	0	868	4432	6378	466	15689	26756	31937	437293	1938812
Other Receipts **7**	4956794	8312	3979	1177	38226	4187	43248	82458	143014	48686	41653	808379	3733474
Total Receipts **8**	390125562	919119	943323	897609	6172269	2456013	5963361	3712589	5119584	8371347	14558459	23659216	317352673
Average Total Receipts **9**	70053	1159	317	2632	6203	14707	41702	78991	176537	270043	1039890	1245222	26446056
Operating Costs/Operating Income (%)													
Cost of Operations **10**	87.1	68.9	67.3	79.1	72.7	70.1	75.1	71.3	79.0	74.9	82.6	41.4	92.0
Salaries and Wages **11**	3.5	6.7	6.1	8.8	6.1	8.2	7.9	8.9	6.7	7.0	6.9	11.8	2.3
Taxes Paid **12**	0.4	1.1	1.3	2.7	1.1	1.4	1.4	0.8	0.7	0.8	0.6	1.1	0.2
Interest Paid **13**	0.5	2.2	0.1	0.9	1.0	1.0	0.5	0.9	0.7	1.3	0.6	1.7	0.4
Depreciation **14**	0.3	0.8	0.5	0.5	1.2	0.6	0.4	0.7	0.4	0.5	0.3	0.9	0.3
Amortization and Depletion **15**	0.3	0.5	0.2	0.3	0.1	0.7	0.1	0.5	0.5	1.0	0.3	0.8	0.2
Pensions and Other Deferred Comp. **16**	0.2	0.1	0.5	0.1	0.1	0.3	0.2	0.1	0.1	0.1	0.1	0.6	0.1
Employee Benefits **17**	0.4	0.4	0.1	1.2	0.4	0.6	0.7	0.9	0.6	0.7	0.3	1.1	0.3
Advertising **18**	0.7	6.8	0.5	1.0	1.6	1.2	1.2	1.3	2.0	2.2	0.7	3.3	0.5
Other Expenses **19**	5.9	14.1	18.1	11.7	11.4	11.6	8.5	13.5	10.5	11.5	5.4	29.9	3.7
Officers' Compensation **20**	0.5	2.2	6.6	5.1	2.4	2.7	1.9	1.5	0.9	0.6	0.2	1.9	0.2
Operating Margin **21**	0.3	•	•	•	1.9	1.7	2.3	•	•	•	2.0	5.5	•
Operating Margin Before Officers' Comp. **22**	0.7	5.3	•	•	4.3	4.4	4.2	1.2	•	0.2	2.3	7.4	0.1

Selected Average Balance Sheet ($ in Thousands)

Net Receivables 23	7020	0	35	226	579	1076	4882	9704	17327	29211	90765	194372	2552745
Inventories 24	5364	0	34	220	654	3425	4100	8062	18033	23495	91141	144250	1853122
Net Property, Plant and Equipment 25	1779	0	4	45	206	346	1096	4176	5455	10065	31031	105277	529833
Total Assets 26	32819	0	110	743	2384	7474	15912	33686	70198	156008	360512	1024406	11943591
Notes and Loans Payable 27	5357	0	44	482	1369	2349	3109	10694	17659	42549	64897	277177	1569089
All Other Liabilities 28	13957	0	25	507	1024	2136	6421	12177	29033	62551	160469	337170	5265032
Net Worth 29	13504	0	41	-246	-10	2989	6383	10815	23505	50909	135146	410060	5109470

Selected Financial Ratios (Times to 1)

Current Ratio 30	1.3	•	3.3	0.7	1.2	1.4	1.6	1.5	1.4	1.5	1.6	1.7	1.3
Quick Ratio 31	0.8	•	2.2	0.4	0.6	0.5	0.8	0.8	0.8	0.9	0.8	0.9	0.8
Net Sales to Working Capital 32	15.5	•	4.9	•	18.6	9.5	8.9	9.9	10.8	8.4	10.9	4.6	20.1
Coverage Ratio 33	7.5	0.5	•	•	3.7	3.2	8.0	4.2	3.1	2.1	6.0	9.2	8.3
Total Asset Turnover 34	2.1	•	2.9	3.5	2.6	2.0	2.6	2.3	2.4	1.7	2.9	1.1	2.2
Inventory Turnover 35	11.1	•	6.2	9.4	6.9	3.0	7.6	6.8	7.5	8.5	9.4	3.3	12.8
Receivables Turnover 36	12.0	•	5.8	11.3	11.1	8.8	10.3	8.3	8.6	10.7	10.4	6.0	13.3
Total Liabilities to Net Worth 37	1.4	•	1.7	•	•	1.5	1.5	2.1	2.0	2.1	1.7	1.5	1.3
Current Assets to Working Capital 38	4.1	•	1.4	•	5.9	3.4	2.7	2.9	3.3	2.9	2.7	2.5	4.9
Current Liabilities to Working Capital 39	3.1	•	0.4	•	4.9	2.4	1.7	1.9	2.3	1.9	1.7	1.5	3.9
Working Capital to Net Sales 40	0.1	•	0.2	•	0.1	0.1	0.1	0.1	0.1	0.1	0.1	0.2	0.0
Inventory to Working Capital 41	1.2	•	0.5	•	2.2	1.8	1.1	1.1	1.1	0.8	0.9	0.5	1.4
Total Receipts to Cash Flow 42	11.7	8.6	9.2	•	8.3	8.3	9.5	6.8	9.4	8.5	13.4	2.3	17.1
Cost of Goods to Cash Flow 43	10.2	6.0	6.2	•	6.0	5.8	7.1	4.8	7.4	6.4	11.1	1.0	15.7
Cash Flow to Total Debt 44	0.3	•	0.5	•	0.3	0.4	0.5	0.5	0.4	0.3	0.3	0.8	0.2

Selected Financial Factors (in Percentages)

Debt Ratio 45	58.9	•	62.7	133.1	100.4	60.0	59.9	67.9	66.5	67.4	62.5	60.0	57.2
Return on Total Assets 46	7.9	•	•	9.1	•	6.4	10.0	8.7	5.5	4.6	9.6	18.0	6.7
Return on Equity Before Income Taxes 47	16.7	•	•	•	112.6	11.0	21.8	20.7	11.2	7.3	21.3	40.0	13.8
Return on Equity After Income Taxes 48	11.8	•	•	•	113.9	7.9	19.6	17.6	4.3	3.1	15.8	27.8	9.8
Profit Margin (Before Income Tax) 49	3.3	•	•	•	2.6	2.3	3.4	2.9	1.5	1.4	2.8	14.3	2.7
Profit Margin (After Income Tax) 50	2.3	•	2.3	•	2.3	1.6	3.0	2.5	0.6	0.6	2.1	10.0	1.9

Table II
Corporations with Net Income

DRUGS AND DRUGGISTS' SUNDRIES

MONEY AMOUNTS AND SIZE OF ASSETS IN THOUSANDS OF DOLLARS

Item Description for Accounting Period 7/05 Through 6/06	Total	Zero Assets	Under 500	500 to 1,000	1,000 to 5,000	5,000 to 10,000	10,000 to 25,000	25,000 to 50,000	50,000 to 100,000	100,000 to 250,000	250,000 to 500,000	500,000 to 2,500,000	2,500,000 and over
Number of Enterprises 1	3114	527	1421	165	636	139	113	•	18	24	•	15	•
Revenues ($ in Thousands)													
Net Sales 2	285697361	402480	727604	423621	5021874	2166781	4800214	•	3568117	7146509	•	18467162	•
Interest 3	906521	7093	127	1106	1576	4492	7962	•	7441	17019	•	109569	•
Rents 4	485488	0	0	0	131	0	0	•	271	162	•	7670	•
Royalties 5	1849680	49	0	0	0	0	4424	•	3803	43683	•	527865	•
Other Portfolio Income 6	2403638	0	0	0	782	4427	5501	•	15460	7973	•	431692	•
Other Receipts 7	4551341	7069	2512	1156	3708	1171	22966	•	15591	44300	•	788029	•
Total Receipts 8	295894029	416691	730243	425883	5028071	2176871	4841067	•	3610683	7259646	•	20331987	•
Average Total Receipts 9	95021	791	514	2581	7906	15661	42841	•	200594	302485	•	1355466	•
Operating Costs/Operating Income (%)													
Cost of Operations 10	85.2	35.7	68.6	76.1	81.0	69.6	74.6	•	79.3	78.5	•	35.9	•
Salaries and Wages 11	3.7	7.6	3.5	5.7	4.2	7.7	7.4	•	4.0	4.5	•	10.8	•
Taxes Paid 12	0.4	1.8	0.9	4.1	0.8	1.3	1.4	•	0.6	0.6	•	1.2	•
Interest Paid 13	0.5	1.0	0.2	0.3	0.4	1.0	0.4	•	0.4	0.7	•	1.9	•
Depreciation 14	0.4	1.0	0.4	0.2	0.2	0.6	0.4	•	0.3	0.5	•	1.0	•
Amortization and Depletion 15	0.3	0.3	0.2	0.0	0.0	0.6	0.1	•	0.2	0.5	•	0.8	•
Pensions and Other Deferred Comp. 16	0.1	0.0	•	0.0	0.0	0.3	0.2	•	0.1	0.1	•	0.7	•
Employee Benefits 17	0.4	0.9	0.0	0.9	0.2	0.5	0.6	•	0.3	0.6	•	1.2	•
Advertising 18	0.9	15.1	0.1	0.8	0.3	0.8	1.4	•	1.7	1.5	•	3.7	•
Other Expenses 19	6.4	14.1	16.2	5.8	5.9	9.7	8.0	•	7.6	8.9	•	33.8	•
Officers' Compensation 20	0.4	0.2	5.7	5.2	1.4	2.8	1.7	•	0.9	0.5	•	1.4	•
Operating Margin 21	1.4	22.2	4.2	1.0	5.6	5.3	3.7	•	4.5	3.1	•	7.6	•
Operating Margin Before Officers' Comp. 22	1.8	22.4	9.9	6.1	7.0	8.1	5.4	•	5.4	3.6	•	9.1	•

Selected Average Balance Sheet ($ in Thousands)

Net Receivables 23	7035	0	51	180	539	1067	4969	22346	30240	178713
Inventories 24	7943	0	58	179	735	3540	4263	21437	23991	139730
Net Property, Plant and Equipment 25	2771	0	6	16	171	367	1132	4155	11331	125629
Total Assets 26	46080	0	178	812	2190	7386	15649	70480	152714	1029251
Notes and Loans Payable 27	7952	0	33	4	632	1989	2888	14310	36441	317463
All Other Liabilities 28	17155	0	45	724	1037	1801	6776	34877	55874	340846
Net Worth 29	20974	0	100	84	521	3596	5985	21292	60399	370942

Selected Financial Ratios (Times to 1)

Current Ratio 30	1.4	•	2.8	0.6	1.9	1.9	1.7	1.5	1.6	1.5
Quick Ratio 31	0.8	•	1.9	0.4	1.0	0.7	0.9	0.8	0.9	0.9
Net Sales to Working Capital 32	15.4	•	5.6	•	8.8	6.3	7.9	10.9	8.8	5.9
Coverage Ratio 33	11.7	26.4	27.7	5.3	16.5	6.9	11.6	14.6	7.3	10.5
Total Asset Turnover 34	2.0	•	2.9	3.2	3.6	2.1	2.7	2.8	1.9	1.2
Inventory Turnover 35	9.8	•	6.1	10.9	8.7	3.1	7.4	7.3	9.7	3.2
Receivables Turnover 36	12.9	•	9.9	28.6	14.1	9.0	10.6	7.8	12.6	6.5
Total Liabilities to Net Worth 37	1.2	•	0.8	8.7	3.2	1.1	1.6	2.3	1.5	1.8
Current Assets to Working Capital 38	3.8	•	1.5	•	2.1	2.2	2.5	3.1	2.7	2.9
Current Liabilities to Working Capital 39	2.8	•	0.5	•	1.1	1.2	1.5	2.1	1.7	1.9
Working Capital to Net Sales 40	0.1	•	0.2	•	0.1	0.2	0.1	0.1	0.1	0.2
Inventory to Working Capital 41	1.1	•	0.5	•	1.0	1.1	1.0	1.0	0.9	0.5
Total Receipts to Cash Flow 42	9.4	2.6	6.9	17.8	9.7	7.3	9.0	8.1	7.7	2.0
Cost of Goods to Cash Flow 43	8.0	0.9	4.7	13.5	7.8	5.1	6.7	6.4	6.0	0.7
Cash Flow to Total Debt 44	0.4	•	1.0	0.2	0.5	0.6	0.5	0.5	0.4	0.9

Selected Financial Factors (in Percentages)

Debt Ratio 45	54.5	•	43.9	89.6	76.2	51.3	61.8	69.8	60.4	64.0
Return on Total Assets 46	11.1	•	13.6	5.8	22.2	14.1	13.5	17.7	10.6	23.6
Return on Equity Before Income Taxes 47	22.3	•	23.4	45.4	87.5	24.8	32.2	54.7	23.1	59.3
Return on Equity After Income Taxes 48	16.6	•	23.2	38.0	82.6	21.7	29.2	42.4	18.5	42.2
Profit Margin (Before Income Tax) 49	5.1	25.7	4.6	1.5	5.8	5.7	4.5	5.9	4.7	17.9
Profit Margin (After Income Tax) 50	3.8	19.5	4.5	1.2	5.4	5.0	4.1	4.6	3.7	12.7

186

Table I
Corporations with and without Net Income

APPAREL, PIECE GOODS, AND NOTIONS

MONEY AMOUNTS AND SIZE OF ASSETS IN THOUSANDS OF DOLLARS

Item Description for Accounting Period 7/05 Through 6/06	Total	Zero Assets	Under 500	500 to 1,000	1,000 to 5,000	5,000 to 10,000	10,000 to 25,000	25,000 to 50,000	50,000 to 100,000	100,000 to 250,000	250,000 to 500,000	500,000 to 2,500,000	2,500,000 and over
Number of Enterprises 1	25472	4064	16853	1938	1810	361	257	100	34	29	13	13	0
Revenues ($ in Thousands)													
Net Sales 2	87326299	643412	10919426	3925424	10949082	6188146	9487799	8544792	4093014	6441711	3801818	22331675	0
Interest 3	202824	1318	1090	1036	3841	4095	5289	6300	7177	19152	24925	128600	0
Rents 4	36862	122	0	0	0	1168	309	1238	4693	18522	4186	6624	0
Royalties 5	1059818	7114	0	0	6571	20324	38	2749	12671	30491	24051	955807	0
Other Portfolio Income 6	2171811	3786	1173	11	28593	12686	1886	23420	16921	23535	222305	1837495	0
Other Receipts 7	1732822	6424	43262	592956	81503	45039	63328	73207	37380	23869	48325	717532	0
Total Receipts 8	92530436	662176	10964951	4519427	11069590	6271458	9558649	8651706	4171856	6557280	4125610	25977733	0
Average Total Receipts 9	3633	163	651	2332	6116	17372	37193	86517	122702	226113	317355	1998287	·
Operating Costs/Operating Income (%)													
Cost of Operations 10	67.8	60.1	69.5	69.7	72.7	72.6	73.8	73.2	66.7	64.1	60.5	60.8	·
Salaries and Wages 11	9.1	9.8	5.0	13.9	7.6	7.6	7.6	7.6	8.5	8.9	11.4	12.4	·
Taxes Paid 12	2.2	2.2	1.8	1.8	2.0	3.2	1.8	2.9	1.6	2.9	3.3	2.0	·
Interest Paid 13	1.1	0.4	0.2	0.4	1.0	1.0	0.8	1.2	1.3	1.5	2.2	1.5	·
Depreciation 14	0.7	0.6	0.3	0.3	0.3	0.3	0.3	0.5	0.7	0.9	1.2	1.4	·
Amortization and Depletion 15	0.2	0.0	0.0	0.0	0.1	0.2	0.1	0.1	0.3	0.3	0.2	0.5	·
Pensions and Other Deferred Comp. 16	0.3	1.2	0.3	0.7	0.2	0.2	0.1	0.4	0.3	0.3	0.7	0.2	·
Employee Benefits 17	0.5	0.7	0.4	0.2	0.3	0.6	0.4	0.4	0.7	1.0	1.0	0.7	·
Advertising 18	1.9	0.9	0.7	1.5	0.7	0.7	0.9	1.2	1.9	2.4	3.3	3.9	·
Other Expenses 19	13.4	18.8	15.2	16.0	11.7	10.1	8.8	8.5	11.8	12.4	14.2	17.9	·
Officers' Compensation 20	2.5	8.4	5.1	9.0	2.9	1.7	2.4	1.8	2.4	1.5	1.5	0.9	·
Operating Margin 21	0.2	·	1.4	·	0.4	1.8	3.0	2.2	3.8	4.0	0.6	·	·
Operating Margin Before Officers' Comp. 22	2.7	5.3	6.5	·	3.3	3.5	5.3	4.0	6.1	5.5	2.1	·	·

Selected Average Balance Sheet ($ in Thousands)

Net Receivables 23	450	0	21	152	718	1934	4834	11064	18316	31435	57246	322043	•
Inventories 24	447	0	34	308	596	2902	5694	11966	22343	38620	47418	224945	•
Net Property, Plant and Equipment 25	213	0	12	43	130	599	945	2890	6578	19176	46113	213251	•
Total Assets 26	2185	0	125	724	2343	6905	15439	35218	69858	155046	337027	2051054	•
Notes and Loans Payable 27	593	0	58	171	705	1831	4438	12927	21602	42605	99103	475333	•
All Other Liabilities 28	629	0	31	320	997	2987	5548	12636	15531	41067	68587	514769	•
Net Worth 29	962	0	36	232	641	2087	5454	9655	32724	71373	169338	1060952	•

Selected Financial Ratios (Times to 1)

Current Ratio 30	1.8	•	2.7	1.6	1.7	1.5	1.8	1.5	2.1	2.1	2.3	1.7	•
Quick Ratio 31	0.9	•	1.5	0.9	0.9	0.6	0.8	0.7	1.0	1.0	1.1	0.9	•
Net Sales to Working Capital 32	5.7	•	10.4	8.9	7.5	8.2	6.1	9.1	4.6	4.2	2.9	4.1	•
Coverage Ratio 33	7.2	0.3	9.7	4.7	2.5	4.0	5.3	4.1	5.7	4.8	5.0	12.1	•
Total Asset Turnover 34	1.6	•	5.2	2.8	2.6	2.5	2.4	2.4	1.7	1.4	0.9	0.8	•
Inventory Turnover 35	5.2	•	13.2	4.6	7.4	4.3	4.8	5.2	3.6	3.7	3.7	4.6	•
Receivables Turnover 36	8.1	•	32.3	9.5	8.7	8.5	7.4	8.4	6.0	7.5	6.8	6.1	•
Total Liabilities to Net Worth 37	1.3	•	2.5	2.1	2.7	2.3	1.8	2.6	1.1	1.2	1.0	0.9	•
Current Assets to Working Capital 38	2.3	•	1.6	2.8	2.5	2.9	2.2	3.0	1.9	1.9	1.8	2.4	•
Current Liabilities to Working Capital 39	1.3	•	0.6	1.8	1.5	1.9	1.2	2.0	0.9	0.9	0.8	1.4	•
Working Capital to Net Sales 40	0.2	•	0.1	0.1	0.1	0.1	0.2	0.1	0.2	0.2	0.3	0.2	•
Inventory to Working Capital 41	0.8	•	0.5	1.1	0.8	1.3	0.9	1.4	0.8	0.8	0.6	0.6	•
Total Receipts to Cash Flow 42	6.1	6.8	7.9	6.9	9.1	8.9	9.4	9.9	6.8	6.9	5.5	3.5	•
Cost of Goods to Cash Flow 43	4.1	4.1	5.5	4.8	6.6	6.5	7.0	7.2	4.5	4.4	3.3	2.1	•
Cash Flow to Total Debt 44	0.5	•	0.9	0.6	0.4	0.4	0.4	0.3	0.5	0.4	0.3	0.5	•

Selected Financial Factors (in Percentages)

Debt Ratio 45	55.9	71.1	67.9	72.6	69.8	64.7	72.6	53.2	54.0	49.8	48.3	•
Return on Total Assets 46	12.6	10.6	5.1	6.5	10.3	10.8	11.8	12.4	10.4	9.8	15.5	•
Return on Equity Before Income Taxes 47	24.6	33.1	12.4	14.1	25.7	24.9	21.8	17.9	15.7	27.5		•
Return on Equity After Income Taxes 48	18.9	32.5	11.6	12.7	24.1	23.7	28.6	17.8	12.7	12.1	19.7	•
Profit Margin (Before Income Tax) 49	6.9	1.8	1.4	1.5	3.1	3.7	3.7	5.9	5.7	9.1	17.0	•
Profit Margin (After Income Tax) 50	5.3	1.8	1.3	1.4	2.9	3.5	3.2	4.8	5.7	7.0	12.2	•

Table II
Corporations with Net Income

APPAREL, PIECE GOODS, AND NOTIONS

MONEY AMOUNTS AND SIZE OF ASSETS IN THOUSANDS OF DOLLARS

Item Description for Accounting Period 7/05 Through 6/06	Total	Zero Assets	Under 500	500 to 1,000	1,000 to 5,000	5,000 to 10,000	10,000 to 25,000	25,000 to 50,000	50,000 to 100,000	100,000 to 250,000	250,000 to 500,000	500,000 to 2,500,000	2,500,000 and over
Number of Enterprises 1	16212	2030	10589	1509	1440	290	•	83	28	22	10	•	0

Revenues ($ in Thousands)

	Total	Zero Assets	Under 500	500 to 1,000	1,000 to 5,000	5,000 to 10,000	10,000 to 25,000	25,000 to 50,000	50,000 to 100,000	100,000 to 250,000	250,000 to 500,000	500,000 to 2,500,000	2,500,000 and over
Net Sales 2	74637217	551791	8506919	3248202	8889815	4881389	•	7007623	3780044	5034166	3482422	•	0
Interest 3	167231	572	439	763	2901	2078	•	4014	5701	16630	15653	•	0
Rents 4	33313	122	0	0	0	1014	•	1238	4106	18257	3569	•	0
Royalties 5	922534	7114	0	0	6571	20324	•	2749	10417	28675	23665	•	0
Other Portfolio Income 6	2133445	273	1033	11	28593	12686	•	22535	16746	23507	189265	•	0
Other Receipts 7	919536	6441	30914	13994	17311	36407	•	62851	31040	17156	31509	•	0
Total Receipts 8	78813276	566313	8539305	3262970	8945191	4953898	•	7101010	3848054	5138391	3746083	•	0
Average Total Receipts 9	4861	279	806	2162	6212	17082	•	85554	137430	233563	374608	•	•

Operating Costs/Operating Income (%)

	Total	Zero Assets	Under 500	500 to 1,000	1,000 to 5,000	5,000 to 10,000	10,000 to 25,000	25,000 to 50,000	50,000 to 100,000	100,000 to 250,000	250,000 to 500,000	500,000 to 2,500,000	2,500,000 and over
Cost of Operations 10	66.5	58.1	67.7	69.5	71.3	70.5	•	73.2	66.4	59.5	60.0	•	•
Salaries and Wages 11	8.5	9.2	4.6	4.8	6.4	7.3	•	7.3	8.5	9.6	10.0	•	•
Taxes Paid 12	2.1	1.8	1.8	0.9	1.8	3.7	•	2.9	1.6	2.8	3.3	•	•
Interest Paid 13	0.9	0.1	0.1	0.4	0.8	0.9	•	0.9	1.3	1.0	1.4	•	•
Depreciation 14	0.7	0.6	0.3	0.2	0.3	0.3	•	0.4	0.7	1.0	0.8	•	•
Amortization and Depletion 15	0.2	0.0	0.0	0.1	0.1	0.3	•	0.1	0.3	0.3	0.2	•	•
Pensions and Other Deferred Comp. 16	0.3	0.2	0.2	0.9	0.2	0.1	•	0.3	0.3	0.3	0.5	•	•
Employee Benefits 17	0.5	0.7	0.3	0.2	0.3	0.6	•	0.3	0.7	1.0	0.9	•	•
Advertising 18	2.0	0.9	0.6	1.7	0.5	0.7	•	1.1	1.9	2.9	3.4	•	•
Other Expenses 19	12.5	15.9	14.9	10.6	10.6	10.0	•	7.4	11.2	13.8	13.1	•	•
Officers' Compensation 20	2.2	5.5	4.8	4.3	3.0	1.8	•	2.0	2.0	1.7	1.5	•	•
Operating Margin 21	3.4	7.2	4.7	6.5	4.6	3.8	•	4.2	5.1	6.2	4.9	•	•
Operating Margin Before Officers' Comp. 22	5.6	12.6	9.4	10.7	7.6	5.6	•	6.2	7.1	7.8	6.4	•	•

Selected Average Balance Sheet ($ in Thousands)

Net Receivables **23**	570	0	23	155	770	2176	11580	19216	30272	65198	•
Inventories **24**	588	0	41	295	574	2979	12142	21437	41168	72365	•
Net Property, Plant and Equipment **25**	272	0	15	25	132	666	2395	6437	22680	27568	•
Total Assets **26**	2872	0	147	728	2388	6769	34600	69586	160144	340383	•
Notes and Loans Payable **27**	733	0	55	137	578	1662	10284	23251	30679	81982	•
All Other Liabilities **28**	705	0	34	294	997	2661	11814	16683	34974	71635	•
Net Worth **29**	1434	0	58	296	812	2446	12501	29652	94491	186766	•

Selected Financial Ratios (Times to 1)

Current Ratio **30**	2.0	•	3.3	1.9	1.9	1.7	1.6	1.9	2.3	2.3	•
Quick Ratio **31**	1.0	•	2.0	1.0	1.1	0.7	0.7	0.9	1.1	1.0	•
Net Sales to Working Capital **32**	5.2	•	9.9	6.9	6.5	7.1	7.3	5.3	3.8	3.3	•
Coverage Ratio **33**	11.7	138.4	39.2	18.5	7.8	7.1	7.6	6.7	9.2	9.6	•
Total Asset Turnover **34**	1.6	•	5.5	3.0	2.6	2.5	2.4	1.9	1.4	1.0	•
Inventory Turnover **35**	5.2	•	13.3	5.1	7.7	4.0	5.1	4.2	3.3	2.9	•
Receivables Turnover **36**	8.3	•	41.1	12.5	8.5	7.5	7.9	7.7	15.1	10.7	•
Total Liabilities to Net Worth **37**	1.0	•	1.5	1.5	1.9	1.8	1.8	1.3	0.7	0.8	•
Current Assets to Working Capital **38**	2.0	•	1.4	2.1	2.1	2.5	2.6	2.1	1.7	1.8	•
Current Liabilities to Working Capital **39**	1.0	•	0.4	1.1	1.1	1.5	1.6	1.1	0.7	0.8	•
Working Capital to Net Sales **40**	0.2	•	0.1	0.1	0.2	0.1	0.1	0.2	0.3	0.3	•
Inventory to Working Capital **41**	0.7	•	0.5	0.9	0.7	1.0	1.1	0.9	0.7	0.7	•
Total Receipts to Cash Flow **42**	5.4	4.6	6.4	6.8	7.3	7.4	8.8	6.5	5.6	4.8	•
Cost of Goods to Cash Flow **43**	3.6	2.7	4.3	4.7	5.2	5.2	6.5	4.3	3.4	2.9	•
Cash Flow to Total Debt **44**	0.6	•	1.4	0.7	0.5	0.5	0.4	0.5	0.6	0.5	•

Selected Financial Factors (in Percentages)

Debt Ratio **45**	50.1	•	60.4	59.3	66.0	63.9	63.9	57.4	41.0	45.1	•
Return on Total Assets **46**	17.3	•	28.3	21.6	15.5	15.4	16.4	16.3	13.1	14.2	•
Return on Equity Before Income Taxes **47**	31.6	•	69.6	50.3	39.7	36.6	39.4	32.4	19.8	23.2	•
Return on Equity After Income Taxes **48**	25.6	•	69.0	49.5	38.4	34.9	35.8	27.1	14.7	19.1	•
Profit Margin (Before Income Tax) **49**	9.9	9.7	5.0	6.9	5.2	5.3	5.8	7.1	8.2	12.4	•
Profit Margin (After Income Tax) **50**	8.0	8.6	5.0	6.8	5.0	5.1	5.3	6.0	6.1	10.2	•

Table I

Corporations with and without Net Income

GROCERY AND RELATED PRODUCT

MONEY AMOUNTS AND SIZE OF ASSETS IN THOUSANDS OF DOLLARS

Item Description for Accounting Period 7/05 Through 6/06	Total	Zero Assets	Under 500	500 to 1,000	1,000 to 5,000	5,000 to 10,000	10,000 to 25,000	25,000 to 50,000	50,000 to 100,000	100,000 to 250,000	250,000 to 500,000	500,000 to 2,500,000	2,500,000 and over
Number of Enterprises **1**	34280	4633	19910	2725	5145	961	574	173	74	50	15	17	3
Revenues ($ in Thousands)													
Net Sales **2**	441185488	1290485	17607437	9638486	52665265	34395210	38182686	25032793	21853545	25890479	26145917	72474794	116008390
Interest **3**	6169080	1091	6671	2001	18119	10514	18846	11668	6678	26932	9736	141827	5914999
Rents **4**	1054991	15	413	2200	14107	6093	7767	4662	1691	27405	9535	115361	865741
Royalties **5**	967347	0	0	0	0	0	5915	0	263	9794	0	10993	940382
Other Portfolio Income **6**	2992770	8481	29181	3492	28875	7408	18855	13164	3477	23862	36803	657857	2161317
Other Receipts **7**	4232341	62630	112811	41214	423073	119865	212144	127361	151512	265324	218481	992316	1505609
Total Receipts **8**	456602017	1362702	17756513	9687393	53149439	34539090	38446213	25189648	22017166	26243796	26420472	74393148	127396438
Average Total Receipts **9**	13320	294	892	3555	10330	35941	66979	145605	297529	524876	1761365	4376068	42465479
Operating Costs/Operating Income (%)													
Cost of Operations **10**	84.1	76.3	80.6	80.8	84.3	88.3	86.7	85.5	88.2	85.9	83.4	86.9	79.8
Salaries and Wages **11**	5.1	4.4	3.8	4.5	4.3	3.2	4.5	4.9	4.2	4.4	3.7	4.7	7.5
Taxes Paid **12**	1.0	1.0	1.0	1.1	0.9	0.6	0.7	0.8	0.8	1.6	0.6	0.6	1.4
Interest Paid **13**	0.9	0.9	0.3	0.4	0.4	0.4	0.4	0.4	0.4	0.6	0.4	0.4	2.3
Depreciation **14**	0.7	0.8	0.8	0.7	0.6	0.4	0.4	0.6	0.5	0.5	0.7	0.5	1.2
Amortization and Depletion **15**	0.1	0.1	0.0	0.0	0.1	0.0	0.0	0.1	0.1	0.2	0.1	0.2	0.2
Pensions and Other Deferred Comp. **16**	0.3	0.1	0.1	0.1	0.2	0.1	0.2	0.1	0.2	0.1	0.2	0.2	0.2
Employee Benefits **17**	0.5	0.1	0.4	0.3	0.4	0.3	0.5	0.5	0.5	0.5	0.5	0.6	0.5
Advertising **18**	0.5	0.1	0.2	0.3	0.2	0.3	0.3	0.4	0.7	1.1	0.4	0.5	0.7
Other Expenses **19**	6.7	10.8	8.9	7.5	6.4	5.4	4.5	5.0	3.8	4.8	9.1	6.4	8.5
Officers' Compensation **20**	0.8	3.5	3.2	3.9	2.1	0.8	1.0	0.6	0.6	0.7	0.2	0.1	0.2
Operating Margin **21**	•	1.8	0.6	0.3	0.1	0.3	0.7	1.1	0.2	•	0.7	•	•
Operating Margin Before Officers' Comp. **22**	0.0	5.3	3.8	4.2	2.2	1.1	1.7	1.7	0.7	0.3	0.9	•	•

Selected Average Balance Sheet ($ in Thousands)

Net Receivables 23	1040	0	29	171	764	2904	5417	11250	21486	32642	101398	142285	5222591
Inventories 24	684	0	16	169	438	1943	3996	9922	21375	36895	85927	202936	2120051
Net Property, Plant and Equipment 25	734	0	29	144	338	831	2226	6325	10446	26021	88987	222357	4033275
Total Assets 26	11898	0	134	773	2098	7263	15676	34681	68753	145698	358522	1070119	111455627
Notes and Loans Payable 27	1568	0	72	315	694	2176	4470	10310	23059	48167	68818	266317	10590787
All Other Liabilities 28	3244	0	39	238	719	3151	5834	12081	25340	51028	181725	429675	27720162
Net Worth 29	7086	0	23	220	685	1937	5371	12290	20354	46503	107979	374128	73144678

Selected Financial Ratios (Times to 1)

Current Ratio 30	1.4	.	1.5	1.9	1.7	1.3	1.5	1.6	1.5	1.5	1.4	1.3	1.3
Quick Ratio 31	1.0	.	1.1	1.1	1.1	0.8	0.8	0.9	0.7	0.7	0.8	0.4	1.0
Net Sales to Working Capital 32	11.7	.	38.5	15.1	16.5	25.3	17.8	15.0	16.7	16.9	26.5	30.8	5.3
Coverage Ratio 33	4.0	9.2	5.7	3.2	3.8	2.8	4.6	5.2	3.1	2.6	5.8	4.6	3.9
Total Asset Turnover 34	1.1	.	6.6	4.6	4.9	4.9	4.2	4.2	4.3	3.6	4.9	4.0	0.3
Inventory Turnover 35	15.8	.	43.8	16.9	19.7	16.3	14.4	12.5	12.2	12.0	16.9	18.3	14.6
Receivables Turnover 36	12.8	.	33.5	18.8	13.7	12.8	13.1	13.5	14.3	17.4	18.4	29.8	7.6
Total Liabilities to Net Worth 37	0.7	.	4.9	2.5	2.1	2.8	1.9	1.8	2.4	2.1	2.3	1.9	0.5
Current Assets to Working Capital 38	3.6	.	3.0	2.1	2.5	4.1	3.2	2.7	2.9	3.0	3.3	4.0	4.0
Current Liabilities to Working Capital 39	2.6	.	2.0	1.1	1.5	3.1	2.2	1.7	1.9	2.0	2.3	3.0	3.0
Working Capital to Net Sales 40	0.1	.	0.0	0.1	0.1	0.0	0.1	0.1	0.1	0.1	0.0	0.0	0.2
Inventory to Working Capital 41	0.6	.	0.7	0.7	0.7	1.4	1.1	1.0	1.2	1.4	1.3	1.5	0.3
Total Receipts to Cash Flow 42	13.0	6.7	12.0	15.0	16.8	21.9	21.0	18.3	25.6	22.1	10.5	17.1	7.7
Cost of Goods to Cash Flow 43	10.9	5.1	9.7	12.1	14.2	19.3	18.2	15.6	22.6	18.9	8.8	14.9	6.2
Cash Flow to Total Debt 44	0.2	.	0.7	0.4	0.4	0.3	0.3	0.4	0.2	0.2	0.7	0.4	0.1

Selected Financial Factors (in Percentages)

Debt Ratio 45	40.4	.	83.2	71.5	67.3	73.3	65.7	64.6	70.4	68.1	69.9	65.0	34.4
Return on Total Assets 46	3.9	.	11.6	5.4	7.0	5.2	7.8	8.7	5.8	5.5	10.1	7.4	3.2
Return on Equity Before Income Taxes 47	5.0	.	56.9	13.1	15.9	12.6	17.7	19.9	13.2	10.6	27.8	16.6	3.6
Return on Equity After Income Taxes 48	3.6	.	56.4	12.6	14.3	10.9	15.9	17.2	11.4	7.1	18.7	11.2	2.5
Profit Margin (Before Income Tax) 49	2.7	7.4	1.5	0.8	1.1	0.7	1.4	1.7	0.9	1.0	1.7	1.5	6.8
Profit Margin (After Income Tax) 50	2.0	6.9	1.4	0.8	1.0	0.6	1.3	1.5	0.8	0.6	1.0	1.2	4.7

Table II
Corporations with Net Income

GROCERY AND RELATED PRODUCT

MONEY AMOUNTS AND SIZE OF ASSETS IN THOUSANDS OF DOLLARS

Item Description for Accounting Period 7/05 Through 6/06	Total	Zero Assets	Under 500	500 to 1,000	1,000 to 5,000	5,000 to 10,000	10,000 to 25,000	25,000 to 50,000	50,000 to 100,000	100,000 to 250,000	250,000 to 500,000	500,000 to 2,500,000	2,500,000 and over
Number of Enterprises **1**	22535	3166	12312	1447	4132	736	460	150	63	39	•	12	•
Revenues ($ in Thousands)													
Net Sales **2**	375810315	982849	14218366	5845547	44850948	27768181	31270267	21520721	19121531	21425905	•	51573775	•
Interest **3**	6043544	916	5267	1961	14651	9521	13418	10478	5929	20509	•	36482	•
Rents **4**	1001328	15	0	1483	3436	6010	5996	4188	1559	16107	•	87828	•
Royalties **5**	951529	0	0	0	0	0	5906	0	263	324	•	4654	•
Other Portfolio Income **6**	2938662	7984	20055	2129	16264	7345	16791	10508	2387	13565	•	643517	•
Other Receipts **7**	3686782	54980	33915	26399	363134	76699	207912	107379	136272	231200	•	726057	•
Total Receipts **8**	390432160	1046744	14277603	5877519	45248433	27867756	31520290	21653274	19267941	21707610	•	53072313	•
Average Total Receipts **9**	17326	331	1160	4062	10951	37864	68522	144355	305840	556605	•	4422693	•
Operating Costs/Operating Income (%)													
Cost of Operations **10**	84.0	73.7	81.8	82.3	84.4	88.0	86.4	85.2	88.4	85.6	•	86.4	•
Salaries and Wages **11**	5.3	3.7	2.8	3.4	4.0	3.1	4.4	4.9	4.2	4.4	•	5.7	•
Taxes Paid **12**	1.0	1.0	0.8	1.1	0.9	0.6	0.7	0.8	0.9	1.8	•	0.8	•
Interest Paid **13**	1.0	0.2	0.2	0.5	0.3	0.3	0.4	0.4	0.4	0.6	•	0.4	•
Depreciation **14**	0.7	0.3	0.7	0.8	0.6	0.3	0.4	0.5	0.4	0.5	•	0.6	•
Amortization and Depletion **15**	0.1	0.1	0.0	0.0	0.1	0.0	0.0	0.0	0.1	0.1	•	0.2	•
Pensions and Other Deferred Comp. **16**	0.3	0.1	0.1	0.1	0.2	0.1	0.1	0.1	0.2	0.1	•	0.3	•
Employee Benefits **17**	0.6	0.0	0.3	0.4	0.4	0.3	0.5	0.4	0.4	0.5	•	0.7	•
Advertising **18**	0.5	0.1	0.1	0.3	0.1	0.2	0.2	0.4	0.6	0.8	•	0.6	•
Other Expenses **19**	6.1	7.7	7.7	6.5	5.8	5.1	4.3	4.9	3.5	4.5	•	4.9	•
Officers' Compensation **20**	0.7	3.4	2.4	2.0	2.1	0.8	1.1	0.7	0.6	0.8	•	0.1	•
Operating Margin **21**	•	9.6	3.0	2.7	1.1	1.2	1.4	1.6	0.4	0.2	•	•	•
Operating Margin Before Officers' Comp. **22**	0.4	13.0	5.4	4.7	3.3	2.0	2.5	2.3	1.0	1.0	•	1.0	•

Selected Average Balance Sheet ($ in Thousands)

Net Receivables 23	1411	0	34	162	789	2870	5451	11704	22850	33354	•	152599
Inventories 24	906	0	17	187	430	2000	4180	9836	22417	35785	•	242687
Net Property, Plant and Equipment 25	984	0	26	123	354	856	1990	6022	9302	26589	•	244843
Total Assets 26	17317	0	135	807	2090	7355	15370	35045	68078	144292	•	1011316
Notes and Loans Payable 27	2095	0	37	341	584	2249	3910	9918	21460	48596	•	247258
All Other Liabilities 28	4620	0	34	217	677	2900	5811	12365	26121	47909	•	420513
Net Worth 29	10601	0	64	250	829	2206	5649	12762	20497	47787	•	343544

Selected Financial Ratios (Times to 1)

Current Ratio 30	1.4	•	1.9	2.2	1.7	1.4	1.5	1.6	1.6	1.6	•	1.2
Quick Ratio 31	1.0	•	1.4	1.3	1.2	0.8	0.9	0.9	0.8	0.8	•	0.5
Net Sales to Working Capital 32	10.9	•	31.4	12.4	16.7	23.1	15.9	14.3	16.2	16.6	•	48.9
Coverage Ratio 33	4.7	76.2	15.7	7.5	7.8	5.6	7.0	6.8	3.9	3.8	•	6.9
Total Asset Turnover 34	1.0	•	8.5	5.0	5.2	5.1	4.4	4.1	4.5	3.8	•	4.2
Inventory Turnover 35	15.5	•	57.2	17.8	21.3	16.6	14.1	12.4	12.0	13.1	•	15.3
Receivables Turnover 36	12.2	•	35.7	23.9	14.0	13.3	13.0	13.3	14.0	18.9	•	28.9
Total Liabilities to Net Worth 37	0.6	•	1.1	2.2	1.5	2.3	1.7	1.7	2.3	2.0	•	1.9
Current Assets to Working Capital 38	3.6	•	2.1	1.8	2.3	3.7	2.9	2.7	2.8	2.8	•	5.7
Current Liabilities to Working Capital 39	2.6	•	1.1	0.8	1.3	2.7	1.9	1.7	1.8	1.8	•	4.7
Working Capital to Net Sales 40	0.1	•	0.0	0.1	0.1	0.0	0.1	0.1	0.1	0.1	•	0.0
Inventory to Working Capital 41	0.6	•	0.4	0.7	0.6	1.3	1.0	1.0	1.2	1.3	•	2.9
Total Receipts to Cash Flow 42	12.6	4.5	10.6	12.1	15.7	20.1	18.7	16.9	25.6	19.8	•	21.4
Cost of Goods to Cash Flow 43	10.6	3.3	8.7	9.9	13.3	17.7	16.2	14.4	22.6	17.0	•	18.5
Cash Flow to Total Debt 44	0.2	•	1.5	0.6	0.5	0.4	0.4	0.4	0.2	0.3	•	0.3

Selected Financial Factors (in Percentages)

Debt Ratio 45	38.8	•	52.4	69.1	60.3	70.0	63.2	63.6	69.9	66.9	•	66.0
Return on Total Assets 46	4.4	•	31.2	18.8	12.1	9.6	11.4	10.6	7.1	8.1	•	11.5
Return on Equity Before Income Taxes 47	5.6	•	61.3	52.8	26.5	26.3	26.5	24.8	17.6	17.9	•	28.9
Return on Equity After Income Taxes 48	4.3	•	61.1	51.9	25.0	24.4	24.4	21.9	15.6	13.5	•	20.7
Profit Margin (Before Income Tax) 49	3.6	16.1	3.4	3.3	2.0	1.5	2.2	2.2	1.2	1.6	•	2.3
Profit Margin (After Income Tax) 50	2.7	15.5	3.4	3.2	1.9	1.4	2.0	1.9	1.1	1.2	•	1.7

Table I

Corporations with and without Net Income

FARM PRODUCT RAW MATERIAL

MONEY AMOUNTS AND SIZE OF ASSETS IN THOUSANDS OF DOLLARS

Item Description for Accounting Period 7/05 Through 6/06	Total	Zero Assets	Under 500	500 to 1,000	1,000 to 5,000	5,000 to 10,000	10,000 to 25,000	25,000 to 50,000	50,000 to 100,000	100,000 to 250,000	250,000 to 500,000	500,000 to 2,500,000	2,500,000 and over
Number of Enterprises 1	5436	769	2392	796	1023	263	120	29	17	13	5	5	3
Revenues ($ in Thousands)													
Net Sales 2	99483523	190024	2687629	2986547	8309224	6421037	6264590	2923922	3251478	8325042	4643522	7839170	45641339
Interest 3	1438494	320	587	2784	10648	4772	7052	1938	5401	12088	21317	19632	1351956
Rents 4	101094	173	1	1576	12130	3566	655	3315	3677	913	879	2616	71593
Royalties 5	78774	0	0	0	1	303	0	128	0	0	0	20888	57455
Other Portfolio Income 6	824954	2432	5389	11972	19818	7600	2143	1834	4722	63085	950	18690	686318
Other Receipts 7	2245828	1197	25727	128464	142384	70230	107394	39350	35047	31122	20455	57810	1586645
Total Receipts 8	104172667	194146	2719333	3131343	8494205	6507508	6381834	2970487	3300325	8432250	4687123	7958806	49395306
Average Total Receipts 9	19163	252	1137	3934	8303	24743	53182	102431	194137	648635	937425	1591761	16465102
Operating Costs/Operating Income (%)													
Cost of Operations 10	91.4	87.2	84.0	86.5	88.1	89.2	90.9	91.2	92.2	95.9	95.9	87.4	92.4
Salaries and Wages 11	2.6	2.9	2.7	3.9	3.3	2.8	2.7	2.4	2.2	1.3	1.1	4.9	2.4
Taxes Paid 12	0.6	0.7	0.7	0.6	0.6	0.5	1.1	0.6	0.4	0.2	0.2	0.5	0.7
Interest Paid 13	2.1	0.6	0.1	0.2	0.9	0.5	0.5	0.6	0.8	0.4	0.7	1.3	3.8
Depreciation 14	0.8	1.6	0.5	0.6	0.8	0.6	0.5	0.9	0.5	0.3	0.3	0.8	0.9
Amortization and Depletion 15	0.0	•	0.0	0.0	0.0	0.0	0.0	0.0	0.0	0.1	0.0	0.1	0.1
Pensions and Other Deferred Comp. 16	0.3	0.0	0.2	0.2	0.1	0.3	0.1	0.1	0.1	0.1	0.1	0.2	0.4
Employee Benefits 17	0.5	0.1	0.1	0.3	0.4	0.2	0.2	0.3	0.2	0.2	0.1	1.0	0.6
Advertising 18	0.1	0.0	0.2	0.2	0.1	0.2	0.1	0.1	0.1	0.5	0.1	0.1	0.1
Other Expenses 19	3.6	7.9	11.1	6.2	5.1	3.4	3.6	3.9	3.1	1.8	1.3	3.4	3.3
Officers' Compensation 20	0.9	0.8	2.4	2.4	1.5	1.4	0.5	0.4	0.5	0.1	0.4	0.2	0.9
Operating Margin 21	•	•	•	•	•	0.9	•	•	0.1	•	•	0.2	•
Operating Margin Before Officers' Comp. 22	•	•	0.4	1.3	0.5	2.4	0.2	0.1	0.6	•	0.4	0.2	0.4

Selected Average Balance Sheet ($ in Thousands)

Net Receivables 23	3428	0	49	155	718	2586	5039	13848	14808	38869	76889	150609	4692936
Inventories 24	1901	0	4	62	387	1363	3772	7125	26553	41536	78802	269147	2043953
Net Property, Plant and Equipment 25	1253	0	41	165	538	1621	2358	7921	9917	23932	16460	112067	1323087
Total Assets 26	12710	0	190	736	2422	7055	15504	37368	69949	149592	279948	739643	17513477
Notes and Loans Payable 27	4539	0	82	237	1262	1896	4043	10217	21074	36815	128034	271058	6295153
All Other Liabilities 28	4359	0	101	126	686	3092	6785	17390	22037	60343	91755	314603	5776690
Net Worth 29	3812	0	7	373	475	2067	4676	9761	26838	52433	60159	153983	5441635

Selected Financial Ratios (Times to 1)

Current Ratio 30	1.3	•	1.1	1.9	1.7	1.3	1.4	1.2	1.4	1.5	1.4	1.4	1.3
Quick Ratio 31	0.7	•	1.0	1.5	1.0	0.9	0.8	0.7	0.6	0.7	0.5	0.4	0.7
Net Sales to Working Capital 32	10.1	•	90.6	16.7	11.7	21.5	16.0	21.8	14.9	16.7	12.4	10.2	7.3
Coverage Ratio 33	2.2	1.4	•	18.4	2.3	5.8	4.2	3.2	3.0	3.1	1.8	2.4	2.0
Total Asset Turnover 34	1.4	•	5.9	5.1	3.4	3.5	3.4	2.7	2.7	4.3	3.3	2.1	0.9
Inventory Turnover 35	8.8	•	235.3	52.1	18.5	16.0	12.6	12.9	6.6	14.8	11.3	5.1	6.9
Receivables Turnover 36	4.9	•	23.3	23.9	12.2	7.9	11.6	9.2	6.6	15.6	12.5	11.3	2.9
Total Liabilities to Net Worth 37	2.3	•	26.1	1.0	4.1	2.4	2.3	2.8	1.6	1.9	3.7	3.8	2.2
Current Assets to Working Capital 38	3.9	•	9.5	2.2	2.4	4.6	3.7	5.8	3.3	2.8	3.3	3.6	4.2
Current Liabilities to Working Capital 39	2.9	•	8.5	1.2	1.4	3.6	2.7	4.8	2.3	1.8	2.3	2.6	3.2
Working Capital to Net Sales 40	0.1	•	0.0	0.1	0.1	0.0	0.1	0.0	0.1	0.1	0.1	0.1	0.1
Inventory to Working Capital 41	1.1	•	0.2	0.3	0.5	1.2	1.2	1.8	1.8	1.1	1.3	1.9	1.1
Total Receipts to Cash Flow 42	23.4	14.6	12.6	12.0	19.6	19.2	22.9	27.6	24.7	45.2	65.3	32.0	22.7
Cost of Goods to Cash Flow 43	21.4	12.7	10.6	10.4	17.3	17.1	20.8	25.2	22.8	43.3	62.6	28.0	21.0
Cash Flow to Total Debt 44	0.1	0.5	0.9	0.9	0.2	0.3	0.2	0.1	0.2	0.1	0.1	0.1	0.1

Selected Financial Factors (in Percentages)

Debt Ratio 45	70.0	•	96.3	49.3	80.4	70.7	69.8	73.9	61.6	64.9	78.5	79.2	68.9
Return on Total Assets 46	6.6	•	•	20.4	6.8	9.5	7.0	4.8	6.5	5.6	4.1	6.4	6.5
Return on Equity Before Income Taxes 47	11.9	•	•	38.0	19.8	26.9	17.7	12.7	11.3	10.8	8.3	17.9	10.4
Return on Equity After Income Taxes 48	8.4	•	•	35.9	16.8	25.8	15.0	10.0	8.6	7.8	4.0	11.1	6.9
Profit Margin (Before Income Tax) 49	2.5	0.2	3.8	1.2	2.3	1.6	1.2	1.6	0.9	0.5	0.5	1.8	3.7
Profit Margin (After Income Tax) 50	1.8	•	3.6	1.0	2.2	1.3	1.0	1.2	0.6	0.3	0.1	1.1	2.5

Table II

Corporations with Net Income

FARM PRODUCT RAW MATERIAL

MONEY AMOUNTS AND SIZE OF ASSETS IN THOUSANDS OF DOLLARS

Item Description for Accounting Period 7/05 Through 6/06	Total	Zero Assets	Under 500	500 to 1,000	1,000 to 5,000	5,000 to 10,000	10,000 to 25,000	25,000 to 50,000	50,000 to 100,000	100,000 to 250,000	250,000 to 500,000	500,000 to 2,500,000	2,500,000 and over
Number of Enterprises 1	3607	361	1619	555	664	244	101	•	•	•	•	•	0

Revenues ($ in Thousands)

	Total	Zero Assets	Under 500	500 to 1,000	1,000 to 5,000	5,000 to 10,000	10,000 to 25,000	25,000 to 50,000	50,000 to 100,000	100,000 to 250,000	250,000 to 500,000	500,000 to 2,500,000	2,500,000 and over
Net Sales 2	83805793	182465	2079704	1146619	6593671	6188453	5656141	•	•	•	•	•	0
Interest 3	1095502	320	587	2357	7629	4104	6203	•	•	•	•	•	0
Rents 4	96868	173	1	165	11532	3566	617	•	•	•	•	•	0
Royalties 5	78774	0	0	0	1	303	0	•	•	•	•	•	0
Other Portfolio Income 6	720835	2098	5389	3874	16620	7600	1642	•	•	•	•	•	0
Other Receipts 7	1815129	1198	25727	41104	56007	68649	97461	•	•	•	•	•	0
Total Receipts 8	87612901	186254	2111408	1194119	6685460	6272675	5762064	•	•	•	•	•	0
Average Total Receipts 9	24290	516	1304	2152	10068	25708	57050	•	•	•	•	•	•

Operating Costs/Operating Income (%)

	Total	Zero Assets	Under 500	500 to 1,000	1,000 to 5,000	5,000 to 10,000	10,000 to 25,000	25,000 to 50,000	50,000 to 100,000	100,000 to 250,000	250,000 to 500,000	500,000 to 2,500,000	2,500,000 and over
Cost of Operations 10	91.5	88.2	86.1	71.0	87.7	89.1	91.1	•	•	•	•	•	•
Salaries and Wages 11	2.5	2.9	1.1	6.6	2.8	2.8	2.7	•	•	•	•	•	•
Taxes Paid 12	0.6	0.6	0.6	1.1	0.5	0.4	1.2	•	•	•	•	•	•
Interest Paid 13	1.7	0.6	0.1	0.2	0.6	0.4	0.4	•	•	•	•	•	•
Depreciation 14	0.7	1.6	0.4	1.0	0.7	0.5	0.5	•	•	•	•	•	•
Amortization and Depletion 15	0.1	•	0.0	0.0	0.0	0.0	0.0	•	•	•	•	•	•
Pensions and Other Deferred Comp. 16	0.3	•	0.3	0.5	0.2	0.3	0.1	•	•	•	•	•	•
Employee Benefits 17	0.4	0.1	0.1	0.1	0.3	0.2	0.2	•	•	•	•	•	•
Advertising 18	0.1	0.0	0.2	0.2	0.1	0.2	0.1	•	•	•	•	•	•
Other Expenses 19	3.1	5.4	8.3	8.0	4.7	3.4	3.2	•	•	•	•	•	•
Officers' Compensation 20	0.9	0.3	3.0	2.5	1.5	1.5	0.4	•	•	•	•	•	•
Operating Margin 21	•	0.2	•	8.9	0.8	1.1	0.1	•	•	•	•	•	•
Operating Margin Before Officers' Comp. 22	•	0.5	2.8	11.4	2.3	2.6	0.5	•	•	•	•	•	•

Selected Average Balance Sheet ($ in Thousands)

Net Receivables 23	4720	0	72	124	777	2665	4951
Inventories 24	2467	0	5	69	469	1121	3606
Net Property, Plant and Equipment 25	1559	0	48	187	458	1491	2118
Total Assets 26	15405	0	242	714	2530	7083	15566
Notes and Loans Payable 27	4469	0	29	163	1132	1689	3809
All Other Liabilities 28	5840	0	122	46	758	3247	6671
Net Worth 29	5096	0	91	505	641	2147	5086

Selected Financial Ratios (Times to 1)

Current Ratio 30	1.3	•	1.3	2.5	2.2	1.3	1.4
Quick Ratio 31	0.8	•	1.2	2.0	1.2	0.9	0.9
Net Sales to Working Capital 32	11.8	•	35.2	7.2	9.6	20.4	15.5
Coverage Ratio 33	2.9	4.9	9.8	74.1	4.6	7.4	6.3
Total Asset Turnover 34	1.5	•	5.3	2.9	3.9	3.6	3.6
Inventory Turnover 35	8.6	•	209.2	21.2	18.6	20.2	14.2
Receivables Turnover 36	4.5	•	18.2	15.4	12.8	9.6	22.6
Total Liabilities to Net Worth 37	2.0	•	1.7	0.4	3.0	2.3	2.1
Current Assets to Working Capital 38	4.4	•	4.5	1.7	1.8	4.3	3.4
Current Liabilities to Working Capital 39	3.4	•	3.5	0.7	0.8	3.3	2.4
Working Capital to Net Sales 40	0.1	•	0.0	0.1	0.1	0.0	0.1
Inventory to Working Capital 41	1.4	•	0.1	0.3	0.4	1.1	1.0
Total Receipts to Cash Flow 42	22.2	16.3	14.2	5.1	16.9	18.5	22.7
Cost of Goods to Cash Flow 43	20.3	14.4	12.2	3.6	14.8	16.5	20.7
Cash Flow to Total Debt 44	0.1	•	0.6	2.0	0.3	0.3	0.2

Selected Financial Factors (in Percentages)

Debt Ratio 45	66.9	•	62.4	29.2	74.7	69.7	67.3
Return on Total Assets 46	7.4	•	7.5	38.4	11.0	10.3	8.4
Return on Equity Before Income Taxes 47	14.5	•	17.9	53.5	33.9	29.4	21.6
Return on Equity After Income Taxes 48	10.6	•	17.0	51.3	30.5	28.3	18.6
Profit Margin (Before Income Tax) 49	3.2	2.3	1.3	13.1	2.2	2.5	2.0
Profit Margin (After Income Tax) 50	2.3	1.9	1.2	12.5	2.0	2.4	1.7

Table I

Corporations with and without Net Income

CHEMICAL AND ALLIED PRODUCTS

MONEY AMOUNTS AND SIZE OF ASSETS IN THOUSANDS OF DOLLARS

Item Description for Accounting Period 7/05 Through 6/06	Total	Zero Assets	Under 500	500 to 1,000	1,000 to 5,000	5,000 to 10,000	10,000 to 25,000	25,000 to 50,000	50,000 to 100,000	100,000 to 250,000	250,000 to 500,000	500,000 to 2,500,000	2,500,000 and over
Number of Enterprises 1	8943	1265	5118	661	1350	205	217	59	29	23	5	12	0
Revenues ($ in Thousands)													
Net Sales 2	65059163	469340	1511460	1554348	8474503	5297033	8573182	5864811	4394914	6769465	2749991	19400115	0
Interest 3	151887	316	54	248	7639	7504	3524	4496	7567	9472	7593	103475	0
Rents 4	25173	0	0	873	857	454	1336	648	3365	6154	696	10790	0
Royalties 5	124852	0	0	0	0	0	0	985	511	92	0	123264	0
Other Portfolio Income 6	266523	21	603	0	1890	14158	54506	3573	6400	57736	21578	106057	0
Other Receipts 7	1158238	19602	17643	8849	49966	28154	92515	51678	36467	252561	48199	552608	0
Total Receipts 8	66785836	489279	1529760	1564318	8534855	5347303	8725063	5926191	4449224	7095480	2828057	20296309	0
Average Total Receipts 9	7468	387	299	2367	6322	26084	40208	100444	153422	308499	565611	1691359	•
Operating Costs/Operating Income (%)													
Cost of Operations 10	78.3	65.4	58.5	48.3	70.4	82.5	79.9	84.1	83.9	88.6	79.5	77.4	•
Salaries and Wages 11	5.8	4.0	10.7	14.2	7.6	5.1	5.3	5.3	4.2	2.5	3.9	6.4	•
Taxes Paid 12	1.0	1.8	2.2	2.3	1.2	0.8	0.9	0.8	0.9	0.7	0.5	1.2	•
Interest Paid 13	1.0	0.3	1.1	0.5	0.6	0.2	0.5	0.6	0.9	0.6	0.9	2.1	•
Depreciation 14	1.3	0.6	1.0	1.3	0.7	0.5	0.7	0.7	0.9	0.5	0.9	2.6	•
Amortization and Depletion 15	0.2	0.0	0.0	0.0	0.0	0.0	0.1	0.0	0.2	0.2	0.1	0.5	•
Pensions and Other Deferred Comp. 16	0.4	0.4	0.0	1.1	0.5	0.5	0.2	0.4	0.2	0.1	0.6	0.5	•
Employee Benefits 17	0.8	0.9	1.0	2.0	0.7	0.4	0.6	0.6	0.7	0.3	0.3	1.4	•
Advertising 18	0.3	0.3	0.6	0.3	0.8	0.1	0.2	0.2	0.1	0.1	0.8	0.1	•
Other Expenses 19	8.2	14.8	17.4	15.0	10.1	6.2	7.8	4.8	4.5	6.7	10.5	8.8	•
Officers' Compensation 20	1.7	6.7	9.6	8.8	3.3	1.6	1.9	1.0	0.9	0.6	0.2	0.6	•
Operating Margin 21	0.9	4.9	•	6.3	4.0	2.1	2.0	1.6	2.5	•	1.8	•	•
Operating Margin Before Officers' Comp. 22	2.6	11.6	7.3	15.1	7.3	3.8	3.9	2.6	3.4	•	2.0	•	•

Selected Average Balance Sheet ($ in Thousands)

	1	2	3	4	5	6	7	8	9	10	11	12	13
Net Receivables 23	909	0	30	211	833	2850	5570	13522	18804	42067	117853	167850	•
Inventories 24	644	0	17	125	438	1892	4088	8961	18909	28592	46103	146306	•
Net Property, Plant and Equipment 25	739	0	13	170	238	835	2154	4734	13635	17477	45847	347309	•
Total Assets 26	3995	0	90	667	2221	7069	15602	36335	70509	137019	323751	1503330	•
Notes and Loans Payable 27	1170	0	76	277	633	763	4766	9277	21235	25966	85215	471531	•
All Other Liabilities 28	1470	0	34	246	753	3247	5674	12005	23128	58959	136964	539877	•
Net Worth 29	1355	0	-21	144	835	3058	5162	15053	26146	52093	101572	491921	•

Selected Financial Ratios (Times to 1)

	1	2	3	4	5	6	7	8	9	10	11	12	13
Current Ratio 30	1.4	•	1.5	1.6	1.9	1.5	1.5	1.6	1.5	1.4	1.3	1.3	•
Quick Ratio 31	0.8	•	1.1	1.1	1.3	1.1	0.8	0.9	0.9	0.8	0.8	0.6	•
Net Sales to Working Capital 32	11.0	•	11.6	17.8	13.2	7.4	9.5	12.1	9.2	12.2	12.4	12.6	•
Coverage Ratio 33	4.5	27.6	0.1	14.2	8.8	13.8	8.2	5.8	5.1	7.3	6.4	2.6	•
Total Asset Turnover 34	1.8	•	3.3	3.5	2.8	3.7	2.5	2.7	2.1	1.7	1.1	1.1	•
Inventory Turnover 35	8.8	•	10.3	9.1	10.1	11.3	7.7	9.3	6.7	9.1	9.5	8.5	•
Receivables Turnover 36	8.4	•	10.5	9.0	7.8	9.0	7.9	7.3	6.9	8.1	6.0	10.3	•
Total Liabilities to Net Worth 37	1.9	•	•	3.6	1.7	1.3	2.0	1.4	1.7	1.6	2.2	2.1	•
Current Assets to Working Capital 38	3.3	•	2.8	3.0	2.1	2.8	2.9	3.2	2.6	3.6	4.6	4.4	•
Current Liabilities to Working Capital 39	2.3	•	1.8	2.0	1.1	1.8	1.9	2.2	1.6	2.6	3.6	3.4	•
Working Capital to Net Sales 40	0.1	•	0.1	0.1	0.1	0.1	0.1	0.1	0.1	0.1	0.1	0.1	•
Inventory to Working Capital 41	1.0	•	0.6	0.7	0.5	0.7	1.0	1.1	1.0	1.4	1.1	1.2	•
Total Receipts to Cash Flow 42	10.0	8.2	5.2	7.6	12.2	10.1	15.9	13.7	10.2	7.1	10.7	•	•
Cost of Goods to Cash Flow 43	7.8	4.8	2.5	5.4	10.0	8.1	13.4	11.5	9.0	5.6	8.3	•	•
Cash Flow to Total Debt 44	0.3	0.3	0.9	0.6	0.5	0.4	0.3	0.3	0.2	0.3	0.3	0.1	•

Selected Financial Factors (in Percentages)

	1	2	3	4	5	6	7	8	9	10	11	12	13
Debt Ratio 45	66.1	123.2	78.4	62.4	56.7	66.9	58.6	62.9	62.0	68.6	67.3	•	•
Return on Total Assets 46	8.7	0.2	26.2	15.1	11.9	10.8	9.3	10.1	10.0	9.7	5.9	•	•
Return on Equity Before Income Taxes 47	19.9	15.2	112.9	35.7	25.6	28.8	18.5	21.9	22.6	26.1	11.2	•	•
Return on Equity After Income Taxes 48	16.6	16.1	98.2	33.8	21.2	26.6	16.9	18.5	17.0	21.6	8.2	•	•
Profit Margin (Before Income Tax) 49	3.7	9.2	6.9	4.8	3.0	3.8	2.8	3.8	4.0	4.8	3.4	•	•
Profit Margin (After Income Tax) 50	3.1	8.4	6.0	4.5	2.5	3.5	2.6	3.2	3.0	4.0	2.5	•	•

Table II

Corporations with Net Income

CHEMICAL AND ALLIED PRODUCTS

MONEY AMOUNTS AND SIZE OF ASSETS IN THOUSANDS OF DOLLARS

Item Description for Accounting Period 7/05 Through 6/06	Total	Zero Assets	Under 500	500 to 1,000	1,000 to 5,000	5,000 to 10,000	10,000 to 25,000	25,000 to 50,000	50,000 to 100,000	100,000 to 250,000	250,000 to 500,000	500,000 to 2,500,000	2,500,000 and over
Number of Enterprises 1	4558	431	2177	419	1033	•	189	48	23	20	•	•	0
Revenues ($ in Thousands)													
Net Sales 2	58393270	351215	843670	999301	7240257		7878815	4976671	3851142	5675355			0
Interest 3	138400	316	1	211	5501		3193	2638	6607	8936			0
Rents 4	24026	0	0	0	857		1336	473	3267	6154			0
Royalties 5	124852	0	0	0	0		0	985	511	92			0
Other Portfolio Income 6	261296	0	603	0	1777		53397	2974	3014	57736			0
Other Receipts 7	937292	228	17335	8842	48116		86897	49178	36055	65276			0
Total Receipts 8	59879136	351759	861609	1008354	7296508		8023638	5032919	3900596	5813549			0
Average Total Receipts 9	13137	816	396	2407	7063		42453	104852	169591	290677			•
Operating Costs/Operating Income (%)													
Cost of Operations 10	78.8	67.5	54.5	53.5	69.1		80.4	83.3	84.1	88.2			•
Salaries and Wages 11	5.6	1.3	10.3	10.3	7.3		4.9	5.6	4.2	2.7			•
Taxes Paid 12	1.0	0.9	2.4	2.0	1.2		0.9	0.8	0.8	0.8			•
Interest Paid 13	1.0	0.3	1.1	0.6	0.6		0.5	0.6	0.6	0.7			•
Depreciation 14	1.2	0.5	1.1	0.9	0.8		0.6	0.6	0.7	0.5			•
Amortization and Depletion 15	0.2	0.0	0.1	0.0	0.0		0.0	0.0	0.1	0.2			•
Pensions and Other Deferred Comp. 16	0.4	0.0	0.0	1.7	0.5		0.2	0.4	0.2	0.2			•
Employee Benefits 17	0.8	0.2	1.6	0.9	0.7		0.5	0.6	0.5	0.4			•
Advertising 18	0.3	0.2	0.3	0.4	0.9		0.2	0.2	0.1	0.1			•
Other Expenses 19	7.2	11.6	12.6	12.7	10.1		7.4	4.4	4.1	3.2			•
Officers' Compensation 20	1.5	2.6	10.7	5.9	3.5		1.9	1.0	0.8	0.6			•
Operating Margin 21	2.0	14.8	5.3	11.2	5.3		2.5	2.5	3.7	2.4			•
Operating Margin Before Officers' Comp. 22	3.5	17.5	16.0	17.1	8.7		4.4	3.5	4.5	3.1			•

Selected Average Balance Sheet ($ in Thousands)

Net Receivables 23	1604	0	49	180	902	•	5997	14202	20041	39226
Inventories 24	1096	0	22	113	485	•	4250	10007	20405	28483
Net Property, Plant and Equipment 25	1286	0	20	180	277	•	1710	4133	13340	19397
Total Assets 26	7031	0	115	680	2242	•	15828	36826	71409	141743
Notes and Loans Payable 27	1944	0	68	309	654	•	4473	9033	17918	28132
All Other Liabilities 28	2529	0	40	199	764	•	6030	12224	23997	57793
Net Worth 29	2558	0	7	171	825	•	5324	15569	29494	55818

Selected Financial Ratios (Times to 1)

Current Ratio 30	1.4	•	1.3	1.7	1.8	•	1.5	1.5	1.6	1.4
Quick Ratio 31	0.8	•	0.9	1.3	1.2	•	0.8	0.9	0.8	0.7
Net Sales to Working Capital 32	11.0	•	18.1	17.5	8.7	•	9.2	12.7	9.8	12.2
Coverage Ratio 33	5.6	46.1	7.5	22.9	11.0	•	9.4	7.7	9.9	8.4
Total Asset Turnover 34	1.8	•	3.4	3.5	3.1	•	2.6	2.8	2.3	2.0
Inventory Turnover 35	9.2	•	9.6	11.3	10.0	•	7.9	8.6	6.9	8.8
Receivables Turnover 36	8.5	•	8.7	8.9	7.6	•	8.0	6.9	7.7	8.4
Total Liabilities to Net Worth 37	1.7	•	14.6	3.0	1.7	•	2.0	1.4	1.4	1.5
Current Assets to Working Capital 38	3.3	•	4.2	2.5	2.2	•	2.9	3.2	2.7	3.7
Current Liabilities to Working Capital 39	2.3	•	3.2	1.5	1.2	•	1.9	2.2	1.7	2.7
Working Capital to Net Sales 40	0.1	•	0.1	0.1	0.1	•	0.1	0.1	0.1	0.1
Inventory to Working Capital 41	1.0	•	1.0	0.5	0.6	•	1.1	1.1	1.1	1.6
Total Receipts to Cash Flow 42	10.0	4.1	6.0	4.6	6.9	•	9.9	14.6	12.1	13.9
Cost of Goods to Cash Flow 43	7.9	2.8	3.3	2.5	4.8	•	8.0	12.2	10.1	12.3
Cash Flow to Total Debt 44	0.3	•	0.6	1.0	0.7	•	0.4	0.3	0.3	0.2

Selected Financial Factors (in Percentages)

Debt Ratio 45	63.6	•	93.6	74.8	63.2	•	66.4	57.7	58.7	60.6
Return on Total Assets 46	10.4	•	28.9	44.5	20.8	•	12.8	12.1	13.1	11.3
Return on Equity Before Income Taxes 47	23.4	•	389.5	169.1	51.4	•	34.1	24.9	28.5	25.2
Return on Equity After Income Taxes 48	20.0	•	383.2	149.5	48.8	•	31.7	23.0	24.6	19.2
Profit Margin (Before Income Tax) 49	4.7	15.0	7.4	12.1	6.1	•	4.4	3.7	5.0	5.0
Profit Margin (After Income Tax) 50	4.0	14.0	7.3	10.7	5.7	•	4.0	3.4	4.3	3.8

Table I

Corporations with and without Net Income

PETROLEUM AND PETROLEUM PRODUCTS

MONEY AMOUNTS AND SIZE OF ASSETS IN THOUSANDS OF DOLLARS

Item Description for Accounting Period 7/05 Through 6/06		Total	Zero Assets	Under 500	500 to 1,000	1,000 to 5,000	5,000 to 10,000	10,000 to 25,000	25,000 to 50,000	50,000 to 100,000	100,000 to 250,000	250,000 to 500,000	500,000 to 2,500,000	2,500,000 and over
Number of Enterprises	1	9904	844	5026	630	2207	603	363	138	32	33	7	15	6
Revenues ($ in Thousands)														
Net Sales	2	418664089	52944224	2964140	3233411	41516221	36412929	39430235	30683336	13634034	38393024	20185989	65064220	74202326
Interest	3	450020	59541	4450	2283	16126	14314	11425	13141	1764	11255	9253	107298	199170
Rents	4	291203	0	2227	743	31260	50646	35183	25265	8553	15274	10266	104596	7189
Royalties	5	54734	0	0	0	160	150	1209	550	515	1180	8	268	50694
Other Portfolio Income	6	4729247	632428	25499	856	49228	78247	43032	46489	9190	14649	58495	40854	3730282
Other Receipts	7	1381554	275764	1797	2241	179939	145618	167661	137940	53409	141229	-19289	145251	149993
Total Receipts	8	425570847	53911957	2998113	3239534	41792934	36701904	39688745	30906721	13707465	38576611	20244722	65462487	78339654
Average Total Receipts	9	42970	63877	597	5142	18937	60866	109335	223962	428358	1168988	2892103	4364166	13056609
Operating Costs/Operating Income (%)														
Cost of Operations	10	91.0	96.0	78.3	90.5	91.5	91.3	93.1	93.3	93.6	96.5	97.3	96.7	75.4
Salaries and Wages	11	1.7	0.8	7.9	2.0	2.4	1.9	2.0	2.0	2.1	0.7	0.7	0.6	2.9
Taxes Paid	12	0.8	0.3	2.1	1.0	0.5	2.9	0.8	0.4	0.3	0.4	0.2	0.2	1.2
Interest Paid	13	0.6	0.6	0.4	0.2	0.2	0.3	0.2	0.3	0.3	0.2	0.2	0.4	1.7
Depreciation	14	0.6	0.2	1.4	0.8	0.5	0.4	0.5	0.6	0.5	0.2	0.2	0.3	1.7
Amortization and Depletion	15	0.1	0.1	0.1	0.0	0.0	0.0	0.0	0.0	0.1	0.1	0.0	0.1	0.4
Pensions and Other Deferred Comp.	16	0.1	0.1	0.1	0.0	0.1	0.1	0.1	0.0	0.0	0.0	0.0	0.0	0.6
Employee Benefits	17	0.2	0.3	0.2	0.2	0.1	0.1	0.1	0.2	0.1	0.1	0.1	0.1	0.7
Advertising	18	0.1	0.0	0.4	0.2	0.1	0.1	0.1	0.0	0.1	0.0	0.0	0.0	0.4
Other Expenses	19	3.7	1.8	8.9	4.3	3.6	2.5	2.6	2.5	2.3	1.0	0.8	1.3	11.1
Officers' Compensation	20	0.3	0.0	2.9	1.6	0.8	0.4	0.3	0.3	0.7	0.1	0.1	0.3	0.1
Operating Margin	21	0.7	•	•	•	0.1	0.1	0.0	0.3	•	0.6	0.3	0.0	3.8
Operating Margin Before Officers' Comp.	22	1.1	•	0.1	0.8	0.9	0.5	0.4	0.5	0.6	0.7	0.4	0.3	3.9

Selected Average Balance Sheet ($ in Thousands)

Net Receivables 23	2215	0	26	299	934	2744	5062	11647	25454	69338	134888	343008	876746
Inventories 24	869	0	17	92	348	678	1708	3989	9917	24689	76425	181254	288251
Net Property, Plant and Equipment 25	4510	0	29	141	531	1833	4443	10637	20437	24919	61298	218108	5650016
Total Assets 26	13441	0	133	747	2489	7048	15092	35649	67882	156943	334817	1001145	14521877
Notes and Loans Payable 27	3088	0	60	167	744	2426	4394	10978	23417	39072	88682	263810	2891120
All Other Liabilities 28	4428	0	20	308	924	2730	5912	14435	29092	79343	167092	523565	3861139
Net Worth 29	5925	0	53	272	821	1893	4786	10235	15374	38528	79043	213770	7769618

Selected Financial Ratios (Times to 1)

Current Ratio 30	1.4	•	3.3	1.5	1.6	1.4	1.2	1.2	1.3	1.2	1.2	1.2	1.5
Quick Ratio 31	0.7	•	2.4	1.2	1.1	1.1	0.9	0.9	0.9	0.9	0.8	0.7	0.5
Net Sales to Working Capital 32	28.5	•	10.3	30.1	28.4	44.0	66.1	65.9	64.1	39.8	90.9	36.5	9.6
Coverage Ratio 33	5.5	3.9	•	•	5.1	3.9	4.0	2.6	6.9	4.6	2.6	7.0	
Total Asset Turnover 34	3.1	•	4.4	6.9	7.6	8.6	7.2	6.2	7.4	7.4	8.6	4.3	0.9
Inventory Turnover 35	44.3	•	27.1	50.7	49.4	81.3	59.2	52.0	40.2	45.5	36.7	23.2	32.4
Receivables Turnover 36	21.0	•	22.5	17.2	21.0	25.8	22.3	21.4	15.2	20.6	21.8	15.2	14.6
Total Liabilities to Net Worth 37	1.3	•	1.5	1.7	2.0	2.7	2.5	2.2	3.4	3.1	3.2	3.7	0.9
Current Assets to Working Capital 38	3.6	•	1.4	3.0	2.6	3.3	5.4	6.0	6.0	4.0	7.2	5.6	2.9
Current Liabilities to Working Capital 39	2.6	•	0.4	2.0	1.6	2.3	4.4	5.0	5.0	3.0	6.2	4.6	1.9
Working Capital to Net Sales 40	0.0	•	0.1	0.0	0.0	0.0	0.0	0.0	0.0	0.0	0.0	0.0	0.1
Inventory to Working Capital 41	0.7	•	0.4	0.5	0.6	0.6	1.1	1.3	1.2	1.0	1.3	1.8	0.4
Total Receipts to Cash Flow 42	19.3	30.7	19.2	35.6	30.5	37.4	38.9	35.9	46.2	58.2	81.0	64.9	5.6
Cost of Goods to Cash Flow 43	17.6	29.5	15.1	32.3	27.9	34.1	36.2	33.5	43.3	56.2	78.8	62.8	4.2
Cash Flow to Total Debt 44	0.3	•	0.4	0.3	0.4	0.3	0.2	0.2	0.2	0.2	0.1	0.1	0.3

Selected Financial Factors (in Percentages)

Debt Ratio 45	55.9	•	59.8	63.6	67.0	73.1	68.3	71.3	77.4	75.5	76.4	78.6	46.5
Return on Total Assets 46	9.9	•	•	•	7.5	9.8	7.0	8.2	5.2	9.3	7.1	4.4	10.2
Return on Equity Before Income Taxes 47	18.4	•	•	•	18.3	27.8	16.5	21.4	14.0	23.4	12.9		16.4
Return on Equity After Income Taxes 48	13.4	•	•	•	17.1	24.4	15.2	17.8	12.1	27.3	18.4		11.6
Profit Margin (Before Income Tax) 49	2.6	1.9	•	0.8	0.9	0.7	1.0	0.5	1.1	0.6	0.6	0.6	10.3
Profit Margin (After Income Tax) 50	1.9	1.3	•	0.7	0.8	0.7	0.8	0.4	0.9	0.5	0.4	0.4	7.3

Table II

Corporations with Net Income

PETROLEUM AND PETROLEUM PRODUCTS

MONEY AMOUNTS AND SIZE OF ASSETS IN THOUSANDS OF DOLLARS

Item Description for Accounting Period 7/05 Through 6/06	Total	Zero Assets	Under 500	500 to 1,000	1,000 to 5,000	5,000 to 10,000	10,000 to 25,000	25,000 to 50,000	50,000 to 100,000	100,000 to 250,000	250,000 to 500,000	500,000 to 2,500,000	2,500,000 and over
Number of Enterprises **1**	5802	435	2118	493	1752	508	300	119	•	29	•	12	6
Revenues ($ in Thousands)													
Net Sales **2**	352438611	36349237	1876725	2483876	35644633	28424931	34200205	27436128	•	35464225	•	50978892	74202326
Interest **3**	422446	54322	4022	1431	13232	12330	10667	9113	•	6653	•	101427	199170
Rents **4**	178839	0	999	743	28766	30826	33561	23763	•	15274	•	26921	7189
Royalties **5**	54134	0	0	0	160	150	1209	550	•	1180	•	182	50694
Other Portfolio Income **6**	4695155	631772	25499	502	47593	75449	29585	43939	•	13886	•	38841	3730282
Other Receipts **7**	1227766	270184	1485	1585	163004	129014	136002	112918	•	133961	•	115678	149993
Total Receipts **8**	359016951	37305515	1908730	2488137	35897388	28672700	34411229	27626411	•	35634979	•	51261941	78339654
Average Total Receipts **9**	61878	85760	901	5047	20489	56442	114704	232155	•	1228792	•	4271828	13056609
Operating Costs/Operating Income (%)													
Cost of Operations **10**	90.3	94.6	74.9	90.9	91.3	93.2	93.1	93.7	•	96.4	•	96.7	75.4
Salaries and Wages **11**	1.7	1.0	10.7	1.8	2.3	2.0	1.9	1.8	•	0.7	•	0.6	2.9
Taxes Paid **12**	0.6	0.5	1.1	1.1	0.5	0.4	0.9	0.4	•	0.4	•	0.2	1.2
Interest Paid **13**	0.6	0.6	0.5	0.2	0.2	0.3	0.2	0.3	•	0.2	•	0.4	1.7
Depreciation **14**	0.6	0.3	0.6	0.8	0.5	0.4	0.5	0.5	•	0.2	•	0.3	1.7
Amortization and Depletion **15**	0.1	0.2	0.1	0.0	0.0	0.0	0.0	0.0	•	0.1	•	0.1	0.4
Pensions and Other Deferred Comp. **16**	0.2	0.1	0.2	0.0	0.1	0.1	0.1	0.0	•	0.0	•	0.0	0.6
Employee Benefits **17**	0.3	0.4	0.2	0.2	0.1	0.1	0.1	0.1	•	0.1	•	0.1	0.7
Advertising **18**	0.1	0.0	0.5	0.2	0.1	0.0	0.1	0.0	•	0.0	•	0.0	0.4
Other Expenses **19**	4.1	2.5	6.3	2.9	3.9	2.7	2.6	2.3	•	1.0	•	1.1	11.1
Officers' Compensation **20**	0.3	0.1	3.9	1.4	0.6	0.4	0.3	0.3	•	0.1	•	0.3	0.1
Operating Margin **21**	1.1	•	0.8	0.5	0.4	0.3	0.3	0.5	•	0.7	•	0.4	3.8
Operating Margin Before Officers' Comp. **22**	1.4	4.7	1.8	1.0	0.7	0.7	0.7	0.8	•	0.8	•	0.7	3.9

Selected Average Balance Sheet ($ in Thousands)

Net Receivables 23	3330	0	26	296	1003	2558	5200	12153	•	69972	•	359186	876746
Inventories 24	1226	0	30	89	317	728	1557	3636	•	30442	•	179636	499008
Net Property, Plant and Equipment 25	7326	0	11	134	486	1830	4343	10032	•	23425	•	222514	5650016
Total Assets 26	21522	0	168	735	2503	6804	14938	35606	•	156564	•	1023126	14521877
Notes and Loans Payable 27	4590	0	43	142	617	1940	3835	10272	•	37766	•	223730	2891120
All Other Liabilities 28	6953	0	34	312	969	2474	5986	14460	•	81018	•	549571	3861139
Net Worth 29	9979	0	91	282	918	2390	5117	10873	•	37780	•	249825	7769618

Selected Financial Ratios (Times to 1)

Current Ratio 30	1.4	•	3.0	1.5	1.6	1.4	1.3	1.3	•	1.3	•	1.2	1.5
Quick Ratio 31	0.7	•	2.1	1.2	1.1	1.1	1.0	0.9	•	0.9	•	0.6	0.5
Net Sales to Working Capital 32	25.8	•	10.7	33.4	28.2	43.3	62.5	51.9	•	44.0	•	39.3	9.6
Coverage Ratio 33	6.3	5.6	6.1	4.3	7.1	5.6	5.3	5.1	•	7.9	•	3.5	7.0
Total Asset Turnover 34	2.8	•	5.3	6.9	8.1	8.2	7.6	6.5	•	7.8	•	4.2	0.9
Inventory Turnover 35	44.8	•	22.2	51.4	58.6	71.7	68.2	59.4	•	38.7	•	22.9	18.7
Receivables Turnover 36	20.7	•	32.0	16.4	23.4	24.0	23.6	23.0	•	35.0	•	15.1	28.2
Total Liabilities to Net Worth 37	1.2	•	0.8	1.6	1.7	1.8	1.9	2.3	•	3.1	•	3.1	0.9
Current Assets to Working Capital 38	3.5	•	1.5	3.2	2.6	3.3	4.9	4.7	•	4.3	•	6.4	2.9
Current Liabilities to Working Capital 39	2.5	•	0.5	2.2	1.6	2.3	3.9	3.7	•	3.3	•	5.4	1.9
Working Capital to Net Sales 40	0.0	•	0.1	0.0	0.0	0.0	0.0	0.0	•	0.0	•	0.0	0.1
Inventory to Working Capital 41	0.7	•	0.4	0.5	0.6	0.6	0.9	1.0	•	1.1	•	2.1	0.4
Total Receipts to Cash Flow 42	16.6	21.1	14.1	33.6	26.1	31.5	36.4	35.5	•	53.7	•	54.2	5.6
Cost of Goods to Cash Flow 43	15.0	19.9	10.6	30.6	23.9	29.4	33.9	33.3	•	51.7	•	52.4	4.2
Cash Flow to Total Debt 44	0.3	•	0.8	0.3	0.5	0.4	0.3	0.3	•	0.2	•	0.1	0.3

Selected Financial Factors (in Percentages)

Debt Ratio 45	53.6	•	45.7	61.7	63.3	64.9	65.7	69.5	•	75.9	•	75.6	46.5
Return on Total Assets 46	10.7	•	16.0	5.8	10.2	12.0	8.8	9.5	•	10.8	•	5.7	10.2
Return on Equity Before Income Taxes 47	19.4	•	24.6	11.6	24.0	28.1	20.8	24.9	•	39.1	•	16.6	16.4
Return on Equity After Income Taxes 48	14.3	•	24.1	9.4	22.7	24.9	19.2	21.0	•	33.0	•	12.0	11.6
Profit Margin (Before Income Tax) 49	3.2	2.8	2.5	0.6	1.1	1.2	0.9	1.2	•	1.2	•	1.0	10.3
Profit Margin (After Income Tax) 50	2.4	1.9	2.5	0.5	1.0	1.1	0.9	1.0	•	1.0	•	0.7	7.3

Table I

Corporations with and without Net Income

BEER, WINE, AND DISTILLED ALCOHOLIC BEVERAGE

MONEY AMOUNTS AND SIZE OF ASSETS IN THOUSANDS OF DOLLARS

Item Description for Accounting Period 7/05 Through 6/06	Total	Zero Assets	Under 500	500 to 1,000	1,000 to 5,000	5,000 to 10,000	10,000 to 25,000	25,000 to 50,000	50,000 to 100,000	100,000 to 250,000	250,000 to 500,000	500,000 to 2,500,000	2,500,000 and over
Number of Enterprises **1**	3415	117	1421	418	700	380	204	92	41	25	5	12	0
Revenues ($ in Thousands)													
Net Sales **2**	76684795	1155708	368114	1085830	8193305	9255350	9365672	8198317	6898910	8852343	3431606	20079640	0
Interest **3**	293544	6867	105	534	2302	2802	610	3141	3555	6948	3677	263003	0
Rents **4**	147362	1391	0	0	7040	179	137	885	3577	9194	10688	114272	0
Royalties **5**	333026	0	0	0	0	60	0	0	279	121	2186	330380	0
Other Portfolio Income **6**	286094	67831	0	27	41460	75509	13124	2539	7637	20305	2708	54954	0
Other Receipts **7**	1247869	71446	2494	4828	57224	89427	122397	73093	164221	217217	23076	422445	0
Total Receipts **8**	78992690	1303243	370713	1091219	8301331	9423327	9501940	8277975	7078179	8906128	3473941	21264694	0
Average Total Receipts **9**	23131	11139	261	2611	11859	24798	46578	89978	172639	356245	694788	1772058	.
Operating Costs/Operating Income (%)													
Cost of Operations **10**	74.6	75.6	41.4	70.4	76.5	73.2	75.2	74.3	77.0	72.6	81.4	73.9	.
Salaries and Wages **11**	8.2	8.2	3.3	7.1	9.6	8.9	8.4	8.8	7.9	7.6	5.0	8.0	.
Taxes Paid **12**	3.2	3.9	8.5	4.6	1.6	3.1	3.7	3.2	2.2	3.7	1.9	3.8	.
Interest Paid **13**	1.3	2.4	0.4	0.7	0.5	0.6	0.6	0.6	0.6	0.8	0.9	3.1	.
Depreciation **14**	0.6	0.4	0.3	1.5	0.4	0.6	0.6	0.7	0.8	0.5	0.3	0.7	.
Amortization and Depletion **15**	0.5	0.9	0.1	.	0.1	0.2	0.5	0.6	0.4	0.5	0.6	1.0	.
Pensions and Other Deferred Comp. **16**	0.3	0.2	.	0.5	0.4	0.5	0.3	0.3	0.3	0.2	0.6	0.3	.
Employee Benefits **17**	0.8	0.3	0.4	0.2	1.3	0.6	0.8	0.8	0.9	0.7	1.0	0.8	.
Advertising **18**	1.3	0.2	0.0	0.7	0.5	0.5	0.8	1.2	1.6	1.8	2.4	1.8	.
Other Expenses **19**	6.8	5.8	12.0	13.2	6.2	7.6	5.1	6.4	6.0	7.1	5.4	7.6	.
Officers' Compensation **20**	1.3	1.1	12.5	4.3	2.3	2.3	1.3	1.0	0.8	1.4	0.4	0.5	.
Operating Margin **21**	1.1	1.0	21.2	.	0.5	1.9	2.8	2.1	1.7	3.1	0.2	.	.
Operating Margin Before Officers' Comp. **22**	2.4	2.1	33.7	1.1	2.8	4.2	4.1	3.1	2.5	4.5	0.6	.	.

Selected Average Balance Sheet ($ in Thousands)

Net Receivables 23	2638	0	16	88	612	994	2082	5397	12965	29654	47626	475798
Inventories 24	1953	0	10	165	794	1590	3073	6446	15803	32389	83319	194408
Net Property, Plant and Equipment 25	1319	0	3	104	362	1139	2563	5260	10536	17139	13951	152875
Total Assets 26	11145	0	103	657	2411	7269	15480	34052	69592	149143	341153	1551012
Notes and Loans Payable 27	2537	0	27	224	686	1857	4728	9602	20265	36461	150797	250300
All Other Liabilities 28	4766	0	45	279	854	1758	3033	7608	16694	43739	121808	926975
Net Worth 29	3842	0	31	154	871	3655	7720	16842	32633	68943	68548	373736

Selected Financial Ratios (Times to 1)

Current Ratio 30	1.3	•	1.5	1.7	1.5	2.1	1.9	1.7	1.6	1.9	1.0	1.0
Quick Ratio 31	0.7	•	1.3	0.7	0.8	1.2	1.0	0.8	0.8	1.1	0.4	0.6
Net Sales to Working Capital 32	17.6	•	10.2	12.1	23.4	11.2	12.9	13.6	11.1	8.6	143.4	256.4
Coverage Ratio 33	4.2	6.6	60.0	•	4.5	7.6	8.4	5.8	8.2	8.1	2.5	2.5
Total Asset Turnover 34	2.0	•	2.5	4.0	4.9	3.4	3.0	2.6	2.4	2.3	2.0	1.1
Inventory Turnover 35	8.6	•	10.4	11.1	11.3	11.2	11.2	10.3	8.2	7.8	6.7	6.4
Receivables Turnover 36	10.9	•	13.3	42.4	17.8	26.2	19.4	15.1	15.3	11.0	10.5	5.6
Total Liabilities to Net Worth 37	1.9	•	2.3	3.3	1.8	1.0	1.0	1.0	1.1	1.2	4.0	3.2
Current Assets to Working Capital 38	4.5	•	2.8	2.5	3.2	1.9	2.1	2.5	2.6	2.1	29.5	117.3
Current Liabilities to Working Capital 39	3.5	•	1.8	1.5	2.2	0.9	1.1	1.5	1.6	1.1	28.5	116.3
Working Capital to Net Sales 40	0.1	•	0.1	0.1	0.0	0.1	0.1	0.1	0.1	0.1	0.0	0.0
Inventory to Working Capital 41	1.6	•	0.4	1.3	1.4	0.7	0.9	1.0	1.1	0.8	14.8	35.5
Total Receipts to Cash Flow 42	10.7	8.1	3.2	12.3	16.7	10.5	13.0	12.8	11.1	8.1	16.3	9.3
Cost of Goods to Cash Flow 43	8.0	6.1	1.3	8.7	12.8	7.7	9.7	9.5	8.6	5.9	13.3	6.9
Cash Flow to Total Debt 44	0.3	•	1.1	0.4	0.5	0.6	0.5	0.4	0.4	0.5	0.2	0.2

Selected Financial Factors (in Percentages)

Debt Ratio 45	65.5	•	70.1	76.5	63.9	49.7	50.1	50.5	53.1	53.8	79.9	75.9
Return on Total Assets 46	10.9	•	56.2	•	11.5	14.3	14.2	9.7	11.9	15.8	4.7	8.4
Return on Equity Before Income Taxes 47	24.1	•	184.5	•	24.9	24.7	25.1	16.3	22.3	29.9	14.3	21.1
Return on Equity After Income Taxes 48	20.5	•	184.4	•	22.7	23.9	24.8	14.4	20.5	27.9	8.7	14.9
Profit Margin (Before Income Tax) 49	4.1	13.8	21.9	•	1.8	3.7	4.2	3.1	4.3	6.0	1.4	4.7
Profit Margin (After Income Tax) 50	3.5	8.6	21.9	•	1.7	3.6	2.7	4.0	5.6	0.9	3.3

197

WHOLESALE TRADE
424800

Table II
Corporations with Net Income

BEER, WINE, AND DISTILLED ALCOHOLIC BEVERAGE

MONEY AMOUNTS AND SIZE OF ASSETS IN THOUSANDS OF DOLLARS

Item Description for Accounting Period 7/05 Through 6/06	Total	Zero Assets	Under 500	500 to 1,000	1,000 to 5,000	5,000 to 10,000	10,000 to 25,000	25,000 to 50,000	50,000 to 100,000	100,000 to 250,000	250,000 to 500,000	500,000 to 2,500,000	2,500,000 and over
Number of Enterprises **1**	2339	111	617	346	574	362	177	78	38	21	•	•	0

Revenues ($ in Thousands)

	Total	Zero Assets	Under 500	500 to 1,000	1,000 to 5,000	5,000 to 10,000	10,000 to 25,000	25,000 to 50,000	50,000 to 100,000	100,000 to 250,000	250,000 to 500,000	500,000 to 2,500,000	2,500,000 and over
Net Sales **2**	70412639	1058684	220072	1048482	6879732	8881685	8554616	7225829	6521803	7005942	•	•	0
Interest **3**	274568	5464	0	260	2291	2631	594	2856	3555	4997	•	•	0
Rents **4**	136121	1391	0	0	7040	179	137	885	3577	8642	•	•	0
Royalties **5**	330780	0	0	0	0	0	0	0	279	121	•	•	0
Other Portfolio Income **6**	247765	67699	0	27	10353	75429	12840	2009	4111	20305	•	•	0
Other Receipts **7**	1220602	69204	567	1356	55438	88158	117220	68060	161825	213353	•	•	0
Total Receipts **8**	72622475	1202442	220639	1050125	6954854	9048082	8685407	7299639	6695150	7253360	•	•	0
Average Total Receipts **9**	31049	10833	358	3035	12116	24995	49070	93585	176188	345398	•	•	•

Operating Costs/Operating Income (%)

	Total	Zero Assets	Under 500	500 to 1,000	1,000 to 5,000	5,000 to 10,000	10,000 to 25,000	25,000 to 50,000	50,000 to 100,000	100,000 to 250,000	250,000 to 500,000	500,000 to 2,500,000	2,500,000 and over
Cost of Operations **10**	74.5	75.2	24.1	72.8	74.0	73.0	75.5	74.1	77.5	74.2	•	•	•
Salaries and Wages **11**	8.2	8.2	0.1	7.2	10.6	8.9	8.2	8.5	7.7	6.9	•	•	•
Taxes Paid **12**	3.1	4.0	2.1	3.8	1.6	3.2	3.3	3.2	2.2	2.6	•	•	•
Interest Paid **13**	1.3	2.6	0.2	0.4	0.4	0.5	0.5	0.5	0.6	0.9	•	•	•
Depreciation **14**	0.6	0.5	0.3	1.3	0.5	0.6	0.6	0.6	0.6	0.4	•	•	•
Amortization and Depletion **15**	0.5	1.0	0.1	•	0.1	0.2	0.4	0.5	0.3	0.5	•	•	•
Pensions and Other Deferred Comp. **16**	0.3	0.1	•	0.5	0.5	0.5	0.3	0.3	0.3	0.2	•	•	•
Employee Benefits **17**	0.8	0.1	0.1	0.2	1.5	0.6	0.8	0.8	0.8	0.6	•	•	•
Advertising **18**	1.3	0.2	0.0	0.4	0.6	0.5	0.7	1.1	1.6	2.2	•	•	•
Other Expenses **19**	6.5	4.8	15.4	10.7	6.3	7.4	5.0	6.3	5.6	5.1	•	•	•
Officers' Compensation **20**	1.3	0.6	20.9	2.9	2.5	2.3	1.3	0.9	0.8	1.6	•	•	•
Operating Margin **21**	1.7	2.7	36.8	0.3	1.5	2.3	3.3	3.1	2.0	4.8	•	•	•
Operating Margin Before Officers' Comp. **22**	2.9	3.3	57.7	3.3	3.9	4.6	4.6	4.0	2.8	6.4	•	•	•

Selected Average Balance Sheet ($ in Thousands)

Net Receivables 23	3672	0	0	105	586	995	2124	5621	13446	28318
Inventories 24	2686	0	0	186	813	1618	3183	6670	16458	30492
Net Property, Plant and Equipment 25	1797	0	7	125	386	1144	2589	5204	10174	17388
Total Assets 26	14936	0	146	665	2522	7295	15518	34026	69689	148519
Notes and Loans Payable 27	3234	0	36	218	656	1828	4510	7727	19094	35331
All Other Liabilities 28	6411	0	1	275	861	1618	3196	7983	17602	38406
Net Worth 29	5291	0	109	172	1005	3849	7812	18315	32993	74781

Selected Financial Ratios (Times to 1)

Current Ratio 30	1.3	•	41.8	1.7	1.5	2.1	2.0	1.7	1.6	2.1
Quick Ratio 31	0.8	•	36.8	0.5	0.8	1.3	1.0	0.8	0.8	1.3
Net Sales to Working Capital 32	16.9	•	3.5	14.8	20.8	10.9	12.5	13.8	10.5	7.6
Coverage Ratio 33	4.8	7.4	195.1	2.1	7.0	9.0	10.3	9.1	9.3	10.3
Total Asset Turnover 34	2.0	•	2.4	4.6	4.8	3.4	3.1	2.7	2.5	2.2
Inventory Turnover 35	8.4	•	4.6	11.9	10.9	11.1	11.5	10.3	8.1	8.1
Receivables Turnover 36	10.7	•	365.6	55.0	21.6	27.4	20.1	15.6	15.4	23.6
Total Liabilities to Net Worth 37	1.8	•	0.3	2.9	1.5	0.9	1.0	0.9	1.1	1.0
Current Assets to Working Capital 38	4.5	•	1.0	2.5	2.9	1.9	2.0	2.5	2.5	1.9
Current Liabilities to Working Capital 39	3.5	•	0.0	1.5	1.9	0.9	1.0	1.5	1.5	0.9
Working Capital to Net Sales 40	0.1	•	0.3	0.1	0.0	0.1	0.1	0.1	0.1	0.1
Inventory to Working Capital 41	1.6	•	0.1	1.7	1.3	0.7	0.8	1.1	1.1	0.7
Total Receipts to Cash Flow 42	10.2	7.4	2.1	11.3	14.2	10.2	12.3	11.3	11.1	8.0
Cost of Goods to Cash Flow 43	7.6	5.5	0.5	8.2	10.5	7.4	9.3	8.4	8.6	6.0
Cash Flow to Total Debt 44	0.3	•	4.7	0.5	0.6	0.7	0.5	0.5	0.4	0.6

Selected Financial Factors (in Percentages)

Debt Ratio 45	64.6	•	25.5	74.2	60.2	47.2	49.7	46.2	52.7	49.6
Return on Total Assets 46	12.3	•	90.9	4.1	14.2	15.8	16.6	12.6	12.8	20.5
Return on Equity Before Income Taxes 47	27.6	•	121.4	8.4	30.5	26.7	29.7	20.8	24.2	36.7
Return on Equity After Income Taxes 48	23.8	•	121.4	8.0	28.2	26.0	29.4	18.8	22.3	34.6
Profit Margin (Before Income Tax) 49	4.8	16.3	37.0	0.5	2.6	4.2	4.8	4.1	4.7	8.2
Profit Margin (After Income Tax) 50	4.2	10.7	37.0	0.5	2.4	4.1	4.8	3.7	4.3	7.7

Table I

Corporations with and without Net Income

MISCELLANEOUS NONDURABLE GOODS

MONEY AMOUNTS AND SIZE OF ASSETS IN THOUSANDS OF DOLLARS

Item Description for Accounting Period 7/05 Through 6/06	Total	Zero Assets	Under 500	500 to 1,000	1,000 to 5,000	5,000 to 10,000	10,000 to 25,000	25,000 to 50,000	50,000 to 100,000	100,000 to 250,000	250,000 to 500,000	500,000 to 2,500,000	2,500,000 and over
Number of Enterprises 1	33632	5907	19912	3739	2890	628	325	114	59	35	8	11	3
Revenues ($ in Thousands)													
Net Sales 2	135942416	676794	12270509	8355038	19150108	17101262	15484581	10336474	8862911	10032732	7791454	15966474	9914079
Interest 3	218765	4053	4252	6387	16411	12461	9363	9712	16853	25085	18157	67223	28809
Rents 4	34500	1227	3258	1248	2264	2069	4482	1699	1585	3344	0	13228	98
Royalties 5	32840	0	0	0	573	2166	454	10221	4458	7278	1648	3508	2534
Other Portfolio Income 6	976136	11211	37046	36721	55817	12980	16651	5001	10805	50761	38133	650431	50577
Other Receipts 7	1455419	22656	71097	30617	114971	38743	207560	97251	92968	155153	244745	166298	213359
Total Receipts 8	138660076	715941	12386162	8430011	19340144	17169681	15723091	10460358	8989580	10274353	8094137	16867162	10209456
Average Total Receipts 9	4123	121	622	2255	6692	27340	48379	91758	152366	293553	1011767	1533378	3403152
Operating Costs/Operating Income (%)													
Cost of Operations 10	79.3	72.1	77.0	72.6	80.5	84.3	83.4	79.6	82.4	70.0	89.6	78.1	71.7
Salaries and Wages 11	6.1	11.5	4.7	7.9	5.1	4.4	5.5	6.8	5.3	8.9	3.8	7.1	8.6
Taxes Paid 12	1.3	2.3	1.3	2.2	1.8	0.9	1.1	1.9	0.8	1.2	0.6	1.1	1.4
Interest Paid 13	0.7	0.1	0.3	0.5	0.5	0.4	0.5	0.8	0.8	1.2	0.7	1.4	0.6
Depreciation 14	0.7	1.6	0.7	0.4	0.8	0.3	0.5	0.6	0.7	0.8	0.4	1.2	1.6
Amortization and Depletion 15	0.2	0.1	0.2	0.0	0.0	0.0	0.2	0.1	0.2	0.4	0.2	0.4	0.6
Pensions and Other Deferred Comp. 16	0.2	0.0	0.1	0.3	0.2	0.1	0.2	0.2	0.2	0.3	0.1	0.3	0.4
Employee Benefits 17	0.5	1.1	0.4	0.3	0.4	0.2	0.5	0.6	0.5	0.8	0.5	0.8	0.6
Advertising 18	0.7	0.8	0.5	0.6	0.4	0.6	0.5	0.9	1.0	2.0	0.2	0.7	0.4
Other Expenses 19	8.1	22.9	12.1	10.3	7.2	6.2	5.7	6.2	6.4	10.1	5.1	8.0	12.6
Officers' Compensation 20	1.3	2.2	2.7	3.2	2.2	1.1	1.2	1.1	1.0	0.8	0.3	0.2	0.3
Operating Margin 21	0.9	•	•	1.7	0.9	1.5	0.6	1.2	0.8	3.6	•	0.7	1.2
Operating Margin Before Officers' Comp. 22	2.2	•	2.6	4.8	3.1	2.6	1.9	2.3	1.8	4.3	•	0.9	1.6

Selected Average Balance Sheet ($ in Thousands)

Net Receivables 23	456	0	22	256	660	2469	4624	11261	16939	41262	76574	190190	855851
Inventories 24	413	0	35	225	538	2085	4851	9680	17644	34864	66313	218992	533898
Net Property, Plant and Equipment 25	228	0	18	61	274	506	2027	4081	9598	21658	23724	149034	565024
Total Assets 26	1672	0	112	736	2096	6572	15192	33198	69336	164811	388413	938877	3011057
Notes and Loans Payable 27	432	0	60	249	545	2440	4519	9538	23350	53446	117459	148876	310920
All Other Liabilities 28	667	0	34	292	903	2343	5265	14131	22058	69770	141335	454271	1125559
Net Worth 29	573	0	18	195	648	1789	5408	9529	23928	41595	129619	335729	1574577

Selected Financial Ratios (Times to 1)

Current Ratio 30	1.5	•	1.8	2.1	1.5	1.6	1.5	1.5	1.6	1.4	1.0	1.4	1.5
Quick Ratio 31	0.8	•	1.0	1.3	0.9	0.9	0.8	0.8	0.8	0.8	0.6	0.6	0.9
Net Sales to Working Capital 32	11.0	•	16.8	6.5	12.0	14.6	12.9	10.7	7.9	9.4	202.0	10.0	6.1
Coverage Ratio 33	5.5	•	4.0	6.5	4.8	5.2	5.6	4.2	3.9	6.1	4.3	6.1	9.8
Total Asset Turnover 34	2.4	•	5.5	3.0	3.2	4.1	3.1	2.7	2.2	1.7	2.5	1.5	1.1
Inventory Turnover 35	7.8	•	13.6	7.2	9.9	11.0	8.2	7.5	7.0	5.8	13.2	5.2	4.4
Receivables Turnover 36	8.8	•	29.0	8.4	9.6	12.4	9.5	8.4	9.8	6.9	8.5	8.3	3.7
Total Liabilities to Net Worth 37	1.9	•	5.1	2.8	2.2	2.7	1.8	2.5	1.9	3.0	2.0	1.8	0.9
Current Assets to Working Capital 38	3.0	•	2.2	1.9	2.9	2.8	3.1	3.1	2.6	3.5	37.1	3.5	3.2
Current Liabilities to Working Capital 39	2.0	•	1.2	0.9	1.9	1.8	2.1	2.1	1.6	2.5	36.1	2.5	2.2
Working Capital to Net Sales 40	0.1	•	0.1	0.2	0.1	0.1	0.1	0.1	0.1	0.1	0.0	0.1	0.2
Inventory to Working Capital 41	1.1	•	0.9	0.7	1.0	1.0	1.3	1.2	1.0	1.1	14.4	1.2	1.2
Total Receipts to Cash Flow 42	11.0	13.7	10.8	9.8	13.4	14.6	15.2	13.6	13.4	7.1	17.4	7.8	7.4
Cost of Goods to Cash Flow 43	8.8	9.9	8.4	7.1	10.8	12.3	12.7	10.8	11.1	4.9	15.6	6.1	5.3
Cash Flow to Total Debt 44	0.3	•	0.6	0.4	0.3	0.4	0.3	0.3	0.2	0.3	0.2	0.3	0.3

Selected Financial Factors (in Percentages)

Debt Ratio 45	65.8	•	83.7	73.5	69.1	72.8	64.4	71.3	65.5	74.8	66.6	64.2	47.7
Return on Total Assets 46	9.0	•	6.5	9.2	7.4	9.7	8.2	8.6	6.4	12.5	7.5	13.0	6.3
Return on Equity Before Income Taxes 47	21.5	•	30.1	29.4	19.0	28.8	19.0	22.9	13.8	41.4	17.2	30.4	10.8
Return on Equity After Income Taxes 48	17.8	•	27.6	28.6	17.1	26.6	16.9	18.6	11.3	34.4	14.9	24.7	7.0
Profit Margin (Before Income Tax) 49	3.0	•	0.9	2.6	1.9	1.9	2.2	2.4	2.2	6.0	2.3	7.0	5.2
Profit Margin (After Income Tax) 50	2.5	•	0.8	2.5	1.7	1.7	1.9	2.0	1.8	5.0	2.0	5.7	3.4

Table II

Corporations with Net Income

MISCELLANEOUS NONDURABLE GOODS

MONEY AMOUNTS AND SIZE OF ASSETS IN THOUSANDS OF DOLLARS

Item Description for Accounting Period 7/05 Through 6/06	Total	Zero Assets	Under 500	500 to 1,000	1,000 to 5,000	5,000 to 10,000	10,000 to 25,000	25,000 to 50,000	50,000 to 100,000	100,000 to 250,000	250,000 to 500,000	500,000 to 2,500,000	2,500,000 and over
Number of Enterprises **1**	18709	1861	11019	2733	2141	494	275	94	45	27	•	11	•
Revenues ($ in Thousands)													
Net Sales **2**	118653733	490822	9502782	6768768	17235171	14506422	13333935	8628924	7043826	8483363	•	15966474	•
Interest **3**	193297	2193	1921	5219	10558	9416	6511	9604	14035	21817	•	67223	•
Rents **4**	25671	1227	0	1248	2253	592	985	1699	1169	3173	•	13228	•
Royalties **5**	31443	0	0	0	0	2166	454	10221	4139	7247	•	3508	•
Other Portfolio Income **6**	942274	3995	32767	25832	53911	12773	15612	4852	7799	46178	•	650431	•
Other Receipts **7**	1320698	23699	55732	30276	92164	26471	186783	85967	88482	146662	•	166298	•
Total Receipts **8**	121167116	521936	9593202	6831343	17394057	14557840	13544280	8741267	7159450	8708440	•	16867162	•
Average Total Receipts **9**	6476	280	871	2500	8124	29469	49252	92992	159099	322535	•	1533378	•
Operating Costs/Operating Income (%)													
Cost of Operations **10**	79.1	66.3	77.5	70.1	81.4	86.3	82.9	77.9	81.3	67.9	•	78.1	•
Salaries and Wages **11**	6.0	11.6	4.2	8.5	4.9	3.7	5.4	7.1	5.6	9.3	•	7.1	•
Taxes Paid **12**	1.3	2.7	1.2	2.5	1.8	0.8	1.1	2.1	0.9	1.2	•	1.1	•
Interest Paid **13**	0.6	0.1	0.3	0.4	0.3	0.3	0.4	0.7	0.7	1.1	•	1.4	•
Depreciation **14**	0.7	1.0	0.6	0.4	0.6	0.3	0.5	0.6	0.6	0.8	•	1.2	•
Amortization and Depletion **15**	0.2	0.1	0.1	0.0	0.0	0.0	0.3	0.1	0.1	0.3	•	0.4	•
Pensions and Other Deferred Comp. **16**	0.2	0.0	0.2	0.3	0.2	0.1	0.2	0.2	0.2	0.3	•	0.3	•
Employee Benefits **17**	0.5	1.2	0.4	0.2	0.4	0.2	0.4	0.6	0.6	0.9	•	0.8	•
Advertising **18**	0.7	0.6	0.5	0.7	0.3	0.6	0.5	1.0	1.0	2.2	•	0.7	•
Other Expenses **19**	7.4	13.2	9.2	10.5	5.9	4.5	5.5	6.5	6.1	10.3	•	8.0	•
Officers' Compensation **20**	1.2	2.0	2.4	3.2	2.2	0.9	1.3	1.2	1.1	0.7	•	0.2	•
Operating Margin **21**	2.0	1.4	3.4	3.2	2.0	2.3	1.6	1.9	1.8	4.9	•	0.7	•
Operating Margin Before Officers' Comp. **22**	3.2	3.4	5.8	6.3	4.3	3.2	2.8	3.1	2.9	5.6	•	0.9	•

Selected Average Balance Sheet ($ in Thousands)

Net Receivables 23	718	0	30	257	727	2662	4669	11560	17860	45695	190190	•
Inventories 24	622	0	38	258	562	2025	4812	9794	17784	38600	211020	•
Net Property, Plant and Equipment 25	344	0	19	55	207	490	1871	4186	8502	22022	149034	•
Total Assets 26	2565	0	142	724	2172	6485	14984	33504	68166	168045	938877	•
Notes and Loans Payable 27	574	0	60	233	409	2080	4073	8764	22628	51792	148876	•
All Other Liabilities 28	1016	0	43	339	930	2377	5199	13759	19650	57723	454271	•
Net Worth 29	975	0	39	152	834	2028	5712	10981	25889	58529	335729	•

Selected Financial Ratios (Times to 1)

Current Ratio 30	1.6	•	1.9	2.0	1.6	1.7	1.5	1.5	1.7	1.7	1.4	•
Quick Ratio 31	0.8	•	1.0	1.2	0.9	1.0	0.8	0.9	0.9	0.9	0.6	•
Net Sales to Working Capital 32	10.3	•	18.0	7.1	12.0	14.2	12.1	10.2	7.6	6.8	10.0	•
Coverage Ratio 33	7.9	92.3	16.1	12.4	10.5	10.3	8.1	5.3	6.0	7.7	6.1	•
Total Asset Turnover 34	2.5	•	6.1	3.4	3.7	4.5	3.2	2.7	2.3	1.9	1.5	•
Inventory Turnover 35	8.1	•	17.4	6.7	11.7	12.5	8.4	7.3	7.2	5.5	5.4	•
Receivables Turnover 36	9.1	•	29.9	19.3	11.3	12.3	9.9	8.5	10.4	6.7	9.6	•
Total Liabilities to Net Worth 37	1.6	•	2.6	3.7	1.6	2.2	1.6	2.1	1.6	1.9	1.8	•
Current Assets to Working Capital 38	2.8	•	2.2	2.0	2.6	2.5	2.9	2.9	2.4	2.4	3.5	•
Current Liabilities to Working Capital 39	1.8	•	1.2	1.0	1.6	1.5	1.9	1.9	1.4	1.4	2.5	•
Working Capital to Net Sales 40	0.1	•	0.1	0.1	0.1	0.1	0.1	0.1	0.1	0.1	0.1	•
Inventory to Working Capital 41	1.0	•	0.9	0.7	1.0	0.8	1.2	1.1	0.9	0.9	1.2	•
Total Receipts to Cash Flow 42	10.3	6.7	9.4	8.3	13.7	16.1	13.5	11.8	11.9	6.3	7.8	•
Cost of Goods to Cash Flow 43	8.1	4.4	7.3	5.8	11.2	13.9	11.2	9.2	9.7	4.3	6.1	•
Cash Flow to Total Debt 44	0.4	•	0.9	0.5	0.4	0.4	0.3	0.3	0.3	0.5	0.3	•

Selected Financial Factors (in Percentages)

Debt Ratio 45	62.0	•	72.5	78.9	61.6	68.7	61.9	67.2	62.0	65.2	64.2	•
Return on Total Assets 46	12.1	•	28.4	15.3	12.1	13.5	11.6	10.8	9.4	16.4	13.0	•
Return on Equity Before Income Taxes 47	27.9	•	97.0	66.7	28.5	38.9	26.6	26.7	20.7	40.9	30.4	•
Return on Equity After Income Taxes 48	24.0	•	94.9	65.2	26.4	36.5	24.2	22.1	17.6	34.6	24.7	•
Profit Margin (Before Income Tax) 49	4.3	7.6	4.4	4.1	2.9	2.7	3.1	3.2	3.4	7.6	7.0	•
Profit Margin (After Income Tax) 50	3.7	6.8	4.3	4.0	2.7	2.5	2.8	2.6	2.9	6.4	5.7	•

Table I

Corporations with and without Net Income

WHOLESALE ELECTRONIC MARKETS AND AGENTS AND BROKERS

MONEY AMOUNTS AND SIZE OF ASSETS IN THOUSANDS OF DOLLARS

Item Description for Accounting Period 7/05 Through 6/06	Total	Zero Assets	Under 500	500 to 1,000	1,000 to 5,000	5,000 to 10,000	10,000 to 25,000	25,000 to 50,000	50,000 to 100,000	100,000 to 250,000	250,000 to 500,000	500,000 to 2,500,000	2,500,000 and over
Number of Enterprises 1	13907	2494	11239	0	160	0	7	3	0	4	0	0	0
Revenues ($ in Thousands)													
Net Sales 2	5413987	232182	3281788	0	221886	0	33525	41014	0	1603592	0	0	0
Interest 3	17303	230	954	0	248	0	0	0	0	15871	0	0	0
Rents 4	3369	0	0	0	0	0	0	0	0	3369	0	0	0
Royalties 5	9396	0	0	0	0	0	0	0	0	9396	0	0	0
Other Portfolio Income 6	28385	1	58	0	0	0	0	6	0	28321	0	0	0
Other Receipts 7	120905	21	57754	0	-645	0	575	212	0	62987	0	0	0
Total Receipts 8	5593345	232434	3340554	0	221489	0	34100	41232	0	1723536	0	0	0
Average Total Receipts 9	402	93	297	.	1384	.	4871	13744	.	430884	.	.	.
Operating Costs/Operating Income (%)													
Cost of Operations 10	.	.	.	.	.	.	.	.	.	.	.	.	.
Salaries and Wages 11	21.8	0.9	12.3	.	38.9	.	13.2	39.5	.	41.8	.	.	.
Taxes Paid 12	3.3	3.0	2.7	.	2.8	.	1.9	3.4	.	4.8	.	.	.
Interest Paid 13	1.6	1.1	0.4	.	.	.	5.7	8.5	.	4.2	.	.	.
Depreciation 14	1.2	0.1	0.7	.	0.3	.	1.7	0.5	.	2.4	.	.	.
Amortization and Depletion 15	0.8	0.1	0.0	.	.	.	3.3	4.7	.	2.5	.	.	.
Pensions and Other Deferred Comp. 16	1.9	.	1.7	.	14.3	.	0.1	1.5	.	0.8	.	.	.
Employee Benefits 17	2.6	.	2.4	.	2.5	.	1.3	1.9	.	3.2	.	.	.
Advertising 18	1.0	0.1	0.8	.	.	.	15.2	9.5	.	1.2	.	.	.
Other Expenses 19	36.7	42.0	41.6	.	8.6	.	45.1	18.0	.	30.0	.	.	.
Officers' Compensation 20	20.1	32.4	28.8	.	23.9	.	2.3	3.4	.	0.8	.	.	.
Operating Margin 21	9.0	20.3	8.5	.	8.7	.	10.3	9.3	.	8.3	.	.	.
Operating Margin Before Officers' Comp. 22	29.1	52.7	37.3	.	32.6	.	12.6	12.7	.	9.1	.	.	.

Selected Average Balance Sheet ($ in Thousands)

Item	1	2	3	4	5	6	7
Net Receivables 23	46	0	4	179	6566	17831	118970
Inventories 24	1	0	0	1	0	0	1561
Net Property, Plant and Equipment 25	49	0	8	6	1897	4115	141329
Total Assets 26	266	53	1181	•	12414	41340	675918
Notes and Loans Payable 27	95	29	3	•	4196	32943	216618
All Other Liabilities 28	62	15	211	•	9558	4112	143618
Net Worth 29	109	9	967	•	-1340	4285	315682

Selected Financial Ratios (Times to 1)

Item	1	2	3	4	5	6	7
Current Ratio 30	1.2	1.2	2.0	2.0	0.9	1.1	1.3
Quick Ratio 31	1.0	1.2	1.5	1.5	0.8	1.0	1.0
Net Sales to Working Capital 32	19.9	46.8	6.8	6.8	5.8	•	9.6
Coverage Ratio 33	8.7	18.8	28.2	•	3.1	2.2	5.0
Total Asset Turnover 34	1.5	•	5.5	1.2	0.4	0.3	0.6
Inventory Turnover 35	•	•	•	•	•	•	•
Receivables Turnover 36	8.3	159.2	4.4	4.4	0.6	1.5	3.4
Total Liabilities to Net Worth 37	1.4	5.1	0.2	0.2	•	8.6	1.1
Current Assets to Working Capital 38	5.0	5.4	2.0	2.0	•	10.5	4.7
Current Liabilities to Working Capital 39	4.0	4.4	1.0	1.0	•	9.5	3.7
Working Capital to Net Sales 40	0.1	0.0	0.1	0.1	•	0.2	0.1
Inventory to Working Capital 41	0.1	0.1	0.0	0.0	•	•	0.0
Total Receipts to Cash Flow 42	2.2	2.0	6.4	6.4	2.0	4.2	2.5
Cost of Goods to Cash Flow 43	•	1.8	•	•	•	•	•
Cash Flow to Total Debt 44	1.1	3.2	1.0	1.0	0.2	0.1	0.5

Selected Financial Factors (in Percentages)

Item	1	2	3	4	5	6	7
Debt Ratio 45	58.9	83.5	18.1	•	110.8	89.6	53.3
Return on Total Assets 46	20.6	58.6	9.9	•	6.8	6.0	12.3
Return on Equity Before Income Taxes 47	44.5	342.7	12.1	•	31.3	•	21.0
Return on Equity After Income Taxes 48	38.3	341.2	12.0	•	31.3	•	13.7
Profit Margin (Before Income Tax) 49	12.5	20.4	10.3	8.5	12.0	9.8	16.6
Profit Margin (After Income Tax) 50	10.7	20.3	10.2	8.4	11.8	9.8	10.8

WHOLESALE ELECTRONIC MARKETS AND AGENTS AND BROKERS

Table II

Corporations with Net Income

MONEY AMOUNTS AND SIZE OF ASSETS IN THOUSANDS OF DOLLARS

Item Description for Accounting Period 7/05 Through 6/06	Total	Zero Assets	Under 500	500 to 1000	251 to 500	501 to 1,000	1,001 to 5,000	5,001 to 10,000	10,001 to 25,000	25,001 to 50,000	50,001 to 100,000	100,001 to 250,000	250,001 and over
Number of Enterprises **1**	10010	1800	8064	0	133	0	·	0	0	·	0	0	0
Revenues ($ in Thousands)													
Net Sales **2**	4965485	217968	2923131	0	161854	0	·	0	0	·	0	0	0
Interest **3**	16378	0	260	0	247	0	·	0	0	·	0	0	0
Rents **4**	3369	0	0	0	0	0	·	0	0	·	0	0	0
Royalties **5**	9396	0	0	0	0	0	·	0	0	·	0	0	0
Other Portfolio Income **6**	28379	0	58	0	0	0	·	0	0	·	0	0	0
Other Receipts **7**	120752	20	57602	0	-644	0	·	0	0	·	0	0	0
Total Receipts **8**	5143759	217988	2981051	0	161457	0	·	0	0	·	0	0	0
Average Total Receipts **9**	514	121	370	·	1214	·	·	·	·	·	·	·	·
Operating Costs/Operating Income (%)													
Cost of Operations **10**	·	·	·	·	·	·	·	·	·	·	·	·	·
Salaries and Wages **11**	22.6	0.9	12.2	·	49.0	·	·	·	·	·	·	·	·
Taxes Paid **12**	3.2	3.0	2.3	·	3.0	·	·	·	·	·	·	·	·
Interest Paid **13**	1.7	1.2	0.3	·	·	·	·	·	·	·	·	·	·
Depreciation **14**	1.2	0.0	0.7	·	0.5	·	·	·	·	·	·	·	·
Amortization and Depletion **15**	0.9	0.0	0.0	·	·	·	·	·	·	·	·	·	·
Pensions and Other Deferred Comp. **16**	1.3	·	1.7	·	1.8	·	·	·	·	·	·	·	·
Employee Benefits **17**	2.4	·	2.1	·	2.2	·	·	·	·	·	·	·	·
Advertising **18**	1.0	0.1	0.7	·	·	·	·	·	·	·	·	·	·
Other Expenses **19**	37.2	33.0	43.3	·	7.1	·	·	·	·	·	·	·	·
Officers' Compensation **20**	17.2	32.5	25.1	·	21.9	·	·	·	·	·	·	·	·
Operating Margin **21**	11.4	29.2	11.6	·	14.6	·	·	·	·	·	·	·	·
Operating Margin Before Officers' Comp. **22**	28.6	61.8	36.6	·	36.4	·	·	·	·	·	·	·	·

Selected Average Balance Sheet ($ in Thousands)

Net Receivables 23	60	0	3	•	96
Inventories 24	1	0	1	•	2
Net Property, Plant and Equipment 25	65	0	9	•	8
Total Assets 26	342	0	47	•	1188
Notes and Loans Payable 27	115	0	21	•	4
All Other Liabilities 28	78	0	13	•	213
Net Worth 29	149	0	12	•	971

Selected Financial Ratios (Times to 1)

Current Ratio 30	1.2	•	1.2	•	1.3
Quick Ratio 31	1.0	•	1.1	•	1.2
Net Sales to Working Capital 32	23.2	•	72.2	•	22.5
Coverage Ratio 33	10.2	24.9	46.7	•	
Total Asset Turnover 34	1.4	•	7.7	•	1.0
Inventory Turnover 35	•	•	•	•	
Receivables Turnover 36	8.2	•	257.0	•	5.9
Total Liabilities to Net Worth 37	1.3	•	2.8	•	0.2
Current Assets to Working Capital 38	5.6	•	6.1	•	4.9
Current Liabilities to Working Capital 39	4.6	•	5.1	•	3.9
Working Capital to Net Sales 40	0.0	•	0.0	•	0.0
Inventory to Working Capital 41	0.1	•	0.2	•	0.0
Total Receipts to Cash Flow 42	2.1	1.7	1.8	•	4.9
Cost of Goods to Cash Flow 43	•	•	•	•	
Cash Flow to Total Debt 44	1.3	•	5.7	•	1.2

Selected Financial Factors (in Percentages)

Debt Ratio 45	56.4	•	73.5	•	18.2
Return on Total Assets 46	24.5	•	107.0	•	14.7
Return on Equity Before Income Taxes 47	50.6	•	395.0	•	17.9
Return on Equity After Income Taxes 48	44.3	•	393.5	•	17.7
Profit Margin (Before Income Tax) 49	15.2	29.2	13.5	•	14.3
Profit Margin (After Income Tax) 50	13.3	29.1	13.5	•	14.2

202

Table I

Corporations with and without Net Income

NEW AND USED CAR DEALERS

MONEY AMOUNTS AND SIZE OF ASSETS IN THOUSANDS OF DOLLARS

Item Description for Accounting Period 7/05 Through 6/06		Total	Zero Assets	Under 500	500 to 1,000	1,000 to 5,000	5,000 to 10,000	10,000 to 25,000	25,000 to 50,000	50,000 to 100,000	100,000 to 250,000	250,000 to 500,000	500,000 to 2,500,000	2,500,000 and over
Number of Enterprises	1	51472	2795	25055	4901	9024	5169	3555	731	168	53	8	8	4
Revenues ($ in Thousands)														
Net Sales	2	688898331	774295	22867548	12780915	89126416	147743257	208343639	87487685	35903073	21047755	6631778	22539191	33652778
Interest	3	1079988	1556	19112	11040	148597	133613	189845	80209	38329	68913	50947	237184	100644
Rents	4	284752	0	0	0	15947	21376	27335	27348	22875	52859	2972	29133	84906
Royalties	5	9688	0	0	0	0	4789	126	0	0	4060	0	714	0
Other Portfolio Income	6	852232	6718	35652	42958	86178	84390	146163	78540	87830	105886	10134	32916	134867
Other Receipts	7	12534574	3307	2095	101688	1429935	2683995	3756963	1575043	692185	473337	109818	635839	1070369
Total Receipts	8	703659565	785876	22924407	12936601	90807073	150671420	212464071	89248825	36744292	21752810	6805649	23474977	35043564
Average Total Receipts	9	13671	281	915	2640	10063	29149	59765	122091	218716	410430	850706	2934372	8760891
Operating Costs/Operating Income (%)														
Cost of Operations	10	87.8	84.5	84.6	83.6	86.9	88.7	88.6	88.6	87.7	86.3	87.7	87.3	84.7
Salaries and Wages	11	5.0	2.9	2.3	4.7	4.8	4.8	5.0	4.9	5.2	5.6	5.1	6.6	6.3
Taxes Paid	12	0.8	2.7	1.5	1.4	0.9	0.8	0.8	0.7	0.8	0.8	0.8	1.0	0.9
Interest Paid	13	0.7	0.9	0.5	1.2	0.8	0.7	0.6	0.6	0.7	0.9	1.0	1.1	1.3
Depreciation	14	0.4	0.2	0.2	0.7	0.2	0.2	0.3	0.4	0.6	1.1	0.9	0.4	2.0
Amortization and Depletion	15	0.1	0.0	0.0	0.0	0.0	0.0	0.1	0.0	0.0	0.1	0.1	0.2	0.5
Pensions and Other Deferred Comp.	16	0.1	0.0	0.1	0.0	0.1	0.1	0.1	0.1	0.1	0.1	0.1	0.1	0.1
Employee Benefits	17	0.4	0.3	0.2	0.2	0.5	0.5	0.4	0.4	0.4	0.5	0.5	0.5	0.4
Advertising	18	1.1	0.5	0.8	1.0	1.1	1.2	1.1	1.1	1.1	1.1	0.9	0.8	1.0
Other Expenses	19	4.1	10.9	7.0	6.6	5.0	3.7	3.6	3.3	3.5	4.8	3.7	3.9	5.1
Officers' Compensation	20	0.7	0.8	1.9	1.2	1.1	0.9	0.6	0.6	0.5	0.5	0.5	0.1	0.1
Operating Margin	21	•	•	0.9	•	•	•	•	•	•	•	•	•	•
Operating Margin Before Officers' Comp.	22	•	•	2.9	0.5	•	•	•	•	•	•	•	•	•

Selected Average Balance Sheet ($ in Thousands)

Net Receivables 23	430	0	18	122	343	732	1676	4072	8967	16519	50726	82513	459831
Inventories 24	2076	0	72	285	1683	4791	9601	18448	30584	52745	122718	347799	1095431
Net Property, Plant and Equipment 25	438	0	14	103	162	508	1412	4011	10764	30343	71911	187650	1037381
Total Assets 26	3734	0	133	687	2641	7138	14977	33452	65880	139116	307972	1169248	4204569
Notes and Loans Payable 27	2460	0	88	432	1726	5198	10920	23102	42234	90695	199046	420359	1820877
All Other Liabilities 28	468	0	32	141	338	797	1418	3533	8468	15058	36701	310614	700199
Net Worth 29	806	0	13	114	578	1143	2639	6817	15178	33363	72225	438274	1683493

Selected Financial Ratios (Times to 1)

Current Ratio 30	1.3	•	2.4	1.8	1.5	1.2	1.2	1.2	1.2	1.1	1.4	1.2	1.1
Quick Ratio 31	0.3	•	0.8	0.7	0.3	0.3	0.3	0.4	0.4	0.4	0.5	0.3	0.3
Net Sales to Working Capital 32	22.0	•	13.9	10.4	12.9	24.6	27.2	24.3	22.9	33.4	14.3	27.4	44.7
Coverage Ratio 33	2.3	•	3.4	1.4	1.5	1.6	2.6	3.0	3.3	2.9	2.3	3.1	2.3
Total Asset Turnover 34	3.6	•	6.9	3.8	3.7	4.0	3.9	3.6	3.2	2.9	2.7	2.4	2.0
Inventory Turnover 35	5.7	•	10.7	7.6	5.1	5.3	5.4	5.8	6.1	6.5	5.9	7.1	6.5
Receivables Turnover 36	31.4	•	56.8	22.8	27.9	39.9	33.9	29.7	25.2	26.7	16.1	28.3	21.3
Total Liabilities to Net Worth 37	3.6	•	9.2	5.0	3.6	5.2	4.7	3.9	3.3	3.2	3.3	1.7	1.5
Current Assets to Working Capital 38	4.7	•	1.7	2.2	3.1	5.4	5.8	5.4	5.2	7.8	3.3	5.2	9.0
Current Liabilities to Working Capital 39	3.7	•	0.7	1.2	2.1	4.4	4.8	4.4	4.2	6.8	2.3	4.2	8.0
Working Capital to Net Sales 40	0.0	•	0.1	0.1	0.1	0.0	0.0	0.0	0.0	0.0	0.1	0.0	0.0
Inventory to Working Capital 41	3.3	•	1.2	1.3	2.2	4.0	4.2	3.7	3.3	4.8	1.9	3.5	5.9
Total Receipts to Cash Flow 42	26.3	25.7	16.3	18.9	24.0	33.5	29.1	27.6	23.8	22.3	25.0	20.8	18.0
Cost of Goods to Cash Flow 43	23.1	21.8	13.8	15.8	20.9	29.7	25.7	24.5	20.9	19.3	21.9	18.2	15.3
Cash Flow to Total Debt 44	0.2	•	0.5	0.2	0.2	0.1	0.2	0.2	0.2	0.2	0.1	0.2	0.2

Selected Financial Factors (in Percentages)

Debt Ratio 45	78.4	•	90.2	83.4	78.1	84.0	82.4	79.6	77.0	76.0	76.5	62.5	60.0
Return on Total Assets 46	6.0	•	11.6	6.3	4.5	4.4	6.1	6.9	8.0	7.4	5.9	8.0	5.9
Return on Equity Before Income Taxes 47	15.7	•	83.4	11.0	6.7	10.2	21.1	22.6	24.3	20.4	14.1	14.5	8.4
Return on Equity After Income Taxes 48	13.9	•	81.3	10.4	6.1	9.2	20.3	21.2	22.6	18.0	9.6	9.5	5.5
Profit Margin (Before Income Tax) 49	0.9	•	1.2	0.5	0.4	0.4	1.0	1.3	1.7	1.7	1.2	2.3	1.7
Profit Margin (After Income Tax) 50	0.8	•	1.2	0.5	0.4	0.4	0.9	1.2	1.6	1.5	0.8	1.5	1.1

Table II
Corporations with Net Income

NEW AND USED CAR DEALERS

MONEY AMOUNTS AND SIZE OF ASSETS IN THOUSANDS OF DOLLARS

Item Description for Accounting Period 7/05 Through 6/06	Total	Zero Assets	Under 500	500 to 1,000	1,000 to 5,000	5,000 to 10,000	10,000 to 25,000	25,000 to 50,000	50,000 to 100,000	100,000 to 250,000	250,000 to 500,000	500,000 to 2,500,000	2,500,000 and over
Number of Enterprises **1**	30098	807	13733	3551	5291	3294	2618	592	147	49	•	•	•
Revenues ($ in Thousands)													
Net Sales **2**	526911108	547876	17980692	10130673	54655109	100038254	160736057	72663457	32220689	20015819	•	•	•
Interest **3**	906259	1525	12698	10623	98313	92737	138364	75512	30653	68785	•	•	•
Rents **4**	246012	0	0	0	12543	9511	17073	23123	22438	52859	•	•	•
Royalties **5**	9688	0	0	0	0	4789	126	0	0	4060	•	•	•
Other Portfolio Income **6**	627702	841	35541	38400	75376	54922	124882	67748	85299	93983	•	•	•
Other Receipts **7**	9183645	2777	22824	89313	939601	1863301	2927942	1379583	608569	461978	•	•	•
Total Receipts **8**	537891414	553019	18051755	10269009	55780942	102063514	163944444	74209423	32967648	20697484	•	•	•
Average Total Receipts **9**	17871	685	1314	2892	10543	30985	62622	125354	224270	422398	•	•	•
Operating Costs/Operating Income (%)													
Cost of Operations **10**	87.6	85.7	85.6	83.4	86.4	88.5	88.2	88.3	87.6	86.5	•	•	•
Salaries and Wages **11**	5.0	2.6	2.2	3.9	4.9	4.7	5.0	5.0	5.2	5.6	•	•	•
Taxes Paid **12**	0.8	3.2	1.5	1.4	0.9	0.8	0.8	0.7	0.8	0.8	•	•	•
Interest Paid **13**	0.6	0.9	0.4	1.0	0.7	0.6	0.5	0.6	0.7	0.8	•	•	•
Depreciation **14**	0.3	0.1	0.1	0.6	0.2	0.2	0.3	0.4	0.6	0.7	•	•	•
Amortization and Depletion **15**	0.1	0.0	0.0	0.0	0.0	0.0	0.0	0.0	0.0	0.1	•	•	•
Pensions and Other Deferred Comp. **16**	0.1	0.0	0.1	0.0	0.1	0.1	0.1	0.1	0.1	0.1	•	•	•
Employee Benefits **17**	0.4	0.2	0.1	0.1	0.5	0.5	0.4	0.4	0.4	0.5	•	•	•
Advertising **18**	1.1	0.4	0.7	0.7	1.1	1.1	1.1	1.1	1.0	1.1	•	•	•
Other Expenses **19**	3.8	5.9	5.7	6.0	4.3	3.5	3.5	3.3	3.4	4.9	•	•	•
Officers' Compensation **20**	0.7	0.6	1.2	1.1	1.3	0.9	0.6	0.6	0.5	0.5	•	•	•
Operating Margin **21**	•	0.4	2.4	1.7	•	•	•	0.0	•	•	•	•	•
Operating Margin Before Officers' Comp. **22**	0.3	1.0	3.6	2.8	1.0	0.1	0.1	0.2	0.2	•	•	•	•

Selected Average Balance Sheet ($ in Thousands)

Net Receivables 23	553	0	26	135	433	688	1728	3959	9122	16848
Inventories 24	2549	0	80	295	1807	4749	9255	17846	29743	52273
Net Property, Plant and Equipment 25	534	0	16	64	144	525	1454	4111	10710	25556
Total Assets 26	4750	0	168	687	2705	7039	15146	33447	65877	138577
Notes and Loans Payable 27	2882	0	62	332	1558	4787	10605	22323	41395	86792
All Other Liabilities 28	604	0	34	153	342	715	1430	3557	8911	15887
Net Worth 29	1264	0	73	202	805	1537	3112	7567	15571	35897

Selected Financial Ratios (Times to 1)

Current Ratio 30	1.3	·	3.7	2.3	1.7	1.3	1.2	1.3	1.3	1.2
Quick Ratio 31	0.4	·	1.3	0.9	0.5	0.3	0.3	0.4	0.4	0.4
Net Sales to Working Capital 32	20.1	·	12.5	8.4	10.1	22.3	24.5	22.2	22.4	24.8
Coverage Ratio 33	3.6	2.5	7.5	4.2	3.5	3.1	3.9	3.9	3.9	3.4
Total Asset Turnover 34	3.7	·	7.8	4.2	3.8	4.3	4.1	3.7	3.3	2.9
Inventory Turnover 35	6.0	·	14.0	8.1	4.9	5.7	5.9	6.1	6.5	6.8
Receivables Turnover 36	32.4	·	58.7	24.6	22.5	43.6	35.8	31.2	27.3	29.4
Total Liabilities to Net Worth 37	2.8	·	1.3	2.4	2.4	3.6	3.9	3.4	3.2	2.9
Current Assets to Working Capital 38	4.2	·	1.4	1.8	2.4	4.5	5.1	4.8	5.0	5.8
Current Liabilities to Working Capital 39	3.2	·	0.4	0.8	1.4	3.5	4.1	3.8	4.0	4.8
Working Capital to Net Sales 40	0.0	·	0.1	0.1	0.1	0.0	0.0	0.0	0.0	0.0
Inventory to Working Capital 41	2.9	·	0.9	1.1	1.7	3.3	3.6	3.3	3.2	3.6
Total Receipts to Cash Flow 42	23.3	16.5	14.9	13.5	20.4	27.6	25.4	24.9	22.5	21.6
Cost of Goods to Cash Flow 43	20.4	14.1	12.7	11.3	17.6	24.5	22.4	21.9	19.7	18.7
Cash Flow to Total Debt 44	0.2	·	0.9	0.4	0.3	0.2	0.2	0.2	0.2	0.2

Selected Financial Factors (in Percentages)

Debt Ratio 45	73.4	·	56.7	70.6	70.2	78.2	79.5	77.4	76.4	74.1
Return on Total Assets 46	8.6	·	25.0	17.0	9.4	7.7	8.2	8.4	9.1	7.7
Return on Equity Before Income Taxes 47	23.2	·	50.2	44.0	22.6	23.6	29.7	27.6	28.5	21.1
Return on Equity After Income Taxes 48	21.2	·	49.5	43.6	21.8	22.5	28.7	26.1	26.6	18.6
Profit Margin (Before Income Tax) 49	1.7	1.4	2.8	3.1	1.8	1.2	1.5	1.7	2.0	1.9
Profit Margin (After Income Tax) 50	1.5	1.2	2.8	3.1	1.7	1.1	1.5	1.6	1.9	1.6

Table I

Corporations with and without Net Income

OTHER MOTOR VEHICLE AND PARTS DEALERS

MONEY AMOUNTS AND SIZE OF ASSETS IN THOUSANDS OF DOLLARS

Item Description for Accounting Period 7/05 Through 6/06	Total	Zero Assets	Under 500	500 to 1,000	1,000 to 5,000	5,000 to 10,000	10,000 to 25,000	25,000 to 50,000	50,000 to 100,000	100,000 to 250,000	250,000 to 500,000	500,000 to 2,500,000	2,500,000 and over
Number of Enterprises 1	42094	4541	23540	4771	7552	1064	435	106	42	26	7	9	0
Revenues ($ in Thousands)													
Net Sales 2	146678297	1410723	14993199	9018496	43272101	16663476	15117399	8851605	7407372	6020120	3478244	20445563	0
Interest 3	179369	1294	5065	5400	25242	21010	24409	11444	9358	15649	14186	46312	0
Rents 4	75625	209	5142	1965	17732	9064	3638	10222	2581	1718	8842	14511	0
Royalties 5	43377	3408	0	502	1187	0	0	156	0	22410	0	15714	0
Other Portfolio Income 6	300030	24398	38470	353	58571	32294	40029	14885	26657	46272	718	17381	0
Other Receipts 7	1980250	24755	14892	97370	504321	255040	177247	67437	88331	171371	165378	414111	0
Total Receipts 8	149256948	1464787	15056768	9124086	43879154	16980884	15362722	8955749	7534299	6277540	3667368	20953592	0
Average Total Receipts 9	3546	323	640	1912	5810	15959	35317	84488	179388	241444	523910	2328177	•
Operating Costs/Operating Income (%)													
Cost of Operations 10	72.6	64.8	65.7	71.0	76.1	78.9	81.1	79.4	78.6	74.6	67.2	55.5	•
Salaries and Wages 11	9.5	10.5	9.5	8.5	7.9	7.1	6.8	7.5	8.0	9.1	17.1	17.0	•
Taxes Paid 12	1.8	2.9	2.7	2.6	1.4	1.4	1.1	1.2	1.2	1.5	1.4	2.7	•
Interest Paid 13	1.2	2.0	0.8	0.9	1.1	1.4	1.1	1.1	1.1	1.5	1.1	1.2	•
Depreciation 14	1.1	0.9	0.9	1.0	0.6	0.9	1.0	1.1	1.1	2.8	2.1	1.7	•
Amortization and Depletion 15	0.1	0.5	0.1	0.2	0.0	0.1	0.1	0.0	0.1	0.4	1.1	0.2	•
Pensions and Other Deferred Comp. 16	0.2	0.1	0.1	0.2	0.2	0.1	0.1	0.2	0.2	0.5	0.1	0.1	•
Employee Benefits 17	0.7	1.0	0.3	0.5	0.5	0.5	0.7	0.8	1.0	0.9	1.2	1.5	•
Advertising 18	1.3	1.3	1.4	0.9	1.4	1.2	1.0	0.8	0.9	1.6	1.2	1.9	•
Other Expenses 19	8.9	16.0	12.9	11.7	7.7	6.7	5.6	6.1	6.0	6.5	8.3	13.7	•
Officers' Compensation 20	1.7	1.8	5.1	2.9	1.9	1.2	0.9	0.9	0.4	0.7	0.7	0.3	•
Operating Margin 21	1.1	•	0.5	•	1.0	0.4	0.3	1.0	1.3	0.0	•	4.1	•
Operating Margin Before Officers' Comp. 22	2.8	•	5.7	2.6	3.0	1.6	1.3	1.9	1.8	0.7	•	4.4	•

Selected Average Balance Sheet ($ in Thousands)

	•	•	•	•	•	•	•	•	•	•	•	•
Net Receivables 23	158	0	18	77	180	612	1645	5558	10766	20322	33590	149358
Inventories 24	753	0	64	374	1410	3867	8175	16071	38688	37182	78194	581243
Net Property, Plant and Equipment 25	268	0	29	126	277	961	1852	5918	11120	36514	66534	397398
Total Assets 26	1603	0	149	707	2247	7288	14217	34378	72997	151189	349479	1844166
Notes and Loans Payable 27	663	0	77	339	866	3599	7517	18534	38233	72187	94277	526988
All Other Liabilities 28	492	0	39	132	788	2011	3562	8382	18728	33337	68740	721151
Net Worth 29	448	0	32	236	593	1678	3139	7462	16036	45666	186462	596026

Selected Financial Ratios (Times to 1)

	•	•	•	•	•	•	•	•	•	•	•	•
Current Ratio 30	1.4	•	2.1	2.5	1.6	1.4	1.4	1.3	1.2	1.3	1.2	1.1
Quick Ratio 31	0.3	•	0.8	0.7	0.3	0.3	0.3	0.4	0.3	0.5	0.4	0.3
Net Sales to Working Capital 32	10.6	•	11.5	6.2	8.4	9.6	10.3	14.0	16.3	12.3	19.9	22.7
Coverage Ratio 33	3.5	1.9	2.2	2.0	3.1	2.6	2.7	3.0	3.7	4.4	4.5	6.5
Total Asset Turnover 34	2.2	•	4.3	2.7	2.5	2.1	2.4	2.4	2.4	1.5	1.4	1.2
Inventory Turnover 35	3.4	•	6.5	3.6	3.1	3.2	3.4	4.1	3.6	4.6	4.3	2.2
Receivables Turnover 36	24.0	•	36.7	26.1	32.5	30.2	21.1	16.2	17.3	13.0	15.8	18.7
Total Liabilities to Net Worth 37	2.6	•	3.6	2.0	2.8	3.3	3.5	3.6	3.6	2.3	0.9	2.1
Current Assets to Working Capital 38	3.4	•	1.9	1.7	2.7	3.6	3.4	4.4	5.2	3.9	5.3	9.5
Current Liabilities to Working Capital 39	2.4	•	0.9	0.7	1.7	2.6	2.4	3.4	4.2	2.9	4.3	8.5
Working Capital to Net Sales 40	0.1	•	0.1	0.2	0.1	0.1	0.1	0.1	0.1	0.1	0.1	0.0
Inventory to Working Capital 41	2.4	•	1.1	1.2	2.1	2.8	2.6	3.1	3.7	2.2	3.3	6.0
Total Receipts to Cash Flow 42	11.2	8.3	10.1	10.9	12.6	14.2	17.3	15.5	13.8	11.2	11.0	6.6
Cost of Goods to Cash Flow 43	8.2	5.4	6.7	7.7	9.6	11.2	14.0	12.3	10.8	8.3	7.4	3.6
Cash Flow to Total Debt 44	0.3	•	0.5	0.4	0.3	0.2	0.2	0.2	0.2	0.2	0.3	0.3

Selected Financial Factors (in Percentages)

	•	•	•	•	•	•	•	•	•	•	•	•
Debt Ratio 45	72.1	•	78.1	66.6	73.6	77.0	77.9	78.3	78.0	69.8	46.6	67.7
Return on Total Assets 46	8.7	•	7.6	4.9	9.1	8.0	7.5	8.1	10.2	10.3	7.3	9.5
Return on Equity Before Income Taxes 47	22.2	•	18.9	7.2	23.5	21.4	21.4	24.8	33.6	26.2	10.6	24.8
Return on Equity After Income Taxes 48	18.0	•	17.3	5.9	22.3	19.3	19.0	21.8	31.0	19.8	7.9	15.9
Profit Margin (Before Income Tax) 49	2.9	1.8	1.0	0.9	2.4	2.3	1.9	2.2	3.1	5.2	4.0	6.5
Profit Margin (After Income Tax) 50	2.3	1.5	0.9	0.7	2.3	2.1	1.7	1.9	2.8	3.9	3.0	4.2

Table II
Corporations with Net Income

OTHER MOTOR VEHICLE AND PARTS DEALERS

MONEY AMOUNTS AND SIZE OF ASSETS IN THOUSANDS OF DOLLARS

Item Description for Accounting Period 7/05 Through 6/06	Total	Zero Assets	Under 500	500 to 1,000	1,000 to 5,000	5,000 to 10,000	10,000 to 25,000	25,000 to 50,000	50,000 to 100,000	100,000 to 250,000	250,000 to 500,000	500,000 to 2,500,000	2,500,000 and over
Number of Enterprises 1	23550	839	12130	3223	6100	732	366	87	38	19	•	•	0
Revenues ($ in Thousands)													
Net Sales 2	122173194	930098	10174653	6504594	38226345	12314538	13561471	7406976	6868589	4502258	•	•	0
Interest 3	155022	1294	3787	5151	17827	17174	19211	10544	9026	15454	•	•	0
Rents 4	60194	209	4535	1222	14954	3107	3220	10191	1721	245	•	•	0
Royalties 5	20047	3408	0	0	98	0	0	146	0	681	•	•	0
Other Portfolio Income 6	250807	19151	17576	342	51654	31988	33611	13555	24875	45166	•	•	0
Other Receipts 7	1713130	18684	10249	94008	437740	136409	151687	55098	82369	147913	•	•	0
Total Receipts 8	124372394	972844	10210800	6605317	38748618	12503216	13769200	7496510	6986580	4711717	•	•	0
Average Total Receipts 9	5281	1160	842	2049	6352	17081	37621	86167	183857	247985	•	•	•
Operating Costs/Operating Income (%)													
Cost of Operations 10	72.0	69.4	63.5	70.2	75.6	77.3	80.7	79.7	78.5	70.5	•	•	•
Salaries and Wages 11	9.4	9.1	9.8	7.9	7.8	7.1	6.8	7.3	8.1	10.6	•	•	•
Taxes Paid 12	1.7	2.4	2.4	2.7	1.4	1.3	1.1	1.1	1.1	1.7	•	•	•
Interest Paid 13	1.0	1.5	0.5	0.7	1.0	1.3	1.0	1.0	1.1	1.4	•	•	•
Depreciation 14	1.1	0.9	0.9	1.0	0.6	1.0	1.0	0.9	1.0	3.5	•	•	•
Amortization and Depletion 15	0.1	0.2	0.0	0.2	0.0	0.1	0.1	0.0	0.1	0.4	•	•	•
Pensions and Other Deferred Comp. 16	0.2	0.1	0.1	0.2	0.2	0.2	0.1	0.2	0.2	0.6	•	•	•
Employee Benefits 17	0.7	1.1	0.2	0.4	0.5	0.5	0.7	0.7	1.1	1.1	•	•	•
Advertising 18	1.2	1.3	1.3	0.8	1.3	1.1	1.0	0.7	0.9	1.1	•	•	•
Other Expenses 19	8.6	10.3	12.2	11.5	7.6	6.6	5.5	5.5	6.0	6.9	•	•	•
Officers' Compensation 20	1.6	1.0	5.5	2.7	2.0	1.3	0.9	0.9	0.5	0.4	•	•	•
Operating Margin 21	2.4	2.6	3.7	1.6	2.0	2.3	1.0	1.7	1.6	1.8	•	•	•
Operating Margin Before Officers' Comp. 22	4.0	3.6	9.2	4.3	4.0	3.6	1.9	2.6	2.1	2.2	•	•	•

Selected Average Balance Sheet ($ in Thousands)

	•	•	•	•	•	•	•	•	•	•
Net Receivables 23	247	0	27	93	189	712	1700	5723	11001	22483
Inventories 24	1072	0	72	337	1411	4399	7990	16255	37367	33871
Net Property, Plant and Equipment 25	362	0	34	125	266	1045	1897	5631	10260	34521
Total Assets 26	2340	0	173	720	2293	7679	14238	34611	73435	152797
Notes and Loans Payable 27	878	0	58	282	778	3311	7297	18584	37690	71897
All Other Liabilities 28	746	0	48	140	854	2296	3476	8193	19606	32862
Net Worth 29	716	0	67	297	661	2073	3465	7835	16138	48038

Selected Financial Ratios (Times to 1)

	•	•	•	•	•	•	•	•	•	•
Current Ratio 30	1.4	•	2.1	2.4	1.6	1.5	1.5	1.3	1.2	1.6
Quick Ratio 31	0.4	•	0.9	0.8	0.3	0.3	0.3	0.4	0.3	0.6
Net Sales to Working Capital 32	10.7	•	12.9	6.8	8.3	8.8	10.3	14.5	16.4	8.3
Coverage Ratio 33	5.2	5.7	8.8	5.4	4.4	3.9	3.4	3.9	4.0	6.6
Total Asset Turnover 34	2.2	•	4.8	2.8	2.7	2.2	2.6	2.5	2.5	1.6
Inventory Turnover 35	3.5	•	7.4	4.2	3.4	3.0	3.7	4.2	3.8	4.9
Receivables Turnover 36	23.6	•	32.5	23.0	33.6	27.1	22.8	16.7	18.3	11.8
Total Liabilities to Net Worth 37	2.3	•	1.6	1.4	2.5	2.7	3.1	3.4	3.6	2.2
Current Assets to Working Capital 38	3.3	•	1.9	1.7	2.6	3.2	3.2	4.5	5.1	2.8
Current Liabilities to Working Capital 39	2.3	•	0.9	0.7	1.6	2.2	2.2	3.5	4.1	1.8
Working Capital to Net Sales 40	0.1	•	0.1	0.1	0.1	0.1	0.1	0.1	0.1	0.1
Inventory to Working Capital 41	2.4	•	1.0	1.1	2.0	2.4	2.4	3.2	3.7	1.5
Total Receipts to Cash Flow 42	10.0	7.4	8.0	8.8	11.4	11.8	16.0	14.4	13.3	8.9
Cost of Goods to Cash Flow 43	7.2	5.1	5.1	6.2	8.6	9.2	12.9	11.5	10.5	6.3
Cash Flow to Total Debt 44	0.3	•	1.0	0.5	0.3	0.3	0.2	0.2	0.2	0.3

Selected Financial Factors (in Percentages)

	•	•	•	•	•	•	•	•	•	•
Debt Ratio 45	69.4	•	61.4	58.7	71.2	73.0	75.7	77.4	78.0	68.6
Return on Total Assets 46	11.5	•	22.1	11.0	12.0	11.2	9.2	9.8	10.9	13.9
Return on Equity Before Income Taxes 47	30.4	•	50.6	21.7	32.3	30.8	26.6	32.1	37.3	37.4
Return on Equity After Income Taxes 48	25.7	•	49.1	20.1	30.9	28.3	24.1	28.7	34.5	29.0
Profit Margin (Before Income Tax) 49	4.2	7.2	4.0	3.2	3.4	3.8	2.5	3.0	3.3	7.6
Profit Margin (After Income Tax) 50	3.6	6.6	3.9	3.0	3.3	3.5	2.3	2.6	3.1	5.9

Table I
Corporations with and without Net Income

FURNITURE AND HOME FURNISHINGS STORES

MONEY AMOUNTS AND SIZE OF ASSETS IN THOUSANDS OF DOLLARS

Item Description for Accounting Period 7/05 Through 6/06		Total	Zero Assets	Under 500	500 to 1,000	1,000 to 5,000	5,000 to 10,000	10,000 to 25,000	25,000 to 50,000	50,000 to 100,000	100,000 to 250,000	250,000 to 500,000	500,000 to 2,500,000	2,500,000 and over
Number of Enterprises	1	42130	3153	30962	3709	3611	426	175	37	20	23	5	9	0
Revenues ($ in Thousands)														
Net Sales	2	94983666	1130560	17045500	7274037	16993210	7706122	8471587	2615572	3471782	7389671	2904170	19981456	0
Interest	3	244249	1195	1971	15844	57059	4316	3806	11673	201	61887	48589	37708	0
Rents	4	38528	5	1361	1375	7673	5023	1402	1227	470	4432	5982	9578	0
Royalties	5	24521	0	0	0	0	218	4178	0	31	17062	1255	1777	0
Other Portfolio Income	6	225613	83	28592	14740	41559	46206	1435	433	3209	13632	16633	59090	0
Other Receipts	7	668158	10268	15909	22710	71276	56296	114497	62696	58763	127102	25693	102949	0
Total Receipts	8	96184735	1142111	17093333	7328706	17170777	7818181	8596905	2691601	3554456	7613786	3002322	20192558	0
Average Total Receipts	9	2283	362	552	1976	4755	18353	49125	72746	176723	331034	600464	2243618	•
Operating Costs/Operating Income (%)														
Cost of Operations	10	58.3	70.0	60.5	60.3	61.7	63.4	61.5	59.6	53.4	54.8	55.6	51.2	•
Salaries and Wages	11	12.5	9.9	8.5	12.0	12.1	13.1	13.9	15.4	14.8	14.8	14.9	14.0	•
Taxes Paid	12	2.3	1.6	2.2	2.7	2.1	1.7	2.0	2.1	2.1	2.6	3.2	2.7	•
Interest Paid	13	0.6	0.4	0.6	0.7	0.8	0.4	0.5	0.7	0.7	0.8	0.4	0.5	•
Depreciation	14	1.1	0.2	0.8	0.8	0.8	0.7	0.7	1.5	1.2	1.4	1.3	2.0	•
Amortization and Depletion	15	0.2	0.9	0.1	0.0	0.0	0.0	0.5	0.0	0.2	0.4	0.1	0.2	•
Pensions and Other Deferred Comp.	16	0.2	0.0	0.1	0.2	0.2	0.2	0.3	0.2	0.5	0.2	0.4	0.1	•
Employee Benefits	17	0.9	0.3	0.4	1.1	0.7	1.0	0.9	0.9	1.1	0.7	1.4	1.4	•
Advertising	18	4.4	1.5	3.9	4.0	3.3	4.1	4.4	3.7	4.2	6.0	6.7	5.4	•
Other Expenses	19	15.4	21.6	17.2	13.2	14.1	13.2	14.2	15.1	19.5	17.4	17.3	15.1	•
Officers' Compensation	20	2.3	1.5	5.1	4.3	3.1	2.1	1.4	1.0	0.6	0.5	0.6	0.4	•
Operating Margin	21	1.7	•	0.6	0.7	1.1	•	•	•	1.7	0.3	•	7.1	•
Operating Margin Before Officers' Comp.	22	4.0	•	5.7	5.0	4.2	1.9	1.0	0.7	2.2	0.9	•	7.5	•

Selected Average Balance Sheet ($ in Thousands)

		•	•	•	•	•	•	•	•	•	•
Net Receivables 23	119	0	18	98	336	664	2865	6772	5650	24413	68463	91641
Inventories 24	357	0	52	377	840	2921	5900	11150	25230	38747	133050	469674
Net Property, Plant and Equipment 25	264	0	32	115	324	1275	2805	7148	20655	46304	115455	575030
Total Assets 26	1005	0	137	706	1845	6665	15037	32604	74839	161982	337493	1692437
Notes and Loans Payable 27	270	0	68	354	632	1885	4031	9003	12959	40399	59385	263301
All Other Liabilities 28	381	0	37	201	614	2906	7055	12652	31716	61317	143219	695962
Net Worth 29	353	0	32	151	599	1875	3951	10950	30164	60267	134889	733173

Selected Financial Ratios (Times to 1)

		•	•	•	•	•	•	•	•	•	•
Current Ratio 30	1.6	•	1.9	2.4	1.9	1.5	1.2	1.4	1.4	1.5	1.3	1.5
Quick Ratio 31	0.5	•	0.8	0.7	0.7	0.3	0.5	0.6	0.4	0.7	0.5	0.3
Net Sales to Working Capital 32	9.7	•	12.7	6.0	7.1	11.2	27.4	11.7	14.0	11.4	12.3	8.0
Coverage Ratio 33	5.8	•	2.4	3.0	3.6	4.0	3.0	4.8	6.0	5.0	4.7	18.7
Total Asset Turnover 34	2.2	•	4.0	2.8	2.6	2.7	3.2	2.2	2.3	2.0	1.7	1.3
Inventory Turnover 35	3.7	•	6.3	3.1	3.5	3.9	5.0	3.8	3.7	4.5	2.4	2.4
Receivables Turnover 36	18.8	•	27.3	19.0	14.4	30.2	16.3	10.1	23.4	13.9	9.9	23.4
Total Liabilities to Net Worth 37	1.8	•	3.2	3.7	2.1	2.6	2.8	2.0	1.5	1.7	1.5	1.3
Current Assets to Working Capital 38	2.7	•	2.1	1.7	2.1	3.2	6.0	3.7	3.3	3.1	4.4	3.2
Current Liabilities to Working Capital 39	1.7	•	1.1	0.7	1.1	2.2	5.0	2.7	2.3	2.1	3.4	2.2
Working Capital to Net Sales 40	0.1	•	0.1	0.2	0.1	0.1	0.0	0.1	0.1	0.1	0.1	0.1
Inventory to Working Capital 41	1.6	•	1.2	1.2	1.2	2.2	3.2	1.7	2.3	1.4	2.4	1.9
Total Receipts to Cash Flow 42	8.3	13.0	8.5	10.3	9.4	12.3	11.1	8.1	6.4	7.1	7.8	6.2
Cost of Goods to Cash Flow 43	4.8	9.1	5.1	6.2	5.8	7.8	6.8	4.8	3.4	3.9	4.4	3.2
Cash Flow to Total Debt 44	0.4	•	0.6	0.3	0.4	0.3	0.4	0.4	0.6	0.4	0.4	0.4

Selected Financial Factors (in Percentages)

		•	•	•	•	•	•	•	•	•	•
Debt Ratio 45	64.8	•	76.3	78.6	67.5	71.9	73.7	66.4	59.7	62.8	60.0	56.7
Return on Total Assets 46	8.0	•	5.9	6.1	7.6	4.6	5.2	7.3	9.6	8.2	3.0	11.1
Return on Equity Before Income Taxes 47	18.8	•	14.7	18.9	16.9	12.1	13.3	17.2	19.8	17.7	5.9	24.3
Return on Equity After Income Taxes 48	13.9	•	14.0	16.8	14.9	10.4	10.5	15.6	18.7	13.2	4.6	15.9
Profit Margin (Before Income Tax) 49	3.0	•	0.9	1.5	2.2	1.3	1.1	2.7	3.4	3.3	1.4	8.0
Profit Margin (After Income Tax) 50	2.2	•	0.8	1.3	1.9	1.1	0.9	2.4	3.2	2.5	1.1	5.3

Table II

Corporations with Net Income

FURNITURE AND HOME FURNISHINGS STORES

MONEY AMOUNTS AND SIZE OF ASSETS IN THOUSANDS OF DOLLARS

Item Description for Accounting Period 7/05 Through 6/06		Total	Zero Assets	Under 500	500 to 1,000	1,000 to 5,000	5,000 to 10,000	10,000 to 25,000	25,000 to 50,000	50,000 to 100,000	100,000 to 250,000	250,000 to 500,000	500,000 to 2,500,000	2,500,000 and over
Number of Enterprises	1	23041	252	17473	2276	2514	324	126	29	16	18	·	·	0
Revenues ($ in Thousands)														
Net Sales	2	75874064	29108	11339758	5517211	13818708	7130283	6434017	2207526	3054297	5925947	·	·	0
Interest	3	200899	0	617	2333	40136	3381	2094	11598	148	60792	·	·	0
Rents	4	27973	0	0	876	4487	4241	1277	1227	0	3881	·	·	0
Royalties	5	1847	0	0	0	0	218	0	0	31	72	·	·	0
Other Portfolio Income	6	189415	62	26193	14392	39475	44411	736	368	2833	10808	·	·	0
Other Receipts	7	503123	0	7192	16691	41668	47430	75675	38253	56040	93238	·	·	0
Total Receipts	8	76797321	29170	11373760	5551503	13944474	7229964	6513799	2258972	3113349	6094738	·	·	0
Average Total Receipts	9	3333	116	651	2439	5547	22315	51697	77896	194584	338597	·	·	·
Operating Costs/Operating Income (%)														
Cost of Operations	10	57.9	45.8	59.5	61.5	62.1	62.5	62.5	60.2	53.5	53.9	·	·	·
Salaries and Wages	11	12.3	·	8.3	10.7	11.6	13.3	13.2	14.8	15.1	14.8	·	·	·
Taxes Paid	12	2.3	0.8	2.0	2.6	2.0	1.8	1.8	2.0	2.1	2.4	·	·	·
Interest Paid	13	0.5	·	0.4	0.7	0.7	0.4	0.3	0.6	0.7	0.7	·	·	·
Depreciation	14	1.2	5.4	0.8	0.8	0.8	0.7	0.6	1.6	1.0	1.2	·	·	·
Amortization and Depletion	15	0.1	·	0.1	0.0	0.0	0.0	0.0	0.0	0.2	0.4	·	·	·
Pensions and Other Deferred Comp.	16	0.2	·	0.1	0.2	0.2	0.2	0.2	0.2	0.6	0.2	·	·	·
Employee Benefits	17	0.9	·	0.3	0.9	0.6	1.1	1.0	1.0	1.2	0.9	·	·	·
Advertising	18	4.4	0.3	3.8	3.1	3.1	4.4	4.2	3.5	4.5	6.3	·	·	·
Other Expenses	19	14.1	47.7	15.4	11.1	13.1	12.9	11.7	13.9	18.1	16.4	·	·	·
Officers' Compensation	20	2.2	·	5.1	4.2	3.1	2.2	1.5	0.9	0.5	0.6	·	·	·
Operating Margin	21	3.9	0.1	4.2	4.1	2.7	0.5	3.0	1.3	2.6	2.2	·	·	·
Operating Margin Before Officers' Comp.	22	6.0	0.1	9.2	8.3	5.8	2.8	4.5	2.2	3.1	2.9	·	·	·

Selected Average Balance Sheet ($ in Thousands)

Net Receivables 23	165	0	19	109	343	679	3124	6511	6182	25535
Inventories 24	495	0	51	324	883	2541	6381	10882	26147	36347
Net Property, Plant and Equipment 25	398	0	31	141	361	1354	2555	7337	18841	47979
Total Assets 26	1451	0	133	724	1995	6568	15147	32581	74228	162169
Notes and Loans Payable 27	315	0	44	193	618	1673	2722	8475	13006	42172
All Other Liabilities 28	552	0	30	197	680	3108	6679	11347	34047	53610
Net Worth 29	584	0	59	335	696	1787	5747	12760	27175	66387

Selected Financial Ratios (Times to 1)

Current Ratio 30	1.6	•	2.6	2.4	1.9	1.3	1.4	1.6	1.5	1.5
Quick Ratio 31	0.5	•	1.2	0.7	0.7	0.3	0.6	0.7	0.4	0.8
Net Sales to Working Capital 32	9.7	•	11.1	7.7	7.4	22.1	14.6	8.8	14.0	10.5
Coverage Ratio 33	10.5	•	11.8	8.0	6.2	5.6	15.1	7.4	7.5	7.8
Total Asset Turnover 34	2.3	•	4.9	3.3	2.8	3.4	3.4	2.3	2.6	2.0
Inventory Turnover 35	3.8	•	7.6	4.6	3.9	5.4	5.0	4.2	3.9	4.9
Receivables Turnover 36	19.7	•	28.1	26.2	16.7	37.7	14.7	11.1	28.8	14.1
Total Liabilities to Net Worth 37	1.5	•	1.3	1.2	1.9	2.7	1.6	1.6	1.7	1.4
Current Assets to Working Capital 38	2.7	•	1.6	1.7	2.1	4.9	3.2	2.6	3.2	2.9
Current Liabilities to Working Capital 39	1.7	•	0.6	0.7	1.1	3.9	2.2	1.6	2.2	1.9
Working Capital to Net Sales 40	0.1	•	0.1	0.1	0.1	0.0	0.1	0.1	0.1	0.1
Inventory to Working Capital 41	1.6	•	0.9	1.2	1.2	3.2	1.7	1.2	2.1	1.2
Total Receipts to Cash Flow 42	7.4	3.0	7.0	8.5	8.8	11.8	9.2	8.0	6.5	6.2
Cost of Goods to Cash Flow 43	4.3	1.4	4.2	5.2	5.5	7.4	5.8	4.8	3.5	3.4
Cash Flow to Total Debt 44	0.5	•	0.7	0.5	0.5	0.4	0.6	0.5	0.6	0.6

Selected Financial Factors (in Percentages)

Debt Ratio 45	59.8	•	55.9	53.8	65.1	72.8	62.1	60.8	63.4	59.1
Return on Total Assets 46	12.7	•	23.8	18.0	11.9	7.9	15.2	9.8	13.3	11.7
Return on Equity Before Income Taxes 47	28.5	•	49.3	34.1	28.5	23.9	37.3	21.6	31.5	24.9
Return on Equity After Income Taxes 48	23.1	•	48.7	32.6	26.1	21.5	34.7	19.9	29.9	19.6
Profit Margin (Before Income Tax) 49	5.1	0.3	4.5	4.7	3.6	1.9	4.2	3.6	4.5	5.0
Profit Margin (After Income Tax) 50	4.1	0.3	4.4	4.5	3.3	1.7	3.9	3.3	4.3	4.0

Table I

Corporations with and without Net Income

ELECTRONICS AND APPLIANCE STORES

MONEY AMOUNTS AND SIZE OF ASSETS IN THOUSANDS OF DOLLARS

Item Description for Accounting Period 7/05 Through 6/06	Total	Zero Assets	Under 500	500 to 1,000	1,000 to 5,000	5,000 to 10,000	10,000 to 25,000	25,000 to 50,000	50,000 to 100,000	100,000 to 250,000	250,000 to 500,000	500,000 to 2,500,000	2,500,000 and over
Number of Enterprises 1	31164	3804	22215	2053	2634	220	128	49	24	15	11	8	3
Revenues ($ in Thousands)													
Net Sales 2	124004209	965310	10592487	5559530	21103048	3563985	4611058	4589097	4650325	4617888	7545610	14964136	41241735
Interest 3	336858	1007	5313	4948	4919	2285	7190	5414	4982	4343	127514	117993	50951
Rents 4	63488	110	2618	0	2490	0	2178	83	181	2269	3365	8370	41825
Royalties 5	38861	0	0	0	0	0	5268	0	0	97	3916	29530	50
Other Portfolio Income 6	729936	10597	523	551	39938	14568	1202	641	581	5890	36812	517141	101492
Other Receipts 7	1490660	3823	116752	27197	218829	37058	25472	31796	38010	75978	37028	383950	494767
Total Receipts 8	126664012	980847	10717693	5592226	21369224	3617896	4652368	4627031	4694079	4706465	7754245	16021120	41930820
Average Total Receipts 9	4064	258	482	2724	8113	16445	36347	94429	195587	313764	704931	2002640	13976940
Operating Costs/Operating Income (%)													
Cost of Operations 10	70.3	75.3	54.4	46.6	76.1	58.3	68.8	74.2	71.5	77.1	71.6	68.6	74.6
Salaries and Wages 11	10.7	8.9	14.0	20.3	8.3	18.1	11.2	10.5	11.7	9.5	10.9	13.3	8.3
Taxes Paid 12	1.8	3.4	2.8	3.0	1.4	1.9	1.5	1.0	1.3	1.0	1.3	2.8	1.4
Interest Paid 13	0.5	0.9	0.6	0.6	0.5	0.8	0.5	0.5	0.5	0.4	0.9	0.7	0.4
Depreciation 14	0.8	1.0	1.1	0.7	0.5	0.6	1.2	0.5	1.1	1.0	1.0	1.1	0.7
Amortization and Depletion 15	0.1	1.8	0.1	0.2	0.1	0.4	0.2	0.1	0.2	0.1	0.6	0.1	0.0
Pensions and Other Deferred Comp. 16	0.2	0.0	0.2	0.8	0.1	0.6	0.3	0.2	0.1	0.1	0.1	0.1	0.1
Employee Benefits 17	0.6	1.3	0.7	1.5	0.6	1.8	0.6	0.6	0.8	0.6	0.8	0.6	0.4
Advertising 18	2.2	1.2	1.7	2.3	2.4	0.9	1.8	2.2	1.2	1.0	3.9	2.1	2.5
Other Expenses 19	9.6	15.7	17.7	13.8	7.6	11.3	9.2	10.0	8.6	5.7	9.4	9.5	8.5
Officers' Compensation 20	1.7	4.2	5.5	7.0	2.2	3.9	1.7	1.3	0.8	1.2	0.7	0.7	0.2
Operating Margin 21	1.4	•	1.2	3.2	0.3	1.3	3.0	•	2.2	2.4	•	0.3	3.0
Operating Margin Before Officers' Comp. 22	3.1	•	6.7	10.1	2.6	5.3	4.6	0.3	3.0	3.6	0.7	1.0	3.1

Selected Average Balance Sheet ($ in Thousands)

Net Receivables 23	215	0	11	127	417	1585	4322	14968	13985	43789	80873	125608	195189
Inventories 24	367	0	38	188	633	1010	3202	4487	11400	26692	66535	171312	1638274
Net Property, Plant and Equipment 25	240	0	17	104	340	548	1824	2110	10134	14589	45734	147612	1122390
Total Assets 26	1556	0	110	676	2044	6858	15696	33821	73327	165070	354869	1070370	5795991
Notes and Loans Payable 27	318	0	78	198	562	2237	3617	3508	17386	14516	46551	219730	744968
All Other Liabilities 28	672	0	50	225	918	3144	7584	19643	32824	81484	164831	402329	2427065
Net Worth 29	566	0	-18	253	564	1477	4496	10671	23117	69070	143487	448312	2623958

Selected Financial Ratios (Times to 1)

Current Ratio 30	1.4	•	1.1	1.8	1.5	1.2	1.4	1.4	1.2	1.4	1.5	1.6	1.4
Quick Ratio 31	0.6	•	0.5	1.0	0.8	0.8	0.8	1.0	0.7	1.0	0.8	0.7	0.2
Net Sales to Working Capital 32	14.1	•	105.0	14.4	14.9	25.5	9.7	12.9	22.5	12.5	8.8	8.8	14.8
Coverage Ratio 33	7.5	•	5.2	7.7	4.5	4.6	9.0	0.7	6.7	12.4	2.5	11.0	11.5
Total Asset Turnover 34	2.6	•	4.3	4.0	3.9	2.4	2.3	2.8	2.6	1.9	1.9	1.7	2.4
Inventory Turnover 35	7.6	•	6.9	6.7	9.6	9.4	7.7	15.5	12.2	8.9	7.4	7.5	6.3
Receivables Turnover 36	18.6	•	31.7	14.7	19.1	12.9	8.1	7.5	12.8	7.6	7.4	20.7	60.8
Total Liabilities to Net Worth 37	1.7	•	•	1.7	2.6	3.6	2.5	2.2	2.2	1.4	1.5	1.4	1.2
Current Assets to Working Capital 38	3.4	•	14.4	2.3	2.9	7.0	3.3	3.8	5.1	3.8	3.1	2.7	3.5
Current Liabilities to Working Capital 39	2.4	•	13.4	1.3	1.9	6.0	2.3	2.8	4.1	2.8	2.1	1.7	2.5
Working Capital to Net Sales 40	0.1	•	0.0	0.1	0.1	0.0	0.1	0.1	0.0	0.1	0.1	0.1	0.1
Inventory to Working Capital 41	1.3	•	7.0	0.9	1.3	1.6	0.8	0.7	1.6	0.7	0.9	1.0	1.8
Total Receipts to Cash Flow 42	10.1	•	7.2	6.7	13.9	9.5	9.3	16.5	11.0	11.0	14.6	7.6	10.3
Cost of Goods to Cash Flow 43	7.1	•	3.9	3.1	10.6	5.6	6.4	12.3	7.9	8.5	10.4	5.2	7.7
Cash Flow to Total Debt 44	0.4	•	0.5	1.0	0.4	0.3	0.3	0.2	0.4	0.3	0.2	0.4	0.4

Selected Financial Factors (in Percentages)

Debt Ratio 45	63.6	•	116.4	62.6	72.4	78.5	71.4	68.5	68.5	58.2	59.6	58.1	54.7
Return on Total Assets 46	10.3	•	12.7	17.3	8.1	8.6	9.9	1.0	9.7	8.8	4.4	14.1	11.5
Return on Equity Before Income Taxes 47	24.5	•	•	40.2	22.8	31.1	30.8	•	26.0	19.3	6.5	30.6	23.2
Return on Equity After Income Taxes 48	18.5	•	•	39.5	21.1	29.3	27.7	•	24.5	18.6	3.2	23.3	15.1
Profit Margin (Before Income Tax) 49	3.5	•	2.4	3.8	1.6	2.8	3.8	•	3.1	4.3	1.4	7.3	4.4
Profit Margin (After Income Tax) 50	2.6	•	2.3	3.7	1.5	2.7	2.9	•	2.9	4.2	0.7	5.6	2.9

Table II
Corporations with Net Income

ELECTRONICS AND APPLIANCE STORES

MONEY AMOUNTS AND SIZE OF ASSETS IN THOUSANDS OF DOLLARS

Item Description for Accounting Period 7/05 Through 6/06	Total	Zero Assets	Under 500	500 to 1,000	1,000 to 5,000	5,000 to 10,000	10,000 to 25,000	25,000 to 50,000	50,000 to 100,000	100,000 to 250,000	250,000 to 500,000	500,000 to 2,500,000	2,500,000 and over
Number of Enterprises **1**	16950	2276	10657	1631	1992	199	113	38	16	11	•	•	3
Revenues ($ in Thousands)													
Net Sales **2**	108743554	156920	6269242	4934401	17735295	3340196	4292500	4020313	3462333	4282039	•	•	41241735
Interest **3**	299620	0	4822	1433	4008	1819	4580	3951	4165	2086	•	•	50951
Rents **4**	57360	0	2089	0	2490	0	2178	83	181	2269	•	•	41825
Royalties **5**	38764	0	0	0	0	0	5268	0	0	0	•	•	50
Other Portfolio Income **6**	693054	10286	505	551	39120	14568	1157	627	182	4633	•	•	101492
Other Receipts **7**	1241261	8047	96541	14226	82711	33609	23850	18599	28965	53335	•	•	494767
Total Receipts **8**	111073613	175253	6373199	4950611	17863624	3390192	4329533	4043573	3495826	4344362	•	•	41930820
Average Total Receipts **9**	6553	77	598	3035	8968	17036	38314	106410	218489	394942	•	•	13976940
Operating Costs/Operating Income (%)													
Cost of Operations **10**	70.9	36.5	54.2	43.4	76.7	58.8	69.4	74.9	69.5	79.9	•	•	74.6
Salaries and Wages **11**	10.2	5.3	11.5	21.4	7.6	17.5	10.8	9.2	11.9	7.4	•	•	8.3
Taxes Paid **12**	1.7	1.3	2.3	3.2	1.2	1.9	1.5	0.9	1.6	0.9	•	•	1.4
Interest Paid **13**	0.5	•	0.4	0.4	0.4	0.7	0.4	0.2	0.6	0.4	•	•	0.4
Depreciation **14**	0.8	0.7	0.8	0.8	0.4	0.6	0.8	0.3	1.2	1.0	•	•	0.7
Amortization and Depletion **15**	0.1	0.4	0.1	0.2	0.1	0.4	0.2	0.1	0.2	0.1	•	•	0.0
Pensions and Other Deferred Comp. **16**	0.2	•	0.3	0.9	0.1	0.6	0.3	0.1	0.1	0.1	•	•	0.1
Employee Benefits **17**	0.5	•	0.5	1.6	0.4	1.8	0.6	0.5	0.8	0.5	•	•	0.4
Advertising **18**	2.2	0.2	1.7	2.5	2.4	0.9	1.8	1.9	1.1	0.9	•	•	2.5
Other Expenses **19**	8.6	24.0	15.6	14.0	6.5	9.5	8.2	6.2	8.4	4.0	•	•	8.5
Officers' Compensation **20**	1.5	7.3	6.2	7.2	2.0	4.1	1.6	1.2	0.7	1.1	•	•	0.2
Operating Margin **21**	2.9	24.3	6.4	4.3	2.1	3.3	4.3	4.4	4.0	3.6	•	•	3.0
Operating Margin Before Officers' Comp. **22**	4.4	31.6	12.6	11.6	4.2	7.4	5.9	5.7	4.7	4.8	•	•	3.1

Selected Average Balance Sheet ($ in Thousands)

Net Receivables 23	319	0	16	111	403	1648	4438	14099	16616	46449	•	195189
Inventories 24	587	0	38	156	677	1033	3305	4838	19640	30681	•	1638274
Net Property, Plant and Equipment 25	385	0	17	116	322	588	1646	2122	11942	18761	•	1122390
Total Assets 26	2469	0	123	689	2158	6926	15612	33575	73366	163999	•	5795991
Notes and Loans Payable 27	454	0	60	197	488	2195	3610	3094	21872	19739	•	744968
All Other Liabilities 28	1050	0	50	223	911	3310	8073	18748	32570	82727	•	2427065
Net Worth 29	965	0	13	269	759	1421	3928	11732	18924	61533	•	2623958

Selected Financial Ratios (Times to 1)

Current Ratio 30	1.4	•	1.4	1.7	1.2	1.4	1.4	1.3	1.1	•	•	1.4
Quick Ratio 31	0.6	•	0.9	1.0	0.8	0.8	1.0	0.6	0.7	•	•	0.2
Net Sales to Working Capital 32	13.9	•	25.7	17.2	13.0	27.2	10.5	14.3	19.5	63.8	•	14.8
Coverage Ratio 33	11.0	•	19.9	11.6	7.8	7.9	12.9	30.9	8.9	14.0	•	11.5
Total Asset Turnover 34	2.6	•	4.8	4.4	4.1	2.4	2.4	3.2	2.9	2.4	•	2.4
Inventory Turnover 35	7.7	•	8.4	8.4	10.1	9.5	8.0	16.4	7.7	10.1	•	6.3
Receivables Turnover 36	21.3	•	32.6	20.3	24.3	14.7	9.1	8.5	26.0	10.7	•	60.8
Total Liabilities to Net Worth 37	1.6	•	8.6	1.6	1.8	3.9	3.0	1.9	2.9	1.7	•	1.2
Current Assets to Working Capital 38	3.3	•	3.6	2.4	2.4	7.3	3.4	3.7	4.5	15.5	•	3.5
Current Liabilities to Working Capital 39	2.3	•	2.6	1.4	1.4	6.3	2.4	2.7	3.5	14.5	•	2.5
Working Capital to Net Sales 40	0.1	•	0.0	0.1	0.0	0.0	0.1	0.1	0.1	0.0	•	0.1
Inventory to Working Capital 41	1.3	•	1.2	1.0	1.2	1.6	0.9	0.8	1.8	3.7	•	1.8
Total Receipts to Cash Flow 42	9.3	2.2	5.3	6.2	13.2	8.9	8.9	10.1	9.9	12.1	•	10.3
Cost of Goods to Cash Flow 43	6.6	0.8	2.9	2.7	10.1	5.2	6.2	7.5	6.9	9.7	•	7.7
Cash Flow to Total Debt 44	0.5	•	1.0	1.2	0.5	0.3	0.4	0.5	0.4	0.3	•	0.4

Selected Financial Factors (in Percentages)

Debt Ratio 45	60.9	89.6	60.9	64.8	79.5	74.8	65.1	74.2	62.5	•	•	54.7
Return on Total Assets 46	14.3	40.5	22.4	13.4	13.3	13.6	16.2	16.5	13.0	•	•	11.5
Return on Equity Before Income Taxes 47	33.2	370.3	52.4	33.3	56.8	49.7	45.0	56.7	32.2	•	•	23.2
Return on Equity After Income Taxes 48	26.8	366.0	51.6	31.7	54.7	45.7	37.5	53.9	31.2	•	•	15.1
Profit Margin (Before Income Tax) 49	5.0	36.0	8.0	4.7	2.8	5.1	5.0	5.0	5.1	•	•	4.4
Profit Margin (After Income Tax) 50	4.0	35.8	7.9	4.6	2.7	4.7	4.2	4.7	4.9	•	•	2.9

Table I

Corporations with and without Net Income

HOMES CENTERS; PAINT AND WALLPAPER STORES

MONEY AMOUNTS AND SIZE OF ASSETS IN THOUSANDS OF DOLLARS

Item Description for Accounting Period 7/05 Through 6/06	Total	Zero Assets	Under 500	500 to 1,000	1,000 to 5,000	5,000 to 10,000	10,000 to 25,000	25,000 to 50,000	50,000 to 100,000	100,000 to 250,000	250,000 to 500,000	500,000 to 2,500,000	2,500,000 and over
Number of Enterprises 1	3200	254	1943	415	485	38	44	9	6	3	0	0	3
Revenues ($ in Thousands)													
Net Sales 2	139447205	12594	1639811	570163	3185210	791924	1645089	603387	1098265	2344374	0	0	127556388
Interest 3	414810	0	815	100	3290	1544	928	1560	2	2398	0	0	404173
Rents 4	49293	0	0	10	1113	2734	184	0	0	0	0	0	45253
Royalties 5	157734	0	0	0	0	0	0	0	0	0	0	0	157734
Other Portfolio Income 6	49029	0	1726	73	5484	2071	253	119	3460	155	0	0	35688
Other Receipts 7	2115034	10	832	4565	23785	363	18531	2813	9612	59632	0	0	1994890
Total Receipts 8	142233105	12604	1643184	574911	3218882	798636	1664985	607879	1111339	2406559	0	0	130194126
Average Total Receipts 9	44448	50	846	1385	6637	21017	37841	67542	185223	802186	•		•	43398042
Operating Costs/Operating Income (%)													
Cost of Operations 10	66.8	•	64.8	68.7	72.5	74.4	72.1	68.8	71.9	74.1	•	•	66.4
Salaries and Wages 11	10.8	•	12.1	7.2	9.9	9.7	10.1	13.7	10.5	10.0	•	•	10.8
Taxes Paid 12	2.2	1.6	6.2	3.3	2.4	1.5	1.6	1.8	1.7	0.9	•	•	2.2
Interest Paid 13	0.6	•	0.5	2.4	0.7	0.3	0.6	1.0	0.6	0.8	•	•	0.6
Depreciation 14	1.6	0.5	0.5	1.6	0.6	1.0	0.9	1.1	1.0	1.1	•	•	1.6
Amortization and Depletion 15	0.1	•	•	0.0	0.0	0.0	0.0	0.0	0.1	0.3	•	•	0.1
Pensions and Other Deferred Comp. 16	0.2	•	0.0	0.1	0.3	0.3	0.2	0.5	0.4	0.0	•	•	0.2
Employee Benefits 17	0.5	•	0.3	0.6	0.8	0.9	1.1	1.3	0.6	0.4	•	•	0.5
Advertising 18	1.6	1.3	0.9	1.0	0.5	0.7	0.9	0.9	0.7	0.1	•	•	1.6
Other Expenses 19	6.7	97.6	10.4	11.4	6.7	5.3	8.0	10.3	8.4	5.0	•	•	6.6
Officers' Compensation 20	0.2	•	3.0	5.4	3.0	2.0	1.2	0.6	1.1	1.4	•	•	0.0
Operating Margin 21	8.7	•	1.2	•	2.6	3.8	3.4	0.1	2.9	5.8	•	•	9.2
Operating Margin Before Officers' Comp. 22	8.9	•	4.2	3.6	5.6	5.8	4.6	0.7	4.0	7.2	•	•	9.3

Selected Average Balance Sheet ($ in Thousands)

Net Receivables 23	5102	0	33	72	621	1792	4112	6240	13909	131840	•	5048697
Inventories 24	5878	0	96	212	855	2693	4545	10606	24012	81334	•	5777715
Net Property, Plant and Equipment 25	11040	0	8	409	217	1171	2584	7188	12664	95850	•	11483650
Total Assets 26	34742	0	168	791	2324	7107	13912	31794	70167	446004	•	35487797
Notes and Loans Payable 27	10048	0	71	525	768	1449	4014	7721	16766	121825	•	10218473
All Other Liabilities 28	11079	0	77	202	481	1829	3617	10415	9016	138114	•	11399971
Net Worth 29	13615	0	20	64	1075	3830	6281	13658	44385	186064	•	13870354

Selected Financial Ratios (Times to 1)

Current Ratio 30	1.2	•	2.0	1.3	2.9	2.0	2.1	1.9	4.3	2.0	•	1.1
Quick Ratio 31	0.5	•	0.8	0.4	1.3	1.0	1.0	1.0	1.8	1.2	•	0.5
Net Sales to Working Capital 32	27.8	•	10.4	16.0	5.2	8.3	7.3	6.1	5.8	6.2	•	39.6
Coverage Ratio 33	19.3	•	4.1	0.6	6.6	15.5	8.4	1.9	7.7	12.1	•	20.7
Total Asset Turnover 34	1.3	•	5.0	1.7	2.8	2.9	2.7	2.1	2.6	1.8	•	1.2
Inventory Turnover 35	5.0	•	5.7	4.5	5.6	5.8	5.9	4.3	5.5	7.1	•	4.9
Receivables Turnover 36	5.4	•	22.3	19.0	10.5	15.0	10.1	13.0	12.2	6.1	•	5.2
Total Liabilities to Net Worth 37	1.6	•	7.4	11.3	1.2	0.9	1.2	1.3	0.6	1.4	•	1.6
Current Assets to Working Capital 38	7.7	•	2.0	4.1	1.5	2.0	1.9	2.1	1.3	2.0	•	10.9
Current Liabilities to Working Capital 39	6.7	•	1.0	3.1	0.5	1.0	0.9	1.1	0.3	1.0	•	9.9
Working Capital to Net Sales 40	0.0	•	0.1	0.1	0.2	0.1	0.1	0.2	0.2	0.2	•	0.0
Inventory to Working Capital 41	3.9	•	1.1	2.9	0.7	0.9	0.9	1.0	0.7	0.6	•	5.7
Total Receipts to Cash Flow 42	6.4	1.1	11.6	17.0	11.6	12.5	9.4	12.3	9.6	8.2	•	6.2
Cost of Goods to Cash Flow 43	4.3	•	7.5	11.7	8.4	9.3	6.8	8.5	6.9	6.1	•	4.1
Cash Flow to Total Debt 44	0.3	•	0.5	0.1	0.5	0.5	0.3	0.3	0.7	0.4	•	0.3

Selected Financial Factors (in Percentages)

Debt Ratio 45	60.8	•	88.1	91.9	53.7	46.1	54.9	57.0	36.7	58.3	•	60.9
Return on Total Assets 46	14.5	•	9.3	2.6	12.3	14.6	14.1	3.8	12.3	16.2	•	14.6
Return on Equity Before Income Taxes 47	35.0	•	59.1	•	22.6	25.3	27.5	4.2	16.9	35.6	•	35.5
Return on Equity After Income Taxes 48	23.6	•	55.7	•	21.0	18.3	26.4	3.6	15.1	24.4	•	23.7
Profit Margin (Before Income Tax) 49	10.9	•	1.4	•	3.7	4.6	4.6	0.9	4.1	8.5	•	11.6
Profit Margin (After Income Tax) 50	7.4	•	1.3	•	3.4	3.4	4.4	0.7	3.7	5.8	•	7.7

Table II
Corporations with Net Income

HOMES CENTERS; PAINT AND WALLPAPER STORES

MONEY AMOUNTS AND SIZE OF ASSETS IN THOUSANDS OF DOLLARS

Item Description for Accounting Period 7/05 Through 6/06	Total	Zero Assets	Under 500	500 to 1,000	1,000 to 5,000	5,000 to 10,000	10,000 to 25,000	25,000 to 50,000	50,000 to 100,000	100,000 to 250,000	250,000 to 500,000	500,000 to 2,500,000	2,500,000 and over
Number of Enterprises **1**	1527	0	845	213	368	38	44	•	•	3	0	0	3

Revenues ($ in Thousands)

	Total	Zero Assets	Under 500	500 to 1,000	1,000 to 5,000	5,000 to 10,000	10,000 to 25,000	25,000 to 50,000	50,000 to 100,000	100,000 to 250,000	250,000 to 500,000	500,000 to 2,500,000	2,500,000 and over
Net Sales **2**	138438353	0	1425769	342536	2749304	791924	1645089	•	•	2344374	0	0	127556388
Interest **3**	413220	0	815	0	3232	1544	928	•	•	2398	0	0	404173
Rents **4**	49283	0	0	0	1113	2734	184	•	•	0	0	0	45253
Royalties **5**	157734	0	0	0	0	0	0	•	•	0	0	0	157734
Other Portfolio Income **6**	47527	0	331	73	5484	2071	253	•	•	155	0	0	35688
Other Receipts **7**	2108194	0	761	2792	20039	363	18531	•	•	59632	0	0	1994890
Total Receipts **8**	141214311	0	1427676	345401	2779172	798636	1664985	•	•	2406559	0	0	130194126
Average Total Receipts **9**	92478	•	1690	1622	7552	21017	37841	•	•	802186	•	•	43398042

Operating Costs/Operating Income (%)

	Total	Zero Assets	Under 500	500 to 1,000	1,000 to 5,000	5,000 to 10,000	10,000 to 25,000	25,000 to 50,000	50,000 to 100,000	100,000 to 250,000	250,000 to 500,000	500,000 to 2,500,000	2,500,000 and over
Cost of Operations **10**	66.8	•	65.9	68.9	71.4	74.4	72.1	•	•	74.1	•	•	66.4
Salaries and Wages **11**	10.8	•	11.1	5.0	10.4	9.7	10.1	•	•	10.0	•	•	10.8
Taxes Paid **12**	2.2	•	6.8	4.1	2.2	1.5	1.6	•	•	0.9	•	•	2.2
Interest Paid **13**	0.6	•	0.0	2.3	0.5	0.3	0.6	•	•	0.8	•	•	0.6
Depreciation **14**	1.6	•	0.2	1.0	0.6	1.0	0.9	•	•	1.1	•	•	1.6
Amortization and Depletion **15**	0.1	•	•	0.0	0.0	0.0	0.0	•	•	0.3	•	•	0.1
Pensions and Other Deferred Comp. **16**	0.2	•	0.0	0.1	0.3	0.3	0.2	•	•	0.0	•	•	0.2
Employee Benefits **17**	0.5	•	0.4	0.6	0.8	0.9	1.1	•	•	0.4	•	•	0.5
Advertising **18**	1.6	•	0.7	1.1	0.5	0.7	0.9	•	•	0.1	•	•	1.6
Other Expenses **19**	6.6	•	9.6	11.0	6.6	5.3	8.0	•	•	5.0	•	•	6.6
Officers' Compensation **20**	0.2	•	2.7	6.6	3.1	2.0	1.2	•	•	1.4	•	•	0.0
Operating Margin **21**	8.8	•	2.6	•	3.5	3.8	3.4	•	•	5.8	•	•	9.2
Operating Margin Before Officers' Comp. **22**	9.0	•	5.3	6.0	6.6	5.8	4.6	•	•	7.2	•	•	9.3

Selected Average Balance Sheet ($ in Thousands)

Net Receivables 23	10643	74	38	739	1792	4112	131840	5048697
Inventories 24	12156	132	267	914	2388	4218	81334	5777715
Net Property, Plant and Equipment 25	23055	9	489	203	1171	2584	95850	11483650
Total Assets 26	72451	288	897	2525	7107	13912	446004	35487797
Notes and Loans Payable 27	20802	17	547	629	1449	4014	121825	10218473
All Other Liabilities 28	23145	152	279	565	1829	3617	138114	11399971
Net Worth 29	28504	118	70	1331	3830	6281	186064	13870354

Selected Financial Ratios (Times to 1)

Current Ratio 30	1.1	1.8	1.0	3.1	2.0	2.1	2.0	1.1
Quick Ratio 31	0.5	1.0	0.2	1.6	1.0	1.0	1.2	0.5
Net Sales to Working Capital 32	28.8	13.5	•	5.1	8.3	7.3	6.2	39.6
Coverage Ratio 33	19.8	101.2	1.1	9.8	15.5	8.4	12.1	20.7
Total Asset Turnover 34	1.3	5.9	1.8	3.0	2.9	2.7	1.8	1.2
Inventory Turnover 35	5.0	8.4	4.1	5.8	6.5	6.4	7.1	4.9
Receivables Turnover 36	5.4	20.3	20.8	9.9	23.3	10.5	6.1	5.2
Total Liabilities to Net Worth 37	1.5	1.4	11.8	0.9	0.9	1.2	1.4	1.6
Current Assets to Working Capital 38	7.9	2.2	•	1.5	2.0	1.9	2.0	10.9
Current Liabilities to Working Capital 39	6.9	1.2	•	0.5	1.0	0.9	1.0	9.9
Working Capital to Net Sales 40	0.0	0.1	•	0.2	0.1	0.1	0.2	0.0
Inventory to Working Capital 41	4.1	1.0	•	0.6	0.9	0.9	0.6	5.7
Total Receipts to Cash Flow 42	6.4	11.3	14.0	10.7	12.5	9.4	8.2	6.2
Cost of Goods to Cash Flow 43	4.3	7.5	9.6	7.7	9.3	6.8	6.1	4.1
Cash Flow to Total Debt 44	0.3	0.9	0.1	0.6	0.5	0.5	0.4	0.3

Selected Financial Factors (in Percentages)

Debt Ratio 45	60.7	58.9	92.2	47.3	46.1	54.9	58.3	60.9
Return on Total Assets 46	14.6	16.1	4.6	15.0	14.6	14.1	16.2	14.6
Return on Equity Before Income Taxes 47	35.2	38.9	7.0	25.6	25.3	27.5	35.6	35.5
Return on Equity After Income Taxes 48	23.7	37.5	6.7	23.9	18.3	26.4	24.4	23.7
Profit Margin (Before Income Tax) 49	11.1	2.7	0.3	4.6	4.6	4.6	8.5	11.6
Profit Margin (After Income Tax) 50	7.4	2.6	0.3	4.3	3.4	4.4	5.8	7.7

Table I
Corporations with and without Net Income

HARDWARE STORES

MONEY AMOUNTS AND SIZE OF ASSETS IN THOUSANDS OF DOLLARS

Item Description for Accounting Period 7/05 Through 6/06	Total	Zero Assets	Under 500	500 to 1,000	1,000 to 5,000	5,000 to 10,000	10,000 to 25,000	25,000 to 50,000	50,000 to 100,000	100,000 to 250,000	250,000 to 500,000	500,000 to 2,500,000	2,500,000 and over
Number of Enterprises **1**	7487	1001	2913	1510	1880	131	43	10	0	0	0	0	0
Revenues ($ in Thousands)													
Net Sales **2**	17199075	463768	2490794	2454871	7321827	1848027	1826881	792908	0	0	0	0	0
Interest **3**	17053	89	1919	2534	9360	813	1107	1231	0	0	0	0	0
Rents **4**	14165	54	5495	4502	3191	0	535	387	0	0	0	0	0
Royalties **5**	88	0	0	88	0	0	0	0	0	0	0	0	0
Other Portfolio Income **6**	55046	11717	1913	5114	29336	1126	5554	285	0	0	0	0	0
Other Receipts **7**	236156	13725	31327	38046	110708	19617	18332	4403	0	0	0	0	0
Total Receipts **8**	17521583	489353	2531448	2505155	7474422	1869583	1852409	799214	0	0	0	0	0
Average Total Receipts **9**	2340	489	869	1659	3976	14272	43079	79921	•	•	•	•	•
Operating Costs/Operating Income (%)													
Cost of Operations **10**	65.6	76.7	63.5	65.1	65.6	61.2	71.0	64.3	•	•	•	•	•
Salaries and Wages **11**	12.7	17.7	11.3	10.6	13.1	16.0	10.8	12.3	•	•	•	•	•
Taxes Paid **12**	2.3	3.3	2.6	2.4	2.2	2.5	1.6	2.4	•	•	•	•	•
Interest Paid **13**	0.8	0.9	0.7	0.5	1.0	0.4	0.7	0.8	•	•	•	•	•
Depreciation **14**	1.1	0.5	0.5	1.2	1.4	1.1	0.9	1.0	•	•	•	•	•
Amortization and Depletion **15**	0.1	0.4	0.0	0.0	0.1	0.0	0.1	0.1	•	•	•	•	•
Pensions and Other Deferred Comp. **16**	0.3	0.3	0.0	0.3	0.4	0.2	0.3	0.3	•	•	•	•	•
Employee Benefits **17**	1.0	1.3	1.3	1.0	0.9	0.8	1.4	0.9	•	•	•	•	•
Advertising **18**	1.6	2.7	1.1	2.0	1.4	1.8	1.4	2.4	•	•	•	•	•
Other Expenses **19**	10.7	20.9	13.2	11.6	10.0	9.6	7.3	11.2	•	•	•	•	•
Officers' Compensation **20**	3.3	2.4	7.7	4.7	2.7	1.9	0.9	0.8	•	•	•	•	•
Operating Margin **21**	0.6	•	•	0.6	1.2	4.4	3.7	3.6	•	•	•	•	•
Operating Margin Before Officers' Comp. **22**	4.0	•	5.7	5.3	3.9	6.3	4.6	4.4	•	•	•	•	•

Selected Average Balance Sheet ($ in Thousands)

Net Receivables 23	123	0	42	80	243	511	2832	2863
Inventories 24	418	0	145	384	724	1996	6894	20404
Net Property, Plant and Equipment 25	209	0	17	77	382	2495	4996	13547
Total Assets 26	976	0	293	651	1776	7535	17017	41001
Notes and Loans Payable 27	317	0	140	191	656	522	5466	14239
All Other Liabilities 28	171	0	75	94	301	983	3833	6332
Net Worth 29	487	0	78	366	819	6029	7718	20430

Selected Financial Ratios (Times to 1)

Current Ratio 30	3.0	•	2.1	4.8	3.1	4.0	2.2	2.4
Quick Ratio 31	1.0	•	0.6	1.6	1.1	1.0	0.7	0.4
Net Sales to Working Capital 32	5.2	•	7.2	4.0	4.7	4.4	7.3	6.1
Coverage Ratio 33	4.3	•	0.5	6.3	4.4	15.7	8.1	6.8
Total Asset Turnover 34	2.4	•	2.9	2.5	2.2	1.9	2.5	1.9
Inventory Turnover 35	3.6	•	3.7	2.8	3.5	4.3	4.4	2.5
Receivables Turnover 36	17.8	•	16.2	18.7	17.1	19.3	14.2	26.3
Total Liabilities to Net Worth 37	1.0	•	2.8	0.8	1.2	0.2	1.2	1.0
Current Assets to Working Capital 38	1.5	•	1.9	1.3	1.5	1.3	1.8	1.7
Current Liabilities to Working Capital 39	0.5	•	0.9	0.3	0.5	0.3	0.8	0.7
Working Capital to Net Sales 40	0.2	•	0.1	0.2	0.2	0.2	0.1	0.2
Inventory to Working Capital 41	0.9	•	1.3	0.8	0.9	0.6	1.2	1.3
Total Receipts to Cash Flow 42	10.9	•	11.3	10.8	10.7	8.2	10.4	8.0
Cost of Goods to Cash Flow 43	7.1	•	7.2	7.0	7.0	5.0	7.4	5.2
Cash Flow to Total Debt 44	0.4	•	0.4	0.5	0.4	1.1	0.4	0.5

Selected Financial Factors (in Percentages)

Debt Ratio 45	50.1	•	73.4	43.8	53.9	20.0	54.6	50.2
Return on Total Assets 46	7.6	•	0.9	7.8	9.3	11.0	14.5	10.0
Return on Equity Before Income Taxes 47	11.7	•	•	11.7	15.6	12.9	27.9	17.2
Return on Equity After Income Taxes 48	10.5	•	•	11.2	14.1	12.5	27.1	15.1
Profit Margin (Before Income Tax) 49	2.5	•	2.6	3.3	5.5	5.1	4.4	
Profit Margin (After Income Tax) 50	2.2	•	2.5	3.0	5.4	4.9	3.9	

Table II
Corporations with Net Income

HARDWARE STORES

MONEY AMOUNTS AND SIZE OF ASSETS IN THOUSANDS OF DOLLARS

Item Description for Accounting Period 7/05 Through 6/06		Total	Zero Assets	Under 500	500 to 1,000	1,000 to 5,000	5,000 to 10,000	10,000 to 25,000	25,000 to 50,000	50,000 to 100,000	100,000 to 250,000	250,000 to 500,000	500,000 to 2,500,000	2,500,000 and over
Number of Enterprises	1	4718	256	1625	1171	1492	•	43	•	0	0	0	0	0
Revenues ($ in Thousands)														
Net Sales	2	14029664	181043	1678286	1974452	6040110	•	1826881	•	0	0	0	0	0
Interest	3	13521	89	1015	601	8664	•	1107	•	0	0	0	0	0
Rents	4	4185	54	85	235	2888	•	535	•	0	0	0	0	0
Royalties	5	88	0	0	88	0	•	0	•	0	0	0	0	0
Other Portfolio Income	6	51938	11717	1049	4416	28024	•	5554	•	0	0	0	0	0
Other Receipts	7	201391	286	25399	27589	105871	•	18332	•	0	0	0	0	0
Total Receipts	8	14300787	193189	1705834	2007381	6185557	•	1852409	•	0	0	0	0	0
Average Total Receipts	9	3031	755	1050	1714	4146	•	43079	•					
Operating Costs/Operating Income (%)														
Cost of Operations	10	65.0	59.5	62.7	63.7	65.6	•	71.0	•	•	•	•	•	•
Salaries and Wages	11	12.2	14.6	11.3	10.5	12.3	•	10.8	•	•	•	•	•	•
Taxes Paid	12	2.2	2.4	1.9	2.3	2.3	•	1.6	•	•	•	•	•	•
Interest Paid	13	0.6	1.2	0.7	0.4	0.8	•	0.7	•	•	•	•	•	•
Depreciation	14	1.2	1.0	0.5	1.3	1.5	•	0.9	•	•	•	•	•	•
Amortization and Depletion	15	0.1	0.9	0.0	0.0	0.1	•	0.1	•	•	•	•	•	•
Pensions and Other Deferred Comp.	16	0.3	0.7	0.0	0.4	0.4	•	0.3	•	•	•	•	•	•
Employee Benefits	17	1.0	2.1	1.0	1.0	0.9	•	1.4	•	•	•	•	•	•
Advertising	18	1.5	3.8	1.3	2.0	1.2	•	1.4	•	•	•	•	•	•
Other Expenses	19	10.1	11.0	11.9	12.1	9.9	•	7.3	•	•	•	•	•	•
Officers' Compensation	20	3.0	0.0	6.7	4.5	2.9	•	0.9	•	•	•	•	•	•
Operating Margin	21	2.9	2.8	1.9	2.0	2.3	•	3.7	•	•	•	•	•	•
Operating Margin Before Officers' Comp.	22	5.9	2.8	8.7	6.5	5.2	•	4.6	•	•	•	•	•	•

Selected Average Balance Sheet ($ in Thousands)

Net Receivables 23	161	0	47	57	271	·	2832
Inventories 24	500	0	141	360	673	·	6618
Net Property, Plant and Equipment 25	285	0	16	80	374	·	4996
Total Assets 26	1287	0	342	638	1844	·	17017
Notes and Loans Payable 27	343	0	129	161	559	·	5466
All Other Liabilities 28	216	0	88	103	293	·	3833
Net Worth 29	728	0	125	375	992	·	7718

Selected Financial Ratios (Times to 1)

Current Ratio 30	3.2	·	2.5	4.2	3.4	·	2.2
Quick Ratio 31	1.1	·	0.7	1.4	1.3	·	0.7
Net Sales to Working Capital 32	5.0	·	6.5	4.6	4.5	·	7.3
Coverage Ratio 33	8.5	8.9	6.1	10.7	6.9	·	8.1
Total Asset Turnover 34	2.3	·	3.0	2.6	2.2	·	2.5
Inventory Turnover 35	3.9	·	4.6	3.0	3.9	·	4.6
Receivables Turnover 36	18.4	·	25.6	23.4	16.5	·	14.8
Total Liabilities to Net Worth 37	0.8	·	1.7	0.7	0.9	·	1.2
Current Assets to Working Capital 38	1.4	·	1.7	1.3	1.4	·	1.8
Current Liabilities to Working Capital 39	0.4	·	0.7	0.3	0.4	·	0.8
Working Capital to Net Sales 40	0.2	·	0.2	0.2	0.2	·	0.1
Inventory to Working Capital 41	0.9	·	1.1	0.8	0.8	·	1.2
Total Receipts to Cash Flow 42	9.1	6.9	9.1	9.9	9.4	·	10.4
Cost of Goods to Cash Flow 43	5.9	4.1	5.7	6.3	6.2	·	7.4
Cash Flow to Total Debt 44	0.6	·	0.5	0.6	0.5	·	0.4

Selected Financial Factors (in Percentages)

Debt Ratio 45	43.4	·	63.3	41.3	46.2	·	54.6
Return on Total Assets 46	12.6	·	13.0	10.5	12.1	·	14.5
Return on Equity Before Income Taxes 47	19.6	·	29.5	16.3	19.2	·	27.9
Return on Equity After Income Taxes 48	18.3	·	28.2	15.7	17.6	·	27.1
Profit Margin (Before Income Tax) 49	4.8	9.5	3.6	3.6	4.7	·	5.1
Profit Margin (After Income Tax) 50	4.5	7.0	3.4	3.5	4.3	·	4.9

Table I
Corporations with and without Net Income

OTHER BUILDING MATERIAL DEALERS

MONEY AMOUNTS AND SIZE OF ASSETS IN THOUSANDS OF DOLLARS

Item Description for Accounting Period 7/05 Through 6/06	Total	Zero Assets	Under 500	500 to 1,000	1,000 to 5,000	5,000 to 10,000	10,000 to 25,000	25,000 to 50,000	50,000 to 100,000	100,000 to 250,000	250,000 to 500,000	500,000 to 2,500,000	2,500,000 and over
Number of Enterprises **1**	19375	1283	11928	2066	3353	417	235	61	18	10	0	4	0
Revenues ($ in Thousands)													
Net Sales **2**	74626941	241748	8083946	5072267	19611206	8434331	9647988	5109745	3888115	5254743	0	9279853	0
Interest **3**	82977	185	1932	4539	23259	6916	8891	7505	3090	17862	0	8798	0
Rents **4**	25690	6	0	1750	8106	296	5480	7916	1069	897	0	170	0
Royalties **5**	5943	0	0	0	0	0	4006	450	0	1487	0	0	0
Other Portfolio Income **6**	86368	5689	5691	3036	8365	17760	19663	14372	1646	6142	0	4002	0
Other Receipts **7**	440414	26131	6215	64610	102062	23574	93955	36045	48963	23502	0	15359	0
Total Receipts **8**	75268333	273759	8097784	5146202	19755998	8482877	9779983	5176033	3942883	5304633	0	9308182	0
Average Total Receipts **9**	3885	213	679	2491	5892	20343	41617	84853	219049	530463	•	2327046	•
Operating Costs/Operating Income (%)													
Cost of Operations **10**	73.8	55.2	67.6	72.7	72.5	76.3	77.8	74.1	78.1	76.3	•	73.0	•
Salaries and Wages **11**	8.4	8.3	6.5	7.7	8.7	8.0	8.2	9.5	7.6	9.5	•	9.2	•
Taxes Paid **12**	1.5	0.9	2.1	1.5	1.6	1.5	1.2	1.6	1.1	1.5	•	1.0	•
Interest Paid **13**	0.6	0.6	0.5	0.4	0.5	0.4	0.6	0.7	0.4	0.9	•	0.8	•
Depreciation **14**	0.9	3.9	1.2	0.6	0.7	0.7	0.8	0.9	0.7	1.0	•	1.1	•
Amortization and Depletion **15**	0.1	0.0	0.1	0.0	0.0	0.0	0.0	0.0	0.0	0.1	•	0.4	•
Pensions and Other Deferred Comp. **16**	0.3	0.0	0.1	0.3	0.4	0.2	0.3	0.4	0.3	0.3	•	0.3	•
Employee Benefits **17**	0.8	0.1	0.5	0.5	0.8	0.6	0.8	1.0	0.7	0.9	•	1.5	•
Advertising **18**	0.7	0.3	1.5	1.2	0.9	0.3	0.6	0.4	1.1	0.3	•	0.3	•
Other Expenses **19**	7.4	41.6	13.7	7.7	7.4	5.9	5.8	6.8	6.0	5.1	•	6.1	•
Officers' Compensation **20**	2.2	0.5	4.8	4.6	3.2	1.4	1.4	1.1	0.8	0.4	•	0.6	•
Operating Margin **21**	3.4	•	1.6	2.8	3.1	4.8	2.6	3.6	3.2	3.6	•	5.7	•
Operating Margin Before Officers' Comp. **22**	5.6	•	6.4	7.4	6.3	6.1	4.0	4.7	4.0	5.1	•	6.3	•

Selected Average Balance Sheet ($ in Thousands)

	•	•	•	•	•	•	•	•	•	•	•
Net Receivables 23	375	0	177	617	1899	4458	11925	19786	58435	•	241168
Inventories 24	392	0	269	683	2320	3985	8317	15831	37451	•	220894
Net Property, Plant and Equipment 25	221	0	76	249	713	2365	6875	14421	54863	•	198443
Total Assets 26	1308	0	692	1998	7154	14480	34525	66628	203089	•	898556
Notes and Loans Payable 27	342	0	143	523	1349	3714	8245	16524	47749	•	242741
All Other Liabilities 28	369	0	118	592	1954	4256	7476	20106	38900	•	306276
Net Worth 29	598	0	431	883	3852	6510	18804	29997	116440	•	349540

Selected Financial Ratios (Times to 1)

	•	•	•	•	•	•	•	•	•	•	•	•
Current Ratio 30	2.1	•	1.7	3.8	2.3	2.0	1.9	2.1	1.9	2.4	•	1.8
Quick Ratio 31	1.1	•	0.7	1.8	1.3	1.1	1.0	1.3	1.1	1.2	•	0.9
Net Sales to Working Capital 32	7.7	•	14.6	5.7	6.4	6.6	8.3	6.8	10.1	7.6	•	9.6
Coverage Ratio 33	8.6	3.8	4.8	13.0	8.1	15.3	8.0	8.0	13.8	6.2	•	8.7
Total Asset Turnover 34	2.9	•	4.2	3.5	2.9	2.8	2.8	2.4	3.2	2.6	•	2.6
Inventory Turnover 35	7.2	•	8.4	6.6	6.2	6.6	8.0	7.5	10.7	10.7	•	7.7
Receivables Turnover 36	10.4	•	26.2	12.8	9.9	8.8	9.4	8.0	11.3	11.4	•	9.9
Total Liabilities to Net Worth 37	1.2	•	4.6	0.6	1.3	0.9	1.2	0.8	1.2	0.7	•	1.6
Current Assets to Working Capital 38	1.9	•	2.5	1.4	1.8	2.0	2.2	1.9	2.1	1.7	•	2.2
Current Liabilities to Working Capital 39	0.9	•	1.5	0.4	0.8	1.0	1.2	0.9	1.1	0.7	•	1.2
Working Capital to Net Sales 40	0.1	•	0.1	0.2	0.2	0.1	0.1	0.1	0.1	0.1	•	0.1
Inventory to Working Capital 41	0.8	•	1.2	0.7	0.8	0.7	0.9	0.7	0.9	0.7	•	1.0
Total Receipts to Cash Flow 42	10.7	2.9	9.1	9.9	11.2	11.4	12.4	10.0	12.3	12.0	•	9.9
Cost of Goods to Cash Flow 43	7.9	1.6	6.1	7.2	8.1	8.7	9.7	7.4	9.6	9.2	•	7.2
Cash Flow to Total Debt 44	0.5	•	0.6	1.0	0.5	0.5	0.4	0.5	0.5	0.5	•	0.4

Selected Financial Factors (in Percentages)

	•	•	•	•	•	•	•	•	•	•	•
Debt Ratio 45	54.3	82.1	37.8	55.8	46.2	55.0	45.5	55.0	42.7	•	61.1
Return on Total Assets 46	14.1	9.3	16.3	12.6	16.1	12.9	13.4	16.2	14.0	•	17.4
Return on Equity Before Income Taxes 47	27.2	41.2	24.2	25.0	28.0	25.1	21.6	33.3	20.6	•	39.6
Return on Equity After Income Taxes 48	24.2	39.1	23.3	23.3	25.9	22.2	19.3	28.1	14.8	•	33.6
Profit Margin (Before Income Tax) 49	4.2	1.7	4.2	3.8	5.3	4.0	4.8	4.6	4.6	•	6.0
Profit Margin (After Income Tax) 50	3.8	1.4	4.1	3.5	4.9	3.5	4.3	3.9	4.6	•	5.1

Table II
Corporations with Net Income

OTHER BUILDING MATERIAL DEALERS

MONEY AMOUNTS AND SIZE OF ASSETS IN THOUSANDS OF DOLLARS

Item Description for Accounting Period 7/05 Through 6/06		Total	Zero Assets	Under 500	500 to 1,000	1,000 to 5,000	5,000 to 10,000	10,000 to 25,000	25,000 to 50,000	50,000 to 100,000	100,000 to 250,000	250,000 to 500,000	500,000 to 2,500,000	2,500,000 and over
Number of Enterprises	1	16059	1062	9557	1668	3094	374	216	55	•	10	0	•	0
Revenues ($ in Thousands)														
Net Sales	2	69120362	230605	6510604	4527706	18493900	7806659	9267902	4862524	•	5254743	0	•	0
Interest	3	76801	185	483	3549	20637	6470	8547	7401	•	17862	0	•	0
Rents	4	22270	6	0	238	7515	296	4569	7510	•	897	0	•	0
Royalties	5	5943	0	0	0	0	0	4006	450	•	1487	0	•	0
Other Portfolio Income	6	77498	5689	4806	2794	7294	14951	15888	14284	•	6142	0	•	0
Other Receipts	7	372127	5	3053	59489	98927	22056	92573	32963	•	23502	0	•	0
Total Receipts	8	69675001	236490	6518946	4593776	18628273	7850432	9393485	4925132	•	5304633	0	•	0
Average Total Receipts	9	4339	223	682	2754	6021	20990	43488	89548	•	530463	•	•	•
Operating Costs/Operating Income (%)														
Cost of Operations	10	73.4	51.6	66.6	72.9	72.7	75.2	77.7	74.0	•	76.3	•	•	•
Salaries and Wages	11	8.4	5.4	5.8	7.5	8.6	8.2	8.1	9.6	•	9.5	•	•	•
Taxes Paid	12	1.4	0.7	1.8	1.4	1.6	1.6	1.2	1.6	•	1.5	•	•	•
Interest Paid	13	0.5	0.6	0.3	0.3	0.5	0.4	0.5	0.5	•	0.9	•	•	•
Depreciation	14	0.9	3.7	1.1	0.5	0.7	0.7	0.8	0.9	•	1.0	•	•	•
Amortization and Depletion	15	0.1	0.0	0.1	0.0	0.0	0.0	0.0	0.0	•	0.1	•	•	•
Pensions and Other Deferred Comp.	16	0.3	0.0	0.1	0.3	0.4	0.2	0.3	0.4	•	0.3	•	•	•
Employee Benefits	17	0.8	0.1	0.5	0.6	0.8	0.7	0.8	0.9	•	0.9	•	•	•
Advertising	18	0.7	0.3	1.2	1.2	0.9	0.4	0.6	0.4	•	0.3	•	•	•
Other Expenses	19	7.2	34.2	14.0	7.1	7.3	6.0	5.5	6.5	•	5.1	•	•	•
Officers' Compensation	20	2.2	0.5	5.3	4.7	3.0	1.4	1.4	1.1	•	0.4	•	•	•
Operating Margin	21	4.0	2.9	3.2	3.5	3.5	5.2	3.1	4.2	•	3.6	•	•	•
Operating Margin Before Officers' Comp.	22	6.2	3.3	8.5	8.2	6.5	6.7	4.5	5.3	•	4.0	•	•	•

Selected Average Balance Sheet ($ in Thousands)

Net Receivables 23	418	0	23	189	626	1966	4612	12037	58435
Inventories 24	427	0	43	286	663	2315	4131	8426	37451
Net Property, Plant and Equipment 25	246	0	33	73	244	752	2343	6652	54863
Total Assets 26	1444	0	149	692	2005	7105	14460	33937	203089
Notes and Loans Payable 27	357	0	62	131	482	1418	3596	6997	47749
All Other Liabilities 28	405	0	49	130	606	1905	4115	7748	38900
Net Worth 29	682	0	38	431	917	3782	6749	19191	116440

Selected Financial Ratios (Times to 1)

Current Ratio 30	2.1	•	1.9	4.0	2.3	2.0	1.9	2.1	2.4
Quick Ratio 31	1.1	•	0.8	2.0	1.3	1.0	1.0	1.3	1.2
Net Sales to Working Capital 32	7.6	•	13.6	6.1	6.4	7.0	8.0	7.0	7.6
Coverage Ratio 33	10.1	10.2	10.6	15.5	9.4	15.7	9.5	11.7	6.2
Total Asset Turnover 34	3.0	•	4.6	3.9	3.0	2.9	3.0	2.6	2.6
Inventory Turnover 35	7.4	•	10.6	6.9	6.5	6.8	8.1	7.8	10.7
Receivables Turnover 36	10.5	•	35.7	12.4	10.1	9.5	9.8	14.7	11.4
Total Liabilities to Net Worth 37	1.1	•	2.9	0.6	1.2	0.9	1.1	0.8	0.7
Current Assets to Working Capital 38	1.9	•	2.2	1.3	1.8	2.0	2.1	1.9	1.7
Current Liabilities to Working Capital 39	0.9	•	1.2	0.3	0.8	1.0	1.1	0.9	0.7
Working Capital to Net Sales 40	0.1	•	0.1	0.2	0.2	0.1	0.1	0.1	0.1
Inventory to Working Capital 41	0.8	•	1.0	0.6	0.7	0.7	0.9	0.7	0.7
Total Receipts to Cash Flow 42	10.2	3.3	7.8	9.7	10.7	10.8	12.0	9.7	12.0
Cost of Goods to Cash Flow 43	7.5	1.7	5.2	7.0	7.8	8.1	9.3	7.2	9.2
Cash Flow to Total Debt 44	0.6	•	0.8	1.1	0.5	0.6	0.5	0.6	0.5

Selected Financial Factors (in Percentages)

Debt Ratio 45	52.8	•	74.3	37.7	54.3	46.8	53.3	43.4	42.7
Return on Total Assets 46	16.0	•	16.9	20.9	14.0	18.2	14.8	15.7	14.0
Return on Equity Before Income Taxes 47	30.5	•	59.4	31.3	27.4	32.0	28.3	25.4	20.6
Return on Equity After Income Taxes 48	27.3	•	57.5	30.2	25.6	29.7	25.3	23.0	14.8
Profit Margin (Before Income Tax) 49	4.8	5.4	3.3	5.0	4.2	5.8	4.5	5.5	4.6
Profit Margin (After Income Tax) 50	4.3	5.0	3.2	4.8	3.9	5.4	4.0	5.0	3.3

Table I

Corporations with and without Net Income

LAWN AND GARDEN EQUIPMENT AND SUPPLIES STORES

MONEY AMOUNTS AND SIZE OF ASSETS IN THOUSANDS OF DOLLARS

Item Description for Accounting Period 7/05 Through 6/06	Total	Zero Assets	Under 500	500 to 1,000	1,000 to 5,000	5,000 to 10,000	10,000 to 25,000	25,000 to 50,000	50,000 to 100,000	100,000 to 250,000	250,000 to 500,000	500,000 to 2,500,000	2,500,000 and over
Number of Enterprises **1**	9883	2706	4736	1516	774	112	32	8	0	0	0	0	0
Revenues ($ in Thousands)													
Net Sales **2**	12191293	341511	2243195	3041244	3505818	1784738	903842	370945	0	0	0	0	0
Interest **3**	12648	0	434	1135	6947	2087	909	1136	0	0	0	0	0
Rents **4**	9502	0	0	564	8647	0	292	0	0	0	0	0	0
Royalties **5**	0	0	0	0	0	0	0	0	0	0	0	0	0
Other Portfolio Income **6**	40740	16441	182	4345	8756	279	981	9754	0	0	0	0	0
Other Receipts **7**	91297	13146	2013	7151	16700	36927	11238	4123	0	0	0	0	0
Total Receipts **8**	12345480	371098	2245824	3054439	3546868	1824031	917262	385958	0	0	0	0	0
Average Total Receipts **9**	1249	137	474	2015	4583	16286	28664	48245	.	.	.	.	.
Operating Costs/Operating Income (%)													
Cost of Operations **10**	70.6	84.8	68.7	62.0	72.7	83.5	66.9	68.0	.	.	.	.	.
Salaries and Wages **11**	9.8	5.2	9.3	13.9	8.4	6.2	12.1	9.9	.	.	.	.	.
Taxes Paid **12**	2.2	2.9	3.1	2.9	1.8	0.9	1.6	1.5	.	.	.	.	.
Interest Paid **13**	0.9	2.5	0.5	0.8	0.7	1.2	1.3	1.6	.	.	.	.	.
Depreciation **14**	1.3	0.8	1.0	1.2	1.3	0.6	1.9	5.4	.	.	.	.	.
Amortization and Depletion **15**	0.0	0.0	0.0	0.0	0.0	.	0.0	0.1	.	.	.	.	.
Pensions and Other Deferred Comp. **16**	0.3	.	.	0.2	0.3	0.7	0.2	0.2	.	.	.	.	.
Employee Benefits **17**	0.5	.	0.1	0.5	0.6	0.5	0.4	1.6	.	.	.	.	.
Advertising **18**	1.0	1.0	0.9	0.9	1.3	0.8	1.1	1.4	.	.	.	.	.
Other Expenses **19**	9.7	16.6	10.9	10.7	8.7	6.0	12.2	10.8	.	.	.	.	.
Officers' Compensation **20**	3.1	1.4	3.8	4.1	3.6	0.9	1.4	1.7	.	.	.	.	.
Operating Margin **21**	0.6	.	1.7	2.8	0.6	.	0.8	.	.	.	.	.	.
Operating Margin Before Officers' Comp. **22**	3.6	.	5.4	7.0	4.2	.	2.2	.	.	.	.	.	.

Selected Average Balance Sheet ($ in Thousands)

Net Receivables 23	60	0	23	90	217	573	2347	5591
Inventories 24	267	0	74	270	1231	5884	6071	7183
Net Property, Plant and Equipment 25	109	0	33	219	401	321	4286	13310
Total Assets 26	544	0	146	751	2288	7169	14482	62960
Notes and Loans Payable 27	216	0	72	270	644	2462	6970	48968
All Other Liabilities 28	172	0	41	153	758	3429	4015	21841
Net Worth 29	155	0	33	328	887	1278	3498	-7849

Selected Financial Ratios (Times to 1)

Current Ratio 30	1.6	•	2.1	2.5	1.9	1.3	1.3	0.4
Quick Ratio 31	0.4	•	0.7	1.0	0.4	0.2	0.5	0.2
Net Sales to Working Capital 32	8.5	•	8.6	6.5	5.4	9.6	12.7	•
Coverage Ratio 33	3.1	•	4.4	5.3	3.4	1.8	2.8	2.2
Total Asset Turnover 34	2.3	•	3.2	2.7	2.0	2.2	2.0	0.7
Inventory Turnover 35	3.3	•	4.4	4.6	2.7	2.3	3.1	4.4
Receivables Turnover 36	18.2	•	20.1	20.0	21.9	17.6	11.0	14.3
Total Liabilities to Net Worth 37	2.5	•	3.4	1.3	1.6	4.6	3.1	•
Current Assets to Working Capital 38	2.7	•	1.9	1.7	2.1	4.0	4.0	•
Current Liabilities to Working Capital 39	1.7	•	0.9	0.7	1.1	3.0	3.0	•
Working Capital to Net Sales 40	0.1	•	0.1	0.2	0.2	0.1	0.1	•
Inventory to Working Capital 41	1.8	•	1.3	0.9	1.4	3.5	2.4	•
Total Receipts to Cash Flow 42	11.3	14.5	11.3	9.2	11.9	19.2	8.5	11.2
Cost of Goods to Cash Flow 43	8.0	12.3	7.8	5.7	8.6	16.1	5.7	7.6
Cash Flow to Total Debt 44	0.3	•	0.4	0.5	0.3	0.1	0.3	0.1

Selected Financial Factors (in Percentages)

Debt Ratio 45	71.5	•	77.5	56.3	61.2	82.2	75.8	112.5
Return on Total Assets 46	6.1	•	7.5	10.7	5.0	4.6	6.8	2.6
Return on Equity Before Income Taxes 47	14.5	•	25.6	19.9	9.1	11.3	18.1	•
Return on Equity After Income Taxes 48	13.7	•	24.4	19.4	8.2	10.8	17.1	•
Profit Margin (Before Income Tax) 49	1.8	•	1.8	3.3	1.8	0.9	2.2	1.9
Profit Margin (After Income Tax) 50	1.7	•	1.7	3.2	1.6	0.9	2.1	1.8

Table II

Corporations with Net Income

LAWN AND GARDEN EQUIPMENT AND SUPPLIES STORES

MONEY AMOUNTS AND SIZE OF ASSETS IN THOUSANDS OF DOLLARS

Item Description for Accounting Period 7/05 Through 6/06		Total	Zero Assets	Under 500	500 to 1,000	1,000 to 5,000	5,000 to 10,000	10,000 to 25,000	25,000 to 50,000	50,000 to 100,000	100,000 to 250,000	250,000 to 500,000	500,000 to 2,500,000	2,500,000 and over
Number of Enterprises	1	5577	843	2755	1175	668	·	28	·	0	0	0	0	0
Revenues ($ in Thousands)														
Net Sales	2	10543670	88542	1850910	2537207	3187261	·	804814	·	0	0	0	0	0
Interest	3	11908	0	430	703	6774	·	886	·	0	0	0	0	0
Rents	4	5962	0	0	448	5222	·	292	·	0	0	0	0	0
Royalties	5	0	0	0	0	0	·	0	·	0	0	0	0	0
Other Portfolio Income	6	40506	16441	81	4213	8756	·	981	·	0	0	0	0	0
Other Receipts	7	86367	13146	690	6888	15446	·	11221	·	0	0	0	0	0
Total Receipts	8	10688413	118129	1852111	2549459	3223459	·	818194	·	0	0	0	0	0
Average Total Receipts	9	1917	140	672	2170	4826	·	29221	·	·	·	·	·	·
Operating Costs/Operating Income (%)														
Cost of Operations	10	70.4	86.4	70.0	60.5	72.9	·	65.8	·	·	·	·	·	·
Salaries and Wages	11	9.9	3.9	8.5	14.2	8.4	·	13.1	·	·	·	·	·	·
Taxes Paid	12	2.1	4.0	3.1	2.8	1.7	·	1.8	·	·	·	·	·	·
Interest Paid	13	0.8	6.9	0.5	0.5	0.7	·	1.2	·	·	·	·	·	·
Depreciation	14	1.3	1.4	0.8	1.3	1.3	·	1.6	·	·	·	·	·	·
Amortization and Depletion	15	0.0	0.1	0.0	0.0	0.0	·	0.0	·	·	·	·	·	·
Pensions and Other Deferred Comp.	16	0.3	·	·	0.3	0.3	·	0.3	·	·	·	·	·	·
Employee Benefits	17	0.5	·	0.2	0.5	0.6	·	0.5	·	·	·	·	·	·
Advertising	18	1.0	2.0	0.9	0.8	1.3	·	1.0	·	·	·	·	·	·
Other Expenses	19	9.3	11.0	9.5	11.4	8.2	·	12.1	·	·	·	·	·	·
Officers' Compensation	20	3.0	·	3.5	3.8	3.7	·	1.3	·	·	·	·	·	·
Operating Margin	21	1.5	·	3.0	3.8	1.0	·	1.4	·	·	·	·	·	·
Operating Margin Before Officers' Comp.	22	4.5	·	6.5	7.7	4.6	·	2.7	·	·	·	·	·	·

Selected Average Balance Sheet ($ in Thousands)

Line	Item						
23	Net Receivables	92	0	28	108	196	2627
24	Inventories	374	0	72	252	1218	6147
25	Net Property, Plant and Equipment	156	0	46	179	435	3496
26	Total Assets	767	0	180	741	2275	14328
27	Notes and Loans Payable	248	0	86	223	566	6701
28	All Other Liabilities	270	0	52	193	821	4056
29	Net Worth	249	0	42	325	888	3572

Selected Financial Ratios (Times to 1)

Line	Item						
30	Current Ratio	1.7	·	1.9	1.9	2.1	1.4
31	Quick Ratio	0.5	·	0.7	0.9	0.4	0.5
32	Net Sales to Working Capital	8.1	·	10.3	7.5	5.9	11.6
33	Coverage Ratio	4.6	3.6	7.3	9.2	4.2	3.6
34	Total Asset Turnover	2.5	·	3.7	2.9	2.1	2.0
35	Inventory Turnover	3.6	·	6.6	5.2	2.9	3.1
36	Receivables Turnover	20.0	·	32.0	20.0	24.8	10.3
37	Total Liabilities to Net Worth	2.1	·	3.3	1.3	1.6	3.0
38	Current Assets to Working Capital	2.5	·	2.1	1.9	2.1	3.8
39	Current Liabilities to Working Capital	1.5	·	1.1	0.9	1.1	2.8
40	Working Capital to Net Sales	0.1	·	0.1	0.1	0.2	0.1
41	Inventory to Working Capital	1.6	·	1.3	1.0	1.3	2.2
42	Total Receipts to Cash Flow	10.5	4.0	11.0	8.1	11.9	8.0
43	Cost of Goods to Cash Flow	7.4	3.4	7.7	4.9	8.6	5.2
44	Cash Flow to Total Debt	0.3	·	0.4	0.6	0.3	0.3

Selected Financial Factors (in Percentages)

Line	Item						
45	Debt Ratio	67.6	·	76.8	56.1	61.0	75.1
46	Return on Total Assets	9.0	·	13.0	14.1	5.8	8.5
47	Return on Equity Before Income Taxes	21.8	·	48.5	28.7	11.3	24.6
48	Return on Equity After Income Taxes	20.8	·	46.7	27.9	10.2	23.5
49	Profit Margin (Before Income Tax)	2.9	17.7	3.0	4.3	2.1	3.1
50	Profit Margin (After Income Tax)	2.7	17.5	2.9	4.2	1.9	2.9

218

Table I

Corporations with and without Net Income

FOOD AND BEVERAGE STORES

MONEY AMOUNTS AND SIZE OF ASSETS IN THOUSANDS OF DOLLARS

Item Description for Accounting Period 7/05 Through 6/06	Total	Zero Assets	Under 500	500 to 1,000	1,000 to 5,000	5,000 to 10,000	10,000 to 25,000	25,000 to 50,000	50,000 to 100,000	100,000 to 250,000	250,000 to 500,000	500,000 to 2,500,000	2,500,000 and over
Number of Enterprises 1	77920	9444	58390	4886	4432	369	193	84	52	27	10	24	9
Revenues ($ in Thousands)													
Net Sales 2	475962702	1650981	37405168	15414732	35248561	15713249	14022608	12115629	14076840	14925828	6180129	87342986	221865990
Interest 3	754367	398	2397	5631	13107	5554	8719	7026	4194	18008	7490	122468	559375
Rents 4	623362	4223	4780	11517	22573	18134	12370	17004	11292	15973	9095	133846	362553
Royalties 5	1411575	0	0	0	74	0	0	6769	50	29124	19327	182505	1173726
Other Portfolio Income 6	1880752	52156	75104	3772	58279	8734	44661	26372	46744	13859	25664	76503	1448902
Other Receipts 7	5500231	76096	521471	122323	534614	233266	200007	90514	183323	149441	245653	904553	2238975
Total Receipts 8	486132989	1783854	38008920	15557975	35877208	15978937	14288365	12263314	14322443	15152233	6487358	88762861	227649521
Average Total Receipts 9	6239	189	651	3184	8095	43303	74033	145992	275432	561194	648736	3698453	25294391
Operating Costs/Operating Income (%)													
Cost of Operations 10	73.5	67.3	72.7	74.7	74.6	80.3	76.7	75.1	74.0	74.7	76.3	73.2	72.5
Salaries and Wages 11	10.0	12.2	7.3	7.7	9.3	7.9	9.6	9.3	10.5	10.8	8.8	11.1	10.5
Taxes Paid 12	1.7	2.7	2.3	1.5	1.5	1.2	1.5	1.6	2.3	1.6	1.9	1.6	1.6
Interest Paid 13	0.9	0.9	0.5	0.5	0.5	0.4	0.4	0.5	0.5	0.7	0.8	0.6	1.3
Depreciation 14	1.3	1.6	0.9	0.8	0.9	0.8	0.9	1.1	1.2	1.2	1.4	1.3	1.5
Amortization and Depletion 15	0.2	0.2	0.2	0.1	0.1	0.1	0.1	0.1	0.1	0.1	0.1	0.1	0.2
Pensions and Other Deferred Comp. 16	0.4	0.0	0.0	0.0	0.1	0.1	0.2	0.2	0.3	0.4	0.5	0.4	0.6
Employee Benefits 17	1.4	1.5	0.3	0.5	0.9	0.7	1.1	1.0	1.2	1.4	1.7	1.6	1.8
Advertising 18	0.7	0.9	0.6	0.7	1.1	0.7	0.9	0.8	0.8	0.9	0.5	0.8	0.5
Other Expenses 19	9.2	20.6	13.2	10.3	10.0	7.4	8.5	9.4	8.3	7.5	8.2	8.6	8.7
Officers' Compensation 20	0.5	1.8	2.7	1.7	1.1	0.6	0.6	0.7	0.4	0.4	0.3	0.1	0.1
Operating Margin 21	0.4	•	•	1.5	•	•	•	0.1	0.5	0.4	•	0.6	0.7
Operating Margin Before Officers' Comp. 22	0.9	•	2.1	3.3	1.0	0.4	0.1	0.8	0.9	0.7	•	0.7	0.8

Selected Average Balance Sheet ($ in Thousands)

Net Receivables 23	162	0	5	32	127	612	1513	2447	4247	8864	16632	59937	983958
Inventories 24	349	0	36	142	391	1833	3547	6664	10689	24463	47329	199392	1581415
Net Property, Plant and Equipment 25	933	0	36	190	680	3006	5577	14374	30790	70933	122527	609806	4880023
Total Assets 26	2248	0	126	700	1985	7373	16361	34434	69588	160153	366643	1222473	11762977
Notes and Loans Payable 27	702	0	85	359	739	3165	5008	10852	22570	47331	60224	354036	3343343
All Other Liabilities 28	849	0	16	139	435	2029	5235	11223	21016	51327	117829	420882	5129268
Net Worth 29	698	0	26	202	812	2179	6117	12359	26003	61496	188590	447556	3290366

Selected Financial Ratios (Times to 1)

Current Ratio 30	1.1	•	2.9	2.3	2.0	1.4	1.4	1.2	1.1	1.2	1.0	1.3	0.8
Quick Ratio 31	0.4	•	1.0	0.9	0.9	0.6	0.7	0.5	0.5	0.5	0.4	0.6	0.3
Net Sales to Working Capital 32	153.1	•	15.8	15.8	17.0	39.7	33.0	68.0	117.2	59.3	•	32.2	•
Coverage Ratio 33	3.9	•	3.1	6.4	4.6	4.5	4.6	3.5	5.5	3.7	7.1	5.0	3.6
Total Asset Turnover 34	2.7	•	5.1	4.5	4.0	5.8	4.4	4.2	3.9	3.5	1.7	3.0	2.1
Inventory Turnover 35	12.9	•	12.9	16.7	15.2	18.6	15.7	16.3	18.7	16.9	10.0	13.4	11.3
Receivables Turnover 36	41.3	•	127.3	89.2	62.5	49.1	53.8	62.7	67.4	66.7	32.7	63.3	28.7
Total Liabilities to Net Worth 37	2.2	•	3.9	2.5	1.4	2.4	1.7	1.8	1.7	1.6	0.9	1.7	2.6
Current Assets to Working Capital 38	19.1	•	1.5	1.7	2.0	3.4	3.7	7.1	10.7	5.8	•	4.0	•
Current Liabilities to Working Capital 39	18.1	•	0.5	0.7	1.0	2.4	2.7	6.1	9.7	4.8	•	3.0	•
Working Capital to Net Sales 40	0.0	0.0	0.1	0.1	0.1	0.0	0.0	0.0	0.0	0.0	•	0.0	•
Inventory to Working Capital 41	8.7	•	0.9	0.8	0.8	1.7	1.6	3.3	5.2	2.7	•	1.8	•
Total Receipts to Cash Flow 42	11.6	12.3	11.2	10.3	11.6	15.4	15.1	13.1	13.5	16.0	10.4	12.6	10.7
Cost of Goods to Cash Flow 43	8.5	8.3	8.1	7.7	8.6	12.4	11.6	9.8	10.0	11.9	7.9	9.2	7.8
Cash Flow to Total Debt 44	0.3	•	0.6	0.6	0.6	0.5	0.5	0.5	0.5	0.4	0.3	0.4	0.3

Selected Financial Factors (in Percentages)

Debt Ratio 45	69.0	•	79.4	71.2	59.1	70.4	62.6	64.1	62.6	61.6	48.6	63.4	72.0
Return on Total Assets 46	9.3	•	7.5	13.0	8.4	11.4	8.0	7.7	10.8	8.8	9.0	8.3	9.7
Return on Equity Before Income Taxes 47	22.3	•	24.5	38.0	16.1	30.1	16.7	15.5	23.8	16.8	15.0	18.2	24.9
Return on Equity After Income Taxes 48	16.7	•	23.4	37.2	14.8	27.8	15.2	13.1	20.6	13.8	13.9	11.9	17.8
Profit Margin (Before Income Tax) 49	2.5	•	1.0	2.4	1.6	1.5	1.4	1.3	2.3	1.9	4.6	2.2	3.3
Profit Margin (After Income Tax) 50	1.9	•	0.9	2.4	1.5	1.4	1.3	1.1	2.0	1.5	4.2	1.5	2.4

Table II

Corporations with Net Income

FOOD AND BEVERAGE STORES

MONEY AMOUNTS AND SIZE OF ASSETS IN THOUSANDS OF DOLLARS

Item Description for Accounting Period 7/05 Through 6/06	Total	Zero Assets	Under 500	500 to 1,000	1,000 to 5,000	5,000 to 10,000	10,000 to 25,000	25,000 to 50,000	50,000 to 100,000	100,000 to 250,000	250,000 to 500,000	500,000 to 2,500,000	2,500,000 and over
Number of Enterprises **1**	44896	3745	33324	4256	2964	284	•	•	48	23	•	•	9
Revenues ($ in Thousands)													
Net Sales **2**	425795402	1083229	24675939	14291939	27130903	12883356	•	•	13063665	12354212	•	•	221865990
Interest **3**	725597	3	998	3001	11477	4554	•	•	4029	10385	•	•	559375
Rents **4**	572495	0	1970	8438	19663	11306	•	•	11259	11430	•	•	362553
Royalties **5**	1363087	0	0	0	0	0	•	•	50	36	•	•	1173726
Other Portfolio Income **6**	1823488	48205	62674	1275	56328	3459	•	•	43541	7077	•	•	1448902
Other Receipts **7**	4708331	41170	350539	118712	403764	205802	•	•	171256	91903	•	•	2238975
Total Receipts **8**	434988400	1172607	25092120	14423365	27622135	13108477	•	•	13293800	12475043	•	•	227649521
Average Total Receipts **9**	9689	313	753	3389	9319	46157	•	•	276954	542393	•	•	25294391
Operating Costs/Operating Income (%)													
Cost of Operations **10**	73.1	68.0	72.4	74.6	73.4	82.0	•	•	74.1	74.4	•	•	72.5
Salaries and Wages **11**	10.0	9.4	7.0	7.6	9.2	6.8	•	•	10.6	10.6	•	•	10.5
Taxes Paid **12**	1.6	2.4	2.2	1.5	1.6	1.0	•	•	1.7	1.5	•	•	1.6
Interest Paid **13**	0.9	0.4	0.4	0.5	0.4	0.3	•	•	0.5	0.4	•	•	1.3
Depreciation **14**	1.3	1.0	0.7	0.8	0.9	0.6	•	•	1.2	1.2	•	•	1.5
Amortization and Depletion **15**	0.2	0.1	0.2	0.1	0.1	0.1	•	•	0.1	0.1	•	•	0.2
Pensions and Other Deferred Comp. **16**	0.5	•	0.0	0.0	0.1	0.1	•	•	0.3	0.4	•	•	0.6
Employee Benefits **17**	1.5	1.8	0.3	0.5	0.9	0.8	•	•	1.3	1.3	•	•	1.8
Advertising **18**	0.6	0.9	0.5	0.6	1.2	0.6	•	•	0.8	0.8	•	•	0.5
Other Expenses **19**	8.8	13.9	11.8	10.1	10.0	6.7	•	•	8.3	7.3	•	•	8.7
Officers' Compensation **20**	0.4	1.5	2.3	1.7	1.2	0.6	•	•	0.4	0.4	•	•	0.1
Operating Margin **21**	1.0	0.6	2.1	2.1	0.9	0.4	•	•	0.7	1.5	•	•	0.7
Operating Margin Before Officers' Comp. **22**	1.4	2.2	4.4	3.8	2.1	1.0	•	•	1.1	1.9	•	•	0.8

Selected Average Balance Sheet ($ in Thousands)

Net Receivables 23	267	0	•	5	29	154	694	•	4130	8803	•	983958
Inventories 24	505	0	•	41	136	393	1729	•	9480	22248	•	1572598
Net Property, Plant and Equipment 25	1516	0	•	31	199	680	2255	•	30799	73073	•	480023
Total Assets 26	3626	0	•	134	705	2076	7040	•	69492	158634	•	11762977
Notes and Loans Payable 27	1044	0	•	64	342	630	2048	•	21121	36042	•	3343343
All Other Liabilities 28	1378	0	•	14	131	470	1854	•	20779	44308	•	5129268
Net Worth 29	1204	0	•	57	232	976	3137	•	27592	78284	•	3290366

Selected Financial Ratios (Times to 1)

Current Ratio 30	1.0	•	4.0	2.4	2.0	1.7	•	1.1	1.3	•	0.8
Quick Ratio 31	0.4	•	1.4	0.9	1.0	0.8	•	0.5	0.5	•	0.3
Net Sales to Working Capital 32	239.5	•	13.5	16.7	18.4	29.5	•	130.4	43.8	•	•
Coverage Ratio 33	4.6	23.0	10.9	7.7	7.3	8.5	•	6.0	7.4	•	3.6
Total Asset Turnover 34	2.6	•	5.5	4.8	4.4	6.4	•	3.9	3.4	•	2.1
Inventory Turnover 35	13.7	•	13.0	18.5	17.1	21.5	•	21.3	18.0	•	11.4
Receivables Turnover 36	44.2	•	137.3	126.2	73.9	46.0	•	87.0	70.1	•	50.1
Total Liabilities to Net Worth 37	2.0	•	1.4	2.0	1.1	1.2	•	1.5	1.0	•	2.6
Current Assets to Working Capital 38	30.4	•	1.3	1.7	2.0	2.5	•	11.8	4.3	•	•
Current Liabilities to Working Capital 39	29.4	•	0.3	0.7	1.0	1.5	•	10.8	3.3	•	•
Working Capital to Net Sales 40	0.0	•	0.1	0.1	0.1	0.0	•	0.0	0.0	•	•
Inventory to Working Capital 41	13.9	•	0.8	0.8	0.8	1.2	•	5.8	1.9	•	•
Total Receipts to Cash Flow 42	11.0	7.7	9.2	9.8	10.4	15.3	•	13.1	14.5	•	10.7
Cost of Goods to Cash Flow 43	8.0	5.3	6.7	7.3	7.6	12.5	•	9.7	10.8	•	7.8
Cash Flow to Total Debt 44	0.4	•	1.0	0.7	0.8	0.8	•	0.5	0.5	•	0.3

Selected Financial Factors (in Percentages)

Debt Ratio 45	66.8	•	58.0	67.1	53.0	55.4	•	60.3	50.7	•	72.0
Return on Total Assets 46	10.7	•	23.0	16.6	14.0	15.5	•	11.8	9.6	•	9.7
Return on Equity Before Income Taxes 47	25.1	•	49.8	43.8	25.8	30.8	•	24.8	16.8	•	24.9
Return on Equity After Income Taxes 48	19.5	•	48.8	43.1	24.2	28.7	•	21.6	14.0	•	17.8
Profit Margin (Before Income Tax) 49	3.2	8.9	3.8	3.0	2.7	2.1	•	2.5	2.5	•	3.3
Profit Margin (After Income Tax) 50	2.5	8.5	3.7	3.0	2.6	2.0	•	2.2	2.0	•	2.4

Table I

Corporations with and without Net Income

BEER, WINE, AND LIQUOR STORES

MONEY AMOUNTS AND SIZE OF ASSETS IN THOUSANDS OF DOLLARS

Item Description for Accounting Period 7/05 Through 6/06	Total	Zero Assets	Under 500	500 to 1,000	1,000 to 5,000	5,000 to 10,000	10,000 to 25,000	25,000 to 50,000	50,000 to 100,000	100,000 to 250,000	250,000 to 500,000	500,000 to 2,500,000	2,500,000 and over
Number of Enterprises **1**	18636	579	14995	2369	582	88	16	4	3	0	0	0	0
Revenues ($ in Thousands)													
Net Sales **2**	21815724	191920	10662927	4033456	2670229	1898705	897855	478718	981915	0	0	0	0
Interest **3**	3855	0	794	458	1797	208	320	0	278	0	0	0	0
Rents **4**	615	0	1	0	0	0	0	0	614	0	0	0	0
Royalties **5**	0	0	0	0	0	0	0	0	0	0	0	0	0
Other Portfolio Income **6**	71739	10476	30093	16616	13939	366	245	6	0	0	0	0	0
Other Receipts **7**	367767	6281	256562	19778	68006	3801	5865	1863	5609	0	0	0	0
Total Receipts **8**	22259700	208677	10950377	4070308	2753971	1903080	904285	480587	988416	0	0	0	0
Average Total Receipts **9**	1194	360	730	1718	4732	21626	56518	120147	329472	•	•	•	•
Operating Costs/Operating Income (%)													
Cost of Operations **10**	79.2	88.4	78.8	79.6	79.4	81.0	80.2	74.5	77.8	•	•	•	•
Salaries and Wages **11**	5.2	1.6	4.8	4.1	5.8	6.1	6.7	9.3	7.2	•	•	•	•
Taxes Paid **12**	2.3	1.1	2.8	2.8	1.3	0.6	1.3	1.3	1.2	•	•	•	•
Interest Paid **13**	0.7	0.2	0.7	0.7	0.8	0.2	0.5	1.0	0.3	•	•	•	•
Depreciation **14**	0.6	1.2	0.5	0.8	0.4	0.4	0.4	0.7	0.9	•	•	•	•
Amortization and Depletion **15**	0.3	•	0.3	0.6	0.3	0.0	0.1	0.2	0.1	•	•	•	•
Pensions and Other Deferred Comp. **16**	0.1	•	0.0	0.0	0.2	0.5	0.1	0.0	0.1	•	•	•	•
Employee Benefits **17**	0.3	0.1	0.3	0.2	0.3	0.7	0.5	0.6	0.7	•	•	•	•
Advertising **18**	0.5	0.0	0.3	0.6	0.6	0.3	1.0	1.4	1.1	•	•	•	•
Other Expenses **19**	8.6	11.1	9.6	7.6	10.1	3.8	6.6	9.1	8.3	•	•	•	•
Officers' Compensation **20**	2.5	5.5	3.2	1.7	2.4	1.1	2.6	1.1	0.6	•	•	•	•
Operating Margin **21**	•	•	•	1.5	•	5.2	0.2	0.8	1.8	•	•	•	•
Operating Margin Before Officers' Comp. **22**	2.3	1.7	1.7	3.2	0.8	6.3	2.8	1.9	2.4	•	•	•	•

Selected Average Balance Sheet ($ in Thousands)

Net Receivables 23	23	0	2	10	165	2700	721	2445	4062
Inventories 24	139	0	79	176	842	1942	8650	19404	36086
Net Property, Plant and Equipment 25	54	0	26	92	162	934	2222	6492	52165
Total Assets 26	368	0	181	702	1896	6850	18099	41743	109434
Notes and Loans Payable 27	180	0	101	406	845	2002	3666	17091	28128
All Other Liabilities 28	78	0	30	155	378	1882	7020	11333	32735
Net Worth 29	110	0	49	142	674	2967	7414	13319	48571

Selected Financial Ratios (Times to 1)

Current Ratio 30	2.4	•	3.0	2.8	2.1	1.8	1.5	1.8	1.6
Quick Ratio 31	0.7	•	0.9	0.7	0.6	1.2	0.3	0.3	0.3
Net Sales to Working Capital 32	8.4	•	8.8	7.0	6.3	8.7	11.6	11.1	17.5
Coverage Ratio 33	3.8	•	2.6	4.7	3.0	25.4	3.0	2.1	9.3
Total Asset Turnover 34	3.2	•	3.9	2.4	2.4	3.1	3.1	2.9	3.0
Inventory Turnover 35	6.7	•	7.1	7.7	4.3	9.0	5.2	4.6	7.1
Receivables Turnover 36	58.4	•	471.9	335.1	34.4	8.2	88.6	60.0	85.6
Total Liabilities to Net Worth 37	2.4	•	2.7	4.0	1.8	1.3	1.4	2.1	1.3
Current Assets to Working Capital 38	1.7	•	1.5	1.5	1.9	2.2	3.0	2.3	2.7
Current Liabilities to Working Capital 39	0.7	•	0.5	0.5	0.9	1.2	2.0	1.3	1.7
Working Capital to Net Sales 40	0.1	•	0.1	0.1	0.2	0.1	0.1	0.1	0.1
Inventory to Working Capital 41	1.1	•	1.0	1.1	1.3	0.8	2.1	1.8	2.1
Total Receipts to Cash Flow 42	14.7	51.7	15.4	13.8	13.4	11.9	21.2	16.7	14.8
Cost of Goods to Cash Flow 43	11.6	45.7	12.1	11.0	10.6	9.6	17.0	12.5	11.5
Cash Flow to Total Debt 44	0.3	•	0.4	0.2	0.3	0.5	0.2	0.3	0.4

Selected Financial Factors (in Percentages)

Debt Ratio 45	70.2	•	72.8	79.8	64.5	56.7	59.0	68.1	55.6
Return on Total Assets 46	7.9	•	7.5	7.4	5.8	17.7	4.3	6.3	8.1
Return on Equity Before Income Taxes 47	19.7	•	16.8	28.9	11.0	39.3	6.9	10.5	16.4
Return on Equity After Income Taxes 48	18.7	•	16.2	28.3	8.5	38.9	6.9	10.5	13.3
Profit Margin (Before Income Tax) 49	1.8	•	1.2	2.4	1.6	5.4	0.9	1.2	2.4
Profit Margin (After Income Tax) 50	1.7	•	1.1	2.4	1.3	5.4	0.9	1.2	2.0

Table II

Corporations with Net Income

BEER, WINE, AND LIQUOR STORES

MONEY AMOUNTS AND SIZE OF ASSETS IN THOUSANDS OF DOLLARS

Item Description for Accounting Period 7/05 Through 6/06	Total	Zero Assets	Under 500	500 to 1,000	1,000 to 5,000	5,000 to 10,000	10,000 to 25,000	25,000 to 50,000	50,000 to 100,000	100,000 to 250,000	250,000 to 500,000	500,000 to 2,500,000	2,500,000 and over
Number of Enterprises **1**	12233	181	9905	1591	448	88	•	•	3	0	0	0	0

Revenues ($ in Thousands)

Net Sales **2**	17109367	109374	7030251	3503495	2366615	1898705	•	•	981915	0	0	0	0
Interest **3**	3534	0	793	458	1797	208	•	•	278	0	0	0	0
Rents **4**	615	0	1	0	0	0	•	•	614	0	0	0	0
Royalties **5**	0	0	0	0	0	0			0	0	0	0	0
Other Portfolio Income **6**	71503	10476	30093	16616	13939	366	•	•	0	0	0	0	0
Other Receipts **7**	270153	3293	167985	15564	66015	3801	•	•	5609	0	0	0	0
Total Receipts **8**	17455172	123143	7229123	3536133	2448366	1903080	•	•	988416	0	0	0	0
Average Total Receipts **9**	1427	680	730	2223	5465	21626	•	•	329472	•	•	•	•

Operating Costs/Operating Income (%)

Cost of Operations **10**	79.1	84.0	79.0	79.0	79.2	81.0	•	•	77.8	•	•	•	•
Salaries and Wages **11**	4.9	2.8	3.7	4.0	6.3	6.1	•	•	7.2	•	•	•	•
Taxes Paid **12**	1.8	1.4	1.9	2.9	1.3	0.6	•	•	1.2	•	•	•	•
Interest Paid **13**	0.4	•	0.5	0.3	0.6	0.2	•	•	0.3	•	•	•	•
Depreciation **14**	0.5	•	0.4	0.7	0.4	0.4	•	•	0.9	•	•	•	•
Amortization and Depletion **15**	0.2	•	0.3	0.3	0.3	0.0	•	•	0.1	•	•	•	•
Pensions and Other Deferred Comp. **16**	0.1	•	0.1	0.0	0.2	0.5	•	•	0.1	•	•	•	•
Employee Benefits **17**	0.3	0.1	0.3	0.2	0.4	0.7	•	•	0.7	•	•	•	•
Advertising **18**	0.5	0.0	0.3	0.6	0.7	0.3	•	•	1.1	•	•	•	•
Other Expenses **19**	7.9	14.2	8.9	7.2	9.4	3.8	•	•	8.3	•	•	•	•
Officers' Compensation **20**	2.6	9.7	3.7	1.7	2.3	1.1	•	•	0.6	•	•	•	•
Operating Margin **21**	1.6	•	1.0	3.2	•	5.2	•	•	1.8	•	•	•	•
Operating Margin Before Officers' Comp. **22**	4.2	•	4.7	4.9	1.2	6.3	•	•	2.4	•	•	•	•

Selected Average Balance Sheet ($ in Thousands)

Net Receivables 23	33	0	1	15	214	2700	4062
Inventories 24	159	0	81	205	823	1891	39975
Net Property, Plant and Equipment 25	54	0	21	48	185	934	52165
Total Assets 26	423	0	179	736	2047	6850	109434
Notes and Loans Payable 27	157	0	68	315	831	2002	28128
All Other Liabilities 28	102	0	32	212	455	1882	32735
Net Worth 29	163	0	79	209	761	2967	48571

Selected Financial Ratios (Times to 1)

Current Ratio 30	2.4	3.5	3.0	2.0	1.8	1.6
Quick Ratio 31	0.8	1.1	0.8	0.6	1.2	0.3
Net Sales to Working Capital 32	8.0	8.2	6.8	6.4	8.7	17.5
Coverage Ratio 33	9.7	9.4	14.3	4.9	25.4	9.3
Total Asset Turnover 34	3.3	4.0	3.0	2.6	3.1	3.0
Inventory Turnover 35	7.0	6.9	8.5	5.1	9.2	6.4
Receivables Turnover 36	49.4	723.6	291.3	33.3	16.0	161.1
Total Liabilities to Net Worth 37	1.6	1.3	2.5	1.7	1.3	1.3
Current Assets to Working Capital 38	1.7	1.4	1.5	2.0	2.2	2.7
Current Liabilities to Working Capital 39	0.7	0.4	0.5	1.0	1.2	1.7
Working Capital to Net Sales 40	0.1	0.1	0.1	0.2	0.1	0.1
Inventory to Working Capital 41	1.1	0.9	1.0	1.3	0.8	2.1
Total Receipts to Cash Flow 42	12.3	11.8	11.3	12.3	11.9	14.8
Cost of Goods to Cash Flow 43	9.7	9.3	9.0	9.7	9.6	11.5
Cash Flow to Total Debt 44	0.4	0.6	0.4	0.3	0.5	0.4

Selected Financial Factors (in Percentages)

Debt Ratio 45	61.4	55.7	71.6	62.8	56.7	55.6
Return on Total Assets 46	13.4	16.9	13.2	7.5	17.7	8.1
Return on Equity Before Income Taxes 47	31.1	34.1	43.2	16.1	39.3	16.4
Return on Equity After Income Taxes 48	30.0	33.6	42.6	13.3	38.9	13.3
Profit Margin (Before Income Tax) 49	3.6	3.8	4.1	2.3	5.4	2.4
Profit Margin (After Income Tax) 50	3.5	3.7	4.0	1.9	5.4	2.0

Table I

Corporations with and without Net Income

HEALTH AND PERSONAL CARE STORES

MONEY AMOUNTS AND SIZE OF ASSETS IN THOUSANDS OF DOLLARS

Item Description for Accounting Period 7/05 Through 6/06		Total	Zero Assets	Under 500	500 to 1,000	1,000 to 5,000	5,000 to 10,000	10,000 to 25,000	25,000 to 50,000	50,000 to 100,000	100,000 to 250,000	250,000 to 500,000	500,000 to 2,500,000	2,500,000 and over
Number of Enterprises	1	38611	2299	29701	4068	2277	157	44	24	11	12	8	3	7
Revenues ($ in Thousands)														
Net Sales	2	211683325	1965520	26413686	14291281	12986799	3274955	1829111	1732945	2656163	5043292	3792780	5639216	132057577
Interest	3	222667	2408	1353	3195	9306	468	2926	439	785	5388	10088	48176	138136
Rents	4	106848	53	566	5129	5640	3265	237	1811	8	454	2415	3182	84087
Royalties	5	119368	0	0	0	0	0	0	0	0	42	2487	95024	21814
Other Portfolio Income	6	428140	13059	40853	24065	16018	1914	6617	2104	1756	2091	14318	0	305347
Other Receipts	7	1499895	44822	15350	38822	49919	19844	25873	15031	10219	55812	47625	61794	1114781
Total Receipts	8	214060243	2025862	26471808	14362492	13067682	3300446	1864764	1752330	2668931	5107079	3869713	5847392	133721742
Average Total Receipts	9	5544	881	891	3531	5739	21022	42381	73014	242630	425590	483714	1949131	19103106
Operating Costs/Operating Income (%)														
Cost of Operations	10	71.5	62.0	70.2	75.3	69.5	49.6	68.5	60.8	69.4	73.7	61.6	62.8	73.0
Salaries and Wages	11	10.8	17.0	7.0	6.7	12.0	22.6	11.1	16.0	10.4	12.4	12.5	15.2	11.2
Taxes Paid	12	1.3	1.8	1.6	1.2	1.5	2.1	1.6	2.0	1.4	1.7	1.9	2.1	1.2
Interest Paid	13	0.7	1.5	0.3	0.4	0.5	0.5	0.7	1.1	0.8	1.2	2.2	1.5	0.7
Depreciation	14	0.9	1.1	0.5	0.4	0.7	0.9	0.8	1.5	0.7	0.7	1.5	1.5	1.0
Amortization and Depletion	15	0.3	1.0	0.2	0.1	0.2	0.1	0.1	0.2	0.2	0.2	0.6	0.7	0.3
Pensions and Other Deferred Comp.	16	0.3	0.0	0.3	0.5	0.4	0.2	0.2	0.2	0.1	0.4	0.3	0.3	0.3
Employee Benefits	17	0.6	1.0	0.4	0.3	0.6	0.7	0.6	1.1	0.8	1.3	1.1	1.3	0.6
Advertising	18	1.1	1.0	1.0	0.4	1.0	2.4	5.3	1.4	0.9	0.9	1.4	1.8	1.0
Other Expenses	19	9.0	15.3	10.4	6.1	8.2	15.8	10.9	13.7	10.4	8.5	14.2	13.5	8.4
Officers' Compensation	20	1.5	0.9	6.1	5.3	3.9	1.1	1.5	1.1	1.3	0.4	0.5	0.5	0.1
Operating Margin	21	2.1	•	2.2	3.2	1.6	4.0	•	0.8	3.6	•	2.1	•	2.3
Operating Margin Before Officers' Comp.	22	3.6	•	8.3	8.5	5.4	5.1	0.1	2.0	4.8	•	2.6	•	2.4

Selected Average Balance Sheet ($ in Thousands)

Net Receivables 23	289	0	15	86	360	1580	3711	7062	17152	17723	49154	63221	1136067
Inventories 24	564	0	57	239	398	993	3928	7620	21120	49170	63794	231139	2239404
Net Property, Plant and Equipment 25	467	0	20	103	203	1154	2028	10177	10568	26056	63094	277381	2038333
Total Assets 26	2473	0	137	728	1767	6870	14831	35813	75145	153599	342682	1042870	10467079
Notes and Loans Payable 27	580	0	61	151	467	1852	5558	13163	15682	70018	105898	295037	2189036
All Other Liabilities 28	689	0	39	166	498	2565	23919	13291	37127	49719	112047	267207	2735655
Net Worth 29	1204	0	38	412	803	2453	-14645	9359	22336	33862	124737	480625	5542389

Selected Financial Ratios (Times to 1)

Current Ratio 30	1.5	•	2.5	2.8	2.5	2.0	0.4	1.1	1.6	1.7	1.3	2.1	1.4
Quick Ratio 31	0.6	•	1.1	1.5	1.5	1.5	0.2	0.6	0.7	0.5	0.6	0.5	0.5
Net Sales to Working Capital 32	14.1	•	14.4	10.9	7.3	8.4	•	33.3	12.2	12.2	14.7	6.5	15.4
Coverage Ratio 33	5.6	1.2	9.9	10.1	5.8	11.6	1.8	2.7	5.8	0.9	2.9	2.7	5.8
Total Asset Turnover 34	2.2	•	6.5	4.8	3.2	3.0	2.8	2.0	3.2	2.7	1.4	1.8	1.8
Inventory Turnover 35	6.9	•	11.0	11.0	9.9	10.4	7.3	5.8	7.9	6.3	4.6	5.1	6.1
Receivables Turnover 36	19.6	•	59.3	36.7	18.8	15.6	9.4	11.2	14.3	20.5	11.7	15.9	17.3
Total Liabilities to Net Worth 37	1.1	•	2.6	0.8	1.2	1.8	•	2.8	2.4	3.5	1.7	1.2	0.9
Current Assets to Working Capital 38	2.9	•	1.7	1.6	1.7	2.0	•	9.0	2.7	2.5	4.1	1.9	3.4
Current Liabilities to Working Capital 39	1.9	0.7	0.7	0.6	0.7	1.0	•	8.0	1.7	1.5	3.1	0.9	2.4
Working Capital to Net Sales 40	0.1	•	0.1	0.1	0.1	0.1	•	0.0	0.1	0.1	0.1	0.2	0.1
Inventory to Working Capital 41	1.5	•	0.9	0.7	0.5	0.5	•	3.6	1.0	1.4	2.0	0.8	1.9
Total Receipts to Cash Flow 42	11.7	10.0	11.2	13.4	12.2	5.5	11.8	8.3	8.6	20.5	8.5	10.0	12.1
Cost of Goods to Cash Flow 43	8.3	6.2	7.9	10.1	8.5	2.7	8.1	5.0	5.9	15.1	5.2	6.3	8.8
Cash Flow to Total Debt 44	0.4	•	0.8	0.8	0.5	0.9	0.1	0.3	0.5	0.2	0.3	0.3	0.3

Selected Financial Factors (in Percentages)

Debt Ratio 45	51.3	•	72.5	43.5	54.6	64.3	198.7	73.9	70.3	78.0	63.6	53.9	47.0
Return on Total Assets 46	8.6	•	17.3	19.8	8.6	15.8	3.7	6.2	15.7	2.9	8.7	7.1	7.7
Return on Equity Before Income Taxes 47	14.4	•	56.4	31.6	15.6	40.5	•	14.9	43.7	•	15.7	9.7	12.0
Return on Equity After Income Taxes 48	10.6	•	55.4	30.5	13.9	39.1	•	11.5	42.6	•	12.0	6.8	7.8
Profit Margin (Before Income Tax) 49	3.2	0.3	2.4	3.7	2.2	4.8	0.6	1.9	4.0	•	4.1	2.5	3.5
Profit Margin (After Income Tax) 50	2.3	0.3	2.4	3.6	2.0	4.6	0.3	1.5	3.9	•	3.2	1.7	2.3

Table II

Corporations with Net Income

HEALTH AND PERSONAL CARE STORES

MONEY AMOUNTS AND SIZE OF ASSETS IN THOUSANDS OF DOLLARS

Item Description for Accounting Period 7/05 Through 6/06	Total	Zero Assets	Under 500	500 to 1,000	1,000 to 5,000	5,000 to 10,000	10,000 to 25,000	25,000 to 50,000	50,000 to 100,000	100,000 to 250,000	250,000 to 500,000	500,000 to 2,500,000	2,500,000 and over
Number of Enterprises 1	23750	445	17698	3355	2038	138	25	20	8	8	•	•	3
Revenues ($ in Thousands)													
Net Sales 2	190302051	1325986	19244513	13154914	12217719	3173613	1437744	1413505	2064090	4235788	•	•	5639216
Interest 3	187910	2371	952	3086	8259	173	379	159	239	2036	•	•	48176
Rents 4	99854	53	560	2121	5125	3265	237	1811	8	454	•	•	3182
Royalties 5	119326	0	0	0	0	0	0	0	0	0	•	•	95024
Other Portfolio Income 6	350166	0	6046	22051	3874	1914	6612	2104	594	473	•	•	0
Other Receipts 7	1384253	39109	6507	36319	43830	16361	15487	14471	9142	17771	•	•	61794
Total Receipts 8	192443560	1367519	19258578	13218491	12278807	3195326	1460459	1432050	2074073	4256522	•	•	5847392
Average Total Receipts 9	8103	3073	1088	3940	6025	23155	58418	71602	259259	532065	•	•	1949131
Operating Costs/Operating Income (%)													
Cost of Operations 10	71.5	63.2	70.9	74.9	70.3	50.2	71.5	62.1	69.9	74.6	•	•	62.8
Salaries and Wages 11	10.8	17.4	6.1	7.0	11.3	22.8	10.7	14.6	9.2	11.2	•	•	15.2
Taxes Paid 12	1.3	1.7	1.5	1.2	1.4	2.1	1.3	1.8	1.2	1.7	•	•	2.1
Interest Paid 13	0.6	1.8	0.1	0.4	0.4	0.5	0.4	0.4	0.5	0.5	•	•	1.5
Depreciation 14	0.9	1.1	0.3	0.3	0.7	0.9	0.5	1.5	0.5	0.7	•	•	1.5
Amortization and Depletion 15	0.3	1.3	0.1	0.1	0.1	0.1	0.1	0.2	0.2	0.1	•	•	0.7
Pensions and Other Deferred Comp. 16	0.3	•	0.3	0.5	0.4	0.2	0.2	0.2	0.2	0.1	•	•	0.3
Employee Benefits 17	0.6	1.3	0.3	0.3	0.6	0.7	0.5	1.1	0.6	1.3	•	•	1.3
Advertising 18	1.0	0.4	0.8	0.4	1.0	2.4	3.4	1.2	0.6	0.8	•	•	1.8
Other Expenses 19	8.6	10.3	8.7	5.9	7.3	14.2	7.0	12.6	10.7	7.0	•	•	13.5
Officers' Compensation 20	1.4	0.8	6.1	5.2	3.8	1.0	1.6	1.3	1.4	0.2	•	•	0.5
Operating Margin 21	2.8	0.8	4.7	3.8	2.6	5.0	2.9	3.0	5.0	1.6	•	•	•
Operating Margin Before Officers' Comp. 22	4.2	1.6	10.9	9.0	6.4	6.0	4.5	4.3	6.4	1.8	•	•	•

Selected Average Balance Sheet ($ in Thousands)

Net Receivables 23	447	0	20	96	328	1717	3071	6237	19498	22728	63221
Inventories 24	799	0	67	246	389	1355	3916	5647	20115	63555	231139
Net Property, Plant and Equipment 25	642	0	13	70	193	801	2567	11096	9540	31505	277381
Total Assets 26	3634	0	156	740	1710	6705	14647	34456	74786	146606	1042870
Notes and Loans Payable 27	666	0	34	121	394	1454	5556	9583	13998	47177	295037
All Other Liabilities 28	1010	0	44	173	484	2656	4872	10300	34837	53917	267207
Net Worth 29	1958	0	79	447	832	2595	4219	14574	25951	45512	480625

Selected Financial Ratios (Times to 1)

Current Ratio 30	1.5	•	3.0	2.8	2.3	2.2	1.2	1.7	1.9		2.1
Quick Ratio 31	0.6	•	1.4	1.6	1.3	1.1	0.6	0.7	0.6		0.5
Net Sales to Working Capital 32	13.9	•	13.3	11.2	8.5	7.7	32.5	10.9	11.6		6.5
Coverage Ratio 33	7.5	3.2	33.4	12.2	8.2	13.4	12.2	10.5	11.6	5.3	2.7
Total Asset Turnover 34	2.2	•	7.0	5.3	3.5	3.4	3.9	2.1	3.5	3.6	1.8
Inventory Turnover 35	7.2	•	11.6	11.9	10.8	8.5	10.5	7.8	9.0	6.2	5.1
Receivables Turnover 36	18.9	•	52.9	41.5	21.0	26.8	11.4	12.8	26.5	46.6	15.9
Total Liabilities to Net Worth 37	0.9	•	1.0	0.7	1.1	1.6	2.5	1.4	1.9	2.2	1.2
Current Assets to Working Capital 38	2.8	•	1.5	1.5	1.8	1.7	1.8	7.6	2.4	2.2	1.9
Current Liabilities to Working Capital 39	1.8	•	0.5	0.5	0.8	0.7	0.8	6.6	1.4	1.2	0.9
Working Capital to Net Sales 40	0.1	•	0.1	0.1	0.1	0.1	0.1	0.0	0.1	0.1	0.2
Inventory to Working Capital 41	1.4	•	0.8	0.6	0.6	0.5	0.6	2.9	0.8	1.4	0.8
Total Receipts to Cash Flow 42	11.0	9.4	9.5	12.6	12.0	5.7	11.0	7.3	7.0	17.5	10.0
Cost of Goods to Cash Flow 43	7.8	5.9	6.7	9.4	8.4	2.9	7.9	4.5	4.9	13.0	6.3
Cash Flow to Total Debt 44	0.4	•	1.5	1.1	0.6	1.0	0.5	0.5	0.8	0.3	0.3

Selected Financial Factors (in Percentages)

Debt Ratio 45	46.1	•	49.8	39.7	51.3	61.3	71.2	57.7	65.3	69.0	53.9
Return on Total Assets 46	10.0	•	34.5	24.9	12.4	21.0	18.9	9.7	20.8	9.2	7.1
Return on Equity Before Income Taxes 47	16.0	•	66.6	37.8	22.3	50.1	60.2	20.7	54.6	24.0	9.7
Return on Equity After Income Taxes 48	12.2	•	65.7	36.6	20.5	48.6	55.2	18.0	53.2	19.5	6.8
Profit Margin (Before Income Tax) 49	3.9	4.0	4.8	4.3	3.1	5.7	4.4	4.3	5.5	2.1	2.5
Profit Margin (After Income Tax) 50	3.0	3.9	4.7	4.2	2.8	5.5	4.0	3.7	5.4	1.7	1.7

Table I

Corporations with and without Net Income

GASOLINE STATIONS

MONEY AMOUNTS AND SIZE OF ASSETS IN THOUSANDS OF DOLLARS

Item Description for Accounting Period 7/05 Through 6/06	Total	Zero Assets	Under 500	500 to 1,000	1,000 to 5,000	5,000 to 10,000	10,000 to 25,000	25,000 to 50,000	50,000 to 100,000	100,000 to 250,000	250,000 to 500,000	500,000 to 2,500,000	2,500,000 and over
Number of Enterprises **1**	38508	2473	25176	6103	4109	334	179	73	28	19	3	11	0
Revenues ($ in Thousands)													
Net Sales **2**	240598193	1841178	49841633	25047567	39037779	13129924	16621695	16193301	8367054	12377315	6897669	51243078	0
Interest **3**	79485	590	4032	5925	8889	2970	2233	5088	2679	2254	3235	41590	0
Rents **4**	127239	0	9228	6194	23047	12005	6248	18645	10853	2056	2745	36218	0
Royalties **5**	31085	0	0	0	0	0	0	0	434	958	0	29693	0
Other Portfolio Income **6**	339515	8496	63699	90818	49150	10121	40404	24657	8681	12017	1898	29576	0
Other Receipts **7**	1381438	5115	200622	162764	200951	37628	145936	73469	32829	224399	41055	256669	0
Total Receipts **8**	242556955	1855379	50119214	25313268	39319816	13192648	16816516	16315160	8422530	12618999	6946602	51636824	0
Average Total Receipts **9**	6299	750	1991	4148	9569	39499	93947	223495	300805	664158	2315534	4694257	•
Operating Costs/Operating Income (%)													
Cost of Operations **10**	88.9	91.2	87.9	88.7	90.4	86.1	89.7	90.8	91.2	87.4	88.6	88.6	•
Salaries and Wages **11**	3.3	2.6	3.1	2.8	3.0	3.7	3.8	2.7	2.8	3.8	4.1	3.5	•
Taxes Paid **12**	1.1	1.7	1.1	1.6	1.0	2.0	0.7	0.9	0.7	2.8	0.5	0.6	•
Interest Paid **13**	0.5	0.2	0.3	0.6	0.7	0.5	0.5	0.4	0.5	0.6	0.2	0.5	•
Depreciation **14**	0.9	0.5	0.5	0.9	0.7	0.9	0.9	0.8	0.8	1.0	0.9	1.3	•
Amortization and Depletion **15**	0.1	0.0	0.2	0.1	0.1	0.2	0.1	0.0	0.0	0.0	0.0	0.1	•
Pensions and Other Deferred Comp. **16**	0.0	0.0	0.0	0.0	0.0	0.0	0.0	0.0	0.0	0.1	0.3	0.1	•
Employee Benefits **17**	0.2	0.1	0.1	0.1	0.1	0.2	0.2	0.1	0.2	0.2	0.3	0.3	•
Advertising **18**	0.1	0.0	0.1	0.0	0.1	0.1	0.2	0.1	0.1	0.2	0.4	0.1	•
Other Expenses **19**	4.5	6.3	6.0	4.8	4.1	5.1	4.3	3.9	3.4	3.6	3.4	3.5	•
Officers' Compensation **20**	0.5	0.5	1.1	0.8	0.6	0.5	0.2	0.3	0.3	0.2	0.1	0.1	•
Operating Margin **21**	0.1	•	•	•	•	0.6	•	•	•	0.0	1.3	1.2	•
Operating Margin Before Officers' Comp. **22**	0.6	•	0.8	0.5	•	1.2	•	0.2	0.2	0.2	1.4	1.3	•

Selected Average Balance Sheet ($ in Thousands)

Net Receivables 23	99	0	13	34	129	1047	1546	4331	7312	10899	41851	113934
Inventories 24	120	0	50	67	145	808	1623	3198	5543	12931	67672	88623
Net Property, Plant and Equipment 25	540	0	70	394	1088	2868	7975	17936	32583	64787	194565	521944
Total Assets 26	1104	0	214	704	1821	7110	15652	35792	68146	149041	380420	1063310
Notes and Loans Payable 27	518	0	127	461	1275	3020	7643	13880	24042	60926	104331	286672
All Other Liabilities 28	294	0	34	93	399	1571	4035	11674	18209	48463	120610	397663
Net Worth 29	292	0	53	151	146	2520	3974	10239	25895	39651	155480	378975

Selected Financial Ratios (Times to 1)

Current Ratio 30	1.3	•	2.6	2.1	1.4	1.5	1.3	1.0	1.1	1.1	1.0	1.1
Quick Ratio 31	0.8	•	1.2	1.0	0.9	0.9	0.7	0.6	0.7	0.5	0.5	0.7
Net Sales to Working Capital 32	63.5	•	32.0	39.4	61.5	44.1	70.9	407.6	109.6	220.5	887.2	205.7
Coverage Ratio 33	2.8	•	1.7	2.4	1.0	3.3	2.6	2.8	2.3	4.5	11.2	4.7
Total Asset Turnover 34	5.7	•	9.3	5.8	5.2	5.5	5.9	6.2	4.4	4.4	6.0	4.4
Inventory Turnover 35	46.1	•	34.8	54.0	59.4	41.8	51.3	63.0	49.2	44.0	30.1	46.6
Receivables Turnover 36	67.5	•	131.3	171.9	79.3	40.9	59.0	58.9	41.0	68.1	29.8	48.7
Total Liabilities to Net Worth 37	2.8	•	3.1	3.7	11.5	1.8	2.9	2.5	1.6	2.8	1.4	1.8
Current Assets to Working Capital 38	3.9	•	1.6	1.9	3.2	3.2	4.4	24.4	8.3	16.1	39.6	16.4
Current Liabilities to Working Capital 39	2.9	•	0.6	0.9	2.2	2.2	3.4	23.4	7.3	15.1	38.6	15.4
Working Capital to Net Sales 40	0.0	•	0.0	0.0	0.0	0.0	0.0	0.0	0.0	0.0	0.0	0.0
Inventory to Working Capital 41	1.3	•	0.8	0.7	1.0	0.9	1.3	6.1	2.2	4.8	13.6	4.6
Total Receipts to Cash Flow 42	26.9	67.4	27.5	25.5	35.7	23.2	27.0	29.9	34.1	22.0	22.6	23.5
Cost of Goods to Cash Flow 43	23.9	61.5	24.2	22.6	32.2	20.0	24.2	27.2	31.1	19.2	20.0	20.8
Cash Flow to Total Debt 44	0.3	•	0.4	0.3	0.2	0.4	0.3	0.3	0.2	0.3	0.5	0.3

Selected Financial Factors (in Percentages)

Debt Ratio 45	73.5	•	75.4	78.6	92.0	64.6	74.6	71.4	62.0	73.4	59.1	64.4
Return on Total Assets 46	7.6	•	4.6	7.9	3.5	8.8	7.3	7.0	4.9	11.1	13.2	10.7
Return on Equity Before Income Taxes 47	18.4	•	8.0	21.6	•	17.2	17.5	15.8	7.4	32.3	29.5	23.7
Return on Equity After Income Taxes 48	15.7	•	7.6	21.2	•	16.5	16.4	14.6	6.5	29.3	26.3	18.4
Profit Margin (Before Income Tax) 49	0.9	•	0.2	0.8	•	1.1	0.7	0.7	0.6	2.0	2.0	1.9
Profit Margin (After Income Tax) 50	0.7	•	0.2	0.8	•	1.1	0.7	0.7	0.6	1.8	1.8	1.5

Table II

Corporations with Net Income

GASOLINE STATIONS

MONEY AMOUNTS AND SIZE OF ASSETS IN THOUSANDS OF DOLLARS

Item Description for Accounting Period 7/05 Through 6/06		Total	Zero Assets	Under 500	500 to 1,000	1,000 to 5,000	5,000 to 10,000	10,000 to 25,000	25,000 to 50,000	50,000 to 100,000	100,000 to 250,000	250,000 to 500,000	500,000 to 2,500,000	2,500,000 and over
Number of Enterprises	1	21624	428	13870	4414	2416	254	134	58	21	15	3	11	0
Revenues ($ in Thousands)														
Net Sales	2	192752385	517736	33930789	17022660	29516121	9598343	12697657	13716942	6738799	10872590	6897669	51243078	0
Interest	3	69928	0	1824	5114	6220	2538	1678	3618	2114	1996	3235	41590	0
Rents	4	106485	0	7104	6194	20243	11764	4206	6611	9517	1882	2745	36218	0
Royalties	5	30651	0	0	0	0	0	0	0	0	958	0	29693	0
Other Portfolio Income	6	289058	8496	35010	83796	48349	10078	29184	24090	7021	11561	1898	29576	0
Other Receipts	7	1190151	0	120214	153424	168105	35398	113434	53588	25511	222754	41055	256669	0
Total Receipts	8	194438658	526232	34094941	17271188	29759038	9658121	12846159	13804849	6782962	11111741	6946602	51636824	0
Average Total Receipts	9	8992	1230	2458	3913	12317	38024	95867	238015	322998	740783	2315534	4694257	•
Operating Costs/Operating Income (%)														
Cost of Operations	10	89.2	92.1	87.5	89.1	91.9	86.7	89.6	90.8	91.1	88.5	88.6	88.6	•
Salaries and Wages	11	3.1	0.3	2.9	2.2	2.3	3.5	3.4	2.8	3.0	3.7	4.1	3.5	•
Taxes Paid	12	1.0	0.4	1.0	2.0	0.9	2.5	0.7	1.0	0.6	1.9	0.5	0.6	•
Interest Paid	13	0.4	0.3	0.2	0.6	0.5	0.5	0.4	0.3	0.3	0.6	0.2	0.5	•
Depreciation	14	0.8	0.1	0.4	0.7	0.6	0.8	0.8	0.7	0.8	1.0	0.9	1.3	•
Amortization and Depletion	15	0.1	0.1	0.2	0.1	0.1	0.2	0.0	0.0	0.0	0.0	0.0	0.1	•
Pensions and Other Deferred Comp.	16	0.0	•	0.0	0.0	0.0	0.0	0.0	0.0	0.0	0.1	0.3	0.1	•
Employee Benefits	17	0.2	•	0.1	0.0	0.1	0.3	0.2	0.1	0.2	0.2	0.3	0.3	•
Advertising	18	0.1	•	0.1	0.0	0.1	0.1	0.2	0.1	0.1	0.2	0.4	0.1	•
Other Expenses	19	3.9	4.8	5.3	4.1	3.2	4.0	4.3	3.6	3.2	3.3	3.4	3.5	•
Officers' Compensation	20	0.4	0.7	1.1	0.6	0.4	0.4	0.3	0.3	0.3	0.2	0.1	0.1	•
Operating Margin	21	0.7	1.2	1.1	0.4	0.1	1.0	0.1	0.4	0.4	0.3	1.3	1.2	•
Operating Margin Before Officers' Comp.	22	1.1	1.9	2.2	1.0	0.5	1.4	0.3	0.6	0.7	0.5	1.4	1.3	•

Selected Average Balance Sheet ($ in Thousands)

Net Receivables 23	146	0	13	31	152	1099	1461	4674	7502	11930	41851	113934
Inventories 24	162	0	59	61	150	794	1446	3062	5547	12872	35200	104346
Net Property, Plant and Equipment 25	734	0	67	392	972	2788	8105	17593	31469	71541	194565	521944
Total Assets 26	1534	0	234	691	1818	7240	15338	35309	67966	151784	380420	1063310
Notes and Loans Payable 27	581	0	101	449	902	2876	6388	13023	21128	49311	104331	286672
All Other Liabilities 28	423	0	31	63	374	1519	4001	11847	17854	53932	120610	397663
Net Worth 29	531	0	102	180	542	2844	4949	10439	28984	48541	155480	378975

Selected Financial Ratios (Times to 1)

Current Ratio 30	1.4	•	3.1	3.3	1.8	1.6	1.3	1.1	1.3	1.0	1.0	1.1
Quick Ratio 31	0.8	•	1.5	1.6	1.0	1.1	0.8	0.7	0.8	0.5	0.5	0.7
Net Sales to Working Capital 32	58.9	•	30.0	29.1	46.2	34.3	74.2	175.2	62.2	473.7	887.2	205.7
Coverage Ratio 33	4.7	9.9	9.2	3.9	2.9	4.3	4.1	4.0	4.4	5.5	11.2	4.7
Total Asset Turnover 34	5.8	•	10.5	5.6	6.7	5.2	6.2	6.7	4.7	4.8	6.0	4.4
Inventory Turnover 35	49.1	•	36.0	56.6	74.9	41.3	58.7	70.1	52.7	49.8	57.9	39.6
Receivables Turnover 36	71.2	•	149.4	189.7	99.0	38.9	70.2	61.6	48.2	79.8	109.9	81.8
Total Liabilities to Net Worth 37	1.9	•	1.3	2.8	2.4	1.5	2.1	2.4	1.3	2.1	1.4	1.8
Current Assets to Working Capital 38	3.6	•	1.5	1.4	2.2	2.6	4.4	10.4	4.8	33.8	39.6	16.4
Current Liabilities to Working Capital 39	2.6	•	0.5	0.4	1.2	1.6	3.4	9.4	3.8	32.8	38.6	15.4
Working Capital to Net Sales 40	0.0	•	0.0	0.0	0.0	0.0	0.0	0.0	0.0	0.0	0.0	0.0
Inventory to Working Capital 41	1.2	•	0.7	0.5	0.7	0.7	1.4	2.6	1.4	10.7	13.6	4.6
Total Receipts to Cash Flow 42	24.2	19.9	21.1	21.5	33.5	23.7	23.9	29.3	31.0	20.2	22.6	23.5
Cost of Goods to Cash Flow 43	21.6	18.3	18.4	19.1	30.7	20.5	21.4	26.6	28.2	17.9	20.0	20.8
Cash Flow to Total Debt 44	0.4	•	0.9	0.4	0.3	0.4	0.4	0.3	0.3	0.3	0.5	0.3

Selected Financial Factors (in Percentages)

Debt Ratio 45	65.4	•	56.5	74.0	70.2	60.7	67.7	70.4	57.4	68.0	59.1	64.4
Return on Total Assets 46	11.8	•	19.2	14.1	9.4	11.0	10.2	8.8	6.2	14.7	13.2	10.7
Return on Equity Before Income Taxes 47	26.8	•	39.2	40.2	20.6	21.5	23.9	22.4	11.2	37.8	29.5	23.7
Return on Equity After Income Taxes 48	24.2	2.9	38.9	39.7	20.0	20.7	22.7	21.0	10.1	34.7	26.3	18.4
Profit Margin (Before Income Tax) 49	1.6	2.9	1.6	1.9	0.9	1.6	1.2	1.0	1.0	2.5	2.0	1.9
Profit Margin (After Income Tax) 50	1.4	2.9	1.6	1.9	0.9	1.6	1.2	0.9	0.9	2.3	1.8	1.5

Table I

Corporations with and without Net Income

CLOTHING AND CLOTHING ACCESSORIES STORES

MONEY AMOUNTS AND SIZE OF ASSETS IN THOUSANDS OF DOLLARS

Item Description for Accounting Period 7/05 Through 6/06	Total	Zero Assets	Under 500	500 to 1,000	1,000 to 5,000	5,000 to 10,000	10,000 to 25,000	25,000 to 50,000	50,000 to 100,000	100,000 to 250,000	250,000 to 500,000	500,000 to 2,500,000	2,500,000 and over
Number of Enterprises **1**	52049	5365	39224	4333	2570	263	120	50	30	35	22	29	7
Revenues ($ in Thousands)													
Net Sales **2**	170189389	951568	13533976	5665414	8786352	2944334	3829949	3235017	3856546	9936754	13493052	49180481	54775947
Interest **3**	968273	1133	2458	3432	8941	4729	10252	4707	2327	23690	51772	319273	535558
Rents **4**	168669	7029	27	88	4618	864	13403	1705	12	2181	12041	46029	80671
Royalties **5**	979895	0	0	0	0	0	0	0	6330	26259	49442	405939	491925
Other Portfolio Income **6**	1415511	25477	14579	6931	20515	1583	656	2312	11508	5538	15634	473504	837276
Other Receipts **7**	2511622	31277	117348	-10446	114602	104374	33438	29183	82417	110595	126374	1090076	682383
Total Receipts **8**	176233359	1016484	13668388	5665419	8935028	3055884	3887698	3272924	3959140	10105017	13748315	51515302	57403760
Average Total Receipts **9**	3386	189	348	1308	3477	11619	32397	65458	131971	288715	624923	1776390	8200537
Operating Costs/Operating Income (%)													
Cost of Operations **10**	53.8	61.9	50.0	59.0	58.9	53.9	55.4	60.0	49.9	52.2	53.1	53.0	54.2
Salaries and Wages **11**	13.8	14.6	11.5	12.1	12.7	15.0	14.4	13.6	16.4	15.9	14.8	14.1	13.7
Taxes Paid **12**	2.3	2.3	2.6	2.1	2.1	2.4	2.8	2.1	2.9	2.7	2.4	2.5	2.1
Interest Paid **13**	0.8	2.6	0.7	0.8	1.1	0.9	0.8	0.8	1.0	0.8	0.9	0.6	0.9
Depreciation **14**	1.7	1.0	0.6	0.5	0.8	1.3	1.0	1.0	1.6	1.4	2.0	2.1	2.0
Amortization and Depletion **15**	0.3	0.7	0.2	0.1	0.1	0.1	0.2	0.1	0.1	0.3	0.1	0.2	0.6
Pensions and Other Deferred Comp. **16**	0.4	0.2	0.1	0.2	0.5	0.2	0.2	0.1	0.1	0.2	0.2	0.3	0.6
Employee Benefits **17**	1.0	0.7	0.5	0.7	0.6	0.5	0.8	0.7	1.2	0.9	1.0	1.2	1.2
Advertising **18**	2.5	2.9	2.3	3.1	3.2	4.8	3.1	2.3	3.3	2.0	2.4	2.9	2.1
Other Expenses **19**	18.2	27.8	23.2	14.2	15.7	21.0	17.5	14.5	20.8	22.4	19.4	18.4	16.4
Officers' Compensation **20**	1.9	1.0	8.5	5.5	4.6	1.9	2.8	1.6	1.2	0.9	0.7	1.2	0.4
Operating Margin **21**	3.2	•	1.8	•	•	•	1.1	3.3	1.6	0.3	3.1	3.6	5.7
Operating Margin Before Officers' Comp. **22**	5.0	•	8.4	7.3	4.4	1.9	3.9	4.9	2.8	1.2	3.8	4.8	6.1

Selected Average Balance Sheet ($ in Thousands)

Net Receivables 23	99	0	2	33	90	461	1753	3848	6036	7873	12719	45862	299150
Inventories 24	598	0	74	435	1097	3372	7806	15744	34512	48101	105909	287741	1079261
Net Property, Plant and Equipment 25	456	0	10	78	245	1424	2561	5937	16475	34886	120132	267688	1327747
Total Assets 26	1945	0	113	659	1787	6588	14644	34656	67752	151949	335492	1064579	5502082
Notes and Loans Payable 27	342	0	52	226	625	2249	4159	8725	14351	34747	58636	113438	777564
All Other Liabilities 28	811	0	37	161	532	2158	5584	13792	34115	57504	153384	349511	2892993
Net Worth 29	791	0	25	271	630	2181	4901	12139	19285	59698	123473	601629	1831526

Selected Financial Ratios (Times to 1)

Current Ratio 30	1.8	•	2.3	2.9	2.2	1.5	1.7	1.4	1.8	1.4	1.7	1.9	1.6
Quick Ratio 31	0.6	•	0.6	0.7	0.5	0.3	0.4	0.4	0.5	0.3	0.5	0.6	0.7
Net Sales to Working Capital 32	6.9	•	6.9	3.7	4.5	7.1	6.9	10.4	5.9	11.8	8.7	6.1	8.3
Coverage Ratio 33	9.4	•	2.2	3.3	2.3	3.1	4.1	6.4	5.3	3.3	6.7	13.9	13.1
Total Asset Turnover 34	1.7	•	3.0	2.0	1.9	1.7	2.2	1.9	1.9	1.9	1.8	1.6	1.4
Inventory Turnover 35	2.9	•	2.3	1.8	1.8	1.8	2.3	2.5	1.9	3.1	3.1	3.1	3.9
Receivables Turnover 36	28.7	•	110.2	39.6	36.8	13.6	16.3	16.2	24.9	36.7	38.4	40.8	19.6
Total Liabilities to Net Worth 37	1.5	•	3.6	1.4	1.8	2.0	2.0	1.9	2.5	1.5	1.7	0.8	2.0
Current Assets to Working Capital 38	2.3	•	1.8	1.5	1.8	2.9	2.4	3.7	2.3	3.6	2.5	2.1	2.6
Current Liabilities to Working Capital 39	1.3	•	0.8	0.5	0.8	1.9	1.4	2.7	1.3	2.6	1.5	1.1	1.6
Working Capital to Net Sales 40	0.1	•	0.1	0.3	0.2	0.1	0.1	0.1	0.2	0.1	0.1	0.2	0.1
Inventory to Working Capital 41	1.3	•	1.3	1.1	1.4	2.1	1.6	2.2	1.5	2.3	1.4	1.1	1.2
Total Receipts to Cash Flow 42	6.0	19.3	7.1	9.3	8.8	7.7	8.5	8.0	6.6	6.7	6.9	5.6	5.1
Cost of Goods to Cash Flow 43	3.2	11.9	5.5	5.5	5.2	4.1	4.7	4.8	3.3	3.5	3.6	3.0	2.8
Cash Flow to Total Debt 44	0.5	•	0.6	0.4	0.3	0.3	0.4	0.4	0.4	0.5	0.4	0.7	0.4

Selected Financial Factors (in Percentages)

Debt Ratio 45	59.3	•	78.2	58.8	64.7	66.9	66.5	65.0	71.5	60.7	63.2	43.5	66.7
Return on Total Assets 46	13.1	•	4.6	5.2	4.9	4.7	7.5	9.7	10.1	5.3	10.5	14.3	17.5
Return on Equity Before Income Taxes 47	28.9	•	11.5	8.8	8.0	9.6	16.9	23.3	28.9	9.4	24.2	23.5	48.4
Return on Equity After Income Taxes 48	20.2	•	10.5	7.8	5.9	8.3	15.3	21.3	25.0	5.3	14.5	16.2	34.2
Profit Margin (Before Income Tax) 49	7.0	•	0.8	1.8	1.5	1.9	2.6	4.4	4.3	2.0	4.9	8.4	11.3
Profit Margin (After Income Tax) 50	4.9	•	0.8	1.6	1.1	1.6	2.4	4.0	3.7	1.1	2.9	5.7	8.0

Table II

Corporations with Net Income

CLOTHING AND CLOTHING ACCESSORIES STORES

MONEY AMOUNTS AND SIZE OF ASSETS IN THOUSANDS OF DOLLARS

Item Description for Accounting Period 7/05 Through 6/06	Total	Zero Assets	Under 500	500 to 1,000	1,000 to 5,000	5,000 to 10,000	10,000 to 25,000	25,000 to 50,000	50,000 to 100,000	100,000 to 250,000	250,000 to 500,000	500,000 to 2,500,000	2,500,000 and over
Number of Enterprises **1**	27716	1835	19733	3514	2182	•	96	38	25	26	18	•	7
Revenues ($ in Thousands)													
Net Sales **2**	153948068	180548	8063229	4964770	7483496	•	3157682	2561186	3428116	7760458	11193383	•	54775947
Interest **3**	930114	93	982	2830	8207	•	9676	3319	915	6094	42557	•	535558
Rents **4**	159254	0	0	78	4447	•	13399	1616	0	2181	12041	•	80671
Royalties **5**	959667	0	0	0	0	•	0	0	6330	18395	49130	•	491925
Other Portfolio Income **6**	1382533	18347	8033	4423	7664	•	603	2311	11508	5463	15071	•	837276
Other Receipts **7**	2300735	25779	35878	34463	110685	•	28444	45240	57445	64937	106113	•	682383
Total Receipts **8**	159680371	224767	8108122	5006564	7614499	•	3209804	2613672	3504314	7857528	11418295	•	57403760
Average Total Receipts **9**	5761	122	411	1425	3490	•	33435	68781	140173	302213	634350	•	8200537
Operating Costs/Operating Income (%)													
Cost of Operations **10**	53.6	52.1	46.8	59.9	59.0	•	55.2	57.2	49.6	52.7	51.2	•	54.2
Salaries and Wages **11**	13.7	7.8	12.2	11.3	12.3	•	13.5	13.4	16.4	14.5	14.6	•	13.7
Taxes Paid **12**	2.3	1.4	2.6	2.0	2.1	•	2.7	2.3	3.0	2.5	2.4	•	2.1
Interest Paid **13**	0.8	1.5	0.5	0.8	0.9	•	0.8	0.5	0.7	0.6	0.8	•	0.9
Depreciation **14**	1.7	1.0	0.5	0.5	0.7	•	0.8	0.9	1.3	1.4	2.1	•	2.0
Amortization and Depletion **15**	0.3	0.0	0.1	0.0	0.0	•	0.2	0.1	0.1	0.2	0.1	•	0.6
Pensions and Other Deferred Comp. **16**	0.4	0.0	0.2	0.2	0.5	•	0.2	0.1	0.1	0.1	0.2	•	0.6
Employee Benefits **17**	1.0	0.8	0.4	0.7	0.6	•	0.7	0.6	1.2	0.9	1.0	•	1.2
Advertising **18**	2.5	2.6	2.1	3.3	3.1	•	3.0	1.8	3.2	1.7	2.2	•	2.1
Other Expenses **19**	17.5	35.8	22.2	12.7	14.1	•	15.4	15.7	19.8	19.7	19.3	•	16.4
Officers' Compensation **20**	1.6	2.5	6.7	5.7	4.8	•	3.0	1.8	1.1	1.0	0.7	•	0.4
Operating Margin **21**	4.7	•	5.7	3.1	1.9	•	4.5	5.7	3.6	4.8	5.4	•	5.7
Operating Margin Before Officers' Comp. **22**	6.2	•	12.4	8.7	6.6	•	7.5	7.5	4.7	5.8	6.1	•	6.1

Selected Average Balance Sheet ($ in Thousands)

Net Receivables 23	172	0	3	36	93	•	1977	3025	4734	8938	13606	•	299150
Inventories 24	969	0	81	436	1055	•	7680	14869	36714	56123	93938	•	1079261
Net Property, Plant and Equipment 25	800	0	7	85	227	•	2366	6341	16372	36015	128929	•	1327747
Total Assets 26	3354	0	125	671	1748	•	14827	33853	66947	148436	338980	•	5502082
Notes and Loans Payable 27	524	0	40	230	550	•	3614	6956	12095	33511	64153	•	777564
All Other Liabilities 28	1374	0	30	151	448	•	4990	14230	28502	48065	142276	•	2892993
Net Worth 29	1456	0	56	290	750	•	6223	12668	26350	66860	132551	•	1831526

Selected Financial Ratios (Times to 1)

Current Ratio 30	1.8	•	2.9	3.1	2.4	•	1.9	1.3	1.9	1.7	1.7	•	1.6
Quick Ratio 31	0.6	•	0.9	0.8	0.5	•	0.5	0.4	0.5	0.4	0.6	•	0.7
Net Sales to Working Capital 32	6.6	•	6.1	3.8	4.3	•	5.9	12.2	5.4	8.4	8.7	•	8.3
Coverage Ratio 33	12.4	13.9	14.4	5.9	5.0	•	8.6	16.3	9.3	11.6	10.4	•	13.1
Total Asset Turnover 34	1.7	•	3.3	2.1	2.0	•	2.2	2.0	2.0	2.0	1.8	•	1.4
Inventory Turnover 35	3.1	•	2.4	1.9	1.9	•	2.4	2.6	1.9	2.8	3.4	•	3.9
Receivables Turnover 36	28.3	•	109.0	39.3	39.2	•	16.1	19.5	28.9	66.8	39.7	•	19.6
Total Liabilities to Net Worth 37	1.3	•	1.2	1.3	1.3	•	1.4	1.7	1.5	1.2	1.6	•	2.0
Current Assets to Working Capital 38	2.2	•	1.5	1.5	1.7	•	2.1	4.1	2.1	2.5	2.4	•	2.6
Current Liabilities to Working Capital 39	1.2	•	0.5	0.5	0.7	•	1.1	3.1	1.1	1.5	1.4	•	1.6
Working Capital to Net Sales 40	0.2	•	0.2	0.3	0.2	•	0.2	0.1	0.2	0.1	0.1	•	0.1
Inventory to Working Capital 41	1.2	•	1.0	1.1	1.3	•	1.3	2.6	1.4	1.6	1.2	•	1.2
Total Receipts to Cash Flow 42	5.6	3.4	5.3	8.3	7.9	•	7.1	6.0	6.5	5.9	5.8	•	5.1
Cost of Goods to Cash Flow 43	3.0	1.8	2.5	5.0	4.7	•	3.9	3.4	3.2	3.1	3.0	•	2.8
Cash Flow to Total Debt 44	0.5	•	1.1	0.4	0.4	•	0.5	0.5	0.5	0.6	0.5	•	0.4

Selected Financial Factors (in Percentages)

Debt Ratio 45	56.6	•	55.5	56.7	57.1	•	58.0	62.6	60.6	55.0	60.9	•	66.7
Return on Total Assets 46	15.6	•	21.8	9.9	8.8	•	15.4	16.3	13.4	13.3	14.9	•	17.5
Return on Equity Before Income Taxes 47	33.1	•	45.7	19.0	16.5	•	32.3	40.9	30.4	27.0	34.5	•	48.4
Return on Equity After Income Taxes 48	24.2	•	44.8	17.8	14.4	•	30.8	38.3	27.0	22.1	23.4	•	34.2
Profit Margin (Before Income Tax) 49	8.7	19.0	6.2	3.9	3.6	•	6.1	7.7	5.8	6.0	7.3	•	11.3
Profit Margin (After Income Tax) 50	6.4	16.8	6.1	3.7	3.1	•	5.8	7.2	5.2	4.9	6.0	•	8.0

Table I

Corporations with and without Net Income

SPORTING GOODS, HOBBY, BOOK, AND MUSIC STORES

MONEY AMOUNTS AND SIZE OF ASSETS IN THOUSANDS OF DOLLARS

Item Description for Accounting Period 7/05 Through 6/06	Total	Zero Assets	Under 500	500 to 1,000	1,000 to 5,000	5,000 to 10,000	10,000 to 25,000	25,000 to 50,000	50,000 to 100,000	100,000 to 250,000	250,000 to 500,000	500,000 to 2,500,000	2,500,000 and over
Number of Enterprises **1**	30589	3857	21312	3200	1839	228	73	24	15	15	10	14	3
Revenues ($ in Thousands)													
Net Sales **2**	90523813	1971678	8017520	5606858	7498722	2654268	2134244	1364358	2062883	4888707	6430748	26666575	21227251
Interest **3**	160249	2245	4243	2785	6227	4324	1791	1786	4045	13373	16143	27154	76132
Rents **4**	66392	1720	311	409	2032	864	428	3460	1840	3	10091	9390	35845
Royalties **5**	482928	95	0	0	193	0	0	0	0	20459	22009	97718	342455
Other Portfolio Income **6**	768011	3128	7005	180	991	4024	943	979	3196	1636	23158	18529	704241
Other Receipts **7**	152951	149889	84907	12467	51766	92657	16081	15445	18684	271873	74413	393316	371456
Total Receipts **8**	93554344	2128755	8113986	5622699	7559931	2756137	2153487	1386028	2090648	5196051	6576562	27212682	22757380
Average Total Receipts **9**	3058	552	381	1757	4111	12088	29500	57751	139377	346403	657656	1943763	7585793
Operating Costs/Operating Income (%)													
Cost of Operations **10**	62.8	62.4	58.2	62.3	62.9	66.9	65.8	63.6	61.0	62.1	64.2	60.1	67.2
Salaries and Wages **11**	12.3	11.2	9.4	13.5	11.8	12.6	10.6	11.4	13.7	12.9	11.5	12.6	13.0
Taxes Paid **12**	2.2	2.6	2.5	2.2	2.2	1.4	1.5	1.7	2.1	2.2	1.9	2.2	2.4
Interest Paid **13**	1.2	0.2	0.9	0.8	0.8	0.9	0.7	1.4	1.1	1.0	1.6	0.8	2.4
Depreciation **14**	1.7	1.2	1.0	0.9	1.0	0.9	0.7	0.9	1.3	1.1	1.6	1.7	2.8
Amortization and Depletion **15**	0.3	0.3	0.3	0.0	0.1	0.1	0.1	0.5	0.2	0.2	0.6	0.4	0.1
Pensions and Other Deferred Comp. **16**	0.2	0.2	0.0	0.2	0.1	0.1	0.1	0.1	0.1	0.1	0.1	0.2	0.3
Employee Benefits **17**	0.6	0.8	0.8	0.4	0.5	0.5	0.5	0.7	0.7	0.6	0.4	0.8	0.3
Advertising **18**	2.3	1.8	1.8	2.3	2.1	2.6	4.2	2.6	4.0	3.8	2.7	2.5	1.6
Other Expenses **19**	16.1	17.8	20.5	13.1	14.2	13.8	12.4	15.7	14.8	21.1	16.7	15.8	15.7
Officers' Compensation **20**	1.6	2.6	5.9	3.8	3.3	1.6	2.2	0.8	1.1	1.0	0.4	0.6	0.4
Operating Margin **21**	•	0.1	•	0.4	0.8	•	1.0	0.7	•	•	•	2.3	•
Operating Margin Before Officers' Comp. **22**	0.3	2.7	4.7	4.2	4.1	0.4	3.2	1.5	0.9	•	•	2.9	•

Selected Average Balance Sheet ($ in Thousands)

Net Receivables 23	108	0	4	59	116	655	1989	3596	8572	18613	93582	40275	172339
Inventories 24	640	0	82	367	977	3842	6868	12952	26253	54677	212933	559564	1327299
Net Property, Plant and Equipment 25	457	0	25	127	230	624	1640	3919	12580	31302	69915	264851	2401355
Total Assets 26	1761	0	143	699	1921	6327	14624	33865	72772	163096	346867	1069186	6585981
Notes and Loans Payable 27	585	0	87	220	758	1697	3875	10426	23636	36567	124513	184664	2762404
All Other Liabilities 28	629	0	46	212	462	2112	6045	9128	25906	79679	131333	448865	2130372
Net Worth 29	547	0	9	267	701	2518	4704	14311	23230	46850	91020	435657	1693205

Selected Financial Ratios (Times to 1)

Current Ratio 30	1.6	•	1.9	2.1	2.4	1.6	1.5	1.7	1.4	1.8	1.8	1.6	1.3
Quick Ratio 31	0.4	•	0.5	0.6	0.7	0.6	0.5	0.5	0.3	0.6	0.6	0.3	0.3
Net Sales to Working Capital 32	7.4	•	7.0	6.9	4.6	6.5	8.0	5.8	9.9	6.9	4.7	7.7	10.6
Coverage Ratio 33	2.7	49.4	1.0	1.9	2.9	4.1	3.7	2.6	2.0	1.1	1.3	6.4	1.5
Total Asset Turnover 34	1.7	•	2.6	2.5	2.1	1.8	2.0	1.7	1.9	2.0	1.9	1.8	1.1
Inventory Turnover 35	2.9	•	2.7	3.0	2.6	2.0	2.8	2.8	3.2	3.7	1.9	2.0	3.6
Receivables Turnover 36	31.1	•	95.0	37.3	24.8	17.2	14.7	14.8	19.5	19.8	10.4	35.6	82.1
Total Liabilities to Net Worth 37	2.2	14.8	1.6	1.7	1.7	1.5	2.1	1.4	2.1	2.5	2.8	1.5	2.9
Current Assets to Working Capital 38	2.6	•	2.1	1.9	1.7	2.6	3.0	2.3	3.5	2.3	2.3	2.7	3.9
Current Liabilities to Working Capital 39	1.6	•	1.1	0.9	0.7	1.6	2.0	1.3	2.5	1.3	1.3	1.7	2.9
Working Capital to Net Sales 40	0.1	•	0.1	0.1	0.2	0.2	0.1	0.2	0.1	0.1	0.2	0.1	0.1
Inventory to Working Capital 41	1.7	•	1.5	1.4	1.2	1.6	1.9	1.3	2.2	1.3	1.4	2.0	2.0
Total Receipts to Cash Flow 42	8.7	5.3	8.6	10.3	10.2	10.6	9.8	8.0	10.5	7.6	9.9	8.3	8.8
Cost of Goods to Cash Flow 43	5.5	3.3	5.0	6.4	6.4	7.1	6.4	5.1	6.4	4.7	6.4	5.0	5.9
Cash Flow to Total Debt 44	0.3	•	0.3	0.4	0.3	0.3	0.3	0.4	0.3	0.4	0.3	0.4	0.2

Selected Financial Factors (in Percentages)

Debt Ratio 45	68.9	93.7	61.8	63.5	60.2	67.8	57.7	68.1	71.3	73.8	59.3	74.3
Return on Total Assets 46	5.6	2.2	3.6	5.1	6.4	5.3	6.1	4.0	2.2	4.0	8.9	3.9
Return on Equity Before Income Taxes 47	11.4	•	4.5	9.1	12.2	12.0	8.9	6.2	0.6	3.9	18.5	5.2
Return on Equity After Income Taxes 48	7.7	•	4.0	7.7	11.1	10.2	7.3	2.4	•	0.0	13.0	3.5
Profit Margin (Before Income Tax) 49	2.1	8.0	0.7	1.6	2.6	1.9	2.2	1.1	0.1	0.6	4.2	1.2
Profit Margin (After Income Tax) 50	1.4	5.3	0.6	1.3	2.4	1.6	1.8	0.4	•	0.0	3.0	0.8

229

Table II
Corporations with Net Income

SPORTING GOODS, HOBBY, BOOK, AND MUSIC STORES

MONEY AMOUNTS AND SIZE OF ASSETS IN THOUSANDS OF DOLLARS

Item Description for Accounting Period 7/05 Through 6/06	Total	Zero Assets	Under 500	500 to 1,000	1,000 to 5,000	5,000 to 10,000	10,000 to 25,000	25,000 to 50,000	50,000 to 100,000	100,000 to 250,000	250,000 to 500,000	500,000 to 2,500,000	2,500,000 and over
Number of Enterprises **1**	17406	1985	12055	1978	1111	152	62	20	9	•	7	•	0
Revenues ($ in Thousands)													
Net Sales **2**	67096701	1826407	5336945	3457011	5140116	1804903	1938531	1112525	1505494	•	4077966	•	0
Interest **3**	101925	2174	2402	1094	5320	3852	1418	1786	1657	•	2149	•	0
Rents **4**	37528	1360	1	0	2032	517	0	3460	1554	•	1165	•	0
Royalties **5**	250174	95	0	0	0	0	0	0	0	•	10263	•	0
Other Portfolio Income **6**	686246	3128	1418	1418	733	3070	913	912	49	•	21267	•	0
Other Receipts **7**	1139249	149888	79880	5633	22943	70404	14747	9488	6768	•	32690	•	0
Total Receipts **8**	69311823	1983052	5420646	3463738	5171144	1882746	1955609	1128171	1515522	•	4145500	•	0
Average Total Receipts **9**	3982	999	450	1751	4654	12386	31542	56409	168391	•	592214	•	•
Operating Costs/Operating Income (%)													
Cost of Operations **10**	61.8	62.1	58.1	59.1	64.3	61.2	65.1	63.2	62.1	•	63.6	•	•
Salaries and Wages **11**	12.1	12.1	8.5	13.6	10.2	14.4	10.7	10.5	13.2	•	12.0	•	•
Taxes Paid **12**	2.2	2.5	2.2	2.3	2.1	1.0	1.5	1.6	2.0	•	1.9	•	•
Interest Paid **13**	0.8	0.1	0.6	0.6	0.6	0.4	0.7	1.5	0.7	•	0.9	•	•
Depreciation **14**	1.7	1.2	0.9	0.7	0.8	0.8	0.7	0.9	0.8	•	1.6	•	•
Amortization and Depletion **15**	0.3	0.4	0.3	0.0	0.2	0.0	0.1	0.6	0.3	•	0.5	•	•
Pensions and Other Deferred Comp. **16**	0.2	0.2	0.0	0.4	0.5	0.2	0.2	0.1	0.2	•	0.2	•	•
Employee Benefits **17**	0.6	0.9	0.9	0.3	0.4	0.5	0.5	0.5	0.7	•	0.4	•	•
Advertising **18**	2.2	0.6	1.1	2.2	2.1	3.1	4.2	2.7	3.8	•	2.9	•	•
Other Expenses **19**	14.9	17.3	18.0	12.8	11.0	12.8	11.2	15.3	12.2	•	13.2	•	•
Officers' Compensation **20**	1.5	2.1	5.7	4.5	3.8	1.9	1.9	0.9	0.9	•	0.4	•	•
Operating Margin **21**	1.5	0.6	3.6	3.6	3.9	3.6	3.1	2.3	3.1	•	2.4	•	•
Operating Margin Before Officers' Comp. **22**	3.1	2.8	9.3	8.1	7.8	5.5	5.0	3.2	4.0	•	2.7	•	•

Selected Average Balance Sheet ($ in Thousands)

Net Receivables 23	147	0	6	65	124	661	1319	3797	12465	•	113200
Inventories 24	856	0	81	416	1116	3875	6496	13342	28696	•	189145
Net Property, Plant and Equipment 25	542	0	22	102	225	470	1893	4056	9840	•	72154
Total Assets 26	2289	0	153	695	2073	6009	14068	32660	76205	•	327132
Notes and Loans Payable 27	483	0	79	181	443	654	3274	9207	18389	•	81352
All Other Liabilities 28	811	0	40	196	422	1161	4854	9171	26446	•	132846
Net Worth 29	994	0	34	317	1208	4194	5940	14282	31370	•	112934

Selected Financial Ratios (Times to 1)

Current Ratio 30	1.8	•	2.4	2.3	3.1	2.4	1.6	1.8	1.5	•	2.2
Quick Ratio 31	0.5	•	0.7	0.7	1.0	1.0	0.5	0.6	0.4	•	0.9
Net Sales to Working Capital 32	6.3	•	6.1	5.7	4.3	5.3	7.8	5.9	9.8	•	3.3
Coverage Ratio 33	7.0	65.0	9.1	7.6	8.4	21.3	6.4	3.5	6.1	•	5.3
Total Asset Turnover 34	1.7	•	2.9	2.5	2.2	2.0	2.2	1.7	2.2	•	1.8
Inventory Turnover 35	2.8	•	3.2	2.5	2.7	1.9	3.1	2.6	3.6	•	2.0
Receivables Turnover 36	31.9	•	82.7	36.5	22.3	17.2	20.2	13.1	19.9	•	7.7
Total Liabilities to Net Worth 37	1.3	•	3.5	1.2	0.7	0.4	1.4	1.3	1.4	•	1.9
Current Assets to Working Capital 38	2.3	•	1.7	1.8	1.5	1.7	2.6	2.3	3.2	•	1.8
Current Liabilities to Working Capital 39	1.3	•	0.7	0.8	0.5	0.7	1.6	1.3	2.2	•	0.8
Working Capital to Net Sales 40	0.2	•	0.2	0.2	0.2	0.2	0.1	0.2	0.1	•	0.3
Inventory to Working Capital 41	1.4	•	1.2	1.2	1.0	0.9	1.7	1.3	2.0	•	1.0
Total Receipts to Cash Flow 42	7.7	5.1	6.5	8.1	8.9	6.9	9.1	7.3	9.3	•	9.3
Cost of Goods to Cash Flow 43	4.8	3.1	3.8	4.8	5.7	4.2	5.9	4.6	5.8	•	5.9
Cash Flow to Total Debt 44	0.4	•	0.6	0.6	0.6	1.0	0.4	0.4	0.4	•	0.3

Selected Financial Factors (in Percentages)

Debt Ratio 45	56.6	•	78.0	54.3	41.7	30.2	57.8	56.3	58.8	•	65.5
Return on Total Assets 46	9.4	•	17.0	11.1	11.5	16.3	10.5	8.8	9.9	•	8.8
Return on Equity Before Income Taxes 47	18.6	•	68.6	21.0	17.4	22.3	21.0	14.3	20.1	•	20.8
Return on Equity After Income Taxes 48	15.1	•	67.4	20.3	16.0	21.3	19.3	12.4	15.3	•	16.3
Profit Margin (Before Income Tax) 49	4.8	9.2	5.2	3.8	4.5	7.9	4.0	3.7	3.8	•	4.0
Profit Margin (After Income Tax) 50	3.9	6.2	5.1	3.7	4.2	7.5	3.7	3.2	2.9	•	3.2

Table I
Corporations with and without Net Income

GENERAL MERCHANDISE STORES

MONEY AMOUNTS AND SIZE OF ASSETS IN THOUSANDS OF DOLLARS

Item Description for Accounting Period 7/05 Through 6/06	Total	Zero Assets	Under 500	500 to 1,000	1,000 to 5,000	5,000 to 10,000	10,000 to 25,000	25,000 to 50,000	50,000 to 100,000	100,000 to 250,000	250,000 to 500,000	500,000 to 2,500,000	2,500,000 and over
Number of Enterprises **1**	10733	1364	8136	681	443	23	23	17	9	8	6	9	15
Revenues ($ in Thousands)													
Net Sales **2**	586630302	34936723	2801436	864461	2821022	537323	804460	1332587	861888	2359677	4457760	21762694	512776272
Interest **3**	3544787	319180	2500	1207	1653	330	643	1349	19130	3173	22503	71995	3101124
Rents **4**	945536	698	315	0	7716	0	0	792	10688	2368	6692	16985	899282
Royalties **5**	2498022	193596	0	0	360	0	0	23149	0	0	0	57404	2223512
Other Portfolio Income **6**	2073511	139398	0	2457	3288	83	83	1487	36	169	84	19626	1906800
Other Receipts **7**	17520568	338527	34894	24825	44312	2796	6356	57084	15320	31538	34477	408261	16522179
Total Receipts **8**	61289 0726	35928122	2839145	892950	2878351	540532	811542	1416448	907062	2396925	4521516	22336965	537421169
Average Total Receipts **9**	57103	26340	349	1311	6497	23501	35284	83320	100785	299616	753586	2481885	35828078
Operating Costs/Operating Income (%)													
Cost of Operations **10**	72.2	63.2	60.3	75.2	61.6	70.1	68.4	67.8	64.7	63.3	68.1	74.2	72.9
Salaries and Wages **11**	11.3	12.9	10.1	7.7	13.8	8.6	8.7	13.1	14.8	13.9	12.7	10.3	11.2
Taxes Paid **12**	1.9	2.2	3.0	1.7	3.0	1.1	1.7	2.2	2.3	1.9	1.5	1.8	1.8
Interest Paid **13**	1.1	1.9	0.8	0.6	0.8	0.3	0.7	0.6	0.5	0.8	0.9	0.9	1.1
Depreciation **14**	1.5	2.8	0.9	0.3	0.6	1.2	0.7	1.0	1.0	1.3	1.9	1.2	1.4
Amortization and Depletion **15**	0.0	0.1	0.1	0.3	0.0	0.0	0.0	0.3	0.0	0.0	0.0	0.0	0.0
Pensions and Other Deferred Comp. **16**	0.4	1.2	0.0	0.8	0.9	0.2	0.3	0.2	0.1	0.1	0.2	0.2	0.4
Employee Benefits **17**	0.9	0.9	0.1	0.3	0.8	0.9	0.7	1.0	1.1	0.9	1.6	1.4	0.9
Advertising **18**	1.5	1.4	0.4	0.1	1.2	2.1	1.4	2.3	1.9	2.1	1.9	1.8	1.5
Other Expenses **19**	8.7	12.1	22.2	10.0	13.6	19.4	11.0	15.7	17.7	16.8	8.4	8.7	8.2
Officers' Compensation **20**	0.2	0.0	5.0	8.6	3.3	0.8	2.1	0.7	0.6	1.6	0.5	0.3	0.1
Operating Margin **21**	0.4	1.3	•	•	0.4	•	4.5	•	•	•	2.3	•	0.4
Operating Margin Before Officers' Comp. **22**	0.5	1.3	2.1	3.1	3.7	•	6.6	•	•	•	2.8	•	0.5

Selected Average Balance Sheet ($ in Thousands)

Net Receivables 23	1919	0	4	30	68	398	1784	4669	7737	13296	20320	60373	1302827
Inventories 24	6402	0	71	143	1209	2941	8136	11848	21384	61084	158080	406073	4117513
Net Property, Plant and Equipment 25	8722	0	30	28	252	1582	3418	5000	12389	38236	101017	375845	5909013
Total Assets 26	28479	0	138	665	2101	6986	15027	34206	65518	147649	382720	1177680	19160494
Notes and Loans Payable 27	6983	0	72	187	532	508	3065	6114	10925	22285	87385	253393	4716054
All Other Liabilities 28	9855	0	26	58	557	4751	26103	8059	119419	48866	117848	373710	6593420
Net Worth 29	11640	0	41	420	1011	1727	-14141	20034	-64826	76498	177486	550577	7851020

Selected Financial Ratios (Times to 1)

Current Ratio 30	1.1	•	3.0	3.4	2.3	1.1	2.8	2.8	0.4	2.1	1.8	1.4	1.1
Quick Ratio 31	0.3	•	0.6	1.6	0.4	0.4	1.0	0.8	0.2	0.5	0.2	0.2	0.3
Net Sales to Working Capital 32	40.5	•	5.3	4.1	6.8	55.6	5.0	5.5	•	6.1	9.0	14.8	45.7
Coverage Ratio 33	5.5	3.1	•	•	3.9	•	9.2	3.1	1.8	•	5.3	3.0	5.9
Total Asset Turnover 34	1.9	•	2.5	1.9	3.0	3.3	2.3	2.3	1.5	2.0	1.9	2.1	1.8
Inventory Turnover 35	6.2	•	2.9	6.7	3.2	5.6	2.9	4.5	2.9	3.1	3.2	4.4	6.1
Receivables Turnover 36	30.4	•	88.0	76.1	72.3	86.5	20.3	17.7	14.6	16.8	25.0	40.8	28.2
Total Liabilities to Net Worth 37	1.4	•	2.4	0.6	1.1	3.0	•	0.7	•	0.9	1.2	1.1	1.4
Current Assets to Working Capital 38	8.1	•	1.5	1.4	1.8	11.2	1.6	1.5	•	1.9	2.3	3.6	9.5
Current Liabilities to Working Capital 39	7.1	•	0.5	0.4	0.8	10.2	0.6	0.5	•	0.9	1.3	2.6	8.5
Working Capital to Net Sales 40	0.0	•	0.2	0.2	0.1	0.0	0.2	0.2	•	0.2	0.1	0.1	0.0
Inventory to Working Capital 41	5.0	•	1.0	0.6	1.5	6.6	0.9	0.8	•	1.4	1.8	2.8	5.7
Total Receipts to Cash Flow 42	9.5	9.0	12.1	28.6	10.8	19.5	8.2	11.1	9.5	10.4	12.1	16.5	9.4
Cost of Goods to Cash Flow 43	6.9	5.7	7.3	21.5	6.7	13.7	5.6	7.5	6.1	6.6	8.3	12.3	6.8
Cash Flow to Total Debt 44	0.3	•	0.3	0.2	0.5	0.2	0.1	0.5	0.1	0.4	0.3	0.2	0.3

Selected Financial Factors (in Percentages)

Debt Ratio 45	59.1	•	70.2	36.9	51.9	75.3	194.1	41.4	198.9	48.2	53.6	53.2	59.0
Return on Total Assets 46	11.7	•	•	•	9.8	•	14.0	4.6	1.3	•	8.9	5.6	11.4
Return on Equity Before Income Taxes 47	23.4	•	•	•	15.1	•	•	5.2	•	•	15.6	8.1	23.1
Return on Equity After Income Taxes 48	15.9	•	•	•	14.0	•	•	3.1	0.8	•	11.8	4.6	15.4
Profit Margin (Before Income Tax) 49	5.0	4.1	•	•	2.4	•	5.4	1.3	0.4	•	3.7	1.8	5.3
Profit Margin (After Income Tax) 50	3.4	4.0	•	•	2.2	•	5.1	0.8	•	•	2.8	1.1	3.5

Table II
Corporations with Net Income

GENERAL MERCHANDISE STORES

MONEY AMOUNTS AND SIZE OF ASSETS IN THOUSANDS OF DOLLARS

Item Description for Accounting Period 7/05 Through 6/06	Total	Zero Assets	Under 500	500 to 1,000	1,000 to 5,000	5,000 to 10,000	10,000 to 25,000	25,000 to 50,000	50,000 to 100,000	100,000 to 250,000	250,000 to 500,000	500,000 to 2,500,000	2,500,000 and over
Number of Enterprises 1	6379	527	4810	585	369	•	16	12	•	5	6	•	•
Revenues ($ in Thousands)													
Net Sales 2	566111300	27896404	2003821	862167	2373750	•	657681	1038083	•	1593098	4457760	•	•
Interest 3	3034543	110875	2089	1207	1159	•	442	424	•	55	22503	•	•
Rents 4	942839	482	0	0	7490	•	0	792	•	2231	6692	•	•
Royalties 5	2304423	0	0	0	360	•	0	23149	•	0	0	•	•
Other Portfolio Income 6	2061109	130380	0	2457	1917	•	25	559	•	0	84	•	•
Other Receipts 7	17130489	92912	25128	23297	17614	•	4371	30483	•	4830	34477	•	•
Total Receipts 8	591584703	28231053	2031038	889128	2402290	•	662519	1093490	•	1600214	4521516	•	•
Average Total Receipts 9	92739	53569	422	1520	6510	•	41407	91124	•	320043	753586	•	•
Operating Costs/Operating Income (%)													
Cost of Operations 10	72.6	64.2	53.7	75.3	61.0	•	67.4	68.3	•	63.4	68.1	•	•
Salaries and Wages 11	11.0	10.4	10.6	7.2	13.5	•	8.7	12.3	•	13.0	12.7	•	•
Taxes Paid 12	1.8	1.9	2.7	1.4	3.1	•	1.4	2.4	•	1.9	1.5	•	•
Interest Paid 13	1.0	1.5	0.8	0.6	0.9	•	0.6	0.8	•	0.5	0.9	•	•
Depreciation 14	1.4	3.0	0.8	0.3	0.6	•	0.5	0.8	•	1.1	1.9	•	•
Amortization and Depletion 15	0.0	0.1	0.0	0.3	0.0	•	0.1	0.4	•	0.0	0.0	•	•
Pensions and Other Deferred Comp. 16	0.4	1.5	•	0.8	0.4	•	0.1	0.1	•	0.1	0.1	•	•
Employee Benefits 17	0.9	0.8	0.1	0.3	0.5	•	0.4	0.7	•	0.4	1.6	•	•
Advertising 18	1.5	0.9	0.3	0.1	1.3	•	1.4	1.8	•	2.2	1.9	•	•
Other Expenses 19	8.4	9.7	22.1	9.2	13.3	•	10.5	11.5	•	13.3	8.4	•	•
Officers' Compensation 20	0.1	0.0	5.6	3.1	3.1	•	2.4	0.7	•	2.2	0.5	•	•
Operating Margin 21	0.8	5.9	3.4	1.2	2.3	•	6.5	0.3	•	1.8	2.3	•	•
Operating Margin Before Officers' Comp. 22	0.9	5.9	9.0	4.4	5.4	•	8.9	1.1	•	4.0	2.8	•	•

Selected Average Balance Sheet ($ in Thousands)

Net Receivables 23	2658	0	35	70	2037	4861	•	11849	20320
Inventories 24	10208	0	129	1171	10620	11162	•	57540	158080
Net Property, Plant and Equipment 25	14452	0	32	268	1923	5166	•	34494	101017
Total Assets 26	46665	0	683	2020	16433	33728	•	132902	382720
Notes and Loans Payable 27	11407	0	217	538	3192	5313	•	20881	87385
All Other Liabilities 28	16208	0	67	529	36565	6168	•	40923	117848
Net Worth 29	19049	0	399	953	-23324	22247	•	71098	177486

Selected Financial Ratios (Times to 1)

Current Ratio 30	1.1	•	2.3	2.8	2.4	3.0	3.1	•	2.3	1.8
Quick Ratio 31	0.3	•	0.5	1.0	0.3	1.0	1.1	•	0.6	0.2
Net Sales to Working Capital 32	49.7	•	7.3	5.4	6.5	4.6	6.6	•	7.0	9.0
Coverage Ratio 33	6.1	5.7	7.2	8.5	4.7	12.6	8.2	•	5.3	5.3
Total Asset Turnover 34	1.9	•	2.9	2.2	3.2	2.5	2.6	•	2.4	1.9
Inventory Turnover 35	6.3	•	3.0	8.6	3.4	2.6	5.3	•	3.5	3.2
Receivables Turnover 36	33.2	•	157.5	84.7	69.2	22.0	17.0	•	53.8	25.0
Total Liabilities to Net Worth 37	1.4	•	2.5	0.7	1.1	0.5	0.5	•	0.9	1.2
Current Assets to Working Capital 38	9.7	•	1.8	1.5	1.7	1.5	1.5	•	1.8	2.3
Current Liabilities to Working Capital 39	8.7	•	0.8	0.5	0.7	0.5	0.5	•	0.8	1.3
Working Capital to Net Sales 40	0.0	•	0.1	0.2	0.2	0.2	0.2	•	0.1	0.1
Inventory to Working Capital 41	6.2	•	1.2	0.8	1.4	1.0	0.8	•	1.3	1.8
Total Receipts to Cash Flow 42	9.5	9.0	6.8	10.6	9.4	6.9	8.2	•	8.8	12.1
Cost of Goods to Cash Flow 43	6.9	5.8	3.7	8.0	5.8	4.6	5.6	•	5.6	8.3
Cash Flow to Total Debt 44	0.3	•	0.6	0.5	0.6	0.2	0.9	•	0.6	0.3

Selected Financial Factors (in Percentages)

Debt Ratio 45	59.2	•	71.4	41.6	52.8	241.9	34.0	•	46.5	53.6
Return on Total Assets 46	12.2	•	16.1	10.6	14.1	19.6	16.6	•	6.7	8.9
Return on Equity Before Income Taxes 47	24.9	•	48.6	16.1	23.6	•	22.1	•	10.2	15.6
Return on Equity After Income Taxes 48	17.2	•	48.2	13.2	22.1	•	19.4	•	9.4	11.8
Profit Margin (Before Income Tax) 49	5.4	7.1	4.7	4.3	3.5	7.2	5.7	•	2.3	3.7
Profit Margin (After Income Tax) 50	3.7	7.0	4.7	3.6	3.3	6.9	5.0	•	2.1	2.8

Table I

Corporations with and without Net Income

MISCELLANEOUS STORE RETAILERS

MONEY AMOUNTS AND SIZE OF ASSETS IN THOUSANDS OF DOLLARS

Item Description for Accounting Period 7/05 Through 6/06	Total	Zero Assets	Under 500	500 to 1,000	1,000 to 5,000	5,000 to 10,000	10,000 to 25,000	25,000 to 50,000	50,000 to 100,000	100,000 to 250,000	250,000 to 500,000	500,000 to 2,500,000	2,500,000 and over
Number of Enterprises 1	91513	12885	68074	5276	4649	357	148	62	24	22	0	12	4

Revenues ($ in Thousands)

	Total	Zero Assets	Under 500	500 to 1,000	1,000 to 5,000	5,000 to 10,000	10,000 to 25,000	25,000 to 50,000	50,000 to 100,000	100,000 to 250,000	250,000 to 500,000	500,000 to 2,500,000	2,500,000 and over
Net Sales 2	134935400	1474295	32523744	9815874	18066434	5087578	4116524	3129535	3316062	6099686	0	16095788	35209881
Interest 3	537492	275	10795	6205	33972	12257	2433	5559	2779	24431	0	69303	369483
Rents 4	169923	54	3416	3565	10043	179	5354	1761	7110	2930	0	112498	23014
Royalties 5	132337	51	1697	0	744	0	14138	34241	528	11825	0	9781	59332
Other Portfolio Income 6	800279	4768	56131	2818	21011	39681	16023	49634	32926	13508	0	91336	472440
Other Receipts 7	1469462	21150	317982	57933	260077	54905	26773	80672	51033	62858	0	488757	47323
Total Receipts 8	138044893	1500593	32913765	9886395	18392281	5194600	4181245	3301402	3410438	6215238	0	16867463	36181473
Average Total Receipts 9	1508	116	483	1874	3956	14551	28252	53248	142102	282511	•	1405622	9045368

Operating Costs/Operating Income (%)

	Total	Zero Assets	Under 500	500 to 1,000	1,000 to 5,000	5,000 to 10,000	10,000 to 25,000	25,000 to 50,000	50,000 to 100,000	100,000 to 250,000	250,000 to 500,000	500,000 to 2,500,000	2,500,000 and over
Cost of Operations 10	64.4	59.7	60.0	65.2	68.3	63.5	67.8	62.3	64.4	61.4	•	57.3	70.2
Salaries and Wages 11	10.9	13.2	9.9	10.3	9.3	13.2	11.2	11.1	13.0	11.7	•	14.3	10.6
Taxes Paid 12	2.0	2.9	2.3	2.1	1.9	1.9	1.9	2.0	1.6	1.8	•	2.2	1.6
Interest Paid 13	1.1	3.1	0.7	0.7	1.2	1.0	1.0	1.4	1.9	1.3	•	1.1	1.3
Depreciation 14	1.2	1.1	0.8	0.9	0.9	0.9	1.5	1.7	1.2	1.7	•	2.1	1.1
Amortization and Depletion 15	0.2	0.3	0.1	0.1	0.0	0.1	0.1	0.3	0.2	0.1	•	0.4	0.4
Pensions and Other Deferred Comp. 16	0.2	0.0	0.1	0.1	0.3	0.6	0.3	0.3	0.1	0.1	•	0.2	0.2
Employee Benefits 17	0.9	0.3	0.6	0.6	0.7	0.8	0.7	0.8	0.9	1.3	•	2.2	0.8
Advertising 18	1.8	2.0	1.6	1.4	1.1	1.2	1.3	3.0	1.5	2.8	•	1.6	2.3
Other Expenses 19	13.9	29.0	19.0	13.7	12.1	13.5	10.6	15.5	15.0	13.2	•	15.6	9.1
Officers' Compensation 20	2.4	2.6	5.0	4.1	3.8	2.9	2.0	1.5	1.2	1.2	•	0.7	0.2
Operating Margin 21	1.0	•	•	0.8	0.4	0.5	1.7	0.2	•	3.4	•	2.2	2.2
Operating Margin Before Officers' Comp. 22	3.4	•	4.9	4.8	4.2	3.4	3.6	1.7	0.2	4.6	•	2.9	2.4

Selected Average Balance Sheet ($ in Thousands)

Net Receivables 23	97	0	12	86	334	1414	1638	6040	11080	12574	110529	751395
Inventories 24	199	0	40	269	781	2171	6011	11753	27676	54878	208367	873039
Net Property, Plant and Equipment 25	127	0	21	125	384	832	3056	5709	13675	30380	231032	733878
Total Assets 26	725	0	107	680	1980	6641	14831	35864	71616	180622	1006873	5435430
Notes and Loans Payable 27	253	0	70	300	835	1990	5411	10083	28818	65308	205088	1544422
All Other Liabilities 28	251	0	28	152	478	2916	3903	12947	20223	57908	357355	2410254
Net Worth 29	221	0	9	228	667	1735	5517	12834	22574	57406	444431	1480753

Selected Financial Ratios (Times to 1)

Current Ratio 30	1.5	•	2.2	2.5	2.1	1.3	1.6	1.4	1.5	1.9	1.5	1.1
Quick Ratio 31	0.6	•	1.0	0.8	0.8	0.5	0.5	0.6	0.4	0.6	0.6	0.5
Net Sales to Working Capital 32	10.2	•	11.7	6.4	5.4	11.4	7.4	7.3	8.4	5.2	8.6	56.3
Coverage Ratio 33	4.0	•	2.5	3.2	2.8	3.7	4.2	5.3	2.0	5.0	7.1	4.8
Total Asset Turnover 34	2.0	•	4.5	2.7	2.0	2.1	1.9	1.4	1.9	1.5	1.3	1.6
Inventory Turnover 35	4.8	•	7.1	4.5	3.4	4.2	3.1	2.7	3.2	3.1	3.7	7.1
Receivables Turnover 36	12.8	•	39.6	19.6	11.6	11.6	11.9	8.7	11.5	21.7	12.3	7.7
Total Liabilities to Net Worth 37	2.3	•	10.3	2.0	2.0	2.8	1.7	1.8	2.2	2.1	1.3	2.7
Current Assets to Working Capital 38	2.9	•	1.8	1.7	1.9	4.3	2.6	3.4	3.1	2.1	2.9	15.1
Current Liabilities to Working Capital 39	1.9	•	0.8	0.7	0.9	3.3	1.6	2.4	2.1	1.1	1.9	14.1
Working Capital to Net Sales 40	0.1	•	0.1	0.2	0.2	0.1	0.1	0.1	0.1	0.2	0.1	0.0
Inventory to Working Capital 41	1.4	•	1.0	1.0	1.1	2.1	1.6	1.7	1.8	1.2	1.2	5.6
Total Receipts to Cash Flow 42	8.6	25.5	8.1	10.3	9.0	8.3	10.9	5.9	8.8	8.8	6.3	9.9
Cost of Goods to Cash Flow 43	5.5	15.2	4.9	6.7	6.1	5.3	7.4	3.6	5.6	5.4	3.6	7.0
Cash Flow to Total Debt 44	0.3	•	0.6	0.4	0.3	0.4	0.3	0.4	0.3	0.3	0.4	0.2

Selected Financial Factors (in Percentages)

Debt Ratio 45	69.5	•	91.2	66.5	66.3	73.9	62.8	64.2	68.5	68.2	55.9	72.8
Return on Total Assets 46	9.0	•	8.1	5.9	6.6	7.6	8.0	10.2	7.3	10.2	10.8	10.5
Return on Equity Before Income Taxes 47	22.1	•	55.7	12.0	12.5	21.3	16.3	23.0	11.3	25.6	21.0	30.6
Return on Equity After Income Taxes 48	16.5	•	51.6	11.6	11.3	16.2	14.4	20.3	10.5	21.7	14.4	20.7
Profit Margin (Before Income Tax) 49	3.3	•	1.1	1.5	2.2	2.6	3.2	5.8	1.8	5.3	6.9	5.1
Profit Margin (After Income Tax) 50	2.5	•	1.0	1.4	1.9	2.0	2.8	5.2	1.7	4.5	4.8	3.5

Table II
Corporations with Net Income

MISCELLANEOUS STORE RETAILERS

MONEY AMOUNTS AND SIZE OF ASSETS IN THOUSANDS OF DOLLARS

Item Description for Accounting Period 7/05 Through 6/06	Total	Zero Assets	Under 500	500 to 1,000	1,000 to 5,000	5,000 to 10,000	10,000 to 25,000	25,000 to 50,000	50,000 to 100,000	100,000 to 250,000	250,000 to 500,000	500,000 to 2,500,000	2,500,000 and over
Number of Enterprises **1**	47782	2895	37493	3435	3457	312	98	49	14	15	0	•	•
Revenues ($ in Thousands)													
Net Sales **2**	103753364	565129	21119761	6971687	15746366	4363424	3104389	2424806	1996743	5024462			
Interest **3**	311643	130	5281	5575	29859	6566	2274	5083	2154	13300	0		
Rents **4**	160362	54	2536	3565	9058	52	3951	1423	2147	2930	0		
Royalties **5**	118758	51	1697	0	744	0	13877	34241	0	0	0		
Other Portfolio Income **6**	772032	2150	47233	2175	14754	38487	13330	49296	31763	13338	0		
Other Receipts **7**	1284970	17349	255872	41015	239241	50400	34467	48745	34958	55459	0		
Total Receipts **8**	106401129	584863	21432380	7024017	16040022	4458929	3172288	2563594	2067765	5109489	0		
Average Total Receipts **9**	2227	202	572	2045	4640	14291	32370	52318	147698	340633	•		
Operating Costs/Operating Income (%)													
Cost of Operations **10**	63.5	52.0	58.6	66.4	68.7	63.2	69.3	61.2	68.6	60.3	•		
Salaries and Wages **11**	10.9	12.5	8.5	9.7	8.8	12.5	10.8	9.1	11.4	12.8	•		
Taxes Paid **12**	1.9	1.7	2.2	1.9	1.8	1.9	1.9	1.8	1.5	1.8	•		
Interest Paid **13**	0.9	1.9	0.5	0.9	0.9	0.9	0.9	1.3	1.8	1.5	•		
Depreciation **14**	1.2	0.7	0.7	0.8	0.8	0.8	1.5	1.8	1.2	1.7	•		
Amortization and Depletion **15**	0.2	0.2	0.1	0.1	0.0	0.1	0.0	0.3	0.2	0.1	•		
Pensions and Other Deferred Comp. **16**	0.2	0.0	0.2	0.1	0.3	0.6	0.3	0.3	0.1	0.1	•		
Employee Benefits **17**	0.9	0.4	0.5	0.6	0.6	0.7	0.5	0.9	0.7	1.2	•		
Advertising **18**	1.8	1.5	1.1	1.0	1.0	1.1	0.8	3.2	1.0	2.9	•		
Other Expenses **19**	12.8	18.3	18.1	11.9	11.4	12.7	8.3	15.4	10.7	11.3	•		
Officers' Compensation **20**	2.2	1.7	4.8	3.8	3.6	2.9	2.2	1.5	1.2	1.0	•		
Operating Margin **21**	3.5	9.1	4.4	3.1	1.9	2.5	3.4	3.3	1.8	5.4	•		
Operating Margin Before Officers' Comp. **22**	5.7	10.8	9.2	7.0	5.5	5.4	5.6	4.8	3.0	6.5	•		

Selected Average Balance Sheet ($ in Thousands)

Net Receivables 23	158	0	14	112	367	1379	1902	6242	12388	7938
Inventories 24	295	0	41	251	834	2147	6245	9683	31216	70782
Net Property, Plant and Equipment 25	189	0	23	109	327	785	3103	5565	12962	31498
Total Assets 26	1020	0	118	669	2025	6629	14628	34983	69780	177631
Notes and Loans Payable 27	283	0	42	191	737	1933	4787	9375	23702	76867
All Other Liabilities 28	369	0	24	166	540	2631	4054	10899	15428	60493
Net Worth 29	368	0	52	311	748	2065	5788	14709	30650	40271

Selected Financial Ratios (Times to 1)

Current Ratio 30	1.6	•	2.9	2.1	2.3	1.4	1.6	1.6	1.4	1.9
Quick Ratio 31	0.7	•	1.5	0.8	1.0	0.6	0.8	0.8	0.4	0.4
Net Sales to Working Capital 32	9.9	•	9.9	5.8	7.5	8.2	8.4	5.4	10.1	5.9
Coverage Ratio 33	7.8	7.7	13.0	9.0	5.1	6.1	7.4	7.9	4.0	5.9
Total Asset Turnover 34	2.1	•	4.8	3.0	2.2	2.1	2.2	1.4	2.0	1.9
Inventory Turnover 35	4.7	•	8.1	5.4	3.8	4.1	3.5	3.1	3.1	2.9
Receivables Turnover 36	11.2	•	42.8	18.1	12.7	11.6	11.9	8.3	12.6	28.5
Total Liabilities to Net Worth 37	1.8	•	1.3	1.1	1.7	2.2	1.5	1.4	1.3	3.4
Current Assets to Working Capital 38	2.8	•	1.5	1.8	1.9	3.3	2.6	2.6	3.7	2.1
Current Liabilities to Working Capital 39	1.8	•	0.5	0.8	0.9	2.3	1.6	1.6	2.7	1.1
Working Capital to Net Sales 40	0.1	•	0.1	0.1	0.2	0.1	0.1	0.2	0.1	0.2
Inventory to Working Capital 41	1.3	•	0.7	0.9	1.1	1.6	1.4	1.1	2.1	1.4
Total Receipts to Cash Flow 42	7.2	4.7	6.1	8.7	8.1	7.3	9.5	4.6	9.9	8.2
Cost of Goods to Cash Flow 43	4.6	2.4	3.6	5.8	5.6	4.6	6.6	2.8	6.8	4.9
Cash Flow to Total Debt 44	0.5	•	1.4	0.6	0.4	0.4	0.4	0.5	0.4	0.3

Selected Financial Factors (in Percentages)

Debt Ratio 45	63.9	•	56.2	53.4	63.1	68.9	60.4	58.0	56.1	77.3
Return on Total Assets 46	15.0	•	30.4	13.3	10.7	11.8	14.0	14.9	14.7	16.2
Return on Equity Before Income Taxes 47	36.2	•	64.1	25.4	23.2	31.8	30.5	30.9	25.0	59.2
Return on Equity After Income Taxes 48	29.7	•	62.8	24.9	21.7	26.9	27.7	27.9	24.1	51.1
Profit Margin (Before Income Tax) 49	6.1	12.6	5.9	3.9	3.8	4.7	5.6	9.2	5.4	7.1
Profit Margin (After Income Tax) 50	5.0	11.9	5.8	3.8	3.6	4.0	5.1	8.3	5.2	6.1

Table I

Corporations with and without Net Income

NONSTORE RETAILERS

MONEY AMOUNTS AND SIZE OF ASSETS IN THOUSANDS OF DOLLARS

Item Description for Accounting Period 7/05 Through 6/06	Total	Zero Assets	Under 500	500 to 1,000	1,000 to 5,000	5,000 to 10,000	10,000 to 25,000	25,000 to 50,000	50,000 to 100,000	100,000 to 250,000	250,000 to 500,000	500,000 to 2,500,000	2,500,000 and over
Number of Enterprises 1	50352	9948	34772	2549	2438	285	176	84	27	39	14	17	4
Revenues ($ in Thousands)													
Net Sales 2	132436347	921010	16374808	7736582	15948547	8125830	8537131	8007867	2861202	11818499	10493210	27004796	14606864
Interest 3	600490	1044	5753	7123	19205	11025	8928	11771	11228	67780	119352	199769	137513
Rents 4	122909	468	10841	7458	4316	3750	2260	8708	6266	1936	23635	51504	1767
Royalties 5	665589	550	151	0	12440	1893	10548	1660	297	55682	2324	84756	495288
Other Portfolio Income 6	360575	57769	45516	20951	15456	22465	16906	28390	1907	18911	18330	85854	28121
Other Receipts 7	2707132	13875	139522	63462	57914	27217	160555	78982	25904	185455	79734	536200	1338310
Total Receipts 8	136893042	994716	16576591	7835576	16057878	8192180	8736328	8137378	2906804	12148263	10736585	27962879	16607863
Average Total Receipts 9	2719	100	477	3074	6586	28744	49638	96874	107659	311494	766899	1644875	4151966
Operating Costs/Operating Income (%)													
Cost of Operations 10	70.8	53.4	66.0	72.5	68.5	72.3	68.6	68.1	54.0	71.8	69.7	76.8	72.6
Salaries and Wages 11	7.9	8.3	8.2	6.9	8.0	6.7	8.5	7.5	10.3	7.6	5.1	5.9	13.9
Taxes Paid 12	1.2	2.6	1.7	2.0	1.7	1.0	1.3	1.0	1.4	1.1	0.9	0.9	0.8
Interest Paid 13	0.8	2.2	0.4	0.5	0.7	0.4	0.6	0.7	1.1	0.8	1.1	0.9	1.0
Depreciation 14	1.1	2.1	1.0	1.1	1.6	1.3	1.1	1.0	2.4	0.7	1.0	0.8	1.3
Amortization and Depletion 15	0.3	1.0	0.3	0.2	0.2	0.1	0.1	0.3	0.5	0.4	0.5	0.3	0.3
Pensions and Other Deferred Comp. 16	0.2	0.0	0.2	0.2	0.3	0.2	0.1	0.2	0.4	0.2	0.1	0.3	0.1
Employee Benefits 17	0.8	0.6	0.4	1.0	0.8	0.7	0.9	0.8	1.0	0.7	0.7	0.7	1.0
Advertising 18	2.8	2.7	1.9	0.8	2.0	2.5	3.6	4.4	7.3	3.9	4.9	2.2	2.5
Other Expenses 19	13.6	30.1	14.3	11.6	10.7	12.3	29.8	15.5	18.8	11.9	13.6	8.6	16.1
Officers' Compensation 20	1.7	3.4	4.5	4.2	2.7	1.6	1.2	0.8	1.0	0.7	0.4	1.0	0.4
Operating Margin 21	•	•	1.2	•	2.8	1.0	•	•	1.8	0.2	1.8	1.7	•
Operating Margin Before Officers' Comp. 22	0.5	•	5.7	3.2	5.5	2.5	•	0.5	2.8	0.9	2.3	2.6	•

Selected Average Balance Sheet ($ in Thousands)

Net Receivables 23	231	0	16	204	472	1730	3338	7475	15661	31015	61986	111475	822525
Inventories 24	141	0	14	155	308	1385	2945	6720	12735	24780	59653	74383	151865
Net Property, Plant and Equipment 25	156	0	15	149	518	1697	2865	5217	9883	12818	38757	85985	373335
Total Assets 26	1497	0	76	740	2108	7161	15395	36480	72929	147019	331210	1036273	6984833
Notes and Loans Payable 27	300	0	41	355	640	1916	4825	10480	18092	35205	54201	162431	882899
All Other Liabilities 28	438	0	24	301	718	2154	5807	14085	27191	48591	124046	332929	1460373
Net Worth 29	760	0	11	84	749	3091	4762	11916	27646	63223	152963	540914	4641561

Selected Financial Ratios (Times to 1)

Current Ratio 30	1.8	·	1.4	1.6	1.4	2.0	1.4	1.4	1.7	1.6	1.6	1.8	2.8
Quick Ratio 31	1.1	·	1.0	1.1	0.9	1.3	0.8	0.7	0.9	0.9	0.9	0.9	1.8
Net Sales to Working Capital 32	8.7	·	30.0	15.7	19.5	11.7	17.5	13.8	6.3	8.5	10.3	9.6	2.5
Coverage Ratio 33	3.9	1.7	6.9	1.6	6.2	5.9	·	2.8	4.0	4.7	4.6	6.9	4.3
Total Asset Turnover 34	1.8	·	6.2	4.1	3.1	4.0	3.2	2.6	1.5	2.1	2.3	1.5	0.5
Inventory Turnover 35	13.2	·	22.7	14.2	14.5	14.9	11.3	9.7	4.5	8.8	8.8	16.4	17.5
Receivables Turnover 36	13.5	·	28.9	14.6	13.3	16.4	15.2	13.3	7.3	11.7	12.7	20.0	6.4
Total Liabilities to Net Worth 37	1.0	·	5.9	7.9	1.8	1.3	2.2	2.1	1.6	1.3	1.2	0.9	0.5
Current Assets to Working Capital 38	2.3	·	3.3	2.8	3.8	2.0	3.6	3.3	2.5	2.7	2.6	2.2	1.5
Current Liabilities to Working Capital 39	1.3	·	2.3	1.8	2.8	1.0	2.6	2.3	1.5	1.7	1.6	1.2	0.5
Working Capital to Net Sales 40	0.1	·	0.0	0.1	0.1	0.1	0.1	0.1	0.2	0.1	0.1	0.1	0.4
Inventory to Working Capital 41	0.5	·	0.8	0.7	0.9	0.5	1.1	1.1	0.7	0.8	0.9	0.5	0.1
Total Receipts to Cash Flow 42	7.5	3.8	7.1	10.0	7.9	8.1	·	6.5	4.9	7.4	6.1	7.9	5.4
Cost of Goods to Cash Flow 43	5.3	2.0	4.7	7.2	5.4	5.8	·	4.4	2.7	5.3	4.2	6.0	3.9
Cash Flow to Total Debt 44	0.5	·	1.0	0.5	0.6	0.9	·	0.6	0.5	0.5	0.7	0.4	0.3

Selected Financial Factors (in Percentages)

Debt Ratio 45	49.2	·	85.6	88.7	64.5	56.8	69.1	67.3	62.1	57.0	53.8	47.8	33.5
Return on Total Assets 46	5.2	·	17.0	3.3	12.9	8.5	·	5.2	6.5	7.9	12.0	9.7	2.4
Return on Equity Before Income Taxes 47	7.6	·	100.7	10.9	30.6	16.3	·	10.2	12.8	14.4	20.4	15.8	2.8
Return on Equity After Income Taxes 48	5.7	·	97.7	10.1	28.3	14.2	·	7.1	9.5	12.1	18.1	10.8	2.7
Profit Margin (Before Income Tax) 49	2.2	1.5	2.4	0.3	3.5	1.8	·	1.3	3.4	3.0	4.2	5.4	3.5
Profit Margin (After Income Tax) 50	1.7	0.4	2.3	0.3	3.2	1.5	·	0.9	2.5	3.7	3.7	3.7	3.4

Table II

Corporations with Net Income

NONSTORE RETAILERS

MONEY AMOUNTS AND SIZE OF ASSETS IN THOUSANDS OF DOLLARS

Item Description for Accounting Period 7/05 Through 6/06	Total	Zero Assets	Under 500	500 to 1,000	1,000 to 5,000	5,000 to 10,000	10,000 to 25,000	25,000 to 50,000	50,000 to 100,000	100,000 to 250,000	250,000 to 500,000	500,000 to 2,500,000	2,500,000 and over
Number of Enterprises 1	26497	3432	19446	1573	1581	229	105	58	19	·	9	·	0
Revenues ($ in Thousands)													
Net Sales 2	101744406	695319	14034688	5259213	11714932	6851593	5744380	6397514	2438716	·	7439819	·	0
Interest 3	555520	210	2163	6118	16445	8980	2025	9963	9672	·	110973	·	0
Rents 4	85775	0	3407	7001	0	2865	2149	7096	6045	·	5314	·	0
Royalties 5	637088	0	151	0	0	0	0	1660	16	·	2324	·	0
Other Portfolio Income 6	261929	50665	18528	13697	10338	21460	2349	23385	1807	·	17307	·	0
Other Receipts 7	2501399	4702	137814	14566	39896	20027	45134	43375	20935	·	39800	·	0
Total Receipts 8	105786117	750896	14196751	5300595	11781611	6904925	5796037	6482993	2477191	·	7615537	·	0
Average Total Receipts 9	3992	219	730	3370	7452	30153	55200	111776	130378	·	846171	·	·
Operating Costs/Operating Income (%)													
Cost of Operations 10	69.7	54.4	65.9	77.6	68.2	73.6	70.5	71.7	54.2	·	70.0	·	·
Salaries and Wages 11	7.8	6.5	8.2	5.6	6.8	5.7	7.7	5.7	9.4	·	4.4	·	·
Taxes Paid 12	1.2	1.1	1.5	1.5	1.6	0.9	1.3	0.8	1.2	·	0.8	·	·
Interest Paid 13	0.7	2.3	0.3	0.4	0.5	0.3	0.5	0.4	0.7	·	1.1	·	·
Depreciation 14	0.9	1.4	0.7	0.9	1.0	1.3	0.9	0.8	1.0	·	0.4	·	·
Amortization and Depletion 15	0.2	0.9	0.1	0.1	0.2	0.0	0.1	0.2	0.2	·	0.6	·	·
Pensions and Other Deferred Comp. 16	0.2	0.0	0.2	0.3	0.3	0.3	0.1	0.2	0.5	·	0.1	·	·
Employee Benefits 17	0.7	0.3	0.4	1.0	0.8	0.5	0.6	0.7	0.8	·	0.7	·	·
Advertising 18	2.9	1.6	1.9	1.1	2.5	2.7	3.0	3.6	8.0	·	4.8	·	·
Other Expenses 19	12.2	20.8	13.1	5.6	9.6	10.6	11.1	11.9	18.4	·	11.8	·	·
Officers' Compensation 20	1.7	3.0	4.1	2.6	2.9	1.6	1.1	0.7	0.9	·	0.4	·	·
Operating Margin 21	1.9	7.7	3.4	3.2	5.5	2.3	3.2	3.1	4.7	·	4.9	·	·
Operating Margin Before Officers' Comp. 22	3.5	10.7	7.5	5.9	8.4	3.9	4.3	3.8	5.7	·	5.3	·	·

Selected Average Balance Sheet ($ in Thousands)

	1	2	3	4	5	6	7	8	9	10
Net Receivables 23	362	0	19	248	633	1541	4243	9254	20079	73381
Inventories 24	195	0	20	80	343	1028	3383	6725	14117	63747
Net Property, Plant and Equipment 25	189	0	19	119	338	1874	2645	4949	6346	23097
Total Assets 26	2160	0	104	732	2238	6979	15902	36734	73614	339178
Notes and Loans Payable 27	361	0	52	302	435	2029	4549	9479	13039	64915
All Other Liabilities 28	637	0	29	249	767	1741	6215	13956	26378	109540
Net Worth 29	1162	0	23	180	1036	3209	5137	13299	34196	164722

Selected Financial Ratios (Times to 1)

	1	2	3	4	5	6	7	8	9	10
Current Ratio 30	1.9	•	1.5	2.0	1.5	2.1	1.5	1.5	1.8	1.6
Quick Ratio 31	1.2	•	1.1	1.6	1.1	1.4	0.9	0.8	1.0	0.8
Net Sales to Working Capital 32	8.3	•	30.3	11.9	14.2	12.9	15.0	13.8	5.5	11.1
Coverage Ratio 33	9.4	7.8	13.9	12.1	14.0	10.2	9.9	11.6	10.1	7.8
Total Asset Turnover 34	1.8	•	6.9	4.6	3.3	4.3	3.4	3.0	1.7	2.4
Inventory Turnover 35	13.7	•	24.2	32.3	14.7	21.4	11.4	11.8	4.9	9.1
Receivables Turnover 36	14.0	•	40.0	14.1	12.0	18.5	13.5	12.7	8.2	12.4
Total Liabilities to Net Worth 37	0.9	•	3.4	3.1	1.2	1.2	2.1	1.8	1.2	1.1
Current Assets to Working Capital 38	2.1	•	3.0	2.0	2.8	1.9	3.0	3.0	2.2	2.6
Current Liabilities to Working Capital 39	1.1	•	2.0	1.0	1.8	0.9	2.0	2.0	1.2	1.6
Working Capital to Net Sales 40	0.1	•	0.0	0.1	0.1	0.1	0.1	0.1	0.2	0.1
Inventory to Working Capital 41	0.4	•	0.7	0.3	0.6	0.5	0.9	0.9	0.7	0.9
Total Receipts to Cash Flow 42	6.0	3.2	6.4	11.8	6.8	8.2	7.5	6.5	4.3	5.5
Cost of Goods to Cash Flow 43	4.2	1.7	4.2	9.2	4.7	6.1	5.3	4.7	2.3	3.8
Cash Flow to Total Debt 44	0.6	•	1.4	0.5	0.9	1.0	0.7	0.7	0.8	0.9

Selected Financial Factors (in Percentages)

	1	2	3	4	5	6	7	8	9	10
Debt Ratio 45	46.2	•	77.5	75.4	53.7	54.0	67.7	63.8	53.5	51.4
Return on Total Assets 46	11.7	•	33.4	20.0	21.7	14.8	15.5	14.5	12.1	20.3
Return on Equity Before Income Taxes 47	19.5	•	137.4	74.4	43.5	29.0	43.1	36.7	23.6	36.4
Return on Equity After Income Taxes 48	17.1	•	135.0	73.8	40.9	26.4	41.3	32.6	19.7	33.2
Profit Margin (Before Income Tax) 49	5.9	15.7	4.5	4.0	6.1	3.1	4.0	4.4	6.3	7.3
Profit Margin (After Income Tax) 50	5.2	15.6	4.4	4.0	5.7	2.8	3.9	3.9	5.3	6.6

Table I

Corporations with and without Net Income

AIR TRANSPORTATION

MONEY AMOUNTS AND SIZE OF ASSETS IN THOUSANDS OF DOLLARS

Item Description for Accounting Period 7/05 Through 6/06		Total	Zero Assets	Under 500	500 to 1,000	1,000 to 5,000	5,000 to 10,000	10,000 to 25,000	25,000 to 50,000	50,000 to 100,000	100,000 to 250,000	250,000 to 500,000	500,000 to 2,500,000	2,500,000 and over
Number of Enterprises	1	8435	1577	4427	1218	835	155	120	42	17	17	4	12	10
Revenues ($ in Thousands)														
Net Sales	2	136251400	2983168	2060739	891664	1638184	1402804	2270064	1288436	1835034	4488504	2864010	13594013	100934780
Interest	3	831824	7744	93	157	1140	385	3280	2691	3130	21192	9186	107329	675497
Rents	4	320588	0	628	0	996	3255	101	21	743	1678	1441	7540	304184
Royalties	5	26011	0	0	0	0	0	0	0	0	80	63	25865	2
Other Portfolio Income	6	2604531	215745	5724	0	5865	4636	29835	13308	9710	13920	17105	307545	1981138
Other Receipts	7	3644127	19531	15862	2	4586	3132	15969	15372	33666	79599	12157	312939	3131314
Total Receipts	8	143678481	3226188	2083046	891823	1650771	1414212	2319249	1319828	1882283	4604973	2903962	14355231	107026915
Average Total Receipts	9	17034	2046	471	732	1977	9124	19327	31424	110723	270881	725990	1196269	10702692
Operating Costs/Operating Income (%)														
Cost of Operations	10	27.0	25.6	21.6	66.3	65.0	46.1	60.4	52.1	40.0	33.3	36.4	21.8	24.8
Salaries and Wages	11	19.2	13.1	2.6	2.4	9.4	9.9	9.6	8.2	11.5	16.2	18.1	19.2	20.9
Taxes Paid	12	2.7	2.3	1.3	2.7	2.9	2.5	1.4	1.7	1.8	2.1	1.4	3.6	2.8
Interest Paid	13	3.3	2.0	0.7	1.6	1.9	3.8	1.9	2.0	1.7	2.0	0.9	2.6	3.7
Depreciation	14	7.6	3.0	2.9	35.5	8.5	4.5	8.3	8.4	3.9	4.2	2.9	7.9	7.9
Amortization and Depletion	15	0.3	0.1	0.0	0.0	0.1	0.0	0.1	0.3	0.3	0.3	0.4	0.8	0.3
Pensions and Other Deferred Comp.	16	2.3	0.0	2.6	•	0.2	0.0	0.1	0.1	0.3	0.2	0.6	0.8	2.9
Employee Benefits	17	4.8	3.4	0.4	•	0.4	0.8	1.3	1.3	1.3	2.2	1.5	1.8	5.9
Advertising	18	0.8	0.8	0.1	0.0	0.2	0.1	0.3	0.8	0.5	0.6	0.1	0.7	0.8
Other Expenses	19	42.1	53.9	63.2	13.4	18.9	38.0	21.8	32.0	39.8	47.4	43.1	42.4	42.4
Officers' Compensation	20	0.3	0.9	2.2	•	1.6	0.5	1.3	1.2	1.2	0.5	0.4	0.7	0.1
Operating Margin	21	•	2.3	•	•	•	•	•	•	•	•	•	•	•
Operating Margin Before Officers' Comp.	22	•	4.5	•	•	•	•	•	•	•	•	•	•	•

Selected Average Balance Sheet ($ in Thousands)

Net Receivables 23	858	0	28	51	208	2011	1940	2745	11241	19651	47704	69752	466329
Inventories 24	272	0	0	0	41	42	429	671	2137	7224	15911	21580	168984
Net Property, Plant and Equipment 25	10733	0	58	575	1028	1238	9355	18387	27993	53445	97519	548716	7827493
Total Assets 26	17714	0	119	861	1957	6400	15716	32267	69574	163495	295726	1031796	12444943
Notes and Loans Payable 27	7987	0	110	1196	1572	6680	8259	15290	30606	73929	197829	428596	5373214
All Other Liabilities 28	13272	0	48	51	145	1086	3993	8768	40541	96282	387890	320241	10282196
Net Worth 29	-3545	0	-39	-386	240	-1366	3464	8208	-1574	-6716	-289992	282958	-3210467

Selected Financial Ratios (Times to 1)

Current Ratio 30	0.9	•	1.1	3.3	3.4	3.6	1.2	0.6	1.0	0.7	0.5	1.6	0.9
Quick Ratio 31	0.6	•	1.0	2.7	2.3	1.9	0.9	0.5	0.7	0.5	0.3	1.2	0.6
Net Sales to Working Capital 32	•	•	99.4	4.9	3.4	2.8	27.9	•	•	•	•	9.7	•
Coverage Ratio 33	•	2.5	5.5	•	•	•	•	•	1.1	•	•	2.3	•
Total Asset Turnover 34	0.9	•	3.9	0.9	1.0	1.4	1.2	1.0	1.6	1.6	2.4	1.1	0.8
Inventory Turnover 35	16.1	•	12188.4	31.3	99.7	26.7	23.8	20.2	12.2	16.4	•	11.5	14.8
Receivables Turnover 36	19.5	•	21.6	5.7	8.7	4.9	10.0	7.8	13.1	14.3	15.8	15.7	23.1
Total Liabilities to Net Worth 37	•	•	7.2	•	•	3.5	2.9	•	•	•	•	2.6	•
Current Assets to Working Capital 38	•	•	12.1	1.4	1.4	1.4	6.3	•	•	•	•	2.7	•
Current Liabilities to Working Capital 39	•	•	11.1	0.4	0.4	0.4	5.3	•	•	•	•	1.7	•
Working Capital to Net Sales 40	•	•	0.0	0.2	0.3	0.4	0.0	•	•	•	•	0.1	•
Inventory to Working Capital 41	•	•	•	0.1	0.1	0.0	0.5	•	•	•	•	0.2	•
Total Receipts to Cash Flow 42	4.5	3.0	1.9	23.7	•	7.7	9.2	9.5	3.8	5.6	7.7	3.5	4.5
Cost of Goods to Cash Flow 43	1.2	0.8	0.4	15.4	•	3.5	5.6	5.0	1.5	1.9	2.8	0.8	1.1
Cash Flow to Total Debt 44	0.2	•	1.6	0.0	0.0	0.2	0.2	0.1	0.4	0.3	0.2	0.4	0.1

Selected Financial Factors (in Percentages)

Debt Ratio 45	120.0	132.5	144.8	87.8	121.4	78.0	74.6	102.3	104.1	198.1	•	72.6	125.8
Return on Total Assets 46	•	16.2	•	•	•	•	•	2.9	•	•	•	6.7	•
Return on Equity Before Income Taxes 47	22.8	•	41.6	•	34.4	•	•	•	256.0	•	11.1	13.8	20.1
Return on Equity After Income Taxes 48	23.7	•	•	41.6	39.1	•	•	12.4	286.8	•	12.5	9.6	20.2
Profit Margin (Before Income Tax) 49	3.0	•	3.4	•	•	•	•	•	0.2	•	•	3.4	•
Profit Margin (After Income Tax) 50	3.0	•	3.3	•	•	•	•	•	•	•	•	2.4	•

Table II
Corporations with Net Income

AIR TRANSPORTATION

MONEY AMOUNTS AND SIZE OF ASSETS IN THOUSANDS OF DOLLARS

Item Description for Accounting Period 7/05 Through 6/06	Total	Zero Assets	Under 500	500 to 1,000	1,000 to 5,000	5,000 to 10,000	10,000 to 25,000	25,000 to 50,000	50,000 to 100,000	100,000 to 250,000	250,000 to 500,000	500,000 to 2,500,000	2,500,000 and over
Number of Enterprises 1	2760	166	2061	246	•	34	46	12	•	11	0	0	8

Revenues ($ in Thousands)

	Total	Zero Assets	Under 500	500 to 1,000	1,000 to 5,000	5,000 to 10,000	10,000 to 25,000	25,000 to 50,000	50,000 to 100,000	100,000 to 250,000	250,000 to 500,000	500,000 to 2,500,000	2,500,000 and over
Net Sales 2	34819688	2017320	2032775	794252	•	867409	1568528	666455	•	3572040	0	•	8800808
Interest 3	172422	7609	93	157	•	0	996	1716	•	2558	0	•	70477
Rents 4	9356	0	627	0	•	0	0	21	•	1677	0	•	53
Royalties 5	25865	0	0	0	•	0	0	0	•	0	0	•	25865
Other Portfolio Income 6	632806	215688	5724	0	•	164	29384	9607	•	7257	0	•	302705
Other Receipts 7	1390328	19082	15659	2	•	2157	9939	7092	•	34214	0	•	288736
Total Receipts 8	37050465	2259699	2054878	794411	•	869730	1608847	684891	•	3617746	0	•	9488644
Average Total Receipts 9	13424	13613	997	3229	•	25580	34975	57074	•	328886	•	•	1186080

Operating Costs/Operating Income (%)

	Total	Zero Assets	Under 500	500 to 1,000	1,000 to 5,000	5,000 to 10,000	10,000 to 25,000	25,000 to 50,000	50,000 to 100,000	100,000 to 250,000	250,000 to 500,000	500,000 to 2,500,000	2,500,000 and over
Cost of Operations 10	23.4	0.0	21.5	72.8	•	55.3	57.6	62.7	•	30.9	•	•	19.1
Salaries and Wages 11	16.3	18.9	2.6	2.7	•	7.9	9.6	8.7	•	12.2	•	•	18.9
Taxes Paid 12	3.1	3.3	1.3	2.6	•	2.3	1.2	1.5	•	1.6	•	•	3.9
Interest Paid 13	1.7	2.9	0.3	0.0	•	0.1	0.9	1.1	•	1.2	•	•	2.7
Depreciation 14	7.5	1.7	1.2	6.1	•	0.5	3.1	4.8	•	3.1	•	•	7.9
Amortization and Depletion 15	0.4	0.2	0.0	•	•	0.0	0.1	0.1	•	0.2	•	•	1.2
Pensions and Other Deferred Comp. 16	1.2	•	0.0	•	•	0.0	0.1	0.2	•	0.5	•	•	0.4
Employee Benefits 17	8.7	5.0	0.4	•	•	0.3	1.0	1.1	•	1.7	•	•	2.0
Advertising 18	0.8	0.5	0.1	0.0	•	0.0	0.4	0.0	•	0.1	•	•	0.6
Other Expenses 19	37.7	70.3	61.0	6.7	•	28.0	24.0	17.5	•	42.3	•	•	44.1
Officers' Compensation 20	0.7	0.6	2.2	•	•	0.5	1.2	1.4	•	0.5	•	•	0.8
Operating Margin 21	•	•	9.4	9.1	•	4.9	0.7	0.8	•	5.7	•	•	•
Operating Margin Before Officers' Comp. 22	•	•	11.6	9.1	•	5.4	1.9	2.2	•	6.2	•	•	•

Selected Average Balance Sheet ($ in Thousands)

Net Receivables 23	744	0	59	84	3508	3423	5002	28273	92023
Inventories 24	156	0	0	0	12	597	1742	9728	18242
Net Property, Plant and Equipment 25	6866	0	20	458	635	8457	14219	67792	433709
Total Assets 26	12331	0	147	936	5911	16450	32926	192099	962397
Notes and Loans Payable 27	3363	0	59	2	889	5784	12831	82329	343522
All Other Liabilities 28	4498	0	73	211	2988	3954	9817	66584	334772
Net Worth 29	4471	0	15	723	2035	6711	10278	43186	284103

Selected Financial Ratios (Times to 1)

Current Ratio 30	1.2	•	1.6	2.3	1.6	1.4	1.2	1.2	1.6
Quick Ratio 31	0.8	•	1.6	1.4	1.4	1.1	1.0	0.7	1.1
Net Sales to Working Capital 32	19.5	•	22.1	12.1	13.6	20.1	23.0	26.6	9.3
Coverage Ratio 33	4.0	•	33.7	3012.5	55.9	4.6	4.2	6.7	3.4
Total Asset Turnover 34	1.0	•	6.7	3.4	4.3	2.1	1.7	1.7	1.1
Inventory Turnover 35	18.9	•	•	•	1226.2	32.9	20.0	10.3	11.5
Receivables Turnover 36	21.3	•	23.3	31.2	9.7	12.9	10.8	11.9	15.2
Total Liabilities to Net Worth 37	1.8	•	8.9	0.3	1.9	1.5	2.2	3.4	2.4
Current Assets to Working Capital 38	6.1	•	2.6	1.8	2.6	3.6	5.7	6.7	2.7
Current Liabilities to Working Capital 39	5.1	•	1.6	0.8	1.6	2.6	4.7	5.7	1.7
Working Capital to Net Sales 40	0.1	•	0.0	0.1	0.1	0.0	0.0	0.0	0.1
Inventory to Working Capital 41	0.4	•	•	•	•	0.4	0.2	0.9	0.2
Total Receipts to Cash Flow 42	3.7	2.1	1.7	13.8	5.6	4.9	6.9	3.9	3.2
Cost of Goods to Cash Flow 43	0.9	•	0.4	10.0	3.1	2.8	4.3	1.2	0.6
Cash Flow to Total Debt 44	0.4	•	4.4	1.1	1.2	0.7	0.4	0.6	0.5

Selected Financial Factors (in Percentages)

Debt Ratio 45	63.7	•	89.9	22.7	65.6	59.2	68.8	77.5	70.5
Return on Total Assets 46	6.9	•	72.5	31.4	22.6	8.6	7.9	13.8	10.7
Return on Equity Before Income Taxes 47	14.2	•	693.4	40.6	64.4	16.6	19.4	52.4	25.6
Return on Equity After Income Taxes 48	12.0	•	687.0	40.6	50.0	15.4	17.1	41.5	19.4
Profit Margin (Before Income Tax) 49	5.0	8.5	10.5	9.1	5.1	3.3	3.6	7.0	6.6
Profit Margin (After Income Tax) 50	4.3	8.4	10.4	9.1	4.0	3.0	3.2	5.5	5.0

Table I
Corporations with and without Net Income

RAIL TRANSPORTATION

MONEY AMOUNTS AND SIZE OF ASSETS IN THOUSANDS OF DOLLARS

Item Description for Accounting Period 7/05 Through 6/06	Total	Zero Assets	Under 500	500 to 1,000	1,000 to 5,000	5,000 to 10,000	10,000 to 25,000	25,000 to 50,000	50,000 to 100,000	100,000 to 250,000	250,000 to 500,000	500,000 to 2,500,000	2,500,000 and over
Number of Enterprises **1**	451	16	252	0	82	37	26	9	7	8	0	6	7
Revenues ($ in Thousands)													
Net Sales **2**	53072442	5772	123311	0	449876	65221	192089	192432	241683	881724	0	2321058	48599276
Interest **3**	1263562	0	975	0	301	2155	4051	621	1582	1783	0	82747	1169347
Rents **4**	755428	0	880	0	3521	0	511	1901	2985	8088	0	110211	627331
Royalties **5**	29650	0	0	0	222	0	3	0	307	1820	0	0	27298
Other Portfolio Income **6**	1051608	0	0	0	4821	655	2995	1307	4898	9964	0	52064	974903
Other Receipts **7**	2335475	-2585	24	0	4013	2128	1807	4615	6089	3458	0	118672	2197254
Total Receipts **8**	58508165	3187	125190	0	462754	70159	201456	200876	257544	906837	0	2684752	53595409
Average Total Receipts **9**	129730	199	497	•	5643	1896	7748	22320	36792	113355	•	447459	7656487
Operating Costs/Operating Income (%)													
Cost of Operations **10**	26.6	32.3	•	•	8.8	1.2	9.4	24.9	14.4	42.3	•	3.8	27.8
Salaries and Wages **11**	22.5	17.8	7.8	•	2.8	14.8	14.5	12.2	25.2	10.5	•	21.6	23.0
Taxes Paid **12**	5.8	•	3.2	•	2.7	4.6	5.3	4.1	4.9	4.1	•	5.5	5.9
Interest Paid **13**	6.8	•	4.3	•	0.4	1.1	3.6	1.7	3.6	1.7	•	6.0	7.1
Depreciation **14**	7.9	19.5	2.9	•	3.2	10.2	7.4	16.4	10.5	9.4	•	11.7	7.7
Amortization and Depletion **15**	0.2	•	•	•	0.0	0.4	0.1	0.0	0.0	0.2	•	0.4	0.2
Pensions and Other Deferred Comp. **16**	0.8	•	0.1	•	0.1	1.7	0.0	2.4	2.0	0.1	•	1.9	0.7
Employee Benefits **17**	5.0	•	1.3	•	0.8	2.3	2.4	2.7	4.3	1.3	•	5.6	5.1
Advertising **18**	0.1	•	0.0	•	0.3	0.2	0.4	0.1	0.0	0.0	•	0.1	0.1
Other Expenses **19**	23.8	1.3	81.5	•	78.5	55.5	47.4	20.2	34.0	25.3	•	50.4	21.7
Officers' Compensation **20**	0.5	•	•	•	1.4	4.0	0.7	1.4	1.4	0.7	•	0.6	0.5
Operating Margin **21**	0.1	29.2	•	•	0.9	3.8	8.8	13.8	•	4.4	•	•	0.2
Operating Margin Before Officers' Comp. **22**	0.5	29.2	•	•	2.3	7.9	9.6	15.2	1.0	5.1	•	•	0.7

Selected Average Balance Sheet ($ in Thousands)

Net Receivables 23	13187	0	54	432	629	1825	8357	4548	15796	•	122896	693853
Inventories 24	2203	0	0	•	8	194	363	950	2667	•	6216	130049
Net Property, Plant and Equipment 25	273251	0	157	622	3381	7203	25832	45847	151449	•	690652	16703509
Total Assets 26	348756	0	369	2128	5837	14557	40877	73148	200453	•	1236746	20931863
Notes and Loans Payable 27	77176	0	0	548	589	11373	11672	20291	58716	•	302706	4558724
All Other Liabilities 28	150156	0	90	373	1910	2027	12129	29115	67632	•	413617	9172567
Net Worth 29	121424	0	279	1206	3338	1157	17075	23742	74106	•	520422	7200572

Selected Financial Ratios (Times to 1)

Current Ratio 30	0.7	2.4	•	1.8	3.8	0.4	1.4	0.9	0.8	•	0.9	0.6
Quick Ratio 31	0.5	1.1	•	1.5	3.8	0.3	1.0	0.7	0.5	•	0.7	0.4
Net Sales to Working Capital 32	•	4.0	•	17.6	1.0	5.3	•	•	•	•	•	•
Coverage Ratio 33	2.5	1.1	•	9.8	11.3	4.8	11.8	2.9	5.2	•	2.3	2.5
Total Asset Turnover 34	0.3	1.3	•	2.6	0.3	0.5	0.5	0.5	0.5	•	0.3	0.3
Inventory Turnover 35	14.2	•	•	•	2.7	3.6	14.7	5.2	17.5	•	2.4	14.8
Receivables Turnover 36	9.8	10.0	•	11.6	4.3	4.0	3.0	8.2	8.4	•	4.0	10.9
Total Liabilities to Net Worth 37	1.9	0.3	•	0.8	0.7	11.6	1.4	2.1	1.7	•	1.4	1.9
Current Assets to Working Capital 38	•	1.7	•	2.3	1.4	•	3.6	•	•	•	•	•
Current Liabilities to Working Capital 39	•	0.7	•	1.3	0.4	•	2.6	•	•	•	•	•
Working Capital to Net Sales 40	•	0.2	•	0.1	1.0	•	0.2	•	•	•	•	•
Inventory to Working Capital 41	•	•	•	•	•	•	0.0	•	•	•	•	•
Total Receipts to Cash Flow 42	4.5	1.3	•	2.2	1.9	2.0	3.1	3.2	3.8	•	2.6	4.8
Cost of Goods to Cash Flow 43	1.2	•	•	0.2	0.0	0.2	0.8	0.5	1.6	•	0.1	1.3
Cash Flow to Total Debt 44	0.1	4.1	•	2.8	0.4	0.3	0.3	0.2	0.2	•	0.2	0.1

Selected Financial Factors (in Percentages)

Debt Ratio 45	65.2	24.4	•	43.3	42.8	92.1	58.2	67.5	63.0	•	57.9	65.6
Return on Total Assets 46	5.8	6.4	•	10.8	3.8	8.8	10.4	4.9	4.9	•	4.4	5.8
Return on Equity Before Income Taxes 47	10.0	0.8	•	17.1	6.0	87.5	22.8	9.9	10.8	•	5.9	10.2
Return on Equity After Income Taxes 48	6.6	0.7	•	12.1	6.0	78.7	17.8	6.6	8.3	•	4.4	6.6
Profit Margin (Before Income Tax) 49	10.3	0.5	•	3.8	11.4	13.7	18.2	6.8	7.3	•	7.9	10.5
Profit Margin (After Income Tax) 50	6.8	0.4	•	2.7	11.4	12.3	14.2	4.5	5.6	•	6.0	6.9

Table II
Corporations with Net Income

RAIL TRANSPORTATION

MONEY AMOUNTS AND SIZE OF ASSETS IN THOUSANDS OF DOLLARS

Item Description for Accounting Period 7/05 Through 6/06	Total	Zero Assets	Under 500	500 to 1,000	1,000 to 5,000	5,000 to 10,000	10,000 to 25,000	25,000 to 50,000	50,000 to 100,000	100,000 to 250,000	250,000 to 500,000	500,000 to 2,500,000	2,500,000 and over
Number of Enterprises **1**	393	8	252	0	•	5	17	9	•	•	0	•	•
Revenues ($ in Thousands)													
Net Sales **2**	51480865	5772	123311	0	•	65221	177157	192432	•	•	0	•	•
Interest **3**	1245810	0	975	0	•	0	676	621	•	•	0	•	•
Rents **4**	731470	0	880	0	•	0	511	1901	•	•	0	•	•
Royalties **5**	26901	0	0	0	•	0	3	0	•	•	0	•	•
Other Portfolio Income **6**	1036113	0	0	0	•	655	2995	1307	•	•	0	•	•
Other Receipts **7**	2294170	0	24	0	•	2127	162	4615	•	•	0	•	•
Total Receipts **8**	56815329	5772	125190	0	•	68003	181504	200876	•	•	0	•	•
Average Total Receipts **9**	144568	722	497	•	•	13601	10677	22320	•	•	•	•	•
Operating Costs/Operating Income (%)													
Cost of Operations **10**	27.0	32.3	•	•	•	•	5.9	24.9	•	•	•	•	•
Salaries and Wages **11**	22.5	17.8	7.8	•	•	13.7	14.4	12.2	•	•	•	•	•
Taxes Paid **12**	5.8	•	3.2	•	•	4.6	5.5	4.1	•	•	•	•	•
Interest Paid **13**	6.8	•	4.3	•	•	1.1	2.0	1.7	•	•	•	•	•
Depreciation **14**	7.9	19.5	2.9	•	•	7.9	5.0	16.4	•	•	•	•	•
Amortization and Depletion **15**	0.2	•	•	•	•	0.4	0.1	0.0	•	•	•	•	•
Pensions and Other Deferred Comp. **16**	0.8	•	•	•	•	•	0.0	2.4	•	•	•	•	•
Employee Benefits **17**	5.1	•	1.3	•	•	2.1	2.5	2.7	•	•	•	•	•
Advertising **18**	0.1	•	0.0	•	•	0.2	0.4	0.1	•	•	•	•	•
Other Expenses **19**	22.9	81.5	•	•	•	49.7	36.4	20.2	•	•	•	•	•
Officers' Compensation **20**	0.5	1.3	•	•	•	4.0	0.8	1.4	•	•	•	•	•
Operating Margin **21**	0.4	29.2	•	•	•	16.1	27.1	13.8	•	•	•	•	•
Operating Margin Before Officers' Comp. **22**	0.9	29.2	•	•	•	20.1	27.9	15.2	•	•	•	•	•

Selected Average Balance Sheet ($ in Thousands)

Net Receivables 23	14336	0	54	•	577	1210	8357
Inventories 24	2203	0	0	•	57	125	344
Net Property, Plant and Equipment 25	305777	0	157	•	5774	9352	25832
Total Assets 26	386016	0	369	•	7306	15270	40877
Notes and Loans Payable 27	83949	0	0	•	2009	4918	11672
All Other Liabilities 28	167668	0	90	•	412	2840	12129
Net Worth 29	134399	0	279	•	4885	7512	17075

Selected Financial Ratios (Times to 1)

Current Ratio 30	0.7	•	2.4	•	1.3	1.2	1.4
Quick Ratio 31	0.5	•	1.1	•	1.2	1.1	1.0
Net Sales to Working Capital 32	•	•	4.0	•	69.7	20.2	5.3
Coverage Ratio 33	2.6	•	1.1	•	19.4	15.8	11.8
Total Asset Turnover 34	0.3	•	1.3	•	1.8	0.7	0.5
Inventory Turnover 35	16.1	•	•	•	•	4.9	15.5
Receivables Turnover 36	10.7	•	14.3	•	13.6	7.2	3.3
Total Liabilities to Net Worth 37	1.9	•	0.3	•	0.5	1.0	1.4
Current Assets to Working Capital 38	•	•	1.7	•	4.8	6.7	3.6
Current Liabilities to Working Capital 39	•	•	0.7	•	3.8	5.7	2.6
Working Capital to Net Sales 40	•	•	0.2	•	0.0	0.0	0.2
Inventory to Working Capital 41	•	•	•	•	•	0.2	0.0
Total Receipts to Cash Flow 42	4.6	3.4	1.3	•	1.7	1.8	3.1
Cost of Goods to Cash Flow 43	1.2	1.1	•	•	•	0.1	0.8
Cash Flow to Total Debt 44	0.1	•	4.1	•	3.2	0.7	0.3

Selected Financial Factors (in Percentages)

Debt Ratio 45	65.2	•	24.4	•	33.1	50.8	58.2
Return on Total Assets 46	6.0	•	6.4	•	38.3	21.5	10.4
Return on Equity Before Income Taxes 47	10.5	•	0.8	•	54.4	41.0	22.8
Return on Equity After Income Taxes 48	7.0	•	0.7	•	54.4	38.9	17.8
Profit Margin (Before Income Tax) 49	10.8	29.2	0.5	•	20.4	29.5	18.2
Profit Margin (After Income Tax) 50	7.2	29.2	0.4	•	20.4	28.0	14.2

Table I
Corporations with and without Net Income

WATER TRANSPORTATION

MONEY AMOUNTS AND SIZE OF ASSETS IN THOUSANDS OF DOLLARS

Item Description for Accounting Period 7/05 Through 6/06	Total	Zero Assets	Under 500	500 to 1,000	1,000 to 5,000	5,000 to 10,000	10,000 to 25,000	25,000 to 50,000	50,000 to 100,000	100,000 to 250,000	250,000 to 500,000	500,000 to 2,500,000	2,500,000 and over
Number of Enterprises 1	3365	401	1225	787	648	138	83	24	22	18	8	12	0
Revenues ($ in Thousands)													
Net Sales 2	21866148	1358331	594058	1580644	1035403	1810847	1281146	502881	1082342	1873313	1906678	8840507	0
Interest 3	145500	1712	192	0	1049	579	3133	352	4481	3035	20184	110782	0
Rents 4	104953	36	0	0	3070	203	1159	1358	4861	45	0	94221	0
Royalties 5	422	420	0	0	0	0	0	0	0	2	0	0	0
Other Portfolio Income 6	815130	28028	0	0	17955	16677	55323	2000	74317	16558	50676	553598	0
Other Receipts 7	387609	-124564	103922	0	18854	9516	25215	8403	12699	17487	22085	293989	0
Total Receipts 8	23319762	1263963	698172	1580644	1076331	1837822	1365976	514994	1178700	1910440	1999623	9893097	0
Average Total Receipts 9	6930	3152	570	2008	1661	13318	16458	21458	53577	106136	249953	824425	•
Operating Costs/Operating Income (%)													
Cost of Operations 10	40.3	62.3	0.6	53.6	3.3	66.6	52.2	35.4	32.5	49.9	42.9	33.1	•
Salaries and Wages 11	10.1	7.5	17.2	12.8	24.5	3.6	11.1	18.9	10.6	5.9	5.7	10.4	•
Taxes Paid 12	1.7	0.8	3.8	0.8	3.2	0.7	2.1	3.7	2.4	1.6	2.0	1.6	•
Interest Paid 13	2.9	1.0	0.6	1.1	2.6	2.5	2.3	2.4	3.2	2.9	5.8	3.2	•
Depreciation 14	6.4	4.7	1.8	4.1	7.7	1.1	5.3	6.6	7.6	8.8	8.6	7.2	•
Amortization and Depletion 15	0.2	0.0	0.0	0.0	0.0	0.1	0.0	0.1	0.1	0.2	0.5	0.4	•
Pensions and Other Deferred Comp. 16	0.6	0.2	2.4	•	0.1	0.3	0.2	0.8	0.6	0.3	0.7	1.0	•
Employee Benefits 17	1.7	0.5	0.0	0.1	0.2	0.4	1.7	2.8	2.1	1.4	1.1	2.8	•
Advertising 18	0.4	2.9	0.0	0.2	0.1	0.2	0.2	0.7	0.1	0.1	0.0	0.5	•
Other Expenses 19	33.1	10.3	76.0	20.8	43.4	25.2	20.4	22.9	32.8	22.1	31.6	41.4	•
Officers' Compensation 20	1.7	0.7	9.9	3.2	2.7	0.6	2.6	1.9	1.5	1.0	1.4	1.3	•
Operating Margin 21	0.8	9.1	•	3.2	12.3	•	1.9	3.8	6.5	5.7	•	•	•
Operating Margin Before Officers' Comp. 22	2.5	9.9	•	6.3	14.9	•	4.5	5.7	7.9	6.7	1.0	•	•

Selected Average Balance Sheet ($ in Thousands)

Net Receivables 23	826	0	6	0	93	1124	3893	6235	11295	14444	45371	101187	•
Inventories 24	78	0	0	0	0	29	84	251	901	4459	1027	14361	•
Net Property, Plant and Equipment 25	4220	0	34	285	1157	4079	6248	19012	34495	94416	161162	658283	•
Total Assets 26	8243		104	596	2114	7324	15228	32617	69649	152887	367372	1290762	•
Notes and Loans Payable 27	3095	0	52	464	1049	1893	6627	14664	27367	62222	176502	417367	•
All Other Liabilities 28	1897	0	7	79	318	3019	5234	7401	17145	28902	83216	292755	•
Net Worth 29	3251	0	45	52	747	2412	3368	10553	25137	61762	107653	580641	•

Selected Financial Ratios (Times to 1)

Current Ratio 30	1.3	•	1.0	1.7	0.9	0.8	1.1	1.2	1.4	1.1	1.7	1.4	•
Quick Ratio 31	1.0	•	0.9	1.3	0.8	0.5	0.8	1.0	1.0	0.9	1.2	1.2	•
Net Sales to Working Capital 32	15.2	•	1605.6	22.8	•	•	28.2	13.6	7.2	28.4	6.8	9.1	•
Coverage Ratio 33	3.7	3.2	9.8	3.8	7.2	1.1	4.7	3.6	5.8	3.6	1.9	4.1	•
Total Asset Turnover 34	0.8	•	4.7	3.4	0.8	1.8	1.0	0.6	0.7	0.7	0.6	0.6	•
Inventory Turnover 35	33.7	•	•	•	114.0	304.7	95.9	29.6	17.8	50.6	23.0	17.0	•
Receivables Turnover 36	8.1	•	167.7	61.6	22.2	15.2	5.1	3.9	5.4	6.9	6.4	6.4	•
Total Liabilities to Net Worth 37	1.5	•	1.3	10.4	1.8	2.0	3.5	2.1	1.8	1.5	2.4	1.2	•
Current Assets to Working Capital 38	4.7	•	100.8	2.4	•	•	13.8	6.7	3.6	9.0	2.4	3.3	•
Current Liabilities to Working Capital 39	3.7	•	99.8	1.4	•	•	12.8	5.7	2.6	8.0	1.4	2.3	•
Working Capital to Net Sales 40	0.1	•	0.0	0.0	•	•	0.0	0.1	0.1	0.0	0.1	0.1	•
Inventory to Working Capital 41	0.2	•	•	•	•	•	0.0	0.2	0.1	0.2	0.2	0.2	•
Total Receipts to Cash Flow 42	3.2	13.0	2.5	6.1	2.0	24.3	4.0	4.5	2.4	5.0	3.8	2.3	•
Cost of Goods to Cash Flow 43	1.3	8.1	0.0	3.2	0.1	16.2	2.1	1.6	0.8	2.5	1.6	0.8	•
Cash Flow to Total Debt 44	0.4	3.3	0.6	0.6	0.6	0.1	0.3	0.2	0.5	0.2	0.2	0.5	•

Selected Financial Factors (in Percentages)

Debt Ratio 45	60.6	•	57.2	91.2	64.6	67.1	77.9	67.6	63.9	59.6	70.7	55.0	•
Return on Total Assets 46	8.5	•	26.7	14.6	14.2	5.0	10.9	5.6	13.0	7.2	7.1	7.6	•
Return on Equity Before Income Taxes 47	15.7	•	55.9	121.7	34.6	1.6	38.9	12.4	29.8	12.8	11.3	12.7	•
Return on Equity After Income Taxes 48	13.1	•	55.9	121.7	32.7	•	34.1	11.8	21.5	10.8	8.1	10.8	•
Profit Margin (Before Income Tax) 49	7.8	2.2	5.1	3.2	16.2	0.3	8.5	6.2	15.2	7.6	5.1	10.0	•
Profit Margin (After Income Tax) 50	6.5	0.9	5.1	3.2	15.3	•	7.4	6.0	11.0	6.4	3.7	8.5	•

241

Table II

Corporations with Net Income

WATER TRANSPORTATION

MONEY AMOUNTS AND SIZE OF ASSETS IN THOUSANDS OF DOLLARS

Item Description for Accounting Period 7/05 Through 6/06		Total	Zero Assets	Under 500	500 to 1,000	1,000 to 5,000	5,000 to 10,000	10,000 to 25,000	25,000 to 50,000	50,000 to 100,000	100,000 to 250,000	250,000 to 500,000	500,000 to 2,500,000	2,500,000 and over
Number of Enterprises	1	2273	281	786	552	436	87	62	19	18	·	·	·	0
Revenues ($ in Thousands)														
Net Sales	2	18294643	1083096	97909	1439098	1035403	381681	1052486	452326	966926	·	·	·	0
Interest	3	88173	788	0	0	1049	578	1983	352	4040	·	·	·	0
Rents	4	104851	36	0	0	3070	203	1159	1358	4861	·	·	·	0
Royalties	5	422	420	0	0	0	0	0	0	0	·	·	·	0
Other Portfolio Income	6	786617	22796	0	0	17955	16301	55203	2000	73920	·	·	·	0
Other Receipts	7	501999	2779	103880	0	18854	9516	24537	6113	11805	·	·	·	0
Total Receipts	8	19776705	1109915	201789	1439098	1076331	408279	1135368	462149	1061552	·	·	·	0
Average Total Receipts	9	8701	3950	257	2607	2469	4693	18312	24324	58975	·	·	·	·
Operating Costs/Operating Income (%)														
Cost of Operations	10	39.2	69.9	·	58.9	3.3	67.3	46.5	35.9	31.1	·	·	·	·
Salaries and Wages	11	10.1	5.7	2.1	11.3	24.5	6.1	12.1	18.7	11.4	·	·	·	·
Taxes Paid	12	1.7	0.7	6.7	0.8	3.1	1.2	2.3	3.7	2.5	·	·	·	·
Interest Paid	13	2.3	1.0	0.3	1.0	2.6	0.7	2.5	2.0	2.5	·	·	·	·
Depreciation	14	6.2	2.5	0.1	4.4	7.7	1.6	5.8	6.6	6.6	·	·	·	·
Amortization and Depletion	15	0.2	0.0	0.0	·	0.0	0.3	0.0	0.1	0.1	·	·	·	·
Pensions and Other Deferred Comp.	16	0.7	0.1	14.7	·	0.1	0.2	0.2	0.8	0.7	·	·	·	·
Employee Benefits	17	1.7	0.3	0.1	0.1	0.2	0.8	1.9	2.7	2.3	·	·	·	·
Advertising	18	0.3	2.6	·	0.2	0.1	0.1	0.2	0.6	0.1	·	·	·	·
Other Expenses	19	32.6	10.0	86.5	13.6	43.4	10.1	22.4	20.4	32.8	·	·	·	·
Officers' Compensation	20	1.9	0.2	52.8	3.5	2.7	1.2	3.0	2.1	1.5	·	·	·	·
Operating Margin	21	3.0	6.8	·	6.3	12.4	10.5	3.1	6.4	8.3	·	·	·	·
Operating Margin Before Officers' Comp.	22	4.9	7.1	·	9.7	15.1	11.7	6.2	8.5	9.8	·	·	·	·

Selected Average Balance Sheet ($ in Thousands)

Net Receivables 23	1114	0	2	0	139	966	3825	7614	12476
Inventories 24	99	0	0	0	1	45	69	158	1013
Net Property, Plant and Equipment 25	5153	0	0	344	1186	4797	6072	18284	33694
Total Assets 26	10224	0	44	584	2254	7493	15566	31312	68950
Notes and Loans Payable 27	3434	0	8	347	1477	2267	6175	13291	24632
All Other Liabilities 28	2208	0	1	103	419	1391	5320	8444	15466
Net Worth 29	4582	0	36	134	358	3835	4071	9577	28851

Selected Financial Ratios (Times to 1)

Current Ratio 30	1.5	•	34.3	1.3	0.4	1.0	1.1	1.4	1.5
Quick Ratio 31	1.2	•	34.3	1.0	0.4	0.9	0.8	1.2	1.3
Net Sales to Working Capital 32	9.1	10.7	6.8	46.6	•	•	19.9	7.6	6.7
Coverage Ratio 33	6.1	10.7	140.4	7.5	7.3	24.6	5.4	5.2	8.0
Total Asset Turnover 34	0.8	•	2.8	4.5	1.1	0.6	1.1	0.8	0.8
Inventory Turnover 35	31.8	•	•	•	114.0	64.9	114.9	54.0	16.5
Receivables Turnover 36	7.7	•	154.4	•	23.7	4.6	5.5	4.6	5.8
Total Liabilities to Net Worth 37	1.2	•	0.2	3.3	5.3	1.0	2.8	2.3	1.4
Current Assets to Working Capital 38	2.9	•	1.0	4.0	•	•	8.9	3.7	3.0
Current Liabilities to Working Capital 39	1.9	•	0.0	3.0	•	•	7.9	2.7	2.0
Working Capital to Net Sales 40	0.1	•	0.1	0.0	•	•	0.1	0.1	0.1
Inventory to Working Capital 41	0.1	•	•	•	•	•	0.0	0.1	0.1
Total Receipts to Cash Flow 42	2.7	5.8	0.8	6.7	2.0	4.7	3.4	4.4	2.3
Cost of Goods to Cash Flow 43	1.1	4.0	•	3.9	0.1	3.2	1.6	1.6	0.7
Cash Flow to Total Debt 44	0.5	•	18.6	0.9	0.6	0.3	0.4	0.2	0.6

Selected Financial Factors (in Percentages)

Debt Ratio 45	55.2	•	19.5	77.0	84.1	48.8	73.8	69.4	58.2
Return on Total Assets 46	10.8	•	122.3	32.3	20.0	10.7	14.6	8.0	15.9
Return on Equity Before Income Taxes 47	20.2	•	150.8	121.6	108.6	20.0	45.6	21.2	33.3
Return on Equity After Income Taxes 48	17.5	•	150.8	121.6	102.6	17.3	40.3	20.4	24.4
Profit Margin (Before Income Tax) 49	11.5	9.3	43.0	6.3	16.4	17.5	10.9	8.5	17.9
Profit Margin (After Income Tax) 50	10.0	7.6	43.0	6.3	15.1	15.5	9.7	8.2	13.1

Table I

Corporations with and without Net Income

TRUCK TRANSPORTATION

MONEY AMOUNTS AND SIZE OF ASSETS IN THOUSANDS OF DOLLARS

Item Description for Accounting Period 7/05 Through 6/06	Total	Zero Assets	Under 500	500 to 1,000	1,000 to 5,000	5,000 to 10,000	10,000 to 25,000	25,000 to 50,000	50,000 to 100,000	100,000 to 250,000	250,000 to 500,000	500,000 to 2,500,000	2,500,000 and over
Number of Enterprises **1**	100026	18848	68740	5818	4977	899	463	124	71	45	20	21	0
Revenues ($ in Thousands)													
Net Sales **2**	213804445	5535381	36313042	15801461	36176254	13449002	18876410	11111948	9110411	10908536	11033981	45448020	0
Interest **3**	415720	13627	3272	5513	15034	13474	10682	18090	5491	19138	13558	297840	0
Rents **4**	387688	1965	1765	4986	29656	4789	19388	41664	31305	35522	32933	183715	0
Royalties **5**	206298	0	0	0	103	41445	102	6	0	0	19442	145200	0
Other Portfolio Income **6**	1880120	87885	153492	192008	256743	215977	193935	75527	116371	148805	110540	328835	0
Other Receipts **7**	3080325	19839	273962	41721	250818	71680	194900	160095	30152	261264	267465	1508431	0
Total Receipts **8**	219774596	5658897	36745533	16045689	36728608	13796367	19295417	11407330	9293730	11373265	11477919	47952041	0
Average Total Receipts **9**	2197	300	535	2758	7380	15346	41675	91995	130898	252739	573896	2283431	•
Operating Costs/Operating Income (%)													
Cost of Operations **10**	34.4	18.3	38.0	36.5	40.2	28.5	47.5	44.5	29.7	26.9	30.2	25.7	•
Salaries and Wages **11**	17.4	24.3	12.7	14.3	13.1	21.5	12.3	14.9	21.7	17.8	18.3	25.0	•
Taxes Paid **12**	3.8	4.3	3.5	3.7	3.0	4.1	3.5	3.0	4.6	3.6	4.4	4.7	•
Interest Paid **13**	1.0	1.3	0.7	1.0	0.9	1.0	1.0	1.2	1.4	1.6	1.2	1.1	•
Depreciation **14**	4.2	4.7	3.5	4.7	3.6	4.5	3.9	4.4	5.5	4.7	6.2	4.0	•
Amortization and Depletion **15**	0.1	0.4	0.0	0.0	0.1	0.0	0.1	0.2	0.1	0.2	0.2	0.2	•
Pensions and Other Deferred Comp. **16**	0.5	1.1	0.1	0.2	0.3	0.4	0.2	0.2	0.2	0.6	0.8	1.1	•
Employee Benefits **17**	2.6	2.7	1.0	1.1	2.0	1.4	2.0	1.5	3.3	2.2	2.8	5.6	•
Advertising **18**	0.2	0.2	0.2	0.3	0.2	0.3	0.2	0.2	0.2	0.2	0.2	0.2	•
Other Expenses **19**	33.6	38.8	36.5	35.5	33.2	34.0	27.4	28.9	30.9	42.6	33.9	32.1	•
Officers' Compensation **20**	1.7	2.3	3.1	2.9	2.1	1.9	1.3	1.1	0.8	0.6	0.5	0.5	•
Operating Margin **21**	0.6	1.7	0.7	•	1.1	2.2	0.7	•	1.5	1.2	1.3	•	•
Operating Margin Before Officers' Comp. **22**	2.2	4.0	3.7	2.8	3.2	4.1	2.0	0.9	2.3	1.8	1.8	0.5	•

Selected Average Balance Sheet ($ in Thousands)

Net Receivables 23	349497	68387	37467	14627	9976	4398	1785	661	134	11	211
Inventories 24	9409	1793	1159	1289	315	231	57	19	11	2	8
Net Property, Plant and Equipment 25	578368	190992	69872	38891	16864	6791	3058	939	361	48	399
Total Assets 26	1550208	343056	149976	69899	34108	14989	6911	2253	728	85	898
Notes and Loans Payable 27	443861	113812	59438	31828	16523	6741	3155	1080	467	70	374
All Other Liabilities 28	521648	99012	42978	17432	8757	3651	1227	443	115	19	241
Net Worth 29	584699	130232	47560	20639	8827	4597	2529	730	146	-4	282

Selected Financial Ratios (Times to 1)

Current Ratio 30	1.2	1.2	1.2	1.1	1.1	1.2	1.3	1.4	1.2	•	1.2
Quick Ratio 31	1.0	0.9	1.0	0.8	1.0	0.9	1.1	1.2	1.0	•	1.0
Net Sales to Working Capital 32	22.6	30.7	24.7	70.7	61.6	42.0	21.0	22.0	34.3	104.2	32.1
Coverage Ratio 33	5.6	5.4	3.0	3.6	3.1	4.0	5.6	3.8	2.5	3.5	4.2
Total Asset Turnover 34	1.4	1.6	1.6	1.8	2.6	2.7	2.2	3.2	3.7	6.2	2.4
Inventory Turnover 35	59.1	92.9	56.3	29.6	126.3	83.6	75.1	151.0	90.6	119.4	86.5
Receivables Turnover 36	6.4	9.3	7.2	9.2	10.0	10.2	9.7	11.5	22.1	44.5	10.8
Total Liabilities to Net Worth 37	1.7	1.6	2.2	2.4	2.9	2.3	1.7	2.1	4.0	•	2.2
Current Assets to Working Capital 38	5.6	5.8	5.5	13.0	9.6	6.9	4.2	3.2	3.4	6.0	5.1
Current Liabilities to Working Capital 39	4.6	4.8	4.5	12.0	8.6	5.9	3.2	2.2	2.4	5.0	4.1
Working Capital to Net Sales 40	0.0	0.0	0.0	0.0	0.0	0.0	0.0	0.0	0.0	0.0	0.0
Inventory to Working Capital 41	0.1	0.1	0.2	0.2	0.7	0.2	0.3	0.1	0.2	0.4	0.1
Total Receipts to Cash Flow 42	3.1	3.4	3.1	3.9	4.5	5.0	3.7	3.4	3.4	2.9	3.5
Cost of Goods to Cash Flow 43	0.8	1.0	0.8	1.2	2.0	2.4	1.0	1.2	1.3	0.5	1.2
Cash Flow to Total Debt 44	0.7	0.8	0.8	0.7	0.8	0.8	0.9	1.4	1.4	1.7	1.0

Selected Financial Factors (in Percentages)

Debt Ratio 45	62.3	62.0	68.3	70.5	74.1	69.3	63.4	67.6	80.0	104.9	68.6
Return on Total Assets 46	9.0	10.5	8.1	9.0	9.9	10.5	12.7	11.4	8.8	16.2	10.5
Return on Equity Before Income Taxes 47	19.6	22.6	17.1	21.9	25.8	25.7	28.5	25.9	26.2	•	25.6
Return on Equity After Income Taxes 48	13.1	19.0	13.3	19.5	22.1	23.1	25.5	23.9	23.2	•	20.9
Profit Margin (Before Income Tax) 49	5.3	5.3	3.5	2.5	2.9	4.8	2.6	1.4	1.8	3.9	3.4
Profit Margin (After Income Tax) 50	3.5	4.5	3.1	2.2	2.6	4.3	2.4	1.2	1.8	3.5	2.8

Table II
Corporations with Net Income

TRUCK TRANSPORTATION

MONEY AMOUNTS AND SIZE OF ASSETS IN THOUSANDS OF DOLLARS

Item Description for Accounting Period 7/05 Through 6/06	Total	Zero Assets	Under 500	500 to 1,000	1,000 to 5,000	5,000 to 10,000	10,000 to 25,000	25,000 to 50,000	50,000 to 100,000	100,000 to 250,000	250,000 to 500,000	500,000 to 2,500,000	2,500,000 and over
Number of Enterprises **1**	65390	12364	44143	3429	4069	787	360	104	59	37	·	·	0

Revenues ($ in Thousands)

	Total	Zero Assets	Under 500	500 to 1,000	1,000 to 5,000	5,000 to 10,000	10,000 to 25,000	25,000 to 50,000	50,000 to 100,000	100,000 to 250,000	250,000 to 500,000	500,000 to 2,500,000	2,500,000 and over
Net Sales **2**	175348501	22056281	3664123	10873689	30748787	11782093	15235260	9462830	7865793	9184568	·	·	0
Interest **3**	399395	13415	1752	4662	13625	12375	8115	16268	3867	18284	·	·	0
Rents **4**	338481	1817	241	4986	26898	4428	10494	39121	30319	35522	·	·	0
Royalties **5**	206298	0	0	0	103	41445	102	6	0	0	·	·	0
Other Portfolio Income **6**	1631825	54228	128599	104505	231601	209876	170110	58653	107167	133616	·	·	0
Other Receipts **7**	2897837	18904	202134	33493	210674	50380	177820	150619	32966	249542	·	·	0
Total Receipts **8**	180822337	3752487	22389007	11021335	31231688	12100597	15601901	9727497	8040112	9621532	·	·	·
Average Total Receipts **9**	2765	304	507	3214	7676	15376	43339	93534	136273	260041	·	·	·

Operating Costs/Operating Income (%)

	Total	Zero Assets	Under 500	500 to 1,000	1,000 to 5,000	5,000 to 10,000	10,000 to 25,000	25,000 to 50,000	50,000 to 100,000	100,000 to 250,000	250,000 to 500,000	500,000 to 2,500,000	2,500,000 and over
Cost of Operations **10**	33.0	15.8	32.5	36.2	39.4	29.7	45.8	44.2	29.7	28.3	·	·	·
Salaries and Wages **11**	17.5	27.2	12.0	14.3	12.2	21.8	11.9	14.7	20.2	16.0	·	·	·
Taxes Paid **12**	3.8	5.2	3.4	3.4	2.8	4.0	3.4	2.9	4.6	3.3	·	·	·
Interest Paid **13**	1.0	1.0	0.7	0.8	0.9	1.0	0.9	1.0	1.2	1.7	·	·	·
Depreciation **14**	4.0	4.8	3.2	4.2	3.6	4.0	3.9	3.7	5.3	4.4	·	·	·
Amortization and Depletion **15**	0.1	0.0	0.0	0.0	0.1	0.0	0.1	0.1	0.1	0.2	·	·	·
Pensions and Other Deferred Comp. **16**	0.5	1.6	0.1	0.3	0.3	0.4	0.2	0.2	0.2	0.6	·	·	·
Employee Benefits **17**	2.7	3.1	1.0	1.2	1.7	1.5	1.8	1.5	3.3	2.0	·	·	·
Advertising **18**	0.2	0.2	0.3	0.3	0.2	0.3	0.2	0.2	0.2	0.2	·	·	·
Other Expenses **19**	33.6	33.0	38.3	34.6	34.4	32.0	28.7	29.7	31.7	42.8	·	·	·
Officers' Compensation **20**	1.6	1.8	3.5	2.8	2.1	2.0	1.3	1.0	0.8	0.6	·	·	·
Operating Margin **21**	1.9	6.3	5.2	1.8	2.2	3.1	1.8	0.7	2.5	0.1	·	·	·
Operating Margin Before Officers' Comp. **22**	3.5	8.2	8.7	4.6	4.4	5.1	3.1	1.8	3.4	0.6	·	·	·

Selected Average Balance Sheet ($ in Thousands)

Net Receivables 23	286	0	9	131	693	1839	4602	10671	15384	38243
Inventories 24	10	0	2	12	16	48	181	319	1429	993
Net Property, Plant and Equipment 25	515	0	40	374	905	2858	6982	15723	39888	67514
Total Assets 26	1187	0	80	723	2265	6937	15314	34067	70921	151595
Notes and Loans Payable 27	444	0	56	435	1054	2950	6458	14430	30806	56700
All Other Liabilities 28	319	0	11	103	439	1136	3735	9264	16797	44114
Net Worth 29	423	0	14	184	773	2851	5121	10373	23318	50781

Selected Financial Ratios (Times to 1)

Current Ratio 30	1.3	•	1.8	1.4	1.5	1.5	1.2	1.2	1.2	1.3
Quick Ratio 31	1.1	•	1.5	1.2	1.2	1.3	1.0	1.0	0.9	1.1
Net Sales to Working Capital 32	25.5	•	37.5	40.3	21.6	14.4	31.2	34.5	41.5	19.0
Coverage Ratio 33	6.1	9.5	11.2	5.2	5.3	7.1	5.8	4.4	5.0	3.9
Total Asset Turnover 34	2.3	•	6.2	4.4	3.3	2.2	2.8	2.7	1.9	1.6
Inventory Turnover 35	86.2	•	80.1	92.6	186.5	92.7	107.4	125.9	27.7	70.8
Receivables Turnover 36	10.4	•	45.8	22.6	12.0	10.0	11.0	11.1	9.9	7.9
Total Liabilities to Net Worth 37	1.8	•	4.9	2.9	1.9	1.4	2.0	2.3	2.0	2.0
Current Assets to Working Capital 38	4.3	•	2.3	3.4	3.1	3.0	5.2	5.7	7.6	4.2
Current Liabilities to Working Capital 39	3.3	•	1.3	2.4	2.1	2.0	4.2	4.7	6.6	3.2
Working Capital to Net Sales 40	0.0	•	0.0	0.0	0.0	0.1	0.0	0.0	0.0	0.1
Inventory to Working Capital 41	0.1	•	0.2	0.2	0.0	0.1	0.1	0.1	0.4	0.1
Total Receipts to Cash Flow 42	3.3	2.8	2.8	3.4	3.1	3.7	4.6	4.3	3.7	3.0
Cost of Goods to Cash Flow 43	1.1	0.4	0.9	1.2	1.2	1.1	2.1	1.9	1.1	0.8
Cash Flow to Total Debt 44	1.1	•	2.7	1.7	1.6	1.0	0.9	0.9	0.8	0.8

Selected Financial Factors (in Percentages)

Debt Ratio 45	64.4	•	83.1	74.5	65.9	58.9	66.6	69.6	67.1	66.5
Return on Total Assets 46	13.6	•	45.8	17.1	15.7	14.7	14.1	12.1	11.1	10.6
Return on Equity Before Income Taxes 47	31.9	•	246.8	54.3	37.2	30.7	34.8	30.7	27.0	23.6
Return on Equity After Income Taxes 48	27.2	•	242.5	50.3	35.0	27.6	31.8	27.0	24.4	19.2
Profit Margin (Before Income Tax) 49	5.0	8.7	6.7	3.2	3.8	5.8	4.2	3.5	4.7	4.8
Profit Margin (After Income Tax) 50	4.3	8.0	6.6	2.9	3.6	5.2	3.8	3.1	4.3	3.9

Table I

Corporations with and without Net Income

TRANSIT AND GROUND PASSENGER TRANSPORTATION

MONEY AMOUNTS AND SIZE OF ASSETS IN THOUSANDS OF DOLLARS

Item Description for Accounting Period 7/05 Through 6/06	Total	Zero Assets	Under 500	500 to 1,000	1,000 to 5,000	5,000 to 10,000	10,000 to 25,000	25,000 to 50,000	50,000 to 100,000	100,000 to 250,000	250,000 to 500,000	500,000 to 2,500,000	2,500,000 and over
Number of Enterprises **1**	26105	3656	19450	1510	1201	153	110	8	6	7	0	3	0
Revenues ($ in Thousands)													
Net Sales **2**	24246733	278128	3697111	1416836	6300017	1866247	2607504	287348	427701	2043235	0	5322607	0
Interest **3**	235451	98	1410	293	2984	763	2817	420	500	57492	0	168675	0
Rents **4**	26160	0	12	0	3555	1508	505	4667	76	12071	0	3767	0
Royalties **5**	13	0	0	0	0	0	0	0	0	13	0	0	0
Other Portfolio Income **6**	242713	8820	58678	7638	55130	65863	13605	574	533	12437	0	19435	0
Other Receipts **7**	492151	1836	8687	12462	38926	3840	28206	15667	19878	7854	0	354793	0
Total Receipts **8**	25243221	288882	3765898	1437229	6400612	1938221	2652637	308676	448688	2133102	0	5869277	0
Average Total Receipts **9**	967	79	194	952	5329	12668	24115	38584	74781	304729	•	1956426	•
Operating Costs/Operating Income (%)													
Cost of Operations **10**	32.1	32.6	15.5	55.0	33.0	60.3	43.6	10.7	50.7	34.3	•	19.6	•
Salaries and Wages **11**	21.7	21.9	30.5	14.5	16.6	4.7	17.4	34.2	11.8	26.3	•	29.9	•
Taxes Paid **12**	4.4	2.2	3.9	2.5	3.5	5.0	4.1	6.9	4.2	5.9	•	5.7	•
Interest Paid **13**	3.2	•	2.3	2.9	1.3	2.1	1.3	1.4	2.2	6.6	•	6.5	•
Depreciation **14**	5.6	5.5	5.4	5.0	4.4	8.5	5.7	5.7	6.9	4.3	•	6.6	•
Amortization and Depletion **15**	0.6	•	0.6	1.4	0.1	0.0	0.1	0.5	0.5	1.0	•	1.2	•
Pensions and Other Deferred Comp. **16**	0.8	0.0	0.0	0.1	0.5	0.4	1.0	1.0	0.5	0.8	•	2.0	•
Employee Benefits **17**	1.9	0.2	0.4	0.9	0.8	0.9	3.4	5.6	2.9	5.9	•	2.5	•
Advertising **18**	0.6	1.7	0.8	0.2	0.7	0.3	0.6	0.3	0.6	0.3	•	0.5	•
Other Expenses **19**	30.2	47.4	33.9	16.9	34.9	16.8	19.2	30.8	20.1	20.9	•	39.0	•
Officers' Compensation **20**	2.2	1.3	5.4	2.5	3.2	1.2	1.6	0.7	1.1	0.3	•	0.2	•
Operating Margin **21**	•	•	1.3	•	0.8	•	2.1	2.1	•	•	•	•	•
Operating Margin Before Officers' Comp. **22**	•	•	6.6	0.6	4.0	0.9	3.7	2.8	•	•	•	•	•

Selected Average Balance Sheet ($ in Thousands)

Net Receivables 23	72	0	9	72	325	1495	2357	8255	5156	30421	133368
Inventories 24	5	0	0	2	9	90	88	997	2572	1678	20108
Net Property, Plant and Equipment 25	224	0	23	185	942	4350	6170	10579	28604	80065	608982
Total Assets 26	558	0	88	670	1902	6731	14171	34122	64495	226657	1575924
Notes and Loans Payable 27	261	0	74	457	1166	5328	5027	13259	29099	117753	265523
All Other Liabilities 28	103	0	11	42	316	818	3353	4979	11976	56005	351619
Net Worth 29	194	0	3	171	421	584	5791	15884	23421	52898	958782

Selected Financial Ratios (Times to 1)

Current Ratio 30	1.2	•	1.6	1.1	1.2	0.8	1.5	2.1	1.1	0.9	1.2
Quick Ratio 31	0.8	•	1.2	0.9	0.8	0.7	1.0	2.0	0.7	0.6	0.6
Net Sales to Working Capital 32	35.8	•	23.9	75.5	43.6	•	11.7	4.7	44.1	•	29.5
Coverage Ratio 33	1.3	•	2.4	0.8	2.8	2.7	3.9	8.0	2.6	0.7	0.5
Total Asset Turnover 34	1.7	•	2.2	1.4	2.8	1.8	1.7	1.1	1.1	1.3	1.1
Inventory Turnover 35	58.2	•	570.6	226.7	202.1	81.8	117.7	3.9	14.1	59.6	17.3
Receivables Turnover 36	12.2	•	21.6	24.3	11.7	10.6	13.2	4.3	8.1	11.1	9.9
Total Liabilities to Net Worth 37	1.9	•	24.6	2.9	3.5	10.5	1.4	1.1	1.8	3.3	0.6
Current Assets to Working Capital 38	6.7	•	2.8	11.2	6.1	•	3.1	1.9	9.7	•	7.6
Current Liabilities to Working Capital 39	5.7	•	1.8	10.2	5.1	•	2.1	0.9	8.7	•	6.6
Working Capital to Net Sales 40	0.0	•	0.0	0.0	0.0	•	0.1	0.2	0.0	•	0.0
Inventory to Working Capital 41	0.2	•	0.0	0.2	0.0	•	0.0	0.0	1.9	•	0.3
Total Receipts to Cash Flow 42	4.2	3.5	3.2	11.2	3.7	9.7	5.8	2.9	6.1	9.5	3.2
Cost of Goods to Cash Flow 43	1.4	1.1	0.5	6.1	1.2	5.8	2.5	0.3	3.1	3.2	0.6
Cash Flow to Total Debt 44	0.6	•	0.7	0.2	1.0	0.2	0.5	0.7	0.3	0.2	0.9

Selected Financial Factors (in Percentages)

Debt Ratio 45	65.2	•	96.1	74.5	77.9	91.3	59.1	53.5	63.7	76.7	39.2
Return on Total Assets 46	6.9	•	11.6	3.4	10.3	10.2	8.4	11.4	6.3	6.2	3.5
Return on Equity Before Income Taxes 47	4.5	•	173.0	•	29.9	73.9	15.4	21.5	10.6	•	•
Return on Equity After Income Taxes 48	3.5	•	159.2	•	28.3	71.4	11.8	21.5	10.3	•	•
Profit Margin (Before Income Tax) 49	0.9	•	3.1	•	2.4	3.5	3.8	9.5	3.5	•	•
Profit Margin (After Income Tax) 50	0.7	•	2.9	•	2.3	3.4	2.9	9.5	3.4	•	•

Table II

Corporations with Net Income

TRANSIT AND GROUND PASSENGER TRANSPORTATION

MONEY AMOUNTS AND SIZE OF ASSETS IN THOUSANDS OF DOLLARS

Item Description for Accounting Period 7/05 Through 6/06	Total	Zero Assets	Under 500	500 to 1,000	1,000 to 5,000	5,000 to 10,000	10,000 to 25,000	25,000 to 50,000	50,000 to 100,000	100,000 to 250,000	250,000 to 500,000	500,000 to 2,500,000	2,500,000 and over
Number of Enterprises 1	13325	•	10344	727	786	113	93	•	•	4	0	0	0
Revenues ($ in Thousands)													
Net Sales 2	13962051	•	2619961	360407	4833307	1708545	2293212	•	•	1392002	•	•	•
Interest 3	11255	•	879	24	2255	763	1875	•	•	4502	•	•	•
Rents 4	21349	•	0	0	3555	1508	505	•	•	11039	•	•	•
Royalties 5	0	•	0	0	0	0	0	•	•	0	•	•	•
Other Portfolio Income 6	173196	•	27965	3665	47272	65863	6316	•	•	12251	•	•	•
Other Receipts 7	103300	•	-5	9843	27204	2225	25455	•	•	2730	•	•	•
Total Receipts 8	14271151	•	2648800	373939	4913593	1778904	2327363	•	•	1422524	•	•	•
Average Total Receipts 9	1071	•	256	514	6251	15743	25025	•	•	355631	•	•	•
Operating Costs/Operating Income (%)													
Cost of Operations 10	35.1	•	17.5	39.9	37.8	60.5	42.1	•	•	19.2	•	•	•
Salaries and Wages 11	21.5	•	34.6	12.5	17.2	5.1	19.3	•	•	35.8	•	•	•
Taxes Paid 12	4.4	•	3.8	3.3	3.7	5.3	4.4	•	•	6.2	•	•	•
Interest Paid 13	1.6	•	1.6	5.9	1.0	1.1	1.1	•	•	3.6	•	•	•
Depreciation 14	4.7	•	3.5	5.0	4.4	7.0	4.8	•	•	4.4	•	•	•
Amortization and Depletion 15	0.2	•	0.1	0.6	0.0	0.0	0.1	•	•	1.1	•	•	•
Pensions and Other Deferred Comp. 16	0.6	•	0.0	0.0	0.6	0.4	1.1	•	•	0.7	•	•	•
Employee Benefits 17	1.8	•	0.4	0.4	0.9	0.9	3.4	•	•	5.3	•	•	•
Advertising 18	0.5	•	0.3	0.4	0.8	0.3	0.3	•	•	0.1	•	•	•
Other Expenses 19	23.5	•	24.6	23.7	26.9	17.2	17.7	•	•	23.8	•	•	•
Officers' Compensation 20	3.1	•	5.4	5.4	4.1	1.0	1.7	•	•	0.5	•	•	•
Operating Margin 21	3.2	•	8.0	2.9	2.6	1.1	3.9	•	•	•	•	•	•
Operating Margin Before Officers' Comp. 22	6.3	•	13.5	8.3	6.7	2.2	5.7	•	•	•	•	•	•

Selected Average Balance Sheet ($ in Thousands)

Net Receivables 23	86	•	12	12	375	2000	2464	•	40725
Inventories 24	3	•	0	3	7	79	58	•	1482
Net Property, Plant and Equipment 25	193	•	16	229	912	3610	5424	•	99623
Total Assets 26	496	•	87	606	2068	6716	13632	•	258590
Notes and Loans Payable 27	263	•	62	448	952	4840	4250	•	146149
All Other Liabilities 28	90	•	7	35	375	1087	3530	•	63822
Net Worth 29	144	•	18	123	741	789	5852	•	48618

Selected Financial Ratios (Times to 1)

Current Ratio 30	1.4	•	2.7	0.6	1.5	0.8	1.6	•	1.1
Quick Ratio 31	1.0	•	1.9	0.3	1.1	0.7	1.1	•	1.0
Net Sales to Working Capital 32	20.8	•	15.0	•	19.3	•	10.0	•	52.7
Coverage Ratio 33	4.5	•	6.7	2.1	5.2	5.9	6.0	•	1.5
Total Asset Turnover 34	2.1	•	2.9	0.8	3.0	2.3	1.8	•	1.3
Inventory Turnover 35	125.3	•	742.5	62.7	332.7	116.5	180.1	•	45.1
Receivables Turnover 36	13.0	•	23.6	82.9	11.5	10.3	14.0	•	17.1
Total Liabilities to Net Worth 37	2.4	•	4.0	3.9	1.8	7.5	1.3	•	4.3
Current Assets to Working Capital 38	3.5	•	1.6	•	2.8	•	2.6	•	9.0
Current Liabilities to Working Capital 39	2.5	•	0.6	•	1.8	•	1.6	•	8.0
Working Capital to Net Sales 40	0.0	•	0.1	•	0.1	•	0.1	•	0.0
Inventory to Working Capital 41	0.1	•	0.0	•	0.0	•	0.0	•	0.2
Total Receipts to Cash Flow 42	4.7	•	3.4	5.0	4.6	8.2	5.6	•	6.5
Cost of Goods to Cash Flow 43	1.7	•	0.6	2.0	1.7	5.0	2.4	•	1.3
Cash Flow to Total Debt 44	0.6	•	1.1	0.2	1.0	0.3	0.6	•	0.3

Selected Financial Factors (in Percentages)

Debt Ratio 45	71.0	•	79.9	79.8	64.1	88.3	57.1	•	81.2
Return on Total Assets 46	14.8	•	31.2	10.3	15.7	14.3	11.6	•	7.3
Return on Equity Before Income Taxes 47	39.6	•	131.8	27.1	35.3	100.9	22.6	•	12.7
Return on Equity After Income Taxes 48	37.0	•	126.8	26.6	34.0	98.4	18.4	•	8.9
Profit Margin (Before Income Tax) 49	5.5	•	9.1	6.7	4.3	5.3	5.4	•	1.8
Profit Margin (After Income Tax) 50	5.1	•	8.8	6.6	4.1	5.1	4.4	•	1.2

Table I

Corporations with and without Net Income

PIPELINE TRANSPORTATION

MONEY AMOUNTS AND SIZE OF ASSETS IN THOUSANDS OF DOLLARS

Item Description for Accounting Period 7/05 Through 6/06	Total	Zero Assets	Under 500	500 to 1,000	1,000 to 5,000	5,000 to 10,000	10,000 to 25,000	25,000 to 50,000	50,000 to 100,000	100,000 to 250,000	250,000 to 500,000	500,000 to 2,500,000	2,500,000 and over
Number of Enterprises 1	410	5	0	3	320	32	15	12	6	4	6	8	0
Revenues ($ in Thousands)													
Net Sales 2	6118827	50315	0	44316	1048261	199151	119720	1213188	305894	94233	549206	2494544	0
Interest 3	50000	1500	0	0	881	1228	741	681	1212	4942	1600	37215	0
Rents 4	8841	0	0	0	0	1203	0	93	19	5602	0	1924	0
Royalties 5	1959	0	0	0	1959	0	0	0	0	0	0	0	0
Other Portfolio Income 6	152738	7295	0	0	2572	29	1	26656	0	191	65525	50468	0
Other Receipts 7	274107	623	0	0	25156	12321	11489	5644	4803	10169	35421	168481	0
Total Receipts 8	6606472	59733	0	44316	1078829	213932	131951	1246262	311928	115137	651752	2752632	0
Average Total Receipts 9	16113	11947	·	14772	3371	6685	8797	103855	51988	28784	108625	344079	·
Operating Costs/Operating Income (%)													
Cost of Operations 10	42.6	0.0	·	·	62.1	36.7	23.3	59.0	21.2	9.7	10.0	40.5	·
Salaries and Wages 11	7.5	1.2	·	20.0	8.8	6.7	5.7	2.8	22.9	8.5	3.7	8.2	·
Taxes Paid 12	3.7	4.3	·	2.1	1.9	4.8	4.6	1.2	8.4	6.0	4.0	4.9	·
Interest Paid 13	7.2	·	·	·	0.2	0.0	2.3	0.4	1.1	20.3	9.4	14.2	·
Depreciation 14	8.4	19.2	·	0.9	2.8	7.7	5.1	1.3	3.5	21.7	13.5	13.2	·
Amortization and Depletion 15	0.7	0.2	·	·	1.4	0.0	0.1	0.1	0.1	0.0	0.6	0.9	·
Pensions and Other Deferred Comp. 16	0.4	·	·	0.5	·	·	·	0.2	1.0	2.2	0.7	0.6	·
Employee Benefits 17	1.2	0.5	·	3.5	0.1	0.6	1.0	0.6	7.0	·	0.4	1.6	·
Advertising 18	0.0	·	·	·	0.2	0.0	·	0.0	0.0	0.0	0.0	0.0	·
Other Expenses 19	22.4	82.9	·	56.4	13.1	29.7	30.6	28.4	19.1	20.8	39.7	17.4	·
Officers' Compensation 20	0.6	·	·	2.1	2.1	0.9	0.3	0.4	0.2	·	0.1	0.4	·
Operating Margin 21	5.2	·	·	16.6	7.4	12.8	27.1	5.6	15.4	10.6	17.9	·	·
Operating Margin Before Officers' Comp. 22	5.8	·	·	16.6	9.5	13.8	27.3	6.0	15.6	10.6	18.1	·	·

Selected Average Balance Sheet ($ in Thousands)

Net Receivables 23	4574	0	•	428	413	613	983	11449	6849	7046	56094	145552 •
Inventories 24	535	0	•	5003	63	57	409	3518	142	334	2558	15800 •
Net Property, Plant and Equipment 25	23068	0	•	380	692	4373	6698	16662	38266	81330	158748	910955 •
Total Assets 26	43693	0	•	874	2521	6596	13889	39882	63062	166352	313299	1160408 •
Notes and Loans Payable 27	19115	0	•	0	705	14	5409	6939	14873	73430	149028	771169 •
All Other Liabilities 28	11670	0	•	552	814	2760	1916	15687	19392	29024	113247	413173 •
Net Worth 29	12908	0	•	322	1002	3821	6564	17256	28798	63896	51024	476065 •

Selected Financial Ratios (Times to 1)

Current Ratio 30	1.0	•	0.9	1.9	0.7	1.2	1.5	4.4	0.6	0.9	•
Quick Ratio 31	0.8	•	0.8	1.7	0.5	0.8	1.4	2.4	0.6	0.7	•
Net Sales to Working Capital 32	•	•	•	7.8	•	35.5	7.8	1.1	•	•	•
Coverage Ratio 33	2.8	•	•	747.9	17.0	20.5	16.2	2.6	4.9	1.6	•
Total Asset Turnover 34	0.3	•	16.9	0.9	0.6	2.5	0.8	0.1	0.3	0.2	•
Inventory Turnover 35	11.9	•	1.3	40.3	4.5	16.9	76.0	6.8	3.6	8.0	•
Receivables Turnover 36	4.3	•	1.7	13.7	4.5	12.0	8.9	0.6	2.9	3.3	•
Total Liabilities to Net Worth 37	2.4	•	1.7	0.7	1.1	1.3	1.2	1.6	5.1	2.5	•
Current Assets to Working Capital 38	•	•	•	2.1	•	6.9	3.0	1.3	•	•	•
Current Liabilities to Working Capital 39	•	•	•	1.1	•	5.9	2.0	0.3	•	•	•
Working Capital to Net Sales 40	•	•	•	0.1	•	0.0	0.1	0.9	•	•	•
Inventory to Working Capital 41	•	•	•	0.0	•	1.7	0.0	0.0	•	•	•
Total Receipts to Cash Flow 42	3.2	1.1	1.6	2.1	1.5	3.0	3.5	1.9	1.6	4.3	•
Cost of Goods to Cash Flow 43	1.4	0.0	•	0.8	0.3	1.7	0.8	0.2	0.2	1.8	•
Cash Flow to Total Debt 44	0.2	•	16.4	1.1	0.7	1.5	0.4	0.1	0.2	0.1	•

Selected Financial Factors (in Percentages)

Debt Ratio 45	70.5	•	63.1	60.3	42.1	52.7	56.7	54.3	61.6	83.7	71.3 •
Return on Total Assets 46	6.9	•	281.1	13.7	19.1	22.8	22.2	15.0	7.5	13.4	4.2 •
Return on Equity Before Income Taxes 47	15.0	•	762.6	33.9	33.0	45.3	48.7	30.8	12.1	65.6	5.2 •
Return on Equity After Income Taxes 48	9.0	•	762.6	33.1	24.9	27.1	32.0	20.6	7.7	41.8	1.4 •
Profit Margin (Before Income Tax) 49	12.9	10.4	16.6	10.4	20.3	37.3	8.3	17.4	32.8	36.6	8.0 •
Profit Margin (After Income Tax) 50	7.8	8.8	16.6	10.1	15.3	22.3	5.5	11.6	20.9	23.3	2.1 •

Table II

Corporations with Net Income

PIPELINE TRANSPORTATION

MONEY AMOUNTS AND SIZE OF ASSETS IN THOUSANDS OF DOLLARS

Item Description for Accounting Period 7/05 Through 6/06	Total	Zero Assets	Under 500	500 to 1,000	1,000 to 5,000	5,000 to 10,000	10,000 to 25,000	25,000 to 50,000	50,000 to 100,000	100,000 to 250,000	250,000 to 500,000	500,000 to 2,500,000	2,500,000 and over
Number of Enterprises **1**	375	•	0	3	320	12	11	12	•	•	3	3	0
Revenues ($ in Thousands)													
Net Sales **2**	4646056	•	0	44316	1048261	131027	119690	1213188	•	•	382080	1322128	0
Interest **3**	14674	•	0	0	881	511	486	681	•	•	1085	3716	0
Rents **4**	6938	•	0	0	0	1203	0	93	•	•	0	21	0
Royalties **5**	1959	•	0	0	1959	0	0	0	•	•	0	0	0
Other Portfolio Income **6**	119878	•	0	0	2572	29	0	26656	•	•	65525	17610	0
Other Receipts **7**	125670	•	0	0	25156	12316	11326	5644	•	•	35409	20765	0
Total Receipts **8**	4915175	•	0	44316	1078829	145086	131502	1246262	•	•	484099	1364240	0
Average Total Receipts **9**	13107	•	•	14772	3371	12090	11955	103855	•	•	161366	454747	•
Operating Costs/Operating Income (%)													
Cost of Operations **10**	34.3	•	•	•	62.1	40.9	23.3	59.0	•	•	12.2	1.8	
Salaries and Wages **11**	7.1	•	•	20.0	8.8	10.2	5.7	2.8	•	•	4.2	6.3	
Taxes Paid **12**	4.1	•	•	2.1	1.9	4.4	4.3	1.2	•	•	4.4	7.3	
Interest Paid **13**	5.1	•	•	•	0.2	0.0	2.3	0.4	•	•	7.5	13.7	
Depreciation **14**	7.3	•	•	0.9	2.8	3.4	5.1	1.3	•	•	8.0	17.2	
Amortization and Depletion **15**	0.5	•	•	•	1.4	0.1	0.0	0.1	•	•	0.1	0.4	
Pensions and Other Deferred Comp. **16**	0.4	•	•	0.5	•	•	•	0.2	•	•	0.6	0.8	
Employee Benefits **17**	1.1	•	•	3.5	0.1	0.9	1.0	0.6	•	•	0.5	1.0	
Advertising **18**	0.1	•	•	•	0.2	0.0	•	0.0	•	•	•	0.0	
Other Expenses **19**	22.4	•	•	56.4	13.1	14.8	22.3	28.4	•	•	34.5	21.5	
Officers' Compensation **20**	0.8	•	•	•	2.1	1.4	0.3	0.4	•	•	0.2	0.6	
Operating Margin **21**	16.8	•	•	16.6	7.4	23.8	35.8	5.6	•	•	27.7	29.3	
Operating Margin Before Officers' Comp. **22**	17.6	•	•	16.6	9.5	25.2	36.0	6.0	•	•	28.0	29.9	

Selected Average Balance Sheet ($ in Thousands)

Net Receivables 23	1701	•	•	428	413	915	1123	11449	•	15902	84004	•
Inventories 24	250	•	•	0	63	137	451	3518	•	3853	852	•
Net Property, Plant and Equipment 25	16358	•	•	380	692	1703	9109	16662	•	157682	1576489	•
Total Assets 26	22822	•	•	874	2521	6015	14975	39882	•	312941	1770020	•
Notes and Loans Payable 27	10064	•	•	0	705	0	7376	6939	•	161543	872586	•
All Other Liabilities 28	6705	•	•	552	814	905	2583	15687	•	117552	486962	•
Net Worth 29	6054	•	•	322	1002	5110	5016	17256	•	33846	410472	•

Selected Financial Ratios (Times to 1)

Current Ratio 30	1.3	•	•	0.9	3.5	0.6	1.2	•	•	0.6	1.1	•
Quick Ratio 31	1.0	•	•	0.8	3.1	0.5	0.8	•	•	0.4	0.9	•
Net Sales to Working Capital 32	15.4	•	•	•	6.1	•	35.5	•	•	•	31.7	•
Coverage Ratio 33	5.4	•	•	•	68.0	20.6	20.5	•	•	8.2	3.4	•
Total Asset Turnover 34	0.5	•	•	16.9	1.3	0.7	2.5	•	•	0.4	0.2	•
Inventory Turnover 35	17.0	•	•	•	32.2	5.6	16.9	•	•	4.0	9.5	•
Receivables Turnover 36	8.0	•	•	69.1	9.5	10.3	12.0	•	•	16.0	5.6	•
Total Liabilities to Net Worth 37	2.8	•	•	1.7	1.5	2.0	1.3	•	•	8.2	3.3	•
Current Assets to Working Capital 38	4.1	•	•	•	1.2	•	6.9	•	•	•	9.5	•
Current Liabilities to Working Capital 39	3.1	•	•	•	0.2	•	5.9	•	•	•	8.5	•
Working Capital to Net Sales 40	0.1	•	•	•	0.2	•	0.0	•	•	•	0.0	•
Inventory to Working Capital 41	0.3	•	•	•	0.1	•	1.7	•	•	•	•	•
Total Receipts to Cash Flow 42	2.5	•	•	1.6	4.9	1.5	3.0	•	•	1.4	2.0	•
Cost of Goods to Cash Flow 43	0.8	•	•	•	3.0	0.3	1.7	•	•	0.2	0.0	•
Cash Flow to Total Debt 44	0.3	•	•	16.4	5.9	0.7	1.5	•	•	0.3	0.2	•

Selected Financial Factors (in Percentages)

Debt Ratio 45	73.5	•	•	63.1	60.3	15.0	66.5	56.7	•	89.2	76.8	•
Return on Total Assets 46	15.1	•	•	281.1	13.7	62.7	34.9	22.2	•	25.2	11.5	•
Return on Equity Before Income Taxes 47	46.2	•	•	762.6	33.9	73.8	99.0	48.7	•	204.6	34.9	•
Return on Equity After Income Taxes 48	32.3	•	•	762.6	33.1	57.6	66.5	32.0	•	133.0	22.9	•
Profit Margin (Before Income Tax) 49	22.6	•	•	16.6	10.4	34.6	45.7	8.3	•	54.4	32.5	•
Profit Margin (After Income Tax) 50	15.8	•	•	16.6	10.1	27.0	30.7	5.5	•	35.3	21.3	•

Table I

Corporations with and without Net Income

OTHER TRANSPORTATION AND SUPPORT ACTIVITIES

MONEY AMOUNTS AND SIZE OF ASSETS IN THOUSANDS OF DOLLARS

Item Description for Accounting Period 7/05 Through 6/06	Total	Zero Assets	Under 500	500 to 1,000	1,000 to 5,000	5,000 to 10,000	10,000 to 25,000	25,000 to 50,000	50,000 to 100,000	100,000 to 250,000	250,000 to 500,000	500,000 to 2,500,000	2,500,000 and over
Number of Enterprises **1**	40974	7352	27600	2612	2716	325	205	63	42	29	12	14	3
Revenues ($ in Thousands)													
Net Sales **2**	186637765	1418236	14035282	9971095	18868319	7399547	6515652	4863442	6077676	7208620	3253164	16219369	91007363
Interest **3**	660332	429	5819	3138	6978	4432	3126	6561	13472	9587	29552	170541	406698
Rents **4**	245638	1259	923	8421	1509	5676	1115	879	13615	25756	15893	43031	127561
Royalties **5**	1770977	0	0	0	0	0	0	385	783	0	33445	8358	1728006
Other Portfolio Income **6**	941747	32011	9871	20395	21457	3548	38206	5032	192999	44374	18583	515103	40165
Other Receipts **7**	1491538	36880	63069	7245	103409	58158	169940	98409	80940	76044	182512	249452	365481
Total Receipts **8**	191947997	1488815	14114964	10010294	19001672	7471361	6728039	4974708	6379485	7364381	3533149	17205854	93675274
Average Total Receipts **9**	4685	203	511	3832	6996	22989	32820	78964	151892	253944	294429	1228990	31225091
Operating Costs/Operating Income (%)													
Cost of Operations **10**	38.8	37.5	38.0	61.1	62.2	76.1	60.2	62.6	65.3	61.9	47.6	45.3	20.8
Salaries and Wages **11**	17.2	6.6	15.0	9.2	11.0	8.6	11.3	12.0	11.3	11.6	23.6	16.0	22.1
Taxes Paid **12**	2.8	0.8	4.6	3.3	1.4	1.5	1.7	1.7	3.7	2.6	2.1	2.8	3.1
Interest Paid **13**	0.9	0.4	0.7	0.4	0.7	0.2	1.0	0.9	1.1	1.1	1.5	2.4	0.7
Depreciation **14**	2.6	2.2	2.2	1.2	1.9	0.7	2.0	1.7	1.4	2.5	4.1	2.1	3.4
Amortization and Depletion **15**	0.3	0.1	0.0	0.1	0.2	0.2	0.1	0.4	0.3	0.4	1.4	0.6	0.2
Pensions and Other Deferred Comp. **16**	1.9	0.1	0.4	0.2	0.1	0.7	0.7	0.2	0.2	0.4	0.8	0.5	3.6
Employee Benefits **17**	3.4	0.3	0.6	0.7	0.7	1.2	1.3	1.3	1.9	2.1	2.7	3.6	5.3
Advertising **18**	0.5	0.3	0.4	0.2	0.2	0.1	0.3	0.2	0.3	0.2	0.7	0.2	0.8
Other Expenses **19**	28.1	52.4	31.0	18.9	18.0	7.1	20.2	18.1	15.6	15.7	26.2	26.0	35.5
Officers' Compensation **20**	1.3	2.7	5.7	2.8	3.1	1.6	1.4	0.8	1.1	0.9	0.8	0.8	0.2
Operating Margin **21**	2.2	•	1.5	1.9	0.6	2.1	1.4	0.2	•	0.6	•	•	4.3
Operating Margin Before Officers' Comp. **22**	3.5	•	7.2	4.7	3.6	3.7	1.4	1.0	1.5	1.5	•	0.6	4.5

Selected Average Balance Sheet ($ in Thousands)

Net Receivables 23	566	0	18	200	678	2297	5128	9849	22082	36716	78826	247453	3836314
Inventories 24	41	0	4	60	57	313	304	1450	1464	3922	4959	25836	132084
Net Property, Plant and Equipment 25	863	0	31	214	522	1224	5133	9487	17003	45904	63832	228143	8155127
Total Assets 26	2702	0	96	729	1982	6654	15943	34992	69891	166650	336884	1070164	22119424
Notes and Loans Payable 27	609	0	65	318	1006	1893	6625	12322	24457	49127	75294	234911	3403726
All Other Liabilities 28	964	0	26	229	587	2740	5509	13973	27754	49323	127370	464517	7686459
Net Worth 29	1129	0	5	182	389	2021	3810	8697	17679	68200	134220	370736	11029239

Selected Financial Ratios (Times to 1)

Current Ratio 30	1.2	•	1.6	1.3	1.6	1.6	1.1	1.2	1.2	1.3	1.3	1.3	1.1
Quick Ratio 31	1.0	•	1.3	1.0	1.3	1.3	0.9	0.9	0.9	1.0	1.0	1.0	0.9
Net Sales to Working Capital 32	29.2	•	25.6	34.8	16.7	13.6	38.6	23.4	31.9	14.5	8.1	14.3	70.6
Coverage Ratio 33	6.8	4.5	4.0	6.3	2.9	14.4	4.3	3.6	3.6	3.4	•	3.6	11.6
Total Asset Turnover 34	1.7	•	5.3	5.2	3.5	3.4	2.0	2.2	2.1	1.5	0.8	1.1	1.4
Inventory Turnover 35	43.2	•	45.1	39.0	75.4	55.4	62.9	33.3	64.5	39.2	26.0	20.3	47.8
Receivables Turnover 36	8.5	•	25.4	17.8	11.2	11.4	6.2	7.4	7.6	6.8	3.3	5.5	8.2
Total Liabilities to Net Worth 37	1.4	•	18.4	3.0	4.1	2.3	3.2	3.0	3.0	1.4	1.5	1.9	1.0
Current Assets to Working Capital 38	6.3	•	2.6	3.9	2.8	2.7	10.7	5.7	7.6	3.9	4.9	5.0	14.7
Current Liabilities to Working Capital 39	5.3	•	1.6	2.9	1.8	1.7	9.7	4.7	6.6	2.9	3.9	4.0	13.7
Working Capital to Net Sales 40	0.0	•	0.0	0.0	0.1	0.1	0.0	0.0	0.0	0.1	0.1	0.1	0.0
Inventory to Working Capital 41	0.3	•	0.2	0.5	0.2	0.3	0.0	0.5	0.3	0.3	0.1	0.4	0.3
Total Receipts to Cash Flow 42	3.7	2.2	3.9	5.4	6.7	12.6	5.4	6.6	9.4	7.0	5.8	3.9	2.8
Cost of Goods to Cash Flow 43	1.4	0.8	1.5	3.3	4.2	9.6	3.3	4.1	6.2	4.3	2.8	1.8	0.6
Cash Flow to Total Debt 44	0.8	•	1.4	1.3	0.7	0.4	0.5	0.4	0.3	0.4	0.2	0.4	1.0

Selected Financial Factors (in Percentages)

Debt Ratio 45	58.2	•	94.8	75.0	80.4	69.6	76.1	75.1	74.7	59.1	60.2	65.4	50.1
Return on Total Assets 46	9.9	•	14.4	14.0	6.9	11.1	8.4	7.5	8.4	5.8	•	9.3	11.1
Return on Equity Before Income Taxes 47	20.2	•	209.1	47.0	22.9	34.1	27.0	21.7	23.8	10.0	•	19.5	20.4
Return on Equity After Income Taxes 48	13.2	•	203.2	44.5	19.3	29.9	22.9	18.0	14.1	7.0	•	14.2	12.3
Profit Margin (Before Income Tax) 49	5.0	1.6	2.0	2.2	1.3	3.0	3.2	2.4	2.9	2.7	•	6.2	7.4
Profit Margin (After Income Tax) 50	3.3	0.7	2.0	2.1	1.1	2.7	2.7	2.0	1.7	1.9	•	4.6	4.5

Table II
Corporations with Net Income

OTHER TRANSPORTATION AND SUPPORT ACTIVITIES

MONEY AMOUNTS AND SIZE OF ASSETS IN THOUSANDS OF DOLLARS

Item Description for Accounting Period 7/05 Through 6/06	Total	Zero Assets	Under 500	500 to 1,000	1,000 to 5,000	5,000 to 10,000	10,000 to 25,000	25,000 to 50,000	50,000 to 100,000	100,000 to 250,000	250,000 to 500,000	500,000 to 2,500,000	2,500,000 and over
Number of Enterprises 1	23351	3522	15785	1836	1677	269	139	•	32	21	8	•	0
Revenues ($ in Thousands)													
Net Sales 2	160698232	676341	10409901	7334599	14785851	6750493	4981503	•	4770107	6183283	2987215	•	0
Interest 3	594737	293	1709	3062	4644	3840	2439	•	4820	9020	21183	•	0
Rents 4	220159	1258	887	8421	1509	3514	52	•	12723	25148	15858	•	0
Royalties 5	1759924	0	0	0	0	0	0	•	783	0	33445	•	0
Other Portfolio Income 6	897741	31459	2881	20395	15875	1401	37399	•	189882	23547	17534	•	0
Other Receipts 7	1116310	24401	58248	5805	98507	52586	81124	•	63905	42558	132082	•	0
Total Receipts 8	165287103	733752	10473626	7372282	14906386	6811834	5102517	•	5042220	6283556	3207317	•	0
Average Total Receipts 9	7078	208	664	4015	8889	25323	36709	•	157569	299217	400915	•	•
Operating Costs/Operating Income (%)													
Cost of Operations 10	37.5	39.6	41.9	58.0	62.2	75.1	60.8	•	69.1	59.7	47.4	•	•
Salaries and Wages 11	17.6	9.0	13.4	8.3	12.0	8.8	9.5	•	9.3	11.9	23.9	•	•
Taxes Paid 12	2.9	0.8	4.9	4.1	1.3	1.5	1.4	•	4.1	2.6	1.9	•	•
Interest Paid 13	0.7	0.4	0.5	0.3	0.4	0.2	0.6	•	0.8	0.8	0.8	•	•
Depreciation 14	2.6	3.4	1.6	1.2	1.3	0.5	1.4	•	1.1	2.0	1.7	•	•
Amortization and Depletion 15	0.2	0.1	0.1	0.1	0.1	0.0	0.2	•	0.2	0.4	1.3	•	•
Pensions and Other Deferred Comp. 16	2.2	0.2	0.3	0.2	0.1	0.7	0.2	•	0.2	0.4	0.9	•	•
Employee Benefits 17	3.6	0.4	0.6	0.6	0.7	1.2	1.2	•	1.7	2.2	2.5	•	•
Advertising 18	0.5	0.1	0.3	0.2	0.2	0.1	0.1	•	0.2	0.1	0.7	•	•
Other Expenses 19	26.7	36.5	24.9	20.7	15.4	6.8	20.0	•	10.4	16.4	21.6	•	•
Officers' Compensation 20	1.2	2.9	5.7	3.0	3.1	1.7	1.4	•	1.2	0.9	0.7	•	•
Operating Margin 21	4.4	6.7	5.8	3.4	3.1	3.4	3.2	•	1.7	2.7	•	•	•
Operating Margin Before Officers' Comp. 22	5.6	9.6	11.5	6.4	6.2	5.1	4.6	•	2.9	3.6	•	•	•

Selected Average Balance Sheet ($ in Thousands)

Net Receivables 23	870	0	21	243	828	2556	6048	•	24781	38298	117962
Inventories 24	46	0	5	26	71	267	359	•	1368	1003	271
Net Property, Plant and Equipment 25	1296	0	36	137	426	1129	3708	•	14902	38914	50297
Total Assets 26	3907	0	111	696	2106	6682	15495	•	69263	166459	340562
Notes and Loans Payable 27	725	0	64	220	648	1018	4171	•	16494	34764	53063
All Other Liabilities 28	1464	0	30	250	657	3060	5674	•	23630	51265	168978
Net Worth 29	1717	0	16	226	801	2604	5650	•	29139	80429	118522

Selected Financial Ratios (Times to 1)

Current Ratio 30	1.2	•	1.4	1.6	1.8	1.6	1.4	•	1.3	1.5	1.2
Quick Ratio 31	1.0	•	1.1	1.4	1.4	1.3	1.2	•	1.1	1.2	1.0
Net Sales to Working Capital 32	29.3	•	39.2	23.9	14.0	14.2	12.6	•	16.5	12.1	10.0
Coverage Ratio 33	11.6	41.0	12.7	14.2	10.7	22.2	10.7	•	10.7	6.4	5.7
Total Asset Turnover 34	1.8	•	6.0	5.7	4.2	3.8	2.3	•	2.2	1.8	1.1
Inventory Turnover 35	55.7	•	59.5	87.8	77.7	70.5	60.6	•	75.3	175.3	651.6
Receivables Turnover 36	8.6	•	30.4	21.5	11.9	11.1	6.1	•	7.6	8.5	6.3
Total Liabilities to Net Worth 37	1.3	•	5.8	2.1	1.6	1.6	1.7	•	1.4	1.1	1.9
Current Assets to Working Capital 38	6.3	•	3.3	2.7	2.3	2.8	3.5	•	4.1	2.9	5.7
Current Liabilities to Working Capital 39	5.3	•	2.3	1.7	1.3	1.8	2.5	•	3.1	1.9	4.7
Working Capital to Net Sales 40	0.0	•	0.0	0.0	0.1	0.1	0.1	•	0.1	0.1	0.1
Inventory to Working Capital 41	0.2	•	0.3	0.3	0.2	0.3	0.1	•	0.1	0.1	0.0
Total Receipts to Cash Flow 42	3.5	2.5	3.8	4.6	6.1	11.1	4.8	•	9.7	6.1	5.1
Cost of Goods to Cash Flow 43	1.3	1.0	1.6	2.6	3.8	8.3	2.9	•	6.7	3.7	2.4
Cash Flow to Total Debt 44	0.9	•	1.8	1.9	1.1	0.6	0.8	•	0.4	0.6	0.3

Selected Financial Factors (in Percentages)

Debt Ratio 45	56.0	•	85.3	67.5	62.0	61.0	63.5	•	57.9	51.7	65.2
Return on Total Assets 46	14.2	•	41.3	24.2	18.2	16.9	14.3	•	17.5	9.1	5.3
Return on Equity Before Income Taxes 47	29.6	•	258.1	69.1	43.4	41.4	35.6	•	37.8	15.9	12.5
Return on Equity After Income Taxes 48	21.5	•	255.0	66.3	40.5	37.5	31.5	•	30.1	12.5	8.7
Profit Margin (Before Income Tax) 49	7.4	15.2	6.4	3.9	3.9	4.3	5.6	•	7.4	4.3	4.0
Profit Margin (After Income Tax) 50	5.4	13.4	6.3	3.8	3.7	3.9	5.0	•	5.9	3.4	2.8

WAREHOUSING AND STORAGE

Table I

Corporations with and without Net Income

MONEY AMOUNTS AND SIZE OF ASSETS IN THOUSANDS OF DOLLARS

Item Description for Accounting Period 7/05 Through 6/06	Total	Zero Assets	Under 500	500 to 1,000	1,000 to 5,000	5,000 to 10,000	10,000 to 25,000	25,000 to 50,000	50,000 to 100,000	100,000 to 250,000	250,000 to 500,000	500,000 to 2,500,000	2,500,000 and over
Number of Enterprises 1	7287	411	4410	950	1142	163	141	30	17	15	5	3	0
Revenues ($ in Thousands)													
Net Sales 2	16988729	281626	1661865	1654393	3046285	1102177	2378885	775869	1244226	1600711	1191582	2051108	0
Interest 3	254251	24	139	2481	3764	1346	3414	1860	3577	10508	12932	214206	0
Rents 4	22293	0	4247	0	3685	1259	5191	830	610	1428	673	4371	0
Royalties 5	8891	0	0	0	0	0	0	206	8363	0	275	47	0
Other Portfolio Income 6	170051	54548	19380	226	15049	6504	18023	9181	7387	32054	1985	5715	0
Other Receipts 7	569288	7395	3070	4580	189113	6478	27844	66778	17759	47973	100116	98181	0
Total Receipts 8	18013503	343593	1688701	1661680	3257896	1117764	2433357	854724	1281922	1692674	1307563	2373628	0
Average Total Receipts 9	2472	836	383	1749	2853	6857	17258	28491	75407	112845	261513	791209	•
Operating Costs/Operating Income (%)													
Cost of Operations 10	31.3	8.1	48.2	21.2	39.2	45.0	35.3	18.1	41.7	24.9	33.9	7.1	•
Salaries and Wages 11	20.5	36.2	4.7	19.6	20.6	10.3	17.1	29.2	16.5	32.9	16.3	33.1	•
Taxes Paid 12	3.8	3.1	1.8	3.7	4.7	3.5	3.5	4.5	3.0	3.7	4.5	4.7	•
Interest Paid 13	4.0	6.9	0.3	1.7	1.4	1.9	2.2	2.5	2.6	2.7	4.5	17.6	•
Depreciation 14	4.2	1.0	1.4	1.7	4.1	3.1	3.8	4.4	3.1	4.0	8.1	8.3	•
Amortization and Depletion 15	0.8	3.3	0.3	0.0	0.2	0.2	0.1	0.2	1.2	1.1	0.2	4.0	•
Pensions and Other Deferred Comp. 16	0.6	0.1	0.4	0.1	0.6	0.4	0.9	0.5	0.7	1.1	1.4	0.4	•
Employee Benefits 17	2.5	1.7	1.8	1.4	1.4	1.6	2.6	6.3	2.8	4.2	2.4	2.9	•
Advertising 18	0.4	0.0	0.3	1.3	0.3	0.5	0.3	0.2	0.1	0.1	0.1	0.6	•
Other Expenses 19	30.3	53.0	33.4	40.9	28.3	26.0	30.7	35.1	22.6	21.6	35.3	28.1	•
Officers' Compensation 20	1.9	0.1	1.6	1.9	1.8	4.8	2.4	7.1	1.1	0.8	0.5	0.3	•
Operating Margin 21	•	•	6.0	6.4	•	2.7	1.0	•	4.5	3.0	•	•	•
Operating Margin Before Officers' Comp. 22	1.6	•	7.6	8.3	•	7.5	3.5	•	5.7	3.8	•	•	•

Selected Average Balance Sheet ($ in Thousands)

Net Receivables 23	297	0	17	181	368	688	1996	3754	10616	29474	57334	26955	•
Inventories 24	46	0	2	14	81	22	411	569	3941	4212	1004	2684	•
Net Property, Plant and Equipment 25	1064	0	84	258	764	2829	7722	17414	33303	73399	159126	577243	•
Total Assets 26	2591	0	126	709	1825	6501	16071	35028	72793	158291	326804	1981534	•
Notes and Loans Payable 27	1145	0	72	435	628	1957	6607	11837	24910	50788	147784	1122172	•
All Other Liabilities 28	464	0	21	135	242	925	2871	5548	16919	29436	75912	349914	•
Net Worth 29	982	0	32	139	955	3618	6594	17643	30964	78067	103107	509448	•

Selected Financial Ratios (Times to 1)

Current Ratio 30	1.6	•	1.7	1.8	2.5	1.5	1.5	1.7	1.8	1.6	1.0	1.4	•
Quick Ratio 31	1.0	•	1.5	1.6	2.1	1.2	1.1	1.2	1.2	1.2	0.8	0.1	•
Net Sales to Working Capital 32	9.0	•	26.3	12.6	6.0	12.3	10.6	6.4	6.9	5.1	227.6	7.8	•
Coverage Ratio 33	2.4	2.2	29.6	5.0	4.0	3.1	2.5	1.8	3.9	4.3	1.6	1.5	•
Total Asset Turnover 34	0.9	•	3.0	2.5	1.5	1.0	1.0	0.7	1.0	0.7	0.7	0.3	•
Inventory Turnover 35	15.7	•	83.4	25.5	13.0	139.1	14.5	8.2	7.7	6.3	80.4	18.1	•
Receivables Turnover 36	7.7	•	18.9	10.6	7.3	11.2	8.5	6.3	5.6	3.6	4.2	22.8	•
Total Liabilities to Net Worth 37	1.6	•	2.9	4.1	0.9	0.8	1.4	1.0	1.4	1.0	2.2	2.9	•
Current Assets to Working Capital 38	2.7	•	2.5	2.2	1.7	3.1	2.9	2.4	2.2	2.6	68.9	3.8	•
Current Liabilities to Working Capital 39	1.7	•	1.5	1.2	0.7	2.1	1.9	1.4	1.2	1.6	67.9	2.8	•
Working Capital to Net Sales 40	0.1	•	0.0	0.1	0.2	0.1	0.1	0.2	0.1	0.2	0.0	0.1	•
Inventory to Working Capital 41	0.2	•	0.1	0.2	0.1	0.0	0.3	0.1	0.4	0.1	1.5	0.0	•
Total Receipts to Cash Flow 42	4.3	2.9	6.8	3.2	4.6	6.4	4.5	4.0	4.5	4.2	3.2	4.0	•
Cost of Goods to Cash Flow 43	1.3	0.2	3.3	0.7	1.8	2.9	1.6	0.7	1.9	1.0	1.1	0.3	•
Cash Flow to Total Debt 44	0.3	•	0.6	0.9	0.7	0.4	0.4	0.4	0.4	0.3	0.3	0.1	•

Selected Financial Factors (in Percentages)

Debt Ratio 45	62.1	•	74.2	80.4	47.7	44.3	59.0	49.6	57.5	50.7	68.4	74.3	•
Return on Total Assets 46	8.8	•	23.6	20.9	8.3	6.3	5.7	3.3	10.2	7.8	5.2	9.1	•
Return on Equity Before Income Taxes 47	13.7	•	88.5	85.1	11.8	7.7	8.4	2.8	17.8	12.1	6.1	11.8	•
Return on Equity After Income Taxes 48	11.6	•	84.2	84.7	10.1	6.0	7.1	0.4	13.8	8.7	3.9	11.4	•
Profit Margin (Before Income Tax) 49	5.8	8.6	7.6	6.8	4.2	4.1	3.3	1.9	7.5	8.9	2.6	8.8	•
Profit Margin (After Income Tax) 50	4.9	6.9	7.2	6.8	3.6	3.2	2.8	0.2	5.8	6.4	1.7	8.5	•

251

Table II

Corporations with Net Income

WAREHOUSING AND STORAGE

MONEY AMOUNTS AND SIZE OF ASSETS IN THOUSANDS OF DOLLARS

Item Description for Accounting Period 7/05 Through 6/06	Total	Zero Assets	Under 500	500 to 1000	251 to 500	501 to 1,000	1,001 to 5,000	5,001 to 10,000	10,001 to 25,000	25,001 to 50,000	50,001 to 100,000	100,001 to 250,000	250,001 and over
Number of Enterprises **1**	4776	408	2405	863	796	153	94	22	•	•	•	3	0

Revenues ($ in Thousands)

	Total	Zero Assets	Under 500	500 to 1000	251 to 500	501 to 1,000	1,001 to 5,000	5,001 to 10,000	10,001 to 25,000	25,001 to 50,000	50,001 to 100,000	100,001 to 250,000	250,001 and over
Net Sales **2**	13808997	105893	1349556	1362960	2250079	940812	1817092	652269	•	•	•	2051108	0
Interest **3**	252377	2	139	2405	2569	1346	2849	1860	•	•	•	214206	0
Rents **4**	16664	0	0	0	3674	1259	4352	830	•	•	•	4371	0
Royalties **5**	8891	0	0	0	0	0	0	206	•	•	•	47	0
Other Portfolio Income **6**	164221	54540	18262	226	14858	6504	17554	6406	•	•	•	5715	0
Other Receipts **7**	368477	6733	583	4580	32680	3950	23473	39727	•	•	•	98181	0
Total Receipts **8**	14619627	167168	1368540	1370171	2303860	953871	1865320	701298	•	•	•	2373628	0
Average Total Receipts **9**	3061	410	569	1588	2894	6234	19844	31877	•	•	•	791209	•

Operating Costs/Operating Income (%)

	Total	Zero Assets	Under 500	500 to 1000	251 to 500	501 to 1,000	1,001 to 5,000	5,001 to 10,000	10,001 to 25,000	25,001 to 50,000	50,001 to 100,000	100,001 to 250,000	250,001 and over
Cost of Operations **10**	31.3	11.3	46.6	25.7	46.6	44.5	28.4	21.3	•	•	•	7.1	•
Salaries and Wages **11**	18.4	41.2	4.8	16.7	10.0	9.2	19.1	25.4	•	•	•	33.1	•
Taxes Paid **12**	3.7	2.5	1.7	4.3	3.9	3.3	3.8	3.6	•	•	•	4.7	•
Interest Paid **13**	4.2	11.5	0.2	1.9	1.5	2.0	1.6	2.2	•	•	•	17.6	•
Depreciation **14**	3.9	0.6	1.1	1.8	3.1	2.8	4.1	4.0	•	•	•	8.3	•
Amortization and Depletion **15**	0.8	0.6	0.4	0.0	0.2	0.1	0.1	0.2	•	•	•	4.0	•
Pensions and Other Deferred Comp. **16**	0.6	•	0.5	0.2	0.6	0.4	0.7	0.5	•	•	•	0.4	•
Employee Benefits **17**	2.6	1.3	1.9	1.6	1.9	1.3	2.9	6.8	•	•	•	2.9	•
Advertising **18**	0.4	•	0.3	1.1	0.3	0.1	0.3	0.2	•	•	•	0.6	•
Other Expenses **19**	29.4	61.7	30.7	36.5	23.5	27.2	33.6	32.5	•	•	•	28.1	•
Officers' Compensation **20**	1.6	•	1.4	2.4	2.1	4.4	1.7	1.5	•	•	•	0.3	•
Operating Margin **21**	3.1	•	10.3	7.8	6.3	4.7	3.6	1.9	•	•	•	•	•
Operating Margin Before Officers' Comp. **22**	4.6	11.7	11.7	10.2	8.5	9.1	5.4	3.4	•	•	•	•	•

Selected Average Balance Sheet ($ in Thousands)

	•	•	•	•	•	•	•	•	•
Net Receivables 23	386	0	24	163	437	584	2292	3926	26955
Inventories 24	51	0	2	4	105	19	399	664	2781
Net Property, Plant and Equipment 25	1250	0	52	269	806	2788	7556	19119	577243
Total Assets 26	3287	0	116	697	1825	6393	15573	35148	1981534
Notes and Loans Payable 27	1422	0	22	438	752	1802	5147	11179	1122172
All Other Liabilities 28	605	0	20	91	291	832	2493	6096	349914
Net Worth 29	1259	0	74	167	781	3759	7934	17874	509448

Selected Financial Ratios (Times to 1)

	•	•	•	•	•	•	•	•	•
Current Ratio 30	1.6	•	2.0	2.1	2.6	1.5	1.5	2.0	1.4
Quick Ratio 31	1.0	•	1.8	2.0	2.2	1.2	1.3	1.4	0.1
Net Sales to Working Capital 32	8.0	•	21.0	10.9	5.2	10.8	11.8	5.3	7.8
Coverage Ratio 33	3.1	3.4	49.0	5.4	6.9	4.0	4.8	5.3	1.5
Total Asset Turnover 34	0.9	•	4.9	2.3	1.5	1.0	1.2	0.8	0.3
Inventory Turnover 35	17.6	•	123.6	94.8	12.5	146.5	13.7	9.5	17.4
Receivables Turnover 36	8.0	•	22.6	11.5	6.8	11.3	8.7	8.2	50.7
Total Liabilities to Net Worth 37	1.6	•	0.6	3.2	1.3	0.7	1.0	1.0	2.9
Current Assets to Working Capital 38	2.6	•	2.0	1.9	1.6	2.8	2.9	2.0	3.8
Current Liabilities to Working Capital 39	1.6	•	1.0	0.9	0.6	1.8	1.9	1.0	2.8
Working Capital to Net Sales 40	0.1	•	0.0	0.1	0.2	0.1	0.1	0.2	0.1
Inventory to Working Capital 41	0.1	•	0.1	0.0	0.1	0.0	0.2	0.1	0.0
Total Receipts to Cash Flow 42	3.9	2.7	5.8	3.8	4.1	5.3	3.6	3.2	4.0
Cost of Goods to Cash Flow 43	1.2	0.3	2.7	1.0	1.9	2.4	1.0	0.7	0.3
Cash Flow to Total Debt 44	0.4	•	2.3	0.8	0.7	0.4	0.7	0.5	0.1

Selected Financial Factors (in Percentages)

	•	•	•	•	•	•	•	•	•
Debt Ratio 45	61.7	•	36.3	76.0	57.2	41.2	49.1	49.1	74.3
Return on Total Assets 46	11.6	•	57.8	23.2	15.7	7.7	9.8	9.8	9.1
Return on Equity Before Income Taxes 47	20.5	•	88.8	78.7	31.4	9.9	15.2	15.6	11.8
Return on Equity After Income Taxes 48	18.1	•	85.3	78.3	28.3	8.1	13.6	12.4	11.4
Profit Margin (Before Income Tax) 49	8.9	27.1	11.7	8.3	8.7	6.0	6.2	9.4	8.8
Profit Margin (After Income Tax) 50	7.9	22.7	11.2	8.3	7.8	5.0	5.6	7.5	8.5

Table I

Corporations with and without Net Income

NEWSPAPER PUBLISHERS

MONEY AMOUNTS AND SIZE OF ASSETS IN THOUSANDS OF DOLLARS

Item Description for Accounting Period 7/05 Through 6/06	Total	Zero Assets	Under 500	500 to 1,000	1,000 to 5,000	5,000 to 10,000	10,000 to 25,000	25,000 to 50,000	50,000 to 100,000	100,000 to 250,000	250,000 to 500,000	500,000 to 2,500,000	2,500,000 and over
Number of Enterprises 1	6724	986	4382	569	539	47	81	47	24	14	7	17	11
Revenues ($ in Thousands)													
Net Sales 2	52851780	133638	2180862	732803	1907853	572465	1554125	1609635	1461095	1860301	1827327	9296315	29715361
Interest 3	361033	48	203	455	866	51	3695	4742	4634	11641	7974	91725	234998
Rents 4	160716	0	10	0	1314	163	897	7247	4896	4972	6260	20802	114155
Royalties 5	302034	0	0	0	0	0	0	2996	30	0	438	602	297968
Other Portfolio Income 6	1306562	0	0	196	12316	18859	7557	51727	16912	130836	4032	200976	863152
Other Receipts 7	1673600	4927	541	1456	50611	1230	9973	46432	78036	8726	9936	364471	1097260
Total Receipts 8	56655725	138613	2181616	734910	1972960	592768	1576247	1722779	1565603	2016476	1855967	9974891	32322894
Average Total Receipts 9	8426	141	498	1292	3660	12612	19460	36655	65233	144034	265138	586758	2938445
Operating Costs/Operating Income (%)													
Cost of Operations 10	25.5	14.0	37.0	34.1	39.6	10.7	34.9	30.5	37.8	28.0	16.7	18.8	25.0
Salaries and Wages 11	23.2	6.6	13.9	19.5	14.5	49.1	23.5	26.2	20.8	24.1	25.9	25.1	23.3
Taxes Paid 12	3.7	1.5	2.5	4.5	3.3	5.1	3.6	4.1	3.0	4.1	4.3	3.9	3.6
Interest Paid 13	4.0	6.6	1.1	1.0	1.6	0.3	1.2	2.2	2.7	2.3	3.5	6.2	4.2
Depreciation 14	3.0	1.1	0.7	2.1	2.9	1.2	2.9	3.2	3.5	4.3	5.7	3.4	2.8
Amortization and Depletion 15	3.2	0.5	0.1	1.4	0.4	0.2	0.5	2.1	1.5	2.4	5.2	4.3	3.6
Pensions and Other Deferred Comp. 16	1.5	0.1	0.6	0.8	0.2	0.3	0.9	1.7	1.0	1.3	1.6	1.5	1.8
Employee Benefits 17	2.9	0.3	0.8	3.1	1.7	4.1	3.3	3.2	2.5	3.8	3.6	3.1	3.0
Advertising 18	2.0	0.1	5.6	0.6	1.3	0.6	0.7	1.9	1.0	1.4	1.7	1.2	2.3
Other Expenses 19	24.7	68.7	31.5	23.2	32.8	25.8	17.4	25.5	20.6	24.2	24.4	27.4	23.3
Officers' Compensation 20	2.0	4.1	8.9	5.8	3.8	5.2	3.2	2.1	2.2	2.1	1.6	1.4	1.3
Operating Margin 21	4.3	•	•	3.9	•	•	7.8	•	3.4	2.2	5.9	3.7	5.9
Operating Margin Before Officers' Comp. 22	6.3	0.5	6.1	9.7	1.7	2.5	11.0	•	5.6	4.3	7.5	5.1	7.2

Selected Average Balance Sheet ($ in Thousands)

Net Receivables 23	1471	0	28	127	357	1597	2211	5227	7164	15934	32084	77245	643015
Inventories 24	105	0	0	9	20	138	239	403	1113	2646	6249	9733	33708
Net Property, Plant and Equipment 25	2377	0	22	84	1036	1188	4117	10053	18468	47933	103464	189395	850954
Total Assets 26	14673	0	75	636	2712	5593	15692	38115	65444	147786	379341	1079352	6231061
Notes and Loans Payable 27	4089	0	40	226	1292	19	3157	14522	22102	28360	124316	387958	1560059
All Other Liabilities 28	3367	0	85	44	503	2684	3209	8665	14353	34069	98489	282496	1351105
Net Worth 29	7217	0	-51	366	917	2890	9326	14928	28990	85357	156535	408898	3319897

Selected Financial Ratios (Times to 1)

Current Ratio 30	1.1	•	0.5	2.6	1.5	1.8	2.3	1.3	1.4	2.2	1.4	1.5	0.9
Quick Ratio 31	0.8	•	0.5	2.5	1.4	1.4	1.9	1.1	1.0	1.8	0.9	1.2	0.7
Net Sales to Working Capital 32	46.6	•	•	9.5	12.2	9.5	5.9	13.7	11.4	4.9	16.7	9.7	•
Coverage Ratio 33	3.9	1.0	•	5.2	1.8	3.6	8.4	3.0	4.8	5.6	3.1	2.8	4.6
Total Asset Turnover 34	0.5	•	6.6	2.0	1.3	2.2	1.2	0.9	0.9	0.9	0.7	0.5	0.4
Inventory Turnover 35	19.2	•	34323.8	49.7	71.2	9.5	28.0	25.9	20.7	14.1	7.0	10.6	20.1
Receivables Turnover 36	5.7	•	15.7	10.2	9.6	6.4	8.3	7.7	8.2	8.4	6.9	6.7	4.7
Total Liabilities to Net Worth 37	1.0	•	•	0.7	2.0	0.9	0.7	1.6	1.3	0.7	1.4	1.6	0.9
Current Assets to Working Capital 38	15.0	•	•	1.6	3.0	2.2	1.8	4.5	3.6	1.8	3.8	3.2	•
Current Liabilities to Working Capital 39	14.0	•	•	0.6	2.0	1.2	0.8	3.5	2.6	0.8	2.8	2.2	•
Working Capital to Net Sales 40	0.0	•	•	0.1	0.1	0.2	0.2	0.1	0.1	0.2	0.1	0.1	•
Inventory to Working Capital 41	0.6	•	•	0.1	0.1	0.1	0.1	0.2	0.2	0.1	0.3	0.2	•
Total Receipts to Cash Flow 42	3.2	1.5	3.9	4.5	3.3	4.5	4.2	4.0	3.5	4.0	3.5	2.9	3.1
Cost of Goods to Cash Flow 43	0.8	0.2	1.4	1.5	1.3	0.5	1.5	1.2	1.3	1.1	0.6	0.5	0.8
Cash Flow to Total Debt 44	0.3	•	1.0	1.1	0.6	1.0	0.7	0.4	0.5	0.5	0.3	0.3	0.3

Selected Financial Factors (in Percentages)

Debt Ratio 45	50.8	•	167.5	42.4	66.2	48.3	40.6	60.8	55.7	42.2	58.7	62.1	46.7
Return on Total Assets 46	8.3	•	•	10.6	3.7	2.7	12.7	5.9	12.3	11.5	7.5	8.7	8.3
Return on Equity Before Income Taxes 47	12.6	•	26.8	14.8	5.0	3.7	18.8	10.2	22.0	16.4	12.4	14.7	12.1
Return on Equity After Income Taxes 48	8.4	•	30.5	14.5	4.8	1.1	17.4	7.7	18.1	12.8	8.9	8.7	8.0
Profit Margin (Before Income Tax) 49	11.6	0.1	•	4.2	1.3	0.9	9.2	4.4	10.5	10.5	7.4	11.0	14.9
Profit Margin (After Income Tax) 50	7.7	•	•	4.1	1.2	0.3	8.5	3.3	8.6	8.2	5.3	6.5	9.9

Table II
Corporations with Net Income

NEWSPAPER PUBLISHERS

MONEY AMOUNTS AND SIZE OF ASSETS IN THOUSANDS OF DOLLARS

Item Description for Accounting Period 7/05 Through 6/06	Total	Zero Assets	Under 500	500 to 1,000	1,000 to 5,000	5,000 to 10,000	10,000 to 25,000	25,000 to 50,000	50,000 to 100,000	100,000 to 250,000	250,000 to 500,000	500,000 to 2,500,000	2,500,000 and over
Number of Enterprises 1	4818	447	3212	507	469	6	76	39	21	•	•	13	•
Revenues ($ in Thousands)													
Net Sales 2	44352534	46895	1520025	714847	1380977	58744	1513884	1350460	1360250	•	•	7992258	•
Interest 3	336046	48	203	455	740	9	3695	4742	3886	•	•	70511	•
Rents 4	114201	0	10	0	0	163	897	7247	4886	•	•	20665	•
Royalties 5	278254	0	0	0	0	0	0	2908	30	•	•	563	•
Other Portfolio Income 6	1277668	0	0	196	4106	18859	7547	36272	16871	•	•	199941	•
Other Receipts 7	1506897	3903	431	1456	49190	990	21371	45120	77380	•	•	337340	•
Total Receipts 8	47865600	50846	1520669	716954	1435013	78765	1547394	1446749	1463303	•	•	8621278	•
Average Total Receipts 9	9935	114	473	1414	3060	13128	20360	37096	69681	•	•	663175	•
Operating Costs/Operating Income (%)													
Cost of Operations 10	26.3	40.0	38.3	34.0	31.8	39.2	35.6	31.9	34.6	•	•	14.7	•
Salaries and Wages 11	22.6	1.3	12.9	19.3	16.4	22.4	22.8	25.1	21.5	•	•	26.5	•
Taxes Paid 12	3.8	0.7	2.7	4.5	3.1	4.5	3.6	3.9	3.1	•	•	4.1	•
Interest Paid 13	3.8	•	1.5	1.0	2.0	0.3	1.3	1.7	2.3	•	•	3.3	•
Depreciation 14	3.1	0.1	0.9	2.0	3.3	1.1	2.9	3.3	3.5	•	•	3.6	•
Amortization and Depletion 15	3.1	1.3	0.0	1.0	0.3	0.1	0.5	1.1	1.4	•	•	3.0	•
Pensions and Other Deferred Comp. 16	1.3	0.2	0.8	0.8	0.2	0.5	0.9	1.7	1.0	•	•	1.6	•
Employee Benefits 17	2.9	0.7	0.8	3.2	2.3	1.6	3.3	3.1	2.6	•	•	3.4	•
Advertising 18	1.9	0.2	0.5	0.5	0.6	5.3	0.7	2.0	0.9	•	•	1.3	•
Other Expenses 19	21.7	38.3	22.0	23.4	30.7	12.9	16.9	24.0	21.6	•	•	28.6	•
Officers' Compensation 20	2.0	6.2	12.7	5.9	4.4	5.0	3.3	2.4	2.2	•	•	1.5	•
Operating Margin 21	7.6	10.8	6.9	4.4	4.8	7.2	8.3	•	5.2	•	•	8.4	•
Operating Margin Before Officers' Comp. 22	9.6	17.0	19.6	10.3	9.2	12.2	11.6	2.2	7.4	•	•	9.9	•

Selected Average Balance Sheet ($ in Thousands)

Net Receivables 23	1831	0	32	132	370	537	2263	5695	7605	83097
Inventories 24	109	0	0	10	22	679	233	398	1085	8656
Net Property, Plant and Equipment 25	2989	0	28	92	1095	272	4238	10832	19912	226371
Total Assets 26	18258	0	82	630	2583	7282	15434	36960	67058	1075468
Notes and Loans Payable 27	4816	0	8	205	1410	148	3345	13470	20780	256785
All Other Liabilities 28	3744	0	55	43	331	4130	3333	9480	15563	302280
Net Worth 29	9699	0	19	382	842	3004	8756	14010	30715	516403

Selected Financial Ratios (Times to 1)

Current Ratio 30	1.1	•	1.6	2.9	1.5	4.9	2.1	1.3	1.4	1.6
Quick Ratio 31	0.8	•	1.6	2.8	1.4	2.4	1.8	1.0	1.0	1.3
Net Sales to Working Capital 32	51.7	•	28.5	9.1	13.4	2.0	6.6	14.1	11.9	8.7
Coverage Ratio 33	5.1	•	5.5	5.8	5.3	151.7	9.2	5.1	6.6	5.9
Total Asset Turnover 34	0.5	•	5.8	2.2	1.1	1.3	1.3	0.9	1.0	0.6
Inventory Turnover 35	22.2	•	28372.1	48.3	42.5	5.6	30.5	27.8	20.7	10.5
Receivables Turnover 36	5.4	•	15.7	11.1	9.3	1.1	9.6	7.5	8.4	14.8
Total Liabilities to Net Worth 37	0.9	•	3.4	0.6	2.1	1.4	0.8	1.6	1.2	1.1
Current Assets to Working Capital 38	17.2	•	2.6	1.5	2.9	1.3	1.9	4.7	3.8	2.6
Current Liabilities to Working Capital 39	16.2	•	1.6	0.5	1.9	0.3	0.9	3.7	2.8	1.6
Working Capital to Net Sales 40	0.0	•	0.0	0.1	0.1	0.5	0.2	0.1	0.1	0.1
Inventory to Working Capital 41	0.6	•	0.0	0.1	0.1	0.0	0.1	0.2	0.2	0.1
Total Receipts to Cash Flow 42	3.1	1.7	3.9	4.4	2.9	2.9	4.0	3.9	3.2	2.5
Cost of Goods to Cash Flow 43	0.8	0.7	1.5	1.5	0.9	1.1	1.4	1.2	1.1	0.4
Cash Flow to Total Debt 44	0.3	•	1.9	1.3	0.6	0.8	0.7	0.4	0.6	0.4

Selected Financial Factors (in Percentages)

Debt Ratio 45	46.9	•	77.1	39.4	67.4	58.7	43.3	62.1	54.2	52.0
Return on Total Assets 46	9.8	•	48.9	12.6	12.2	55.9	15.1	7.9	14.4	11.2
Return on Equity Before Income Taxes 47	14.8	•	174.2	17.3	30.5	134.6	23.7	16.9	26.6	19.3
Return on Equity After Income Taxes 48	10.5	•	160.7	17.0	30.2	114.6	22.0	13.9	22.4	13.1
Profit Margin (Before Income Tax) 49	15.6	19.3	6.9	4.7	8.7	41.3	10.4	6.8	12.6	16.2
Profit Margin (After Income Tax) 50	11.0	18.7	6.4	4.6	8.6	35.2	9.7	5.6	10.6	11.0

254

Table I

Corporations with and without Net Income

PERIODICAL PUBLISHERS

MONEY AMOUNTS AND SIZE OF ASSETS IN THOUSANDS OF DOLLARS

Item Description for Accounting Period 7/05 Through 6/06	Total	Zero Assets	Under 500	500 to 1,000	1,000 to 5,000	5,000 to 10,000	10,000 to 25,000	25,000 to 50,000	50,000 to 100,000	100,000 to 250,000	250,000 to 500,000	500,000 to 2,500,000	2,500,000 and over
Number of Enterprises 1	8041	543	5975	632	707	27	76	28	19	11	11	11	0
Revenues ($ in Thousands)													
Net Sales 2	26596281	8814	2231393	624230	4305429	336080	1537047	1105477	1517230	1512239	1928164	11490179	0
Interest 3	567833	0	383	2191	2084	0	4967	1611	6663	4946	15562	529427	0
Rents 4	69394	0	0	0	8713	0	1885	10125	3130	621	20572	24348	0
Royalties 5	286542	0	0	0	0	0	0	23	989	4047	127781	153703	0
Other Portfolio Income 6	538594	0	2	0	3759	196	18778	6018	41676	41389	69800	356976	0
Other Receipts 7	408886	0	3499	1375	32530	54136	11761	23212	40056	50230	23678	168405	0
Total Receipts 8	28467530	8814	2235277	627796	4352515	390412	1574438	1146466	1609744	1613472	2185557	12723038	0
Average Total Receipts 9	3540	16	374	993	6156	14460	20716	40945	84723	146679	198687	1156640	•
Operating Costs/Operating Income (%)													
Cost of Operations 10	39.3	80.1	29.0	21.3	61.6	21.3	39.7	40.5	47.8	40.6	32.8	34.2	•
Salaries and Wages 11	16.9	•	16.0	24.8	9.9	28.2	15.3	18.6	15.0	19.5	24.3	17.6	•
Taxes Paid 12	2.4	•	2.3	3.4	2.2	3.1	2.9	2.4	2.4	2.8	3.1	2.1	•
Interest Paid 13	6.2	•	0.1	1.2	0.3	2.6	1.0	1.2	0.9	6.0	7.2	11.7	•
Depreciation 14	1.5	•	0.8	1.0	0.7	0.7	1.6	1.5	1.2	1.5	3.2	1.7	•
Amortization and Depletion 15	3.9	•	0.1	1.9	0.9	1.0	1.0	1.3	2.0	4.4	3.6	6.7	•
Pensions and Other Deferred Comp. 16	0.8	•	1.3	•	0.4	1.2	0.7	0.4	0.5	1.3	2.0	0.8	•
Employee Benefits 17	1.7	•	1.3	2.2	1.1	1.3	2.0	2.0	1.3	1.8	3.1	1.8	•
Advertising 18	1.8	•	2.3	0.1	1.3	3.6	1.6	1.6	3.2	1.7	4.3	1.5	•
Other Expenses 19	25.2	0.7	34.0	36.4	16.6	42.7	29.2	21.6	22.5	23.0	27.8	25.7	•
Officers' Compensation 20	3.1	24.4	11.5	10.3	3.3	7.0	3.9	3.3	2.0	3.0	2.6	1.0	•
Operating Margin 21	•	•	1.2	•	1.7	•	1.2	5.7	1.3	•	•	•	•
Operating Margin Before Officers' Comp. 22	0.2	19.2	12.8	7.6	5.0	•	5.1	9.0	3.3	•	•	•	•

Selected Average Balance Sheet ($ in Thousands)

Net Receivables 23	482	0	13	243	1169	1314	2618	5684	13286	19790	30566	146963	•
Inventories 24	83	0	5	22	70	669	720	841	2268	4551	2561	33564	•
Net Property, Plant and Equipment 25	234	0	9	53	186	386	2511	6022	6222	17657	16942	72360	•
Total Assets 26	4480	0	79	680	2940	8398	15118	32421	68440	168136	324282	2185368	•
Notes and Loans Payable 27	2463	0	33	153	477	7157	2960	6888	14099	91173	109091	1463093	•
All Other Liabilities 28	1422	0	31	354	1952	1604	6771	15817	35477	56655	82253	585897	•
Net Worth 29	594	0	15	173	511	-363	5387	9717	18864	20309	132939	136378	•

Selected Financial Ratios (Times to 1)

Current Ratio 30	1.1	•	1.3	1.1	1.3	1.2	1.5	1.6	1.1	1.1	2.0	0.9	•
Quick Ratio 31	0.8	•	0.9	1.0	1.0	1.0	1.0	1.1	0.8	0.7	1.6	0.5	•
Net Sales to Working Capital 32	28.5	•	27.2	36.1	16.1	18.6	9.1	6.3	20.7	24.3	3.3	•	•
Coverage Ratio 33	1.7	•	15.4	•	9.1	2.3	4.8	8.7	8.8	1.2	0.9	1.5	•
Total Asset Turnover 34	0.7	•	4.7	1.5	2.1	1.5	1.3	1.2	1.2	0.8	0.5	0.5	•
Inventory Turnover 35	15.8	•	23.0	9.7	53.8	4.0	11.1	19.0	16.8	12.3	22.5	10.6	•
Receivables Turnover 36	7.8	•	42.1	3.8	5.1	6.1	7.5	6.9	7.5	7.0	6.2	9.7	•
Total Liabilities to Net Worth 37	6.5	•	4.2	2.9	4.8	•	1.8	2.3	2.6	7.3	1.4	15.0	•
Current Assets to Working Capital 38	9.9	•	4.4	13.5	4.9	6.0	3.2	2.8	8.2	10.4	2.0	•	•
Current Liabilities to Working Capital 39	8.9	•	3.4	12.5	3.9	5.0	2.2	1.8	7.2	9.4	1.0	•	•
Working Capital to Net Sales 40	0.0	•	0.0	0.0	0.1	0.1	0.1	0.2	0.0	0.0	0.3	•	•
Inventory to Working Capital 41	0.9	•	0.3	0.6	0.2	0.2	0.3	0.1	0.6	0.9	0.0	•	•
Total Receipts to Cash Flow 42	4.0	•	3.1	3.4	6.2	2.3	3.4	3.5	4.0	5.1	5.1	3.7	•
Cost of Goods to Cash Flow 43	1.6	•	0.9	0.7	3.8	0.5	1.4	1.4	1.9	2.1	1.7	1.3	•
Cash Flow to Total Debt 44	0.2	•	1.9	0.6	0.4	0.6	0.6	0.5	0.4	0.2	0.2	0.1	•

Selected Financial Factors (in Percentages)

Debt Ratio 45	86.7	•	80.7	74.6	82.6	104.3	64.4	70.0	72.4	87.9	59.0	93.8	•
Return on Total Assets 46	7.8	•	7.1	•	6.5	9.0	6.2	12.6	9.5	6.0	3.4	8.7	•
Return on Equity Before Income Taxes 47	24.2	•	34.5	33.4	13.8	•	37.2	30.7	9.5	•	•	48.8	•
Return on Equity After Income Taxes 48	18.0	•	34.5	31.4	11.1	•	34.8	21.2	1.4	•	•	38.5	•
Profit Margin (Before Income Tax) 49	4.3	•	1.4	•	2.8	3.5	3.7	9.2	7.2	1.4	•	6.4	•
Profit Margin (After Income Tax) 50	3.2	•	1.4	•	2.6	3.0	3.0	8.6	5.0	0.2	•	5.0	•

Table II
Corporations with Net Income

PERIODICAL PUBLISHERS

MONEY AMOUNTS AND SIZE OF ASSETS IN THOUSANDS OF DOLLARS

Item Description for Accounting Period 7/05 Through 6/06	Total	Zero Assets	Under 500	500 to 1,000	1,000 to 5,000	5,000 to 10,000	10,000 to 25,000	25,000 to 50,000	50,000 to 100,000	100,000 to 250,000	250,000 to 500,000	500,000 to 2,500,000	2,500,000 and over
Number of Enterprises 1	3615	0	2539	556	398	15	51	19	16	5	•	•	0
Revenues ($ in Thousands)													
Net Sales 2	21304312	0	1321174	473107	2653887	267301	1265940	849814	1231279	886358	•	•	0
Interest 3	554617	0	382	2183	1078	0	4623	1167	6136	4606	•	•	0
Rents 4	39708	0	0	0	0	0	1884	10125	346	621	•	•	0
Royalties 5	167571	0	0	0	0	0	0	0	311	415	•	•	0
Other Portfolio Income 6	511473	0	0	0	3759	173	13637	3283	38701	25270	•	•	0
Other Receipts 7	308787	0	148	643	30728	5904	6223	10372	35208	47072	•	•	0
Total Receipts 8	22886468	0	1321704	475933	2689452	273378	1292307	874761	1311981	964342	•	•	0
Average Total Receipts 9	6331	•	521	856	6757	18225	25339	46040	81999	192868	•	•	•
Operating Costs/Operating Income (%)													
Cost of Operations 10	35.9	•	21.7	18.2	54.3	17.7	39.7	39.3	40.1	34.4	•	•	•
Salaries and Wages 11	16.9	•	19.7	23.2	9.6	18.3	14.0	18.4	16.5	17.4	•	•	•
Taxes Paid 12	2.4	•	1.9	2.9	2.8	2.6	2.7	2.3	2.7	2.7	•	•	•
Interest Paid 13	6.5	•	•	1.0	0.4	0.0	0.7	0.6	0.9	0.8	•	•	•
Depreciation 14	1.5	•	0.4	1.1	1.1	0.7	1.3	1.8	1.3	1.5	•	•	•
Amortization and Depletion 15	4.0	•	0.1	2.4	0.5	0.5	1.1	1.1	1.6	1.8	•	•	•
Pensions and Other Deferred Comp. 16	0.8	•	•	•	0.4	1.2	0.8	0.5	0.5	1.7	•	•	•
Employee Benefits 17	1.7	•	0.4	2.8	1.1	0.8	2.3	2.2	1.5	1.2	•	•	•
Advertising 18	1.6	•	0.9	0.0	1.6	0.9	1.2	1.3	3.4	1.8	•	•	•
Other Expenses 19	25.3	•	34.2	35.0	17.7	41.0	25.0	18.2	23.2	28.7	•	•	•
Officers' Compensation 20	2.1	•	3.5	11.0	2.6	8.6	4.1	3.6	1.9	3.7	•	•	•
Operating Margin 21	1.4	•	17.2	2.4	7.9	7.7	7.1	10.7	6.3	4.2	•	•	•
Operating Margin Before Officers' Comp. 22	3.5	•	20.7	13.4	10.5	16.3	11.2	14.3	8.2	7.9	•	•	•

Selected Average Balance Sheet ($ in Thousands)

Net Receivables 23	770	22	244	1107	1831	2846	6013	13466	26363
Inventories 24	148	0	16	63	1203	757	1068	2146	8689
Net Property, Plant and Equipment 25	425	9	38	304	512	2643	7646	6093	24534
Total Assets 26	8316	94	693	3405	9154	15463	33851	67198	156073
Notes and Loans Payable 27	4808	35	123	505	2673	3190	5297	14229	29287
All Other Liabilities 28	2214	12	294	1513	2627	5853	17774	32822	60112
Net Worth 29	1294	46	277	1388	3854	6420	10780	20147	66675

Selected Financial Ratios (Times to 1)

Current Ratio 30	1.2	1.9	1.2	1.7	1.4	1.6	1.6	1.2	1.2
Quick Ratio 31	0.8	1.6	1.1	1.3	1.3	1.2	1.1	0.8	0.9
Net Sales to Working Capital 32	16.9	13.4	17.2	8.5	9.1	9.5	6.4	15.0	14.8
Coverage Ratio 33	2.4		3.9	27.4	309.0	13.5	24.7	14.7	17.8
Total Asset Turnover 34	0.7	5.6	1.2	2.0	1.9	1.6	1.3	1.1	1.1
Inventory Turnover 35	14.3		9.7	57.4	2.6	13.0	16.4	14.4	7.0
Receivables Turnover 36	8.9	48.1	3.7	4.1	6.0	8.7	6.9	7.3	6.6
Total Liabilities to Net Worth 37	5.4	1.0	1.5	1.5	1.4	1.4	2.1	2.3	1.3
Current Assets to Working Capital 38	5.6	2.1	7.4	2.5	3.2	2.8	2.6	6.1	5.9
Current Liabilities to Working Capital 39	4.6	1.1	6.4	1.5	2.2	1.8	1.6	5.1	4.9
Working Capital to Net Sales 40	0.1	0.1	0.1	0.1	0.1	0.1	0.2	0.1	0.1
Inventory to Working Capital 41	0.5		0.4	0.0	0.1	0.3	0.2	0.4	0.8
Total Receipts to Cash Flow 42	3.4	2.1	3.1	4.4	2.1	3.2	3.4	3.3	2.6
Cost of Goods to Cash Flow 43	1.2	0.4	0.6	2.4	0.4	1.3	1.3	1.3	0.9
Cash Flow to Total Debt 44	0.2	5.3	0.7	0.7	1.6	0.8	0.6	0.5	0.8

Selected Financial Factors (in Percentages)

Debt Ratio 45	84.4	50.6	60.1	59.2	57.9	58.5	68.2	70.0	57.3
Return on Total Assets 46	11.0	95.8	4.9	18.9	19.4	15.9	18.7	15.6	15.8
Return on Equity Before Income Taxes 47	41.2	193.9	9.2	44.6	45.8	35.4	56.4	48.5	35.0
Return on Equity After Income Taxes 48	34.9	193.9	8.7	43.3	43.0	32.0	53.7	37.9	29.5
Profit Margin (Before Income Tax) 49	9.0	17.3	3.0	9.3	9.9	9.2	13.6	12.7	13.1
Profit Margin (After Income Tax) 50	7.7	17.3	2.8	9.0	9.3	8.3	12.9	9.9	11.1

Table I

Corporations with and without Net Income

BOOK PUBLISHERS

MONEY AMOUNTS AND SIZE OF ASSETS IN THOUSANDS OF DOLLARS

Item Description for Accounting Period 7/05 Through 6/06	Total	Zero Assets	Under 500	500 to 1,000	1,000 to 5,000	5,000 to 10,000	10,000 to 25,000	25,000 to 50,000	50,000 to 100,000	100,000 to 250,000	250,000 to 500,000	500,000 to 2,500,000	2,500,000 and over
Number of Enterprises 1	5445	1007	3590	315	374	73	29	28	7	9	3	6	5
Revenues ($ in Thousands)													
Net Sales 2	27657034	118469	491321	260967	960479	1054149	421661	1159013	443210	1442065	375765	4435609	16494329
Interest 3	1145394	1868	516	1136	479	301	312	1586	2154	8679	1464	9028	1117869
Rents 4	68656	0	0	0	225	0	334	1587	966	26	927	5308	59284
Royalties 5	480477	2602	0	0	8	0	0	4053	5274	4528	87	59407	404518
Other Portfolio Income 6	940193	0	0	0	58	22203	16	7194	1653	140293	36	4843	763898
Other Receipts 7	1003695	5099	28827	0	1050	7403	2405	33646	4676	90065	3501	70836	756185
Total Receipts 8	31295449	128038	520664	262103	962299	1084056	424728	1207079	457933	1685656	381780	4585031	19596083
Average Total Receipts 9	5748	127	145	832	2573	14850	14646	43110	65419	187295	127260	764172	3919217
Operating Costs/Operating Income (%)													
Cost of Operations 10	31.4	51.0	61.6	42.0	36.3	18.2	56.4	41.6	37.4	33.8	26.0	38.6	27.2
Salaries and Wages 11	20.9	35.5	10.2	5.6	8.9	36.1	14.0	15.1	20.9	21.6	16.2	18.4	22.5
Taxes Paid 12	2.7	3.4	3.7	1.3	1.4	3.9	2.8	2.1	1.9	2.3	1.9	2.1	2.9
Interest Paid 13	8.0	9.6	0.3	10.5	1.3	1.4	2.0	2.3	2.1	4.7	14.3	4.8	10.7
Depreciation 14	3.0	0.5	0.5	0.2	0.8	1.7	1.3	1.3	1.1	0.7	0.7	2.1	4.0
Amortization and Depletion 15	3.1	2.0	•	6.1	0.3	0.0	0.3	1.8	2.4	4.0	13.3	4.1	3.1
Pensions and Other Deferred Comp. 16	1.1	0.6	2.0	0.1	1.9	1.4	0.3	0.5	0.9	0.9	0.1	1.0	1.2
Employee Benefits 17	2.6	1.7	2.4	0.7	0.4	4.1	1.7	1.6	2.1	1.8	1.2	4.3	2.5
Advertising 18	2.8	2.4	0.8	•	0.8	1.0	4.4	9.8	4.8	2.3	1.7	2.8	2.5
Other Expenses 19	26.1	25.0	16.3	39.3	21.1	22.4	13.8	24.7	23.8	32.1	38.2	20.4	27.8
Officers' Compensation 20	2.1	0.7	8.2	10.4	9.9	2.8	3.4	3.3	1.6	2.2	0.6	1.6	1.3
Operating Margin 21	•	•	•	•	17.1	6.9	•	•	1.0	•	•	•	•
Operating Margin Before Officers' Comp. 22	•	•	2.2	•	26.9	9.7	3.1	•	2.6	•	•	1.3	•

Selected Average Balance Sheet ($ in Thousands)

Net Receivables 23	848	0	8	109	317	3460	4006	5837	11141	38362	27306	129799	523855
Inventories 24	568	0	10	478	364	558	5607	7035	14903	16560	35195	103875	278175
Net Property, Plant and Equipment 25	549	0	19	0	219	1000	964	2988	6066	7166	13813	123044	353860
Total Assets 26	9626	0	60	743	1929	7855	13666	34950	63757	162180	417689	1306302	7659304
Notes and Loans Payable 27	3417	0	29	1491	609	2407	4759	10411	46860	71951	362247	604746	2301636
All Other Liabilities 28	2905	0	29	303	276	2296	5747	16385	28127	62531	64650	344324	2340349
Net Worth 29	3303	0	1	-1050	1044	3152	3160	8154	-11230	27698	-9208	357233	3017318

Selected Financial Ratios (Times to 1)

Current Ratio 30	1.3	•	1.1	3.0	2.0	1.2	1.6	1.7	1.7	1.2	1.7	1.1	1.2
Quick Ratio 31	0.5	•	0.3	1.6	1.4	0.6	0.5	0.7	0.7	0.7	1.1	0.6	0.5
Net Sales to Working Capital 32	7.9	•	18.3	3.5	5.2	8.2	4.6	3.5	3.5	12.5	3.4	17.4	7.8
Coverage Ratio 33	2.2	0.9	•	13.9	8.1	1.2	1.1	3.1	3.2	3.2	0.1	1.6	2.2
Total Asset Turnover 34	0.5	•	2.3	1.1	1.3	1.8	1.1	1.2	1.0	1.0	0.3	0.6	0.4
Inventory Turnover 35	2.8	8.8	0.7	2.6	4.7	1.5	2.4	1.6	3.3	3.3	0.9	2.7	3.2
Receivables Turnover 36	5.7	17.8	6.2	7.6	5.2	2.6	9.5	5.8	5.2	5.2	1.9	5.1	5.9
Total Liabilities to Net Worth 37	1.9	•	57.4	•	0.8	1.5	3.3	3.3	•	4.9	•	2.7	1.5
Current Assets to Working Capital 38	4.7	•	12.0	1.5	2.0	5.5	2.6	2.4	2.4	6.3	2.4	8.7	5.1
Current Liabilities to Working Capital 39	3.7	•	11.0	0.5	1.0	4.5	1.6	1.4	1.4	5.3	1.4	7.7	4.1
Working Capital to Net Sales 40	0.1	•	0.1	0.3	0.2	0.1	0.2	0.3	0.3	0.1	0.3	0.1	0.1
Inventory to Working Capital 41	0.9	•	8.7	0.5	0.4	2.0	1.1	0.9	0.9	1.5	0.5	2.6	0.7
Total Receipts to Cash Flow 42	3.3	7.5	4.8	2.9	3.9	9.1	4.6	3.9	3.9	3.3	6.1	5.2	2.8
Cost of Goods to Cash Flow 43	1.0	4.6	2.0	1.0	0.7	5.1	1.9	1.5	1.5	1.1	1.6	2.0	0.8
Cash Flow to Total Debt 44	0.2	0.3	0.1	1.0	0.8	0.2	0.3	0.2	0.2	0.4	0.0	0.2	0.3

Selected Financial Factors (in Percentages)

Debt Ratio 45	65.7		98.3	241.4	45.9	59.9	76.9	76.7	117.6	82.9	102.2	72.7	60.6
Return on Total Assets 46	9.2		0.6	•	24.7	20.4	2.7	3.0	6.2	15.1	0.5	4.4	10.3
Return on Equity Before Income Taxes 47	14.6		•	12.4	42.4	44.7	2.2	1.2	•	60.9	171.7	6.2	14.4
Return on Equity After Income Taxes 48	11.0		•	12.4	41.8	43.9	2.0	•	•	54.8	171.7	3.8	10.7
Profit Margin (Before Income Tax) 49	9.5		•	•	17.2	9.7	0.5	0.2	4.2	10.5	•	3.0	13.1
Profit Margin (After Income Tax) 50	7.2		•	•	17.0	9.6	0.4	•	3.2	9.5	•	1.8	9.8

Table II
Corporations with Net Income

BOOK PUBLISHERS

MONEY AMOUNTS AND SIZE OF ASSETS IN THOUSANDS OF DOLLARS

Item Description for Accounting Period 7/05 Through 6/06	Total	Zero Assets	Under 500	500 to 1,000	1,000 to 5,000	5,000 to 10,000	10,000 to 25,000	25,000 to 50,000	50,000 to 100,000	100,000 to 250,000	250,000 to 500,000	500,000 to 2,500,000	2,500,000 and over
Number of Enterprises 1	2180	490	1142	123	308	62	18	20	3	5	0	3	5
Revenues ($ in Thousands)													
Net Sales 2	23678440	112019	159536	148274	864591	1054070	279625	771263	207714	661544	0	2925476	16649329
Interest 3	1135508	1868	515	1136	460	301	21	1332	1215	6647	0	4143	1117869
Rents 4	67083	0	0	0	225	0	334	965	966	0	0	5308	59284
Royalties 5	456124	2602	0	0	0	0	0	2884	1206	1181	0	43734	404518
Other Portfolio Income 6	937091	0	0	0	41	22203	16	4954	1653	140026	0	4299	763898
Other Receipts 7	890062	4842	567	0	910	7403	2236	11657	2259	45947	0	58057	756185
Total Receipts 8	27164308	121331	160618	149410	866227	1083977	282232	793055	215013	855345	0	3041017	19596083
Average Total Receipts 9	12461	248	141	1215	2812	17484	15680	39653	71671	171069	•	1013672	3919217
Operating Costs/Operating Income (%)													
Cost of Operations 10	30.8	53.1	27.3	46.1	37.8	18.2	50.9	43.8	26.6	39.7	•	44.6	27.2
Salaries and Wages 11	21.3	10.9	•	3.8	8.6	36.1	13.7	18.0	20.6	20.6	•	17.2	22.5
Taxes Paid 12	2.8	1.5	8.7	1.4	1.2	3.9	3.0	2.7	2.5	2.4	•	2.2	2.9
Interest Paid 13	8.2	10.1	•	1.5	1.4	1.4	2.0	1.9	0.1	7.8	•	2.3	10.7
Depreciation 14	3.3	0.5	0.1	0.1	0.8	1.7	1.0	1.7	1.3	0.5	•	2.1	4.0
Amortization and Depletion 15	2.7	1.7	•	•	0.0	0.0	0.2	2.6	3.8	7.0	•	1.4	3.1
Pensions and Other Deferred Comp. 16	1.1	0.4	6.2	0.1	1.8	1.4	0.4	0.6	1.4	1.0	•	0.7	1.2
Employee Benefits 17	2.4	1.8	2.5	1.2	0.3	4.1	1.5	1.9	1.2	1.7	•	2.6	2.5
Advertising 18	2.4	2.6	0.8	•	0.9	1.0	1.9	3.9	6.8	3.7	•	1.6	2.5
Other Expenses 19	25.7	22.2	20.5	26.2	19.1	22.4	17.4	15.7	22.1	16.8	•	22.7	27.8
Officers' Compensation 20	2.1	0.7	25.2	18.2	8.6	2.8	4.0	2.8	1.3	2.6	•	1.5	1.3
Operating Margin 21	•	•	8.6	1.3	19.4	7.1	4.0	4.4	12.4	•	•	1.1	•
Operating Margin Before Officers' Comp. 22	•	•	33.8	19.5	28.0	9.8	8.0	7.3	13.7	•	•	2.6	•

Selected Average Balance Sheet ($ in Thousands)

Net Receivables 23	1734	0	0	272	357	4072	4570	5458	7534	36259	•	123044	523855
Inventories 24	1003	0	11	6	334	1143	7146	6511	10571	17196	•	145122	286545
Net Property, Plant and Equipment 25	1153	0	29	0	260	1177	1317	3808	11128	1948	•	138484	353860
Total Assets 26	20977	0	70	625	2099	8350	14025	33265	65100	159168	•	1401265	7659304
Notes and Loans Payable 27	6367	0	0	498	665	2832	5538	8506	866	70458	•	434966	2301636
All Other Liabilities 28	6212	0	9	36	291	2704	3339	14970	15825	46782	•	309290	2340349
Net Worth 29	8398	0	61	91	1143	2814	5147	9790	48410	41928	•	657010	3017318

Selected Financial Ratios (Times to 1)

Current Ratio 30	1.3	•	3.7	0.6	3.3	2.0	1.8	1.7	2.8	1.8	•	1.3	1.2
Quick Ratio 31	0.5	•	3.4	0.6	1.8	1.4	0.9	0.6	1.4	1.0	•	0.6	0.5
Net Sales to Working Capital 32	7.0	•	5.5	•	3.4	5.2	3.2	4.0	2.6	3.8	•	10.7	7.8
Coverage Ratio 33	2.5	1.3	•	2.3	15.1	8.2	3.5	4.7	155.6	4.2	•	3.2	2.2
Total Asset Turnover 34	0.5	•	2.0	1.9	1.3	2.0	1.1	1.2	1.1	0.8	•	0.7	0.4
Inventory Turnover 35	3.3	•	3.6	99.8	3.2	2.7	1.1	2.6	1.7	3.1	•	3.0	3.1
Receivables Turnover 36	6.5	•	102.3	8.7	7.2	8.4	2.2	8.7	18.4	4.2	•	15.9	12.6
Total Liabilities to Net Worth 37	1.5	•	0.2	5.9	0.8	2.0	1.7	2.4	0.3	2.8	•	1.1	1.5
Current Assets to Working Capital 38	4.2	•	1.4	•	1.4	2.0	2.2	2.4	1.6	2.2	•	4.5	5.1
Current Liabilities to Working Capital 39	3.2	•	0.4	•	0.4	1.0	1.2	1.4	0.6	1.2	•	3.5	4.1
Working Capital to Net Sales 40	0.1	•	0.2	•	0.3	0.2	0.3	0.2	0.4	0.3	•	0.1	0.1
Inventory to Working Capital 41	0.7	•	0.1	•	0.4	0.4	1.0	0.9	0.4	0.5	•	1.6	0.7
Total Receipts to Cash Flow 42	3.1	4.2	4.2	3.7	2.8	3.9	5.2	5.1	2.8	5.4	•	4.2	2.8
Cost of Goods to Cash Flow 43	0.9	2.2	1.1	1.7	1.1	0.7	2.7	2.2	0.8	2.2	•	1.9	0.8
Cash Flow to Total Debt 44	0.3	•	3.6	0.6	1.0	0.8	0.3	0.3	1.5	0.2	•	0.3	0.3

Selected Financial Factors (in Percentages)

Debt Ratio 45	60.0	•	13.4	85.5	45.5	66.3	63.3	70.6	25.6	73.7	•	53.1	60.6
Return on Total Assets 46	10.6	•	18.5	6.9	28.0	22.9	7.6	10.7	16.9	27.6	•	5.1	10.3
Return on Equity Before Income Taxes 47	15.7	•	21.3	27.0	48.0	59.7	14.8	28.6	22.6	80.1	•	7.4	14.4
Return on Equity After Income Taxes 48	12.2	•	21.2	26.4	47.3	58.8	14.6	21.8	19.3	72.7	•	4.8	10.7
Profit Margin (Before Income Tax) 49	12.1	2.8	9.3	2.0	19.5	9.9	4.9	7.3	15.8	25.4	•	5.0	13.1
Profit Margin (After Income Tax) 50	9.4	2.0	9.2	2.0	19.3	9.7	4.8	5.5	13.5	23.0	•	3.3	9.8

Table I

Corporations with and without Net Income

DATABASE, DIRECTORY, AND OTHER PUBLISHERS

MONEY AMOUNTS AND SIZE OF ASSETS IN THOUSANDS OF DOLLARS

Item Description for Accounting Period 7/05 Through 6/06	Total	Zero Assets	Under 500	500 to 1,000	1,000 to 5,000	5,000 to 10,000	10,000 to 25,000	25,000 to 50,000	50,000 to 100,000	100,000 to 250,000	250,000 to 500,000	500,000 to 2,500,000	2,500,000 and over
Number of Enterprises **1**	5317	1204	3462	315	180	92	27	12	7	7	3	3	5
Revenues ($ in Thousands)													
Net Sales **2**	18437021	89847	347521	905645	1414059	1380901	604067	573577	478548	867537	304791	2009372	9461157
Interest **3**	225101	149	2071	119	846	712	677	864	2394	3509	439	1187	212136
Rents **4**	57922	0	0	0	0	0	0	2052	39	37	0	0	55794
Royalties **5**	107005	0	0	0	0	0	0	0	0	13927	0	0	93078
Other Portfolio Income **6**	203007	15604	8515	0	45	198	35238	501	4344	7446	6126	53164	71825
Other Receipts **7**	283093	19699	1892	1979	2805	4051	1588	185	14343	22512	4994	151262	57781
Total Receipts **8**	19313149	125299	359999	907743	1417755	1385862	641570	577179	499668	914968	316350	2214985	9951771
Average Total Receipts **9**	3632	104	104	2882	7876	15064	23762	48098	71381	130710	105450	738328	1990354
Operating Costs/Operating Income (%)													
Cost of Operations **10**	26.8	23.4	13.4	19.9	31.6	47.2	38.8	17.8	49.9	16.1	34.4	22.5	24.6
Salaries and Wages **11**	20.2	19.2	8.5	19.7	21.8	22.9	17.5	34.1	12.2	23.6	21.1	37.8	15.8
Taxes Paid **12**	4.0	2.9	2.8	3.4	2.1	2.7	3.0	3.3	1.1	2.3	1.8	2.9	5.3
Interest Paid **13**	6.2	2.9	0.0	0.5	0.4	0.7	0.9	1.0	2.3	3.6	6.5	1.3	10.8
Depreciation **14**	1.7	0.4	0.1	0.5	1.8	1.3	1.6	1.5	2.1	2.0	1.6	2.2	1.8
Amortization and Depletion **15**	3.5	10.3	4.1	0.0	0.2	0.2	0.4	0.5	1.4	4.6	8.8	2.0	5.2
Pensions and Other Deferred Comp. **16**	0.5	•	•	0.4	0.4	0.4	0.5	1.1	0.3	0.2	•	0.6	0.6
Employee Benefits **17**	1.7	0.3	1.3	0.9	0.5	1.7	1.2	3.1	1.5	3.0	2.4	3.9	1.3
Advertising **18**	2.8	0.3	0.4	0.3	1.6	1.6	2.4	2.2	4.1	4.8	0.3	1.6	3.7
Other Expenses **19**	30.0	108.1	65.7	45.7	14.9	13.5	21.2	26.8	19.1	44.8	27.6	21.1	33.0
Officers' Compensation **20**	3.7	1.8	22.4	8.2	22.3	3.0	6.7	2.5	1.3	1.6	0.7	1.1	0.7
Operating Margin **21**	•	•	•	0.5	2.4	4.8	5.8	6.1	4.7	•	•	3.0	•
Operating Margin Before Officers' Comp. **22**	2.5	•	3.7	8.8	24.7	7.8	12.5	8.6	6.0	•	•	4.0	•

Selected Average Balance Sheet ($ in Thousands)

Item	1	2	3	4	5	6	7	8	9	10	11	12	13
Net Receivables **23**	754	0	0	358	1053	4139	3251	6801	16797	28483	29225	150499	460376
Inventories **24**	412	0	0	0	35	234	1484	1883	922	6297	2692	5352	405358
Net Property, Plant and Equipment **25**	347	0	0	55	489	901	1087	4360	5700	10803	9217	67213	245502
Total Assets **26**	5601	0	24	760	2163	7734	14413	32431	86949	167520	331575	698393	4541454
Notes and Loans Payable **27**	2207	0	66	100	268	1373	2861	5698	16861	58634	76164	72228	2036133
All Other Liabilities **28**	1916	0	11	547	911	4710	5404	24221	20715	106247	104014	344938	1341135
Net Worth **29**	1477	0	-54	112	983	1650	6148	2512	49373	2639	151397	281228	1164186

Selected Financial Ratios (Times to 1)

Item	1	2	3	4	5	6	7	8	9	10	11	12	13
Current Ratio **30**	0.9	•	0.2	0.9	1.7	1.4	1.3	1.7	1.9	0.8	0.6	0.8	0.8
Quick Ratio **31**	0.5	•	0.1	0.8	1.5	1.2	0.9	1.4	1.4	0.4	0.3	0.7	0.4
Net Sales to Working Capital **32**	1.7	•	•	•	11.9	9.4	11.3	6.0	3.7	•	•	•	•
Coverage Ratio **33**	1.7	•	2.6	2.6	8.3	8.0	14.4	7.8	5.0	0.7	0.8	11.7	1.3
Total Asset Turnover **34**	0.6	•	4.3	3.8	3.6	1.9	1.6	1.5	0.8	0.7	0.3	1.0	0.4
Inventory Turnover **35**	2.3	•	28.7	•	71.7	30.3	5.9	4.5	37.0	3.2	13.0	28.2	1.1
Receivables Turnover **36**	4.2	•	45.9	8.6	7.4	3.6	4.9	5.1	4.2	2.6	7.0	2.9	4.1
Total Liabilities to Net Worth **37**	2.8	•	•	5.8	1.2	3.7	1.3	11.9	0.8	62.5	1.2	1.5	2.9
Current Assets to Working Capital **38**	•	•	•	•	2.5	3.7	4.2	2.4	2.1	•	•	•	•
Current Liabilities to Working Capital **39**	•	•	•	•	1.5	2.7	3.2	1.4	1.1	•	•	•	•
Working Capital to Net Sales **40**	•	•	•	•	0.1	0.1	0.1	0.2	0.3	•	•	•	•
Inventory to Working Capital **41**	•	•	•	•	0.1	0.2	0.6	0.2	0.0	•	•	•	•
Total Receipts to Cash Flow **42**	4.0	5.4	2.2	7.1	7.4	6.5	4.2	3.4	4.0	2.5	5.3	3.3	3.8
Cost of Goods to Cash Flow **43**	1.1	1.3	0.3	1.4	2.3	3.1	1.6	0.6	2.0	0.4	1.8	0.8	0.9
Cash Flow to Total Debt **44**	0.2	0.6	0.6	0.9	0.4	0.6	0.5	0.5	0.3	0.1	0.5	0.1	0.1

Selected Financial Factors (in Percentages)

Item	1	2	3	4	5	6	7	8	9	10	11	12	13
Debt Ratio **45**	73.6	•	330.5	85.2	54.5	78.7	57.3	92.3	43.2	98.4	54.3	59.7	74.4
Return on Total Assets **46**	6.3	•	•	4.6	10.9	11.4	20.0	11.3	9.0	1.9	1.6	15.0	5.7
Return on Equity Before Income Taxes **47**	9.5	•	27.9	19.5	21.0	46.7	43.5	126.7	12.6	•	•	34.1	4.8
Return on Equity After Income Taxes **48**	7.1	•	27.9	18.6	20.0	44.1	35.1	126.2	10.8	•	•	23.4	3.7
Profit Margin (Before Income Tax) **49**	4.0	•	•	0.8	2.6	5.1	12.0	6.7	9.1	•	•	14.3	3.0
Profit Margin (After Income Tax) **50**	3.0	•	•	0.7	2.5	4.9	9.6	6.6	7.8	•	•	9.8	2.3

259

Table II
Corporations with Net Income

DATABASE, DIRECTORY, AND OTHER PUBLISHERS

MONEY AMOUNTS AND SIZE OF ASSETS IN THOUSANDS OF DOLLARS

Item Description for Accounting Period 7/05 Through 6/06	Total	Zero Assets	Under 500	500 to 1,000	1,000 to 5,000	5,000 to 10,000	10,000 to 25,000	25,000 to 50,000	50,000 to 100,000	100,000 to 250,000	250,000 to 500,000	500,000 to 2,500,000	2,500,000 and over
Number of Enterprises **1**	2429	9	1891	254	147	80	24	9	3	•	0	•	5
Revenues ($ in Thousands)													
Net Sales **2**	17243291	28216	284683	841053	1288432	1369608	502631	513861	218642	•	0	•	9461157
Interest **3**	219774	104	436	4	83	665	529	309	1086	•	0	•	212136
Rents **4**	57751	0	0	0	0	0	0	1918	39	•	0	•	55794
Royalties **5**	106986	0	0	0	0	0	0	0	0	•	0	•	93078
Other Portfolio Income **6**	182965	0	8515	0	45	130	35233	477	6	•	0	•	71825
Other Receipts **7**	233836	462	27	1804	171	4010	1546	134	1656	•	0	•	57781
Total Receipts **8**	18044603	28782	293661	842861	1288731	1374413	539939	516699	221429	•	0	•	9951771
Average Total Receipts **9**	7429	3198	155	3318	8767	17180	22497	57411	73810	•	•	•	1990354
Operating Costs/Operating Income (%)													
Cost of Operations **10**	26.1	31.0	1.4	21.5	31.8	47.1	35.1	18.4	33.3	•	•	•	24.6
Salaries and Wages **11**	20.2	2.6	6.6	18.5	20.9	22.7	17.9	33.0	9.6	•	•	•	15.8
Taxes Paid **12**	4.1	0.5	2.2	3.3	2.0	2.6	2.4	3.2	1.3	•	•	•	5.3
Interest Paid **13**	6.4	•	0.0	0.4	0.2	0.7	0.8	0.7	0.7	•	•	•	10.8
Depreciation **14**	1.6	0.1	0.1	0.6	1.4	1.3	1.2	1.4	0.7	•	•	•	1.8
Amortization and Depletion **15**	3.4	2.6	•	0.0	0.1	0.2	0.5	0.2	0.1	•	•	•	5.2
Pensions and Other Deferred Comp. **16**	0.5	•	•	•	0.4	0.4	0.4	1.2	0.1	•	•	•	0.6
Employee Benefits **17**	1.7	0.4	1.6	0.6	0.3	1.7	1.2	3.0	2.2	•	•	•	1.3
Advertising **18**	2.8	0.2	0.3	0.2	1.5	1.6	2.5	2.3	8.9	•	•	•	3.7
Other Expenses **19**	29.1	26.0	64.7	46.7	12.5	13.3	22.9	24.0	19.9	•	•	•	33.0
Officers' Compensation **20**	3.6	•	20.0	6.2	24.5	3.0	7.5	2.2	1.5	•	•	•	0.7
Operating Margin **21**	0.5	36.7	3.2	2.1	4.4	5.3	7.6	10.4	21.8	•	•	•	•
Operating Margin Before Officers' Comp. **22**	4.1	36.7	23.2	8.3	28.9	8.3	15.1	12.6	23.2	•	•	•	•

Selected Average Balance Sheet ($ in Thousands)

	C1	C2	C3	C4	C5	C6	C7	C8	C9	C10
Net Receivables 23	1556	0	0	444	1209	4685	3459	8292	20840	460376
Inventories 24	455	0	0	0	24	366	1570	1772	476	358175
Net Property, Plant and Equipment 25	726	0	0	68	518	994	1121	4226	1572	245502
Total Assets 26	11534	•	21	762	2363	7871	14398	33558	79873	4541454
Notes and Loans Payable 27	4591	•	9	94	206	1507	2013	5770	5670	2036133
All Other Liabilities 28	3751	•	6	596	902	5196	5629	24088	15356	1341135
Net Worth 29	3193	•	7	72	1255	1168	6756	3701	58848	1164186

Selected Financial Ratios (Times to 1)

	C1	C2	C3	C4	C5	C6	C7	C8	C9	C10
Current Ratio 30	0.9	•	11.3	0.8	1.8	1.3	1.4	1.8	3.8	0.8
Quick Ratio 31	0.5	•	5.1	0.8	1.7	1.1	1.1	1.5	2.1	0.4
Net Sales to Working Capital 32	•	•	9.6	•	10.6	10.7	8.1	6.1	1.8	•
Coverage Ratio 33	1.9	•	413.7	6.2	20.9	8.8	20.6	17.4	34.8	1.3
Total Asset Turnover 34	0.6	•	7.1	4.3	3.7	2.2	1.5	1.7	0.9	0.4
Inventory Turnover 35	4.1	•	206.7	•	118.3	22.0	4.7	5.9	50.9	1.3
Receivables Turnover 36	5.1	•	40669.0	14.0	7.2	7.3	5.5	5.5	7.0	8.2
Total Liabilities to Net Worth 37	2.6	•	2.2	9.6	0.9	5.7	1.1	8.1	0.4	2.9
Current Assets to Working Capital 38	•	•	1.1	•	2.2	4.0	3.2	2.3	1.4	•
Current Liabilities to Working Capital 39	•	•	0.1	•	1.2	3.0	2.2	1.3	0.4	•
Working Capital to Net Sales 40	•	•	0.1	•	0.1	0.1	0.1	0.2	0.6	•
Inventory to Working Capital 41	•	•	•	•	0.0	0.2	0.5	0.2	0.0	•
Total Receipts to Cash Flow 42	3.9	1.6	1.5	6.7	7.7	6.3	3.6	3.1	2.5	3.8
Cost of Goods to Cash Flow 43	1.0	0.5	0.0	1.4	2.4	3.0	1.2	0.6	0.8	0.9
Cash Flow to Total Debt 44	0.2	•	7.0	0.7	1.0	0.4	0.8	0.6	1.4	0.1

Selected Financial Factors (in Percentages)

	C1	C2	C3	C4	C5	C6	C7	C8	C9	C10
Debt Ratio 45	72.3	69.0	90.6	46.9	85.2	53.1	89.0	26.3	74.4	
Return on Total Assets 46	7.4	45.4	12.1	17.2	14.0	22.8	19.6	21.6	5.7	
Return on Equity Before Income Taxes 47	12.4	146.1	107.5	30.8	83.3	46.2	167.7	28.5	4.8	
Return on Equity After Income Taxes 48	10.0	145.6	105.9	29.8	79.3	37.5	167.2	25.0	3.7	
Profit Margin (Before Income Tax) 49	5.6	38.7	6.4	2.3	4.4	5.7	14.9	10.9	23.0	3.0
Profit Margin (After Income Tax) 50	4.5	38.0	6.4	2.3	4.3	5.4	12.1	10.8	20.2	2.3

Table I

Corporations with and without Net Income

SOFTWARE PUBLISHERS

MONEY AMOUNTS AND SIZE OF ASSETS IN THOUSANDS OF DOLLARS

Item Description for Accounting Period 7/05 Through 6/06	Total	Zero Assets	Under 500	500 to 1,000	1,000 to 5,000	5,000 to 10,000	10,000 to 25,000	25,000 to 50,000	50,000 to 100,000	100,000 to 250,000	250,000 to 500,000	500,000 to 2,500,000	2,500,000 and over
Number of Enterprises **1**	8541	1953	4524	655	679	283	190	89	53	44	31	29	11
Revenues ($ in Thousands)													
Net Sales **2**	86483239	983457	1504674	1490464	2174969	1725749	2603138	3002024	2512196	3853250	5123614	16069145	45440558
Interest **3**	1841988	10609	1710	2330	14203	20151	24156	33906	28956	71508	90350	353740	1190370
Rents **4**	101721	0	0	0	0	1096	351	93	181	4997	9987	37848	47167
Royalties **5**	6013677	8139	15077	0	5279	2975	849	117884	19677	132016	103986	1115985	4491812
Other Portfolio Income **6**	8483632	32675	65	13294	130719	16636	138969	50580	25168	15862	82773	1840780	6136113
Other Receipts **7**	22304503	50029	14404	12824	31515	44067	50936	39553	54116	102985	74264	984673	20845135
Total Receipts **8**	125228760	1084909	1535930	1518912	2356685	1810674	2818399	3244040	2640294	4180618	5484974	20402171	78151155
Average Total Receipts **9**	14662	556	340	2319	3471	6398	14834	36450	49817	95014	176935	703523	7104650
Operating Costs/Operating Income (%)													
Cost of Operations **10**	27.4	40.2	3.0	43.5	28.1	21.4	18.1	25.0	20.9	18.7	17.9	26.3	30.8
Salaries and Wages **11**	36.4	31.6	47.5	19.8	44.2	52.4	45.3	32.8	39.1	36.2	37.9	37.1	34.9
Taxes Paid **12**	3.3	4.1	5.2	2.9	4.4	4.2	4.2	3.9	4.0	3.2	3.7	2.9	3.1
Interest Paid **13**	2.0	0.8	2.8	0.6	1.8	1.8	1.3	0.9	1.7	1.7	0.6	2.2	2.3
Depreciation **14**	2.5	1.3	1.0	1.6	2.6	2.7	2.5	2.2	2.1	2.1	2.2	2.7	2.5
Amortization and Depletion **15**	1.8	2.2	1.1	0.5	1.6	1.1	1.7	0.9	3.8	2.8	1.8	2.1	1.6
Pensions and Other Deferred Comp. **16**	0.4	0.0	0.3	3.6	0.2	0.5	0.4	1.0	0.5	0.3	0.8	1.0	0.0
Employee Benefits **17**	3.5	2.4	3.6	1.5	4.5	4.4	3.0	2.7	3.0	2.8	3.4	3.7	3.6
Advertising **18**	5.5	1.0	1.2	0.7	2.6	2.7	2.4	2.0	2.0	3.0	1.6	4.9	7.6
Other Expenses **19**	34.8	40.2	33.0	22.2	38.3	36.6	35.5	32.0	29.2	37.9	26.4	24.0	40.0
Officers' Compensation **20**	2.5	7.9	16.2	9.1	9.3	7.4	6.0	3.5	2.9	2.3	2.1	2.3	1.0
Operating Margin **21**	•	•	•	•	•	•	•	•	•	•	1.7	•	•
Operating Margin Before Officers' Comp. **22**	•	•	1.4	3.1	•	•	•	•	•	•	3.8	•	•

Selected Average Balance Sheet ($ in Thousands)

Net Receivables 23	4698	0	8	152	556	1542	3763	8667	13195	28851	69175	174312	2593210
Inventories 24	202	0	4	54	38	153	243	279	402	1091	923	16768	85811
Net Property, Plant and Equipment 25	1231	0	19	66	198	615	871	2421	3391	6040	18663	62597	623436
Total Assets 26	22254	0	73	709	2452	7281	15440	36564	70756	160277	366087	1232294	11043393
Notes and Loans Payable 27	2402	0	101	419	1865	1542	2825	4414	12816	24709	20143	132465	992884
All Other Liabilities 28	8555	0	115	429	1089	4165	7530	18068	28804	60062	101096	384479	4441042
Net Worth 29	11297	0	-143	-139	-502	1575	5085	14082	29136	75506	244847	715350	5609468

Selected Financial Ratios (Times to 1)

Current Ratio 30	1.3	•	0.9	1.4	1.7	1.7	1.4	1.4	1.8	2.1	1.9	1.1	
Quick Ratio 31	1.0	•	0.6	1.2	1.6	1.5	1.1	1.1	1.3	1.6	1.2	0.8	
Net Sales to Working Capital 32	4.3	•	•	6.7	2.7	3.3	5.0	4.9	2.5	1.7	1.8	10.9	
Coverage Ratio 33	14.3	•	•	•	•	•	2.5	•	•	14.8	9.7	21.6	
Total Asset Turnover 34	0.5	•	4.6	3.2	1.3	0.8	0.9	0.9	0.5	0.5	0.4	0.4	
Inventory Turnover 35	13.8	•	2.5	18.3	23.9	8.5	10.2	30.2	24.7	15.0	32.0	8.7	14.8
Receivables Turnover 36	2.7	•	28.7	8.6	6.2	4.0	3.7	4.3	3.8	3.1	2.6	3.3	2.2
Total Liabilities to Net Worth 37	1.0	•	•	•	3.6	2.0	1.6	1.4	1.1	0.5	0.7	1.0	
Current Assets to Working Capital 38	4.2	•	•	3.8	2.4	2.5	3.6	3.7	2.3	1.9	2.1	11.6	
Current Liabilities to Working Capital 39	3.2	•	•	2.8	1.4	1.5	2.6	2.7	1.3	0.9	1.1	10.6	
Working Capital to Net Sales 40	0.2	•	•	0.1	0.4	0.3	0.2	0.2	0.4	0.6	0.6	0.1	
Inventory to Working Capital 41	0.1	•	•	0.1	0.0	0.1	0.0	0.0	0.0	0.0	0.1	0.3	
Total Receipts to Cash Flow 42	1.9	10.1	6.1	6.9	•	43.6	5.8	3.6	4.8	3.1	3.2	2.7	1.3
Cost of Goods to Cash Flow 43	0.5	4.1	0.2	3.0	•	9.3	1.0	0.9	1.0	0.6	0.6	0.7	0.4
Cash Flow to Total Debt 44	0.5	•	0.3	0.4	0.0	0.2	0.4	0.4	0.3	0.4	0.6	0.6	

Selected Financial Factors (in Percentages)

Debt Ratio 45	49.2	•	296.4	119.6	120.5	78.4	67.1	61.5	58.8	52.9	33.1	41.9	49.2
Return on Total Assets 46	13.0	•	•	•	•	2.1	•	•	•	•	4.2	9.4	18.7
Return on Equity Before Income Taxes 47	23.8	•	29.5	66.7	187.2	66.7	3.3	•	•	•	5.9	14.5	35.0
Return on Equity After Income Taxes 48	16.3	•	29.5	66.7	194.3	66.7	0.6	•	•	•	4.1	12.0	24.6
Profit Margin (Before Income Tax) 49	26.6	•	•	•	•	1.4	•	•	•	2.7	8.8	18.7	47.6
Profit Margin (After Income Tax) 50	18.2	•	•	•	•	0.2	•	•	•	0.6	6.0	15.5	33.5

Table II

Corporations with Net Income

SOFTWARE PUBLISHERS

MONEY AMOUNTS AND SIZE OF ASSETS IN THOUSANDS OF DOLLARS

Item Description for Accounting Period 7/05 Through 6/06		Total	Zero Assets	Under 500	500 to 1,000	1,000 to 5,000	5,000 to 10,000	10,000 to 25,000	25,000 to 50,000	50,000 to 100,000	100,000 to 250,000	250,000 to 500,000	500,000 to 2,500,000	2,500,000 and over
Number of Enterprises	1	3679	1404	1337	366	278	54	92	54	24	•	20	19	•
Revenues ($ in Thousands)														
Net Sales	2	71809909	749357	906974	1254608	1202013	605965	1852991	1991526	1318735	•	4249598	12434775	•
Interest	3	1556709	1259	1060	123	5011	2126	8430	23383	16775	•	51564	276474	•
Rents	4	66227	0	0	0	0	119	0	24	179	•	9620	6323	•
Royalties	5	5515683	0	0	0	0	2975	0	60873	14816	•	68755	916190	•
Other Portfolio Income	6	8314228	32471	0	6534	130660	11741	137307	32061	17673	•	63872	1752775	•
Other Receipts	7	21994571	47270	12700	7066	9958	21961	37655	27965	27945	•	12495	962893	•
Total Receipts	8	109257327	830357	920734	1268331	1347642	644887	2036383	2135832	1396123	•	4455904	16349430	•
Average Total Receipts	9	29698	591	689	3465	4848	11942	22135	39552	58172	•	222795	860496	•
Operating Costs/Operating Income (%)														
Cost of Operations	10	28.8	47.0	2.3	51.4	29.5	23.1	19.6	26.6	19.2	•	17.6	25.5	•
Salaries and Wages	11	33.2	4.0	50.6	12.2	24.9	28.5	31.6	25.0	36.6	•	35.1	37.0	•
Taxes Paid	12	3.1	3.7	4.4	2.2	3.1	2.7	2.9	3.3	4.5	•	3.4	3.1	•
Interest Paid	13	2.0	0.2	0.3	0.2	0.5	1.6	0.4	0.7	1.6	•	0.7	2.4	•
Depreciation	14	2.3	0.4	0.5	0.5	1.8	0.9	1.7	1.7	2.1	•	2.0	2.7	•
Amortization and Depletion	15	1.3	0.3	0.0	0.2	0.2	0.1	0.5	0.8	2.4	•	1.4	1.4	•
Pensions and Other Deferred Comp.	16	0.3	0.0	0.4	1.3	0.4	0.2	0.4	1.4	0.6	•	0.8	0.7	•
Employee Benefits	17	3.4	1.7	2.6	0.8	3.3	3.7	2.3	2.2	2.6	•	3.1	3.7	•
Advertising	18	6.0	0.8	0.2	0.6	0.8	1.2	1.8	2.0	2.3	•	1.5	5.4	•
Other Expenses	19	34.1	27.6	21.0	10.9	18.2	26.1	28.2	29.1	23.3	•	21.9	23.0	•
Officers' Compensation	20	1.7	5.0	7.8	7.5	5.7	3.3	4.4	3.2	2.1	•	1.6	1.5	•
Operating Margin	21	•	9.2	10.0	12.3	11.7	8.6	6.2	3.9	2.7	•	10.9	•	•
Operating Margin Before Officers' Comp.	22	•	14.3	17.7	19.8	17.3	11.9	10.6	7.1	4.8	•	12.5	•	•

Selected Average Balance Sheet ($ in Thousands)

Net Receivables 23	9002	0	1	242	790	2284	4256	8254	13047	83185	139140
Inventories 24	402	0	10	95	52	710	363	209	203	615	19644
Net Property, Plant and Equipment 25	2416	0	16	35	174	254	1013	2518	4430	26071	76209
Total Assets 26	42107	0	98	774	2539	6771	15169	37456	73346	377039	1345039
Notes and Loans Payable 27	3890	0	126	148	1626	1036	2129	4753	7358	29512	117118
All Other Liabilities 28	16383	0	13	267	967	3769	7151	15724	29717	124514	403333
Net Worth 29	21834	0	-41	359	-54	1966	5889	16980	36271	223013	824587

Selected Financial Ratios (Times to 1)

Current Ratio 30	1.3		5.7	1.8	2.4	1.5	1.5	1.6	1.4	1.9	2.0
Quick Ratio 31	1.0		4.0	1.3	2.0	1.3	1.3	1.3	1.2	1.5	1.3
Net Sales to Working Capital 32	5.3		11.1	11.8	3.4	7.9	6.4	4.0	4.9	2.3	2.0
Coverage Ratio 33	20.5	90.0	41.8	63.7	49.6	10.3	38.6	16.6	6.4	24.5	11.7
Total Asset Turnover 34	0.5		6.9	4.4	1.7	1.7	1.3	1.0	0.7	0.6	0.5
Inventory Turnover 35	14.0		1.7	18.5	24.7	3.7	10.9	47.0	52.0	60.7	8.5
Receivables Turnover 36	2.9		139.1	9.2	5.9	3.9	5.6	5.2	4.6	5.1	4.5
Total Liabilities to Net Worth 37	0.9			1.2		2.4	1.6	1.2	1.0	0.7	0.6
Current Assets to Working Capital 38	4.9		1.2	2.2	1.7	3.1	3.0	2.7	3.5	2.1	2.0
Current Liabilities to Working Capital 39	3.9		0.2	1.2	0.7	2.1	2.0	1.7	2.5	1.1	1.0
Working Capital to Net Sales 40	0.2		0.1	0.1	0.3	0.1	0.1	0.3	0.2	0.4	0.5
Inventory to Working Capital 41	0.1		0.2	0.3	0.0	0.1	0.2	0.0	0.0	0.0	0.1
Total Receipts to Cash Flow 42	1.6	2.4	3.4	4.6	3.6	2.5	2.6	2.8	3.6	2.9	2.3
Cost of Goods to Cash Flow 43	0.5	1.1	2.4	1.1	0.6	0.6	0.5	0.7	0.7	0.5	0.6
Cash Flow to Total Debt 44	0.6		1.5	1.8	0.5	0.9	0.8	0.6	0.4	0.5	0.5

Selected Financial Factors (in Percentages)

Debt Ratio 45	48.1		141.4	53.6	102.1	71.0	61.2	54.7	50.5	40.9	38.7
Return on Total Assets 46	18.6		81.0	60.5	41.3	27.5	21.9	12.1	7.5	9.2	13.9
Return on Equity Before Income Taxes 47	34.0			128.3		85.5	55.0	25.0	12.8	15.0	20.7
Return on Equity After Income Taxes 48	25.0			128.3		77.4	49.2	21.3	11.0	11.8	17.4
Profit Margin (Before Income Tax) 49	38.1	20.0	11.5	13.4	23.8	15.0	16.1	11.5	8.4	11.8	15.7
Profit Margin (After Income Tax) 50	28.0	17.5	11.5	13.4	21.8	13.6	14.4	9.8	7.3	12.4	21.9

Table I

Corporations with and without Net Income

MOTION PICTURE AND VIDEO INDUSTRIES (EXCEPT VIDEO RENTAL)

MONEY AMOUNTS AND SIZE OF ASSETS IN THOUSANDS OF DOLLARS

Item Description for Accounting Period 7/05 Through 6/06	Total	Zero Assets	Under 500	500 to 1,000	1,000 to 5,000	5,000 to 10,000	10,000 to 25,000	25,000 to 50,000	50,000 to 100,000	100,000 to 250,000	250,000 to 500,000	500,000 to 2,500,000	2,500,000 and over
Number of Enterprises 1	24886	4266	18779	869	687	97	91	38	20	15	6	13	5
Revenues ($ in Thousands)													
Net Sales 2	42616875	574107	5036336	1956430	2098983	662851	1813320	1146714	720675	760936	1558536	5498693	20789294
Interest 3	5526810	20676	8732	378	5991	2604	380	6784	3581	16626	42459	86707	5331892
Rents 4	135697	15384	0	0	0	597	0	215	289	3736	2162	8408	104907
Royalties 5	797458	301076	14914	0	3639	0	4270	3	0	3641	4339	116864	348711
Other Portfolio Income 6	1644318	17009	1403	146	30883	18253	8897	809	3954	1420	82624	63258	1415664
Other Receipts 7	1308894	51281	10024	-14718	11213	45806	41833	15175	10637	38204	57206	109415	932816
Total Receipts 8	52030052	979533	5071409	1942236	2150709	730111	1868700	1169700	739136	824563	1747326	5883345	28923284
Average Total Receipts 9	2091	230	270	2235	3131	7527	20535	30782	36957	54971	291221	452565	5784657
Operating Costs/Operating Income (%)													
Cost of Operations 10	30.4	43.2	27.9	16.6	49.1	31.1	30.1	48.0	39.5	21.6	29.4	40.8	26.4
Salaries and Wages 11	9.9	21.3	3.9	20.4	10.8	16.7	12.5	9.3	11.9	9.4	11.0	8.8	9.6
Taxes Paid 12	2.2	2.3	1.9	2.2	3.2	2.6	2.1	2.6	3.1	1.8	2.6	1.6	2.3
Interest Paid 13	15.1	6.8	0.6	1.1	1.1	2.4	1.2	2.2	3.5	6.3	2.4	3.2	28.7
Depreciation 14	8.9	38.7	2.6	3.8	4.6	3.4	5.0	4.2	3.5	2.2	4.3	2.5	13.8
Amortization and Depletion 15	9.0	3.0	0.2	0.0	1.7	0.0	3.4	7.4	8.7	22.4	13.8	10.3	12.6
Pensions and Other Deferred Comp. 16	0.5	2.3	2.0	1.3	0.4	0.4	0.1	0.2	0.0	0.0	0.1	0.1	0.2
Employee Benefits 17	1.3	1.0	1.2	1.3	0.8	0.9	1.2	1.0	1.4	0.6	0.8	1.5	1.3
Advertising 18	3.9	26.0	0.3	1.3	1.0	1.5	1.9	0.5	3.2	1.3	0.8	1.4	6.2
Other Expenses 19	29.8	70.6	29.4	33.3	26.3	33.3	25.6	23.7	25.0	39.1	21.9	19.9	32.5
Officers' Compensation 20	5.6	13.1	27.8	11.4	6.1	10.6	11.2	2.9	2.9	0.7	10.6	1.0	0.1
Operating Margin 21	•	•	2.2	7.3	•	•	5.6	•	•	•	2.2	8.8	•
Operating Margin Before Officers' Comp. 22	•	•	30.0	18.7	1.2	7.7	16.8	1.0	0.1	•	12.8	9.8	•

Selected Average Balance Sheet ($ in Thousands)

Net Receivables 23	326	0	4	70	260	1296	1584	3310	8141	27402	29608	115303	1028440
Inventories 24	273	0	2	33	192	75	1006	1333	5978	10042	29817	9828	1175215
Net Property, Plant and Equipment 25	553	0	10	348	522	1480	4768	7989	13984	18218	133310	154099	1732881
Total Assets 26	17942	52	810	2063	7210	14721	37121	69286	139788	406346	1109899		83920024
Notes and Loans Payable 27	4313	138	552	1303	2567	6612	21521	22928	49208	127746	332810		19084566
All Other Liabilities 28	900	17	149	495	3071	5531	7931	27545	45814	107892	200866		3200789
Net Worth 29	12729	-103	108	266	1573	2578	7668	18814	44766	170707	576223		61634668

Selected Financial Ratios (Times to 1)

Current Ratio 30	1.1	•	1.5	1.5	1.4	1.3	0.9	1.1	1.2	2.4	1.2	2.2	1.0
Quick Ratio 31	0.8	•	1.3	1.1	0.8	0.8	0.6	0.7	0.6	1.3	0.6	0.9	0.8
Net Sales to Working Capital 32	10.4	•	24.5	20.4	12.7	6.7	•	32.7	7.7	1.4	14.2	2.0	429.4
Coverage Ratio 33	1.4	•	6.0	7.2	•	4.1	8.1	1.1	0.9	1.5	6.7	5.8	1.2
Total Asset Turnover 34	0.1	•	5.1	2.8	1.5	0.9	1.4	0.8	0.5	0.4	0.6	0.4	0.0
Inventory Turnover 35	1.9	•	41.2	11.3	7.8	28.4	6.0	10.9	2.4	1.1	2.6	17.6	0.9
Receivables Turnover 36	3.2	•	56.2	27.6	11.7	3.4	12.3	6.8	4.5	2.8	11.7	4.1	1.9
Total Liabilities to Net Worth 37	0.4	•	•	6.5	6.8	3.6	4.7	3.8	2.7	2.1	1.4	0.9	0.4
Current Assets to Working Capital 38	8.8	•	3.0	3.0	3.9	4.1	•	11.7	5.8	1.7	6.3	1.8	537.3
Current Liabilities to Working Capital 39	7.8	•	2.0	2.0	2.9	3.1	•	10.7	4.8	0.7	5.3	0.8	536.3
Working Capital to Net Sales 40	0.1	•	0.0	0.0	0.1	0.1	•	0.0	0.1	0.7	0.1	0.5	0.0
Inventory to Working Capital 41	0.9	•	0.1	0.4	0.8	0.0	•	2.5	1.9	0.4	1.5	0.1	53.2
Total Receipts to Cash Flow 42	4.0	•	3.6	2.9	6.2	2.9	3.3	8.0	9.5	2.7	4.3	3.7	4.0
Cost of Goods to Cash Flow 43	1.2	•	1.0	0.5	3.0	0.9	1.0	3.9	3.8	0.6	1.3	1.5	1.1
Cash Flow to Total Debt 44	0.1	•	0.5	1.1	0.3	0.4	0.5	0.1	0.1	0.2	0.3	0.2	0.0

Selected Financial Factors (in Percentages)

Debt Ratio 45	29.1	•	296.5	86.6	87.1	78.2	82.5	79.3	72.8	68.0	58.0	48.1	26.6
Return on Total Assets 46	2.0	•	17.6	21.3	9.1	13.3	1.9	3.3	10.5	7.1	1.7		
Return on Equity Before Income Taxes 47	0.7	•	•	137.3	31.4	66.7	0.5	3.2	21.3	11.3	0.4		
Return on Equity After Income Taxes 48	0.6	•	•	137.3	29.6	66.0	0.2	2.6	18.3	9.6	0.3		
Profit Margin (Before Income Tax) 49	5.5	•	2.9	6.6	7.2	8.6	0.1	2.8	14.0	15.4	5.6		
Profit Margin (After Income Tax) 50	4.5	•	2.7	6.6	6.8	8.5	0.0	2.3	12.0	13.1	4.5		

263

Table II

Corporations with Net Income

MOTION PICTURE AND VIDEO INDUSTRIES (EXCEPT VIDEO RENTAL)

MONEY AMOUNTS AND SIZE OF ASSETS IN THOUSANDS OF DOLLARS

Item Description for Accounting Period 7/05 Through 6/06	Total	Zero Assets	Under 500	500 to 1,000	1,000 to 5,000	5,000 to 10,000	10,000 to 25,000	25,000 to 50,000	50,000 to 100,000	100,000 to 250,000	250,000 to 500,000	500,000 to 2,500,000	2,500,000 and over
Number of Enterprises 1	12059	1342	9846	406	324	40	51	16	11	7	•	8	•
Revenues ($ in Thousands)													
Net Sales 2	33807996	112514	3648035	1353909	1105381	377494	1395945	888172	523441	489246	•	3990533	•
Interest 3	5384895	14187	3236	337	2756	72	184	478	3376	7508	•	57801	•
Rents 4	114686	0	0	0	0	0	0	0	289	1192	•	6967	•
Royalties 5	153591	45387	0	0	3444	0	0	0	0	3641	•	86835	•
Other Portfolio Income 6	1620534	16932	1267	146	22539	17987	1254	718	2554	182	•	58666	•
Other Receipts 7	1247010	87572	16855	373	3489	41324	25035	10952	10081	33231	•	83475	•
Total Receipts 8	42328712	276592	3669393	1354765	1137609	436877	1422418	900320	539741	535000	•	4284277	•
Average Total Receipts 9	3510	206	373	3337	3511	10922	27891	56270	49067	76429	•	535535	•
Operating Costs/Operating Income (%)													
Cost of Operations 10	30.0	13.1	25.9	11.7	38.5	28.8	36.5	50.9	49.6	23.9	•	35.8	•
Salaries and Wages 11	9.4	11.1	3.3	27.8	8.2	18.8	11.2	8.8	10.8	4.1	•	8.1	•
Taxes Paid 12	2.1	3.8	1.9	2.5	2.4	2.3	2.2	2.3	3.1	1.9	•	1.6	•
Interest Paid 13	17.2	0.0	0.1	0.7	1.2	3.5	0.9	1.3	3.6	7.5	•	3.5	•
Depreciation 14	8.0	10.1	0.9	3.9	3.6	2.3	5.5	3.2	3.3	2.6	•	2.3	•
Amortization and Depletion 15	9.9	0.4	0.1	0.0	0.6	0.0	0.1	4.5	5.4	29.1	•	10.0	•
Pensions and Other Deferred Comp. 16	0.5	11.9	2.0	1.8	0.7	0.6	0.1	0.2	0.1	0.0	•	0.0	•
Employee Benefits 17	0.9	0.8	0.9	1.8	0.9	1.0	0.5	1.0	1.7	0.3	•	1.0	•
Advertising 18	3.8	1.5	0.2	1.8	0.5	0.7	0.6	0.4	1.2	2.0	•	1.7	•
Other Expenses 19	25.6	141.4	25.4	20.0	22.1	13.8	14.2	15.2	13.9	21.8	•	19.1	•
Officers' Compensation 20	5.6	12.3	28.2	15.8	9.1	15.9	14.2	2.4	3.3	1.0	•	1.2	•
Operating Margin 21	•	•	11.1	12.2	12.2	12.4	14.1	9.9	3.9	5.8	•	15.6	•
Operating Margin Before Officers' Comp. 22	•	•	39.3	28.1	21.3	28.3	28.3	12.3	7.2	6.9	•	16.8	•

Selected Average Balance Sheet ($ in Thousands)

Net Receivables 23	555	0	4	149	357	1130	2327	3438	5634	30201	149754
Inventories 24	523	0	1	0	146	115	318	4325	9998	12416	8571
Net Property, Plant and Equipment 25	605	0	6	339	461	1022	6786	14403	14092	30882	149060
Total Assets 26	35304	0	61	864	2118	7245	14047	37368	72002	155154	1138926
Notes and Loans Payable 27	7816	0	22	303	1361	2104	6364	13205	23686	70286	310835
All Other Liabilities 28	1485	0	13	143	356	1028	4027	11584	27281	45446	249236
Net Worth 29	26003	0	26	418	401	4113	3656	12579	21035	39423	578855

Selected Financial Ratios (Times to 1)

Current Ratio 30	1.3	•	2.9	2.4	1.7	2.9	1.1	1.0	1.2	2.8	3.0
Quick Ratio 31	1.0	•	2.6	2.4	1.3	2.9	0.9	0.6	0.3	1.4	1.3
Net Sales to Working Capital 32	4.7	•	12.1	10.8	9.6	4.3	73.0	213.0	10.8	1.5	1.8
Coverage Ratio 33	1.7	22190.5	98.3	18.7	13.7	9.0	19.1	9.5	2.9	3.0	7.4
Total Asset Turnover 34	0.1	•	6.0	3.9	1.6	1.3	1.9	1.5	0.7	0.5	0.4
Inventory Turnover 35	1.6	•	73.1	•	9.0	23.5	31.4	6.5	2.4	1.3	20.8
Receivables Turnover 36	2.8	•	64.2	44.7	12.2	2.7	12.7	32.3	16.9	2.9	3.5
Total Liabilities to Net Worth 37	0.4	•	1.4	1.1	4.3	0.8	2.8	2.0	2.4	2.9	1.0
Current Assets to Working Capital 38	4.3	•	1.5	1.7	2.4	1.5	15.8	58.1	6.4	1.5	1.5
Current Liabilities to Working Capital 39	3.3	•	0.5	0.7	1.4	0.5	14.8	57.1	5.4	0.5	0.5
Working Capital to Net Sales 40	0.2	•	0.1	0.1	0.1	0.2	0.0	0.0	0.1	0.6	0.6
Inventory to Working Capital 41	0.4	•	0.1	•	0.4	0.0	0.0	16.6	2.3	0.3	0.0
Total Receipts to Cash Flow 42	3.4	0.8	3.0	3.4	3.6	3.0	3.8	5.2	6.4	3.3	3.0
Cost of Goods to Cash Flow 43	1.0	0.1	0.8	0.4	1.4	0.9	1.4	2.6	3.2	0.8	1.1
Cash Flow to Total Debt 44	0.1	•	3.5	2.2	0.6	1.0	0.7	0.4	0.1	0.2	0.3

Selected Financial Factors (in Percentages)

Debt Ratio 45	26.3	•	58.0	51.6	81.1	43.2	74.0	66.3	70.8	74.6	49.2
Return on Total Assets 46	2.3	•	71.2	50.2	26.3	41.2	32.8	18.6	7.0	10.2	11.4
Return on Equity Before Income Taxes 47	1.3	•	167.9	98.2	128.5	64.5	119.4	49.3	15.8	26.9	19.4
Return on Equity After Income Taxes 48	1.2	•	165.7	98.2	123.7	62.8	118.5	48.9	14.2	25.4	16.6
Profit Margin (Before Income Tax) 49	12.3	39.4	11.7	12.3	15.1	28.1	16.0	11.2	7.0	15.1	22.5
Profit Margin (After Income Tax) 50	11.1	39.0	11.5	12.3	14.5	27.4	15.8	11.1	6.3	14.3	19.3

Table I

Corporations with and without Net Income

SOUND RECORDING INDUSTRIES

MONEY AMOUNTS AND SIZE OF ASSETS IN THOUSANDS OF DOLLARS

Item Description for Accounting Period 7/05 Through 6/06	Total	Zero Assets	Under 500	500 to 1,000	1,000 to 5,000	5,000 to 10,000	10,000 to 25,000	25,000 to 50,000	50,000 to 100,000	100,000 to 250,000	250,000 to 500,000	500,000 to 2,500,000	2,500,000 and over
Number of Enterprises **1**	7069	1407	5251	55	240	81	16	10	6	0	0	3	0
Revenues ($ in Thousands)													
Net Sales **2**	8187905	38573	1288927	27964	109530	146757	224822	196751	278164	0	0	5876416	0
Interest **3**	101068	79	81	242	563	1850	2435	1768	5848	0	0	88203	0
Rents **4**	1647	0	0	622	0	0	0	568	20	0	0	437	0
Royalties **5**	2128912	5154	0	0	10961	0	0	100348	6	0	0	2012444	0
Other Portfolio Income **6**	639314	38	0	0	0	0	16333	2618	4425	0	0	615902	0
Other Receipts **7**	945213	3682	24589	1133	44087	19	111183	7888	11805	0	0	740825	0
Total Receipts **8**	12004059	47526	1313597	29961	165141	148626	354773	309941	300268	0	0	9334227	0
Average Total Receipts **9**	1698	34	250	545	688	1835	22173	30994	50045	•	•	3111409	•
Operating Costs/Operating Income (%)													
Cost of Operations **10**	39.2	46.9	14.3	42.9	7.2	41.0	38.9	45.9	53.3	•	•	44.3	•
Salaries and Wages **11**	15.4	11.1	12.0	16.0	22.6	6.0	12.1	19.5	12.0	•	•	16.5	•
Taxes Paid **12**	1.7	0.7	2.4	2.4	5.2	0.8	1.0	2.8	1.9	•	•	1.5	•
Interest Paid **13**	4.0	0.0	0.4	•	0.0	1.6	1.6	3.1	2.9	•	•	5.1	•
Depreciation **14**	6.6	4.9	2.3	7.0	6.6	5.1	0.9	1.8	1.0	•	•	8.3	•
Amortization and Depletion **15**	2.6	3.5	0.2	•	33.8	3.8	0.9	4.0	1.3	•	•	2.6	•
Pensions and Other Deferred Comp. **16**	0.7	0.5	0.7	•	1.7	•	0.3	1.3	0.2	•	•	0.8	•
Employee Benefits **17**	1.6	2.5	0.8	•	0.7	•	2.0	3.3	1.3	•	•	1.8	•
Advertising **18**	3.8	3.4	1.0	2.0	7.1	0.1	9.8	3.6	2.6	•	•	4.3	•
Other Expenses **19**	53.9	42.3	40.9	21.9	51.1	58.6	73.9	60.3	16.7	•	•	57.7	•
Officers' Compensation **20**	2.8	6.6	11.9	12.6	5.8	•	6.1	9.3	3.1	•	•	0.3	•
Operating Margin **21**	•	•	13.0	•	•	•	•	•	3.7	•	•	•	•
Operating Margin Before Officers' Comp. **22**	•	•	25.0	7.8	•	•	•	•	6.8	•	•	•	•

Selected Average Balance Sheet ($ in Thousands)

Net Receivables 23	499	0	2	230	163	360	1368	2564	9255	1112120
Inventories 24	83	0	4	227	3	57	1803	1468	5686	148025
Net Property, Plant and Equipment 25	92	0	15	149	171	1420	1889	4707	2872	105122
Total Assets 26	4099	0	53	748	1632	6161	15411	34336	80894	8896888
Notes and Loans Payable 27	801	0	31	184	267	3833	9786	9370	31250	1559706
All Other Liabilities 28	1735	0	9	8	504	16729	4921	12126	19055	3476252
Net Worth 29	1563	0	14	556	861	-14402	704	12840	30588	3860930

Selected Financial Ratios (Times to 1)

Current Ratio 30	0.6	•	5.6	70.5	6.3	0.3	0.9	1.1	1.3	0.6
Quick Ratio 31	0.4	•	5.2	44.0	5.0	0.1	0.4	0.4	0.9	0.4
Net Sales to Working Capital 32	•	•	8.5	0.9	1.2	•	•	13.0	10.4	•
Coverage Ratio 33	4.9	34.2	34.3	•	363.4	•	9.6	2.3	5.0	4.4
Total Asset Turnover 34	0.3	•	4.6	0.7	0.3	0.3	0.9	0.6	0.6	0.2
Inventory Turnover 35	5.5	•	10.0	1.0	10.5	13.0	3.0	6.1	4.3	5.9
Receivables Turnover 36	2.0	•	36.0	1.7	2.4	6.8	7.5	10.5	2.1	3.5
Total Liabilities to Net Worth 37	1.6	•	2.9	0.3	0.9	•	20.9	1.7	1.6	1.3
Current Assets to Working Capital 38	•	•	1.2	1.0	1.2	•	•	10.7	4.6	•
Current Liabilities to Working Capital 39	•	•	0.2	0.0	0.2	•	•	9.7	3.6	•
Working Capital to Net Sales 40	•	•	0.1	1.2	0.8	•	•	0.1	0.1	•
Inventory to Working Capital 41	•	•	0.0	0.4	•	•	•	1.3	1.0	•
Total Receipts to Cash Flow 42	1.6	3.6	2.2	4.8	1.7	2.6	1.2	1.7	4.1	1.4
Cost of Goods to Cash Flow 43	0.6	1.7	0.3	2.0	0.1	1.1	0.5	0.8	2.2	0.6
Cash Flow to Total Debt 44	0.3	•	2.8	0.6	0.3	0.0	0.8	0.5	0.2	0.3

Selected Financial Factors (in Percentages)

Debt Ratio 45	61.9	•	74.4	25.7	47.2	333.8	95.4	62.6	62.2	56.6
Return on Total Assets 46	5.6	•	71.4	1.6	2.5	•	13.9	4.1	8.3	5.0
Return on Equity Before Income Taxes 47	11.6	•	271.1	2.1	4.7	2.0	273.4	6.1	17.7	8.9
Return on Equity After Income Taxes 48	11.3	•	267.8	1.8	4.2	2.0	180.6	2.8	17.6	8.8
Profit Margin (Before Income Tax) 49	15.7	1.0	14.9	2.3	8.9	•	13.7	4.0	11.7	17.5
Profit Margin (After Income Tax) 50	15.3	0.8	14.8	2.0	7.9	•	9.0	1.8	11.6	17.4

Table II

Corporations with Net Income

SOUND RECORDING INDUSTRIES

MONEY AMOUNTS AND SIZE OF ASSETS IN THOUSANDS OF DOLLARS

Item Description for Accounting Period 7/05 Through 6/06	Total	Zero Assets	Under 500	500 to 1,000	1,000 to 5,000	5,000 to 10,000	10,000 to 25,000	25,000 to 50,000	50,000 to 100,000	100,000 to 250,000	250,000 to 500,000	500,000 to 2,500,000	2,500,000 and over
Number of Enterprises **1**	4011	369	3379	55	176	10	8	7	6	0	0	0	0
Revenues ($ in Thousands)													
Net Sales **2**	6587238	18024	1268393	27964	97256	58939	160946	157995	4797722	0	0	0	0
Interest **3**	81723	62	81	242	563	1427	2435	1491	75423	0	0	0	0
Rents **4**	1442	0	0	622	0	0	0	568	252	0	0	0	0
Royalties **5**	1501181	5154	0	0	10961	0	0	82150	1402916	0	0	0	0
Other Portfolio Income **6**	635736	38	0	0	0	0	16291	2463	616945	0	0	0	0
Other Receipts **7**	528467	39	24589	1133	44087	12	4474	7454	446677	0	0	0	0
Total Receipts **8**	9335787	23317	1293063	29961	152867	60378	184146	252121	7339935	0	0	0	0
Average Total Receipts **9**	2328	63	383	545	869	6038	23018	36017	1223322	•	•	•	•
Operating Costs/Operating Income (%)													
Cost of Operations **10**	40.7	8.1	14.5	42.9	•	78.6	35.4	51.6	47.9	•	•	•	•
Salaries and Wages **11**	14.0	5.6	12.0	16.0	12.3	•	8.2	19.1	14.8	•	•	•	•
Taxes Paid **12**	1.3	0.7	2.4	2.4	3.7	0.2	0.2	2.8	1.0	•	•	•	•
Interest Paid **13**	2.5	•	0.4	•	0.0	•	1.1	0.7	3.2	•	•	•	•
Depreciation **14**	2.8	8.9	2.3	7.0	1.2	0.0	0.3	1.4	3.1	•	•	•	•
Amortization and Depletion **15**	0.7	•	0.1	•	0.0	9.5	1.3	3.5	0.7	•	•	•	•
Pensions and Other Deferred Comp. **16**	0.9	1.1	0.8	1.9	0.0	•	0.0	1.1	0.9	•	•	•	•
Employee Benefits **17**	1.8	2.6	0.8	0.8	0.8	•	1.9	3.1	2.1	•	•	•	•
Advertising **18**	2.7	4.5	0.8	2.0	•	•	12.9	2.1	3.0	•	•	•	•
Other Expenses **19**	49.1	67.1	40.3	21.9	17.2	13.6	30.2	54.5	53.1	•	•	•	•
Officers' Compensation **20**	3.1	9.0	11.6	12.6	6.6	3.8	3.8	7.3	0.6	•	•	•	•
Operating Margin **21**	•	•	14.1	•	56.3	•	4.6	•	•	•	•	•	•
Operating Margin Before Officers' Comp. **22**	•	1.3	25.6	7.8	62.8	•	8.4	•	•	•	•	•	•

Selected Average Balance Sheet ($ in Thousands)

Net Receivables 23	265	0	3	230	218	1088	1819	2315	160364
Inventories 24	128	0	0	225	4	101	1453	2430	76792
Net Property, Plant and Equipment 25	88	0	23	149	35	0	312	5207	37001
Total Assets 26	5572	0	78	748	1436	6644	17743	34126	3557610
Notes and Loans Payable 27	680	0	22	184	127	0	12075	5361	414479
All Other Liabilities 28	1974	0	11	8	614	1715	2700	12200	1274232
Net Worth 29	2919	0	45	556	695	4928	2968	16565	1868898

Selected Financial Ratios (Times to 1)

Current Ratio 30	0.4	•	6.5	70.5	6.1	2.9	0.8	1.3	0.4
Quick Ratio 31	0.2	•	5.9	44.0	6.1	2.6	0.2	0.5	0.2
Net Sales to Working Capital 32	•	•	8.8	0.9	1.5	1.8	•	6.3	•
Coverage Ratio 33	10.7	•	39.0	•	4087.6	•	21.9	20.3	8.7
Total Asset Turnover 34	0.3	•	4.8	0.7	0.4	0.9	1.1	0.7	0.2
Inventory Turnover 35	5.2	•	291.9	1.0	•	45.7	4.9	4.8	5.0
Receivables Turnover 36	4.7	•	141.7	4.4	2.2	5.1	9.1	19.5	10.0
Total Liabilities to Net Worth 37	0.9	•	0.7	0.3	1.1	0.3	5.0	1.1	0.9
Current Assets to Working Capital 38	•	•	1.2	1.0	1.2	1.5	•	4.6	•
Current Liabilities to Working Capital 39	•	•	0.2	0.0	0.2	0.5	•	3.6	•
Working Capital to Net Sales 40	•	•	0.1	1.2	0.7	0.6	•	0.2	•
Inventory to Working Capital 41	•	•	0.0	0.4	•	•	•	0.7	•
Total Receipts to Cash Flow 42	1.5	1.7	2.2	4.8	0.8	7.1	2.1	1.6	1.4
Cost of Goods to Cash Flow 43	0.6	0.1	0.3	2.0	•	5.6	0.7	0.8	0.7
Cash Flow to Total Debt 44	0.4	•	5.1	0.6	1.0	0.5	0.6	0.8	0.3

Selected Financial Factors (in Percentages)

Debt Ratio 45	47.6	•	42.7	25.7	51.6	25.8	83.3	51.5	47.5
Return on Total Assets 46	7.8	•	78.9	1.6	43.7	0.5	28.2	9.7	6.3
Return on Equity Before Income Taxes 47	13.5	•	134.3	2.1	90.3	0.6	161.0	19.0	10.7
Return on Equity After Income Taxes 48	13.2	•	132.8	1.8	89.3	0.4	117.1	15.4	10.6
Profit Margin (Before Income Tax) 49	23.9	22.0	16.0	2.3	113.5	0.5	23.8	14.0	24.9
Profit Margin (After Income Tax) 50	23.5	21.6	15.8	2.0	112.2	0.3	17.3	11.3	24.7

Table I

Corporations with and without Net Income

BROADCASTING (EXCEPT INTERNET)

MONEY AMOUNTS AND SIZE OF ASSETS IN THOUSANDS OF DOLLARS

Item Description for Accounting Period 7/05 Through 6/06	Total	Zero Assets	Under 500	500 to 1,000	1,000 to 5,000	5,000 to 10,000	10,000 to 25,000	25,000 to 50,000	50,000 to 100,000	100,000 to 250,000	250,000 to 500,000	500,000 to 2,500,000	2,500,000 and over
Number of Enterprises 1	6321	417	4153	473	839	152	126	42	29	35	14	30	11
Revenues ($ in Thousands)													
Net Sales 2	106916847	125215	733230	631290	2678590	906383	1145632	625594	844912	2954524	2080282	9035740	85155457
Interest 3	2629668	564	39	2162	5997	4663	6590	3607	14629	18681	19251	372374	2181111
Rents 4	485899	174	551	4	2168	632	38	1855	1030	13048	3382	22242	440775
Royalties 5	6391401	0	0	0	48736	0	0	1	403	18	31738	27239	6283267
Other Portfolio Income 6	2084215	1496	2460	8010	32102	22829	20424	6584	75546	80289	26536	826379	981567
Other Receipts 7	3988118	-36118	3599	199	49400	12848	15487	17866	30944	64073	51832	810618	2968360
Total Receipts 8	122497148	91331	739879	641665	2816993	947355	1188171	655507	967464	3130633	2213021	11094592	98010537
Average Total Receipts 9	19379	219	178	1357	3358	6233	9430	15607	33361	89447	158073	369820	8910049
Operating Costs/Operating Income (%)													
Cost of Operations 10	19.8	4.5	18.3	25.6	22.3	46.4	14.8	18.6	10.0	52.3	14.1	10.3	19.7
Salaries and Wages 11	14.3	26.6	25.1	38.6	23.9	12.4	23.0	20.4	30.8	11.3	20.1	23.6	12.4
Taxes Paid 12	2.8	4.7	13.5	4.9	3.6	2.2	3.8	3.3	3.5	1.9	4.5	4.4	2.4
Interest Paid 13	7.0	99.3	1.3	0.8	2.3	1.7	2.7	5.3	5.8	6.9	12.3	16.2	6.1
Depreciation 14	4.3	12.3	1.6	1.8	3.1	2.3	4.0	5.0	7.4	4.8	11.8	6.1	4.0
Amortization and Depletion 15	12.3	1.0	1.4	1.2	1.4	2.2	6.2	6.1	7.0	3.4	11.9	16.5	13.0
Pensions and Other Deferred Comp. 16	0.6	0.0	0.1	•	0.1	0.2	1.0	0.2	0.5	0.2	0.3	0.5	0.7
Employee Benefits 17	2.7	1.9	0.6	2.0	2.1	1.3	1.3	1.2	2.6	0.8	2.3	1.6	3.0
Advertising 18	3.3	1.0	1.9	1.3	0.9	1.6	3.1	3.1	2.4	1.7	1.6	2.9	3.6
Other Expenses 19	42.2	71.0	44.6	34.2	42.8	15.2	36.0	43.0	38.9	21.3	32.7	51.2	42.6
Officers' Compensation 20	1.4	0.3	15.6	2.0	3.9	6.0	3.1	2.4	3.6	1.4	1.7	2.2	1.0
Operating Margin 21	•	•	•	•	•	8.5	0.9	•	•	•	•	•	•
Operating Margin Before Officers' Comp. 22	•	•	•	•	•	14.5	4.0	•	•	•	•	•	•

Selected Average Balance Sheet ($ in Thousands)

Net Receivables 23	3912	0	10	101	681	874	1628	2614	7067	18129	35708	114753	1712663
Inventories 24	373	0	0	2	37	7	529	555	374	1789	1512	546	192956
Net Property, Plant and Equipment 25	5701	0	20	145	381	1234	2767	3622	12442	20806	93228	109483	2654599
Total Assets 26	49820	0	71	666	2094	6450	15375	37408	68882	156312	364110	1345081	23194642
Notes and Loans Payable 27	18938	0	125	869	1750	4680	5117	12322	24366	137596	245523	586548	8080048
All Other Liabilities 28	12256	0	19	257	795	2008	3141	6337	21827	54590	67080	488880	5226105
Net Worth 29	18626	0	-74	-460	-451	-239	7116	18748	22689	-35873	51507	269654	9888489

Selected Financial Ratios (Times to 1)

Current Ratio 30	1.0	•	0.9	1.2	1.8	1.6	1.9	1.3	1.0	2.4	0.9
Quick Ratio 31	0.7	•	0.5	1.0	1.7	1.1	1.3	0.9	0.8	1.7	0.6
Net Sales to Working Capital 32	146.9	•	•	17.9	3.6	3.8	3.2	6.6	481.3	1.9	•
Coverage Ratio 33	1.6	•	•	0.5	8.8	2.7	0.2	1.1	1.0	0.2	2.2
Total Asset Turnover 34	0.3	2.5	2.0	1.5	0.9	0.6	0.4	0.4	0.5	0.2	0.3
Inventory Turnover 35	9.0	•	178.3	19.1	371.6	2.5	5.0	7.8	24.7	56.9	7.9
Receivables Turnover 36	5.0	11.9	5.4	5.4	7.5	5.5	5.6	4.5	4.9	3.4	5.2
Total Liabilities to Net Worth 37	1.7	•	•	•	1.0	1.2	1.0	2.0	6.1	4.0	1.3
Current Assets to Working Capital 38	70.9	•	•	6.1	2.3	2.6	2.1	4.6	220.6	1.7	•
Current Liabilities to Working Capital 39	69.9	•	•	5.1	1.3	1.6	1.1	3.6	219.6	0.7	•
Working Capital to Net Sales 40	0.0	•	•	0.1	0.3	0.3	0.3	0.2	0.0	0.5	•
Inventory to Working Capital 41	5.0	•	•	0.2	0.0	0.3	0.1	0.1	3.3	0.0	•
Total Receipts to Cash Flow 42	2.4	•	6.8	2.8	4.0	2.7	2.9	3.2	5.5	3.5	2.2
Cost of Goods to Cash Flow 43	0.5	•	1.2	0.6	1.8	0.4	0.5	0.3	2.9	0.4	0.4
Cash Flow to Total Debt 44	0.2	0.2	0.2	0.5	0.2	0.4	0.3	0.2	0.1	0.1	0.3

Selected Financial Factors (in Percentages)

Debt Ratio 45	62.6	•	203.6	169.1	121.5	103.7	53.7	49.9	67.1	122.9	85.9	80.0	57.4
Return on Total Assets 46	3.8	•	•	1.6	13.4	4.2	0.5	2.8	3.8	1.9	0.7	4.5	
Return on Equity Before Income Taxes 47	3.9	•	55.3	31.4	8.7	•	5.7	•	1.0	3.8	1.9	5.7	
Return on Equity After Income Taxes 48	1.7	•	55.3	31.5	11.4	4.4	•	•	•	3.3	•	3.7	
Profit Margin (Before Income Tax) 49	4.3	•	•	•	12.9	4.5	•	•	0.8	0.1	•	7.3	
Profit Margin (After Income Tax) 50	1.9	•	•	•	11.4	3.5	•	•	•	•	•	4.7	

267

Table II

Corporations with Net Income

BROADCASTING (EXCEPT INTERNET)

MONEY AMOUNTS AND SIZE OF ASSETS IN THOUSANDS OF DOLLARS

Item Description for Accounting Period 7/05 Through 6/06	Total	Zero Assets	Under 500	500 to 1,000	1,000 to 5,000	5,000 to 10,000	10,000 to 25,000	25,000 to 50,000	50,000 to 100,000	100,000 to 250,000	250,000 to 500,000	500,000 to 2,500,000	2,500,000 and over
Number of Enterprises **1**	2984	394	1897	58	379	104	70	23	14	17	5	14	8
Revenues ($ in Thousands)													
Net Sales **2**	88508309	101322	272669	3597	1384806	901036	963024	521538	489615	2222476	838265	5648684	75161276
Interest **3**	2219385	499	0	2118	2232	1893	4751	2278	4620	11824	14049	122661	2052461
Rents **4**	407583	95	0	4	2168	632	25	1635	611	11575	2452	8403	379983
Royalties **5**	6315619	0	0	0	48736	0	0	1	0	3	0	26650	6240229
Other Portfolio Income **6**	1906157	1496	0	5095	25682	22460	18416	1045	49887	62803	9243	803534	906501
Other Receipts **7**	3407028	37628	7	194	12767	12649	12689	14886	25633	46893	32079	596021	2615576
Total Receipts **8**	102764081	141040	272676	11008	1476391	938670	998905	541383	570366	2355574	896088	7205953	87356026
Average Total Receipts **9**	34438	358	144	190	3895	9026	14270	23538	40740	138563	179218	514711	10919503
Operating Costs/Operating Income (%)													
Cost of Operations **10**	22.3	•	0.0	36.4	22.8	46.7	15.2	19.2	12.8	66.1	18.7	9.4	22.1
Salaries and Wages **11**	12.4	8.4	17.8	10.3	26.4	12.4	19.7	13.5	26.5	7.7	14.1	24.1	11.1
Taxes Paid **12**	2.1	3.0	4.4	0.5	4.0	2.2	3.4	2.3	3.6	1.3	3.6	4.5	1.9
Interest Paid **13**	5.9	•	2.6	5.4	1.0	1.4	2.5	2.1	2.9	2.3	4.8	12.0	5.8
Depreciation **14**	3.7	14.1	0.5	13.6	1.4	2.3	3.4	3.7	4.2	3.0	9.7	3.7	3.8
Amortization and Depletion **15**	11.9	0.0	•	1.5	0.1	2.2	3.4	3.3	4.4	1.0	4.1	13.0	12.8
Pensions and Other Deferred Comp. **16**	0.7	•	0.1	•	0.2	0.1	0.9	0.3	0.5	0.3	0.4	0.5	0.7
Employee Benefits **17**	3.0	1.1	0.0	1.1	3.4	1.3	1.0	0.9	2.1	0.5	2.3	1.8	3.2
Advertising **18**	3.3	0.6	0.6	0.0	1.1	1.6	3.1	2.5	2.2	1.3	1.1	3.4	3.5
Other Expenses **19**	40.1	70.5	33.8	16.9	31.2	14.7	33.7	39.1	29.4	12.0	34.0	34.5	42.1
Officers' Compensation **20**	1.2	•	29.9	2.9	5.1	6.0	2.1	1.9	3.8	1.4	1.7	0.9	0.9
Operating Margin **21**	•	2.3	10.2	11.3	3.4	9.2	11.4	11.1	7.6	2.9	5.3	•	•
Operating Margin Before Officers' Comp. **22**	•	2.3	40.1	14.2	8.4	15.2	13.5	13.0	11.4	4.3	7.1	•	•

Selected Average Balance Sheet ($ in Thousands)

Net Receivables 23	6055	0	17	7	623	1275	1744	3925	8508	18463	51735	93892	1930830
Inventories 24	741	0	0	0	33	7	90	607	721	3708	2667	198	261904
Net Property, Plant and Equipment 25	9376	0	4	4	256	1799	3264	5274	10597	22765	98083	89320	3132390
Total Assets 26	85561	0	75	810	1762	6060	15277	38345	69210	163820	355932	1393573	28355377
Notes and Loans Payable 27	28464	0	130	5	1338	4240	5370	7504	15622	46471	186035	442167	9383060
All Other Liabilities 28	20964	0	8	3	998	3110	3570	7856	13331	56759	38777	428603	6757706
Net Worth 29	36133	0	-64	801	-575	-1289	6337	22986	40257	60590	129120	522803	12214610

Selected Financial Ratios (Times to 1)

Current Ratio 30	1.0	•	4.3	217.6	1.2	0.8	1.4	2.2	2.5	1.1	2.2	2.1	0.9
Quick Ratio 31	0.7	•	4.3	5.9	1.0	0.7	1.1	1.5	1.8	0.8	1.6	1.8	0.6
Net Sales to Working Capital 32	•	•	5.1	0.1	22.2	•	7.2	3.5	2.9	28.8	3.0	3.4	•
Coverage Ratio 33	2.7	•	4.9	41.1	10.5	10.6	7.0	7.9	9.4	5.1	3.5	2.6	2.5
Total Asset Turnover 34	0.3	•	1.9	0.1	2.1	1.4	0.9	0.6	0.5	0.8	0.5	0.3	0.3
Inventory Turnover 35	8.9	•	•	•	25.6	604.0	23.2	7.2	6.2	23.3	11.7	191.6	7.9
Receivables Turnover 36	5.6	•	5.3	0.1	7.0	7.8	6.5	6.8	4.2	7.0	6.5	5.4	5.6
Total Liabilities to Net Worth 37	1.4	•	•	0.0	•	•	0.7	0.7	0.7	1.7	1.7	1.7	1.3
Current Assets to Working Capital 38	•	•	1.3	1.0	7.2	•	3.4	1.8	1.7	10.0	1.8	1.9	•
Current Liabilities to Working Capital 39	•	•	0.3	0.0	6.2	•	2.4	0.8	0.7	9.0	0.8	0.9	•
Working Capital to Net Sales 40	•	•	0.2	12.8	0.0	•	0.1	0.3	0.3	0.0	0.3	0.3	•
Inventory to Working Capital 41	•	•	•	•	0.2	•	0.0	0.0	0.1	0.2	0.0	0.0	•
Total Receipts to Cash Flow 42	2.2	0.9	2.6	0.4	2.8	4.0	2.2	1.9	2.2	5.4	2.3	2.4	2.1
Cost of Goods to Cash Flow 43	0.5	•	0.0	0.2	0.6	1.9	0.3	0.4	0.3	3.6	0.4	0.2	0.5
Cash Flow to Total Debt 44	0.3	•	0.4	16.8	0.6	0.3	0.7	0.8	0.5	0.2	0.3	0.2	0.3

Selected Financial Factors (in Percentages)

Debt Ratio 45	57.8	•	186.4	1.1	132.6	121.3	58.5	40.1	41.8	63.0	63.5	62.5	56.9
Return on Total Assets 46	5.5	•	24.8	17.1	22.8	20.9	15.8	10.1	13.6	9.2	8.0	9.2	4.9
Return on Equity Before Income Taxes 47	8.2	•	•	16.8	•	•	32.6	14.7	20.9	20.1	15.8	15.1	6.9
Return on Equity After Income Taxes 48	5.8	•	•	16.1	•	•	30.0	12.2	17.0	15.8	11.1	12.7	4.6
Profit Margin (Before Income Tax) 49	10.0	40.0	10.2	217.3	10.0	13.2	15.0	14.9	24.0	9.3	12.1	19.6	9.0
Profit Margin (After Income Tax) 50	7.1	29.2	10.2	208.4	9.2	11.8	13.8	12.4	19.6	7.3	8.5	16.5	6.0

Table I

Corporations with and without Net Income

INTERNET PUBLISHING AND BROADCASTING

MONEY AMOUNTS AND SIZE OF ASSETS IN THOUSANDS OF DOLLARS

Item Description for Accounting Period 7/05 Through 6/06	Total	Zero Assets	Under 500	500 to 1,000	1,000 to 5,000	5,000 to 10,000	10,000 to 25,000	25,000 to 50,000	50,000 to 100,000	100,000 to 250,000	250,000 to 500,000	500,000 to 2,500,000	2,500,000 and over
Number of Enterprises 1	6396	2505	3590	146	47	58	13	14	8	11	3	0	0
Revenues ($ in Thousands)													
Net Sales 2	11773839	197518	1098158	351444	171651	490024	201690	483478	380836	664777	7734263	0	0
Interest 3	38269	75	61	0	1048	2472	2185	4274	975	5741	21437	0	0
Rents 4	37332	264	0	0	0	0	0	0	0	0	37068	0	0
Royalties 5	172125	0	0	0	0	0	15370	0	2015	2131	152609	0	0
Other Portfolio Income 6	73840	1	0	546	0	219	0	4151	0	29109	39812	0	0
Other Receipts 7	127389	274	149	1	702	2677	4065	502	52106	10937	55980	0	0
Total Receipts 8	12222794	198132	1098368	351991	173401	495392	223310	492405	435932	712695	8041169	0	0
Average Total Receipts 9	1911	79	306	2411	3689	8541	17178	35172	54492	64790	2680390	•	•
Operating Costs/Operating Income (%)													
Cost of Operations 10	22.0	18.5	43.4	12.0	9.9	34.2	16.4	14.3	9.0	14.3	20.9	•	•
Salaries and Wages 11	21.1	26.4	12.9	15.5	59.2	20.5	27.5	28.7	42.3	26.9	19.5	•	•
Taxes Paid 12	3.2	2.1	2.3	2.5	5.6	3.3	2.6	3.1	4.3	4.2	3.2	•	•
Interest Paid 13	5.8	0.5	0.8	1.6	5.0	0.1	3.4	0.7	1.4	5.2	7.8	•	•
Depreciation 14	4.0	0.2	0.9	0.4	2.9	2.3	1.3	3.5	4.3	3.1	5.0	•	•
Amortization and Depletion 15	3.1	1.9	0.0	0.1	5.1	0.8	0.3	1.7	3.0	5.1	3.8	•	•
Pensions and Other Deferred Comp. 16	1.1	0.1	0.8	2.4	•	0.5	•	0.0	1.2	0.1	1.3	•	•
Employee Benefits 17	1.4	1.0	0.1	0.8	4.8	2.8	2.0	1.9	2.4	2.5	1.2	•	•
Advertising 18	2.1	5.1	4.8	9.7	14.2	2.5	3.4	7.0	2.9	1.3	0.7	•	•
Other Expenses 19	30.6	38.0	28.0	21.4	47.7	17.9	29.3	27.9	42.3	35.1	30.9	•	•
Officers' Compensation 20	2.4	3.3	4.5	13.4	11.1	6.2	6.5	3.6	2.6	2.0	1.0	•	•
Operating Margin 21	3.2	2.8	1.5	20.2	•	9.0	7.3	7.4	•	0.3	4.6	•	•
Operating Margin Before Officers' Comp. 22	5.6	6.1	6.0	33.7	•	15.2	13.8	11.1	•	2.2	5.6	•	•

Selected Average Balance Sheet ($ in Thousands)

Net Receivables 23	321	0	5	49	585	1415	2043	5016	25156	24378	449535	•
Inventories 24	40	0	0	5	105	5	259	76	48	2	81395	•
Net Property, Plant and Equipment 25	251	0	12	27	227	334	463	5390	6181	10627	426842	•
Total Assets 26	3108	0	66	655	2825	6175	13799	34011	69085	157119	5372232	•
Notes and Loans Payable 27	566	0	62	26	2254	554	3342	4133	23704	20344	913837	•
All Other Liabilities 28	1703	0	19	1761	1423	2822	5457	5678	14750	20828	3280121	•
Net Worth 29	839	0	-14	-1132	-851	2799	5001	24200	30632	115947	1178274	•

Selected Financial Ratios (Times to 1)

Current Ratio 30	1.3	•	0.6	0.7	1.0	1.3	5.4	1.6	1.8	3.1	1.1	•
Quick Ratio 31	0.9	•	0.4	0.6	1.0	1.1	5.4	1.5	1.7	2.5	0.7	•
Net Sales to Working Capital 32	11.5	•	•	•	72.4	9.0	1.5	4.6	3.3	1.6	26.8	•
Coverage Ratio 33	2.2	7.2	3.0	14.0	•	107.9	6.3	13.8	0.2	2.4	2.1	•
Total Asset Turnover 34	0.6	•	4.6	3.7	1.3	1.4	1.1	1.0	0.7	0.4	0.5	•
Inventory Turnover 35	10.2	•	2967.8	60.0	3.4	575.6	9.8	64.8	88.8	5134.5	6.6	•
Receivables Turnover 36	6.1	•	35.9	70.9	4.5	8.1	6.1	6.7	2.1	3.3	5.9	•
Total Liabilities to Net Worth 37	2.7	•	•	•	•	1.2	1.8	0.4	1.3	0.4	3.6	•
Current Assets to Working Capital 38	4.7	•	•	•	41.5	3.9	1.2	2.7	2.2	1.5	10.4	•
Current Liabilities to Working Capital 39	3.7	•	•	•	40.5	2.9	0.2	1.7	1.2	0.5	9.4	•
Working Capital to Net Sales 40	0.1	•	•	•	0.0	0.1	0.7	0.2	0.3	0.6	0.0	•
Inventory to Working Capital 41	0.2	•	•	•	0.5	•	•	•	0.0	0.0	0.9	•
Total Receipts to Cash Flow 42	2.9	2.6	3.8	•	•	4.1	2.2	3.0	2.8	2.9	2.8	•
Cost of Goods to Cash Flow 43	0.6	0.5	1.7	0.3	•	1.4	0.4	0.4	0.3	0.4	0.6	•
Cash Flow to Total Debt 44	0.3	•	1.0	0.5	•	0.6	0.8	1.2	0.4	0.5	0.2	•

Selected Financial Factors (in Percentages)

Debt Ratio 45	73.0	•	121.6	272.8	130.1	54.7	63.8	28.8	55.7	26.2	78.1	•
Return on Total Assets 46	7.5	•	10.6	80.0	•	13.9	24.1	10.1	0.2	4.9	7.9	•
Return on Equity Before Income Taxes 47	15.3	•	•	•	277.5	30.4	56.0	13.1	•	3.9	18.7	•
Return on Equity After Income Taxes 48	10.3	•	•	•	277.5	23.4	36.9	10.2	•	2.8	12.6	•
Profit Margin (Before Income Tax) 49	7.0	3.1	1.5	20.2	•	10.1	18.0	9.2	•	7.4	8.5	•
Profit Margin (After Income Tax) 50	4.7	2.7	1.5	20.2	•	7.8	11.9	7.1	•	5.4	5.8	•

Table II
Corporations with Net Income

INTERNET PUBLISHING AND BROADCASTING

MONEY AMOUNTS AND SIZE OF ASSETS IN THOUSANDS OF DOLLARS

Item Description for Accounting Period 7/05 Through 6/06	Total	Zero Assets	Under 500	500 to 1,000	1,000 to 5,000	5,000 to 10,000	10,000 to 25,000	25,000 to 50,000	50,000 to 100,000	100,000 to 250,000	250,000 to 500,000	500,000 to 2,500,000	2,500,000 and over
Number of Enterprises 1	4104	1726	2180	115	21	30	13	10	3	7	0	0	0
Revenues ($ in Thousands)													
Net Sales 2	10141894	159247	390864	351357	131511	251145	201690	365818	215684	8074578	0	0	0
Interest 3	30654	5	0	0	175	1023	2185	2224	110	24931	0	0	0
Rents 4	37332	264	0	0	0	0	0	0	0	37068	0	0	0
Royalties 5	167979	0	0	0	0	0	15370	0	0	152609	0	0	0
Other Portfolio Income 6	73726	1	0	546	0	219	0	4125	0	68833	0	0	0
Other Receipts 7	67519	85	29	1	1	394	4065	-297	543	62702	0	0	0
Total Receipts 8	10519104	159602	390893	351904	131687	252781	223310	371870	216337	8420721	0	0	0
Average Total Receipts 9	2563	92	179	3060	6271	8426	17178	37187	72112	1202960	•	•	•
Operating Costs/Operating Income (%)													
Cost of Operations 10	19.0	22.9	6.0	12.0	1.0	19.3	16.4	13.9	1.7	20.9	•	•	•
Salaries and Wages 11	20.1	13.1	8.8	15.5	44.4	18.1	27.5	27.0	43.1	19.5	•	•	•
Taxes Paid 12	3.2	1.7	3.9	2.4	3.7	1.8	2.6	3.0	4.8	3.3	•	•	•
Interest Paid 13	6.2	0.6	0.8	0.2	2.1	0.1	3.4	0.7	1.9	7.5	•	•	•
Depreciation 14	4.1	0.2	0.9	0.4	1.4	0.8	1.3	2.6	0.9	4.9	•	•	•
Amortization and Depletion 15	3.3	0.2	•	0.1	1.5	0.1	0.3	1.0	0.6	4.0	•	•	•
Pensions and Other Deferred Comp. 16	1.2	•	2.2	2.4	•	0.9	•	0.1	0.6	1.3	•	•	•
Employee Benefits 17	1.3	•	0.1	0.8	3.4	1.1	2.0	1.8	1.9	1.3	•	•	•
Advertising 18	1.6	6.0	4.6	9.7	1.9	3.0	3.4	8.0	1.1	0.7	•	•	•
Other Expenses 19	30.1	40.2	42.7	19.5	20.6	12.5	29.3	24.8	33.8	30.6	•	•	•
Officers' Compensation 20	2.3	3.6	11.8	13.5	9.0	2.8	6.5	2.9	2.6	1.0	•	•	•
Operating Margin 21	7.6	11.5	18.3	23.5	11.0	39.4	7.3	14.2	7.1	5.0	•	•	•
Operating Margin Before Officers' Comp. 22	9.9	15.1	30.1	37.0	20.1	42.3	13.8	17.1	9.6	6.0	•	•	•

Selected Average Balance Sheet ($ in Thousands)

Net Receivables 23	408	0	7	34	1025	1164	2043	6039	17702	208642
Inventories 24	61	0	0	6	203	0	64	7	101	34885
Net Property, Plant and Equipment 25	343	0	5	34	134	155	463	4789	3395	188704
Total Assets 26	4299	59	579	3640	6124	13799	33109	64446		2354909
Notes and Loans Payable 27	780	36	20	1860	1049	3342	5043	33476		408086
All Other Liabilities 28	2371	25	616	1726	1010	5457	4107	18190		1338768
Net Worth 29	1148	-2	-57	55	4066	5001	23959	12780		608055

Selected Financial Ratios (Times to 1)

Current Ratio 30	1.2	•	0.5	0.7	1.3	3.8	5.4	1.4	0.9	1.2
Quick Ratio 31	1.0	•	0.2	0.7	1.3	2.4	5.4	1.3	0.8	0.9
Net Sales to Working Capital 32	15.2	•	•	•	9.8	3.1	1.5	6.4	•	17.4
Coverage Ratio 33	2.8	21.8	24.3	130.0	6.3	388.1	6.3	22.1	4.8	2.2
Total Asset Turnover 34	0.6	•	3.0	5.3	1.7	1.4	1.1	1.1	1.1	0.5
Inventory Turnover 35	7.7	•	190.3	60.0	0.3	•	39.8	738.0	11.8	6.9
Receivables Turnover 36	6.4	•	43.7	177.7	4.0	12.9	7.8	5.1	8.1	5.8
Total Liabilities to Net Worth 37	2.7	•	•	•	65.1	0.5	1.8	0.4	4.0	2.9
Current Assets to Working Capital 38	5.2	•	•	•	4.1	1.4	1.2	3.4	•	6.0
Current Liabilities to Working Capital 39	4.2	•	•	•	3.1	0.4	0.2	2.4	•	5.0
Working Capital to Net Sales 40	0.1	•	•	•	0.1	0.4	0.7	0.2	•	0.1
Inventory to Working Capital 41	0.4	•	•	•	•	0.3	•	•	•	0.5
Total Receipts to Cash Flow 42	2.6	2.0	1.8	2.5	3.5	2.0	2.2	2.7	2.9	2.8
Cost of Goods to Cash Flow 43	0.5	0.5	0.1	0.3	0.0	0.4	0.4	0.4	0.0	0.6
Cash Flow to Total Debt 44	0.3	•	1.6	2.0	0.5	2.0	0.8	1.5	0.5	0.2

Selected Financial Factors (in Percentages)

Debt Ratio 45	73.3	•	102.6	109.9	98.5	33.6	63.8	27.6	80.2	74.2
Return on Total Assets 46	10.1	•	57.8	125.0	22.9	54.9	24.1	18.3	10.4	8.2
Return on Equity Before Income Taxes 47	24.3	•	•	•	1270.4	82.5	56.0	24.1	41.4	17.5
Return on Equity After Income Taxes 48	18.7	•	•	•	1270.4	73.3	36.9	19.9	36.0	12.2
Profit Margin (Before Income Tax) 49	11.3	11.7	18.3	23.5	11.2	40.1	18.0	15.8	7.4	9.2
Profit Margin (After Income Tax) 50	8.7	11.3	18.3	23.5	11.2	35.6	11.9	13.0	6.4	6.4

Table I

Corporations with and without Net Income

TELECOMMUNICATIONS

MONEY AMOUNTS AND SIZE OF ASSETS IN THOUSANDS OF DOLLARS

Item Description for Accounting Period 7/05 Through 6/06	Total	Zero Assets	Under 500	500 to 1,000	1,000 to 5,000	5,000 to 10,000	10,000 to 25,000	25,000 to 50,000	50,000 to 100,000	100,000 to 250,000	250,000 to 500,000	500,000 to 2,500,000	2,500,000 and over
Number of Enterprises 1	17565	2570	11290	1113	1422	284	349	196	134	92	34	42	40
Revenues ($ in Thousands)													
Net Sales 2	389278110	1403013	5398811	2566089	9213674	2750665	4639068	5501946	6470532	9966017	8624677	19794961	312948657
Interest 3	15365981	25776	1502	1035	14613	11387	40829	36315	50668	114903	82986	451805	14534162
Rents 4	11492072	83	0	4474	4422	3048	5874	7942	11363	34805	18628	48147	11353285
Royalties 5	1466675	0	0	0	0	0	580	758	5946	176560	5255	25695	1251881
Other Portfolio Income 6	11541210	13879	139	0	175129	24338	105964	116494	60227	240662	58750	1428889	9316739
Other Receipts 7	22386437	217669	173768	9831	174327	40193	294930	154427	538505	155541	141103	429207	20056935
Total Receipts 8	451530485	1660420	5574220	2581429	9582165	2829631	5087245	5817882	7137241	10688488	8931399	22178704	369461659
Average Total Receipts 9	25706	646	494	2319	6739	9963	14577	29683	53263	116179	262688	528064	9236541
Operating Costs/Operating Income (%)													
Cost of Operations 10	22.9	41.6	63.0	57.8	72.7	63.4	43.1	42.8	45.3	53.9	37.4	33.3	16.9
Salaries and Wages 11	13.5	19.1	5.9	11.2	10.1	10.6	15.0	13.9	11.9	11.3	16.9	13.2	13.8
Taxes Paid 12	3.1	5.5	1.4	1.9	1.4	1.9	2.5	2.5	2.3	2.0	2.6	2.3	3.4
Interest Paid 13	9.2	9.4	0.8	2.7	0.5	0.9	2.5	3.9	3.2	3.6	6.4	19.7	9.6
Depreciation 14	10.6	9.8	1.4	3.0	2.5	4.2	6.4	8.1	11.0	7.1	15.8	13.7	11.0
Amortization and Depletion 15	1.5	4.3	0.1	0.4	0.2	0.6	1.5	1.4	2.0	1.0	2.0	3.9	1.4
Pensions and Other Deferred Comp. 16	1.3	1.7	1.2	0.0	0.1	0.2	1.0	0.1	0.2	0.3	0.3	0.4	1.5
Employee Benefits 17	2.1	1.7	0.3	0.3	0.8	1.0	1.6	1.1	1.5	1.5	1.9	1.6	2.3
Advertising 18	1.9	1.6	0.7	0.8	0.6	0.4	1.4	1.1	1.3	1.7	1.5	4.0	1.9
Other Expenses 19	42.8	43.1	17.1	16.0	13.5	22.4	32.8	58.4	38.7	21.4	27.5	30.3	46.3
Officers' Compensation 20	0.5	3.2	6.1	2.8	2.7	2.4	2.3	1.5	1.2	1.0	0.9	1.5	0.2
Operating Margin 21	•	•	2.0	3.2	•	•	•	•	•	•	•	•	•
Operating Margin Before Officers' Comp. 22	•	•	8.1	6.0	•	•	•	•	•	•	•	•	•

Selected Average Balance Sheet ($ in Thousands)

Net Receivables 23	6514	0	8	208	535	1137	1947	3730	7593	22581	49256	105293	2560126
Inventories 24	418	0	7	32	122	185	580	760	1726	3180	3359	16539	132980
Net Property, Plant and Equipment 25	18022	0	16	144	676	2241	5205	11567	23411	50303	142953	329050	7102299
Total Assets 26	74041	0	84	712	2442	7401	16110	34303	67698	161558	348401	1187327	29980524
Notes and Loans Payable 27	22137	0	54	1210	765	2166	7245	15263	25396	52252	170986	500496	8615515
All Other Liabilities 28	20727	0	49	507	978	2058	-277	12656	15564	45018	76278	325553	8402662
Net Worth 29	31176	0	-19	-1006	699	3176	9141	6385	26738	64288	101138	361278	12862348

Selected Financial Ratios (Times to 1)

Current Ratio 30	0.9	•	1.0	1.5	1.5	1.8	1.5	1.2	1.1	1.4	1.0	1.3	0.8
Quick Ratio 31	0.7	•	0.8	1.1	1.1	1.5	1.1	0.8	0.8	1.1	0.8	0.9	0.6
Net Sales to Working Capital 32	•	2040.4	13.9	6.2	6.4	17.0	25.6	6.4	6.4	7.6	•		•
Coverage Ratio 33	1.7	7.8	2.4	•	•	0.8	•	•	1.8	•	2.0		
Total Asset Turnover 34	0.3	5.7	3.2	2.7	1.3	0.8	0.7	0.7	0.7	0.4	0.4		0.3
Inventory Turnover 35	12.2	45.7	41.8	38.6	33.1	15.8	12.7	18.4	28.3	9.5	9.5		9.9
Receivables Turnover 36	3.4	58.9	14.8	13.7	7.1	7.3	6.7	5.2	5.8	4.2	2.3		3.1
Total Liabilities to Net Worth 37	1.4	•	2.5	1.3	0.8	4.4	1.5	1.5	2.4	2.3	1.3		
Current Assets to Working Capital 38	•	228.8	3.1	2.3	2.9	7.4	12.2	3.3	4.9	•			•
Current Liabilities to Working Capital 39	•	227.8	2.1	1.3	1.9	6.4	11.2	2.3	3.9	•			•
Working Capital to Net Sales 40	•	0.0	0.1	0.2	0.2	0.1	0.0	0.2	0.1	•			•
Inventory to Working Capital 41	•	35.8	0.3	0.1	0.3	0.5	1.1	0.2	0.3	•			•
Total Receipts to Cash Flow 42	2.4	9.8	5.0	12.3	7.8	3.7	•	6.2	5.3	8.3	17.9		2.0
Cost of Goods to Cash Flow 43	0.5	4.1	3.1	9.0	4.9	1.6	•	2.8	2.8	3.1	6.0		0.3
Cash Flow to Total Debt 44	0.2	0.9	0.2	0.3	0.3	0.5	•	0.2	0.2	0.1	0.0		0.2

Selected Financial Factors (in Percentages)

Debt Ratio 45	57.9	•	122.4	241.4	71.4	57.1	43.3	81.4	60.5	60.2	71.0	69.6	57.0
Return on Total Assets 46	4.7	•	34.3	20.8	•	•	1.6	•	•	4.4	•	3.1	5.1
Return on Equity Before Income Taxes 47	4.7	•	•	•	•	•	•	•	•	4.9	•	•	6.0
Return on Equity After Income Taxes 48	3.0	•	•	•	•	•	•	•	•	1.2	•	•	4.3
Profit Margin (Before Income Tax) 49	6.6	•	5.2	3.8	•	•	•	•	•	2.9	•	•	9.9
Profit Margin (After Income Tax) 50	4.2	•	5.2	3.5	•	•	•	0.7	•	0.7	•	•	7.1

Table II

Corporations with Net Income

TELECOMMUNICATIONS

MONEY AMOUNTS AND SIZE OF ASSETS IN THOUSANDS OF DOLLARS

Item Description for Accounting Period 7/05 Through 6/06		Total	Zero Assets	Under 500	500 to 1,000	1,000 to 5,000	5,000 to 10,000	10,000 to 25,000	25,000 to 50,000	50,000 to 100,000	100,000 to 250,000	250,000 to 500,000	500,000 to 2,500,000	2,500,000 and over
Number of Enterprises	1	9280	1555	5465	761	773	188	220	127	77	58	16	16	24
Revenues ($ in Thousands)														
Net Sales	2	309333444	525422	3053548	1447230	4584076	2025604	3307286	3288284	4072609	6907282	3468958	7184316	269468831
Interest	3	13611357	13762	381	429	6490	7644	26667	20299	30674	55677	59763	90270	13299303
Rents	4	10805487	42	0	0	2792	2987	4096	5506	7416	31586	18357	41511	10691195
Royalties	5	1422707	0	0	0	0	0	580	174	0	175327	1672	25695	1219257
Other Portfolio Income	6	9281303	13256	117	0	164724	19422	99562	90834	45482	162536	27890	46755	8610725
Other Receipts	7	19994436	42397	100367	1786	134621	29204	268732	117931	461998	130941	52086	203370	18451001
Total Receipts	8	364448734	594879	3154413	1449445	4892703	2084861	3706923	3523028	4618179	7463349	3628726	7591917	321740312
Average Total Receipts	9	39272	383	577	1905	6329	11090	16850	27740	59976	128678	226795	474495	13405846
Operating Costs/Operating Income (%)														
Cost of Operations	10	15.9	21.1	51.6	54.1	55.5	65.1	41.2	38.8	50.1	54.9	19.5	23.4	11.9
Salaries and Wages	11	13.9	11.6	7.1	6.8	13.4	7.9	10.2	12.2	8.0	9.3	17.6	9.1	14.5
Taxes Paid	12	3.2	6.4	1.6	2.0	1.8	1.7	2.2	2.8	1.9	1.8	2.9	1.9	3.3
Interest Paid	13	8.6	14.2	0.3	0.3	0.6	0.5	1.7	2.0	1.9	2.1	4.2	8.2	9.4
Depreciation	14	9.8	11.3	0.7	1.9	3.5	3.2	5.2	7.4	9.0	6.6	9.9	10.4	10.3
Amortization and Depletion	15	1.1	4.5	0.0	0.0	0.1	0.3	0.5	0.5	0.8	0.6	2.0	1.8	1.2
Pensions and Other Deferred Comp.	16	1.5	3.2	2.0	•	0.2	0.2	0.4	0.2	0.2	0.3	0.6	0.2	1.6
Employee Benefits	17	2.3	2.3	0.2	0.2	1.2	0.6	1.0	1.1	1.0	1.3	1.9	1.3	2.4
Advertising	18	1.9	1.2	0.6	1.1	1.1	0.2	0.9	0.7	0.9	0.9	1.9	3.0	2.0
Other Expenses	19	46.0	22.4	17.6	20.5	19.1	11.6	32.8	26.2	27.2	19.2	31.1	34.1	49.1
Officers' Compensation	20	0.4	2.5	7.1	2.0	3.0	1.9	2.1	1.7	1.2	0.7	1.4	0.8	0.1
Operating Margin	21	•	•	11.3	11.1	0.6	6.7	1.8	6.3	•	2.3	7.1	5.8	•
Operating Margin Before Officers' Comp.	22	•	1.8	18.4	13.1	3.6	8.7	3.9	8.0	•	3.1	8.5	6.6	•

Selected Average Balance Sheet ($ in Thousands)

Net Receivables 23	10444	0	6	189	645	1127	2090	3078	7830	19718	35627	114203	3793260
Inventories 24	602	0	4	38	128	134	475	651	1669	3348	1523	18412	191000
Net Property, Plant and Equipment 25	28525	0	15	97	874	2021	5512	12839	24625	51448	136618	262992	10391151
Total Assets 26	123193	72	72	679	2523	7255	15962	33307	69123	149250	323439	1024799	45654841
Notes and Loans Payable 27	32743	24	—	174	389	1214	3170	9642	16979	38637	95190	424155	12053709
All Other Liabilities 28	34578	31	—	149	876	2233	3577	6907	14827	38521	79752	230454	12896104
Net Worth 29	55872	18	—	357	1258	3808	9215	16759	37317	72092	148498	370190	20705028

Selected Financial Ratios (Times to 1)

Current Ratio 30	0.8	•	1.7	2.9	1.7	1.8	1.8	1.7	1.7	1.7	1.3	1.2	0.8
Quick Ratio 31	0.6	•	1.4	1.6	1.3	1.4	1.4	1.3	1.3	1.2	1.0	1.0	0.6
Net Sales to Working Capital 32	•	•	31.5	5.4	10.5	6.3	5.5	5.4	5.5	5.7	10.8	11.7	•
Coverage Ratio 33	2.5	1.9	55.9	36.0	14.2	20.8	9.1	7.6	7.0	6.4	3.8	2.4	2.4
Total Asset Turnover 34	0.3	•	7.7	2.8	2.4	1.5	0.9	0.8	0.8	0.8	0.7	0.4	0.2
Inventory Turnover 35	8.8	•	66.7	27.1	25.7	52.4	13.0	15.4	15.9	19.5	27.7	5.7	7.0
Receivables Turnover 36	3.4	•	69.8	14.9	11.1	10.9	7.1	8.9	8.1	7.5	8.4	3.6	3.1
Total Liabilities to Net Worth 37	1.2	•	3.0	0.9	1.0	0.9	0.7	1.0	0.9	1.1	1.2	1.8	1.2
Current Assets to Working Capital 38	2.4	•	2.4	1.5	2.5	2.3	2.2	2.4	2.4	2.4	4.4	5.3	•
Current Liabilities to Working Capital 39	•	•	1.4	0.5	1.5	1.3	1.2	1.4	1.4	1.4	3.4	4.3	•
Working Capital to Net Sales 40	•	•	0.0	0.2	0.2	0.2	0.2	0.2	0.2	0.2	0.1	0.1	•
Inventory to Working Capital 41	•	•	0.3	0.2	0.1	0.2	0.2	0.2	0.2	0.2	0.1	0.3	•
Total Receipts to Cash Flow 42	1.9	3.4	3.3	3.7	5.0	5.9	2.4	3.0	3.2	3.9	2.7	2.4	1.8
Cost of Goods to Cash Flow 43	0.3	0.7	1.7	2.0	2.8	3.8	1.0	1.2	1.6	2.2	0.5	0.6	0.2
Cash Flow to Total Debt 44	0.3	•	3.1	1.6	0.9	0.5	0.9	0.5	0.5	0.4	0.5	0.3	0.3

Selected Financial Factors (in Percentages)

Debt Ratio 45	54.6	•	74.7	47.5	50.2	47.5	42.3	49.7	46.0	51.7	54.1	63.9	54.6
Return on Total Assets 46	5.9	•	115.2	32.4	18.5	15.0	14.6	12.0	10.0	10.5	10.7	8.8	5.7
Return on Equity Before Income Taxes 47	7.9	•	447.2	60.0	34.4	27.2	22.5	20.7	15.8	18.3	17.2	14.3	7.4
Return on Equity After Income Taxes 48	6.1	•	446.2	57.6	31.8	22.8	18.0	17.1	11.2	13.3	13.8	12.3	5.6
Profit Margin (Before Income Tax) 49	13.3	12.4	14.7	11.3	7.3	9.6	13.8	13.4	11.2	13.8	11.1	11.8	13.6
Profit Margin (After Income Tax) 50	10.2	11.8	14.6	10.8	6.7	8.1	11.0	11.1	7.9	8.1	9.4	10.1	10.3

Table I
Corporations with and without Net Income

INTERNET SERVICE PROVIDERS, WEB PORTALS, AND D.P. SERVICES

MONEY AMOUNTS AND SIZE OF ASSETS IN THOUSANDS OF DOLLARS

Item Description for Accounting Period 7/05 Through 6/06	Total	Zero Assets	Under 500	500 to 1,000	1,000 to 5,000	5,000 to 10,000	10,000 to 25,000	25,000 to 50,000	50,000 to 100,000	100,000 to 250,000	250,000 to 500,000	500,000 to 2,500,000	2,500,000 and over
Number of Enterprises 1	15850	3293	11194	462	551	129	100	35	34	20	13	11	8
Revenues ($ in Thousands)													
Net Sales 2	89361364	382259	5075086	325767	2098579	1132923	2828972	2304553	1895528	2035480	2436171	5335177	63510869
Interest 3	6162838	2634	1694	1299	4277	3317	5761	17388	18545	25119	31829	80450	5970525
Rents 4	609743	0	5386	529	0	271	5298	0	2944	232	14686	550	579847
Royalties 5	8905165	0	0	0	0	30641	82	1922	391	5945	3274	3001	8859908
Other Portfolio Income 6	1520283	86140	48930	0	10708	850	995	2528	6188	17581	35051	304428	1006885
Other Receipts 7	5028574	27771	43151	9	13437	22464	70069	303804	36040	61647	48983	89336	4311863
Total Receipts 8	111587967	498804	5174247	327604	2127001	1190466	2911177	2630195	1959636	2146004	2569994	5812942	84239897
Average Total Receipts 9	7040	151	462	709	3860	9228	29112	75148	57636	107300	197692	528449	10529987
Operating Costs/Operating Income (%)													
Cost of Operations 10	17.2	8.8	38.3	25.4	41.2	37.6	17.7	69.1	34.1	16.6	30.4	16.8	11.6
Salaries and Wages 11	21.7	37.9	14.0	19.1	21.9	20.9	28.2	10.6	22.5	35.1	23.9	25.7	21.5
Taxes Paid 12	2.7	3.5	2.1	4.7	2.4	4.9	2.9	1.1	3.6	2.8	3.7	2.4	2.7
Interest Paid 13	8.4	0.6	0.7	1.1	1.3	3.2	1.8	1.2	1.7	1.8	4.1	3.5	10.9
Depreciation 14	4.4	2.4	1.6	7.7	3.7	3.2	3.3	2.5	3.2	4.1	10.0	5.7	4.6
Amortization and Depletion 15	5.5	1.3	0.2	1.7	1.3	0.4	2.2	3.0	2.1	2.4	2.1	4.3	6.9
Pensions and Other Deferred Comp. 16	0.6	0.2	0.1	2.6	0.1	0.4	0.6	0.2	0.7	0.5	0.1	0.2	0.7
Employee Benefits 17	2.1	4.4	0.5	2.4	1.8	3.0	3.4	1.4	2.7	2.9	2.5	2.1	2.1
Advertising 18	4.6	3.2	1.5	6.8	2.8	1.2	0.5	1.3	2.1	2.2	0.6	7.4	5.3
Other Expenses 19	49.9	57.0	30.7	25.5	28.1	36.2	45.5	12.7	24.1	33.0	25.8	30.8	57.9
Officers' Compensation 20	2.1	16.7	8.1	10.2	5.4	5.5	3.5	1.8	3.3	1.6	1.8	1.1	1.4
Operating Margin 21	•	•	2.2	•	•	•	•	•	•	•	•	0.0	•
Operating Margin Before Officers' Comp. 22	•	•	10.3	2.9	•	•	•	•	3.3	•	•	1.1	•

Selected Average Balance Sheet ($ in Thousands)

Net Receivables 23	2182	0	12	48	438	611	2150	5546	8502	25681	49582	78659	3923463
Inventories 24	399	0	1	36	20	11	182	625	603	404	1575	2651	770601
Net Property, Plant and Equipment 25	1248	0	14	277	764	589	3283	5845	6573	12573	109297	138241	1880618
Total Assets 26	22352	0	70	807	2269	6793	15355	34247	70737	160125	362791	1058878	40787101
Notes and Loans Payable 27	2417	0	98	687	1996	1006	6496	14327	15005	38187	131401	362347	3443866
All Other Liabilities 28	11213	0	41	137	672	2924	5950	16376	19578	51241	62652	189575	21336241
Net Worth 29	8722	0	-69	-16	-399	2863	2908	3544	36154	70698	168738	506956	16006994

Selected Financial Ratios (Times to 1)

Current Ratio 30	1.1	•	0.8	1.0	1.4	1.8	0.9	1.0	1.7	1.8	1.3	1.8	1.1
Quick Ratio 31	0.4	•	0.6	0.9	1.3	1.6	0.7	0.8	1.3	1.5	1.0	1.4	0.4
Net Sales to Working Capital 32	7.1	•	•	101.9	12.4	4.0	•	104.2	4.0	3.2	9.4	4.0	6.7
Coverage Ratio 33	1.8	—	7.0	•	•	•	•	8.6	3.0	2.4	1.1	3.5	1.8
Total Asset Turnover 34	0.3	•	6.5	0.9	1.7	1.3	1.8	1.9	0.8	0.6	0.5	0.5	0.2
Inventory Turnover 35	2.4	•	122.4	4.9	79.1	294.7	27.6	72.8	31.5	41.8	36.1	30.6	1.2
Receivables Turnover 36	2.6	•	56.4	13.8	8.3	16.1	11.8	12.6	8.0	5.5	4.5	6.8	2.0
Total Liabilities to Net Worth 37	1.6	•	•	•	•	1.4	4.3	8.7	1.0	1.3	1.2	1.1	1.5
Current Assets to Working Capital 38	10.8	•	•	38.8	3.9	2.3	•	35.0	2.4	2.2	4.8	2.2	13.2
Current Liabilities to Working Capital 39	9.8	•	•	37.8	2.9	1.3	•	34.0	1.4	1.2	3.8	1.2	12.2
Working Capital to Net Sales 40	0.1	•	•	0.0	0.1	0.3	•	0.0	0.2	0.3	0.1	0.3	0.1
Inventory to Working Capital 41	0.6	•	•	5.2	0.1	0.0	•	1.2	0.1	0.0	0.1	0.0	0.8
Total Receipts to Cash Flow 42	2.0	3.9	3.3	6.2	6.5	5.4	2.9	4.9	4.5	3.4	5.3	3.2	1.7
Cost of Goods to Cash Flow 43	0.3	0.3	1.3	1.6	2.7	2.0	0.5	3.4	1.5	0.6	1.6	0.5	0.2
Cash Flow to Total Debt 44	0.2	•	1.0	0.1	0.2	0.4	0.8	0.4	0.4	0.3	0.2	0.3	0.2

Selected Financial Factors (in Percentages)

Debt Ratio 45	61.0	•	198.9	102.0	117.6	57.9	81.1	89.7	48.9	55.8	53.5	52.1	60.8
Return on Total Assets 46	3.7	•	31.3	•	•	•	•	19.9	3.9	2.7	2.3	5.7	3.7
Return on Equity Before Income Taxes 47	4.2	•	•	298.1	82.3	•	•	170.0	5.1	3.5	0.5	8.5	4.1
Return on Equity After Income Taxes 48	3.0	•	•	439.4	86.9	•	•	162.1	3.4	2.6	•	7.3	3.1
Profit Margin (Before Income Tax) 49	6.4	•	4.1	•	•	•	•	9.2	3.3	2.4	0.4	8.9	8.3
Profit Margin (After Income Tax) 50	4.7	•	3.9	•	•	•	•	8.7	2.2	1.8	•	7.7	6.2

Table II
Corporations with Net Income

INTERNET SERVICE PROVIDERS, WEB PORTALS, AND D.P. SERVICES

MONEY AMOUNTS AND SIZE OF ASSETS IN THOUSANDS OF DOLLARS

Item Description for Accounting Period 7/05 Through 6/06	Total	Zero Assets	Under 500	500 to 1,000	1,000 to 5,000	5,000 to 10,000	10,000 to 25,000	25,000 to 50,000	50,000 to 100,000	100,000 to 250,000	250,000 to 500,000	500,000 to 2,500,000	2,500,000 and over
Number of Enterprises **1**	8923	2217	6263	125	148	62	35	21	22	10	•	•	6

Revenues ($ in Thousands)

	Total	Zero Assets	Under 500	500 to 1,000	1,000 to 5,000	5,000 to 10,000	10,000 to 25,000	25,000 to 50,000	50,000 to 100,000	100,000 to 250,000	250,000 to 500,000	500,000 to 2,500,000	2,500,000 and over
Net Sales **2**	75353412	194348	3895273	276197	1177118	867552	860023	836220	1326280	1251474	•	•	3729790
Interest **3**	2182787	918	1537	241	818	150	983	4849	15618	8949	•	•	34228
Rents **4**	427649	0	5386	0	0	271	4877	0	1140	0	•	•	258
Royalties **5**	8867218	0	0	0	0	0	0	1922	284	5945	•	•	0
Other Portfolio Income **6**	1394812	82227	13175	0	10670	717	567	762	3333	14161	•	•	284437
Other Receipts **7**	4855446	4354	30075	210	4431	613	32595	299552	26574	48738	•	•	62377
Total Receipts **8**	93081324	281847	3945446	276648	1193037	869303	899045	1143305	1373229	1329267	•	•	4111090
Average Total Receipts **9**	10432	127	630	2213	8061	14021	25687	54443	62420	132927	•	•	685182

Operating Costs/Operating Income (%)

	Total	Zero Assets	Under 500	500 to 1,000	1,000 to 5,000	5,000 to 10,000	10,000 to 25,000	25,000 to 50,000	50,000 to 100,000	100,000 to 250,000	250,000 to 500,000	500,000 to 2,500,000	2,500,000 and over
Cost of Operations **10**	12.5	1.2	38.0	26.3	55.5	46.0	20.6	41.9	34.5	7.8	•	•	20.8
Salaries and Wages **11**	21.4	6.0	11.3	9.3	7.1	9.1	22.3	16.9	19.3	37.8	•	•	21.9
Taxes Paid **12**	2.7	2.2	1.9	3.0	0.9	4.6	2.4	1.8	3.8	3.1	•	•	2.2
Interest Paid **13**	3.7	0.1	0.3	0.7	0.3	0.1	0.6	0.9	1.3	2.2	•	•	2.2
Depreciation **14**	3.4	1.9	1.1	5.5	1.8	3.4	3.1	2.2	2.7	3.1	•	•	4.7
Amortization and Depletion **15**	6.1	0.4	0.2	0.1	0.4	0.0	1.4	6.6	1.5	3.0	•	•	3.3
Pensions and Other Deferred Comp. **16**	0.7	0.0	0.2	3.1	0.2	0.5	0.9	0.4	0.9	0.7	•	•	0.3
Employee Benefits **17**	2.0	3.8	0.5	1.7	0.4	2.8	2.4	2.9	2.5	3.0	•	•	1.6
Advertising **18**	5.1	4.4	1.2	7.2	1.8	0.0	0.5	2.4	2.0	0.7	•	•	9.6
Other Expenses **19**	53.2	41.0	25.3	20.0	16.3	24.5	36.8	20.1	20.0	33.2	•	•	24.7
Officers' Compensation **20**	2.1	28.9	8.4	7.6	4.0	4.0	3.3	4.0	4.1	1.6	•	•	1.1
Operating Margin **21**	•	10.0	11.7	15.6	11.4	5.0	5.6	•	7.3	3.9	•	•	7.4
Operating Margin Before Officers' Comp. **22**	•	38.8	20.0	23.2	15.4	8.9	8.9	4.0	11.4	5.5	•	•	8.6

Selected Average Balance Sheet ($ in Thousands)

Net Receivables 23	3276	0	16	64	723	681	2439	4495	9842	19434	72319
Inventories 24	693	0	1	0	9	0	272	236	594	240	2222
Net Property, Plant and Equipment 25	1200	0	13	301	421	869	3756	5522	6572	12083	161300
Total Assets 26	30889	0	88	641	2218	6217	15544	33601	71873	177855	870772
Notes and Loans Payable 27	2749	0	60	437	471	487	2086	17329	12804	52395	114600
All Other Liabilities 28	12817	0	45	157	852	1127	5478	13358	17895	49162	174979
Net Worth 29	15323	0	-17	47	895	4602	7979	2914	41174	76299	581194

Selected Financial Ratios (Times to 1)

Current Ratio 30	1.2	•	1.4	2.1	1.7	3.7	1.4	1.2	2.1	2.6	2.0
Quick Ratio 31	0.8	•	0.9	2.1	1.5	3.4	1.2	0.9	1.7	2.2	1.7
Net Sales to Working Capital 32	6.1	•	38.1	12.5	13.7	3.7	10.7	10.0	3.3	2.9	4.4
Coverage Ratio 33	4.1	1038.8	48.3	23.9	38.8	52.2	17.1	42.7	9.7	5.7	8.9
Total Asset Turnover 34	0.3	•	7.1	3.4	3.6	2.3	1.6	1.2	0.8	0.7	0.7
Inventory Turnover 35	1.5	•	179.0	•	466.4	•	18.6	70.7	35.0	40.6	58.2
Receivables Turnover 36	2.6	•	63.9	24.0	14.1	29.1	7.8	9.8	9.3	10.2	10.9
Total Liabilities to Net Worth 37	1.0	•	•	12.8	1.5	0.4	0.9	10.5	0.7	1.3	0.5
Current Assets to Working Capital 38	5.9	•	3.8	1.9	2.5	1.4	3.3	5.9	1.9	1.6	2.0
Current Liabilities to Working Capital 39	4.9	•	2.8	0.9	1.5	0.4	2.3	4.9	0.9	0.6	1.0
Working Capital to Net Sales 40	0.2	•	0.0	0.1	0.1	0.3	0.1	0.1	0.3	0.3	0.2
Inventory to Working Capital 41	0.6	•	0.1	•	0.0	•	0.1	0.1	0.1	0.0	0.0
Total Receipts to Cash Flow 42	1.7	2.0	2.9	2.9	4.0	4.2	2.4	1.8	3.7	2.7	3.1
Cost of Goods to Cash Flow 43	0.2	0.0	1.1	0.8	2.2	1.9	0.5	0.8	1.3	0.2	0.6
Cash Flow to Total Debt 44	0.3	•	2.1	1.3	1.5	2.1	1.4	0.7	0.5	0.5	0.7

Selected Financial Factors (in Percentages)

Debt Ratio 45	50.4	•	119.7	92.7	59.7	26.0	48.7	91.3	42.7	57.1	33.3
Return on Total Assets 46	4.2	•	93.7	56.7	46.9	11.8	17.0	44.5	10.1	8.6	14.1
Return on Equity Before Income Taxes 47	6.4	•	•	748.1	113.4	15.7	31.2	501.6	15.9	16.5	18.8
Return on Equity After Income Taxes 48	5.2	•	•	568.0	105.8	12.8	27.7	485.6	13.6	14.9	16.9
Profit Margin (Before Income Tax) 49	11.6	55.0	12.9	15.8	12.8	5.2	10.1	36.7	10.8	10.1	17.5
Profit Margin (After Income Tax) 50	9.5	52.4	12.7	12.0	11.9	4.2	9.0	35.5	9.3	9.1	15.8

274

Table I

Corporations with and without Net Income

OTHER INFORMATION SERVICES, NEWS SYNDICATES, LIBRARIES

MONEY AMOUNTS AND SIZE OF ASSETS IN THOUSANDS OF DOLLARS

Item Description for Accounting Period 7/05 Through 6/06	Total	Zero Assets	Under 500	500 to 1,000	1,000 to 5,000	5,000 to 10,000	10,000 to 25,000	25,000 to 50,000	50,000 to 100,000	100,000 to 250,000	250,000 to 500,000	500,000 to 2,500,000	2,500,000 and over
Number of Enterprises 1	10670	1088	8685	253	397	128	49	21	10	14	8	12	5
Revenues ($ in Thousands)													
Net Sales 2	26848564	668811	2401583	419127	878783	1717275	1256907	668748	431598	1617862	1739514	8538132	6510224
Interest 3	256390	2096	1277	214	3074	7006	7797	5888	8418	14600	18535	87500	99985
Rents 4	34118	0	0	0	205	3322	2109	207	204	0	0	11188	16884
Royalties 5	138254	1485	0	0	0	0	14518	9	4755	4521	1281	109278	2407
Other Portfolio Income 6	845239	75	3343	0	21859	0	1354	503	252	120958	7131	157676	532087
Other Receipts 7	2295585	268	33699	1024	16728	2738	31480	5964	17836	27599	72423	783818	1302007
Total Receipts 8	30418150	672735	2439902	420365	920649	1730341	1314165	681319	463063	1785540	2550279	8976197	8463594
Average Total Receipts 9	2851	618	281	1662	2319	13518	26820	32444	46306	127539	318785	748016	1692719
Operating Costs/Operating Income (%)													
Cost of Operations 10	21.2	38.6	46.7	3.7	33.1	34.3	33.7	15.9	16.1	10.9	37.9	16.8	8.3
Salaries and Wages 11	25.9	15.2	8.0	57.9	29.7	29.2	20.4	20.3	33.8	28.1	22.8	26.1	31.2
Taxes Paid 12	2.8	1.7	2.5	5.4	3.4	4.2	2.0	2.9	3.7	3.5	3.3	3.3	1.6
Interest Paid 13	4.0	1.4	1.7	0.8	3.0	0.4	1.2	0.9	2.4	2.5	5.6	1.7	10.5
Depreciation 14	2.5	2.4	0.9	9.2	2.6	2.0	2.2	4.2	3.2	3.4	3.5	1.8	3.3
Amortization and Depletion 15	2.8	2.0	0.4	0.4	3.2	0.1	1.4	1.4	2.2	3.7	5.5	2.3	4.6
Pensions and Other Deferred Comp. 16	1.0	0.1	1.8	0.3	0.2	1.1	0.3	0.3	0.2	2.1	0.2	1.1	1.0
Employee Benefits 17	2.5	0.5	1.2	2.0	2.0	3.0	1.8	1.8	5.1	2.0	2.7	2.0	3.9
Advertising 18	3.2	5.2	4.6	1.2	1.9	0.5	10.9	12.5	1.8	3.0	7.0	0.9	3.2
Other Expenses 19	39.2	31.9	21.5	42.8	43.3	25.7	28.7	27.7	40.0	40.7	70.9	34.9	49.3
Officers' Compensation 20	3.4	2.4	14.2	6.0	7.4	4.5	4.5	4.2	2.5	3.0	1.8	1.7	0.9
Operating Margin 21	•	•	•	•	•	•	•	7.9	•	•	7.3	•	•
Operating Margin Before Officers' Comp. 22	•	0.8	10.6	0.2	•	•	•	12.1	•	0.2	•	9.0	•

Selected Average Balance Sheet ($ in Thousands)

Net Receivables 23	557	0	9	196	534	2091	2361	4168	8320	22536	51801	114226	589379
Inventories 24	15	0	0	0	43	14	154	235	524	1227	1097	7371	1280
Net Property, Plant and Equipment 25	246	0	5	209	169	793	1719	3797	6283	18355	44103	64875	149090
Total Assets 26	4391	0	53	708	2392	6859	14834	35638	76028	164129	363196	1042112	4887791
Notes and Loans Payable 27	1459	0	98	778	976	451	3224	14994	7268	48762	80429	213204	1929868
All Other Liabilities 28	1300	0	35	1069	759	3366	9398	7830	38578	41942	178412	351718	1063508
Net Worth 29	1632	0	-80	-1139	657	3042	2212	12814	30183	73425	104354	477191	1894415

Selected Financial Ratios (Times to 1)

Current Ratio 30	0.7	•	0.8	0.4	1.5	1.3	1.0	1.8	0.7	1.1	0.8	1.2	0.5
Quick Ratio 31	0.6	•	0.7	0.4	1.4	1.1	0.8	1.6	0.5	0.9	0.6	0.9	0.3
Net Sales to Working Capital 32	•	•	•	•	4.3	14.5	•	4.9	15.8	•	•	12.7	•
Coverage Ratio 33	2.2	0.3	•	•	•	•	•	12.1	4.1	•	•	8.6	2.2
Total Asset Turnover 34	0.6	•	5.2	2.3	0.9	2.0	1.7	0.9	0.7	0.7	0.6	0.7	0.3
Inventory Turnover 35	36.0	•	312.8	•	17.1	336.5	56.3	21.6	13.3	10.3	75.2	16.2	84.0
Receivables Turnover 36	5.4	•	37.6	12.0	4.4	6.9	13.1	5.2	3.6	5.3	3.5	4.8	4.4
Total Liabilities to Net Worth 37	1.7	•	•	•	2.6	1.3	5.7	1.8	1.5	1.2	2.5	1.2	1.6
Current Assets to Working Capital 38	•	•	•	•	2.9	4.7	•	2.3	9.6	•	•	5.5	•
Current Liabilities to Working Capital 39	•	•	•	•	1.9	3.7	•	1.3	8.6	•	•	4.5	•
Working Capital to Net Sales 40	•	•	•	•	0.2	0.1	•	0.2	0.1	•	•	0.1	•
Inventory to Working Capital 41	•	•	•	•	0.2	0.0	•	0.1	0.2	•	•	0.1	•
Total Receipts to Cash Flow 42	2.6	3.5	20.8	12.9	5.6	4.3	2.9	3.1	2.7	2.0	•	2.3	1.9
Cost of Goods to Cash Flow 43	0.6	1.3	3.0	0.8	1.9	1.4	0.5	0.5	0.3	0.7	•	0.4	0.2
Cash Flow to Total Debt 44	0.4	0.3	0.3	0.0	0.6	0.5	0.5	0.3	0.5	0.4	•	0.6	0.2

Selected Financial Factors (in Percentages)

Debt Ratio 45	62.8	•	249.2	260.9	55.7	72.5	85.1	64.0	60.3	55.3	71.3	54.2	61.2
Return on Total Assets 46	5.1	•	•	•	•	•	•	9.5	7.1	•	•	9.9	6.1
Return on Equity Before Income Taxes 47	7.6	•	6.7	42.7	•	•	•	24.1	11.9	•	•	19.2	8.5
Return on Equity After Income Taxes 48	4.2	•	7.5	42.7	•	•	•	18.4	7.7	•	•	12.5	7.7
Profit Margin (Before Income Tax) 49	4.9	•	•	•	•	•	•	9.7	7.6	•	•	12.9	7.7
Profit Margin (After Income Tax) 50	2.7	•	•	•	•	•	•	7.4	4.9	•	•	8.4	11.2

Table II
Corporations with Net Income

OTHER INFORMATION SERVICES, NEWS SYNDICATES, LIBRARIES

MONEY AMOUNTS AND SIZE OF ASSETS IN THOUSANDS OF DOLLARS

Item Description for Accounting Period 7/05 Through 6/06	Total	Zero Assets	Under 500	500 to 1,000	1,000 to 5,000	5,000 to 10,000	10,000 to 25,000	25,000 to 50,000	50,000 to 100,000	100,000 to 250,000	250,000 to 500,000	500,000 to 2,500,000	2,500,000 and over
Number of Enterprises 1	3577	535	2804	0	95	74	27	10	4	11	4	9	5
Revenues ($ in Thousands)													
Net Sales 2	21923377	611615	1466141	0	475276	1309114	1036681	511408	242400	1246766	1017370	7496383	6510224
Interest 3	217671	1944	134	0	611	2352	3695	2651	7159	9090	7470	82581	99985
Rents 4	30377	0	0	0	0	0	2109	0	196	0	0	11188	16884
Royalties 5	130938	1485	0	0	0	0	13885	0	4755	4521	13	103872	2407
Other Portfolio Income 6	768408	75	26	0	9747	0	1351	129	9	120562	3069	101352	532087
Other Receipts 7	2273109	396	33611	0	15753	238	29352	1410	19980	27723	766116	76522	1302007
Total Receipts 8	25343880	615515	1499912	0	501387	1311704	1087073	515598	274499	1408662	1794038	7871898	8463594
Average Total Receipts 9	7085	1150	535	•	5278	17726	40262	51560	68625	128060	448510	874655	1692719
Operating Costs/Operating Income (%)													
Cost of Operations 10	21.0	42.2	62.0	•	26.7	44.9	37.2	10.4	6.5	6.5	21.4	19.1	8.3
Salaries and Wages 11	23.3	9.6	4.1	•	15.4	22.2	14.2	16.6	31.1	25.9	23.2	23.0	31.2
Taxes Paid 12	2.6	1.3	1.9	•	2.3	4.4	2.1	2.4	4.0	3.4	4.1	3.2	1.6
Interest Paid 13	4.3	1.4	0.3	•	1.2	0.1	1.1	0.8	1.9	2.9	3.8	1.9	10.5
Depreciation 14	2.3	2.5	0.5	•	2.3	0.8	1.3	3.3	3.3	3.5	2.1	1.9	3.3
Amortization and Depletion 15	2.7	1.6	0.1	•	0.0	0.0	0.1	0.4	0.9	3.5	3.5	2.5	4.6
Pensions and Other Deferred Comp. 16	1.1	0.1	2.8	•	0.3	1.3	0.4	0.4	0.4	1.7	0.3	1.2	1.0
Employee Benefits 17	2.4	0.5	0.6	•	1.5	1.9	1.4	1.7	5.3	1.8	2.1	2.1	3.9
Advertising 18	2.5	5.7	0.1	•	1.4	0.0	10.9	15.6	1.1	1.8	3.4	0.7	3.2
Other Expenses 19	38.4	25.8	10.9	•	27.6	17.2	25.7	23.0	43.2	45.5	102.8	32.6	49.3
Officers' Compensation 20	2.5	2.4	11.2	•	6.2	3.6	4.0	2.9	2.7	2.6	2.2	1.7	0.9
Operating Margin 21	•	6.9	5.4	•	15.1	3.7	1.6	22.6	•	0.9	•	10.1	•
Operating Margin Before Officers' Comp. 22	•	9.3	16.6	•	21.3	7.3	5.6	25.5	2.3	3.5	•	11.8	•

Selected Average Balance Sheet ($ in Thousands)

Net Receivables 23	1389	0	2	•	204	2123	•	2884	4601	13194	25243	6028	124360	589379
Inventories 24	28	0	1	•	19	0	•	108	33	0	122	223	9790	1280
Net Property, Plant and Equipment 25	561	0	5	•	243	692	•	1335	5995	7873	15379	31435	83462	149090
Total Assets 26	11096	0	45	•	2266	6557	•	14773	39831	73636	165239	358350	1120256	4887791
Notes and Loans Payable 27	3469	0	15	•	1052	435	•	3548	7289	6789	41185	11079	210118	1929868
All Other Liabilities 28	2841	0	29	•	435	1966	•	7880	9831	48455	29712	216128	320116	1063508
Net Worth 29	4786	0	1	•	778	4156	•	3346	22711	18392	94342	131142	590022	1894415

Selected Financial Ratios (Times to 1)

Current Ratio 30	0.7	•	0.8	•	1.1	1.8	1.1	1.7	0.9	1.3	0.7	1.4	0.5	
Quick Ratio 31	0.5	•	0.7	•	1.0	1.7	0.8	1.7	0.8	1.0	0.5	0.9	0.3	
Net Sales to Working Capital 32	•	•	•	38.0	8.9	42.5	6.5	•	7.3	•	9.5			
Coverage Ratio 33	3.9	6.3	25.0	18.3	35.0	6.6	29.6	7.7	5.8	2.9	9.1	2.2		
Total Asset Turnover 34	0.6	•	11.6	2.2	2.7	2.6	1.3	0.8	0.7	0.7	0.7	0.3		
Inventory Turnover 35	46.0	•	617.1	68.6	•	132.6	160.9	•	60.6	244.0	16.3	84.0		
Receivables Turnover 36	5.9	•	62.3	18.0	7.5	17.7	7.8	2.9	6.4	4.9	5.2	4.4		
Total Liabilities to Net Worth 37	1.3	•	51.3	1.9	0.6	3.4	0.8	3.0	0.8	1.7	0.9	1.6		
Current Assets to Working Capital 38	•	•	•	10.0	2.2	10.1	2.3	•	4.4	3.7	•			
Current Liabilities to Working Capital 39	•	•	•	9.0	1.2	9.1	1.3	•	3.4	2.7	•			
Working Capital to Net Sales 40	•	•	•	0.0	0.1	0.0	0.2	•	0.1	0.1	•			
Inventory to Working Capital 41	•	•	•	0.1	0.2	0.0	•	0.1	0.1	•				
Total Receipts to Cash Flow 42	2.2	3.2	6.3	2.4	5.3	3.3	2.3	1.9	2.2	1.0	2.3	1.9		
Cost of Goods to Cash Flow 43	0.5	1.3	3.9	0.6	2.4	1.2	0.2	0.1	0.1	0.2	0.4	0.2		
Cash Flow to Total Debt 44	0.4	•	1.9	1.4	1.4	1.0	1.3	0.6	0.7	1.2	0.7	0.2		

Selected Financial Factors (in Percentages)

Debt Ratio 45	56.9	•	98.1	65.7	36.6	77.4	43.0	75.0	42.9	63.4	47.3	61.2	
Return on Total Assets 46	9.3	•	93.4	48.0	10.8	19.4	31.1	12.4	11.5	7.8	13.1	6.1	
Return on Equity Before Income Taxes 47	16.1	•	4687.1	132.1	16.5	72.9	52.7	43.1	16.6	14.1	22.2	8.5	
Return on Equity After Income Taxes 48	12.6	•	4457.0	109.9	14.0	68.5	45.9	28.6	12.5	10.2	15.0	7.7	
Profit Margin (Before Income Tax) 49	12.6	7.5	7.7	20.6	3.9	6.3	23.4	13.1	13.8	7.3	15.7	12.4	
Profit Margin (After Income Tax) 50	9.9	6.2	7.3	17.1	3.3	6.0	20.4	8.7	10.4	5.3	10.6	11.2	

Table I

Corporations with and without Net Income

CREDIT INTERMEDIATION

MONEY AMOUNTS AND SIZE OF ASSETS IN THOUSANDS OF DOLLARS

Item Description for Accounting Period 7/05 Through 6/06	Total	Zero Assets	Under 500	500 to 1,000	1,000 to 5,000	5,000 to 10,000	10,000 to 25,000	25,000 to 50,000	50,000 to 100,000	100,000 to 250,000	250,000 to 500,000	500,000 to 2,500,000	2,500,000 and over
Number of Enterprises 1	60399	7215	39048	3846	4432	1507	998	740	802	857	419	389	145
Revenues ($ in Thousands)													
Net Sales 2	534167311	61107783	16073839	7176697	7359704	4295258	6518493	5477743	6005000	13312552	11316329	36375318	359148595
Interest 3	324113343	41928442	44273	37893	283316	204628	396319	828877	1999625	5310089	6316396	17516564	249246920
Rents 4	1546733	188888	401	1524	3193	1070	1214	17235	17508	22144	18051	173946	1101560
Royalties 5	532503	0	2332	0	82	0	96	32	20	44054	1045	5223	479619
Other Portfolio Income 6	10714768	1730046	7419	195	21173	30187	170051	84591	112260	301383	280653	1701533	6275277
Other Receipts 7	197259964	17260407	16019414	7137085	7051940	4059373	5950813	4547008	3875587	7634882	4700184	16978052	102045219
Total Receipts 8	534167311	61107783	16073839	7176697	7359704	4295258	6518493	5477743	6005000	13312552	11316329	36375318	359148595
Average Total Receipts 9	8844	8470	412	1866	1661	2850	6532	7402	7488	15534	27008	93510	2476887
Operating Costs/Operating Income (%)													
Cost of Operations 10	2.2	0.1	10.2	0.3	3.4	13.0	8.8	8.0	2.7	4.4	0.5	2.1	1.9
Salaries and Wages 11	9.9	8.0	21.7	27.1	30.9	17.1	29.8	27.5	22.0	16.9	17.3	15.8	7.0
Taxes Paid 12	1.4	1.5	2.5	1.6	3.4	2.4	3.3	2.8	3.2	2.6	2.7	2.4	1.0
Interest Paid 13	48.1	62.1	1.1	0.9	4.4	10.9	7.7	12.8	19.9	20.4	29.7	25.0	55.8
Depreciation 14	1.7	1.0	0.8	0.6	1.0	0.9	0.9	1.8	1.9	2.2	1.7	2.3	1.8
Amortization and Depletion 15	0.6	0.3	0.1	0.1	0.1	0.2	0.2	0.5	0.4	0.9	0.9	1.3	0.7
Pensions and Other Deferred Comp. 16	0.5	0.3	0.5	0.3	0.4	0.5	0.3	0.6	0.7	1.0	1.1	1.1	0.4
Employee Benefits 17	0.9	0.6	0.8	0.6	0.9	1.0	1.1	1.4	2.0	1.9	2.3	1.6	0.7
Advertising 18	1.5	0.2	1.8	0.9	3.5	1.6	3.6	3.0	1.7	1.8	1.5	2.8	1.4
Other Expenses 19	21.3	18.6	44.6	28.0	37.2	38.3	34.0	29.0	26.9	28.9	21.6	26.4	18.8
Officers' Compensation 20	1.3	0.8	7.8	2.1	5.8	6.6	4.3	4.5	5.8	4.4	3.3	1.9	0.5
Operating Margin 21	10.7	6.5	8.0	37.6	9.0	7.5	5.9	8.1	12.8	14.7	17.5	17.3	10.1
Operating Margin Before Officers' Comp. 22	12.0	7.3	15.8	39.6	14.8	14.1	10.2	12.6	18.6	19.1	20.8	19.3	10.6

Selected Average Balance Sheet ($ in Thousands)

Item	1	2	3	4	5	6	7	8	9	10	11	12
Net Receivables 23	12912	0	236	713	2676	7014	14615	31633	59671	111393	243728	3693046
Inventories 24	•	•	•	•	•	•	•	•	•	•	•	•
Net Property, Plant and Equipment 25	729	14	64	192	265	456	868	1460	3306	5279	13793	202285
Total Assets 26	77121	94	692	2176	7073	16041	36167	71744	157148	347778	975640	2697552
Notes and Loans Payable 27	43226	41	309	1056	4099	6799	9247	10926	23089	64540	236388	16799830
All Other Liabilities 28	28297	126	313	511	2673	6934	21618	50223	112580	239235	590030	8325949
Net Worth 29	5598	-73	71	608	301	2309	5302	10595	21479	44003	149222	1571773

Selected Financial Ratios (Times to 1)

Item	1	2	3	4	5	6	7	8	9	10	11	12
Current Ratio 30	0.5	1.4	3.8	1.5	0.9	1.2	0.9	0.9	0.7	0.6	0.6	0.5
Quick Ratio 31	0.4	1.1	3.3	1.3	0.8	1.0	0.8	0.8	0.7	0.6	0.5	0.4
Net Sales to Working Capital 32	•	25.5	4.3	4.0	•	4.1	•	•	•	•	•	•
Coverage Ratio 33	1.2	1.1	8.2	41.1	3.0	1.8	1.6	1.6	1.6	1.7	1.7	1.2
Total Asset Turnover 34	0.1	•	4.4	2.7	0.8	0.4	0.2	0.1	0.1	0.1	0.1	0.1
Inventory Turnover 35	•	•	•	•	•	•	•	•	•	•	•	•
Receivables Turnover 36	•	•	•	•	•	•	•	•	•	•	•	•
Total Liabilities to Net Worth 37	12.8	•	8.8	2.6	22.5	5.9	5.8	5.8	6.3	6.9	5.5	16.0
Current Assets to Working Capital 38	•	3.7	1.4	3.0	6.7	•	•	•	•	•	•	•
Current Liabilities to Working Capital 39	•	2.7	0.4	2.0	5.7	•	•	•	•	•	•	•
Working Capital to Net Sales 40	•	0.0	0.2	0.2	0.2	•	•	•	•	•	•	•
Inventory to Working Capital 41	•	0.0	0.0	0.0	•	•	•	•	•	•	•	•
Total Receipts to Cash Flow 42	3.4	4.5	1.6	2.4	2.9	3.1	2.8	2.8	2.5	2.8	2.5	3.7
Cost of Goods to Cash Flow 43	0.1	0.0	0.0	0.1	0.3	0.2	0.1	0.1	0.1	0.0	0.1	0.1
Cash Flow to Total Debt 44	0.0	1.1	1.9	0.4	0.2	0.1	0.0	0.0	0.0	0.0	0.0	0.0

Selected Financial Factors (in Percentages)

Item	1	2	3	4	5	6	7	8	9	10	11	12
Debt Ratio 45	92.7	177.4	89.8	72.0	95.7	85.6	85.3	85.2	86.3	87.3	84.7	94.1
Return on Total Assets 46	6.7	39.6	103.8	10.2	7.3	5.5	4.2	3.3	3.4	3.6	4.0	6.1
Return on Equity Before Income Taxes 47	16.0	•	992.9	24.5	68.8	16.3	10.7	8.4	10.0	10.2	10.6	15.1
Return on Equity After Income Taxes 48	11.1	•	988.9	22.7	63.4	14.6	9.0	6.5	7.4	7.4	7.2	9.8
Profit Margin (Before Income Tax) 49	10.1	8.0	37.6	9.0	7.3	5.8	7.7	11.9	13.9	16.6	16.9	9.6
Profit Margin (After Income Tax) 50	7.0	7.8	37.4	8.3	6.7	5.2	6.5	9.1	10.2	12.1	11.5	6.2

Table II

Corporations with Net Income

CREDIT INTERMEDIATION

MONEY AMOUNTS AND SIZE OF ASSETS IN THOUSANDS OF DOLLARS

Item Description for Accounting Period 7/05 Through 6/06	Total	Zero Assets	Under 500	500 to 1,000	1,000 to 5,000	5,000 to 10,000	10,000 to 25,000	25,000 to 50,000	50,000 to 100,000	100,000 to 250,000	250,000 to 500,000	500,000 to 2,500,000	2,500,000 and over
Number of Enterprises 1	38626	3481	24423	3239	2911	1010	736	547	663	757	381	354	124
Revenues ($ in Thousands)													
Net Sales 2	487972834	45008231	13491179	6777927	5389344	3685252	4856954	4272966	5092653	11405678	10410918	33253229	34432803
Interest 3	303207548	29760819	97402	31734	158759	117406	220281	586681	1675938	4764220	5797457	16091499	243905353
Rents 4	1484823	150125	584	1524	1147	461	748	10592	16707	19932	17557	164084	1101362
Royalties 5	528909	0	0	0	33	0	96	20	20	44054	21	5044	479619
Other Portfolio Income 6	9492065	993464	2077	194	11898	5308	151344	51143	105618	279291	268739	1435947	6187041
Other Receipts 7	173259489	14103823	13391116	6744475	5217507	3562077	4484485	3624529	3294370	6298181	4327144	15556655	92655128
Total Receipts 8	487972834	45008231	13491179	6777927	5389344	3685252	4856954	4272966	5092653	11405678	10410918	33253229	34432803
Average Total Receipts 9	12633	12930	552	2093	1851	3649	6599	7812	7681	15067	27325	93936	2776843
Operating Costs/Operating Income (%)													
Cost of Operations 10	2.2	0.0	9.4	0.3	3.1	13.1	8.2	8.3	2.8	4.6	0.6	2.0	2.0
Salaries and Wages 11	9.4	7.6	21.1	28.1	24.6	16.0	30.1	25.3	20.2	16.8	17.5	15.3	6.7
Taxes Paid 12	1.4	1.7	2.3	1.6	3.0	2.2	3.4	2.6	2.9	2.7	2.9	2.3	1.0
Interest Paid 13	48.3	58.1	0.5	0.8	3.7	8.1	7.6	12.0	19.1	20.5	27.8	23.2	56.3
Depreciation 14	1.0	1.1	0.6	0.6	0.8	0.9	0.9	1.3	1.8	1.9	1.7	2.0	0.8
Amortization and Depletion 15	0.6	0.3	0.1	0.0	0.1	0.1	0.2	0.3	0.2	0.6	0.9	1.3	0.6
Pensions and Other Deferred Comp. 16	0.5	0.3	0.6	0.3	0.3	0.6	0.4	0.6	0.8	1.1	1.2	0.9	0.4
Employee Benefits 17	0.8	0.6	0.5	0.6	0.7	0.9	1.2	1.3	1.9	1.9	2.4	1.7	0.7
Advertising 18	1.5	0.2	1.4	0.8	4.2	1.2	3.0	3.0	1.0	1.9	1.4	2.8	1.4
Other Expenses 19	20.3	16.9	44.1	24.8	34.7	34.6	28.1	24.3	24.1	24.4	20.3	25.6	18.5
Officers' Compensation 20	1.2	0.8	6.1	1.8	5.5	6.7	4.4	4.5	5.7	4.7	3.4	1.8	0.5
Operating Margin 21	12.9	12.5	13.4	40.4	19.2	15.6	12.6	16.4	19.4	18.9	19.9	21.0	11.0
Operating Margin Before Officers' Comp. 22	14.1	13.3	19.5	42.1	24.7	22.4	17.0	21.0	25.1	23.6	23.3	22.8	11.4

Selected Average Balance Sheet ($ in Thousands)

Net Receivables 23	17007	0	7	239	843	2900	7315	14760	31395	60420	111271	250738	3543753
Inventories 24	•	•	•	•	•	•	•	•	•	•	•	•	•
Net Property, Plant and Equipment 25	716	0	13	68	148	302	453	700	1396	3128	5551	13840	123765
Total Assets 26	112569	0	97	692	2191	7101	16251	36342	71890	157935	349113	980811	29440686
Notes and Loans Payable 27	64060	0	16	298	1008	3781	6735	9328	10200	19678	54825	211800	1886213
All Other Liabilities 28	40711	0	18	362	484	1317	6065	20802	51012	116312	250763	614560	9010884
Net Worth 29	7798	0	63	32	698	2003	3451	6211	10678	21945	43525	154451	1569589

Selected Financial Ratios (Times to 1)

Current Ratio 30	0.5	•	5.4	4.2	1.9	1.4	1.2	0.9	0.8	0.7	0.6	0.6	0.4
Quick Ratio 31	0.4	•	4.7	3.6	1.7	1.2	1.0	0.8	0.8	0.7	0.6	0.5	0.3
Net Sales to Working Capital 32	•	•	11.6	4.6	2.8	3.5	3.8	•	•	•	•	•	•
Coverage Ratio 33	1.3	1.2	29.4	50.7	6.1	2.9	2.6	2.3	2.0	1.9	1.7	1.9	1.2
Total Asset Turnover 34	0.1	•	5.7	3.0	0.8	0.5	0.4	0.2	0.1	0.1	0.1	0.1	0.1
Inventory Turnover 35	•	•	•	•	•	•	•	•	•	•	•	•	•
Receivables Turnover 36	•	•	•	•	•	•	•	•	•	•	•	•	•
Total Liabilities to Net Worth 37	13.4	•	0.5	20.8	2.1	2.5	3.7	4.9	5.7	6.2	7.0	5.4	17.8
Current Assets to Working Capital 38	•	•	1.2	1.3	2.1	3.8	6.4	•	•	•	•	•	•
Current Liabilities to Working Capital 39	•	•	0.2	0.3	1.1	2.8	5.4	•	•	•	•	•	•
Working Capital to Net Sales 40	0.1	•	0.1	0.2	0.4	0.3	0.3	•	•	•	•	•	•
Inventory to Working Capital 41	•	•	•	•	•	•	•	•	•	•	•	•	•
Total Receipts to Cash Flow 42	3.2	3.7	1.9	1.6	2.0	2.1	2.7	2.7	2.5	2.5	2.7	2.3	3.6
Cost of Goods to Cash Flow 43	0.1	0.0	0.2	0.0	0.1	0.3	0.2	0.2	0.1	0.1	0.0	0.0	0.1
Cash Flow to Total Debt 44	0.0	•	8.4	2.0	0.6	0.3	0.2	0.1	0.1	0.0	0.0	0.0	0.0

Selected Financial Factors (in Percentages)

Debt Ratio 45	93.1	•	35.0	95.4	68.1	71.8	78.8	82.9	85.1	86.1	87.5	84.3	94.7
Return on Total Assets 46	6.8	•	78.6	124.5	19.4	12.2	8.1	6.0	4.0	3.7	3.7	4.2	6.3
Return on Equity Before Income Taxes 47	20.1	•	116.7	2656.9	50.8	28.5	23.8	20.1	13.2	12.3	11.9	12.5	18.4
Return on Equity After Income Taxes 48	14.6	•	114.1	2646.1	48.9	27.3	22.4	18.2	10.9	9.4	8.8	8.9	12.2
Profit Margin (Before Income Tax) 49	12.4	12.4	13.4	40.4	19.2	15.6	12.4	16.0	18.3	18.0	18.9	20.5	10.4
Profit Margin (After Income Tax) 50	9.0	10.0	13.1	40.2	18.4	15.0	11.7	14.4	15.1	13.7	14.1	14.6	6.9

Table I

Corporations with and without Net Income

COMMERCIAL BANKING

MONEY AMOUNTS AND SIZE OF ASSETS IN THOUSANDS OF DOLLARS

Item Description for Accounting Period 7/05 Through 6/06	Total	Zero Assets	Under 500	500 to 1,000	1,000 to 5,000	5,000 to 10,000	10,000 to 25,000	25,000 to 50,000	50,000 to 100,000	100,000 to 250,000	250,000 to 500,000	500,000 to 2,500,000	2,500,000 and over
Number of Enterprises **1**	1990	357	0	•	•	78	205	286	439	382	128	59	10
Revenues ($ in Thousands)													
Net Sales **2**	72138757	55406597	0	•	•	13308	380291	645922	1791435	3547612	2722181	3302859	2009540
Interest **3**	48879073	39949922	0	•	•	9128	173427	345998	1091468	2051321	1649608	2157729	1449933
Rents **4**	333258	183237	0	•	•	1	259	534	1728	5655	5108	22286	114449
Royalties **5**	185	0	0	•	•	0	0	0	20	118	0	0	46
Other Portfolio Income **6**	1887025	1341592	0	•	•	237	6783	18987	57631	106463	102263	161362	91707
Other Receipts **7**	21039216	13931846	0	•	•	3942	199822	280403	640588	1384055	965202	961482	353405
Total Receipts **8**	72138757	55406597	0	•	•	13308	380291	645922	1791435	3547612	2722181	3302859	2009540
Average Total Receipts **9**	36251	155201	•	•	•	171	1855	2258	4081	9287	21267	55981	200954
Operating Costs/Operating Income (%)													
Cost of Operations **10**	•	•	•	•	•	•	•	•	•	•	•	•	•
Salaries and Wages **11**	8.5	7.3	•	•	•	48.5	13.4	12.9	15.4	14.8	14.7	15.1	12.3
Taxes Paid **12**	1.7	1.5	•	•	•	10.6	2.2	2.9	3.2	2.9	2.9	3.1	3.1
Interest Paid **13**	56.0	65.7	•	•	•	11.2	11.1	21.5	26.4	27.2	28.2	27.9	34.5
Depreciation **14**	1.3	1.0	•	•	•	7.6	1.4	2.3	2.8	2.3	2.1	2.1	7.4
Amortization and Depletion **15**	0.2	0.1	•	•	•	1.2	0.2	0.7	0.7	1.1	0.4	0.2	0.4
Pensions and Other Deferred Comp. **16**	0.4	0.3	•	•	•	•	0.4	0.9	0.8	0.8	0.7	0.9	1.6
Employee Benefits **17**	0.9	0.5	•	•	•	2.2	2.4	2.9	2.9	2.4	2.5	2.0	1.5
Advertising **18**	0.3	0.2	•	•	•	3.9	0.8	1.1	1.1	1.1	0.9	0.8	0.9
Other Expenses **19**	17.9	17.7	•	•	•	117.9	67.8	42.8	22.4	21.5	18.0	16.8	14.3
Officers' Compensation **20**	1.8	0.7	•	•	•	14.6	7.5	11.1	9.4	6.9	5.3	3.1	4.7
Operating Margin **21**	10.8	4.9	•	•	•	•	•	0.9	14.8	19.1	24.4	28.1	19.3
Operating Margin Before Officers' Comp. **22**	12.6	5.6	•	•	•	•	0.2	12.0	24.2	26.0	29.7	31.2	24.0

Selected Average Balance Sheet ($ in Thousands)

Net Receivables 23	61672	0	•	2348	8887	20948	43022	90719	205192	440089	895007
Inventories 24	•	•	•	•	•	•	•	•	•	•	•
Net Property, Plant and Equipment 25	1766	0	•	231	311	706	1378	2632	5472	11837	17888
Total Assets 26	12996	0	•	7576	17848	36959	71360	153390	346408	852375	4729980
Notes and Loans Payable 27	5593	0	•	0	200	495	1473	5314	15047	54071	313140
All Other Liabilities 28	105724	0	•	4083	15323	33904	60598	132156	296293	709763	3933024
Net Worth 29	12679	0	•	3494	2325	2560	9289	15919	35067	88541	483816

Selected Financial Ratios (Times to 1)

Current Ratio 30	0.9	•	•	1.7	1.2	1.0	1.0	0.9	0.9	0.9	0.9
Quick Ratio 31	0.9	•	•	1.7	1.1	1.0	1.0	0.9	0.9	0.9	0.6
Net Sales to Working Capital 32	•	•	•	0.1	0.8	14.4	7.7	•	•	•	•
Coverage Ratio 33	1.2	1.1	•	•	0.2	0.9	1.5	1.6	1.8	1.9	1.5
Total Asset Turnover 34	0.3	•	•	0.0	0.1	0.1	0.1	0.1	0.1	0.1	0.0
Inventory Turnover 35	•	•	•	•	•	•	•	•	•	•	•
Receivables Turnover 36	•	•	•	•	•	•	•	•	•	•	•
Total Liabilities to Net Worth 37	8.8	•	•	1.2	6.7	13.4	6.7	8.6	8.9	8.6	8.8
Current Assets to Working Capital 38	•	•	•	2.4	6.9	208.8	116.8	•	•	•	•
Current Liabilities to Working Capital 39	•	•	•	1.4	5.9	207.8	115.8	•	•	•	•
Working Capital to Net Sales 40	•	•	•	17.3	1.2	0.1	0.1	•	•	•	•
Inventory to Working Capital 41	•	•	•	•	•	0.0	0.0	•	•	•	•
Total Receipts to Cash Flow 42	3.9	5.1	•	•	2.9	2.9	3.0	2.7	2.6	2.5	3.3
Cost of Goods to Cash Flow 43	•	•	•	•	•	•	•	•	•	•	•
Cash Flow to Total Debt 44	0.1	•	•	0.0	0.0	0.0	0.0	0.0	0.0	0.0	0.0

Selected Financial Factors (in Percentages)

Debt Ratio 45	89.8	•	•	53.9	87.0	93.1	87.0	89.6	89.9	89.6	89.8
Return on Total Assets 46	19.2	•	•	•	0.2	1.2	2.2	2.7	3.1	3.6	2.2
Return on Equity Before Income Taxes 47	27.6	•	•	•	•	•	5.4	9.9	13.4	16.6	7.6
Return on Equity After Income Taxes 48	20.8	•	•	•	•	•	4.0	7.7	10.0	11.8	4.9
Profit Margin (Before Income Tax) 49	9.6	3.8	•	•	•	•	12.3	17.0	22.1	26.2	18.3
Profit Margin (After Income Tax) 50	7.3	2.1	•	•	•	•	9.2	13.2	16.5	18.7	11.9

Table II

Corporations with Net Income

COMMERCIAL BANKING

MONEY AMOUNTS AND SIZE OF ASSETS IN THOUSANDS OF DOLLARS

Item Description for Accounting Period 7/05 Through 6/06	Total	Zero Assets	Under 500	500 to 1,000	1,000 to 5,000	5,000 to 10,000	10,000 to 25,000	25,000 to 50,000	50,000 to 100,000	100,000 to 250,000	250,000 to 500,000	500,000 to 2,500,000	2,500,000 and over
Number of Enterprises 1	1458	181	0	•	29	9	144	206	356	343	121	•	10
Revenues ($ in Thousands)													
Net Sales 2	55719332	40303072	0	•	96815	5758	213631	452392	1538906	3181453	2603413	•	2009540
Interest 3	36224963	28173796	0	•	491	4533	79087	214653	901504	1894293	1559275	•	1449933
Rents 4	294486	145959	0	•	0	0	82	496	1257	4926	5036	•	114449
Royalties 5	185	0	0	•	0	0	0	0	20	118	0	•	46
Other Portfolio Income 6	1238321	707468	0	•	0	156	5466	17335	53746	102470	98616	•	91707
Other Receipts 7	17961377	11275849	0	•	96324	1069	128996	219908	582379	1179646	940486	•	353405
Total Receipts 8	55719332	40303072	0	•	96815	5758	213631	452392	1538906	3181453	2603413	•	2009540
Average Total Receipts 9	38216	222669	•	•	3338	640	1484	2196	4323	9275	21516	•	200954
Operating Costs/Operating Income (%)													
Cost of Operations 10	•	•	•	•	•	•	•	•	•	•	•	•	•
Salaries and Wages 11	8.5	7.1	•	•	12.1	11.1	20.0	12.1	13.9	14.5	14.5	•	12.3
Taxes Paid 12	2.0	1.7	•	•	1.2	3.4	3.2	3.1	3.1	3.0	2.9	•	3.1
Interest Paid 13	51.4	62.1	•	•	•	19.1	17.4	23.3	25.9	27.8	27.6	•	34.5
Depreciation 14	1.5	1.1	•	•	•	0.5	1.7	2.2	2.6	2.3	2.1	•	7.4
Amortization and Depletion 15	0.1	0.1	•	•	•	•	0.3	0.4	0.4	0.4	0.4	•	0.4
Pensions and Other Deferred Comp. 16	0.5	0.3	•	•	1.4	•	0.8	1.0	0.8	0.8	0.7	•	1.6
Employee Benefits 17	0.9	0.5	•	•	4.9	3.2	3.7	3.3	2.8	2.4	2.4	•	1.5
Advertising 18	0.4	0.2	•	•	5.6	1.3	1.0	1.0	1.0	1.1	0.9	•	0.9
Other Expenses 19	16.3	16.8	•	•	56.3	27.1	27.9	19.4	19.7	17.8	17.6	•	14.3
Officers' Compensation 20	1.9	0.7	•	•	6.8	21.2	10.0	11.9	8.9	7.0	5.3	•	4.7
Operating Margin 21	16.5	9.3	•	•	11.7	13.1	14.1	22.2	20.8	23.0	25.7	•	19.3
Operating Margin Before Officers' Comp. 22	18.4	10.1	•	•	18.6	34.3	24.1	34.1	29.7	30.0	30.9	•	24.0

Selected Average Balance Sheet ($ in Thousands)

Net Receivables 23	76794	0	324	8006	9085	20731	42864	92500	207472	•	895007
Inventories 24	•	•	•	•	•	•	•	•	•	•	•
Net Property, Plant and Equipment 25	2096	0	20	201	579	1297	2673	5499	•	17888	
Total Assets 26	156157	0	1182	10208	18515	36999	71331	154862	347257	•	4729980
Notes and Loans Payable 27	7174	0	0	218	577	1647	5049	13793	•	313140	
All Other Liabilities 28	133002	0	136	8662	15644	31731	61011	133708	297936	•	3933024
Net Worth 29	15980	0	1046	1546	2654	4690	8673	16104	35527	•	483816

Selected Financial Ratios (Times to 1)

Current Ratio 30	0.9	•	62.6	1.2	1.1	1.0	1.0	1.0	0.9	•	0.9
Quick Ratio 31	0.9	•	57.2	1.2	1.0	1.0	1.0	0.9	0.9	•	0.6
Net Sales to Working Capital 32	•	•	3.0	0.4	1.2	1.4	6.2	•	•	•	•
Coverage Ratio 33	1.3	1.1	•	1.5	1.7	1.8	1.7	1.7	1.8	•	1.5
Total Asset Turnover 34	0.2	•	2.8	0.1	0.1	0.1	0.1	0.1	0.1	•	0.0
Inventory Turnover 35	•	•	•	•	•	•	•	•	•	•	•
Receivables Turnover 36	•	•	•	•	•	•	•	•	•	•	•
Total Liabilities to Net Worth 37	8.8	•	0.1	5.6	6.0	6.9	7.2	8.6	8.8	•	8.8
Current Assets to Working Capital 38	•	•	1.0	6.9	13.5	21.9	89.0	•	•	•	•
Current Liabilities to Working Capital 39	•	•	0.0	5.9	12.5	20.9	88.0	•	•	•	•
Working Capital to Net Sales 40	•	•	0.3	2.3	0.8	0.7	0.2	•	•	•	•
Inventory to Working Capital 41	•	•	•	•	•	•	0.0	•	•	•	•
Total Receipts to Cash Flow 42	3.3	4.2	1.5	2.6	2.6	2.6	2.7	2.6	2.5	•	3.3
Cost of Goods to Cash Flow 43	•	•	•	•	•	•	•	•	•	•	•
Cash Flow to Total Debt 44	0.1	•	16.1	0.0	0.0	0.0	0.0	0.0	0.0	•	0.0

Selected Financial Factors (in Percentages)

Debt Ratio 45	89.8	•	11.5	84.9	85.7	87.3	87.8	89.6	89.8	•	89.8
Return on Total Assets 46	16.5	•	33.2	1.8	2.3	2.5	2.7	2.9	3.2	•	2.2
Return on Equity Before Income Taxes 47	38.0	•	37.5	4.3	6.5	9.0	9.0	11.9	14.1	•	7.6
Return on Equity After Income Taxes 48	30.9	•	36.7	3.6	5.7	7.5	7.2	9.5	10.6	•	4.9
Profit Margin (Before Income Tax) 49	15.9	9.3	11.7	10.4	11.7	19.2	18.0	20.7	23.4	•	18.3
Profit Margin (After Income Tax) 50	12.9	7.0	11.5	8.6	10.3	16.1	14.4	16.5	17.5	•	11.9

Table I

Corporations with and without Net Income

SAVINGS INSTITUTIONS AND OTHER DEPOSITORY CREDIT

MONEY AMOUNTS AND SIZE OF ASSETS IN THOUSANDS OF DOLLARS

Item Description for Accounting Period 7/05 Through 6/06	Total	Zero Assets	Under 500	500 to 1,000	1,000 to 5,000	5,000 to 10,000	10,000 to 25,000	25,000 to 50,000	50,000 to 100,000	100,000 to 250,000	250,000 to 500,000	500,000 to 2,500,000	2,500,000 and over
Number of Enterprises 1	1236	29	9	0	30	15	48	118	179	320	212	219	57
Revenues ($ in Thousands)													
Net Sales 2	86432686	3588827	249479	0	121374	11756	44325	246300	782187	3168471	4106747	12521091	61592128
Interest 3	58860129	1305537	483	0	62537	3665	38944	197962	597001	2423880	3307327	8889768	42033025
Rents 4	398003	4391	0	0	182	28	128	3627	1611	8092	8378	96225	275342
Royalties 5	4794	0	0	0	0	0	0	21	0	0	895	3689	189
Other Portfolio Income 6	2414639	238280	314	0	108	13	697	15068	27069	97549	145678	496443	1393418
Other Receipts 7	24755121	2040619	248682	0	58547	8050	4556	29622	156506	638950	644469	3034966	17890154
Total Receipts 8	86432686	3588827	249479	0	121374	11756	44325	246300	782187	3168471	4106747	12521091	61592128
Average Total Receipts 9	69929	123753	27720	•	4046	784	923	2087	4370	9901	19371	57174	1080564
Operating Costs/Operating Income (%)													
Cost of Operations 10	0.1	0.0	•	•	•	•	•	•	0.1	•	•	0.4	0.1
Salaries and Wages 11	15.7	9.6	•	•	25.6	6.1	15.9	12.9	15.7	16.7	15.9	15.0	16.2
Taxes Paid 12	2.4	1.7	0.0	•	4.6	1.0	3.6	3.2	3.1	3.0	3.0	2.4	2.3
Interest Paid 13	38.0	23.0	39.8	•	14.4	457.7	32.7	31.9	32.1	32.8	35.7	35.6	39.8
Depreciation 14	1.9	1.2	•	•	1.8	0.6	1.6	2.4	2.5	2.3	2.1	2.9	1.7
Amortization and Depletion 15	1.1	2.0	•	•	0.1	0.7	0.0	0.1	0.2	0.2	0.3	1.1	1.2
Pensions and Other Deferred Comp. 16	1.0	0.6	•	•	1.3	0.2	1.8	2.1	1.7	2.0	1.8	1.4	0.8
Employee Benefits 17	1.7	0.9	•	•	2.9	0.1	3.8	2.9	2.5	2.7	2.6	2.2	1.5
Advertising 18	1.3	0.6	•	•	0.4	0.2	0.9	1.1	1.4	1.5	1.4	1.2	1.4
Other Expenses 19	16.7	22.5	21.0	•	27.4	72.7	27.7	19.3	19.6	18.9	17.2	17.0	16.1
Officers' Compensation 20	1.4	1.6	•	•	2.7	0.7	8.8	8.5	6.3	5.0	3.8	2.3	0.8
Operating Margin 21	18.6	36.2	39.2	•	18.7	•	3.2	15.7	14.8	14.9	16.3	18.3	18.1
Operating Margin Before Officers' Comp. 22	20.1	37.8	39.2	•	21.4	•	11.9	24.2	21.1	19.9	20.1	20.6	18.9

Selected Average Balance Sheet ($ in Thousands)

Net Receivables 23	71170	0	0	•	157	1836	1067	1285	6083	17211	35703	68866	1026042
Inventories 24	•	•	•	•	•	•	•	•	•	•	•	•	•
Net Property, Plant and Equipment 25	11531	0	0	•	42	29	207	560	1385	3120	5847	14170	150621
Total Assets 26	1067191	0	266	•	1903	7217	17243	37446	73072	163180	343727	947078	16983437
Notes and Loans Payable 27	230762	0	12	•	2	1515	715	2126	4783	14289	30888	116152	4342087
All Other Liabilities 28	801617	0	492227	•	120	150749	13421	28322	57774	128444	273858	724870	12488937
Net Worth 29	34812	0	-491973	•	1780	-145046	3107	6998	10515	20446	38981	106056	152412

Selected Financial Ratios (Times to 1)

Current Ratio 30	0.2	•	0.0	•	14.9	0.0	0.3	0.3	0.3	0.3	0.3	0.3	0.2
Quick Ratio 31	0.2	•	0.0	•	14.6	0.0	0.3	0.3	0.3	0.3	0.2	0.2	0.1
Net Sales to Working Capital 32	•	•	•	•	2.4	•	•	•	•	•	•	•	•
Coverage Ratio 33	1.5	2.6	2.0	•	2.3	0.0	1.5	1.4	1.4	1.4	1.4	1.5	1.4
Total Asset Turnover 34	0.1	•	104.3	•	2.1	0.1	0.1	0.1	0.1	0.1	0.1	0.1	0.1
Inventory Turnover 35	•	•	•	•	•	•	•	•	•	•	•	•	•
Receivables Turnover 36	•	•	•	•	•	•	•	•	•	•	•	•	•
Total Liabilities to Net Worth 37	29.7	•	•	•	0.1	4.5	4.4	5.9	7.0	7.8	7.9	•	110.4
Current Assets to Working Capital 38	•	•	•	•	1.1	•	•	•	•	•	•	•	•
Current Liabilities to Working Capital 39	•	•	•	•	0.1	•	•	•	•	•	•	•	•
Working Capital to Net Sales 40	•	•	•	•	0.4	•	•	•	•	•	•	•	•
Inventory to Working Capital 41	•	•	•	•	•	•	•	•	•	•	•	•	•
Total Receipts to Cash Flow 42	3.2	1.8	•	•	2.6	1.7	3.5	3.5	3.3	3.3	3.3	3.2	3.3
Cost of Goods to Cash Flow 43	0.0	0.0	•	•	•	•	•	•	•	•	0.0	0.0	0.0
Cash Flow to Total Debt 44	0.0	•	•	•	12.6	0.0	0.0	0.0	0.0	0.0	0.0	0.0	0.0

Selected Financial Factors (in Percentages)

Debt Ratio 45	96.7	•	185284.1	•	6.4	2109.7	82.0	81.3	85.6	87.5	88.7	88.8	99.1
Return on Total Assets 46	3.7	•	8244.0	•	70.5	1.9	1.9	2.6	2.7	2.8	2.9	3.2	3.7
Return on Equity Before Income Taxes 47	36.5	•	•	•	42.6	0.8	4.3	4.3	5.7	6.7	7.6	9.4	125.9
Return on Equity After Income Taxes 48	25.0	•	•	•	27.3	2.4	3.0	3.0	3.9	4.6	5.0	6.5	83.7
Profit Margin (Before Income Tax) 49	18.2	36.0	39.2	•	18.7	2.6	14.4	14.4	13.8	13.9	15.3	17.5	17.8
Profit Margin (After Income Tax) 50	12.5	31.7	38.7	•	12.0	•	10.1	10.1	9.3	9.5	10.1	12.0	11.8

Table II
Corporations with Net Income

SAVINGS INSTITUTIONS AND OTHER DEPOSITORY CREDIT

MONEY AMOUNTS AND SIZE OF ASSETS IN THOUSANDS OF DOLLARS

Item Description for Accounting Period 7/05 Through 6/06	Total	Zero Assets	Under 500	500 to 1,000	1,000 to 5,000	5,000 to 10,000	10,000 to 25,000	25,000 to 50,000	50,000 to 100,000	100,000 to 250,000	250,000 to 500,000	500,000 to 2,500,000	2,500,000 and over
Number of Enterprises 1	1071	12	4	•	•	0	38	90	162	297	203	212	53
Revenues ($ in Thousands)													
Net Sales 2	83065203	3348906	305068	0	•	0	37369	205059	714988	2929585	3981164	11948438	59594625
Interest 3	56817295	1084512	62620	0	•	0	35220	165897	550502	2245602	3225525	8572629	40874788
Rents 4	391670	4108	183	0	•	0	73	3472	1489	7352	8114	91672	275206
Royalties 5	3740	0	0	0	•	0	0	21	0	0	21	3509	189
Other Portfolio Income 6	2361007	237003	121	0	•	0	571	11730	25707	92350	137447	478660	1377416
Other Receipts 7	23491491	2023283	242144	0	•	0	1505	23939	137290	584281	610057	2801968	17067026
Total Receipts 8	83065203	3348906	305068	0	•	0	37369	205059	714988	2929585	3981164	11948438	59594625
Average Total Receipts 9	77559	279076	76267	•	•	•	983	2278	4414	9864	19612	56361	1124427
Operating Costs/Operating Income (%)													
Cost of Operations 10	0.1	0.0	•	•	•	•	•	•	0.1	•	•	0.2	0.1
Salaries and Wages 11	15.7	9.2	3.2	•	•	•	14.8	11.5	15.1	16.4	15.8	15.0	16.3
Taxes Paid 12	2.4	1.7	1.2	•	•	•	3.3	3.2	3.1	3.1	3.0	2.5	2.4
Interest Paid 13	37.5	18.8	5.8	•	•	•	32.7	31.2	31.8	32.5	35.4	35.6	39.6
Depreciation 14	1.8	1.2	0.6	•	•	•	1.5	2.2	2.3	2.2	2.1	2.1	1.7
Amortization and Depletion 15	0.9	2.2	0.0	•	•	•	0.0	0.1	0.1	0.2	0.2	1.1	0.9
Pensions and Other Deferred Comp. 16	1.0	0.6	0.5	•	•	•	1.7	2.3	1.8	1.9	1.9	1.4	0.8
Employee Benefits 17	1.7	0.9	0.0	•	•	•	3.6	2.7	2.4	2.6	2.6	2.2	1.5
Advertising 18	1.3	0.7	0.2	•	•	•	1.0	1.1	1.3	1.5	1.3	1.3	1.4
Other Expenses 19	15.9	12.2	4.0	•	•	•	20.1	17.8	18.2	17.8	15.6	16.8	15.9
Officers' Compensation 20	1.3	1.4	0.4	•	•	•	8.7	9.1	6.2	4.9	3.8	2.1	0.7
Operating Margin 21	20.4	51.1	84.2	•	•	•	12.6	18.9	17.6	16.8	18.2	19.6	18.9
Operating Margin Before Officers' Comp. 22	21.7	52.5	84.6	•	•	•	21.3	28.0	23.8	21.7	22.0	21.7	19.6

Selected Average Balance Sheet ($ in Thousands)

Net Receivables 23	79522	0	0	1198	1482	5902	17093	35208	69487	1076940
Inventories 24	•	•	•	•	•	•	•	•	•	•
Net Property, Plant and Equipment 25	12687	0	44	199	532	1367	3050	5958	13679	156513
Total Assets 26	1183369	0	2653	17442	37443	73541	163337	344704	946639	17589761
Notes and Loans Payable 27	257345	0	18	804	2051	4628	13268	30446	111685	4544405
All Other Liabilities 28	884316	0	44239	13922	28989	58338	129610	275619	732515	12916952
Net Worth 29	41707	0	-41604	2716	6402	10575	20459	38639	102439	128404

Selected Financial Ratios (Times to 1)

Current Ratio 30	0.2	•	0.4	0.3	0.3	0.3	0.3	0.3	0.3	0.2
Quick Ratio 31	0.2	•	0.4	0.2	0.3	0.3	0.3	0.3	0.2	0.1
Net Sales to Working Capital 32	•	•	•	•	•	•	•	•	•	•
Coverage Ratio 33	1.5	3.7	15.6	1.4	1.6	1.5	1.5	1.5	1.5	1.5
Total Asset Turnover 34	0.1	•	28.7	0.1	0.1	0.1	0.1	0.1	0.1	0.1
Inventory Turnover 35	•	•	•	•	•	•	•	•	•	•
Receivables Turnover 36	•	•	•	•	•	•	•	•	•	•
Total Liabilities to Net Worth 37	27.4	•	•	5.4	4.8	6.0	7.0	7.9	8.2	136.0
Current Assets to Working Capital 38	•	•	•	•	•	•	•	•	•	•
Current Liabilities to Working Capital 39	•	•	•	•	•	•	•	•	•	•
Working Capital to Net Sales 40	•	•	•	•	•	•	•	•	•	•
Inventory to Working Capital 41	•	•	•	•	•	•	•	•	•	•
Total Receipts to Cash Flow 42	3.1	1.6	•	3.3	3.3	3.1	3.2	3.2	3.1	3.3
Cost of Goods to Cash Flow 43	0.0	0.0	•	0.0	0.0	0.0	•	•	0.0	0.0
Cash Flow to Total Debt 44	1.5	•	•	0.0	0.0	0.0	0.0	0.0	0.0	0.0

Selected Financial Factors (in Percentages)

Debt Ratio 45	96.5	1668.0	•	84.4	82.9	85.6	87.5	88.8	89.2	99.3
Return on Total Assets 46	3.8	2586.7	•	2.5	3.0	2.9	2.9	3.0	3.2	3.7
Return on Equity Before Income Taxes 47	37.1	•	•	4.4	6.4	6.9	7.6	8.7	10.3	162.4
Return on Equity After Income Taxes 48	26.1	•	•	3.2	4.6	4.9	5.3	6.0	7.2	108.5
Profit Margin (Before Income Tax) 49	19.9	50.9	84.2	12.1	18.0	16.6	15.8	17.2	18.8	18.5
Profit Margin (After Income Tax) 50	14.0	46.4	81.2	8.9	12.9	11.7	11.0	11.8	13.0	12.4

Table I

Corporations with and without Net Income

CREDIT CARD ISSUING AND OTHER CONSUMER CREDIT

MONEY AMOUNTS AND SIZE OF ASSETS IN THOUSANDS OF DOLLARS

Item Description for Accounting Period 7/05 Through 6/06	Total	Zero Assets	Under 500	500 to 1,000	1,000 to 5,000	5,000 to 10,000	10,000 to 25,000	25,000 to 50,000	50,000 to 100,000	100,000 to 250,000	250,000 to 500,000	500,000 to 2,500,000	2,500,000 and over
Number of Enterprises 1	8560	261	4951	1088	1234	547	239	76	48	39	26	28	21
Revenues ($ in Thousands)													
Net Sales 2	94787413	397859	818194	312057	1442133	1113539	1143964	807577	771316	1709863	1852773	8411349	76006788
Interest 3	33517047	12561	4639	2084	80902	111771	39471	129731	83665	326317	699513	2907689	29118704
Rents 4	267951	0	92	0	38	288	332	667	305	1756	58	16901	247513
Royalties 5	42922	0	0	0	82	0	0	0	0	42840	0	0	0
Other Portfolio Income 6	2030695	795	232	11	4621	4666	8780	11914	4514	31023	346	251211	1712581
Other Receipts 7	58928798	384503	813231	309962	1356490	996814	1095381	665265	682832	1307927	1152856	5235548	44927990
Total Receipts 8	94787413	397859	818194	312057	1442133	1113539	1143964	807577	771316	1709863	1852773	8411349	76006788
Average Total Receipts 9	11073	1524	165	287	1169	2036	4786	10626	16069	43843	71260	300405	3619371
Operating Costs/Operating Income (%)													
Cost of Operations 10	6.1	•	•	•	•	•	•	•	1.4	0.5	0.1	0.3	7.6
Salaries and Wages 11	8.7	28.1	14.8	21.1	14.7	12.8	19.3	20.2	16.1	16.3	14.8	13.0	7.2
Taxes Paid 12	1.2	2.6	2.0	3.6	2.3	2.2	2.5	2.6	2.1	3.2	2.1	1.8	1.0
Interest Paid 13	19.6	4.5	1.5	9.5	7.5	17.5	13.0	17.1	15.2	12.4	27.9	16.8	20.7
Depreciation 14	4.1	2.3	1.1	1.0	0.8	2.1	1.5	4.0	1.7	1.8	1.1	1.7	4.7
Amortization and Depletion 15	1.0	0.7	0.0	0.1	0.2	0.5	0.5	0.5	0.5	1.5	0.9	2.3	0.9
Pensions and Other Deferred Comp. 16	0.4	0.1	0.9	•	0.1	0.8	0.6	0.8	0.4	0.4	0.2	0.4	0.4
Employee Benefits 17	0.9	0.7	1.7	0.0	0.8	0.7	1.3	1.3	1.2	1.4	1.5	0.9	0.8
Advertising 18	3.3	0.6	2.4	1.0	9.0	2.7	3.1	2.6	0.6	3.7	2.5	3.8	3.2
Other Expenses 19	43.0	56.7	50.0	47.1	50.3	39.2	39.3	28.3	37.3	33.4	32.7	43.6	43.4
Officers' Compensation 20	1.1	0.0	20.1	5.6	3.8	9.5	6.5	3.5	4.7	5.0	1.1	1.0	0.5
Operating Margin 21	10.5	3.7	5.4	10.9	10.4	12.0	12.5	19.0	18.8	20.3	15.0	14.5	9.6
Operating Margin Before Officers' Comp. 22	11.6	3.7	25.6	16.6	14.2	21.5	19.0	22.5	23.4	25.4	16.1	15.5	10.1

Selected Average Balance Sheet ($ in Thousands)

Net Receivables 23	36886	0	28	438	1300	5211	11854	25757	48799	95578	202159	590778	13238620
Inventories 24	•	•	•	•	•	•	•	•	•	•	•	•	•
Net Property, Plant and Equipment 25	1957	0	9	21	55	123	363	661	1890	4600	4718	13143	745591
Total Assets 26	69682	0	133	722	2135	6658	15639	36344	70491	151509	360790	1078195	25399752
Notes and Loans Payable 27	35771	0	84	453	1115	4451	9326	21293	40142	85333	248754	523151	12917189
All Other Liabilities 28	23584	0	10	64	498	916	2563	5513	13900	14617	49729	294381	8992433
Net Worth 29	10326	0	38	206	521	1292	3749	9538	16449	51559	62307	260663	3490130

Selected Financial Ratios (Times to 1)

Current Ratio 30	1.6	•	30.9	2.8	2.3	2.7	1.9	2.4	2.2	3.0	1.2	1.5	1.6
Quick Ratio 31	1.6	•	22.3	2.5	2.2	2.5	1.8	2.3	2.1	2.6	1.1	1.4	1.6
Net Sales to Working Capital 32	0.7	•	1.6	0.6	1.4	0.5	0.8	0.6	0.5	0.5	1.7	1.2	0.6
Coverage Ratio 33	1.5	1.8	4.7	2.2	2.4	1.7	2.0	2.1	2.2	2.6	1.5	1.9	1.5
Total Asset Turnover 34	0.2	•	1.2	0.4	0.5	0.3	0.3	0.3	0.2	0.3	0.2	0.3	0.1
Inventory Turnover 35	•	•	•	•	•	•	•	•	•	•	•	•	•
Receivables Turnover 36	•	•	•	•	•	•	•	•	•	•	•	•	•
Total Liabilities to Net Worth 37	5.7	•	2.5	2.5	3.1	4.2	3.2	2.8	3.3	1.9	4.8	3.1	6.3
Current Assets to Working Capital 38	2.6	•	1.0	1.6	1.8	1.6	2.1	1.7	1.8	1.5	5.7	3.0	2.6
Current Liabilities to Working Capital 39	1.6	•	0.0	0.6	0.8	0.6	1.1	0.7	0.8	0.5	4.7	2.0	1.6
Working Capital to Net Sales 40	1.5	•	0.6	1.6	0.7	1.9	1.3	1.6	1.9	1.8	0.6	0.8	1.6
Inventory to Working Capital 41	0.0	•	•	•	0.0	0.0	•	•	0.0	0.0	0.0	0.0	0.0
Total Receipts to Cash Flow 42	1.9	1.7	2.0	1.9	1.8	2.0	2.0	2.3	1.9	2.1	2.3	1.8	1.9
Cost of Goods to Cash Flow 43	0.1	•	•	•	•	•	•	•	0.0	0.0	0.0	0.0	0.0
Cash Flow to Total Debt 44	0.1	•	0.9	0.3	0.4	0.2	0.2	0.2	0.2	0.2	0.1	0.2	0.1

Selected Financial Factors (in Percentages)

Debt Ratio 45	85.2	•	71.4	71.5	75.6	80.6	76.0	73.8	76.7	66.0	82.7	75.8	86.3
Return on Total Assets 46	4.8	•	8.5	8.1	9.8	9.0	7.8	10.5	7.7	9.4	8.5	8.7	4.3
Return on Equity Before Income Taxes 47	11.4	•	23.4	15.3	23.3	18.9	15.8	20.9	18.3	17.1	17.2	16.6	10.2
Return on Equity After Income Taxes 48	7.8	•	22.9	14.6	22.3	17.0	14.5	18.5	15.5	12.8	12.8	12.1	6.6
Profit Margin (Before Income Tax) 49	10.7	3.7	5.4	10.9	10.4	12.0	12.4	18.7	18.7	20.1	15.0	14.4	9.8
Profit Margin (After Income Tax) 50	7.3	2.9	5.3	10.5	9.9	10.8	11.4	16.6	15.9	15.1	11.2	10.5	6.3

Table II
Corporations with Net Income

CREDIT CARD ISSUING AND OTHER CONSUMER CREDIT

MONEY AMOUNTS AND SIZE OF ASSETS IN THOUSANDS OF DOLLARS

Item Description for Accounting Period 7/05 Through 6/06	Total	Zero Assets	Under 500	500 to 1,000	1,000 to 5,000	5,000 to 10,000	10,000 to 25,000	25,000 to 50,000	50,000 to 100,000	100,000 to 250,000	250,000 to 500,000	500,000 to 2,500,000	2,500,000 and over
Number of Enterprises 1	5402	•	2462	973	932	385	191	68	40	32	19	22	•
Revenues ($ in Thousands)													
Net Sales 2	85496593	•	245974	288949	1308742	854496	1029837	767487	672681	1588290	1498875	7653931	•
Interest 3	32956883	•	4627	2084	61555	69902	31546	126010	52219	270723	575875	2712304	•
Rents 4	267437	•	92	0	9	0	183	667	258	1756	58	16901	•
Royalties 5	42874	•	0	0	33	0	0	0	0	42840	0	0	•
Other Portfolio Income 6	1830523	•	232	11	3848	4486	8074	8052	4396	29403	346	127974	•
Other Receipts 7	50398876	•	241023	286854	1243297	780108	990034	632758	615808	1243568	922596	4796752	•
Total Receipts 8	85496593	•	245974	288949	1308742	854496	1029837	767487	672681	1588290	1498875	7653931	•
Average Total Receipts 9	15827	•	100	297	1404	2219	5392	11287	16817	49634	78888	347906	•
Operating Costs/Operating Income (%)													
Cost of Operations 10	6.7	•	•	•	•	•	•	•	1.4	0.6	0.1	0.3	•
Salaries and Wages 11	8.4	•	2.7	22.0	13.3	10.2	19.4	20.8	15.5	15.8	15.6	13.0	•
Taxes Paid 12	1.2	•	0.9	3.6	2.1	2.2	2.5	2.6	2.1	3.2	2.3	1.9	•
Interest Paid 13	18.5	•	1.7	6.9	6.4	14.6	11.7	16.4	13.8	11.3	21.3	12.0	•
Depreciation 14	1.0	•	1.6	1.1	0.8	2.4	1.5	2.5	1.9	1.3	1.2	1.2	•
Amortization and Depletion 15	1.1	•	•	0.1	0.2	0.3	0.5	0.6	0.2	1.5	1.1	2.4	•
Pensions and Other Deferred Comp. 16	0.4	•	•	•	0.0	1.0	0.6	0.8	0.4	0.4	0.1	0.2	•
Employee Benefits 17	0.9	•	0.0	0.0	0.7	0.4	1.3	1.3	1.3	1.3	1.8	0.9	•
Advertising 18	3.6	•	1.2	1.0	9.8	3.2	3.4	2.8	0.5	3.8	2.7	4.1	•
Other Expenses 19	44.3	•	66.3	48.0	43.9	32.2	36.1	27.6	31.3	32.1	33.8	44.8	•
Officers' Compensation 20	1.0	•	0.0	5.0	3.3	11.2	6.5	3.4	4.7	5.2	1.0	1.0	•
Operating Margin 21	12.8	•	25.5	12.4	19.5	22.3	16.6	21.3	26.8	23.6	19.0	18.0	•
Operating Margin Before Officers' Comp. 22	13.8	•	25.6	17.4	22.8	33.5	23.1	24.7	31.5	28.8	20.0	19.1	•

Selected Average Balance Sheet ($ in Thousands)

Net Receivables 23	642974	•	240252	100403	50876	26043	12340	5696	1424	395	0	49332
Inventories 24	•	•	•	•	•	•	•	•	•	•	•	•
Net Property, Plant and Equipment 25	13161	•	6052	4017	2206	550	382	139	46	23	4	555
Total Assets 26	1130329	•	364183	155350	70989	35881	15541	6700	2128	710	107	95298
Notes and Loans Payable 27	409538	•	232397	81404	40238	21202	9607	4028	951	412	9	47378
All Other Liabilities 28	368386	•	51023	16129	12883	5485	2458	1232	343	70	0	32496
Net Worth 29	352405	•	80763	57817	17869	9194	3476	1440	834	227	98	15424

Selected Financial Ratios (Times to 1)

Current Ratio 30	1.7	•	1.3	2.9	2.3	2.3	1.9	3.2	2.5	3.5	66.8	1.5
Quick Ratio 31	1.6	•	1.3	2.5	2.3	2.2	1.8	3.1	2.4	3.0	56.4	1.5
Net Sales to Working Capital 32	1.1	•	1.3	0.6	0.5	0.7	0.8	0.5	1.4	0.6	1.3	0.8
Coverage Ratio 33	2.5	•	1.9	3.1	2.9	2.3	2.4	2.5	4.1	2.8	15.7	1.7
Total Asset Turnover 34	0.3	•	0.2	0.3	0.2	0.3	0.3	0.3	0.7	0.4	0.9	0.2
Inventory Turnover 35	•	•	•	•	•	•	•	•	•	•	•	•
Receivables Turnover 36	•	•	•	•	•	•	•	•	•	•	•	•
Total Liabilities to Net Worth 37	2.2	•	3.5	1.7	3.0	2.9	3.5	3.7	1.6	2.1	0.1	5.2
Current Assets to Working Capital 38	2.4	•	4.2	1.5	1.7	1.7	2.1	1.5	1.7	1.4	1.0	2.9
Current Liabilities to Working Capital 39	1.4	•	3.2	0.5	0.7	0.7	1.1	0.5	0.7	0.4	0.0	1.9
Working Capital to Net Sales 40	0.9	•	0.8	1.7	1.9	1.5	1.2	1.9	0.7	1.7	0.8	1.3
Inventory to Working Capital 41	0.0	•	0.0	0.0	0.0	•	•	•	•	•	•	0.0
Total Receipts to Cash Flow 42	1.6	•	2.1	2.0	1.8	2.2	2.0	1.9	1.7	1.8	1.1	1.8
Cost of Goods to Cash Flow 43	0.0	•	0.0	0.0	0.0	•	•	•	•	•	•	0.1
Cash Flow to Total Debt 44	0.3	•	0.1	0.3	0.2	0.2	0.2	0.2	0.6	0.3	10.0	0.1

Selected Financial Factors (in Percentages)

Debt Ratio 45	68.8	•	77.8	62.8	74.8	74.4	77.6	78.5	60.8	68.0	8.3	83.8
Return on Total Assets 46	9.2	•	8.7	11.1	9.6	11.8	9.8	12.2	17.0	8.1	25.4	5.2
Return on Equity Before Income Taxes 47	17.8	•	18.5	20.1	25.1	25.8	25.7	34.4	32.8	16.2	25.9	13.4
Return on Equity After Income Taxes 48	13.6	•	13.9	15.4	22.1	23.1	23.9	31.9	31.9	15.5	25.5	9.5
Profit Margin (Before Income Tax) 49	18.0	•	19.0	23.4	26.7	21.0	16.5	22.3	19.5	12.4	25.4	13.0
Profit Margin (After Income Tax) 50	13.7	•	14.2	18.0	23.5	18.8	15.4	20.7	18.9	11.9	25.0	9.3

Table I

Corporations with and without Net Income

REAL ESTATE CREDIT INCL. MORTGAGE BANKERS AND ORIGINATORS

MONEY AMOUNTS AND SIZE OF ASSETS IN THOUSANDS OF DOLLARS

Item Description for Accounting Period 7/05 Through 6/06		Total	Zero Assets	Under 500	500 to 1,000	1,000 to 5,000	5,000 to 10,000	10,000 to 25,000	25,000 to 50,000	50,000 to 100,000	100,000 to 250,000	250,000 to 500,000	500,000 to 2,500,000	2,500,000 and over
Number of Enterprises	1	15801	2269	9846	819	1643	659	272	134	62	40	16	30	11
Revenues ($ in Thousands)														
Net Sales	2	50028370	516706	4593944	1914175	2620755	1656959	2954679	2088504	1289814	1227457	1263124	4354014	25548238
Interest	3	13245214	90874	17106	2004	75725	52435	84931	76081	65678	131496	161573	1319004	11168308
Rents	4	271981	1095	309	0	1443	197	311	11666	11660	2152	94	9096	233960
Royalties	5	497	0	0	0	0	0	83	0	0	414	0	0	0
Other Portfolio Income	6	1017157	100277	0	1	2982	20341	57271	23976	20590	52828	30635	587120	121141
Other Receipts	7	35493521	324460	4576529	1912170	2540605	1583986	2812083	1976781	1191886	1040567	1070822	2438794	14024829
Total Receipts	8	50028370	516706	4593944	1914175	2620755	1656959	2954679	2088504	1289814	1227457	1263124	4354014	25548238
Average Total Receipts	9	3166	228	467	2337	1595	2514	10863	15586	20803	30686	78945	145134	2322567
Operating Costs/Operating Income (%)														
Cost of Operations	10	3.3	11.6	3.0	0.0	1.6	8.2	7.0	8.0	6.5	5.8	4.4	1.2	2.5
Salaries and Wages	11	26.6	29.9	19.9	66.7	43.0	21.4	38.0	39.3	32.0	36.2	29.5	25.2	20.5
Taxes Paid	12	3.3	3.3	3.5	2.8	4.1	2.9	4.3	3.0	3.4	2.8	3.1	4.0	3.1
Interest Paid	13	21.6	20.1	0.3	0.5	4.3	9.0	6.2	8.2	12.3	15.6	18.5	22.0	33.4
Depreciation	14	1.4	1.5	0.9	0.7	1.0	0.2	0.5	0.8	0.7	1.1	0.5	1.5	2.0
Amortization and Depletion	15	1.6	3.2	0.1	0.1	0.1	0.2	0.0	0.4	0.0	1.0	0.1	1.1	2.8
Pensions and Other Deferred Comp.	16	0.6	0.1	0.2	0.5	0.3	0.8	0.3	0.2	0.4	0.2	1.5	0.4	0.8
Employee Benefits	17	1.5	1.6	1.1	1.0	0.9	0.6	1.0	1.1	1.4	1.6	1.0	1.5	1.8
Advertising	18	2.3	0.4	2.6	1.6	3.1	1.8	5.5	4.4	3.3	1.3	1.8	4.6	1.4
Other Expenses	19	29.5	31.9	51.7	19.0	33.9	36.2	29.3	28.8	29.8	22.8	18.8	27.1	26.7
Officers' Compensation	20	2.6	1.0	6.5	2.4	5.8	6.2	3.2	3.2	3.8	5.0	3.5	3.4	0.9
Operating Margin	21	5.5	•	10.3	4.8	1.8	12.6	4.7	2.4	6.3	6.5	17.1	7.8	4.2
Operating Margin Before Officers' Comp.	22	8.1	•	16.8	7.2	7.6	18.8	7.8	5.6	10.1	11.6	20.6	11.2	5.1

Selected Average Balance Sheet ($ in Thousands)

Net Receivables 23	1364	0	4	157	567	1201	3844	5647	11561	23442	43495	149963	1000885
Inventories 24	•	•	•	•	•	•	•	•	•	•	•	•	•
Net Property, Plant and Equipment 25	264	0	17	94	209	384	476	1506	896	3584	2534	12707	216254
Total Assets 26	19600	0	111	626	2240	7395	15535	34787	69128	150384	361362	1024340	22166481
Notes and Loans Payable 27	9316	0	29	171	944	4485	10403	18721	33314	94355	268118	531340	10078803
All Other Liabilities 28	8195	0	11	24	537	877	5458	10791	23850	50979	70596	367030	9937956
Net Worth 29	2088	0	72	430	759	2033	-325	5275	11964	5050	22648	125970	2149722

Selected Financial Ratios (Times to 1)

Current Ratio 30	0.4	•	5.1	4.2	1.2	0.6	0.8	0.5	0.6	0.6	0.5	0.4	0.3
Quick Ratio 31	0.3	•	4.2	4.0	1.0	0.5	0.6	0.3	0.5	0.4	0.3	0.3	0.2
Net Sales to Working Capital 32	•	•	8.9	7.5	7.8	•	•	•	•	•	•	•	•
Coverage Ratio 33	1.3	0.8	35.5	11.6	1.4	2.4	1.8	1.3	1.5	1.9	1.4	1.4	1.1
Total Asset Turnover 34	0.2	•	4.2	3.7	0.7	0.3	0.7	0.4	0.3	0.2	0.2	0.1	0.1
Inventory Turnover 35	•	•	•	•	•	•	•	•	•	•	•	•	•
Receivables Turnover 36	•	•	•	•	•	•	•	•	•	•	•	•	•
Total Liabilities to Net Worth 37	8.4	•	0.5	0.5	1.9	2.6	•	5.6	4.8	28.8	15.0	7.1	9.3
Current Assets to Working Capital 38	•	•	1.2	1.3	5.6	•	•	•	•	•	•	•	•
Current Liabilities to Working Capital 39	•	•	0.2	0.3	4.6	•	•	•	•	•	•	•	•
Working Capital to Net Sales 40	•	•	0.1	0.1	0.1	•	•	•	•	•	•	•	•
Inventory to Working Capital 41	•	•	0.0	•	0.0	•	•	•	•	•	•	•	•
Total Receipts to Cash Flow 42	3.3	4.6	1.8	4.8	3.3	2.2	3.4	3.9	3.1	3.9	3.0	3.2	4.0
Cost of Goods to Cash Flow 43	0.1	0.5	0.1	0.0	0.1	0.2	0.2	0.3	0.2	0.2	0.1	0.0	0.1
Cash Flow to Total Debt 44	0.1	•	6.7	2.5	0.3	0.2	0.2	0.1	0.1	0.1	0.1	0.1	0.0

Selected Financial Factors (in Percentages)

Debt Ratio 45	89.3	•	35.4	31.2	66.1	72.5	102.1	84.8	82.7	96.6	93.7	87.7	90.3
Return on Total Assets 46	4.4	•	44.5	19.6	4.3	7.2	7.6	4.8	5.5	4.5	7.7	4.2	3.9
Return on Equity Before Income Taxes 47	8.3	•	66.9	26.1	3.7	15.0	•	7.1	10.7	38.6	58.4	9.1	4.5
Return on Equity After Income Taxes 48	6.2	•	66.5	25.6	2.8	14.9	•	6.0	7.8	35.2	55.7	4.1	2.6
Profit Margin (Before Income Tax) 49	5.5	•	10.3	4.8	1.8	12.1	4.7	2.4	6.1	6.4	16.8	7.9	4.1
Profit Margin (After Income Tax) 50	4.1	•	10.3	4.7	1.3	12.0	4.1	2.0	4.5	5.8	16.0	3.6	2.4

Table II
Corporations with Net Income

REAL ESTATE CREDIT INCL. MORTGAGE BANKERS AND ORIGINATORS

MONEY AMOUNTS AND SIZE OF ASSETS IN THOUSANDS OF DOLLARS

Item Description for Accounting Period 7/05 Through 6/06	Total	Zero Assets	Under 500	500 to 1,000	1,000 to 5,000	5,000 to 10,000	10,000 to 25,000	25,000 to 50,000	50,000 to 100,000	100,000 to 250,000	250,000 to 500,000	500,000 to 2,500,000	2,500,000 and over
Number of Enterprises 1	9004	293	6137	•	1092	465	195	89	48	29	•	18	7
Revenues ($ in Thousands)													
Net Sales 2	41610792	97966	3658352	•	1724094	1399333	2227450	1473829	959451	956276	•	3271825	22971576
Interest 3	10981054	4690	15882	•	68319	32962	45906	44311	39497	95734	•	856829	9669659
Rents 4	263513	58	309	•	1137	93	227	5228	11560	2130	•	8780	233898
Royalties 5	497	0	0	•	0	0	83	0	0	414	•	0	0
Other Portfolio Income 6	756885	765	0	•	2569	436	45645	9401	19314	44155	•	483352	120615
Other Receipts 7	29608843	92453	3642161	•	1652069	1364842	2135589	1414889	889080	813843	•	1922864	12947404
Total Receipts 8	41610792	97966	3658352	•	1724094	1399333	2227450	1473829	959451	956276	•	3271825	22971576
Average Total Receipts 9	4621	334	596	•	1579	3007	11423	16560	19989	32975	•	181768	3281654
Operating Costs/Operating Income (%)													
Cost of Operations 10	3.1	1.8	1.7	•	1.8	6.1	9.2	6.4	6.6	4.4	•	•	2.7
Salaries and Wages 11	24.4	28.6	15.8	•	32.4	20.7	38.5	37.3	29.6	33.6	•	21.9	18.9
Taxes Paid 12	3.1	6.2	3.5	•	3.7	2.7	4.3	2.6	3.2	2.4	•	3.7	2.9
Interest Paid 13	21.1	11.1	0.3	•	4.0	9.4	5.4	8.0	13.1	14.5	•	18.2	31.7
Depreciation 14	1.5	1.0	0.6	•	0.8	0.1	0.5	0.7	0.6	0.7	•	1.5	2.1
Amortization and Depletion 15	1.8	0.6	0.0	•	0.0	0.1	0.0	0.2	0.0	1.3	•	1.2	3.0
Pensions and Other Deferred Comp. 16	0.6	0.0	0.2	•	0.2	0.8	0.3	0.2	0.4	0.3	•	0.4	0.8
Employee Benefits 17	1.3	3.8	0.4	•	0.5	0.4	0.9	0.9	1.1	1.5	•	1.5	1.7
Advertising 18	1.8	0.9	1.8	•	3.6	0.8	3.6	4.9	1.2	1.0	•	4.2	1.2
Other Expenses 19	28.6	17.3	53.1	•	34.6	37.3	26.2	26.1	26.7	21.9	•	20.2	27.6
Officers' Compensation 20	2.4	0.6	6.9	•	4.3	5.7	2.7	3.3	3.6	5.5	•	3.2	0.9
Operating Margin 21	10.3	28.2	15.7	•	14.1	15.8	8.3	9.5	13.8	12.8	•	23.9	6.6
Operating Margin Before Officers' Comp. 22	12.7	28.8	22.6	•	18.4	21.6	11.0	12.8	17.3	18.3	•	27.2	7.5

Selected Average Balance Sheet ($ in Thousands)

Net Receivables 23	1309	0	•	693	1140	4120	4714	13698	31491	•	236796	370473
Inventories 24	•	•	4	•	•	•	•	•	•	•	•	•
Net Property, Plant and Equipment 25	368	0	16	101	458	526	1023	781	2450	•	16008	314880
Total Assets 26	29953	0	131	2269	7385	15798	35782	69397	149157	•	1070255	32051691
Notes and Loans Payable 27	14023	0	16	947	4043	9854	18956	34950	79776	•	526363	1644802
All Other Liabilities 28	12491	0	7	626	1013	2435	11878	21073	54960	•	371551	14185241
Net Worth 29	3440	0	108	696	2329	3510	4949	13373	14421	•	172342	3220647

Selected Financial Ratios (Times to 1)

Current Ratio 30	0.3	•	10.8	1.4	0.5	0.8	0.5	0.6	0.6	•	0.5	0.3
Quick Ratio 31	0.2	•	9.4	1.2	0.5	0.6	0.3	0.5	0.4	•	0.4	0.1
Net Sales to Working Capital 32	•	•	8.9	4.4	•	•	•	•	•	•	•	•
Coverage Ratio 33	1.5	3.5	60.6	4.5	2.7	2.6	2.2	2.0	1.9	•	2.3	1.2
Total Asset Turnover 34	0.2	•	4.5	0.7	0.4	0.7	0.5	0.3	0.2	•	0.2	0.1
Inventory Turnover 35	•	•	•	•	•	•	•	•	•	•	•	•
Receivables Turnover 36	•	•	•	•	•	•	•	•	•	•	•	•
Total Liabilities to Net Worth 37	7.7	•	0.2	2.3	2.2	3.5	6.2	4.2	9.3	•	5.2	9.0
Current Assets to Working Capital 38	•	•	1.1	3.5	•	•	•	•	•	•	•	•
Current Liabilities to Working Capital 39	•	•	0.1	2.5	•	•	•	•	•	•	•	•
Working Capital to Net Sales 40	•	•	0.1	0.2	•	•	•	•	•	•	•	•
Inventory to Working Capital 41	•	•	•	•	•	•	•	•	•	•	•	•
Total Receipts to Cash Flow 42	2.9	2.4	1.6	2.2	2.2	3.3	3.2	2.7	3.2	•	2.4	3.5
Cost of Goods to Cash Flow 43	0.1	0.0	0.0	0.0	0.1	0.3	0.2	0.2	0.1	•	•	0.1
Cash Flow to Total Debt 44	0.1	•	16.5	0.4	0.3	0.3	0.2	0.1	0.1	•	0.1	0.0

Selected Financial Factors (in Percentages)

Debt Ratio 45	88.5	•	17.8	69.3	68.5	77.8	86.2	80.7	90.3	•	83.9	90.0
Return on Total Assets 46	4.8	•	72.5	12.5	10.3	9.9	8.1	7.7	6.0	•	7.1	3.9
Return on Equity Before Income Taxes 47	13.7	•	86.7	31.8	20.4	27.1	31.6	20.3	28.8	•	25.1	6.7
Return on Equity After Income Taxes 48	11.5	•	86.3	30.2	20.3	24.8	29.7	17.1	27.2	•	19.5	4.8
Profit Margin (Before Income Tax) 49	10.2	28.2	15.7	14.0	15.8	8.3	9.5	13.6	12.6	•	23.8	6.6
Profit Margin (After Income Tax) 50	8.6	27.4	15.6	13.3	15.7	7.6	8.9	11.4	11.9	•	18.5	4.7

286

Table I

Corporations with and without Net Income

INTL. TRADE, SECONDARY FINANCING, OTHER NONDEPOSITORY CREDIT

MONEY AMOUNTS AND SIZE OF ASSETS IN THOUSANDS OF DOLLARS

Item Description for Accounting Period 7/05 Through 6/06	Total	Zero Assets	Under 500	500 to 1,000	1,000 to 5,000	5,000 to 10,000	10,000 to 25,000	25,000 to 50,000	50,000 to 100,000	100,000 to 250,000	250,000 to 500,000	500,000 to 2,500,000	2,500,000 and over
Number of Enterprises 1	4637	833	2403	•	•	36	99	60	38	50	29	42	38
Revenues ($ in Thousands)													
Net Sales 2	184695466	667428	229988	•	•	193504	785699	493274	386855	945437	548404	3685127	175643058
Interest 3	167289896	545125	16605	•	•	10983	18707	51958	111570	326220	386175	1984669	163791355
Rents 4	102486	0	0	•	•	0	0	608	455	2652	3003	8834	84699
Royalties 5	4748	0	2332	•	•	0	11	10	0	681	151	1534	29
Other Portfolio Income 6	2560375	326	4313	•	•	2993	76410	4876	318	6777	1300	154261	2301705
Other Receipts 7	14737961	121977	206738	•	•	179528	690571	435822	274512	609107	157775	1535829	9465270
Total Receipts 8	184695466	667428	229988	•	•	193504	785699	493274	386855	945437	548404	3685127	175643058
Average Total Receipts 9	39831	801	96	•	•	5375	7936	8221	10180	18909	18910	87741	4622186
Operating Costs/Operating Income (%)													
Cost of Operations 10	0.3	•	•	•	•	2.3	22.0	4.8	6.1	2.0	0.3	7.5	0.0
Salaries and Wages 11	1.7	5.0	27.5	•	•	24.2	22.4	18.6	16.4	13.7	7.6	9.4	1.1
Taxes Paid 12	0.2	0.8	8.5	•	•	5.7	2.2	2.3	5.2	1.1	0.8	1.5	0.1
Interest Paid 13	82.1	79.9	4.0	•	•	10.4	5.9	17.6	25.2	22.2	51.5	32.6	84.9
Depreciation 14	0.3	0.1	1.9	•	•	2.4	0.7	1.2	1.1	1.4	1.2	3.4	0.2
Amortization and Depletion 15	0.0	0.0	0.8	•	•	0.2	0.3	0.5	0.2	0.8	0.1	0.7	0.0
Pensions and Other Deferred Comp. 16	0.2	0.0	•	•	•	•	0.1	0.8	0.4	0.8	2.2	1.0	0.1
Employee Benefits 17	0.2	0.0	0.6	•	•	1.0	0.9	0.7	1.4	0.6	0.8	0.7	0.1
Advertising 18	0.1	0.0	1.2	•	•	0.3	0.9	0.4	0.8	0.7	0.4	0.6	0.0
Other Expenses 19	6.3	16.3	46.0	•	•	93.8	30.7	30.8	28.4	35.0	23.8	19.1	5.0
Officers' Compensation 20	0.3	0.1	9.1	•	•	11.3	3.0	3.3	2.5	2.1	0.7	1.0	0.2
Operating Margin 21	8.3	•	0.6	•	•	•	10.8	19.0	12.4	19.4	10.7	22.5	8.1
Operating Margin Before Officers' Comp. 22	8.7	•	9.6	•	•	•	13.8	22.3	14.9	21.5	11.5	23.5	8.3

Selected Average Balance Sheet ($ in Thousands)

Net Receivables 23	40324	0	28	•	1666	7590	20214	47665	106505	231502	686664	3730705
Inventories 24	•	•	•	•	•	•	•	•	•	•	•	•
Net Property, Plant and Equipment 25	493	0	7	•	1008	272	675	1600	1550	1390	9561	34968
Total Assets 26	442272	0	108	•	7077	15416	33704	77049	159941	362214	1179283	51955572
Notes and Loans Payable 27	393178	0	41	•	7989	8459	19487	50650	94784	227304	702075	46758492
All Other Liabilities 28	26800	0	10	•	1473	2657	6662	9952	15781	26328	151897	3029429
Net Worth 29	22294	0	57	•	-2385	4300	7555	16447	49377	108582	325311	2171650

Selected Financial Ratios (Times to 1)

Current Ratio 30	0.5	27.5	•	0.8	1.6	1.5	1.3	1.3	1.3	1.3	1.8	0.4
Quick Ratio 31	0.3	17.4	•	0.6	1.3	1.3	1.1	1.2	1.2	1.2	1.5	0.3
Net Sales to Working Capital 32	•	1.1	•	•	2.1	0.9	0.8	0.7	0.3	0.3	0.2	•
Coverage Ratio 33	1.1	1.1	1.0	•	2.8	2.1	1.5	1.9	1.9	1.2	1.7	1.1
Total Asset Turnover 34	0.1	0.9	•	0.8	0.5	0.2	0.1	0.1	0.1	0.1	0.1	0.1
Inventory Turnover 35	•	•	•	•	•	•	•	•	•	•	•	•
Receivables Turnover 36	•	•	•	•	•	•	•	•	•	•	•	•
Total Liabilities to Net Worth 37	18.8	0.9	•	•	2.6	3.5	3.7	2.2	2.3	2.3	2.6	22.9
Current Assets to Working Capital 38	•	1.0	•	•	2.8	2.9	4.6	4.3	4.6	4.6	2.3	•
Current Liabilities to Working Capital 39	•	0.0	•	•	1.8	1.9	3.6	3.3	3.6	3.6	1.3	•
Working Capital to Net Sales 40	•	0.9	•	•	0.5	1.1	1.2	1.5	2.9	2.9	4.3	•
Inventory to Working Capital 41	•	•	•	•	•	0.0	0.0	0.0	•	•	0.0	•
Total Receipts to Cash Flow 42	7.0	3.3	7.2	2.6	2.7	2.1	2.6	2.0	2.9	2.9	2.5	7.7
Cost of Goods to Cash Flow 43	0.0	•	•	0.1	0.6	0.1	0.2	0.0	0.0	0.0	0.2	0.0
Cash Flow to Total Debt 44	0.0	0.6	•	0.2	0.3	0.1	0.1	0.1	0.1	0.0	0.0	0.0

Selected Financial Factors (in Percentages)

Debt Ratio 45	95.0	47.1	•	133.7	72.1	77.6	78.7	69.1	70.0	72.4	95.8
Return on Total Assets 46	8.1	4.0	•	•	8.6	8.8	5.0	4.9	3.2	4.1	8.2
Return on Equity Before Income Taxes 47	13.4	0.9	•	115.9	19.8	20.2	7.7	7.4	1.9	6.0	15.3
Return on Equity After Income Taxes 48	8.8	0.4	•	116.9	19.1	19.4	3.8	5.3	1.1	4.0	10.0
Profit Margin (Before Income Tax) 49	7.5	0.6	•	•	10.7	18.6	12.4	19.4	10.7	22.2	7.2
Profit Margin (After Income Tax) 50	4.9	0.2	•	•	10.3	17.8	6.1	13.8	6.6	15.0	4.7

Table II

Corporations with Net Income

INTL. TRADE, SECONDARY FINANCING, OTHER NONDEPOSITORY CREDIT

MONEY AMOUNTS AND SIZE OF ASSETS IN THOUSANDS OF DOLLARS

Item Description for Accounting Period 7/05 Through 6/06	Total	Zero Assets	Under 500	500 to 1,000	1,000 to 5,000	5,000 to 10,000	10,000 to 25,000	25,000 to 50,000	50,000 to 100,000	100,000 to 250,000	250,000 to 500,000	500,000 to 2,500,000	2,500,000 and over
Number of Enterprises 1	2813	413	1452	456	209	11	74	45	28	39	18	36	30
Revenues ($ in Thousands)													
Net Sales 2	181572426	579344	165481	622562	350472	174759	546029	412225	357323	833196	380189	3357524	173793321
Interest 3	164860658	480339	9471	22592	7432	255	12413	23410	89850	239383	237147	1805580	161932785
Rents 4	100955	0	0	1524	0	0	0	596	455	1931	2916	8834	84699
Royalties 5	2255	0	0	0	0	0	11	0	0	681	0	1534	29
Other Portfolio Income 6	2538873	0	3	0	4341	0	76150	2189	318	6512	1264	149214	2298880
Other Receipts 7	14069685	99005	156007	598446	338699	174504	457455	386030	266700	584689	138862	1392362	9476928
Total Receipts 8	181572426	579344	165481	622562	350472	174759	546029	412225	357323	833196	380189	3357524	173793321
Average Total Receipts 9	64548	1403	114	1365	1677	15887	7379	9161	12762	21364	21122	93265	5793111
Operating Costs/Operating Income (%)													
Cost of Operations 10	0.2	•	•	0.6	6.6	2.5	7.6	5.7	6.6	2.3	0.4	8.2	0.0
Salaries and Wages 11	1.6	5.7	24.6	6.0	27.3	26.7	26.8	17.1	17.0	14.6	7.5	8.4	1.1
Taxes Paid 12	0.2	0.9	9.3	1.5	3.0	3.6	2.3	2.4	2.1	1.2	1.0	1.4	0.1
Interest Paid 13	82.3	79.7	4.9	1.5	8.0	0.6	7.0	11.3	15.0	18.4	51.4	31.4	84.8
Depreciation 14	0.3	0.1	2.3	1.4	1.0	2.7	0.5	0.7	1.0	1.6	0.8	3.7	0.2
Amortization and Depletion 15	0.0	0.0	0.5	0.0	0.0	0.0	0.4	0.2	0.2	0.9	0.1	0.5	0.0
Pensions and Other Deferred Comp. 16	0.2	0.0	•	0.1	0.3	•	0.2	0.9	0.4	0.7	2.2	1.0	0.1
Employee Benefits 17	0.2	0.0	0.4	0.0	0.6	1.1	1.0	0.6	1.3	0.6	0.9	0.7	0.1
Advertising 18	0.1	0.0	1.5	1.2	1.1	0.3	0.9	0.5	0.8	0.8	0.4	0.5	0.0
Other Expenses 19	6.0	10.8	36.9	83.2	20.3	46.8	27.2	28.3	24.8	34.2	17.4	17.6	5.0
Officers' Compensation 20	0.3	0.1	10.4	2.3	4.2	12.5	3.8	3.3	2.7	2.0	0.6	1.0	0.2
Operating Margin 21	8.7	2.6	9.2	2.2	27.6	3.2	22.3	29.1	28.1	22.8	17.2	25.5	8.2
Operating Margin Before Officers' Comp. 22	9.0	2.7	19.6	4.5	31.8	15.7	26.1	32.5	30.8	24.8	17.8	26.6	8.4

Selected Average Balance Sheet ($ in Thousands)

Net Receivables 23	61517	0	40	337	358	1604	8796	20264	52669	107743	262062	761140	4446197
Inventories 24	•	•	•	•	•	•	•	•	•	•	•	•	•
Net Property, Plant and Equipment 25	745	0	7	32	937	1636	255	565	1068	1913	1318	9865	44293
Total Assets 26	705769	0	103	593	2236	7251	15831	33107	76796	160675	384379	1204279	64100362
Notes and Loans Payable 27	630204	0	37	322	2989	1605	8334	18114	43791	96222	233281	748537	57812104
All Other Liabilities 28	39849	0	2	46	102	4614	2911	6178	11679	12301	37461	103686	3543100
Net Worth 29	35716	0	64	225	-855	1032	4586	8816	21326	52152	113637	352055	2745158

Selected Financial Ratios (Times to 1)

Current Ratio 30	0.5	•	39.4	3.6	2.3	0.9	1.7	1.7	1.5	1.4	1.3	2.0	0.4
Quick Ratio 31	0.3	•	24.3	2.7	1.3	0.6	1.5	1.4	1.4	1.3	1.2	1.8	0.3
Net Sales to Working Capital 32	•	•	1.3	3.5	3.4	•	1.5	0.9	0.6	0.6	0.3	0.2	•
Coverage Ratio 33	1.1	1.0	2.9	2.4	4.5	6.7	4.2	3.6	2.9	2.2	1.3	1.8	1.1
Total Asset Turnover 34	0.1	•	1.1	2.3	0.7	2.2	0.5	0.3	0.2	0.1	0.1	0.1	0.1
Inventory Turnover 35	•	•	•	•	•	•	•	•	•	•	•	•	•
Receivables Turnover 36	•	•	•	•	•	•	•	•	•	•	•	•	•
Total Liabilities to Net Worth 37	18.8	•	0.6	1.6	•	6.0	2.5	2.8	2.6	2.1	2.4	2.4	22.4
Current Assets to Working Capital 38	•	•	1.0	1.4	1.8	•	2.4	2.5	3.0	3.3	4.3	2.0	•
Current Liabilities to Working Capital 39	•	•	0.0	0.4	0.8	•	1.4	1.5	2.0	2.3	3.3	1.0	•
Working Capital to Net Sales 40	•	0.8	0.3	•	0.3	•	0.7	1.1	1.5	1.8	3.1	4.8	•
Inventory to Working Capital 41	•	•	•	•	•	•	0.0	0.0	•	0.0	0.0	0.0	•
Total Receipts to Cash Flow 42	6.9	7.5	3.4	1.2	2.3	2.1	2.3	1.8	2.0	1.9	2.9	2.4	7.7
Cost of Goods to Cash Flow 43	0.0	•	•	0.0	0.1	0.1	0.2	0.1	0.1	0.0	0.0	0.2	0.0
Cash Flow to Total Debt 44	0.0	•	0.9	3.0	0.2	1.2	0.3	0.2	0.1	0.1	0.0	0.0	0.0

Selected Financial Factors (in Percentages)

Debt Ratio 45	94.9	•	38.4	62.0	138.2	85.8	71.0	73.4	72.2	67.5	70.4	70.8	95.7
Return on Total Assets 46	8.2	•	15.5	8.6	26.7	8.1	13.6	11.1	7.2	5.5	3.8	4.4	8.3
Return on Equity Before Income Taxes 47	14.2	•	16.5	13.2	•	48.6	35.7	30.1	16.8	9.3	3.2	6.6	15.5
Return on Equity After Income Taxes 48	9.4	•	15.6	10.7	•	48.2	34.8	29.2	12.8	6.7	2.1	4.5	10.1
Profit Margin (Before Income Tax) 49	7.9	2.6	9.2	2.2	27.6	3.2	22.2	29.0	28.1	22.7	17.2	25.1	7.3
Profit Margin (After Income Tax) 50	5.2	2.2	8.7	1.8	26.8	3.1	21.6	28.1	21.3	16.4	11.2	17.1	4.8

Table I

Corporations with and without Net Income

ACTIVITIES RELATED TO CREDIT INTERMEDIATION

MONEY AMOUNTS AND SIZE OF ASSETS IN THOUSANDS OF DOLLARS

Item Description for Accounting Period 7/05 Through 6/06	Total	Zero Assets	Under 500	500 to 1,000	1,000 to 5,000	5,000 to 10,000	10,000 to 25,000	25,000 to 50,000	50,000 to 100,000	100,000 to 250,000	250,000 to 500,000	500,000 to 2,500,000	2,500,000 and over
Number of Enterprises 1	28177	3466	21839	1423	987	172	135	67	36	25	8	11	8
Revenues ($ in Thousands)													
Net Sales 2	46084619	530365	10182234	2103236	2586967	1306191	1209534	1196166	983392	2713712	823100	4100878	18348844
Interest 3	2321984	24424	5440	9712	41177	16647	40838	27147	50242	50856	112201	257705	1685596
Rents 4	173053	164	0	0	819	556	183	133	1749	1837	1410	20605	145597
Royalties 5	479358	0	0	0	0	0	2	0	0	0	0	0	479356
Other Portfolio Income 6	804878	48777	2560	183	6370	1936	20115	9772	2135	6742	433	51132	654723
Other Receipts 7	42305346	457000	10174234	2093341	2538601	1287052	1148396	1159114	929266	2654277	709056	3771436	15383572
Total Receipts 8	46084619	530365	10182234	2103236	2586967	1306191	1209534	1196166	983392	2713712	823100	4100878	18348844
Average Total Receipts 9	1636	153	466	1478	2621	7594	8960	17853	27316	108548	102888	372807	2293606
Operating Costs/Operating Income (%)													
Cost of Operations 10	8.3	0.4	14.8	0.8	7.3	32.2	16.1	20.6	4.6	17.8	•	8.6	2.1
Salaries and Wages 11	18.7	36.9	23.5	27.0	28.4	13.9	30.1	26.4	33.0	12.6	25.8	19.9	11.9
Taxes Paid 12	2.3	3.1	2.0	2.0	3.3	1.4	2.5	2.6	2.9	1.6	3.4	1.8	2.6
Interest Paid 13	5.3	6.0	0.4	0.9	1.5	3.7	5.5	7.4	9.7	3.3	11.7	3.5	9.2
Depreciation 14	2.5	0.6	0.8	0.9	0.9	0.6	1.1	2.0	1.6	3.2	1.4	1.9	4.4
Amortization and Depletion 15	0.9	1.0	0.1	0.1	0.1	0.0	0.2	0.6	0.2	0.8	6.9	1.4	1.4
Pensions and Other Deferred Comp. 16	0.8	0.0	0.7	0.4	0.4	0.1	0.3	0.4	0.7	1.1	0.1	2.5	0.7
Employee Benefits 17	1.4	1.1	0.6	1.0	0.8	1.6	0.8	1.1	1.7	1.3	4.6	2.3	1.7
Advertising 18	4.4	7.3	1.5	1.2	1.3	0.5	2.5	3.3	1.9	2.5	1.5	7.3	7.1
Other Expenses 19	41.4	45.0	41.4	46.4	34.3	30.7	32.4	23.5	28.3	48.0	32.6	32.9	46.2
Officers' Compensation 20	3.0	3.4	7.6	3.4	7.1	4.0	4.6	3.7	3.9	0.7	1.3	0.9	0.4
Operating Margin 21	10.8	•	6.5	15.8	14.5	11.2	3.8	8.4	11.5	7.3	10.8	17.0	12.2
Operating Margin Before Officers' Comp. 22	13.8	•	14.1	19.3	21.6	15.2	8.4	12.2	15.4	7.9	12.1	17.9	12.6

Selected Average Balance Sheet ($ in Thousands)

Item	Total												
Net Receivables 23	1594	0	10	97	347	696	3680	11118	14558	39430	21788	352989	4658707
Inventories 24	•	•	•	•	•	•	•	•	•	•	•	•	•
Net Property, Plant and Equipment 25	108	0	14	92	160	142	1029	1216	3090	17176	8534	37550	150262
Total Assets 26	4800	0	76	737	2207	6919	15064	34764	70402	157693	355293	1034021	13012446
Notes and Loans Payable 27	1344	0	37	287	678	2767	6029	17234	37292	53737	152308	295626	3299298
All Other Liabilities 28	1856	0	15	56	689	1845	5736	10359	22526	59892	133778	296886	5348260
Net Worth 29	1599	0	25	394	840	2306	3299	7171	10584	44064	69207	441509	4364887

Selected Financial Ratios (Times to 1)

Item	Total												
Current Ratio 30	1.0	•	1.9	5.2	1.3	1.1	1.3	1.0	0.8	0.9	0.8	1.5	0.9
Quick Ratio 31	0.8	•	1.8	4.2	1.1	0.5	0.9	0.8	0.6	0.9	0.3	1.3	0.8
Net Sales to Working Capital 32	•	•	23.4	3.1	9.7	21.9	4.7	•	•	•	•	2.0	•
Coverage Ratio 33	2.9	0.2	15.9	18.3	10.5	4.0	1.7	2.1	2.2	3.2	2.0	5.8	2.1
Total Asset Turnover 34	0.3	•	6.1	2.0	1.2	1.1	0.6	0.5	0.4	0.7	0.3	0.4	0.2
Inventory Turnover 35	•	•	•	•	•	•	•	•	•	•	•	•	•
Receivables Turnover 36	•	•	•	•	•	•	•	•	•	•	•	•	•
Total Liabilities to Net Worth 37	2.0	•	2.1	0.9	1.6	2.0	3.6	3.8	5.7	2.6	4.1	1.3	2.0
Current Assets to Working Capital 38	•	•	2.2	1.2	4.4	11.5	4.6	•	•	•	•	3.1	•
Current Liabilities to Working Capital 39	•	•	1.2	0.2	3.4	10.5	3.6	•	•	•	•	2.1	•
Working Capital to Net Sales 40	•	•	0.0	0.3	0.1	0.0	0.2	•	•	•	•	0.5	•
Inventory to Working Capital 41	•	•	•	•	•	0.0	•	•	•	•	•	0.0	•
Total Receipts to Cash Flow 42	2.1	3.5	2.4	1.8	2.3	2.6	3.1	3.6	2.8	1.9	2.7	2.1	1.8
Cost of Goods to Cash Flow 43	0.2	0.0	0.4	0.0	0.2	0.8	0.5	0.7	0.1	0.3	•	0.2	0.0
Cash Flow to Total Debt 44	0.2	•	3.8	2.4	0.8	0.6	0.2	0.2	0.2	0.5	0.1	0.3	0.1

Selected Financial Factors (in Percentages)

Item	Total												
Debt Ratio 45	66.7	•	67.6	46.6	61.9	66.7	78.1	79.4	85.0	72.1	80.5	57.3	66.5
Return on Total Assets 46	5.2	•	42.4	33.6	19.1	16.2	5.5	8.1	8.2	7.3	6.8	7.4	3.4
Return on Equity Before Income Taxes 47	10.1	•	122.7	59.5	45.3	36.4	10.2	21.0	29.6	18.0	17.7	14.3	5.2
Return on Equity After Income Taxes 48	7.6	•	117.6	58.5	43.2	34.4	9.9	18.5	28.0	12.1	10.7	9.3	3.2
Profit Margin (Before Income Tax) 49	9.9	•	6.5	15.8	14.5	11.1	3.7	8.4	11.5	7.3	11.9	16.9	10.0
Profit Margin (After Income Tax) 50	7.5	•	6.2	15.6	13.8	10.4	3.6	7.4	10.9	4.9	7.2	11.0	6.1

Table II
Corporations with Net Income

ACTIVITIES RELATED TO CREDIT INTERMEDIATION

MONEY AMOUNTS AND SIZE OF ASSETS IN THOUSANDS OF DOLLARS

Item Description for Accounting Period 7/05 Through 6/06	Total	Zero Assets	Under 500	500 to 1,000	1,000 to 5,000	5,000 to 10,000	10,000 to 25,000	25,000 to 50,000	50,000 to 100,000	100,000 to 250,000	250,000 to 500,000	500,000 to 2,500,000	2,500,000 and over
Number of Enterprises 1	18878	•	14367	1192	649	139	93	50	29	16	•	•	•
Revenues ($ in Thousands)													
Net Sales 2	40508489	•	9116304	1980121	1909222	1251905	802638	961974	849303	1916878	•	•	•
Interest 3	1366696	•	4802	5727	20962	9754	16110	12400	42368	18485	•	•	•
Rents 4	166762	•	0	0	0	368	183	133	1689	1837	•	•	•
Royalties 5	479358	•	0	0	0	0	2	0	0	0	•	•	•
Other Portfolio Income 6	766457	•	1720	183	1141	230	15440	2437	2133	4400	•	•	•
Other Receipts 7	37729216	•	9109782	1974211	1887119	1241553	770903	947004	803113	1892156	•	•	•
Total Receipts 8	40508489	•	9116304	1980121	1909222	1251905	802638	961974	849303	1916878	•	•	•
Average Total Receipts 9	2146	•	635	1661	2942	9007	8631	19239	29286	119805	•	•	•
Operating Costs/Operating Income (%)													
Cost of Operations 10	8.2	•	13.2	0.9	5.8	31.4	18.7	24.4	5.3	23.4	•	•	•
Salaries and Wages 11	18.9	•	24.2	27.3	25.5	13.3	26.1	22.9	30.5	14.7	•	•	•
Taxes Paid 12	2.4	•	1.8	1.8	3.0	1.3	2.8	2.5	2.7	2.0	•	•	•
Interest Paid 13	4.2	•	0.3	0.9	1.1	3.1	5.3	5.4	8.7	1.4	•	•	•
Depreciation 14	1.3	•	0.6	0.9	0.9	0.6	1.2	1.0	1.4	1.9	•	•	•
Amortization and Depletion 15	1.0	•	0.1	0.1	0.0	0.0	0.1	0.5	0.2	0.5	•	•	•
Pensions and Other Deferred Comp. 16	0.8	•	0.8	0.4	0.5	0.1	0.4	0.4	0.8	1.5	•	•	•
Employee Benefits 17	1.5	•	0.6	1.0	0.8	1.6	0.9	1.0	1.8	1.4	•	•	•
Advertising 18	4.7	•	1.2	1.2	1.5	0.5	2.7	2.9	1.3	3.5	•	•	•
Other Expenses 19	40.2	•	41.3	45.0	30.1	31.5	24.2	21.1	28.1	36.1	•	•	•
Officers' Compensation 20	2.6	•	6.0	2.6	8.3	3.9	5.3	3.4	4.1	0.7	•	•	•
Operating Margin 21	14.3	•	9.8	17.9	22.5	12.6	12.2	14.4	15.0	12.9	•	•	•
Operating Margin Before Officers' Comp. 22	16.9	•	15.9	20.4	30.7	16.5	17.4	17.8	19.1	13.6	•	•	•

Selected Average Balance Sheet ($ in Thousands)

Net Receivables 23	448	•	6	90	439	839	2356	11350	14889	37863
Inventories 24	•	•	•	•	•	•	•	•	•	•
Net Property, Plant and Equipment 25	138	•	15	108	125	150	1101	1237	2996	16951
Total Assets 26	4407	•	80	743	2181	7099	15177	35457	70156	147807
Notes and Loans Payable 27	1766	•	16	265	600	2663	5613	17103	31479	34531
All Other Liabilities 28	1662	•	14	46	588	1840	5618	10502	27466	68912
Net Worth 29	979	•	50	433	993	2596	3946	7853	11211	44364

Selected Financial Ratios (Times to 1)

Current Ratio 30	0.5	•	3.1	5.1	2.1	1.2	1.3	0.9	0.8	0.9
Quick Ratio 31	0.4	•	2.9	4.2	1.7	0.5	0.8	0.8	0.6	0.8
Net Sales to Working Capital 32	•	•	20.8	3.5	3.8	11.9	5.3	•	•	•
Coverage Ratio 33	4.2	•	38.4	20.6	21.2	5.1	3.3	3.7	2.7	10.0
Total Asset Turnover 34	0.5	•	7.9	2.2	1.3	1.3	0.6	0.5	0.4	0.8
Inventory Turnover 35	•	•	•	•	•	•	•	•	•	•
Receivables Turnover 36	•	•	•	•	•	•	•	•	5.3	2.3
Total Liabilities to Net Worth 37	3.5	•	0.6	0.7	1.2	1.7	2.8	3.5	•	•
Current Assets to Working Capital 38	•	•	1.5	1.2	1.9	6.3	4.8	•	•	•
Current Liabilities to Working Capital 39	•	•	0.5	0.2	0.9	5.3	3.8	•	•	•
Working Capital to Net Sales 40	•	•	0.0	0.3	0.3	0.1	0.2	•	•	•
Inventory to Working Capital 41	•	•	•	•	•	•	•	•	•	•
Total Receipts to Cash Flow 42	2.0	•	2.2	1.8	2.1	2.4	3.1	3.1	2.6	2.2
Cost of Goods to Cash Flow 43	0.2	•	0.3	0.0	0.1	0.8	0.6	0.8	0.1	0.5
Cash Flow to Total Debt 44	0.3	•	9.6	3.0	1.2	0.8	0.2	0.2	0.2	0.5

Selected Financial Factors (in Percentages)

Debt Ratio 45	77.8	•	37.6	41.8	54.5	63.4	74.0	77.9	84.0	70.0
Return on Total Assets 46	8.5	•	80.1	42.0	31.8	20.0	9.9	10.7	9.9	11.5
Return on Equity Before Income Taxes 47	29.2	•	125.0	68.6	66.6	43.8	26.4	35.3	39.1	34.5
Return on Equity After Income Taxes 48	23.1	•	121.1	67.5	63.8	41.5	26.1	32.3	37.2	25.3
Profit Margin (Before Income Tax) 49	13.3	•	9.8	17.9	22.5	12.6	12.1	14.4	15.0	12.8
Profit Margin (After Income Tax) 50	10.5	•	9.5	17.6	21.5	12.0	11.9	13.2	14.2	9.4

Table I

Corporations with and without Net Income

INVESTMENT BANKING AND SECURITIES DEALING

MONEY AMOUNTS AND SIZE OF ASSETS IN THOUSANDS OF DOLLARS

Item Description for Accounting Period 7/05 Through 6/06	Total	Zero Assets	Under 500	500 to 1,000	1,000 to 5,000	5,000 to 10,000	10,000 to 25,000	25,000 to 50,000	50,000 to 100,000	100,000 to 250,000	250,000 to 500,000	500,000 to 2,500,000	2,500,000 and over
Number of Enterprises 1	3423	869	2110	111	186	15	63	23	7	12	4	10	14
Revenues ($ in Thousands)													
Net Sales 2	171241881	274161	497486	49591	372894	61900	350681	421535	126031	249859	274531	2479815	166083398
Interest 3	106250190	17587	2362	374	2685	1342	5514	3206	889	15579	43111	279179	105878360
Rents 4	902405	5580	0	0	3617	0	874	0	0	502	0	99	891733
Royalties 5	5852	0	0	0	0	0	0	0	0	0	0	1	5851
Other Portfolio Income 6	9926149	30686	103	212	286	694	32252	6328	3184	15881	450	284577	9551495
Other Receipts 7	54157285	220308	495021	49005	366306	59864	312041	412001	121958	217897	230970	1915959	49755959
Total Receipts 8	171241881	274161	497486	49591	372894	61900	350681	421535	126031	249859	274531	2479815	166083398
Average Total Receipts 9	50027	315	236	447	2005	4127	5566	18328	18004	20822	68633	247982	11863100
Operating Costs/Operating Income (%)													
Cost of Operations 10	0.1	•	3.5	•	•	•	1.8	•	•	0.6	•	•	0.1
Salaries and Wages 11	14.1	28.8	17.2	17.1	36.5	11.6	44.8	24.8	46.2	35.8	30.5	26.5	13.7
Taxes Paid 12	1.0	1.4	5.6	1.3	3.6	2.6	2.9	2.5	3.5	2.7	2.6	2.9	0.9
Interest Paid 13	55.6	42.6	0.0	0.0	0.6	0.1	2.2	1.7	2.7	4.1	11.6	15.9	57.0
Depreciation 14	1.2	0.5	0.1	0.3	0.8	0.6	1.6	1.0	0.3	1.4	5.7	1.6	1.2
Amortization and Depletion 15	0.2	0.2	0.0	1.0	•	•	0.9	0.1	0.3	0.1	0.6	0.2	0.2
Pensions and Other Deferred Comp. 16	0.5	0.3	0.3	•	0.4	2.8	0.3	0.2	1.9	1.3	0.3	0.5	0.5
Employee Benefits 17	0.7	0.2	1.3	0.5	2.0	1.9	1.6	3.1	2.3	1.5	1.2	1.4	0.6
Advertising 18	0.2	0.3	3.7	0.1	0.3	0.2	0.4	0.1	0.1	0.6	0.6	1.1	0.1
Other Expenses 19	14.1	31.5	50.1	44.8	29.6	20.6	36.8	48.8	18.9	33.1	35.7	32.4	13.4
Officers' Compensation 20	2.2	18.9	4.6	3.7	13.4	45.2	2.5	5.0	16.0	9.5	4.1	2.7	2.1
Operating Margin 21	10.1	•	13.6	31.1	12.7	14.3	4.1	12.7	7.9	9.2	7.1	14.8	10.1
Operating Margin Before Officers' Comp. 22	12.3	•	18.2	34.8	26.2	59.6	6.6	17.7	23.9	18.7	11.1	17.5	12.2

Selected Average Balance Sheet ($ in Thousands)

Net Receivables 23	232394	0	0	278	305	925	12096	13148	49879	69260	236917	56551689
Inventories 24	•	•	•	•	•	•	•	•	•	•	•	•
Net Property, Plant and Equipment 25	3416	•	2	25	192	734	939	441	865	15412	16426	810064
Total Assets 26	962615	0	80	804	1534	15742	33824	67025	160136	346059	1250002	234023161
Notes and Loans Payable 27	158212	0	14	156	324	5739	2948	13250	17168	71707	203609	38457371
All Other Liabilities 28	750754	0	11	151	195	2753	9710	17045	68651	187908	419099	183100216
Net Worth 29	53649	0	56	496	1015	7250	21166	36730	74317	86444	627294	12465574

Selected Financial Ratios (Times to 1)

Current Ratio 30	0.8	•	2.3	4.1	5.5	0.3	2.2	1.6	1.3	0.9	1.3	0.8
Quick Ratio 31	0.4	•	1.9	4.1	5.0	0.3	1.4	1.0	1.0	0.8	1.1	0.4
Net Sales to Working Capital 32	•	•	7.6	0.9	2.2	•	1.5	1.2	1.0	•	1.8	•
Coverage Ratio 33	1.2	0.4	1827.8	1543.7	20.8	102.5	8.2	3.0	3.2	1.6	1.9	1.2
Total Asset Turnover 34	0.1	•	2.9	0.6	1.3	0.5	0.5	0.3	0.1	0.2	0.2	0.1
Inventory Turnover 35	•	•	•	•	•	•	•	•	•	•	•	•
Receivables Turnover 36	•	•	•	•	•	•	•	•	•	•	•	•
Total Liabilities to Net Worth 37	16.9	•	0.4	0.6	0.5	1.4	0.6	0.8	1.2	3.0	1.0	17.8
Current Assets to Working Capital 38	•	•	1.7	1.3	1.2	•	1.9	2.7	4.0	•	4.6	•
Current Liabilities to Working Capital 39	•	•	0.7	0.3	0.2	•	0.9	1.7	3.0	•	3.6	•
Working Capital to Net Sales 40	•	•	0.1	1.1	0.4	•	0.6	0.8	1.0	•	0.6	•
Inventory to Working Capital 41	•	•	•	•	•	•	0.0	0.0	•	•	•	•
Total Receipts to Cash Flow 42	4.8	•	1.9	1.3	2.7	3.1	1.7	4.4	3.0	2.6	3.0	4.9
Cost of Goods to Cash Flow 43	0.0	•	0.1	•	•	•	0.1	0.0	0.0	•	0.0	0.0
Cash Flow to Total Debt 44	0.0	•	5.0	1.1	1.5	0.3	0.8	0.1	0.1	0.1	0.1	0.0

Selected Financial Factors (in Percentages)

Debt Ratio 45	94.4	•	30.6	38.3	33.8	58.8	37.4	45.2	53.6	75.0	49.8	94.7
Return on Total Assets 46	3.5	•	39.9	17.3	17.4	7.6	7.7	2.2	1.7	3.7	5.9	3.4
Return on Equity Before Income Taxes 47	10.2	•	57.5	28.0	25.1	18.3	10.8	2.6	2.5	5.5	5.6	10.5
Return on Equity After Income Taxes 48	7.3	•	56.4	28.0	22.1	18.3	8.4	2.1	1.8	3.3	2.3	7.6
Profit Margin (Before Income Tax) 49	11.0	•	13.6	31.1	12.7	14.3	12.5	5.3	8.9	6.9	14.1	11.0
Profit Margin (After Income Tax) 50	7.9	•	13.3	31.1	11.2	14.3	9.7	4.2	6.5	4.1	5.8	8.0

Table II
Corporations with Net Income

INVESTMENT BANKING AND SECURITIES DEALING

MONEY AMOUNTS AND SIZE OF ASSETS IN THOUSANDS OF DOLLARS

Item Description for Accounting Period 7/05 Through 6/06	Total	Zero Assets	Under 500	500 to 1,000	1,000 to 5,000	5,000 to 10,000	10,000 to 25,000	25,000 to 50,000	50,000 to 100,000	100,000 to 250,000	250,000 to 500,000	500,000 to 2,500,000	2,500,000 and over
Number of Enterprises **1**	2297	441	1627	57	83	12	27	12	•	•	•	•	•
Revenues ($ in Thousands)													
Net Sales **2**	170031388	179777	475832	49269	142224	61899	245949	347730	•	•	•	•	•
Interest **3**	105977584	567	2362	264	681	1342	5001	3069	•	•	•	•	•
Rents **4**	893208	0	0	0	0	0	874	0	•	•	•	•	•
Royalties **5**	5852	0	0	0	0	0	0	0	•	•	•	•	•
Other Portfolio Income **6**	9902746	29193	103	0	212	694	15726	5417	•	•	•	•	•
Other Receipts **7**	53251998	150017	473367	49005	141331	59863	224348	339244	•	•	•	•	•
Total Receipts **8**	170031388	179777	475832	49269	142224	61899	245949	347730	•	•	•	•	•
Average Total Receipts **9**	74023	408	292	864	1714	5158	9109	28978	•	•	•	•	•
Operating Costs/Operating Income (%)													
Cost of Operations **10**	0.1	•	3.6	•	•	•	•	•	•	•	•	•	•
Salaries and Wages **11**	14.0	•	16.9	17.2	13.6	11.6	36.6	25.7	•	•	•	•	•
Taxes Paid **12**	1.0	0.2	5.7	1.0	2.6	2.6	2.4	2.6	•	•	•	•	•
Interest Paid **13**	55.7	59.4	0.0	0.0	0.2	0.1	2.0	1.5	•	•	•	•	•
Depreciation **14**	1.2	•	0.0	0.3	0.1	0.6	1.5	1.1	•	•	•	•	•
Amortization and Depletion **15**	0.2	•	0.0	1.0	•	•	0.0	0.1	•	•	•	•	•
Pensions and Other Deferred Comp. **16**	0.5	•	0.3	•	0.9	2.8	0.2	0.2	•	•	•	•	•
Employee Benefits **17**	0.7	•	1.4	0.6	1.3	1.9	1.5	3.6	•	•	•	•	•
Advertising **18**	0.2	•	3.9	0.1	0.3	0.2	0.1	0.2	•	•	•	•	•
Other Expenses **19**	13.8	9.1	48.4	44.4	19.3	20.6	23.7	39.7	•	•	•	•	•
Officers' Compensation **20**	2.1	•	2.4	3.7	22.3	45.2	2.1	5.9	•	•	•	•	•
Operating Margin **21**	10.5	31.3	17.3	31.7	39.4	14.4	29.9	19.3	•	•	•	•	•
Operating Margin Before Officers' Comp. **22**	12.7	31.3	19.7	35.4	61.7	59.6	32.0	25.3	•	•	•	•	•

Selected Average Balance Sheet ($ in Thousands)

Item								
Net Receivables 23	344252	0	0	541	44	99	1850	9757
Inventories 24								
Net Property, Plant and Equipment 25	5057		2	48	30	182	444	1576
Total Assets 26	1430221		57	937	1501	7282	16103	33555
Notes and Loans Payable 27	233617	0	0	4	0	0	2702	4510
All Other Liabilities 28	1117732		14	294	241	3493	3703	13652
Net Worth 29	78871		43	639	1260	3790	9699	15392

Selected Financial Ratios (Times to 1)

Item								
Current Ratio 30	0.8		1.9	2.6	4.2	0.6	1.4	1.6
Quick Ratio 31	0.4		0.9	2.5	3.8	0.6	1.0	1.1
Net Sales to Working Capital 32			25.4	1.9	2.2		4.8	3.4
Coverage Ratio 33	1.2	1.5	5868.8	7814.5	158.5	102.6	15.9	13.8
Total Asset Turnover 34	0.1		5.2	0.9	1.1	0.7	0.6	0.9
Inventory Turnover 35								
Receivables Turnover 36								
Total Liabilities to Net Worth 37	17.1		0.3	0.5	0.2	0.9	0.7	1.2
Current Assets to Working Capital 38			2.1	1.6	1.3		3.6	2.6
Current Liabilities to Working Capital 39			1.1	0.6	0.3		2.6	1.6
Working Capital to Net Sales 40			0.0	0.5	0.4		0.2	0.3
Inventory to Working Capital 41							0.0	0.0
Total Receipts to Cash Flow 42	4.8		4.1	1.9	1.8	3.1	2.0	1.8
Cost of Goods to Cash Flow 43	0.0		0.1					
Cash Flow to Total Debt 44	0.0		11.4	2.2	4.1	0.5	0.7	0.9

Selected Financial Factors (in Percentages)

Item								
Debt Ratio 45	94.5		24.3	31.9	16.1	48.0	39.8	54.1
Return on Total Assets 46	3.5		89.3	29.3	45.2	10.2	17.9	17.9
Return on Equity Before Income Taxes 47	10.7		118.0	42.9	53.5	19.4	27.8	36.1
Return on Equity After Income Taxes 48	7.7		116.2	42.9	48.1	19.4	22.9	29.9
Profit Margin (Before Income Tax) 49	11.4	31.3	17.3	31.7	39.3	14.3	29.6	19.2
Profit Margin (After Income Tax) 50	8.2	26.2	17.0	35.3	31.7	14.3	24.3	15.9

Table I

Corporations with and without Net Income

SECURITIES BROKERAGE

MONEY AMOUNTS AND SIZE OF ASSETS IN THOUSANDS OF DOLLARS

Item Description for Accounting Period 7/05 Through 6/06	Total	Zero Assets	Under 500	500 to 1,000	1,000 to 5,000	5,000 to 10,000	10,000 to 25,000	25,000 to 50,000	50,000 to 100,000	100,000 to 250,000	250,000 to 500,000	500,000 to 2,500,000	2,500,000 and over
Number of Enterprises 1	8015	1070	5325	412	849	143	91	32	14	23	7	15	35
Revenues ($ in Thousands)													
Net Sales 2	185755351	929151	1853075	1336097	2563191	968815	2137981	1029374	561872	1487801	831058	4648706	167408230
Interest 3	95497313	137922	193	5213	12652	10557	12058	16723	10781	51711	58925	950729	94429848
Rents 4	589320	0	0	0	0	0	417	0	2260	1909	325	491	583919
Royalties 5	29501	0	0	0	0	0	3906	0	146	1680	2433	1263	20073
Other Portfolio Income 6	8842796	23435	5242	20	16166	4108	40187	26472	22650	63376	25070	150752	8465318
Other Receipts 7	80796421	767794	1847640	1330864	2534373	954150	2081413	986179	526035	1369125	744305	3545471	64109072
Total Receipts 8	185755351	929151	1853075	1336097	2563191	968815	2137981	1029374	561872	1487801	831058	4648706	167408230
Average Total Receipts 9	23176	868	348	3243	3019	6775	23494	32168	40134	64687	118723	309914	4783092
Operating Costs/Operating Income (%)													
Cost of Operations 10	1.3	•	9.9	•	•	1.6	2.4	3.1	3.7	0.0	•	0.1	1.2
Salaries and Wages 11	15.6	36.0	16.4	18.1	34.3	28.6	27.1	36.5	37.7	36.7	52.2	36.4	13.8
Taxes Paid 12	1.3	2.3	2.9	1.3	4.3	2.9	1.9	3.4	2.9	3.0	3.7	2.3	1.1
Interest Paid 13	47.7	6.1	1.1	0.0	0.4	0.6	0.6	1.5	1.1	2.9	5.2	18.7	52.3
Depreciation 14	0.7	0.4	0.6	0.5	0.5	0.6	0.4	1.2	0.6	1.3	1.0	0.8	0.7
Amortization and Depletion 15	0.4	0.5	0.0	0.0	0.1	0.3	0.1	0.0	0.0	0.2	0.2	3.6	0.4
Pensions and Other Deferred Comp. 16	0.6	0.2	1.3	0.0	0.7	0.2	0.3	1.7	0.5	0.7	0.4	0.8	0.6
Employee Benefits 17	0.8	1.0	1.7	1.4	2.0	1.8	1.2	1.4	2.0	1.3	2.0	1.6	0.7
Advertising 18	0.4	3.2	2.2	0.0	0.4	0.2	0.1	0.6	1.0	1.0	0.4	0.6	0.4
Other Expenses 19	20.1	37.9	41.3	77.7	33.9	51.6	53.7	32.1	32.6	34.0	28.0	21.7	18.2
Officers' Compensation 20	3.3	2.3	16.1	5.1	18.7	8.2	4.3	5.8	15.5	11.3	2.1	3.4	2.7
Operating Margin 21	7.8	10.1	6.6	•	4.7	3.3	7.7	12.7	2.3	7.5	4.8	9.9	8.0
Operating Margin Before Officers' Comp. 22	11.1	12.4	22.7	1.0	23.4	11.5	12.0	18.5	17.8	18.8	6.9	13.3	10.7

Selected Average Balance Sheet ($ in Thousands)

Net Receivables 23	55376	0	6	176	235	888	2018	3996	17510	21217	68820	316702	12489571
Inventories 24	·	·	·	·	·	·	·	·	·	·	·	·	·
Net Property, Plant and Equipment 25	663	0	8	41	63	140	839	2308	2957	4947	8670	9575	133576
Total Assets 26	267926	0	102	720	1891	7075	15127	35270	73431	157808	386686	1105646	60500423
Notes and Loans Payable 27	75193	0	41	0	498	304	1550	3425	8113	11462	52581	118041	17120531
All Other Liabilities 28	167800	0	13	406	739	1904	5994	15141	29119	82861	236309	696086	37952641
Net Worth 29	24932	0	47	313	654	4867	7582	16703	36199	63485	97796	291520	5427251

Selected Financial Ratios (Times to 1)

Current Ratio 30	1.1	·	6.6	1.4	2.2	2.5	1.5	1.6	1.4	1.1	1.0	1.0	1.1
Quick Ratio 31	0.4	·	4.5	1.1	1.6	1.9	1.1	1.2	1.0	0.7	0.4	0.7	0.4
Net Sales to Working Capital 32	2.0	·	6.4	19.5	4.3	3.1	7.2	3.7	3.2	6.7	87.7	·	1.8
Coverage Ratio 33	1.2	2.6	7.2	·	11.8	6.1	14.2	9.5	3.1	3.3	1.8	1.5	1.2
Total Asset Turnover 34	0.1	·	3.4	4.5	1.6	1.0	1.6	0.9	0.5	0.4	0.3	0.3	0.1
Inventory Turnover 35	·	·	·	·	·	·	·	·	·	·	·	·	·
Receivables Turnover 36	·	·	·	·	·	·	·	·	·	·	·	·	·
Total Liabilities to Net Worth 37	9.7	·	1.2	1.3	1.9	0.5	1.0	1.1	1.0	1.5	3.0	2.8	10.1
Current Assets to Working Capital 38	15.7	·	1.2	3.4	1.9	1.7	2.8	2.7	3.6	9.9	187.3	·	15.9
Current Liabilities to Working Capital 39	14.7	·	0.2	2.4	0.9	0.7	1.8	1.7	2.6	8.9	186.3	·	14.9
Working Capital to Net Sales 40	0.5	·	0.2	0.1	0.2	0.3	0.1	0.3	0.3	0.1	0.0	·	0.5
Inventory to Working Capital 41	0.0	·	·	·	·	·	·	·	0.1	0.1	0.0	·	·
Total Receipts to Cash Flow 42	4.1	2.5	2.5	1.5	2.9	1.9	1.7	2.6	3.7	2.9	3.6	3.7	4.4
Cost of Goods to Cash Flow 43	0.1	0.2	0.2	·	0.0	0.0	0.0	0.1	0.1	0.0	0.0	0.0	0.1
Cash Flow to Total Debt 44	0.0	·	2.6	5.5	0.8	1.6	1.8	0.7	0.3	0.2	0.1	0.1	0.0

Selected Financial Factors (in Percentages)

Debt Ratio 45	90.7	·	53.9	56.5	65.4	31.2	49.9	52.6	50.7	59.8	74.7	73.6	91.0
Return on Total Assets 46	4.8	·	26.3	·	8.1	3.4	12.8	12.7	4.0	1.8	2.8	8.1	4.8
Return on Equity Before Income Taxes 47	7.2	·	49.2	·	21.5	4.2	23.7	23.9	2.5	6.9	4.8	10.7	7.0
Return on Equity After Income Taxes 48	5.3	·	47.5	·	21.0	3.0	19.7	16.9	0.5	2.9	4.8	7.4	5.1
Profit Margin (Before Income Tax) 49	7.8	10.1	6.6	·	4.6	3.0	7.7	12.4	2.3	6.7	4.0	10.0	7.9
Profit Margin (After Income Tax) 50	5.7	8.8	6.4	·	4.6	2.1	6.4	8.8	0.4	2.9	1.6	6.9	5.8

Table II

Corporations with Net Income

SECURITIES BROKERAGE

MONEY AMOUNTS AND SIZE OF ASSETS IN THOUSANDS OF DOLLARS

Item Description for Accounting Period 7/05 Through 6/06	Total	Zero Assets	Under 500	500 to 1,000	1,000 to 5,000	5,000 to 10,000	10,000 to 25,000	25,000 to 50,000	50,000 to 100,000	100,000 to 250,000	250,000 to 500,000	500,000 to 2,500,000	2,500,000 and over
Number of Enterprises 1	5308	590	3684	166	620	93	64	21	8	16	4	12	29
Revenues ($ in Thousands)													
Net Sales 2	162344235	796467	1344079	631787	1534130	927111	1980706	702070	323376	1025646	486689	3902025	148690148
Interest 3	81992837	83570	62	874	9079	10250	8164	9633	5483	41164	34922	272313	81517324
Rents 4	324833	0	0	0	0	0	417	0		0	0	491	323926
Royalties 5	27817	0	0	0	0	0	3906	0	146	0	2433	1263	20068
Other Portfolio Income 6	8853426	23363	4854	0	1278	2640	13517	17047	22650	36035	5924	144711	8381405
Other Receipts 7	71345322	689534	1339163	630913	1523773	914221	1954702	675390	295097	948447	443410	3483247	58447425
Total Receipts 8	162344235	796467	1344079	631787	1534130	927111	1980706	702070	323376	1025646	486689	3902025	148690148
Average Total Receipts 9	30585	1350	365	3806	2474	9969	30949	33432	40422	64103	121672	325169	5127246
Operating Costs/Operating Income (%)													
Cost of Operations 10	1.4	•	13.6	•	•	1.7	2.6	4.5	•	0.0	•	0.1	1.4
Salaries and Wages 11	16.0	42.0	10.1	8.4	26.7	24.6	25.3	26.7	45.0	35.3	48.8	42.2	14.6
Taxes Paid 12	1.3	2.6	2.1	0.9	5.1	2.8	1.8	3.7	3.1	3.1	4.1	2.8	1.2
Interest Paid 13	46.7	1.1	0.2	•	0.5	0.6	0.2	0.8	0.8	2.0	5.1	5.3	50.8
Depreciation 14	0.7	0.5	0.1	0.2	0.4	0.5	0.3	0.8	0.5	1.3	0.8	0.7	0.7
Amortization and Depletion 15	0.5	0.6	0.0	•	0.0	0.3	0.1	0.1	0.0	0.1	0.2	4.3	0.4
Pensions and Other Deferred Comp. 16	0.6	0.2	1.8	•	1.1	0.2	0.3	2.5	0.4	0.6	0.3	1.0	0.6
Employee Benefits 17	0.8	1.2	1.4	1.1	1.3	1.7	0.9	1.4	1.4	1.2	2.1	1.9	0.7
Advertising 18	0.4	3.7	2.3	•	0.6	0.2	0.1	0.4	0.3	1.1	0.2	0.8	0.4
Other Expenses 19	18.6	30.6	37.6	84.3	21.4	49.6	54.6	28.2	24.7	19.8	24.0	24.7	17.2
Officers' Compensation 20	3.4	2.7	13.2	3.5	26.4	8.5	2.9	6.1	10.2	13.1	2.5	4.0	2.9
Operating Margin 21	9.5	14.7	17.5	1.5	16.5	9.0	11.0	25.0	13.5	22.2	11.9	12.4	9.1
Operating Margin Before Officers' Comp. 22	12.9	17.4	30.7	5.1	43.0	17.5	13.9	31.1	23.7	35.4	14.3	16.4	12.1

Selected Average Balance Sheet ($ in Thousands)

Item													
Net Receivables 23	80044	0	5	194	225	1306	1734	3345	17048	18749	76255	259116	14500958
Inventories 24	•	•	•	•	•	•	•	•	•	•	•	•	•
Net Property, Plant and Equipment 25	882	0	0	35	53	195	936	1834	774	5223	8846	11304	147064
Total Assets 26	353869	93	725	1938	6884	15284	35840	74048	153993	357371	1055737		64039466
Notes and Loans Payable 27	101435	4	0	193	468	1312	2503	8266	13109	39286	120840		18490458
All Other Liabilities 28	217302	8	276	714	2798	5528	12347	38981	85854	211310	646484		39371001
Net Worth 29	35132	82	449	1031	3618	8443	20990	26800	55031	106774	288414		6178007

Selected Financial Ratios (Times to 1)

Item													
Current Ratio 30	1.1	•	9.3	2.4	3.8	2.3	2.0	2.0	1.2	1.2	1.3	1.0	1.1
Quick Ratio 31	0.5	•	6.8	2.2	2.9	1.9	1.5	1.5	0.8	0.7	0.6	0.7	0.5
Net Sales to Working Capital 32	2.1	•	5.9	10.0	2.7	3.8	6.0	2.8	5.6	3.9	1.8	•	2.0
Coverage Ratio 33	1.2	14.0	76.0	•	37.2	16.2	49.8	33.9	17.6	11.8	3.3	3.4	1.2
Total Asset Turnover 34	0.1	•	3.9	5.3	1.3	1.4	2.0	0.9	0.5	0.4	0.3	0.3	0.1
Inventory Turnover 35	•	•	•	•	•	•	•	•	•	•	•	•	•
Receivables Turnover 36	•	•	•	•	•	•	•	•	•	•	•	•	•
Total Liabilities to Net Worth 37	9.1	•	0.1	0.6	0.9	0.9	0.8	0.7	1.8	1.8	2.3	2.7	9.4
Current Assets to Working Capital 38	16.0	•	1.1	1.7	1.4	1.8	2.0	2.0	7.4	6.0	3.9	•	16.3
Current Liabilities to Working Capital 39	15.0	•	0.1	0.7	0.4	0.8	1.0	1.0	6.4	5.0	2.9	•	15.3
Working Capital to Net Sales 40	0.5	•	0.2	0.1	0.4	0.3	0.2	0.4	0.2	0.3	0.5	•	0.5
Inventory to Working Capital 41	0.0	•	•	•	•	•	•	•	0.2	0.2	•	•	0.0
Total Receipts to Cash Flow 42	4.1	2.7	2.0	1.2	2.8	1.8	1.6	2.1	3.6	2.8	3.0	3.1	4.4
Cost of Goods to Cash Flow 43	0.1	•	0.3	•	•	0.0	0.0	0.1	0.0	0.0	•	0.0	0.1
Cash Flow to Total Debt 44	0.0	•	16.3	11.4	1.0	1.7	2.9	1.1	0.2	0.2	0.2	0.1	0.0

Selected Financial Factors (in Percentages)

Item													
Debt Ratio 45	90.1	•	12.2	38.0	47.4	44.8	41.4	63.8	64.3	70.1	72.7		90.4
Return on Total Assets 46	4.9	•	69.3	8.0	21.7	22.7	24.0	7.8	9.7	5.7	5.5		4.8
Return on Equity Before Income Taxes 47	8.3	•	77.8	12.9	39.7	40.3	39.8	20.2	24.8	13.3	14.2		7.5
Return on Equity After Income Taxes 48	6.2	•	76.4	10.3	39.3	35.1	31.3	15.4	18.3	8.6	10.0		5.5
Profit Margin (Before Income Tax) 49	9.5	14.7	17.5	1.5	16.5	8.8	11.0	25.0	13.4	21.3	11.6	12.6	9.1
Profit Margin (After Income Tax) 50	7.1	13.2	17.2	1.2	16.4	7.9	9.6	19.6	10.2	15.7	7.6	8.9	6.7

Table I

Corporations with and without Net Income

COMMODITY CONTRACTS DEALING AND BROKERAGE

MONEY AMOUNTS AND SIZE OF ASSETS IN THOUSANDS OF DOLLARS

Item Description for Accounting Period 7/05 Through 6/06	Total	Zero Assets	Under 500	500 to 1,000	1,000 to 5,000	5,000 to 10,000	10,000 to 25,000	25,000 to 50,000	50,000 to 100,000	100,000 to 250,000	250,000 to 500,000	500,000 to 2,500,000	2,500,000 and over
Number of Enterprises 1	2238	4	1906	92	120	15	47	22	7	12	4	4	5
Revenues ($ in Thousands)													
Net Sales 2	6687700	95519	221162	25584	264625	82228	185095	743114	83599	254002	425736	359421	3947615
Interest 3	2071879	390	1298	0	2848	393	506	4998	2609	19301	10166	14203	2015266
Rents 4	17894	0	0	0	470	0	0	11235	21	70	0	0	6099
Royalties 5	13265	0	0	0	0	0	0	13265	0	0	0	0	0
Other Portfolio Income 6	337842	27389	0	0	22571	0	1356	2	11764	6545	684	108	267421
Other Receipts 7	4246820	67740	219864	25584	238736	81835	183233	713714	69205	228086	414886	345110	1658829
Total Receipts 8	6687700	95519	221162	25584	264625	82228	185095	743114	83599	254002	425736	359421	3947615
Average Total Receipts 9	2988	23880	116	278	2205	5482	3938	33778	11943	21167	106434	89855	789523
Operating Costs/Operating Income (%)													
Cost of Operations 10	11.1	40.7	•	•	35.4	•	•	42.9	•	8.4	63.8	•	•
Salaries and Wages 11	16.0	6.1	2.1	18.4	9.7	16.3	56.8	10.9	26.5	17.6	7.1	41.9	14.7
Taxes Paid 12	1.4	1.9	2.3	7.3	2.6	2.6	4.0	1.1	5.0	1.9	1.5	1.7	1.0
Interest Paid 13	29.9	3.1	3.1	21.8	4.9	0.1	4.5	1.5	6.6	6.0	5.6	12.0	47.2
Depreciation 14	0.9	0.2	0.4	10.3	1.3	0.4	0.7	1.5	1.3	0.7	0.4	0.4	0.8
Amortization and Depletion 15	1.1	0.1	•	•	2.4	0.2	0.0	0.1	0.4	0.1	0.1	0.6	1.6
Pensions and Other Deferred Comp. 16	0.4	0.0	•	10.8	1.0	0.2	0.8	0.6	0.6	0.3	0.6	0.3	0.2
Employee Benefits 17	1.2	0.1	0.2	•	1.5	0.1	3.2	1.4	2.0	1.2	0.7	0.6	1.2
Advertising 18	0.3	0.0	0.5	•	0.0	1.7	0.1	0.7	1.3	0.4	0.0	0.2	0.1
Other Expenses 19	32.8	12.9	36.1	219.4	13.3	82.6	24.9	36.5	35.6	37.3	12.3	26.5	34.3
Officers' Compensation 20	3.2	1.7	22.5	32.3	18.8	5.7	8.9	1.5	20.8	3.0	0.7	4.7	0.7
Operating Margin 21	1.8	33.3	32.7	•	9.1	•	•	1.3	•	23.1	7.2	11.2	•
Operating Margin Before Officers' Comp. 22	5.0	35.0	55.3	•	27.9	•	4.9	2.8	20.8	26.1	7.8	15.8	•

Selected Average Balance Sheet ($ in Thousands)

Net Receivables 23	7435	0	18	4	595	859	3183	9351	9444	17978	45867	475926	2759301
Inventories 24	•	•	•	•	•	•	•	•	•	•	•	•	•
Net Property, Plant and Equipment 25	133	0	5	277	245	109	564	1301	856	500	25158	1441	11563
Total Assets 26	31248	0	113	677	2236	7457	16531	36372	64661	144567	321163	1242438	11851145
Notes and Loans Payable 27	5271	0	39	109	948	19	6481	8226	20756	8240	91058	114706	2009034
All Other Liabilities 28	24637	0	3	179	624	4984	4475	18021	21838	117947	195470	1073877	9542482
Net Worth 29	1340	0	70	390	664	2454	5575	10125	22066	18380	34635	53856	299629

Selected Financial Ratios (Times to 1)

Current Ratio 30	0.9	•	12.0	0.2	1.7	1.3	1.0	1.2	1.3	0.9	0.9	1.0	0.9
Quick Ratio 31	0.6	•	10.7	0.2	1.3	1.0	0.6	0.9	0.9	0.5	0.3	0.7	0.6
Net Sales to Working Capital 32	•	•	1.6	•	4.2	3.7	•	9.0	1.3	•	•	5.3	•
Coverage Ratio 33	1.1	11.7	11.6	•	2.8	•	0.1	1.9	1.0	4.8	2.3	1.9	1.0
Total Asset Turnover 34	0.1	•	1.0	0.4	1.0	0.7	0.2	0.9	0.2	0.1	0.3	0.1	0.1
Inventory Turnover 35	•	•	•	•	•	•	•	•	•	•	•	•	•
Receivables Turnover 36	•	•	•	•	•	•	•	•	•	•	•	•	•
Total Liabilities to Net Worth 37	22.3	•	0.6	0.7	2.4	2.0	2.6	1.9	6.9	8.3	22.1	•	38.6
Current Assets to Working Capital 38	•	•	1.1	•	2.4	4.4	6.9	4.9	•	•	60.1	•	•
Current Liabilities to Working Capital 39	•	•	0.1	•	1.4	3.4	5.9	3.9	•	•	59.1	•	•
Working Capital to Net Sales 40	•	0.6	0.6	•	0.2	0.3	0.1	0.8	•	•	0.2	•	•
Inventory to Working Capital 41	•	•	•	•	•	•	•	1.0	•	•	•	•	•
Total Receipts to Cash Flow 42	3.5	6.0	1.6	•	8.3	1.4	6.7	2.7	3.2	1.8	5.5	2.9	4.0
Cost of Goods to Cash Flow 43	0.4	2.4	•	•	2.9	•	•	1.2	•	0.2	3.5	•	•
Cash Flow to Total Debt 44	0.0	•	1.7	•	0.2	0.8	0.1	0.5	0.1	0.1	0.0	•	0.0

Selected Financial Factors (in Percentages)

Debt Ratio 45	95.7	•	37.9	42.4	70.3	67.1	66.3	72.2	65.9	87.3	89.2	95.7	97.5
Return on Total Assets 46	3.0	•	36.8	•	13.8	•	0.1	2.5	1.2	4.3	4.2	1.7	3.0
Return on Equity Before Income Taxes 47	4.0	•	54.1	•	30.2	•	•	4.3	•	26.6	22.1	18.6	•
Return on Equity After Income Taxes 48	•	•	53.4	•	20.9	•	•	•	•	18.7	14.4	13.8	•
Profit Margin (Before Income Tax) 49	1.8	33.3	32.7	•	9.1	•	•	1.3	•	23.1	7.2	11.1	•
Profit Margin (After Income Tax) 50	•	21.7	32.3	•	6.3	•	•	•	•	16.2	4.7	8.3	•

Table II
Corporations with Net Income

COMMODITY CONTRACTS DEALING AND BROKERAGE

MONEY AMOUNTS AND SIZE OF ASSETS IN THOUSANDS OF DOLLARS

Item Description for Accounting Period 7/05 Through 6/06	Total	Zero Assets	Under 500	500 to 1,000	1,000 to 5,000	5,000 to 10,000	10,000 to 25,000	25,000 to 50,000	50,000 to 100,000	100,000 to 250,000	250,000 to 500,000	500,000 to 2,500,000	2,500,000 and over
Number of Enterprises **1**	1673	4	1503	0	93	4	31	14	•	9	•	•	•
Revenues ($ in Thousands)													
Net Sales **2**	4039330	95519	233303	0	249011	33158	213098	678030	•	227228	•	•	•
Interest **3**	550493	390	1298	0	2801	217	506	4232	•	12430	•	•	•
Rents **4**	16861	0	0	0	0	0	0	11235	•	70	•	•	•
Royalties **5**	13265	0	0	0	0	0	0	13265	•	0	•	•	•
Other Portfolio Income **6**	122097	27389	0	0	22558	0	1125	2	•	5383	•	•	•
Other Receipts **7**	3336614	67740	232005	0	223652	32941	211467	649296	•	209345	•	•	•
Total Receipts **8**	4039330	95519	233303	0	249011	33158	213098	678030	•	227228	•	•	•
Average Total Receipts **9**	2414	23880	155	•	2678	8290	6874	48431	•	25248	•	•	•
Operating Costs/Operating Income (%)													
Cost of Operations **10**	16.8	40.7	•	•	36.9	•	•	37.8	•	9.4	•	•	•
Salaries and Wages **11**	16.1	6.1	2.1	•	8.4	21.4	46.0	11.1	•	14.2	•	•	•
Taxes Paid **12**	1.6	1.9	2.3	•	1.9	4.3	2.6	1.2	•	1.6	•	•	•
Interest Paid **13**	14.7	3.1	2.9	•	4.8	•	3.2	1.4	•	5.0	•	•	•
Depreciation **14**	1.0	0.2	0.4	•	0.7	0.3	0.6	1.6	•	0.5	•	•	•
Amortization and Depletion **15**	0.3	0.1	•	•	2.6	0.1	•	0.1	•	0.0	•	•	•
Pensions and Other Deferred Comp. **16**	0.5	0.0	0.2	•	0.5	0.5	0.5	0.7	•	0.3	•	•	•
Employee Benefits **17**	1.0	0.1	0.2	•	1.1	0.3	2.5	1.5	•	0.7	•	•	•
Advertising **18**	0.2	0.0	0.5	•	0.0	0.0	0.0	0.8	•	0.3	•	•	•
Other Expenses **19**	28.4	12.9	34.2	•	8.0	7.8	19.0	36.1	•	35.6	•	•	•
Officers' Compensation **20**	4.7	1.7	21.5	•	18.8	12.8	3.7	1.6	•	3.2	•	•	•
Operating Margin **21**	14.7	33.3	35.8	•	16.4	52.5	21.9	6.1	•	29.1	•	•	•
Operating Margin Before Officers' Comp. **22**	19.3	35.0	57.2	•	35.2	65.3	25.6	7.7	•	32.3	•	•	•

Selected Average Balance Sheet ($ in Thousands)

Account	1	2	3	4	5	6	7	8	9
Net Receivables 23	3982	0	23	768	209	3019	13402	•	15508
Inventories 24	•	•	•	•	•	•	•	•	•
Net Property, Plant and Equipment 25	120	0	7	27	144	341	2020	•	554
Total Assets 26	18790	0	144	2170	8834	16314	36659	•	132694
Notes and Loans Payable 27	1723	0	49	1194	0	4769	7672	•	10490
All Other Liabilities 28	15620	0	5	355	3754	5846	21251	•	104740
Net Worth 29	1447	0	91	622	5080	5699	7736	•	17464

Selected Financial Ratios (Times to 1)

Ratio	1	2	3	4	5	6	7	8	9
Current Ratio 30	1.1	11.8	•	2.5	1.8	0.7	1.1	•	0.9
Quick Ratio 31	0.7	10.6	•	2.3	0.9	0.5	1.0	•	0.5
Net Sales to Working Capital 32	1.8	1.6	11.7	3.6	2.6	•	34.9	•	•
Coverage Ratio 33	2.0	13.2	•	4.4	•	7.9	5.3	•	6.8
Total Asset Turnover 34	0.1	1.1	•	1.2	0.9	0.4	1.3	•	0.2
Inventory Turnover 35	•	•	•	•	•	•	•	•	•
Receivables Turnover 36	•	•	•	•	•	•	•	•	•
Total Liabilities to Net Worth 37	12.0	0.6	•	2.5	0.7	1.9	3.7	•	6.6
Current Assets to Working Capital 38	10.0	1.1	•	1.7	2.2	•	18.8	•	18.8
Current Liabilities to Working Capital 39	9.0	0.1	•	0.7	1.2	•	17.8	•	•
Working Capital to Net Sales 40	0.6	0.6	•	0.3	0.4	•	0.0	•	•
Inventory to Working Capital 41	0.1	•	•	•	•	•	•	•	•
Total Receipts to Cash Flow 42	2.6	6.0	•	1.5	7.3	1.7	2.8	2.4	1.6
Cost of Goods to Cash Flow 43	0.4	2.4	•	•	•	2.7	•	0.9	0.2
Cash Flow to Total Debt 44	0.1	1.9	•	0.2	1.3	0.2	•	0.7	0.1

Selected Financial Factors (in Percentages)

Factor	1	2	3	4	5	6	7	8	9
Debt Ratio 45	92.3	•	37.1	71.4	42.5	65.1	78.9	•	86.8
Return on Total Assets 46	3.8	•	41.6	26.1	49.3	10.5	9.9	•	6.5
Return on Equity Before Income Taxes 47	24.5	•	61.1	70.5	85.6	26.4	38.2	•	42.1
Return on Equity After Income Taxes 48	19.0	•	60.4	57.7	85.4	26.0	26.6	•	31.0
Profit Margin (Before Income Tax) 49	14.7	33.3	35.8	16.4	52.5	21.9	6.1	•	29.1
Profit Margin (After Income Tax) 50	11.4	21.7	35.4	13.4	52.4	21.6	4.3	•	21.4

Table I

Corporations with and without Net Income

SECURITIES & COMMODITY EXCHANGES, OTHER FINANCIAL INVESTMENT

MONEY AMOUNTS AND SIZE OF ASSETS IN THOUSANDS OF DOLLARS

Item Description for Accounting Period 7/05 Through 6/06	Total	Zero Assets	Under 500	500 to 1,000	1,000 to 5,000	5,000 to 10,000	10,000 to 25,000	25,000 to 50,000	50,000 to 100,000	100,000 to 250,000	250,000 to 500,000	500,000 to 2,500,000	2,500,000 and over
1 Number of Enterprises	37211	4754	27905	1103	2120	389	490	176	102	73	27	51	20
Revenues ($ in Thousands)													
2 Net Sales	93225544	789665	9410541	897808	4231536	2657500	5840841	2599263	3388835	3043279	1861349	16457994	42046933
3 Interest	8909700	41314	12468	2919	50578	17600	37577	53746	70921	157968	84995	756270	7623344
4 Rents	76987	47	3202	0	403	498	2179	8440	283	3809	373	16277	41476
5 Royalties	183509	0	62612	0	1948	0	4756	1738	239	21797	247	58781	31391
6 Other Portfolio Income	1993182	37729	37482	2199	165256	65214	206308	95798	83929	169998	28447	675484	425336
7 Other Receipts	82062166	710575	9294777	892690	4013351	2574188	5590021	2439541	3233463	2689707	1688753	15009716	33925386
8 Total Receipts	93225544	789665	9410541	897808	4231536	2657500	5840841	2599263	3388835	3043279	1861349	16457994	42046933
9 Average Total Receipts	2505	166	337	814	1996	6832	11920	14769	33224	41689	68939	322706	2102347
Operating Costs/Operating Income (%)													
10 Cost of Operations	0.6	0.5	1.3	•	1.0	0.5	0.9	1.5	2.1	1.2	•	0.1	0.4
11 Salaries and Wages	20.8	14.0	22.4	28.9	28.6	32.7	26.3	25.7	20.6	34.0	17.6	22.4	16.4
12 Taxes Paid	2.3	4.4	2.7	3.0	2.7	3.1	2.3	3.8	2.0	4.4	3.1	2.1	1.8
13 Interest Paid	6.5	21.5	0.5	0.3	1.6	1.3	1.6	2.3	3.2	5.4	5.0	3.5	11.1
14 Depreciation	1.2	1.6	0.8	0.3	1.5	0.9	1.1	1.6	1.4	2.0	1.5	1.4	1.1
15 Amortization and Depletion	1.0	8.4	0.1	0.0	0.6	0.2	0.4	0.6	0.6	2.2	5.1	2.6	0.5
16 Pensions and Other Deferred Comp.	1.6	3.3	2.6	4.1	1.7	0.6	0.8	1.3	0.7	0.8	0.9	1.1	1.8
17 Employee Benefits	1.7	0.6	1.7	0.6	1.7	1.1	1.0	1.7	0.9	1.5	1.5	2.4	1.7
18 Advertising	1.1	0.7	1.1	0.4	0.2	0.4	0.4	1.4	0.1	1.3	0.1	1.7	1.1
19 Other Expenses	35.5	30.2	30.0	47.4	32.7	26.3	31.3	26.3	26.7	29.5	28.5	32.8	41.1
20 Officers' Compensation	9.7	3.9	24.7	20.9	18.2	18.7	21.8	19.7	18.9	9.4	6.7	6.4	3.1
21 Operating Margin	18.0	10.9	12.0	•	9.3	14.2	12.2	14.1	22.9	8.3	30.1	23.5	19.8
22 Operating Margin Before Officers' Comp.	27.7	14.8	36.8	15.0	27.5	32.9	34.0	33.8	41.8	17.7	36.9	29.9	22.9

Selected Average Balance Sheet ($ in Thousands)

Net Receivables 23	1956	0	7	5	219	650	1706	3040	6403	16591	53576	137660	3008054
Inventories 24	•	•	•	•	•	•	•	•	•	•	•	•	•
Net Property, Plant and Equipment 25	242	•	12	22	348	314	957	2375	4016	9412	3821	35701	194494
Total Assets 26	12247	0	72	708	2350	7396	15578	34897	70189	158906	370590	1077990	17378273
Notes and Loans Payable 27	4797	0	31	201	1105	1770	4364	7488	20810	38385	86671	228230	7600935
All Other Liabilities 28	3414	0	15	160	529	1884	2520	9124	12825	33427	102148	267869	5079372
Net Worth 29	4036	0	25	346	717	3742	8694	18285	36555	87093	181771	581891	4697966

Selected Financial Ratios (Times to 1)

Current Ratio 30	1.0	•	2.4	1.5	1.6	1.4	1.9	1.6	1.5	1.4	1.6	1.7	0.9
Quick Ratio 31	0.8	•	1.9	1.1	1.1	0.9	1.4	1.2	1.0	0.9	1.1	1.1	0.8
Net Sales to Working Capital 32	36.5	•	13.4	10.5	5.3	8.2	3.9	3.0	3.8	2.5	1.6	2.0	•
Coverage Ratio 33	3.8	1.5	24.6	•	6.6	11.5	8.5	7.0	8.1	2.5	6.9	7.6	2.8
Total Asset Turnover 34	0.2	•	4.7	1.1	0.8	0.9	0.8	0.4	0.5	0.3	0.2	0.3	0.1
Inventory Turnover 35	•	•	•	•	•	•	•	•	•	•	•	•	•
Receivables Turnover 36	•	•	•	•	•	•	•	•	•	•	•	•	•
Total Liabilities to Net Worth 37	2.0	•	1.9	1.0	2.3	1.0	0.8	0.9	0.9	0.8	1.0	0.9	2.7
Current Assets to Working Capital 38	70.2	•	1.7	3.2	2.8	3.4	2.1	2.6	3.0	3.4	2.8	2.4	•
Current Liabilities to Working Capital 39	69.2	•	0.7	2.2	1.8	2.4	1.1	1.6	2.0	2.4	1.8	1.4	•
Working Capital to Net Sales 40	0.0	•	0.1	0.1	0.2	0.1	0.3	0.3	0.3	0.4	0.6	0.5	•
Inventory to Working Capital 41	0.0	•	•	0.0	0.0	0.0	0.0	0.0	0.0	0.0	0.0	0.0	•
Total Receipts to Cash Flow 42	2.0	2.8	2.7	2.6	3.2	2.8	2.5	3.0	2.1	3.3	1.8	2.0	1.7
Cost of Goods to Cash Flow 43	0.0	0.0	0.0	•	0.0	0.0	0.0	0.0	0.0	0.0	•	0.0	0.0
Cash Flow to Total Debt 44	0.1	•	2.7	0.9	0.4	0.7	0.7	0.3	0.5	0.2	0.2	0.3	0.1

Selected Financial Factors (in Percentages)

Debt Ratio 45	67.0	•	64.9	51.1	69.5	49.4	44.2	47.6	47.9	45.2	51.0	46.0	73.0
Return on Total Assets 46	5.1	•	58.6	•	9.3	14.2	10.4	6.9	12.2	3.6	6.4	8.1	3.8
Return on Equity Before Income Taxes 47	11.3	•	160.3	•	25.8	25.7	16.4	11.3	20.5	4.0	11.2	13.0	9.1
Return on Equity After Income Taxes 48	8.1	•	158.0	•	20.8	23.7	14.9	9.6	19.1	2.1	9.4	8.5	6.1
Profit Margin (Before Income Tax) 49	18.2	10.9	12.0	•	9.3	14.1	12.0	14.1	22.5	8.3	29.4	23.5	20.3
Profit Margin (After Income Tax) 50	13.1	5.8	11.8	•	7.5	13.0	10.9	11.9	21.0	4.4	24.7	15.3	13.6

SECURITIES & COMMODITY EXCHANGES, OTHER FINANCIAL INVESTMENT

Table II

Corporations with Net Income

MONEY AMOUNTS AND SIZE OF ASSETS IN THOUSANDS OF DOLLARS

Item Description for Accounting Period 7/05 Through 6/06	Total	Zero Assets	Under 500	500 to 1,000	1,000 to 5,000	5,000 to 10,000	10,000 to 25,000	25,000 to 50,000	50,000 to 100,000	100,000 to 250,000	250,000 to 500,000	500,000 to 2,500,000	2,500,000 and over
Number of Enterprises 1	21713	1738	18077	441	741	183	262	103	54	•	18	39	•
Revenues ($ in Thousands)													
Net Sales 2	84766700	596915	7799177	787210	3113428	2542180	4750888	2083279	2760098	•	1672665	15546766	•
Interest 3	8546567	28139	7961	963	25177	11373	27294	29834	49719	•	82417	681841	•
Rents 4	66376	0	3202	0	0	498	783	257	270	•	0	16254	•
Royalties 5	178307	0	62430	0	1948	0	0	1708	6	•	58781	247	•
Other Portfolio Income 6	1738466	32888	37259	950	149263	60887	94473	87950	71742	•	14984	636129	•
Other Receipts 7	74236984	535888	7688325	785297	2937040	2469422	4628338	1963530	2638361	•	1516483	14212295	•
Total Receipts 8	84766700	596915	7799177	787210	3113428	2542180	4750888	2083279	2760098	•	1672665	15546766	•
Average Total Receipts 9	3904	343	431	1785	4202	13892	18133	20226	51113	•	92926	398635	•
Operating Costs/Operating Income (%)													
Cost of Operations 10	0.4	•	1.3	•	0.5	0.4	1.0	1.4	1.9	•	•	0.1	•
Salaries and Wages 11	19.0	6.4	20.7	24.7	26.1	31.6	22.7	24.2	17.8	•	15.3	20.9	•
Taxes Paid 12	2.1	1.4	2.6	2.4	2.3	2.3	2.2	3.0	1.8	•	2.8	2.2	•
Interest Paid 13	6.6	16.1	0.5	0.0	0.9	0.6	1.2	2.3	2.6	•	4.3	3.3	•
Depreciation 14	1.1	0.8	0.7	0.3	1.1	0.5	0.7	1.4	1.3	•	1.0	1.2	•
Amortization and Depletion 15	0.9	2.1	0.1	0.0	0.4	0.1	0.2	0.3	0.3	•	2.5	2.7	•
Pensions and Other Deferred Comp. 16	1.6	0.2	2.2	4.7	2.2	0.6	0.7	1.2	0.7	•	0.9	1.2	•
Employee Benefits 17	1.5	0.3	1.9	0.4	1.5	1.0	0.7	1.4	0.7	•	1.6	1.5	•
Advertising 18	1.1	0.9	1.1	0.5	0.2	0.4	0.4	1.7	0.1	•	0.1	1.8	•
Other Expenses 19	33.6	14.4	27.3	18.8	19.9	24.5	23.7	19.8	20.4	•	27.7	33.0	•
Officers' Compensation 20	8.6	4.8	24.2	20.1	18.8	18.7	23.3	16.3	16.4	•	7.1	4.6	•
Operating Margin 21	23.4	52.5	17.4	28.1	26.2	19.3	23.0	26.9	36.0	•	36.7	27.5	•
Operating Margin Before Officers' Comp. 22	32.0	57.4	41.5	48.2	45.0	38.1	46.3	43.2	52.4	•	43.8	32.2	•

Selected Average Balance Sheet ($ in Thousands)

Net Receivables 23	3159	0	7	9	174	1158	2365	3652	7681	47229	158366
Inventories 24	•	•	•	•	•	•	•	•	•	•	•
Net Property, Plant and Equipment 25	318	0	16	47	303	359	912	2648	4975	4008	39938
Total Assets 26	18159	0	86	746	2523	7615	16081	34596	70089	343886	1094318
Notes and Loans Payable 27	7592	0	34	351	639	1374	3771	7708	20550	65263	200783
All Other Liabilities 28	4833	0	16	164	563	3638	2883	9571	14540	103517	263640
Net Worth 29	5734	0	36	230	1321	2603	9427	17317	34999	175107	629895

Selected Financial Ratios (Times to 1)

Current Ratio 30	1.0	•	3.1	1.8	1.8	1.4	2.2	1.7	1.2	2.1	1.6
Quick Ratio 31	0.8	•	2.4	1.5	1.3	0.9	1.5	1.4	0.8	1.6	1.2
Net Sales to Working Capital 32	•	•	11.6	14.2	7.5	10.5	4.6	3.6	10.0	1.4	2.8
Coverage Ratio 33	4.6	4.3	35.7	662.4	31.5	35.1	19.3	12.8	14.7	9.4	9.3
Total Asset Turnover 34	0.2	•	5.0	2.4	1.7	1.8	1.1	0.6	0.7	0.3	0.4
Inventory Turnover 35	•	•	•	•	•	•	•	•	•	•	•
Receivables Turnover 36	•	•	•	•	•	•	•	•	•	•	•
Total Liabilities to Net Worth 37	2.2	•	1.4	2.2	0.9	1.9	0.7	1.0	1.0	1.0	0.7
Current Assets to Working Capital 38	•	•	1.5	2.3	2.3	3.8	1.9	2.4	5.1	1.9	2.7
Current Liabilities to Working Capital 39	•	•	0.5	1.3	1.3	2.8	0.9	1.4	4.1	0.9	1.7
Working Capital to Net Sales 40	•	•	0.1	0.1	0.1	0.1	0.2	0.3	0.1	0.7	0.4
Inventory to Working Capital 41	•	•	•	•	•	•	0.0	•	•	•	0.0
Total Receipts to Cash Flow 42	1.9	1.5	2.5	2.3	2.5	2.5	2.3	2.5	1.8	1.6	1.8
Cost of Goods to Cash Flow 43	0.0	0.0	0.0	0.0	0.0	0.0	0.0	0.0	0.0	0.0	0.0
Cash Flow to Total Debt 44	0.2	•	3.5	1.5	1.4	1.1	1.2	0.5	0.8	0.3	0.5

Selected Financial Factors (in Percentages)

Debt Ratio 45	68.4	•	58.4	69.1	47.7	65.8	41.4	49.9	50.1	49.1	42.4
Return on Total Assets 46	6.5	•	89.3	67.3	44.9	36.2	27.2	17.1	28.0	11.0	11.3
Return on Equity Before Income Taxes 47	16.1	•	208.6	217.6	83.0	103.0	44.0	31.5	52.3	19.3	17.5
Return on Equity After Income Taxes 48	12.3	•	206.2	213.1	75.3	97.1	41.5	28.3	49.7	16.7	12.1
Profit Margin (Before Income Tax) 49	23.6	52.5	17.3	28.1	26.1	19.3	22.9	26.9	35.8	36.4	27.7
Profit Margin (After Income Tax) 50	18.0	45.8	17.1	27.5	23.7	18.2	21.6	24.2	34.0	31.4	19.0

Table I

Corporations with and without Net Income

LIFE INSURANCE

MONEY AMOUNTS AND SIZE OF ASSETS IN THOUSANDS OF DOLLARS

Item Description for Accounting Period 7/05 Through 6/06	Total	Zero Assets	Under 500	500 to 1,000	1,000 to 5,000	5,000 to 10,000	10,000 to 25,000	25,000 to 50,000	50,000 to 100,000	100,000 to 250,000	250,000 to 500,000	500,000 to 2,500,000	2,500,000 and over
Number of Enterprises 1	1146	55	272	102	216	72	80	56	42	42	44	70	94
Revenues ($ in Thousands)													
Net Sales 2	888817466	21370549	47166	277975	204848	170658	552788	873644	1349284	2108909	3993640	22750396	835117609
Interest 3	158745516	1651831	1426	26182	15654	15355	47381	85198	100715	257807	709075	3156006	152678887
Rents 4	3774774	5958	0	0	0	585	2256	845	6953	8798	13766	41528	3694085
Royalties 5	16508	0	0	0	0	0	0	0	0	482	0	990	15036
Other Portfolio Income 6	21777948	1896355	43	276	10164	7254	17033	12624	40595	52114	33038	410211	19298242
Other Receipts 7	704502720	17816405	45697	251517	179030	147464	486118	774977	1201021	1789708	3237761	19141661	659431359
Total Receipts 8	888817466	21370549	47166	277975	204848	170658	552788	873644	1349284	2108909	3993640	22750396	835117609
Average Total Receipts 9	775582	388555	173	2725	948	2370	6910	15601	32126	50212	90765	325006	8884230
Operating Costs/Operating Income (%)													
Cost of Operations 10	51.6	79.1	27.9	51.2	19.4	44.4	40.2	47.1	39.6	46.6	45.9	49.9	51.0
Salaries and Wages 11	1.8	0.1	•	•	•	•	0.1	•	0.2	0.5	0.7	0.3	1.9
Taxes Paid 12	0.8	0.2	0.6	0.1	0.7	1.9	1.6	1.2	1.4	1.6	1.3	0.9	0.8
Interest Paid 13	3.0	0.1	0.7	0.1	0.1	0.3	0.1	0.4	0.1	0.4	1.4	0.5	3.2
Depreciation 14	0.6	0.0	0.0	0.0	0.0	0.4	0.4	0.2	0.3	0.4	0.3	0.3	0.6
Amortization and Depletion 15	0.9	0.3	0.8	0.9	0.8	1.2	2.1	1.6	2.5	3.3	2.5	1.8	0.9
Pensions and Other Deferred Comp. 16	0.4	0.0	•	•	0.1	1.0	0.5	0.4	1.4	0.7	0.6	0.5	0.4
Employee Benefits 17	0.2	0.1	0.1	•	0.0	0.3	0.2	0.3	0.2	0.2	0.2	0.2	0.2
Advertising 18	0.3	0.0	•	0.0	0.0	0.1	0.3	0.1	1.5	0.1	0.5	0.6	0.3
Other Expenses 19	37.1	18.7	59.2	46.1	78.4	36.9	40.5	39.8	47.2	41.8	39.5	45.4	37.3
Officers' Compensation 20	0.1	0.0	0.0	•	•	•	0.0	0.1	•	0.1	0.1	0.1	0.1
Operating Margin 21	3.3	1.4	10.7	1.6	0.4	13.5	13.9	8.9	5.6	4.2	7.1	•	3.4
Operating Margin Before Officers' Comp. 22	3.3	1.4	10.7	1.6	0.4	13.5	14.0	9.0	5.6	4.3	7.2	•	3.5

Selected Average Balance Sheet ($ in Thousands)

Net Receivables 23	81690	0	8	35	112	1039	1650	413	1348	5073	298	6672	985376
Inventories 24	•	•	•	•	•	•	•	•	•	•	•	•	•
Net Property, Plant and Equipment 25	47065	0	0	0	3	151	114	852	762	1994	98	3751	569071
Total Assets 26	4500080	186	745	2503	6983	16440	36571	74271	164046	361488	•	1162370	53673171
Notes and Loans Payable 27	135567	0	0	0	0	0	0	160	1384	2789	•	5309	1646819
All Other Liabilities 28	3666995	235	453	1334	3454	10542	23730	51484	136286	299532	•	978539	43723335
Net Worth 29	697518	-49	292	1168	3530	5898	12841	22627	26376	59166	•	178522	8303018

Selected Financial Ratios (Times to 1)

Current Ratio 30	0.5	4.2	6.2	10.0	4.7	3.1	3.1	2.1	1.1	1.6	0.9	0.5
Quick Ratio 31	0.4	3.1	4.5	8.1	3.7	2.4	2.4	1.6	0.9	1.3	0.7	0.4
Net Sales to Working Capital 32	•	1.4	5.5	0.6	0.8	1.3	1.4	2.0	14.2	1.9	•	0.4
Coverage Ratio 33	2.1	17.0	25.5	5.9	49.9	98.7	22.2	102.0	10.3	6.0	0.3	2.1
Total Asset Turnover 34	0.2	0.9	3.7	0.4	0.3	0.4	0.4	0.4	0.3	0.3	0.3	0.2
Inventory Turnover 35	•	•	•	•	•	•	•	•	•	•	•	•
Receivables Turnover 36	•	•	•	•	•	•	•	•	•	•	•	•
Total Liabilities to Net Worth 37	5.5	1.6	•	1.0	1.8	2.3	1.8	2.3	5.2	5.1	5.5	5.5
Current Assets to Working Capital 38	•	1.3	1.2	•	1.1	1.5	1.5	1.9	16.0	2.8	•	•
Current Liabilities to Working Capital 39	•	0.3	0.2	0.1	0.3	0.5	0.5	0.9	15.0	1.8	•	•
Working Capital to Net Sales 40	•	0.7	0.2	1.5	1.3	0.8	0.7	0.5	0.1	0.5	•	•
Inventory to Working Capital 41	•	•	•	•	•	•	•	•	•	•	•	•
Total Receipts to Cash Flow 42	2.6	5.1	2.1	1.3	2.2	2.0	2.1	2.0	2.3	1.8	2.3	2.6
Cost of Goods to Cash Flow 43	1.3	4.0	1.1	0.3	1.0	0.8	1.0	0.8	1.1	1.0	1.1	1.3
Cash Flow to Total Debt 44	0.1	0.5	2.9	0.5	0.3	0.3	0.3	0.3	0.2	0.1	0.1	0.1

Selected Financial Factors (in Percentages)

Debt Ratio 45	84.5	126.4	60.8	53.3	49.5	64.1	64.9	69.5	83.9	83.6	84.6	84.5
Return on Total Assets 46	1.1	10.6	6.2	0.2	4.6	5.9	3.9	2.4	1.4	2.1	0.0	1.1
Return on Equity Before Income Taxes 47	3.8	•	•	15.1	8.9	16.3	10.5	7.9	7.9	10.9	•	3.8
Return on Equity After Income Taxes 48	2.5	•	12.9	•	6.9	12.9	7.9	4.9	3.9	7.4	•	2.5
Profit Margin (Before Income Tax) 49	3.4	10.7	1.6	•	13.3	13.9	8.6	5.6	4.1	7.1	7.1	3.5
Profit Margin (After Income Tax) 50	2.2	10.1	1.4	•	10.2	11.0	6.5	3.5	2.0	4.8	4.8	2.3

Table II
Corporations with Net Income

LIFE INSURANCE

MONEY AMOUNTS AND SIZE OF ASSETS IN THOUSANDS OF DOLLARS

Item Description for Accounting Period 7/05 Through 6/06	Total	Zero Assets	Under 500	500 to 1,000	1,000 to 5,000	5,000 to 10,000	10,000 to 25,000	25,000 to 50,000	50,000 to 100,000	100,000 to 250,000	250,000 to 500,000	500,000 to 2,500,000	2,500,000 and over
Number of Enterprises 1	882	39	177	85	187	49	68	46	32	32	39	55	74
Revenues ($ in Thousands)													
Net Sales 2	746336251	2481546	31560	26737	186765	148536	481796	671156	954259	1609897	3676596	18674791	717392612
Interest 3	138927026	512091	1216	1775	14019	11626	42448	68353	75441	202572	626443	2550448	134820596
Rents 4	3461987	5958	0	0	0	103	1391	722	2347	7906	12716	39223	3391621
Royalties 5	16079	0	0	0	0					53		990	15036
Other Portfolio Income 6	19509878	70576	23	135	10122	6664	16711	11636	36515	17233	29569	319290	18991404
Other Receipts 7	584421281	1892921	30321	24827	162624	130143	421246	590445	839956	1382133	3007868	15764840	560173955
Total Receipts 8	746336251	2481546	31560	26737	186765	148536	481796	671156	954259	1609897	3676596	18674791	717392612
Average Total Receipts 9	846186	63629	178	315	999	3031	7085	14590	29821	50309	94272	339542	9694495
Operating Costs/Operating Income (%)													
Cost of Operations 10	52.9	59.0	30.6	24.5	18.8	45.6	41.9	50.1	33.6	48.8	44.5	50.7	53.0
Salaries and Wages 11	2.0	0.8	•	•	•	•	0.1	•	0.2	0.3	0.5	0.3	2.1
Taxes Paid 12	0.9	1.3	0.7	0.7	0.7	1.4	1.6	1.1	1.3	1.8	1.3	0.9	0.9
Interest Paid 13	3.5	1.2	0.2	0.7	0.1	0.3	0.1	0.1	0.0	0.4	1.5	0.5	3.6
Depreciation 14	0.7	0.2	0.0	0.0	0.0	0.3	0.4	0.2	0.2	0.4	0.3	0.3	0.7
Amortization and Depletion 15	1.0	2.2	1.2	0.7	0.8	0.9	1.8	1.3	2.1	3.6	2.5	1.6	1.0
Pensions and Other Deferred Comp. 16	0.4	0.1	•	•	0.0	0.9	0.4	0.5	1.7	0.6	0.5	0.5	0.4
Employee Benefits 17	0.2	0.4	•	•	0.0	0.2	0.2	0.3	0.1	0.2	0.1	0.2	0.2
Advertising 18	0.3	0.2	•	•	0.0	0.1	0.1	0.1	2.1	0.1	0.4	0.4	0.3
Other Expenses 19	33.4	22.5	34.9	38.9	52.5	31.9	35.5	33.7	47.1	34.2	40.3	39.1	33.2
Officers' Compensation 20	0.1	0.1	•	0.7	•	•	0.0	0.1	•	0.1	0.1	0.1	0.1
Operating Margin 21	4.6	11.7	32.4	34.5	26.9	18.4	18.0	12.6	11.6	9.5	8.1	5.4	4.5
Operating Margin Before Officers' Comp. 22	4.8	11.9	32.4	34.5	26.9	18.4	18.0	12.7	11.6	9.6	8.2	5.5	4.6

Selected Average Balance Sheet ($ in Thousands)

Net Receivables 23	104394	0	9	42	128	438	1213	1325	466	1522	5663	2289	1236090
Inventories 24	•	•	•	•	•	•	•	•	•	•	•	•	•
Net Property, Plant and Equipment 25	55700	0	0	0	2	75	96	125	535	714	1828	4535	658791
Total Assets 26	5253908	0	211	747	2531	6913	16448	36558	72138	160628	363575	1148650	61424726
Notes and Loans Payable 27	168569	0	0	0	0	0	0	0	210	249	2785	3757	2004704
All Other Liabilities 28	4237498	0	236	380	1254	3554	10161	21995	47964	134185	300001	946625	49536407
Net Worth 29	847841	0	-25	367	1277	3359	6287	14564	23963	26194	60789	198267	9883614

Selected Financial Ratios (Times to 1)

Current Ratio 30	0.6	•	5.7	9.3	10.6	4.4	3.5	3.8	2.4	1.1	1.4	1.2	0.6
Quick Ratio 31	0.4	•	4.2	6.7	8.3	2.9	2.6	2.9	1.8	1.0	1.2	0.8	0.4
Net Sales to Working Capital 32	•	•	1.2	0.6	1.2	1.2	1.1	1.7	7.2	2.6	6.5	•	•
Coverage Ratio 33	2.4	10.4	168.7	51.0	333.0	59.2	188.5	138.8	334.1	21.9	6.2	11.0	2.3
Total Asset Turnover 34	0.2	•	0.8	0.4	0.4	0.4	0.4	0.4	0.4	0.3	0.3	0.3	0.2
Inventory Turnover 35	•	•	•	•	•	•	•	•	•	•	•	•	•
Receivables Turnover 36	•	•	•	•	•	•	•	•	•	•	•	•	•
Total Liabilities to Net Worth 37	5.2	•	•	1.0	1.0	1.1	1.6	1.5	2.0	5.1	5.0	4.8	5.2
Current Assets to Working Capital 38	•	•	1.2	1.1	1.1	1.3	1.4	1.7	7.7	3.7	6.7	5.2	•
Current Liabilities to Working Capital 39	•	•	0.2	0.1	0.1	0.3	0.4	0.7	6.7	2.7	5.7	•	•
Working Capital to Net Sales 40	•	•	0.9	1.8	1.4	0.8	0.9	0.6	0.1	0.4	0.2	•	•
Inventory to Working Capital 41	•	•	•	•	•	•	•	•	•	•	•	•	•
Total Receipts to Cash Flow 42	2.8	3.2	1.4	1.3	2.2	2.2	2.0	1.8	2.4	2.1	2.3	2.8	2.8
Cost of Goods to Cash Flow 43	1.5	1.9	0.3	0.3	1.0	1.0	0.8	0.6	1.2	0.9	1.2	1.5	1.5
Cash Flow to Total Debt 44	0.1	0.5	0.6	0.6	0.4	0.3	0.3	0.3	0.2	0.1	0.2	0.1	0.1

Selected Financial Factors (in Percentages)

Debt Ratio 45	83.9	•	112.0	50.9	49.5	51.4	61.8	60.2	66.8	83.7	83.3	82.7	83.9
Return on Total Assets 46	1.3	•	27.6	14.8	10.6	8.1	7.8	4.9	4.8	3.1	2.5	1.8	1.3
Return on Equity Before Income Taxes 47	4.8	•	•	29.5	21.0	16.4	20.2	12.3	14.3	18.0	12.4	9.3	4.6
Return on Equity After Income Taxes 48	3.4	•	•	27.3	18.1	13.2	16.4	9.5	10.6	12.8	8.6	6.5	3.3
Profit Margin (Before Income Tax) 49	4.8	11.7	32.4	34.4	26.8	18.1	17.9	12.3	11.5	9.4	8.0	5.4	4.7
Profit Margin (After Income Tax) 50	3.4	8.3	31.4	31.9	23.1	14.6	14.6	9.5	8.5	6.7	5.6	3.8	3.3

Table I

Corporations with and without Net Income

LIFE INSURANCE, STOCK COMPANIES (FORM 1120L)

MONEY AMOUNTS AND SIZE OF ASSETS IN THOUSANDS OF DOLLARS

Item Description for Accounting Period 7/05 Through 6/06	Total	Zero Assets	Under 500	500 to 1,000	1,000 to 5,000	5,000 to 10,000	10,000 to 25,000	25,000 to 50,000	50,000 to 100,000	100,000 to 250,000	250,000 to 500,000	500,000 to 2,500,000	2,500,000 and over
Number of Enterprises **1**	1088	55	267	100	208	67	80	51	42	36	38	58	86
Revenues ($ in Thousands)													
Net Sales **2**	796292315	21370549	47058	277896	201188	109688	552788	800801	1349284	1709933	3527486	19808213	746537430
Interest **3**	139000913	1651831	1417	26111	14774	11961	47381	73275	100715	215482	598434	2371207	133888325
Rents **4**	2835925	5958	0	0	0	585	2256	760	6953	7788	11589	25172	2774862
Royalties **5**	11462	0	0	0	0	0	0	0	0	53	0	937	10472
Other Portfolio Income **6**	18271991	1896355	43	276	9810	6922	17033	12091	40595	41648	21725	377067	15848423
Other Receipts **7**	636172024	17816405	45598	251509	176604	90220	486118	714675	1201021	1444962	2895738	17033830	594015348
Total Receipts **8**	796292315	21370549	47058	277896	201188	109688	552788	800801	1349284	1709933	3527486	19808213	746537430
Average Total Receipts **9**	731886	388555	176	2779	967	1637	6910	15702	32126	47498	92829	341521	8680668
Operating Costs/Operating Income (%)													
Cost of Operations **10**	52.3	79.1	27.7	51.2	19.4	31.9	40.2	45.8	39.6	43.9	44.1	50.2	51.7
Salaries and Wages **11**	1.9	0.1	•	•	•	•	0.1	•	0.2	0.7	0.8	0.4	2.0
Taxes Paid **12**	0.8	0.2	0.6	0.1	0.7	2.6	1.6	1.1	1.4	1.4	1.3	0.8	0.8
Interest Paid **13**	3.2	0.1	0.7	0.1	0.1	0.4	0.1	0.4	0.1	0.5	1.6	0.5	3.4
Depreciation **14**	0.6	0.0	0.0	0.0	0.0	0.4	0.4	0.1	0.3	0.4	0.3	0.2	0.7
Amortization and Depletion **15**	0.9	0.3	0.9	0.9	0.8	1.4	2.1	1.5	2.5	3.4	2.1	1.7	0.9
Pensions and Other Deferred Comp. **16**	0.3	0.0	•	•	0.1	1.5	0.5	0.3	1.4	0.7	0.4	0.4	0.3
Employee Benefits **17**	0.2	0.1	•	•	0.0	0.2	0.2	0.2	0.2	0.1	0.1	0.2	0.2
Advertising **18**	0.3	0.0	•	0.0	0.0	0.1	0.3	0.1	1.5	0.1	0.5	0.6	0.3
Other Expenses **19**	36.4	18.7	59.3	46.1	78.5	43.1	40.5	41.0	47.2	43.9	41.2	46.0	36.6
Officers' Compensation **20**	0.1	0.0	•	•	•	•	0.0	0.1	•	0.1	0.0	0.1	0.1
Operating Margin **21**	3.1	1.4	10.8	1.6	0.4	18.5	13.9	9.3	5.6	4.9	7.6	•	3.2
Operating Margin Before Officers' Comp. **22**	3.2	1.4	10.8	1.6	0.4	18.5	14.0	9.4	5.6	5.0	7.6	•	3.3

Selected Average Balance Sheet ($ in Thousands)

Net Receivables 23	82647	0	8	36	117	318	1039	1811	413	1099	5652	7705	1034584
Inventories 24	•	•	•	•	•	•	•	•	•	•	•	•	•
Net Property, Plant and Equipment 25	47644	•	0	0	73	151	852	86	563	1841	3604	•	598597
Total Assets 26	4264180	•	188	736	2486	6682	16440	35504	74271	161347	358802	1150115	5285918
Notes and Loans Payable 27	141666	•	0	0	0	0	0	160	0	0	1614	3230	6403
All Other Liabilities 28	3436269	•	238	457	1273	2922	10542	22557	51484	131176	293996	958486	42586606
Net Worth 29	686245	•	-50	279	1213	3760	5898	12947	22627	28557	61576	185227	8487466

Selected Financial Ratios (Times to 1)

Current Ratio 30	0.5	•	4.2	6.2	11.8	6.8	3.1	3.1	2.1	1.0	1.3	0.8	0.5
Quick Ratio 31	0.4	•	3.1	4.6	9.6	5.4	2.3	2.4	1.6	0.8	1.1	0.6	0.4
Net Sales to Working Capital 32	•	•	1.4	5.6	0.6	0.5	1.3	1.4	2.0	•	3.1	•	•
Coverage Ratio 33	2.0	10.4	17.2	25.3	5.4	44.2	98.7	21.4	102.0	10.5	5.7	•	2.0
Total Asset Turnover 34	0.2	•	0.9	3.8	0.4	0.2	0.4	0.4	0.4	0.3	0.3	0.3	0.2
Inventory Turnover 35	•	•	•	•	•	•	•	•	•	•	•	•	•
Receivables Turnover 36	•	•	•	•	•	•	•	•	•	•	•	•	•
Total Liabilities to Net Worth 37	5.2	•	•	•	•	1.0	1.8	1.7	2.3	4.7	4.8	•	5.2
Current Assets to Working Capital 38	1.3	•	•	1.2	•	1.5	1.5	1.9	•	4.4	•	4.4	•
Current Liabilities to Working Capital 39	•	•	0.3	0.3	0.2	0.2	0.5	0.5	0.9	•	3.4	•	•
Working Capital to Net Sales 40	•	•	0.7	0.2	1.6	2.0	0.8	0.5	0.7	0.3	•	•	•
Inventory to Working Capital 41	•	•	•	•	•	•	•	•	•	•	•	•	•
Total Receipts to Cash Flow 42	2.6	5.1	•	2.1	1.4	1.8	2.0	2.0	2.2	2.1	2.3	•	2.6
Cost of Goods to Cash Flow 43	1.4	4.0	•	1.1	0.3	0.6	0.9	0.8	0.9	0.9	1.2	•	1.3
Cash Flow to Total Debt 44	0.1	0.5	2.9	0.6	0.3	0.3	0.3	0.2	•	0.2	•	•	0.1

Selected Financial Factors (in Percentages)

Debt Ratio 45	83.9	•	126.6	62.1	51.2	43.7	64.1	63.5	69.5	82.3	82.8	83.9	83.9
Return on Total Assets 46	1.1	•	10.8	6.3	0.2	4.6	5.9	4.2	2.4	1.6	2.4	•	1.1
Return on Equity Before Income Taxes 47	3.5	•	•	16.0	8.0	16.3	11.0	7.9	8.1	11.3	•	•	3.5
Return on Equity After Income Taxes 48	2.3	•	13.6	•	6.1	12.9	8.2	3.8	•	7.7	•	•	2.3
Profit Margin (Before Income Tax) 49	3.3	•	1.4	1.6	10.8	0.3	18.3	13.9	9.0	5.6	4.9	7.5	3.4
Profit Margin (After Income Tax) 50	2.1	•	1.0	1.4	10.2	•	14.0	11.0	6.8	3.5	2.3	5.1	2.2

Table II

Corporations with Net Income

LIFE INSURANCE, STOCK COMPANIES (FORM 1120L)

MONEY AMOUNTS AND SIZE OF ASSETS IN THOUSANDS OF DOLLARS

Item Description for Accounting Period 7/05 Through 6/06	Total	Zero Assets	Under 500	500 to 1000	251 to 500	501 to 1,000	1,001 to 5,000	5,001 to 10,000	10,001 to 25,000	25,001 to 50,000	50,001 to 100,000	100,001 to 250,000	250,001 and over
Number of Enterprises 1	840	39	177	82	182	•	68	41	32	29	•	•	•
Revenues ($ in Thousands)													
Net Sales 2	656045536	2481546	31560	26658	183489	•	481796	598313	954259	1375695			
Interest 3	119577469	512091	1216	1705	13332	•	42448	56429	75441	184930			
Rents 4	2554020	5958	0	0	0	•	1391	637	2347	7788			
Royalties 5	11462	0	0	0	0	•	0	0	0	53			
Other Portfolio Income 6	16045679	70576	23	135	9793	•	16711	11105	36515	14823			
Other Receipts 7	517856906	1892921	30321	24818	160364	•	421246	530142	839956	1168101			
Total Receipts 8	656045536	2481546	31560	26658	183489	•	481796	598313	954259	1375695			
Average Total Receipts 9	781007	63629	178	325	1008	•	7085	14593	29821	47438			
Operating Costs/Operating Income (%)													
Cost of Operations 10	54.0	59.0	30.6	24.5	18.8	•	41.9	48.6	33.6	47.5			
Salaries and Wages 11	2.2	0.8	•	•	•	•	0.1	•	0.2	0.3			
Taxes Paid 12	0.9	1.3	0.7	0.7	0.7	•	1.6	1.0	1.3	1.6			
Interest Paid 13	3.8	1.2	0.2	0.7	0.1	•	0.1	0.1	0.0	0.5			
Depreciation 14	0.7	0.2	0.0	0.0	0.0	•	0.4	0.1	0.2	0.4			
Amortization and Depletion 15	0.9	2.2	1.2	0.7	0.8	•	1.8	1.1	2.1	3.6			
Pensions and Other Deferred Comp. 16	0.3	0.1	•	•	0.0	•	0.4	0.4	1.7	0.7			
Employee Benefits 17	0.2	0.4	•	•	0.0	•	0.2	0.2	0.1	0.1			
Advertising 18	0.3	0.2	•	•	0.0	•	0.1	0.1	2.1	0.1			
Other Expenses 19	31.9	22.5	34.9	38.9	52.2	•	35.5	34.6	47.1	34.7			
Officers' Compensation 20	0.1	0.1	•	•	•	•	0.0	0.1	0.1	0.2			
Operating Margin 21	4.6	11.7	32.4	34.5	27.3	•	18.0	13.6	11.6	10.4			
Operating Margin Before Officers' Comp. 22	4.7	11.9	32.4	34.5	27.3	•	18.0	13.8	11.6	10.5			

Selected Average Balance Sheet ($ in Thousands)

Net Receivables 23	105217	0	9	43	132	1213	1487	466	1118
Inventories 24									
Net Property, Plant and Equipment 25	56381	0	0	0	2	96	92	535	654
Total Assets 26	4917781	0	211	745	2496	16448	35229	72138	158423
Notes and Loans Payable 27	175537	0	0	0	0	0	0	210	275
All Other Liabilities 28	3913283	0	236	388	1183	10161	20323	47964	129551
Net Worth 29	828961	0	-25	358	1312	6287	14906	23963	28597

Selected Financial Ratios (Times to 1)

Current Ratio 30	0.5		5.7	9.3	12.1	3.5	3.9	2.4	1.1
Quick Ratio 31	0.4		4.2	6.8	9.5	2.6	2.9	1.8	0.9
Net Sales to Working Capital 32			1.2	0.6	0.7	1.2	1.1	1.7	17.6
Coverage Ratio 33	2.3	10.4	168.7	50.9	331.7	188.5	133.9	334.1	21.5
Total Asset Turnover 34	0.2		0.8	0.4	0.4	0.4	0.4	0.4	0.3
Inventory Turnover 35									
Receivables Turnover 36									
Total Liabilities to Net Worth 37	4.9			1.1	0.9	1.6	1.4	2.0	4.5
Current Assets to Working Capital 38			1.2	1.1	1.1	1.4	1.3	1.7	19.4
Current Liabilities to Working Capital 39			0.2	0.1	0.1	0.4	0.3	0.7	18.4
Working Capital to Net Sales 40			0.9	1.8	1.4	0.8	0.9	0.6	0.1
Inventory to Working Capital 41									
Total Receipts to Cash Flow 42	2.9	3.2	1.5	1.4	1.3	2.0	2.1	1.8	2.3
Cost of Goods to Cash Flow 43	1.5	1.9	0.5	0.3	0.3	0.8	1.0	0.6	1.1
Cash Flow to Total Debt 44	0.1	0.5	0.5	0.6	0.6	0.3	0.3	0.3	0.2

Selected Financial Factors (in Percentages)

Debt Ratio 45	83.1		112.0	52.0	47.4	61.8	57.7	66.8	81.9
Return on Total Assets 46	1.4		27.6	15.3	11.0	7.8	5.5	4.8	3.2
Return on Equity Before Income Taxes 47	4.6			31.3	20.9	20.2	13.0	14.3	17.0
Return on Equity After Income Taxes 48	3.2			29.0	18.0	16.4	10.0	10.6	11.7
Profit Margin (Before Income Tax) 49	4.8	11.7	32.4	34.4	27.2	17.9	13.3	11.5	10.2
Profit Margin (After Income Tax) 50	3.4	8.3	31.4	31.9	23.4	14.6	10.2	8.5	7.1

Table I

Corporations with and without Net Income

LIFE INSURANCE, MUTUAL COMPANIES (FORM 1120L)

MONEY AMOUNTS AND SIZE OF ASSETS IN THOUSANDS OF DOLLARS

Item Description for Accounting Period 7/05 Through 6/06	Total	Zero Assets	Under 500	500 to 1,000	1,000 to 5,000	5,000 to 10,000	10,000 to 25,000	25,000 to 50,000	50,000 to 100,000	100,000 to 250,000	250,000 to 500,000	500,000 to 2,500,000	2,500,000 and over
Number of Enterprises **1**	57	0	5	3	8	5	0	5	0	6	6	12	8
Revenues ($ in Thousands)													
Net Sales **2**	92525152	0	109	79	3660	60970	0	72843	0	398976	466154	2942184	88580178
Interest **3**	19744604	0	9	71	879	3394	0	11923	0	42325	110642	784799	18790562
Rents **4**	938849	0	0	0	0	0	0	85	0	1010	2177	16356	919222
Royalties **5**	5045	0	0	0	0	0	0	0	0	429	0	52	4564
Other Portfolio Income **6**	3505958	0	0	0	354	331	0	531	0	10465	11312	33144	3449819
Other Receipts **7**	68330696	0	100	8	2427	57245	0	60304	0	344747	342023	2107833	65416011
Total Receipts **8**	92525152	0	109	79	3660	60970	0	72843	0	398976	466154	2942184	88580178
Average Total Receipts **9**	1623248	·	22	26	458	12194	·	14569	·	66496	77692	245182	11072522
Operating Costs/Operating Income (%)													
Cost of Operations **10**	45.8	·	101.8	26.6	20.3	67.0	·	62.1	·	58.3	59.3	47.6	45.6
Salaries and Wages **11**	0.9	·	·	·	·	·	·	·	·	·	0.0	0.0	1.0
Taxes Paid **12**	1.0	·	·	1.3	1.7	0.6	·	2.2	·	2.5	1.7	1.3	0.9
Interest Paid **13**	1.1	·	·	·	·	·	·	·	·	0.2	·	0.6	1.2
Depreciation **14**	0.4	·	·	·	·	0.5	·	1.0	·	0.5	0.4	0.5	0.4
Amortization and Depletion **15**	1.5	·	·	·	1.4	0.9	·	2.4	·	3.0	5.7	2.7	1.5
Pensions and Other Deferred Comp. **16**	0.9	·	·	·	·	0.1	·	1.2	·	0.8	1.7	1.2	0.9
Employee Benefits **17**	0.1	·	26.6	·	·	0.4	·	0.8	·	0.6	0.3	0.1	0.1
Advertising **18**	0.2	·	·	·	·	0.0	·	0.1	·	0.4	0.0	0.2	0.2
Other Expenses **19**	43.5	·	13.8	32.9	73.0	25.8	·	26.3	·	32.8	26.7	41.5	43.7
Officers' Compensation **20**	0.1	·	3.7	·	·	·	·	·	·	·	0.3	·	0.1
Operating Margin **21**	4.5	·	·	39.2	3.7	4.6	·	4.1	·	1.0	3.9	4.2	4.5
Operating Margin Before Officers' Comp. **22**	4.6	·	·	39.2	3.7	4.6	·	4.1	·	1.0	4.2	4.2	4.6

Selected Average Balance Sheet ($ in Thousands)

	1	2	3	4	5	6	7	8	9	10	11
Net Receivables 23	64857	•	0	0	36	•	0	2840	1403	1675	456386
Inventories 24	•	•	•	•	•	•	•	•	•	•	•
Net Property, Plant and Equipment 25	36851	•	0	0	429	•	394	•	1960	4457	251670
Total Assets 26	9081827	•	88	2938	11023	789	47460	180238	378500	1221601	62416718
Notes and Loans Payable 27	21527	•	0	0	0	•	0	•	0	0	153346
All Other Liabilities 28	8135369	•	88	2938	10586	173	35700	166950	334593	1075462	55943168
Net Worth 29	924931	•	0	0	437	616	11760	13288	43906	146118	6320204

Selected Financial Ratios (Times to 1)

	1	2	3	4	5	6	7	8	9	10	11
Current Ratio 30	0.8	•	2.5	0.7	9.0	3.1	•	1.9	16.2	1.5	0.8
Quick Ratio 31	0.6	•	2.5	0.0	•	2.6	•	1.6	14.2	1.3	0.6
Net Sales to Working Capital 32	•	•	0.5	•	0.3	1.1	•	2.0	0.5	2.0	0.6
Coverage Ratio 33	4.9	•	•	•	•	7.3	•	•	7.5	•	4.9
Total Asset Turnover 34	0.2	•	0.2	0.2	0.0	0.3	•	0.4	0.2	0.2	0.2
Inventory Turnover 35	•	•	•	•	•	•	•	•	•	•	•
Receivables Turnover 36	•	•	•	•	•	•	•	•	•	•	•
Total Liabilities to Net Worth 37	8.8	•	•	•	24.2	0.3	3.0	12.6	7.6	7.4	8.9
Current Assets to Working Capital 38	•	•	1.6	1.1	1.1	1.5	•	2.1	1.1	2.9	•
Current Liabilities to Working Capital 39	•	•	0.6	0.1	0.1	0.5	•	1.1	0.1	1.9	•
Working Capital to Net Sales 40	2.2	•	2.2	3.0	3.0	0.9	•	0.5	2.1	0.5	•
Inventory to Working Capital 41	•	•	•	•	•	•	•	•	0.0	•	•
Total Receipts to Cash Flow 42	2.2	•	1.4	1.4	1.4	3.4	•	3.3	3.5	2.2	2.2
Cost of Goods to Cash Flow 43	1.0	•	0.4	0.3	0.3	2.1	•	1.9	2.1	1.1	1.0
Cash Flow to Total Debt 44	0.1	•	0.1	0.1	0.1	0.3	•	0.1	0.1	0.1	0.1

Selected Financial Factors (in Percentages)

	1	2	3	4	5	6	7	8	9	10	11
Debt Ratio 45	89.8	•	100.0	100.0	96.0	22.0	75.2	92.6	88.4	88.0	89.9
Return on Total Assets 46	1.0	•	•	0.3	4.8	1.3	1.2	0.4	•	0.8	1.0
Return on Equity Before Income Taxes 47	7.8	•	•	1.7	121.1	5.0	5.1	6.7	7.1	7.1	7.8
Return on Equity After Income Taxes 48	5.2	•	•	1.7	98.7	4.2	4.4	4.7	4.4	4.4	5.2
Profit Margin (Before Income Tax) 49	4.4	•	39.2	39.2	2.2	4.3	4.0	3.8	1.0	4.2	4.5
Profit Margin (After Income Tax) 50	3.0	•	39.2	39.2	2.2	3.5	3.4	2.7	0.9	2.6	3.0

Table II
Corporations with Net Income

LIFE INSURANCE, MUTUAL COMPANIES (FORM 1120L)

MONEY AMOUNTS AND SIZE OF ASSETS IN THOUSANDS OF DOLLARS

Item Description for Accounting Period 7/05 Through 6/06	Total	Zero Assets	Under 500	500 to 1,000	1,000 to 5,000	5,000 to 10,000	10,000 to 25,000	25,000 to 50,000	50,000 to 100,000	100,000 to 250,000	250,000 to 500,000	500,000 to 2,500,000	2,500,000 and over
Number of Enterprises 1	42	0	0	3	5	•	0	5	0	3	•	•	•
Revenues ($ in Thousands)													
Net Sales 2	90290715	0	0	79	3276	•	0	72843	0	234202	•	•	•
Interest 3	19349557	0	0	71	686	•	0	11923	0	17642	•	•	•
Rents 4	907967	0	0	0	0	•	0	85	0	118	•	•	•
Royalties 5	4616	0	0	0	0	•	0	0	0	0	•	•	•
Other Portfolio Income 6	3464201	0	0	0	328	•	0	531	0	2412	•	•	•
Other Receipts 7	66564374	0	0	8	2262	•	0	60304	0	214030	•	•	•
Total Receipts 8	90290715	0	0	79	3276	•	0	72843	0	234202	•	•	•
Average Total Receipts 9	2149779	•	•	26	655	•	•	14569	•	78067	•	•	•
Operating Costs/Operating Income (%)													
Cost of Operations 10	45.2	•	•	26.6	16.5	•	•	62.1	•	56.1	•	•	•
Salaries and Wages 11	1.0	•	•	•	•	•	•	•	•	•	•	•	•
Taxes Paid 12	0.9	•	•	1.3	1.6	•	•	2.2	•	3.0	•	•	•
Interest Paid 13	1.1	•	•	•	•	•	•	•	•	0.2	•	•	•
Depreciation 14	0.4	•	•	•	•	•	•	1.0	•	0.4	•	•	•
Amortization and Depletion 15	1.5	•	•	•	1.3	•	•	2.4	•	3.6	•	•	•
Pensions and Other Deferred Comp. 16	0.9	•	•	•	•	•	•	1.2	•	0.2	•	•	•
Employee Benefits 17	0.1	•	•	•	•	•	•	0.8	•	0.7	•	•	•
Advertising 18	0.2	•	•	•	•	•	•	0.1	•	0.0	•	•	•
Other Expenses 19	43.9	•	•	32.9	72.6	•	•	26.3	•	31.3	•	•	•
Officers' Compensation 20	0.1	•	•	•	•	•	•	•	•	•	•	•	•
Operating Margin 21	4.7	•	•	39.2	8.0	•	•	4.1	•	4.5	•	•	•
Operating Margin Before Officers' Comp. 22	4.8	•	•	39.2	8.0	•	•	4.1	•	4.5	•	•	•

Selected Average Balance Sheet ($ in Thousands)

Item					
Net Receivables 23	87914		0	0	5424
Inventories 24					
Net Property, Plant and Equipment 25	42090	0	0	394	1298
Total Assets 26	11976444	789	3821	47460	181946
Notes and Loans Payable 27	29215		0	0	0
All Other Liabilities 28	10721791	173	3821	35700	178985
Net Worth 29	1225438	616	0	11760	2960

Selected Financial Ratios (Times to 1)

Item					
Current Ratio 30	0.8	9.0	1.0	3.1	4.2
Quick Ratio 31	0.5	0.0		2.6	3.4
Net Sales to Working Capital 32		0.3		1.1	1.6
Coverage Ratio 33	5.1				29.2
Total Asset Turnover 34	0.2	0.0	0.2	0.3	0.4
Inventory Turnover 35					
Receivables Turnover 36					
Total Liabilities to Net Worth 37	8.8	0.3		3.0	60.5
Current Assets to Working Capital 38		1.1		1.5	1.3
Current Liabilities to Working Capital 39	0.1			0.5	0.3
Working Capital to Net Sales 40		3.0		0.9	0.6
Inventory to Working Capital 41					
Total Receipts to Cash Flow 42	2.2	1.4		3.4	3.0
Cost of Goods to Cash Flow 43	1.0	0.4		2.1	1.7
Cash Flow to Total Debt 44	0.1	0.1		0.1	0.1

Selected Financial Factors (in Percentages)

Item					
Debt Ratio 45	89.8	22.0	100.0	75.2	98.4
Return on Total Assets 46	1.0	1.3	1.1	1.2	2.0
Return on Equity Before Income Taxes 47	8.2	1.7		5.0	117.3
Return on Equity After Income Taxes 48	5.5	1.7		4.2	111.5
Profit Margin (Before Income Tax) 49	4.7	39.2	6.4	4.0	4.4
Profit Margin (After Income Tax) 50	3.2	39.2	6.4	3.4	4.2

Table I

Corporations with and without Net Income

MUTUAL PROPERTY AND CASUALTY COMPANIES (FORM 1120-PC)

MONEY AMOUNTS AND SIZE OF ASSETS IN THOUSANDS OF DOLLARS

Item Description for Accounting Period 7/05 Through 6/06	Total	Zero Assets	Under 500	500 to 1,000	1,000 to 5,000	5,000 to 10,000	10,000 to 25,000	25,000 to 50,000	50,000 to 100,000	100,000 to 250,000	250,000 to 500,000	500,000 to 2,500,000	2,500,000 and over
Number of Enterprises **1**	1514	31	92	71	530	159	220	115	76	74	53	70	23
Revenues ($ in Thousands)													
Net Sales **2**	218313517	966107	9043	42908	432858	542803	1643117	2063249	2141515	5868777	9960423	46249327	148393390
Interest **3**	12630524	10039	337	1370	35299	23173	79137	93959	142548	300294	434880	1803725	9705761
Rents **4**	504649	0	0	9	1341	619	2484	1851	2776	13490	14352	80126	387604
Royalties **5**	604	0	0	0	0	0	0	0	0	0	0	508	95
Other Portfolio Income **6**	7203176	4951	72	16	8160	12712	30789	32072	57758	221691	224311	1080786	5529856
Other Receipts **7**	197974564	951117	8634	41513	388058	506299	1530707	1935367	1938433	5333302	9286880	43284182	132770074
Total Receipts **8**	218313517	966107	9043	42908	432858	542803	1643117	2063249	2141515	5868777	9960423	46249327	148393390
Average Total Receipts **9**	144197	31165	98	604	817	3414	7469	17941	28178	79308	187933	660705	6451887
Operating Costs/Operating Income (%)													
Cost of Operations **10**	58.3	74.7	59.2	41.6	47.8	49.5	55.1	55.1	48.3	57.1	55.3	64.1	57.0
Salaries and Wages **11**	12.3	7.4	4.2	13.0	15.3	9.5	9.7	12.6	15.8	17.6	16.3	13.0	11.6
Taxes Paid **12**	2.4	1.4	0.0	1.6	3.8	6.5	2.9	3.9	2.8	3.1	2.3	2.0	2.4
Interest Paid **13**	0.6	0.1	0.8	0.4	0.1	0.2	0.2	0.2	0.4	0.2	0.2	0.2	0.8
Depreciation **14**	0.9	0.6	•	0.4	0.5	0.3	0.4	0.4	0.8	1.1	0.6	0.7	1.0
Amortization and Depletion **15**	0.2	0.0	0.0	0.1	0.1	0.0	1.0	0.0	0.0	0.0	0.2	0.1	0.2
Pensions and Other Deferred Comp. **16**	0.4	2.7	•	•	0.1	0.3	0.1	0.2	0.5	0.2	0.6	0.5	0.4
Employee Benefits **17**	1.5	1.0	•	0.2	1.1	0.6	0.6	1.5	1.3	2.2	1.6	1.6	1.5
Advertising **18**	0.4	0.1	•	0.6	0.3	0.2	0.2	0.2	0.4	0.4	0.2	0.2	0.4
Other Expenses **19**	12.3	6.9	332.0	34.0	18.2	21.1	20.9	17.5	18.9	11.6	11.7	8.0	13.3
Officers' Compensation **20**	0.2	0.7	•	1.2	2.8	1.2	0.6	0.8	1.0	0.6	0.6	0.3	0.2
Operating Margin **21**	10.5	4.3	7.0	10.0	10.7	8.2	8.2	7.4	9.8	5.9	10.2	9.2	11.2
Operating Margin Before Officers' Comp. **22**	10.7	5.0	•	8.2	12.8	11.9	8.8	8.3	10.9	6.5	10.9	9.5	11.4

Selected Average Balance Sheet ($ in Thousands)

Item	1	2	3	4	5	6	7	8	9	10	11	12
Net Receivables 23	30080	0	42	79	519	1194	2861	4667	15358	36541	112626	1456972
Inventories 24	•	•	•	•	•	•	•	•	•	•	•	•
Net Property, Plant and Equipment 25	5241	0	7	63	73	127	253	815	2780	7080	19193	254165
Total Assets 26	352850	98	833	2487	6823	15670	35124	69087	162377	330588	1170352	17719316
Notes and Loans Payable 27	9583	33	28	7	29	42	113	523	343	1920	6575	601981
All Other Liabilities 28	213353	109	621	1025	3592	10512	24375	42812	101431	210754	722602	10618296
Net Worth 29	129914	-45	184	1455	3202	5116	10636	25752	60604	117914	441175	6499039

Selected Financial Ratios (Times to 1)

Item	1	2	3	4	5	6	7	8	9	10	11	12
Current Ratio 30	0.9	0.5	1.0	1.8	1.4	1.0	0.9	0.9	1.0	0.9	0.8	0.8
Quick Ratio 31	0.8	0.5	0.9	1.6	1.2	0.9	0.8	0.7	0.9	0.8	0.8	0.8
Net Sales to Working Capital 32	•	•	1.1	•	2.5	50.8	•	•	23.9	•	•	•
Coverage Ratio 33	15.7	38.7	19.6	174.3	48.5	38.9	38.6	26.0	32.8	42.8	13.1	•
Total Asset Turnover 34	0.4	1.0	0.7	0.3	0.5	0.5	0.5	0.4	0.5	0.6	0.4	•
Inventory Turnover 35	•	•	•	•	•	•	•	•	•	•	•	•
Receivables Turnover 36	•	•	•	•	•	•	•	•	•	•	•	•
Total Liabilities to Net Worth 37	1.7	•	3.5	0.7	1.1	2.1	2.3	1.7	1.7	1.8	1.7	•
Current Assets to Working Capital 38	•	•	•	2.3	3.3	68.8	•	•	25.7	•	•	•
Current Liabilities to Working Capital 39	•	•	•	1.3	2.3	67.8	•	•	24.7	•	•	•
Working Capital to Net Sales 40	•	•	•	0.9	0.4	0.0	•	•	0.0	•	•	•
Inventory to Working Capital 41	•	•	•	•	•	•	•	•	•	•	•	•
Total Receipts to Cash Flow 42	4.8	9.5	2.5	3.7	3.3	3.6	4.2	3.8	4.9	6.5	4.5	•
Cost of Goods to Cash Flow 43	2.8	7.1	1.0	1.8	1.6	2.0	2.3	1.8	2.7	4.2	2.5	•
Cash Flow to Total Debt 44	0.1	0.2	0.4	0.2	0.3	0.2	0.2	0.2	0.2	0.1	0.1	•

Selected Financial Factors (in Percentages)

Item	1	2	3	4	5	6	7	8	9	10	11	12
Debt Ratio 45	63.2	145.8	78.0	41.5	53.1	67.4	69.7	62.7	•	64.3	62.3	63.3
Return on Total Assets 46	4.0	•	5.3	3.1	5.1	3.7	3.6	3.9	•	5.5	4.8	3.9
Return on Equity Before Income Taxes 47	10.2	653.0	23.0	5.3	10.5	11.1	11.7	10.1	6.4	14.9	12.3	9.7
Return on Equity After Income Taxes 48	6.6	653.0	14.3	3.6	7.6	7.3	7.0	6.8	1.6	10.0	8.0	6.4
Profit Margin (Before Income Tax) 49	9.2	4.3	7.0	9.4	9.9	7.6	6.9	9.3	•	9.4	8.2	9.8
Profit Margin (After Income Tax) 50	6.0	3.0	4.3	6.4	7.1	5.0	4.2	6.2	•	6.3	5.3	6.4

Table II
Corporations with Net Income

MUTUAL PROPERTY AND CASUALTY COMPANIES (FORM 1120-PC)

MONEY AMOUNTS AND SIZE OF ASSETS IN THOUSANDS OF DOLLARS

Item Description for Accounting Period 7/05 Through 6/06	Total	Zero Assets	Under 500	500 to 1,000	1,000 to 5,000	5,000 to 10,000	10,000 to 25,000	25,000 to 50,000	50,000 to 100,000	100,000 to 250,000	250,000 to 500,000	500,000 to 2,500,000	2,500,000 and over
Number of Enterprises **1**	1199	21	50	50	437	137	159	87	58	•	50	63	•
Revenues ($ in Thousands)													
Net Sales **2**	210076215	966081	9023	33452	331606	456308	1243060	1651258	1831857	•	9764421	41464352	•
Interest **3**	12020148	10013	330	1158	28475	21012	58553	73128	107302	•	394919	1643660	•
Rents **4**	491649	0	0	0	1013	572	2036	1851	2203	•	14231	72564	•
Royalties **5**	604	0	0	0	0	0	0	0	0	•	0	508	•
Other Portfolio Income **6**	7015305	4951	63	0	7669	9655	24447	25875	44621	•	222114	1000891	•
Other Receipts **7**	190548509	951117	8630	32294	294449	425069	1158024	1550404	1677731	•	9133157	38746729	•
Total Receipts **8**	210076215	966081	9023	33452	331606	456308	1243060	1651258	1831857	•	9764421	41464352	•
Average Total Receipts **9**	175210	46004	180	669	759	3331	7818	18980	31584	•	195288	658164	•
Operating Costs/Operating Income (%)													
Cost of Operations **10**	57.4	74.7	53.0	35.3	37.1	44.0	50.9	52.3	45.8	•	55.4	61.9	•
Salaries and Wages **11**	12.5	7.4	4.2	15.8	16.6	10.6	10.4	14.0	16.7	•	16.5	13.7	•
Taxes Paid **12**	2.4	1.4	•	1.8	4.2	5.6	2.7	3.5	2.8	•	2.3	2.1	•
Interest Paid **13**	0.6	0.1	0.8	0.5	0.0	0.2	0.2	0.1	0.3	•	0.2	0.2	•
Depreciation **14**	0.9	0.6	•	0.5	0.5	0.4	0.4	0.5	0.8	•	0.7	0.8	•
Amortization and Depletion **15**	0.1	0.0	•	0.2	0.0	0.0	0.0	0.0	0.0	•	0.2	0.0	•
Pensions and Other Deferred Comp. **16**	0.4	2.7	•	•	0.1	0.3	0.2	0.2	0.4	•	0.7	0.5	•
Employee Benefits **17**	1.5	1.0	•	0.2	1.1	0.7	0.7	1.7	1.3	•	1.6	1.7	•
Advertising **18**	0.4	0.1	•	0.8	0.3	0.2	0.1	0.2	0.3	•	0.2	0.3	•
Other Expenses **19**	11.9	6.6	10.5	29.0	16.1	22.6	18.2	14.1	16.7	•	11.2	7.7	•
Officers' Compensation **20**	0.3	0.7	•	1.5	2.8	1.3	0.7	1.0	1.1	•	0.6	0.3	•
Operating Margin **21**	11.5	4.6	31.5	14.5	21.1	14.0	15.3	12.3	13.7	•	10.5	10.8	•
Operating Margin Before Officers' Comp. **22**	11.7	5.3	31.5	16.0	23.9	15.3	16.0	13.3	14.8	•	11.1	11.1	•

Selected Average Balance Sheet ($ in Thousands)

Item											
Net Receivables 23	36466	0	0	40	53	318	1162	3023	4322	34099	116793
Inventories 24	•	•	•	•	•	•	•	•	•	•	•
Net Property, Plant and Equipment 25	6478	0	0	10	61	83	145	324	959	7485	19417
Total Assets 26	42203	0	149	863	2476	6742	16243	35931	69449	331121	1210201
Notes and Loans Payable 27	11990	0	50	40	4	34	54	95	398	2034	6315
All Other Liabilities 28	255594	0	132	631	827	3259	9570	23106	43403	208347	743701
Net Worth 29	160619	0	-33	192	1645	3450	6618	12729	25647	120740	460186

Selected Financial Ratios (Times to 1)

Item											
Current Ratio 30	0.9	•	0.5	0.9	1.5	1.1	0.9	0.9	1.1	1.1	0.9
Quick Ratio 31	0.8	•	0.5	0.8	1.3	1.0	0.8	0.8	0.7	1.0	0.8
Net Sales to Working Capital 32	•	•	•	•	2.2	7.6	•	•	•	16.3	•
Coverage Ratio 33	17.0	41.3	40.5	31.2	581.4	54.5	62.4	107.8	45.7	44.2	41.7
Total Asset Turnover 34	0.4	1.2	0.8	0.3	0.5	•	0.5	0.5	0.5	0.6	0.5
Inventory Turnover 35	•	•	•	•	•	•	•	•	•	•	•
Receivables Turnover 36	•	•	•	•	•	•	•	•	•	•	•
Total Liabilities to Net Worth 37	1.7	•	•	3.5	0.5	1.0	1.5	1.8	1.7	1.7	1.6
Current Assets to Working Capital 38	•	•	•	•	1.9	2.9	9.8	•	•	16.9	•
Current Liabilities to Working Capital 39	•	•	•	•	0.9	1.9	8.8	•	•	15.9	•
Working Capital to Net Sales 40	•	•	•	1.1	0.5	0.1	•	•	•	0.1	•
Inventory to Working Capital 41	•	•	•	•	•	•	•	•	•	•	•
Total Receipts to Cash Flow 42	4.7	9.5	2.4	2.3	2.8	3.1	2.8	4.0	3.5	5.0	6.0
Cost of Goods to Cash Flow 43	2.7	7.1	1.3	0.8	1.0	1.6	1.2	2.1	1.6	2.7	3.7
Cash Flow to Total Debt 44	0.1	•	0.4	0.4	0.3	0.3	0.4	0.2	0.2	0.2	0.1

Selected Financial Factors (in Percentages)

Item											
Debt Ratio 45	62.5	•	122.3	77.8	33.6	48.8	59.3	64.6	63.1	63.5	62.0
Return on Total Assets 46	4.4	•	39.1	11.6	6.2	6.6	7.2	6.3	6.1	5.8	5.4
Return on Equity Before Income Taxes 47	11.1	•	•	50.7	9.4	12.8	17.3	17.5	16.2	15.5	13.9
Return on Equity After Income Taxes 48	7.4	•	38.9	7.5	9.6	13.3	12.4	11.8	10.4	9.3	
Profit Margin (Before Income Tax) 49	10.2	4.6	31.5	14.5	20.3	13.2	14.7	11.7	13.1	9.6	9.7
Profit Margin (After Income Tax) 50	6.8	3.2	31.5	11.1	16.3	9.9	11.3	8.3	9.6	6.4	6.5

Table I

Corporations with and without Net Income

STOCK PROPERTY AND CASUALTY COMPANIES (FORM 1120-PC)

MONEY AMOUNTS AND SIZE OF ASSETS IN THOUSANDS OF DOLLARS

Item Description for Accounting Period 7/05 Through 6/06	Total	Zero Assets	Under 500	500 to 1,000	1,000 to 5,000	5,000 to 10,000	10,000 to 25,000	25,000 to 50,000	50,000 to 100,000	100,000 to 250,000	250,000 to 500,000	500,000 to 2,500,000	2,500,000 and over
Number of Enterprises **1**	4402	195	1475	465	1008	359	275	129	134	130	56	93	82
Revenues ($ in Thousands)													
Net Sales **2**	628287624	16096665	54439	35778	655811	1166550	4068834	2619229	8541463	16717734	8657099	64769563	504901459
Interest **3**	30211264	111285	8518	8101	56008	59378	96425	98461	206269	458293	2276807	26405660	
Rents **4**	833893	1725	0	0	1555	294	576	3891	5372	14274	7211	66892	732102
Royalties **5**	566738	0	0	0	0	0	3	3238	0	2251	1405	8662	551179
Other Portfolio Income **6**	15937235	44752	2801	3733	17943	18252	23124	35401	81453	176882	179077	856016	14497798
Other Receipts **7**	580738494	15938903	43120	23944	583305	1088626	3948706	2478238	8248369	16066034	8043347	61561186	462714720
Total Receipts **8**	628287624	16096665	54439	35778	655811	1166550	4068834	2619229	8541463	16717734	8657099	64769563	504901459
Average Total Receipts **9**	142728	82547	37	77	654	3249	14796	20304	63742	128598	154591	696447	6157335
Operating Costs/Operating Income (%)													
Cost of Operations **10**	58.5	81.9	56.6	55.2	61.0	51.1	57.1	50.4	63.0	60.1	51.3	60.3	57.6
Salaries and Wages **11**	12.7	5.5	16.3	4.9	30.0	22.0	10.1	16.7	10.1	12.8	16.5	15.1	12.6
Taxes Paid **12**	2.1	0.9	1.0	1.5	1.1	1.5	1.4	3.1	2.2	1.8	2.9	2.2	2.1
Interest Paid **13**	1.3	0.6	0.0	0.1	0.2	0.4	0.1	0.3	0.4	0.7	0.7	0.7	1.5
Depreciation **14**	0.7	0.3	*	0.0	0.1	0.5	0.2	0.5	0.6	0.5	0.6	1.0	0.7
Amortization and Depletion **15**	0.3	0.1	0.1	0.0	0.1	0.1	0.0	0.1	0.1	0.2	0.2	0.2	0.3
Pensions and Other Deferred Comp. **16**	0.4	0.2	*	*	0.0	0.1	0.1	0.1	0.1	0.2	0.5	0.4	0.5
Employee Benefits **17**	1.4	0.3	0.8	*	0.2	0.4	0.3	0.6	1.6	0.9	1.4	1.1	1.5
Advertising **18**	0.4	0.4	*	*	0.1	0.4	0.2	0.6	0.4	0.3	0.8	0.5	0.4
Other Expenses **19**	14.8	6.8	22.2	69.9	11.5	18.7	27.1	19.3	14.7	14.7	14.0	13.4	15.1
Officers' Compensation **20**	0.4	1.9	*	*	0.3	0.8	0.6	1.0	0.6	0.5	0.5	0.5	0.3
Operating Margin **21**	6.9	1.2	2.9	*	*	4.1	2.7	7.1	6.3	7.5	10.4	4.6	7.4
Operating Margin Before Officers' Comp. **22**	7.3	3.1	2.9	*	*	4.9	3.3	8.1	6.9	7.9	10.9	5.1	7.7

Selected Average Balance Sheet ($ in Thousands)

Net Receivables 23	22713	0	2	5	115	338	1318	3195	6768	14918	31628	95973	1041713
Inventories 24	•	•	•	•	•	•	•	•	•	•	•	•	•
Net Property, Plant and Equipment 25	3646	0	0	14	93	411	897	3158	•	4718	22513	•	158966
Total Assets 26	366502	204	745	2401	7043	16041	34943	70151	161523	344573	1124088	•	17616985
Notes and Loans Payable 27	26210	0	5	3	17	134	228	745	2441	7084	13695	70858	1299283
All Other Liabilities 28	194026	253	552	1776	4939	12239	22700	47419	103755	227718	659933	•	9142040
Net Worth 29	146266	-54	190	607	1971	3574	11499	20290	50683	103160	393297	•	7175662

Selected Financial Ratios (Times to 1)

Current Ratio 30	0.8	•	0.6	0.8	0.9	0.9	0.9	1.0	1.0	0.9	0.9	0.8	0.8
Quick Ratio 31	0.7	•	0.5	0.6	0.7	0.7	0.8	0.9	0.8	0.7	0.7
Net Sales to Working Capital 32	•	•	266.5	•	•	•	11905.6	65.6	•	•	•
Coverage Ratio 33	5.7	2.9	•	•	11.0	19.8	20.3	16.3	11.9	14.8	6.9	5.5
Total Asset Turnover 34	0.4	•	0.2	0.1	0.3	0.5	0.9	0.6	0.9	0.8	0.4	0.6	0.3
Inventory Turnover 35	•	•	•	•	•	•	•	•	•	•	•
Receivables Turnover 36	•	•	•	•	•	•	•	•	•	•	•
Total Liabilities to Net Worth 37	1.5	•	2.9	•	3.0	2.6	3.5	2.0	2.5	2.2	2.3	1.9	1.5
Current Assets to Working Capital 38	•	•	•	•	•	•	12330.2	45.4	•	•	•
Current Liabilities to Working Capital 39	•	•	•	•	•	•	12329.2	44.4	•	•	•
Working Capital to Net Sales 40	•	•	•	•	•	•	0.0	0.0	•	•	•
Inventory to Working Capital 41	•	•	•	•	•	•	0.1	0.1	•	•	•
Total Receipts to Cash Flow 42	5.1	13.5	3.0	18.2	4.7	3.4	4.0	5.0	4.8	5.0	4.5	6.1	5.0
Cost of Goods to Cash Flow 43	3.0	11.0	1.7	11.1	2.4	2.0	2.0	3.2	2.9	2.9	2.3	3.7	2.9
Cash Flow to Total Debt 44	0.1	•	0.0	0.0	0.1	0.3	0.2	0.3	0.2	0.2	0.1	0.2	0.1

Selected Financial Factors (in Percentages)

Debt Ratio 45	60.1	•	126.3	74.5	74.7	72.0	77.7	67.1	71.1	68.6	70.1	65.0	59.3
Return on Total Assets 46	3.0	•	0.5	•	•	1.8	2.4	4.1	5.8	6.2	4.7	2.9	2.9
Return on Equity Before Income Taxes 47	6.2	•	•	•	•	5.9	10.3	11.7	18.7	18.1	14.7	7.2	5.8
Return on Equity After Income Taxes 48	4.0	•	•	•	1.1	2.7	6.3	12.4	12.3	9.3	4.0	3.9
Profit Margin (Before Income Tax) 49	6.3	1.1	2.9	•	3.6	2.5	6.6	6.0	7.1	9.8	4.1	6.8
Profit Margin (After Income Tax) 50	4.1	0.7	0.2	0.7	0.7	3.6	3.6	3.9	4.9	6.2	2.3	4.5

Table II
Corporations with Net Income

STOCK PROPERTY AND CASUALTY COMPANIES (FORM 1120-PC)

MONEY AMOUNTS AND SIZE OF ASSETS IN THOUSANDS OF DOLLARS

Item Description for Accounting Period 7/05 Through 6/06	Total	Zero Assets	Under 500	500 to 1,000	1,000 to 5,000	5,000 to 10,000	10,000 to 25,000	25,000 to 50,000	50,000 to 100,000	100,000 to 250,000	250,000 to 500,000	500,000 to 2,500,000	2,500,000 and over
Number of Enterprises **1**	3682	149	1309	399	868	256	211	96	110	105	42	69	67
Revenues ($ in Thousands)													
Net Sales **2**	565125870	16094265	31083	14563	341031	767066	3282282	2085775	7094856	14339787	7025374	55265588	45784199
Interest **3**	26145721	110921	7937	7670	49078	44387	78348	79017	174314	379520	327504	1694959	23192067
Rents **4**	764961	1718	0	0	1238	294	567	3169	3761	11647	6760	45223	690585
Royalties **5**	563500	0	0	0	0	0	3	0	0	2251	1405	8662	551179
Other Portfolio Income **6**	14608618	44580	2698	3732	17493	17185	19216	26459	66587	165568	166946	718206	13359950
Other Receipts **7**	523043070	15937046	20448	3161	273222	705200	3184148	1977130	6850194	13780801	6522759	52798538	42090418
Total Receipts **8**	565125870	16094265	31083	14563	341031	767066	3282282	2085775	7094856	14339787	7025374	55265588	45784199
Average Total Receipts **9**	153483	108015	24	36	393	2996	15556	21727	64499	136569	167271	800951	6847525
Operating Costs/Operating Income (%)													
Cost of Operations **10**	57.1	81.9	28.5	12.7	43.3	49.3	51.6	45.8	61.9	57.7	45.7	58.9	56.2
Salaries and Wages **11**	12.6	5.4	12.2	7.9	10.0	14.2	10.0	19.2	10.5	12.8	17.6	14.9	12.6
Taxes Paid **12**	2.0	0.9	0.7	0.6	1.3	1.6	1.4	3.2	2.2	1.8	2.8	2.2	2.0
Interest Paid **13**	1.2	0.6	0.0	0.2	0.2	0.3	0.1	0.4	0.3	0.3	0.7	0.6	1.3
Depreciation **14**	0.7	0.3	*	*	0.1	0.1	0.2	0.5	0.6	0.5	0.6	0.9	0.7
Amortization and Depletion **15**	0.3	0.1	0.2	*	0.2	0.1	0.0	0.1	0.1	0.2	0.2	0.2	0.3
Pensions and Other Deferred Comp. **16**	0.4	0.2	*	*	0.1	0.0	0.1	0.2	0.1	0.2	0.4	0.4	0.3
Employee Benefits **17**	1.4	0.3	*	*	0.1	0.3	0.3	0.6	1.0	1.0	1.5	1.0	1.6
Advertising **18**	0.5	0.4	*	*	0.1	0.1	0.2	0.8	0.4	0.3	1.0	0.5	0.5
Other Expenses **19**	14.8	6.8	9.2	5.1	12.4	15.6	27.4	15.0	13.5	14.8	13.9	12.9	15.3
Officers' Compensation **20**	0.4	1.9	*	*	*	0.8	0.5	1.1	0.5	0.5	0.6	0.5	0.3
Operating Margin **21**	8.6	1.3	49.2	73.5	32.3	17.6	8.3	13.2	9.0	9.8	14.9	6.9	8.8
Operating Margin Before Officers' Comp. **22**	9.0	3.1	49.2	73.5	32.3	18.4	8.8	14.3	9.6	10.3	15.5	7.3	9.2

Selected Average Balance Sheet ($ in Thousands)

	1	2	3	4	5	6	7	8	9	10	11	12	13
Net Receivables 23	21217	0	2	6	101	272	1290	3350	6588	14135	35629	101551	994831
Inventories 24	·	·	·	·	·	·	·	·	·	·	·	·	·
Net Property, Plant and Equipment 25	3990	0	0	0	4	87	66	429	740	3628	5877	20766	186078
Total Assets 26	367894	0	219	748	2307	7143	15992	35186	70184	165856	351253	1125996	18296061
Notes and Loans Payable 27	24356	0	1	3	4	86	164	888	2212	7233	13106	52312	1259201
All Other Liabilities 28	190175	0	174	539	1376	4645	10044	20997	45597	106536	208939	614924	9341154
Net Worth 29	153363	0	44	206	927	2412	5784	13302	22375	52087	129208	458760	7695706

Selected Financial Ratios (Times to 1)

	1	2	3	4	5	6	7	8	9	10	11	12	13
Current Ratio 30	0.8	·	1.0	0.7	1.0	1.1	1.1	1.0	1.0	·	·	0.9	0.8
Quick Ratio 31	0.7	·	0.8	0.6	0.9	0.9	0.9	0.9	0.8	·	·	0.8	0.7
Net Sales to Working Capital 32	·	·	·	29.8	12.1	20.9	8.9	·	·	·	·	·	·
Coverage Ratio 33	7.7	3.0	2551.3	354.7	153.7	66.0	71.9	33.5	33.5	28.7	21.4	12.3	7.0
Total Asset Turnover 34	0.4	·	0.1	0.0	0.2	0.4	1.0	0.6	0.9	0.8	0.5	0.7	0.4
Inventory Turnover 35	·	·	·	·	·	·	·	·	·	·	·	·	·
Receivables Turnover 36	·	·	·	·	·	·	·	·	·	·	·	·	·
Total Liabilities to Net Worth 37	1.4	·	4.0	2.6	1.5	2.0	1.8	1.6	2.1	2.2	1.7	1.5	1.4
Current Assets to Working Capital 38	·	·	·	41.7	19.2	8.8	14.3	·	·	·	·	·	·
Current Liabilities to Working Capital 39	·	·	·	40.7	18.2	7.8	13.3	·	·	·	·	·	·
Working Capital to Net Sales 40	·	·	·	0.1	0.0	0.1	0.0	·	·	·	·	·	·
Inventory to Working Capital 41	·	·	·	·	0.0	0.0	·	·	·	·	·	·	·
Total Receipts to Cash Flow 42	4.7	13.4	1.9	1.5	2.4	2.9	3.7	2.9	4.7	4.3	3.8	5.5	4.6
Cost of Goods to Cash Flow 43	2.7	11.0	0.5	0.2	1.0	1.6	1.7	1.5	2.9	2.5	1.7	3.2	2.6
Cash Flow to Total Debt 44	0.2	0.1	0.0	0.1	0.2	0.5	0.3	0.3	0.3	0.2	0.2	0.2	0.1

Selected Financial Factors (in Percentages)

	1	2	3	4	5	6	7	8	9	10	11	12	13
Debt Ratio 45	58.3	·	80.0	72.4	59.8	66.2	63.8	62.2	68.1	68.6	63.2	59.3	57.9
Return on Total Assets 46	3.8	·	5.3	3.6	5.5	7.2	7.9	8.1	8.2	8.1	7.1	4.9	3.6
Return on Equity Before Income Taxes 47	7.9	·	26.6	12.9	13.6	21.0	21.6	20.8	25.0	24.8	18.5	11.0	7.3
Return on Equity After Income Taxes 48	5.5	·	24.1	11.1	10.5	15.5	15.5	14.6	18.0	17.9	12.8	7.4	5.0
Profit Margin (Before Income Tax) 49	7.9	1.1	49.2	72.9	32.1	16.9	8.0	12.8	8.7	9.5	14.3	6.3	8.1
Profit Margin (After Income Tax) 50	5.5	0.8	44.5	62.7	24.8	12.5	5.7	8.9	6.3	6.8	9.9	4.2	5.7

Table I

Corporations with and without Net Income

INSURANCE AGENCIES AND BROKERAGES

MONEY AMOUNTS AND SIZE OF ASSETS IN THOUSANDS OF DOLLARS

Item Description for Accounting Period 7/05 Through 6/06	Total	Zero Assets	Under 500	500 to 1,000	1,000 to 5,000	5,000 to 10,000	10,000 to 25,000	25,000 to 50,000	50,000 to 100,000	100,000 to 250,000	250,000 to 500,000	500,000 to 2,500,000	2,500,000 and over
Number of Enterprises 1	86716	10977	65020	5762	3892	646	249	91	37	21	3	12	6
Revenues ($ in Thousands)													
Net Sales 2	92919436	2079321	23006718	11338807	12876450	5550809	4562979	2857408	2426276	2915225	481370	5708932	19115141
Interest 3	1053634	5144	13547	17746	28731	23974	25082	15100	23493	61388	3169	65748	770513
Rents 4	57062	0	6833	3907	6185	11051	4688	302	1244	8745	0	1014	13093
Royalties 5	14219	0	0	0	0	34	0	210	0	0	0	2047	11928
Other Portfolio Income 6	3091679	105957	60192	21664	35619	5515	38285	29752	9199	13072	3378	438187	2330856
Other Receipts 7	88702842	1968220	22926146	11295490	12805915	5510235	4494924	2812044	2392340	2832020	474823	5201936	15988751
Total Receipts 8	92919436	2079321	23006718	11338807	12876450	5550809	4562979	2857408	2426276	2915225	481370	5708932	19115141
Average Total Receipts 9	1072	189	354	1968	3308	8593	18325	31400	65575	138820	160457	475744	3185857
Operating Costs/Operating Income (%)													
Cost of Operations 10	14.7	4.5	14.7	40.4	7.6	12.1	27.0	23.3	22.3	3.0	20.1	0.1	6.8
Salaries and Wages 11	26.8	29.4	21.3	17.7	33.3	32.1	25.9	28.1	27.4	33.5	32.5	30.1	30.2
Taxes Paid 12	2.8	2.8	2.8	2.1	2.9	3.0	2.3	2.8	2.3	2.3	2.9	3.2	3.1
Interest Paid 13	1.9	2.1	0.5	0.7	0.7	1.3	0.6	1.2	0.7	1.3	1.8	3.3	5.5
Depreciation 14	0.9	1.7	0.8	0.6	1.0	1.0	0.8	1.4	0.9	0.8	1.5	0.9	0.8
Amortization and Depletion 15	1.0	0.7	0.4	0.6	0.7	0.6	0.3	0.6	0.8	0.4	0.4	4.4	1.5
Pensions and Other Deferred Comp. 16	1.5	0.4	1.6	0.8	1.1	1.6	1.0	1.1	1.1	0.4	2.3	0.5	3.0
Employee Benefits 17	1.8	1.9	1.2	1.8	1.8	1.7	1.7	2.1	1.9	1.8	3.4	2.9	2.3
Advertising 18	1.1	3.0	1.6	0.8	1.3	0.9	0.9	0.5	1.0	1.4	0.6	1.4	0.4
Other Expenses 19	26.4	37.9	24.8	15.4	25.6	24.2	24.6	23.3	28.6	44.4	24.1	34.9	30.0
Officers' Compensation 20	9.4	4.9	14.8	10.4	12.8	12.7	6.7	7.8	5.2	2.2	6.0	4.0	3.8
Operating Margin 21	11.8	10.8	15.3	8.7	11.2	8.8	8.2	7.9	7.8	8.8	4.5	14.4	12.5
Operating Margin Before Officers' Comp. 22	21.2	15.7	30.1	19.1	24.1	21.4	14.9	15.7	13.0	10.9	10.5	18.4	16.3

Selected Average Balance Sheet ($ in Thousands)

Net Receivables 23	335	•	7	89	491	1765	4093	9777	17449	37491	100806	153386	3263303
Inventories 24	•	•	•	•	•	•	•	•	•	•	•	•	•
Net Property, Plant and Equipment 25	51	0	12	59	181	597	647	2224	3540	6805	7979	29671	199553
Total Assets 26	1495	76	719	2241	7049	15941	35477	70955	148940	392986	1028092		13467714
Notes and Loans Payable 27	224	0	26	224	505	2166	2483	5841	9426	23333	197249	295416	1169884
All Other Liabilities 28	760	0	26	275	1143	4665	9080	21675	45965	88437	176855	337202	7129478
Net Worth 29	511	0	25	221	594	217	4379	7961	15565	37169	18881	395474	5168352

Selected Financial Ratios (Times to 1)

Current Ratio 30	1.0	•	1.4	1.2	1.2	1.1	1.1	1.1	0.9	1.0	0.8	1.0	1.0
Quick Ratio 31	0.9	•	1.3	1.1	1.1	0.9	1.0	0.9	0.8	0.8	0.4	0.8	0.9
Net Sales to Working Capital 32	36.8	•	33.6	28.3	11.2	20.7	15.0	14.3	11.5	•	•	•	•
Coverage Ratio 33	7.4	6.1	29.8	13.2	17.4	7.6	13.9	7.8	11.5	7.7	3.5	5.3	3.8
Total Asset Turnover 34	0.7	•	4.6	2.7	1.5	1.2	1.1	0.9	0.9	0.9	0.4	0.5	0.2
Inventory Turnover 35	•	•	•	•	•	•	•	•	•	•	•	•	•
Receivables Turnover 36	•	•	•	•	•	•	•	•	•	•	•	•	•
Total Liabilities to Net Worth 37	1.9	•	2.0	2.3	2.8	31.4	2.6	3.5	3.6	3.0	19.8	1.6	1.6
Current Assets to Working Capital 38	21.4	•	3.7	5.0	5.1	12.7	8.9	11.1	11.1	•	•	•	•
Current Liabilities to Working Capital 39	20.4	•	2.7	4.0	4.1	11.7	7.9	10.1	10.1	•	•	•	•
Working Capital to Net Sales 40	0.0	•	0.0	0.0	0.1	0.0	0.1	0.1	0.1	•	•	•	•
Inventory to Working Capital 41	0.0	•	•	•	•	0.1	0.0	0.0	0.0	•	•	•	•
Total Receipts to Cash Flow 42	3.0	2.5	2.8	4.9	3.1	3.5	3.4	3.7	3.0	3.0	4.3	2.6	2.8
Cost of Goods to Cash Flow 43	0.4	0.1	0.4	2.0	0.2	0.4	0.9	0.9	0.7	0.9	0.9	0.0	0.2
Cash Flow to Total Debt 44	0.4	•	2.4	0.8	0.6	0.4	0.5	0.3	0.4	0.6	0.1	0.3	0.1

Selected Financial Factors (in Percentages)

Debt Ratio 45	65.8	•	67.2	69.3	73.5	96.9	72.5	77.6	78.1	75.0	95.2	61.5	61.6
Return on Total Assets 46	10.2	•	73.3	25.8	17.6	12.3	10.1	8.0	7.8	9.3	2.6	8.2	5.0
Return on Equity Before Income Taxes 47	26.0	•	215.9	77.6	62.6	346.0	34.1	31.0	32.3	32.5	38.5	17.2	9.6
Return on Equity After Income Taxes 48	22.6	•	213.7	75.2	60.3	311.1	29.0	24.2	25.7	27.1	38.5	10.5	7.0
Profit Margin (Before Income Tax) 49	12.4	10.8	15.3	8.7	11.2	8.7	8.2	7.9	7.7	8.7	4.5	14.3	15.5
Profit Margin (After Income Tax) 50	10.8	10.3	15.1	8.4	10.8	7.9	6.9	6.1	6.1	7.3	4.5	8.7	11.4

Table II

Corporations with Net Income

INSURANCE AGENCIES AND BROKERAGES

MONEY AMOUNTS AND SIZE OF ASSETS IN THOUSANDS OF DOLLARS

Item Description for Accounting Period 7/05 Through 6/06	Total	Zero Assets	Under 500	500 to 1,000	1,000 to 5,000	5,000 to 10,000	10,000 to 25,000	25,000 to 50,000	50,000 to 100,000	100,000 to 250,000	250,000 to 500,000	500,000 to 2,500,000	2,500,000 and over
Number of Enterprises **1**	69852	7134	53426	4980	3474	484	212	76	33	•	0	0	8
Revenues ($ in Thousands)													
Net Sales **2**	82121966	1811961	20599575	8229448	11666926	4624795	3918402	2654148	2340004	•	0	0	4696605
Interest **3**	1020473	3899	11196	12537	26723	22663	22746	12302	23049	•	0	0	58708
Rents **4**	45629	0	6126	3907	2217	9526	4678	302	1244	•	0	0	954
Royalties **5**	12172	0	0	0	0	34	0	210	0	•	0	0	0
Other Portfolio Income **6**	3075387	102954	59051	19976	35619	4933	37739	29000	5575	•	0	0	438180
Other Receipts **7**	77968305	1705108	20523202	8193028	11602367	4587639	3853239	2612334	2310136	•	0	0	419763
Total Receipts **8**	82121966	1811961	20599575	8229448	11666926	4624795	3918402	2654148	2340004	•	0	0	4696605
Average Total Receipts **9**	1176	254	386	1652	3358	9555	18483	34923	70909	•	•	•	587076
Operating Costs/Operating Income (%)													
Cost of Operations **10**	12.9	4.9	13.8	25.6	8.4	14.6	31.4	24.7	22.7	•	•	•	0.1
Salaries and Wages **11**	26.7	24.6	21.8	22.2	29.3	30.1	23.4	27.0	26.6	•	•	•	27.1
Taxes Paid **12**	2.8	2.3	2.8	2.5	2.9	2.8	2.3	2.6	2.1	•	•	•	3.2
Interest Paid **13**	2.0	1.0	0.5	0.9	0.5	1.5	0.5	0.9	0.6	•	•	•	2.9
Depreciation **14**	0.8	1.7	0.7	0.7	0.8	0.8	0.7	1.2	0.9	•	•	•	0.9
Amortization and Depletion **15**	0.9	0.1	0.4	0.8	0.5	0.4	0.3	0.5	0.4	•	•	•	4.0
Pensions and Other Deferred Comp. **16**	1.6	0.5	1.4	1.0	1.2	1.7	1.0	1.1	1.1	•	•	•	0.5
Employee Benefits **17**	1.9	2.2	1.0	2.4	1.8	1.4	1.7	2.0	1.9	•	•	•	3.0
Advertising **18**	1.0	3.3	1.6	0.9	1.2	0.8	0.6	0.5	0.6	•	•	•	0.5
Other Expenses **19**	25.6	36.2	23.9	17.6	25.7	21.7	19.8	20.6	28.7	•	•	•	33.9
Officers' Compensation **20**	9.5	4.4	14.2	13.1	13.9	11.4	7.1	7.9	5.3	•	•	•	3.4
Operating Margin **21**	14.4	18.8	17.8	12.4	13.7	12.8	11.2	11.0	9.0	•	•	•	20.5
Operating Margin Before Officers' Comp. **22**	23.9	23.2	32.0	25.5	27.5	24.1	18.2	18.9	14.4	•	•	•	23.9

Selected Average Balance Sheet ($ in Thousands)

Net Receivables 23	395	0	6	93	519	1462	4066	10823	19047	183119
Inventories 24	•	•	•	•	•	•	•	•	•	•
Net Property, Plant and Equipment 25	52	0	12	63	134	488	591	2445	3841	26118
Total Assets 26	1708	0	80	732	2147	7313	15487	35346	69588	976205
Notes and Loans Payable 27	216	0	24	224	342	2215	2025	5629	8853	189635
All Other Liabilities 28	888	0	28	278	1099	4496	9202	24124	49280	372241
Net Worth 29	603	0	28	230	706	601	4259	5594	11454	414328

Selected Financial Ratios (Times to 1)

Current Ratio 30	1.0	•	1.3	1.2	1.3	1.2	1.1	1.1	0.9	1.0
Quick Ratio 31	0.9	•	1.3	1.1	1.2	0.9	1.0	0.9	0.8	0.7
Net Sales to Working Capital 32	35.0	•	37.5	26.1	9.1	12.4	13.6	26.1	•	•
Coverage Ratio 33	8.7	19.0	37.4	15.4	26.4	9.3	21.5	13.4	14.8	8.2
Total Asset Turnover 34	0.7	•	4.8	2.3	1.6	1.3	1.2	1.0	1.0	0.6
Inventory Turnover 35	•	•	•	•	•	•	•	•	•	•
Receivables Turnover 36	•	•	•	•	•	•	•	•	•	•
Total Liabilities to Net Worth 37	1.8	•	1.9	2.2	2.0	11.2	2.6	5.3	5.1	1.4
Current Assets to Working Capital 38	21.3	•	4.0	5.3	4.1	7.2	8.2	19.5	•	•
Current Liabilities to Working Capital 39	20.3	•	3.0	4.3	3.1	6.2	7.2	18.5	•	•
Working Capital to Net Sales 40	0.0	•	0.0	0.0	0.1	0.1	0.1	0.0	0.0	•
Inventory to Working Capital 41	0.0	•	•	•	0.1	0.0	0.0	0.0	•	•
Total Receipts to Cash Flow 42	2.9	2.2	2.7	3.9	2.8	3.2	3.6	3.6	2.8	2.3
Cost of Goods to Cash Flow 43	0.4	0.1	0.4	1.0	0.2	0.5	1.1	0.9	0.6	0.0
Cash Flow to Total Debt 44	0.4	•	2.7	0.8	0.8	0.4	0.5	0.3	0.4	0.4

Selected Financial Factors (in Percentages)

Debt Ratio 45	64.7	•	65.3	68.6	67.1	91.8	72.5	84.2	83.5	57.6
Return on Total Assets 46	11.7	•	88.1	30.0	22.2	18.7	13.9	11.7	9.8	14.0
Return on Equity Before Income Taxes 47	29.4	•	247.3	89.4	64.9	202.5	48.2	68.5	55.4	29.0
Return on Equity After Income Taxes 48	25.9	•	244.9	86.8	62.7	185.7	41.9	56.9	48.9	19.4
Profit Margin (Before Income Tax) 49	15.1	18.8	17.8	12.4	13.6	12.7	11.1	11.0	8.9	20.5
Profit Margin (After Income Tax) 50	13.3	18.2	17.6	12.1	13.2	11.7	9.7	9.1	7.9	13.7

Table I

Corporations with and without Net Income

OTHER INSURANCE RELATED ACTIVITIES

MONEY AMOUNTS AND SIZE OF ASSETS IN THOUSANDS OF DOLLARS

Item Description for Accounting Period 7/05 Through 6/06	Total	Zero Assets	Under 500	500 to 1,000	1,000 to 5,000	5,000 to 10,000	10,000 to 25,000	25,000 to 50,000	50,000 to 100,000	100,000 to 250,000	250,000 to 500,000	500,000 to 2,500,000	2,500,000 and over
Number of Enterprises **1**	13361	1950	9814	504	650	209	112	43	30	22	14	11	3
Revenues ($ in Thousands)													
Net Sales **2**	38637392	521040	3213016	1054404	2192881	2991625	2698316	2408981	1819622	3232564	5106789	5152537	8245618
Interest **3**	1137825	3646	2858	3403	7769	6967	14236	18883	17920	16106	82800	218080	745157
Rents **4**	97295	0	0	4355	6581	381	1641	129	1115	10179	871	1276	70766
Royalties **5**	25481	0	0	0	0	0	0	0	3094	10678	0	11709	0
Other Portfolio Income **6**	326974	27789	3296	343	2192	16840	6896	12727	8781	96717	23647	60492	67254
Other Receipts **7**	37049817	489605	3206862	1046303	2176339	2967437	2675543	2377242	1788712	3098884	4999471	4860980	7362441
Total Receipts **8**	38637392	521040	3213016	1054404	2192881	2991625	2698316	2408981	1819622	3232564	5106789	5152537	8245618
Average Total Receipts **9**	2892	267	327	2092	3374	14314	24092	56023	60654	146935	364771	468412	2748539
Operating Costs/Operating Income (%)													
Cost of Operations **10**	18.9	20.6	4.2	0.7	1.8	4.8	14.3	20.4	14.5	22.6	40.1	43.9	8.3
Salaries and Wages **11**	19.3	36.4	43.5	14.3	27.5	14.3	24.1	24.8	29.3	21.8	12.5	12.7	11.0
Taxes Paid **12**	2.6	2.0	2.8	1.9	3.3	2.1	2.1	2.1	3.2	2.1	1.9	1.4	4.1
Interest Paid **13**	1.7	0.8	0.4	0.0	0.6	0.7	0.6	0.2	2.4	1.4	1.6	4.1	2.4
Depreciation **14**	0.9	1.8	0.6	0.9	1.1	1.4	0.5	0.3	1.6	0.9	0.8	1.0	1.1
Amortization and Depletion **15**	0.8	1.5	0.0	*	0.7	0.2	0.2	0.2	1.8	1.4	0.4	1.6	1.1
Pensions and Other Deferred Comp. **16**	1.1	1.3	0.8	0.4	2.4	0.3	0.7	0.3	0.9	2.0	0.3	0.3	2.5
Employee Benefits **17**	2.4	1.5	1.7	1.5	2.8	1.1	6.7	10.1	2.5	2.1	1.2	1.7	1.0
Advertising **18**	0.8	1.0	0.5	0.8	0.9	0.3	0.6	0.2	0.7	0.3	1.6	0.5	1.0
Other Expenses **19**	39.4	40.7	30.5	62.1	44.2	69.7	42.8	31.9	38.0	39.1	32.4	19.3	46.0
Officers' Compensation **20**	3.4	6.5	12.9	5.6	13.1	2.3	3.0	4.9	2.3	1.4	0.9	1.4	0.4
Operating Margin **21**	8.7	*	1.9	11.8	1.5	2.8	4.5	4.5	2.8	4.8	6.3	12.0	21.1
Operating Margin Before Officers' Comp. **22**	12.0	*	14.9	17.4	14.6	5.0	7.5	9.4	5.1	6.3	7.2	13.4	21.5

Selected Average Balance Sheet ($ in Thousands)

Net Receivables 23	474	0	5	215	426	2127	3063	5133	10244	13361	47360	236084	344341
Inventories 24	•	•	•	•	•	•	•	•	•	•	•	•	•
Net Property, Plant and Equipment 25	154	0	12	96	439	679	743	1061	5393	8727	8773	25143	195499
Total Assets 26	5814	58	703	2319	6246	15518	32654	73980	159793	328006	927972		16757368
Notes and Loans Payable 27	734	36	1	615	1310	2505	2488	16802	29556	68188	227484		1260244
All Other Liabilities 28	2389	13	361	1367	3554	9312	24148	33365	76951	176547	273999		6572223
Net Worth 29	2692	10	340	1382	3702	6018	23813	53286	83270	426489			8924901

Selected Financial Ratios (Times to 1)

Current Ratio 30	1.1	2.0	1.5	1.4	1.3	1.4	1.2	1.2	1.2	1.4	1.2	1.4	0.9
Quick Ratio 31	0.9	1.7	1.2	1.1	1.3	1.2	0.8	1.0	0.9	0.8	1.1		0.7
Net Sales to Working Capital 32	15.2	16.3	11.4	8.2	11.6	8.7	15.1	11.6	7.5	16.8	4.7		•
Coverage Ratio 33	6.1	5.4	905.7	3.6	4.8	7.8	20.6	2.1	4.4	5.2	3.9		9.9
Total Asset Turnover 34	0.5	5.6	3.0	1.5	2.3	1.6	1.7	0.8	0.9	1.1	0.5		0.2
Inventory Turnover 35	•	•	•	•	•	•	•	•	•	•	•		•
Receivables Turnover 36	•	•	•	•	•	•	•	•	•	•	•		•
Total Liabilities to Net Worth 37	1.2	5.0	1.1	5.9	3.5	3.2	4.4	2.1	2.0	2.9	3.8		0.9
Current Assets to Working Capital 38	8.0	2.0	2.9	3.7	3.9	3.8	7.1	6.2	3.5	6.4	3.8		•
Current Liabilities to Working Capital 39	7.0	1.0	1.9	2.7	2.9	2.8	6.1	5.2	2.5	5.4	2.8		•
Working Capital to Net Sales 40	0.1	0.1	0.1	0.1	0.1	0.1	0.1	0.1	0.1	0.1	0.2		•
Inventory to Working Capital 41	0.0	0.0	0.0	0.0	0.0	0.0	•	0.0	0.0	0.1	0.0		•
Total Receipts to Cash Flow 42	2.2	3.7	1.4	2.6	1.4	2.2	2.9	2.4	2.7	2.7	3.5	4.5	1.5
Cost of Goods to Cash Flow 43	0.4	0.2	0.0	0.0	0.1	0.3	0.6	0.5	1.1	0.9	0.1		•
Cash Flow to Total Debt 44	0.4	1.8	4.1	0.7	2.1	0.9	0.7	0.6	0.6	0.4	0.3		0.2

Selected Financial Factors (in Percentages)

Debt Ratio 45	53.7	83.3	51.6	85.5	77.9	76.1	81.6	67.8	66.7	74.6	54.0		46.7
Return on Total Assets 46	5.1	13.4	2.9	8.0	7.8	4.2	5.6	9.4	8.0	3.8			
Return on Equity Before Income Taxes 47	9.3	65.6	35.3	14.6	28.7	28.5	6.9	13.1	29.7	6.5			
Return on Equity After Income Taxes 48	6.6	61.6	72.8	68.8	18.7	25.6	34.8	3.7	8.6	24.8	8.6		4.3
Profit Margin (Before Income Tax) 49	8.6	1.9	11.8	1.5	2.8	4.4	4.3	2.7	4.8	6.8	11.8		21.0
Profit Margin (After Income Tax) 50	6.1	1.8	11.2	1.3	1.8	3.9	3.7	1.5	3.1	5.7	7.8		14.1

311

Table II
Corporations with Net Income

OTHER INSURANCE RELATED ACTIVITIES

MONEY AMOUNTS AND SIZE OF ASSETS IN THOUSANDS OF DOLLARS

Item Description for Accounting Period 7/05 Through 6/06	Total	Zero Assets	Under 500	500 to 1,000	1,000 to 5,000	5,000 to 10,000	10,000 to 25,000	25,000 to 50,000	50,000 to 100,000	100,000 to 250,000	250,000 to 500,000	500,000 to 2,500,000	2,500,000 and over
Number of Enterprises 1	8877	1466	6310	475	286	172	81	31	22	15	8	8	3
Revenues ($ in Thousands)													
Net Sales 2	32136073	228392	2247506	1054365	1418200	2349717	1701295	2209209	1500121	2718012	4012494	4451144	8245618
Interest 3	1048575	773	2734	3380	4676	5105	9134	9447	12066	11049	40131	204922	745157
Rents 4	93962	0	0	4355	4561	381	1159	129	1115	10116	871	509	70766
Royalties 5	25481	0	0	0	0	0	0	0	3094	10678	0	11709	0
Other Portfolio Income 6	296249	27787	1547	327	2073	16840	5783	8187	8140	91913	12876	53522	67254
Other Receipts 7	30671806	199832	2243225	1046303	1406890	2327391	1685219	2191446	1475706	2594256	3958616	4180482	7362441
Total Receipts 8	32136073	228392	2247506	1054365	1418200	2349717	1701295	2209209	1500121	2718012	4012494	4451144	8245618
Average Total Receipts 9	3620	156	356	2220	4959	13661	21004	71265	68187	181201	501562	556393	2748539
Operating Costs/Operating Income (%)													
Cost of Operations 10	21.0	•	6.1	0.7	0.9	1.8	19.1	21.7	16.3	19.6	50.2	50.8	8.3
Salaries and Wages 11	16.8	7.4	35.3	14.3	22.3	16.8	32.7	24.2	28.2	22.1	6.0	10.1	11.0
Taxes Paid 12	2.6	1.4	3.4	1.9	3.0	2.5	2.7	2.0	3.3	1.6	1.2	1.3	4.1
Interest Paid 13	1.5	0.3	0.1	0.0	0.5	0.6	0.9	0.1	2.5	1.4	1.0	3.0	2.4
Depreciation 14	0.8	1.8	0.8	0.9	1.0	0.7	0.7	0.3	1.6	0.9	0.3	0.9	1.1
Amortization and Depletion 15	0.6	0.0	0.0	•	0.1	0.0	0.0	0.1	1.8	1.1	0.2	0.6	1.1
Pensions and Other Deferred Comp. 16	1.3	0.3	1.0	0.4	3.2	0.4	1.0	0.3	0.8	2.3	0.2	0.2	2.5
Employee Benefits 17	2.4	0.4	2.1	1.5	2.4	1.3	10.1	11.0	2.3	1.7	0.5	1.3	1.0
Advertising 18	0.6	2.3	0.7	0.8	0.4	0.3	0.2	0.2	0.7	0.3	0.1	0.5	1.0
Other Expenses 19	36.0	26.5	25.2	61.9	43.7	66.4	17.8	28.0	33.4	37.4	29.9	15.3	46.0
Officers' Compensation 20	3.4	12.7	16.3	5.6	15.5	2.1	4.5	5.2	2.3	1.5	0.4	1.1	0.4
Operating Margin 21	13.1	47.1	9.1	12.1	7.1	7.1	10.4	6.8	6.8	10.0	9.9	15.0	21.1
Operating Margin Before Officers' Comp. 22	16.5	59.7	25.4	17.7	22.6	9.2	14.9	12.1	9.1	11.5	10.3	16.1	21.5

Selected Average Balance Sheet ($ in Thousands)

Net Receivables 23	622	0	4	228	758	2259	3582	6108	8606	13035	50108	309965	344341
Inventories 24	•	•	•	•	•	•	•	•	•	•	•	•	•
Net Property, Plant and Equipment 25	180	0	14	102	234	439	889	1212	6317	11370	7782	31133	195499
Total Assets 26	7641	0	66	688	2536	6058	16118	31501	72618	159545	311622	784935	16757368
Notes and Loans Payable 27	812	0	20	1	494	819	2353	2389	20079	34215	44551	179444	1260244
All Other Liabilities 28	3149	0	5	376	1343	3189	9033	22163	27910	83412	163910	312205	6572223
Net Worth 29	3680	0	40	311	698	2049	4732	6949	24629	41917	103161	293286	8924901

Selected Financial Ratios (Times to 1)

Current Ratio 30	1.2	•	4.5	1.5	2.4	1.6	1.7	1.1	1.3	1.3	1.3	1.4	0.9
Quick Ratio 31	0.9	•	4.4	1.2	2.0	1.6	1.4	0.8	1.0	0.8	0.8	1.1	0.7
Net Sales to Working Capital 32	13.2	•	9.5	11.3	4.6	7.6	4.7	27.1	11.5	11.3	11.7	4.2	•
Coverage Ratio 33	9.7	1229.2	76.3	13.9	13.4	13.1	61.7	3.7	8.0	11.4	•	6.0	9.9
Total Asset Turnover 34	0.5	183.1	5.4	3.2	2.0	2.3	1.3	2.3	0.9	1.1	1.6	0.7	0.2
Inventory Turnover 35	•	•	•	•	•	•	•	•	•	•	•	•	•
Receivables Turnover 36	•	•	•	•	•	•	•	•	•	•	•	•	•
Total Liabilities to Net Worth 37	1.1	•	0.6	1.2	2.6	2.0	2.4	3.5	1.9	2.8	2.0	1.7	0.9
Current Assets to Working Capital 38	7.2	•	1.3	2.9	1.7	2.7	2.5	9.1	4.9	4.6	4.0	3.7	•
Current Liabilities to Working Capital 39	6.2	•	0.3	1.9	0.7	1.7	1.5	8.1	3.9	3.6	3.0	2.7	•
Working Capital to Net Sales 40	0.1	•	0.1	0.1	0.2	0.1	0.0	0.0	0.1	0.1	0.1	0.2	•
Inventory to Working Capital 41	0.0	•	0.0	0.0	•	•	•	•	0.0	0.0	0.1	0.0	•
Total Receipts to Cash Flow 42	2.1	1.4	3.5	1.4	2.2	1.4	3.9	3.0	2.7	2.2	2.6	3.6	1.5
Cost of Goods to Cash Flow 43	0.4	•	0.2	0.0	0.0	0.0	0.7	0.7	0.4	0.4	1.3	1.8	0.1
Cash Flow to Total Debt 44	0.4	•	4.0	4.2	1.2	2.4	0.5	1.0	0.5	0.7	0.9	0.3	0.2

Selected Financial Factors (in Percentages)

Debt Ratio 45	51.8	•	38.9	54.8	72.5	66.2	70.6	77.9	66.1	73.7	66.9	62.6	46.7
Return on Total Assets 46	6.9	•	49.9	39.1	14.8	17.3	14.5	15.7	8.6	12.9	18.7	12.5	3.8
Return on Equity Before Income Taxes 47	12.9	•	80.6	86.4	49.7	47.3	45.7	69.8	18.6	42.9	51.6	27.9	6.5
Return on Equity After Income Taxes 48	9.9	•	79.1	81.8	47.4	39.1	42.6	63.2	14.4	34.5	44.6	19.2	4.3
Profit Margin (Before Income Tax) 49	13.1	47.1	9.1	12.1	7.0	7.1	10.3	6.8	6.7	9.9	10.6	14.7	21.0
Profit Margin (After Income Tax) 50	10.1	46.8	8.9	11.5	6.7	5.9	9.6	6.2	5.2	8.0	9.2	10.1	14.1

Table I

Corporations with and without Net Income

OPEN-END INVESTMENT FUNDS (FORM 1120-RIC)

MONEY AMOUNTS AND SIZE OF ASSETS IN THOUSANDS OF DOLLARS

Item Description for Accounting Period 7/05 Through 6/06	Total	Zero Assets	Under 500	500 to 1,000	1,000 to 5,000	5,000 to 10,000	10,000 to 25,000	25,000 to 50,000	50,000 to 100,000	100,000 to 250,000	250,000 to 500,000	500,000 to 2,500,000	2,500,000 and over
Number of Enterprises **1**	10959	•	41	55	337	282	721	861	1292	2056	1544	2296	792
Revenues ($ in Thousands)													
Net Sales **2**	309790417	•	16134	857	34430	48877	366674	1034965	3204892	11579150	18411141	80229046	189800724
Interest **3**	137906644		1702	157	12166	10673	113153	297663	1131590	4078877	6805144	30818684	92188233
Rents **4**	0		0	0	0	0	0	0	0	0	0	0	0
Royalties **5**	0		0	0	0	0	0	0	0	0	0	0	0
Other Portfolio Income **6**	62550799	•	9665	175	9472	16313	157698	397571	1200096	4272671	6176207	22958021	25546008
Other Receipts **7**	109332974	•	4767	525	12792	21891	95823	339731	873206	3227602	5429790	26452341	72066483
Total Receipts **8**	309790417	•	16134	857	34430	48877	366674	1034965	3204892	11579150	18411141	80229046	189800724
Average Total Receipts **9**	28268	•	394	16	102	173	509	1202	2481	5632	11924	34943	239647
Operating Costs/Operating Income (%)													
Cost of Operations **10**	•	•	•	•	•	•	•	•	•	•	•	•	•
Salaries and Wages **11**	0.0		•	•	0.1	0.5	0.3	0.1	0.1	0.1	0.0	•	0.0
Taxes Paid **12**	0.2		0.1	0.4	0.3	0.4	0.3	0.3	0.3	0.4	0.3	0.2	0.2
Interest Paid **13**	0.3		•	•	•	0.5	0.4	0.1	0.9	0.4	0.7	0.4	0.2
Depreciation **14**	0.0		•	•	•	•	•	•	0.0	0.0	0.0	0.0	0.0
Amortization and Depletion **15**	0.0		•	2.6	0.8	0.4	0.1	0.0	0.0	0.0	0.0	0.0	0.0
Pensions and Other Deferred Comp. **16**	•		•	•	•	•	•	•	•	•	•	•	•
Employee Benefits **17**	•		•	•	•	•	•	•	•	•	•	•	•
Advertising **18**	0.0		•	•	•	•	0.0	•	0.0	0.0	0.0	0.0	0.0
Other Expenses **19**	20.6		19.7	60.1	33.6	29.2	32.8	27.7	24.8	24.1	23.0	21.9	19.5
Officers' Compensation **20**	0.0		•	•	•	•	0.0	0.0	0.0	0.0	0.0	0.0	0.0
Operating Margin **21**	78.9		80.2	37.0	65.2	69.1	66.1	71.8	73.7	75.0	75.9	77.4	80.1
Operating Margin Before Officers' Comp. **22**	78.9		80.2	37.0	65.2	69.1	66.1	71.8	73.8	75.0	75.9	77.4	80.1

Selected Average Balance Sheet ($ in Thousands)

Item	Total												
Net Receivables 23	13892	•	4	3	139	110	246	700	1227	2696	4849	15359	128164
Inventories 24	•	•	•	•	•	•	•	•	•	•	•	•	•
Net Property, Plant and Equipment 25	0	•	0	0	0	0	0	0	0	0	0	1	1
Total Assets 26	956343	•	315	691	2989	7169	16825	36636	72857	166712	359372	1101283	8729174
Notes and Loans Payable 27	970	•	0	0	0	34	28	5	245	163	1449	1540	5273
All Other Liabilities 28	48721	•	78	94	137	208	534	1493	3282	9025	20985	74422	386459
Net Worth 29	906652	•	237	597	2851	6926	16263	35138	69330	157524	336939	1025320	8337442

Selected Financial Ratios (Times to 1)

Item	Total												
Current Ratio 30	2.7	•	2.2	•	3.0	4.3	5.3	5.0	4.5	4.1	3.3	2.6	2.7
Quick Ratio 31	2.5	•	1.5	0.0	2.8	4.0	4.5	4.6	4.1	3.8	3.0	2.3	2.4
Net Sales to Working Capital 32	0.3	•	4.3	•	0.4	0.2	0.2	0.2	0.2	0.2	0.2	0.3	0.4
Coverage Ratio 33	231.4	•	•	•	•	120.8	116.9	392.5	55.7	126.7	79.1	146.6	400.0
Total Asset Turnover 34	0.0	•	1.3	0.0	0.0	0.0	0.0	0.0	0.0	0.0	0.0	0.0	0.0
Inventory Turnover 35	•	•	•	•	•	•	•	•	•	•	•	•	•
Receivables Turnover 36	•	•	•	•	•	•	•	•	•	•	•	•	•
Total Liabilities to Net Worth 37	0.1	•	0.3	0.2	0.0	0.0	0.0	0.0	0.1	0.1	0.1	0.1	0.0
Current Assets to Working Capital 38	1.6	•	1.8	•	1.5	1.3	1.2	1.2	1.3	1.3	1.4	1.6	1.6
Current Liabilities to Working Capital 39	0.6	•	0.8	•	0.5	0.3	0.2	0.2	0.3	0.3	0.4	0.6	0.6
Working Capital to Net Sales 40	3.0	•	0.2	0.0	2.6	4.6	4.7	4.8	4.5	4.9	4.1	3.3	2.6
Inventory to Working Capital 41	•	•	•	•	•	•	•	•	•	•	•	•	•
Total Receipts to Cash Flow 42	1.1	•	2.5	1.3	1.4	1.3	1.4	1.2	1.2	1.2	1.2	1.2	1.1
Cost of Goods to Cash Flow 43	•	•	•	•	•	•	•	•	•	•	•	•	•
Cash Flow to Total Debt 44	0.5	•	2.0	0.1	0.5	0.5	0.6	0.7	0.6	0.5	0.4	0.4	0.6

Selected Financial Factors (in Percentages)

Item	Total												
Debt Ratio 45	5.2	•	24.7	13.6	4.6	3.4	3.3	4.1	4.8	5.5	6.2	6.9	4.5
Return on Total Assets 46	2.1	•	100.3	0.8	2.2	1.4	1.6	1.7	1.8	1.8	1.9	2.0	2.0
Return on Equity Before Income Taxes 47	2.2	•	133.2	1.0	2.3	1.5	1.6	1.8	1.8	1.9	2.0	2.2	2.1
Return on Equity After Income Taxes 48	2.2	•	133.2	1.0	2.3	1.5	1.6	1.8	1.8	1.9	2.0	2.2	2.1
Profit Margin (Before Income Tax) 49	69.4	•	80.2	37.1	65.2	59.3	50.9	51.4	51.1	54.1	56.4	63.9	74.4
Profit Margin (After Income Tax) 50	69.4	•	80.2	37.1	65.2	59.3	50.9	51.4	51.1	54.0	56.4	63.9	74.4

Table II
Corporations with Net Income

OPEN-END INVESTMENT FUNDS (FORM 1120-RIC)

MONEY AMOUNTS AND SIZE OF ASSETS IN THOUSANDS OF DOLLARS

Item Description for Accounting Period 7/05 Through 6/06	Total	Zero Assets	Under 500	500 to 1,000	1,000 to 5,000	5,000 to 10,000	10,000 to 25,000	25,000 to 50,000	50,000 to 100,000	100,000 to 250,000	250,000 to 500,000	500,000 to 2,500,000	2,500,000 and over
Number of Enterprises **1**	8818	•	28	34	255	227	515	641	1000	1655	1257	1998	717
Revenues ($ in Thousands)													
Net Sales **2**	293186879	•	16082	703	32304	40581	311394	866521	2733100	10285333	16294610	75057368	182794443
Interest **3**	137354381	•	1652	30	11955	9915	109758	292565	1104427	4034241	6761385	30575634	92007889
Rents **4**	0	•	0	0	0	0	0	0	0	0	0	0	0
Royalties **5**	0	•	0	0	0	0	0	0	0	0	0	0	0
Other Portfolio Income **6**	5032832	•	9665	175	9312	11506	108300	269632	842972	3298027	4490245	19254954	20373963
Other Receipts **7**	105504166	•	4765	498	11037	19160	93336	304324	785701	2953065	5042980	25226780	70412591
Total Receipts **8**	293186879	•	16082	703	32304	40581	311394	866521	2733100	10285333	16294610	75057368	182794443
Average Total Receipts **9**	33249	•	574	21	127	179	605	1352	2733	6215	12963	37566	254943
Operating Costs/Operating Income (%)													
Cost of Operations **10**	•	•	•	•	•	•	•	•	•	•	•	•	•
Salaries and Wages **11**	0.0	•	•	•	0.0	0.6	0.3	0.1	0.1	0.1	0.0	0.1	0.0
Taxes Paid **12**	0.2	•	0.1	•	0.1	0.2	0.3	0.3	0.2	0.3	0.3	0.2	0.2
Interest Paid **13**	0.3	•	•	•	•	0.4	0.0	0.2	0.7	0.5	0.8	0.5	0.2
Depreciation **14**	0.0	•	•	•	•	•	•	•	0.0	0.0	0.0	0.0	0.0
Amortization and Depletion **15**	0.0	•	•	1.7	0.9	0.4	0.1	0.0	0.0	0.0	0.0	0.0	0.0
Pensions and Other Deferred Comp. **16**	•	•	•	•	•	•	•	•	•	•	•	•	•
Employee Benefits **17**	•	•	•	•	•	•	•	•	•	•	•	•	•
Advertising **18**	0.0	•	•	•	•	•	0.0	•	0.0	0.0	0.0	0.0	0.0
Other Expenses **19**	19.2	•	19.1	44.1	21.7	21.5	26.6	24.7	22.3	21.6	21.0	20.1	18.7
Officers' Compensation **20**	0.0	•	•	•	•	•	0.0	0.0	0.0	0.0	0.0	0.0	0.0
Operating Margin **21**	80.2	•	80.9	54.2	77.2	76.9	72.6	74.8	76.5	77.5	77.8	79.1	80.9
Operating Margin Before Officers' Comp. **22**	80.2	•	80.9	54.2	77.2	76.9	72.7	74.8	76.6	77.5	77.8	79.1	80.9

Selected Average Balance Sheet ($ in Thousands)													
Net Receivables 23	16165	•	6	0	165	133	220	739	1248	2962	4765	15958	136490
Inventories 24	•	•	•	•	•	•	•	•	•	•	•	•	•
Net Property, Plant and Equipment 25	0	•	0	0	0	0	0	0	0	0	0	1	1
Total Assets 26	1080232	•	288	680	2966	7238	16699	36584	73148	167636	359039	1109879	9025903
Notes and Loans Payable 27	1131	•	0	0	0	42	0	7	210	167	1767	1648	5526
All Other Liabilities 28	55255	•	26	37	136	201	501	1455	3167	9092	21261	75800	403868
Net Worth 29	1023846	•	262	643	2830	6995	16198	35122	69770	158377	336010	1032431	8616510
Selected Financial Ratios (Times to 1)													
Current Ratio 30	2.4	•	5.0	0.1	3.6	3.3	4.2	3.8	3.6	3.5	2.6	2.3	2.3
Quick Ratio 31	2.1	•	4.5	0.0	3.4	3.2	3.4	3.3	3.2	3.3	2.3	2.1	2.0
Net Sales to Working Capital 32	0.5	•	5.5	•	0.4	0.3	0.4	0.3	0.3	0.3	0.4	0.4	0.5
Coverage Ratio 33	240.9	•	•	•	•	206.4	4522.7	416.0	85.1	138.3	81.8	149.4	415.9
Total Asset Turnover 34	0.0	•	2.0	0.0	0.0	0.0	0.0	0.0	0.0	0.0	0.0	0.0	0.0
Inventory Turnover 35	•	•	•	•	•	•	•	•	•	•	•	•	•
Receivables Turnover 36	•	•	•	•	•	•	•	•	•	•	•	•	•
Total Liabilities to Net Worth 37	0.1	•	0.1	0.1	0.0	0.0	0.0	0.0	0.0	0.1	0.1	0.1	0.0
Current Assets to Working Capital 38	1.7	•	1.2	•	1.4	1.4	1.3	1.4	1.4	1.4	1.6	1.8	1.8
Current Liabilities to Working Capital 39	0.7	•	0.2	•	0.4	0.4	0.3	0.4	0.4	0.4	0.6	0.8	0.8
Working Capital to Net Sales 40	2.2	•	0.2	•	2.8	3.1	2.6	3.0	3.0	3.7	2.8	2.6	2.0
Inventory to Working Capital 41	•	•	•	•	•	•	•	•	•	•	•	•	•
Total Receipts to Cash Flow 42	1.1	•	2.5	1.4	1.4	1.4	1.5	1.3	1.2	1.2	1.2	1.2	1.1
Cost of Goods to Cash Flow 43	•	•	•	•	•	•	•	•	•	•	•	•	•
Cash Flow to Total Debt 44	0.5	•	8.8	0.4	0.7	0.5	0.8	0.7	0.7	0.5	0.5	0.4	0.6
Selected Financial Factors (in Percentages)													
Debt Ratio 45	5.2	•	9.0	5.4	4.6	3.4	3.0	4.0	4.6	5.5	6.4	7.0	4.5
Return on Total Assets 46	2.3	•	161.4	1.6	3.3	1.9	2.5	2.4	2.4	2.4	2.4	2.4	2.2
Return on Equity Before Income Taxes 47	2.4	•	177.3	1.7	3.5	2.0	2.6	2.5	2.5	2.5	2.5	2.5	2.3
Return on Equity After Income Taxes 48	2.4	•	177.3	1.7	3.5	2.0	2.6	2.5	2.5	2.5	2.5	2.5	2.3
Profit Margin (Before Income Tax) 49	74.3	•	80.9	54.2	77.2	76.9	69.7	65.0	62.9	63.3	65.9	69.5	77.8
Profit Margin (After Income Tax) 50	74.3	•	80.9	54.2	77.2	76.9	69.7	65.0	62.9	63.3	65.8	69.5	77.8

Table I

Corporations with and without Net Income

REAL ESTATE INVESTMENT TRUSTS (FORM 1120-REIT)

MONEY AMOUNTS AND SIZE OF ASSETS IN THOUSANDS OF DOLLARS

Item Description for Accounting Period 7/05 Through 6/06	Total	Zero Assets	Under 500	500 to 1,000	1,000 to 5,000	5,000 to 10,000	10,000 to 25,000	25,000 to 50,000	50,000 to 100,000	100,000 to 250,000	250,000 to 500,000	500,000 to 2,500,000	2,500,000 and over
Number of Enterprises 1	1251	100	57	7	53	43	97	104	129	163	133	229	136
Revenues ($ in Thousands)													
Net Sales 2	11408999	14052587	371492	119158	453841	330318	450646	1080747	3040063	3052398	4368347	21166954	65594448
Interest 3	42384038	610148	198800	210	762	4964	81408	154006	269424	692424	953309	7195897	32222686
Rents 4	38440462	530647	30491	0	27634	70617	193975	322016	526265	1713831	2327862	9512181	23184942
Royalties 5	0	0	0	0	0	0	0	0	0	0	0	0	0
Other Portfolio Income 6	22905106	12546252	37642	118242	422605	159617	180841	554350	2197104	498503	268999	1826665	4094285
Other Receipts 7	10351393	365540	104559	706	2840	95120	-5578	50375	47270	147640	818177	2632211	6092535
Total Receipts 8	11408999	14052587	371492	119158	453841	330318	450646	1080747	3040063	3052398	4368347	21166954	65594448
Average Total Receipts 9	91192	140526	6517	17023	8563	7682	4646	10392	23566	18726	32845	92432	482312
Operating Costs/Operating Income (%)													
Cost of Operations 10	•	•	•	•	•	•	•	•	•	•	•	•	•
Salaries and Wages 11	1.4	1.0	0.4	•	0.1	0.0	0.4	0.5	0.2	1.1	1.2	1.9	1.5
Taxes Paid 12	2.3	0.4	0.1	0.1	0.3	2.2	2.4	3.2	1.1	3.5	3.9	3.9	2.1
Interest Paid 13	14.5	11.7	11.7	•	0.6	4.1	5.6	15.2	5.7	11.5	10.1	13.5	18.6
Depreciation 14	5.6	0.7	0.1	•	0.6	3.6	3.4	3.2	2.8	7.2	6.8	8.2	5.9
Amortization and Depletion 15	0.8	0.3	0.5	•	0.1	1.0	0.7	0.7	0.4	0.6	0.6	0.8	0.9
Pensions and Other Deferred Comp. 16	•	•	•	•	•	•	•	•	•	•	•	•	•
Employee Benefits 17	•	•	•	•	•	•	•	•	•	•	•	•	•
Advertising 18	0.1	0.0	0.0	0.0	0.0	0.0	0.2	0.1	0.0	0.2	0.2	0.2	0.1
Other Expenses 19	13.0	2.7	34.7	0.1	4.6	18.7	30.4	23.9	9.9	33.3	28.4	14.8	12.4
Officers' Compensation 20	0.3	0.2	0.0	0.0	0.1	0.0	0.1	0.1	0.1	0.3	0.4	0.7	0.2
Operating Margin 21	61.9	93.0	52.6	99.9	93.7	70.4	56.8	53.1	79.9	42.3	48.5	55.8	58.1
Operating Margin Before Officers' Comp. 22	62.2	93.2	52.6	99.9	93.8	70.4	57.0	53.2	79.9	42.6	48.9	56.6	58.3

Selected Average Balance Sheet ($ in Thousands)

Net Receivables 23	48559	0	2	0	61	87	176	611	2382	7093	6782	39844	361545
Inventories 24	•	•	•	•	•	•	•	•	•	•	•	•	•
Net Property, Plant and Equipment 25	226045	0	30	0	345	915	4948	12492	22255	51613	96177	346706	1304945
Total Assets 26	1067206	0	179	866	2685	6334	16844	35650	71988	167170	359075	1166596	7190142
Notes and Loans Payable 27	231025	0	69	0	277	2220	3228	7239	14332	40784	67618	253528	1560919
All Other Liabilities 28	145228	0	27	9	67	1082	1379	3600	1389	4927	17482	73887	1183035
Net Worth 29	690952	0	84	857	2341	3033	12237	24810	56267	121459	273974	839181	4446188

Selected Financial Ratios (Times to 1)

Current Ratio 30	0.9	•	1.6	88.7	10.1	0.6	2.3	1.6	4.0	3.7	2.8	2.5	0.7
Quick Ratio 31	0.8	•	1.2	43.4	8.9	0.6	1.4	1.2	3.5	2.5	2.4	1.7	0.7
Net Sales to Working Capital 32	•	•	285.5	21.2	34.4	3.2	6.4	5.1	5.1	1.3	1.6	1.2	•
Coverage Ratio 33	5.3	56.1	5.5	•	161.7	18.1	11.1	4.4	14.9	4.7	5.8	5.1	4.1
Total Asset Turnover 34	0.1	•	36.4	19.7	3.2	1.2	0.3	0.3	0.3	0.1	0.1	0.1	0.1
Inventory Turnover 35	•	•	•	•	•	•	•	•	•	•	•	•	•
Receivables Turnover 36	•	•	•	•	•	•	•	•	•	•	•	•	•
Total Liabilities to Net Worth 37	0.5	•	1.1	0.0	0.1	1.1	0.4	0.4	0.3	0.4	0.3	0.4	0.6
Current Assets to Working Capital 38	•	•	2.8	1.0	1.1	1.7	2.6	1.3	1.3	1.4	1.6	1.7	•
Current Liabilities to Working Capital 39	•	•	1.8	0.0	0.1	0.7	1.6	0.3	0.4	0.4	0.6	0.7	•
Working Capital to Net Sales 40	•	•	0.0	0.0	0.0	0.3	0.2	0.8	0.8	0.8	0.6	0.8	•
Inventory to Working Capital 41	•	•	•	•	•	•	•	•	•	•	•	•	•
Total Receipts to Cash Flow 42	1.9	5.5	1.3	143.7	19.2	2.5	3.7	6.1	1.8	6.1	1.5	1.7	1.6
Cost of Goods to Cash Flow 43	•	•	•	•	•	•	•	•	•	•	•	•	•
Cash Flow to Total Debt 44	0.1	•	52.6	13.0	1.3	0.9	0.4	0.3	0.2	0.2	0.3	0.2	0.1

Selected Financial Factors (in Percentages)

Debt Ratio 45	35.3	•	53.3	1.1	12.8	52.1	27.3	30.4	21.8	27.3	23.7	28.1	38.2
Return on Total Assets 46	6.5	•	2343.7	1962.1	300.7	90.4	17.2	19.4	28.0	6.0	5.4	5.5	5.1
Return on Equity Before Income Taxes 47	8.2	•	4102.5	1983.0	342.8	178.4	21.6	21.5	33.4	6.5	5.8	6.1	6.3
Return on Equity After Income Taxes 48	8.2	•	4102.3	1983.0	342.8	178.4	21.6	21.5	33.4	6.5	5.8	6.1	6.3
Profit Margin (Before Income Tax) 49	61.9	93.0	52.6	99.9	93.7	70.4	56.8	51.4	79.8	42.3	48.4	55.8	58.1
Profit Margin (After Income Tax) 50	61.8	92.6	52.6	99.9	93.7	70.4	56.8	51.4	79.8	42.3	48.4	55.7	58.0

Table II
Corporations with Net Income

REAL ESTATE INVESTMENT TRUSTS (FORM 1120-REIT)

MONEY AMOUNTS AND SIZE OF ASSETS IN THOUSANDS OF DOLLARS

Item Description for Accounting Period 7/05 Through 6/06	Total	Zero Assets	Under 500	500 to 1,000	1,000 to 5,000	5,000 to 10,000	10,000 to 25,000	25,000 to 50,000	50,000 to 100,000	100,000 to 250,000	250,000 to 500,000	500,000 to 2,500,000	2,500,000 and over
Number of Enterprises **1**	994	91	23	•	23	30	65	75	95	127	110	215	•
Revenues ($ in Thousands)													
Net Sales **2**	111419230	13960528	371024	•	446567	319702	413528	984087	2903451	2744305	3829992	20188838	•
Interest **3**	41921057	524375	198732	•	669	4668	79810	146078	262537	664864	922625	6895330	•
Rents **4**	36107875	526515	29956	•	20454	60298	153053	230603	395618	1350076	1837789	8772711	•
Royalties **5**	0	0	0	•	0	0	0	0	0	0	0	0	•
Other Portfolio Income **6**	22860089	12546252	37642	•	422605	159617	177783	542556	2191789	496766	253446	1819108	•
Other Receipts **7**	10530209	363386	104694	•	2839	95119	2882	64850	53507	232599	816132	2701689	•
Total Receipts **8**	111419230	13960528	371024	•	446567	319702	413528	984087	2903451	2744305	3829992	20188838	•
Average Total Receipts **9**	112092	153412	16131	•	19416	10657	6362	13121	30563	21609	34818	93902	•
Operating Costs/Operating Income (%)													
Cost of Operations **10**	•	•	•	•	•	•	•	•	•	•	•	•	•
Salaries and Wages **11**	1.4	1.0	0.2	•	•	0.0	0.4	0.5	0.2	0.9	0.9	1.7	•
Taxes Paid **12**	2.2	0.4	0.1	•	0.3	2.2	2.1	2.3	0.9	2.5	3.1	3.8	•
Interest Paid **13**	13.9	1.1	11.8	•	0.4	4.3	4.5	11.8	4.6	8.2	7.6	12.4	•
Depreciation **14**	5.3	0.7	0.1	•	0.2	3.7	2.7	2.5	2.3	5.1	5.1	7.5	•
Amortization and Depletion **15**	0.8	0.2	0.5	•	0.1	1.0	0.4	0.6	0.2	0.5	0.5	0.8	•
Pensions and Other Deferred Comp. **16**	•	•	•	•	•	•	•	•	•	•	•	•	•
Employee Benefits **17**	•	•	•	•	•	•	•	•	•	•	•	•	•
Advertising **18**	0.1	0.0	0.0	•	0.0	•	0.2	0.1	0.0	0.1	0.1	0.2	•
Other Expenses **19**	12.0	2.3	34.4	•	2.7	13.2	20.1	16.5	4.9	28.9	24.4	13.0	•
Officers' Compensation **20**	0.3	0.2	•	•	•	•	0.1	0.1	0.0	0.3	0.4	0.6	•
Operating Margin **21**	64.1	94.0	53.1	•	96.2	75.6	69.5	65.7	86.8	53.6	57.8	59.8	•
Operating Margin Before Officers' Comp. **22**	64.4	94.2	53.1	•	96.2	75.6	69.6	65.8	86.8	53.9	58.2	60.4	•

Selected Average Balance Sheet ($ in Thousands)

Item											
Net Receivables 23	60865	0	0	•	134	167	832	3160	8782	7685	41828
Inventories 24	•	•	•	•	•	•	•	•	•	•	•
Net Property, Plant and Equipment 25	265383	0	42	763	5248	13041	22071	41438	76681	338335	•
Total Assets 26	1303636	0	188	2946	5999	16951	35958	72526	169141	359093	1161636
Notes and Loans Payable 27	269299	0	48	609	2952	3320	6124	12615	30513	47837	227097
All Other Liabilities 28	180300	0	56	134	1507	1741	4346	1029	5502	18924	69862
Net Worth 29	854036	0	83	2203	1540	11890	25487	58881	133126	292332	864678

Selected Financial Ratios (Times to 1)

Item											
Current Ratio 30	0.9	•	1.2	14.9	0.6	2.6	1.7	4.7	4.2	3.2	2.7
Quick Ratio 31	0.8	•	0.8	13.3	0.6	1.5	1.2	4.1	2.9	2.9	1.9
Net Sales to Working Capital 32	•	•	864.9	37.2	•	3.3	5.8	5.2	1.2	1.4	1.1
Coverage Ratio 33	5.6	83.0	5.5	218.4	18.8	16.4	6.4	19.8	7.5	8.6	5.8
Total Asset Turnover 34	0.1	•	85.9	6.6	1.8	0.4	0.4	0.1	0.1	0.1	0.1
Inventory Turnover 35	•	•	•	•	•	•	•	•	•	•	•
Receivables Turnover 36	•	•	•	•	•	•	•	•	•	•	•
Total Liabilities to Net Worth 37	0.5	•	1.3	0.3	2.9	0.4	0.4	0.2	0.3	0.2	0.3
Current Assets to Working Capital 38	•	•	6.3	1.1	•	1.6	2.5	1.3	1.3	1.4	1.6
Current Liabilities to Working Capital 39	•	•	5.3	0.1	•	0.6	1.5	0.3	0.3	0.4	0.6
Working Capital to Net Sales 40	•	•	0.0	0.0	•	0.3	0.2	0.2	0.9	0.7	0.9
Inventory to Working Capital 41	•	•	•	•	•	•	•	•	•	•	•
Total Receipts to Cash Flow 42	1.8	5.5	1.3	23.3	2.6	2.6	3.5	6.3	1.6	1.4	1.6
Cost of Goods to Cash Flow 43	•	•	•	•	•	•	•	•	•	•	•
Cash Flow to Total Debt 44	0.1	•	119.2	1.1	0.9	0.5	0.4	0.4	0.4	0.4	0.2

Selected Financial Factors (in Percentages)

Item											
Debt Ratio 45	34.5	•	55.7	25.2	74.3	29.9	29.1	18.8	21.3	18.6	25.6
Return on Total Assets 46	6.7	•	5572.4	637.1	141.9	27.8	27.6	38.5	7.9	6.3	5.8
Return on Equity Before Income Taxes 47	8.4	•	10293.1	848.2	523.4	37.2	32.9	45.0	8.7	6.9	6.5
Return on Equity After Income Taxes 48	8.4	•	10292.7	848.1	523.4	37.1	32.9	45.0	8.7	6.9	6.5
Profit Margin (Before Income Tax) 49	64.1	94.0	53.1	96.2	75.6	69.5	63.9	86.7	53.6	57.7	59.7
Profit Margin (After Income Tax) 50	64.0	93.5	53.1	96.2	75.6	69.4	63.9	86.7	53.6	57.7	59.7

Table I

Corporations with and without Net Income

OTHER FINANCIAL VEHICLES

MONEY AMOUNTS AND SIZE OF ASSETS IN THOUSANDS OF DOLLARS

Item Description for Accounting Period 7/05 Through 6/06	Total	Zero Assets	Under 500	500 to 1,000	1,000 to 5,000	5,000 to 10,000	10,000 to 25,000	25,000 to 50,000	50,000 to 100,000	100,000 to 250,000	250,000 to 500,000	500,000 to 2,500,000	2,500,000 and over
Number of Enterprises **1**	12051	1547	8253	360	1280	116	150	53	40	58	46	101	47

Revenues ($ in Thousands)

	Total	Zero Assets	Under 500	500 to 1,000	1,000 to 5,000	5,000 to 10,000	10,000 to 25,000	25,000 to 50,000	50,000 to 100,000	100,000 to 250,000	250,000 to 500,000	500,000 to 2,500,000	2,500,000 and over
Net Sales **2**	19718348	1177091	272947	67367	374548	103770	351232	89933	206541	424831	1230113	5077734	10342241
Interest **3**	14028858	810239	31060	17748	20295	26651	39596	38102	105882	271211	1060153	4078244	7529376
Rents **4**	36780	35	93	5001	2953	1558	943	14	0	22421	0	3764	0
Royalties **5**	22957	0	0	0	0	0	12874	0	10062	21	0	0	0
Other Portfolio Income **6**	1767990	102838	99	17279	32336	20162	22275	1923	5366	86736	42199	270679	1166099
Other Receipts **7**	3862063	263979	241695	27339	318964	55399	275544	49894	85231	44442	127761	725047	1646766
Total Receipts **8**	19718348	1177091	272947	67367	374548	103770	351232	89933	206541	424831	1230113	5077734	10342241
Average Total Receipts **9**	1636	761	33	187	293	895	2342	1697	5164	7325	26742	50275	220048

Operating Costs/Operating Income (%)

	Total	Zero Assets	Under 500	500 to 1,000	1,000 to 5,000	5,000 to 10,000	10,000 to 25,000	25,000 to 50,000	50,000 to 100,000	100,000 to 250,000	250,000 to 500,000	500,000 to 2,500,000	2,500,000 and over
Cost of Operations **10**	0.0	0.4	0.4	•	•	•	•	•	0.1	0.0	•	0.0	•
Salaries and Wages **11**	0.2	0.0	4.4	•	0.8	3.6	2.3	2.4	0.2	1.1	0.1	0.0	0.0
Taxes Paid **12**	0.3	0.4	2.5	6.4	2.7	2.4	1.9	2.6	1.8	1.4	0.3	0.1	0.0
Interest Paid **13**	51.7	62.1	12.1	23.4	5.2	27.1	13.4	35.7	26.3	58.8	71.5	48.1	54.7
Depreciation **14**	0.5	0.0	0.5	2.0	0.3	0.0	0.4	0.5	0.0	8.5	5.2	0.0	0.0
Amortization and Depletion **15**	0.1	0.0	0.3	•	0.2	0.4	0.6	0.0	1.3	0.1	0.1	0.0	0.0
Pensions and Other Deferred Comp. **16**	1.1	0.0	•	•	0.2	0.1	0.1	0.0	0.0	0.1	0.0	•	2.1
Employee Benefits **17**	0.1	0.0	3.1	0.0	1.1	0.2	0.1	0.1	0.1	0.1	0.0	0.0	0.0
Advertising **18**	0.0	1.3	•	•	0.1	•	0.1	0.4	•	0.0	0.0	•	0.0
Other Expenses **19**	12.3	21.5	64.4	89.8	41.5	37.9	43.1	38.9	44.1	39.9	8.1	4.6	9.2
Officers' Compensation **20**	0.5	0.0	11.7	1.2	14.4	0.5	4.2	0.6	0.1	0.3	0.0	0.0	0.0
Operating Margin **21**	33.2	15.4	•	•	33.4	27.9	33.7	18.6	25.9	•	14.7	47.2	33.8
Operating Margin Before Officers' Comp. **22**	33.7	15.4	11.1	•	47.8	28.4	37.9	19.2	26.0	•	14.7	47.2	33.8

Selected Average Balance Sheet ($ in Thousands)

Net Receivables 23	6525	0	29	110	42	1310	2397	4342	24601	37325	217335	1124841
Inventories 24	·	·	·	·	·	·	·	·	·	·	·	·
Net Property, Plant and Equipment 25	35	0	3	1	221	1449	55	1741	803	4	10	0
Total Assets 26	36422	80	766	2007	6874	16926	34704	67986	157120	356103	1059298	6277382
Notes and Loans Payable 27	20728	247	1305	741	1924	6337	11346	17525	71637	175979	430012	4003790
All Other Liabilities 28	3618	330	7	148	513	2954	7046	8950	18027	50410	155573	433375
Net Worth 29	12076	-497	-546	1118	4436	7636	16312	41511	67456	129714	473713	1840217

Selected Financial Ratios (Times to 1)

Current Ratio 30	0.6	0.1	0.5	8.2	10.1	1.3	3.5	3.1	0.8	0.8	1.0	0.5
Quick Ratio 31	0.5	0.1	0.5	7.1	4.9	1.0	1.4	2.1	0.7	0.7	0.7	0.4
Net Sales to Working Capital 32	·	·	·	0.5	0.4	2.0	0.2	0.3	·	·	·	·
Coverage Ratio 33	1.6	1.2	·	7.1	2.0	3.7	1.5	1.9	0.8	1.2	2.0	1.5
Total Asset Turnover 34	0.0	·	0.2	0.1	0.1	0.1	0.0	0.1	0.0	0.1	0.0	0.0
Inventory Turnover 35	·	·	·	·	·	·	·	·	·	·	·	·
Receivables Turnover 36	·	·	·	·	·	·	·	·	·	·	·	·
Total Liabilities to Net Worth 37	2.0	·	·	0.8	0.5	1.2	1.1	0.6	1.3	1.7	1.2	2.4
Current Assets to Working Capital 38	·	·	·	1.1	1.1	4.3	1.4	1.5	·	·	·	·
Current Liabilities to Working Capital 39	·	·	·	0.1	0.1	3.3	0.4	0.5	·	·	·	·
Working Capital to Net Sales 40	·	·	·	2.1	2.3	0.5	6.3	3.2	·	·	·	·
Inventory to Working Capital 41	·	·	·	·	·	·	·	·	·	·	·	·
Total Receipts to Cash Flow 42	2.3	3.7	1.6	1.4	1.8	1.4	1.8	1.5	7.7	4.4	2.0	2.4
Cost of Goods to Cash Flow 43	0.0	0.0	0.0	·	·	·	·	0.0	0.0	·	0.0	·
Cash Flow to Total Debt 44	0.0	·	0.1	0.2	0.2	0.2	0.1	0.1	0.0	0.0	0.0	0.0

Selected Financial Factors (in Percentages)

Debt Ratio 45	66.8	720.1	171.4	44.3	35.5	54.9	53.0	38.9	57.1	63.6	55.3	70.7
Return on Total Assets 46	3.6	4.7	·	5.4	6.9	2.5	6.9	3.9	2.2	6.5	4.5	2.9
Return on Equity Before Income Taxes 47	4.0	·	·	8.9	8.3	5.2	1.7	11.1	3.0	3.0	4.9	3.2
Return on Equity After Income Taxes 48	2.6	·	·	11.2	7.9	4.2	1.0	7.9	1.9	2.2	3.3	2.2
Profit Margin (Before Income Tax) 49	29.3	15.4	·	31.9	25.8	36.2	16.4	24.5	14.7	·	46.6	26.9
Profit Margin (After Income Tax) 50	19.6	6.8	·	30.3	20.8	25.6	10.1	14.9	10.5	·	31.3	18.2

Table II
Corporations with Net Income

OTHER FINANCIAL VEHICLES

MONEY AMOUNTS AND SIZE OF ASSETS IN THOUSANDS OF DOLLARS

Item Description for Accounting Period 7/05 Through 6/06	Total	Zero Assets	Under 500	500 to 1,000	1,000 to 5,000	5,000 to 10,000	10,000 to 25,000	25,000 to 50,000	50,000 to 100,000	100,000 to 250,000	250,000 to 500,000	500,000 to 2,500,000	2,500,000 and over
Number of Enterprises **1**	4003	607	2522	•	466	69	95	26	18	20	24	68	•
Revenues ($ in Thousands)													
Net Sales **2**	14243648	977402	203454	•	334452	85878	334521	76666	147594	211138	633751	3465139	•
Interest **3**	9418014	648673	28932	•	12104	16247	32896	29773	50983	80335	557977	2673680	•
Rents **4**	3584	34	93	•	278	0	943	14	0	2021	0	46	•
Royalties **5**	22957	0	0	•	0	0	12874	0	10062	21	0	0	•
Other Portfolio Income **6**	1545469	102146	98	•	28975	18029	22091	169	2166	80129	36318	218614	•
Other Receipts **7**	3253624	226549	174331	•	293095	51602	265717	46710	84383	48632	39456	572799	•
Total Receipts **8**	14243648	977402	203454	•	334452	85878	334521	76666	147594	211138	633751	3465139	•
Average Total Receipts **9**	3558	1610	81	•	718	1245	3521	2949	8200	10557	26406	50958	•
Operating Costs/Operating Income (%)													
Cost of Operations **10**	0.0	0.5	0.4	•	•	•	•	•	0.1	0.1	•	0.0	•
Salaries and Wages **11**	0.1	0.0	2.3	•	0.1	0.0	2.2	2.2	0.3	1.1	•	0.0	•
Taxes Paid **12**	0.3	0.5	0.6	•	2.5	2.6	1.8	2.8	2.4	1.1	0.0	0.1	•
Interest Paid **13**	37.9	56.7	10.1	•	3.4	16.5	7.4	29.7	7.1	32.6	64.6	26.0	•
Depreciation **14**	0.0	0.0	0.2	•	0.2	•	0.4	0.0	0.0	0.2	0.0	•	•
Amortization and Depletion **15**	0.1	0.0	0.4	•	0.0	0.0	0.5	0.0	1.7	0.1	0.2	0.0	•
Pensions and Other Deferred Comp. **16**	1.6	0.0	•	•	0.2	0.0	0.1	0.0	0.0	0.1	•	0.0	•
Employee Benefits **17**	0.0	0.0	0.1	•	0.9	0.1	0.1	0.0	0.1	0.2	0.0	0.0	•
Advertising **18**	0.0	•	0.6	•	0.0	•	0.1	0.1	•	0.0	•	•	•
Other Expenses **19**	8.7	9.1	26.9	•	13.5	2.4	32.7	9.0	42.1	26.1	4.3	2.0	•
Officers' Compensation **20**	0.5	0.0	4.6	•	13.3	•	4.3	0.7	0.1	0.4	0.0	0.0	•
Operating Margin **21**	50.8	33.2	53.9	•	65.9	78.4	50.3	55.6	46.1	38.1	30.8	71.8	•
Operating Margin Before Officers' Comp. **22**	51.3	33.2	58.5	•	79.2	78.4	54.6	56.3	46.2	38.5	30.8	71.8	•

Selected Average Balance Sheet ($ in Thousands)

Net Receivables 23	17133	0	0	290	21	1844	3084	3973	30677	19215	254950	•
Inventories 24	•	•	•	•	•	•	•	•	•	•	•	•
Net Property, Plant and Equipment 25	41	0	7	1	0	1123	101	67	1732	0	2	•
Total Assets 26	73766	92	6695	1779	17173	33463	64901	166901	384245	1052128		•
Notes and Loans Payable 27	31851	4	1448	674	4727	10541	3793	55896	161189	238464		•
All Other Liabilities 28	7392	1	557	236	3764	5871	3547	16681	4558	124177		•
Net Worth 29	34524	88	4690	868	8683	17051	57561	94324	218499	689486		•

Selected Financial Ratios (Times to 1)

Current Ratio 30	0.9	•	21.6	•	17.8	3.2	6.8	1.4	0.7	2.0	•
Quick Ratio 31	0.7	•	20.9	•	12.6	1.1	4.2	1.2	0.7	1.5	•
Net Sales to Working Capital 32	•	•	5.1	•	0.6	0.4	0.5	0.7	•	0.3	•
Coverage Ratio 33	2.2	1.6	6.3	•	5.7	2.9	7.5	2.2	1.5	3.7	•
Total Asset Turnover 34	0.0	•	0.9	•	0.2	0.1	0.1	0.1	0.1	0.0	•
Inventory Turnover 35	•	•	•	•	•	•	•	•	•	•	•
Receivables Turnover 36	•	•	•	•	•	•	•	•	•	•	•
Total Liabilities to Net Worth 37	1.1	•	0.1	•	1.0	1.0	0.1	0.8	0.8	0.5	•
Current Assets to Working Capital 38	•	•	1.0	•	3.8	1.5	1.2	3.6	•	2.1	•
Current Liabilities to Working Capital 39	•	•	0.0	•	2.8	0.5	0.2	2.6	•	1.1	•
Working Capital to Net Sales 40	•	•	0.2	•	0.4	2.5	2.2	1.4	•	4.0	•
Inventory to Working Capital 41	•	•	•	•	•	•	•	•	•	•	•
Total Receipts to Cash Flow 42	1.7	3.0	1.3	•	1.3	1.6	1.2	3.0	2.9	1.4	•
Cost of Goods to Cash Flow 43	0.0	0.0	0.0	•	•	•	0.0	0.0	•	0.0	•
Cash Flow to Total Debt 44	0.1	•	13.2	•	0.6	0.1	1.0	0.0	0.1	0.1	•

Selected Financial Factors (in Percentages)

Debt Ratio 45	53.2	•	4.9	51.2	29.9	49.4	49.0	11.3	43.5	43.1	34.5
Return on Total Assets 46	4.0	•	56.1	27.6	17.6	12.4	7.5	6.7	4.4	6.6	4.7
Return on Equity Before Income Taxes 47	4.7	•	49.7	53.8	20.8	21.5	9.6	6.6	4.2	3.7	5.3
Return on Equity After Income Taxes 48	3.4	•	49.1	52.4	19.2	17.0	8.3	4.6	3.6	2.7	3.6
Profit Margin (Before Income Tax) 49	46.1	33.2	53.9	65.1	78.4	53.1	55.3	46.0	37.6	30.8	71.4
Profit Margin (After Income Tax) 50	32.5	22.8	53.4	48.3	72.5	41.9	48.3	32.6	32.2	22.6	48.9

318

Table I

Corporations with and without Net Income

LESSORS OF BUILDINGS

MONEY AMOUNTS AND SIZE OF ASSETS IN THOUSANDS OF DOLLARS

Item Description for Accounting Period 7/05 Through 6/06	Total	Zero Assets	Under 500	500 to 1,000	1,000 to 5,000	5,000 to 10,000	10,000 to 25,000	25,000 to 50,000	50,000 to 100,000	100,000 to 250,000	250,000 to 500,000	500,000 to 2,500,000	2,500,000 and over
Number of Enterprises **1**	216362	24391	110798	34818	39157	4262	2107	513	181	89	28	15	3
Revenues ($ in Thousands)													
Net Sales **2**	40265793	2697300	3711046	3106653	10530008	3476097	4285440	2787793	1993731	1611729	2144803	2442862	1478333
Interest **3**	807403	26944	27320	35384	139577	50626	76206	58076	50012	61465	81712	129293	70789
Rents **4**	172358	12025	27930	7527	26208	6295	19493	27597	7021	4016	2062	239	31946
Royalties **5**	30400	31	78	172	9060	269	2729	5507	24	12227	295	8	0
Other Portfolio Income **6**	4355135	943635	313081	293769	917074	257226	333995	167566	472743	277755	116724	88561	173004
Other Receipts **7**	34900497	1714665	3342637	2769801	9438089	3161681	3853017	2529047	1463931	1256266	1944010	2224761	1202594
Total Receipts **8**	40265793	2697300	3711046	3106653	10530008	3476097	4285440	2787793	1993731	1611729	2144803	2442862	1478333
Average Total Receipts **9**	186	111	33	89	269	816	2034	5434	11015	18109	76600	162857	492778
Operating Costs/Operating Income (%)													
Cost of Operations **10**	14.3	6.1	6.5	4.6	18.5	4.0	19.3	18.0	10.3	14.1	35.1	19.5	8.5
Salaries and Wages **11**	8.8	2.2	10.0	5.9	10.1	12.4	9.3	9.2	8.4	7.4	8.4	9.5	6.0
Taxes Paid **12**	10.1	9.4	10.4	11.0	11.6	15.3	12.5	10.1	8.5	7.5	5.4	3.1	3.2
Interest Paid **13**	12.0	10.3	8.8	9.9	10.1	12.9	13.8	13.4	14.9	17.5	10.4	18.5	12.0
Depreciation **14**	7.8	7.7	6.7	8.0	7.3	10.8	9.7	8.3	7.3	8.5	5.1	9.3	2.7
Amortization and Depletion **15**	0.7	0.9	0.2	0.4	0.5	0.5	0.8	0.6	1.4	1.1	0.8	1.6	0.2
Pensions and Other Deferred Comp. **16**	0.3	0.3	0.0	0.1	0.6	0.5	0.4	0.4	0.2	0.2	0.2	0.0	0.0
Employee Benefits **17**	1.2	0.4	1.2	1.1	1.5	2.2	1.2	1.3	1.0	0.6	0.9	1.0	0.3
Advertising **18**	0.5	0.1	1.0	0.8	0.4	0.6	0.3	0.4	0.4	0.6	0.8	0.7	0.5
Other Expenses **19**	32.6	28.6	50.1	41.7	33.2	31.9	27.8	29.5	40.5	25.6	19.9	29.9	13.4
Officers' Compensation **20**	2.9	1.8	2.5	7.9	3.0	3.8	2.1	2.4	1.6	2.4	3.1	1.1	0.8
Operating Margin **21**	8.8	32.3	2.5	8.5	3.3	5.1	2.9	6.3	5.6	14.3	9.9	5.8	52.4
Operating Margin Before Officers' Comp. **22**	11.7	34.1	5.0	16.5	6.3	8.9	5.0	8.7	7.1	16.8	13.0	6.9	53.2

Selected Average Balance Sheet ($ in Thousands)

Net Receivables 23	40	0	3	21	44	168	419	1092	2832	7436	29729	35813	414186
Inventories 24	•	•	•	•	•	•	•	•	•	•	•	•	•
Net Property, Plant and Equipment 25	800	0	130	528	1485	4655	9846	20863	40213	82485	133504	492924	1713876
Total Assets 26	1255	0	179	712	2080	6747	15100	34528	66739	148328	336698	1071273	5485818
Notes and Loans Payable 27	798	0	122	514	1442	4470	9862	19834	38748	85569	156264	655621	1959787
All Other Liabilities 28	101	0	11	39	137	400	1160	3410	5162	18034	63028	144018	496695
Net Worth 29	357	0	46	159	501	1876	4077	11284	22829	44725	117405	271634	3029336

Selected Financial Ratios (Times to 1)

Current Ratio 30	2.0	•	2.4	2.2	1.8	2.0	1.9	2.3	2.1	1.5	2.5	0.7	5.2
Quick Ratio 31	1.3	•	1.7	1.6	1.2	1.5	1.3	1.6	1.6	1.3	1.7	0.4	1.1
Net Sales to Working Capital 32	1.7	•	2.1	1.7	1.9	1.6	1.8	1.6	1.7	2.1	1.4	•	0.3
Coverage Ratio 33	1.7	4.1	1.3	1.8	1.3	1.4	1.2	1.4	1.4	1.8	1.9	1.3	5.3
Total Asset Turnover 34	0.1	•	0.2	0.1	0.1	0.1	0.2	0.2	0.2	0.1	0.2	0.2	0.1
Inventory Turnover 35	•	•	•	•	•	•	•	•	•	•	•	•	•
Receivables Turnover 36	•	•	•	•	•	•	•	•	•	•	•	•	•
Total Liabilities to Net Worth 37	2.5	•	2.9	3.5	3.2	2.6	2.7	2.1	1.9	2.3	1.9	2.9	0.8
Current Assets to Working Capital 38	2.0	•	1.7	1.8	2.2	2.0	2.1	1.8	1.9	2.9	1.7	•	1.2
Current Liabilities to Working Capital 39	1.0	•	0.7	0.8	1.2	1.0	1.1	0.8	0.9	1.9	0.7	•	0.2
Working Capital to Net Sales 40	0.6	•	0.5	0.6	0.5	0.6	0.6	0.6	0.6	0.5	0.7	•	3.4
Inventory to Working Capital 41	0.0	•	•	•	0.0	0.0	0.0	0.0	0.0	0.0	0.0	•	0.0
Total Receipts to Cash Flow 42	4.4	3.6	3.4	3.8	5.8	4.2	5.4	3.9	5.3	4.5	5.1	4.8	2.0
Cost of Goods to Cash Flow 43	0.6	0.2	0.2	0.2	1.1	0.2	1.1	0.7	0.5	0.6	1.8	0.9	0.2
Cash Flow to Total Debt 44	0.0	•	0.1	0.0	0.0	0.0	0.0	0.1	0.0	0.0	0.1	0.0	0.1

Selected Financial Factors (in Percentages)

Debt Ratio 45	71.6	•	74.4	77.7	75.9	72.2	73.0	67.3	65.8	69.8	65.1	74.6	44.8
Return on Total Assets 46	3.0	•	2.1	2.3	1.7	2.2	2.2	3.1	3.3	3.9	4.6	3.7	5.8
Return on Equity Before Income Taxes 47	4.5	•	1.8	4.7	1.7	2.2	1.3	2.9	2.6	5.7	6.4	3.4	8.5
Return on Equity After Income Taxes 48	2.9	•	0.9	3.5	0.5	1.1	•	1.0	1.0	4.4	4.1	2.3	7.3
Profit Margin (Before Income Tax) 49	8.6	32.3	2.4	8.4	3.1	4.9	2.6	6.0	5.3	14.1	9.8	5.8	52.4
Profit Margin (After Income Tax) 50	5.5	23.8	1.2	6.2	0.9	2.5	•	2.1	2.1	10.8	6.3	3.8	44.9

319

Table II

Corporations with Net Income

LESSORS OF BUILDINGS

MONEY AMOUNTS AND SIZE OF ASSETS IN THOUSANDS OF DOLLARS

Item Description for Accounting Period 7/05 Through 6/06	Total	Zero Assets	Under 500	500 to 1,000	1,000 to 5,000	5,000 to 10,000	10,000 to 25,000	25,000 to 50,000	50,000 to 100,000	100,000 to 250,000	250,000 to 500,000	500,000 to 2,500,000	2,500,000 and over
Number of Enterprises 1	46633	7234	21520	7212	8547	1130	628	193	86	54	19	8	3
Revenues ($ in Thousands)													
Net Sales 2	26298310	1978177	2179625	2149200	6012318	1916637	2636332	1701323	1068624	1166707	1733470	2277565	1478333
Interest 3	610285	20426	18375	24941	81853	38469	54434	37818	42159	50615	52740	117667	70789
Rents 4	137519	12025	27930	6984	22170	5825	10617	11008	4993	3150	632	239	31946
Royalties 5	19484	31	25	172	3643	269	2729	65	24	12223	295	8	0
Other Portfolio Income 6	3542073	934183	134448	286400	682916	244131	311101	151228	173923	259543	113406	77793	173004
Other Receipts 7	21988949	1011512	1998847	1830703	5221736	1627943	2257451	1501204	847525	841176	1556397	2081858	1202594
Total Receipts 8	26298310	1978177	2179625	2149200	6012318	1916637	2636332	1701323	1068624	1166707	1733470	2277565	1478333
Average Total Receipts 9	564	273	101	298	703	1696	4198	8815	12426	21606	91235	284696	492778
Operating Costs/Operating Income (%)													
Cost of Operations 10	14.8	0.5	6.6	6.1	17.3	5.5	25.7	19.6	12.1	5.0	39.7	19.6	8.5
Salaries and Wages 11	7.5	1.0	10.0	6.4	10.3	8.3	6.6	5.6	7.7	5.4	5.6	9.8	6.0
Taxes Paid 12	6.7	7.8	9.0	6.4	7.0	8.3	7.6	6.9	8.7	7.3	5.0	3.0	3.2
Interest Paid 13	8.8	7.2	3.2	6.9	6.3	10.5	8.9	7.9	12.9	17.3	8.0	15.5	12.0
Depreciation 14	5.5	6.3	4.7	4.2	4.4	8.6	6.1	5.2	6.9	8.4	3.8	8.1	2.7
Amortization and Depletion 15	0.6	0.7	0.1	0.2	0.3	0.3	0.8	0.6	1.6	1.0	0.5	1.7	0.2
Pensions and Other Deferred Comp. 16	0.3	0.2	0.1	0.1	0.5	0.7	0.3	0.4	0.2	0.1	0.1	0.0	0.0
Employee Benefits 17	0.7	0.1	0.9	1.2	0.7	0.9	0.8	0.7	0.5	0.4	0.4	1.0	0.3
Advertising 18	0.6	0.1	1.2	1.1	0.4	0.7	0.2	0.3	0.5	0.5	0.8	0.7	0.5
Other Expenses 19	25.7	18.2	37.5	36.3	27.7	25.4	19.9	24.4	21.7	25.9	16.3	30.4	13.4
Officers' Compensation 20	3.3	2.2	2.2	9.1	3.9	4.6	2.4	2.4	1.5	2.5	3.8	1.1	0.8
Operating Margin 21	25.5	55.7	24.6	22.1	21.1	26.4	20.5	25.9	25.6	26.2	16.0	9.1	52.4
Operating Margin Before Officers' Comp. 22	28.8	58.0	26.8	31.2	25.0	31.0	22.9	28.3	27.1	28.8	19.8	10.2	53.2

Selected Average Balance Sheet ($ in Thousands)

Net Receivables 23	95	0	7	22	95	151	449	1156	3082	6096	26989	35665	414186
Inventories 24	•	•	•	•	•	•	•	•	•	•	•	•	•
Net Property, Plant and Equipment 25	1015	0	99	416	1170	4032	8369	19326	36710	81231	132125	434828	1713876
Total Assets 26	2070	0	177	697	2084	6673	15347	34994	66526	146994	341302	1167606	5485818
Notes and Loans Payable 27	1052	0	89	394	1120	3581	8706	16635	36140	82774	139211	736084	1959787
All Other Liabilities 28	202	0	11	69	190	276	1599	4254	6022	13889	46635	158538	496695
Net Worth 29	816	0	76	234	775	2816	5042	14105	24363	50330	155455	272984	3029336

Selected Financial Ratios (Times to 1)

Current Ratio 30	2.4	•	4.1	3.0	2.3	2.5	1.7	2.2	2.3	1.7	2.8	0.5	5.2
Quick Ratio 31	1.4	•	3.2	2.4	1.8	2.0	1.2	1.5	1.8	1.4	1.8	0.3	1.1
Net Sales to Working Capital 32	2.1	•	3.0	2.8	2.5	2.7	3.3	2.2	1.7	2.1	1.5	•	0.3
Coverage Ratio 33	3.9	8.8	8.7	4.2	4.3	3.5	3.3	4.3	3.0	2.5	3.0	1.6	5.3
Total Asset Turnover 34	0.3	•	0.6	0.4	0.3	0.3	0.3	0.3	0.2	0.1	0.3	0.2	0.1
Inventory Turnover 35	•	•	•	•	•	•	•	•	•	•	•	•	•
Receivables Turnover 36	•	•	•	•	•	•	•	•	•	•	•	•	•
Total Liabilities to Net Worth 37	1.5	•	1.3	2.0	1.7	1.4	2.0	1.5	1.7	1.9	1.2	3.3	0.8
Current Assets to Working Capital 38	1.7	•	1.3	1.5	1.7	1.6	2.5	1.8	1.7	2.4	1.5	•	1.2
Current Liabilities to Working Capital 39	0.7	•	0.3	0.5	0.7	0.6	1.5	0.8	0.7	1.4	0.5	•	0.2
Working Capital to Net Sales 40	0.5	•	0.3	0.4	0.4	0.4	0.3	0.4	0.6	0.5	0.7	•	3.4
Inventory to Working Capital 41	0.0	•	•	0.0	0.0	0.0	0.0	0.0	0.0	0.0	0.0	•	0.0
Total Receipts to Cash Flow 42	3.1	2.8	2.1	3.3	3.6	2.8	3.9	2.5	3.1	3.3	4.4	4.1	2.0
Cost of Goods to Cash Flow 43	0.5	0.0	0.1	0.2	0.6	0.2	1.0	0.5	0.4	0.2	1.7	0.8	0.2
Cash Flow to Total Debt 44	0.1	•	0.5	0.2	0.1	0.2	0.1	0.2	0.1	0.1	0.1	0.1	0.1

Selected Financial Factors (in Percentages)

Debt Ratio 45	60.6	•	56.9	66.4	62.8	57.8	67.1	59.7	63.4	65.8	54.5	76.6	44.8
Return on Total Assets 46	9.3	•	15.9	12.4	9.2	9.3	7.9	8.5	7.2	6.4	6.4	6.0	5.8
Return on Equity Before Income Taxes 47	17.6	•	32.7	28.1	19.0	15.8	16.8	16.1	13.0	11.3	9.3	9.5	8.5
Return on Equity After Income Taxes 48	14.3	•	30.0	23.9	15.5	13.2	13.2	12.2	10.0	9.5	6.8	7.4	7.3
Profit Margin (Before Income Tax) 49	25.4	55.7	24.6	22.1	21.0	26.2	20.2	25.8	25.4	26.3	15.9	9.1	52.4
Profit Margin (After Income Tax) 50	20.8	44.1	22.6	18.8	17.1	21.9	15.9	19.6	22.0	11.6	15.9	7.1	44.9

Table I

Corporations with and without Net Income

LESSORS OF MINIWAREHOUSES, SELF-STORAGE, OTHER REAL ESTATE

MONEY AMOUNTS AND SIZE OF ASSETS IN THOUSANDS OF DOLLARS

Item Description for Accounting Period 7/05 Through 6/06	Total	Zero Assets	Under 500	500 to 1,000	1,000 to 5,000	5,000 to 10,000	10,000 to 25,000	25,000 to 50,000	50,000 to 100,000	100,000 to 250,000	250,000 to 500,000	500,000 to 2,500,000	2,500,000 and over
Number of Enterprises **1**	67563	7545	40890	8965	8241	1076	563	145	75	39	11	13	0
Revenues ($ in Thousands)													
Net Sales **2**	18225105	561280	2660630	1155124	3021865	799632	1465657	602459	837061	4646737	605922	1868739	0
Interest **3**	506334	14843	12232	33567	59443	25883	40073	21473	41580	36669	23774	196799	0
Rents **4**	81530	4162	5442	2333	4878	2233	5344	6324	8036	296	20842	21640	0
Royalties **5**	69985	0	607	8714	307	10052	36449	2292	11565	0	0	0	0
Other Portfolio Income **6**	2370161	257851	162720	138913	395948	251189	218954	103398	131537	131600	111432	466618	0
Other Receipts **7**	15197095	284424	2479629	971597	2561289	510275	1164837	468972	644343	4478172	449874	1183682	0
Total Receipts **8**	18225105	561280	2660630	1155124	3021865	799632	1465657	602459	837061	4646737	605922	1868739	0
Average Total Receipts **9**	270	74	65	129	367	743	2603	4155	11161	119147	55084	143749	•
Operating Costs/Operating Income (%)													
Cost of Operations **10**	19.4	0.1	3.0	1.4	8.2	0.5	13.6	0.3	6.8	58.5	13.9	7.1	•
Salaries and Wages **11**	8.5	2.1	14.1	3.7	10.0	6.9	10.3	16.8	12.6	2.1	16.9	11.2	•
Taxes Paid **12**	4.4	6.2	6.1	5.9	5.9	7.2	5.0	6.0	3.7	1.1	3.3	5.0	•
Interest Paid **13**	8.0	4.4	2.9	7.5	8.2	8.3	9.5	11.3	10.7	2.7	7.6	25.9	•
Depreciation **14**	4.6	2.7	3.2	5.1	6.9	7.1	4.3	6.5	6.9	1.2	9.0	7.7	•
Amortization and Depletion **15**	0.7	0.0	0.1	0.2	0.2	0.8	1.0	0.7	0.8	1.0	0.7	1.3	•
Pensions and Other Deferred Comp. **16**	0.7	0.0	2.3	1.7	0.6	0.9	0.5	0.4	0.2	0.1	0.2	0.1	•
Employee Benefits **17**	0.7	0.7	1.7	0.5	0.3	2.3	1.4	1.2	0.9	0.1	0.3	0.6	•
Advertising **18**	0.8	0.7	1.0	3.9	1.1	0.3	0.5	0.4	1.2	0.0	1.0	0.3	•
Other Expenses **19**	35.3	42.5	42.3	48.5	43.1	24.9	24.6	26.3	28.5	31.4	37.8	30.3	•
Officers' Compensation **20**	5.0	0.2	10.4	6.6	4.7	15.1	3.6	5.4	4.4	0.2	8.6	6.2	•
Operating Margin **21**	11.8	40.5	12.9	15.0	10.9	25.7	25.9	24.6	23.2	1.4	0.5	4.4	•
Operating Margin Before Officers' Comp. **22**	16.8	40.7	23.3	21.5	15.6	40.7	29.5	30.0	27.6	1.7	9.1	10.6	•

Selected Average Balance Sheet ($ in Thousands)

Net Receivables **23**	54	0	5	17	90	360	801	1254	5072	4442	11621	66452
Inventories **24**	•	•	•	•	•	•	•	•	•	•	•	•
Net Property, Plant and Equipment **25**	531	0	95	413	972	2969	5923	13776	24659	52126	189260	446853
Total Assets **26**	1221	0	151	693	1825	7218	15283	34196	69803	154278	359727	1426757
Notes and Loans Payable **27**	555	0	72	410	1057	3423	7668	16438	32240	74599	115826	396433
All Other Liabilities **28**	184	0	22	54	193	536	1833	4393	10189	15101	68299	393377
Net Worth **29**	482	0	56	230	576	3259	5783	13364	27375	64578	175602	636947

Selected Financial Ratios (Times to 1)

Current Ratio **30**	2.5	•	1.7	4.7	2.1	1.9	1.9	2.3	2.0	0.7	5.3
Quick Ratio **31**	1.6	•	1.1	3.4	1.5	1.3	1.0	1.5	1.6	0.5	2.7
Net Sales to Working Capital **32**	1.7	•	5.8	1.2	1.8	1.6	1.0	1.0	11.9	•	0.5
Coverage Ratio **33**	2.5	10.3	5.4	3.0	2.3	4.0	3.7	3.1	3.2	1.5	1.0	1.2
Total Asset Turnover **34**	0.2	•	0.4	0.2	0.2	0.2	0.2	0.2	0.8	0.2	0.1
Inventory Turnover **35**	•	•	•	•	•	•	•	•	•	•	•
Receivables Turnover **36**	•	•	•	•	•	•	•	•	•	•	•
Total Liabilities to Net Worth **37**	1.5	•	1.7	2.0	2.2	1.6	1.5	1.4	1.0	•	1.2
Current Assets to Working Capital **38**	1.7	•	2.5	1.3	1.9	2.1	1.8	1.8	2.0	•	1.2
Current Liabilities to Working Capital **39**	0.7	•	1.5	0.3	0.9	1.1	0.8	0.8	1.0	•	0.2
Working Capital to Net Sales **40**	0.6	•	0.2	0.8	0.5	0.6	1.0	1.0	0.1	•	1.8
Inventory to Working Capital **41**	0.0	•	•	•	0.0	0.0	0.0	0.0	0.0	•	0.0
Total Receipts to Cash Flow **42**	4.0	3.4	2.2	2.8	2.6	3.2	2.9	2.9	23.7	5.5	12.2
Cost of Goods to Cash Flow **43**	0.8	0.0	0.1	0.0	0.2	0.4	0.0	0.2	13.8	0.8	0.9
Cash Flow to Total Debt **44**	0.1	•	0.3	0.1	0.1	0.1	0.1	0.1	0.1	0.1	0.0

Selected Financial Factors (in Percentages)

Debt Ratio **45**	60.5	•	62.6	66.8	68.5	62.2	60.9	60.8	58.1	51.2	55.4
Return on Total Assets **46**	4.3	•	6.8	4.1	3.8	5.9	4.3	5.4	3.2	1.2	3.0
Return on Equity Before Income Taxes **47**	6.5	•	14.8	8.3	7.0	11.4	7.4	9.5	2.6	0.1	1.0
Return on Equity After Income Taxes **48**	4.8	•	14.1	6.6	5.0	9.7	5.5	7.3	0.9	0.1	0.1
Profit Margin (Before Income Tax) **49**	11.7	40.5	12.8	14.9	10.9	25.4	24.0	23.2	1.4	0.3	4.4
Profit Margin (After Income Tax) **50**	8.6	27.4	12.2	11.8	7.8	21.5	17.8	17.9	0.5	•	0.5

Table II

Corporations with Net Income

LESSORS OF MINIWAREHOUSES, SELF-STORAGE, OTHER REAL ESTATE

MONEY AMOUNTS AND SIZE OF ASSETS IN THOUSANDS OF DOLLARS

Item Description for Accounting Period 7/05 Through 6/06		Total	Zero Assets	Under 500	500 to 1,000	1,000 to 5,000	5,000 to 10,000	10,000 to 25,000	25,000 to 50,000	50,000 to 100,000	100,000 to 250,000	250,000 to 500,000	500,000 to 2,500,000	2,500,000 and over
Number of Enterprises	1	23916	2928	14854	2778	2602	361	258	63	42	•	3	•	0
Revenues ($ in Thousands)														
Net Sales	2	14729818	431558	2093741	898749	2282388	692453	1229850	440446	604862	•	228629	•	0
Interest	3	368630	8051	6347	28595	49142	23604	26776	18347	27681	•	12759	•	0
Rents	4	51261	4162	3137	2231	4823	2098	4065	70	8036	•	3624	•	0
Royalties	5	67727	0	607	8714	307	10052	36449	34	11565	•	0	•	0
Other Portfolio Income	6	2209457	240941	151538	138815	371810	247728	212012	92298	128854	•	68179	•	0
Other Receipts	7	12032743	178404	1932112	720394	1856306	408971	950548	329697	428726	•	144067	•	0
Total Receipts	8	14729818	431558	2093741	898749	2282388	692453	1229850	440446	604862	•	228629	•	0
Average Total Receipts	9	616	147	141	324	877	1918	4767	6991	14401	•	76210	•	•
Operating Costs/Operating Income (%)														
Cost of Operations	10	21.6	0.1	3.8	0.0	6.9	0.1	16.1	0.3	2.5	•	•	•	•
Salaries and Wages	11	7.1	0.3	15.4	3.7	4.5	5.9	8.3	7.9	11.6	•	28.0	•	•
Taxes Paid	12	3.7	5.7	5.3	5.9	3.9	6.2	3.6	5.6	4.1	•	4.4	•	•
Interest Paid	13	5.1	3.7	1.8	5.8	4.6	6.4	5.1	6.6	7.6	•	2.6	•	•
Depreciation	14	3.0	2.7	2.6	4.8	5.6	4.7	2.6	4.6	4.7	•	4.3	•	•
Amortization and Depletion	15	0.6	0.0	0.1	0.3	0.1	0.5	0.9	0.6	0.8	•	0.5	•	•
Pensions and Other Deferred Comp.	16	0.6	0.0	2.5	0.1	0.3	0.6	0.4	0.5	0.2	•	0.2	•	•
Employee Benefits	17	0.6	0.0	1.3	0.5	0.2	2.4	1.4	1.2	0.6	•	0.2	•	•
Advertising	18	0.6	0.1	0.9	2.8	0.7	0.2	0.4	0.3	1.2	•	0.1	•	•
Other Expenses	19	27.4	13.9	21.3	40.3	40.7	15.2	18.5	18.6	20.7	•	22.4	•	•
Officers' Compensation	20	3.8	•	12.6	1.1	2.6	2.9	2.6	5.2	4.5	•	8.2	•	•
Operating Margin	21	25.9	73.4	32.4	34.6	30.0	55.0	40.0	48.5	41.7	•	29.2	•	•
Operating Margin Before Officers' Comp.	22	29.7	73.4	45.0	35.7	32.6	57.9	42.6	53.7	46.2	•	37.3	•	•

Selected Average Balance Sheet ($ in Thousands)

	1	2	3	4	5	6	7	8	9	10
Net Receivables 23	72	0	12	27	112	185	904	1200	3573	8164
Inventories 24	•	•	•	•	•	•	•	•	•	•
Net Property, Plant and Equipment 25	561	0	77	390	802	3136	5289	12097	19475	104861
Total Assets 26	1644	0	136	688	1922	7003	15317	35410	70051	330648
Notes and Loans Payable 27	503	0	37	292	896	3171	6265	12503	25101	18452
All Other Liabilities 28	334	0	24	80	201	463	1828	4585	10444	107501
Net Worth 29	807	0	75	315	825	3368	7223	18322	34506	204694

Selected Financial Ratios (Times to 1)

	1	2	3	4	5	6	7	8	9	10
Current Ratio 30	2.7	•	1.4	5.8	3.2	3.1	2.5	2.2	1.9	0.4
Quick Ratio 31	1.8	•	1.2	4.8	2.4	2.0	1.8	1.4	1.3	0.3
Net Sales to Working Capital 32	2.4	•	12.6	2.2	2.4	1.7	1.8	1.3	1.4	•
Coverage Ratio 33	6.0	20.8	18.8	6.9	7.6	9.5	8.7	8.3	6.5	12.3
Total Asset Turnover 34	0.4	•	1.0	0.5	0.5	0.3	0.3	0.2	0.2	0.2
Inventory Turnover 35	0.0	•	•	•	•	•	•	•	•	•
Receivables Turnover 36	•	•	•	•	•	•	•	•	•	•
Total Liabilities to Net Worth 37	1.0	•	0.8	1.2	1.3	1.1	1.1	0.9	1.0	0.6
Current Assets to Working Capital 38	1.6	•	3.5	1.2	1.5	1.5	1.7	1.8	2.1	•
Current Liabilities to Working Capital 39	0.6	•	2.5	0.2	0.5	0.5	0.7	0.8	0.8	1.1
Working Capital to Net Sales 40	0.4	•	0.1	0.5	0.4	0.6	0.5	0.8	0.7	0.7
Inventory to Working Capital 41	0.0	•	0.0	0.0	0.0	0.0	0.0	0.0	0.0	0.0
Total Receipts to Cash Flow 42	3.4	3.3	2.2	2.3	1.8	2.9	2.6	2.1	2.4	4.7
Cost of Goods to Cash Flow 43	0.7	0.0	0.1	0.0	0.0	0.0	0.4	0.0	0.1	0.1
Cash Flow to Total Debt 44	0.2	•	1.1	0.4	0.4	0.2	0.2	0.2	0.2	0.1

Selected Financial Factors (in Percentages)

	1	2	3	4	5	6	7	8	9	10
Debt Ratio 45	50.9	•	44.9	54.2	57.1	51.9	52.8	48.3	50.7	38.1
Return on Total Assets 46	11.6	•	35.3	18.9	15.8	16.7	13.9	10.8	10.1	7.3
Return on Equity Before Income Taxes 47	19.7	•	60.7	35.3	31.9	31.1	26.1	18.3	17.4	10.8
Return on Equity After Income Taxes 48	16.8	•	59.2	31.3	27.4	24.9	23.1	15.1	14.3	8.9
Profit Margin (Before Income Tax) 49	25.8	73.4	32.4	34.4	30.0	54.7	39.6	48.1	41.8	29.0
Profit Margin (After Income Tax) 50	22.0	56.4	31.6	30.5	25.8	43.7	35.0	39.7	34.3	23.8

Table I

Corporations with and without Net Income

OFFICES OF REAL ESTATE AGENTS AND BROKERS

MONEY AMOUNTS AND SIZE OF ASSETS IN THOUSANDS OF DOLLARS

Item Description for Accounting Period 7/05 Through 6/06	Total	Zero Assets	Under 500	500 to 1,000	1,000 to 5,000	5,000 to 10,000	10,000 to 25,000	25,000 to 50,000	50,000 to 100,000	100,000 to 250,000	250,000 to 500,000	500,000 to 2,500,000	2,500,000 and over
Number of Enterprises 1	116523	18000	91232	3921	3011	199	98	37	10	8	3	5	0
Revenues ($ in Thousands)													
Net Sales 2	73690794	1426397	41453204	6038910	11976797	1220169	2637803	1971549	889543	293944	1336791	4445687	0
Interest 3	234240	1751	29671	8262	29031	9061	15128	11737	2316	8059	4919	114305	0
Rents 4	307031	1416	25492	18295	33939	7148	41751	12257	206	13190	167	153169	0
Royalties 5	171524	0	0	2	33	0	0	3997	0	0	0	167492	0
Other Portfolio Income 6	402156	10560	34389	12035	54368	48423	11029	10288	1331	14403	29115	176212	0
Other Receipts 7	72575843	1412670	41363652	6000316	11859426	1155537	2569895	1933270	885690	258292	1302590	3834509	0
Total Receipts 8	73690794	1426397	41453204	6038910	11976797	1220169	2637803	1971549	889543	293944	1336791	4445687	0
Average Total Receipts 9	632	79	454	1540	3978	6132	26916	53285	88954	36743	445597	889137	•
Operating Costs/Operating Income (%)													
Cost of Operations 10	17.1	1.2	16.2	18.8	14.1	22.8	29.3	45.2	37.6	0.3	57.7	0.5	•
Salaries and Wages 11	29.2	6.0	24.9	32.7	41.5	29.0	31.5	14.7	21.3	31.8	9.2	51.7	•
Taxes Paid 12	1.6	1.8	1.3	1.8	1.3	2.6	1.2	2.5	2.1	3.7	1.6	3.2	•
Interest Paid 13	0.8	0.3	0.2	0.6	1.2	3.7	1.1	1.3	1.3	7.9	0.7	3.3	•
Depreciation 14	0.8	1.3	0.6	0.9	0.7	1.4	0.9	1.3	1.3	4.6	0.7	1.2	•
Amortization and Depletion 15	0.1	0.0	0.0	0.0	0.1	0.3	0.1	0.2	0.1	0.1	0.3	0.4	•
Pensions and Other Deferred Comp. 16	1.2	0.0	1.6	1.9	0.5	0.3	0.1	0.1	0.4	0.1	0.6	0.2	•
Employee Benefits 17	0.7	0.7	0.6	0.2	0.7	0.5	0.7	0.5	1.0	1.5	0.6	2.5	•
Advertising 18	3.2	5.0	3.6	3.3	2.6	1.4	3.1	2.3	3.9	6.4	2.8	1.0	•
Other Expenses 19	26.1	46.0	29.0	22.3	23.3	20.2	18.9	20.7	12.2	25.2	9.8	21.5	•
Officers' Compensation 20	8.3	11.3	11.1	7.7	4.7	2.4	3.0	1.6	7.2	0.9	1.0	2.4	•
Operating Margin 21	11.0	26.3	10.9	9.7	9.2	15.6	10.1	9.7	11.7	17.4	15.1	12.0	•
Operating Margin Before Officers' Comp. 22	19.3	37.6	21.9	17.4	13.9	17.9	13.0	11.3	18.9	18.3	16.1	14.4	•

Selected Average Balance Sheet ($ in Thousands)

	•	•	•	•	•	•	•	•	•	•	•	•
Net Receivables 23	26	0	3	39	118	571	2384	3481	7635	14130	54799	287354
Inventories 24	•	•	•	•	•	•	•	•	•	•	•	•
Net Property, Plant and Equipment 25	62	0	19	220	605	3084	3896	6671	21226	32365	31723	211449
Total Assets 26	262	0	75	723	1987	8107	15763	36617	66774	133298	303423	1558096
Notes and Loans Payable 27	110	0	31	316	1241	4051	8225	17615	25515	50964	4684	410937
All Other Liabilities 28	66	0	14	148	334	1091	2996	6661	15490	23713	129047	657739
Net Worth 29	87	0	29	259	412	2965	4542	12341	25769	58621	169692	489420

Selected Financial Ratios (Times to 1)

	•	•	•	•	•	•	•	•	•	•	•	•
Current Ratio 30	2.0	•	2.1	2.3	2.0	2.7	1.3	1.5	1.6	1.7	2.2	2.0
Quick Ratio 31	1.4	•	1.8	1.4	1.2	1.1	0.9	0.7	1.0	0.6	1.8	1.4
Net Sales to Working Capital 32	10.3	•	21.9	7.7	9.9	3.0	14.6	10.7	7.4	1.5	4.0	2.4
Coverage Ratio 33	15.1	103.7	47.4	16.1	8.6	5.2	10.3	8.6	10.0	3.2	23.7	4.6
Total Asset Turnover 34	2.4	•	6.1	2.1	2.0	0.8	1.7	1.5	1.3	0.3	1.5	0.6
Inventory Turnover 35	•	•	•	•	•	•	•	•	•	•	•	•
Receivables Turnover 36	•	•	•	•	•	•	•	•	•	•	•	•
Total Liabilities to Net Worth 37	2.0	•	1.6	1.8	3.8	1.7	2.5	2.0	1.6	1.3	0.8	2.2
Current Assets to Working Capital 38	2.0	•	1.9	1.8	2.0	1.6	4.0	2.9	2.7	2.4	1.9	2.0
Current Liabilities to Working Capital 39	1.0	•	0.9	0.8	1.0	0.6	3.0	1.9	1.7	1.4	0.9	1.0
Working Capital to Net Sales 40	0.1	•	0.0	0.1	0.1	0.3	0.1	0.1	0.1	0.7	0.3	0.4
Inventory to Working Capital 41	0.0	•	•	0.0	0.0	•	0.0	0.0	0.0	•	0.0	0.0
Total Receipts to Cash Flow 42	3.1	1.5	2.8	3.5	3.5	3.5	4.1	3.8	5.3	2.5	4.6	3.7
Cost of Goods to Cash Flow 43	0.5	0.0	0.5	0.7	0.5	0.8	1.2	1.7	2.0	0.0	2.6	0.0
Cash Flow to Total Debt 44	1.2	•	3.5	1.0	0.7	0.3	0.6	0.6	0.4	0.2	0.7	0.2

Selected Financial Factors (in Percentages)

	•	•	•	•	•	•	•	•	•	•	•	•
Debt Ratio 45	67.0	•	60.9	64.2	79.3	63.4	71.2	66.3	61.4	56.0	44.1	68.6
Return on Total Assets 46	28.4	•	67.6	22.1	20.9	14.6	19.0	16.0	17.1	7.0	22.8	8.8
Return on Equity Before Income Taxes 47	80.4	•	169.2	57.9	88.9	32.1	59.5	41.8	39.8	10.9	39.1	22.0
Return on Equity After Income Taxes 48	77.2	•	167.9	55.9	87.5	27.9	57.5	40.8	37.7	10.9	36.9	14.4
Profit Margin (Before Income Tax) 49	11.0	26.3	10.9	9.7	9.2	15.5	10.0	9.7	11.5	17.4	14.9	12.1
Profit Margin (After Income Tax) 50	10.6	26.1	10.8	9.4	9.1	13.5	9.7	9.4	10.9	17.3	14.0	7.9

Table II

Corporations with Net Income

OFFICES OF REAL ESTATE AGENTS AND BROKERS

MONEY AMOUNTS AND SIZE OF ASSETS IN THOUSANDS OF DOLLARS

Item Description for Accounting Period 7/05 Through 6/06	Total	Zero Assets	Under 500	500 to 1,000	1,000 to 5,000	5,000 to 10,000	10,000 to 25,000	25,000 to 50,000	50,000 to 100,000	100,000 to 250,000	250,000 to 500,000	500,000 to 2,500,000	2,500,000 and over
Number of Enterprises **1**	84324	10444	68980	2225	2371	185	71	25	10	•	3	•	0
Revenues ($ in Thousands)													
Net Sales **2**	66230961	1149438	36428677	5183849	11455529	1213995	2448281	1793498	889543	•	1336791	•	0
Interest **3**	166182	333	20829	3863	21268	9061	14961	9625	2316	•	4919	•	0
Rents **4**	222267	0	18561	4186	19330	7148	1777	12257	206	•	167	•	0
Royalties **5**	171497	0	0	2	6	0	0	3997	0	•	0	•	0
Other Portfolio Income **6**	353129	5436	29299	9302	48609	48423	11011	5381	1331	•	29115	•	0
Other Receipts **7**	65317886	1143669	36359988	5166496	11366316	1149363	2420532	1762238	885690	•	1302590	•	0
Total Receipts **8**	66230961	1149438	36428677	5183849	11455529	1213995	2448281	1793498	889543	•	1336791	•	0
Average Total Receipts **9**	785	110	528	2330	4832	6562	34483	71740	88954	•	445597	•	•
Operating Costs/Operating Income (%)													
Cost of Operations **10**	16.5	1.3	15.3	17.5	13.2	22.9	28.8	46.8	37.6	•	57.7	•	•
Salaries and Wages **11**	30.5	4.4	25.8	36.3	43.1	29.1	32.4	14.8	21.3	•	9.2	•	•
Taxes Paid **12**	1.4	1.5	1.2	1.2	1.3	2.6	1.0	2.7	2.1	•	1.6	•	•
Interest Paid **13**	0.6	0.2	0.2	0.3	1.0	3.5	0.5	0.9	1.3	•	0.7	•	•
Depreciation **14**	0.7	0.6	0.6	0.7	0.6	1.4	0.8	1.3	1.3	•	0.7	•	•
Amortization and Depletion **15**	0.1	0.0	0.0	0.0	0.1	0.3	0.1	0.2	0.1	•	0.3	•	•
Pensions and Other Deferred Comp. **16**	1.1	0.0	1.6	0.8	0.5	0.3	0.1	0.1	0.4	•	0.6	•	•
Employee Benefits **17**	0.7	0.4	0.6	0.2	0.7	0.5	0.5	0.5	1.0	•	0.6	•	•
Advertising **18**	3.1	4.5	3.5	3.4	2.7	1.4	3.0	2.4	3.9	•	2.8	•	•
Other Expenses **19**	24.2	40.6	27.3	18.8	21.9	19.1	17.2	17.5	12.2	•	9.8	•	•
Officers' Compensation **20**	7.6	9.7	10.0	7.6	4.7	2.4	2.9	1.7	7.2	•	1.0	•	•
Operating Margin **21**	13.5	36.8	13.9	13.2	10.2	16.5	12.6	11.1	11.7	•	15.1	•	•
Operating Margin Before Officers' Comp. **22**	21.1	46.5	23.9	20.8	14.9	18.9	15.5	12.7	18.9	•	16.1	•	•

Selected Average Balance Sheet ($ in Thousands)

	•	•	•	•	•	•	•	•	•	•	•
Net Receivables 23	31	•	0	2	20	134	615	2634	3275	7635	54799
Inventories 24	•	•	•	•	•	•	•	•	•	•	•
Net Property, Plant and Equipment 25	65	•	0	18	167	551	2905	3010	9020	21226	31723
Total Assets 26	288	•	78	678	1828	8203	16351	36008	66774	•	303423
Notes and Loans Payable 27	98	•	22	153	1094	4003	5783	14086	25515	•	4684
All Other Liabilities 28	81	•	15	205	373	1170	3455	7238	15490	•	129047
Net Worth 29	108	•	40	320	362	3030	7114	14684	25769	•	169692

Selected Financial Ratios (Times to 1)

	•	•	•	•	•	•	•	•	•	•
Current Ratio 30	2.0	•	2.4	1.9	2.0	3.3	1.4	1.6	1.6	2.2
Quick Ratio 31	1.4	•	2.1	1.2	1.2	1.4	1.0	0.8	1.0	1.8
Net Sales to Working Capital 32	11.3	•	20.8	12.7	11.7	2.7	15.0	12.1	7.4	4.0
Coverage Ratio 33	22.0	183.6	72.9	47.8	11.1	5.7	26.8	12.7	10.0	23.7
Total Asset Turnover 34	2.7	•	6.8	3.4	2.6	0.8	2.1	2.0	1.3	1.5
Inventory Turnover 35	•	•	•	•	•	•	•	•	•	•
Receivables Turnover 36	•	•	•	•	•	•	•	•	•	•
Total Liabilities to Net Worth 37	1.7	•	0.9	1.1	4.1	1.7	1.3	1.5	1.6	0.8
Current Assets to Working Capital 38	2.0	•	1.7	2.2	2.0	1.4	3.6	2.6	2.7	1.9
Current Liabilities to Working Capital 39	1.0	•	0.7	1.2	1.0	0.4	2.6	1.6	1.7	0.9
Working Capital to Net Sales 40	0.1	•	0.0	0.1	0.1	0.4	0.1	0.1	0.1	0.3
Inventory to Working Capital 41	0.0	•	0.0	0.0	0.0	•	0.0	0.0	0.0	•
Total Receipts to Cash Flow 42	3.0	1.4	2.7	3.5	3.5	3.9	4.0		5.3	4.6
Cost of Goods to Cash Flow 43	0.5	0.0	0.6	0.5	0.8	1.1	1.9	2.0		2.6
Cash Flow to Total Debt 44	1.5	5.2	1.9	0.9	0.4	0.9	0.8	0.4		0.7

Selected Financial Factors (in Percentages)

	•	•	•	•	•	•	•	•	•	•
Debt Ratio 45	62.5	•	48.5	52.8	80.2	63.1	56.5	59.2	61.4	44.1
Return on Total Assets 46	38.7	•	96.0	46.4	29.6	16.0	27.6	23.9	17.1	22.8
Return on Equity Before Income Taxes 47	98.6	•	184.1	96.3	136.3	35.8	61.1	54.1	39.8	39.1
Return on Equity After Income Taxes 48	95.3	•	182.9	93.5	134.3	31.3	59.4	52.8	37.7	36.9
Profit Margin (Before Income Tax) 49	13.5	36.8	13.9	13.2	10.2	16.5	12.6	11.1	11.5	14.9
Profit Margin (After Income Tax) 50	13.1	36.5	13.8	12.8	10.0	14.4	12.2	10.8	10.9	14.0

Table I

Corporations with and without Net Income

OTHER REAL ESTATE ACTIVITIES

MONEY AMOUNTS AND SIZE OF ASSETS IN THOUSANDS OF DOLLARS

Item Description for Accounting Period 7/05 Through 6/06	Total	Zero Assets	Under 500	500 to 1,000	1,000 to 5,000	5,000 to 10,000	10,000 to 25,000	25,000 to 50,000	50,000 to 100,000	100,000 to 250,000	250,000 to 500,000	500,000 to 2,500,000	2,500,000 and over
Number of Enterprises 1	187051	36874	124416	10199	12426	1334	1217	319	168	75	12	11	0
Revenues ($ in Thousands)													
Net Sales 2	68583845	3231392	21637062	7960321	10390593	3807395	5800177	3458971	2961194	3777306	701245	4858190	0
Interest 3	987531	55267	107970	31429	79818	41607	99619	103128	76308	63817	38965	289600	0
Rents 4	1534600	85184	173572	163151	211153	81838	229763	183864	122618	125503	16231	141724	0
Royalties 5	37252	0	881	0	12393	2828	12867	10	124	2433	0	5716	0
Other Portfolio Income 6	3372526	704757	281199	152955	553861	128768	246611	361895	319397	234212	71020	317850	0
Other Receipts 7	62651936	2386184	21073440	7612786	9533368	3552354	5211317	2810074	2442747	3351341	575029	4103300	0
Total Receipts 8	68583845	3231392	21637062	7960321	10390593	3807395	5800177	3458971	2961194	3777306	701245	4858190	0
Average Total Receipts 9	367	88	174	781	836	2854	4766	10843	17626	50364	58437	441654	•
Operating Costs/Operating Income (%)													
Cost of Operations 10	12.7	16.9	5.0	7.3	13.4	21.3	25.5	15.0	17.1	27.8	0.4	15.3	•
Salaries and Wages 11	24.7	6.8	25.2	44.5	25.0	14.1	13.9	15.6	18.4	32.8	15.3	27.0	•
Taxes Paid 12	3.5	3.3	3.4	4.0	4.7	3.1	3.1	3.2	3.7	2.2	2.7	1.9	•
Interest Paid 13	3.1	3.8	0.8	1.5	3.0	4.2	5.4	6.1	6.3	4.3	10.2	5.6	•
Depreciation 14	1.6	1.6	1.0	1.3	1.8	1.5	2.6	2.6	2.9	1.9	3.8	1.2	•
Amortization and Depletion 15	0.2	•	0.1	0.1	0.2	0.2	0.3	0.6	0.5	0.3	0.5	0.8	•
Pensions and Other Deferred Comp. 16	0.9	0.8	1.8	1.2	0.3	0.3	0.3	0.2	0.2	0.7	1.0	0.4	•
Employee Benefits 17	1.5	0.3	1.6	2.5	1.3	1.0	0.8	1.1	1.5	1.5	1.0	2.8	•
Advertising 18	1.0	1.2	1.1	0.3	1.1	0.5	0.7	1.8	2.1	1.4	0.6	0.2	•
Other Expenses 19	30.4	27.4	34.2	28.0	31.5	37.4	29.0	33.9	33.6	16.3	54.8	15.8	•
Officers' Compensation 20	8.1	5.4	15.5	5.7	6.3	4.4	4.9	4.3	2.7	3.1	3.5	1.4	•
Operating Margin 21	12.4	32.7	10.3	3.6	11.3	12.2	13.4	15.7	10.9	7.9	6.3	27.7	•
Operating Margin Before Officers' Comp. 22	20.5	38.1	25.8	9.3	17.6	16.5	18.3	19.9	13.6	11.0	9.8	29.1	•

Selected Average Balance Sheet ($ in Thousands)

	•	•	•	•	•	•	•	•	•	•	•	•
Net Receivables 23	55	4	59	143	588	814	2619	5037	9705	19786	273941	•
Inventories 24	•	0	•	•	•	•	•	•	•	•	•	•
Net Property, Plant and Equipment 25	184	24	254	670	1890	4786	9626	23184	34522	60972	173398	•
Total Assets 26	669	83	686	2166	6880	15188	34909	70594	151124	348711	1329284	•
Notes and Loans Payable 27	321	56	391	1084	4344	7938	16637	31160	46178	162735	380969	•
All Other Liabilities 28	140	17	91	372	1536	2814	7181	17218	42975	64146	347271	•
Net Worth 29	208	10	204	711	1000	4436	11091	22216	61971	121830	601043	•

Selected Financial Ratios (Times to 1)

	•	•	•	•	•	•	•	•	•	•	•	•
Current Ratio 30	1.7	2.2	2.5	2.3	1.9	1.6	1.7	1.3	1.1	1.1	1.7	•
Quick Ratio 31	1.1	1.5	1.9	1.3	1.2	0.8	0.9	0.8	0.8	0.6	1.1	•
Net Sales to Working Capital 32	3.8	8.4	4.8	1.9	2.6	2.9	2.2	3.7	14.0	4.7	2.3	•
Coverage Ratio 33	5.0	9.6	14.3	3.4	4.5	3.8	3.5	2.7	2.8	1.6	6.0	•
Total Asset Turnover 34	0.5	2.1	1.1	0.4	0.4	0.3	0.3	0.2	0.2	0.2	0.3	•
Inventory Turnover 35	•	•	•	•	•	•	•	•	•	•	•	•
Receivables Turnover 36	•	•	•	•	•	•	•	•	•	•	•	•
Total Liabilities to Net Worth 37	2.2	7.3	2.4	2.0	5.9	2.4	2.1	2.2	1.4	1.9	1.2	•
Current Assets to Working Capital 38	2.4	1.9	1.7	1.8	2.1	2.8	2.5	4.3	11.4	8.6	2.4	•
Current Liabilities to Working Capital 39	1.4	0.9	0.7	0.8	1.1	1.8	1.5	3.3	10.4	7.6	1.4	•
Working Capital to Net Sales 40	0.3	0.1	0.2	0.5	0.4	0.3	0.5	0.3	0.1	0.2	0.4	•
Inventory to Working Capital 41	0.1	•	•	0.0	0.0	0.0	0.0	0.1	0.3	0.0	0.7	•
Total Receipts to Cash Flow 42	3.1	2.6	3.9	3.1	4.0	3.3	3.1	3.3	6.3	2.2	2.5	•
Cost of Goods to Cash Flow 43	0.4	0.4	0.3	0.4	0.9	0.8	0.5	0.6	1.7	0.0	0.4	•
Cash Flow to Total Debt 44	0.3	0.9	0.4	0.2	0.1	0.1	0.1	0.1	0.1	0.1	0.2	•

Selected Financial Factors (in Percentages)

	•	•	•	•	•	•	•	•	•	•	•	•
Debt Ratio 45	68.9	87.9	70.3	67.2	85.5	70.8	68.2	68.5	59.0	65.1	54.8	•
Return on Total Assets 46	8.4	23.0	5.7	5.3	6.6	5.9	6.7	4.2	4.1	2.8	11.1	•
Return on Equity Before Income Taxes 47	21.7	177.7	13.7	12.7	33.4	14.3	15.0	8.4	6.4	3.0	20.4	•
Return on Equity After Income Taxes 48	18.4	172.4	10.9	11.6	29.8	12.3	12.2	5.5	5.0	1.9	13.8	•
Profit Margin (Before Income Tax) 49	12.3	32.7	10.3	3.6	10.8	11.7	13.3	15.4	10.6	7.9	6.3	27.7
Profit Margin (After Income Tax) 50	10.4	27.5	10.0	2.8	9.9	10.5	11.4	12.5	6.9	6.1	4.0	18.8

Table II
Corporations with Net Income

OTHER REAL ESTATE ACTIVITIES

MONEY AMOUNTS AND SIZE OF ASSETS IN THOUSANDS OF DOLLARS

Item Description for Accounting Period 7/05 Through 6/06	Total	Zero Assets	Under 500	500 to 1,000	1,000 to 5,000	5,000 to 10,000	10,000 to 25,000	25,000 to 50,000	50,000 to 100,000	100,000 to 250,000	250,000 to 500,000	500,000 to 2,500,000	2,500,000 and over
Number of Enterprises **1**	91107	14013	65702	4372	5464	719	541	164	80	37	7	8	0
Revenues ($ in Thousands)													
Net Sales **2**	52735833	2455858	16828482	5882407	7561720	3267824	4659280	2603937	2345379	2649555	406530	4074861	0
Interest **3**	720618	25344	85416	21114	69659	22582	74551	36617	36989	46267	30510	271571	0
Rents **4**	1081041	75960	124598	128904	145733	55281	126226	99964	102918	63640	16093	141724	0
Royalties **5**	30819	0	176	0	12393	2828	12867	10	124	2420	0	0	0
Other Portfolio Income **6**	3070845	691770	262061	145390	489391	104237	222432	334112	292786	153441	62428	312797	0
Other Receipts **7**	47832510	1662784	16356231	5586999	6844544	3082896	4223204	2133234	1912562	2383787	297499	3348769	0
Total Receipts **8**	52735833	2455858	16828482	5882407	7561720	3267824	4659280	2603937	2345379	2649555	406530	4074861	0
Average Total Receipts **9**	579	175	256	1345	1384	4545	8612	15878	29317	71610	58076	509358	•
Operating Costs/Operating Income (%)													
Cost of Operations **10**	11.9	10.3	4.4	6.0	16.4	21.2	29.2	12.8	15.2	7.6	•	17.9	•
Salaries and Wages **11**	22.8	3.7	21.9	50.1	19.8	12.0	12.6	15.2	16.9	44.5	6.3	21.2	•
Taxes Paid **12**	2.9	2.9	2.8	4.2	3.5	2.3	2.6	3.3	3.4	2.2	3.3	1.5	•
Interest Paid **13**	2.1	2.7	0.5	0.6	2.1	1.8	3.4	3.4	3.9	3.7	5.5	5.4	•
Depreciation **14**	1.1	1.4	0.9	0.3	1.4	0.8	1.5	2.1	1.6	1.8	1.7	1.3	•
Amortization and Depletion **15**	0.1	•	0.0	0.0	0.1	0.1	0.2	0.4	0.6	0.3	0.1	0.4	•
Pensions and Other Deferred Comp. **16**	1.0	1.0	1.9	1.5	0.3	0.3	0.2	0.2	0.2	0.4	1.7	0.4	•
Employee Benefits **17**	1.4	0.3	1.1	3.0	1.5	0.7	0.7	0.9	1.0	2.0	0.5	2.1	•
Advertising **18**	0.9	1.0	0.9	0.1	1.2	0.2	0.7	1.1	2.2	1.8	0.5	0.3	•
Other Expenses **19**	24.8	16.7	31.1	13.8	23.8	36.0	19.5	28.1	32.3	15.4	61.8	14.4	•
Officers' Compensation **20**	7.9	4.8	15.3	6.3	5.2	3.5	5.2	3.7	2.3	3.9	3.3	1.7	•
Operating Margin **21**	23.1	55.4	19.3	14.0	24.7	21.0	24.1	28.7	20.5	16.4	15.3	33.4	•
Operating Margin Before Officers' Comp. **22**	31.0	60.2	34.6	20.3	29.8	24.6	29.3	32.4	22.8	20.3	18.6	35.1	•

Selected Average Balance Sheet ($ in Thousands)

Net Receivables 23	78	0	5	67	168	776	1161	2371	5141	17415	16566	356192	•
Inventories 24	•	0	•	•	•	•	•	•	•	•	•	•	•
Net Property, Plant and Equipment 25	159	0	15	211	548	1778	3355	9334	21405	30419	35477	233655	•
Total Assets 26	721	0	82	709	2196	7106	15219	35253	72410	155997	341538	1519614	•
Notes and Loans Payable 27	258	0	37	242	866	3052	6049	14084	26738	46407	132022	337833	•
All Other Liabilities 28	167	0	14	152	385	1369	3297	7084	21896	50595	73752	432472	•
Net Worth 29	297	0	31	315	945	2685	5873	14084	23776	58996	135764	749310	•

Selected Financial Ratios (Times to 1)

Current Ratio 30	1.8	•	3.1	2.5	2.6	2.5	1.6	1.6	1.2	1.0	1.2	1.7	•
Quick Ratio 31	1.1	•	2.3	1.9	1.4	1.5	0.9	1.0	0.7	0.7	0.5	1.1	•
Net Sales to Working Capital 32	4.5	•	8.4	6.4	2.3	2.9	4.1	3.1	9.7	•	2.1	2.1	•
Coverage Ratio 33	12.1	21.4	37.8	24.0	12.5	12.6	8.1	9.4	6.2	5.4	3.8	7.2	•
Total Asset Turnover 34	0.8	•	3.1	1.9	0.6	0.6	0.6	0.5	0.4	0.5	0.2	0.3	•
Inventory Turnover 35	•	•	•	•	•	•	•	•	•	•	•	•	•
Receivables Turnover 36	•	•	•	•	•	•	•	•	•	•	•	•	•
Total Liabilities to Net Worth 37	1.4	•	1.6	1.3	1.3	1.6	1.6	1.5	2.0	1.6	1.5	1.0	•
Current Assets to Working Capital 38	2.3	•	1.5	1.7	1.6	1.7	2.7	2.5	7.1	•	5.5	2.5	•
Current Liabilities to Working Capital 39	1.3	•	0.5	0.7	0.6	0.7	1.7	1.5	6.1	•	4.5	1.5	•
Working Capital to Net Sales 40	0.2	•	0.1	0.2	0.4	0.3	0.2	0.3	0.1	•	0.5	0.5	•
Inventory to Working Capital 41	0.1	•	•	•	•	0.0	0.0	0.0	0.3	0.0	0.0	0.8	•
Total Receipts to Cash Flow 42	2.6	2.1	2.2	4.3	2.6	3.4	2.8	2.7	2.7	4.2	1.9	2.3	•
Cost of Goods to Cash Flow 43	0.3	0.2	0.1	0.3	0.4	0.7	0.8	0.3	0.4	0.3	•	0.4	•
Cash Flow to Total Debt 44	0.5	•	2.3	0.8	0.4	0.3	0.3	0.3	0.2	0.2	0.2	0.3	•

Selected Financial Factors (in Percentages)

Debt Ratio 45	58.9	•	61.9	55.6	57.0	62.2	61.4	60.0	67.2	62.2	60.2	50.7	•
Return on Total Assets 46	20.2	•	62.1	27.7	16.9	14.6	15.6	14.4	9.8	9.3	3.5	13.0	•
Return on Equity Before Income Taxes 47	45.1	•	158.6	59.7	36.1	35.5	35.3	32.3	25.1	19.9	6.6	22.8	•
Return on Equity After Income Taxes 48	40.4	•	155.4	55.4	34.3	33.1	31.9	28.0	19.7	16.9	4.9	15.5	•
Profit Margin (Before Income Tax) 49	23.1	55.4	19.3	14.0	24.7	21.0	24.1	28.7	20.3	16.4	15.3	33.5	•
Profit Margin (After Income Tax) 50	20.7	48.5	18.9	13.0	23.4	19.5	21.8	24.8	16.0	13.9	11.4	22.9	•

Table I

Corporations with and without Net Income

AUTOMOTIVE EQUIPMENT RENTAL AND LEASING

MONEY AMOUNTS AND SIZE OF ASSETS IN THOUSANDS OF DOLLARS

Item Description for Accounting Period 7/05 Through 6/06		Total	Zero Assets	Under 500	500 to 1,000	1,000 to 5,000	5,000 to 10,000	10,000 to 25,000	25,000 to 50,000	50,000 to 100,000	100,000 to 250,000	250,000 to 500,000	500,000 to 2,500,000	2,500,000 and over
Number of Enterprises	1	8759	1180	5418	694	1006	194	158	63	23	10	4	3	6
Revenues ($ in Thousands)														
Net Sales	2	37597789	114093	1083987	538576	1337016	646789	2130859	1681373	1152000	1021808	843642	1652640	25395006
Interest	3	845083	8	1402	102	1033	2296	4858	2110	1797	4552	13254	4240	809431
Rents	4	114149	0	0	584	821	0	2330	665	1577	0	954	545	106673
Royalties	5	26823	0	0	0	0	0	0	0	0	0	0	0	26823
Other Portfolio Income	6	2798216	459	26222	4676	123148	50985	169168	165142	102641	136892	108684	2892	1907306
Other Receipts	7	33813518	113626	1056363	533214	1212014	593508	1954503	1513456	1045985	880364	720750	1644963	22544773
Total Receipts	8	37597789	114093	1083987	538576	1337016	646789	2130859	1681373	1152000	1021808	843642	1652640	25395006
Average Total Receipts	9	4292	97	200	776	1329	3334	13486	26688	50087	102181	210910	550880	4232501
Operating Costs/Operating Income (%)														
Cost of Operations	10	17.7	47.3	14.4	35.3	11.3	19.5	36.0	34.3	46.3	32.4	1.6	0.2	14.9
Salaries and Wages	11	12.0	0.2	3.3	9.4	11.8	6.7	10.9	6.8	6.8	5.8	6.6	4.2	14.3
Taxes Paid	12	2.7	3.2	1.6	2.1	3.0	3.7	2.2	2.8	1.7	2.8	1.1	0.4	3.0
Interest Paid	13	6.4	3.9	3.5	3.5	4.8	3.9	3.8	5.6	5.2	4.1	4.8	6.8	7.1
Depreciation	14	23.7	17.1	14.1	11.4	27.6	24.9	19.4	28.4	19.4	29.3	44.7	76.6	20.1
Amortization and Depletion	15	0.1	0.0	0.0	0.0	0.0	0.0	0.0	0.1	0.1	0.1	0.1	0.3	0.1
Pensions and Other Deferred Comp.	16	0.4	•	0.1	•	0.3	0.2	0.2	0.2	0.3	0.1	0.1	0.2	0.6
Employee Benefits	17	1.5	•	0.5	0.8	0.5	0.2	0.9	0.6	0.6	0.8	0.8	0.4	2.0
Advertising	18	0.9	0.5	0.4	3.2	2.3	0.6	0.7	0.6	0.5	0.5	0.8	0.1	0.9
Other Expenses	19	25.5	22.0	67.3	24.1	26.2	22.7	18.8	12.8	11.2	14.7	21.7	4.7	27.8
Officers' Compensation	20	1.0	1.2	2.8	7.4	2.9	2.1	1.6	1.5	1.1	1.2	0.7	0.4	0.7
Operating Margin	21	7.9	4.6	•	3.0	9.3	15.6	5.5	6.3	6.7	8.1	17.1	5.8	8.6
Operating Margin Before Officers' Comp.	22	8.9	5.8	•	10.4	12.2	17.7	7.1	7.9	7.8	9.4	17.8	6.2	9.3

Selected Average Balance Sheet ($ in Thousands)

Net Receivables **23**	610	0	16	30	296	1105	1022	3916	6909	10573	103702	49886	580453
Inventories **24**	•	•	•	•	•	•	•	•	•	•	•	•	•
Net Property, Plant and Equipment **25**	4674	0	74	448	1363	5261	10576	23022	46545	100341	289991	736469	4878810
Total Assets **26**	7441	0	125	800	2053	7425	16346	35474	74528	140695	363138	1401494	7807568
Notes and Loans Payable **27**	3922	0	139	459	1159	4573	11122	23250	54252	98318	298348	798660	3698349
All Other Liabilities **28**	2166	0	7	28	132	657	1385	10864	8594	15768	33012	542192	2606025
Net Worth **29**	1353	0	-21	313	762	2195	3839	1360	11682	26608	31778	60643	1503193

Selected Financial Ratios (Times to 1)

Current Ratio **30**	0.5	•	1.4	3.2	1.8	1.9	0.7	0.5	1.1	0.6	0.7	0.1	0.4
Quick Ratio **31**	0.4	•	1.0	2.1	1.7	1.8	0.4	0.4	0.7	0.3	0.7	0.1	0.3
Net Sales to Working Capital **32**	•	•	24.4	3.3	5.5	4.3	•	•	47.6	•	•	•	•
Coverage Ratio **33**	2.3	2.2	•	1.9	2.9	4.9	2.5	2.1	2.3	3.0	4.5	1.9	2.2
Total Asset Turnover **34**	0.6	•	1.6	1.0	0.6	0.4	0.8	0.8	0.7	0.7	0.6	0.4	0.5
Inventory Turnover **35**	•	•	•	•	•	•	•	•	•	•	•	•	•
Receivables Turnover **36**	•	•	•	•	•	•	•	•	•	•	•	•	•
Total Liabilities to Net Worth **37**	4.5	•	•	1.6	1.7	2.4	3.3	25.1	5.4	4.3	10.4	22.1	4.2
Current Assets to Working Capital **38**	•	•	3.6	1.5	2.2	2.1	•	•	15.1	•	•	•	•
Current Liabilities to Working Capital **39**	•	•	2.6	0.5	1.2	1.1	•	•	14.1	•	•	•	•
Working Capital to Net Sales **40**	•	•	0.0	0.3	0.2	0.2	•	•	0.0	•	•	•	•
Inventory to Working Capital **41**	•	•	0.0	0.3	0.0	0.0	•	•	3.3	•	•	•	•
Total Receipts to Cash Flow **42**	3.9	•	6.6	8.8	4.4	3.6	6.6	7.1	7.7	6.0	2.7	11.6	3.5
Cost of Goods to Cash Flow **43**	0.7	•	0.3	3.1	0.5	0.7	2.4	2.4	3.6	1.9	0.0	0.0	0.5
Cash Flow to Total Debt **44**	0.2	•	0.6	0.2	0.2	0.2	0.2	0.1	0.1	0.2	0.2	0.0	0.2

Selected Financial Factors (in Percentages)

Debt Ratio **45**	81.8	•	116.9	60.8	62.9	70.4	76.5	96.2	84.3	81.1	91.2	95.7	80.7
Return on Total Assets **46**	8.3	•	•	6.3	9.2	8.8	7.7	9.0	7.9	8.9	12.7	4.9	8.6
Return on Equity Before Income Taxes **47**	25.4	•	76.0	7.4	16.3	23.7	19.4	124.3	28.6	31.3	113.3	52.7	24.6
Return on Equity After Income Taxes **48**	23.0	•	76.0	6.9	15.0	21.9	18.5	121.2	26.3	30.8	109.6	49.7	22.0
Profit Margin (Before Income Tax) **49**	8.0	4.6	•	3.0	9.3	15.6	5.5	6.3	6.7	8.1	17.1	5.8	8.7
Profit Margin (After Income Tax) **50**	7.3	4.5	•	2.8	8.6	14.4	5.3	6.2	6.1	8.0	16.5	5.5	7.8

Table II

Corporations with Net Income

AUTOMOTIVE EQUIPMENT RENTAL AND LEASING

MONEY AMOUNTS AND SIZE OF ASSETS IN THOUSANDS OF DOLLARS

Item Description for Accounting Period 7/05 Through 6/06	Total	Zero Assets	Under 500	500 to 1,000	1,000 to 5,000	5,000 to 10,000	10,000 to 25,000	25,000 to 50,000	50,000 to 100,000	100,000 to 250,000	250,000 to 500,000	500,000 to 2,500,000	2,500,000 and over
Number of Enterprises 1	4059	923	1865	426	550	115	104	38	18	•	•	0	•
Revenues ($ in Thousands)													
Net Sales 2	34274999	106910	280311	159530	939264	493766	1728166	1054414	984225	•	•	0	•
Interest 3	825359	0	104	0	1033	2260	3966	1410	1547	•	•	0	•
Rents 4	113460	0	0	0	821	0	2292	665	1577	•	•	0	•
Royalties 5	26823	0	0	0	0	0	0	0	0	•	•	0	•
Other Portfolio Income 6	2671034	0	25689	2309	117278	43308	143949	119154	86036	•	•	0	•
Other Receipts 7	30638323	106910	254518	157221	820132	448198	1577959	933185	895065	•	•	0	•
Total Receipts 8	34274999	106910	280311	159530	939264	493766	1728166	1054414	984225	•	•	0	•
Average Total Receipts 9	8444	116	150	374	1708	4294	16617	27748	54679	•	•	•	•
Operating Costs/Operating Income (%)													
Cost of Operations 10	17.3	50.4	•	•	11.2	14.8	40.8	38.5	49.3	•	•	•	•
Salaries and Wages 11	12.3	•	11.0	•	7.4	7.3	8.9	7.6	7.0	•	•	•	•
Taxes Paid 12	2.7	3.3	2.1	1.4	2.4	3.2	2.1	2.1	1.5	•	•	•	•
Interest Paid 13	6.4	2.0	4.6	4.5	4.8	3.1	3.5	4.2	4.3	•	•	•	•
Depreciation 14	23.2	15.9	20.1	25.2	31.5	22.6	17.8	23.2	15.9	•	•	•	•
Amortization and Depletion 15	0.1	0.0	0.0	•	0.0	•	0.0	0.1	0.0	•	•	•	•
Pensions and Other Deferred Comp. 16	0.5	•	0.3	•	0.5	0.1	0.2	0.1	0.3	•	•	•	•
Employee Benefits 17	1.6	•	1.8	2.6	0.7	0.2	0.9	0.6	0.6	•	•	•	•
Advertising 18	0.8	0.6	0.3	1.1	0.8	0.6	0.7	0.7	0.6	•	•	•	•
Other Expenses 19	24.2	21.3	33.8	27.6	22.6	22.8	15.6	8.7	10.4	•	•	•	•
Officers' Compensation 20	0.9	0.7	10.9	9.5	3.0	1.8	1.4	1.6	1.1	•	•	•	•
Operating Margin 21	10.0	5.8	15.0	28.1	15.1	23.5	8.2	12.7	9.1	•	•	•	•
Operating Margin Before Officers' Comp. 22	11.0	6.5	26.0	37.5	18.1	25.2	9.6	14.2	10.2	•	•	•	•

Selected Average Balance Sheet ($ in Thousands)

Net Receivables 23	865	0	18	19	102	1717	1160	4725	7822
Inventories 24	•	•	•	•	•	•	•	•	•
Net Property, Plant and Equipment 25	7172	0	73	517	1659	4608	10312	23489	43734
Total Assets 26	10827	0	114	911	2141	7174	16741	36688	76138
Notes and Loans Payable 27	4963	0	71	292	1363	3106	10876	23659	53795
All Other Liabilities 28	3665	0	11	6	110	716	1554	3185	8546
Net Worth 29	2199	0	32	612	669	3352	4311	9844	13797

Selected Financial Ratios (Times to 1)

Current Ratio 30	0.4	•	0.6	368.2	1.3	3.7	0.6	0.8	1.2
Quick Ratio 31	0.3	•	0.6	264.9	1.1	3.3	0.4	0.6	0.7
Net Sales to Working Capital 32	•	•	•	1.0	26.7	2.5	•	•	19.2
Coverage Ratio 33	2.6	3.9	4.3	7.2	4.2	8.4	3.4	4.0	3.1
Total Asset Turnover 34	0.8	•	1.3	0.4	0.8	0.6	1.0	0.8	0.7
Inventory Turnover 35	•	•	•	•	•	•	•	•	•
Receivables Turnover 36	•	•	•	•	•	•	•	•	•
Total Liabilities to Net Worth 37	3.9	•	2.6	0.5	2.2	1.1	2.9	2.7	4.5
Current Assets to Working Capital 38	•	•	•	1.0	4.9	1.4	•	•	6.3
Current Liabilities to Working Capital 39	•	•	•	0.0	3.9	0.4	•	•	5.3
Working Capital to Net Sales 40	•	•	•	1.0	0.0	0.4	•	•	0.1
Inventory to Working Capital 41	•	•	•	0.0	0.0	0.0	•	•	1.5
Total Receipts to Cash Flow 42	3.8	6.6	3.3	3.1	4.3	2.8	6.4	5.6	6.9
Cost of Goods to Cash Flow 43	0.7	3.4	•	•	0.5	0.4	2.6	2.1	3.4
Cash Flow to Total Debt 44	0.3	•	0.6	0.4	0.3	0.4	0.2	0.2	0.1

Selected Financial Factors (in Percentages)

Debt Ratio 45	79.7	•	72.1	32.8	68.8	53.3	74.3	73.2	81.9
Return on Total Assets 46	12.8	•	25.8	13.4	15.9	15.9	11.6	12.8	9.6
Return on Equity Before Income Taxes 47	38.5	•	71.0	17.2	38.6	30.0	31.6	35.6	36.0
Return on Equity After Income Taxes 48	35.5	•	70.9	16.8	36.0	28.1	30.4	34.9	33.6
Profit Margin (Before Income Tax) 49	10.0	5.8	15.0	28.1	15.1	23.5	8.2	12.6	9.1
Profit Margin (After Income Tax) 50	9.2	5.8	15.0	27.4	14.1	21.9	7.9	12.4	8.5

Table I

Corporations with and without Net Income

OTHER CONSUMER GOODS AND GENERAL RENTAL CENTERS

MONEY AMOUNTS AND SIZE OF ASSETS IN THOUSANDS OF DOLLARS

Item Description for Accounting Period 7/05 Through 6/06	Total	Zero Assets	Under 500	500 to 1,000	1,000 to 5,000	5,000 to 10,000	10,000 to 25,000	25,000 to 50,000	50,000 to 100,000	100,000 to 250,000	250,000 to 500,000	500,000 to 2,500,000	2,500,000 and over
Number of Enterprises **1**	14282	754	11709	1008	601	134	49	12	0	5	5	5	0
Revenues ($ in Thousands)													
Net Sales **2**	22750100	83678	3090500	2226561	1261028	1105223	1079535	286012	0	602889	1829947	11184726	0
Interest **3**	19084	149	421	276	2462	1004	703	0	0	2275	580	11214	0
Rents **4**	6360	0	1433	2567	0	0	0	0	0	0	1949	412	0
Royalties **5**	115825	0	0	0	0	0	0	0	0	0	0	115825	0
Other Portfolio Income **6**	117861	18902	19944	23925	13367	10682	14952	6828	0	4059	353	4849	0
Other Receipts **7**	22490970	64627	3068702	2199793	1245199	1093537	1063880	279184	0	596555	1827065	11052426	0
Total Receipts **8**	22750100	83678	3090500	2226561	1261028	1105223	1079535	286012	0	602889	1829947	11184726	0
Average Total Receipts **9**	1593	111	264	2209	2098	8248	22031	23834	•	120578	365989	2236945	•
Operating Costs/Operating Income (%)													
Cost of Operations **10**	26.4	20.4	24.9	26.3	30.9	32.4	44.4	15.9	•	23.7	35.8	22.9	
Salaries and Wages **11**	20.7	1.1	20.3	23.5	18.9	18.2	12.4	18.0	•	22.3	12.7	22.9	
Taxes Paid **12**	3.8	2.9	3.8	4.3	4.6	4.1	2.1	3.4	•	2.8	3.2	3.9	
Interest Paid **13**	2.4	•	1.7	1.4	3.6	1.6	1.8	6.6	•	7.7	3.3	2.2	
Depreciation **14**	9.0	3.5	5.1	6.3	10.9	11.5	9.7	25.1	•	14.9	14.2	8.5	
Amortization and Depletion **15**	1.5	0.4	0.0	0.2	1.1	0.3	1.0	0.1	•	1.3	5.1	1.8	
Pensions and Other Deferred Comp. **16**	0.1	•	0.1	0.2	0.2	0.4	0.0	0.2	•	0.4	0.1	0.0	
Employee Benefits **17**	1.1	0.2	1.2	0.5	1.0	2.4	0.9	2.6	•	0.8	1.4	1.0	
Advertising **18**	3.2	3.2	2.6	2.7	1.7	2.9	1.3	1.1	•	7.4	8.0	2.9	
Other Expenses **19**	28.0	45.6	30.6	27.7	26.3	16.9	24.1	22.5	•	20.7	14.1	31.7	
Officers' Compensation **20**	1.7	•	4.3	4.5	2.9	3.3	1.6	2.7	•	1.4	0.6	0.2	
Operating Margin **21**	2.2	22.5	5.3	2.3	•	6.1	0.8	2.0	•	•	1.5	1.9	
Operating Margin Before Officers' Comp. **22**	3.9	22.5	9.6	6.8	0.8	9.4	2.4	4.7	•	•	2.1	2.2	

Selected Average Balance Sheet ($ in Thousands)

Line Item	1	2	3	4	5	6	7	8	9	10	11
Net Receivables 23	84	0	4	48	102	710	2765	1810	22371	2466	134952
Inventories 24											
Net Property, Plant and Equipment 25	509	0	64	398	965	3194	7217	27513	50748	107297	727718
Total Assets 26	1207	0	116	678	1524	5774	15514	38486	170086	373273	1912253
Notes and Loans Payable 27	637	0	116	443	1447	2453	7769	25976	109727	160776	810323
All Other Liabilities 28	300	0	20	103	314	615	3290	6280	32442	79819	575861
Net Worth 29	269	0	-20	131	-236	2706	4455	6230	27917	132678	526069

Selected Financial Ratios (Times to 1)

Line Item	1	2	3	4	5	6	7	8	9	10	11
Current Ratio 30	1.3		1.4	1.6	1.9	3.2	1.5	0.4	1.2	1.6	1.0
Quick Ratio 31	0.7		0.7	0.9	1.3	1.2	1.1	0.3	1.1	0.5	0.6
Net Sales to Working Capital 32	25.0		21.1	23.4	12.3	5.2	10.8		18.0	5.3	
Coverage Ratio 33	1.9		4.0	2.7	0.4	4.9	1.4	1.3	0.6	1.5	1.9
Total Asset Turnover 34	1.3		2.3	3.3	1.4	1.4	1.4	0.6	0.7	1.0	1.2
Inventory Turnover 35											
Receivables Turnover 36											
Total Liabilities to Net Worth 37	3.5			4.2		1.1	2.5	5.2	5.1	1.8	2.6
Current Assets to Working Capital 38	4.9		3.4	2.6	2.2	1.5	2.8		5.5	2.5	
Current Liabilities to Working Capital 39	3.9		2.4	1.6	1.2	0.5	1.8		4.5	1.5	
Working Capital to Net Sales 40	0.0		0.0	0.0	0.1	0.2	0.1		0.1	0.2	
Inventory to Working Capital 41	1.4		1.1	1.0	1.0	0.5	0.6		0.2	0.9	
Total Receipts to Cash Flow 42	5.4	1.8	4.3	5.9	6.3	6.8	6.1	5.6	8.8	11.2	4.9
Cost of Goods to Cash Flow 43	1.4	0.4	1.1	1.5	1.9	2.2	2.7	0.9	2.1	4.0	1.1
Cash Flow to Total Debt 44	0.3		0.4	0.7	0.2	0.4	0.3	0.1	0.1	0.1	0.3

Selected Financial Factors (in Percentages)

Line Item	1	2	3	4	5	6	7	8	9	10	11
Debt Ratio 45	77.7		117.3	80.6	115.5	53.1	71.3	83.8	83.6	64.5	72.5
Return on Total Assets 46	6.1		15.9	11.9	1.9	11.0	3.7	5.3	3.2	4.7	4.8
Return on Equity Before Income Taxes 47	13.2			38.5	19.3	18.7	3.8	7.6		4.1	8.1
Return on Equity After Income Taxes 48	8.3			38.3	24.5	18.7	3.7	7.3		2.8	2.0
Profit Margin (Before Income Tax) 49	2.2	22.5	5.3	2.3	6.1	0.8	2.0	2.3		1.5	1.9
Profit Margin (After Income Tax) 50	1.4	18.2	5.1	2.3	6.1	0.7	1.9	2.3		1.0	0.5

REAL ESTATE AND RENTAL AND LEASING
532215

Table II
Corporations with Net Income

OTHER CONSUMER GOODS AND GENERAL RENTAL CENTERS

MONEY AMOUNTS AND SIZE OF ASSETS IN THOUSANDS OF DOLLARS

Item Description for Accounting Period 7/05 Through 6/06	Total	Zero Assets	Under 500	500 to 1,000	1,000 to 5,000	5,000 to 10,000	10,000 to 25,000	25,000 to 50,000	50,000 to 100,000	100,000 to 250,000	250,000 to 500,000	500,000 to 2,500,000	2,500,000 and over
Number of Enterprises **1**	6965	715	5409	550	152	97	27	•	0	0	•	•	0
Revenues ($ in Thousands)													
Net Sales **2**	12334929	82551	2260362	1405913	672734	696525	686566	•	0	0	•	•	0
Interest **3**	10850	149	129	275	2327	1004	499	•	0	0	•	•	0
Rents **4**	5043	0	125	2567	0	0	0	•	0	0	•	•	0
Royalties **5**	36335	0	0	0	0	0	0	•	0	0	•	•	0
Other Portfolio Income **6**	79328	18902	11417	10484	7984	10682	13364	•	0	0	•	•	0
Other Receipts **7**	12203373	63500	2248691	1392587	662423	684839	672703	•	0	0	•	•	0
Total Receipts **8**	12334929	82551	2260362	1405913	672734	696525	686566	•	0	0	•	•	0
Average Total Receipts **9**	1771	115	418	2556	4426	7181	25428	•	•	•	•	•	•
Operating Costs/Operating Income (%)													
Cost of Operations **10**	23.6	19.9	23.0	35.2	41.8	14.3	41.7	•	•	•	•	•	•
Salaries and Wages **11**	21.1	0.8	19.2	16.2	15.9	26.3	13.3	•	•	•	•	•	•
Taxes Paid **12**	4.0	2.9	3.8	4.0	2.7	2.9	2.4	•	•	•	•	•	•
Interest Paid **13**	2.1	•	1.7	1.1	0.7	1.8	1.8	•	•	•	•	•	•
Depreciation **14**	10.0	2.4	4.2	5.8	3.0	15.0	11.8	•	•	•	•	•	•
Amortization and Depletion **15**	1.4	0.4	0.0	0.0	0.8	0.0	0.3	•	•	•	•	•	•
Pensions and Other Deferred Comp. **16**	0.2	•	0.0	0.4	0.4	0.7	0.0	•	•	•	•	•	•
Employee Benefits **17**	1.4	0.2	0.9	0.5	1.0	2.4	0.8	•	•	•	•	•	•
Advertising **18**	1.8	3.3	2.4	1.5	0.6	3.1	1.7	•	•	•	•	•	•
Other Expenses **19**	23.7	45.7	30.4	25.2	20.4	19.5	18.1	•	•	•	•	•	•
Officers' Compensation **20**	2.2	•	3.7	4.9	5.0	3.7	1.5	•	•	•	•	•	•
Operating Margin **21**	8.6	24.3	10.6	5.2	7.8	10.2	6.6	•	•	•	•	•	•
Operating Margin Before Officers' Comp. **22**	10.7	24.3	14.3	10.1	12.8	13.8	8.1	•	•	•	•	•	•

Selected Average Balance Sheet ($ in Thousands)

Net Receivables 23	117			0	18	343	749	3874
Inventories 24								
Net Property, Plant and Equipment 25	571		70	490	640	2997	7163
Total Assets 26	1379		149	771	1780	5767	15571
Notes and Loans Payable 27	710		178	395	391	2549	7402
All Other Liabilities 28	363		17	65	650	543	3248
Net Worth 29	306		-46	311	740	2675	4921

Selected Financial Ratios (Times to 1)

Current Ratio 30	1.4		1.7	2.9	2.3	3.3	1.5
Quick Ratio 31	0.8		1.0	1.8	1.9	1.2	1.2
Net Sales to Working Capital 32	16.8		15.8	14.5	7.8	4.0	13.1
Coverage Ratio 33	5.1		7.3	5.5	12.2	6.7	4.8
Total Asset Turnover 34	1.3		2.8	3.3	2.5	1.2	1.6
Inventory Turnover 35							
Receivables Turnover 36							
Total Liabilities to Net Worth 37	3.5			1.5	1.4	1.2	2.2
Current Assets to Working Capital 38	3.5		2.5	1.5	1.8	1.4	3.1
Current Liabilities to Working Capital 39	2.5		1.5	0.5	0.8	0.4	2.1
Working Capital to Net Sales 40	0.1		0.1	0.1	0.1	0.3	0.1
Inventory to Working Capital 41	1.0		0.8	0.5	0.1	0.5	0.3
Total Receipts to Cash Flow 42	4.8	1.7	3.6	5.9	4.1	4.6	6.7
Cost of Goods to Cash Flow 43	1.1	0.3	0.8	2.1	1.7	0.7	2.8
Cash Flow to Total Debt 44	0.3		0.6	0.9	1.0	0.5	0.4

Selected Financial Factors (in Percentages)

Debt Ratio 45	77.8		130.5	59.7	58.5	53.6	68.4
Return on Total Assets 46	13.7		34.5	21.1	21.2	14.9	13.6
Return on Equity Before Income Taxes 47	49.5			42.8	47.0	27.3	34.0
Return on Equity After Income Taxes 48	40.6			42.6	40.3	27.3	33.7
Profit Margin (Before Income Tax) 49	8.6	24.3	10.6	5.2	7.8	10.2	6.6
Profit Margin (After Income Tax) 50	7.0	19.9	10.4	6.7	5.2	10.2	6.5

COMMERCIAL AND INDUSTRIAL MACHINERY AND EQUIPMENT RENTAL

Table I
Corporations with and without Net Income

MONEY AMOUNTS AND SIZE OF ASSETS IN THOUSANDS OF DOLLARS

Item Description for Accounting Period 7/05 Through 6/06	Total	Zero Assets	Under 500	500 to 1,000	1,000 to 5,000	5,000 to 10,000	10,000 to 25,000	25,000 to 50,000	50,000 to 100,000	100,000 to 250,000	250,000 to 500,000	500,000 to 2,500,000	2,500,000 and over
Number of Enterprises 1	29453	4087	17787	2643	3932	474	270	110	56	38	23	23	11
Revenues ($ in Thousands)													
Net Sales 2	54043471	616013	3633634	1865189	4240708	3342940	2872773	2663443	2139637	2093466	4345470	6689013	19541186
Interest 3	5339378	4604	12920	2588	11546	3660	51776	17107	18392	85344	131674	388466	4611302
Rents 4	342656	60	0	18	159	288	113	9732	6636	187	16911	48618	259936
Royalties 5	7677	0	0	0	244	950	0	844	0	2780	2176	199	485
Other Portfolio Income 6	3627446	72092	43927	90320	112690	68503	130047	92989	118710	223638	138339	1099144	1437049
Other Receipts 7	44726314	539257	3576787	1772263	4116069	3269539	2690837	2542771	1995899	1781517	4056370	5152586	13232414
Total Receipts 8	54043471	616013	3633634	1865189	4240708	3342940	2872773	2663443	2139637	2093466	4345470	6689013	19541186
Average Total Receipts 9	1835	151	204	706	1079	7053	10640	24213	38208	55091	188933	290827	1776471
Operating Costs/Operating Income (%)													
Cost of Operations 10	23.6	26.7	28.2	24.8	28.8	44.0	40.0	50.4	33.7	27.6	41.0	16.2	8.9
Salaries and Wages 11	10.3	6.3	17.4	12.1	13.2	7.4	9.2	8.6	8.2	8.0	9.4	10.8	9.8
Taxes Paid 12	2.0	1.3	3.6	2.6	2.7	3.7	1.9	1.7	1.6	1.4	1.8	1.5	1.6
Interest Paid 13	12.2	4.4	1.8	4.0	2.9	2.2	5.2	3.5	5.1	9.9	7.3	10.7	23.7
Depreciation 14	19.7	13.2	7.7	14.9	13.4	13.8	17.4	13.6	18.7	16.3	21.4	25.1	24.4
Amortization and Depletion 15	0.8	0.7	0.0	0.0	0.1	0.2	0.3	0.5	0.4	0.9	1.3	0.5	1.4
Pensions and Other Deferred Comp. 16	0.5	0.0	0.1	0.5	0.3	1.8	0.2	0.3	0.2	0.4	0.4	0.5	0.5
Employee Benefits 17	1.3	0.4	1.5	0.5	0.8	0.9	0.8	0.8	1.0	1.0	1.3	2.0	1.6
Advertising 18	0.5	0.3	1.1	0.9	0.5	0.4	0.3	0.5	0.3	0.2	0.4	0.3	0.4
Other Expenses 19	19.7	28.2	26.9	26.2	31.5	16.5	16.4	12.7	19.2	23.5	18.2	18.9	17.2
Officers' Compensation 20	2.1	3.5	8.5	3.9	5.2	4.5	2.6	1.5	1.4	1.4	1.3	0.6	0.5
Operating Margin 21	7.3	14.9	3.2	9.7	0.6	4.7	5.7	5.8	10.2	9.4	•	12.8	10.0
Operating Margin Before Officers' Comp. 22	9.4	18.5	11.7	13.6	5.8	9.2	8.3	7.3	11.5	10.8	•	13.4	10.5

Selected Average Balance Sheet ($ in Thousands)

Net Receivables 23	1970	0	20	49	354	787	2066	5047	12358	22268	88565	154588	4321167
Inventories 24	•	•	•	•	•	•	•	•	•	•	•	•	•
Net Property, Plant and Equipment 25	1630	0	46	421	815	4099	7414	15084	25579	57472	99969	292340	2239995
Total Assets 26	5799	0	118	745	1862	6711	15626	33767	64989	146731	352911	1039628	9731155
Notes and Loans Payable 27	3527	0	88	869	1165	3163	7731	17082	35723	84622	163687	363849	6603120
All Other Liabilities 28	950	0	12	43	310	774	3054	7255	13515	32404	98587	292945	1223275
Net Worth 29	1322	0	19	-167	387	2774	4841	9431	15752	29705	90638	382834	1904761

Selected Financial Ratios (Times to 1)

Current Ratio 30	1.7	•	2.6	2.5	2.5	1.1	1.4	1.1	1.6	1.1	1.5	1.6	1.8
Quick Ratio 31	1.4	•	2.3	2.0	1.8	0.8	0.8	0.7	1.1	0.8	1.2	1.1	1.6
Net Sales to Working Capital 32	1.6	•	5.7	6.5	2.2	56.4	7.1	18.5	4.1	9.3	4.1	2.6	0.8
Coverage Ratio 33	1.6	4.4	2.8	3.4	1.2	3.2	2.1	2.7	3.0	1.9	0.5	1.9	1.4
Total Asset Turnover 34	0.3	•	1.7	0.9	0.6	1.1	0.7	0.7	0.6	0.4	0.5	0.3	0.2
Inventory Turnover 35	•	•	•	•	•	•	•	•	•	•	•	•	•
Receivables Turnover 36	•	•	•	•	•	•	•	•	•	•	•	•	•
Total Liabilities to Net Worth 37	3.4	•	5.4	3.8	1.4	2.2	2.6	3.1	3.9	2.9	1.7	2.7	4.1
Current Assets to Working Capital 38	2.4	•	1.6	1.7	1.7	14.7	3.7	8.9	2.5	7.8	3.0	2.7	2.3
Current Liabilities to Working Capital 39	1.4	•	0.6	0.7	0.7	13.7	2.7	7.9	1.5	6.8	2.0	1.7	1.3
Working Capital to Net Sales 40	0.6	•	0.2	0.2	0.5	0.0	0.1	0.1	0.2	0.1	0.2	0.4	1.3
Inventory to Working Capital 41	0.1	•	0.1	0.2	0.2	2.2	0.5	1.8	0.4	0.8	0.5	0.2	0.0
Total Receipts to Cash Flow 42	5.5	3.1	4.5	4.2	5.4	7.1	6.0	7.1	5.3	4.9	14.8	4.5	5.2
Cost of Goods to Cash Flow 43	1.3	0.8	1.3	1.1	1.6	3.1	2.4	3.6	1.8	1.4	6.1	0.7	0.5
Cash Flow to Total Debt 44	0.1	•	0.5	0.2	0.1	0.3	0.2	0.1	0.1	0.1	0.0	0.1	0.0

Selected Financial Factors (in Percentages)

Debt Ratio 45	77.2	•	84.3	122.4	79.2	58.7	69.0	72.1	75.8	79.8	74.3	63.2	80.4
Return on Total Assets 46	6.0	•	8.6	12.9	2.0	7.2	7.3	6.6	9.0	7.2	1.8	5.7	6.1
Return on Equity Before Income Taxes 47	9.5	•	35.0	•	1.5	12.0	12.2	14.8	24.6	17.3	•	7.4	9.1
Return on Equity After Income Taxes 48	7.9	•	32.1	•	•	10.8	10.6	12.6	22.0	10.7	•	5.7	8.3
Profit Margin (Before Income Tax) 49	6.8	14.9	3.2	9.7	0.5	4.7	5.5	5.8	10.2	9.3	•	9.7	9.8
Profit Margin (After Income Tax) 50	5.7	12.7	2.9	9.1	•	4.3	4.8	4.9	9.1	5.8	•	7.4	8.9

Table II
Corporations with Net Income

COMMERCIAL AND INDUSTRIAL MACHINERY AND EQUIPMENT RENTAL

MONEY AMOUNTS AND SIZE OF ASSETS IN THOUSANDS OF DOLLARS

Item Description for Accounting Period 7/05 Through 6/06	Total	Zero Assets	Under 500	500 to 1,000	1,000 to 5,000	5,000 to 10,000	10,000 to 25,000	25,000 to 50,000	50,000 to 100,000	100,000 to 250,000	250,000 to 500,000	500,000 to 2,500,000	2,500,000 and over
Number of Enterprises 1	12208	1580	6580	1513	1843	348	175	73	38	11	•	•	•
Revenues ($ in Thousands)													
Net Sales 2	42093032	509880	1868834	1153572	3308284	2940494	1975028	2158072	1847347	1885984	•	•	•
Interest 3	5131079	820	9862	2094	7668	3381	26469	10083	16491	66313	•	•	•
Rents 4	279074	60	0	18	23	0	96	9359	6636	1811	•	•	•
Royalties 5	5302	0	0	0	244	950	0	844	0	0	•	•	•
Other Portfolio Income 6	3250331	63884	40572	60447	88860	54776	117619	80391	74120	23061	•	•	•
Other Receipts 7	33427246	445116	1818400	1091013	3211489	2881387	1830844	2057395	1750100	1794799	•	•	•
Total Receipts 8	42093032	509880	1868834	1153572	3308284	2940494	1975028	2158072	1847347	1885984	•	•	•
Average Total Receipts 9	3448	323	284	762	1795	8450	11286	29563	48614	171453	•	•	•
Operating Costs/Operating Income (%)													
Cost of Operations 10	20.6	30.2	28.0	14.9	26.5	46.6	35.4	52.6	37.8	53.7	•	•	•
Salaries and Wages 11	9.6	6.2	11.8	10.7	11.6	6.9	9.6	7.4	7.8	4.8	•	•	•
Taxes Paid 12	1.9	1.1	2.9	2.4	2.5	3.8	2.2	1.6	1.6	1.7	•	•	•
Interest Paid 13	12.8	2.7	1.7	3.4	2.0	2.1	3.3	2.6	4.4	3.2	•	•	•
Depreciation 14	17.6	8.3	8.7	14.5	10.5	11.0	15.6	11.2	17.1	10.3	•	•	•
Amortization and Depletion 15	0.8	0.2	0.0	0.0	0.0	0.0	0.2	0.2	0.1	0.9	•	•	•
Pensions and Other Deferred Comp. 16	0.5	0.0	0.1	0.7	0.3	2.0	0.3	0.4	0.2	0.1	•	•	•
Employee Benefits 17	1.3	0.5	1.0	0.1	0.8	0.9	0.9	0.6	1.0	1.0	•	•	•
Advertising 18	0.4	0.3	0.4	0.9	0.4	0.3	0.4	0.6	0.3	0.3	•	•	•
Other Expenses 19	18.6	19.3	19.2	23.4	28.5	14.9	14.9	10.4	14.6	10.5	•	•	•
Officers' Compensation 20	1.9	3.8	10.1	4.6	5.1	4.8	2.7	1.4	1.4	1.5	•	•	•
Operating Margin 21	14.2	27.4	16.1	24.5	11.8	6.8	14.6	11.1	13.6	12.0	•	•	•
Operating Margin Before Officers' Comp. 22	16.1	31.1	26.2	29.0	16.9	11.6	17.3	12.5	15.0	13.5	•	•	•

Selected Average Balance Sheet ($ in Thousands)

Net Receivables 23	4442	•	44	0	30	534	929	2496	4993	15735	81883
Inventories 24	•	•	•	•	•	•	•	•	•	•	•
Net Property, Plant and Equipment 25	2403	•	59	457	679	3649	7105	14865	27224	•	43152
Total Assets 26	11253	•	162	732	1797	6416	15527	33194	65543	•	341960
Notes and Loans Payable 27	6621	•	96	614	599	2941	6969	15405	36340	•	76402
All Other Liabilities 28	1799	•	13	20	256	913	3451	6850	10361	•	121529
Net Worth 29	2833	•	54	97	942	2562	5106	10939	18841	•	144030

Selected Financial Ratios (Times to 1)

Current Ratio 30	1.8	•	2.9	4.2	2.4	1.1	1.7	1.3	1.8	•	2.8
Quick Ratio 31	1.6	•	2.7	3.7	2.1	0.8	1.2	0.7	1.2	•	2.0
Net Sales to Working Capital 32	1.3	•	4.9	5.4	3.3	37.7	4.3	11.8	4.1	•	1.7
Coverage Ratio 33	2.1	11.0	10.6	8.1	6.9	4.2	5.4	5.3	4.1	•	4.7
Total Asset Turnover 34	0.3	•	1.8	1.0	1.0	1.3	0.7	0.9	0.7	•	0.5
Inventory Turnover 35	•	•	•	•	•	•	•	•	•	•	•
Receivables Turnover 36	•	•	•	•	•	•	•	•	•	•	•
Total Liabilities to Net Worth 37	3.0	•	2.0	6.5	0.9	1.5	2.0	2.0	2.5	•	1.4
Current Assets to Working Capital 38	2.2	•	1.5	1.3	1.7	9.0	2.4	5.0	2.3	•	1.6
Current Liabilities to Working Capital 39	1.2	•	0.5	0.3	0.7	8.0	1.4	4.0	1.3	•	0.6
Working Capital to Net Sales 40	0.8	•	0.2	0.2	0.3	0.0	0.2	0.1	0.2	•	0.6
Inventory to Working Capital 41	0.1	•	0.0	0.1	0.1	1.4	0.4	1.3	0.5	•	0.4
Total Receipts to Cash Flow 42	4.1	2.5	3.3	2.5	4.0	6.7	4.0	5.6	4.6	•	5.3
Cost of Goods to Cash Flow 43	0.8	0.8	0.9	0.4	1.1	3.1	1.4	2.9	1.7	•	2.8
Cash Flow to Total Debt 44	0.1	•	0.8	0.5	0.5	0.3	0.3	0.2	0.2	•	0.2

Selected Financial Factors (in Percentages)

Debt Ratio 45	74.8	•	66.9	86.7	47.6	60.1	67.1	67.0	71.3	•	57.9
Return on Total Assets 46	8.1	•	31.1	29.0	13.7	11.7	13.0	12.2	13.3	•	7.6
Return on Equity Before Income Taxes 47	16.5	•	84.9	190.9	22.4	22.4	32.2	30.0	35.0	•	14.1
Return on Equity After Income Taxes 48	14.7	•	82.1	183.9	20.2	20.7	29.9	27.2	31.7	•	9.9
Profit Margin (Before Income Tax) 49	13.6	27.4	16.1	24.4	11.8	6.8	14.6	11.1	13.6	•	11.8
Profit Margin (After Income Tax) 50	12.1	24.8	15.5	23.5	10.6	6.3	13.5	10.1	12.3	•	8.4

Table I

Corporations with and without Net Income

LESSORS OF NONFINAN. INTANGIBLE ASSETS (EX. COPYRIGHTED WORKS)

MONEY AMOUNTS AND SIZE OF ASSETS IN THOUSANDS OF DOLLARS

Item Description for Accounting Period 7/05 Through 6/06	Total	Zero Assets	Under 500	500 to 1,000	1,000 to 5,000	5,000 to 10,000	10,000 to 25,000	25,000 to 50,000	50,000 to 100,000	100,000 to 250,000	250,000 to 500,000	500,000 to 2,500,000	2,500,000 and over
Number of Enterprises 1	1954	396	1309	178	30	14	11	7	3	3	4	0	0
Revenues ($ in Thousands)													
Net Sales 2	1421570	6738	292114	12949	174023	98358	58279	172003	39833	159428	407844	0	0
Interest 3	28397	564	269	0	1658	461	129	581	0	7997	16739	0	0
Rents 4	39	0	0	0	0	13	0	26	0	0	0	0	0
Royalties 5	579828	2647	30897	0	50531	8886	0	55370	6088	132802	292608	0	0
Other Portfolio Income 6	14571	0	0	0	311	4847	5773	1	833	1595	1211	0	0
Other Receipts 7	798735	3527	260948	12949	121523	84151	52377	116025	32912	17034	97286	0	0
Total Receipts 8	1421570	6738	292114	12949	174023	98358	58279	172003	39833	159428	407844	0	0
Average Total Receipts 9	728	17	223	73	5801	7026	5298	24572	13278	53143	101961	•	
Operating Costs/Operating Income (%)													
Cost of Operations 10	8.3	•	10.3	•	1.4	35.6	5.3	27.4	•	•	•	•	
Salaries and Wages 11	15.4	•	9.1	1.2	32.5	13.8	14.9	6.6	•	0.1	25.1	•	
Taxes Paid 12	2.2	15.1	1.7	0.3	3.5	1.4	3.0	2.8	2.3	1.3	2.1	•	
Interest Paid 13	1.3	0.3	0.6	•	0.1	1.3	2.3	4.3	7.8	•	0.9	•	
Depreciation 14	1.6	0.2	0.1	•	1.2	0.5	1.3	0.5	•	0.0	4.6	•	
Amortization and Depletion 15	3.8	30.9	3.4	•	0.4	4.6	3.7	9.3	13.7	4.7	1.4	•	
Pensions and Other Deferred Comp. 16	0.4	•	0.0	•	2.5	•	0.6	0.0	•	•	0.3	•	
Employee Benefits 17	1.1	•	0.1	•	1.2	1.6	0.7	0.6	•	0.0	2.5	•	
Advertising 18	3.0	0.1	5.0	•	1.7	0.1	0.9	1.9	•	12.9	0.1	•	
Other Expenses 19	28.2	22.3	25.4	50.1	25.8	9.7	49.2	44.5	1.4	47.4	20.2	•	
Officers' Compensation 20	4.0	•	5.0	0.6	13.3	0.9	16.9	1.9	•	•	1.1	•	
Operating Margin 21	30.7	31.2	39.3	47.9	16.4	30.3	1.3	0.2	74.8	33.5	41.7	•	
Operating Margin Before Officers' Comp. 22	34.6	31.2	44.3	48.4	29.7	31.3	18.1	2.1	74.8	33.5	42.8	•	

Selected Average Balance Sheet ($ in Thousands)

Line Item														
Net Receivables 23	130	•	0	14	1	•	1721	242	3140	3555	•	0	28388	9234
Inventories 24	•	•	•	•	•	•	•	•	•	•	•	•	•	•
Net Property, Plant and Equipment 25	195	•	0	90	315	619	7532	1295	456	•	0	2	•	86319
Total Assets 26	1696	580	3427	7532	18607	36661	66657	120636	465447					
Notes and Loans Payable 27	142	0	0	56	0	128	1546	3501	9758	0	18120			
All Other Liabilities 28	357	0	35	13	1266	1015	6089	16536	23324	-12793	95834			
Net Worth 29	1197	0	-1	567	2033	4971	9016	10366	43334	133429	351493			

Selected Financial Ratios (Times to 1)

Line Item														
Current Ratio 30	1.7	•	0.8	1.4	2.3	3.1	0.8	1.9	•	0.5	•	1.8		
Quick Ratio 31	1.2	•	0.8	1.2	1.9	2.6	0.7	1.6	•	0.1	•	0.6		
Net Sales to Working Capital 32	5.3	•	14.6	3.4	2.8	•	5.0	•	1.7	4.6				
Coverage Ratio 33	24.0	92.3	63.4	•	129.8	24.9	1.5	1.0	10.3	46.8				
Total Asset Turnover 34	0.4	•	2.5	0.1	1.7	0.9	0.3	0.7	0.2	0.4	0.2			
Inventory Turnover 35	•	•	•	•	•	•	•	•	•	•	•			
Receivables Turnover 36	•	•	•	•	•	•	•	•	•	•	0.3			
Total Liabilities to Net Worth 37	0.4	•	0.0	0.7	0.5	1.1	2.5	0.5	0.5	0.3				
Current Assets to Working Capital 38	2.4	•	3.6	1.8	1.5	2.2	2.2	1.0	2.2					
Current Liabilities to Working Capital 39	1.4	•	2.6	0.8	0.5	1.2	•	1.2						
Working Capital to Net Sales 40	0.2	•	0.1	0.3	0.4	0.2	•	0.6	0.2					
Inventory to Working Capital 41	0.0	•	•	0.0	0.0	0.1	•	0.0						
Total Receipts to Cash Flow 42	1.8	2.1	1.6	1.0	2.6	2.9	2.0	2.3	1.3	1.2	1.7			
Cost of Goods to Cash Flow 43	0.1	0.2	•	0.0	1.0	0.1	0.6	•						
Cash Flow to Total Debt 44	0.8	•	1.6	5.5	1.6	0.9	0.3	0.4	•	0.5				

Selected Financial Factors (in Percentages)

Line Item												
Debt Ratio 45	29.4	•	100.6	2.2	40.7	34.0	51.5	71.7	35.0	•	24.5	
Return on Total Assets 46	13.6	98.6	6.0	27.9	29.5	1.0	3.0	16.0	14.3	9.3		
Return on Equity Before Income Taxes 47	18.5	•	•	6.1	46.7	42.8	0.7	0.4	22.3	12.9	12.1	
Return on Equity After Income Taxes 48	14.7	•	•	6.1	39.1	39.2	0.7	22.3	8.4	8.3		
Profit Margin (Before Income Tax) 49	30.5	31.2	39.3	47.9	16.4	30.3	1.3	0.2	72.7	32.5	41.7	
Profit Margin (After Income Tax) 50	24.2	16.2	37.8	47.9	13.7	27.7	1.3	72.7	21.2	28.6		

Table II
Corporations with Net Income

LESSORS OF NONFINAN. INTANGIBLE ASSETS (EX. COPYRIGHTED WORKS)

MONEY AMOUNTS AND SIZE OF ASSETS IN THOUSANDS OF DOLLARS

Item Description for Accounting Period 7/05 Through 6/06	Total	Zero Assets	Under 500	500 to 1,000	1,000 to 5,000	5,000 to 10,000	10,000 to 25,000	25,000 to 50,000	50,000 to 100,000	100,000 to 250,000	250,000 to 500,000	500,000 to 2,500,000	2,500,000 and over
Number of Enterprises 1	870	17	793	0	30	11	7	•	3	0	•	0	0
Revenues ($ in Thousands)													
Net Sales 2	1374605	4091	290453	0	174023	82162	51828	•	192819	0	0	0	0
Interest 3	28269	564	269	0	1658	461	0	•	7997	0	•	0	0
Rents 4	39	0	0	0	0	13	0	•	0	0	0	0	0
Royalties 5	571094	0	30897	0	50531	8886	0	•	132802	0	•	0	0
Other Portfolio Income 6	14218	0	0	0	311	4847	5773	•	2074	0	0	0	0
Other Receipts 7	760985	3527	259287	0	121523	67955	46055	•	49946	0	•	0	0
Total Receipts 8	1374605	4091	290453	0	174023	82162	51828	•	192819	0	0	0	0
Average Total Receipts 9	1580	241	366	•	5801	7469	7404	•	64273	•	•	•	•
Operating Costs/Operating Income (%)													
Cost of Operations 10	7.7	•	8.7	•	1.4	38.4	•	•	•	•	•	•	•
Salaries and Wages 11	14.6	•	7.9	•	32.5	1.4	16.8	•	0.1	0	•	•	•
Taxes Paid 12	2.1	7.8	1.6	•	3.5	0.8	3.3	•	1.4	0	•	•	•
Interest Paid 13	0.7	0.6	0.3	•	0.1	1.0	1.6	•	•	•	•	•	•
Depreciation 14	1.6	0.3	0.1	•	1.2	0.2	1.4	•	0.0	•	•	•	•
Amortization and Depletion 15	2.9	3.8	2.8	•	0.4	2.2	4.1	•	3.9	•	•	•	•
Pensions and Other Deferred Comp. 16	0.4	•	•	•	2.5	•	0.7	•	•	•	•	•	•
Employee Benefits 17	1.0	•	0.0	•	1.2	0.0	0.6	•	0.0	•	•	•	•
Advertising 18	3.0	0.2	4.5	•	1.7	0.2	1.0	•	10.7	•	•	•	•
Other Expenses 19	24.1	13.7	15.3	•	25.8	7.5	17.0	•	39.3	•	•	•	•
Officers' Compensation 20	3.6	•	5.0	•	13.3	1.1	5.5	•	•	•	•	•	•
Operating Margin 21	38.1	73.7	54.0	•	16.4	47.2	48.1	•	44.6	•	•	•	•
Operating Margin Before Officers' Comp. 22	41.7	73.7	59.0	•	29.7	48.4	53.5	•	44.6	•	•	•	•

Selected Average Balance Sheet ($ in Thousands)

Line Item									
Net Receivables 23	190	0	23	•	1721	144	4316	•	1521
Inventories 24	•	•	•	•	•	•	•	•	•
Net Property, Plant and Equipment 25	431	0	0	•	315	695	1376	•	2
Total Assets 26	3207	0	111	•	3427	7728	23398	•	100672
Notes and Loans Payable 27	186	0	27	•	128	1227	1916	•	0
All Other Liabilities 28	595	0	58	•	1266	274	1306	•	-12793
Net Worth 29	2425	0	27	•	2033	6227	20176	•	113465

Selected Financial Ratios (Times to 1)

Line Item									
Current Ratio 30	2.1	•	1.2	•	2.3	9.0	3.2	•	•
Quick Ratio 31	1.4	•	1.2	•	1.9	7.8	3.2	•	•
Net Sales to Working Capital 32	5.1	•	24.7	•	3.4	2.0	1.8	•	18.1
Coverage Ratio 33	51.8	132.0	212.8	•	129.8	48.8	31.9	•	•
Total Asset Turnover 34	0.5	•	3.3	•	1.7	1.0	0.3	•	0.6
Inventory Turnover 35	•	•	•	•	•	•	•	•	•
Receivables Turnover 36	•	•	•	•	•	•	•	•	•
Total Liabilities to Net Worth 37	0.3	•	3.1	•	0.7	0.2	0.2	•	•
Current Assets to Working Capital 38	1.9	•	5.4	•	1.8	1.1	1.4	•	1.0
Current Liabilities to Working Capital 39	0.9	•	4.4	•	0.8	0.1	0.4	•	•
Working Capital to Net Sales 40	0.2	•	0.0	•	0.3	0.5	0.5	•	0.1
Inventory to Working Capital 41	0.0	•	0.0	•	0.0	0.0	0.0	•	•
Total Receipts to Cash Flow 42	1.7	1.3	1.5	•	2.6	2.0	1.6	•	1.2
Cost of Goods to Cash Flow 43	0.1	•	0.1	•	0.0	0.8	0.0	•	•
Cash Flow to Total Debt 44	1.2	•	3.0	•	1.6	2.4	1.5	•	•

Selected Financial Factors (in Percentages)

Line Item									
Debt Ratio 45	24.4	•	75.9	•	40.7	19.4	13.8	•	•
Return on Total Assets 46	19.1	•	178.8	•	27.9	46.6	15.7	•	27.8
Return on Equity Before Income Taxes 47	24.7	•	737.6	•	46.7	56.6	17.6	•	24.7
Return on Equity After Income Taxes 48	20.5	•	716.8	•	39.1	52.9	17.6	•	19.4
Profit Margin (Before Income Tax) 49	38.0	73.7	54.0	•	16.4	47.2	48.1	•	43.5
Profit Margin (After Income Tax) 50	31.5	49.1	52.4	•	13.7	44.1	48.1	•	34.2

Table I

Corporations with and without Net Income

LEGAL SERVICES

MONEY AMOUNTS AND SIZE OF ASSETS IN THOUSANDS OF DOLLARS

Item Description for Accounting Period 7/05 Through 6/06		Total	Zero Assets	Under 500	500 to 1,000	1,000 to 5,000	5,000 to 10,000	10,000 to 25,000	25,000 to 50,000	50,000 to 100,000	100,000 to 250,000	250,000 to 500,000	500,000 to 2,500,000	2,500,000 and over
Number of Enterprises	1	104389	16062	83284	2401	2289	189	110	38	10	5	0	0	0
Revenues ($ in Thousands)														
Net Sales	2	83136775	3050364	47099980	6050218	10740977	5207256	5102540	3332763	647596	1905080	0	0	0
Interest	3	102133	772	23514	7116	11437	5261	5113	6916	5468	36535	0	0	0
Rents	4	63675	0	13613	17077	19690	6797	2900	1366	0	2233	0	0	0
Royalties	5	5270	0	4525	0	735	0	0	10	0	0	0	0	0
Other Portfolio Income	6	52233	1	23505	6224	3314	6268	2530	1869	3369	5151	0	0	0
Other Receipts	7	3665388	17814	2569849	99657	441771	304148	103829	70919	41785	15617	0	0	0
Total Receipts	8	87025474	3068951	49734986	6180292	11217924	5529730	5216912	3413843	698218	1964616	0	0	0
Average Total Receipts	9	834	191	597	2574	4901	29258	47426	89838	69822	392923	·	·	·
Operating Costs/Operating Income (%)														
Cost of Operations	10	6.1	12.2	6.1	12.6	3.6	0.3	4.4	1.1	6.0	19.0	·	·	·
Salaries and Wages	11	29.6	9.2	26.0	24.8	30.2	41.4	50.7	48.1	38.1	40.2	·	·	·
Taxes Paid	12	3.4	1.9	3.5	4.0	3.3	3.2	3.2	3.4	2.9	3.1	·	·	·
Interest Paid	13	0.5	0.2	0.4	0.5	0.4	0.9	0.4	0.4	1.1	0.3	·	·	·
Depreciation	14	0.8	0.1	0.7	0.7	1.0	1.0	1.0	1.5	1.5	1.3	·	·	·
Amortization and Depletion	15	0.1	0.0	0.0	0.0	0.0	0.0	0.1	0.1	0.3	0.8	·	·	·
Pensions and Other Deferred Comp.	16	1.9	1.4	1.7	1.9	2.5	2.3	2.0	3.0	0.8	0.6	·	·	·
Employee Benefits	17	2.0	0.3	1.8	2.4	2.3	1.9	2.0	2.8	1.7	2.7	·	·	·
Advertising	18	2.0	1.3	2.3	2.1	2.4	1.1	0.7	0.4	2.3	0.9	·	·	·
Other Expenses	19	26.9	53.4	28.1	21.0	25.5	18.5	22.0	26.1	23.8	21.6	·	·	·
Officers' Compensation	20	21.9	10.0	24.0	24.2	23.2	31.0	9.2	11.9	14.0	1.7	·	·	·
Operating Margin	21	4.9	9.9	5.3	5.6	5.6	·	4.3	1.2	7.5	7.7	·	·	·
Operating Margin Before Officers' Comp.	22	26.8	19.9	29.4	29.8	28.9	29.3	13.5	13.1	21.5	9.5	·	·	·

Selected Average Balance Sheet ($ in Thousands)

Item	C1	C2	C3	C4	C5	C6	C7	C8	C9	C10
Net Receivables 23	9	0	1	54	117	39	412	3367	10596	25646
Inventories 24	1	0	0	2	0	0	157	128	0	10670
Net Property, Plant and Equipment 25	28	0	16	73	187	1503	2620	5725	4340	25263
Total Assets 26		171	75	702	1651	7264	15577	33861	67851	225017
Notes and Loans Payable 27		59	39	232	296	3304	4053	5009	20305	36904
All Other Liabilities 28		79	35	218	836	2307	9012	16872	25794	111557
Net Worth 29		33	1	252	519	1654	2511	11980	21752	76557

Selected Financial Ratios (Times to 1)

Item	1	2	3	4	5	6	7	8
Current Ratio 30	1.2	1.0	1.4	1.3	1.5	1.1	1.3	1.3
Quick Ratio 31	0.8	0.7	0.8	1.0	0.7	0.6	1.0	0.8
Net Sales to Working Capital 32	48.0	•	19.8	15.8	18.5	38.2	17.6	14.4
Coverage Ratio 33	22.4	26.3	16.1	28.5	6.0	15.7	11.1	31.9
Total Asset Turnover 34	4.6	7.5	3.6	2.8	3.8	3.0	2.6	1.7
Inventory Turnover 35	86.3	751.1	141.7	402.6	219.1	12.9	7.7	6.8
Receivables Turnover 36	95.9	330.1	50.0	49.2	192.1	76.8	31.0	18.2
Total Liabilities to Net Worth 37	4.1	148.2	1.8	2.2	3.4	5.2	1.8	1.9
Current Assets to Working Capital 38	6.3	•	3.4	4.0	3.0	8.5	4.2	4.8
Current Liabilities to Working Capital 39	5.3	•	2.4	3.0	2.0	7.5	3.2	3.8
Working Capital to Net Sales 40	0.0	•	0.1	0.1	0.1	0.0	0.1	0.1
Inventory to Working Capital 41	0.0	•	0.0	0.0	0.0	0.1	0.0	0.4
Total Receipts to Cash Flow 42	3.3	3.1	4.4	3.4	5.8	4.5	4.6	3.5
Cost of Goods to Cash Flow 43	0.2	0.2	0.6	0.1	0.0	0.2	0.1	0.7
Cash Flow to Total Debt 44	1.7	2.5	1.3	1.2	0.9	0.8	0.9	0.7

Selected Financial Factors (in Percentages)

Item	C1	C2	C3	C4	C5	C6	C7	C8	C9	C10
Debt Ratio 45	80.6	•	99.3	64.1	68.6	77.2	83.9	64.6	67.9	66.0
Return on Total Assets 46	46.7	•	85.3	29.8	29.6	20.4	20.9	10.3	15.4	18.5
Return on Equity Before Income Taxes 47	229.7	•	12232.5	77.8	90.9	74.6	121.3	26.5	44.7	52.8
Return on Equity After Income Taxes 48	223.1	•	12047.8	76.4	87.8	68.6	112.4	21.5	41.3	45.5
Profit Margin (Before Income Tax) 49	9.6	10.5	10.9	7.8	10.1	4.5	6.6	3.6	15.0	10.6
Profit Margin (After Income Tax) 50	9.3	10.4	10.7	7.6	9.7	4.1	6.1	2.9	13.9	9.1

Table II
Corporations with Net Income

LEGAL SERVICES

MONEY AMOUNTS AND SIZE OF ASSETS IN THOUSANDS OF DOLLARS

Item Description for Accounting Period 7/05 Through 6/06	Total	Zero Assets	Under 500	500 to 1,000	1,000 to 5,000	5,000 to 10,000	10,000 to 25,000	25,000 to 50,000	50,000 to 100,000	100,000 to 250,000	250,000 to 500,000	500,000 to 2,500,000	2,500,000 and over
Number of Enterprises **1**	72369	10643	57781	1765	1922	111	98	•	•	•	0	0	0
Revenues ($ in Thousands)													
Net Sales **2**	66691846	2044395	37300259	4835659	8952907	3602517	4372743	•	•	•	0	0	0
Interest **3**	83534	317	13205	3191	9974	3678	5113	•	•	•	0	0	0
Rents **4**	57421	0	13033	12312	18781	6797	2900	•	•	•	0	0	0
Royalties **5**	10	0	0	0	0	0	0	0	0	0	0	0	0
Other Portfolio Income **6**	46327	1	20541	3323	3289	6257	2530	•	•	•	0	0	0
Other Receipts **7**	1890237	17815	1344728	90726	164865	43484	103549	•	•	•	0	0	0
Total Receipts **8**	68769375	2062528	38691766	4945211	9149816	3662733	4486835	•	•	•	0	0	0
Average Total Receipts **9**	950	194	670	2802	4761	32998	45784	•	•	•	•	•	•
Operating Costs/Operating Income (%)													
Cost of Operations **10**	7.0	18.3	6.7	15.7	4.3	0.5	4.9	•	•	•	•	•	•
Salaries and Wages **11**	28.2	13.2	23.9	21.9	26.1	44.5	50.9	•	•	•	•	•	•
Taxes Paid **12**	3.2	2.7	3.2	3.9	3.1	3.5	3.3	•	•	•	•	•	•
Interest Paid **13**	0.4	0.2	0.4	0.4	0.4	1.0	0.5	•	•	•	•	•	•
Depreciation **14**	0.8	0.2	0.7	0.6	1.0	1.2	1.1	•	•	•	•	•	•
Amortization and Depletion **15**	0.1	•	0.0	0.0	0.0	0.0	0.1	•	•	•	•	•	•
Pensions and Other Deferred Comp. **16**	1.8	2.1	1.5	1.8	2.3	2.8	2.2	•	•	•	•	•	•
Employee Benefits **17**	1.7	0.4	1.4	2.3	2.2	1.9	2.1	•	•	•	•	•	•
Advertising **18**	2.1	1.9	2.3	2.4	2.8	0.9	0.8	•	•	•	•	•	•
Other Expenses **19**	25.0	31.3	26.2	19.2	25.6	19.3	22.1	•	•	•	•	•	•
Officers' Compensation **20**	19.6	12.1	22.0	23.8	22.0	19.3	6.9	•	•	•	•	•	•
Operating Margin **21**	10.0	17.6	11.7	8.0	10.2	5.2	5.2	•	•	•	•	•	•
Operating Margin Before Officers' Comp. **22**	29.6	29.7	33.6	31.8	32.2	24.6	12.1	•	•	•	•	•	•

Selected Average Balance Sheet ($ in Thousands)

Net Receivables 23	11	0	1	63	139	51	459
Inventories 24	1	0	0	0	0	1	148
Net Property, Plant and Equipment 25	30	0	15	54	196	2115	2547
Total Assets 26	196	0	79	726	1682	7130	15703
Notes and Loans Payable 27	52	0	31	184	272	2337	3894
All Other Liabilities 28	92	0	36	251	811	2893	9077
Net Worth 29	52	0	11	291	599	1900	2731

Selected Financial Ratios (Times to 1)

Current Ratio 30	1.2	•	1.1	1.4	1.5	1.2	1.2
Quick Ratio 31	0.9	•	0.8	0.7	1.2	0.7	0.6
Net Sales to Working Capital 32	38.3	•	279.8	19.5	11.5	42.2	33.1
Coverage Ratio 33	33.8	122.1	44.1	23.9	35.5	8.0	17.3
Total Asset Turnover 34	4.7	•	8.2	3.8	2.8	4.6	2.8
Inventory Turnover 35	102.1	•	695.2	866.0	•	219.1	14.7
Receivables Turnover 36	89.2	•	362.1	49.7	44.9	137.7	75.9
Total Liabilities to Net Worth 37	2.7	•	6.1	1.5	1.8	2.8	4.7
Current Assets to Working Capital 38	5.1	•	18.4	3.4	3.0	5.4	7.7
Current Liabilities to Working Capital 39	4.1	•	17.4	2.4	2.0	4.4	6.7
Working Capital to Net Sales 40	0.0	•	0.0	0.1	0.1	0.0	0.0
Inventory to Working Capital 41	0.0	•	•	0.0	•	0.0	0.1
Total Receipts to Cash Flow 42	3.1	2.4	2.8	4.2	3.1	5.0	4.2
Cost of Goods to Cash Flow 43	0.2	0.4	0.2	0.7	0.1	0.0	0.2
Cash Flow to Total Debt 44	2.1	•	3.4	1.5	1.4	1.2	0.8

Selected Financial Factors (in Percentages)

Debt Ratio 45	73.3	•	86.0	59.9	64.4	73.4	82.6
Return on Total Assets 46	63.5	•	129.3	40.4	35.4	36.0	23.6
Return on Equity Before Income Taxes 47	231.0	•	900.5	96.5	96.5	118.4	128.0
Return on Equity After Income Taxes 48	225.0	•	888.4	94.8	93.3	109.5	118.8
Profit Margin (Before Income Tax) 49	13.1	18.5	15.4	10.3	12.4	6.9	7.8
Profit Margin (After Income Tax) 50	12.8	18.3	15.2	10.1	12.0	6.4	7.3

Table I

Corporations with and without Net Income

ACCOUNTING, TAX PREPARATION, BOOKKEEPING, AND PAYROLL SERVICES

MONEY AMOUNTS AND SIZE OF ASSETS IN THOUSANDS OF DOLLARS

Item Description for Accounting Period 7/05 Through 6/06	Total	Zero Assets	Under 500	500 to 1,000	1,000 to 5,000	5,000 to 10,000	10,000 to 25,000	25,000 to 50,000	50,000 to 100,000	100,000 to 250,000	250,000 to 500,000	500,000 to 2,500,000	2,500,000 and over
Number of Enterprises 1	66627	11592	53314	713	828	96	54	11	8	7	0	4	0
Revenues ($ in Thousands)													
Net Sales 2	34946064	717991	16484196	2837636	5941526	472237	267625	145204	2403142	930618	0	4745887	0
Interest 3	1006929	6	9510	5307	5043	2037	6431	4428	1982	12725	0	959460	0
Rents 4	18257	0	2173	8435	2477	0	0	0	0	0	0	5171	0
Royalties 5	304899	0	0	0	0	0	0	0	0	0	0	294504	0
Other Portfolio Income 6	69289	17191	14394	474	1358	2	163	517	0	194	0	34991	0
Other Receipts 7	584082	92926	174142	14190	80196	4852	5256	9971	887	2603	0	199069	0
Total Receipts 8	36929520	828114	16684415	2866042	6030600	479128	279475	160120	2406011	956534	0	6239082	0
Average Total Receipts 9	554	71	313	4020	7283	4991	5175	14556	300751	136648	·	1559770	·
Operating Costs/Operating Income (%)													
Cost of Operations 10	12.0	1.6	2.5	9.3	19.2	15.2	8.1	46.6	83.5	1.3	·	3.8	·
Salaries and Wages 11	33.8	26.3	33.0	40.6	44.0	31.5	39.8	13.7	5.2	36.6	·	35.2	·
Taxes Paid 12	4.5	5.3	4.4	5.5	3.1	3.6	4.5	6.7	4.1	2.3	·	6.3	·
Interest Paid 13	1.8	0.3	0.6	0.7	0.4	1.6	2.5	2.9	0.1	3.4	·	9.0	·
Depreciation 14	1.1	0.9	1.0	1.1	0.5	1.0	2.7	0.7	0.2	1.9	·	2.2	·
Amortization and Depletion 15	0.6	0.1	0.3	0.0	0.3	0.3	1.5	0.4	0.1	1.7	·	2.5	·
Pensions and Other Deferred Comp. 16	1.3	0.5	1.5	3.5	1.1	1.1	0.6	4.0	0.2	0.1	·	0.9	·
Employee Benefits 17	2.4	2.7	2.5	4.9	1.3	2.6	3.0	1.9	1.5	3.3	·	2.3	·
Advertising 18	2.4	0.9	0.7	0.3	9.7	0.8	0.9	0.1	0.0	1.2	·	2.5	·
Other Expenses 19	24.4	39.5	23.5	14.8	11.9	26.1	35.6	13.4	2.7	57.7	·	50.4	·
Officers' Compensation 20	14.1	19.4	22.9	18.4	6.2	10.3	7.0	10.4	0.4	0.7	·	0.4	·
Operating Margin 21	1.7	2.6	7.1	1.1	2.3	5.9	·	·	2.1	·	·	·	·
Operating Margin Before Officers' Comp. 22	15.8	22.0	30.0	19.5	8.5	16.2	0.7	9.7	2.5	·	·	·	·

Selected Average Balance Sheet ($ in Thousands)

Net Receivables 23	•	255180	26685	12581	1729	2796	661	333	144	4	32
Inventories 24	•	121958	1293	440	2562	8	9	1	0	0	5
Net Property, Plant and Equipment 25	•	121020	10610	2358	746	478	286	299	339	10	25
Total Assets 26	•	4770222	183054	57329	33898	15527	5635	1791	664	55	412
Notes and Loans Payable 27	•	3628086	42574	8194	1386	2467	1487	464	554	31	264
All Other Liabilities 28	•	577274	106515	42892	24602	9224	3160	272	252	19	88
Net Worth 29	•	564862	33966	6242	7910	3836	988	1055	-142	6	60

Selected Financial Ratios (Times to 1)

Current Ratio 30	0.3	1.3	0.9	1.4	0.5	1.5	•	0.9	•	0.9	0.4
Quick Ratio 31	0.1	0.8	0.7	0.7	0.3	1.2	•	0.5	•	0.8	0.3
Net Sales to Working Capital 32	•	6.7	•	•	•	1.5	•	22.0	•	•	•
Coverage Ratio 33	2.8	•	41.4	4.3	5.6	0.2	11.5	4.2	14.8	71.1	5.1
Total Asset Turnover 34	0.2	0.7	5.2	0.4	0.9	0.3	4.0	6.0	5.6	1.3	
Inventory Turnover 35	0.4	1.3	570.6	2.4	49.9	82.3	1520.3	2038.9	1255.6	12.9	
Receivables Turnover 36	9.3	10.0	23.3	2.6	2.2	11.9	28.3	27.8	78.0	16.1	
Total Liabilities to Net Worth 37	7.4	4.4	8.2	3.3	3.0	4.7	0.7	8.6	5.8		
Current Assets to Working Capital 38	•	4.2	•	•	3.4	3.1	•	•			
Current Liabilities to Working Capital 39	•	3.2	•	2.4	2.4	2.1	•	•			
Working Capital to Net Sales 40	•	0.2	0.2	0.7	0.7	0.0	•	•			
Inventory to Working Capital 41	•	0.1	•	0.0	0.0	0.0	•	•			
Total Receipts to Cash Flow 42	1.7	2.2	2.2	4.7	3.5	3.5	7.8	7.1	4.0	2.2	3.8
Cost of Goods to Cash Flow 43	0.1	0.0	18.3	2.2	0.3	0.5	1.5	0.7	0.1	0.0	0.5
Cash Flow to Total Debt 44	0.2	0.4	0.3	0.1	0.1	0.3	1.2	0.7	1.6	•	0.4

Selected Financial Factors (in Percentages)

Debt Ratio 45	•	88.2	81.4	89.1	76.7	75.3	82.5	41.1	121.5	89.6	85.4
Return on Total Assets 46	•	6.2	11.8	4.8	7.8	0.2	16.5	16.5	50.1	•	11.6
Return on Equity Before Income Taxes 47	•	33.8	•	15.6	106.0	36.4	25.6	•	447.0	•	64.1
Return on Equity After Income Taxes 48	•	21.5	•	15.2	84.9	36.4	22.9	•	441.1	•	55.5
Profit Margin (Before Income Tax) 49	•	16.1	2.2	9.4	3.8	7.3	2.1	8.3	17.9	•	7.4
Profit Margin (After Income Tax) 50	•	10.2	1.8	9.1	3.4	7.3	2.0	8.2	17.3	•	6.4

337

Table II
Corporations with Net Income

ACCOUNTING, TAX PREPARATION, BOOKKEEPING, AND PAYROLL SERVICES

MONEY AMOUNTS AND SIZE OF ASSETS IN THOUSANDS OF DOLLARS

Item Description for Accounting Period 7/05 Through 6/06	Total	Zero Assets	Under 500	500 to 1,000	1,000 to 5,000	5,000 to 10,000	10,000 to 25,000	25,000 to 50,000	50,000 to 100,000	100,000 to 250,000	250,000 to 500,000	500,000 to 2,500,000	2,500,000 and over
Number of Enterprises **1**	46735	6872	38554	540	655	66	25	8	·	4	0	·	0
Revenues ($ in Thousands)													
Net Sales **2**	28651950	485039	14214940	1940745	3990738	376548	147310	141301	·	416647	0	·	0
Interest **3**	978195	5	6578	2217	3172	922	1479	978	·	11256	0	·	0
Rents **4**	18199	0	2173	8435	2477	0	0	0	·	0	0	·	0
Royalties **5**	273211	0	0	0	0	0	0	0	·	0	0	·	0
Other Portfolio Income **6**	65327	17096	11650	150	1326	0	162	0	·	10394	0	·	0
Other Receipts **7**	443275	1508	140710	12603	76775	4851	2861	9931	·	1938	0	·	0
Total Receipts **8**	30430157	503648	14376051	1964150	4074488	382323	151812	152210	·	440235	0	·	0
Average Total Receipts **9**	651	73	373	3637	6221	5793	6072	19026	·	110059	·	·	·
Operating Costs/Operating Income (%)													
Cost of Operations **10**	13.2	0.2	2.1	11.4	23.8	18.7	1.8	47.8	·	0.3	·	·	·
Salaries and Wages **11**	28.8	12.0	29.2	41.3	28.9	24.5	26.7	12.5	·	36.3	·	·	·
Taxes Paid **12**	4.5	5.8	4.2	6.1	4.1	3.1	2.9	6.8	·	1.2	·	·	·
Interest Paid **13**	2.0	0.2	0.5	0.8	0.5	0.3	3.3	0.8	·	5.5	·	·	·
Depreciation **14**	1.0	0.6	0.9	0.9	0.5	1.1	2.6	0.7	·	1.2	·	·	·
Amortization and Depletion **15**	0.7	·	0.3	0.0	0.2	0.3	2.2	0.4	·	2.9	·	·	·
Pensions and Other Deferred Comp. **16**	1.2	0.8	1.5	2.8	0.6	1.3	0.7	3.9	·	0.1	·	·	·
Employee Benefits **17**	2.3	2.2	2.4	4.9	1.7	2.1	1.6	1.8	·	2.0	·	·	·
Advertising **18**	2.8	0.7	0.6	0.1	14.4	0.9	0.4	0.1	·	2.6	·	·	·
Other Expenses **19**	25.0	34.7	25.3	13.0	14.1	25.1	29.5	12.9	·	47.7	·	·	·
Officers' Compensation **20**	14.4	17.5	23.6	16.0	6.6	12.4	8.4	9.2	·	1.4	·	·	·
Operating Margin **21**	4.3	25.5	9.4	2.7	4.6	10.1	19.8	3.1	·	·	·	·	·
Operating Margin Before Officers' Comp. **22**	18.7	42.9	33.0	18.7	11.2	22.5	28.2	12.3	·	0.0	·	·	·

Selected Average Balance Sheet ($ in Thousands)

Net Receivables 23	38	0	4	136	237	752	3190	2377	26821
Inventories 24	7	0	0	0	2	2	4	3455	2262
Net Property, Plant and Equipment 25	27	0	9	377	218	350	546	918	9284
Total Assets 26	517	0	60	647	1803	5769	15727	35285	152602
Notes and Loans Payable 27	350	0	24	494	431	630	2299	1905	47521
All Other Liabilities 28	83	0	16	194	154	3478	8990	27137	82440
Net Worth 29	84	0	20	-41	1218	1661	4438	6242	22642

Selected Financial Ratios (Times to 1)

Current Ratio 30	0.4	•	1.2	0.6	1.7	0.4	1.6	1.0	1.4
Quick Ratio 31	0.3	•	1.1	0.5	1.3	0.3	1.5	0.8	0.8
Net Sales to Working Capital 32	•	•	73.1	•	14.4	•	1.6	21.8	4.7
Coverage Ratio 33	6.4	135.7	22.6	6.0	15.1	39.3	8.0	14.6	1.8
Total Asset Turnover 34	1.2	•	6.1	5.6	3.4	1.0	0.4	0.5	0.7
Inventory Turnover 35	11.7	•	•	1720.1	698.2	498.8	27.9	2.4	0.1
Receivables Turnover 36	15.7	•	95.2	27.4	32.1	12.1	3.7	3.6	7.8
Total Liabilities to Net Worth 37	5.2	•	2.0	•	0.5	2.5	2.5	4.7	5.7
Current Assets to Working Capital 38	•	•	5.8	•	2.4	•	2.7	33.6	3.7
Current Liabilities to Working Capital 39	•	•	4.8	•	1.4	•	1.7	32.6	2.7
Working Capital to Net Sales 40	•	•	0.0	•	0.1	•	0.6	0.0	0.2
Inventory to Working Capital 41	•	•	•	•	0.0	•	0.0	0.5	0.1
Total Receipts to Cash Flow 42	3.3	1.9	3.4	6.7	5.9	3.1	2.1	4.5	2.1
Cost of Goods to Cash Flow 43	0.4	0.0	0.1	0.8	1.4	0.6	0.0	2.1	0.0
Cash Flow to Total Debt 44	0.4	•	2.7	0.8	1.8	0.5	0.3	0.1	0.4

Selected Financial Factors (in Percentages)

Debt Ratio 45	83.8	•	66.9	106.3	32.5	71.2	71.8	82.3	85.2
Return on Total Assets 46	14.8	•	67.2	25.8	24.1	11.8	9.8	5.8	6.7
Return on Equity Before Income Taxes 47	76.9	•	193.8	•	33.3	39.8	30.3	30.5	19.8
Return on Equity After Income Taxes 48	68.1	•	191.4	•	30.3	39.7	25.9	29.8	13.9
Profit Margin (Before Income Tax) 49	10.5	29.3	10.5	3.9	6.7	11.6	22.8	10.8	4.3
Profit Margin (After Income Tax) 50	9.3	28.4	10.4	3.8	6.1	11.6	19.5	10.5	3.0

Table I

Corporations with and without Net Income

ARCHITECTURAL, ENGINEERING, AND RELATED SERVICES

MONEY AMOUNTS AND SIZE OF ASSETS IN THOUSANDS OF DOLLARS

Item Description for Accounting Period 7/05 Through 6/06		Total	Zero Assets	Under 500	500 to 1,000	1,000 to 5,000	5,000 to 10,000	10,000 to 25,000	25,000 to 50,000	50,000 to 100,000	100,000 to 250,000	250,000 to 500,000	500,000 to 2,500,000	2,500,000 and over
Number of Enterprises	1	91377	10302	73105	3493	3371	589	292	93	51	39	22	17	3
Revenues ($ in Thousands)														
Net Sales	2	174121304	1904954	55131119	9289775	19435594	11141672	10123851	5709516	6048293	10489480	8531038	19780808	16535204
Interest	3	544587	3219	47765	16479	20170	13528	53287	12701	11728	35000	60716	198362	71632
Rents	4	129130	28	6894	626	11558	172	1137	2227	8143	6040	11903	66316	14085
Royalties	5	155632	0	0	0	2936	0	175	2494	594	13458	1086	11402	123487
Other Portfolio Income	6	543253	3406	16590	33014	12669	60690	9988	17573	44279	36031	11635	218543	78837
Other Receipts	7	1789272	32201	154339	125164	119846	112498	189203	51937	75330	114625	127061	464093	222974
Total Receipts	8	177283178	1943808	55356707	9465058	19602773	11328560	10377641	5796448	6188367	10694634	8743439	20739524	17046219
Average Total Receipts	9	1940	189	757	2710	5815	19234	35540	62327	121341	274221	397429	1219972	5682073
Operating Costs/Operating Income (%)														
Cost of Operations	10	40.2	18.2	23.1	33.8	32.7	36.3	39.6	48.3	45.3	48.3	55.8	61.4	72.4
Salaries and Wages	11	18.9	23.4	20.9	20.9	23.5	25.0	22.0	17.0	21.2	19.8	18.0	5.7	14.3
Taxes Paid	12	3.0	3.2	3.3	3.3	4.0	3.6	3.6	3.1	2.5	2.8	1.9	2.4	1.1
Interest Paid	13	0.8	2.0	0.4	0.4	0.8	0.5	0.7	0.6	1.0	0.5	2.2	1.8	0.6
Depreciation	14	1.2	1.9	0.9	2.1	1.5	1.5	1.4	1.4	1.7	1.1	1.4	1.5	0.4
Amortization and Depletion	15	0.2	0.1	0.0	0.0	0.1	0.2	0.4	0.2	0.4	0.3	•	0.9	0.2
Pensions and Other Deferred Comp.	16	1.1	1.1	1.1	1.0	1.7	1.6	1.2	1.2	1.5	1.4	0.9	1.0	0.2
Employee Benefits	17	2.4	1.7	1.6	1.8	2.4	3.1	3.0	2.6	1.9	2.9	2.3	3.8	3.5
Advertising	18	0.3	0.4	0.6	0.3	0.3	0.4	0.3	0.4	0.2	0.2	0.2	0.1	0.0
Other Expenses	19	20.7	24.9	22.3	22.3	20.7	18.2	21.1	20.7	19.7	18.9	15.8	21.6	8.4
Officers' Compensation	20	8.6	9.2	18.6	10.3	7.5	5.5	4.8	2.9	2.9	1.8	0.9	1.9	0.3
Operating Margin	21	2.5	6.1	4.6	3.7	4.8	4.1	2.0	1.6	1.6	2.1	0.7	•	•
Operating Margin Before Officers' Comp.	22	11.1	15.3	23.2	14.0	12.3	9.6	6.8	4.6	4.5	3.9	1.6	•	•

Selected Average Balance Sheet ($ in Thousands)

Net Receivables **23**	244	0	8	143	758	2241	7097	14198	26907	48865	99985	354494	808734
Inventories **24**	31	0	1	17	62	140	593	1423	3455	5866	7270	27342	356449
Net Property, Plant and Equipment **25**	106	0	29	149	387	1206	2637	4915	11602	18932	31737	62279	234543
Total Assets **26**	840	0	78	701	2040	6528	15780	35708	69550	160493	360008	1180878	4071496
Notes and Loans Payable **27**	239	0	50	237	660	2764	3601	7127	17698	24095	114884	376130	336643
All Other Liabilities **28**	326	0	20	163	632	1744	7073	16041	30974	66685	140033	497993	1779372
Net Worth **29**	275	0	8	300	748	2020	5107	12540	20879	69713	105092	306755	1955481

Selected Financial Ratios (Times to 1)

Current Ratio **30**	1.4	•	1.5	1.7	1.9	1.5	1.4	1.4	1.6	1.2	1.2	1.3	
Quick Ratio **31**	1.0	•	1.1	1.4	1.5	1.2	1.0	1.1	1.2	0.9	0.8	0.6	
Net Sales to Working Capital **32**	15.0	79.5	19.4	10.0	9.8	9.2	10.3	8.4	7.0	15.2	12.3	12.7	
Coverage Ratio **33**	6.5	5.1	13.6	14.2	8.0	7.8	4.8	6.0	8.3	2.5	2.6	4.3	
Total Asset Turnover **34**	2.3	•	9.7	3.8	2.8	2.2	1.7	1.7	1.7	1.1	1.0	1.4	
Inventory Turnover **35**	24.8	173.5	53.3	30.2	49.1	23.1	15.5	20.8	22.1	29.8	26.1	11.2	
Receivables Turnover **36**	8.8	93.9	20.9	7.9	9.2	5.3	4.4	4.7	5.5	5.1	4.1	7.7	
Total Liabilities to Net Worth **37**	2.1	9.2	1.3	1.7	2.2	2.1	2.3	1.8	1.3	2.4	2.8	1.1	
Current Assets to Working Capital **38**	3.7	3.8	2.9	2.4	2.1	3.0	3.7	3.4	2.6	6.6	6.3	4.8	
Current Liabilities to Working Capital **39**	2.7	2.8	1.9	1.4	1.1	2.0	2.7	2.4	1.6	5.6	5.3	3.8	
Working Capital to Net Sales **40**	0.1	0.0	0.1	0.1	0.1	0.1	0.1	0.1	0.1	0.1	0.1	0.1	
Inventory to Working Capital **41**	0.3	0.1	0.1	0.1	0.1	0.2	0.3	0.2	0.2	0.4	0.4	1.0	
Total Receipts to Cash Flow **42**	4.7	2.8	3.8	4.3	4.5	5.2	4.5	5.2	5.0	5.2	6.4	4.8	11.9
Cost of Goods to Cash Flow **43**	1.9	0.5	0.9	1.4	1.5	1.9	1.8	2.4	2.4	2.5	3.6	2.9	8.6
Cash Flow to Total Debt **44**	0.7	2.8	1.6	1.0	0.8	0.7	0.5	0.5	0.6	0.2	0.3	0.2	

Selected Financial Factors (in Percentages)

Debt Ratio **45**	67.2	•	90.2	57.2	63.3	69.1	67.6	70.0	64.9	56.6	70.8	74.0	52.0
Return on Total Assets **46**	11.6	•	52.1	22.8	18.2	17.3	11.4	8.5	6.5	7.7	5.8	4.5	3.4
Return on Equity Before Income Taxes **47**	30.1	•	490.8	49.6	43.5	51.0	30.6	22.5	15.5	15.6	11.8	10.6	5.4
Return on Equity After Income Taxes **48**	26.8	•	485.8	47.0	39.9	46.7	24.2	16.5	11.6	11.4	10.1	7.2	4.0
Profit Margin (Before Income Tax) **49**	4.3	8.2	5.0	5.6	5.4	4.5	3.2	4.0	4.0	3.2	2.8	1.9	
Profit Margin (After Income Tax) **50**	3.9	7.1	4.9	5.3	5.2	3.6	2.3	3.0	2.9	2.7	1.9	1.4	

Table II

Corporations with Net Income

ARCHITECTURAL, ENGINEERING, AND RELATED SERVICES

MONEY AMOUNTS AND SIZE OF ASSETS IN THOUSANDS OF DOLLARS

Item Description for Accounting Period 7/05 Through 6/06	Total	Zero Assets	Under 500	500 to 1,000	1,000 to 5,000	5,000 to 10,000	10,000 to 25,000	25,000 to 50,000	50,000 to 100,000	100,000 to 250,000	250,000 to 500,000	500,000 to 2,500,000	2,500,000 and over
Number of Enterprises 1	60986	5050	50062	2508	2490	474	233	63	44	33	16	10	3
Revenues ($ in Thousands)													
Net Sales 2	133583737	1638099	33307755	7837858	14321154	8679809	8562383	4605387	5514948	9737639	7060129	15783374	16535204
Interest 3	410010	1588	6847	15348	15355	12023	49650	6712	10748	28353	52043	139710	71632
Rents 4	111719	28	4226	626	9153	172	1137	2221	4736	6040	9662	59633	14085
Royalties 5	143008	0	0	0	2936	0	175	2413	179	13458	0	359	123487
Other Portfolio Income 6	301666	1201	11456	22241	5138	57725	9841	17550	43351	35002	9232	10093	78837
Other Receipts 7	1555597	31902	149107	122601	110137	110495	117720	51354	68731	95049	112326	363201	222974
Total Receipts 8	136105737	1672818	33479391	7998674	14463873	8860224	8740906	4685637	5642693	9915541	7243392	16356370	17046219
Average Total Receipts 9	2232	331	669	3189	5809	18692	37515	74375	128243	300471	452712	1635637	5682073
Operating Costs/Operating Income (%)													
Cost of Operations 10	40.9	18.8	17.7	34.1	32.5	32.8	39.0	47.6	44.6	49.4	54.8	61.1	72.4
Salaries and Wages 11	19.0	22.2	22.8	21.7	22.9	26.1	22.4	16.0	21.4	19.0	17.6	5.5	14.3
Taxes Paid 12	2.9	3.2	3.7	3.4	3.6	3.7	3.5	2.9	2.5	2.8	2.0	2.0	1.1
Interest Paid 13	0.6	1.1	0.5	0.3	0.4	0.3	0.6	0.5	1.0	0.4	1.9	1.0	0.6
Depreciation 14	1.1	1.5	1.0	1.5	1.5	1.3	1.5	1.1	1.5	1.1	1.5	1.2	0.4
Amortization and Depletion 15	0.2	0.1	0.0	0.0	0.0	0.1	0.2	0.1	0.3	0.3	0.7	0.3	0.2
Pensions and Other Deferred Comp. 16	1.1	1.2	1.4	1.0	1.8	1.4	1.1	1.1	0.9	1.5	1.0	0.8	0.2
Employee Benefits 17	2.5	1.7	1.7	2.0	1.8	3.1	2.9	2.3	1.9	2.5	2.1	4.0	3.5
Advertising 18	0.3	0.4	0.7	0.3	0.4	0.4	0.3	0.2	0.2	0.2	0.3	0.1	0.0
Other Expenses 19	19.2	28.6	24.2	18.6	19.4	18.0	19.5	20.8	19.7	18.0	15.1	21.6	8.4
Officers' Compensation 20	7.1	9.3	16.6	11.3	7.4	6.3	4.4	2.6	2.9	1.8	0.9	2.1	0.3
Operating Margin 21	5.0	11.9	9.7	5.9	8.4	6.5	4.6	4.9	3.1	3.1	2.0	0.4	•
Operating Margin Before Officers' Comp. 22	12.1	21.2	26.4	17.2	15.7	12.8	8.9	7.5	5.9	4.9	3.0	2.5	•

Selected Average Balance Sheet ($ in Thousands)

Net Receivables 23	299	0	7	99	747	2483	6828	15391	28382	50188	103333	500668	808734
Inventories 24	37	0	1	11	65	117	599	1635	3266	5695	7469	47835	421975
Net Property, Plant and Equipment 25	120	0	31	127	395	1153	2859	4561	11472	17585	37919	53590	234543
Total Assets 26	968	0	79	686	2018	6533	15652	36122	68818	157700	353227	1322876	4071496
Notes and Loans Payable 27	224	0	41	158	520	2572	3389	5107	16994	14524	107186	363176	336643
All Other Liabilities 28	368	0	17	167	540	1885	6002	15929	28825	65301	152474	534364	1779372
Net Worth 29	376	0	20	361	958	2076	6261	15086	22999	77875	93568	425335	1955481

Selected Financial Ratios (Times to 1)

Current Ratio 30	1.5	•	1.5	1.5	2.1	1.9	1.7	1.6	1.4	1.6	1.1	1.4	1.3
Quick Ratio 31	1.0	•	1.3	1.2	1.8	1.5	1.4	1.2	1.1	1.2	0.9	1.0	0.6
Net Sales to Working Capital 32	12.0	•	53.2	25.9	7.8	8.6	7.8	7.2	9.8	7.7	27.2	7.1	12.7
Coverage Ratio 33	12.1	13.2	23.5	25.0	22.7	25.6	12.2	14.9	6.5	14.4	3.4	5.2	4.3
Total Asset Turnover 34	2.3	•	8.4	4.6	2.9	2.8	2.3	2.0	1.8	1.9	1.2	1.2	1.4
Inventory Turnover 35	24.0	•	127.3	93.1	28.8	51.2	23.9	21.3	17.1	25.6	32.4	20.2	9.5
Receivables Turnover 36	8.6	•	103.0	33.2	8.0	8.7	6.0	9.5	4.5	6.6	5.9	6.3	13.6
Total Liabilities to Net Worth 37	1.6	•	2.9	0.9	1.1	2.1	1.5	1.4	2.0	1.0	2.8	2.1	1.1
Current Assets to Working Capital 38	3.2	•	2.9	3.0	1.9	2.1	2.4	2.6	3.4	2.7	11.0	3.6	4.8
Current Liabilities to Working Capital 39	2.2	•	1.9	2.0	0.9	1.1	1.4	1.6	2.4	1.7	10.0	2.6	3.8
Working Capital to Net Sales 40	0.1	•	0.0	0.0	0.1	0.1	0.1	0.1	0.1	0.1	0.0	0.1	0.1
Inventory to Working Capital 41	0.3	•	0.1	0.1	0.1	0.1	0.2	0.2	0.3	0.2	0.6	0.2	1.0
Total Receipts to Cash Flow 42	4.4	2.6	3.3	4.5	4.0	4.5	4.4	4.2	4.9	5.3	6.1	4.5	11.9
Cost of Goods to Cash Flow 43	1.8	0.5	0.6	1.5	1.3	1.5	1.7	2.0	2.2	2.6	3.3	2.7	8.6
Cash Flow to Total Debt 44	0.8	•	3.5	2.1	1.4	0.9	0.9	0.8	0.6	0.7	0.3	0.4	0.2

Selected Financial Factors (in Percentages)

Debt Ratio 45	61.2	•	74.1	47.4	52.5	68.2	60.0	58.2	66.6	50.6	73.5	67.8	52.0
Return on Total Assets 46	17.1	•	90.4	37.9	27.9	23.7	17.1	14.4	11.6	9.9	8.2	6.1	3.4
Return on Equity Before Income Taxes 47	40.5	•	334.2	69.1	56.2	71.7	39.3	32.1	29.5	18.7	22.0	15.3	5.4
Return on Equity After Income Taxes 48	36.8	•	331.5	66.1	52.4	66.5	32.7	27.1	23.1	14.5	19.3	11.1	4.0
Profit Margin (Before Income Tax) 49	6.9	14.0	10.3	8.0	9.4	8.1	6.7	6.6	5.4	4.9	4.7	4.1	1.9
Profit Margin (After Income Tax) 50	6.3	12.8	10.2	7.6	8.7	7.5	5.6	5.6	4.2	3.8	4.9	3.0	1.4

Table I

Corporations with and without Net Income

SPECIALIZED DESIGN SERVICES

MONEY AMOUNTS AND SIZE OF ASSETS IN THOUSANDS OF DOLLARS

Item Description for Accounting Period 7/05 Through 6/06	Total	Zero Assets	Under 500	500 to 1,000	1,000 to 5,000	5,000 to 10,000	10,000 to 25,000	25,000 to 50,000	50,000 to 100,000	100,000 to 250,000	250,000 to 500,000	500,000 to 2,500,000	2,500,000 and over
Number of Enterprises 1	40654	5229	33525	1115	672	81	15	10	4	0	4	0	0
Revenues ($ in Thousands)													
Net Sales 2	20261526	566362	11308224	1824718	2733078	1089697	439084	411861	339704	0	1548798	0	0
Interest 3	28685	179	3907	1343	2438	1539	198	1703	2651	0	14727	0	0
Rents 4	5914	761	20	0	777	3517	0	255	75	0	510	0	0
Royalties 5	32622	0	0	0	24118	0	0	0	8504	0	0	0	0
Other Portfolio Income 6	461026	0	522	29583	263	500	25	43	2289	0	427800	0	0
Other Receipts 7	251235	265	17677	54569	5581	3207	12416	12778	964	0	143778	0	0
Total Receipts 8	21041008	567567	11330350	1910213	2766255	1098460	451723	426640	354187	0	2135613	0	0
Average Total Receipts 9	518	109	338	1713	4116	13561	30115	42664	88547	•	533903	•	•
Operating Costs/Operating Income (%)													
Cost of Operations 10	48.4	34.8	44.2	70.7	60.5	58.7	46.7	72.0	68.9	•	18.3	•	•
Salaries and Wages 11	13.7	1.5	9.0	8.9	12.5	18.3	19.2	13.0	11.7	•	56.1	•	•
Taxes Paid 12	2.6	1.9	2.5	3.1	1.9	2.3	2.5	2.1	1.0	•	5.1	•	•
Interest Paid 13	0.7	0.6	0.8	0.5	0.2	0.8	0.5	1.3	1.5	•	0.9	•	•
Depreciation 14	1.4	1.3	1.1	0.9	0.6	1.4	0.6	1.1	2.2	•	5.6	•	•
Amortization and Depletion 15	0.1	0.0	0.0	0.0	0.0	0.1	0.0	0.2	1.9	•	0.1	•	•
Pensions and Other Deferred Comp. 16	0.6	0.4	0.7	0.1	1.1	0.7	0.4	0.7	0.0	•	0.4	•	•
Employee Benefits 17	1.1	0.6	0.7	0.3	1.0	0.8	1.5	2.6	0.4	•	5.7	•	•
Advertising 18	0.9	1.0	1.0	0.4	1.4	0.3	0.4	0.3	1.5	•	0.6	•	•
Other Expenses 19	21.0	36.3	25.7	12.2	13.3	12.1	14.5	7.1	16.2	•	17.3	•	•
Officers' Compensation 20	6.9	15.5	8.1	6.7	6.5	2.6	4.4	2.8	1.8	•	2.4	•	•
Operating Margin 21	2.5	6.0	6.1	•	1.0	2.1	9.3	•	•	•	•	•	•
Operating Margin Before Officers' Comp. 22	9.5	21.5	14.2	2.8	7.6	4.7	13.7	•	•	•	•	•	•

Selected Average Balance Sheet ($ in Thousands)

Net Receivables 23	55	0	17	149	492	1552	5609	5447	20966	207572	•
Inventories 24	23	0	6	164	580	320	1536	1696	10440	7140	•
Net Property, Plant and Equipment 25	34	0	16	175	190	1046	1200	2317	16716	84510	•
Total Assets 26	212	0	76	679	1834	7159	17823	33142	83158	644484	•
Notes and Loans Payable 27	68	0	51	197	439	1416	2487	7284	35926	42324	•
All Other Liabilities 28	85	0	28	371	1078	5409	8978	19172	28843	127516	•
Net Worth 29	60	0	-2	111	318	335	6358	6685	18388	474644	•

Selected Financial Ratios (Times to 1)

Current Ratio 30	1.6	•	1.6	1.1	1.4	0.7	1.5	0.9	1.4	4.0	•
Quick Ratio 31	1.2	•	1.4	0.5	0.7	0.7	1.0	0.4	0.9	3.7	•
Net Sales to Working Capital 32	8.5	•	16.4	55.2	8.6	•	6.0	7.3	1.1	•	•
Coverage Ratio 33	10.1	12.3	9.1	2.5	10.6	4.8	25.3	1.3	•	28.7	•
Total Asset Turnover 34	2.3	•	4.4	2.4	2.2	1.9	1.6	1.2	1.0	0.6	•
Inventory Turnover 35	10.7	•	23.9	7.1	4.2	24.7	8.9	17.5	5.6	10.0	•
Receivables Turnover 36	10.6	•	23.3	11.9	8.7	7.8	5.0	8.0	3.6	2.7	•
Total Liabilities to Net Worth 37	2.6	•	•	5.1	4.8	20.4	1.8	4.0	3.5	0.4	•
Current Assets to Working Capital 38	2.6	•	2.6	15.2	3.4	•	2.9	•	3.6	1.3	•
Current Liabilities to Working Capital 39	1.6	•	1.6	14.2	2.4	•	1.9	•	2.6	0.3	•
Working Capital to Net Sales 40	0.1	•	0.1	0.0	0.1	•	0.2	•	0.1	0.9	•
Inventory to Working Capital 41	0.3	•	0.2	5.6	1.1	•	0.1	•	1.0	0.0	•
Total Receipts to Cash Flow 42	4.5	3.1	3.8	10.7	8.7	8.6	4.2	28.7	9.6	2.8	•
Cost of Goods to Cash Flow 43	2.2	1.1	1.7	7.5	5.3	5.0	2.0	20.6	6.6	0.5	•
Cash Flow to Total Debt 44	0.7	•	1.1	0.3	0.3	0.2	0.6	0.1	0.1	0.8	•

Selected Financial Factors (in Percentages)

Debt Ratio 45	71.9	•	103.0	83.6	82.7	95.3	64.3	79.8	77.9	26.4	•
Return on Total Assets 46	16.7	•	31.3	3.2	5.6	6.8	20.9	2.1	•	16.0	•
Return on Equity Before Income Taxes 47	53.5	•	•	11.9	29.3	115.0	56.2	2.2	•	20.9	•
Return on Equity After Income Taxes 48	51.1	•	•	7.1	28.4	88.9	52.7	•	•	19.6	•
Profit Margin (Before Income Tax) 49	6.4	6.2	6.3	0.8	2.3	2.9	12.2	0.4	•	25.6	•
Profit Margin (After Income Tax) 50	6.1	6.1	6.2	0.5	2.2	2.2	11.4	•	•	24.1	•

Table II

Corporations with Net Income

SPECIALIZED DESIGN SERVICES

MONEY AMOUNTS AND SIZE OF ASSETS IN THOUSANDS OF DOLLARS

Item Description for Accounting Period 7/05 Through 6/06	Total	Zero Assets	Under 500	500 to 1,000	1,000 to 5,000	5,000 to 10,000	10,000 to 25,000	25,000 to 50,000	50,000 to 100,000	100,000 to 250,000	250,000 to 500,000	500,000 to 2,500,000	2,500,000 and over
Number of Enterprises **1**	26788	3670	21819	751	492	33	11	•	0	0	•	•	0
Revenues ($ in Thousands)													
Net Sales **2**	14871087	443740	7936280	1527044	1914988	602864	426455	•	0	0	•	•	0
Interest **3**	24523	179	3705	1343	1626	558	197	•	0	0	•	•	0
Rents **4**	2397	761	20	0	777	0	0	•	0	0	•	•	0
Royalties **5**	24118	0	0	0	24118	0	0	•	0	0	•	•	0
Other Portfolio Income **6**	458518	0	522	29423	89	27	25	•	0	0	•	•	0
Other Receipts **7**	219564	0	11722	45475	3341	1100	9663	•	0	0	•	•	0
Total Receipts **8**	15600207	444680	7952249	1603285	1944939	604549	436340	•	0	0	•	•	0
Average Total Receipts **9**	582	121	364	2135	3953	18320	39667	•	•	•	•	•	•
Operating Costs/Operating Income (%)													
Cost of Operations **10**	45.2	33.2	40.4	66.4	60.7	57.0	48.1	•	•	•	•	•	•
Salaries and Wages **11**	14.7	1.1	9.2	10.6	11.9	10.7	18.4	•	•	•	•	•	•
Taxes Paid **12**	2.7	1.8	2.4	3.5	1.6	2.4	2.4	•	•	•	•	•	•
Interest Paid **13**	0.6	0.3	0.6	0.6	0.2	0.4	0.5	•	•	•	•	•	•
Depreciation **14**	1.3	1.4	0.7	0.8	0.6	1.2	0.6	•	•	•	•	•	•
Amortization and Depletion **15**	0.1	0.0	0.1	0.0	0.0	0.1	0.0	•	•	•	•	•	•
Pensions and Other Deferred Comp. **16**	0.6	0.5	0.7	0.1	1.0	1.2	0.4	•	•	•	•	•	•
Employee Benefits **17**	1.2	0.5	0.6	0.4	0.9	1.4	1.4	•	•	•	•	•	•
Advertising **18**	0.8	0.6	1.0	0.4	1.0	0.6	0.5	•	•	•	•	•	•
Other Expenses **19**	19.7	30.5	25.0	11.6	11.1	14.3	13.0	•	•	•	•	•	•
Officers' Compensation **20**	6.2	14.5	7.3	5.8	5.6	4.2	4.3	•	•	•	•	•	•
Operating Margin **21**	6.9	15.4	11.9	•	5.4	6.6	10.4	•	•	•	•	•	•
Operating Margin Before Officers' Comp. **22**	13.2	29.9	19.3	5.6	11.1	10.8	14.7	•	•	•	•	•	•

Selected Average Balance Sheet ($ in Thousands)

	•	•	•	•	•	•	•
Net Receivables 23	59	0	15	157	512	2128	6879
Inventories 24	23	0	3	238	574	608	854
Net Property, Plant and Equipment 25	33	0	14	129	225	703	1558
Total Assets 26	228	0	75	735	1936	6547	17503
Notes and Loans Payable 27	47	0	30	154	260	1244	2973
All Other Liabilities 28	80	0	27	347	1082	3343	5952
Net Worth 29	102	0	18	233	595	1960	8578

Selected Financial Ratios (Times to 1)

	•	•	•	•	•	•	•
Current Ratio 30	2.0	•	1.7	1.3	1.5	1.3	2.1
Quick Ratio 31	1.5	•	1.5	0.6	0.8	1.0	1.8
Net Sales to Working Capital 32	6.7	•	16.3	16.7	7.2	17.4	5.5
Coverage Ratio 33	21.0	46.5	19.7	8.8	40.8	19.9	25.7
Total Asset Turnover 34	2.4	•	4.8	2.8	2.0	2.8	2.2
Inventory Turnover 35	11.0	•	43.4	5.7	4.1	17.1	21.8
Receivables Turnover 36	11.7	•	24.5	13.0	7.7	7.4	11.3
Total Liabilities to Net Worth 37	1.2	•	3.2	2.1	2.3	2.3	1.0
Current Assets to Working Capital 38	2.1	•	2.3	4.4	3.1	4.6	1.9
Current Liabilities to Working Capital 39	1.1	•	1.3	3.4	2.1	3.6	0.9
Working Capital to Net Sales 40	0.1	•	0.1	0.1	0.1	0.1	0.2
Inventory to Working Capital 41	0.3	•	0.3	2.0	0.8	0.6	0.1
Total Receipts to Cash Flow 42	3.7	2.9	3.1	8.0	6.6	6.0	4.3
Cost of Goods to Cash Flow 43	1.7	1.0	1.2	5.3	4.0	3.4	2.1
Cash Flow to Total Debt 44	1.2	•	2.1	0.5	0.4	0.7	1.0

Selected Financial Factors (in Percentages)

	•	•	•	•	•	•	•
Debt Ratio 45	55.5	•	76.2	68.2	69.3	70.1	51.0
Return on Total Assets 46	30.3	•	61.9	14.8	14.6	20.3	29.4
Return on Equity Before Income Taxes 47	64.9	•	247.0	41.4	46.3	64.3	57.6
Return on Equity After Income Taxes 48	62.8	•	244.8	38.1	45.6	53.4	54.0
Profit Margin (Before Income Tax) 49	11.9	15.7	12.1	4.8	7.1	6.9	12.7
Profit Margin (After Income Tax) 50	11.5	15.5	12.0	4.4	7.0	5.7	12.0

Table I
Corporations with and without Net Income

COMPUTER SYSTEMS DESIGN AND RELATED SERVICES

MONEY AMOUNTS AND SIZE OF ASSETS IN THOUSANDS OF DOLLARS

Item Description for Accounting Period 7/05 Through 6/06	Total	Zero Assets	Under 500	500 to 1,000	1,000 to 5,000	5,000 to 10,000	10,000 to 25,000	25,000 to 50,000	50,000 to 100,000	100,000 to 250,000	250,000 to 500,000	500,000 to 2,500,000	2,500,000 and over
Number of Enterprises 1	108521	20124	79770	3006	3899	869	471	157	76	81	32	31	6
Revenues ($ in Thousands)													
Net Sales 2	154336295	6962850	25958528	5758971	23257494	10461503	9567151	5941636	5410474	8943450	9965954	17967275	24141010
Interest 3	1421148	45089	9001	11160	41371	27064	43511	50242	34884	100321	78641	194285	785579
Rents 4	142651	1386	7916	66	971	506	2064	3748	2964	5591	5512	47175	64751
Royalties 5	1719799	4082	2868	2393	69371	3676	457	33215	2685	44672	115979	837904	602497
Other Portfolio Income 6	1666381	381360	20632	71938	225939	68107	50231	50463	6114	140411	85142	315257	250782
Other Receipts 7	2440117	66005	98625	80045	211296	151123	81775	128813	23381	385586	182585	730181	300707
Total Receipts 8	161726391	7460772	26097570	5924573	23806442	10711979	9745189	6208117	5480502	9620031	10433813	20092077	26145326
Average Total Receipts 9	1490	371	327	1971	6106	12327	20690	39542	72112	118766	326057	648132	4357554
Operating Costs/Operating Income (%)													
Cost of Operations 10	31.1	10.0	22.5	29.8	36.0	43.7	43.0	35.3	43.2	37.9	44.8	41.5	12.0
Salaries and Wages 11	26.9	28.1	19.9	28.5	30.7	27.5	28.0	30.6	24.4	29.4	17.2	28.5	31.1
Taxes Paid 12	3.8	3.1	3.7	3.0	3.7	3.3	3.3	3.1	2.8	3.0	2.1	3.2	6.9
Interest Paid 13	1.8	2.9	0.8	1.1	0.6	0.9	1.1	1.8	1.3	1.8	1.2	1.4	4.9
Depreciation 14	1.6	0.7	0.8	0.8	1.1	1.3	1.8	1.9	2.1	2.3	1.7	1.8	2.5
Amortization and Depletion 15	1.4	0.4	0.1	0.3	0.6	0.9	1.0	1.4	1.4	2.3	2.4	1.6	3.7
Pensions and Other Deferred Comp. 16	0.7	0.8	0.9	0.9	0.8	1.3	0.6	0.4	0.2	0.3	0.5	0.6	0.5
Employee Benefits 17	2.5	1.1	1.5	1.7	2.2	2.7	2.4	2.5	1.9	2.6	1.6	3.3	4.3
Advertising 18	0.7	0.3	0.7	0.8	1.0	1.1	1.1	1.2	0.6	0.6	0.3	0.6	0.4
Other Expenses 19	28.6	56.7	29.6	26.5	18.9	19.2	23.3	26.2	64.5	21.7	27.0	22.0	36.3
Officers' Compensation 20	5.3	5.1	14.4	11.3	6.7	3.8	3.4	2.8	1.7	2.2	1.1	1.2	1.6
Operating Margin 21	•	•	5.1	•	•	•	•	•	•	•	•	•	•
Operating Margin Before Officers' Comp. 22	0.9	•	19.4	6.5	4.4	•	•	•	•	•	1.1	•	•

Selected Average Balance Sheet ($ in Thousands)

Item	C1	C2	C3	C4	C5	C6	C7	C8	C9	C10	C11	C12	C13
Net Receivables 23	330	0	9	208	846	2122	4017	9622	17638	28862	64433	165336	2511291
Inventories 24	15	0	1	45	57	162	379	719	1297	2282	3021	6973	28626
Net Property, Plant and Equipment 25	84	0	10	64	183	458	1238	2755	4403	8183	20628	59487	421585
Total Assets 26	1378	0	48	682	2282	7018	15250	35408	73099	153709	345706	991138	9355369
Notes and Loans Payable 27	365	0	35	300	618	1725	3975	7250	24196	26871	67866	152988	3017328
All Other Liabilities 28	424	0	20	265	1188	3215	6595	14583	30232	47939	103457	300091	2002454
Net Worth 29	589	0	-6	118	476	2079	4679	13574	18671	78900	174383	538060	4335587

Selected Financial Ratios (Times to 1)

Item	C1	C2	C3	C4	C5	C6	C7	C8	C9	C10	C11	C12	C13
Current Ratio 30	1.5	•	1.3	1.3	1.4	1.4	1.5	1.4	1.3	1.9	1.5	2.2	1.4
Quick Ratio 31	1.2	•	1.1	1.1	1.2	1.2	1.2	1.1	1.0	1.5	1.3	1.6	1.1
Net Sales to Working Capital 32	6.0	•	47.9	20.1	12.1	8.4	5.8	6.6	8.3	3.0	7.0	2.2	4.2
Coverage Ratio 33	1.3	0.3	8.4	•	1.0	•	•	•	•	3.0	4.9	5.6	1.9
Total Asset Turnover 34	1.0	•	6.7	2.8	2.6	1.7	1.3	1.1	1.0	0.7	0.9	0.6	0.4
Inventory Turnover 35	28.7	•	52.0	12.6	37.9	32.4	23.0	18.6	23.7	18.4	46.2	34.5	16.9
Receivables Turnover 36	4.7	•	38.7	9.0	8.1	7.3	5.4	4.2	4.1	4.2	5.2	4.1	1.7
Total Liabilities to Net Worth 37	1.3	•	•	4.8	3.8	2.4	2.3	1.6	2.9	0.9	1.0	0.8	1.2
Current Assets to Working Capital 38	2.8	•	4.8	4.8	3.5	3.5	3.0	3.5	4.8	2.1	3.1	1.8	3.6
Current Liabilities to Working Capital 39	1.8	•	3.8	3.8	2.5	2.5	2.0	2.5	3.8	1.1	2.1	0.8	2.6
Working Capital to Net Sales 40	0.2	•	0.0	0.0	0.1	0.1	0.2	0.2	0.1	0.3	0.1	0.5	0.2
Inventory to Working Capital 41	0.1	•	0.2	0.4	0.2	0.2	0.1	0.2	0.2	0.1	0.1	0.0	0.0
Total Receipts to Cash Flow 42	4.0	2.2	3.1	5.1	6.7	7.7	8.0	5.0	5.4	4.7	3.4	4.1	2.7
Cost of Goods to Cash Flow 43	1.2	0.2	0.7	1.5	2.4	3.4	3.4	1.8	2.3	1.8	1.5	1.7	0.3
Cash Flow to Total Debt 44	0.5	•	1.9	0.7	0.5	0.3	0.2	0.3	0.2	0.3	0.5	0.3	0.3

Selected Financial Factors (in Percentages)

Item	C1	C2	C3	C4	C5	C6	C7	C8	C9	C10	C11	C12	C13
Debt Ratio 45	57.3	•	113.2	82.7	79.1	70.4	69.3	61.7	74.5	48.7	49.6	45.7	53.7
Return on Total Assets 46	2.3	•	42.8	•	1.7	•	•	•	•	3.8	5.2	4.7	4.0
Return on Equity Before Income Taxes 47	1.2	•	•	•	0.2	•	•	•	•	5.0	8.3	7.2	4.2
Return on Equity After Income Taxes 48	•	•	•	•	•	•	•	•	•	3.4	5.6	5.4	2.5
Profit Margin (Before Income Tax) 49	0.5	•	5.6	•	0.0	•	•	•	•	3.6	4.6	6.7	4.5
Profit Margin (After Income Tax) 50	•	•	5.5	•	•	•	•	•	•	2.4	3.2	5.1	2.7

Table II
Corporations with Net Income

COMPUTER SYSTEMS DESIGN AND RELATED SERVICES

MONEY AMOUNTS AND SIZE OF ASSETS IN THOUSANDS OF DOLLARS

Item Description for Accounting Period 7/05 Through 6/06	Total	Zero Assets	Under 500	500 to 1,000	1,000 to 5,000	5,000 to 10,000	10,000 to 25,000	25,000 to 50,000	50,000 to 100,000	100,000 to 250,000	250,000 to 500,000	500,000 to 2,500,000	2,500,000 and over
Number of Enterprises 1	62135	8360	48409	1769	2733	426	228	71	•	51	18	21	•
Revenues ($ in Thousands)													
Net Sales 2	117805495	3760594	21205830	4421796	19566494	7759098	6373016	3528175	•	6115160	7885563	13623110	•
Interest 3	849203	4817	2355	7496	15855	7877	14879	11151	•	77717	49091	147016	•
Rents 4	73101	0	0	66	0	406	817	2690	•	3620	5417	45870	•
Royalties 5	908054	0	2868	263	1467	139	426	19636	•	34675	101	837468	•
Other Portfolio Income 6	1331783	123120	19934	71280	222100	62875	47503	38851	•	133354	69283	308635	•
Other Receipts 7	1737917	48752	143024	19540	169663	80322	40399	67232	•	71828	113396	701101	•
Total Receipts 8	122705553	3937283	21374011	4520441	19975579	7910717	6477040	3667735	•	6436354	8122851	15663200	•
Average Total Receipts 9	1975	471	442	2555	7309	18570	28408	51658	•	126203	451270	745867	•
Operating Costs/Operating Income (%)													
Cost of Operations 10	29.3	12.1	21.6	29.6	35.5	45.8	48.7	34.0	•	34.7	49.8	40.4	•
Salaries and Wages 11	25.4	41.9	19.0	26.5	27.4	21.9	17.9	28.2	•	27.2	12.8	27.3	•
Taxes Paid 12	3.9	4.5	3.4	2.5	3.5	2.9	2.8	3.0	•	2.8	1.8	3.4	•
Interest Paid 13	1.3	0.4	0.6	0.7	0.4	0.4	0.7	0.6	•	1.6	0.6	1.1	•
Depreciation 14	1.3	0.6	0.6	0.7	0.7	0.7	1.4	1.4	•	1.9	1.4	1.6	•
Amortization and Depletion 15	1.2	0.1	0.0	0.0	0.3	0.3	0.4	0.8	•	1.5	1.3	1.7	•
Pensions and Other Deferred Comp. 16	0.7	0.7	0.9	0.8	0.9	1.5	0.7	0.6	•	0.3	0.4	0.6	•
Employee Benefits 17	2.3	1.0	1.4	1.4	1.9	2.5	1.8	2.0	•	2.4	1.2	3.2	•
Advertising 18	0.5	0.2	0.5	0.6	0.6	0.7	0.8	1.0	•	0.5	0.2	0.7	•
Other Expenses 19	23.9	23.6	27.7	23.1	15.4	13.7	14.0	19.4	•	21.0	25.1	22.1	•
Officers' Compensation 20	4.8	5.4	12.6	8.5	6.5	3.1	3.1	2.6	•	1.4	0.8	1.0	•
Operating Margin 21	5.3	9.5	11.5	5.6	7.0	6.4	7.7	6.4	•	4.7	4.5	•	•
Operating Margin Before Officers' Comp. 22	10.2	14.9	24.2	14.1	13.4	9.5	10.9	9.0	•	6.1	5.4	•	•

Selected Average Balance Sheet ($ in Thousands)

Net Receivables 23	359	0	11	234	985	3255	5232	11770	·	30002	83295	154806
Inventories 24	12	0	1	63	43	191	381	791	·	1846	2832	1768
Net Property, Plant and Equipment 25	107	0	11	73	163	378	1415	2642	·	8394	25250	74485
Total Assets 26	1633	0	55	715	2219	7330	15199	35660	·	160500	352285	1070168
Notes and Loans Payable 27	373	0	26	224	399	1661	4211	7132	·	30348	70519	171098
All Other Liabilities 28	454	0	15	254	1081	3377	6843	14483	·	40146	116063	254464
Net Worth 29	805	0	14	236	738	2292	4145	14045	·	90006	165703	644606

Selected Financial Ratios (Times to 1)

Current Ratio 30	1.7	·	2.0	1.7	1.5	1.4	1.4	1.5	·	2.2	1.4	2.4
Quick Ratio 31	1.4	·	1.8	1.4	1.3	1.2	1.2	1.3	·	1.6	1.2	1.9
Net Sales to Working Capital 32	6.5	·	22.2	12.3	13.2	10.5	9.0	6.3	·	2.5	9.0	2.3
Coverage Ratio 33	8.4	36.2	20.6	12.3	26.5	19.9	14.3	17.0	·	7.3	13.4	12.6
Total Asset Turnover 34	1.2	·	7.9	3.5	3.2	2.5	1.8	1.4	·	0.7	1.2	0.6
Inventory Turnover 35	44.9	·	118.8	11.7	59.1	43.6	35.8	21.4	·	22.5	77.0	148.1
Receivables Turnover 36	6.0	·	42.8	10.1	8.6	7.4	5.9	4.6	·	4.7	10.5	5.4
Total Liabilities to Net Worth 37	1.0	·	2.9	2.0	2.0	2.2	2.7	1.5	·	0.8	1.1	0.7
Current Assets to Working Capital 38	2.4	·	2.0	2.4	3.1	3.4	3.3	2.9	·	1.8	3.3	1.7
Current Liabilities to Working Capital 39	1.4	·	1.0	1.4	2.1	2.4	2.3	1.9	·	0.8	2.3	0.7
Working Capital to Net Sales 40	0.2	·	0.0	0.1	0.1	0.1	0.1	0.2	·	0.4	0.1	0.4
Inventory to Working Capital 41	0.0	·	0.1	0.3	0.1	0.1	0.2	0.1	·	0.0	0.1	0.0
Total Receipts to Cash Flow 42	3.3	3.0	2.7	3.8	4.8	5.1	4.9	3.8	·	3.7	3.2	3.2
Cost of Goods to Cash Flow 43	1.0	0.4	0.6	1.1	1.7	2.3	2.4	1.3	·	1.3	1.6	1.3
Cash Flow to Total Debt 44	0.7	·	3.9	1.4	1.0	0.7	0.5	0.6	·	0.5	0.7	0.5

Selected Financial Factors (in Percentages)

Debt Ratio 45	50.7	·	74.3	66.9	66.7	68.7	72.7	60.6	·	43.9	53.0	39.8
Return on Total Assets 46	12.7	·	102.5	29.8	30.4	21.8	18.5	15.3	·	8.9	10.1	8.3
Return on Equity Before Income Taxes 47	22.6	·	379.8	82.7	87.8	66.3	63.0	36.5	·	13.8	19.9	12.7
Return on Equity After Income Taxes 48	19.9	·	377.5	79.7	83.7	61.0	55.4	31.5	·	11.5	14.9	10.6
Profit Margin (Before Income Tax) 49	9.6	14.2	12.3	7.8	9.1	8.3	9.3	10.3	·	10.3	7.5	12.6
Profit Margin (After Income Tax) 50	8.5	12.1	12.2	7.5	8.6	7.7	8.2	8.9	·	8.7	5.6	10.5

Table I

Corporations with and without Net Income

MANAGEMENT, SCIENTIFIC, AND TECHNICAL CONSULTING SERVICES

MONEY AMOUNTS AND SIZE OF ASSETS IN THOUSANDS OF DOLLARS

Item Description for Accounting Period 7/05 Through 6/06	Total	Zero Assets	Under 500	500 to 1,000	1,000 to 5,000	5,000 to 10,000	10,000 to 25,000	25,000 to 50,000	50,000 to 100,000	100,000 to 250,000	250,000 to 500,000	500,000 to 2,500,000	2,500,000 and over
Number of Enterprises 1	225775	38956	174322	6515	4598	624	452	128	78	46	24	28	4
Revenues ($ in Thousands)													
Net Sales 2	163949961	3265799	50077337	20195249	20446461	6025744	8848191	4674630	5455182	10319482	3927668	23971381	6742836
Interest 3	874414	7848	39470	25487	39416	20386	29496	17961	50486	32651	84426	353328	173459
Rents 4	84104	208	505	5013	5395	2223	2965	2882	12171	3963	2404	31707	14666
Royalties 5	828516	0	628	83	42278	738	15056	84	154877	8462	1765	604457	89
Other Portfolio Income 6	2084640	65568	112990	50362	69882	82716	145017	70674	35319	25516	22696	1253123	150780
Other Receipts 7	5536517	-35643	2483382	326796	576172	185223	479567	221559	192538	249604	118225	741668	-2576
Total Receipts 8	173358152	3303780	52714312	20602990	21179604	6317030	9520292	4987790	5900573	10639678	4157184	26955664	7079254
Average Total Receipts 9	768	85	302	3162	4606	10123	21063	38967	75648	231297	173216	962702	1769814
Operating Costs/Operating Income (%)													
Cost of Operations 10	26.7	11.9	29.8	10.2	48.3	33.3	35.2	26.9	31.3	50.4	21.0	9.7	0.7
Salaries and Wages 11	25.7	10.5	17.4	30.9	18.5	22.4	24.7	30.3	28.7	20.7	37.7	38.8	53.4
Taxes Paid 12	3.0	2.6	2.9	2.7	2.4	3.6	2.9	3.4	2.9	2.3	4.0	3.6	3.7
Interest Paid 13	1.0	1.4	0.6	0.5	0.7	0.9	1.0	1.2	1.3	1.3	2.1	1.9	1.0
Depreciation 14	1.1	1.3	0.9	0.5	0.6	1.3	1.4	2.6	1.6	1.0	1.5	2.0	1.6
Amortization and Depletion 15	0.4	0.1	0.1	0.1	0.1	0.2	0.4	0.5	0.7	0.8	2.1	1.1	0.6
Pensions and Other Deferred Comp. 16	1.6	2.0	1.8	1.1	0.8	1.1	1.1	0.9	1.2	0.6	0.7	2.4	4.4
Employee Benefits 17	2.0	5.4	1.4	2.2	1.2	2.1	2.2	2.4	3.5	1.9	1.5	2.4	3.5
Advertising 18	0.9	1.2	0.8	0.4	0.4	0.4	2.5	0.4	0.3	0.7	0.3	2.2	0.1
Other Expenses 19	28.6	41.5	26.6	41.7	16.0	21.5	23.7	27.9	25.6	18.6	36.7	36.4	35.6
Officers' Compensation 20	7.7	19.1	14.6	5.7	6.4	9.0	4.3	4.6	3.3	0.9	3.4	2.5	0.7
Operating Margin 21	1.4	3.1	3.2	3.9	4.7	4.4	0.4	•	•	0.9	•	•	•
Operating Margin Before Officers' Comp. 22	9.0	22.2	17.8	9.6	11.0	13.4	4.8	3.6	3.0	1.8	•	•	•

Selected Average Balance Sheet ($ in Thousands)

Net Receivables 23	101	0	6	146	521	1820	3933	7958	14468	41885	47004	283561	604882
Inventories 24	6	0	2	9	55	49	228	619	1302	3328	764	10652	1723
Net Property, Plant and Equipment 25	48	0	10	75	252	638	2018	4046	8169	15274	23166	117245	96841
Total Assets 26	487	0	52	692	1990	7012	15696	35814	71668	143050	352388	1107004	4881214
Notes and Loans Payable 27	146	0	39	288	748	1542	4460	10106	18387	35511	189130	300423	157184
All Other Liabilities 28	180	0	16	206	527	2156	4958	9206	22100	51128	124372	483902	2187388
Net Worth 29	161	0	-3	198	716	3314	6277	16502	31182	56412	38887	322679	2536642

Selected Financial Ratios (Times to 1)

Current Ratio 30	1.4	•	1.3	2.3	2.4	1.6	1.6	1.7	1.6	1.3	1.3	1.3	0.8
Quick Ratio 31	1.0	•	1.1	1.9	1.9	1.1	1.3	1.2	1.3	1.0	1.0	1.0	0.5
Net Sales to Working Capital 32	11.8	•	44.5	12.8	5.9	6.1	6.2	5.1	5.5	13.8	5.8	6.5	•
Coverage Ratio 33	8.3	4.1	14.6	13.2	13.5	10.9	8.7	5.6	7.3	4.1	•	6.1	0.6
Total Asset Turnover 34	1.5	•	5.5	4.5	2.2	1.4	1.2	1.0	1.0	1.6	0.5	0.8	0.3
Inventory Turnover 35	32.0	•	55.4	36.4	39.2	66.1	30.2	15.9	16.8	34.0	45.1	7.8	7.1
Receivables Turnover 36	7.2	•	51.3	24.4	8.4	5.0	5.0	4.2	3.9	6.3	3.0	3.2	2.7
Total Liabilities to Net Worth 37	2.0	•	•	2.5	1.8	1.1	1.5	1.2	1.3	1.5	8.1	2.4	0.9
Current Assets to Working Capital 38	3.7	•	4.7	1.7	1.7	2.7	2.6	2.5	2.6	4.2	4.6	4.1	•
Current Liabilities to Working Capital 39	2.7	•	3.7	0.7	0.7	1.7	1.6	1.5	1.6	3.2	3.6	3.1	•
Working Capital to Net Sales 40	0.1	•	0.0	0.1	0.2	0.2	0.2	0.2	0.2	0.1	0.2	0.2	•
Inventory to Working Capital 41	0.1	•	0.2	0.0	0.0	0.0	0.1	0.1	0.1	0.2	0.0	0.1	•
Total Receipts to Cash Flow 42	3.2	2.6	3.2	2.2	4.6	3.8	3.7	3.4	3.4	5.0	3.7	2.5	3.2
Cost of Goods to Cash Flow 43	0.8	0.3	1.0	0.2	2.2	1.3	1.3	0.9	1.1	2.5	0.8	0.2	0.0
Cash Flow to Total Debt 44	0.7	•	1.6	2.8	0.8	0.7	0.6	0.5	0.5	0.5	0.1	0.4	0.2

Selected Financial Factors (in Percentages)

Debt Ratio 45	67.0	•	104.8	71.4	64.0	52.7	60.0	53.9	56.5	60.6	89.0	70.9	48.0
Return on Total Assets 46	12.1	•	50.2	28.9	19.9	13.6	11.3	7.0	8.9	8.2	•	8.9	0.2
Return on Equity Before Income Taxes 47	32.3	•	•	93.2	51.2	26.2	25.0	12.5	17.7	15.9	•	25.6	•
Return on Equity After Income Taxes 48	28.8	•	•	91.8	49.0	24.8	22.0	10.1	14.3	11.4	•	19.7	•
Profit Margin (Before Income Tax) 49	7.1	4.3	8.5	6.0	8.2	9.0	8.0	5.6	7.9	4.0	•	9.7	•
Profit Margin (After Income Tax) 50	6.4	3.4	8.4	5.9	7.9	8.5	7.0	4.6	6.4	2.9	•	7.4	•

MANAGEMENT, SCIENTIFIC, AND TECHNICAL CONSULTING SERVICES

Table II

Corporations with Net Income

MONEY AMOUNTS AND SIZE OF ASSETS IN THOUSANDS OF DOLLARS

Item Description for Accounting Period 7/05 Through 6/06	Total	Zero Assets	Under 500	500 to 1,000	1,000 to 5,000	5,000 to 10,000	10,000 to 25,000	25,000 to 50,000	50,000 to 100,000	100,000 to 250,000	250,000 to 500,000	500,000 to 2,500,000	2,500,000 and over
Number of Enterprises 1	134243	18321	106942	4623	3365	465	316	94	50	30	•	•	24
Revenues ($ in Thousands)													
Net Sales 2	138713088	2393512	41368329	19262350	17604730	5540175	7734159	3912619	4208842	7787734	•	•	20718178
Interest 3	645492	1752	20715	24018	26695	4507	19002	15823	19133	16360	•	•	308569
Rents 4	66450	208	498	5013	1913	2222	2746	2816	12114	7	•	•	23281
Royalties 5	822107	0	590	63	41993	738	15056	84	154877	4160	•	•	604457
Other Portfolio Income 6	1889751	63240	66020	47523	66098	60388	137219	57533	31629	11102	•	•	1202263
Other Receipts 7	5320731	46589	2488691	311501	544418	157895	416626	166725	211756	232850	•	•	702354
Total Receipts 8	147457619	2505301	43943043	19650468	18285847	5765925	8324808	4155600	4638351	8052213	•	•	23559102
Average Total Receipts 9	1098	137	411	4251	5434	12400	26344	44209	92767	268407	•	•	981629
Operating Costs/Operating Income (%)													
Cost of Operations 10	26.4	14.3	29.0	10.1	49.9	34.6	36.3	28.3	28.2	52.0	•	•	10.7
Salaries and Wages 11	24.8	11.0	17.2	29.4	16.4	19.2	22.5	29.7	29.2	16.2	•	•	38.1
Taxes Paid 12	3.0	2.5	2.9	2.5	2.3	3.4	2.8	3.4	3.0	2.4	•	•	3.8
Interest Paid 13	0.8	0.9	0.6	0.4	0.2	0.4	0.8	1.0	0.8	0.9	•	•	1.9
Depreciation 14	1.0	0.7	0.8	0.4	0.5	0.9	1.2	1.4	1.4	0.7	•	•	2.0
Amortization and Depletion 15	0.3	0.0	0.0	0.0	0.1	0.1	0.2	0.3	0.6	0.6	•	•	1.2
Pensions and Other Deferred Comp. 16	1.5	2.1	1.5	1.0	0.8	1.1	1.1	0.9	1.2	0.6	•	•	2.5
Employee Benefits 17	1.8	1.2	1.4	2.1	1.0	1.9	2.2	2.2	3.6	1.7	•	•	2.2
Advertising 18	0.9	1.5	0.7	0.4	0.4	0.3	2.8	0.4	0.3	0.6	•	•	2.4
Other Expenses 19	26.7	27.5	24.9	42.3	13.2	19.0	22.1	24.3	25.4	19.6	•	•	34.2
Officers' Compensation 20	7.5	19.2	14.1	5.5	6.6	8.4	4.0	4.8	3.4	0.8	•	•	2.9
Operating Margin 21	5.3	19.2	7.1	5.7	8.7	10.6	4.1	3.4	3.1	4.1	•	•	•
Operating Margin Before Officers' Comp. 22	12.7	38.4	21.2	11.2	15.2	19.1	8.1	8.1	6.4	4.9	•	•	1.0

Selected Average Balance Sheet ($ in Thousands)

Net Receivables 23	124	0	6	187	490	2292	3958	8707	17055	45229	•	221265
Inventories 24	8	0	2	10	66	56	294	726	1466	2725	•	11205
Net Property, Plant and Equipment 25	57	0	11	47	214	385	2226	3535	7412	12705	•	122726
Total Assets 26	564	0	58	696	1936	7065	16131	35833	71093	142976	•	1018445
Notes and Loans Payable 27	125	0	34	261	421	640	4462	9476	12400	31544	•	221668
All Other Liabilities 28	235	0	17	213	447	2212	5106	10139	24043	49342	•	471084
Net Worth 29	204	0	7	222	1068	4213	6564	16218	34650	62090	•	325693

Selected Financial Ratios (Times to 1)

Current Ratio 30	1.3	•	1.3	2.3	2.7	1.7	1.7	1.7	1.7	1.5	•	1.2
Quick Ratio 31	1.0	•	1.2	2.1	2.2	1.5	1.4	1.3	1.4	1.2	•	0.9
Net Sales to Working Capital 32	14.8	27.8	47.9	15.0	6.2	6.8	6.6	5.3	5.4	11.2	•	13.8
Coverage Ratio 33	15.8	27.8	24.7	19.9	59.9	37.5	15.4	10.4	17.8	9.5	•	7.4
Total Asset Turnover 34	1.8	•	6.6	6.0	2.7	1.7	1.5	1.2	1.2	1.8	•	0.8
Inventory Turnover 35	33.9	•	67.2	40.6	39.4	74.3	30.2	16.2	16.2	49.6	•	8.2
Receivables Turnover 36	8.8	•	61.6	25.8	11.4	5.4	6.3	4.9	4.3	7.6	•	4.2
Total Liabilities to Net Worth 37	1.8	•	7.0	2.1	0.8	0.7	1.5	1.2	1.1	1.3	•	2.1
Current Assets to Working Capital 38	4.0	•	4.2	1.7	1.6	2.3	2.4	2.5	2.4	3.2	•	7.3
Current Liabilities to Working Capital 39	3.0	•	3.2	0.7	0.6	1.3	1.4	1.5	1.4	2.2	•	6.3
Working Capital to Net Sales 40	0.1	•	0.0	0.1	0.2	0.1	0.2	0.2	0.2	0.1	•	0.1
Inventory to Working Capital 41	0.1	•	0.1	0.0	0.1	0.1	0.1	0.1	0.1	0.1	•	0.2
Total Receipts to Cash Flow 42	2.9	2.2	2.9	2.1	4.3	3.3	3.4	3.4	2.9	4.1	•	2.5
Cost of Goods to Cash Flow 43	0.8	0.3	0.8	0.2	2.1	2.1	1.2	1.0	0.8	2.1	•	0.3
Cash Flow to Total Debt 44	1.0	•	2.6	4.2	1.4	1.3	0.7	0.6	0.8	0.8	•	0.5

Selected Financial Factors (in Percentages)

Debt Ratio 45	63.8	•	87.5	68.1	44.8	40.4	59.3	54.7	51.3	56.6	•	68.0
Return on Total Assets 46	22.7	•	91.8	48.6	34.4	25.4	19.1	12.3	16.7	15.1	•	11.9
Return on Equity Before Income Taxes 47	58.8	•	705.8	144.8	61.4	41.5	43.9	24.7	32.4	31.2	•	32.1
Return on Equity After Income Taxes 48	54.3	•	696.5	143.1	59.4	40.1	39.7	21.3	27.6	24.9	•	25.2
Profit Margin (Before Income Tax) 49	11.6	23.9	13.3	7.7	12.5	14.7	11.8	9.6	13.3	7.5	•	12.1
Profit Margin (After Income Tax) 50	10.7	22.6	13.1	7.6	12.1	14.2	10.7	8.3	11.4	6.0	•	9.5

Table I

Corporations with and without Net Income

SCIENTIFIC RESEARCH AND DEVELOPMENT SERVICES

MONEY AMOUNTS AND SIZE OF ASSETS IN THOUSANDS OF DOLLARS

Item Description for Accounting Period 7/05 Through 6/06	Total	Zero Assets	Under 500	500 to 1,000	1,000 to 5,000	5,000 to 10,000	10,000 to 25,000	25,000 to 50,000	50,000 to 100,000	100,000 to 250,000	250,000 to 500,000	500,000 to 2,500,000	2,500,000 and over
Number of Enterprises 1	11453	1602	6411	1106	1335	363	300	135	86	62	28	20	4
Revenues ($ in Thousands)													
Net Sales 2	38181353	252920	3865400	2112956	2374863	2225639	1540458	1935932	1989376	2442942	3287190	2823167	13330509
Interest 3	1029377	6018	2232	3868	27857	23437	73879	72312	104335	180943	112550	215678	206267
Rents 4	22346	0	0	0	1843	176	2490	284	1442	2710	1394	0	12006
Royalties 5	2622380	0	0	0	2051	17431	6315	23571	25767	121797	487242	437138	1501069
Other Portfolio Income 6	1445858	33645	42030	12394	45932	32440	25473	51691	84204	132804	64398	160799	760045
Other Receipts 7	2580022	83764	133527	1156	724417	68489	243493	43868	127778	204779	204779	668458	67287
Total Receipts 8	45581336	376347	4043189	2130374	3176963	2367612	1892108	2127658	2332902	3094208	4157553	4305240	15877183
Average Total Receipts 9	4006	235	631	1926	2380	6522	6307	15760	27127	49907	148484	215262	3969296
Operating Costs/Operating Income (%)													
Cost of Operations 10	39.7	20.8	9.1	31.9	26.1	26.2	45.2	31.6	42.8	14.7	30.4	23.0	65.5
Salaries and Wages 11	28.7	77.4	26.5	17.2	53.7	36.6	47.9	38.4	38.4	49.0	28.6	50.0	11.1
Taxes Paid 12	4.2	6.1	3.0	4.5	10.0	4.4	6.9	5.3	5.7	5.3	2.8	6.3	2.4
Interest Paid 13	3.0	5.3	0.5	0.9	3.3	1.8	3.6	2.0	2.1	4.7	3.4	7.5	3.0
Depreciation 14	3.4	5.0	1.1	1.3	4.7	3.3	6.4	4.8	4.9	6.0	3.9	8.8	1.7
Amortization and Depletion 15	3.0	16.4	0.1	0.3	2.8	1.1	4.9	3.8	5.5	5.6	4.4	4.7	2.5
Pensions and Other Deferred Comp. 16	1.4	0.4	1.6	2.2	2.6	0.8	1.5	1.1	1.8	1.4	0.5	2.0	1.2
Employee Benefits 17	3.1	2.3	2.2	2.2	8.6	3.7	5.9	4.3	5.3	5.5	3.5	6.9	0.4
Advertising 18	1.0	0.5	2.2	0.1	0.9	1.6	1.9	0.7	1.8	1.5	0.7	1.7	0.4
Other Expenses 19	47.2	84.1	46.9	31.0	60.6	43.2	86.3	74.3	68.1	89.2	56.6	70.7	20.9
Officers' Compensation 20	5.8	25.4	10.8	11.0	16.1	7.0	11.9	7.0	7.6	5.9	4.6	5.7	0.3
Operating Margin 21	•	•	•	•	•	•	•	•	•	•	•	•	•
Operating Margin Before Officers' Comp. 22	•	6.7	8.5	•	•	•	•	•	•	•	•	•	•

Selected Average Balance Sheet ($ in Thousands)

Net Receivables 23	808	0	5	204	550	1183	1584	3612	6372	9577	33712	74550	824288
Inventories 24	176	0	0	24	74	318	410	591	1163	2071	6868	11679	228715
Net Property, Plant and Equipment 25	803	0	17	95	256	1051	1592	3880	6649	13804	41287	134872	494200
Total Assets 26	7461	0	70	727	2265	7134	15898	35048	70468	160550	345658	870545	6495087
Notes and Loans Payable 27	1802	0	133	312	730	1547	2268	4657	5902	34682	88658	298444	1372165
All Other Liabilities 28	1665	0	46	203	1013	1934	4486	7692	16331	37341	66435	140411	1431438
Net Worth 29	3994	0	-109	212	521	3653	9144	22699	48235	88526	190565	431690	3691484

Selected Financial Ratios (Times to 1)

Current Ratio 30	2.3	•	0.5	1.6	1.3	2.5	2.6	3.0	3.9	3.9	2.6	2.7	1.5
Quick Ratio 31	1.6	•	0.4	1.4	1.1	2.0	2.0	2.2	2.9	2.7	1.6	1.6	0.9
Net Sales to Working Capital 32	1.6	•	•	10.9	4.7	2.1	0.7	0.9	0.6	0.5	1.0	0.7	5.0
Coverage Ratio 33	•	2.0	•	•	•	•	•	•	•	•	•	•	4.4
Total Asset Turnover 34	0.4	•	8.6	2.6	0.8	0.9	0.3	0.4	0.3	0.2	0.3	0.2	0.5
Inventory Turnover 35	7.5	•	1043.9	25.0	6.3	5.0	5.7	7.7	8.5	2.8	5.2	2.8	9.5
Receivables Turnover 36	4.4	•	46.9	12.1	3.5	6.5	3.3	4.7	4.2	3.8	4.0	2.6	3.8
Total Liabilities to Net Worth 37	0.9	•	•	2.4	3.3	1.0	0.7	0.5	0.5	0.8	0.8	1.0	0.8
Current Assets to Working Capital 38	1.8	•	•	2.7	4.2	1.7	1.6	1.5	1.3	1.3	1.6	1.6	3.2
Current Liabilities to Working Capital 39	0.8	•	•	1.7	3.2	0.7	0.6	0.5	0.3	0.3	0.6	0.6	2.2
Working Capital to Net Sales 40	0.6	•	•	0.1	0.2	0.5	1.3	1.1	1.5	1.9	1.0	1.4	0.2
Inventory to Working Capital 41	0.1	•	•	0.2	0.1	0.2	0.1	0.0	0.0	0.0	0.1	0.1	0.4
Total Receipts to Cash Flow 42	5.8	•	2.7	4.2	•	9.6	•	196.2	•	8.7	2.9	3.7	4.4
Cost of Goods to Cash Flow 43	2.3	•	0.2	1.3	•	2.5	•	62.0	•	1.3	0.9	0.9	2.9
Cash Flow to Total Debt 44	0.2	•	1.3	0.9	•	0.2	•	0.0	•	0.1	0.3	0.1	0.3

Selected Financial Factors (in Percentages)

Debt Ratio 45	46.5	•	255.6	70.8	77.0	48.8	42.5	35.2	31.6	44.9	44.9	50.4	43.2
Return on Total Assets 46	•	9.0	•	•	•	•	•	•	•	•	•	•	6.7
Return on Equity Before Income Taxes 47	•	•	•	•	•	•	•	•	•	•	•	•	9.2
Return on Equity After Income Taxes 48	•	•	•	•	•	•	•	•	•	•	•	•	6.6
Profit Margin (Before Income Tax) 49	•	•	0.5	•	•	•	•	•	•	•	•	•	10.2
Profit Margin (After Income Tax) 50	•	•	0.4	•	•	•	•	•	•	•	•	•	7.3

Table II
Corporations with Net Income

SCIENTIFIC RESEARCH AND DEVELOPMENT SERVICES

MONEY AMOUNTS AND SIZE OF ASSETS IN THOUSANDS OF DOLLARS

Item Description for Accounting Period 7/05 Through 6/06	Total	Zero Assets	Under 500	500 to 1,000	1,000 to 5,000	5,000 to 10,000	10,000 to 25,000	25,000 to 50,000	50,000 to 100,000	100,000 to 250,000	250,000 to 500,000	500,000 to 2,500,000	2,500,000 and over
Number of Enterprises **1**	5402	118	4127	528	318	173	53	27	16	17	13	•	•
Revenues ($ in Thousands)													
Net Sales **2**	29421294	77505	3673948	973305	1366407	1941543	700528	1238312	793265	1393943	2493140	•	•
Interest **3**	344423	67	1791	1186	6754	7229	6797	11784	6379	42095	27735	•	•
Rents **4**	15206	0	0	0	1812	176	0	27	7	529	648	•	•
Royalties **5**	2038280	0	0	0	0	14519	1064	3115	884	98680	469709	•	•
Other Portfolio Income **6**	1172128	32295	11085	11889	16366	31637	18733	51241	72936	13075	7640	•	•
Other Receipts **7**	1064919	27127	40274	151	143410	54927	82068	8479	20004	114301	21668	•	•
Total Receipts **8**	34056250	136994	3727098	986531	1534749	2050031	809190	1312958	893475	1662623	3020540	•	•
Average Total Receipts **9**	6304	1161	903	1868	4826	11850	15268	48628	55842	97801	232349	•	•
Operating Costs/Operating Income (%)													
Cost of Operations **10**	42.1	49.1	7.7	1.2	34.1	23.6	36.6	30.7	48.6	15.4	32.7	•	•
Salaries and Wages **11**	18.8	14.8	25.0	27.3	29.8	28.5	16.2	20.3	15.8	30.1	16.5	•	•
Taxes Paid **12**	2.9	4.4	2.7	3.9	4.1	3.4	3.7	3.6	3.5	3.2	1.9	•	•
Interest Paid **13**	2.0	3.9	0.1	1.0	0.3	0.5	0.5	1.0	0.3	1.6	2.0	•	•
Depreciation **14**	2.0	3.0	0.7	1.1	1.7	2.1	3.4	1.7	2.0	3.5	2.7	•	•
Amortization and Depletion **15**	1.2	2.0	0.1	0.0	0.1	0.1	0.1	0.5	0.2	1.8	4.2	•	•
Pensions and Other Deferred Comp. **16**	1.2	1.4	1.7	3.8	1.3	0.8	2.0	1.4	2.8	0.7	0.4	•	•
Employee Benefits **17**	1.9	1.3	2.1	1.6	4.3	2.9	4.3	2.7	3.5	4.1	2.5	•	•
Advertising **18**	0.6	0.4	2.3	0.1	0.2	0.8	0.0	0.1	0.2	0.8	0.5	•	•
Other Expenses **19**	25.9	28.4	37.3	28.2	15.3	24.2	24.8	27.8	17.2	38.6	37.0	•	•
Officers' Compensation **20**	3.5	3.0	9.4	13.5	8.3	5.0	4.3	2.5	2.6	2.6	4.3	•	•
Operating Margin **21**	•	•	11.0	18.3	0.5	8.0	3.8	7.6	3.2	•	•	•	•
Operating Margin Before Officers' Comp. **22**	1.4	•	20.4	31.8	8.8	13.0	8.2	10.1	5.8	0.1	•	•	•

Selected Average Balance Sheet ($ in Thousands)

Net Receivables 23	1205	0	6	192	607	1980	2551	10304	13767	17778	52684
Inventories 24	190	0	0	6	155	218	655	1011	2935	3266	9247
Net Property, Plant and Equipment 25	790	0	17	66	234	1302	2332	5154	5929	16275	47307
Total Assets 26	7993	0	68	681	1824	7040	16960	35715	64228	167004	355230
Notes and Loans Payable 27	1685	0	14	65	277	812	137	4092	4224	20765	87595
All Other Liabilities 28	1699	0	30	73	751	1657	5145	12548	18897	40236	54778
Net Worth 29	4608	0	24	543	796	4570	11678	19075	41107	106004	212857

Selected Financial Ratios (Times to 1)

Current Ratio 30	1.7	•	1.2	6.7	1.3	2.7	2.7	1.7	2.4	3.7	1.9
Quick Ratio 31	1.1	•	1.1	6.6	1.1	2.3	2.1	1.4	1.9	2.2	1.3
Net Sales to Working Capital 32	4.1	18.5	141.0	4.4	14.6	3.5	2.3	5.0	2.0	1.2	2.3
Coverage Ratio 33	8.1	•	130.7	19.9	40.4	28.8	40.6	14.2	72.2	11.3	9.0
Total Asset Turnover 34	0.7	•	13.0	2.7	2.4	1.6	0.8	1.3	0.8	0.5	0.5
Inventory Turnover 35	12.1	•	4981.8	3.7	9.5	12.2	7.4	13.9	8.2	3.9	6.8
Receivables Turnover 36	5.4	•	126.5	9.7	5.4	7.8	3.7	5.0	4.0	3.9	4.0
Total Liabilities to Net Worth 37	0.7	•	1.9	0.3	1.3	0.5	0.5	0.9	0.6	0.6	0.7
Current Assets to Working Capital 38	2.4	•	6.0	1.2	4.7	1.6	1.6	2.4	1.7	1.4	2.1
Current Liabilities to Working Capital 39	1.4	•	5.0	0.2	3.7	0.6	0.6	1.4	0.7	0.4	1.1
Working Capital to Net Sales 40	0.2	•	0.0	0.2	0.1	0.3	0.4	0.2	0.5	0.8	0.4
Inventory to Working Capital 41	0.2	•	0.0	0.0	0.1	0.1	0.1	0.1	0.2	0.0	0.1
Total Receipts to Cash Flow 42	3.1	2.4	2.4	2.3	4.4	3.3	2.7	2.9	4.7	2.1	2.0
Cost of Goods to Cash Flow 43	1.3	1.2	0.2	0.0	1.5	0.8	1.0	0.9	2.3	0.3	0.7
Cash Flow to Total Debt 44	0.5	•	8.3	5.8	1.0	1.4	0.9	1.0	0.5	0.7	0.7

Selected Financial Factors (in Percentages)

Debt Ratio 45	42.3	•	65.1	20.3	56.4	35.1	31.1	46.6	36.0	36.5	40.1
Return on Total Assets 46	10.8	•	163.6	55.9	30.8	22.4	15.4	18.8	16.0	9.1	9.8
Return on Equity Before Income Taxes 47	16.4	•	465.4	66.7	68.9	33.3	21.9	32.8	24.7	13.1	14.6
Return on Equity After Income Taxes 48	13.5	•	459.0	66.1	63.6	29.8	19.6	29.0	21.0	11.1	10.6
Profit Margin (Before Income Tax) 49	13.9	68.0	12.5	19.6	12.8	13.6	19.3	13.6	20.5	16.9	16.2
Profit Margin (After Income Tax) 50	11.5	66.4	12.3	19.5	11.8	12.1	17.3	12.1	17.4	14.4	11.8

Table I

Corporations with and without Net Income

ADVERTISING AND RELATED SERVICES

MONEY AMOUNTS AND SIZE OF ASSETS IN THOUSANDS OF DOLLARS

Item Description for Accounting Period 7/05 Through 6/06		Total	Zero Assets	Under 500	500 to 1,000	1,000 to 5,000	5,000 to 10,000	10,000 to 25,000	25,000 to 50,000	50,000 to 100,000	100,000 to 250,000	250,000 to 500,000	500,000 to 2,500,000	2,500,000 and over
Number of Enterprises	1	47070	8547	34954	1799	1238	244	166	52	28	18	8	8	8
Revenues ($ in Thousands)														
Net Sales	2	69139095	1086972	18113911	3126146	7279078	2613299	4471967	3180288	2064156	2345216	3212297	4506631	17139134
Interest	3	927474	2911	6396	2488	14539	6773	11743	9802	5213	10979	19387	57227	780015
Rents	4	82800	0	1816	1877	651	0	30	198	0	919	0	50	77259
Royalties	5	96101	39	0	0	0	0	0	32578	104	11563	16167	5481	30169
Other Portfolio Income	6	422001	700	23594	323	8809	799	775	5836	8435	64507	764	44089	263371
Other Receipts	7	1930198	175269	207872	129225	136876	446235	77481	24459	21167	79751	20512	-10457	621808
Total Receipts	8	72597669	1265891	18353589	3260059	7439953	3067106	4561996	3253161	2099075	2512935	3269127	4603021	18911756
Average Total Receipts	9	1542	148	525	1812	6010	12570	27482	62561	74967	139608	408641	575378	2363970
Operating Costs/Operating Income (%)														
Cost of Operations	10	31.9	27.8	33.4	35.6	43.5	53.2	57.7	54.8	42.2	43.7	51.9	34.0	3.5
Salaries and Wages	11	21.0	23.2	8.1	20.3	12.5	16.4	11.4	11.8	21.1	22.7	11.1	30.0	42.2
Taxes Paid	12	2.5	3.0	1.8	2.6	1.6	1.8	1.5	1.5	1.9	2.6	1.0	3.3	4.1
Interest Paid	13	3.4	7.2	0.3	0.9	0.5	0.5	0.4	0.4	0.9	2.9	1.0	4.1	10.7
Depreciation	14	1.4	1.2	0.7	1.2	0.8	1.2	0.6	0.9	1.1	1.4	1.5	4.0	2.2
Amortization and Depletion	15	1.3	2.0	0.1	0.2	0.4	0.1	0.2	0.7	1.2	1.7	0.8	2.5	3.6
Pensions and Other Deferred Comp.	16	0.7	0.2	0.4	1.3	0.5	0.8	0.3	0.2	0.5	1.3	0.2	1.9	1.1
Employee Benefits	17	1.3	0.5	0.9	1.8	0.6	0.9	0.8	1.0	1.3	1.5	2.0	2.1	1.9
Advertising	18	4.3	1.2	5.0	6.0	10.6	2.9	7.3	10.8	2.9	1.2	0.5	4.1	0.4
Other Expenses	19	27.7	34.6	37.7	18.7	19.7	27.3	12.0	13.5	24.0	19.5	24.7	15.2	33.9
Officers' Compensation	20	5.3	7.5	9.1	8.5	5.8	4.1	2.9	2.6	2.3	3.6	0.9	1.8	3.9
Operating Margin	21	•	•	2.6	3.1	3.6	•	4.9	1.6	0.6	•	4.3	•	•
Operating Margin Before Officers' Comp.	22	4.5	•	11.7	11.6	9.4	•	7.8	4.3	2.9	1.6	5.2	•	•

Selected Average Balance Sheet ($ in Thousands)

Net Receivables 23	650	0	13	143	819	1868	5832	12686	21874	29041	100332	215423	2890484
Inventories 24	34	0	4	70	94	157	338	1594	753	1936	760	8820	113807
Net Property, Plant and Equipment 25	129	0	18	114	294	801	1271	3512	4297	12964	44235	99563	349297
Total Assets 26	2393	0	71	754	2300	6542	14941	34605	69412	160768	312286	1038725	10553620
Notes and Loans Payable 27	408	0	44	212	438	777	1790	3354	14519	48957	50424	272014	1523998
All Other Liabilities 28	1186	0	27	357	1297	2962	9672	20707	40006	51668	154010	374993	5368463
Net Worth 29	799	0	-0	186	565	2803	3479	10544	14887	60143	107852	391718	3661160

Selected Financial Ratios (Times to 1)

Current Ratio 30	0.9	•	1.4	1.1	1.2	1.8	1.3	1.0	1.4	1.2	1.2	1.2	0.8
Quick Ratio 31	0.8	•	1.2	0.9	1.0	1.5	1.1	1.0	0.8	1.1	1.1	0.9	0.7
Net Sales to Working Capital 32	•	•	42.4	34.1	26.5	5.1	14.1	9.3	•	6.1	16.3	10.5	•
Coverage Ratio 33	2.3	2.1	14.3	9.7	12.9	18.6	18.9	10.3	3.4	2.7	7.0	0.8	1.4
Total Asset Turnover 34	0.6	•	7.3	2.3	2.6	1.6	1.8	1.8	1.1	0.8	1.3	0.5	0.2
Inventory Turnover 35	13.7	•	41.6	8.9	27.2	36.3	46.0	21.0	41.3	29.4	274.4	21.7	0.7
Receivables Turnover 36	2.5	•	34.8	10.6	7.3	4.5	4.4	4.8	4.0	3.2	5.7	2.4	0.8
Total Liabilities to Net Worth 37	2.0	•	•	3.1	1.3	3.3	2.3	3.7	1.7	1.7	1.9	1.7	1.9
Current Assets to Working Capital 38	•	•	3.6	10.7	7.3	2.3	5.9	3.9	•	3.3	7.0	7.3	•
Current Liabilities to Working Capital 39	•	•	2.6	9.7	6.3	1.3	4.9	2.9	•	2.3	6.0	6.3	•
Working Capital to Net Sales 40	•	•	0.0	0.0	0.0	0.2	0.1	0.1	•	0.2	0.1	0.1	•
Inventory to Working Capital 41	•	•	0.2	2.0	0.6	0.0	0.0	0.3	•	0.1	0.0	0.2	•
Total Receipts to Cash Flow 42	3.6	2.9	2.6	4.4	4.4	3.3	5.9	6.9	4.3	5.5	3.4	10.0	3.4
Cost of Goods to Cash Flow 43	1.2	0.8	0.9	1.6	1.9	1.7	3.4	3.8	1.8	2.4	1.8	3.4	0.1
Cash Flow to Total Debt 44	0.3	•	2.8	0.7	0.8	0.9	0.4	0.4	0.3	0.2	0.6	0.1	0.1

Selected Financial Factors (in Percentages)

Debt Ratio 45	66.6	•	100.3	75.4	75.4	57.2	76.7	69.5	78.6	62.6	65.5	62.3	65.3
Return on Total Assets 46	4.9	•	30.9	19.0	16.0	14.1	13.0	7.7	3.3	6.4	9.1	1.8	3.1
Return on Equity Before Income Taxes 47	8.5	•	•	69.3	60.1	31.2	53.1	22.7	10.9	10.8	22.6	•	2.6
Return on Equity After Income Taxes 48	7.3	•	•	68.5	57.5	29.3	51.1	21.5	8.4	8.5	16.4	•	1.7
Profit Margin (Before Income Tax) 49	4.6	8.1	3.9	7.4	5.8	8.2	6.9	3.9	2.2	5.0	6.1	•	4.5
Profit Margin (After Income Tax) 50	4.0	7.3	3.9	7.3	5.5	7.7	6.6	3.7	1.7	3.9	4.4	•	2.9

Table II
Corporations with Net Income

ADVERTISING AND RELATED SERVICES

MONEY AMOUNTS AND SIZE OF ASSETS IN THOUSANDS OF DOLLARS

Item Description for Accounting Period 7/05 Through 6/06	Total	Zero Assets	Under 500	500 to 1,000	1,000 to 5,000	5,000 to 10,000	10,000 to 25,000	25,000 to 50,000	50,000 to 100,000	100,000 to 250,000	250,000 to 500,000	500,000 to 2,500,000	2,500,000 and over
Number of Enterprises **1**	30281	4934	22964	1074	918	168	132	45	20	•	•	3	5
Revenues ($ in Thousands)													
Net Sales **2**	53453822	889344	13740113	2463648	6441762	2048637	3939118	3018998	1646266	•	•	2020486	12561950
Interest **3**	766794	536	4977	1644	9958	4656	9842	7516	3222	•	•	37988	660624
Rents **4**	80278	0	1816	4	127	0	0	198	0	•	•	0	77255
Royalties **5**	63560	0	0	0	0	0	0	32578	104	•	•	0	3673
Other Portfolio Income **6**	373127	73	18421	323	8401	731	564	3957	1821	•	•	42404	231225
Other Receipts **7**	1039314	161334	111955	124218	130297	13559	33323	23339	21020	•	•	-23148	375222
Total Receipts **8**	55775895	1051287	13877282	2589837	6590545	2067583	3982847	3086586	1672433	•	•	2077730	13909949
Average Total Receipts **9**	1842	213	604	2411	7179	12307	30173	68591	83622	•	•	692577	2781990
Operating Costs/Operating Income (%)													
Cost of Operations **10**	31.4	26.9	28.5	29.5	46.4	48.5	56.1	56.9	44.6	•	•	21.8	4.8
Salaries and Wages **11**	19.5	26.5	7.0	22.0	11.1	13.7	11.3	10.6	20.7	•	•	34.3	40.8
Taxes Paid **12**	2.3	3.4	1.6	2.7	1.6	1.9	1.5	1.4	1.9	•	•	3.0	4.0
Interest Paid **13**	2.8	4.5	0.2	0.9	0.3	0.4	0.2	0.4	0.4	•	•	1.7	10.3
Depreciation **14**	1.2	1.2	0.7	1.1	0.5	0.9	0.6	0.8	0.9	•	•	2.1	2.3
Amortization and Depletion **15**	0.9	0.9	0.0	0.0	0.0	0.1	0.1	0.7	0.7	•	•	3.8	2.7
Pensions and Other Deferred Comp. **16**	0.7	0.1	0.5	1.3	0.3	0.9	0.4	0.2	0.5	•	•	0.4	1.4
Employee Benefits **17**	1.1	0.4	0.7	2.0	0.6	1.0	0.8	1.0	1.1	•	•	2.0	1.3
Advertising **18**	3.6	0.7	2.5	4.8	8.3	0.9	7.3	11.4	0.5	•	•	8.8	0.4
Other Expenses **19**	27.9	30.4	43.8	19.3	18.2	16.2	11.2	11.1	23.1	•	•	18.7	32.3
Officers' Compensation **20**	4.7	8.8	7.5	9.7	5.9	4.0	2.5	2.5	2.1	•	•	0.8	3.1
Operating Margin **21**	3.8	•	7.0	6.7	6.8	11.5	8.1	2.9	3.6	•	•	2.5	•
Operating Margin Before Officers' Comp. **22**	8.5	5.0	14.5	16.4	12.7	15.5	10.5	5.5	5.7	•	•	3.3	•

Selected Average Balance Sheet ($ in Thousands)

Net Receivables **23**	767	0	11	158	950	2006	6425	13768	24326	•	214297	3559060
Inventories **24**	44	0	2	37	126	194	329	1664	866	•	10789	209582
Net Property, Plant and Equipment **25**	129	0	16	79	188	746	748	3677	3870	•	51430	435221
Total Assets **26**	2618	66	761	2200	6404	15210	34595	67776	•	1231410	12227929	
Notes and Loans Payable **27**	297	0	27	274	350	828	1066	3470	7960	•	51684	1285763
All Other Liabilities **28**	1299	0	20	337	1305	2618	9984	20489	45764	•	412614	6103596
Net Worth **29**	1022	0	20	150	545	2958	4160	10636	14053	•	767112	4838570

Selected Financial Ratios (Times to 1)

Current Ratio **30**	0.8	•	2.0	1.1	1.4	1.6	1.2	1.4	0.9	•	1.0	0.7
Quick Ratio **31**	0.7	•	1.8	1.0	1.2	1.4	1.1	1.1	0.8	•	0.7	0.6
Net Sales to Working Capital **32**	•	•	26.7	57.0	14.0	6.9	12.4	9.7	•	•	53.7	•
Coverage Ratio **33**	4.0	4.2	37.5	13.5	36.6	31.1	44.5	14.9	14.0	•	4.0	1.9
Total Asset Turnover **34**	0.7	•	9.0	3.0	3.2	1.9	2.0	1.9	1.2	•	0.5	0.2
Inventory Turnover **35**	12.5	•	107.4	18.4	25.9	30.5	50.8	23.0	42.4	•	13.6	0.6
Receivables Turnover **36**	2.4	•	48.0	12.6	8.1	4.2	4.6	5.8	6.8	•	3.2	1.4
Total Liabilities to Net Worth **37**	1.6	•	2.3	4.1	3.0	1.2	2.7	2.3	3.8	•	0.6	1.5
Current Assets to Working Capital **38**	•	•	2.0	14.4	3.7	2.6	5.1	3.7	•	•	32.2	•
Current Liabilities to Working Capital **39**	•	•	1.0	13.4	2.7	1.6	4.1	2.7	•	•	31.2	•
Working Capital to Net Sales **40**	•	•	0.0	0.0	0.1	0.1	0.1	0.1	•	•	0.0	•
Inventory to Working Capital **41**	•	•	0.0	0.9	0.3	0.1	0.0	0.3	•	•	0.5	•
Total Receipts to Cash Flow **42**	3.2	2.8	2.0	3.6	4.0	4.4	5.4	7.4	3.9	•	5.5	3.1
Cost of Goods to Cash Flow **43**	1.0	0.8	0.6	1.1	1.9	2.1	3.0	4.2	1.7	•	1.2	0.1
Cash Flow to Total Debt **44**	0.4	•	6.3	1.0	1.1	0.8	0.5	0.4	0.4	•	0.3	0.1

Selected Financial Factors (in Percentages)

Debt Ratio **45**	61.0	•	69.7	80.3	75.2	53.8	72.6	69.3	79.3	•	37.7	60.4
Return on Total Assets **46**	7.7	•	74.0	38.5	29.8	24.4	18.4	10.7	6.7	•	3.8	4.0
Return on Equity Before Income Taxes **47**	14.8	•	238.1	180.8	116.8	51.1	65.7	32.5	30.2	•	4.6	4.8
Return on Equity After Income Taxes **48**	13.4	•	235.8	179.2	113.1	48.4	63.6	31.1	26.4	•	4.5	3.7
Profit Margin (Before Income Tax) **49**	8.6	14.3	8.0	11.8	9.1	12.4	9.2	5.2	5.2	•	5.2	9.2
Profit Margin (After Income Tax) **50**	7.8	13.4	7.9	11.7	8.8	11.7	8.9	4.9	4.5	•	5.1	7.1

Table I
Corporations with and without Net Income

OTHER PROFESSIONAL, SCIENTIFIC, AND TECHNICAL SERVICES

MONEY AMOUNTS AND SIZE OF ASSETS IN THOUSANDS OF DOLLARS

Item Description for Accounting Period 7/05 Through 6/06	Total	Zero Assets	Under 500	500 to 1,000	1,000 to 5,000	5,000 to 10,000	10,000 to 25,000	25,000 to 50,000	50,000 to 100,000	100,000 to 250,000	250,000 to 500,000	500,000 to 2,500,000	2,500,000 and over
Number of Enterprises **1**	90409	14009	70656	3053	1950	288	271	79	40	35	12	12	3
Revenues ($ in Thousands)													
Net Sales **2**	76426865	3896305	29060580	3814994	6699970	3374309	5852352	5035984	2701347	5096950	2081026	5400686	3412363
Interest **3**	309409	21993	9175	1653	6685	6759	26212	30082	28196	68424	12373	50099	47758
Rents **4**	52342	0	3260	0	3087	65	31822	3287	1207	1623	2291	538	5162
Royalties **5**	135039	0	29581	1844	22	0	185	70	27	38981	17171	4233	42925
Other Portfolio Income **6**	759217	70890	55148	3405	52241	19682	54607	7924	24839	87204	8079	77107	298088
Other Receipts **7**	1982020	181940	804649	15599	138554	84929	104935	174673	23995	99144	115274	167314	71016
Total Receipts **8**	7964892	4171128	2996393	3837495	6900559	3485744	6070113	5252020	2779611	5392326	2236214	5699977	3877312
Average Total Receipts **9**	881	298	424	1257	3539	12103	22399	66481	69490	154066	186351	474998	1292437
Operating Costs/Operating Income (%)													
Cost of Operations **10**	25.6	13.9	17.7	42.8	45.2	43.2	41.6	15.5	39.1	42.5	28.8	8.4	7.9
Salaries and Wages **11**	22.5	27.4	21.5	12.4	18.1	20.1	20.4	17.0	24.4	19.7	33.1	36.2	34.4
Taxes Paid **12**	3.3	3.7	3.7	3.0	3.3	3.3	3.2	2.1	3.0	2.7	3.5	3.3	3.2
Interest Paid **13**	1.7	0.2	0.6	2.0	1.4	1.4	1.0	1.0	1.6	2.5	2.0	4.4	9.1
Depreciation **14**	1.5	1.5	1.3	1.3	1.3	1.8	1.3	1.3	2.0	1.6	1.7	1.6	3.5
Amortization and Depletion **15**	1.0	0.2	0.2	0.9	0.6	0.2	0.4	0.7	0.5	1.4	3.3	3.9	4.7
Pensions and Other Deferred Comp. **16**	1.1	1.0	1.0	0.6	1.4	0.2	0.5	1.1	0.6	0.8	4.9	1.5	1.8
Employee Benefits **17**	1.8	1.1	1.2	1.1	0.8	2.3	2.0	1.8	2.1	1.9	3.1	5.7	3.5
Advertising **18**	0.8	1.1	0.8	0.5	1.1	0.8	0.9	0.5	0.5	0.5	2.0	0.8	0.2
Other Expenses **19**	33.2	54.2	35.0	16.8	22.0	19.2	28.7	60.5	23.4	22.5	22.3	36.3	39.9
Officers' Compensation **20**	7.1	6.4	10.8	17.9	8.0	4.7	4.1	2.0	2.1	1.9	0.9	2.2	1.1
Operating Margin **21**	0.4	•	6.2	0.7	•	2.8	•	•	0.7	1.8	•	•	•
Operating Margin Before Officers' Comp. **22**	7.6	•	17.1	18.6	4.8	7.5	•	•	2.8	3.8	•	•	•

Selected Average Balance Sheet ($ in Thousands)

Net Receivables 23	110	0	7	124	309	3710	3736	7655	13176	41365	58551	134544	492146
Inventories 24	11	0	4	45	41	261	479	310	781	4535	3154	3952	3501
Net Property, Plant and Equipment 25	64	0	24	132	339	681	1911	3613	7258	14832	24872	40112	144373
Total Assets 26	636	0	84	677	1903	6796	15347	35760	68043	164370	321010	1031323	4060829
Notes and Loans Payable 27	248	0	57	517	2223	1929	2910	9375	17356	47843	117571	262147	1161103
All Other Liabilities 28	214	0	19	186	625	2540	6801	14854	9439	50122	103113	355727	1627853
Net Worth 29	174	0	8	-26	-946	2327	5637	11531	41248	66405	100326	413449	1271873

Selected Financial Ratios (Times to 1)

Current Ratio 30	1.3	•	1.4	1.2	1.7	1.4	1.4	1.6	1.5	0.9	1.1	1.1	
Quick Ratio 31	1.0	•	1.1	1.0	1.5	1.1	0.9	1.2	1.1	0.5	0.8	0.8	
Net Sales to Working Capital 32	16.6	•	45.5	25.9	26.6	5.7	9.0	10.3	5.3	5.8	•	19.6	12.2
Coverage Ratio 33	3.8	•	15.8	1.7	0.9	5.3	0.6	1.7	3.2	4.0	1.9	1.3	1.5
Total Asset Turnover 34	1.3	•	4.9	1.8	1.8	1.7	1.4	1.8	1.0	0.9	0.5	0.4	0.3
Inventory Turnover 35	19.8	•	20.2	11.8	37.7	19.4	18.8	32.0	33.8	13.7	15.9	9.5	25.8
Receivables Turnover 36	8.7	•	72.4	9.8	10.6	3.3	6.1	8.4	4.4	3.9	4.2	4.8	2.8
Total Liabilities to Net Worth 37	2.7	•	9.1	•	1.9	1.7	2.1	0.6	1.5	2.2	1.5	2.2	
Current Assets to Working Capital 38	4.6	•	3.8	6.7	6.7	2.5	3.8	3.2	2.6	3.2	•	9.6	9.0
Current Liabilities to Working Capital 39	3.6	•	2.8	5.7	5.7	1.5	2.8	2.2	1.6	2.2	•	8.6	8.0
Working Capital to Net Sales 40	0.1	•	0.0	0.0	0.2	0.1	0.1	0.2	0.1	•	0.1	0.1	
Inventory to Working Capital 41	0.2	•	0.4	0.4	0.1	0.1	0.0	0.1	0.3	•	0.2	0.0	
Total Receipts to Cash Flow 42	3.1	2.2	2.7	7.0	5.6	4.5	4.3	1.7	4.4	3.8	4.9	3.1	2.7
Cost of Goods to Cash Flow 43	0.8	0.3	0.5	3.0	2.5	2.0	1.8	0.3	1.7	1.6	1.4	0.3	0.2
Cash Flow to Total Debt 44	0.6	•	2.0	0.3	0.2	0.6	0.5	1.5	0.6	0.4	0.2	0.2	0.1

Selected Financial Factors (in Percentages)

Debt Ratio 45	72.7	•	90.1	103.8	149.7	65.8	63.3	67.8	39.4	59.6	68.7	59.9	68.7
Return on Total Assets 46	8.4	•	49.0	6.1	2.2	13.0	0.9	3.1	5.2	8.8	2.1	2.5	3.9
Return on Equity Before Income Taxes 47	22.7	•	462.5	0.5	30.7	•	3.9	6.0	16.2	3.2	1.4	4.1	
Return on Equity After Income Taxes 48	20.2	•	455.4	1.5	24.3	•	•	4.7	13.2	2.6	•	3.8	
Profit Margin (Before Income Tax) 49	4.7	•	9.3	1.3	6.1	•	•	0.7	3.6	7.4	1.8	1.3	4.6
Profit Margin (After Income Tax) 50	4.2	•	9.2	1.3	4.8	•	•	•	2.9	6.0	1.5	•	4.3

Table II
Corporations with Net Income

OTHER PROFESSIONAL, SCIENTIFIC, AND TECHNICAL SERVICES

MONEY AMOUNTS AND SIZE OF ASSETS IN THOUSANDS OF DOLLARS

Item Description for Accounting Period 7/05 Through 6/06	Total	Zero Assets	Under 500	500 to 1000	251 to 500	501 to 1,000	1,001 to 5,000	5,001 to 10,000	10,001 to 25,000	25,001 to 50,000	50,001 to 100,000	100,001 to 250,000	250,001 and over
Number of Enterprises **1**	58324	6294	48864	1703	1023	180	143	43	28	25	7	9	3
Revenues ($ in Thousands)													
Net Sales **2**	56983376	909592	23013081	2379554	4529837	3082360	4003910	4051824	2095881	3270569	1163462	5070943	3412363
Interest **3**	230173	963	7984	823	3325	5917	10246	24106	25428	51608	7876	44140	47758
Rents **4**	11327	0	82	0	146	0	117	2395	1207	528	1153	538	5162
Royalties **5**	116631	0	29581	1844	0	0	0	0	27	38021	0	4233	42925
Other Portfolio Income **6**	693874	70273	53322	3213	1872	19682	53466	7386	22725	79953	6786	77106	298088
Other Receipts **7**	1016145	8457	318434	12000	76020	66252	58638	62872	21856	72034	82014	166553	71016
Total Receipts **8**	59051526	989285	23422484	2397434	4611200	3174211	4126377	4148583	2167124	3512713	1261291	5363513	3877312
Average Total Receipts **9**	1012	157	479	1408	4508	17635	28856	96479	77397	140509	180184	595946	1292437
Operating Costs/Operating Income (%)													
Cost of Operations **10**	24.4	15.9	19.8	31.2	38.0	45.2	43.1	16.2	40.0	33.7	32.4	7.7	7.9
Salaries and Wages **11**	21.3	23.3	20.1	13.7	15.6	17.6	20.3	11.1	22.6	21.8	25.5	35.5	34.4
Taxes Paid **12**	3.2	3.3	3.5	3.5	3.3	3.2	3.0	1.6	3.0	2.9	3.3	3.3	3.2
Interest Paid **13**	1.7	0.3	0.6	1.9	1.3	0.7	0.6	1.0	1.4	2.4	1.7	4.0	9.1
Depreciation **14**	1.4	1.8	1.2	1.0	0.9	1.5	0.8	0.7	1.3	1.7	2.0	1.6	3.5
Amortization and Depletion **15**	1.0	0.6	0.1	1.2	0.6	0.2	0.2	0.7	0.4	1.6	2.5	4.0	4.7
Pensions and Other Deferred Comp. **16**	1.1	2.1	1.1	0.5	1.6	0.2	0.6	0.4	0.6	1.2	0.4	1.6	1.8
Employee Benefits **17**	1.8	1.0	1.0	1.3	0.6	2.2	1.8	1.5	1.8	2.1	1.3	5.8	3.5
Advertising **18**	0.7	0.7	0.7	0.4	0.6	0.8	1.0	0.4	0.4	0.7	3.3	0.8	0.2
Other Expenses **19**	29.1	28.5	29.3	14.5	19.9	16.2	18.9	63.1	23.0	21.9	28.7	31.9	39.9
Officers' Compensation **20**	7.3	13.4	10.6	23.0	9.4	4.9	3.7	1.4	1.6	2.7	0.8	1.5	1.1
Operating Margin **21**	7.1	9.0	12.1	7.8	8.1	7.3	5.9	1.9	3.9	7.2	•	2.2	•
Operating Margin Before Officers' Comp. **22**	14.3	22.4	22.6	30.8	17.5	12.2	9.6	3.4	5.5	9.9	•	3.7	•

Selected Average Balance Sheet ($ in Thousands)

Net Receivables 23	121	0	5	75	344	2718	4933	7020	14465	45115	40486	172380	492146
Inventories 24	11	0	4	58	46	309	652	209	414	1322	3729	6277	3697
Net Property, Plant and Equipment 25	68	0	26	133	319	773	1602	4310	5638	14585	29472	49549	144373
Total Assets 26	736	0	91	625	2124	6860	15614	40941	68512	171384	317352	1043842	4060829
Notes and Loans Payable 27	241	0	47	497	1575	1991	3053	9023	14100	36649	112161	281687	1161103
All Other Liabilities 28	244	0	20	107	596	2381	7630	17066	3702	56476	77262	363158	1627853
Net Worth 29	251	0	24	21	-48	2488	4931	14852	50710	78258	127929	398998	1271873

Selected Financial Ratios (Times to 1)

Current Ratio 30	1.3	•	1.7	2.1	1.0	1.5	1.2	1.4	2.0	1.5	1.0	1.1	1.1
Quick Ratio 31	1.0	•	1.3	1.9	0.9	1.3	1.0	0.8	1.4	1.2	0.5	0.8	0.8
Net Sales to Working Capital 32	16.2	•	30.4	9.2	130.5	11.3	16.9	13.3	4.3	5.0	54.5	24.7	12.2
Coverage Ratio 33	7.4	55.2	26.0	5.6	8.8	14.8	15.1	5.5	6.3	7.0	5.1	3.0	1.5
Total Asset Turnover 34	1.3	•	5.2	2.2	2.1	2.5	1.8	2.3	1.1	0.8	0.5	0.5	0.3
Inventory Turnover 35	22.0	•	21.4	7.5	36.7	25.0	18.5	73.0	72.4	33.4	14.4	7.0	24.4
Receivables Turnover 36	10.0	•	111.3	12.2	9.8	4.9	6.1	12.2	5.4	3.2	8.2	6.5	4.6
Total Liabilities to Net Worth 37	1.9	•	2.8	28.9	•	1.8	2.2	1.8	0.4	1.2	1.5	1.6	2.2
Current Assets to Working Capital 38	4.4	•	2.5	1.9	28.0	2.9	6.1	3.4	2.0	2.9	39.2	12.2	9.0
Current Liabilities to Working Capital 39	3.4	•	1.5	0.9	27.0	1.9	5.1	2.4	1.0	1.9	38.2	11.2	8.0
Working Capital to Net Sales 40	0.1	•	0.0	0.1	0.0	0.1	0.1	0.1	0.2	0.2	0.0	0.0	0.1
Inventory to Working Capital 41	0.2	•	0.3	0.1	1.1	0.2	0.3	0.0	0.0	0.1	1.2	0.3	0.0
Total Receipts to Cash Flow 42	2.9	2.6	2.7	5.2	3.8	4.3	4.3	1.5	3.9	3.1	3.3	2.9	2.7
Cost of Goods to Cash Flow 43	0.7	0.4	0.5	1.6	1.4	1.9	1.9	0.2	1.6	1.0	1.1	0.2	0.2
Cash Flow to Total Debt 44	0.7	•	2.6	0.4	0.5	0.9	0.6	2.4	1.1	0.5	0.3	0.3	0.1

Selected Financial Factors (in Percentages)

Debt Ratio 45	65.9	•	73.5	96.7	102.2	63.7	68.4	63.7	26.0	54.3	59.7	61.8	68.7
Return on Total Assets 46	16.5	•	74.3	23.3	23.1	27.5	17.2	12.1	9.5	12.6	4.4	6.5	3.9
Return on Equity Before Income Taxes 47	41.7	•	268.9	570.9	•	70.7	50.9	27.3	10.8	23.7	8.8	11.3	4.1
Return on Equity After Income Taxes 48	39.1	•	265.4	569.0	•	61.1	45.9	20.4	9.3	20.1	8.1	8.9	3.8
Profit Margin (Before Income Tax) 49	10.7	17.8	13.8	8.5	9.8	10.3	9.0	4.3	7.3	14.2	6.8	8.0	4.6
Profit Margin (After Income Tax) 50	10.0	17.0	13.6	8.5	9.5	8.9	8.1	3.2	6.3	12.0	6.2	6.3	4.3

Table I

Corporations with and without Net Income

OFFICES OF BANK HOLDING COMPANIES

MONEY AMOUNTS AND SIZE OF ASSETS IN THOUSANDS OF DOLLARS

Item Description for Accounting Period 7/05 Through 6/06	Total	Zero Assets	Under 500	500 to 1,000	1,000 to 5,000	5,000 to 10,000	10,000 to 25,000	25,000 to 50,000	50,000 to 100,000	100,000 to 250,000	250,000 to 500,000	500,000 to 2,500,000	2,500,000 and over
Number of Enterprises 1	5064	89	•	0	31	•	270	605	1059	1463	752	567	168
Revenues ($ in Thousands)													
Net Sales 2	138401423	2183715	•	0	11361	•	76512	325802	1449421	3263625	3251128	7300605	120530669
Interest 3	519055661	3855868	•	0	66696	•	151302	576064	2265063	8022312	10035696	23385103	470684213
Rents 4	25665891	1932	•	0	608	•	292	1691	15440	39473	51902	182292	25362234
Royalties 5	356629	0	•	0	0	•	0	9	415	191	322	6041	349651
Other Portfolio Income 6	48308308	219778	•	0	6380	•	14903	59078	193500	617502	897374	1379119	44911700
Other Receipts 7	138499191	297877	•	0	3101	•	65068	388094	1147884	2611148	2778739	5297496	125905371
Total Receipts 8	870277103	6559170	•	0	88146	•	308077	1350738	5071723	14554251	17015161	37550656	787743838
Average Total Receipts 9	171856	73699	•	•	2843	•	1141	2233	4789	9948	22627	66227	4688951
Operating Costs/Operating Income (%)													
Cost of Operations 10	3.9	•	•	•	•	•	•	•	0.1	0.3	0.0	0.1	4.4
Salaries and Wages 11	82.7	25.6	•	•	45.2	•	47.6	55.3	48.8	65.5	81.7	83.3	84.7
Taxes Paid 12	11.1	3.4	•	•	21.2	•	12.3	12.8	10.5	13.1	15.3	14.5	10.9
Interest Paid 13	210.8	163.3	•	•	201.4	•	93.1	105.6	90.3	125.8	149.1	143.8	221.5
Depreciation 14	18.6	3.0	•	•	16.7	•	8.4	10.0	9.3	11.4	12.2	11.8	19.8
Amortization and Depletion 15	4.1	0.5	•	•	0.2	•	5.5	1.7	1.2	1.3	2.0	2.4	4.4
Pensions and Other Deferred Comp. 16	5.0	2.2	•	•	9.8	•	4.7	4.1	4.1	4.2	5.0	6.0	5.0
Employee Benefits 17	11.9	2.5	•	•	12.7	•	15.7	13.6	9.6	11.5	11.8	10.7	12.2
Advertising 18	6.9	3.1	•	•	8.7	•	3.6	4.5	4.9	4.7	5.7	6.4	7.1
Other Expenses 19	158.4	99.5	•	•	140.2	•	84.7	89.8	71.4	81.9	92.2	99.0	168.2
Officers' Compensation 20	7.0	2.7	•	•	89.2	•	58.2	47.5	34.2	31.6	26.2	19.8	4.6
Operating Margin 21	•	•	•	•	•	•	•	•	•	•	•	•	•
Operating Margin Before Officers' Comp. 22	•	•	•	•	•	•	•	•	•	•	•	•	•

Selected Average Balance Sheet ($ in Thousands)

	1	2	3	4	5	6	7	8	9	10	11
Net Receivables 23	928182	0	408	•	9881	22253	45224	101231	220105	591754	23732525
Inventories 24	62	0	0	•	0	0	1	0	2	21	1795
Net Property, Plant and Equipment 25	19492	0	24	•	212	601	1526	3317	7155	18355	452507
Total Assets 26	2593072	0	2190	•	19021	37054	73865	159342	351162	993462	71217482
Notes and Loans Payable 27	294800	0	1	•	424	938	2901	7600	19858	73322	8461123
All Other Liabilities 28	1981111	0	33	•	14244	31280	63524	136173	299626	832442	53843297
Net Worth 29	317162	0	2155	•	4353	4836	7440	15570	31678	87698	8913062

Selected Financial Ratios (Times to 1)

	1	2	3	4	5	6	7	8	9	10	11
Current Ratio 30	0.8	•	61.8	•	1.1	1.0	1.0	1.0	1.0	0.9	0.7
Quick Ratio 31	0.6	•	61.7	•	1.1	1.0	1.0	0.9	0.9	0.9	0.6
Net Sales to Working Capital 32	•	•	0.2	•	0.2	0.5	1.7	2.9	•	•	•
Coverage Ratio 33	1.5	1.0	2.1	•	1.6	1.5	1.6	1.6	1.7	1.7	1.5
Total Asset Turnover 34	0.0	•	0.2	•	0.0	0.0	0.0	0.0	0.0	0.0	0.0
Inventory Turnover 35	17.0	•	•	•	•	•	2.7	15.3	0.0	0.8	17.7
Receivables Turnover 36	0.0	•	0.9	•	0.0	0.0	0.0	0.0	0.0	0.0	0.0
Total Liabilities to Net Worth 37	7.2	•	0.0	•	3.4	6.7	8.9	9.2	10.1	10.3	7.0
Current Assets to Working Capital 38	•	•	1.0	•	9.8	30.7	79.1	182.6	•	•	•
Current Liabilities to Working Capital 39	•	•	0.0	•	8.8	29.7	78.1	181.6	•	•	•
Working Capital to Net Sales 40	5.5	1.0	5.7	•	5.7	2.0	0.6	0.3	0.0	•	1.5
Inventory to Working Capital 41	0.0	•	•	•	0.0	•	0.0	0.0	0.0	•	0.0
Total Receipts to Cash Flow 42	0.4	1.2	0.3	•	0.7	0.7	0.8	0.6	0.5	0.5	0.4
Cost of Goods to Cash Flow 43	0.0	•	•	•	0.0	•	0.0	0.0	0.0	0.0	0.0
Cash Flow to Total Debt 44	0.0	•	37.2	•	0.0	0.0	0.0	0.0	0.0	0.0	0.0

Selected Financial Factors (in Percentages)

	1	2	3	4	5	6	7	8	9	10	11
Debt Ratio 45	87.8	•	1.6	•	77.1	86.9	89.9	90.2	91.0	91.2	87.5
Return on Total Assets 46	3.4	•	70.5	•	2.3	2.4	2.7	2.9	3.2	3.2	3.4
Return on Equity Before Income Taxes 47	9.3	•	37.3	•	3.8	6.3	10.1	11.5	14.6	15.4	9.0
Return on Equity After Income Taxes 48	6.3	•	27.0	•	3.0	5.3	8.2	8.9	10.8	11.0	6.1
Profit Margin (Before Income Tax) 49	108.4	•	219.6	•	58.1	56.8	54.8	80.1	107.1	105.0	112.3
Profit Margin (After Income Tax) 50	73.4	•	158.8	•	46.4	47.5	44.7	61.9	79.5	74.8	75.5

Table II
Corporations with Net Income

OFFICES OF BANK HOLDING COMPANIES

MONEY AMOUNTS AND SIZE OF ASSETS IN THOUSANDS OF DOLLARS

Item Description for Accounting Period 7/05 Through 6/06	Total	Zero Assets	Under 500	500 to 1,000	1,000 to 5,000	5,000 to 10,000	10,000 to 25,000	25,000 to 50,000	50,000 to 100,000	100,000 to 250,000	250,000 to 500,000	500,000 to 2,500,000	2,500,000 and over
Number of Enterprises 1	4664	47	0	0	•	21	232	534	977	1398	733	554	•
Revenues ($ in Thousands)													
Net Sales 2	137010849	1276606	0	0	•	8067	63538	300629	1376862	3140811	3169660	7169635	•
Interest 3	514779795	1233605	0	0	•	11387	140319	495563	2087225	7698424	9775529	22782237	•
Rents 4	25631520	860	0	0	•	26	256	1561	8127	33823	50858	174164	•
Royalties 5	356599	0	0	0	•	0	0	9	399	191	322	6041	•
Other Portfolio Income 6	48003141	53587	0	0	•	8276	14355	56227	177373	580438	879945	1330550	•
Other Receipts 7	137797980	201343	0	0	•	267	64517	363502	993520	2521870	2755030	5054613	•
Total Receipts 8	863579884	2766001	0	0	•	28023	282985	1217491	4643506	13975557	16631344	36517240	•
Average Total Receipts 9	185159	58851	•	•	•	1334	1220	2280	4753	9997	22689	65916	•
Operating Costs/Operating Income (%)													
Cost of Operations 10	3.9	•	•	•	•	•	•	•	0.1	0.1	0.0	0.1	•
Salaries and Wages 11	82.9	22.5	•	•	•	32.5	45.2	50.5	45.1	63.7	81.2	81.9	•
Taxes Paid 12	11.2	3.8	•	•	•	9.0	13.4	12.2	10.1	13.1	15.3	14.4	•
Interest Paid 13	210.0	39.5	•	•	•	40.7	104.5	101.6	87.5	124.9	149.0	140.9	•
Depreciation 14	18.7	1.4	•	•	•	6.8	9.1	9.0	8.8	11.2	12.3	11.6	•
Amortization and Depletion 15	4.1	0.4	•	•	•	•	0.8	1.0	1.0	1.2	2.0	2.4	•
Pensions and Other Deferred Comp. 16	5.0	0.7	•	•	•	0.7	5.6	4.1	4.1	4.3	5.0	6.0	•
Employee Benefits 17	12.0	2.5	•	•	•	3.0	16.9	12.9	9.2	11.4	11.7	10.5	•
Advertising 18	6.9	5.1	•	•	•	0.7	3.7	3.9	3.7	4.6	5.7	6.4	•
Other Expenses 19	158.6	96.6	•	•	•	104.3	85.1	77.7	63.7	79.1	90.1	94.6	•
Officers' Compensation 20	6.9	2.2	•	•	•	22.6	64.6	46.0	31.8	31.4	26.1	19.6	•
Operating Margin 21	•	•	•	•	•	•	•	•	•	•	•	•	•
Operating Margin Before Officers' Comp. 22	•	•	•	•	•	•	•	•	•	•	•	•	•

Selected Average Balance Sheet ($ in Thousands)

Net Receivables 23	1002798	0	3335	10560	22640	45591	101582	221142	593491
Inventories 24	68	0	0	0	0	1	0	2	21
Net Property, Plant and Equipment 25	20940	0	433	217	540	1498	3290	7159	18286
Total Assets 26	2805838	0	7981	19597	37136	74054	159480	351848	989688
Notes and Loans Payable 27	319472	0	483	338	947	2921	7503	19785	72548
All Other Liabilities 28	2143185	0	3831	15372	31525	63809	136469	300220	829756
Net Worth 29	343181	0	3667	3887	4664	7323	15508	31843	87384

Selected Financial Ratios (Times to 1)

Current Ratio 30	0.8	•	1.7	1.1	1.0	1.0	1.0	1.0	0.9
Quick Ratio 31	0.6	•	1.0	1.1	1.0	1.0	1.0	0.9	0.9
Net Sales to Working Capital 32	•	•	0.1	0.2	0.4	1.3	3.1	•	•
Coverage Ratio 33	1.5	2.0	4.1	1.8	1.7	1.7	1.7	1.7	1.8
Total Asset Turnover 34	0.0	•	0.0	0.0	0.0	0.0	0.0	0.0	0.0
Inventory Turnover 35	17.0	•	•	•	2.7	•	6.3	0.0	0.6
Receivables Turnover 36	0.0	•	0.2	0.0	0.0	0.0	0.0	0.0	0.0
Total Liabilities to Net Worth 37	7.2	•	1.2	4.0	7.0	9.1	9.3	10.0	10.3
Current Assets to Working Capital 38	•	•	2.4	9.9	23.3	59.7	192.3	•	•
Current Liabilities to Working Capital 39	•	•	1.4	8.9	22.3	58.7	191.3	•	•
Working Capital to Net Sales 40	•	•	8.2	6.3	2.5	0.8	0.3	•	•
Inventory to Working Capital 41	•	•	•	0.0	0.0	0.0	0.0	•	•
Total Receipts to Cash Flow 42	0.4	0.8	0.8	0.6	0.7	0.8	0.6	0.5	0.5
Cost of Goods to Cash Flow 43	0.0	•	0.0	0.0	0.0	0.0	0.0	0.0	0.0
Cash Flow to Total Debt 44	0.0	•	0.1	0.0	0.0	0.0	0.0	0.0	0.0

Selected Financial Factors (in Percentages)

Debt Ratio 45	87.8	•	54.1	80.2	87.4	90.1	90.3	90.9	91.2
Return on Total Assets 46	3.4	•	8.0	2.6	2.6	2.8	3.0	3.2	3.3
Return on Equity Before Income Taxes 47	9.4	•	13.2	5.9	8.8	11.9	12.4	15.1	16.2
Return on Equity After Income Taxes 48	6.4	•	9.3	5.0	7.6	9.8	9.7	11.3	11.7
Profit Margin (Before Income Tax) 49	110.3	41.4	126.4	84.3	72.7	61.6	85.8	111.3	109.5
Profit Margin (After Income Tax) 50	74.9	27.3	89.1	70.3	62.6	51.0	66.9	83.0	78.7

Table I
Corporations with and without Net Income

OFFICES OF OTHER HOLDING COMPANIES

MONEY AMOUNTS AND SIZE OF ASSETS IN THOUSANDS OF DOLLARS

Item Description for Accounting Period 7/05 Through 6/06	Total	Zero Assets	Under 500	500 to 1,000	1,000 to 5,000	5,000 to 10,000	10,000 to 25,000	25,000 to 50,000	50,000 to 100,000	100,000 to 250,000	250,000 to 500,000	500,000 to 2,500,000	2,500,000 and over
Number of Enterprises **1**	45857	6898	•	3953	4275	•	887	430	200	173	68	76	24
Revenues ($ in Thousands)													
Net Sales **2**	923938	55928	•	2579	23559	•	65442	71284	97561	139886	80164	274917	61539
Interest **3**	7505621	317122	•	19256	279613	•	148212	133504	140232	225144	461884	2080388	3608952
Rents **4**	157708	7772	•	50	10008	•	6684	30387	32728	4276	1728	49246	10699
Royalties **5**	261674	23143	•	58	11073	•	143	9361	3909	20071	119023	58052	0
Other Portfolio Income **6**	6801876	705054	•	128641	711378	•	312886	543310	439382	867281	377014	1571518	404856
Other Receipts **7**	9393603	830435	•	105009	505048	•	1113569	728673	476235	1067422	579592	3146411	334718
Total Receipts **8**	25044420	1939454	•	255593	1540679	•	1646936	1516519	1190047	2324080	1619405	7180532	4420764
Average Total Receipts **9**	546	281	•	65	360	•	1857	3527	5950	13434	23815	94481	184198
Operating Costs/Operating Income (%)													
Cost of Operations **10**	29.7	1.7	•	•	5.7	•	18.8	18.9	38.3	21.1	17.4	4.1	250.3
Salaries and Wages **11**	98.1	21.1	•	91.8	136.9	•	80.3	95.2	55.1	85.3	239.2	98.5	32.7
Taxes Paid **12**	86.9	86.5	•	246.1	177.4	•	56.5	52.2	22.7	39.5	49.1	47.7	529.8
Interest Paid **13**	586.3	278.1	•	604.9	1080.4	•	175.3	235.7	178.5	197.9	388.3	516.2	3812.2
Depreciation **14**	13.9	9.5	•	82.8	44.7	•	19.9	11.2	20.9	4.5	21.7	8.3	6.7
Amortization and Depletion **15**	32.4	53.0	•	85.5	69.8	•	67.9	45.3	19.7	10.7	6.9	46.6	0.3
Pensions and Other Deferred Comp. **16**	11.3	0.0	•	•	238.6	•	8.9	2.9	1.2	17.1	2.5	2.3	2.5
Employee Benefits **17**	10.6	3.3	•	37.7	21.0	•	9.7	3.2	3.8	10.8	12.5	10.7	5.5
Advertising **18**	1.7	0.0	•	0.1	2.0	•	2.4	1.7	1.5	0.4	0.1	0.6	8.2
Other Expenses **19**	569.1	1354.2	•	2707.3	1541.2	•	680.8	560.8	487.3	357.2	451.2	322.4	222.4
Officers' Compensation **20**	62.6	7.2	•	189.2	581.6	•	57.4	43.2	16.5	20.3	70.4	72.2	1.2
Operating Margin **21**	•	•	•	•	•	•	•	•	•	•	•	•	•
Operating Margin Before Officers' Comp. **22**	•	•	•	•	•	•	•	•	•	•	•	•	•

Selected Average Balance Sheet ($ in Thousands)

Net Receivables 23	647	0	35	96	538	1751	5372	4260	3879	103854	731513
Inventories 24	2	0	0	6	11	34	72	22	341	12	0
Net Property, Plant and Equipment 25	67	0	25	116	389	980	2569	2215	2570	2539	3077
Total Assets 26	7757	0	669	2333	15748	35841	71870	152615	353484	1121085	6382436
Notes and Loans Payable 27	1439	0	118	691	3263	6735	14691	22360	72238	208840	1055961
All Other Liabilities 28	1467	0	60	234	2434	38134	6448	21256	42003	177198	1058368
Net Worth 29	4851	0	491	1408	10051	-9028	50731	109000	239243	735047	4268107

Selected Financial Ratios (Times to 1)

Current Ratio 30	2.0	•	3.8	3.8	1.5	3.0	4.0	2.4	1.4	1.7	1.9
Quick Ratio 31	1.6	•	2.1	2.5	1.1	2.0	2.6	1.3	0.7	1.4	1.8
Net Sales to Working Capital 32	0.0	6.9	0.0	0.0	0.1	0.0	0.0	0.0	0.1	0.0	0.0
Coverage Ratio 33	3.1	•	10.4	2.9	8.4	5.5	2.9	5.7	3.0	4.0	1.7
Total Asset Turnover 34	0.0	•	•	0.0	0.0	0.0	0.0	0.0	0.0	0.0	0.0
Inventory Turnover 35	2.9	•	•	0.0	1.2	0.9	2.6	7.6	0.6	12.8	•
Receivables Turnover 36	0.0	•	0.0	0.1	0.1	0.1	0.1	0.2	0.1	0.0	0.0
Total Liabilities to Net Worth 37	0.6	•	0.4	0.7	0.6	•	0.4	0.4	0.5	0.5	0.5
Current Assets to Working Capital 38	2.0	•	1.4	1.4	2.8	1.5	1.3	1.7	3.5	2.5	2.1
Current Liabilities to Working Capital 39	1.0	0.1	0.4	0.4	1.8	0.5	0.3	0.7	2.5	1.5	1.1
Working Capital to Net Sales 40	44.1	0.0	267.1	76.1	15.8	35.4	27.3	20.7	13.7	29.1	288.2
Inventory to Working Capital 41	0.0	•	•	0.0	0.0	0.0	0.0	0.0	0.0	0.0	0.0
Total Receipts to Cash Flow 42	0.1	0.1	0.0	0.0	0.1	0.1	0.2	0.1	0.1	0.1	0.0
Cost of Goods to Cash Flow 43	0.0	0.0	•	0.0	0.0	0.0	0.0	0.0	0.0	0.0	0.1
Cash Flow to Total Debt 44	0.1	•	0.2	0.2	0.2	0.0	0.1	0.2	0.1	0.1	0.0

Selected Financial Factors (in Percentages)

Debt Ratio 45	37.5	•	26.6	39.6	36.2	125.2	29.4	28.6	32.3	34.4	33.1
Return on Total Assets 46	4.7	•	6.1	7.5	6.9	6.0	3.6	6.0	3.9	6.6	2.6
Return on Equity Before Income Taxes 47	5.1	•	7.5	8.2	9.5	•	3.3	6.9	3.9	7.5	1.7
Return on Equity After Income Taxes 48	3.7	•	6.0	6.0	8.0	•	2.2	5.2	2.5	5.8	1.2
Profit Margin (Before Income Tax) 49	1235.8	1640.8	5658.8	2103.9	1292.2	1063.0	346.5	929.7	785.7	1531.7	2762.7
Profit Margin (After Income Tax) 50	888.5	842.0	4530.8	1530.4	1086.7	814.8	228.7	704.4	506.7	1177.2	1971.6

Table II
Corporations with Net Income

OFFICES OF OTHER HOLDING COMPANIES

MONEY AMOUNTS AND SIZE OF ASSETS IN THOUSANDS OF DOLLARS

Item Description for Accounting Period 7/05 Through 6/06	Total	Zero Assets	Under 500	500 to 1,000	1,000 to 5,000	5,000 to 10,000	10,000 to 25,000	25,000 to 50,000	50,000 to 100,000	100,000 to 250,000	250,000 to 500,000	500,000 to 2,500,000	2,500,000 and over
Number of Enterprises **1**	14734	956	8205	2339	•	434	426	225	107	96	39	53	•
Revenues ($ in Thousands)													
Net Sales **2**	660971	42605	0	2579	•	40535	50754	64483	45559	104798	52580	226070	•
Interest **3**	4681395	238878	21712	16143	•	36574	119476	94808	97475	177492	358361	1588072	•
Rents **4**	106893	5926	0	50	•	1041	3586	5978	24425	4056	812	46513	•
Royalties **5**	124920	23021	812	58	•	15966	11	8833	3638	10785	249	54717	•
Other Portfolio Income **6**	6186855	666657	184807	126702	•	466537	286384	499066	396848	850689	330364	1532314	•
Other Receipts **7**	9602505	1091358	126332	148090	•	417235	1097774	729627	446835	980973	458280	3055593	•
Total Receipts **8**	21363539	2068445	333663	293622	•	977888	1557985	1402795	1014780	2128793	1200646	6503279	•
Average Total Receipts **9**	1450	2164	41	126	•	2253	3657	6235	9484	22175	30786	122703	•
Operating Costs/Operating Income (%)													
Cost of Operations **10**	12.3	2.2	•	•	•	•	18.5	20.8	13.7	28.2	16.7	5.0	•
Salaries and Wages **11**	51.5	18.8	•	61.0	•	45.2	53.1	33.9	59.8	29.6	17.8	80.0	•
Taxes Paid **12**	106.5	99.3	•	202.8	•	66.4	57.6	48.8	37.9	48.2	51.5	52.6	•
Interest Paid **13**	302.8	234.7	•	353.5	•	158.4	94.6	105.7	206.5	127.1	327.1	289.8	•
Depreciation **14**	11.2	7.0	•	32.8	•	10.6	7.7	5.2	21.3	4.6	12.3	9.4	•
Amortization and Depletion **15**	28.1	42.6	•	80.5	•	6.2	7.9	21.7	25.8	1.3	3.5	56.4	•
Pensions and Other Deferred Comp. **16**	4.4	0.0	•	•	•	10.7	10.7	2.6	2.1	1.9	1.0	2.3	•
Employee Benefits **17**	6.0	1.0	•	13.0	•	1.3	4.4	2.3	5.3	1.9	1.3	12.0	•
Advertising **18**	1.4	0.0	•	0.1	•	9.5	2.1	1.3	2.8	0.3	0.0	0.7	•
Other Expenses **19**	304.2	423.6	•	1327.1	•	287.4	184.6	207.6	378.2	194.1	244.5	330.5	•
Officers' Compensation **20**	49.9	9.4	•	189.2	•	46.2	30.3	31.7	23.6	15.1	57.7	72.2	•
Operating Margin **21**	•	•	•	•	•	•	•	•	•	•	•	•	•
Operating Margin Before Officers' Comp. **22**	•	•	•	•	•	•	•	•	•	•	•	•	•

Selected Average Balance Sheet ($ in Thousands)

Net Receivables 23	1717	0	6	13	•	412	528	1812	6433	4444	2347	119202	•
Inventories 24	5	0	0	0	•	0	16	64	3	10	555	32	•
Net Property, Plant and Equipment 25	79	0	1	14	•	523	246	683	1647	797	1866	2467	•
Total Assets 26	16172	0	127	676	•	6617	15553	35707	72666	156347	342426	1112395	•
Notes and Loans Payable 27	2621	0	23	112	•	1295	2486	5911	12963	25231	62208	167271	•
All Other Liabilities 28	1499	0	1	41	•	697	974	3478	6373	19824	32766	146910	•
Net Worth 29	12052	0	103	523	•	4624	12094	26317	53330	111292	247452	808214	•

Selected Financial Ratios (Times to 1)

Current Ratio 30	2.1	38.3	•	5.9	•	2.9	3.1	2.6	5.5	2.5	1.1	2.2	•
Quick Ratio 31	1.9	29.2	•	3.3	•	2.1	2.4	1.7	3.6	1.6	0.5	1.8	•
Net Sales to Working Capital 32	0.0	•	•	0.0	•	0.1	0.1	0.0	0.0	0.1	0.3	0.0	•
Coverage Ratio 33	9.0	18.3	128.7	26.3	•	12.2	28.3	17.6	7.9	13.8	5.9	8.0	•
Total Asset Turnover 34	0.0	•	•	0.0	•	0.0	0.0	0.0	0.0	0.0	0.0	0.0	•
Inventory Turnover 35	1.1	•	•	•	•	•	1.4	0.9	22.9	31.5	0.4	6.6	•
Receivables Turnover 36	0.0	•	•	0.1	•	0.5	0.2	0.2	0.1	0.3	0.2	0.0	•
Total Liabilities to Net Worth 37	0.3	0.2	•	0.3	•	0.4	0.3	0.4	0.4	0.4	0.4	0.4	•
Current Assets to Working Capital 38	1.9	1.0	•	1.2	•	1.5	1.5	1.6	1.2	1.6	9.5	1.9	•
Current Liabilities to Working Capital 39	0.9	0.0	•	0.2	•	0.5	0.5	0.6	0.2	0.6	8.5	0.9	•
Working Capital to Net Sales 40	50.9	•	•	183.6	•	15.3	18.5	22.4	39.3	14.7	3.4	32.9	•
Inventory to Working Capital 41	0.0	•	•	•	•	•	0.0	0.0	0.0	0.0	0.2	0.0	•
Total Receipts to Cash Flow 42	0.1	0.0	•	0.0	•	0.1	0.0	0.1	0.1	0.1	0.1	0.1	•
Cost of Goods to Cash Flow 43	0.0	0.0	•	•	•	•	0.0	0.0	0.0	0.0	0.0	0.0	•
Cash Flow to Total Debt 44	0.2	•	0.8	0.5	•	0.5	0.8	0.4	0.2	0.3	0.2	0.2	•

Selected Financial Factors (in Percentages)

Debt Ratio 45	25.5	•	18.9	22.6	•	30.1	22.2	26.3	26.6	28.8	27.7	28.0	•
Return on Total Assets 46	7.6	•	27.0	15.2	•	27.3	20.5	14.9	9.5	12.3	7.5	8.8	•
Return on Equity Before Income Taxes 47	9.1	•	33.0	18.9	•	35.9	25.4	19.1	11.3	16.0	8.7	10.7	•
Return on Equity After Income Taxes 48	7.3	•	26.9	16.5	•	29.9	22.9	16.1	9.3	13.1	6.3	8.4	•
Profit Margin (Before Income Tax) 49	2435.2	4051.4	•	8961.6	•	1776.2	2582.3	1750.9	1417.8	1631.7	1589.0	2026.2	•
Profit Margin (After Income Tax) 50	1950.4	3003.8	•	7833.7	•	1481.5	2319.5	1478.1	1166.6	1330.9	1163.5	1595.3	•

EMPLOYMENT SERVICES

Table I
Corporations with and without Net Income

MONEY AMOUNTS AND SIZE OF ASSETS IN THOUSANDS OF DOLLARS

Item Description for Accounting Period 7/05 Through 6/06	Total	Zero Assets	Under 500	500 to 1,000	1,000 to 5,000	5,000 to 10,000	10,000 to 25,000	25,000 to 50,000	50,000 to 100,000	100,000 to 250,000	250,000 to 500,000	500,000 to 2,500,000	2,500,000 and over
Number of Enterprises 1	24630	1531	20229	1495	933	280	72	27	22	18	10	13	0
Revenues ($ in Thousands)													
Net Sales 2	136284129	579710	20277572	6124989	21192252	11883672	7882243	4270440	8307695	11397711	17462707	26905137	0
Interest 3	245565	512	3839	2669	2326	5311	5249	3037	5603	12959	24680	179380	0
Rents 4	3169	0	0	579	26	0	507	1150	10	233	0	663	0
Royalties 5	306095	0	0	0	0	0	0	0	453	14629	32652	258361	0
Other Portfolio Income 6	226038	153	6777	2780	18748	82	1602	7505	36821	4711	17625	129235	0
Other Receipts 7	2002403	966	116003	6395	57911	11373	14772	30985	58654	22677	13134	1669534	0
Total Receipts 8	139067399	581341	20404191	6137412	21271263	11900438	7904373	4313117	8409236	11452920	17550798	29142310	0
Average Total Receipts 9	5646	380	1009	4105	22799	42502	109783	159745	382238	636273	1755080	2241716	•
Operating Costs/Operating Income (%)													
Cost of Operations 10	56.2	53.4	26.6	34.4	76.3	55.6	73.8	44.7	59.6	32.8	77.0	59.8	•
Salaries and Wages 11	23.8	26.3	42.7	41.0	8.3	28.6	10.3	36.2	23.5	46.9	6.9	18.9	•
Taxes Paid 12	6.1	7.7	6.4	7.1	5.5	5.6	5.3	6.6	6.3	6.0	5.7	6.8	•
Interest Paid 13	0.4	0.2	0.3	0.2	0.1	0.3	0.3	0.3	0.5	0.9	0.2	1.0	•
Depreciation 14	0.3	0.2	0.2	0.1	0.1	0.2	0.1	0.2	0.3	0.3	0.2	0.6	•
Amortization and Depletion 15	0.3	0.1	0.1	0.1	0.0	0.1	0.1	0.2	0.3	0.6	0.5	0.8	•
Pensions and Other Deferred Comp. 16	0.2	0.0	0.6	0.2	0.0	0.0	0.1	0.2	0.0	0.0	0.1	0.1	•
Employee Benefits 17	2.9	2.9	2.3	0.9	4.2	2.1	3.0	2.2	3.4	2.0	5.5	1.9	•
Advertising 18	0.4	0.2	0.7	0.5	0.2	0.4	0.2	0.3	0.2	0.2	0.1	0.5	•
Other Expenses 19	7.4	6.0	10.2	9.2	3.8	5.0	5.3	5.5	4.5	8.6	3.3	13.0	•
Officers' Compensation 20	1.8	4.2	7.5	2.2	1.2	1.1	0.6	0.7	0.4	0.2	0.3	0.6	•
Operating Margin 21	0.2	•	2.3	4.2	0.4	1.1	0.9	2.7	0.8	1.5	0.2	•	•
Operating Margin Before Officers' Comp. 22	2.0	2.9	9.8	6.4	1.6	2.2	1.4	3.4	1.3	1.8	0.5	•	•

Selected Average Balance Sheet ($ in Thousands)

Line Item												
Net Receivables 23	399	27	224	853	3225	5482	13158	20831	38424	110546	327144	•
Inventories 24	2	0	0	0	1	17	241	364	120	101	2281	•
Net Property, Plant and Equipment 25	66	9	35	108	418	572	2112	4832	8860	19836	45977	•
Total Assets 26	1340	96	632	2087	7181	14627	33306	65412	157376	375075	1245288	•
Notes and Loans Payable 27	315	59	149	323	5145	3780	8172	23139	63941	42849	154878	•
All Other Liabilities 28	505	33	174	929	1863	6285	14263	29182	62655	162155	453779	•
Net Worth 29	520	4	309	836	174	4561	10872	13091	30780	170070	636632	•

Selected Financial Ratios (Times to 1)

Ratio												
Current Ratio 30	1.3	1.2	2.5	1.8	0.9	1.4	1.5	1.0	1.2	1.5	1.3	•
Quick Ratio 31	1.1	1.0	2.3	1.6	0.7	1.0	1.3	0.8	0.9	1.2	1.1	•
Net Sales to Working Capital 32	33.7	92.1	13.8	36.4	•	37.9	20.1	450.9	41.5	29.0	16.8	•
Coverage Ratio 33	6.1	9.8	27.7	9.4	5.1	4.9	11.7	5.3	3.2	4.4	5.5	•
Total Asset Turnover 34	4.1	10.4	6.5	10.9	5.9	7.5	4.7	5.8	4.0	4.7	1.7	•
Inventory Turnover 35	1562.8	•	851010.7	16597.1	4742.8	293.7	618.1	1735.7	13309.1	542.8	•	•
Receivables Turnover 36	14.4	40.7	18.7	24.1	20.0	18.2	12.5	19.8	16.3	19.2	6.2	•
Total Liabilities to Net Worth 37	1.6	24.9	1.0	1.5	40.2	2.2	2.1	4.0	4.1	1.2	1.0	•
Current Assets to Working Capital 38	4.1	5.8	1.7	2.3	•	3.6	2.8	37.8	5.1	3.2	4.1	•
Current Liabilities to Working Capital 39	3.1	4.8	0.7	1.3	•	2.6	1.8	36.8	4.1	2.2	3.1	•
Working Capital to Net Sales 40	0.0	0.0	0.1	0.0	0.0	0.0	0.0	0.0	0.0	0.0	0.1	•
Inventory to Working Capital 41	0.0	0.0	•	0.0	•	0.0	0.0	0.9	0.0	0.0	0.0	•
Total Receipts to Cash Flow 42	11.8	9.0	8.0	24.6	18.0	17.1	12.4	17.3	10.7	31.9	6.5	27.3
Cost of Goods to Cash Flow 43	6.6	2.4	2.7	18.8	10.0	12.6	5.5	10.3	3.5	24.6	3.9	14.6
Cash Flow to Total Debt 44	0.6	1.2	1.6	0.7	0.3	0.6	0.6	0.6	0.4	0.5	0.3	0.5

Selected Financial Factors (in Percentages)

Factor												
Debt Ratio 45	61.2	96.1	51.1	60.0	97.6	68.8	67.4	80.0	80.4	54.7	48.9	•
Return on Total Assets 46	11.2	33.4	29.6	9.5	9.1	10.7	19.1	14.6	11.7	3.9	8.8	•
Return on Equity Before Income Taxes 47	24.1	778.2	58.3	21.2	302.5	27.1	53.5	59.0	41.5	6.7	14.1	•
Return on Equity After Income Taxes 48	19.8	769.9	57.8	20.7	295.9	23.9	50.1	53.6	34.9	4.8	8.9	•
Profit Margin (Before Income Tax) 49	2.3	2.9	4.4	0.8	1.2	1.1	3.7	2.0	2.0	0.7	4.3	•
Profit Margin (After Income Tax) 50	1.9	2.8	4.4	0.8	1.2	1.0	3.4	1.9	1.7	0.5	2.7	•

Table II
Corporations with Net Income

EMPLOYMENT SERVICES

MONEY AMOUNTS AND SIZE OF ASSETS IN THOUSANDS OF DOLLARS

Item Description for Accounting Period 7/05 Through 6/06	Total	Zero Assets	Under 500	500 to 1,000	1,000 to 5,000	5,000 to 10,000	10,000 to 25,000	25,000 to 50,000	50,000 to 100,000	100,000 to 250,000	250,000 to 500,000	500,000 to 2,500,000	2,500,000 and over
Number of Enterprises 1	15884	86	13854	1013	613	187	58	27	19	•	•	8	0
Revenues ($ in Thousands)													
Net Sales 2	108866782	341145	13163016	4579581	18529666	9978881	7199281	4270440	7781610	•	•	17419720	0
Interest 3	223977	143	2655	913	1472	5176	2498	3037	4867	•	•	168748	0
Rents 4	2590	0	0	0	26	0	507	1150	10	•	•	663	0
Royalties 5	287909	0	0	0	0	0	0	0	0	•	•	240629	0
Other Portfolio Income 6	218151	153	6777	2749	17816	82	174	7505	36617	•	•	125765	0
Other Receipts 7	1939846	904	113759	5883	57344	4772	14526	30985	51990	•	•	1630754	0
Total Receipts 8	111339255	342345	13288207	4589126	18606324	9988911	7216986	4313117	7875094	•	•	19586279	0
Average Total Receipts 9	7010	3981	959	4530	30353	53417	124431	159745	414479	•	•	2448285	•
Operating Costs/Operating Income (%)													
Cost of Operations 10	56.5	32.8	25.0	23.0	75.8	56.0	74.7	44.7	58.4	•	•	59.7	•
Salaries and Wages 11	22.5	41.1	36.7	51.3	7.9	28.4	9.9	36.2	24.7	•	•	17.5	•
Taxes Paid 12	6.2	7.4	5.8	6.5	6.0	5.2	4.9	6.6	6.5	•	•	7.5	•
Interest Paid 13	0.4	0.1	0.4	0.2	0.1	0.3	0.3	0.3	0.5	•	•	1.0	•
Depreciation 14	0.2	0.2	0.2	0.1	0.1	0.2	0.1	0.2	0.2	•	•	0.5	•
Amortization and Depletion 15	0.3	0.0	0.1	0.0	0.0	0.1	0.1	0.2	0.3	•	•	0.8	•
Pensions and Other Deferred Comp. 16	0.2	0.0	0.9	0.3	0.0	0.0	0.1	0.2	0.0	•	•	0.1	•
Employee Benefits 17	3.2	3.7	2.7	0.2	2.2	2.2	3.0	2.2	3.6	•	•	2.0	•
Advertising 18	0.4	0.2	0.9	0.4	0.2	0.4	0.2	0.3	0.2	•	•	0.6	•
Other Expenses 19	7.2	4.0	11.2	9.5	3.6	4.3	4.9	5.5	4.0	•	•	14.6	•
Officers' Compensation 20	1.9	5.4	10.4	1.7	1.2	0.6	0.4	0.7	0.4	•	•	0.7	•
Operating Margin 21	1.1	5.0	5.8	6.9	2.4	0.9	1.4	2.7	1.1	•	•	•	•
Operating Margin Before Officers' Comp. 22	3.0	10.4	16.2	8.6	3.0	2.0	1.8	3.4	1.5	•	•	•	•

Selected Average Balance Sheet ($ in Thousands)

Net Receivables **23**	451	0	29	274	879	2543	5830	13158	20441	·	395656
Inventories **24**	3	0	0	0	0	0	3	241	202	·	3657
Net Property, Plant and Equipment **25**	74	0	10	15	114	454	547	2112	4763	·	46928
Total Assets **26**	1560	0	99	640	2028	6822	14348	33306	65007	·	1545683
Notes and Loans Payable **27**	338	0	50	158	367	5017	3283	8172	25359	·	152553
All Other Liabilities **28**	528	0	23	85	916	2062	7139	14263	30753	·	461004
Net Worth **29**	695	0	26	398	745	-258	3926	10872	8895	·	932126

Selected Financial Ratios (Times to 1)

Current Ratio **30**	1.4	·	1.6	5.0	1.7	0.8	1.4	1.5	1.0	·	1.4
Quick Ratio **31**	1.1	·	1.3	4.5	1.5	0.6	1.0	1.3	0.8	·	1.2
Net Sales to Working Capital **32**	31.9	80.3	37.0	10.5	44.7	·	40.6	20.1	·	·	12.0
Coverage Ratio **33**	9.6	·	18.9	47.9	15.7	10.2	7.3	11.7	5.7	·	8.5
Total Asset Turnover **34**	4.4	·	9.6	7.1	14.9	7.8	8.7	4.7	6.3	·	1.4
Inventory Turnover **35**	1536.0	·	·	739170.6	·	·	30923.3	293.7	1184.4	·	355.7
Receivables Turnover **36**	15.8	·	36.3	21.0	31.2	26.7	20.8	14.6	24.8	·	5.2
Total Liabilities to Net Worth **37**	1.2	·	2.8	0.6	1.7	2.7	2.7	2.1	6.3	·	0.7
Current Assets to Working Capital **38**	3.7	·	2.7	1.3	2.4	3.5	3.5	2.8	·	·	3.4
Current Liabilities to Working Capital **39**	2.7	·	1.7	0.3	1.4	2.5	2.5	1.8	·	·	2.4
Working Capital to Net Sales **40**	0.0	·	0.0	0.1	0.0	0.0	0.0	0.0	·	·	0.1
Inventory to Working Capital **41**	0.0	·	·	·	0.0	·	0.0	0.0	·	·	0.0
Total Receipts to Cash Flow **42**	10.4	11.8	6.5	6.3	22.5	16.0	16.4	12.4	17.6	·	5.0
Cost of Goods to Cash Flow **43**	5.9	3.9	1.6	1.5	17.0	9.0	12.3	5.5	10.3	·	3.0
Cash Flow to Total Debt **44**	0.8	·	2.0	2.9	1.0	0.5	0.7	0.6	0.4	·	0.7

Selected Financial Factors (in Percentages)

Debt Ratio **45**	55.5	·	73.4	37.8	63.3	103.8	72.6	67.4	86.3	·	39.7
Return on Total Assets **46**	17.6	·	68.3	51.6	20.5	21.6	16.5	19.1	17.6	·	12.1
Return on Equity Before Income Taxes **47**	35.4	·	243.4	81.3	52.2	·	52.1	53.5	105.7	·	17.7
Return on Equity After Income Taxes **48**	30.4	·	241.7	80.6	51.5	·	47.4	50.1	96.5	·	11.9
Profit Margin (Before Income Tax) **49**	3.6	5.3	6.7	7.2	1.3	2.5	1.6	3.7	2.3	·	7.6
Profit Margin (After Income Tax) **50**	3.1	5.1	6.7	7.1	1.3	2.5	1.5	3.4	2.1	·	5.1

Table I

Corporations with and without Net Income

TRAVEL ARRANGEMENT AND RESERVATION SERVICES

MONEY AMOUNTS AND SIZE OF ASSETS IN THOUSANDS OF DOLLARS

Item Description for Accounting Period 7/05 Through 6/06	Total	Zero Assets	Under 500	500 to 1,000	1,000 to 5,000	5,000 to 10,000	10,000 to 25,000	25,000 to 50,000	50,000 to 100,000	100,000 to 250,000	250,000 to 500,000	500,000 to 2,500,000	2,500,000 and over
Number of Enterprises **1**	22649	2901	18882	417	252	39	74	29	25	16	8	6	0
Revenues ($ in Thousands)													
Net Sales **2**	38627752	244401	14783608	1559085	1713205	818798	2413099	1377523	2756726	2266492	2830744	7864072	0
Interest **3**	606688	13	1496	908	2859	2462	7029	5089	7718	7696	35062	536357	0
Rents **4**	47045	0	2409	0	0	2220	175	168	7117	817	2007	32133	0
Royalties **5**	13152	0	0	0	0	0	0	3	2472	0	0	10677	0
Other Portfolio Income **6**	2404008	175	1210	4	488	497	19311	13858	41413	15532	22907	2288613	0
Other Receipts **7**	1521251	1202	47006	4203	3687	1949	66149	109888	112916	98650	351643	723954	0
Total Receipts **8**	43219896	245791	14835729	1564200	1720239	825926	2505763	1506529	2928362	2389187	3242363	11455806	0
Average Total Receipts **9**	1908	85	786	3751	6826	21178	33862	51949	117134	149324	405295	1909301	•
Operating Costs/Operating Income (%)													
Cost of Operations **10**	54.9	34.6	76.0	69.2	45.6	79.1	59.4	37.1	62.2	44.1	71.2	8.8	•
Salaries and Wages **11**	13.6	0.7	5.6	5.9	23.7	9.0	15.7	19.5	12.8	20.2	16.1	24.7	•
Taxes Paid **12**	2.1	1.5	1.2	0.8	2.7	1.5	3.1	2.6	2.4	2.3	1.4	3.4	•
Interest Paid **13**	1.6	0.5	0.2	0.2	0.4	0.2	0.5	0.5	1.4	0.6	1.3	5.8	•
Depreciation **14**	0.9	1.6	0.5	0.6	0.9	0.5	0.8	1.3	1.0	1.3	1.0	1.8	•
Amortization and Depletion **15**	0.6	0.1	0.0	•	0.0	0.0	0.1	0.7	0.6	1.7	0.4	2.1	•
Pensions and Other Deferred Comp. **16**	0.5	•	0.1	0.7	0.1	0.1	0.4	0.6	1.0	0.3	0.7	1.0	•
Employee Benefits **17**	1.2	•	0.3	0.5	1.6	0.7	1.4	1.7	2.2	1.8	1.7	2.0	•
Advertising **18**	3.4	1.3	0.8	0.0	0.8	0.3	2.6	2.7	2.9	1.4	3.4	10.9	•
Other Expenses **19**	22.2	44.4	12.3	16.2	19.5	7.2	17.5	37.0	17.1	25.1	16.6	45.3	•
Officers' Compensation **20**	2.7	3.9	2.8	7.9	4.7	2.6	1.3	1.2	1.1	0.8	0.5	3.7	•
Operating Margin **21**	•	11.4	0.1	•	•	•	•	•	•	0.3	•	•	•
Operating Margin Before Officers' Comp. **22**	•	15.2	3.0	4.7	4.7	1.5	•	•	•	1.1	•	•	•

Selected Average Balance Sheet ($ in Thousands)

Net Receivables 23	163	0	3	49	410	2792	4971	5326	9913	13429	23269	370755	•
Inventories 24	6	0	1	0	14	13	44	334	1005	312	2475	9676	•
Net Property, Plant and Equipment 25	105	0	13	138	303	1435	1360	3946	10033	17047	30364	162280	•
Total Assets 26	1645	0	63	712	2592	7608	16737	37785	75020	142223	321907	4293604	•
Notes and Loans Payable 27	242	0	50	113	316	1161	1758	6785	13529	21585	90838	437163	•
All Other Liabilities 28	828	0	31	280	2183	5108	11112	17493	42503	62979	126558	2150305	•
Net Worth 29	575	0	-18	319	93	1339	3866	13507	18988	57659	104510	1706136	•

Selected Financial Ratios (Times to 1)

Current Ratio 30	1.1	•	1.0	1.8	0.7	0.8	1.1	0.9	1.0	1.0	1.1	1.4	•
Quick Ratio 31	0.8	•	0.8	1.6	0.5	0.7	0.9	0.6	0.7	0.7	0.6	0.9	•
Net Sales to Working Capital 32	32.1	•	912.5	18.2	•	•	24.5	•	438.1	•	42.0	6.3	•
Coverage Ratio 33	6.2	23.6	3.3	•	2.1	•	4.5	9.8	2.1	9.9	1.1	7.2	•
Total Asset Turnover 34	1.0	•	12.4	5.3	2.6	2.8	1.9	1.3	1.5	1.0	1.1	0.3	•
Inventory Turnover 35	145.7	•	547.8	•	223.2	1261.7	442.2	52.7	68.3	200.5	101.8	11.9	•
Receivables Turnover 36	9.1	•	175.9	83.3	11.0	8.5	8.3	9.8	12.3	9.6	12.0	2.8	•
Total Liabilities to Net Worth 37	1.9	•	•	1.2	26.9	4.7	3.3	1.8	3.0	1.5	2.1	1.5	•
Current Assets to Working Capital 38	8.5	•	43.6	2.2	•	•	9.0	•	145.7	•	14.4	3.7	•
Current Liabilities to Working Capital 39	7.5	•	42.6	1.2	•	•	8.0	•	144.7	•	13.4	2.7	•
Working Capital to Net Sales 40	0.0	•	0.0	0.1	•	•	0.0	•	0.0	•	0.0	0.2	•
Inventory to Working Capital 41	0.2	•	1.4	•	•	•	0.0	•	5.6	•	0.3	0.1	•
Total Receipts to Cash Flow 42	4.5	2.0	9.3	7.9	6.2	18.0	6.3	2.6	6.3	3.6	7.0	2.0	•
Cost of Goods to Cash Flow 43	2.5	0.7	7.1	5.4	2.8	14.2	3.7	1.0	3.9	1.6	5.0	0.2	•
Cash Flow to Total Debt 44	0.4	•	1.0	1.2	0.4	0.2	0.4	0.8	0.3	0.5	0.2	0.3	•

Selected Financial Factors (in Percentages)

Debt Ratio 45	65.0	•	127.8	55.2	96.4	82.4	76.9	64.3	74.7	59.5	67.5	60.3	•
Return on Total Assets 46	10.1	•	8.7	•	2.1	•	3.1	6.1	4.2	5.8	1.6	12.7	•
Return on Equity Before Income Taxes 47	24.3	•	•	•	30.0	•	10.4	15.4	8.7	12.9	0.3	27.6	•
Return on Equity After Income Taxes 48	16.6	•	•	•	0.3	•	8.0	12.4	2.7	9.7	0.2	18.7	•
Profit Margin (Before Income Tax) 49	8.2	11.9	0.5	•	0.4	•	1.2	4.4	1.5	5.2	0.1	36.0	•
Profit Margin (After Income Tax) 50	5.6	11.8	0.5	•	0.0	•	0.9	3.5	0.5	3.9	0.1	24.4	•

Table II
Corporations with Net Income

TRAVEL ARRANGEMENT AND RESERVATION SERVICES

MONEY AMOUNTS AND SIZE OF ASSETS IN THOUSANDS OF DOLLARS

Item Description for Accounting Period 7/05 Through 6/06	Total	Zero Assets	Under 500	500 to 1,000	1,000 to 5,000	5,000 to 10,000	10,000 to 25,000	25,000 to 50,000	50,000 to 100,000	100,000 to 250,000	250,000 to 500,000	500,000 to 2,500,000	2,500,000 and over
Number of Enterprises 1	11256	1139	9483	350	156	19	50	19	17	•	4	•	0
Revenues ($ in Thousands)													
Net Sales 2	23382530	155777	5623938	1213730	1032674	370605	1848173	975812	1904878	•	942261	•	0
Interest 3	583009	13	662	908	2112	579	4901	4488	7293	•	28750	•	0
Rents 4	30532	0	49	0	0	0	175	121	7117	•	1854	•	0
Royalties 5	13106	0	0	0	0	0	0	0	2429	•	0	•	0
Other Portfolio Income 6	2362535	175	0	4	488	497	14625	12450	24413	•	15123	•	0
Other Receipts 7	1150279	1202	39158	119	2398	1892	55234	107372	92517	•	41195	•	0
Total Receipts 8	27521991	157167	5663807	1214761	1037672	375793	1923108	1100243	2038647	•	1029183	•	0
Average Total Receipts 9	2445	138	597	3471	6652	19779	38462	57908	119920	•	257296	•	•
Operating Costs/Operating Income (%)													
Cost of Operations 10	42.0	23.0	63.0	73.1	40.5	78.9	55.0	25.2	58.1	•	67.0	•	•
Salaries and Wages 11	15.2	1.0	4.1	4.6	25.0	9.6	15.6	19.5	12.7	•	14.5	•	•
Taxes Paid 12	2.4	1.1	1.5	0.6	3.2	1.5	3.1	3.0	2.1	•	1.6	•	•
Interest Paid 13	2.3	0.8	0.2	0.2	0.5	0.1	0.3	0.5	0.5	•	3.6	•	•
Depreciation 14	1.2	2.5	1.0	0.6	1.1	0.6	0.6	1.3	1.1	•	0.7	•	•
Amortization and Depletion 15	0.9	•	0.1	•	0.1	0.1	0.1	0.7	0.4	•	0.2	•	•
Pensions and Other Deferred Comp. 16	0.5	•	0.0	0.9	0.2	0.2	0.4	0.8	1.4	•	0.8	•	•
Employee Benefits 17	1.4	•	0.4	0.3	2.0	0.5	1.5	1.6	2.7	•	1.6	•	•
Advertising 18	4.9	0.5	1.6	0.1	1.2	0.1	2.8	3.3	2.3	•	5.7	•	•
Other Expenses 19	28.1	35.7	20.9	9.9	18.4	4.8	19.2	46.7	19.6	•	9.1	•	•
Officers' Compensation 20	3.1	5.7	3.9	6.1	4.7	3.5	1.2	1.5	1.4	•	0.5	•	•
Operating Margin 21	•	29.7	3.3	3.5	3.3	0.3	0.2	•	•	•	•	•	•
Operating Margin Before Officers' Comp. 22	1.1	35.4	7.2	9.6	8.0	3.7	1.4	•	•	•	•	•	•

Selected Average Balance Sheet ($ in Thousands)

Net Receivables 23	284	0	4	58	417	2861	5391	3472	10630	•	32570
Inventories 24	9	0	2	0	20	25	52	317	390	•	3458
Net Property, Plant and Equipment 25	168	0	19	123	412	2384	1536	4910	11119	•	19776
Total Assets 26	2909	0	70	716	3162	7798	17206	39448	75848	•	350908
Notes and Loans Payable 27	362	0	35	112	230	0	1413	7223	7103	•	102896
All Other Liabilities 28	1430	0	14	214	2304	2907	12219	16665	44338	•	110185
Net Worth 29	1118	0	21	389	628	4891	3575	15560	24406	•	137826

Selected Financial Ratios (Times to 1)

Current Ratio 30	1.3	•	2.7	2.5	0.8	1.9	1.0	0.9	1.0	•	1.4
Quick Ratio 31	0.9	•	2.3	2.5	0.7	1.6	0.8	0.5	0.7	•	0.6
Net Sales to Working Capital 32	13.5	•	23.6	12.6	•	8.3	98.1	•	•	•	6.3
Coverage Ratio 33	7.7	38.0	18.8	21.4	9.2	14.2	15.6	18.7	11.3	•	2.1
Total Asset Turnover 34	0.7	•	8.5	4.8	2.1	2.5	2.1	1.3	1.5	•	0.7
Inventory Turnover 35	93.1	•	197.4	•	131.7	606.9	389.8	40.9	167.1	•	45.7
Receivables Turnover 36	6.3	•	103.3	64.8	11.0	6.5	9.0	15.2	10.9	•	14.5
Total Liabilities to Net Worth 37	1.6	•	2.4	0.8	4.0	0.6	3.8	1.5	2.1	•	1.5
Current Assets to Working Capital 38	4.6	•	1.6	1.6	•	2.1	32.7	•	•	•	3.5
Current Liabilities to Working Capital 39	3.6	•	0.6	0.6	•	1.1	31.7	•	•	•	2.5
Working Capital to Net Sales 40	0.1	•	0.0	0.1	•	0.1	0.0	•	•	•	0.2
Inventory to Working Capital 41	0.1	•	0.1	•	•	0.0	0.2	•	•	•	0.1
Total Receipts to Cash Flow 42	3.2	1.7	4.5	8.1	5.4	18.9	4.9	1.9	4.8	•	9.6
Cost of Goods to Cash Flow 43	1.3	0.4	2.8	5.9	2.2	14.9	2.7	0.5	2.8	•	6.4
Cash Flow to Total Debt 44	0.4	•	2.7	1.3	0.5	0.4	0.6	1.1	0.5	•	0.1

Selected Financial Factors (in Percentages)

Debt Ratio 45	61.6	•	70.2	45.6	80.1	37.3	79.2	60.6	67.8	•	60.7
Return on Total Assets 46	12.7	•	35.8	18.4	8.8	4.5	9.5	11.8	7.6	•	5.0
Return on Equity Before Income Taxes 47	28.8	•	113.8	32.2	39.6	6.6	42.9	28.3	21.5	•	6.6
Return on Equity After Income Taxes 48	20.9	•	113.5	32.0	32.5	4.3	39.0	24.4	14.7	•	6.5
Profit Margin (Before Income Tax) 49	15.5	30.6	4.0	3.6	3.8	1.7	4.1	8.6	4.7	•	3.8
Profit Margin (After Income Tax) 50	11.3	30.4	4.0	3.6	3.1	1.1	3.8	7.4	3.2	•	3.8

Table I

Corporations with and without Net Income

OTHER ADMINISTRATIVE AND SUPPORT SERVICES

MONEY AMOUNTS AND SIZE OF ASSETS IN THOUSANDS OF DOLLARS

Item Description for Accounting Period 7/05 Through 6/06	Total	Zero Assets	Under 500	500 to 1,000	1,000 to 5,000	5,000 to 10,000	10,000 to 25,000	25,000 to 50,000	50,000 to 100,000	100,000 to 250,000	250,000 to 500,000	500,000 to 2,500,000	2,500,000 and over
Number of Enterprises 1	195813	37851	146022	5228	5539	529	354	123	63	49	28	24	4
Revenues ($ in Thousands)													
Net Sales 2	19005439	3354564	56213716	11057715	32159477	9642468	8955238	7613611	6328644	7687346	10822539	22633312	21536808
Interest 3	1445151	20415	47286	6371	30486	8395	25661	12713	23180	124565	130279	217412	798388
Rents 4	298368	0	10343	8234	5379	0	5817	13932	2050	4345	10134	22777	215357
Royalties 5	1211349	0	0	0	0	141	527	1103	6933	7908	14956	27972	1151809
Other Portfolio Income 6	4907636	73789	101438	27266	57365	15527	37211	36188	13025	51141	95584	337922	4061183
Other Receipts 7	5462745	96128	687770	26029	255671	198913	429390	422892	102924	448171	371665	985131	1438058
Total Receipts 8	211330688	3544896	57060553	11125615	32508378	9865444	9453844	8100439	6476756	8323476	11445157	24224526	29201603
Average Total Receipts 9	1079	94	391	2128	5869	18649	26706	65857	102806	169867	408756	1009355	7300401
Operating Costs/Operating Income (%)													
Cost of Operations 10	38.7	25.0	35.8	43.4	52.4	48.6	49.4	51.6	40.4	34.6	20.8	30.3	30.9
Salaries and Wages 11	19.3	11.7	17.9	15.0	15.2	17.5	21.9	17.7	17.3	28.6	32.2	25.1	17.6
Taxes Paid 12	3.6	3.3	3.6	3.6	3.3	3.2	3.9	2.7	3.2	3.8	4.5	4.7	2.9
Interest Paid 13	2.1	1.6	0.8	0.7	1.0	0.8	1.2	1.4	1.7	3.6	3.5	2.5	7.3
Depreciation 14	2.1	3.5	2.1	2.7	1.4	1.4	1.5	1.4	1.5	1.8	1.7	2.1	3.5
Amortization and Depletion 15	1.1	0.5	0.1	0.1	0.2	0.1	0.4	0.5	1.1	1.1	2.0	2.2	4.8
Pensions and Other Deferred Comp. 16	0.4	0.3	0.3	0.3	0.3	0.5	0.4	0.6	0.2	0.9	0.3	1.0	0.4
Employee Benefits 17	1.8	1.3	0.9	1.5	1.5	2.0	2.3	2.7	2.1	2.6	3.1	2.7	1.9
Advertising 18	1.4	3.2	1.4	1.2	0.6	0.5	0.9	1.9	0.5	0.8	3.1	0.4	3.0
Other Expenses 19	25.5	40.2	25.0	21.6	16.4	21.8	17.7	20.7	28.2	25.0	31.1	27.4	41.8
Officers' Compensation 20	4.0	9.2	7.6	6.2	5.0	2.2	2.3	1.8	1.5	2.1	1.1	0.6	0.1
Operating Margin 21	0.1	0.1	4.4	3.8	2.8	1.4	*	*	2.3	*	*	1.0	*
Operating Margin Before Officers' Comp. 22	4.1	9.3	12.0	10.0	7.8	3.6	0.5	*	3.8	*	*	1.6	*

Selected Average Balance Sheet ($ in Thousands)

Net Receivables 23	111	0	10	160	622	1706	3981	8927	17362	37811	54706	247537	543646
Inventories 24	13	0	2	31	73	60	399	1110	2709	3291	3229	8201	165260
Net Property, Plant and Equipment 25	106	0	27	228	358	2310	2448	4632	10318	18543	42324	157826	1114475
Total Assets 26	713		78	718	1986	6765	14934	34512	71373	160504	362927	1084559	12961116
Notes and Loans Payable 27	251		50	274	824	2868	5041	13092	24059	61429	142755	332965	3610257
All Other Liabilities 28	227		19	317	739	2281	4973	12939	23460	52300	110963	271671	4402922
Net Worth 29	235		9	127	423	1615	4920	8480	23854	46775	109209	479922	4947936

Selected Financial Ratios (Times to 1)

Current Ratio 30	1.2	•	1.2	1.3	1.4	1.3	1.4	1.3	1.3	1.6	1.4	1.3	0.7
Quick Ratio 31	0.9	•	1.0	1.0	1.1	1.1	1.0	1.0	1.0	1.1	0.9	1.1	0.4
Net Sales to Working Capital 32	28.0	•	77.4	21.6	17.2	22.0	9.9	12.9	11.3	5.2	10.0	12.3	•
Coverage Ratio 33	4.3	4.6	8.7	7.7	4.7	6.0	4.2	3.4	3.8	2.0	1.7	4.3	3.9
Total Asset Turnover 34	1.4	•	4.9	2.9	2.9	2.7	1.7	1.8	1.4	1.0	1.1	0.9	0.4
Inventory Turnover 35	31.0	•	63.8	29.1	41.6	147.3	31.3	28.7	15.0	16.5	24.9	34.8	10.1
Receivables Turnover 36	10.3	•	38.9	12.2	11.0	10.0	6.9	6.9	6.4	4.6	8.0	5.1	9.7
Total Liabilities to Net Worth 37	2.0	•	8.0	4.6	3.7	3.2	2.0	3.1	2.0	2.4	2.3	1.3	1.6
Current Assets to Working Capital 38	6.4	•	6.4	4.0	3.7	4.6	3.3	3.9	3.9	2.6	3.6	4.9	•
Current Liabilities to Working Capital 39	5.4	•	5.4	3.0	2.7	3.6	2.3	2.9	2.9	1.6	2.6	3.9	•
Working Capital to Net Sales 40	0.0	•	0.0	0.0	0.1	0.0	0.1	0.1	0.1	0.2	0.1	0.1	•
Inventory to Working Capital 41	0.4	•	0.2	0.2	0.2	0.1	0.2	0.2	0.1	0.1	0.1	0.1	•
Total Receipts to Cash Flow 42	3.9	2.7	4.7	4.7	5.9	4.6	5.6	4.8	3.3	4.3	3.4	3.2	2.7
Cost of Goods to Cash Flow 43	1.5	0.7	2.0	2.0	3.1	2.2	2.8	2.5	1.3	1.5	0.7	1.0	0.8
Cash Flow to Total Debt 44	0.5	•	1.4	0.8	0.6	0.8	0.5	0.5	0.6	0.3	0.4	0.5	0.3

Selected Financial Factors (in Percentages)

Debt Ratio 45	67.0	•	88.9	82.3	78.7	76.1	67.1	75.4	66.6	70.9	69.9	55.7	61.8
Return on Total Assets 46	12.6	•	33.1	15.1	14.3	12.1	8.4	8.7	8.9	6.9	6.2	9.3	11.9
Return on Equity Before Income Taxes 47	29.4	•	264.2	73.9	52.9	42.1	19.4	25.0	19.6	11.7	8.4	16.1	23.4
Return on Equity After Income Taxes 48	26.3	•	260.2	72.6	50.7	38.5	17.1	20.8	16.4	7.2	4.5	10.9	21.8
Profit Margin (Before Income Tax) 49	6.8	5.7	5.9	4.4	3.9	3.7	3.8	3.4	4.7	3.5	2.4	8.2	21.5
Profit Margin (After Income Tax) 50	6.1	5.0	5.9	4.4	3.7	3.4	3.3	2.9	3.9	2.2	1.3	5.5	20.1

Table II

Corporations with Net Income

ADMINISTRATIVE AND SUPPORT AND WASTE MANAGEMENT AND REMEDIATION SERVICES
561905

OTHER ADMINISTRATIVE AND SUPPORT SERVICES

MONEY AMOUNTS AND SIZE OF ASSETS IN THOUSANDS OF DOLLARS

Item Description for Accounting Period 7/05 Through 6/06	Total	Zero Assets	Under 500	500 to 1,000	1,000 to 5,000	5,000 to 10,000	10,000 to 25,000	25,000 to 50,000	50,000 to 100,000	100,000 to 250,000	250,000 to 500,000	500,000 to 2,500,000	2,500,000 and over
Number of Enterprises 1	133335	22951	101114	3890	4513	451	224	81	42	28	17	20	4
Revenues ($ in Thousands)													
Net Sales 2	16454322	2397602	40961980	9313412	28897384	7992835	7558782	6294154	5315862	5156734	7439693	21681077	21536808
Interest 3	1204712	2633	14169	4456	16307	5267	12252	8455	14660	48529	82268	197329	798388
Rents 4	283674	0	5364	4522	4453	0	5142	13529	2050	1306	9334	22618	215357
Royalties 5	1210718	0	0	0	0	0	527	733	6838	7884	14956	27972	1151809
Other Portfolio Income 6	4807950	69566	78825	24820	52813	11829	22659	27925	10585	44661	65203	337884	4061183
Other Receipts 7	5063890	107718	611847	21668	251399	176965	344007	327046	97707	423602	313838	950029	1438058
Total Receipts 8	177117266	2577519	41672185	9368878	29222356	8186896	7943369	6671842	5447702	5682716	7925292	23216909	29201603
Average Total Receipts 9	1328	112	412	2408	6475	18153	35461	82368	129707	202954	466194	1160845	7300401
Operating Costs/Operating Income (%)													
Cost of Operations 10	39.3	19.2	33.7	40.3	54.2	58.0	49.4	54.1	45.8	35.6	20.0	31.4	30.9
Salaries and Wages 11	18.5	10.8	17.2	15.9	14.3	15.4	21.1	16.2	14.1	25.9	34.0	24.1	17.6
Taxes Paid 12	3.5	3.2	3.5	3.7	3.3	3.2	3.9	2.3	3.2	3.4	4.2	4.8	2.9
Interest Paid 13	2.0	0.8	0.7	0.6	0.7	0.7	0.6	0.9	1.4	2.6	3.0	2.3	7.3
Depreciation 14	2.0	2.1	2.0	2.7	1.3	1.3	1.4	1.3	1.2	1.7	1.5	2.1	3.5
Amortization and Depletion 15	1.0	0.1	0.1	0.1	0.1	0.1	0.2	0.3	0.8	0.5	1.1	1.8	4.8
Pensions and Other Deferred Comp. 16	0.4	0.3	0.3	0.3	0.3	0.5	0.4	0.7	0.2	1.2	0.3	1.0	0.4
Employee Benefits 17	1.8	1.1	1.6	1.6	1.5	1.8	2.2	3.0	1.9	2.9	2.6	2.7	1.9
Advertising 18	1.4	1.0	0.9	1.3	0.6	0.6	0.5	2.2	0.5	1.1	4.4	0.4	3.0
Other Expenses 19	24.0	37.2	23.7	19.4	14.2	12.8	16.4	16.9	25.9	24.2	28.5	26.9	41.8
Officers' Compensation 20	3.8	9.1	7.3	6.6	5.2	2.2	2.2	1.6	1.4	2.6	0.8	0.6	0.1
Operating Margin 21	2.4	15.0	9.1	7.6	4.4	3.6	1.7	0.4	3.8	•	•	1.9	•
Operating Margin Before Officers' Comp. 22	6.2	24.1	16.4	14.2	9.6	5.7	3.9	2.0	5.2	0.9	0.4	2.5	•

Selected Average Balance Sheet ($ in Thousands)

Net Receivables 23	122	0	10	182	615	1722	4378	9749	21141	39990	60366	199631	543646
Inventories 24	14	0	2	39	63	50	495	1293	3652	5309	5591	9947	180388
Net Property, Plant and Equipment 25	129	0	27	253	336	2356	3097	5578	9142	23631	32609	184300	1114475
Total Assets 26	875	0	79	739	1914	6674	15339	34462	71659	165945	352683	1123228	12961116
Notes and Loans Payable 27	270	0	39	273	761	2713	3932	10826	21133	63640	107114	282214	3610257
All Other Liabilities 28	271	0	16	169	663	1820	4691	12555	29528	40300	107754	307277	4402922
Net Worth 29	335	0	24	297	490	2140	6716	11082	20997	62005	137815	533737	4947936

Selected Financial Ratios (Times to 1)

Current Ratio 30	1.2	•	1.6	1.9	1.5	1.4	1.6	1.3	1.4	2.0	1.4	1.4	0.7
Quick Ratio 31	0.9	•	1.3	1.5	1.2	1.2	1.2	1.1	1.0	1.4	0.8	1.1	0.4
Net Sales to Working Capital 32	24.6	•	31.7	11.9	15.7	16.1	10.2	16.0	10.8	4.7	10.1	12.4	•
Coverage Ratio 33	6.2	28.8	17.2	14.1	8.8	10.1	12.4	8.2	5.6	4.3	3.0	5.0	3.9
Total Asset Turnover 34	1.4	•	5.1	3.2	3.3	2.7	2.2	2.3	1.8	1.1	1.2	1.0	0.4
Inventory Turnover 35	34.7	•	65.5	24.7	55.1	206.3	33.7	32.5	15.9	12.4	15.7	34.2	9.2
Receivables Turnover 36	11.8	•	42.5	12.3	12.8	11.8	8.6	8.0	7.3	4.8	14.5	10.9	19.8
Total Liabilities to Net Worth 37	1.6	•	2.3	1.5	2.9	2.1	1.3	2.1	2.4	1.7	1.6	1.1	1.6
Current Assets to Working Capital 38	5.2	•	2.7	2.1	3.0	3.4	2.8	4.2	3.7	2.0	3.4	3.8	•
Current Liabilities to Working Capital 39	4.2	•	1.7	1.1	2.0	2.4	1.8	3.2	2.7	1.0	2.4	2.8	•
Working Capital to Net Sales 40	0.0	•	0.0	0.1	0.1	0.1	0.1	0.1	0.1	0.2	0.1	0.1	•
Inventory to Working Capital 41	0.3	•	0.2	0.1	0.2	0.1	0.2	0.3	0.2	0.1	0.1	0.1	•
Total Receipts to Cash Flow 42	3.7	2.0	3.4	4.2	6.0	6.7	5.1	4.8	3.3	3.6	3.2	3.1	2.7
Cost of Goods to Cash Flow 43	1.4	0.4	1.1	1.7	3.3	3.9	2.5	2.6	1.5	1.3	0.6	1.0	0.8
Cash Flow to Total Debt 44	0.6	•	2.2	1.3	0.7	0.6	0.8	0.7	0.8	0.5	0.6	0.6	0.3

Selected Financial Factors (in Percentages)

Debt Ratio 45	61.8	•	69.4	59.9	74.4	67.9	56.2	67.8	70.7	62.6	60.9	52.5	61.8
Return on Total Assets 46	16.9	•	58.7	28.4	20.9	17.8	16.3	16.4	13.7	12.4	11.1	11.1	11.9
Return on Equity Before Income Taxes 47	37.1	•	180.8	65.7	72.3	49.9	34.2	44.8	38.4	25.5	18.8	18.6	23.4
Return on Equity After Income Taxes 48	33.9	•	178.8	65.0	69.9	46.8	31.5	39.9	32.9	19.6	13.7	13.0	21.8
Profit Margin (Before Income Tax) 49	10.1	22.5	10.8	8.1	5.5	6.0	6.8	6.4	6.4	8.6	5.9	9.2	21.5
Profit Margin (After Income Tax) 50	9.2	21.5	10.7	8.1	5.4	5.7	6.3	5.7	5.5	6.6	4.3	6.4	20.1

Table I

Corporations with and without Net Income

WASTE MANAGEMENT AND REMEDIATION SERVICES

MONEY AMOUNTS AND SIZE OF ASSETS IN THOUSANDS OF DOLLARS

Item Description for Accounting Period 7/05 Through 6/06	Total	Zero Assets	Under 500	500 to 1,000	1,000 to 5,000	5,000 to 10,000	10,000 to 25,000	25,000 to 50,000	50,000 to 100,000	100,000 to 250,000	250,000 to 500,000	500,000 to 2,500,000	2,500,000 and over
Number of Enterprises 1	14531	1525	8860	2052	1650	187	156	45	21	14	11	6	6
Revenues ($ in Thousands)													
Net Sales 2	58428486	293098	6375848	3143684	8459602	2347877	3851880	1379449	1585723	2489469	2789498	3898534	21813825
Interest 3	773808	0	731	933	2028	1139	5042	6738	5029	2963	11746	87062	650398
Rents 4	70970	0	1689	253	2157	1046	1397	1294	321	449	6	1294	61064
Royalties 5	25683	0	0	0	7239	0	0	1041	286	3160	0	731	13227
Other Portfolio Income 6	959527	14064	14918	35778	9747	17558	18429	10880	3981	1661	5407	29617	797488
Other Receipts 7	1456048	52839	8733	14619	41854	13645	67828	31026	14041	24906	54148	22526	1109880
Total Receipts 8	61714522	360001	6401919	3195267	8522627	2381265	3944576	1430428	1609381	2522608	2860805	4039764	24445882
Average Total Receipts 9	4247	236	723	1557	5165	12734	25286	31787	76637	180186	260073	673294	4074314
Operating Costs/Operating Income (%)													
Cost of Operations 10	40.8	25.8	36.1	37.6	45.1	58.9	59.1	51.1	50.5	25.6	40.0	30.6	38.3
Salaries and Wages 11	14.6	15.3	13.2	16.3	10.2	6.2	8.0	10.1	11.3	25.7	11.1	17.9	17.6
Taxes Paid 12	3.9	3.5	3.1	3.3	2.9	2.5	2.3	3.2	2.6	3.6	3.0	3.4	5.4
Interest Paid 13	4.9	1.2	0.7	1.4	1.5	1.0	1.1	2.4	1.9	1.9	5.2	7.3	9.4
Depreciation 14	5.3	2.9	3.2	3.4	3.8	2.8	3.8	4.3	5.1	4.4	5.0	5.8	7.4
Amortization and Depletion 15	1.6	0.0	0.1	0.9	0.1	0.1	0.2	1.1	0.5	1.2	2.6	3.7	2.8
Pensions and Other Deferred Comp. 16	0.4	0.0	0.2	0.3	0.5	0.2	0.5	0.3	0.4	1.0	1.2	0.4	0.4
Employee Benefits 17	2.0	3.3	0.9	1.1	1.6	0.6	2.3	1.9	1.9	3.7	3.0	2.4	2.3
Advertising 18	0.4	1.2	0.9	0.4	0.4	0.1	0.5	0.2	0.4	0.3	0.1	0.4	0.2
Other Expenses 19	24.4	49.5	32.3	25.7	26.9	22.3	17.3	22.5	24.7	28.7	23.9	30.3	20.7
Officers' Compensation 20	1.8	13.6	5.4	4.5	2.7	1.6	2.7	2.0	1.0	0.9	1.9	0.5	0.1
Operating Margin 21	•	•	3.9	5.1	4.4	3.6	2.3	1.1	•	3.2	2.9	•	•
Operating Margin Before Officers' Comp. 22	1.7	•	9.3	9.5	7.0	5.0	5.0	3.0	0.6	4.1	4.8	•	•

Selected Average Balance Sheet ($ in Thousands)

Net Receivables 23	551	0	11	52	597	2136	3650	5023	13442	22604	77879	91701	603450
Inventories 24	41	0	5	10	34	261	369	684	538	439	1796	19996	31001
Net Property, Plant and Equipment 25	1824	0	57	228	996	2308	5467	10494	22999	52728	89978	356584	2962393
Total Assets 26	4941	0	122	654	2374	6430	14457	36103	71284	145159	341902	933916	7913529
Notes and Loans Payable 27	1947	0	72	384	1185	2514	5145	13567	33872	58352	152978	292099	3011691
All Other Liabilities 28	1730	0	19	139	680	1803	5963	10500	24961	43845	109425	298771	2947018
Net Worth 29	1264	0	31	131	509	2112	3349	12035	12452	42962	79498	343046	1954821

Selected Financial Ratios (Times to 1)

Current Ratio 30	1.0	•	2.0	1.9	1.4	1.6	1.3	1.4	1.2	1.1	1.2	0.6	0.9
Quick Ratio 31	0.7	•	1.5	1.4	1.1	1.2	1.0	1.0	0.9	0.9	1.1	0.5	0.6
Net Sales to Working Capital 32	1275.3	•	34.1	11.0	15.6	10.1	17.5	9.6	16.3	78.8	11.6	•	•
Coverage Ratio 33	2.1	6.3	7.0	5.8	4.5	6.1	5.2	3.0	1.6	3.4	2.1	1.1	1.8
Total Asset Turnover 34	0.8	•	5.9	2.3	2.2	2.0	1.7	0.8	1.1	1.2	0.7	0.7	0.5
Inventory Turnover 35	39.6	•	50.6	58.8	68.5	28.3	39.5	22.9	70.9	103.6	56.5	9.9	44.9
Receivables Turnover 36	7.3	•	83.1	20.4	9.8	5.1	7.2	5.9	6.0	7.5	4.6	5.7	5.8
Total Liabilities to Net Worth 37	2.9	•	2.9	4.0	3.7	2.0	3.3	2.0	4.7	2.4	3.3	1.7	3.0
Current Assets to Working Capital 38	344.2	•	2.0	2.1	3.3	2.8	4.9	3.8	5.8	14.6	5.4	•	•
Current Liabilities to Working Capital 39	343.2	•	1.0	1.1	2.3	1.8	3.9	2.8	4.8	13.6	4.4	•	•
Working Capital to Net Sales 40	0.0	•	0.0	0.1	0.1	0.1	0.1	0.1	0.1	0.0	0.1	•	•
Inventory to Working Capital 41	11.2	•	0.3	0.0	0.1	0.2	0.3	0.2	0.2	0.1	0.1	•	•
Total Receipts to Cash Flow 42	4.1	2.0	3.1	3.7	3.8	4.5	5.5	4.5	4.6	4.0	4.1	3.9	4.5
Cost of Goods to Cash Flow 43	1.7	0.5	1.1	1.4	1.7	2.7	3.2	2.3	2.3	1.0	1.6	1.2	1.7
Cash Flow to Total Debt 44	0.3	•	2.5	0.8	0.7	0.6	0.4	0.3	0.3	0.4	0.2	0.3	0.1

Selected Financial Factors (in Percentages)

Debt Ratio 45	74.4	•	74.3	79.9	78.6	67.1	76.8	66.7	82.5	70.4	76.7	63.3	75.3
Return on Total Assets 46	8.5	•	29.6	19.0	14.2	11.8	9.9	6.0	3.2	7.9	8.1	5.8	7.6
Return on Equity Before Income Taxes 47	17.4	•	98.7	78.1	51.6	30.1	34.5	11.9	6.6	18.9	18.4	1.8	13.4
Return on Equity After Income Taxes 48	14.3	•	98.2	77.7	49.2	27.8	31.5	8.9	5.3	15.7	15.4	•	9.9
Profit Margin (Before Income Tax) 49	5.5	6.4	4.3	6.7	5.1	5.1	4.7	4.7	1.1	4.6	5.8	1.0	7.2
Profit Margin (After Income Tax) 50	4.5	6.2	4.3	6.7	4.9	4.7	4.3	3.5	0.9	3.8	4.8	•	5.3

Table II

Corporations with Net Income

ADMINISTRATIVE AND SUPPORT AND WASTE MANAGEMENT AND REMEDIATION SERVICES
562000

WASTE MANAGEMENT AND REMEDIATION SERVICES

MONEY AMOUNTS AND SIZE OF ASSETS IN THOUSANDS OF DOLLARS

Item Description for Accounting Period 7/05 Through 6/06	Total	Zero Assets	Under 500	500 to 1,000	1,000 to 5,000	5,000 to 10,000	10,000 to 25,000	25,000 to 50,000	50,000 to 100,000	100,000 to 250,000	250,000 to 500,000	500,000 to 2,500,000	2,500,000 and over
Number of Enterprises **1**	9599	417	6280	1416	1191	106	120	27	13	•	8	•	•
Revenues ($ in Thousands)													
Net Sales **2**	48042478	159460	5444280	2720556	6931200	1498191	3235096	947832	1141461	•	2141248	•	•
Interest **3**	668619	0	71	915	885	1045	3704	6239	4697	•	9957	•	•
Rents **4**	62492	0	0	253	108	1046	1389	848	321	•	0	•	•
Royalties **5**	24357	0	0	0	7239	0	0	0	0	•	0	•	•
Other Portfolio Income **6**	802809	13831	14903	28934	7580	17558	17943	5670	3120	•	2445	•	•
Other Receipts **7**	1228888	52776	8509	11837	39515	10268	57838	29501	9065	•	59980	•	•
Total Receipts **8**	50829643	226067	5467763	2762495	6986527	1528108	3315970	990090	1158664	•	2213630	•	•
Average Total Receipts **9**	5295	542	871	1951	5866	14416	27633	36670	89128	•	276704	•	•
Operating Costs/Operating Income (%)													
Cost of Operations **10**	41.5	39.8	37.6	35.2	39.8	52.3	59.6	55.5	54.3	•	39.0	•	•
Salaries and Wages **11**	14.3	2.3	13.2	17.1	11.2	6.7	7.9	7.7	10.5	•	10.9	•	•
Taxes Paid **12**	4.0	0.8	3.1	2.7	2.9	2.4	2.1	3.0	2.8	•	3.3	•	•
Interest Paid **13**	4.7	2.0	0.8	0.9	1.2	1.0	1.0	1.1	1.9	•	3.3	•	•
Depreciation **14**	5.3	4.3	3.1	3.4	3.1	2.4	3.4	3.3	5.1	•	4.4	•	•
Amortization and Depletion **15**	1.4	0.0	0.1	0.1	0.1	0.1	0.1	0.6	0.6	•	1.4	•	•
Pensions and Other Deferred Comp. **16**	0.5	0.0	0.2	0.3	0.6	0.2	0.5	0.4	0.5	•	1.6	•	•
Employee Benefits **17**	2.0	0.1	0.9	0.8	1.8	0.9	1.9	1.5	2.5	•	3.5	•	•
Advertising **18**	0.4	0.5	0.8	0.3	0.5	0.1	0.5	0.2	0.5	•	0.1	•	•
Other Expenses **19**	21.4	56.7	29.1	23.9	28.7	23.2	15.6	18.9	15.5	•	22.7	•	•
Officers' Compensation **20**	1.8	8.2	5.6	4.7	2.7	1.5	2.9	1.9	1.2	•	2.2	•	•
Operating Margin **21**	2.8	•	5.4	10.5	7.6	9.2	4.6	6.1	4.5	•	7.7	•	•
Operating Margin Before Officers' Comp. **22**	4.6	•	11.0	15.2	10.3	10.7	7.5	8.0	5.7	•	9.8	•	•

Selected Average Balance Sheet ($ in Thousands)

Net Receivables 23	625	0	11	70	556	1789	3648	6320	16450	94153
Inventories 24	42	0	5	10	38	313	414	767	593	1485
Net Property, Plant and Equipment 25	2182	0	69	242	899	2465	5269	9525	28470	75770
Total Assets 26	6014	0	137	687	2274	6381	14064	37034	74342	334654
Notes and Loans Payable 27	2338	0	89	228	988	1901	4767	8778	22897	109256
All Other Liabilities 28	2046	0	22	168	722	1891	5288	11432	22311	138806
Net Worth 29	1630	0	27	291	564	2590	4009	16823	29134	86592

Selected Financial Ratios (Times to 1)

Current Ratio 30	1.2	•	1.7	2.1	1.4	1.4	1.4	1.9	1.3	1.5
Quick Ratio 31	0.9	•	1.4	1.5	1.1	1.0	1.1	1.5	1.1	1.3
Net Sales to Working Capital 32	24.6	•	44.4	9.7	18.6	16.6	13.3	5.0	13.8	6.4
Coverage Ratio 33	2.8	14.4	8.6	14.0	8.1	11.8	7.8	10.9	4.2	4.3
Total Asset Turnover 34	0.8	•	6.3	2.8	2.6	2.2	1.9	0.9	1.2	0.8
Inventory Turnover 35	49.4	•	64.3	67.8	61.5	23.6	38.8	25.4	80.3	70.3
Receivables Turnover 36	8.4	•	101.8	23.0	11.3	8.5	8.1	5.8	5.9	5.7
Total Liabilities to Net Worth 37	2.7	•	4.1	1.4	3.0	1.5	2.5	1.2	1.6	2.9
Current Assets to Working Capital 38	6.2	•	2.4	1.9	3.4	3.7	3.4	2.1	4.1	3.1
Current Liabilities to Working Capital 39	5.2	•	1.4	0.9	2.4	2.7	2.4	1.1	3.1	2.1
Working Capital to Net Sales 40	0.0	•	0.0	0.1	0.1	0.1	0.1	0.2	0.1	0.2
Inventory to Working Capital 41	0.2	•	0.4	0.0	0.0	0.4	0.3	0.1	0.1	0.0
Total Receipts to Cash Flow 42	4.0	1.2	3.3	3.2	3.2	3.6	5.1	4.0	5.6	3.5
Cost of Goods to Cash Flow 43	1.7	0.5	1.2	1.1	1.3	1.9	3.1	2.2	3.0	1.4
Cash Flow to Total Debt 44	0.3	•	2.4	1.5	1.1	1.0	0.5	0.4	0.3	0.3

Selected Financial Factors (in Percentages)

Debt Ratio 45	72.9	•	80.5	57.6	75.2	59.4	71.5	54.6	60.8	74.1
Return on Total Assets 46	11.0	•	41.5	36.4	24.4	27.0	15.5	10.9	9.3	11.5
Return on Equity Before Income Taxes 47	25.9	•	188.4	79.7	86.2	60.9	47.5	21.9	18.2	34.1
Return on Equity After Income Taxes 48	22.2	•	187.6	79.5	83.1	57.6	44.3	18.3	17.3	30.3
Profit Margin (Before Income Tax) 49	8.4	27.1	5.8	12.1	8.4	11.2	7.1	10.5	6.0	11.0
Profit Margin (After Income Tax) 50	7.2	26.7	5.8	12.0	8.1	10.6	6.6	8.8	5.7	9.8

Table I

Corporations with and without Net Income

EDUCATIONAL SERVICES

MONEY AMOUNTS AND SIZE OF ASSETS IN THOUSANDS OF DOLLARS

Item Description for Accounting Period 7/05 Through 6/06	Total	Zero Assets	Under 500	500 to 1,000	1,000 to 5,000	5,000 to 10,000	10,000 to 25,000	25,000 to 50,000	50,000 to 100,000	100,000 to 250,000	250,000 to 500,000	500,000 to 2,500,000	2,500,000 and over
Number of Enterprises 1	44885	8251	34467	649	1266	83	83	24	25	25	6	7	0
Revenues ($ in Thousands)													
Net Sales 2	33247315	654381	8864547	633491	4043334	771304	1897087	1144556	1918184	4275192	1288922	7756317	0
Interest 3	129748	449	5989	1240	6498	2422	5495	3020	5076	32410	6684	60464	0
Rents 4	21288	217	2	0	1094	955	319	0	344	6528	952	10878	0
Royalties 5	214600	0	0	0	67957	105	772	0	61	786	67008	77912	0
Other Portfolio Income 6	123840	8598	1424	378	43627	1403	1007	179	13533	6489	4371	42827	0
Other Receipts 7	560570	609	111243	1793	62975	13952	37087	16433	46009	30421	14460	225592	0
Total Receipts 8	34297361	664254	8983205	636902	4225485	790141	1941767	1164188	1983207	4351826	1382397	8173990	0
Average Total Receipts 9	764	81	261	981	3338	9520	23395	48508	79328	174073	230400	1167713	•
Operating Costs/Operating Income (%)													
Cost of Operations 10	14.4	7.9	9.9	26.4	9.5	30.8	28.7	25.4	28.2	25.7	17.7	4.5	•
Salaries and Wages 11	28.0	13.8	23.0	20.6	31.3	31.8	25.2	29.1	27.3	25.5	32.4	34.6	•
Taxes Paid 12	3.5	4.4	4.0	3.3	4.2	4.2	3.1	4.2	3.1	2.9	3.8	2.6	•
Interest Paid 13	1.3	0.6	0.7	1.6	0.8	2.0	0.9	0.6	1.7	2.1	6.4	0.8	•
Depreciation 14	2.0	1.5	1.4	1.9	1.8	1.6	1.9	2.3	2.2	2.4	2.0	2.5	•
Amortization and Depletion 15	0.8	0.2	0.3	0.1	0.2	1.2	0.2	1.1	1.7	1.1	5.2	0.7	•
Pensions and Other Deferred Comp. 16	0.5	0.3	0.7	0.8	0.4	0.6	0.5	0.5	0.4	0.5	0.3	0.3	•
Employee Benefits 17	2.3	1.4	1.8	1.1	3.1	1.1	1.8	1.9	1.9	1.5	4.0	3.3	•
Advertising 18	5.6	2.5	2.0	1.1	5.0	2.1	5.6	5.7	4.6	5.1	2.6	12.1	•
Other Expenses 19	31.6	54.3	40.2	30.1	32.8	24.2	25.4	25.8	24.8	25.7	29.9	27.6	•
Officers' Compensation 20	5.2	10.5	11.6	11.2	5.6	4.4	4.1	1.0	1.7	1.2	1.9	1.5	•
Operating Margin 21	5.0	2.7	4.4	1.7	5.3	•	2.6	2.3	2.4	6.2	•	9.6	•
Operating Margin Before Officers' Comp. 22	10.2	13.1	16.0	13.0	10.9	0.4	6.7	3.3	4.1	7.4	•	11.1	•

Selected Average Balance Sheet ($ in Thousands)

Net Receivables 23	83	0	10	92	360	1755	3107	7009	12822	32443	81041	98382	•
Inventories 24	7	0	2	6	16	582	237	1204	899	1589	2566	5208	•
Net Property, Plant and Equipment 25	120	0	24	306	581	892	3850	7989	14756	30395	53941	225612	•
Total Assets 26	579	0	76	625	1893	7393	16234	32847	66774	159031	388998	1406499	•
Notes and Loans Payable 27	194	0	59	550	808	2448	3509	5023	18313	30536	123177	390480	•
All Other Liabilities 28	190	0	21	409	1085	4015	5485	10296	22968	61874	129287	316420	•
Net Worth 29	195	0	-4	-334	-0	929	7241	17529	25493	66621	136534	699600	•

Selected Financial Ratios (Times to 1)

Current Ratio 30	1.2	•	1.2	0.6	1.1	0.9	1.6	1.6	1.3	1.4	0.9	1.2	•
Quick Ratio 31	0.9	•	1.0	0.5	1.0	0.7	1.2	1.2	1.0	1.2	0.7	0.8	•
Net Sales to Working Capital 32	21.0	•	48.2	•	49.7	•	7.3	8.2	11.0	8.9	•	14.7	•
Coverage Ratio 33	7.4	7.7	8.9	2.4	13.1	0.3	6.5	7.9	4.2	4.7	1.1	20.3	•
Total Asset Turnover 34	1.3	•	3.4	1.6	1.7	1.3	1.4	1.5	1.1	1.1	0.6	0.8	•
Inventory Turnover 35	15.8	•	13.0	46.1	19.3	4.9	27.6	10.1	24.1	27.7	14.8	9.7	•
Receivables Turnover 36	8.6	•	24.6	14.8	8.9	4.2	7.7	7.2	6.8	6.0	3.2	7.7	•
Total Liabilities to Net Worth 37	2.0	•	•	•	•	7.0	1.2	0.9	1.6	1.4	1.8	1.0	•
Current Assets to Working Capital 38	6.4	•	6.1	•	17.3	•	2.6	2.8	4.2	3.7	•	5.4	•
Current Liabilities to Working Capital 39	5.4	•	5.1	•	16.3	•	1.6	1.8	3.2	2.7	•	4.4	•
Working Capital to Net Sales 40	0.0	•	0.0	•	0.0	•	0.1	0.1	0.1	0.1	•	0.1	•
Inventory to Working Capital 41	0.2	•	0.3	•	0.3	•	0.1	0.2	0.2	0.1	•	0.1	•
Total Receipts to Cash Flow 42	3.2	2.5	2.7	5.5	3.2	6.2	4.1	4.4	4.3	3.5	3.9	2.9	•
Cost of Goods to Cash Flow 43	0.5	0.2	0.3	1.5	0.3	1.9	1.2	1.1	1.2	0.9	0.7	0.1	•
Cash Flow to Total Debt 44	0.6	•	1.2	0.2	0.5	0.2	0.6	0.7	0.4	0.5	0.2	0.5	•

Selected Financial Factors (in Percentages)

Debt Ratio 45	66.3	•	105.4	153.4	100.0	87.4	55.4	46.6	61.8	58.1	64.9	50.3	•
Return on Total Assets 46	11.8	•	21.8	6.1	17.9	0.6	8.1	6.7	8.5	10.8	4.1	12.1	•
Return on Equity Before Income Taxes 47	30.4	•	•	•	•	•	15.4	11.0	17.0	20.3	1.5	23.1	•
Return on Equity After Income Taxes 48	23.4	•	•	•	•	•	12.7	9.4	14.4	13.8	0.9	14.8	•
Profit Margin (Before Income Tax) 49	8.0	4.1	5.7	2.3	9.8	4.9	4.0	5.6	7.9	0.9	0.9	14.6	•
Profit Margin (After Income Tax) 50	6.2	3.7	5.6	2.0	9.1	4.0	3.4	4.8	5.4	0.6	0.6	9.3	•

Table II

Corporations with Net Income

EDUCATIONAL SERVICES

MONEY AMOUNTS AND SIZE OF ASSETS IN THOUSANDS OF DOLLARS

Item Description for Accounting Period 7/05 Through 6/06		Total	Zero Assets	Under 500	500 to 1,000	1,000 to 5,000	5,000 to 10,000	10,000 to 25,000	25,000 to 50,000	50,000 to 100,000	100,000 to 250,000	250,000 to 500,000	500,000 to 2,500,000	2,500,000 and over
Number of Enterprises	1	24708	3300	19925	436	878	48	63	16	17	16	•	•	0
Revenues ($ in Thousands)														
Net Sales	2	27000218	402336	6525963	431841	3482534	622789	1559543	878938	1454695	3050897	•	•	0
Interest	3	104704	314	5148	1239	5450	1592	4396	1884	3230	23315	•	•	0
Rents	4	14693	217	2	0	1045	955	319	0	308	19	•	•	0
Royalties	5	213776	0	0	0	67957	105	772	0	61	786	•	•	0
Other Portfolio Income	6	112859	8580	1424	376	43627	235	580	122	13063	6072	•	•	0
Other Receipts	7	523229	578	99155	1058	59781	10656	39141	15169	42619	22920	•	•	0
Total Receipts	8	27969479	412025	6631692	434514	3660394	636332	1604751	896113	1513976	3104009	•	•	0
Average Total Receipts	9	1132	125	333	997	4169	13257	25472	56007	89057	194001	•	•	•
Operating Costs/Operating Income (%)														
Cost of Operations	10	14.0	7.7	9.1	24.3	10.1	32.1	33.1	20.3	28.1	28.4	•	•	•
Salaries and Wages	11	28.0	6.4	23.0	12.8	31.9	27.8	21.8	30.4	27.1	23.8	•	•	•
Taxes Paid	12	3.4	3.1	4.0	3.4	4.3	4.0	3.1	4.0	3.3	2.7	•	•	•
Interest Paid	13	0.8	0.3	0.5	1.7	0.5	0.3	0.5	0.7	1.6	1.1	•	•	•
Depreciation	14	1.7	0.3	1.0	2.6	1.5	1.0	1.2	2.2	1.9	1.8	•	•	•
Amortization and Depletion	15	0.5	0.1	0.2	0.2	0.0	1.4	0.1	0.5	0.9	0.6	•	•	•
Pensions and Other Deferred Comp.	16	0.5	0.2	0.9	1.2	0.5	0.7	0.6	0.7	0.4	0.2	•	•	•
Employee Benefits	17	2.5	1.2	1.9	0.3	3.4	0.5	1.8	1.9	1.9	1.4	•	•	•
Advertising	18	6.1	1.7	1.8	1.5	4.8	1.9	5.6	6.0	4.5	6.3	•	•	•
Other Expenses	19	28.0	49.6	34.6	31.2	27.7	18.4	20.0	27.2	24.0	20.9	•	•	•
Officers' Compensation	20	5.1	12.3	11.8	12.0	6.4	3.6	4.6	1.1	1.8	1.2	•	•	•
Operating Margin	21	9.5	17.1	11.1	8.8	9.0	8.3	7.6	5.0	4.6	11.7	•	•	•
Operating Margin Before Officers' Comp.	22	14.6	29.4	22.9	20.8	15.3	11.9	12.1	6.2	6.3	12.9	•	•	•

Selected Average Balance Sheet ($ in Thousands)

Net Receivables 23	107	0	15	111	436	2596	3680	6942	12091	37556
Inventories 24	9	0	2	7	22	900	238	1718	709	1444
Net Property, Plant and Equipment 25	167	0	23	183	691	796	3347	10248	16886	30399
Total Assets 26	785	0	84	601	2039	7671	14994	34447	66466	155495
Notes and Loans Payable 27	219	0	40	269	743	1059	2752	6671	15843	20576
All Other Liabilities 28	226	0	24	235	677	3383	5255	9072	25230	66690
Net Worth 29	341	0	19	97	619	3228	6987	18705	25393	68228

Selected Financial Ratios (Times to 1)

Current Ratio 30	1.4	•	1.3	1.1	1.7	1.5	1.8	1.7	1.2	1.4
Quick Ratio 31	1.1	•	1.2	0.9	1.6	1.1	1.4	1.3	0.9	1.3
Net Sales to Working Capital 32	11.9	•	30.4	37.5	8.3	6.6	6.8	6.9	16.6	7.6
Coverage Ratio 33	16.4	61.1	26.6	6.5	31.2	36.7	20.0	11.3	6.3	13.0
Total Asset Turnover 34	1.4	•	3.9	1.6	1.9	1.7	1.7	1.6	1.3	1.2
Inventory Turnover 35	16.1	•	12.8	32.2	18.6	4.6	34.3	6.5	33.9	37.5
Receivables Turnover 36	10.4	•	25.4	12.3	9.0	3.8	7.3	8.8	6.6	5.5
Total Liabilities to Net Worth 37	1.3	•	3.4	5.2	2.3	1.4	1.1	0.8	1.6	1.3
Current Assets to Working Capital 38	3.4	•	3.9	11.8	2.4	3.1	2.3	2.3	5.5	3.3
Current Liabilities to Working Capital 39	2.4	•	2.9	10.8	1.4	2.1	1.3	1.3	4.5	2.3
Working Capital to Net Sales 40	0.1	•	0.0	0.0	0.1	0.2	0.1	0.1	0.1	0.1
Inventory to Working Capital 41	0.1	•	0.2	0.1	0.1	0.3	0.1	0.2	0.2	0.1
Total Receipts to Cash Flow 42	3.0	2.0	2.5	4.0	3.2	4.4	4.0	3.8	4.0	3.4
Cost of Goods to Cash Flow 43	0.4	0.2	0.2	1.0	0.3	1.4	1.3	0.8	1.1	1.0
Cash Flow to Total Debt 44	0.8	•	2.0	0.5	0.9	0.7	0.8	0.9	0.5	0.6

Selected Financial Factors (in Percentages)

Debt Ratio 45	56.6	•	77.2	83.9	69.6	57.9	53.4	45.7	61.8	56.1
Return on Total Assets 46	19.2	•	51.7	18.3	28.4	18.1	18.1	12.2	13.1	17.8
Return on Equity Before Income Taxes 47	41.5	•	218.2	95.9	90.4	41.9	37.0	20.5	28.8	37.4
Return on Equity After Income Taxes 48	34.3	•	216.2	91.8	85.1	35.6	33.2	18.2	25.0	27.5
Profit Margin (Before Income Tax) 49	12.9	19.5	12.7	9.4	14.1	10.4	10.4	7.0	8.6	13.4
Profit Margin (After Income Tax) 50	10.7	18.8	12.6	9.0	13.3	8.9	9.4	6.2	7.4	9.9

Table I

Corporations with and without Net Income

OFFICES OF PHYSICIANS

MONEY AMOUNTS AND SIZE OF ASSETS IN THOUSANDS OF DOLLARS

Item Description for Accounting Period 7/05 Through 6/06	Total	Zero Assets	Under 500	500 to 1,000	1,000 to 5,000	5,000 to 10,000	10,000 to 25,000	25,000 to 50,000	50,000 to 100,000	100,000 to 250,000	250,000 to 500,000	500,000 to 2,500,000	2,500,000 and over
Number of Enterprises **1**	142409	15998	120232	3455	2217	318	99	53	21	12	0	4	0
Revenues ($ in Thousands)													
Net Sales **2**	212443149	4743455	124088955	17818552	33496915	9871360	4933117	4768764	2825061	2407082	0	7489887	0
Interest **3**	152149	1590	41447	14005	24809	10156	8299	7477	7397	13188	0	23779	0
Rents **4**	117716	157	58225	1518	12773	5803	1507	18472	9551	8284	0	1425	0
Royalties **5**	13324	0	0	0	0	0	983	0	12341	0	0	0	0
Other Portfolio Income **6**	205646	1979	47031	3265	29560	10763	732	21431	14560	2333	0	73990	0
Other Receipts **7**	5241690	194505	3231344	278125	656156	174862	97432	149567	107954	50503	0	301247	0
Total Receipts **8**	218173674	4941686	127467002	18115465	34220213	10072944	5042070	4965711	2976864	2481390	0	7890328	0
Average Total Receipts **9**	1532	309	1060	5243	15435	31676	50930	93693	141755	206782	•	1972582	•
Operating Costs/Operating Income (%)													
Cost of Operations **10**	4.7	9.3	2.9	2.3	8.5	8.1	14.6	11.5	10.9	9.8	•	1.0	•
Salaries and Wages **11**	27.3	15.3	24.2	24.9	34.8	24.7	32.0	37.8	31.8	35.4	•	46.7	•
Taxes Paid **12**	3.0	3.2	3.1	2.8	2.7	2.5	2.5	2.5	2.2	3.2	•	3.9	•
Interest Paid **13**	0.4	0.3	0.2	0.4	0.3	0.5	0.5	0.7	0.8	1.8	•	1.2	•
Depreciation **14**	1.0	0.8	0.8	0.8	1.4	1.9	1.1	1.4	1.2	2.3	•	0.3	•
Amortization and Depletion **15**	0.1	0.1	0.0	0.1	0.0	0.1	0.2	0.3	0.3	0.7	•	0.6	•
Pensions and Other Deferred Comp. **16**	3.4	2.2	3.8	2.6	3.3	1.9	1.8	2.4	0.9	1.8	•	5.8	•
Employee Benefits **17**	2.0	1.2	1.7	1.6	2.2	1.9	1.7	3.0	3.4	2.6	•	5.3	•
Advertising **18**	0.6	0.5	0.6	0.8	0.7	0.2	0.4	0.3	0.2	2.2	•	0.1	•
Other Expenses **19**	32.0	33.0	30.1	33.5	28.0	47.2	41.8	39.6	51.0	36.6	•	36.9	•
Officers' Compensation **20**	23.7	34.8	29.4	27.0	16.8	12.7	5.3	2.3	0.8	1.2	•	0.5	•
Operating Margin **21**	2.0	•	3.1	3.1	1.3	•	•	•	•	2.5	•	•	•
Operating Margin Before Officers' Comp. **22**	25.7	34.0	32.5	30.1	18.1	11.1	3.6	0.7	•	3.7	•	•	•

Selected Average Balance Sheet ($ in Thousands)

Net Receivables 23	22	0	2	34	261	1363	4401	9297	13430	26818	•	65628
Inventories 24	1	0	0	2	29	17	219	362	1070	673	•	1358
Net Property, Plant and Equipment 25	58	0	26	229	710	2894	3055	10804	18204	35788	•	29611
Total Assets 26	213	0	89	697	1981	7035	14487	35312	66797	174490	•	936487
Notes and Loans Payable 27	100	0	45	335	1063	4512	7649	13275	21384	54037	•	311022
All Other Liabilities 28	84	0	34	222	801	2016	6742	17171	29393	33385	•	524657
Net Worth 29	29	0	9	140	117	507	96	4866	16021	87068	•	100808

Selected Financial Ratios (Times to 1)

Current Ratio 30	1.0	•	1.0	1.3	0.9	1.3	1.1	0.8	1.2	1.2	•	0.7
Quick Ratio 31	0.9	•	0.9	1.1	0.8	1.1	0.8	0.7	0.9	1.1	•	0.5
Net Sales to Working Capital 32	•	•	•	66.6	•	40.5	113.8	•	30.3	21.5	•	2.7
Coverage Ratio 33	14.2	12.7	25.7	12.2	11.0	1.9	2.1	4.7	3.3	4.1	•	2.7
Total Asset Turnover 34	7.0	•	11.6	7.4	7.6	4.4	3.4	2.5	2.0	1.1	•	2.0
Inventory Turnover 35	52.7	•	93.5	78.9	44.3	143.6	33.3	28.6	13.7	29.1	•	13.7
Receivables Turnover 36	68.5	•	448.3	130.3	52.2	26.7	11.4	10.3	11.7	9.5	•	57.1
Total Liabilities to Net Worth 37	6.4	•	8.6	4.0	15.9	12.9	149.6	6.3	3.2	1.0	•	8.3
Current Assets to Working Capital 38	•	•	•	4.3	•	4.2	18.5	•	6.5	5.6	•	
Current Liabilities to Working Capital 39	•	•	3.3	3.3	•	3.2	17.5	•	5.5	4.6	•	
Working Capital to Net Sales 40	•	•	0.0	0.0	0.0	0.0	0.0	0.0	0.0	0.0	•	
Inventory to Working Capital 41	•	•	•	0.0	•	0.0	0.4	•	0.4	0.1	•	
Total Receipts to Cash Flow 42	3.1	3.1	3.2	3.0	3.7	2.4	2.6	2.6	2.0	2.6	•	2.9
Cost of Goods to Cash Flow 43	0.1	0.3	0.1	0.1	0.3	0.2	0.4	0.3	0.2	0.3	•	0.0
Cash Flow to Total Debt 44	2.6	•	4.0	3.1	2.2	2.0	1.3	1.1	1.3	0.9	•	0.8

Selected Financial Factors (in Percentages)

Debt Ratio 45	86.6	•	89.6	79.9	94.1	92.8	99.3	86.2	76.0	50.1	•	89.2
Return on Total Assets 46	35.3	•	70.5	38.5	28.8	3.9	3.5	8.0	5.3	8.5	•	6.4
Return on Equity Before Income Taxes 47	243.8	•	650.9	175.6	441.8	25.7	280.5	45.9	15.5	12.8	•	37.8
Return on Equity After Income Taxes 48	236.4	•	641.0	174.2	437.6	18.1	214.4	29.0	8.8	9.5	•	24.1
Profit Margin (Before Income Tax) 49	4.7	3.4	5.8	4.8	3.4	0.4	0.5	2.5	1.8	5.6	•	2.0
Profit Margin (After Income Tax) 50	4.5	3.4	5.7	4.7	3.4	0.3	0.4	1.6	1.0	4.1	•	1.3

Table II

Corporations with Net Income

OFFICES OF PHYSICIANS

MONEY AMOUNTS AND SIZE OF ASSETS IN THOUSANDS OF DOLLARS

Item Description for Accounting Period 7/05 Through 6/06		Total	Zero Assets	Under 500	500 to 1,000	1,000 to 5,000	5,000 to 10,000	10,000 to 25,000	25,000 to 50,000	50,000 to 100,000	100,000 to 250,000	250,000 to 500,000	500,000 to 2,500,000	2,500,000 and over
Number of Enterprises	1	97120	8357	84864	2165	1436	184	54	34	13	•	0	•	0
Revenues ($ in Thousands)														
Net Sales	2	144195738	2812752	86666950	11158896	18794574	7263292	2844180	3406015	1939458	•	0	•	0
Interest	3	102765	541	26355	7208	10094	8444	3468	7154	6313	•	0	•	0
Rents	4	92640	157	54400	722	9854	5741	143	14718	3394	•	0	•	0
Royalties	5	983	0	0	0	0	0	983	0	0	•	0	•	0
Other Portfolio Income	6	164796	1933	27986	2019	29026	852	723	14952	12139	•	0	•	0
Other Receipts	7	3901826	48087	2394999	170175	568468	149474	69278	68750	91448	•	0	•	0
Total Receipts	8	148458748	2863470	89170690	11339020	19412016	7427803	2918775	3511589	2052752	•	0	•	0
Average Total Receipts	9	1529	343	1051	5237	13518	40368	54051	103282	157904	•	•	•	•
Operating Costs/Operating Income (%)														
Cost of Operations	10	4.0	1.5	3.3	3.1	6.6	0.9	7.6	15.2	14.2	•	•	•	•
Salaries and Wages	11	24.9	15.4	20.7	22.9	31.6	27.1	38.2	35.5	27.2	•	•	•	•
Taxes Paid	12	3.0	3.7	3.0	2.7	3.0	2.0	2.8	2.5	2.4	•	•	•	•
Interest Paid	13	0.3	0.1	0.2	0.3	0.3	0.3	0.5	0.6	0.5	•	•	•	•
Depreciation	14	1.0	0.3	0.8	0.7	1.9	1.5	1.3	1.2	1.2	•	•	•	•
Amortization and Depletion	15	0.1	0.1	0.0	0.0	0.1	0.1	0.1	0.2	0.2	•	•	•	•
Pensions and Other Deferred Comp.	16	3.1	2.5	3.1	2.1	3.1	2.2	2.4	2.8	1.2	•	•	•	•
Employee Benefits	17	1.9	1.1	1.7	0.9	2.1	2.1	1.5	2.2	2.6	•	•	•	•
Advertising	18	0.7	0.5	0.7	0.7	1.1	0.3	0.6	0.3	0.2	•	•	•	•
Other Expenses	19	30.9	32.6	28.9	32.2	26.2	48.1	35.8	35.3	51.2	•	•	•	•
Officers' Compensation	20	25.1	32.8	31.2	26.9	20.3	14.9	8.2	2.5	0.6	•	•	•	•
Operating Margin	21	5.0	9.2	6.2	7.5	3.7	0.4	0.9	1.9	•	•	•	•	•
Operating Margin Before Officers' Comp.	22	30.1	42.1	37.4	34.3	24.0	15.3	9.2	4.5	•	•	•	•	•

Selected Average Balance Sheet ($ in Thousands)

Net Receivables 23	22	0	2	23	274	1107	3664	10700	11915
Inventories 24	1	0	0	2	20	23	316	439	2562
Net Property, Plant and Equipment 25	55	0	27	161	721	3064	3468	8386	17755
Total Assets 26	223	0	96	672	2017	7445	13212	35680	69151
Notes and Loans Payable 27	86	0	42	248	910	2996	5519	10554	12112
All Other Liabilities 28	78	0	30	149	791	1758	6039	12542	28724
Net Worth 29	59	0	23	275	316	2691	1654	12584	28315

Selected Financial Ratios (Times to 1)

Current Ratio 30	1.2	•	1.2	2.1	1.0	1.8	1.1	1.2	1.5
Quick Ratio 31	1.0	•	1.1	1.6	0.9	1.6	0.9	1.0	1.1
Net Sales to Working Capital 32	95.4	•	154.4	25.4	424.5	25.3	54.3	32.1	14.8
Coverage Ratio 33	24.7	93.5	40.4	28.9	22.0	9.6	7.5	10.0	10.7
Total Asset Turnover 34	6.7	•	10.7	7.7	6.5	5.3	4.0	2.8	2.2
Inventory Turnover 35	45.4	•	96.2	66.8	44.3	15.9	12.6	34.6	8.3
Receivables Turnover 36	80.6	•	398.9	155.6	51.9	61.6	14.6	10.3	25.0
Total Liabilities to Net Worth 37	2.8	•	3.2	1.4	5.4	1.8	7.0	1.8	1.4
Current Assets to Working Capital 38	6.3	•	7.1	1.9	29.3	2.3	8.4	6.7	3.2
Current Liabilities to Working Capital 39	5.3	•	6.1	0.9	28.3	1.3	7.4	5.7	2.2
Working Capital to Net Sales 40	0.0	•	0.0	0.0	0.0	0.0	0.0	0.0	0.1
Inventory to Working Capital 41	0.1	•	0.1	0.0	0.8	0.0	0.3	0.2	0.3
Total Receipts to Cash Flow 42	3.0	2.5	3.1	2.7	3.6	2.2	2.9	2.7	1.9
Cost of Goods to Cash Flow 43	0.1	0.0	0.1	0.1	0.2	0.0	0.2	0.4	0.3
Cash Flow to Total Debt 44	3.1	•	4.6	4.8	2.1	3.7	1.6	1.6	1.9

Selected Financial Factors (in Percentages)

Debt Ratio 45	73.7	•	76.1	59.1	84.3	63.9	87.5	64.7	59.1
Return on Total Assets 46	54.9	•	99.6	72.0	47.7	16.0	16.3	15.6	10.4
Return on Equity Before Income Taxes 47	200.6	•	407.1	170.1	290.1	39.6	112.7	39.9	23.0
Return on Equity After Income Taxes 48	195.2	•	401.4	169.0	287.7	37.2	105.6	29.7	16.9
Profit Margin (Before Income Tax) 49	7.9	11.0	9.1	9.1	7.0	2.7	3.5	5.0	4.4
Profit Margin (After Income Tax) 50	7.7	11.0	9.0	9.0	7.0	2.5	3.3	3.7	3.2

Table I

Corporations with and without Net Income

OFFICES OF DENTISTS

MONEY AMOUNTS AND SIZE OF ASSETS IN THOUSANDS OF DOLLARS

Item Description for Accounting Period 7/05 Through 6/06	Total	Zero Assets	Under 500	500 to 1,000	1,000 to 5,000	5,000 to 10,000	10,000 to 25,000	25,000 to 50,000	50,000 to 100,000	100,000 to 250,000	250,000 to 500,000	500,000 to 2,500,000	2,500,000 and over
Number of Enterprises **1**	69682	5677	59844	3535	614	0	3	6	0	3	0	0	0
Revenues ($ in Thousands)													
Net Sales **2**	52885586	1388040	41485435	6437181	2474027	0	114737	164377	0	821789	0	0	0
Interest **3**	15494	442	11341	3427	174	0	0	51	0	60	0	0	0
Rents **4**	8490	2080	5332	805	41	0	0	0	0	233	0	0	0
Royalties **5**	0	0	0	0	0	0	0	0	0	0	0	0	0
Other Portfolio Income **6**	76178	31367	35488	8744	98	0	263	218	0	1	0	0	0
Other Receipts **7**	593809	-813	521733	30451	39190	0	-1	3013	0	232	0	0	0
Total Receipts **8**	53579557	1421116	42059329	6480608	2513530	0	114999	167659	0	822315	0	0	0
Average Total Receipts **9**	769	250	703	1833	4094	•	38333	27943	•	274105	•	•	•
Operating Costs/Operating Income (%)													
Cost of Operations **10**	5.0	1.2	4.9	4.1	6.6	•	•	7.0	•	18.4	•	•	•
Salaries and Wages **11**	23.7	17.7	22.6	26.9	26.2	•	73.9	26.0	•	44.5	•	•	•
Taxes Paid **12**	3.7	3.8	3.7	3.8	3.9	•	4.4	4.5	•	3.8	•	•	•
Interest Paid **13**	0.9	0.1	0.8	1.9	0.9	•	•	3.1	•	1.4	•	•	•
Depreciation **14**	1.6	0.4	1.6	2.5	1.7	•	•	3.5	•	1.6	•	•	•
Amortization and Depletion **15**	0.4	•	0.3	0.9	0.2	•	•	1.6	•	2.1	•	•	•
Pensions and Other Deferred Comp. **16**	2.1	2.5	2.1	2.6	1.1	•	15.7	0.2	•	0.0	•	•	•
Employee Benefits **17**	1.0	0.6	1.0	0.9	0.5	•	5.1	2.2	•	1.6	•	•	•
Advertising **18**	1.5	0.6	1.5	1.7	1.0	•	•	5.9	•	2.2	•	•	•
Other Expenses **19**	33.7	54.5	33.7	27.0	43.9	•	5.4	42.2	•	21.4	•	•	•
Officers' Compensation **20**	20.1	16.1	21.3	21.2	7.0	•	1.1	9.9	•	0.1	•	•	•
Operating Margin **21**	6.3	2.5	6.5	6.5	7.3	•	•	•	•	3.0	•	•	•
Operating Margin Before Officers' Comp. **22**	26.4	18.7	27.8	27.7	14.2	•	3.9	•	•	3.2	•	•	•

Selected Average Balance Sheet ($ in Thousands)

Net Receivables 23	6	0	3	23	73	12009	4101	33058
Inventories 24	1	0	1	0	1	87	346	2859
Net Property, Plant and Equipment 25	64	0	52	228	573	0	8488	45669
Total Assets 26	166	0	129	640	1483	15867	32598	145866
Notes and Loans Payable 27	107	0	87	459	662	0	15634	39305
All Other Liabilities 28	27	0	20	74	288	12673	12107	47072
Net Worth 29	32	0	22	107	534	3195	4858	59489

Selected Financial Ratios (Times to 1)

Current Ratio 30	1.2	•	1.1	1.1	2.0	1.0	1.0	1.6
Quick Ratio 31	1.0	•	1.0	0.9	1.9	1.0	0.7	1.2
Net Sales to Working Capital 32	122.9	77.6	218.3	131.8	17.3	•	•	16.8
Coverage Ratio 33	9.1	•	10.7	4.8	11.3	•	•	3.3
Total Asset Turnover 34	4.6	•	5.4	2.8	2.7	2.4	0.8	1.9
Inventory Turnover 35	43.8	•	42.1	421.1	225.0	•	5.5	17.7
Receivables Turnover 36	120.6	•	257.7	94.7	49.4	3.7	6.5	16.6
Total Liabilities to Net Worth 37	4.2	•	4.9	5.0	1.8	4.0	5.7	1.5
Current Assets to Working Capital 38	7.4	•	11.5	9.8	2.0	•	•	2.8
Current Liabilities to Working Capital 39	6.4	•	10.5	8.8	1.0	•	•	1.8
Working Capital to Net Sales 40	0.0	•	0.0	0.0	0.1	•	•	0.1
Inventory to Working Capital 41	0.1	•	0.2	0.0	0.0	•	•	0.2
Total Receipts to Cash Flow 42	2.9	2.1	2.9	3.7	2.0	2048.9	3.4	5.5
Cost of Goods to Cash Flow 43	0.1	0.0	0.1	0.2	0.1	•	0.2	1.0
Cash Flow to Total Debt 44	2.0	•	2.3	0.9	2.1	0.0	0.3	0.6

Selected Financial Factors (in Percentages)

Debt Ratio 45	80.8	•	83.1	83.2	64.0	79.9	85.1	59.2
Return on Total Assets 46	39.0	•	46.5	25.8	26.4	•	•	8.4
Return on Equity Before Income Taxes 47	180.5	•	250.0	121.8	66.9	•	•	14.3
Return on Equity After Income Taxes 48	178.3	•	247.1	120.6	66.4	•	•	12.1
Profit Margin (Before Income Tax) 49	7.6	4.9	7.9	7.2	8.9	•	•	3.1
Profit Margin (After Income Tax) 50	7.5	4.8	7.8	7.1	8.8	•	•	2.6

369

Table II

Corporations with Net Income

OFFICES OF DENTISTS

MONEY AMOUNTS AND SIZE OF ASSETS IN THOUSANDS OF DOLLARS

Item Description for Accounting Period 7/05 Through 6/06	Total	Zero Assets	Under 500	500 to 1,000	1,000 to 5,000	5,000 to 10,000	10,000 to 25,000	25,000 to 50,000	50,000 to 100,000	100,000 to 250,000	250,000 to 500,000	500,000 to 2,500,000	2,500,000 and over
Number of Enterprises **1**	48333	2214	43222	2434	457	0	0	6	0	0	0	0	0
Revenues ($ in Thousands)													
Net Sales **2**	37907381	577424	30408092	4173344	2152438	0	0	596083	0	0	0	0	0
Interest **3**	6954	140	6364	288	152	0	0	10	0	0	0	0	0
Rents **4**	3314	0	3080	0	0	0	0	233	0	0	0	0	0
Royalties **5**	0	0	0	0	0	0	0	0	0	0	0	0	0
Other Portfolio Income **6**	42819	14520	27512	470	98	0	0	218	0	0	0	0	0
Other Receipts **7**	386065	123	313827	29850	39180	0	0	3088	0	0	0	0	0
Total Receipts **8**	38346533	592207	30758875	4203952	2191868	0	0	599632	0	0	0	0	0
Average Total Receipts **9**	793	267	712	1727	4796	.	.	99939	.	.	.	.	.
Operating Costs/Operating Income (%)													
Cost of Operations **10**	4.9	0.0	4.8	5.5	6.0	.	.	4.3	.	.	.	.	.
Salaries and Wages **11**	23.9	21.0	22.5	29.6	26.2	.	.	47.9	.	.	.	.	.
Taxes Paid **12**	3.6	4.5	3.5	4.0	3.9	.	.	4.3	.	.	.	.	.
Interest Paid **13**	0.9	0.0	0.8	2.0	0.3	.	.	0.8	.	.	.	.	.
Depreciation **14**	1.3	0.6	1.3	1.8	0.7	.	.	2.2	.	.	.	.	.
Amortization and Depletion **15**	0.4	.	0.3	0.8	0.2	.	.	1.4	.	.	.	.	.
Pensions and Other Deferred Comp. **16**	1.7	3.0	1.7	2.3	0.9	.	.	0.0	.	.	.	.	.
Employee Benefits **17**	0.9	0.4	0.9	0.8	0.5	.	.	1.3	.	.	.	.	.
Advertising **18**	1.5	0.2	1.5	1.8	1.0	.	.	2.9	.	.	.	.	.
Other Expenses **19**	32.9	39.5	33.0	24.8	46.5	.	.	29.1	.	.	.	.	.
Officers' Compensation **20**	17.4	14.6	19.0	15.0	4.7	.	.	0.5	.	.	.	.	.
Operating Margin **21**	10.6	16.1	10.5	11.6	9.1	.	.	5.5	.	.	.	.	.
Operating Margin Before Officers' Comp. **22**	27.9	30.8	29.5	26.5	13.8	.	.	6.0	.	.	.	.	.

Selected Average Balance Sheet ($ in Thousands)

Net Receivables 23	8	0	3	30	98	18479
Inventories 24	1	0	1	0	2	552
Net Property, Plant and Equipment 25	57	0	49	163	237	23201
Total Assets 26	173	0	133	630	1426	69381
Notes and Loans Payable 27	96	0	80	399	285	14748
All Other Liabilities 28	27	0	18	71	365	28561
Net Worth 29	50	0	35	160	776	26072

Selected Financial Ratios (Times to 1)

Current Ratio 30	1.4	•	1.3	1.3	2.1	1.6
Quick Ratio 31	1.2	•	1.2	1.0	2.0	1.2
Net Sales to Working Capital 32	55.6	•	77.3	49.2	14.5	10.8
Coverage Ratio 33	14.0	557.6	15.3	7.3	34.7	9.0
Total Asset Turnover 34	4.5	•	5.3	2.7	3.3	1.4
Inventory Turnover 35	45.3	•	43.6	518.3	177.7	7.7
Receivables Turnover 36	98.7	•	196.3	74.9	43.0	10.8
Total Liabilities to Net Worth 37	2.5	•	2.8	2.9	0.8	1.7
Current Assets to Working Capital 38	3.8	•	4.5	4.8	1.9	2.7
Current Liabilities to Working Capital 39	2.8	•	3.5	3.8	0.9	1.7
Working Capital to Net Sales 40	0.0	•	0.0	0.0	0.1	0.1
Inventory to Working Capital 41	0.1	•	0.1	•	•	0.1
Total Receipts to Cash Flow 42	2.6	2.2	2.6	3.3	1.8	3.7
Cost of Goods to Cash Flow 43	0.1	0.0	0.1	0.2	0.1	0.2
Cash Flow to Total Debt 44	2.4	•	2.7	1.1	4.0	0.6

Selected Financial Factors (in Percentages)

Debt Ratio 45	71.2	•	73.9	74.7	45.6	62.4
Return on Total Assets 46	57.3	•	66.0	38.8	37.1	9.8
Return on Equity Before Income Taxes 47	184.8	•	236.0	132.2	66.2	23.2
Return on Equity After Income Taxes 48	182.7	•	233.4	131.0	65.8	20.5
Profit Margin (Before Income Tax) 49	11.7	18.7	11.7	12.3	10.9	6.1
Profit Margin (After Income Tax) 50	11.6	18.5	11.5	12.2	10.8	5.4

Table I

Corporations with and without Net Income

OFFICES OF OTHER HEALTH PRACTITIONERS

MONEY AMOUNTS AND SIZE OF ASSETS IN THOUSANDS OF DOLLARS

Item Description for Accounting Period 7/05 Through 6/06		Total	Zero Assets	Under 500	500 to 1,000	1,000 to 5,000	5,000 to 10,000	10,000 to 25,000	25,000 to 50,000	50,000 to 100,000	100,000 to 250,000	250,000 to 500,000	500,000 to 2,500,000	2,500,000 and over
Number of Enterprises	1	92004	15317	75044	594	951	16	34	22	15	12	0	0	0
Revenues ($ in Thousands)														
Net Sales	2	41464457	1289722	24627609	1187785	5413544	291865	1752403	778380	1146453	4976694	0	0	0
Interest	3	69508	434	3000	183	3878	3425	2535	6085	5982	43987	0	0	0
Rents	4	12984	0	3430	329	2448	0	618	3339	2268	554	0	0	0
Royalties	5	83	0	83	0	0	0	0	0	0	0	0	0	0
Other Portfolio Income	6	76460	14101	4085	0	3190	515	821	17509	1179	35062	0	0	0
Other Receipts	7	1119644	25778	90368	17327	39254	829	70688	687570	132856	54971	0	0	0
Total Receipts	8	42743136	1330035	24728575	1205624	5462314	296634	1827065	1492883	1288738	5111268	0	0	0
Average Total Receipts	9	465	87	330	2030	5744	18540	53737	67858	85916	425939	.	.	.
Operating Costs/Operating Income (%)														
Cost of Operations	10	12.6	10.3	13.0	6.2	11.5	14.4	39.9	6.9	2.2	7.5	.	.	.
Salaries and Wages	11	22.6	14.9	20.2	32.7	32.1	24.8	8.7	41.3	24.6	25.3	.	.	.
Taxes Paid	12	3.1	3.2	3.5	4.0	2.8	4.6	1.8	3.9	2.6	1.5	.	.	.
Interest Paid	13	0.8	0.8	0.5	0.6	0.7	0.5	0.7	2.1	2.3	1.8	.	.	.
Depreciation	14	1.1	1.0	1.1	0.9	1.2	1.6	0.4	2.4	1.5	0.7	.	.	.
Amortization and Depletion	15	0.3	0.3	0.1	0.1	0.2	0.0	0.1	0.7	0.6	0.9	.	.	.
Pensions and Other Deferred Comp.	16	1.0	0.2	1.3	1.0	1.2	0.5	0.2	1.5	0.2	0.1	.	.	.
Employee Benefits	17	1.8	0.5	1.2	1.5	3.4	1.6	1.5	5.7	1.7	3.0	.	.	.
Advertising	18	1.4	1.2	1.8	1.3	1.0	1.5	0.7	0.4	0.8	0.7	.	.	.
Other Expenses	19	39.2	52.2	30.3	26.5	41.8	25.5	45.5	117.1	72.9	59.1	.	.	.
Officers' Compensation	20	11.6	14.5	16.8	15.3	3.9	15.0	0.4	1.3	1.1	0.2	.	.	.
Operating Margin	21	4.4	0.8	10.0	9.7	0.1	10.1	0.1	.	.	.	.	.	.
Operating Margin Before Officers' Comp.	22	16.0	15.4	26.9	25.1	4.0	25.1	0.5	.	.	.	.	.	.

Selected Average Balance Sheet ($ in Thousands)

Net Receivables 23	21	0	5	136	371	2875	4200	8148	10276	45985
Inventories 24	2	0	2	34	7	99	432	458	277	1078
Net Property, Plant and Equipment 25	29	0	20	112	474	1021	2429	5950	13548	20232
Total Assets 26	124	0	61	597	1707	6930	15159	33683	66538	207184
Notes and Loans Payable 27	54	0	30	208	889	1222	4313	8648	22095	91044
All Other Liabilities 28	38	0	13	40	347	2412	7073	18323	19091	98984
Net Worth 29	32	0	18	349	471	3296	3773	6712	25352	17156

Selected Financial Ratios (Times to 1)

Current Ratio 30	1.5	•	1.7	8.7	1.5	2.0	1.5	1.2	1.8	1.1
Quick Ratio 31	1.2	•	1.4	7.8	1.2	1.9	1.2	0.8	1.3	0.8
Net Sales to Working Capital 32	22.3	•	28.3	6.3	20.7	6.7	14.6	12.1	7.0	34.5
Coverage Ratio 33	10.4	5.8	21.3	18.5	2.4	25.5	7.2	5.0	1.9	2.1
Total Asset Turnover 34	3.6	•	5.4	3.4	3.3	2.6	3.4	1.1	1.1	2.0
Inventory Turnover 35	24.1	•	21.8	3.6	98.8	26.6	47.6	5.3	6.0	28.7
Receivables Turnover 36	23.2	•	67.9	9.9	19.3	4.1	10.7	4.7	8.1	10.3
Total Liabilities to Net Worth 37	2.9	•	2.3	0.7	2.6	1.1	3.0	4.0	1.6	11.1
Current Assets to Working Capital 38	3.0	•	2.5	1.1	3.1	2.0	2.9	6.7	2.3	8.3
Current Liabilities to Working Capital 39	2.0	•	1.5	0.1	2.1	1.0	1.9	5.7	1.3	7.3
Working Capital to Net Sales 40	0.0	•	0.0	0.2	0.0	0.1	0.1	0.1	0.1	0.0
Inventory to Working Capital 41	0.1	•	0.2	0.1	0.0	0.0	0.2	0.2	0.0	0.1
Total Receipts to Cash Flow 42	2.5	2.3	3.1	3.0	2.6	3.1	2.1	0.9	1.4	1.7
Cost of Goods to Cash Flow 43	0.3	0.2	0.4	0.2	0.3	0.5	0.8	0.1	0.0	0.1
Cash Flow to Total Debt 44	1.9	•	2.4	2.7	1.7	1.6	2.2	1.5	1.3	1.3

Selected Financial Factors (in Percentages)

Debt Ratio 45	74.2	•	70.0	41.5	72.4	52.4	75.1	80.1	61.9	91.7
Return on Total Assets 46	30.1	•	58.7	39.8	5.8	32.1	17.2	11.2	4.9	7.5
Return on Equity Before Income Taxes 47	105.3	•	186.1	64.4	12.1	64.9	59.6	44.9	6.0	47.8
Return on Equity After Income Taxes 48	102.2	•	184.6	64.4	11.5	46.9	48.2	40.4	2.3	37.6
Profit Margin (Before Income Tax) 49	7.5	4.0	10.4	11.2	1.0	11.7	4.4	8.5	2.0	2.0
Profit Margin (After Income Tax) 50	7.3	3.9	10.4	11.2	1.0	8.5	3.5	7.7	0.8	1.6

371

Table II
Corporations with Net Income

OFFICES OF OTHER HEALTH PRACTITIONERS

MONEY AMOUNTS AND SIZE OF ASSETS IN THOUSANDS OF DOLLARS

Item Description for Accounting Period 7/05 Through 6/06	Total	Zero Assets	Under 500	500 to 1,000	1,000 to 5,000	5,000 to 10,000	10,000 to 25,000	25,000 to 50,000	50,000 to 100,000	100,000 to 250,000	250,000 to 500,000	500,000 to 2,500,000	2,500,000 and over
Number of Enterprises **1**	65369	•	55834	484	556	•	28	•	10	9	0	0	0
Revenues ($ in Thousands)													
Net Sales **2**	27272768	•	18036868	1158259	1921613	•	1214171	•	670509	2597648	0	0	0
Interest **3**	25562	•	2426	1	1358	•	1916	•	4769	8261	0	0	0
Rents **4**	4630	•	8	0	0	•	618	•	2058	554	0	0	0
Royalties **5**	83	•	83	0	0	•	0	•	0	0	0	0	0
Other Portfolio Income **6**	68731	•	4084	0	2821	•	821	•	826	28126	0	0	0
Other Receipts **7**	524207	•	79963	17327	28740	•	47582	•	127114	44648	0	0	0
Total Receipts **8**	27895981	•	18123432	1175587	1954532	•	1265108	•	805276	2679237	0	0	0
Average Total Receipts **9**	427	•	325	2429	3515	•	45182	•	80528	297693	•	•	•
Operating Costs/Operating Income (%)													
Cost of Operations **10**	13.3	•	10.6	6.4	25.7	•	57.6	•	0.8	13.9	•	•	•
Salaries and Wages **11**	21.0	•	18.6	32.9	20.3	•	12.0	•	28.4	32.9	•	•	•
Taxes Paid **12**	3.2	•	3.4	3.9	3.1	•	2.6	•	3.1	1.9	•	•	•
Interest Paid **13**	0.7	•	0.4	0.4	0.9	•	1.0	•	2.5	1.2	•	•	•
Depreciation **14**	1.1	•	1.0	0.9	1.6	•	0.6	•	2.0	1.1	•	•	•
Amortization and Depletion **15**	0.3	•	0.2	0.1	0.6	•	0.1	•	0.7	0.9	•	•	•
Pensions and Other Deferred Comp. **16**	1.1	•	1.3	1.0	1.1	•	0.3	•	0.2	0.1	•	•	•
Employee Benefits **17**	1.7	•	1.1	1.5	1.9	•	2.1	•	2.6	5.1	•	•	•
Advertising **18**	1.7	•	1.9	1.2	2.2	•	1.0	•	0.3	1.2	•	•	•
Other Expenses **19**	31.8	•	29.1	26.1	30.2	•	18.8	•	70.5	39.9	•	•	•
Officers' Compensation **20**	12.7	•	16.7	15.4	5.7	•	0.5	•	1.2	0.5	•	•	•
Operating Margin **21**	11.4	•	15.7	10.2	6.6	•	3.3	•	•	1.4	•	•	•
Operating Margin Before Officers' Comp. **22**	24.1	•	32.4	25.6	12.3	•	3.8	•	•	1.9	•	•	•

Selected Average Balance Sheet ($ in Thousands)

Net Receivables 23	19	5	167	250	3375	11170	39030
Inventories 24	3	2	42	19	444	333	1165
Net Property, Plant and Equipment 25	29	19	82	379	2922	18179	24526
Total Assets 26	126	65	605	1598	15853	68716	176260
Notes and Loans Payable 27	41	21	187	688	5237	25425	49678
All Other Liabilities 28	36	12	47	397	7420	16646	77318
Net Worth 29	49	31	371	514	3195	26645	49263

Selected Financial Ratios (Times to 1)

Current Ratio 30	1.7	1.9	8.6	1.5	1.5	1.6	1.3
Quick Ratio 31	1.3	1.7	7.7	1.1	1.1	1.4	0.9
Net Sales to Working Capital 32	15.9	21.5	6.4	15.1	11.8	7.6	14.3
Coverage Ratio 33	21.9	39.0	32.4	10.0	8.4	4.1	4.9
Total Asset Turnover 34	3.3	5.0	4.0	2.2	2.7	1.0	1.6
Inventory Turnover 35	21.2	16.6	3.6	46.8	56.3	1.7	34.4
Receivables Turnover 36	23.5	65.6	12.4	18.1	12.9	7.0	14.8
Total Liabilities to Net Worth 37	1.6	1.1	0.6	2.1	4.0	1.6	2.6
Current Assets to Working Capital 38	2.5	2.1	1.1	3.2	2.9	2.7	4.9
Current Liabilities to Working Capital 39	1.5	1.1	0.1	2.2	1.9	1.7	3.9
Working Capital to Net Sales 40	0.1	0.0	0.2	0.1	0.1	0.1	0.1
Inventory to Working Capital 41	0.1	0.2	0.1	0.1	0.2	0.0	0.1
Total Receipts to Cash Flow 42	2.6	2.7	3.0	3.0	4.0	1.4	2.4
Cost of Goods to Cash Flow 43	0.3	0.3	0.2	0.8	2.3	0.0	0.3
Cash Flow to Total Debt 44	2.1	3.6	3.4	1.1	0.8	1.2	1.0

Selected Financial Factors (in Percentages)

Debt Ratio 45	61.1	51.6	38.7	67.9	79.8	61.2	72.1
Return on Total Assets 46	47.7	83.3	47.7	20.1	23.3	9.8	9.4
Return on Equity Before Income Taxes 47	117.0	167.8	75.5	56.2	101.6	19.2	26.8
Return on Equity After Income Taxes 48	114.2	166.5	75.5	55.3	85.3	13.9	22.0
Profit Margin (Before Income Tax) 49	13.7	16.2	11.7	8.4	7.5	7.6	4.6
Profit Margin (After Income Tax) 50	13.4	16.1	11.7	8.2	6.3	5.5	3.8

Table I

Corporations with and without Net Income

OUTPATIENT CARE CENTERS

MONEY AMOUNTS AND SIZE OF ASSETS IN THOUSANDS OF DOLLARS

Item Description for Accounting Period 7/05 Through 6/06	Total	Zero Assets	Under 500	500 to 1,000	1,000 to 5,000	5,000 to 10,000	10,000 to 25,000	25,000 to 50,000	50,000 to 100,000	100,000 to 250,000	250,000 to 500,000	500,000 to 2,500,000	2,500,000 and over
Number of Enterprises **1**	6393	240	5526	162	361	28	33	14	8	4	9	4	4

Revenues ($ in Thousands)

	Total	Zero Assets	Under 500	500 to 1,000	1,000 to 5,000	5,000 to 10,000	10,000 to 25,000	25,000 to 50,000	50,000 to 100,000	100,000 to 250,000	250,000 to 500,000	500,000 to 2,500,000	2,500,000 and over
Net Sales **2**	29457648	16407	3418736	396967	2591422	1192471	706473	1576495	700283	1202320	2633391	3471308	11551374
Interest **3**	126861	17	205	5	6558	1672	1950	5942	4532	344	21184	18362	66091
Rents **4**	86536	336	0	0	695	0	0	535	679	0	1469	531	82291
Royalties **5**	77462	0	0	0	0	0	1136	0	0	0	0	73000	3326
Other Portfolio Income **6**	840942	14443	0	10	3016	5543	1076	151	195	213	8523	544	807231
Other Receipts **7**	750036	9	23081	278	8343	3041	111268	18814	24818	125	129723	278235	152296
Total Receipts **8**	31339485	31212	3442022	397260	2610034	1202727	821903	1601937	730507	1203002	2794290	3841980	12662609
Average Total Receipts **9**	4902	130	623	2452	7230	42955	24906	114424	91313	300750	310477	960495	3165652

Operating Costs/Operating Income (%)

	Total	Zero Assets	Under 500	500 to 1,000	1,000 to 5,000	5,000 to 10,000	10,000 to 25,000	25,000 to 50,000	50,000 to 100,000	100,000 to 250,000	250,000 to 500,000	500,000 to 2,500,000	2,500,000 and over
Cost of Operations **10**	31.3	•	12.0	37.2	15.7	0.1	32.9	48.6	20.3	0.4	40.7	42.6	39.5
Salaries and Wages **11**	21.0	57.1	16.0	19.6	32.7	34.1	21.6	13.2	19.4	14.7	29.0	21.0	18.4
Taxes Paid **12**	3.5	9.4	2.8	3.9	3.4	1.6	2.5	1.1	2.5	1.3	2.5	7.4	3.6
Interest Paid **13**	2.9	1.3	0.7	1.7	0.7	0.4	2.4	0.2	1.6	2.2	1.5	2.2	5.5
Depreciation **14**	1.6	3.7	0.8	3.4	0.9	0.3	2.2	0.5	2.8	1.0	1.5	1.6	2.2
Amortization and Depletion **15**	1.5	0.4	0.0	0.1	0.1	0.0	0.7	0.0	1.1	0.5	2.1	1.7	2.6
Pensions and Other Deferred Comp. **16**	0.5	0.2	0.4	0.2	1.1	3.8	0.2	0.1	1.8	0.0	0.2	0.1	0.4
Employee Benefits **17**	2.5	3.6	2.1	3.7	4.2	1.7	2.1	1.4	1.4	0.8	1.4	1.9	3.2
Advertising **18**	0.4	2.1	1.0	0.3	0.4	0.1	1.0	0.7	0.8	0.4	1.0	0.2	0.1
Other Expenses **19**	31.6	106.7	43.5	21.2	29.1	58.0	62.0	30.9	52.7	74.1	16.6	24.1	24.3
Officers' Compensation **20**	2.1	19.2	8.7	2.2	7.1	1.0	1.9	0.6	1.0	0.3	1.3	0.5	0.3
Operating Margin **21**	1.0	•	12.0	6.6	4.6	•	•	2.7	•	4.5	2.2	•	•
Operating Margin Before Officers' Comp. **22**	3.1	•	20.7	8.8	11.8	•	3.3	4.8	4.8	3.4	•	•	0.1

Selected Average Balance Sheet ($ in Thousands)

Net Receivables 23	678	5	0	520	139	3995	6566	6240	8242	40624	298280	562774
Inventories 24	65	1	0	87	0	808	364	650	739	2141	3533	75637
Net Property, Plant and Equipment 25	664	42	501	319	277	4216	3739	14320	57988	30651	157717	592374
Total Assets 26	5882	97	781	1968	7013	15584	33485	71064	196069	344909	1169034	6480362
Notes and Loans Payable 27	1786	108	590	573	3672	7221	1746	20462	75177	85776	487398	1741543
All Other Liabilities 28	2185	14	61	650	3844	5328	21774	28541	73913	62064	236256	2758722
Net Worth 29	1911	-25	129	746	-503	3035	9965	22061	46978	197069	445380	1980096

Selected Financial Ratios (Times to 1)

Current Ratio 30	1.4	0.4	0.4	1.8	0.8	1.3	1.1	0.7	1.1	1.8	1.4	1.7
Quick Ratio 31	1.2	0.4	0.4	1.3	0.5	1.0	0.9	0.6	1.0	1.3	1.2	1.4
Net Sales to Working Capital 32	9.1	•	•	10.9	•	10.5	74.9	•	37.8	7.9	6.8	4.8
Coverage Ratio 33	3.5	18.2	5.0	9.0	0.4	•	26.5	0.4	3.1	6.4	4.3	2.7
Total Asset Turnover 34	0.8	6.4	3.1	3.6	6.1	1.4	3.4	1.2	1.5	0.8	0.7	0.4
Inventory Turnover 35	22.3	66.2	•	12.9	•	8.7	150.2	27.3	1.5	55.6	104.7	15.1
Receivables Turnover 36	6.9	146.1	55.8	14.3	139.0	5.9	18.7	15.2	28.0	8.9	2.7	5.2
Total Liabilities to Net Worth 37	2.1	5.0	5.0	1.6	•	4.1	2.4	2.2	3.2	0.8	1.6	2.3
Current Assets to Working Capital 38	3.2	•	•	2.3	•	4.3	12.9	•	8.0	2.3	3.7	2.5
Current Liabilities to Working Capital 39	2.2	•	•	1.3	•	3.3	11.9	•	7.0	1.3	2.7	1.5
Working Capital to Net Sales 40	0.1	•	•	0.1	•	0.1	0.0	•	0.0	0.1	0.1	0.2
Inventory to Working Capital 41	0.1	•	•	0.2	•	0.7	0.2	•	0.1	0.1	0.0	0.1
Total Receipts to Cash Flow 42	3.1	2.1	4.3	3.3	1.7	2.2	3.0	2.1	1.3	4.4	3.4	4.5
Cost of Goods to Cash Flow 43	1.0	0.3	1.6	0.5	0.0	0.7	1.5	0.4	0.0	1.8	1.5	1.8
Cash Flow to Total Debt 44	0.4	2.4	0.9	1.8	3.2	0.8	1.6	0.9	1.5	0.4	0.3	0.1

Selected Financial Factors (in Percentages)

Debt Ratio 45	67.5	125.3	83.4	62.1	107.2	80.5	70.2	69.0	76.0	42.9	61.9	69.4
Return on Total Assets 46	8.1	85.4	26.4	22.0	1.0	•	14.9	0.7	10.2	8.2	7.1	6.7
Return on Equity Before Income Taxes 47	17.8	•	127.0	51.6	•	20.6	•	48.2	28.9	12.1	14.4	13.7
Return on Equity After Income Taxes 48	11.8	•	94.6	50.9	•	21.1	•	43.2	26.6	7.7	10.0	7.1
Profit Margin (Before Income Tax) 49	7.4	12.6	6.7	5.4	•	4.3	•	4.5	8.2	7.4	9.4	
Profit Margin (After Income Tax) 50	4.9	12.5	5.0	5.3	•	3.8	•	4.2	5.2	5.1	4.9	

Table II
Corporations with Net Income

OUTPATIENT CARE CENTERS

MONEY AMOUNTS AND SIZE OF ASSETS IN THOUSANDS OF DOLLARS

Item Description for Accounting Period 7/05 Through 6/06	Total	Zero Assets	Under 500	500 to 1,000	1,000 to 5,000	5,000 to 10,000	10,000 to 25,000	25,000 to 50,000	50,000 to 100,000	100,000 to 250,000	250,000 to 500,000	500,000 to 2,500,000	2,500,000 and over
Number of Enterprises 1	4453	•	4017	109	277	•	6	•	0	•	6	4	•
Revenues ($ in Thousands)													
Net Sales 2	24780533	•	3306812	273796	2087360	•	130513	•	0	•	2306027	3471308	•
Interest 3	82791	•	191	5	2201	•	361	•	0	•	19946	18362	•
Rents 4	3907	•	0	0	95	•	0	•	0	•	1469	531	•
Royalties 5	76326	•	0	0	0	•	0	•	0	•	0	73000	•
Other Portfolio Income 6	832651	•	0	10	0	•	395	•	0	•	8436	544	•
Other Receipts 7	478147	•	23082	22	7303	•	3	•	0	•	127445	278235	•
Total Receipts 8	26254355	•	3330085	273833	2096959	•	131272	•	0	•	2463323	3841980	•
Average Total Receipts 9	5896	•	829	2512	7570	•	21879	•	•	•	410554	960495	•
Operating Costs/Operating Income (%)													
Cost of Operations 10	34.6	•	12.5	24.6	19.4	•	4.3	•	•	•	42.6	42.6	•
Salaries and Wages 11	19.6	•	15.0	27.7	34.2	•	45.7	•	•	•	28.5	21.0	•
Taxes Paid 12	3.5	•	2.5	3.4	3.6	•	4.4	•	•	•	2.5	7.4	•
Interest Paid 13	2.1	•	0.6	2.0	0.4	•	1.3	•	•	•	1.3	2.2	•
Depreciation 14	1.4	•	0.7	3.9	0.7	•	3.8	•	•	•	1.2	1.6	•
Amortization and Depletion 15	1.3	•	0.0	0.1	0.0	•	0.5	•	•	•	1.6	1.7	•
Pensions and Other Deferred Comp. 16	0.6	•	0.4	•	1.2	•	0.2	•	•	•	0.2	0.1	•
Employee Benefits 17	2.6	•	2.2	4.9	4.8	•	3.2	•	•	•	1.2	1.9	•
Advertising 18	0.4	•	1.0	0.2	0.3	•	1.2	•	•	•	1.1	0.2	•
Other Expenses 19	25.5	•	41.6	23.3	18.5	•	27.1	•	•	•	15.6	24.1	•
Officers' Compensation 20	2.2	•	9.0	0.0	7.3	•	1.1	•	•	•	1.0	0.5	•
Operating Margin 21	6.2	•	14.7	9.9	9.4	•	7.3	•	•	•	3.2	•	•
Operating Margin Before Officers' Comp. 22	8.4	•	23.7	9.9	16.8	•	8.4	•	•	•	4.2	•	•

Selected Average Balance Sheet ($ in Thousands)

Net Receivables 23	822	7	0	456	3970	41958	298280
Inventories 24	71	2	0	113	449	1749	24794
Net Property, Plant and Equipment 25	715	46	399	326	8123	33576	157717
Total Assets 26	7285	110	746	1711	15553	346767	1169034
Notes and Loans Payable 27	1532	44	726	394	10153	62615	487398
All Other Liabilities 28	2706	12	91	508	3156	74008	236256
Net Worth 29	3047	53	-71	810	2245	210144	445380

Selected Financial Ratios (Times to 1)

Current Ratio 30	1.7	1.5	0.4	1.6	1.6	1.7	1.4
Quick Ratio 31	1.4	1.2	0.4	1.3	1.3	1.2	1.2
Net Sales to Working Capital 32	7.4	70.3		15.6	9.1	9.7	6.8
Coverage Ratio 33	6.7	28.2	5.9	26.5	7.3	8.5	4.3
Total Asset Turnover 34	0.8	7.5	3.4	4.4	1.4	1.1	0.7
Inventory Turnover 35	27.1	66.3		12.9	2.1	93.6	14.9
Receivables Turnover 36	7.8	235.9	30421.8	17.4	3.1	9.6	2.1
Total Liabilities to Net Worth 37	1.4	1.1	5.9	1.1	5.9	0.7	1.6
Current Assets to Working Capital 38	2.5	3.1	2.6	2.6	2.7	2.4	3.7
Current Liabilities to Working Capital 39	1.5	2.1	1.6	1.6	1.7	1.4	2.7
Working Capital to Net Sales 40	0.1	0.0	0.1	0.1	0.1	0.1	0.1
Inventory to Working Capital 41	0.1	0.1	0.3	0.3	0.3	0.0	0.0
Total Receipts to Cash Flow 42	3.3	2.0	3.9	3.9	3.9	4.3	3.4
Cost of Goods to Cash Flow 43	1.1	0.2	0.8	0.8	0.8	1.8	1.5
Cash Flow to Total Debt 44	0.4	7.2	2.1	2.1	2.1	0.7	0.3

Selected Financial Factors (in Percentages)

Debt Ratio 45	58.2	51.8	109.6	52.7	85.6	39.4	61.9
Return on Total Assets 46	10.8	119.6	40.1	45.3	12.7	12.5	7.1
Return on Equity Before Income Taxes 47	22.0	239.3	92.2	76.1		18.1	14.4
Return on Equity After Income Taxes 48	16.8	236.5		91.4	74.8	11.8	10.0
Profit Margin (Before Income Tax) 49	12.1	15.4	9.9	9.9	7.9	9.9	7.4
Profit Margin (After Income Tax) 50	9.2	15.2	7.4	9.8	7.7	6.5	5.1

Table I

Corporations with and without Net Income

MISC. HEALTH CARE AND SOCIAL ASSISTANCE

MONEY AMOUNTS AND SIZE OF ASSETS IN THOUSANDS OF DOLLARS

Item Description for Accounting Period 7/05 Through 6/06	Total	Zero Assets	Under 500	500 to 1,000	1,000 to 5,000	5,000 to 10,000	10,000 to 25,000	25,000 to 50,000	50,000 to 100,000	100,000 to 250,000	250,000 to 500,000	500,000 to 2,500,000	2,500,000 and over
Number of Enterprises 1	52189	9192	38275	2610	1596	231	132	55	39	34	14	12	0
Revenues ($ in Thousands)													
Net Sales 2	75996856	1400041	22130658	4513241	5823223	4065041	4212453	3282843	3856223	4159821	5742988	16810322	0
Interest 3	243647	2852	3959	1227	4380	7201	8053	12640	29676	43559	22370	107731	0
Rents 4	26116	56	9423	0	3364	822	278	579	3970	2123	4173	1329	0
Royalties 5	79139	2510	0	0	0	0	2620	2064	38211	28602	1131	4001	0
Other Portfolio Income 6	233119	52306	46263	1002	2696	2107	3924	45314	6969	8313	5365	58860	0
Other Receipts 7	1410764	7001	152546	75791	122695	272235	53869	47815	87722	187760	41059	362270	0
Total Receipts 8	77989641	1464766	22342849	4591261	5956358	4347406	4281197	3391255	4022771	4430178	5817086	17344513	0
Average Total Receipts 9	1494	159	584	1759	3732	18820	32433	61659	103148	130299	415506	1445376	·
Operating Costs/Operating Income (%)													
Cost of Operations 10	20.5	17.6	13.2	10.5	22.4	50.8	29.0	35.1	20.0	17.5	20.0	20.9	·
Salaries and Wages 11	30.9	32.7	34.3	38.8	31.9	19.8	25.9	29.6	30.7	33.9	31.7	26.9	·
Taxes Paid 12	4.0	3.3	4.5	4.9	5.0	1.9	3.7	4.0	3.9	3.6	3.8	3.5	·
Interest Paid 13	1.9	1.1	0.5	1.5	2.0	0.8	1.0	1.3	1.7	5.0	2.7	3.5	·
Depreciation 14	2.2	1.6	1.1	2.8	2.4	1.0	2.0	1.4	2.1	3.5	2.0	3.8	·
Amortization and Depletion 15	0.9	0.7	0.1	0.6	0.3	0.1	0.3	0.6	1.1	2.5	1.8	1.8	·
Pensions and Other Deferred Comp. 16	0.5	0.7	0.9	0.3	0.8	0.1	0.2	0.3	0.5	0.3	0.3	0.2	·
Employee Benefits 17	2.7	2.2	1.2	1.3	2.7	2.3	2.7	5.4	2.3	2.8	3.1	4.7	·
Advertising 18	0.6	1.0	0.7	0.6	0.6	0.4	0.4	0.4	0.7	0.5	0.2	0.5	·
Other Expenses 19	30.0	38.5	29.9	27.2	26.7	27.4	33.2	23.2	39.1	42.2	32.8	26.3	·
Officers' Compensation 20	4.6	8.8	10.1	6.4	5.1	0.9	1.9	1.6	2.6	1.7	0.6	0.9	·
Operating Margin 21	1.4	·	3.6	5.1	0.2	·	·	·	·	·	1.0	6.9	·
Operating Margin Before Officers' Comp. 22	6.0	0.4	13.6	11.5	5.2	·	1.8	·	·	·	1.5	7.8	·

Selected Average Balance Sheet ($ in Thousands)

Net Receivables 23	138	0	7	111	428	1379	4534	9363	13408	19475	64424	204890
Inventories 24	13	0	2	4	49	132	275	593	2586	2434	3892	14974
Net Property, Plant and Equipment 25	185	0	35	282	698	852	2740	6176	11606	27789	57915	279013
Total Assets 26	903	0	79	768	1992	6473	14569	37050	70514	166048	328213	1704393
Notes and Loans Payable 27	390	0	62	506	1078	2464	5277	12226	17455	65960	144543	671495
All Other Liabilities 28	231	0	13	195	400	2681	5228	11521	25497	40120	65639	433803
Net Worth 29	281	0	3	66	515	1328	4064	13302	27561	59968	118031	599094

Selected Financial Ratios (Times to 1)

Current Ratio 30	1.4	•	1.2	1.5	1.5	1.0	1.5	1.4	1.5	1.3	1.6	1.3
Quick Ratio 31	0.9	•	1.1	1.4	1.2	0.8	1.2	1.2	1.0	0.8	1.2	0.7
Net Sales to Working Capital 32	17.1	•	124.0	21.0	10.7	•	11.4	13.1	7.7	9.6	8.3	13.0
Coverage Ratio 33	3.1	•	9.8	5.5	2.2	2.9	2.5	1.3	0.6	•	1.8	3.9
Total Asset Turnover 34	1.6	•	7.3	2.3	1.8	2.7	2.2	1.6	1.4	0.7	1.2	0.8
Inventory Turnover 35	22.7	•	37.5	45.9	16.8	67.8	33.6	35.3	7.7	8.8	21.1	19.5
Receivables Turnover 36	10.8	•	87.7	18.0	6.6	11.1	7.0	7.2	7.0	6.1	7.6	7.6
Total Liabilities to Net Worth 37	2.2	•	22.4	10.6	2.9	3.9	2.6	1.8	1.6	1.8	1.8	1.8
Current Assets to Working Capital 38	3.8	•	6.4	3.0	2.9	•	3.2	3.7	2.8	4.7	2.5	4.2
Current Liabilities to Working Capital 39	2.8	•	5.4	2.0	1.9	•	2.2	2.7	1.8	3.7	1.5	3.2
Working Capital to Net Sales 40	0.1	•	0.0	0.0	0.1	•	0.1	0.1	0.1	0.1	0.1	0.1
Inventory to Working Capital 41	0.2	•	0.4	0.0	0.2	•	0.1	0.2	0.2	0.2	0.1	0.1
Total Receipts to Cash Flow 42	3.5	•	3.6	3.7	4.2	4.0	3.4	5.3	3.1	3.7	3.2	3.2
Cost of Goods to Cash Flow 43	0.7	3.7	0.5	0.4	0.9	2.0	1.0	1.9	0.6	0.7	0.6	0.7
Cash Flow to Total Debt 44	0.7	0.7	2.1	0.7	0.6	0.9	0.9	0.5	0.7	0.3	0.6	0.4

Selected Financial Factors (in Percentages)

Debt Ratio 45	68.9	•	95.7	91.4	74.2	79.5	72.1	64.1	60.9	63.9	64.0	64.8
Return on Total Assets 46	9.5	•	36.8	18.8	8.0	5.9	5.5	2.8	1.5	•	6.1	11.2
Return on Equity Before Income Taxes 47	20.7	•	773.0	178.4	17.2	18.8	11.9	1.9	•	•	7.7	23.6
Return on Equity After Income Taxes 48	15.2	•	759.5	170.9	14.0	16.3	8.0	•	•	•	4.2	15.8
Profit Margin (Before Income Tax) 49	4.0	•	4.5	6.8	2.4	1.4	1.5	0.4	•	•	2.2	10.1
Profit Margin (After Income Tax) 50	2.9	•	4.4	6.5	2.0	1.2	1.0	•	•	•	1.2	6.8

Table II
Corporations with Net Income

MISC. HEALTH CARE AND SOCIAL ASSISTANCE

MONEY AMOUNTS AND SIZE OF ASSETS IN THOUSANDS OF DOLLARS

Item Description for Accounting Period 7/05 Through 6/06	Total	Zero Assets	Under 500	500 to 1,000	1,000 to 5,000	5,000 to 10,000	10,000 to 25,000	25,000 to 50,000	50,000 to 100,000	100,000 to 250,000	250,000 to 500,000	500,000 to 2,500,000	2,500,000 and over
Number of Enterprises 1	30534	3984	23083	2018	1121	147	93	30	•	15	9	•	0
Revenues ($ in Thousands)													
Net Sales 2	55432131	608334	15282728	3890069	4052357	2100861	3493396	2503346	•	2068369	3616632	•	0
Interest 3	161741	182	2230	318	1495	2261	3684	8391	•	19306	17510	•	0
Rents 4	14517	56	0	0	3282	600	181	97	•	1801	3200	•	0
Royalties 5	52482	2510	0	0	0	0	0	2064	•	4788	909	•	0
Other Portfolio Income 6	142125	15104	44815	190	1686	1281	1991	24740	•	3293	3563	•	0
Other Receipts 7	1056853	2918	66222	43777	96197	268523	19958	34210	•	56940	27354	•	0
Total Receipts 8	56859849	629104	15395995	3934354	4155017	2373526	3519210	2572848	•	2154497	3669168	•	0
Average Total Receipts 9	1862	158	667	1950	3707	16146	37841	85762	•	143633	407685	•	•
Operating Costs/Operating Income (%)													
Cost of Operations 10	19.4	9.7	13.8	11.9	22.8	25.1	28.4	34.1	•	11.0	19.7	•	•
Salaries and Wages 11	29.6	16.3	33.5	37.5	29.2	29.6	22.5	28.9	•	32.6	31.5	•	•
Taxes Paid 12	3.8	3.0	4.2	4.4	4.5	2.7	3.4	4.4	•	3.2	3.9	•	•
Interest Paid 13	1.6	0.4	0.4	1.2	2.0	0.7	0.6	0.9	•	3.3	2.1	•	•
Depreciation 14	1.9	1.5	0.8	1.6	2.7	1.3	1.9	1.3	•	2.8	1.6	•	•
Amortization and Depletion 15	0.7	0.2	0.1	0.4	0.3	0.1	0.1	0.3	•	1.6	1.2	•	•
Pensions and Other Deferred Comp. 16	0.5	0.1	0.8	0.3	0.8	0.2	0.2	0.2	•	0.3	0.5	•	•
Employee Benefits 17	3.0	0.9	1.2	1.2	2.8	3.7	2.5	6.5	•	2.6	3.7	•	•
Advertising 18	0.5	1.9	0.8	0.4	0.5	0.5	0.4	0.4	•	0.4	0.2	•	•
Other Expenses 19	28.3	47.7	27.8	25.3	20.5	40.0	33.2	17.6	•	37.7	31.0	•	•
Officers' Compensation 20	3.6	7.1	7.6	6.0	4.5	1.1	1.9	1.3	•	1.1	0.6	•	•
Operating Margin 21	7.1	11.1	9.0	9.8	9.4	•	4.9	4.2	•	3.5	3.9	•	•
Operating Margin Before Officers' Comp. 22	10.6	18.2	16.7	15.8	13.9	•	6.8	5.5	•	4.6	4.5	•	•

Selected Average Balance Sheet ($ in Thousands)

Net Receivables 23	•	58594	25795	10861	4787	1822	358	136	8	0	182
Inventories 24	•	3656	1672	348	188	167	44	3	1	0	13
Net Property, Plant and Equipment 25	•	60320	26545	7709	3106	948	834	255	26	0	206
Total Assets 26	•	319153	171848	36073	14687	5972	2083	767	78	0	1112
Notes and Loans Payable 27	•	130037	53203	10139	4701	2392	945	455	40	0	422
All Other Liabilities 28	•	67335	44046	13503	5198	1944	274	138	12	0	285
Net Worth 29	•	121781	74599	12431	4788	1636	865	174	26	0	405

Selected Financial Ratios (Times to 1)

Current Ratio 30	•	1.3	2.0	1.6	1.4	1.0	1.7	2.2	1.4	•	1.4
Quick Ratio 31	•	1.1	1.3	1.4	1.1	0.8	1.4	2.0	1.3	•	1.0
Net Sales to Working Capital 32	•	16.2	4.4	12.5	14.6	•	9.0	12.0	63.5	•	14.6
Coverage Ratio 33	•	3.5	3.3	9.1	10.1	12.5	6.9	10.0	23.5	33.6	7.1
Total Asset Turnover 34	•	1.3	0.8	2.3	2.6	2.4	1.7	2.5	8.5	•	1.6
Inventory Turnover 35	•	21.7	9.0	81.7	56.8	21.5	18.7	72.1	61.2	•	27.6
Receivables Turnover 36	•	7.5	5.8	8.5	8.2	9.3	8.6	18.8	77.4	•	11.1
Total Liabilities to Net Worth 37	•	1.6	1.3	1.9	2.1	2.7	1.4	3.4	2.0	•	1.7
Current Assets to Working Capital 38	•	4.1	2.1	2.6	3.5	•	2.4	1.8	3.5	•	3.2
Current Liabilities to Working Capital 39	•	3.1	1.1	1.6	2.5	•	1.4	0.8	2.5	•	2.2
Working Capital to Net Sales 40	•	0.1	0.2	0.1	0.1	•	0.1	0.1	0.0	•	0.1
Inventory to Working Capital 41	•	0.2	0.1	0.0	0.1	•	0.1	0.0	0.1	•	0.1
Total Receipts to Cash Flow 42	•	3.0	2.5	4.9	2.9	2.4	3.5	3.3	3.2	1.9	3.1
Cost of Goods to Cash Flow 43	•	0.6	0.3	1.7	0.8	0.6	0.8	0.4	0.4	0.2	0.6
Cash Flow to Total Debt 44	•	0.7	0.6	0.7	1.3	1.4	0.8	1.0	4.0	•	0.8

Selected Financial Factors (in Percentages)

Debt Ratio 45	•	61.8	56.6	65.5	67.4	72.6	58.5	77.4	67.0	•	63.5
Return on Total Assets 46	•	9.4	8.7	18.1	16.0	20.6	24.1	30.6	86.6	•	18.3
Return on Equity Before Income Taxes 47	•	17.5	14.0	46.7	44.3	69.2	49.8	121.6	251.2	•	43.1
Return on Equity After Income Taxes 48	•	12.3	10.9	37.2	39.6	66.0	47.1	117.8	248.2	•	36.5
Profit Margin (Before Income Tax) 49	•	5.3	7.6	7.0	5.6	7.9	11.9	10.9	9.7	14.6	9.6
Profit Margin (After Income Tax) 50	•	3.7	5.9	5.5	5.1	7.6	11.3	10.6	9.6	14.5	8.2

Table I

Corporations with and without Net Income

HOSPITALS, NURSING, AND RESIDENTIAL CARE FACILITIES

MONEY AMOUNTS AND SIZE OF ASSETS IN THOUSANDS OF DOLLARS

Item Description for Accounting Period 7/05 Through 6/06	Total	Zero Assets	Under 500	500 to 1,000	1,000 to 5,000	5,000 to 10,000	10,000 to 25,000	25,000 to 50,000	50,000 to 100,000	100,000 to 250,000	250,000 to 500,000	500,000 to 2,500,000	2,500,000 and over
Number of Enterprises 1	18263	2617	12299	1085	1703	214	155	80	35	38	8	21	7
Revenues ($ in Thousands)													
Net Sales 2	102300229	1718119	7344513	1833252	7527254	2693488	4393652	4121089	3773379	8026956	2537595	23228456	35102477
Interest 3	742281	5137	4461	783	1845	2070	4301	15124	5834	51086	14052	320713	316875
Rents 4	379571	4496	0	0	2077	0	4274	2874	8253	41679	16813	63984	235120
Royalties 5	10296	0	0	0	0	0	0	0	0	0	0	10296	0
Other Portfolio Income 6	1298505	23685	20195	79221	13609	75803	108613	30705	1930	163825	7723	142355	630844
Other Receipts 7	3343911	111446	11314	130269	31869	301904	85953	81022	64794	324149	31203	690584	1479400
Total Receipts 8	108074793	1862883	7380483	2043525	7576654	3073265	4596793	4250814	3854190	8607695	2607386	24456388	37764716
Average Total Receipts 9	5918	712	600	1883	4449	14361	29657	53135	110120	226518	325923	1164590	5394959
Operating Costs/Operating Income (%)													
Cost of Operations 10	8.1	4.6	7.1	8.3	3.9	8.2	17.8	5.7	14.9	10.0	5.1	15.6	2.7
Salaries and Wages 11	40.7	39.2	36.8	40.3	41.8	37.4	34.9	40.3	39.9	42.9	45.1	33.3	46.6
Taxes Paid 12	5.4	4.8	5.5	5.9	6.8	6.1	7.2	6.1	5.3	5.6	6.6	4.4	5.3
Interest Paid 13	3.2	2.9	1.4	2.4	1.9	1.8	2.1	2.6	2.2	2.8	3.4	3.3	4.2
Depreciation 14	2.5	3.0	1.2	2.3	1.5	1.2	1.6	1.7	1.5	1.8	2.5	2.2	3.7
Amortization and Depletion 15	0.7	1.5	0.0	0.1	0.1	0.1	1.6	0.7	0.6	0.5	0.9	1.0	0.8
Pensions and Other Deferred Comp. 16	0.6	0.2	0.1	0.1	0.1	0.2	0.5	0.2	0.2	0.3	0.0	0.2	1.4
Employee Benefits 17	4.1	3.9	2.0	1.5	2.5	4.7	5.0	3.3	3.3	4.3	4.2	3.1	5.7
Advertising 18	0.4	0.8	0.3	0.7	0.5	0.2	0.3	0.3	0.3	0.3	0.4	0.5	0.4
Other Expenses 19	34.2	51.5	34.2	39.0	38.0	48.1	30.1	38.0	33.3	36.9	37.7	37.9	28.1
Officers' Compensation 20	1.2	3.8	5.5	2.5	1.0	1.2	0.9	0.9	0.7	0.7	0.3	1.0	0.6
Operating Margin 21	*	*	5.8	*	1.8	*	*	0.4	*	*	*	*	0.6
Operating Margin Before Officers' Comp. 22	0.0	*	11.3	*	2.8	*	*	1.3	*	*	*	*	1.2

Selected Average Balance Sheet ($ in Thousands)

Net Receivables 23	681	0	6	174	476	1808	3651	6216	11502	28865	47446	118574	793080
Inventories 24	15	0	0	1	3	13	106	131	1351	1266	1234	2555	10087
Net Property, Plant and Equipment 25	2061	0	78	306	1031	3344	6378	14924	27026	75122	189539	419880	2508073
Total Assets 26	6239	0	137	713	2272	7497	15495	34488	68256	159336	356373	1238407	9078339
Notes and Loans Payable 27	2515	0	223	301	1686	3076	9186	18787	38913	78912	162358	518323	2837612
All Other Liabilities 28	1576	0	19	373	643	3128	5674	9516	22593	58424	130272	330641	1963546
Net Worth 29	2148	0	-105	40	-56	1293	634	6184	6750	22000	63744	389443	4277181

Selected Financial Ratios (Times to 1)

Current Ratio 30	1.1	•	0.4	1.2	1.1	0.9	1.3	1.3	1.1	0.7	1.3	1.3	1.1
Quick Ratio 31	0.8	•	0.4	1.1	0.9	0.8	1.0	1.0	0.9	0.6	0.9	0.9	0.7
Net Sales to Working Capital 32	51.7	•	•	45.5	41.3	•	18.7	15.5	36.3	•	18.4	15.0	41.7
Coverage Ratio 33	2.4	•	5.7	4.6	2.3	3.7	2.2	2.3	1.0	1.4	•	1.8	2.9
Total Asset Turnover 34	0.9	•	4.3	2.4	1.9	1.7	1.8	1.5	1.6	1.3	0.9	0.9	0.6
Inventory Turnover 35	31.4	•	7360.1	157.1	60.4	78.3	47.8	22.3	11.9	16.6	13.0	67.5	13.3
Receivables Turnover 36	8.3	•	71.0	9.9	8.8	8.3	6.9	8.5	9.9	7.6	5.9	8.8	6.8
Total Liabilities to Net Worth 37	1.9	•	•	16.8	•	4.8	23.4	4.6	9.1	6.2	4.6	2.2	1.1
Current Assets to Working Capital 38	12.3	•	•	5.6	8.6	•	4.6	3.9	8.6	•	5.0	4.3	10.6
Current Liabilities to Working Capital 39	11.3	•	•	4.6	7.6	•	3.6	2.9	7.6	•	4.0	3.3	9.6
Working Capital to Net Sales 40	0.0	•	•	0.0	0.0	•	0.1	0.1	0.0	•	0.1	0.0	0.0
Inventory to Working Capital 41	0.2	•	•	0.0	0.0	•	0.1	0.0	0.8	•	0.1	0.0	0.1
Total Receipts to Cash Flow 42	3.1	2.8	3.3	2.4	3.3	2.1	3.8	2.8	3.8	3.2	4.3	2.9	3.2
Cost of Goods to Cash Flow 43	0.3	0.1	0.2	0.2	0.1	0.2	0.7	0.2	0.6	0.3	0.2	0.4	0.1
Cash Flow to Total Debt 44	0.4	•	0.7	1.0	0.6	0.9	0.5	0.7	0.5	0.5	0.2	0.5	0.3

Selected Financial Factors (in Percentages)

Debt Ratio 45	65.6	•	176.1	94.4	102.5	82.8	95.9	82.1	90.1	86.2	82.1	68.6	52.9
Return on Total Assets 46	6.8	•	33.3	25.8	8.4	11.4	8.6	8.7	3.4	5.3	•	5.5	6.8
Return on Equity Before Income Taxes 47	11.5	•	•	358.5	•	48.2	116.7	27.2	11.6	•	•	7.9	9.4
Return on Equity After Income Taxes 48	8.0	•	•	354.4	•	45.7	89.8	22.1	•	5.5	•	6.5	5.6
Profit Margin (Before Income Tax) 49	4.4	•	6.3	8.5	2.4	5.0	2.6	3.3	1.2	•	•	2.8	8.1
Profit Margin (After Income Tax) 50	3.1	•	6.2	8.4	2.3	4.7	2.0	2.7	0.6	•	•	2.3	4.8

377

Table II
Corporations with Net Income

HOSPITALS, NURSING, AND RESIDENTIAL CARE FACILITIES

MONEY AMOUNTS AND SIZE OF ASSETS IN THOUSANDS OF DOLLARS

Item Description for Accounting Period 7/05 Through 6/06	Total	Zero Assets	Under 500	500 to 1,000	1,000 to 5,000	5,000 to 10,000	10,000 to 25,000	25,000 to 50,000	50,000 to 100,000	100,000 to 250,000	250,000 to 500,000	500,000 to 2,500,000	2,500,000 and over
Number of Enterprises 1	10498	436	7718	867	1056	188	113	54	23	23	0	•	•
Revenues ($ in Thousands)													
Net Sales 2	75963270	86172	6178273	1463484	4284839	2339062	3504595	2979376	2656847	5500818	0	•	•
Interest 3	590043	1020	551	777	855	1848	3805	9249	4773	35438	0	•	•
Rents 4	260227	0	0	0	505	0	4274	1687	7608	26989	0	•	•
Royalties 5	5165	0	0	0	0	0	0	0	0	0	0		
Other Portfolio Income 6	1083682	19955	415	79221	13438	75640	88811	29980	943	8442	0		
Other Receipts 7	2885145	39810	11312	130261	16022	300883	76465	73292	36882	197118	0		
Total Receipts 8	80787532	146957	6190551	1673743	4315659	2717433	3677950	3093584	2707053	5768805	0		
Average Total Receipts 9	7696	337	802	1930	4087	14454	32548	57289	117698	250818	•		
Operating Costs/Operating Income (%)													
Cost of Operations 10	9.3	•	8.1	10.4	5.1	6.5	20.8	5.5	18.0	8.7			
Salaries and Wages 11	40.8	31.1	36.5	38.5	41.7	39.2	33.1	42.9	36.4	41.3			
Taxes Paid 12	5.4	8.6	5.3	4.8	6.7	6.5	7.0	7.0	5.0	5.9			
Interest Paid 13	3.0	6.3	1.3	2.2	1.9	1.7	1.7	2.1	1.6	2.3			
Depreciation 14	2.5	2.1	1.0	2.3	1.8	1.1	1.5	1.6	1.4	2.2			
Amortization and Depletion 15	0.6	0.1	0.0	0.1	0.1	0.1	0.2	0.7	0.4	0.5			
Pensions and Other Deferred Comp. 16	0.6	0.5	0.1	0.1	0.1	0.2	0.5	0.2	0.3	0.2			
Employee Benefits 17	4.2	2.9	2.0	1.4	3.1	4.7	4.1	3.9	3.1	4.0			
Advertising 18	0.4	0.1	0.4	0.6	0.4	0.2	0.3	0.3	0.3	0.3			
Other Expenses 19	29.7	34.8	32.4	34.2	31.7	46.7	28.0	32.1	30.7	33.9			
Officers' Compensation 20	1.2	25.6	4.4	2.9	1.4	1.3	1.0	0.9	0.9	0.5			
Operating Margin 21	2.2	•	8.4	2.5	6.0	•	1.8	2.9	1.9	0.1			
Operating Margin Before Officers' Comp. 22	3.4	13.6	12.9	5.4	7.3	•	2.7	3.8	2.8	0.6			

Selected Average Balance Sheet ($ in Thousands)

Net Receivables 23	907	0	9	186	448	1908	3681	8170	12398	35080
Inventories 24	19	0	0	2	2	13	122	134	1837	1517
Net Property, Plant and Equipment 25	2557	0	71	248	999	3323	6605	14651	25890	84930
Total Assets 26	8398	0	155	703	2142	7694	15768	35595	69476	173601
Notes and Loans Payable 27	3121	0	299	210	1552	2801	8535	18189	34475	80508
All Other Liabilities 28	1597	0	20	191	289	2944	4900	9880	23584	42443
Net Worth 29	3680	0	-164	302	301	1948	2333	7526	11418	50650

Selected Financial Ratios (Times to 1)

Current Ratio 30	1.1	•	0.5	1.3	2.1	1.0	1.4	1.4	1.2	1.2
Quick Ratio 31	0.9	•	0.4	1.3	1.9	0.8	1.2	1.1	1.0	1.0
Net Sales to Working Capital 32	38.0	•	•	32.1	9.1	•	15.1	12.5	21.8	20.6
Coverage Ratio 33	3.9	10.4	7.5	8.7	4.6	5.8	4.9	4.0	3.3	3.1
Total Asset Turnover 34	0.9	•	5.2	2.4	1.9	1.6	2.0	1.6	1.7	1.4
Inventory Turnover 35	35.1	•	•	81.6	95.4	61.2	52.7	22.7	11.3	13.8
Receivables Turnover 36	8.5	•	124.9	12.4	9.8	10.0	7.4	7.5	9.6	7.0
Total Liabilities to Net Worth 37	1.3	•	•	1.3	6.1	2.9	5.8	3.7	5.1	2.4
Current Assets to Working Capital 38	8.4	•	•	4.1	1.9	•	3.4	3.4	5.3	5.4
Current Liabilities to Working Capital 39	7.4	•	•	3.1	0.9	•	2.4	2.4	4.3	4.4
Working Capital to Net Sales 40	0.0	•	•	0.0	0.1	•	0.1	0.1	0.0	0.0
Inventory to Working Capital 41	0.1	•	•	0.0	0.0	•	0.1	0.0	0.6	0.1
Total Receipts to Cash Flow 42	3.1	1.5	3.1	2.2	3.1	2.1	3.5	3.1	3.5	3.0
Cost of Goods to Cash Flow 43	0.3	•	0.3	0.2	0.2	0.1	0.7	0.2	0.6	0.3
Cash Flow to Total Debt 44	0.5	•	0.8	1.9	0.7	1.0	0.7	0.6	0.6	0.7

Selected Financial Factors (in Percentages)

Debt Ratio 45	56.2	•	206.2	57.1	85.9	74.7	85.2	78.9	83.6	70.8
Return on Total Assets 46	9.8	•	51.6	45.7	16.3	15.7	16.5	13.0	9.0	10.0
Return on Equity Before Income Taxes 47	16.6	•	•	94.2	90.2	51.3	88.9	46.0	38.3	23.4
Return on Equity After Income Taxes 48	13.0	•	•	93.5	87.6	49.5	78.9	39.8	32.0	19.0
Profit Margin (Before Income Tax) 49	8.5	58.6	8.6	16.9	6.7	8.0	6.7	6.3	3.8	5.0
Profit Margin (After Income Tax) 50	6.6	58.3	8.5	16.7	6.5	7.7	5.9	5.4	3.2	4.0

Table I
Corporations with and without Net Income

OTHER ARTS, ENTERTAINMENT, AND RECREATION

MONEY AMOUNTS AND SIZE OF ASSETS IN THOUSANDS OF DOLLARS

Item Description for Accounting Period 7/05 Through 6/06	Total	Zero Assets	Under 500	500 to 1,000	1,000 to 5,000	5,000 to 10,000	10,000 to 25,000	25,000 to 50,000	50,000 to 100,000	100,000 to 250,000	250,000 to 500,000	500,000 to 2,500,000	2,500,000 and over
Number of Enterprises **1**	63581	12506	47818	1968	929	158	88	42	24	27	9	10	0
Revenues ($ in Thousands)													
Net Sales **2**	35542084	832067	11139790	4457395	3431661	1712266	1194368	1138916	1253726	4040062	2121317	4220517	0
Interest **3**	213882	241	5808	1993	10953	4923	10515	6094	14229	31937	19087	108101	0
Rents **4**	83801	0	2430	783	2046	728	843	673	917	18443	14025	42914	0
Royalties **5**	105272	0	0	22	0	12596	0	0	0	51288	38327	3040	0
Other Portfolio Income **6**	296178	219	4491	7007	14972	14529	16227	9244	3085	48070	39848	138485	0
Other Receipts **7**	2089502	146654	94381	99315	73598	173653	312081	152417	119325	443069	365599	109408	0
Total Receipts **8**	38830719	979181	11246900	4566515	3533230	1918695	1534034	1307344	1391282	4632869	2598203	4622465	0
Average Total Receipts **9**	603	78	235	2320	3803	12144	17432	31127	57970	171588	288689	462246	•
Operating Costs/Operating Income (%)													
Cost of Operations **10**	15.8	18.9	10.1	15.2	14.1	8.6	22.1	17.7	24.1	17.5	38.3	17.8	•
Salaries and Wages **11**	19.3	16.9	13.2	5.5	19.2	31.1	37.3	34.0	31.6	36.3	24.6	13.9	•
Taxes Paid **12**	3.0	1.9	2.3	3.0	2.4	3.3	6.7	2.5	2.9	4.0	4.4	3.1	•
Interest Paid **13**	1.7	0.5	0.5	0.3	0.2	2.3	2.0	1.2	3.1	3.4	3.1	5.2	•
Depreciation **14**	2.2	1.1	1.1	1.1	2.6	2.3	2.6	2.7	2.7	2.8	2.7	4.9	•
Amortization and Depletion **15**	0.9	0.1	0.2	0.0	0.0	0.1	0.1	0.6	2.6	3.7	1.1	2.1	•
Pensions and Other Deferred Comp. **16**	1.8	1.5	3.0	2.4	0.7	0.1	0.7	0.6	1.0	1.9	1.5	0.9	•
Employee Benefits **17**	1.1	2.2	0.6	0.2	0.4	0.3	1.9	1.8	0.9	1.9	3.0	1.4	•
Advertising **18**	2.1	1.6	1.0	3.5	2.2	2.6	1.8	3.1	2.1	3.0	2.1	2.4	•
Other Expenses **19**	40.8	64.0	41.2	58.4	26.6	44.4	39.1	44.7	32.8	33.1	23.1	44.6	•
Officers' Compensation **20**	11.5	11.9	22.6	10.9	15.4	5.9	5.1	1.7	7.5	1.6	2.1	1.9	•
Operating Margin **21**	•	•	4.3	•	16.1	•	•	•	•	•	•	1.9	•
Operating Margin Before Officers' Comp. **22**	11.2	•	26.9	10.3	31.6	4.8	•	•	•	•	3.8	•	•

Selected Average Balance Sheet ($ in Thousands)

Net Receivables 23	42	0	2	18	213	927	2461	4163	6927	16355	27232	96809	•
Inventories 24	8	0	4	27	112	219	365	1088	1521	2289	3741		•
Net Property, Plant and Equipment 25	130	0	9	122	283	1716	4475	6474	12801	42941	101171	399733	•
Total Assets 26	637	0	52	671	1913	7741	15706	35470	65416	172997	368410	2128009	•
Notes and Loans Payable 27	203	0	49	260	876	4646	5892	11676	34336	63690	92607	412391	•
All Other Liabilities 28	176	0	17	573	435	3292	5012	14719	23195	69482	97366	397050	•
Net Worth 29	258	0	-14	-162	603	-196	4803	9074	7885	39825	178437	1318568	•

Selected Financial Ratios (Times to 1)

Current Ratio 30	1.1	•	1.7	1.2	1.8	1.4	1.2	1.4	1.2	1.1	1.5	0.7	•
Quick Ratio 31	0.8	•	1.2	1.0	1.2	1.3	1.0	0.9	0.9	0.8	1.0	0.5	•
Net Sales to Working Capital 32	27.9	•	16.4	36.2	6.7	7.1	11.4	7.0	14.9	49.6	6.3		•
Coverage Ratio 33	5.3	•	12.4	6.4	91.5	5.7	5.5	4.3	0.9	2.5	6.3	3.2	•
Total Asset Turnover 34	0.9	•	4.5	3.4	1.9	1.4	0.9	0.8	0.8	0.9	0.6	0.2	•
Inventory Turnover 35	11.4	•	6.4	12.9	4.7	55.9	13.6	13.2	11.5	17.2	39.5	20.0	•
Receivables Turnover 36	14.9	•	99.0	122.6	21.7	20.8	4.8	8.0	7.9	7.9	8.0	6.4	•
Total Liabilities to Net Worth 37	1.5	•	•	2.2	2.2	2.3	2.9	•	3.3	1.1	0.6		•
Current Assets to Working Capital 38	8.4	•	2.4	5.4	2.2	3.2	5.3	3.7	5.7	19.3	3.0		•
Current Liabilities to Working Capital 39	7.4	•	1.4	4.4	1.2	2.2	4.3	2.7	4.7	18.3	2.0		•
Working Capital to Net Sales 40	0.0	•	0.1	0.0	0.1	0.1	0.1	0.1	0.1	0.0	0.2		•
Inventory to Working Capital 41	0.5	•	0.3	0.3	0.4	0.0	0.1	0.1	0.3	0.4	0.1		•
Total Receipts to Cash Flow 42	2.3	1.9	2.4	1.7	2.4	1.9	2.4	2.3	3.5	3.1	2.8	2.0	•
Cost of Goods to Cash Flow 43	0.4	0.4	0.2	0.3	0.3	0.2	0.5	0.4	0.9	0.5	1.1	0.4	•
Cash Flow to Total Debt 44	0.6	•	1.5	1.6	1.2	0.7	0.5	0.4	0.3	0.4	0.4	0.3	•

Selected Financial Factors (in Percentages)

Debt Ratio 45	59.5	•	127.8	124.2	68.5	102.5	69.4	74.4	87.9	77.0	51.6	38.0	•
Return on Total Assets 46	8.1	•	25.7	7.5	37.3	18.5	9.4	4.0	2.2	7.5	12.3	3.3	•
Return on Equity Before Income Taxes 47	16.3	•	•	•	116.9	•	25.0	12.0	•	19.7	21.3	3.7	•
Return on Equity After Income Taxes 48	13.9	•	•	•	114.6	•	23.3	11.5	•	14.8	16.1	2.3	•
Profit Margin (Before Income Tax) 49	7.5	•	5.2	1.9	19.1	10.9	8.9	4.0	•	5.2	16.1	11.6	•
Profit Margin (After Income Tax) 50	6.4	•	5.1	1.8	18.7	10.1	8.2	3.8	•	4.0	12.2	7.3	•

379

Table II
Corporations with Net Income

OTHER ARTS, ENTERTAINMENT, AND RECREATION

MONEY AMOUNTS AND SIZE OF ASSETS IN THOUSANDS OF DOLLARS

Item Description for Accounting Period 7/05 Through 6/06	Total	Zero Assets	Under 500	500 to 1,000	1,000 to 5,000	5,000 to 10,000	10,000 to 25,000	25,000 to 50,000	50,000 to 100,000	100,000 to 250,000	250,000 to 500,000	500,000 to 2,500,000	2,500,000 and over
Number of Enterprises **1**	32651	6016	24678	1143	639	60	50	17	•	21	•	6	0
Revenues ($ in Thousands)													
Net Sales **2**	27453412	654749	8451597	3305729	3172031	738510	906895	689006	•	3393249	•	3442652	0
Interest **3**	124903	75	3402	1211	7615	2843	8085	1179	•	22427	•	59085	0
Rents **4**	58864	0	0	783	1363	728	0	0	•	14264	•	28040	0
Royalties **5**	100027	0	0	0	0	7372	0	0	•	51288	•	3040	0
Other Portfolio Income **6**	275090	0	3246	2906	14923	14315	11090	6311	•	47968	•	134379	0
Other Receipts **7**	1382298	15533	31603	86581	99064	51802	109401	64068	•	329370	•	90686	0
Total Receipts **8**	29394594	670357	8489848	3397210	3294996	815570	1035471	760564	•	3858566	•	3757882	0
Average Total Receipts **9**	900	111	344	2972	5156	13593	20709	44739	•	183741	•	626314	•
Operating Costs/Operating Income (%)													
Cost of Operations **10**	15.7	23.0	6.6	18.8	13.1	19.8	21.4	14.7	•	20.8	•	15.3	•
Salaries and Wages **11**	16.5	3.0	12.6	5.9	19.1	6.3	22.2	15.6	•	30.9	•	13.0	•
Taxes Paid **12**	2.8	1.4	1.9	3.3	2.1	1.7	4.1	1.9	•	3.7	•	3.4	•
Interest Paid **13**	1.1	0.4	0.1	0.2	0.1	0.2	0.7	0.7	•	2.5	•	3.9	•
Depreciation **14**	1.9	1.0	0.8	0.9	1.0	1.0	2.4	2.0	•	3.1	•	5.2	•
Amortization and Depletion **15**	0.9	0.0	0.0	0.0	0.0	0.0	0.1	0.3	•	3.4	•	2.5	•
Pensions and Other Deferred Comp. **16**	1.9	1.0	3.4	1.9	0.5	0.1	0.6	0.4	•	1.7	•	0.9	•
Employee Benefits **17**	1.0	0.5	0.6	0.3	0.5	0.3	1.9	0.8	•	1.9	•	0.9	•
Advertising **18**	2.1	1.9	0.7	4.4	2.2	4.6	2.0	2.2	•	3.4	•	1.7	•
Other Expenses **19**	35.5	45.5	38.1	46.4	23.0	25.8	31.6	39.3	•	32.2	•	43.7	•
Officers' Compensation **20**	11.9	8.6	23.1	11.1	16.1	13.6	6.6	1.2	•	1.8	•	1.7	•
Operating Margin **21**	8.8	13.6	12.1	6.9	22.3	26.5	6.3	20.9	•	•	•	7.8	•
Operating Margin Before Officers' Comp. **22**	20.7	22.2	35.2	18.0	38.4	40.1	12.9	22.1	•	•	•	9.5	•

Selected Average Balance Sheet ($ in Thousands)

Net Receivables 23	46	0	3	31	278	730	2653	2634	·	13489	·	74662 ·
Inventories 24	8	0	2	13	135	23	145	496	·	1256	·	6962 ·
Net Property, Plant and Equipment 25	170	0	9	109	213	731	3757	5518	·	50310	·	484702 ·
Total Assets 26	567	0	60	684	1958	6979	16661	36394	·	178351	·	1023297 ·
Notes and Loans Payable 27	155	0	21	128	560	1232	3862	4746	·	61006	·	248788 ·
All Other Liabilities 28	196	0	21	294	413	1336	6070	8601	·	73150	·	385871 ·
Net Worth 29	216	0	18	262	985	4411	6729	23047	·	44195	·	388638 ·

Selected Financial Ratios (Times to 1)

Current Ratio 30	1.3	·	1.9	1.4	2.0	3.1	1.9	1.4	·	1.0	·	0.8 ·
Quick Ratio 31	1.0	·	1.5	1.2	1.5	2.8	1.5	1.2	·	0.7	·	0.6 ·
Net Sales to Working Capital 32	17.4	·	16.8	24.1	6.7	3.8	7.8	4.9	·	·	·	·
Coverage Ratio 33	15.3	43.6	115.6	48.8	212.4	243.9	29.0	46.6	·	4.5	·	5.3 ·
Total Asset Turnover 34	1.5	·	5.7	4.2	2.5	1.8	1.1	1.1	·	0.9	·	0.6 ·
Inventory Turnover 35	16.3	·	11.1	42.9	4.8	104.0	26.7	12.1	·	26.7	·	12.6 ·
Receivables Turnover 36	20.5	·	160.0	91.4	24.1	29.3	6.5	16.5	·	12.0	·	15.4 ·
Total Liabilities to Net Worth 37	1.6	·	2.4	1.6	1.0	0.6	1.5	0.6	·	3.0	·	1.6 ·
Current Assets to Working Capital 38	4.5	·	2.1	3.6	2.0	1.5	3.3	2.1	·	·	·	·
Current Liabilities to Working Capital 39	3.5	·	1.1	2.6	1.0	0.5	2.3	1.1	·	·	·	·
Working Capital to Net Sales 40	0.1	·	0.1	0.0	0.1	0.3	0.1	0.2	·	·	·	·
Inventory to Working Capital 41	0.2	·	0.2	0.0	0.4	0.0	0.1	0.0	·	·	·	·
Total Receipts to Cash Flow 42	2.1	1.8	2.1	1.9	2.2	1.7	2.1	1.5	·	2.9	·	1.8 ·
Cost of Goods to Cash Flow 43	0.3	0.4	0.1	0.3	0.3	0.3	0.5	0.2	·	0.6	·	0.3 ·
Cash Flow to Total Debt 44	1.1	·	3.8	3.7	2.3	2.9	0.9	2.1	·	0.4	·	0.5 ·

Selected Financial Factors (in Percentages)

Debt Ratio 45	61.8	·	70.2	61.6	49.7	36.8	59.6	36.7	·	75.2	·	62.0 ·
Return on Total Assets 46	25.1	·	72.2	41.6	66.6	65.3	23.0	35.4	·	9.9	·	11.8 ·
Return on Equity Before Income Taxes 47	61.5	·	239.8	106.2	131.8	102.9	55.1	54.7	·	31.1	·	25.2 ·
Return on Equity After Income Taxes 48	56.0	·	236.6	105.6	129.7	97.6	52.8	54.3	·	25.5	·	17.5 ·
Profit Margin (Before Income Tax) 49	15.8	16.0	12.5	9.6	26.2	36.9	20.4	31.1	·	8.5	·	17.1 ·
Profit Margin (After Income Tax) 50	14.4	15.5	12.4	9.6	25.7	35.0	19.6	30.9	·	7.0	·	11.8 ·

Table I
Corporations with and without Net Income

AMUSEMENT, GAMBLING, AND RECREATION INDUSTRIES

MONEY AMOUNTS AND SIZE OF ASSETS IN THOUSANDS OF DOLLARS

Item Description for Accounting Period 7/05 Through 6/06	Total	Zero Assets	Under 500	500 to 1,000	1,000 to 5,000	5,000 to 10,000	10,000 to 25,000	25,000 to 50,000	50,000 to 100,000	100,000 to 250,000	250,000 to 500,000	500,000 to 2,500,000	2,500,000 and over
Number of Enterprises 1	52870	6812	36971	3360	4473	693	348	125	42	25	10	12	0
Revenues ($ in Thousands)													
Net Sales 2	44606796	627506	9976355	2591541	7474135	4311497	3212968	2217516	1474659	2214740	2361671	8144207	0
Interest 3	443203	515	4187	6661	12278	6562	8562	6095	8904	21092	35099	333249	0
Rents 4	154803	0	4191	3272	12273	16044	3517	10286	4844	6655	11551	82169	0
Royalties 5	84264	3	0	0	4729	0	0	0	325	3863	1987	73358	0
Other Portfolio Income 6	601479	13547	134232	13801	117616	18409	34411	23872	29525	8165	6931	200988	0
Other Receipts 7	3749143	-22593	391681	136589	434870	211553	284886	205891	331803	89177	178176	1507113	0
Total Receipts 8	49639688	618978	10510646	2751864	8055901	4564065	3544344	2463660	1850060	2343692	2595415	10341064	0
Average Total Receipts 9	939	91	284	819	1801	6586	10185	19709	44049	93748	259542	861755	•
Operating Costs/Operating Income (%)													
Cost of Operations 10	22.8	15.7	22.9	17.7	30.4	24.4	33.3	22.9	14.4	30.0	11.4	15.8	•
Salaries and Wages 11	22.5	11.9	16.6	20.4	21.0	27.1	22.2	26.1	33.8	18.5	29.2	26.3	•
Taxes Paid 12	7.1	12.4	4.8	6.0	5.8	7.2	7.3	7.0	12.4	5.2	6.1	10.6	•
Interest Paid 13	5.0	3.2	1.8	2.0	3.9	2.5	4.1	3.2	4.2	5.0	6.6	12.7	•
Depreciation 14	6.0	5.8	3.9	5.2	6.2	6.4	6.0	6.9	6.1	5.5	6.7	8.2	•
Amortization and Depletion 15	0.7	1.0	0.4	0.6	0.4	0.7	0.3	0.6	0.9	1.2	1.1	1.2	•
Pensions and Other Deferred Comp. 16	0.3	0.5	0.1	0.8	0.3	0.6	0.2	0.2	0.5	0.2	0.4	0.2	•
Employee Benefits 17	1.7	0.6	0.9	0.8	1.8	1.2	2.2	1.7	1.7	1.8	1.2	3.3	•
Advertising 18	2.7	5.0	2.5	1.9	1.8	2.6	2.6	3.4	5.1	2.6	2.2	3.6	•
Other Expenses 19	35.9	44.8	41.6	38.6	30.2	31.2	27.4	33.5	37.5	29.2	42.7	38.5	•
Officers' Compensation 20	3.3	0.4	7.3	4.4	3.1	2.3	2.0	1.7	1.5	1.5	1.3	1.6	•
Operating Margin 21	•	•	•	1.5	•	•	•	•	•	•	•	•	•
Operating Margin Before Officers' Comp. 22	•	•	4.4	5.9	•	•	•	•	0.9	•	•	•	•

Selected Average Balance Sheet ($ in Thousands)

	•	•	•	•	•	•	•	•	•	•	•	•
Net Receivables 23	58	0	2	12	94	664	675	2107	2286	8505	7426	96256
Inventories 24	29	0	5	20	70	363	437	753	418	1680	4724	27651
Net Property, Plant and Equipment 25	596	0	53	426	1419	4500	8960	20553	38688	63099	169448	671625
Total Assets 26	1136	0	91	714	2177	7278	14856	35180	68782	147609	338819	1663766
Notes and Loans Payable 27	635	0	80	323	1431	3513	7388	10827	30128	59543	180099	1015756
All Other Liabilities 28	246	0	23	58	262	1766	2620	6925	11481	54339	122983	391892
Net Worth 29	255	0	-12	332	483	1999	4848	17428	27173	33727	35737	256118

Selected Financial Ratios (Times to 1)

	•	•	•	•	•	•	•	•	•	•	•	•
Current Ratio 30	1.0	•	1.1	1.7	1.1	0.8	1.2	1.1	1.0	1.0	0.5	1.2
Quick Ratio 31	0.7	•	0.7	1.5	0.6	0.5	0.7	0.8	0.7	0.6	0.3	0.9
Net Sales to Working Capital 32	101.7	•	124.5	11.2	66.7	•	20.6	26.3	•	95.7	•	12.9
Coverage Ratio 33	1.7	0.2	2.3	4.8	1.8	0.8	1.7	2.3	2.7	2.0	1.2	1.4
Total Asset Turnover 34	0.7	•	3.0	1.1	0.8	0.9	0.6	0.5	0.5	0.6	0.7	0.4
Inventory Turnover 35	6.7	•	13.1	6.7	7.2	4.2	7.0	5.4	12.1	15.8	5.7	3.9
Receivables Turnover 36	13.0	•	133.2	25.9	17.0	9.8	13.0	10.1	17.8	11.0	32.8	7.4
Total Liabilities to Net Worth 37	3.4	•	1.1	1.1	3.5	2.6	2.1	1.0	1.5	3.4	8.5	5.5
Current Assets to Working Capital 38	28.8	•	12.9	2.5	20.0	•	7.5	11.4	39.9	•	•	5.6
Current Liabilities to Working Capital 39	27.8	•	11.9	1.5	19.0	•	6.5	10.4	38.9	•	•	4.6
Working Capital to Net Sales 40	0.0	•	0.0	0.1	0.0	0.0	0.0	0.0	0.0	0.0	0.0	0.1
Inventory to Working Capital 41	3.9	•	2.1	0.1	3.9	•	1.2	1.3	1.6	•	•	0.8
Total Receipts to Cash Flow 42	3.8	3.8	3.9	2.9	4.4	4.6	4.7	3.4	3.0	4.9	3.9	3.2
Cost of Goods to Cash Flow 43	0.9	0.6	0.9	0.5	1.3	1.1	1.6	0.8	0.4	1.5	0.4	0.5
Cash Flow to Total Debt 44	0.3	•	0.7	0.7	0.2	0.3	0.2	0.3	0.3	0.2	0.2	0.2

Selected Financial Factors (in Percentages)

	•	•	•	•	•	•	•	•	•	•	•	•
Debt Ratio 45	77.5	•	113.1	53.5	77.8	72.5	67.4	50.5	60.5	77.2	89.5	84.6
Return on Total Assets 46	6.1	•	12.6	10.5	5.3	1.6	4.2	3.7	5.9	6.1	5.4	7.2
Return on Equity Before Income Taxes 47	10.7	•	•	17.9	10.1	•	5.1	4.3	9.5	13.5	7.8	12.9
Return on Equity After Income Taxes 48	8.1	•	•	17.1	9.0	•	4.1	3.2	7.6	11.1	•	6.8
Profit Margin (Before Income Tax) 49	3.2	•	2.4	7.7	2.9	•	2.7	4.2	7.3	5.1	1.2	4.9
Profit Margin (After Income Tax) 50	2.5	•	2.3	7.4	2.6	•	2.1	3.2	5.9	4.2	•	2.6

Table II

Corporations with Net Income

AMUSEMENT, GAMBLING, AND RECREATION INDUSTRIES

MONEY AMOUNTS AND SIZE OF ASSETS IN THOUSANDS OF DOLLARS

Item Description for Accounting Period 7/05 Through 6/06	Total	Zero Assets	Under 500	500 to 1,000	1,000 to 5,000	5,000 to 10,000	10,000 to 25,000	25,000 to 50,000	50,000 to 100,000	100,000 to 250,000	250,000 to 500,000	500,000 to 2,500,000	2,500,000 and over
Number of Enterprises 1	25999	2104	19491	1861	2039	245	153	59	•	15	•	8	0
Revenues ($ in Thousands)													
Net Sales 2	27194288	408409	6360440	1705535	5201658	2522188	2056028	1527011	•	1475439	•	4040444	0
Interest 3	224689	500	2414	4693	5269	2717	3831	4095	•	5582	•	181804	0
Rents 4	104731	0	773	2002	3764	4485	2396	8291	•	5811	•	68093	0
Royalties 5	80785	3	0	0	4729	0	0	0	•	3863	•	70365	0
Other Portfolio Income 6	499746	13165	69006	13790	113335	12897	20598	20080	•	7486	•	200448	0
Other Receipts 7	3007982	19538	341614	129226	277847	132396	235194	90862	•	40279	•	1325145	0
Total Receipts 8	31112221	441615	6774247	1855246	5606602	2674683	2318047	1650339	•	1538460	•	5886299	0
Average Total Receipts 9	1197	210	348	997	2750	10917	15151	27972	•	102564	•	735787	•
Operating Costs/Operating Income (%)													
Cost of Operations 10	25.3	8.2	21.5	14.6	31.0	28.4	34.1	21.0	•	38.5	•	26.6	•
Salaries and Wages 11	21.0	10.4	16.7	21.9	17.6	26.9	21.3	23.3	•	16.0	•	25.6	•
Taxes Paid 12	7.2	16.2	4.4	5.7	5.6	7.2	6.7	7.0	•	5.4	•	12.7	•
Interest Paid 13	3.4	2.9	1.4	1.7	2.4	0.6	2.3	1.8	•	2.0	•	11.8	•
Depreciation 14	5.1	2.7	3.0	4.8	4.5	3.9	4.9	5.0	•	4.3	•	9.8	•
Amortization and Depletion 15	0.5	1.4	0.2	0.4	0.1	0.3	0.2	0.3	•	0.3	•	1.6	•
Pensions and Other Deferred Comp. 16	0.4	0.2	0.1	1.0	0.4	0.9	0.2	0.3	•	0.2	•	0.2	•
Employee Benefits 17	1.7	0.4	0.8	0.8	1.6	1.4	2.0	1.2	•	1.9	•	4.0	•
Advertising 18	2.2	3.8	1.8	2.0	1.8	2.2	2.8	3.3	•	2.4	•	1.8	•
Other Expenses 19	30.2	39.5	36.7	35.0	25.6	23.5	25.1	28.5	•	18.3	•	32.6	•
Officers' Compensation 20	3.3	0.2	6.6	4.3	3.1	2.4	1.7	1.8	•	1.8	•	1.6	•
Operating Margin 21	•	13.9	6.8	7.8	6.2	2.2	•	6.3	•	8.9	•	•	•
Operating Margin Before Officers' Comp. 22	3.1	14.1	13.4	12.1	9.3	4.7	0.5	8.1	•	10.6	•	•	•

Selected Average Balance Sheet ($ in Thousands)

Net Receivables 23	70	•	0	3	8	120	371	758	1629	•	7513	•	125771
Inventories 24	37	•	0	4	33	52	913	517	619	•	1723	•	54146
Net Property, Plant and Equipment 25	548	•	0	45	459	1266	3609	8830	18492	•	56144	•	533455
Total Assets 26	1238	•	0	90	743	2017	7409	14844	34091	•	146601	•	1728266
Notes and Loans Payable 27	520	•	0	49	230	1023	1049	5323	9567	•	38725	•	837734
All Other Liabilities 28	270	•	0	17	66	254	2252	3027	6580	•	57109	•	395272
Net Worth 29	447	•	0	24	447	739	4109	6494	17944	•	50767	•	495261

Selected Financial Ratios (Times to 1)

Current Ratio 30	1.2	•	1.4	2.4	1.3	0.8	1.3	1.0	•	1.1	•	1.3
Quick Ratio 31	0.8	•	1.0	2.1	1.1	0.3	0.8	0.7	•	0.5	•	1.0
Net Sales to Working Capital 32	20.1	•	34.4	7.6	20.1	•	17.5	236.2	•	31.3	•	6.2
Coverage Ratio 33	5.2	8.5	10.7	10.8	7.0	14.6	6.0	9.1	•	7.7	•	2.5
Total Asset Turnover 34	0.8	•	3.6	1.2	1.3	1.4	0.9	0.8	•	0.7	•	0.3
Inventory Turnover 35	7.2	•	17.4	4.0	15.1	3.2	8.9	8.8	•	22.0	•	2.5
Receivables Turnover 36	14.7	•	176.7	31.9	24.9	37.9	19.1	14.7	•	14.2	•	8.0
Total Liabilities to Net Worth 37	1.8	•	2.8	0.7	1.7	0.8	1.3	0.9	•	1.9	•	2.5
Current Assets to Working Capital 38	5.6	•	3.3	1.7	4.4	•	4.9	76.8	•	12.0	•	4.3
Current Liabilities to Working Capital 39	4.6	•	2.3	0.7	3.4	•	3.9	75.8	•	11.0	•	3.3
Working Capital to Net Sales 40	0.0	•	0.0	0.1	0.0	•	0.1	0.0	•	0.0	•	0.2
Inventory to Working Capital 41	0.8	•	0.4	0.1	0.5	•	0.8	8.8	•	0.5	•	0.7
Total Receipts to Cash Flow 42	2.9	1.9	2.8	2.4	3.4	3.7	3.4	2.7	•	3.7	•	2.5
Cost of Goods to Cash Flow 43	0.7	0.2	0.6	0.4	1.0	1.0	1.2	0.6	•	1.4	•	0.7
Cash Flow to Total Debt 44	0.5	•	1.8	1.3	0.6	0.9	0.5	0.6	•	0.3	•	0.2

Selected Financial Factors (in Percentages)

Debt Ratio 45	63.9	•	73.7	39.9	63.4	44.5	56.3	47.4	•	65.4	•	71.3
Return on Total Assets 46	14.8	•	53.1	22.5	20.7	12.2	12.4	12.6	•	10.1	•	8.5
Return on Equity Before Income Taxes 47	33.2	•	183.4	33.9	48.3	20.5	23.6	21.4	•	25.3	•	17.8
Return on Equity After Income Taxes 48	30.2	•	181.4	32.9	46.7	20.3	21.9	19.2	•	22.7	•	13.1
Profit Margin (Before Income Tax) 49	14.2	22.0	13.3	16.5	14.0	8.2	11.4	14.8	•	13.1	•	17.5
Profit Margin (After Income Tax) 50	12.9	21.7	13.2	16.0	13.5	8.1	10.6	13.3	•	11.7	•	12.8

Table I
Corporations with and without Net Income

ACCOMMODATION

MONEY AMOUNTS AND SIZE OF ASSETS IN THOUSANDS OF DOLLARS

Item Description for Accounting Period 7/05 Through 6/06		Total	Zero Assets	Under 500	500 to 1,000	1,000 to 5,000	5,000 to 10,000	10,000 to 25,000	25,000 to 50,000	50,000 to 100,000	100,000 to 250,000	250,000 to 500,000	500,000 to 2,500,000	2,500,000 and over
Number of Enterprises	1	33923	4413	17650	3101	7447	671	353	120	59	45	24	22	18
Revenues ($ in Thousands)														
Net Sales	2	81938623	3879988	3756326	1903052	8217448	2381444	3591361	2698416	4644737	4590311	3591271	7611343	35072924
Interest	3	2589574	134696	6824	6090	13090	13440	9530	19572	24832	39210	90860	296849	1934579
Rents	4	568869	51220	517	3333	6885	5525	11343	2717	10050	31351	24200	96299	325429
Royalties	5	1644668	5514	0	0	0	3	905	0	76	5780	179149	28503	1424737
Other Portfolio Income	6	5503008	750187	200762	11155	90374	63776	116389	54022	394534	165945	30859	1452263	2172743
Other Receipts	7	10228812	112918	59155	44489	85258	42236	187549	110169	393872	341194	189597	498565	8163814
Total Receipts	8	102473554	4934523	4023584	1968119	8413055	2506424	3917077	2884896	5468101	5173791	4105936	9983822	49094226
Average Total Receipts	9	3021	1118	228	635	1130	3735	11097	24041	92680	114973	171081	453810	2727457
Operating Costs/Operating Income (%)														
Cost of Operations	10	15.5	6.8	12.3	2.3	15.8	16.3	22.3	25.5	31.5	19.2	14.0	16.0	13.5
Salaries and Wages	11	27.3	24.5	16.5	16.9	18.7	14.4	20.9	15.9	12.7	16.8	20.7	20.5	39.1
Taxes Paid	12	7.9	11.2	10.1	9.4	7.5	5.6	5.4	5.1	3.2	5.7	6.7	9.0	8.6
Interest Paid	13	9.2	12.5	3.2	7.9	9.0	7.9	5.1	4.8	2.7	4.6	6.3	8.1	12.3
Depreciation	14	5.5	5.2	3.7	5.4	7.2	5.7	4.7	5.4	2.7	5.7	6.2	5.8	5.7
Amortization and Depletion	15	0.9	0.9	0.2	2.1	0.7	0.3	0.7	0.4	0.5	0.6	0.6	1.0	1.0
Pensions and Other Deferred Comp.	16	0.5	0.3	0.5	•	0.1	0.1	0.2	0.1	0.1	0.2	0.7	0.3	0.8
Employee Benefits	17	2.6	4.4	0.3	0.4	0.9	0.9	1.8	1.7	1.5	2.3	1.9	1.7	3.9
Advertising	18	3.4	2.0	1.5	2.1	2.1	3.1	2.1	1.9	2.8	3.0	3.3	3.6	4.5
Other Expenses	19	40.3	47.1	59.3	46.6	35.0	42.5	41.1	41.4	55.2	45.7	42.2	41.7	34.9
Officers' Compensation	20	1.8	1.3	3.7	1.9	2.5	2.6	0.9	0.7	0.4	0.9	1.2	0.8	2.1
Operating Margin	21	•	•	•	5.0	0.4	0.7	•	•	•	•	•	•	•
Operating Margin Before Officers' Comp.	22	•	•	•	6.9	3.0	3.3	•	•	•	•	•	•	•

Selected Average Balance Sheet ($ in Thousands)

Net Receivables 23	411	0	11	22	46	362	767	1269	6074	5739	31074	91984	515171
Inventories 24	82	0	3	6	17	63	120	360	1185	1471	6304	23765	90768
Net Property, Plant and Equipment 25	2788	0	75	502	1607	4496	9254	19720	35209	94649	170227	418676	2858497
Total Assets 26	6542	0	137	715	2171	6428	14926	32882	67838	164634	338762	991669	8125024
Notes and Loans Payable 27	3157	0	113	729	1838	5035	9175	22560	32169	70445	154453	367023	3498132
All Other Liabilities 28	1520	0	22	48	156	1049	2526	7154	18270	28320	48496	211794	2179554
Net Worth 29	1866	0	2	-62	177	345	3225	3167	17399	65869	135813	412852	2447338

Selected Financial Ratios (Times to 1)

Current Ratio 30	1.3	•	1.7	1.4	1.7	1.2	1.0	0.8	1.3	1.4	1.7	1.4	1.3
Quick Ratio 31	1.0	•	1.4	1.3	1.0	1.0	0.7	0.6	0.9	0.8	1.2	0.9	1.0
Net Sales to Working Capital 32	8.7	•	11.0	18.2	9.4	13.2	•	•	16.6	9.4	4.2	5.0	7.1
Coverage Ratio 33	2.1	2.0	•	2.1	1.3	1.7	1.7	1.9	2.7	2.8	2.7	3.8	2.1
Total Asset Turnover 34	0.4	•	1.6	0.9	0.5	0.6	0.7	0.7	1.2	0.6	0.4	0.3	0.2
Inventory Turnover 35	4.6	•	9.1	2.3	10.0	9.2	19.0	15.9	20.9	13.3	3.3	2.3	2.9
Receivables Turnover 36	7.3	•	29.0	26.3	23.5	10.4	12.5	14.1	15.9	13.1	3.7	4.7	5.2
Total Liabilities to Net Worth 37	2.5	•	89.0	•	11.3	17.7	3.6	9.4	2.9	1.5	1.5	1.4	2.3
Current Assets to Working Capital 38	3.9	•	2.4	3.4	2.4	5.0	•	•	4.3	3.6	2.4	3.5	4.2
Current Liabilities to Working Capital 39	2.9	•	1.4	2.4	1.4	4.0	•	•	3.3	2.6	1.4	2.5	3.2
Working Capital to Net Sales 40	0.1	•	0.1	0.1	0.1	0.1	•	•	0.1	0.1	0.2	0.2	0.1
Inventory to Working Capital 41	0.3	•	0.2	0.2	0.1	0.2	•	•	0.3	0.1	0.2	0.3	0.4
Total Receipts to Cash Flow 42	2.8	3.0	3.8	2.5	3.3	2.7	3.7	3.7	3.4	2.5	2.3	2.6	2.6
Cost of Goods to Cash Flow 43	0.4	0.2	0.5	0.1	0.5	0.4	0.8	0.9	1.1	0.5	0.3	0.4	0.3
Cash Flow to Total Debt 44	0.2	•	0.4	0.3	0.2	0.2	0.2	0.2	0.5	0.4	0.3	0.2	0.1

Selected Financial Factors (in Percentages)

Debt Ratio 45	71.5	•	98.9	108.7	91.9	94.6	78.4	90.4	74.4	60.0	59.9	58.4	69.9
Return on Total Assets 46	7.3	•	•	14.0	6.0	7.6	6.0	6.1	8.2	7.8	7.4	10.7	6.3
Return on Equity Before Income Taxes 47	13.6	•	•	•	17.6	61.0	11.7	29.2	20.0	12.4	11.6	18.9	11.0
Return on Equity After Income Taxes 48	10.0	•	•	•	15.6	54.4	9.0	24.5	19.0	9.6	9.1	17.0	7.6
Profit Margin (Before Income Tax) 49	10.5	12.4	•	8.4	2.8	5.9	3.7	4.1	4.4	8.0	10.5	22.6	13.8
Profit Margin (After Income Tax) 50	7.8	5.2	7.9	•	2.5	5.3	2.8	3.4	4.2	6.2	8.3	20.2	9.5

383

Table II

Corporations with Net Income

ACCOMMODATION

ACCOMMODATION

MONEY AMOUNTS AND SIZE OF ASSETS IN THOUSANDS OF DOLLARS

Item Description for Accounting Period 7/05 Through 6/06	Total	Zero Assets	Under 500	500 to 1,000	1,000 to 5,000	5,000 to 10,000	10,000 to 25,000	25,000 to 50,000	50,000 to 100,000	100,000 to 250,000	250,000 to 500,000	500,000 to 2,500,000	2,500,000 and over
Number of Enterprises **1**	16184	1777	7348	1817	4404	438	210	77	35	31	17	16	15
Revenues ($ in Thousands)													
Net Sales **2**	63161930	3253160	1699570	1289123	5539231	1504240	2362210	1280383	1834632	3526840	2421744	5752365	32698432
Interest **3**	2437423	101325	5382	4655	11975	9472	7473	19030	17281	33978	83111	286071	1857670
Rents **4**	524685	50022	24	2408	5063	5525	6291	1961	6142	28128	22326	80561	316233
Royalties **5**	1639214	985	0	0	0	3	905	0	76	5780	179149	28503	1423813
Other Portfolio Income **6**	5405746	702854	186188	11022	89022	61402	114805	53241	391053	158806	29449	1440143	2167759
Other Receipts **7**	9716342	93847	29590	29654	114686	36447	87261	71636	351187	334185	108681	461022	7998149
Total Receipts **8**	82885340	4202193	1920754	1336862	5759977	1617089	2578945	1426251	2600371	4087717	2844460	8048665	46462056
Average Total Receipts **9**	5121	2365	261	736	1308	3692	12281	18523	74296	131862	167321	503042	3097470
Operating Costs/Operating Income (%)													
Cost of Operations **10**	14.6	7.6	10.4	2.1	15.4	20.0	22.4	16.6	32.4	19.4	13.5	13.1	13.9
Salaries and Wages **11**	30.1	20.8	10.7	16.8	16.5	14.2	25.6	24.9	17.6	17.6	24.6	22.4	39.9
Taxes Paid **12**	8.3	11.7	6.4	8.4	6.9	6.7	5.8	6.8	4.6	5.2	6.2	10.7	8.8
Interest Paid **13**	9.9	10.0	1.4	5.9	8.3	7.9	4.8	7.2	4.4	4.2	6.5	9.0	12.6
Depreciation **14**	5.1	5.7	3.2	4.9	6.1	6.1	4.3	6.6	4.4	4.8	6.5	5.5	4.8
Amortization and Depletion **15**	0.8	0.6	0.1	0.6	0.7	0.4	0.2	0.4	0.5	0.6	0.7	1.2	1.0
Pensions and Other Deferred Comp. **16**	0.6	0.3	1.0	•	0.1	0.1	0.3	0.2	0.2	0.2	0.9	0.3	0.9
Employee Benefits **17**	2.8	5.1	0.4	0.5	0.8	1.1	2.1	2.8	1.1	2.5	2.4	1.8	3.7
Advertising **18**	3.6	1.9	1.2	1.5	1.8	1.8	2.2	2.8	2.6	3.2	4.0	2.8	4.7
Other Expenses **19**	36.0	37.1	50.1	41.0	30.5	30.7	28.6	28.0	56.6	45.2	32.3	38.0	34.7
Officers' Compensation **20**	2.0	0.6	6.0	2.0	3.2	3.4	0.9	1.1	0.6	0.8	1.6	0.9	2.2
Operating Margin **21**	•	•	9.2	16.5	9.8	7.7	2.8	2.6	•	•	0.7	•	•
Operating Margin Before Officers' Comp. **22**	•	•	15.2	18.4	13.0	11.2	3.7	3.6	•	•	2.3	•	•

Selected Average Balance Sheet ($ in Thousands)

Net Receivables 23	756	0	11	27	56	372	990	824	3923	6916	40285	90405	595591
Inventories 24	138	0	4	5	18	64	106	266	740	1068	8029	27578	116563
Net Property, Plant and Equipment 25	4551	0	99	445	1606	4689	9013	19901	34158	90345	163951	434903	3054858
Total Assets 26	11605	0	182	697	2194	6467	15218	32245	64784	166931	356181	1057972	9107293
Notes and Loans Payable 27	5298	0	81	653	1769	4814	8877	23091	30444	74106	162238	390041	3870767
All Other Liabilities 28	2774	0	14	29	125	938	1525	6001	12470	30725	40121	178718	2538069
Net Worth 29	3532	0	88	14	299	715	4816	3153	21870	62100	153822	489213	2698458

Selected Financial Ratios (Times to 1)

Current Ratio 30	1.4	•	3.1	1.9	2.0	1.5	1.8	0.9	1.5	1.3	2.2	1.5	1.2
Quick Ratio 31	1.0	•	2.5	1.7	1.1	1.2	1.4	0.6	1.0	0.8	1.6	1.0	0.9
Net Sales to Working Capital 32	8.0	•	5.9	15.0	6.9	7.9	7.7	•	9.3	14.0	2.6	4.4	9.1
Coverage Ratio 33	2.8	3.9	16.6	4.4	2.7	2.9	3.5	2.9	4.9	3.9	3.8	4.8	2.2
Total Asset Turnover 34	0.3	•	1.3	1.0	0.6	0.5	0.7	0.5	0.8	0.7	0.4	0.3	0.2
Inventory Turnover 35	4.1	•	5.8	2.7	10.6	10.7	23.7	10.4	22.9	20.7	2.4	1.7	2.6
Receivables Turnover 36	7.0	•	24.1	22.9	27.0	14.7	12.3	14.6	19.8	15.6	3.4	8.0	7.3
Total Liabilities to Net Worth 37	2.3	•	1.1	47.1	6.3	8.0	2.2	9.2	2.0	1.7	1.3	1.2	2.4
Current Assets to Working Capital 38	3.8	•	1.5	2.2	2.0	3.0	2.3	•	3.1	5.0	1.8	3.1	5.2
Current Liabilities to Working Capital 39	2.8	•	0.5	1.2	1.0	2.0	1.3	•	2.1	4.0	0.8	2.1	4.2
Working Capital to Net Sales 40	0.1	•	0.2	0.1	0.1	0.1	0.1	•	0.1	0.1	0.4	0.2	0.1
Inventory to Working Capital 41	0.3	•	0.2	0.0	0.1	0.2	0.1	•	0.2	0.1	0.2	0.3	0.5
Total Receipts to Cash Flow 42	2.5	2.3	2.3	2.2	2.6	2.6	3.5	3.0	2.4	2.3	2.2	2.1	2.5
Cost of Goods to Cash Flow 43	0.4	0.2	0.2	0.0	0.4	0.5	0.8	0.5	0.8	0.5	0.3	0.3	0.3
Cash Flow to Total Debt 44	0.2	•	1.1	0.5	0.3	0.2	0.3	0.2	0.5	0.5	0.3	0.3	0.1

Selected Financial Factors (in Percentages)

Debt Ratio 45	69.6	•	51.9	97.9	86.4	88.9	68.4	90.2	66.2	62.8	56.8	53.8	70.4
Return on Total Assets 46	9.3	•	30.0	26.5	12.7	12.3	12.4	10.9	17.3	11.2	9.8	14.6	6.7
Return on Equity Before Income Taxes 47	19.7	•	58.5	988.1	57.9	73.0	27.8	73.0	40.9	22.4	16.7	25.0	12.5
Return on Equity After Income Taxes 48	15.7	•	55.9	954.2	56.0	68.2	24.7	65.7	39.4	18.2	13.7	22.8	8.8
Profit Margin (Before Income Tax) 49	17.8	28.9	22.2	20.2	13.8	15.2	11.9	13.9	17.1	12.2	18.1	34.1	15.5
Profit Margin (After Income Tax) 50	14.3	20.3	21.2	19.5	13.3	14.2	10.6	12.5	16.4	9.9	14.8	31.0	10.9

Table I
Corporations with and without Net Income

FOOD SERVICES AND DRINKING PLACES

MONEY AMOUNTS AND SIZE OF ASSETS IN THOUSANDS OF DOLLARS

Item Description for Accounting Period 7/05 Through 6/06	Total	Zero Assets	Under 500	500 to 1,000	1,000 to 5,000	5,000 to 10,000	10,000 to 25,000	25,000 to 50,000	50,000 to 100,000	100,000 to 250,000	250,000 to 500,000	500,000 to 2,500,000	2,500,000 and over
Number of Enterprises 1	253567	30504	199114	13842	8734	654	413	140	56	48	23	28	11
Revenues ($ in Thousands)													
Net Sales 2	313792833	4776583	99610831	25825780	37748318	10266341	11738806	8008824	7324986	10688596	10849209	34189952	52764608
Interest 3	1405856	8117	13420	11537	12738	5854	11080	7155	8931	17125	11930	330856	967113
Rents 4	655123	6963	23815	7857	12884	13012	6859	11111	18114	45021	45269	244940	219278
Royalties 5	4387658	20631	5718	0	51	448	34084	89047	59071	163570	578574	889622	2546843
Other Portfolio Income 6	6951140	208396	438990	49737	94537	27918	56612	27836	52767	489221	43009	201697	5260416
Other Receipts 7	8904552	177479	480720	239519	426947	278415	247760	200861	35976	214727	632741	875272	5094137
Total Receipts 8	336097162	5198169	100573494	26134430	38295475	10591988	12095201	8344834	7499845	11618260	12160732	36732339	66852395
Average Total Receipts 9	1325	170	505	1888	4385	16196	29286	59606	133926	242047	528727	1311869	6077490
Operating Costs/Operating Income (%)													
Cost of Operations 10	41.4	43.5	42.1	36.7	40.6	40.2	44.2	43.9	39.7	42.7	38.0	41.2	42.6
Salaries and Wages 11	19.9	17.7	16.8	21.1	18.9	21.3	19.3	19.5	17.8	20.3	26.5	23.2	22.4
Taxes Paid 12	4.3	4.7	4.4	4.5	3.7	3.9	3.7	3.7	3.7	3.9	3.5	4.4	4.8
Interest Paid 13	1.7	2.7	0.6	0.9	1.1	1.6	1.7	2.1	1.4	2.6	2.9	2.6	3.6
Depreciation 14	2.3	3.0	1.6	2.2	2.1	2.0	2.4	2.4	2.4	3.0	3.2	3.3	2.7
Amortization and Depletion 15	0.5	0.6	0.3	0.3	0.5	0.6	0.5	0.7	0.5	0.6	0.7	0.5	0.6
Pensions and Other Deferred Comp. 16	0.2	0.0	0.1	0.1	0.0	0.3	0.3	0.2	0.2	0.3	0.3	0.4	0.3
Employee Benefits 17	1.2	0.6	0.5	0.8	0.8	1.3	1.1	1.3	1.2	1.7	1.5	1.6	2.8
Advertising 18	2.4	2.4	1.7	2.8	3.3	3.2	2.9	2.8	2.5	3.0	2.8	2.9	2.2
Other Expenses 19	24.8	37.2	25.9	25.2	23.7	24.6	22.7	22.7	29.7	23.6	26.4	20.8	25.1
Officers' Compensation 20	2.5	3.2	4.7	2.7	2.1	1.5	1.3	1.5	0.9	1.2	0.9	0.9	0.8
Operating Margin 21	•	•	1.2	2.9	3.3	•	•	•	•	•	•	•	•
Operating Margin Before Officers' Comp. 22	1.3	•	5.9	5.5	5.3	1.2	1.3	0.9	0.8	•	•	•	•

Selected Average Balance Sheet ($ in Thousands)

Net Receivables 23	57	0	3	24	109	171	676	2563	4728	6855	30637	81560	732301
Inventories 24	21	0	7	26	53	416	442	859	2026	3657	8786	23259	125079
Net Property, Plant and Equipment 25	280	0	51	365	936	3626	7571	16147	35999	72280	169335	495515	1509451
Total Assets 26	731	111	664	1892	6691	14975	35444	69602	150818	352112	1056976	6654266	
Notes and Loans Payable 27	296	89	406	1050	3262	7589	17574	24998	59909	168703	328950	1579228	
All Other Liabilities 28	223	23	105	362	1568	3683	11196	20851	48275	100241	371074	2447978	
Net Worth 29	213	-1	152	480	1861	3703	6674	23752	42634	83168	356951	2627060	

Selected Financial Ratios (Times to 1)

Current Ratio 30	1.0	•	1.2	1.2	0.8	0.9	0.9	0.8	0.8	0.8	0.9	0.9
Quick Ratio 31	0.7	•	0.8	0.8	0.4	0.6	0.6	0.5	0.6	0.6	0.6	0.7
Net Sales to Working Capital 32	•	91.3	70.3	62.7	•	•	•	•	•	•	•	•
Coverage Ratio 33	4.6	4.6	5.5	5.2	2.8	2.6	2.5	3.2	3.2	2.8	3.2	6.5
Total Asset Turnover 34	1.7	4.5	2.8	2.3	1.9	1.6	1.9	1.5	1.3	1.3	1.2	0.7
Inventory Turnover 35	24.6	30.9	26.1	33.2	28.4	29.2	25.7	26.0	20.4	21.6	16.3	
Receivables Turnover 36	25.6	147.7	76.8	48.8	37.9	22.6	31.5	27.0	19.6	19.2	7.8	
Total Liabilities to Net Worth 37	2.4	•	3.4	2.9	3.0	4.3	1.9	2.5	3.2	2.0	1.5	
Current Assets to Working Capital 38	•	6.3	5.8	7.5	•	•	•	•	•	•	•	•
Current Liabilities to Working Capital 39	•	5.3	4.8	6.5	•	•	•	•	•	•	•	•
Working Capital to Net Sales 40	•	0.0	0.0	0.0	•	•	•	•	•	•	•	•
Inventory to Working Capital 41	•	1.3	0.9	0.8	•	•	•	•	•	•	•	•
Total Receipts to Cash Flow 42	4.7	5.6	4.9	5.2	5.8	5.5	4.2	5.6	4.3	5.3	3.0	
Cost of Goods to Cash Flow 43	1.9	2.4	1.8	2.1	2.6	2.4	1.7	2.4	1.6	2.2	1.3	
Cash Flow to Total Debt 44	0.5	0.8	0.7	0.6	0.4	0.4	0.7	0.4	0.4	0.3	0.4	

Selected Financial Factors (in Percentages)

Debt Ratio 45	70.9	101.2	77.0	74.6	72.2	75.3	81.2	65.9	71.7	76.4	66.2	60.5
Return on Total Assets 46	13.3	12.6	13.9	13.3	10.4	8.9	9.1	6.8	12.2	10.8	9.4	16.7
Return on Equity Before Income Taxes 47	35.6	•	49.6	42.5	23.9	23.1	30.1	12.1	29.8	29.2	19.2	35.8
Return on Equity After Income Taxes 48	29.1	•	48.2	40.7	22.7	20.6	26.9	9.8	23.9	19.4	12.7	28.0
Profit Margin (Before Income Tax) 49	6.1	2.2	4.1	4.7	2.8	3.0	3.5	2.2	5.7	5.1	5.6	19.6
Profit Margin (After Income Tax) 50	5.0	2.1	3.9	4.5	2.7	3.1	3.4	1.8	4.6	3.4	5.6	15.3

385

Table II
Corporations with Net Income

FOOD SERVICES AND DRINKING PLACES

MONEY AMOUNTS AND SIZE OF ASSETS IN THOUSANDS OF DOLLARS

Item Description for Accounting Period 7/05 Through 6/06		Total	Zero Assets	Under 500	500 to 1,000	1,000 to 5,000	5,000 to 10,000	10,000 to 25,000	25,000 to 50,000	50,000 to 100,000	100,000 to 250,000	250,000 to 500,000	500,000 to 2,500,000	2,500,000 and over
Number of Enterprises	1	133397	9672	106242	9678	6737	530	304	101	44	35	17	24	11
Revenues ($ in Thousands)														
Net Sales	2	251903741	1511757	69043678	18484843	31760358	8181106	8843802	6002772	6082522	8463933	8881800	31882562	52764608
Interest	3	1285225	3343	9485	9444	10117	3194	8776	3408	5578	14168	10429	240170	967113
Rents	4	577639	1010	9636	3642	10757	11299	5498	10451	11169	44781	13355	236763	219278
Royalties	5	4186117	0	5718	0	51	0	22173	84687	50855	156533	538791	780468	2546843
Other Portfolio Income	6	6673439	154989	328974	43844	82572	26179	55220	26180	51412	473874	41199	128577	5260416
Other Receipts	7	8328712	120971	320469	183988	339133	220286	199228	167415	29562	202107	610952	840464	5094137
Total Receipts	8	272954873	1792070	69717960	18725761	32202988	8442064	9134697	6294913	6231098	9355396	10096526	34109004	66852395
Average Total Receipts	9	2046	185	656	1935	4780	15928	30048	62326	141616	267297	593913	1421208	6077490
Operating Costs/Operating Income (%)														
Cost of Operations	10	40.9	43.9	41.4	36.8	39.5	40.5	44.9	43.0	36.6	41.3	36.9	41.5	42.6
Salaries and Wages	11	19.9	12.8	16.0	20.4	19.1	19.9	19.2	19.2	18.4	21.4	28.6	22.7	22.4
Taxes Paid	12	4.2	4.8	4.1	4.4	3.7	3.8	3.6	3.8	3.7	4.0	3.7	4.5	4.8
Interest Paid	13	1.7	2.1	0.5	0.8	1.0	1.5	1.4	2.0	1.3	2.1	2.3	2.1	3.6
Depreciation	14	2.2	1.8	1.4	2.0	1.9	1.8	2.2	2.4	2.3	3.1	3.4	3.4	2.7
Amortization and Depletion	15	0.4	0.3	0.3	0.3	0.4	0.6	0.4	0.6	0.4	0.5	0.5	0.3	0.6
Pensions and Other Deferred Comp.	16	0.2	0.0	0.2	0.1	0.0	0.1	0.1	0.1	0.2	0.3	0.4	0.3	0.3
Employee Benefits	17	1.3	0.6	0.5	0.5	0.8	1.0	1.1	1.2	1.1	1.9	1.6	1.4	2.8
Advertising	18	2.4	2.2	1.7	2.2	3.5	3.1	2.8	3.0	2.6	3.1	2.8	3.0	2.2
Other Expenses	19	23.6	29.9	23.6	23.9	22.8	24.4	20.4	21.7	31.3	23.6	26.0	20.7	25.1
Officers' Compensation	20	2.3	2.8	4.9	2.7	2.1	1.3	1.5	1.4	1.0	1.3	1.1	0.6	0.8
Operating Margin	21	0.8	•	5.6	6.0	5.2	1.9	2.4	1.5	1.1	•	•	•	•
Operating Margin Before Officers' Comp.	22	3.1	1.7	10.4	8.7	7.2	3.2	3.8	2.9	2.1	•	•	0.3	•

Selected Average Balance Sheet ($ in Thousands)

	1	2	3	4	5	6	7	8	9	10	11	12	13
Net Receivables 23	91	0	4	23	125	123	698	2171	5013	8177	12803	55588	732301
Inventories 24	32	0	8	25	56	410	428	779	1898	3771	10048	30365	124288
Net Property, Plant and Equipment 25	437	0	54	347	906	3343	7426	16078	36938	81275	190222	547324	1509451
Total Assets 26	1181	0	128	660	1948	6375	14770	35283	69610	155646	352530	1055773	6654266
Notes and Loans Payable 27	402	0	74	331	987	2860	6172	16293	26023	56225	142249	330839	1579228
All Other Liabilities 28	350	0	20	78	369	1317	3642	13067	21011	50912	94977	285891	2447978
Net Worth 29	430	0	34	252	592	2198	4955	5923	22576	48509	115303	439044	2627060

Selected Financial Ratios (Times to 1)

	1	2	3	4	5	6	7	8	9	10	11	12	13
Current Ratio 30	1.0	•	1.7	1.6	1.3	0.9	1.1	0.9	0.8	0.9	0.7	0.8	0.9
Quick Ratio 31	0.7	•	1.2	1.2	1.0	0.5	0.7	0.6	0.5	0.6	0.5	0.4	0.7
Net Sales to Working Capital 32	594.5	•	32.5	28.7	35.5	•	110.1	•	•	•	•	•	•
Coverage Ratio 33	6.5	9.4	14.3	10.0	7.6	4.4	5.1	4.1	3.6	4.7	3.8	4.2	6.5
Total Asset Turnover 34	1.6	•	5.1	2.9	2.4	2.4	2.0	1.7	2.0	1.6	1.5	1.3	0.7
Inventory Turnover 35	24.5	•	34.6	27.9	33.5	15.3	30.6	32.8	26.7	26.5	19.2	18.2	16.4
Receivables Turnover 36	25.3	•	151.6	82.2	47.9	95.3	40.2	28.4	36.1	31.2	29.6	47.8	13.1
Total Liabilities to Net Worth 37	1.7	•	2.8	1.6	2.3	1.9	2.0	5.0	2.1	2.2	2.1	1.4	1.5
Current Assets to Working Capital 38	88.3	•	2.4	2.6	4.5	•	15.4	•	•	•	•	•	•
Current Liabilities to Working Capital 39	87.3	•	1.4	1.6	3.5	•	14.4	•	•	•	•	•	•
Working Capital to Net Sales 40	0.0	•	0.0	0.0	0.0	•	0.0	•	•	•	•	•	•
Inventory to Working Capital 41	10.4	•	0.4	0.3	0.4	•	1.9	•	•	•	•	•	•
Total Receipts to Cash Flow 42	4.2	3.4	4.7	4.6	4.9	4.9	5.5	5.0	3.7	5.0	4.2	5.0	3.0
Cost of Goods to Cash Flow 43	1.7	1.5	2.0	1.7	1.9	2.0	2.5	2.1	1.4	2.1	1.5	2.1	1.3
Cash Flow to Total Debt 44	0.6	•	1.5	1.0	0.7	0.8	0.5	0.4	0.8	0.4	0.5	0.4	0.4

Selected Financial Factors (in Percentages)

	1	2	3	4	5	6	7	8	9	10	11	12	13
Debt Ratio 45	63.6	•	73.6	61.8	69.6	65.5	66.5	83.2	67.6	68.8	67.3	58.4	60.5
Return on Total Assets 46	17.6	•	35.7	23.4	18.3	16.0	13.8	14.2	9.6	15.5	13.1	11.0	16.7
Return on Equity Before Income Taxes 47	40.8	•	125.8	55.1	52.2	36.0	33.1	64.0	21.6	39.1	29.6	20.2	35.8
Return on Equity After Income Taxes 48	34.8	•	124.3	53.9	50.4	34.8	30.5	58.9	18.5	32.0	20.0	14.1	28.0
Profit Margin (Before Income Tax) 49	9.3	17.5	6.5	7.3	6.6	5.1	5.6	6.4	3.5	7.8	6.5	6.7	19.6
Profit Margin (After Income Tax) 50	7.9	16.9	6.5	7.1	6.3	5.0	5.2	5.9	3.0	6.4	4.4	4.7	15.3

Table I

Corporations with and without Net Income

AUTOMOTIVE REPAIR AND MAINTENANCE

MONEY AMOUNTS AND SIZE OF ASSETS IN THOUSANDS OF DOLLARS

Item Description for Accounting Period 7/05 Through 6/06	Total	Zero Assets	Under 500	500 to 1,000	1,000 to 5,000	5,000 to 10,000	10,000 to 25,000	25,000 to 50,000	50,000 to 100,000	100,000 to 250,000	250,000 to 500,000	500,000 to 2,500,000	2,500,000 and over
Number of Enterprises **1**	105596	9630	87215	6154	2319	203	51	6	11	4	3	0	0
Revenues ($ in Thousands)													
Net Sales **2**	64398524	1545085	39363224	10284120	7687480	1398462	1139882	177752	1162771	793186	846561	0	0
Interest **3**	37137	2041	10103	4580	7052	452	438	1759	5178	5136	399	0	0
Rents **4**	33979	119	14471	9182	5381	1172	1194	0	1903	114	442	0	0
Royalties **5**	67509	0	115	0	296	0	0	0	1551	63786	1761	0	0
Other Portfolio Income **6**	213460	52692	51123	36035	4557	30393	23130	4395	1193	8060	1883	0	0
Other Receipts **7**	187954	7273	83069	30809	33908	11266	10953	525	4399	2235	3517	0	0
Total Receipts **8**	64938563	1607210	39552105	10364726	7738674	1441745	1175597	184431	1176995	872517	854563	0	0
Average Total Receipts **9**	615	167	453	1684	3337	7102	23051	30738	107000	218129	284854	·	·
Operating Costs/Operating Income (%)													
Cost of Operations **10**	50.3	38.8	47.3	60.2	53.8	50.6	51.3	36.9	53.2	60.5	48.7	·	·
Salaries and Wages **11**	12.1	13.5	12.7	7.9	14.8	8.2	14.2	23.2	15.7	8.5	8.5	·	·
Taxes Paid **12**	3.7	4.1	3.7	3.0	3.7	12.0	3.2	3.5	3.5	1.1	3.0	·	·
Interest Paid **13**	1.2	1.2	0.8	1.3	1.8	1.9	2.0	2.3	3.0	3.7	6.0	·	·
Depreciation **14**	1.9	2.2	1.8	1.7	2.3	2.2	2.9	4.5	2.3	3.3	3.1	·	·
Amortization and Depletion **15**	0.4	0.5	0.2	0.5	0.4	0.2	1.6	1.0	1.2	3.7	1.9	·	·
Pensions and Other Deferred Comp. **16**	0.1	0.0	0.1	0.1	0.2	0.6	0.2	0.2	0.0	0.3	0.1	·	·
Employee Benefits **17**	1.1	0.7	1.1	1.3	0.9	0.7	1.2	3.3	1.1	3.3	1.4	·	·
Advertising **18**	1.6	1.9	1.6	1.6	1.6	1.0	2.8	2.0	1.1	1.7	1.6	·	·
Other Expenses **19**	19.8	39.1	21.0	17.0	14.2	17.1	19.1	20.1	19.1	25.3	19.2	·	·
Officers' Compensation **20**	6.0	6.0	7.6	3.9	4.0	2.3	1.5	2.1	0.6	0.7	1.0	·	·
Operating Margin **21**	1.7	·	2.3	1.6	2.3	3.2	·	0.9	·	·	5.6	·	·
Operating Margin Before Officers' Comp. **22**	7.7	·	9.9	5.5	6.3	5.6	1.5	3.0	·	·	6.5	·	·

Selected Average Balance Sheet ($ in Thousands)

Net Receivables 23	19	0	9	77	149	711	936	2190	10146	12836	5903	•
Inventories 24	21	0	12	55	196	716	1286	2417	2373	8353	35148	•
Net Property, Plant and Equipment 25	87	0	40	300	866	3182	6301	7088	20679	44760	117560	•
Total Assets 26	207	0	100	696	1750	6554	15290	33215	70504	189484	314743	•
Notes and Loans Payable 27	124	0	67	409	1034	3480	6037	15112	30277	101299	181467	•
All Other Liabilities 28	40	0	25	103	234	1040	1325	7235	17946	37080	57667	•
Net Worth 29	42	0	8	184	482	2034	7928	10868	22280	51105	75610	•

Selected Financial Ratios (Times to 1)

Current Ratio 30	1.5	•	1.4	1.8	1.8	1.3	1.0	0.8	1.5	1.2	1.2	•
Quick Ratio 31	0.9	•	0.9	1.2	1.2	0.6	0.6	0.2	1.1	0.4	0.3	•
Net Sales to Working Capital 32	25.7	•	36.3	16.4	13.5	11.1	•	•	16.7	20.8	32.4	•
Coverage Ratio 33	3.1	•	4.3	2.8	2.7	4.4	2.6	2.8	1.1	0.4	2.1	•
Total Asset Turnover 34	3.0	•	4.5	2.4	1.9	1.1	1.5	0.9	1.5	1.0	0.9	•
Inventory Turnover 35	14.4	•	17.4	18.4	9.1	4.9	8.9	4.5	23.7	14.4	3.9	•
Receivables Turnover 36	31.6	•	46.4	23.8	19.5	10.8	16.3	7.6	17.2	16.9	29.7	•
Total Liabilities to Net Worth 37	3.9	•	11.8	2.8	2.6	2.2	0.9	2.1	2.2	2.7	3.2	•
Current Assets to Working Capital 38	3.1	•	3.5	2.3	2.3	4.0	•	•	3.2	5.7	5.9	•
Current Liabilities to Working Capital 39	2.1	•	2.5	1.3	1.3	3.0	•	•	2.2	4.7	4.9	•
Working Capital to Net Sales 40	0.0	•	0.0	0.1	0.1	0.1	•	•	0.1	0.0	0.0	•
Inventory to Working Capital 41	0.9	•	1.0	0.6	0.7	1.7	•	•	0.5	1.2	3.2	•
Total Receipts to Cash Flow 42	6.3	5.0	6.0	7.0	8.1	5.5	6.6	6.5	6.5	6.4	5.8	•
Cost of Goods to Cash Flow 43	3.2	1.9	2.8	4.2	4.4	2.8	3.4	2.4	3.5	3.9	2.8	•
Cash Flow to Total Debt 44	0.6	•	0.8	0.5	0.3	0.3	0.5	0.2	0.3	0.2	0.2	•

Selected Financial Factors (in Percentages)

Debt Ratio 45	79.4	•	92.2	73.5	72.5	69.0	48.2	67.3	68.4	73.0	76.0	•
Return on Total Assets 46	11.0	•	15.7	8.9	8.9	8.6	7.5	5.8	4.9	1.7	11.3	•
Return on Equity Before Income Taxes 47	36.4	•	155.5	21.4	20.3	21.4	8.8	11.6	1.2	•	24.9	•
Return on Equity After Income Taxes 48	34.2	•	152.2	19.4	19.2	19.6	8.4	8.4	0.7	•	18.3	•
Profit Margin (Before Income Tax) 49	2.5	•	2.7	2.4	2.9	6.3	3.1	4.2	0.2	•	6.7	•
Profit Margin (After Income Tax) 50	2.4	•	2.6	2.1	2.8	5.8	3.0	3.1	0.1	•	4.9	•

Table II

Corporations with Net Income

AUTOMOTIVE REPAIR AND MAINTENANCE

MONEY AMOUNTS AND SIZE OF ASSETS IN THOUSANDS OF DOLLARS

Item Description for Accounting Period 7/05 Through 6/06	Total	Zero Assets	Under 500	500 to 1,000	1,000 to 5,000	5,000 to 10,000	10,000 to 25,000	25,000 to 50,000	50,000 to 100,000	100,000 to 250,000	250,000 to 500,000	500,000 to 2,500,000	2,500,000 and over
Number of Enterprises **1**	63291	3806	53462	4295	1559	119	37	•	5	0	•	0	0
Revenues ($ in Thousands)													
Net Sales **2**	46165297	661442	26260885	8728538	6813142	997486	1006039	•	673451	0	•	0	0
Interest **3**	24023	1758	7898	2418	5057	438	347	•	3950	0	•	0	0
Rents **4**	17480	0	5803	6207	3063	1172	791	•	2	0	•	0	0
Royalties **5**	67213	0	115	0	0	0	0	•	65337	0	•	0	0
Other Portfolio Income **6**	171738	30383	39110	30487	4322	30363	22980	•	7816	0	•	0	0
Other Receipts **7**	149463	5108	61831	26722	29670	10443	9622	•	2025	0	•	0	0
Total Receipts **8**	46595214	698691	26375642	8794372	6855254	1039902	1039779	•	752581	0	•	0	0
Average Total Receipts **9**	736	184	493	2048	4397	8739	28102	•	150516	•	•	•	•
Operating Costs/Operating Income (%)													
Cost of Operations **10**	50.0	47.3	45.3	60.2	53.3	55.0	50.7	•	66.7	•	•	•	•
Salaries and Wages **11**	11.7	3.9	12.4	7.5	14.6	10.0	14.3	•	14.6	•	•	•	•
Taxes Paid **12**	3.4	4.1	3.6	2.6	3.7	2.8	3.2	•	2.7	•	•	•	•
Interest Paid **13**	0.9	0.6	0.6	1.0	1.3	2.3	1.7	•	1.5	•	•	•	•
Depreciation **14**	1.6	1.3	1.4	1.4	1.8	2.5	2.4	•	2.3	•	•	•	•
Amortization and Depletion **15**	0.3	0.9	0.1	0.2	0.3	0.3	1.6	•	0.7	•	•	•	•
Pensions and Other Deferred Comp. **16**	0.1	0.0	0.1	0.1	0.2	0.1	0.3	•	0.1	•	•	•	•
Employee Benefits **17**	1.1	0.9	1.0	1.2	1.0	0.7	1.2	•	2.5	•	•	•	•
Advertising **18**	1.7	1.3	1.7	1.6	1.6	1.3	2.8	•	0.6	•	•	•	•
Other Expenses **19**	18.5	23.1	20.3	17.2	13.6	15.6	15.9	•	14.9	•	•	•	•
Officers' Compensation **20**	5.8	9.3	7.5	3.8	4.1	2.3	1.5	•	1.0	•	•	•	•
Operating Margin **21**	4.9	7.3	5.9	3.0	4.4	7.2	4.4	•	•	•	•	•	•
Operating Margin Before Officers' Comp. **22**	10.8	16.5	13.4	6.8	8.5	9.5	5.9	•	•	•	•	•	•

Selected Average Balance Sheet ($ in Thousands)

Net Receivables 23	22	0	9	93	185	784	1251	9472
Inventories 24	20	0	10	47	216	430	1520	3101
Net Property, Plant and Equipment 25	90	0	34	300	860	4025	5768	33003
Total Assets 26	222	0	96	714	1835	6869	15085	97771
Notes and Loans Payable 27	109	0	50	331	896	3813	5224	28736
All Other Liabilities 28	40	0	18	110	255	1326	2758	35212
Net Worth 29	73	0	27	273	684	1730	7103	33823

Selected Financial Ratios (Times to 1)

Current Ratio 30	1.7	•	1.7	1.9	1.9	1.4	1.2	1.0
Quick Ratio 31	1.1	•	1.3	1.4	1.2	0.9	0.7	0.6
Net Sales to Working Capital 32	21.1	•	26.0	15.7	13.3	15.6	29.3	187.5
Coverage Ratio 33	7.2	21.0	12.3	4.7	4.9	5.9	5.4	3.6
Total Asset Turnover 34	3.3	•	5.1	2.8	2.4	1.2	1.8	1.4
Inventory Turnover 35	17.9	•	22.1	25.8	10.8	10.7	9.1	29.0
Receivables Turnover 36	36.4	•	51.9	26.5	29.0	11.7	17.4	28.4
Total Liabilities to Net Worth 37	2.0	•	2.5	1.6	1.7	3.0	1.1	1.9
Current Assets to Working Capital 38	2.4	•	2.3	2.1	2.1	3.4	5.3	29.0
Current Liabilities to Working Capital 39	1.4	•	1.3	1.1	1.1	2.4	4.3	28.0
Working Capital to Net Sales 40	0.0	•	0.0	0.1	0.1	0.1	0.0	0.0
Inventory to Working Capital 41	0.6	•	0.5	0.4	0.6	1.0	1.8	4.3
Total Receipts to Cash Flow 42	5.5	3.6	5.0	6.3	7.2	4.8	5.9	8.5
Cost of Goods to Cash Flow 43	2.8	1.7	2.3	3.8	3.8	2.6	3.0	5.7
Cash Flow to Total Debt 44	0.9	•	1.4	0.7	0.5	0.3	0.6	0.2

Selected Financial Factors (in Percentages)

Debt Ratio 45	67.1	•	71.4	61.8	62.7	74.8	52.9	65.4
Return on Total Assets 46	22.4	•	35.6	13.6	15.1	16.8	17.1	7.7
Return on Equity Before Income Taxes 47	58.6	•	114.2	28.1	32.2	55.4	29.6	16.1
Return on Equity After Income Taxes 48	56.8	•	112.7	26.2	31.1	51.7	29.0	15.4
Profit Margin (Before Income Tax) 49	5.9	12.9	6.4	3.8	5.0	11.4	7.7	4.0
Profit Margin (After Income Tax) 50	5.7	12.8	6.3	3.5	4.9	10.7	7.6	3.9

Table I

Corporations with and without Net Income

OTHER REPAIR AND MAINTENANCE

MONEY AMOUNTS AND SIZE OF ASSETS IN THOUSANDS OF DOLLARS

Item Description for Accounting Period 7/05 Through 6/06	Total	Zero Assets	Under 500	500 to 1,000	1,000 to 5,000	5,000 to 10,000	10,000 to 25,000	25,000 to 50,000	50,000 to 100,000	100,000 to 250,000	250,000 to 500,000	500,000 to 2,500,000	2,500,000 and over
Number of Enterprises 1	58770	12735	42569	1811	1397	112	114	12	15	5	0	0	0
Revenues ($ in Thousands)													
Net Sales 2	34129962	972716	15432971	2722076	6409465	1567125	3344089	798870	1910257	972394	0	0	0
Interest 3	17845	539	2003	1257	3724	1844	5405	454	1273	1346	0	0	0
Rents 4	5236	0	551	811	1362	60	769	262	375	1045	0	0	0
Royalties 5	818	0	0	0	0	0	0	0	573	245	0	0	0
Other Portfolio Income 6	79225	12187	9566	1866	11616	26704	6647	184	3256	7198	0	0	0
Other Receipts 7	156298	2699	31529	-10414	47033	8809	49026	5197	19597	2822	0	0	0
Total Receipts 8	34389384	988141	15476620	2715596	6473200	1604542	3405936	804967	1935331	985050	0	0	0
Average Total Receipts 9	585	78	364	1500	4634	14326	29877	67081	129022	197010	•	•	•
Operating Costs/Operating Income (%)													
Cost of Operations 10	53.2	41.1	47.9	53.2	50.1	53.6	67.6	72.9	69.2	70.9	•	•	•
Salaries and Wages 11	12.7	6.9	13.2	11.5	16.7	12.8	7.7	5.3	15.2	6.7	•	•	•
Taxes Paid 12	2.8	2.3	2.6	3.3	3.0	2.5	2.9	2.2	3.3	2.1	•	•	•
Interest Paid 13	0.8	0.9	0.5	0.8	1.3	0.5	0.7	0.9	1.5	3.1	•	•	•
Depreciation 14	1.5	2.5	1.5	1.9	1.3	1.8	1.6	0.8	1.2	1.0	•	•	•
Amortization and Depletion 15	0.3	0.6	0.1	1.0	0.3	0.0	0.2	0.2	1.2	1.6	•	•	•
Pensions and Other Deferred Comp. 16	0.4	0.1	0.2	0.4	0.3	1.0	0.6	0.3	0.9	0.3	•	•	•
Employee Benefits 17	2.2	1.3	0.8	1.9	4.9	2.7	2.2	4.1	3.9	1.2	•	•	•
Advertising 18	0.7	2.7	1.0	0.3	0.4	0.6	0.3	0.3	0.3	0.3	•	•	•
Other Expenses 19	16.4	41.9	20.1	14.1	13.9	14.7	9.8	5.4	6.0	11.8	•	•	•
Officers' Compensation 20	5.7	6.2	8.1	6.6	3.8	4.2	2.7	2.0	0.7	1.2	•	•	•
Operating Margin 21	3.4	•	4.1	5.0	4.0	5.6	3.6	5.6	•	•	•	•	•
Operating Margin Before Officers' Comp. 22	9.0	•	12.2	11.6	7.7	9.8	6.3	7.6	•	0.9	•	•	•

Selected Average Balance Sheet ($ in Thousands)

Net Receivables 23	50	0	13	152	507	2000	4938	8470	19371	37423
Inventories 24	35	0	12	84	458	1301	2764	11189	8793	12149
Net Property, Plant and Equipment 25	37	0	19	121	359	1100	2728	4542	9625	9513
Total Assets 26	193	0	67	651	1822	6170	15848	31589	75868	147979
Notes and Loans Payable 27	81	0	39	263	875	1390	3647	7683	22996	78925
All Other Liabilities 28	52	0	15	122	380	2445	4817	12332	31036	50792
Net Worth 29	60	0	13	266	567	2335	7384	11574	21836	18262

Selected Financial Ratios (Times to 1)

Current Ratio 30	1.8	•	2.3	2.4	1.8	1.7	2.1	1.8	1.4	0.7
Quick Ratio 31	1.1	•	1.5	1.7	1.0	1.2	1.3	0.8	0.8	0.4
Net Sales to Working Capital 32	10.8	•	15.7	7.2	8.7	7.1	5.1	6.0	9.5	•
Coverage Ratio 33	6.0	•	10.4	6.9	5.0	17.5	9.4	8.3	•	1.4
Total Asset Turnover 34	3.0	•	5.4	2.3	2.5	2.3	1.9	2.1	1.7	1.3
Inventory Turnover 35	8.7	•	14.9	9.6	5.0	5.8	7.2	4.3	10.0	11.3
Receivables Turnover 36	12.1	•	29.6	8.4	9.0	6.7	7.2	6.6	9.6	4.0
Total Liabilities to Net Worth 37	2.2	•	4.0	1.4	2.2	1.6	1.1	1.7	2.5	7.1
Current Assets to Working Capital 38	2.3	•	1.8	1.7	2.2	2.4	1.9	2.2	3.4	•
Current Liabilities to Working Capital 39	1.3	•	0.8	0.7	1.2	1.4	0.9	1.2	2.4	•
Working Capital to Net Sales 40	0.1	•	0.1	0.1	0.1	0.1	0.2	0.2	0.1	•
Inventory to Working Capital 41	0.7	•	0.5	0.4	0.8	0.7	0.6	1.2	0.9	•
Total Receipts to Cash Flow 42	6.0	3.5	5.0	6.7	6.0	5.1	8.1	10.0	187.9	11.0
Cost of Goods to Cash Flow 43	3.2	1.4	2.4	3.6	3.0	2.7	5.5	7.3	130.0	7.8
Cash Flow to Total Debt 44	0.7	•	1.4	0.6	0.6	0.7	0.4	0.3	0.0	0.1

Selected Financial Factors (in Percentages)

Debt Ratio 45	69.0	•	80.0	59.1	68.9	62.2	53.4	63.4	71.2	87.7
Return on Total Assets 46	14.9	•	26.5	12.8	15.6	19.2	11.3	15.3	•	5.5
Return on Equity Before Income Taxes 47	40.2	•	119.3	26.8	40.1	48.0	21.6	36.8	•	11.8
Return on Equity After Income Taxes 48	36.8	•	115.2	25.4	38.2	40.4	17.6	33.4	•	2.5
Profit Margin (Before Income Tax) 49	4.1	•	4.4	4.8	4.9	8.0	5.4	6.4	•	1.1
Profit Margin (After Income Tax) 50	3.8	•	4.2	4.5	4.7	6.7	4.4	5.8	•	0.2

Table II
Corporations with Net Income

OTHER REPAIR AND MAINTENANCE

MONEY AMOUNTS AND SIZE OF ASSETS IN THOUSANDS OF DOLLARS

Item Description for Accounting Period 7/05 Through 6/06		Total	Zero Assets	Under 500	500 to 1,000	1,000 to 5,000	5,000 to 10,000	10,000 to 25,000	25,000 to 50,000	50,000 to 100,000	100,000 to 250,000	250,000 to 500,000	500,000 to 2,500,000	2,500,000 and over
Number of Enterprises	1	31006	5683	22640	1251	1206	112	93	•	7	•	0	0	0
Revenues ($ in Thousands)														
Net Sales	2	26327960	494471	10774239	2022194	5826115	1567125	3056256	•	953889	•	0	0	0
Interest	3	14821	0	1965	488	3537	1844	5309	•	434	•	0	0	0
Rents	4	3723	0	551	811	133	60	769	•	91	•	0	0	0
Royalties	5	245	0	0	0	0	0	0	•	0	•	0	0	0
Other Portfolio Income	6	74627	12034	9093	1734	10383	26704	6592	•	703	•	0	0	0
Other Receipts	7	131056	2652	14752	1323	44017	8809	50789	•	522	•	0	0	0
Total Receipts	8	26552432	509157	10800600	2026550	5884185	1604542	3119715	•	955639	•	0	0	0
Average Total Receipts	9	856	90	477	1620	4879	14326	33545	•	136520	•	•	•	•
Operating Costs/Operating Income (%)														
Cost of Operations	10	52.6	35.3	47.8	43.3	49.3	53.6	66.9	•	73.1	•	•	•	•
Salaries and Wages	11	12.8	3.1	13.5	13.6	17.2	12.8	7.9	•	8.3	•	•	•	•
Taxes Paid	12	2.8	2.1	2.6	3.9	3.0	2.5	3.0	•	2.6	•	•	•	•
Interest Paid	13	0.7	0.8	0.4	1.0	1.2	0.5	0.6	•	1.3	•	•	•	•
Depreciation	14	1.4	1.8	1.3	2.4	1.3	1.8	1.5	•	0.4	•	•	•	•
Amortization and Depletion	15	0.2	0.3	0.0	0.3	0.3	0.0	0.1	•	0.4	•	•	•	•
Pensions and Other Deferred Comp.	16	0.4	0.1	0.2	0.5	0.3	1.0	0.7	•	0.2	•	•	•	•
Employee Benefits	17	2.1	0.6	0.5	1.6	5.2	2.7	2.3	•	1.2	•	•	•	•
Advertising	18	0.4	2.1	0.5	0.3	0.4	0.6	0.4	•	0.4	•	•	•	•
Other Expenses	19	14.9	34.5	17.3	16.8	13.6	14.7	9.7	•	9.3	•	•	•	•
Officers' Compensation	20	5.3	8.5	7.4	7.7	3.7	4.2	2.7	•	0.6	•	•	•	•
Operating Margin	21	6.5	10.8	8.4	8.7	4.6	5.6	4.4	•	2.2	•	•	•	•
Operating Margin Before Officers' Comp.	22	11.8	19.3	15.9	16.4	8.3	9.8	7.1	•	2.8	•	•	•	•

Selected Average Balance Sheet ($ in Thousands)

Net Receivables 23	76	0	·	15	195	538	2000	5228	22172
Inventories 24	48	0	·	11	56	434	1249	3000	10816
Net Property, Plant and Equipment 25	53	0	·	21	168	361	1100	2789	8261
Total Assets 26	270	0	·	78	620	1863	6170	16556	77147
Notes and Loans Payable 27	93	0	·	29	268	861	1390	3543	22355
All Other Liabilities 28	69	0	·	13	84	404	2445	5114	26907
Net Worth 29	108	0	·	35	268	597	2335	7898	27885

Selected Financial Ratios (Times to 1)

Current Ratio 30	2.1	·	3.1	3.4	1.8	1.7	2.2	·	1.4
Quick Ratio 31	1.3	·	2.2	2.6	1.1	1.2	1.3	·	0.9
Net Sales to Working Capital 32	9.2	·	14.5	5.7	8.7	7.1	5.2	·	12.2
Coverage Ratio 33	11.3	19.2	22.6	10.1	5.8	17.5	12.4	·	2.9
Total Asset Turnover 34	3.1	·	6.1	2.6	2.6	2.3	2.0	·	1.8
Inventory Turnover 35	9.3	·	20.5	12.4	5.5	6.0	7.3	·	9.2
Receivables Turnover 36	11.9	·	31.9	8.1	9.6	6.9	7.6	·	12.3
Total Liabilities to Net Worth 37	1.5	·	1.2	1.3	2.1	1.6	1.1	·	1.8
Current Assets to Working Capital 38	1.9	·	1.5	1.4	2.2	2.4	1.9	·	3.6
Current Liabilities to Working Capital 39	0.9	·	0.5	0.4	1.2	1.4	0.9	·	2.6
Working Capital to Net Sales 40	0.1	·	0.1	0.2	0.1	0.1	0.2	·	0.1
Inventory to Working Capital 41	0.6	·	0.3	0.2	0.8	0.7	0.6	·	1.0
Total Receipts to Cash Flow 42	5.2	2.5	4.5	4.7	5.8	5.1	7.5	·	11.5
Cost of Goods to Cash Flow 43	2.8	0.9	2.1	2.1	2.9	2.7	5.0	·	8.4
Cash Flow to Total Debt 44	1.0	·	2.5	1.0	0.7	0.7	0.5	·	0.2

Selected Financial Factors (in Percentages)

Debt Ratio 45	59.8	·	54.8	56.8	67.9	62.2	52.3	·	63.9
Return on Total Assets 46	25.3	·	55.3	25.7	17.5	19.2	14.1	·	6.5
Return on Equity Before Income Taxes 47	57.5	·	117.0	53.7	45.2	48.0	27.1	·	11.8
Return on Equity After Income Taxes 48	54.1	·	114.0	51.6	43.2	40.4	22.5	·	9.5
Profit Margin (Before Income Tax) 49	7.3	13.7	8.7	8.9	5.6	8.0	6.5	·	2.4
Profit Margin (After Income Tax) 50	6.9	13.5	8.5	8.5	5.3	6.7	5.4	·	2.0

Table I

Corporations with and without Net Income

PERSONAL AND LAUNDRY SERVICES

MONEY AMOUNTS AND SIZE OF ASSETS IN THOUSANDS OF DOLLARS

Item Description for Accounting Period 7/05 Through 6/06	Total	Zero Assets	Under 500	500 to 1,000	1,000 to 5,000	5,000 to 10,000	10,000 to 25,000	25,000 to 50,000	50,000 to 100,000	100,000 to 250,000	250,000 to 500,000	500,000 to 2,500,000	2,500,000 and over
Number of Enterprises 1	140302	24167	106067	5101	4360	388	128	36	24	13	4	10	3
Revenues ($ in Thousands)													
Net Sales 2	75091070	2157683	30280169	5545802	11912449	4137821	1764578	1505501	2066646	1980772	1525627	5156055	7057967
Interest 3	190054	5822	8234	7178	13862	5420	11785	5691	7143	7518	4850	70400	42150
Rents 4	59755	10	514	4099	5390	348	6228	611	1420	258	7777	20306	12795
Royalties 5	118839	0	0	0	0	0	125	0	234	12177	0	50136	56167
Other Portfolio Income 6	612842	66793	75878	27435	115646	13834	8612	9305	57199	33522	11947	123411	69262
Other Receipts 7	1273650	82093	226025	38396	325683	61262	58992	28069	58025	157225	29615	193879	14384
Total Receipts 8	77346210	2312401	30590820	5622910	12373030	4218685	1850320	1549177	2190667	2191472	1579816	5614187	7252725
Average Total Receipts 9	551	96	288	1102	2838	10873	14456	43033	91278	168575	394954	561419	2417575
Operating Costs/Operating Income (%)													
Cost of Operations 10	29.0	22.0	25.6	29.2	29.1	43.5	23.0	32.5	26.1	41.4	45.6	20.9	37.2
Salaries and Wages 11	20.5	19.2	19.6	19.8	23.0	15.5	25.8	24.6	20.2	21.5	22.6	22.6	19.8
Taxes Paid 12	4.2	4.0	4.0	4.8	4.8	4.5	3.8	3.9	3.0	3.0	3.7	4.5	4.5
Interest Paid 13	1.9	2.0	1.0	1.8	2.3	1.5	2.4	2.0	1.8	5.2	2.1	4.5	2.6
Depreciation 14	3.0	2.3	2.4	5.1	2.7	4.7	5.4	2.5	2.6	2.7	5.2	3.6	2.6
Amortization and Depletion 15	1.0	0.6	0.4	0.6	0.5	0.3	0.7	0.3	0.4	2.5	3.7	5.9	1.1
Pensions and Other Deferred Comp. 16	0.4	0.6	0.2	0.6	0.4	0.3	0.8	0.6	0.8	0.3	0.6	0.6	0.8
Employee Benefits 17	1.6	0.9	0.8	1.5	1.8	1.4	2.9	3.4	5.0	1.6	2.5	3.3	2.1
Advertising 18	2.1	2.3	2.5	2.0	1.2	2.6	0.9	2.9	1.5	4.8	0.4	1.7	1.4
Other Expenses 19	30.8	39.3	34.3	27.2	32.7	20.9	30.9	25.0	38.1	29.4	16.3	32.1	20.4
Officers' Compensation 20	5.1	9.1	7.7	8.0	4.6	2.7	2.5	2.3	1.0	1.4	0.5	0.5	0.4
Operating Margin 21	0.3	•	1.4	•	•	2.0	0.9	•	•	•	•	•	7.0
Operating Margin Before Officers' Comp. 22	5.4	6.7	9.1	7.4	1.6	4.7	3.4	2.1	0.4	•	•	0.2	7.5

Selected Average Balance Sheet ($ in Thousands)

Net Receivables 23	40	0	5	77	208	1052	2437	5711	7393	20186	40554	127074	325594
Inventories 24	18	0	3	22	57	350	610	1472	5244	9901	12303	81712	243612
Net Property, Plant and Equipment 25	140	0	38	350	867	2869	4754	8988	25683	33492	123447	246014	1315897
Total Assets 26	403	0	85	713	1778	7208	14823	34299	71095	152421	340343	1097400	4719576
Notes and Loans Payable 27	175	0	68	340	1122	2772	4929	10477	23121	91256	85820	297013	1166694
All Other Liabilities 28	111	0	15	99	335	2234	4539	18893	19942	64084	138745	442566	1180149
Net Worth 29	117	0	1	275	321	2202	5354	4930	28031	-2919	115778	357821	2372732

Selected Financial Ratios (Times to 1)

Current Ratio 30	1.5	•	1.4	1.8	1.4	1.4	1.6	1.2	1.4	0.9	1.1	1.7	1.9
Quick Ratio 31	1.0	•	1.0	1.4	0.9	1.1	1.1	0.7	0.7	0.6	0.7	1.1	0.8
Net Sales to Working Capital 32	15.0	•	41.8	12.5	18.8	15.2	6.3	12.2	11.9	•	84.4	4.4	5.9
Coverage Ratio 33	2.7	3.4	3.5	1.5	1.3	3.5	3.4	2.3	4.0	0.4	1.1	2.9	4.8
Total Asset Turnover 34	1.3	•	3.4	1.5	1.5	1.5	0.9	1.2	1.2	1.0	1.1	0.5	0.5
Inventory Turnover 35	8.8	•	21.9	14.3	14.0	13.3	5.2	9.2	4.3	6.4	14.1	1.3	3.6
Receivables Turnover 36	12.7	•	64.1	17.7	13.3	11.0	5.8	8.2	11.8	7.8	6.3	2.3	14.4
Total Liabilities to Net Worth 37	2.4	•	81.7	1.6	4.5	2.3	1.8	6.0	1.5	•	1.9	2.1	1.0
Current Assets to Working Capital 38	3.0	•	3.7	2.2	3.8	3.7	2.7	5.1	3.2	•	17.9	2.4	2.1
Current Liabilities to Working Capital 39	2.0	•	2.7	1.2	2.8	2.7	1.7	4.1	2.2	•	16.9	1.4	1.1
Working Capital to Net Sales 40	0.1	•	0.0	0.1	0.1	0.1	0.2	0.1	0.1	•	0.0	0.2	0.2
Inventory to Working Capital 41	0.5	•	0.5	0.3	0.4	0.6	0.2	0.4	1.0	•	4.5	0.4	0.6
Total Receipts to Cash Flow 42	4.5	3.4	4.1	5.6	6.4	5.4	4.1	5.0	3.3	7.1	7.4	3.2	4.7
Cost of Goods to Cash Flow 43	1.3	0.8	1.0	1.6	1.8	2.4	0.9	1.6	0.9	2.9	3.4	0.7	1.7
Cash Flow to Total Debt 44	0.4	•	0.8	0.4	0.3	0.4	0.4	0.3	0.6	0.1	0.2	0.2	0.2

Selected Financial Factors (in Percentages)

Debt Ratio 45	70.9	•	98.8	61.5	81.9	69.5	63.9	85.6	60.6	101.9	66.0	67.4	49.7
Return on Total Assets 46	6.9	•	11.4	4.0	4.7	8.0	7.5	5.7	8.7	2.1	2.6	6.3	6.1
Return on Equity Before Income Taxes 47	15.1	•	677.3	3.3	6.4	18.8	14.7	22.5	16.5	161.3	0.9	12.7	9.6
Return on Equity After Income Taxes 48	12.1	•	664.7	2.3	4.8	17.7	13.0	17.2	14.0	242.9	•	9.2	6.6
Profit Margin (Before Income Tax) 49	3.3	4.8	2.4	0.8	0.7	3.9	5.7	2.7	5.4	•	0.3	8.8	9.7
Profit Margin (After Income Tax) 50	2.7	4.6	2.4	0.6	0.6	3.6	5.0	2.0	4.6	•	•	6.4	6.7

Table II
Corporations with Net Income

PERSONAL AND LAUNDRY SERVICES

MONEY AMOUNTS AND SIZE OF ASSETS IN THOUSANDS OF DOLLARS

Item Description for Accounting Period 7/05 Through 6/06	Total	Zero Assets	Under 500	500 to 1,000	1,000 to 5,000	5,000 to 10,000	10,000 to 25,000	25,000 to 50,000	50,000 to 100,000	100,000 to 250,000	250,000 to 500,000	500,000 to 2,500,000	2,500,000 and over
Number of Enterprises **1**	76589	11776	58904	3223	2226	312	86	•	21	10	0	•	3
Revenues ($ in Thousands)													
Net Sales **2**	53210338	1105972	19249828	4148910	7668012	3225244	1401083	•	1975305	1894776	0	•	7057967
Interest **3**	162769	3774	4844	5278	12593	4388	7886	•	6833	7408	0	•	42150
Rents **4**	53948	0	175	2703	4159	310	5332	•	1420	6256	0	•	12795
Royalties **5**	112643	0	0	0	0	0	125	•	0	6215	0	•	56167
Other Portfolio Income **6**	558474	66793	44642	26456	108895	7452	6139	•	57117	44422	0	•	69262
Other Receipts **7**	887478	56766	175197	27808	98152	51897	61197	•	57250	140730	0	•	14384
Total Receipts **8**	54985650	1233305	19474686	4211155	7891811	3289291	1481762	•	2097925	2099807	0	•	7252725
Average Total Receipts **9**	718	105	331	1307	3545	10543	17230	•	99901	209981	•	•	2417575
Operating Costs/Operating Income (%)													
Cost of Operations **10**	27.6	8.0	22.8	33.5	26.2	40.6	22.7	•	26.5	32.5	•	•	37.2
Salaries and Wages **11**	18.9	16.8	17.2	16.1	19.1	16.2	27.4	•	19.4	25.4	•	•	19.8
Taxes Paid **12**	4.0	3.9	3.3	3.9	4.8	4.5	3.7	•	3.0	3.2	•	•	4.5
Interest Paid **13**	1.5	1.9	0.8	1.0	1.4	1.1	2.0	•	1.6	2.3	•	•	2.6
Depreciation **14**	2.6	1.2	2.0	4.0	2.1	4.8	5.5	•	2.5	3.7	•	•	2.6
Amortization and Depletion **15**	0.9	0.6	0.4	0.3	0.3	0.4	0.4	•	0.4	1.5	•	•	1.1
Pensions and Other Deferred Comp. **16**	0.4	0.9	0.2	0.6	0.5	0.2	0.8	•	0.4	0.4	•	•	0.8
Employee Benefits **17**	1.7	0.4	0.6	1.6	2.1	0.8	3.2	•	5.0	3.0	•	•	2.1
Advertising **18**	1.9	1.3	2.3	1.6	1.1	1.7	0.9	•	1.4	3.5	•	•	1.4
Other Expenses **19**	30.1	34.7	33.8	24.0	36.1	21.8	28.5	•	38.9	25.8	•	•	20.4
Officers' Compensation **20**	4.8	11.8	7.6	8.7	4.7	2.6	2.1	•	0.9	1.1	•	•	0.4
Operating Margin **21**	5.5	18.4	8.9	4.5	1.5	5.3	2.7	•	•	•	•	•	7.0
Operating Margin Before Officers' Comp. **22**	10.3	30.2	16.6	13.2	6.2	7.8	4.9	•	0.8	•	•	•	7.5

Selected Average Balance Sheet ($ in Thousands)

Net Receivables 23	58	0	5	88	268	857	2605	7689	28480	•	325694
Inventories 24	25	0	4	28	58	404	651	5300	9352	•	243612
Net Property, Plant and Equipment 25	177	0	37	337	800	2792	4583	24679	49114	•	1315897
Total Assets 26	558	0	88	710	1880	7094	14864	72376	172921	•	4719576
Notes and Loans Payable 27	180	0	51	266	863	2344	4796	21772	54062	•	1166694
All Other Liabilities 28	151	0	12	106	340	1928	4262	20924	60156	•	1180149
Net Worth 29	227	0	25	339	677	2823	5806	29680	58703	•	2372732

Selected Financial Ratios (Times to 1)

Current Ratio 30	1.7	•	2.0	2.0	1.4	1.8	•	1.5	1.1	•	1.9
Quick Ratio 31	1.1	•	1.6	1.6	1.0	1.3	•	0.7	0.8	•	0.8
Net Sales to Working Capital 32	10.7	•	19.7	11.5	14.3	5.9	•	11.3	61.4	•	5.9
Coverage Ratio 33	6.8	17.0	13.0	7.0	7.7	5.3	•	4.8	4.7	•	4.8
Total Asset Turnover 34	1.2	•	3.7	1.8	1.5	1.1	•	1.3	1.1	•	0.5
Inventory Turnover 35	7.6	•	19.7	15.5	10.4	5.7	•	4.7	6.6	•	3.6
Receivables Turnover 36	13.7	•	84.1	19.0	13.0	6.2	•	13.1	13.3	•	14.4
Total Liabilities to Net Worth 37	1.5	•	2.5	1.1	1.5	1.6	•	1.4	1.9	•	1.0
Current Assets to Working Capital 38	2.4	•	2.0	2.0	3.4	2.2	•	3.0	17.0	•	2.1
Current Liabilities to Working Capital 39	1.4	•	1.0	1.0	2.4	1.2	•	2.0	16.0	•	1.1
Working Capital to Net Sales 40	0.1	•	0.1	0.1	0.1	0.2	•	0.1	0.0	•	0.2
Inventory to Working Capital 41	0.4	•	0.2	0.3	0.7	0.2	•	0.9	3.0	•	0.6
Total Receipts to Cash Flow 42	3.7	2.0	3.1	4.7	5.1	3.7	•	3.2	4.3	•	4.7
Cost of Goods to Cash Flow 43	1.0	0.2	0.7	1.6	1.3	1.8	•	0.8	1.4	•	1.7
Cash Flow to Total Debt 44	0.6	•	1.7	0.7	0.6	0.5	•	0.7	0.4	•	0.2

Selected Financial Factors (in Percentages)

Debt Ratio 45	59.3	•	71.1	52.3	64.0	60.9	•	59.0	66.1	•	49.7
Return on Total Assets 46	12.9	•	40.6	12.8	10.3	11.5	•	10.1	11.7	•	6.1
Return on Equity Before Income Taxes 47	27.1	•	130.0	22.9	21.2	23.8	•	19.4	27.1	•	9.6
Return on Equity After Income Taxes 48	24.4	•	129.1	21.6	19.7	21.5	•	16.7	20.9	•	6.6
Profit Margin (Before Income Tax) 49	8.9	29.9	10.1	6.0	4.2	8.5	•	6.1	8.4	•	9.7
Profit Margin (After Income Tax) 50	8.0	29.4	10.0	5.7	3.9	7.7	•	5.3	6.5	•	6.7

Table I

Corporations with and without Net Income

RELIGIOUS, GRANTMAKING, CIVIC AND PROFESSIONAL ORGANIZATIONS

MONEY AMOUNTS AND SIZE OF ASSETS IN THOUSANDS OF DOLLARS

Item Description for Accounting Period 7/05 Through 6/06	Total	Zero Assets	Under 500	500 to 1,000	1,000 to 5,000	5,000 to 10,000	10,000 to 25,000	25,000 to 50,000	50,000 to 100,000	100,000 to 250,000	250,000 to 500,000	500,000 to 2,500,000	2,500,000 and over
Number of Enterprises **1**	40209	3029	32250	2667	1989	173	80	9	7	5	0	0	0
Revenues ($ in Thousands)													
Net Sales **2**	10366018	141890	3291327	984124	2227876	663454	406132	200541	225720	2224953	0	0	0
Interest **3**	153549	836	41069	25950	51333	12812	5516	2931	3161	9942	0	0	0
Rents **4**	33871	0	15287	3110	11096	1823	148	7	78	2321	0	0	0
Royalties **5**	5694	0	0	0	0	0	5694	0	0	0	0	0	0
Other Portfolio Income **6**	44223	11037	8518	9441	6256	169	2937	2412	2274	1180	0	0	0
Other Receipts **7**	1596990	3592	474074	317571	214206	336880	152300	19366	59977	19023	0	0	0
Total Receipts **8**	12200345	157355	3830275	1340196	2510767	1015138	572727	225257	291210	2257419	0	0	0
Average Total Receipts **9**	303	52	119	503	1262	5868	7159	25029	41601	451484	·	·	·
Operating Costs/Operating Income (%)													
Cost of Operations **10**	29.2	45.1	10.1	5.7	19.5	33.0	37.0	3.9	2.5	78.8	·	·	·
Salaries and Wages **11**	10.8	1.6	5.1	8.1	18.5	12.6	23.5	39.3	26.7	6.4	·	·	·
Taxes Paid **12**	2.0	3.0	1.7	0.9	3.0	2.2	4.8	3.4	5.2	0.7	·	·	·
Interest Paid **13**	0.5	·	0.4	0.4	0.4	1.9	3.0	0.5	0.4	0.1	·	·	·
Depreciation **14**	1.7	0.1	0.9	0.9	2.0	3.8	6.0	4.4	8.3	0.5	·	·	·
Amortization and Depletion **15**	0.1	0.0	0.0	0.0	0.0	0.1	0.1	0.9	0.0	0.3	·	·	·
Pensions and Other Deferred Comp. **16**	0.3	·	0.1	·	0.1	0.1	0.3	3.1	1.5	0.4	·	·	·
Employee Benefits **17**	1.5	·	0.3	0.2	3.7	2.0	2.6	3.2	2.2	1.0	·	·	·
Advertising **18**	0.4	1.1	0.2	0.0	0.5	0.3	0.9	0.5	0.4	0.7	·	·	·
Other Expenses **19**	67.4	37.8	91.4	115.6	63.1	94.1	59.9	45.4	76.9	11.0	·	·	·
Officers' Compensation **20**	2.4	7.1	6.0	·	0.7	0.5	1.2	2.0	1.4	0.5	·	·	·
Operating Margin **21**	·	4.3	·	·	·	·	·	·	·	·	·	·	·
Operating Margin Before Officers' Comp. **22**	·	11.3	·	·	·	·	·	·	·	0.1	·	·	·

Selected Average Balance Sheet ($ in Thousands)

Net Receivables 23	20	0	2	26	140	424	819	3590	3538	40209
Inventories 24	2	0	0	0	13	19	326	165	127	2688
Net Property, Plant and Equipment 25	84	0	8	62	523	3263	9792	14203	36708	37533
Total Assets 26	312	0	89	667	1908	7054	16034	32749	61968	175097
Notes and Loans Payable 27	32	0	8	105	132	1068	2785	2398	2416	13217
All Other Liabilities 28	82	0	18	180	517	1614	3449	6111	12706	102297
Net Worth 29	198	0	64	381	1259	4373	9800	24241	46846	59583

Selected Financial Ratios (Times to 1)

Current Ratio 30	2.9	•	4.8	3.6	2.7	2.0	2.1	4.1	4.5	1.3
Quick Ratio 31	2.6	•	4.5	3.4	2.5	1.6	1.7	2.7	2.7	0.9
Net Sales to Working Capital 32	2.0	•	1.7	1.0	1.5	2.4	1.9	1.9	2.4	20.8
Coverage Ratio 33	3.7	•	0.8	11.5	3.5	2.2	1.5	12.6	10.3	12.9
Total Asset Turnover 34	0.8	•	1.1	0.6	0.6	0.5	0.3	0.7	0.5	2.5
Inventory Turnover 35	40.9	•	151.4	152.0	16.6	67.4	5.8	5.3	6.4	130.4
Receivables Turnover 36	12.1	•	35.0	11.7	9.2	13.9	4.9	7.7	4.0	9.9
Total Liabilities to Net Worth 37	0.6	•	0.4	0.7	0.5	0.6	0.6	0.4	0.3	1.9
Current Assets to Working Capital 38	1.5	•	1.3	1.4	1.6	2.0	1.9	1.3	1.3	4.8
Current Liabilities to Working Capital 39	0.5	•	0.3	0.4	0.6	1.0	0.9	0.3	0.3	3.8
Working Capital to Net Sales 40	0.5	•	0.6	1.1	0.7	0.4	0.5	0.5	0.4	0.0
Inventory to Working Capital 41	0.0	•	0.0	•	0.0	0.0	0.2	0.0	0.0	0.1
Total Receipts to Cash Flow 42	1.8	2.6	1.4	1.2	1.9	1.2	1.8	2.3	1.4	8.9
Cost of Goods to Cash Flow 43	0.5	1.2	0.1	0.1	0.4	0.4	0.7	0.1	0.0	7.0
Cash Flow to Total Debt 44	1.2	•	2.8	1.0	0.9	1.2	0.4	1.1	1.5	0.4

Selected Financial Factors (in Percentages)

Debt Ratio 45	36.6	•	28.7	42.8	34.0	38.0	38.9	26.0	24.4	66.0
Return on Total Assets 46	1.6	•	0.4	2.6	0.9	2.3	1.4	3.9	2.0	2.9
Return on Equity Before Income Taxes 47	1.9	•	•	4.1	1.0	2.1	0.7	4.8	2.4	7.7
Return on Equity After Income Taxes 48	1.3	•	•	3.8	0.6	1.3	0.5	3.2	1.5	5.5
Profit Margin (Before Income Tax) 49	1.4	15.2	•	4.3	1.1	2.3	1.4	5.2	3.5	1.0
Profit Margin (After Income Tax) 50	1.0	12.7	•	3.9	0.6	1.5	0.9	3.4	2.1	0.7

Table II
Corporations with Net Income

RELIGIOUS, GRANTMAKING, CIVIC AND PROFESSIONAL ORGANIZATIONS

MONEY AMOUNTS AND SIZE OF ASSETS IN THOUSANDS OF DOLLARS

Item Description for Accounting Period 7/05 Through 6/06	Total	Zero Assets	Under 500	500 to 1,000	1,000 to 5,000	5,000 to 10,000	10,000 to 25,000	25,000 to 50,000	50,000 to 100,000	100,000 to 250,000	250,000 to 500,000	500,000 to 2,500,000	2,500,000 and over
Number of Enterprises **1**	22333	1727	17078	1939	1436	90	49	•	3	•	0	0	0
Revenues ($ in Thousands)													
Net Sales **2**	6081187	95461	2249327	684189	1461912	390617	320098	•	187671	•	0	0	0
Interest **3**	122072	73	34588	24867	38608	8665	4323	•	1646	•	0	0	0
Rents **4**	27400	0	10722	2949	10710	583	29	•	78	•	0	0	0
Royalties **5**	5694	0	0	0	0	0	5694	•	0	•	0	0	0
Other Portfolio Income **6**	42640	11037	8501	9441	4842	61	2913	•	2274	•	0	0	0
Other Receipts **7**	1058244	3538	400779	178411	75429	254844	85575	•	21953	•	0	0	0
Total Receipts **8**	7337237	110109	2703917	899857	1591501	654770	418632	•	213622	•	0	0	0
Average Total Receipts **9**	329	64	158	464	1108	7275	8544	•	71207	•	•	•	•
Operating Costs/Operating Income (%)													
Cost of Operations **10**	16.4	33.2	11.9	8.2	7.0	52.6	43.5	•	0.8	•	•	•	•
Salaries and Wages **11**	13.4	2.3	4.8	10.0	22.2	12.4	14.6	•	22.6	•	•	•	•
Taxes Paid **12**	2.3	4.3	1.5	1.3	3.6	2.0	2.1	•	4.6	•	•	•	•
Interest Paid **13**	0.4	•	0.1	0.1	0.3	2.0	1.7	•	0.0	•	•	•	•
Depreciation **14**	1.6	0.1	0.8	0.7	1.9	2.3	3.1	•	4.3	•	•	•	•
Amortization and Depletion **15**	0.1	•	0.0	0.0	0.1	0.0	0.1	•	0.0	•	•	•	•
Pensions and Other Deferred Comp. **16**	0.4	•	0.1	•	0.1	0.1	0.4	•	1.8	•	•	•	•
Employee Benefits **17**	1.2	•	0.2	0.2	2.0	1.1	1.6	•	2.6	•	•	•	•
Advertising **18**	0.4	1.7	0.1	0.0	0.7	0.4	0.9	•	0.5	•	•	•	•
Other Expenses **19**	74.7	36.3	87.1	103.7	65.3	85.7	55.8	•	70.1	•	•	•	•
Officers' Compensation **20**	3.8	10.5	8.5	•	0.7	0.7	1.6	•	1.7	•	•	•	•
Operating Margin **21**	•	11.6											
Operating Margin Before Officers' Comp. **22**	•	22.1											

Selected Average Balance Sheet ($ in Thousands)

Net Receivables 23	17	0	2	27	74	389	1300	7647
Inventories 24	3	0	0	0	15	17	493	119
Net Property, Plant and Equipment 25	79	0	8	38	413	2620	7094	18622
Total Assets 26	379	0	124	686	1834	7130	16226	63684
Notes and Loans Payable 27	25	0	7	10	113	1168	2179	314
All Other Liabilities 28	88	0	18	104	427	2175	5115	22632
Net Worth 29	266	0	99	572	1294	3787	8933	40737

Selected Financial Ratios (Times to 1)

Current Ratio 30	3.8	•	6.5	8.3	3.2	1.8	2.1	5.7
Quick Ratio 31	3.5	•	6.2	8.0	2.9	1.6	1.7	3.7
Net Sales to Working Capital 32	1.4	•	1.4	0.7	1.2	2.5	1.7	2.6
Coverage Ratio 33	15.4	•	41.1	123.0	15.7	5.1	4.2	207.2
Total Asset Turnover 34	0.7	•	1.1	0.5	0.6	0.6	0.4	1.0
Inventory Turnover 35	16.9	•	387.1	860.7	4.7	132.6	5.8	4.1
Receivables Turnover 36	13.8	•	55.9	10.8	14.6	17.0	4.8	11.6
Total Liabilities to Net Worth 37	0.4	•	0.3	0.2	0.4	0.9	0.8	0.6
Current Assets to Working Capital 38	1.4	•	1.2	1.1	1.5	2.3	1.9	1.2
Current Liabilities to Working Capital 39	0.4	•	0.2	0.1	0.5	1.3	0.9	0.2
Working Capital to Net Sales 40	0.7	•	0.7	1.4	0.8	0.4	0.6	0.4
Inventory to Working Capital 41	0.0	•	0.0	•	0.0	0.0	0.2	0.0
Total Receipts to Cash Flow 42	1.6	2.2	1.4	1.3	1.8	1.2	1.8	1.4
Cost of Goods to Cash Flow 43	0.3	0.7	0.2	0.1	0.1	0.6	0.8	0.0
Cash Flow to Total Debt 44	1.5	•	3.9	2.3	1.1	1.1	0.5	1.9

Selected Financial Factors (in Percentages)

Debt Ratio 45	29.8	•	20.0	16.7	29.4	46.9	44.9	36.0
Return on Total Assets 46	4.4	•	5.0	3.8	3.0	6.2	2.8	4.8
Return on Equity Before Income Taxes 47	5.8	•	6.2	4.5	4.0	9.5	3.9	7.4
Return on Equity After Income Taxes 48	5.0	•	5.5	4.2	3.4	7.9	3.5	5.0
Profit Margin (Before Income Tax) 49	5.7	27.0	4.6	7.2	5.0	8.3	5.4	4.8
Profit Margin (After Income Tax) 50	4.9	23.4	4.2	6.7	4.3	6.9	4.7	3.2

Index

Index